An Assessment of Marketing Thought & Practice

An Assessment of Marketing Thought & Practice

1982 Educators' Conference Proceedings
Series No. 48

Editors

Bruce J. Walker
Arizona State University

William O. Bearden
University of South Carolina

William R. Darden
University of Arkansas

Patrick E. Murphy
Marquette University

John R. Nevin
University of Wisconsin

Jerry C. Olson
Marketing Science Institute

Barton A. Weitz
University of California at Los Angeles

AMERICAN MARKETING ASSOCIATION
250 South Wacker Drive • Chicago, Illinois 60606 • (312) 648-0536

Cover design by Mary Jo Krysinski

LIBRARY OF CONGRESS CATALOGING IN PUBLICATION DATA
Main entry under title:

An assessment of marketing thought and practice.
  (Series/American Marketing Association/no. 48)

  1. Marketing--Congresses. I. Walker, Bruce J.
II. American Marketing Association. III. Series:
American Marketing Association. Proceedings series,
no. 48.
HF5411.A83   658.8   82-6693
ISBN 0-87757-158-9   AACR2

This Proceedings was prepared from camera-ready copy
supplied by the authors. In case of a chart's
illegibility the reader should contact the author
of the particular article.

TABLE OF CONTENTS

Marketing educators convened in Chicago from August 1st to 4th for "An Assessment of Marketing Thought and Practice," which was the theme of the 1982 Educators' Conference. This theme recognized that it is healthy--perhaps even imperative for the advancement of our discipline--that marketing educators periodically scrutinize and debate important issues, concepts, techniques and trends in the field of marketing.

To stimulate this spirit of inquiry, several features were added to this annual conference. For the first time, at least in recent years, a keynote session kicked off the conference. Professor Philip Kotler of Northwestern University delivered the keynote address. Also, awards were presented to the six papers that were judged to be the best of the 237 papers submitted to the competitive-review process. A best paper was selected in each of the six tracks and then one of these six papers was selected as the best overall paper. The award-winning papers are designated in this volume's Table of Contents.

A long-standing feature of the Educators' Conference is a set of Special Sessions, which are intended to familiarize educators with techniques, perspectives, and concepts that can enhance their development as teachers and researchers. Besides the keynote session, the Special Sessions at this year's conference included panel discussions, a tutorial, and presentations on a diverse set of topics ranging from doctoral education to Japanese marketing strategies. The entire set of 18 Special Sessions is listed on pages 461 and 462 of this volume.

A total of 237 papers were submitted to a competitive-review process in the six tracks. The papers selected for presentation at the conference were organized in 35 Competitive Sessions. All 102 of these papers are presented in this proceedings.

Developing the program and compiling the proceedings for the annual educators' conference certainly must be a team effort. I feel most fortunate because I have been so capably assisted by a team that I think has been of "world championship" caliber. I would like to acknowledge their contributions.

First, I am grateful to Stephen W. Brown, AMA Vice President--Marketing Education in 1981-82, for asking me to serve as program chair for the conference. Steve has also been a valuable sounding board throughout the program-development process.

In my opinion, the key to a stimulating, productive conference is the program committee assembled by the program chair. With this in mind, I want to give the largest thank-you possible to the seven professors who chaired the six Competitive Sessions tracks and the Special Sessions portion of the program: Jerry C. Olson, Pennsylvania State University--Buyer Behavior Track; William O. Bearden, University of South Carolina--Marketing Education Track; Barton A. Weitz, University of Pennsylvania--Marketing Mix and Marketing Institutions Track; John R. Nevin, University of Wisconsin--Marketing Strategy and Special Markets Track; Patrick E. Murphy, Marquette University--Public Policy and Macromarketing Track; William R. Darden, University of Arkansas--Research Methodology Track; and Joseph P. Guiltinan, University of Kentucky--Special Sessions. Each was tireless and completely effective in his efforts to organize a successful conference. I also want to thank Robert E. Weigand of the University of Illinois at Chicago Circle for his assistance in bringing an added measure of industry participation to the conference.

A stimulating, productive conference also requires high-quality papers and Special Sessions, efficiently moderated sessions, and thoughtful dialogue. Therefore, our thanks are expressed to the numerous people who submitted papers or proposals to the conference and/or served as a session chair or discussant.

The reviewers, who are listed on pages xi - xiii of this volume, were an essential part of the program-development process. The track chairs and I express our appreciation to them for their objective, constructive, and punctual reviews.

The educators' conferences, all AMA conferences in fact, benefit greatly from the vital behind-the-scenes efforts of the AMA staff. The specific contributions of the following staff members are noteworthy: Robert F. Schlax, Director of Education and Professional Development; Pam Stoehr, Conference Coordinator; Joan Perell, Professional Publications Manager; and Thomas E. Caruso, <u>Marketing News</u> editor.

On behalf of all nine members of the program committee, I want to express our appreciation to the administrators, secretarial staffs, and graduate assistants at our respective universities for their support and assistance. My personal thanks go to the following people at Arizona State University: Kenneth L. Rowe, department chair; Connie Niedner, administrative assistant; the student secretaries; and Dave Gale and Nader Shooshtari, graduate assistants. Myrna Bowman, secretary in the Marketing Department at Arizona State University, deserves special recognition--and thanks--for both her very capable efforts and her patience in organizing the multitude of typing and clerical tasks connected with my role in developing the program and compiling the proceedings.

I hope that you have benefited--and will continue to benefit--from the assessment of marketing thought and practice conducted at the 1982 Educators' Conference and compiled in this proceedings. Lastly, I encourage you to continue this assessment--and subsequent development--of the marketing discipline.

Bruce J. Walker
Arizona State University
Program Chair
1982 Educators' Conference

REVIEWERS FOR 1982 MARKETING EDUCATORS' CONFERENCE

Members of blue-ribbon panels that reviewed the papers selected as semifinalists in the Best Paper Awards competition:

Andreasen, Alan R.	University of Illinois-Urbana	Newman, Joseph W.	University of Arizona
Bucklin, Louis P.	University of California - Berkeley	Peterson, Robert A.	University of Texas - Austin
		Roering, Kenneth J.	University of Minnesota - Twin Cities
Churchill, Gilbert, Jr.	University of Wisconsin		
Cravens, David W.	Texas Christian University	Scott, Carol A.	University of California - Los Angeles
Enis, Ben M.	Univerisity of Southern California		
		Staelin, Richard	Duke University
Greyser, Stephen A.	Harvard University	Stern, Louis W.	Northwestern University
Klompmaker, Jay E.	University of North Carolina- Chapel Hill	Walker, Orville C.	University of Minnesota - Twin Cities
Mitchell, Andrew A.	Carnegie Mellon University	Wilson, David T.	Pensylvania State University
Myers, John G.	University of California - Berkeley	Zaltman, Gerald	University of Pittsburgh

Reviewers of papers submitted to the six tracks comprising the Competitive Sessions portion of the program:

Achabal, Dale D.	University of Santa Clara	Cox, Keith K.	University of Houston
Acito, Franklin	Indiana University - Indianapolis	Craig, C. Samuel	New York University
		Crask, Melvin R.	Indiana University - Bloomington
Adler, Roy	Xavier University		
Albaum, Gerald S.	University of Oregon	Cravens, David W.	Texas Christian University
Allen, Chris T.	University of Massachusetts	Cromartie, Jane S.	University of New Orleans
Alpert, Mark I.	University of Texas - Austin	Crosby, Lawrence A.	University of Nebraska - Lincoln
Anderson, Erin	University of Pennsylvania		
Ashton, Dub	University of Arkansas	Curham, Ronald	Boston University
Barnes, James H., Jr.	University of Georgia	Dalrymple, Douglas J.	Indiana University - Bloomington
Bart, Barbara D.	Georgia Southern College		
Batory, Stephen S.	Bloomsburg State College	Darmon, Rene	McGill University, Montreal, Canada
Beisel, John	Pittsburg State University		
Bellenger, Danny	Texas Tech University	Della Bitta, Albert J.	University of Rhode Island - Kingston
Beltramini, Richard F.	Arizona State University		
Berkowitz, Eric N.	University of Minnesota	DeLozier, Wayne M.	Florida State University
Berman, Barry	Hofstra University	Deshpande, Rohit	University of Texas - Austin
Bernhardt, Kenneth L.	Georgia State University	Dholakia, Nikhilesh	University of Rhode Island - Kingston
Berry, Leonard L.	Texas A & M University		
Biehal, Gabe	University of Houston	Dillon, William R.	University of Massachusetts
Bloch, Peter H.	Portland State University	Dixon, Peter	Ohio State University
Bloom, Paul N.	University of Maryland	Donnelly, James H., Jr.	University of Kentucky
Bonoma, Thomas V.	Harvard University	Douglas, Susan P.	New York University
Bozinoff, Lorne	Bell Canada, Willowdale, Canada	Dubinsky, Alan J.	University of Kentucky
		Duncan, Calvin P.	University of Colorado
Brooks, John R.	West Texas State University	Durand, Richard M.	Auburn University
Brown, James R.	University of Nebraska - Lincoln	Dwyer, Robert	University of Cincinnati
		Edell, Julie	Duke University
Burke, Marian	Duke University	Enis, Ben M.	University of Southern California
Burnett, John J.	Texas Tech University		
Burnkrant, Robert E.	Ohio State University	Erickson, Gary	University of Washington
Busch, Paul	University of Wisconsin - Madison	Etzel, Michael J.	University of Notre Dame
		Evans, Richard H.	Syracuse University
Bush, Ronald	Louisiana State University	Farley, John U.	Columbia University
Buzzell, Robert D.	Harvard University	Farris, Paul	Harvard University
Cagley, James	University of Tulsa	Ferrell, O.C.	Illinois State University
Calatone, Roger	McGill University, Montreal, Canada	Fine, Seymour	Rutgers University
		Ford, Gary T.	University of Maryland
Capon, Noel	Columbia University	Ford, Neil M.	University of Wisconsin - Madison
Cattin Philippe J.	University of Connecticut		
Cavusgil, Tamer S.	University of Wisconsin - Whitewater	Fornell, Claes	University of Michigan - Ann Arbor
Chakravarti, Dipankar	University of Florida	Futrell, Charles M.	Texas A & M University
Clapper, James	Wake Forest University	Gardner, Meryl P.	New York University
Clarke, Roberta N.	Boston University	Gatignon, Hubert	University of Pennsylvania
Coe, Barbara	North Texas State University	Gaulden, Corbett	Permian Business Group, Midland, TX
Cohen, Dorothy	Hofstra University		
Comer, James M.	University of Cincinnati	Gelb, Betsy D.	University of Houston
Conover, Jerry	University of Arizona	Gerber, Linder	American University
Cooper, Lee	University of California - Los Angeles	Gilly, Mary C.	Southern Methodist University
		Goldberg, Marvin	McGill University, Montreal, Canada
Cosmas, Stephen C.	DePaul University		

Goodwin, Stephen A.   Bowling Green State
                             University
Gorn, Gerald   University of British
                             Columbia
Grant, Jim   University of South Alabama
Granzin, Kent L.   University of Utah
Green, Paul E.   University of Pennsylvania
Grikscheit, Gary   University of Utah
Hair, Joe, Jr.   Louisiana State University
Hanssens, Dominique M.   University of California -
                             Los Angeles
Harrell, Steven   Black & Decker Manufacturing
                             Company
Harris, Brian   University of Southern
                             California
Harvey, Michael G.   Southern Methodist University
Hempel, Donald J.   University of Connecticut
Henion, Karl E., II   University of Texas - Austin
Henry, Walter   University of California -
                             Riverside
Herberger, Roy   Southern Methodist
                             University
Hill, Richard M.   University of Illinois -
                             Urbana
Hirschman, Elizabeth C.   New York University
Hise, Richard T.   Texas A & M University
Holbrook, Morris B.   Columbia University
Holman, Rebecca H.   Young & Rubicam
Houston, Michael J.   University of Wisconsin -
                             Madison
Huber, Joel C.   Duke University
Hughes, David G.   University of North Carolina
Hunt, James M.   University of Florida
Hunt, Keith H.   Brigham Young University
Hutt, Michael D.   Arizona State University
Hutton, Bruce R.   University of Denver
Ingram, Thomas N.   University of Kentucky
Jain, Arun K.   State University of New
                             York - Buffalo
Jain, Subash C.   University of Connecticut
Johansson, J. K.   University of Washington
John, George   University of Wisconsin -
                             Madison
Johnson, Eric   Carnegie-Mellon University
Johnston, Wesley J.   Ohio State University
Jolson, Marvin A.   University of Maryland -
                             College Park
Jones, J. Morgan   University of North Carolina
Kamen, Joseph M.   Indiana University Northwest
Kangun, Norman   University of Nebraska
Keegan, Warren J.   New York University
Kehoe, William J.   University of Virginia
Kehret, Trudy   Northwestern University
Keon, John   New York University
Kerin, Roger A.   Southern Methodist University
King, Robert L.   Virginia Polytechnic Insti-
                             tute & State University
Kinnear, Thomas C.   University of Michigan -
                             Ann Arbor
Laczniak, Eugene R.   Marquette University
Lamb, Charles W.   Texas A & M University
Lambert, Zarrel V.   Auburn University
Lammers, H. Bruce   California State University-
                             Northridge
Langely, John   University of Tennessee
Langrehr, Fred   Marquette University
La Placa, Peter J.   University of Connecticut
Laroche, Michael   Concordia University
Lastovicka, John L.   University of Kansas
Lehmann, Donald R.   Columbia University
Leigh, Jim   Texas A & M University
Leigh, Thomas W.   Pennsylvania State University
Lindgren, John H. Jr.   University of Virginia
Lindquist, Jay D.   Western Michigan University
Locander, William B.   University of Houston
Loken, Barbara   University of Minnesota

Lumpkin, James R.   North Texas State University
Lupul, Max E.   California State University -
                             Northridge
Lutz, Richard J.   University of Florida
Lynch, John   University of Florida
MacKay, David B.   University of Pittsburgh
Madden, Charles S.   Texas A & M University
Malhotra, Naresh K.   Georgia Institute of
                             Technology
Mason, J. Barry   University of Alabama
Mazis, Michael B.   American University
McAlister, Leigh M.   Massachusetts Institute of
                             Technology
McCrohan, Kevin   George Mason University
McDonald, John P.   Wayne State University
McIntyre, Shelby   University of Santa Clara
McNeal, James U.   Texas A & M University
McNeill, Dennis   University of Denver
Michie, Donald A.   New Mexico State University
Michman, Ronald D.   Shippensburg State College
Mills, Michael K.   University of Southern
                             California
Miniard, Paul W.   Ohio State University
Mokwa, Michael P.   Arizona State University
Morgan, Fred W., Jr.   Wayne State University
Moschis, George P.   Georgia State University
Mowen, John C.   Oklahoma State University
Naor, Jacob   University of Maine
Neidell, Lester A.   University of Tulsa
O'Connor, P.J.   University of Kentucky
Oliver, Richard   Washington University
Paksoy, Christie H.   University of North Carolina
Park, C. Whan   University of Pittsburgh
Parsons, Leonard   Georgia Institute of
                             Technology
Patzer, Gordon   University of North Dakota
Peat, Nancy C.   University of Cincinnati
Permut, Steven E.   Yale University
Peter, Paul J.   University of Wisconsin -
                             Madison
Peterson, Robert A.   University of Texas - Austin
Popper, Ed   Northeastern University
Powell, Terry E.   Georgia State University
Preston, Ivan L.   University of Wisconsin
Rao, Chatrathi   University of Arkansas
Rao, Vithala R.   Cornell University
Rausch, Bernard A.   Signode Corporation
Reibstein, David   University of Pennsylvania
Reid, Leonard   University of Georgia
Reingen, Peter H.   Arizona State University
Resnick, Alan J.   Portland State University
Rethans, Arno J.   Pennsylvania State University
Reve, Torger   Norwegian School of Economics
                             & Business Administration
Richins, Marsha L.   Portland State University
Robertson, Dan H.   Texas A & M University
Robicheaux, Robert A.   University of Alabama
Roedder, Deborah H.   University of California -
                             Los Angeles
Roering, Kenneth J.   University of Minnesota -
                             Twin Cities
Ronkainen, Ilkka A.   Georgetown University
Rothe, James T.   Southern Methodist University
Rothschild, Michael L.   University of Wisconsin -
                             Madison
Ruekert, Robert W.   University of Minnesota
Rust, Roland T.   University of Texas - Austin
Ryan, Michael J.   University of Michigan -
                             Ann Arbor
Sawyer, Alan   Ohio State University
Scammon, Debra L.   University of Utah
Scott, Carol A.   University of California -
                             Los Angeles
Sen, Subrata K.   University of Rochester
Sewall, Murphy   University of Connecticut
Sharma, Subhash   University of South Carolina

Sherrell, Daniel L. — Louisiana State University

Shimp, Terence A. — University of South Carolina

Shocker, Alan — Vanderbilt University

Sirgy, Joseph M. — University of Missouri - St. Louis

Solomon, Paul J. — University of Texas - Arlington

Spekman, Robert E. — University of Maryland - College Park

Spiro, Rosann — University of Tennessee

Spivey, W. Austin — University of Texas - San Antonio

Staelin, Richard — Duke University

Stampfl, Ronald — University of Wisconsin - Madison

Strang, Roger — New York University

Staples, William A. — University of Houston - Clear Lake

Stem, Donald E., Jr. — Washington State University

Stewart, David W. — Vanderbilt University

Stiff, Ronald M. — University of Baltimore

Swan, John E. — University of Alabama - Birmingham

Swasy, John — Pennsylvania State University

Swinyard, William R. — Brigham Young University

Teel, Jesse E., Jr. — University of South Carolina

Terpstra, Vern — University of Michigan

Thorelli, Hans B. — Indiana University - Bloomington

Toy, Daniel — Pennsylvania State University

Twedt, Dik W. — University of Missouri - St. Louis

Tyagi, Pradeep K. — San Diego State University

Tyebjee, Tyzoon T. — University of Santa Clara

Upah, Gregory — Young and Rubicam, New York

Wallendorf, Melanie R. — University of Arizona

Webb, Peter — Pacific Consulting Group

Weinberg, Charles — University of British Columbia

White, Phillip D. — University of Colorado

Wildt, Albert R. — University of Georgia

Wilkie, William L. — University of Florida

William, Ray J. — Pennsylvania State University

Wilson, Dale R. — Batten, Barton, Durstine, & Osborn Inc.

Winer, Russell S. — Columbia University

Wittink, Dik — Cornell University

Woodside, Arch G., Jr. — University of South Carolina

Wotruba, Thomas — San Diego State University

Yalch, Richard F. — University of Washington

Zeithaml, Valarie A. — Texas A & M University

Zikmund, William G. — Oklahoma State University

Zinkhan, George M. — University of Houston

PATTERNS OF INFLUENCE IN THE PURCHASE OF CONSUMER
DURABLES BY MEXICAN HOUSEHOLDS

Sandra M. Huszagh, University of Georgia
Arthur D. Murphy, University of Georgia

ABSTRACT

This paper examines influence in husband/wife purchasing
decisions among Mexican consumers in three income groups.
Results indicate dominance of husbands within subsistence
and marginal income groups and a syncratic pattern within
the middle class. Findings suggest that influence varies
by product. A fairly stable influence pattern is found for
each stage of the decision process.

INTRODUCTION

Historically, overseas markets have served as outlets for
the surplus production of U.S. firms. As major suppliers
of the world's industrial goods and services, U.S. firms
treated foreign nations as undifferentiated markets. In
the past ten years changes in the competitive nature of the
international market, bilateral and multilateral agreements, and anti-protectionist U.S. laws opened the American market to relatively uninhibited foreign competition,
requiring U.S. firms to approach foreign locations as discrete markets. Consequently, knowledge of the cultural
context in a given foreign market will be needed if U.S.
firms are to compete successfully with minimum risk.

During the sixties and seventies most U.S. firms concentrated efforts at foreign expansion on European markets.
Today, entry into or expansion within those markets is far
more hazardous because of competition from domestic producers and market saturation for many products. Consequently, U.S. firms have shifted their attention to nations
in Asia, Africa, and Latin America where populations are
large and rapidly growing, market saturation for a wide
range of consumer products is low, and per capita income
is rising above subsistence levels. While the Peoples'
Republic of China, Japan, and the oil-rich Middle East have
captured the media spotlight as top markets for the eight-
ies, Latin American countries deserve equal attention from
U.S. firms. This is especially true if they hope to stem
the growing encroachment by Japanese and Western and Eastern European firms into a region which the U.S. has long
dominated, because of geographic proximity and historic
ties.

Mexico, with its accessibility, trade linkages, and large
population, warrants special attention by U.S. firms. However, Mexico's development plans and recent balance-of-
payment considerations precipitated by the falling price
of oil on the world market discourage substantial imports
of foreign goods. These factors require that U.S. firms
carefully evaluate the Mexican market when formulating
strategies for entrance into that growing economy. This
evaluation must include not only a collection of data on
the legal and economic environment, but also an examination of consumer segments. A focus on households as basic
consuming units is a logical starting point for such data
collection efforts (Murphy 1979; Musgrove 1978, 1980).
Within this context the marketing research interest in the
influence of husbands and wives in purchasing decisions is
relevant (Cox 1975; Cunningham and Green 1974; Davis 1970,
1971; Davis and Rigaux 1974; Green and Cunningham 1975;
Shuptrine and Samuelson 1976; Wilkes 1975), given the
changing nature of sex roles in the modernizing world
(Higgs 1979; Inkles and Smith 1974; Kahl 1959, 1970; Rosen
and LaRaia 1972).

This paper deals with the pattern of influence in the purchase of consumer durables by Mexican households. Interdisciplinary support for this concentration derives from
sociological and anthropological studies revealing a
country-by-country variation in the relative influence of
family members across a wide spectrum of decisions (Lupri
1969; Queen, Habenstein, and Adams 1961; Safilios-Rothschild 1969; Rodman 1967). The paper fills a critical research gap in the marketing literature, since cross-cultural and country-specific studies of consumer behavior
have largely overlooked Mexico (Belisario 1982; Green and
Cunningham 1980; Davis and Rigaux 1974; Hempel 1974). With
respect to the role of women in Mexico, social science
studies have pointed to their evolving participatory role
in industrial centers (Johnson 1972; Kahl 1959, 1970; Rosen
and LaRaia 1972) and to a slow trend toward egalitarian
husband-wife decision making (Cromwell, Corrales, and
Tonsiello 1973; Ma. deLenero 1969 as reported in Cromwell
et al., based on the authors' translation). However, data
in these sociological studies relate to family problem
solving rather than specific products. In general, the
marketing literature has reflected the traditonal literary
and social science view of the Mexican male as the dominant
influence in the household (Fayerweather 1965; Diaz-
Guerrero 1979; Lewis 1963; Paz 1961).

The present paper brings empirical research to bear on this
stereotype and explores the variation in influence of family
members both in the purchase of different types of products
(Davis 1970; Davis and Rigaux 1974; Ferber 1974; Cunningham
and Green 1974; Sharp and Mott 1956; Wolgast 1958; Woodside
1972) and at different stages of the decision process
(Davis 1970; Davis and Rigaux 1974; Munsinger, Weber and
Hansen 1975; Wilkes 1975). This study concentrates on
household income as a significant stratification variable
(Dominguez and Page 1981) which can contribute to explaining differences in influence patterns. Specifically, three
questions are addressed:

1. Do perceptions of influence in family decision making
differ by income group?
2. Do perceptions of influence in family decision making
differ among income groups by product type?
3. Do perceptions of influence in family decision making
differ by income group at various stages in the decision
process?

The utility of this study to marketing is that it provides
an objective basis for segmenting the Mexican market and
evidence to modify the outmoded notion of overarching male
dominance within the Mexican household (Penalosa 1968).
Study results are useful in identifying the family members
to whom marketing efforts should be directed, in suggesting
product and packaging features appealing to the partner
with the dominant influence, in designing an appropriate
promotion strategy, and in selecting optimal retail outlets
(Engel and Blackwell 1982). For disciplines such as eco-
omics, sociology, and anthropology, which are concerned
with the effects of rising economic status on household and
individual behavior patterns, this study provides insight
into the relationship between household income and perceived
decision making influence within the household.

METHODOLOGY

Field Location

The data for this study were gathered in the state of
Oaxaca during the summer of 1981. To reflect the various
levels of modernization and industrialization within the
state, four cities were chosen for inclusion in the survey.
These cities were Oaxaca (pop. 185,000), Salina Cruz (pop.
65,000), Tehuantepec (pop. 24,000), and Etla (pop. 8,000).
Oaxaca, the state capital, represents a traditional administrative city where service and governmental occupations
predominate (Unikel 1976). Salina Cruz and Tehuantepec
are rapidly growing cities in a region impacted by the
current oil boom in Mexico. Salina Cruz is the location
of a new refinery and a refurbished port designed to export petroleum products and transship containerized cargo.
Tehuantepec, long the commercial center of the isthmus that
shares its name, is experiencing secondary growth in its
commercial and service sectors because of its proximity to
Salina Cruz. Finally, Etla is a district capital in the
valley of Oaxaca dominated by petty commercial and agricultural entrepreneurs. Because of the recent arrival of a
wood processing plant and an equipment depot for the federal electric commission, Etla is presently experiencing
moderate growth. The locations, then, represent the full
range of development activity to be found in the state.

Within each city an area was chosen for study which housed
workers in a major sector of the Mexican economy. Taken
together, the areas provide a representative sample of the
labor force in the state. Three of the four communities
studied (in Oaxaca, Salina Cruz, and Tehuantepec) were
government housing projects, where the opportunity to move
in and the actual lot assigned a family were determined by
lottery (Stepick and Murphy 1980). Thus, for example,
while the PEMEX (Petroleos Mexicanos, the national oil company) neighborhood housed only PEMEX workers, it represented a cross-section of the petroleum industry labor force-1
from night watchmen to accountants. This means that given
the use of a lottery to assign houses, neighborhoods do
not reflect homogeneous clusterings common in the United
States. Etla, a very old and traditional community, was,
of course, not laid out by lottery; but clustering of families by income or occupation is rare in traditional regions in Mexico. A convenience sample based on house location could thus be expected to yield a reasonably unbiased data set in each area. The number of households
interviewed in each area were: Oaxaca, 139; Salina Cruz,
43; Tehuantepec, 44; and Etla, 40.

Instrument and Sample

The survey instrument used gathered three types of information: (1) basic socio-economic data on each household
in the sample, (2) information on the household's standard
of living, and (3) perceptions of respondents regarding
who had most influenced each of three decision stages in
the purchase of twenty different consumer durables. This
paper focuses on data collected in the third part of the
questionnaire, in which one question dealt with the initiation phase of the purchase process; two questions probed
influence in the search stage; and one dealt with the final
decision stage. The English translation of these questions
and the decision stage they represent are as follows:

Question	Decision Stage
1. Who suggested the purchase of ________ ?	Initiation
2. Who investigated the brand?	Search
Who investigated the price?	Search
3. Who decided to purchase ________ ?	Final Decision

For each of the twenty items, the respondents were requested to indicate if the major influence at each stage
of the purchase decision had been the husband (_jefe_), the
wife (_jefa_), joint (_los dos_), or another (_otro_). In the
analysis presented here we have dropped the category
"another" because of its infrequence in the sample--less
than 3 percent of all responses. We are therefore using
a three-point scale in which husband = -1, wife = 0, and
joint = 1.

In each location the instrument was administered by trained female Mexican interviewers who were natives of the
cities under study, although not residents of the specific
area in which the instrument was being applied. Their
familiarity with the region and experience in the application of survey instruments made it possible for them to
speak comfortably with respondents, who were required to
be adult members of the household being visited. Most respondents were non-working women, who were married to the
male household head. The usual time and money constraints
required a household-based sample which to a large extent
excluded males who are generally either working or social-
izing with "male friendship groups." (Olien 1973, pp. 222-
224. Given that prior research has shown a strong agreement at the aggregate level between data obtained from
husbands and wives (Davis 1970; Granbois and Willett 1970)
and that our interest was in the cognitive perception of
influence, the responses obtained were judged capable of
yielding valid results.

Households fall into three income groups: subsistence-
level incomes, marginal incomes, and middle-class incomes. These three categories correspond to the three
major divisions used by the Mexican government and its
development agencies to classify households as to economic
potential and ability to enter into the modern commercial
market (Murphy and Selby 1980). Subsistence-level households are unable to apply for any type of aid program requiring the repayment of principle or interest. In 1981
in the state of Oaxaca these households earned less than
U.S. $200 (4500 pesos) per month. These households were
included in our survey for two reasons: (1) they represent the majority of the total Mexican population and (2)
they have the potential of becoming an attractive market
for a wide range of consumer durables in the coming years
because of the Mexican government's commitment to use its
oil resources to upgrade this group's economic position.
Households in the next income group, the marginals, have
sufficient resources to apply for government subsidized
consumer loans for such items as refrigerators, automobiles, and housing. Much of the current development money
in Mexico is flowing to this group, which has a monthly
household income of between U.S. $200 and U.S. $530 (4500
pesos and 12,000 pesos). The middle class is that group
which is qualified by the commercial banking industry to
apply for consumer loans directly from the banks without
the aid of government subsidies. Households in this group
are earning over U.S. $530 per month. In the city of
Oaxaca, where the predominant segment of the sample was
drawn, these groups represent 65 percent, 28 percent, and
7 percent of the households, respectively.

Of the twenty durables included in the original instrument,
eight were identified for further analysis and inclusion
in this paper, based on their uniform ownership across the
sample. The eight products vary in terms of cost and
their meaning in the Mexican national culture. However,
the infrequency of purchase is fairly consistent across
all products (Safilios-Rothschild 1969), which supports
extended problem solving with at least a three-stage decision process. A description of these consumer durables
follows:

1. Bed frame with mattress (_cama con colchon_). The bed
is traditionally part of the household furnishings provided by the husband and his family upon the patrilocal

marriage of the couple. It is a product that belongs to
the household and not to an individual. Prices range from
U.S. $150 to U.S. $600 for a regular double-bed size.
2. Stove--gas or electric (_estufa de gas o electrica_). The
stove, like the bed, is an item owned by the household and
not the wife or husband. This is especially true of the
larger gas and electric stoves, which require an investment of between U.S. $170 and U.S. $350.
3. Tape recorder (_grabadora_). A wide range of types and
prices is available for this product. In general, the tape
recorder is associated with the purchase of a second or
third portable radio for the household and is clearly an
entertainment item. Prices at the time of the study ranged from U.S. $20 to U.S. $200.
4. Blender (_liquadora_). In Mexico the blender has become
a required household item for any home that can afford one.
It functionally replaces the stone grinder (_mano_ and _met-
ate_), which was formerly used in making most of the dishes
commonly served. Like the _mano_ and _metate_, the blender is
considered the wife's property. Traditionally, a woman
was given a grinder at marriage, and it often lasted
throughout her entire life. The relatively low price of
blenders (U.S. $30 to U.S. $130) makes it possible for
women to purchase these directly and for most homes to
have one regardless of income category.
5. Electric iron (_plancha electrica_). As with the blender,
this is the wife's property, and given the low cost (U.S.
$15 to U.S. $40), most women can own one.
6. Radio (_radio_). Today in Mexico it is a virtual necessity for a home to have a radio. When new they range upward in price from U.S. $20, making them within reach of
almost any household. Unlike the tape recorder and television, which are entertainment items, the radio is the
household's link to the outside world. It is the major
source of news and information concerning events in the
town and neighborhood.
7. Refrigerator (_refrigerador_). This is the most expansive
consumer durable among the eight products, and the one owned by the fewest number of households. Prices begin at
U.S. $400 for a small apartment sized unit and rise to over
U.S. $2500 for the larger models. For those households
that can afford one, a refrigerator represents a signif-
cant step up in consumption patterns.
8. Television (_televisor_). With the least expensive televisions priced around U.S. $200, this item represents a
major investment in entertainment by the household. The
proliferation of TVs often noted in the literature on
Mexico is largely due to a flourishing market in used sets.
These second-hand sets are purchased on time at heavy interest rates from repair shops selling sets that have not
been claimed after repair.

FINDINGS

Income Group

Our first question asks whether a significant difference
exists in husbands' and wives' perceptions of influence after controlling for household income. The answer is une-
quivocably affirmative. Among subsistence-level households
there is a marked male dominance, with respondents in this
group indicating that males are the dominant influencers
for 76 percent (745) of all decision stages concerning the
purchase of the products under investigation. As the
household's ability to participate in the monetary economy
increases, a reduction in the dominant position of males
appears. At first the change is not dramatic with 64 percent (1893) of the decisions in the marginal group still
being made by males alone; but among the middle class,
males alone make only 19 percent (293) of all product decisions. This finding is consistent with research on family influence in Greece and Yugoslavia which revealed a
negative correlation between the husband's income and authority score, but is in contrast with data on the United
States and France showing a positive association between

husband's influence and income (Rodman 1967).

Of particular interest is the fact that little or no difference is evident in the level of independent female decision making across groups. The percentage of decisions
made by women alone stays fairly constant, at 11 percent
(113), 14 percent (418), and 13 percent (191) for the subsistence, marginal, and middle income households, respectively. This, coupled with the observed rise in joint decision making--from 13 percent (127) in the poorest group
and 22 percent (637) in the marginal group to 68 percent
(1024) in the middle income group--suggests that while respondents in the middle class see women as having a greater
role in the purchase of consumer durables, these women are
not making decisions without the husband's influence. Thus
while women are perceived as more important in the decision making process among the more affluent households,
their role is not seen as independent.

Product Type

Table 1 addresses the second question, which deals with the
influence of husbands and wives in the purchase of specific
products, controlling for household income. Overall findings confirm variations in family influence by product category found in studies of U.S. consumers (Cunningham and
Green 1974; Davis and Rigaux 1974; Woodside 1972). The
first feature emerging from the table is that women are
seen as exerting a disproportionate influence over the decision process for electric blenders and irons regardless
of income group. This tendency is most marked in the upper
two income groups, where household income is sufficient to
allow the woman to purchase a product considered her property (as opposed to the household's) without consulting her
husband or other family members. The only other product
perceived as consistently dominated by a single individual
across all income groups is the radio. Now considered a
basic necessity, this item can be purchased by the male
household head without disrupting the family's budget. The
other product traditionally provided by the male head--the
bed--is skewed towards the male among the two lower-income
groups, as would be expected. In contrast, among the middle class we find a joint pattern of influence.

In the sample over 75 percent (99) of the decisions concerning stoves purchased by subsistence-level households
were dominated by men. As indicated by Table 1, this figure is close to the expected value, especially given the
fact that stoves are also seen as part of the household
furnishings provided by the husband. The interesting feature with stoves is that respondents among the marginal and
middle-income populations perceive females as making a disproportionate number of the decisions related to the stove
purchase, indicating that women in households with incomes
above the subsistence level may be acquiring greater power
over the purchase of consumer durables for which they are
the primary users. That this trend is occurring with
stoves is significant because it provides evidence that women are also exerting influence over items not only defined
as having household ownership, but requiring a relatively
high level of investment.

Among the durable goods discussed in this paper, two are
essentially household entertainment items: the tape recorder and the television. In general, entertainment items
which would consume a substantial share of the household
budget either are the prerogative of the male household
head or, more commonly, are purchased as the result of a
syncratic decision process. Table 1 illustrates that this
is the case for both tape recorders and televisions, with
the exception of tape recorders purchased by middle-class
households. In the latter case, men are seen as dominating
somewhat more than their expected share of the decision
process, which may relate to the fact that household incomes are of sufficient magnitude that the purchase does
not strain the family's resources.

3

TABLE 1

DEVIATION FROM EXPECTED VALUE IN INFLUENCE PATTERNS
ACROSS CONSUMER DURABLE PURCHASES FOR THREE INCOME GROUPS

Income Group	Bed	Stove	Tape Recorder	Blender	Iron	Radio	Refrigerator	TV	N
Subsistence $x^2 = 68.26$; $p \leq .001$.									
Male	12	2	−1	−12	−9	17	−9	0	(745)
Female	0	−3	−5	9	8	−4	−2	−3	(113)
Joint	−11	0	6	3	1	−13	11	−3	(127)
N	(187)	(128)	(44)	(111)	(132)	(243)	(40)	(100)	
Marginal $x^2 = 224.44$; $p \leq .001$.									
Male	20	−10	5	−17	−38	64	−37	14	(1893)
Female	−25	15	−14	29	61	−26	−7	−33	(418)
Joint	5	−5	9	−12	−23	−38	44	20	(637)
N	(491)	(411)	(147)	(374)	(434)	(508)	(243)	(340)	
Middle Class $x^2 = 197.67$; $p \leq .001$.									
Male	−11	−1	23	−17	−17	21	1	0	(293)
Female	−20	8	−18	17	45	−7	−9	−15	(191)
Joint	31	−7	−5	0	−28	−14	8	15	(1024)
N	(205)	(119)	(183)	(207)	(209)	(206)	(196)	(183)	

The tendency in households towards joint decision making
when purchasing big-ticket items is most notably illustrated in the case of refrigerators. The expense of this
item, together with the fact that the purchase usually involves consumer credit, means that its purchase probably
demands input from all major household members.

Decision Stages

Our third question asks whether or not the perceptions of
influence change in the various stages of the decision
process. Figure 1 represents the total mean influence for
the eight consumer durables plotted for each income group.
The figure illustrates the more syncratic nature of decision making among the middle class households when compared to the marginal and subsistence level households.
However, in contrast with other studies which have shown
influence shifting from one decision phase to another
(Belisario 1982; Davis 1970; Davis and Rigaux 1974: Wilkes
1975), we find little difference among the three decision
stages.

CONCLUSIONS AND IMPLICATIONS FOR FURTHER RESEARCH

While the study's results cannot be generalized to the entire Mexican population, selection of a traditional state
like Oaxaca provide evidence that a patriarchal pattern
should not be attributed to all consumer segments within
this market. With rising income, perceptions of influence shift from male-dominant to syncratic. Within each
income group differences in relative influence are associated with high cost in the case of the refrigerator and
female use in the case of the electric iron and blender.
These differences underscore the need to research the
cultural context as well as objective criteria such as
price and usage patterns of consumer goods before designing marketing strategies.

Further research is needed to determine why contrasts in
relative influence by decision stage do not appear in

FIGURE 1

MEAN INFLUENCE IN EIGHT CONSUMER DURABLE
PURCHASES AT THREE DECISION PROCESS STAGES

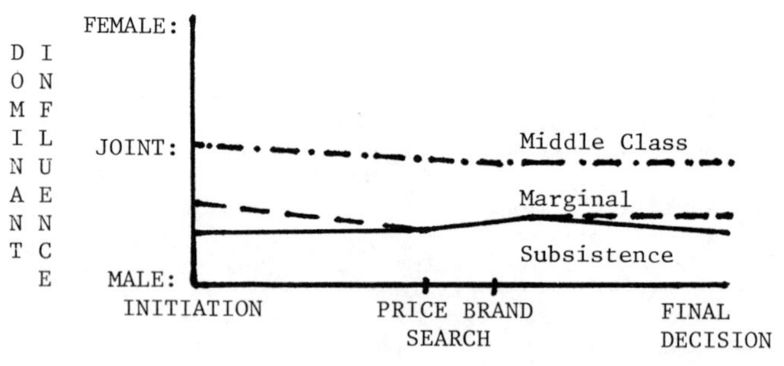

this sample, although they are frequently found in consumer research studies within other developed and developing countries. A possible explanation may be the limited
educational background and experience with consumer durable purchases by this population segment, which could account for minimum role specialization. Further research
should include higher income segments, greater representation of male household heads, and less traditional areas
of Mexico. Products selected should incorporate a similar
range of household expenditures and use conditions congruent with living standards within this rapidly growing
market. The marketing implications of this study are that
marketing programs must be differentiated by income group
and product category to reach the most influential family
member. Continued reliance on the traditional male stereotype or substitution of a female-dominant model will
fail to win a sizable proportion of the Mexican population.

REFERENCES

Belisario, G. Cabrejos (1982), "Family Role Structure: A Comparative Analysis Between the U.S.A. and Colombia," unpublished Ph.D. dissertation, Department of Marketing, University of Georgia.

Cox, E. P. (1975), "Family Purchase Decision Making and the Process of Adjustment," Journal of Marketing Research, 12 (May), 189-95.

Cromwell, R. E., Ramon Corrales, and Peter M. Torsiello (1973), "Normative Patterns of Marital Decision Making Power and Influence in Mexico and the United States: A Partial Test of Resources and Ideology Theory," Journal of Comparative Family Studies, August, 177-96.

Cunningham, Isabella C. M. and Robert T. Green (1974), "Purchasing Roles in the U.S. Family, 1955 and 1973." Journal of Marketing, 38 (October), 61-81.

Davis, Harry L. (1970), "Dimensions of Marital Roles in Consumer Decision Making," Journal of Marketing Research, 7 (May), 168-77.

__________ (1971), "Measurement of Husband-Wife Influence in Consumer Purchase Decisions," Journal of Marketing Research, 8 (August), 305-312.

__________, and Benny P. Rigaux (1974), "Perception of Marital Roles in Decision Processes," Journal of Consumer Research, 1 (June), 51-62.

Diaz-Guerrero, Rogelio (1979), Estudios de Psicologia del Mexicano, Mexico City: Editorial Trillas.

Dominquez, Louis V. and Albert L. Page (1981), "Stratification in Consumer Behavior Research: A Re-Examination," Journal of the Academy of Marketing Science, 9 (Summer), 250-273.

Engel, James F., and Roger D. Blackwell (1982), Consumer Behavior, 4th ed., New York: Holt Rinehart and Winston.

Fayerweather, John (1965), International Marketing, Englewood Cliffs, N.J.: Prentice-Hall.

Ferber, Robert, and Lucy Chao Lee (1974), "Husband-Wife Influence in Family Purchasing Behavior," Journal of Consumer Research, 1 (June), 43-50.

Granbois, D. H., and Ronald P. Willett (1970), "Equivalence of Family Role Measures Based on Husband and Wife Data," Journal of Marriage and the Family, February, 68-72.

Green, Robert T., and Isabella C. M. Cunningham (1975), "Feminine Role Perception and Family Purchasing Decisions," Journal of Marketing Research, 12 (August), 325-32.

__________, and __________ (1980), "Family Purchasing Roles in Two Countries," Journal of International Business Studies, Spring/Summer, 92-97.

Hempel, Donald J. (1974), "Family Buying Decisions: A Cross-Cultural Perspective," Journal of Marketing Research, 11 (August), 295-302.

Higgs, Elizabeth W. (1979), "Value Modification Among Contemporary Brazilian Women: A Case Study of Urban Protestant Women in Sao Paulo," unpublished Master's thesis, Department of Anthropology, University of Georgia.

Inkeles, Alex, and David H. Smith (1974), Becoming Modern: Individual Change in Six Developing Countries, Cambridge, Mass.: Harvard University Press.

Johnson, Allan (1972), "Modernization and Social Change: Attitudes Toward Women's Roles in Mexico City," unpublished Ph.D. dissertation, Department of Sociology, University of Michigan.

Kahl, Joseph A. (1959), "Some Social Concomitants of Industrialization and Urbanization," Human Organization, 18, 53-74.

__________ (1970), The Measurement of Modernism: A Study of Values in Brazil and Mexico, Austin: University of Texas Press.

Lewis, Oscar (1963), The Children of Sanchez: Autobiography of a Mexican Family, New York: Random House.

Lupri, Eugene (1969), "Contemporary Authority Patterns in the West German Family: A Study in Cross-National Validation," Journal of Marriage and the Family, 31 (February), 134-44.

Munsinger, Gary M., Jean E. Weber and Richard W. Hansen (1975), "Joint Home Purchasing Decisions by Husbands and Wives," Journal of Consumer Research, (March), 60-66.

Murphy, Arthur D. (1979), "Urbanization, Development, and Household Adaptive Strategies in Oaxaca, a Secondary City of Mexico," unpublished Ph.D. dissertation, Department of Anthropology, Temple University.

__________, and Henry A. Selby (1980), "Proverty and the Domestic Life Cycle in Oaxaca, an Intermediate City of Mexico," paper presented at the Intermediate Cities in Asia meeting, East-West Center, Honolulu, Hawaii, July.

Musgrove, Philip (1978), "Determinants of Urban Household Consumption in Latin America: A Summary of Evidence from the ECIEL Surveys," Economic Development and Cultural Change, 26 (3), 441-65.

__________ (1980), "Household Size and Composition, Employment, and Poverty in Urban Latin America," Economic Development and Cultural Change, 28 (2), 249-66.

Olien, Michael D. (1973), Latin Americans: Contemporary Peoples and Their Cultural Traditions, New York: Holt, Rinehart and Winston, Inc.

Paz, Octavio (1961), The Labyrinth of Solitude: Life and Thought in Mexico, New York: Grove Press, Inc.

Penalosa, Fernado (1968), "Mexican Family Role," Journal of Marriage and the Family, November, 680-89.

Queen, Stuart A., Robert W. Habenstein, and John B. Adams (1961), The Family in Various Cultures, J. B. Lippincott Company.

Rodman, Hyman (1967), "Marital Power in France, Greece, Yugoslavia, and the United States: A Cross-National Discussion," Journal of Marriage and the Family, 29 (May), 320-24.

Rosen, Bernard C., and Anita L. LaRaia (1972), "Modernity in Women: An Index of Social Change in Brazil," Journal of Marriage and the Family. 34 (May), 353-60.

Safilios-Rothschild, Constantina (1969), "Family Sociology or Wives' Family Sociology? A Cross-Cultural Examination of Decision Making," Journal of Marriage and the Family 31 (May), 290-301.

Sharp, Harry, and Paul Mott (1956), "Consumer Decisions
in the Metroplitan Family," <u>Journal of Marketing</u>, 21
(October), 149-56.

Shuptrine, F. K., and G. Samuelson (1976), "Dimensions of
Martial Roles in Consumer Decision Making: Revisited,"
"<u>Journal of Marketing Research</u>, 13 (February), 87-91.

Stepick, Alex, and Arthur D. Murply (1980), "Comparing
Squatter Settlements and Government Self-Help Projects
as Housing Solutions in Oaxaca, Mexico," <u>Human Organiza-
tion</u>, 39 (4), 339-43.

Unikel, Luis (1976), <u>El desarrollo urbano de Mexico</u>, Mexi-:
co, D. F.: Colegio de Mexico.

Wilkes, Robert E. (1975), "Husband-Wife Influence in Purchase Decisions--A Confirmation and Extension," <u>Journal
of Marketing Research</u>, 12 (May), 224-27.

Wolgast, Elizabeth H. (1958), "Do Husbands or Wives Make
Purchasing Decisions?" <u>Journal of Marketing</u>, 23 (October)
151-58.

Woodside, Arch G. (1972), "Dominance and Conflict in Family
Purchasing Decisions," <u>Association for Consumer Research
Proceedings</u>, 650-659.

A CONCEPTUAL MODEL OF INTERPERSONAL
PURCHASE INFLUENCE IN ORGANIZATIONS

Robert J. Thomas, University of Pennsylvania

ABSTRACT

Interpersonal purchase influence is viewed as a concept important to the understanding of multiple-person aspects of organizational buying behavior. Influence is defined as a process between persons rather than as a characteristic of a person. A multi-level conceptual model of interpersonal purchase influence is developed, hypothesizing that the role expectations of one member for another will explain the outcome of the influence process. Alternative model formulations involving various sets of factors are presented for empirical testing. An empirical comparison of four such models is briefly presented to illustrate the modeling approach.

INTRODUCTION

The marketing of products and services to organizations involves understanding the purchase behavior of organizations as "consumers," and developing a marketing program to satisfy their needs. An implementation of this approach is especially complicated in organizational buying decision processes due to the involvement of multiple persons. This complexity is evident in the macro-models of Webster and Wind (1972), Sheth (1973), and Bonoma, Zaltman, and Johnston (1977). While these models recognize and depict some of the multiple-person complexities of organizational buying behavior, they provide few guidelines for their operationalization and empirical testing. An alternative to this macro-modeling approach is through the modeling of selected concepts which are central to organizational buying behavior; i.e., a micro-modeling approach. These concepts (when operationally defined), become the major dependent variable. Each has the potential of being explained by numerous other factors (independent variables) which are theoretically relevant to the concept.

There are two objectives of this paper: (a) to develop a micro-model of _interpersonal_ _purchase_ _influence_, a concept which assumes central importance when considering multi-person buying situations in organizations, and (b) to suggest alternative hypotheses (or model formulations) which may be the bases for empirical tests. Besides the recognition of interpersonal influence in macro-models, its importance in organizational buying is evidenced by the concern among practitioners to identify "key buying influentials" (Weigand 1968). In the first part of this paper, the concept of interpersonal purchase influence is defined. The realization of this definition in a conceptual model is presented in the second part. Alternative hypotheses and conclusions are then presented in the final parts of this paper, along with a brief presentation of an empirical example.

DEFINING INTERPERSONAL PURCHASE INFLUENCE

Consistent with social influence theorists, interpersonal influence is defined as a _process_ between persons rather than as a characteristic of a person (Cartwright 1965; Dahl 1968; Tedeschi, Schlenker, and Lindskold 1972; Nagel 1975). An influence process involves a focal person called the receiver (denoted by an R), whose state is affected by the _state_ of another person, called the _source_ (denoted by an S). A person's state refers to any attribute or set of attributes characterizing the person (e.g. resources, attitude, behavior, etc.). The influence process may or may not involve interpersonal interaction, however some form of communication (one or two-way) between R and S is a necessary condition. Robertson (1971, p. 170) provides a comprehensive classification of the types of communications leading to influence possibilities.

In the influence process, R's state may be changed through some "method" of influence associated with S. Influence methods can run the gamut from the relatively inert method based solely on R's awareness of S's state (the case of anticipated reactions discussed by Nagel 1975) to the more active methods involving social pressure (Asch 1953; Mowday 1978) and explicit influencing strategies (Perreault and Miles 1978).

The nature of change in R's state caused by S's state is viewed as the "outcome" of the interpersonal influence process. In a dyadic situation, sequentially, the two persons involved may be sources _and_ receivers of influence. In this case, the outcome would reflect the effects of their interaction on each other.

One of the important aspects of a decision-maker's state in organizational buying is multiattribute product evaluations. It is in this sense that S's effect on R is referred to as interpersonal _purchase_ influence. More specifically, interpersonal purchase influence is defined as _the outcome on R's state_ (e.g., the change in multiattribute product evaluations of a person involved in organizational buying) _brought about by the state of another_ _organization member through some method_. Each component of this definition can be operationalized using various influence measurement approaches (Wind 1976, Thomas 1980). In addition to being operational, an advantage of this conceptual definition is that it links a measurable outcome variable (e.g., change in product evaluations) to a social system of interest. The nature of the social system and its linkage to the outcome are critical to developing a conceptual model of interpersonal purchase influence in organizations.

A MODEL OF INTERPERSONAL PURCHASE INFLUENCE

The definition of interpersonal purchase influence presented above derives meaning from its relationship to other concepts. For example, the change in R's state, caused by S's state immediately implies the use of certain concepts from the behavioral sciences to describe the states of the parties involved. In an organizational setting, the relationship between R and S may be affected by their respective department's, the characteristics of the organizations of which they are members, and various environmental factors. A diagram of the model used to conceptualize interpersonal purchase influence, and the major factors involved, is presented in Figure 1.

The model depicted in Figure 1 is based on a role-theoretic view of organizations presented by Katz and Kahn (1978). The role relations between a focal person and others involved in buying are hypothesized to explain the outcome of the interpersonal influence process. The outcome of the influence process (however defined) is hypothesized to _partly_ explain the organizational purchase decision; partly, since other concepts or factors may also contribute to explaining the purchase decision.

7

FIGURE 1

A CONCEPTUAL MODEL OF INTERPERSONAL
PURCHASE INFLUENCE IN ORGANIZATIONS

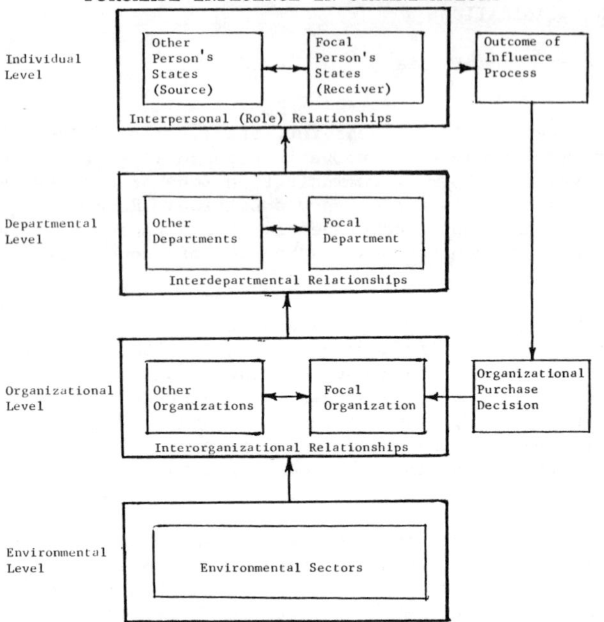

Katz and Kahn (1978) also recognize the possibility that organizational and environmental factors may have an effect on role relations. In Figure 1, these factors are hypothesized to hierarchically affect role relationships. That is, factors at the environmental level are hypothesized to explain factors at the organizational level, which are in turn hypothesized to explain factors at the departmental level, which are hypothesized to explain factors at the individual level. An alternative set of hypotheses suggests that factors at each level may have a direct affect on factors beyond the next level. For example, environmental factors may explain departmental or individual level factors beyond the next level. For example, environmental factors may explain departmental or individual level factors, and organizational factors may explain individual level factors.

Within each of the levels, in Figure 1 (except at the environmental level) the interrelationships among the various units are the basis for describing behavioral processes. For example, role theory will be used below to further model the interpersonal influence process at the individual level. At the organization level, Evan (1966) uses an "organization-set" model (based on role theory) to explain inter-organizational relationships. This is a useful conceptualization in organizational buying since a "focal" organization (the buyer) may engage in relationships with various suppliers and other organizations. At the departmental level, the same conceptual modeling approach can be taken to depict interdepartmental relations. An example is provided by Hickson, et al (1971) in explaining the power of organizational subunits, or departments. In their "strategic contingencies theory," they hypothesize that the power of subunits results from contingent dependencies among them created by unspecified combinations of (a) coping with uncertainty, (b) work flow centrality, and (c) nonsubstitutability of a particular activity. Hinings, et al (1974) found support for these hypotheses.

With respect to environmental factors, Katz and Kahn (1978, p. 124) consider five environmental sectors with which organizations may establish relationships. They suggest that all organizations function (1) within the value patterns of the cultural environment in which they are embedded, (2) within the political structure or pattern of legal norms and statutes that define their formal

legitimacy and limit their activities, (3) within the economic environment of competitive markets and competitive sources of input such as labor force and materials, (4) within the informational and technological environment, and (5) within the natural or physical environment of geography, natural resources, and climate. The consequences of the effects of these environmental factors are the situations created within an organization which are related to purchasing. For example, changing regulatory requirements which affect production processes may alter purchasing patterns.

Thus, while the model in Figure 1 hypothesizes that role relationships among individuals explain the outcome of influence processes, departmental, organizational, and environmental factors are hypothesized to impinge on role relationships. However, according to Katz and Kahn (1978), p. 186), the concept of a role "is the summation of the requirements with which the system confronts the individual member." That is, the role concept includes the effects of departmental, organizational, and environmental factors. It is this role-theoretic view (which should be subject to empirical testing) that is the basis for the model of interpersonal purchase influence. Given this overview of the model, more specific components are considered in the following sections.

Outcome of the Influence Process

The outcome of the influence process can be defined at the individual or interactional level. The interactional unit of analysis focuses on the interpersonal relations of individuals involved in a social situation. Theorizing by Thibaut and Kelley (1959) and Blau (1964), provide descriptive analyses of interpersonal relations as the important feature of the influence process. With this unit of analysis, influence is a function of the outcome matrix of an interpersonal relationship. More specifically, each individual involved in the relationship has a repetoire of behavior sequences which consist of all the responses a person is capable of enacting. Interaction is composed of two or more persons performing some sequences from their repetoire. The successive pairing of sequences produces an outcome or series of outcomes which has a subjective value as the ability of one person to affect the quality of his partner's outcomes (Thibaut and Kelley 1959).

While the interactional unit of analysis provides the ability to develop a more detailed and realistic depiction of interpersonal influence, this detail makes it difficult to operationalize for purposes of measurement. This is recognized by Zaltman and Bonoma (1977) who propose that organizational buying behavior be conceptualized as an exchange process based on interaction. Further, when considering organizational buying in many new task and modified rebuy purchase situations, interaction among buying center participants may be negligible. Consequently, for the remainder of this discussion, the individual will be the focal unit of analysis in the outcome of the influence process.

Consistent with the definition of interpersonal purchase influence, the outcome can be described in terms of the effects of the interpersonal relations on R, the receiver of influence. The outcome effect of interest is on R's product evaluations. If R is assumed to be the focal decision-maker in the organizational buying process, then R's product evaluations (or utility function) is predicitive of the organizational purchase decision (brand choice, supplier selection, etc.). As R is exposed to other members of the organization involved in buying, R's product evaluations over time are, therefore, viewed as the dependent variable in the model. The independent variables are derived from the relationship between R and S (where S can be one person, a group, or a sequence of persons).

The Relationship Between the Source and Receiver of Influence

In a role-oriented view of interpersonal purchase influence in organizations, as summarized from Katz and Kahn (1978), each person involved in buying is linked to a set of relevant others involved in buying because of the functional requirement of the system, i.e., the buying task. These requirements are implemented through the expectations which other members have of the "focal person." Thus, the focal person and relevant others make up a role-set (Merton, 1957), and the "buying center" (Wind 1967) is viewed as a number of such role-sets, one for each person in the buying center.

The expectations of role-set members are linked to the focal person through the role "episode." It consists of a sequence of events involving members of a role-set and the focal person. The sequence begins with "role expectations" held by members of the role-set for the focal person. These role expectations are evaluative standards applied to the behavior of the focal person. These expectations are then "sent" or communicated (as attempts to influence) to the focal person; i.e., the act of "role-sending."

The second part of the role episode involves the perceptions and behavior of the focal person; i.e., the "received role." This received role is hypothesized to be the immediate source of influence and motivation of behavior from other members of the role-set. Since it is based on the focal person's perceptions of the expectations of other role-set members, they are referred to as "role-set expectations." Finally, the actual role behavior of the focal person represents the response to the complex of information received. The response can be varying combinations of compliance or noncompliance with respect to the expectations of the role-set. The role-set members evaluate the focal person's reaction in terms of their expectations, and the cycle moves to another episode.

It should be noted from Katz and Kahn (1978, p. 191) that, "as a communicative and influential process, acts of role-sending can be characterized in terms of any of the dimensions appropriate to the measurement of communication and influence." Therefore, influence has been defined as a process, which is similar to the communication process, and is now anchored to the social system of interest (the organization) via role theory. Specific variables in the model are considered in the following section.

Variables Describing Source and Receiver States

Figure 2 more explicitly characterizes the variables involved in explaining the outcome of the interpersonal purchase influence process. It is magnification of the "individual level" presented in Figure 1. Four role factors are selected which are essential to the characterization of role relationships between R and S (Katz and Kahn 1978) --however, there are at least 20 other possible role variables defined by Alutto (1968) which can be used. In Katz and Kahn's theory, S's expectations, with respect to R, are hypothesized to explain the outcome of the influence process.

S's expectations for R in a purchase situation are defined by S's product preferences (evaluation, utility function, etc.) and "bases of social power." French and Raven (1959) define bases of power or influence in terms of R's perceptions that S has abilities to mediate the outcome of their relationship. Reward, coercive, legitimate, referent, and expert bases provide a taxonomy of the kinds of factors in S which, if perceived as such by R, can influence R's behavior. These bases of influence in S are assumed to reflect many of S's personal characteristics and position in the organization. For example, S's expertise may be derived from S's education,

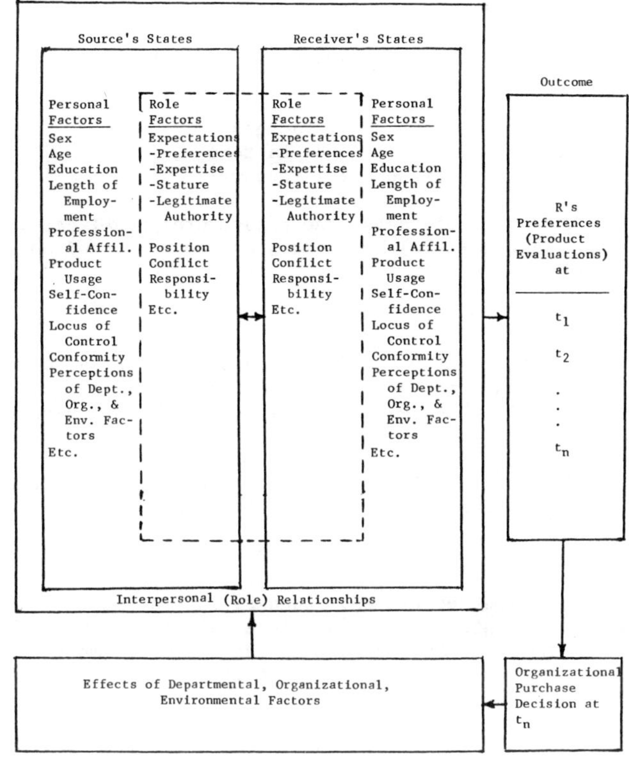

experience, length of employment in the organization, and so on.

Katz and Kahn (1978) also suggests that the extent to which R accepts a sent role may depend on other aspects of R's state besides S's expectations. Some of these personal factors are indicated in Figure 2. They are selected from reviews of several influence-related literatures (organizational, family, group, and community decision-making), however, they are by no means an exhaustive list. These personal factors of R can be hypothesized to mediate the extent to which R is influenced by S's expectations for R. However, other hypothesized formulations of the relationships among variables and variable sets in the model are possible, and considered in the next part of the paper.

ALTERNATIVE MODEL FORMULATIONS

The variables and variable sets presented in the preceding sections, which are assumed to conceptualize a general model of interpersonal purchase influence defined earlier, can now be considered in more specific formulations. These specific formulations, or hypotheses about interpersonal purchase influence in organizations, are presented in terms of a dependent variable and explanatory independent variables which can be empirically tested. As the model, the hypotheses are derived from the theoretical presentation by Katz and Kahn (1978).

In these formulations the dependent variable is the outcome of the influence process on an assumed decision-maker, R (or receiver of influence), and the independent variables are sets of factors relevant to S (the source of influence), R, and their respective departments, organizations, and environments. (It should be noted that S can be a member of an organization, other than R's, yet still be a participant in the buying process.)

To depict alternative hypotheses, let:

Y = outcome of the influence process
(e.g., R's change in multiattribute
product evaluations from t_1 to t_n.)

r = role factors

$S_{E(r)}$ = S's role expectations for R

p = personal factors
d = departmental factors
o = organizational factors
e = environmental factors

Using these variable sets, the fundamental model based on
Katz and Kahn's (1978) hypothesis can be expressed as
follows:

$$Y = f(S_{E(r)}). \tag{1}$$

That is, changes in R's product evaluations are a function
of S's role expectations for R. As discussed in the conceptual model, these expectations could be S's preferences
and bases of power.

A second model formulation which accounts for other factors
relevant to R can be expressed as follows:

$$Y = f(S_{E(r)} | R_r, R_p, R_d, R_o, R_e). \tag{2}$$

This model hypothesizes that changes in R's product evaluations are a function of S's role expectations for R, however, as mediated by R's role, personal, departmental, organizational, and environmental factors. The last three
sets of factors would be defined in terms of R's <u>percep-
tion</u>; e.g., perceived organizational size, rather than an
objective measure of size. Using objective measures of departmental, organizational, and environmental factors rather than perceived measures would result in the following
model:

$$Y = f(S_{E(r)} | R_r, R_p, d, o, e). \tag{3}$$

While formulations (2) and (3) above hypothesize that the
outcome of the influence process is mediated by other fac-
tors--that is, their effects on y are accounted for before
evaluating the effects of $S_{E(r)}$ (in an analysis of covariance sense)--an alternative hypothesis is that the outcome is explained by all factors simultaneously. That is,

$$Y = f(S_{E(r)}, R_r, R_p, d, o, e). \tag{4}$$

This model suggests that all the factors involved might independently affect R's product evaluations rather than
working through role-set expectations as hypothesized by
Katz and Kahn (1978).

Clearly, there are other model formulations which can be
considered, especially if consistent with extant theories,
hypotheses, and findings from the behavioral science literatures. For example, effects at the interpersonal level
can be hypothesized to be caused by effects from the departmental level, which can be caused by effects from the
organizational level, and so on. The model could then be
operationalized as a system of simultaneous equations.

An Empirical Example

Thus far, the discussion has focused on variable sets at a
conceptual level. The design of research to test the above
models would necessitate the selection of specific variables within these sets (based on past findings), their
conceptual and operational definition, the collection of
data to provide valid and reliable measures, and the analytical procedures to test the models. This is beyond the
scope of this paper although the results of one set of
model comparisons are presented in Table 1 to illustrate
the approach. The variables, data collection methods, and

TABLE 1

STANDARDIZED REGRESSION COEFFICIENTS AND R^2 VALUES
FOR FOUR REGRESSION EQUATIONS*:
MAD CHANGE SCORES AGAINST INFLUENCE CORRELATES**

Set #	Independent Variables	Total Sample (N=144) Variable Sets Included In Regression Equations			
		I Only	I+II Only	I+II+III Only	I+II+III+IV
I	S=Stature	.16a	.16a	.17a	.17a
	E=Expertise	.19a	.19a	.18a	.18a
	A=Authority	.19a	.20a	.19a	.18a
	P=Preference	.14b	.12	.06	.06
	SE=Interaction	.04	.04	.03	.04
	SA "	-.07	-.07	-.07	-.07
	SP "	-.02	-.02	-.02	-.06
	EA "	-.25a	-.25a	-.23a	-.24a
	EP "	.02	.03	.05	.06
	AP "	.02	.01	-.01	-.02
	SEA "	.09	.10	.08	.08
	SEP "	.01	.01	-.05	-.08
	SAP "	.01	.01	-.02	-.01
	EAP "	.18a	.17a	.16a	.19a
	SEAP "	.12	.13	.08	.12
II	S-R Conflict		.03	.03	-.02
	Role Responsibility		.04	-.00	.03
III	Locus of Control(Luck,Fate)			.04	.01
	Locus of Control(Planning)			-.07	-.06
	Conformity(Org.Oriented)			.10	.11
	Conformity(Self-Oriented)			.08	.06
	Gen. Self Confidence			.14	.15b
	Spec. Self Confidence			.07	.05
	Age			-.23a	-.20
	Education			.05	.06
	Prof. Affiliation			.04	.03
	Sex			-.04	-.01
	Authority Self-Attribution			-.29b	-.23
	Expertise Self-Attribution			-.28b	-.23
	Stature Self-Attribution			-.22b	-.22b
IV	Centralization				-.16
	Innovativeness				.08
	Size				.04
	Effectiveness				-.07
	R^2	.24	.24	.33	.35
	Adjusted R^2	.16	.14	.16	.16
	Change in R^2		(-)	(.02)	(-)
	p for Equation	.001	.003	.01	.02

* The cell values are standardized regression coefficients
obtained from the BMDPIR program (Dixon, 1975). The letter
<u>a</u> by a value denotes the variable is significant at the .05
level; the letter <u>b</u> denotes the variable is significant at
the .10 level.

** I= Role-set expectation variables
II= Other role correlates
III= Personal correlates
IV= Organizational correlates

analytical procedures from which this table is derived, are
presented by Thomas (1980). The four models tested in
Table 1 are presented below:

$$Y = f(S_{E(r)})$$

$$Y = f(S_{E(r)}, R_r)$$

$$Y = f(S_{E(r)}, R_r, R_p)$$

$$Y = f(S_{E(r)}, R_r, R_p, R_o),$$

where Y is defined as the mean absolute deviation (MAD) of
changes in R's evaluations of five product attributes before and after exposure to an S with selected expectations
for R. In this field experiment involving 144 respondents
in 63 organizations, the Stimulus S was defined to the respondent as another organization member with certain characteristics. These characteristics were three bases of
social power (Stature, Expertise, Authority) and S's preferences. These four factors, each at two levels, were
used to make up 16 profiles of S which were randomly assigned to 16 treatment groups. The independent variables
in Table 1 are a subset of 62 variables factor analyzed to
reduce multicollinearity.

Briefly, the regression results reveal that the successive
addition of R's role, personal, and perceived organizational factors adds little to the explanation of R's change
in product evaluations; this is evidenced by the miniscule
change in R^2. This finding would tend to support Katz and
Kahn's (1978) hypothesis that S's expectations for R are
the immediate motivations of R's behavior; i.e.,
$Y = f(S_{E(r)})$.

SUMMARY AND CONCLUSION

Organizational buying behavior is indeed complex, as are
attempts to model it at a macro-level. In this paper a
micro-modeling approach has been used as a tool to begin to
manage some of the complexity. Interpersonal purchase influence is considered an important concept in organizational buying and was briefly defined. Subsequently, a conceptual model of interpersonal purchase influence was developed from the definition and accepted role theory of organizations. From this conceptual model, more specific
model formulations were developed which represent empirically testable hypotheses.

The conceptual model presented focused primarily on the effects of an influence source on a receiver, who is assumed
to be an individual decision-maker. Extensions and further
developments of the model should consider the outcome in
terms of joint decision-making. Certain products and services require multiple decision-makers; i.e., how participants influence each other reciprocally in a buying situation needs additional modeling and hypotheses. Nevertheless, a first step is taken here in accounting for the
effects of one person on another.

The value of this conceptual approach is that it helps to
better define an organizational buying center. If a person influences a decision-maker's evaluation function,
then that person can be considered a participant in the
buying center. This may lead to buying center definitions
which include non-organizational members. Future substantive research might catalogue the kinds of interpersonal
influences on key organizational positions to develop a
more descriptive understanding of organizational buying
processes.

Finally, while this micro-modeling approach may not explain all the variation in organizational buying behavior
(since only one major concept is the focus of interest), it
provides a tractable approach for developing empirically
testable models. Accumulated findings from substantive research used to test these models, and other more specific
hypotheses, may build a body of knowledge which will facilitate the future development of more empirically testable
macro-models of organizational buying behavior. Extensions
of the modeling approach, and perhaps substantive findings,
may also be relevant to other multiple-person buying situ-
ations---e.g., family buying behavior.

REFERENCES

Alutto, A. (1968) "Role Theory in Propositional Form."
P.h.D. Dissertation. Cornell University.

Asch, S. E. (1951), "Effects of Group Pressure Upon the
Modification and Distortion of Judgements." In Groups,
Leadership, and Men, Guetzkow (ed.). Pittsburgh, Penn-
sylvania: Carnegie Press, 177-196.

Blau, M. (1964), Exchange and Power In Social Life. New
York: John Wiley & Sons.

Bonoma, T., Zaltman, G., and Johnston, W. (1977), Industrial Buying Behavior, Cambridge, MA: Marketing
Science Institute.

Cartwright, D. (1965), "Influence, Leadership, Control."
In Handbook of Organizations. J. March (ed.). Chicago:
Rand McNally.

Dahl, R. A. (1968), "Power." In International Encyclo-
pedia of the Social Sciences." New York: The Free
Press.

Dixon, W. J. (ed.). Biomedical Computer Programs: P-Se-
ries. Los Angeles: University of California Press,
1975.

Evan, M. (1966) "The Organization-Set: Toward a Theory
of Interorganizational Relations." In Approaches to
Organizational Design, J. Thompkins (ed.). Pittsburgh:
University of Pittsburgh Press, 175-191.

French, J. R. P. and Raven, B. (1959), "The Bases of Social Power." Studies in Social Power. Cartwright
(ed.). Ann Arbor, Michigan: University of Michigan
Press, 150-167.

Hickson, D. J., Hinings, C. R., Lee, C. A., Schneck, R. E.
and Pennings, J. M. (1971), " A Strategic Contingencies
Theory of Intraorganizational Power." Administrative
Science Quarterly, 16 (June) 216-229.

Hinings, C. R., Hickson, D. J., Pennings, J. M., and
Schneck, R. E. (1974), "Structural Conditions of Intraorganizational Power." Administrative Science Quarterly, 19 (March) 22-44.

Katz, D. and Kahn, R. L. (1978), The Social Psychology of
Organizations. 2nd ed. New York: John Wiley & Sons.

Merton, K. (1957), Social Theory and Social Structure.
Rev. ed. Glencoe, Illinois: The Free Press.

Mowday, R. T. (1978), "The Exercise of Upward Influence in
Organizations." Administrative Science Quarterly.
23 (March), 137-155.

Nagel, J. H. (1975), The Descriptive Analysis of Power.
New Haven, Connecticut: Yale University Press.

Nunnally, J. (1967), Psychometric Methods. New York:
McGraw-Hill.

Perreault, W. and Miles, R. (1978), "Influence Strategy
Mixes in Complex Organizations." Behavioral Science.
23 (March), 86-98.

Robertson, T. (1971), Innovative Behavior and Communication. New York: Holt, Rinehart & Winston.

Sheth, J. N. (1973), "A Model of Industrial Buyer Behavior." Journal of Marketing. 37 (October), 50-56.

Tedeschi, J. T., Schlenker, B. R. and Lindskold, S. (1972),
"The Exercise of Power and Influence: The Source of Influence." In The Social Influence Processes. J. Tedeschi (ed.). Chicago, Illinois: Aldine-Atherton.
346-418.

Thibaut, W. and Kelley, H. (1959), The Social Psychology
of Groups. New York: John Wiley & Sons.

Thomas, R. J. (1980) Correlates of Interpersonal Purchase
Influence in Organizations, Ph.D. Dissertation, University of Pennsylvania.

Webster, Jr., F. E. and Wind, Y. (1972), Organizational
Buying Behavior. Englewood Cliffs, New Jersey:
Prentice-Hall, Inc.

Weigand, R. E. (1968), "Why Studying the Purchasing Agent
is Not Enough." Journal of Marketing. 31 (January),
41-45.

Wind, Y. (1967), "The determinants of Industrial Buyers'
Behavior." In Industrial Buying and Creative Marketing.
Robinson and Faris (eds.). Boston, Massachusetts:
Allyn and Bacon.

__________(1976), "Preference of Relevant Others and In-
dividual Choice Models". Journal of Consumers Research.
3 (June), 50-57.

Zaltman, G. and Bonoma, T. (1977), "Organizational Buying
Behavior: Hypotheses and Directions." Industrial
Marketing Management. 6, 53-60.

FACIAL EXPRESSION AND MAKETING NEGOTIATIONS

John L. Graham, University of Southern California

ABSTRACT

Using a negotiation simulation and videotaping, measures
of facial expression and movement are compared to other
aspects of marketing negotiations. An exploratory analysis reveals relationships among three nonverbal behaviors
(i.e., frequency of smiles, brow wrinkles, and facial
gazing) and negotiation outcomes, process-related
measures, situational constraints, and negotiator characteristics.

BACKGROUND

Face-to-face negotiation is a key aspect of the industrial purchasing process. Buying and selling professionals often meet to resolve such conflicts as pricing,
delivery, service contracts, and the like. Efficient
exchange of information during such negotiations is
necessary to minimize the costs of such transactions.
Experienced salespeople and negotiators emphasize the
importance of being attuned to both verbal and nonverbal
aspects of communication (Grikscheit and Crissy 1973).
They suggest that key client responses are often not
verbalized (Graham 1980b). Yet almost no work has been
done investigating the role of nonverbal communication in
marketing negotiations (Bonoma and Felder 1977).

The present study specifically addresses the relationships of facial expression and facial gazing to other
aspects of marketing negotiations. The primary contribution is methodological--methods for coding and quanti-
fying facial expressions and movements are presented.
Because there has been almost no theoretical development
in this area, no hypotheses are tested. Rather, an
exploratory approach is taken in analysis of the data to
maximize information for future theory building.

The remainder of the paper is divided into four sections.
First, the laboratory procedures and methods of self-
report data collection are briefly described. Next, the
analysis of facial expression is explained, including
methods of coding and findings. The third section is
comprised of an analysis of facial gazing and its relation to other marketing negotiation variables. The paper
is concluded with a presentation of theoretical implications and directions for future research.

LABORATORY METHODS

The data analyzed here is derived from a behavioral
science negotiation simulation. The participants, tasks,
and data-collection instruments are now delineated.

Participants

The participants in the experiment are 12 Japanese
businessmen and 12 American businessmen. All have been
members of graduate business classes at the University of
Southern California; and all have at least two years
business experience in their respective countries. The
participants were asked to play the role of either buyer
or seller in a negotiation game. Three kinds of interactions were staged--3 Japanese/ Japanese, 3 American/
American, and 6 American/Japanese.

Negotiation Task

The negotiation simulation developed by Kelley (1966)
involves bargaining for the prices of three commodities.
Differing amounts and types of background information can
be included with the basic payoff matrices, depending on
the focus of the research. The game is simple enough to
be learned quickly, but complex enough to provide usually
one-half hour of face-to-face interaction. Several other
negotiation and bargaining games were reviewed. Kelley's
game was selected primarily because it simulates the
essential elements of actual sales negotiations observed
in the preliminary field research.

Data Collection

A combination of methods was used in collecting data for
analysis. First, each participant was asked to complete
a questionnaire following the bargaining sessions.
Second, each interaction was videotaped, thus allowing
for a series of observational methodologies to be
applied.

Questionnaire Data. Several measures of negotiation
outcomes, process-related measures, and individual characteristics were derived from responses to the questionnaire. The following are the four outcome variables
associated with Kelley's (1966) negotiation simulation:
1. Individual profit levels (buyer and seller)
2. Joint profit level
3. Time of negotiations (0-60 minutes)
4. Expressed satisfaction with the agreement (buyer and
    seller) (one Likert item)
The outcome variables along with the other variables
developed in the study are listed in Table 1.

Process-related measures were derived from participants'
responses to the post-game questionnaires. The bargaining strategies of the participants were rated on
three dimensions--representational/instrumental (i.e.,
representational bargaining strategies are problem-
solving oriented and high in information content), power,
and credibility, using single- and multiple-item Likert
scales answered by both participants (representational/
instrumental, four items; power, one item; credibility,
one item). Interpersonal attraction was measured using a
three-item Likert scale. All scales were developed
specifically for this research.

The last process-related measure, impression-formation
accuracy, was determined by summing differences in
responses to questions (regarding the strategy ratings
above) asked both participants. For example, both buyer
and seller were asked to rate the buyer's strategies on a
five-point scale ranging from "honest" to "deceptive."

Table 1
Variables Derived From Questionnaires

Category	Symbol	Variables	Description and Measure*
Outcome Variables	IP	Individual profit level	Profit level associated with final agreement in Kelley's (1966) negotiation game for either buyer or seller, range = 28 to 80
	JP	Joint profit level	Profit level for dyad, range = 56 to 104
	T	Time	Time spent in negotiation, range = 0 to 60 minutes
	S	Satisfaction	Expressed satisfaction by either buyer or seller, one five-point Likert item, range = 1 to 5
Process-Related Measures	RI	Representational/ Instrumental strategies	Buyer and seller ratings of strategies along representational/instrumental continuum, four Likert items, range = 8 to +8, Cronbach α = .71
	A	Attractiveness	Ratings of interpersonal attraction, three Likert items, range = 4 to 20, Cronbach α = .66
	P	Power	Ratings of power of one another's bargaining strategies, one Likert item, range = 1 to 5
	C	Credibility	Ratings of credibility of one another's bargaining strategies, one Likert item, range = 1 to 5
	IFA	Impression formation accuracy	Comparison of one another's ratings on three items, range = 0 to 12, low values indicate high accuracy, Cronbach α = .35
Situational Constraints	X	Cultural variation of the dyads	Experimental treatment intracultural dyads = 1, cross-cultural = 0
	JA	Culture of individuals	Experimental treatment, Japanese negotiators = 0, American negotiators = 1
	SB	Role of Player	Seller = 0, Buyer = 1
Individual	GE	Generalized self-esteem	Jackson Personality Inventory, 20 Likert items, range = 20 to 100, Cronbach = α .87
	SE	Task-specific self-esteem	Buyer and seller ratings of their own bargaining skill, three five-point Likert items, range = 3 to 15, Cronbach α = .79
	IE	Extroversion	Introversion/extroversion, six Likert items (Eysenck scale, 1958), range = 5 to +6, Cronbach α = .58
	IW	Interorganizational contact	Percentage of work involving contact outside the participants' company, range = 0 to 90%
	WE	Work experience	Number of years work experience
	AGE	Age	Age of the participants

*Cronbach α coefficients were calculated using a larger sample size (N=110) which includes the 24 participants in this study.

The sum of these differences on all three items can vary from 0 to 12, 12 being the lowest impression-formation accuracy.

Cultural variation of the parties was the experimental manipulation. Each participant was asked to list his city of residence, location of education, and the extent of previous overseas residence. The responses to these questions served as a check and documentation of the manipulation.

Measures of individual characteristics were also derived from the post-game questionnaires and are listed in Table 1.

The focus of this work is on the development and clarification of measures of nonverbal behaviors in marketing negotiations. Consequently, the measures derived from the questionnaires will be compared to those measures of facial expression and facial gazing derived from analysis of the videotapes. The questionnaire data has been analyzed using a variety of statistical techniques using much larger sample sizes. A complete conceptual discussion of these variables and the results of that work are reported in my other work (Graham 1980b).

Videotape Data. The twelve interactions between Japanese and American businessmen were videotaped. Three cameras were used--one to record the interactions from a wide-angle, side view to capture postures, body movements, and interpersonal distrances; and two other cameras to focus on the faces of the participants to capture facial expressions. All cameras were mounted in the ceiling of a behavior science laboratory and operated by remote control, thereby minimizing obtrusions. Additionally, all participants were asked to evaluate the obtrusiveness of the setting on questionnaires following the negotiation game. All participants reported a minimum of discomfort.

FACIAL EXPRESSION

Work in facial expression as a communicational behavior is just beginning (Ekman 1980). Therefore, the simplest analysis of the videotape data was performed in this study.

Ten-minute excerpts were selected from each of the twelve videotaped interactions. Using Ekman and Friesen's (1976) scheme, as described in my previous work (Graham 1980a), the movement of two action units (AU 4 and AU 12) were coded for each participant during the ten-minute periods. Action Unit 12 might be thought roughly as corresponding to a smile and positive responses. Action Unit 4 might be thought roughly as corresponding to a brow wrinkle and negative responses. A note was made each time the action unit moved. If the expression was held more than five seconds, the duration of the expression was recorded. All such movements were totaled for each participant. For those expressions which lasted longer than five seconds, a count was added for each five-second interval. Thus expressions lasting 0-9 seconds were counted as 1. Expressions lasting 10-14 seconds were counted as 2, and so on. The total count for each individual for each ten-minute excerpt provides the measures, AU 12 and AU 4, listed in individual Table 2.

This investigator coded all the excerpts of the twelve interactions. Another uninformed coder scored one entire interaction to provide a crude check on reliability and generality. Intercoder reliability proved to be good, at 6% (calculated using the forumla--the difference in the number of units between the coders as a percentage of the total number of units).

Action Unit 12 (smiles). As indicated in Table 2, AU 12 is unrelated to most variables in the study. High levels of AU 12 are negatively related to accuracy of impressions for some players (r = .291, p < 0.10). Smiling is more typical of cross-cultural negotiations (ANOVA R^2 = .11, p < 0.10).

Action Unit 4 (brow wrinkles). AU 4 appears to have a greater impact on sales negotiations. Notice the negative relationships with all outcome variables listed in Table 2. AU 4 is strongly negatively associated with

TABLE 2
Relations of Nonverbal Variables to Other Variables
(Correlation Coefficients, N = 24)[2]

Variable[1]	AU12 (smiles)	AU4 (brow wrinkles)	% shared AU12 (SFE)	Time of Facial Gazing
Outcome Measures				
IP_p	-.096	-.122	.244	-.111
IP_o		-.343[3]	.390[4]	
JP_o			.275[3]	-.225
IP_p/T		-.329[3]	.312[3]	.373[4]
S_p	-.096	-.133	-.100	-.637[5]
S_o		-.384[4]		-.586[5]
Process-Related Measures				
A_p				-.534[5]
A_o		-.283[3]		-.275[3]
C_o		-.381[4]		
C_p		-.343[4]		
IFA_p	.291[3]	.409[4]		
T_p		.393[4]		-.224
Situational Constraints (ANOVA R^2)				
JA			.14[4]	.09
X	.11[3]			.20[4]
Individual Characteristics				
GE_p			.400[4]	
SE_o				-.350[4]
IE_p		.415[4]		
WE_p			-.436[4]	-.310[3]
WE_o				-.277[3]
AGE_p		-.309[3]	-.342[3]	-.328[3]

[1] Variable Symbol (see Table 1).
Subscript p = player
Subscript o = opponent
[2] Sample included 3 Japanese dyads, 3 American dyads, and 6 cross-cultural dyads.
[3] p < 0.10.   [4] p < 0.05.   [5] p < 0.01.

players' impression-formation accuracy (r = .409, p < 0.05.). Brow wrinkles are also associated with longer negotiation periods (T) and reduced opponent credibility (C_o). Extroverts (EI_p) and younger players (AGE_p) displayed more brow wrinkles.

Synchrony of Facial Expressions. Communication theory suggests that when two people are effectively sharing ideas their communication behaviors are rhythmically coordinated or "synchronous." A measure of interactional synchrony has been developed here by comparing two participants' facial expressions. The facial expressions of each participant in the twelve interactions were coded separately (as described above). Then the timing of expressions of bargaining partners was compared and periods of shared facial expressions or "mirroring" were identified. Finally, the number of expressions shared was divided by the total number of expressions for individual participants, giving a value termed "percent shared" (SFE). SFE can be thought of as a measure of synchrony or communicational effectiveness--the higher the percent, the more effective the communication.

The values for shared AU 4 expressions were very low and precluded useful comparisons to other variables. The values for shared AU 12 expressions have been compared to other variables in the study, and they are reported below. As indicated in Table 2, the percent of shared AU 12 facial expressions is associated with several variables in the study. Most importantly, strong positive relationships were discovered with profit variables including individual profits for both players and opponents and joint profits. Shared facial expressions were found to be negatively associated with three process-related measures--time (T), credibility (C_o) and attractiveness (A_o). The only situational constraint related to SFE was the culture of the individuals (JA). Americans were found to share a higher percentage of smiles (ANOVA R^2 = .14, p < 0.05). Finally, players with higher generalized self-esteem and younger, less-experienced players were found to share higher percentages of facial expressions.

FACIAL GAZING

The final nonverbal variable to be considered is facial gazing. Other researchers have found significant relationships between facial gazing and outcomes of negotiation games (Lewis and Fry 1977). Moreover, several authors have suggested differences in gazing behavior across cultures (Argyle and Cook 1976).

In this study, facial gazing is defined as the percentage of time a bargainer gazes at the face of his opponent. The same randomly selected, ten-minute videotape excerpts used in developing facial expression measures served as data here. Using a stopwatch, two observers recorded the time each participant spent gazing at his opponent's face during the ten minutes, thus giving the measure facial gazing (FG). The method used was very similar to that reported by Lewis and Fry (1978), except that videotapes were reviewed rather than real-time interactions. Using videotapes is a more reliable technique, allowing reviews and reliability checks. Intercoder reliability (calculated using the formula--the difference in the number of units between coders as a percentage of the sum of the units) was found to be 9%, an adequate level.

Comparing the time of facial gazing to other variables in the study yields several interesting relationships (see Table 2). Facial gazing is associated with higher profit levels per unit of time (r = .374, p < 0.05). However, it is inversely related to all other outcome measures. Particularly striking are the strong negative associations with expressed satisfaction of both participants. Facial gazing is also inversely related to attractiveness of both player and opponent. Differences were found across both cultural variables. Americans appear to gaze at opponents' faces more than Japanese (ANOVA R^2 = .09, n.s.), although the relationship is only borderline statistically significant. Additionally, it was found that facial gazing increases during cross-cultural negotiation (ANOVA R^2 = .20, p < 0.05). This latter difference is even more pronounced if only the Japanese groups are compared. The average time of facial gazing for Japanese during intracultural negotiations is 1.3 minutes (N = 6), and in cross-cultural negotiations is 3.9 minutes (N = 6). Finally, facial gazing was found to be negatively related to four individual characteristics-- players' age and work experience and opponents' work experience and task-specific self-esteem (all relationships are statistically significant, p < 0.10).

CONCLUSIONS

Implications for Theory

No hypotheses were tested in the present work. Instead, the study has been exploratory in nature. The results of the correlation analysis and analysis of variance suggest several relationships between constructs which might be studied in future work. There is not space in this paper to fully discuss all the suggested relations and possible causal mechanisms. However, four of the relationships deserve special attention.

AU 4 and Process-Related Measures. Brow wrinkles (AU 4) appear to be related to several of the self-report process-related measures in the study. Negotiators tended to display brow wrinkles more frequently when they had difficulty sizing up opponents (r_{IFA_p} = .409, p< 0.05), when opponents used deceptive bargaining strategies (r_{C_o} = -.343, p < 0.05), and when negotiations took longer (r_{T}^{o} = .393, p < 0.05). Certainly causality is an issue here, but a hypothesis is suggested by the strong associations. It appears that negotiators display brow wrinkles more frequently when things are going wrong for them. Or stated more precisely:

Proposition I--Higher frequencies of brow wrinkles (AU 4) are inversely related to efficient reception of information during marketing negotiations.

Indeed, this hypothesis is consistent with some of Ekman's more recent findings (1980).

Facial Gazing, AU 4, and Expressed Satisfaction. Frequency of facial gazing appears to have relatively strong negative effects on opponent satisfaction (r_{S_o} = -.586, p < 0.01) and opponent's ratings of players' attractiveness (r_{A_p} = -.534, p < 0.01). Brow wrinkles (AU 4) evidently influences both opponents' profits (r_{IP_o} = -.343, p < 0.10) and opponents' satisfaction ($r_{S_p}^{o}$ = .334, p < 0.05). Others (e.g., Lewis and Fry 1977) have suggested facial gazing to be aggressive behavior, which tends to reduce joint negotiation outcomes. Causality is less an issue here because negotiation behaviors are associated with negotiation outcomes in a sequential way. Thus, the following proposition is indicated:

Proposition II--Higher frequencies of brow wrinkles and facial gazing by bargainers will negatively affect opponent negotiation outcomes.

Shared Facial Expressions and Joint Profits. Another series of relationships with a common thread are those between shared facial expressions (SFE) and profit levels for both players. For the negotiation exercise higher joint profits can be attained when bargainers exchange information efficiently. Thus, the idea that SFE might be used as a measure of interactional synchrony receives support in this exploratory work. Here causality is not suggested. Instead, both more frequently shared facial expressions (SFE) and higher joint negotiation outcomes result from a third construct--efficient exchange of information. The important point here is:

Proposition III--Higher levels of SFE will precede higher joint negotiation outcomes.

Extroversion and Facial Expression. The final relationship to be discussed is that between frequency of brow wrinkles and extroversion. Ekman (1980) suggests the importance of controlling for levels of extroversion in studies of facial expression. The findings reported in Table 2 appear to support that proposition. Therefore a fourth proposition is suggested:

Proposition IV--Extroverted bargainers will tend to display more facial expressions than introverted bargainers.

Limitations

There are several limitations of the study which deserve brief mention.

1. The correlations and ANOVA R^2 comprising the results of this work are far from conclusive. Sample size is small, an inductive approach was taken, and only two-way relations were explored. Inferences were made about causality and spurious relations.
2. The sample of negotiators was far from ideal -- 12 Japanese business men and 12 American businessmen. Indeed, the results in Table 2 indicate cultural differences between groups.
3. The laboratory setting may have influenced behaviors.

Future Research

This work might be improved upon in several ways. Here I will mention only three. First, a more complete study would consider the antecedents and consequences of facial expressions. For example, what verbal behaviors precede brow wrinkles or smiles? What verbal behaviors coincide with periods of facial gazing? Second, larger samples would allow for more powerful statistical tests of relations. And third, the use of facial expression in other marketing settings should be explored (e.g., new-product concept testing or response to TV advertising).

REFERENCES

Argyle, M. and M. Cook (1976), Gaze and Mutual Gaze, Cambridge, England: Cambridge University Press.

Bonoma, T. V. and L. C. Felder (1977), "Nonverbal Communication in Marketing: Toward a Communicational Analysis," Journal of Marketing Research, XIV (May), 169-180.

Ekman, P. (1980), "About Brows," in J. Aschoff, M. von Cranach, I. Eibl-Eibesfeldt, W. Lepenies (eds.), Human Ethology, Cambridge: University Press.

Ekman, P. and W. V. Friesen (1976), "Measuring Facial Movement," Environmental Psychology and Nonverbal Behavior, 1 (Fall).

Eysenck, H. J. (1958), "A Short Questionnaire for the Measurement of Two Dimensions of Personality," Journal of Applied Psychology, 42, 14-17.

Graham, J. L. (1980a), "A New System for Measuring Non-verbal Responses to Marketing Appeals," 1980 AMA Educators' Conference Proceedings, 46, 340-343.

Graham, J. L. (1980b), "Cross-Cultural Sales Negotiations: A Multilevel Analysis," unpublished doctoral dissertation, U. C. Berkeley.

Grikscheit, G. M. and W. J. E. Crissy (1973, "Improving Interpersonal Communication Skill," MSU Business Topics, (Autumn), 62-68.

Kelley, H. H. (1966), "A Classroom Study of the Dilemmas in Interpersonal Negotiations," in K. Archibald (ed.), Strategic Interaction and Conflict, Berkeley: Institute of International Studies, University of California.

Lewis, S. A. and W. R. Fry (1977), "Effects of Visual Access and Orientation on the Discovery of Integrative Bargaining Alternatives," Organizational Behavior and Human Performance, 20, 75-92.

Priki, M. (1973), "Perception of Role Strain by Outside Salesmen," unpublished doctoral dissertation, Ohio State University.

Pruitt, D. G. and S. A. Lewis (1975), "Development of Integrative Solutions in Bilateral Negotiation," Journal of Personality and Social Psychology, 31 (Number 4), 621-633.

SELF-BRAND IMAGE CONGRUENCY AND THE EFFECTS OF TRAIT DESIRABILITY

Ishmael P. Akaah, Wayne State University, Detroit
Edward A. Riordan, Wayne State University, Detroit

ABSTRACT

This paper presents the results of an empirical study regarding the effects of trait desirability on self-concepts (actual and ideal), brand images, and self-brand image congruency. The results indicate that not only does trait desirability influence self-concept and brand evaluations, but also it confounds the relationship between the self-concept and brand preferences.

INTRODUCTION

Research of the proposition that consumers patronize products and services to enhance or maintain their self-concepts (i.e., seek self-brand image congruency) has followed two methodological paths. First, there are self-concept studies that examine the congruency proposition by eliciting in a "global" sense the extent to which consumers perceive products/brands as congruent with their actual and/or ideal self-concepts (Belch and Landon 1977; Landon 1974). As reflected in Landon's (1974) study, this approach requires consumers to rate their self-concepts (actual and ideal) in direct relation to a list of consumer products (one at a time) on a Likert-type scale ranging from "very strongly like me" to "very strongly unlike me" for the actual self-concept measure and from "very strongly like I want to be" to "very strongly unlike I want to be" for the ideal self-concept measure. This is then followed by consumers' purchase-intention ratings for the same set of products (one at a time) using an appropriately labeled Likert-type scale.

Reflective of the second methodological approach are self-concept studies that utilize bipolar (i.e., the semantic differential) or unipolar adjectives in eliciting consumers' self-concept and brand image evaluations (Birdwell 1968; Dolich 1969; Grubb and Hupp 1968; Hughes and Guerrero 1971). The procedure commonly employed consists in having consumers make repeated judgments of their self-concepts (actual and/or ideal) in terms of the bipolar or unipolar adjectives along a graduated scale. The self-concept evaluations are then followed by similar repeated judgments of their brand preferences. The brand evaluation task either takes the form of direct application of traits to brands (e.g., Birdwell 1968; Dolich 1969; Green et al. 1969; Ross 1971) or the application of traits to the stereotypical image of a given brand's users (e.g., Grubb and Hupp 1968; Wells et al. 1957). The format for the latter brand evaluation task deals with critics' concern about the meaningfulness/appropriateness of certain adjectival traits (e.g., optimistic, shy, sociable, introverted) when used to describe products directly.

Inherent in both methodological paths are social desirability problems. First, both suffer from possible limitations stemming from the social desirability of products/brands. That is, to the extent that a product/brand is perceived as more socially desirable than another, this increases the likelihood of that product/brand being evaluated as reflective of the self-concept or as the most preferred product/ brand (Belch and Landon 1977). Additionally, the second approach suffers from limitations of social desirability relative to the adjectival traits utilized. The trait desirability issue stems from research evidence to the effect that respondents tend to give what are considered socially acceptable responses to adjectival traits in personality assessment tasks. That is, the more socially desirable a trait is, the greater is the probability that respondents would endorse it as reflecting their self-concepts and the image of their preferred brands (Edwards 1953; Kenny 1956).

Despite the apparent influence of social desirability on self-concept and brand image evaluations, only Belch and Landon (1977) have dealt with the issue. They hypothesized that:

1. Social desirability for a product is related significantly to self-concept score for the product.

2. Self-concept score for a product is related significantly to purchase behavior, accounting for social desirability.

Underlying their hypotheses was the rationale that the influence of social desirability may have both valid and invalid construct components and that social norms, if they have any meaning at all, should influence the way consumers perceive themselves. They, however, argued that a response which is totally determined by the social desirability of the product, and not at all by individual predispositions, is artificial and certainly not a valid measure of self-concept. Thus, Belch and Landon reasoned that for the self-concept measure to be valid some correlation between self-concept and social desirability must be expected. However, self-concept should be a better predictor of purchase behavior than social desirability alone.

Belch and Landon found social desirability to have a significant effect on the self-concept ratings given to a product (i.e., the more desirable products being perceived as more like the individual or like he wants to be than products of low social desirability). However, the relationship between self-concept and purchase intention was found to be unaffected by social desirability. In particular, the hypothesized relationship held for five of the eight products examined. Although they did not consider the evidence strong enough to support generalizations concerning the effect of social desirability, their research findings, nonetheless, suggested social desirability to be a problem with some products.

Given that Belch and Landon's (1977) study derived from the first methodological path, they did not examine the problem of social desirability as it relates to adjectival traits. As a result, it is unclear as to the extent to which trait desirability influences self-concept and brand image evaluations, and, hence, the congruency between self-concept and purchase behavior. The only literature evidence which bears somewhat on the possible confounding influence of trait/desirability is contained in the study by Grubb and Hupp (1968). However, since Grubb and Hupp did not test for the possible confounding effects of the social desirability of traits, it is unclear as to the extent to which trait desirability must have influenced the significantly positive relationship they found regarding self-concept and purchase behavior.

In light of the absence of research dealing specifically with the issue of trait desirability, the present study was designed to examine whether trait desirability influences self-concept and brand image evaluations, and, hence, the congruency between self-concepts and brand preferences.

HYPOTHESES

The following research hypotheses were formulated and
tested based on the preceding discussion:

H_1: (a) The more socially desirable an adjectival trait
is, the greater is the likelihood that it would be
perceived as reflecting the actual or the ideal
self-concept.

   (b) The more socially desirable an adjectival trait
is, the greater is the likelihood that it would be
perceived as reflecting the image of one's preferred brand of product.

H_2: (a) The relationship between actual self-concept and
preferred brand image is stronger under high
social desirability conditions than under low
social desirability conditions.

   (b) The relationship between ideal self-concept and
preferred brand image is stronger under high
social desirability conditions than under low
social desirability conditions.

Hypothesis 1(a) derives from the notion that the scores
individuals give to trait items may be a function of what
they interpret as socially acceptable or ideal than a true
reflection of how they perceive themselves or want to perceive themselves. Hypothesis 1(b) is a logical extension
of the notion to individuals' preferred brands/models.
That is, to the extent that a trait is socially desirable,
the individual would be more likely to perceive it as reflecting the image of his/her preferred brand.

Hypothesis 2 follows directly from the congruency proposi-
tion--that is, consumers patronize products and services
to enhance or maintain their self-concepts (Grubb and
Grathwohl 1967). However, if the earlier discussion were
correct, one would expect the relationship between self-
concept (actual and ideal) and brand image to be much
stronger (statistically) for socially desirable traits
than it would be for traits that are not so desirable
socially. Since Kenny's (1956) research suggested the
ideal self-concept to be more sensitive to trait desirability than the actual self-concept, the hypotheses were
formulated in terms of the two self-concept definitions.
Moreover, both self-concept definitions have formed the
basis of several previous research studies regarding the
congruency proposition.

METHOD

The Sample

Responses to a questionnaire were obtained from 111 undergraduate business students (56 male, 55 female) attending
a large urban state university. To minimize possible
demand characteristics, the students were assigned at random to two treatment groups--actual self-concept group
(n_1=57), and ideal self-concept group (n_2=54). Respondents
assigned to the actual self-concept group provided, in
addition to their preferred automobile brand evaluations,
only their actual self-concept ratings. Similarly, respondents assigned to the ideal self-concept group provided, in
addition to their preferred automobile ratings, only their
ideal self-concept ratings. Furthermore, an effort was
made to minimize possible order effects (i.e., bias in response styles stemming from the order in which the tasks
were performed) by requiring half of the respondents in
each treatment group to give their self-concept ratings
first, followed by their brand image ratings, and the other
half, their brand image ratings first, followed by their
self-concept ratings.

Measuring Instrument

A total of 16 adjectival traits (8 socially neutral and 8

socially desirable) formed the basis of respondents' self-
concept and brand ratings. The traits were chosen based
on the following four-step approach. First, a master list
of 214 adjectival traits was developed from several literature sources (Birdwell 1968; Dolich 1969; Grubb and Hupp
1968; Hughes and Gruerrero 1971; Ross 1971; Wells et al.
1957). Second, a separate sample of 150 undergraduate
students (other than those used in the present study) was
used to prescreen the list in terms of whether each trait
is appropriate or not when used directly to describe both
self-concepts and automobiles. A "yes"-"no" checklist
approach (with "yes" coded as 2 and "no" coded as 1) was
used for the prescreening task. Traits with mean scores of
at least 1.50 were characterized as having met the "applicability" criterion.

Third, the 125 traits that met the applicability criterion
were evaluated three weeks later (by the same 150-respon-
dent group) in terms of their social desirability. A
seven-point scale ranging from 1 (not at all desirable
socially) through 4 (neither desirable/undesirable socially)
to 7 (extremely desirable socially) was used. Given the
nature of the scale, adjectival traits with mean scores of
5 or greater were characterized as "socially desirable,"
those with mean scores of 3 or less as "socially undesirable," and those with mean scores of between 3 and 5 (i.e.,
reflecting the mid-range of the scale) as "socially neutral." The decision was made at this point to drop the
fifteen traits that fell into the socially undesirable
trait category in an attempt to reduce the trait list to a
manageable size.

Finally another separate group of 384 students (other than
the 150 described earlier) was asked to rate the remaining
110 traits in terms of the extent to which each reflected
their actual self-concepts. A seven-point scale ranging
from 1 (does not at all describe what I am) to 7 (completely describes what I am) was used. The self-concept ratings
were then submitted to a factor analysis program to identify the principal dimensions underlying the respondents'
evaluations, and the loadings of the traits on those principal dimensions identified (Barr et al. 1979). From the
analysis emerged nineteen factors with eigenvalues greater
than 1.0, accounting for 67% of the variance in the ratings.
After a varimax rotation, a table was developed of the
factors and the trait loadings (of .50 or higher).

Three of the nineteen factors did not exhibit "clear" or
unambiguous trait loadings and were therefore dropped. Of
the remainder, eight exhibited high loadings on basically
only socially desirable traits. Hence, one socially desirable trait each (with a very high loading) was chosen to
represent each of the eight factors. The remaining eight
factors also reflected high loadings by largely neutral
traits. One neutral trait each (with a very high loading)
was chosen to represent each of the remaining eight factors.
The list of the 16 adjectival traits chosen for the study
is presented in Table 1.

Questionnaire and Tasks

The questionnaire for the study consisted of two main
tasks--self-concept (actual or ideal) and brand image
ratings. The actual self-concept measure focused on how
respondents of the actual self-concept treatment group
actually perceived themselves to be in terms of each of the
16 adjectival traits of Table 1. A seven-point scale ranging from 1 (does not at all describe what I am) to 7 (completely describes what I am) was used to elicit the actual
self-concept ratings. The ideal self-concept measure concerned how respondents of the ideal self-concept treatment
group would ideally like to perceive themselves to be in
relation to the 16 adjectival traits. The ideal self-
concept was measured using a similar seven-point scale that
ranged from 1 (does not at all describe what I want to be)
to 7 (completely describes what I want to be).

MEAN SOCIAL DESIRABILITY, SELF-CONCEPT, AND BRAND IMAGE SCORES

Trait	Mean Social Desirability Rating (1)	Actual Self-Concept Treatment Group — Mean Actual Self-Concept Rating (2)	Mean Brand Image Rating (3)	Mean Congruence Score (4)	Ideal Self-Concept Treatment Group — Mean Ideal Self-Concept Rating (5)	Mean Brand Image Rating (6)	Mean Congruence Score (7)
I. Socially Desirable							
Fashionable	6.1	4.97	6.05	1.26	4.74	5.37	1.48
Dependable	6.6	6.19	5.58	1.07	6.50	5.65	1.07
Natural Looking	5.8	4.58	3.84	1.51	5.30	3.91	1.72
Stable	5.8	5.53	5.12	1.53	5.41	4.43	1.43
Practical	5.8	5.26	4.56	1.82	5.07	4.37	1.26
Youthful	6.0	5.56	4.92	1.40	4.80	4.26	1.24
Sporty	5.6	5.14	5.49	1.40	4.69	5.22	1.57
Exciting	6.3	5.25	5.70	1.09	5.22	5.41	1.15
II. Socially Neutral							
Rugged	4.5	3.09	3.77	1.49	2.48	3.48	1.63
Ordinary	3.5	2.60	2.07	1.05	3.26	2.91	1.39
Complex	4.0	5.00	4.37	1.40	3.69	3.44	1.54
Foreign	3.4	1.82	4.40	3.07	1.91	3.61	2.59
Middle-Class	4.4	4.49	3.35	1.84	4.20	3.65	1.56
Extravagant	4.5	4.12	4.63	1.49	3.83	3.89	1.54
Big	4.2	2.49	2.02	1.60	2.35	2.50	1.33
Conservative	4.2	3.72	3.05	1.72	4.17	3.52	1.35

In addition to the self-concept ratings, all respondents provided, in terms of the 16 adjectival traits, brand image ratings for their most preferred automobile brands or models. The choice of automobiles for the brand evaluation task stemmed from the fact that they have formed the basis of many previous self-concept studies. A seven-point scale ranging from 1 (does not at all describe my most preferred brand/model) to 7 (completely describes my most preferred brand/model) was used for the brand evaluation task. Respondents also provided data regarding whether they owned the brands they indicated as most preferred or not. To minimize halo and response-style biases, two randomized trait list orders were utilized for the self-concept and the brand image tasks, respectively.

Statistical Analysis

The first step in the analysis was to determine whether (a) the two random orders in which the traits appeared and (b) the two orders for the self-concept and the brand rating tasks (i.e., self-concept ratings first, followed by brand ratings and vice-versa) influenced self-concept and brand image scores. To do this, the self-concept and brand ratings were utilized separately in four 2x2 (i.e., descriptor order by task order) analysis of variance designs. That is, the analysis was done separately for the (a) self and brand ratings and (b) the actual and the ideal self-concept groups--hence implying four separate ANOVAs. None of the F-values from the analysis was statistically significant. Furthermore, since brand ownership has been posited or found to influence self-brand image congruency (Belch and Landon 1977; Evans 1968), the examination of the hypotheses was preceded by ANOVA (based on congruence scores for each respondent) designed to test for differences across those who owned their preferred brands and those who did not. The F-value from the analysis was, however, not statistically significant. Therefore, the self-concept and

brand ratings for each treatment group were pooled together in the statistical analyses described below.

To test Hypothesis 1, the mean social desirability scores obtained during the prescreening, were compiled (Table 1, column 1). Also, the mean self-concept and brand image scores were computed separately (across the respondents) for each treatment group (Columns 2, 3, 5 and 6 of Table 1). The hypothesis was then examined by computing, separately for each treatment group, the Pearson's product moment correlation coefficient between (a) the mean social desirability scores and the mean self-concept scores, and (b) the mean social desirability scores and the mean brand image scores.

To test Hypothesis 2, two methods of analysis were used. The first involved calculating the partial correlation coefficients between the mean self-concept scores and the mean brand image scores (i.e., controlling for trait desirability) (Afifi and Azen 1972). The second involved computing 16 congruence scores (i.e., the absolute arithmetic differences, trait by trait, between self-concept and brand ratings) separately for each respondent. (Analytically, the smaller the congruence score is, the greater is the match between a respondent's self-concept and brand image for that particular trait descriptor). Next, the mean congruence scores for each trait was computed separately (across the respondents) for each treatment group (Columns 4 and 7 of Table 1). The resulting mean congruence scores were then utilized in a 2x2 covariance analysis--i.e., the two trait categories (socially desirable and socially neutral) by the two treatment groups (actual self-concept and the ideal self-concept group), with the mean social desirability scores (Column 1, Table 1) serving as covariate.

RESULTS

Table 2 presents the trait desirability/self-concept and trait desirability/brand image correlation coefficients. As the table indicates, the correlation between social desirability and actual self-concept was .844 (both significant beyond the .0001 level). This relationship indicates that the more socially desirable the adjectival trait, the greater the respondents' tendency to see the adjectival trait as being like what they are or like what they want to be. The rather small difference between the correlations of trait desirability with actual self-concept and with ideal self-concept suggests that trait desirability appears to influence both self-concepts equally--a finding which is consistent with that of Belch and Landon (1977).

TABLE 2

SIMPLE AND PARTIAL CORRELATIONS BETWEEN TRAIT
DESIRABILITY/SELF-CONCEPTS AND BRAND IMAGES

	Simple Correlations[a]		Partial Correlations[a]
Treatment	Self-Concept/ Social Desirability	Brand Image/ Social Desirability	Self-Concept/ Brand-Image
Actual Self-Concept Group	.844[c]	.736[b]	.253[d]
Ideal Self-Concept Group	.866[c]	.847[c]	.130[d]

[a]Based on n = 16 (traits)   [c]p < .0001
[b]p < .001   [d]n.s.

Table 2 also shows the correlation of trait desirability with brand image to be .736 and .847 for the actual self-concept and the ideal self-concept treatment groups, respectively. Both correlations were significant at the .001 level or better. This relationship thus supports the hypothesis that the more socially desirable the adjectival trait, the greater the likelihood that respondents would perceive it as reflecting the image of their preferred brand/model of automobile.

The partial correlation coefficients for examining the relationship between self-concept (actual or brand image)-- under high and low social desirability conditions--are presented in Table 2. As the table indicates neither the partial correlation of actual self-concept with brand image nor the partial correlation of ideal self-concept with brand image was statistically significant. The lack of significance means that social desirability of traits not only affects mean self-concept (actual and ideal) and brand ratings, but also confounds the relationship between the two.

As further confirmation, the mean congruence scores were utilized in covariance analysis. As Table 3(a) indicates, only a marginal difference (p < .10) remains between the two trait categories after the effect of trait desirability is removed or partialled out. This becomes clearer when the results of Table 3(a) are compared to a similar analysis where trait desirability was not included as a covariate (Table 3(b)). The much stronger statistical significance for trait group effect (p < .05) in Table 3(b), as compared to that of Table 3(a), indicates that in the absence of socially desirable traits the strength of self-brand image congruency diminshes to a point where it is virtually the same for the two trait categories. The lack of statistically significant effect for the treatment group terms Table 3(a) and (b) indicates that support for the congruency proposition remains unchanged whether measured in terms of the actual self-concept or the ideal self-concept. Furthermore, the fact that the treatment group by trait group interaction terms of both Table 3(a) and 3 (b) were not significant confirms the earlier conclusion that there is little variation in how the actual and the ideal self-concepts are affected by trait desirability.

TABLE 3

ANOVA ON MEAN CONGRUENCE SCORES WITH AND WITHOUT
TRAIT DESIRABILITY AS COVARIATE

a. ANOVA With Trait Desirability as Covariate

Source of Variation	d.f.	MS.	F	p<
Covariate				
Social Desirability	1	1.107	8.95	.01
Main Effects				
Treatment Group	1	.025	.20	n.s.
Trait Group	1	.494	3.99	.10
Interaction				
Treatment x Trait	1	.010	.08	n.s.
Residual	27	.124		

b. ANOVA Without Trait Desirability as Covariate

Source of Variation	d.f.	MS.	F	p<
Main Effects				
Treatment Group	1	.025	.16	n.s.
Trait Group	1	.658	4.14	.05
Interaction				
Treatment x Trait	1	.010	.06	n.s.
Residual	28	.159		

CONCLUSIONS

The basic conclusions from the study findings are that:

1. Social desirability of traits significantly influences both self-concept (actual or ideal) and brand image ratings; the more desirable the trait, the greater the likelihood that it would be seen as reflecting the self-concept (actual or ideal) and the brand image of respondents' most preferred brands.

2. Social desirability of traits not only affects self-concept and brand ratings but also confounds the relationship between the self-concept (actual or ideal) and brand preferences. In the absence of socially desirable traits, the strength of self-brand image congruency diminishes considerably to a point where the relationship between self-concept and the image of preferred brand ceases to be statistically significant.

3. Social desirability appears to influence about equally actual self-concept and ideal self-concept ratings. That is, there is little variation in terms of how social desirability impacts the two self-concepts.

The conclusions from the study should not necessarily be interpreted as an indictment of the congruency proposition--especially because (a) the social desirability scale used lacks reliability and validity tests, and (b) there was some degree of arbitrariness regarding the manner in which the traits were extracted from the factor analysis results. Despite these study limitations, the fact that the relationship between self-concept and brand preference is not significant, after partialling out the effect of trait desirability has some implication for congruency research.

In the context of the present study, the results suggest that researchers ought to be cognizant of the confounding effects of the social desirability of traits. For

example, it may be easier to establish empirical support
for the congruency proposition by using a trait list that
is "loaded" with highly desirable traits than another that
is not so highly loaded. Thus, if the primary research
goal is to prove/refute the empirical validity of the congruency proposition, then every effort should be made to
control for the effects of trait desirability. One way of
doing this is to ensure that the trait list used spans the
whole desirable/undesirable continuum. Or, the final trait
list should exclude adjectival descriptors which are so
extremely desirable socially that what is captured are
basically only stereotypic responses which do not truly
reflect individuals' self and brand concepts. The other
way is to use Landon's methodology (Belch and Landon 1977;
Landon 1974) since this does not suffer from the limitations of trait desirability.

REFERENCES

Afifi, A.A., and S.P. Azen (1972), _Statistical Analysis:
    A Computer Oriented Approach_, New York: Academic
    Press.

Barr, A.J., J.H. Goodnight, and J.P. Sall (1979), _SAS
    User's Guide_, Raleigh, North Carolina: SAS Institute
    Inc.

Belch, G.E. and E.L. Landon, Jr. (1977), "Discriminant
    Validity of a Product-Anchored Self-Concept Measure,"
    Journal of Marketing Research, 14 (May), 252-56.

Birdwell, A.E. (1968), "A Study of the Influence of Image
    Congruence on Consumer Choice," _Journal of Business_,
    41 (January), 76-88.

Dolich, I.J. (1969), "Congruence Relationships Between Self
    Images and Product Brands," _Journal of Marketing
    Research_, 6 (February), 80-84.

Edwards, A.L. (1953), "The Relationships Between the Judged
    Desirability of a Trait and the Probability That the
    Trait Will Be Endorsed," _Journal of Applied Psychology_,
    37, 90-3.

Green, P.E., A. Maheshwari, and V.R. Rao (1969), "Self-
    Concept and Brand Preference: An Empirical Applica-
    tion of Multidimensional Scaling," _Journal of the
    Marketing Research Society_, 4 (October), 343-60.

Grubb, E.L., and H.L. Grathwohl (1967), "Consumer Self-
    Concept, Symbolism and Market Behavior: A Theoretical
    Approach," _Journal of Marketing_, 31 (October), 22-7.

Grubb, E.L., and G. Hupp (1968), "Perception of Self,
    Generalized Stereotypes, and Brand Selection,"
    Journal of Marketing Research, 5 (February), 58-63.

Hughes, D., and J.L. Guerrero (1971), "Automobile Self-
    Congruity Models Re-examined," _Journal of Marketing
    Research_, 8 (February), 125-27.

Kenny, D.T. (1956), "The Influence of Social Desirability
    on Discrepancy Measures Between Real and Ideal Self,"
    Journal of Consulting Psychology, 20 (August), 315-18.

Landon, E.L., Jr. (1974), "Self-Concept, Ideal Self Concept
    and Consumer Purchase Intentions," _Journal of Consumer
    Research_, 1 (September), 44-51.

Ross, I. (1971), "Self-Concept and Brand Preference,"
    Journal of Business, 44 (January), 38-50.

Wells, W.F., F.J. Andriuli, F.J. Goi, and S. Seader (1957),
    "An Adjective Check List for the Study of Product Per-
    sonality," _Journal of Applied Psychology_, 41, 317-19.

THE INFLUENCE OF PERSONAL VALUES ON
ATTITUDE AND STORE CHOICE BEHAVIOR

Boris W. Becker, Oregon State University, Corvallis
Patrick E. Connor, Willamette University, Salem

ABSTRACT

Value systems of individuals who are price-sensitive purchasers of furniture are compared with value systems of
price-insensitive purchasers. Price-sensitivity, in turn,
is found to be significantly related to actual store
choice behavior. This research supports the contention
that values underlie consumer attitudes, and that attitudes in turn influence behavior. The importance of
values, as fundamental and parsimonious predictors of
consumer behavior, is emphasized.

INTRODUCTION

Over a decade ago, in a wide-ranging and imaginative paper,
Nicosia and Glock (1968) suggested that "values" is a
potentially useful construct in the theory of consumer
behavior. Their conceptualization, however, has provoked
only modest interest in expanding the theoretical connection of values to consumer behavior, or in performing
empirical tests on limited hypotheses.

The basic purpose of this paper is to present the findings
of such an empirical test. Specifically, we first evaluate the relationship between individuals' personal values
and attitudes, the latter operationalized as importance of
price in the retail store selection decision. Second, we
relate consumer attitudes to actual store choice behavior.
In short, we examine the potential links between values
and attitudes, attitudes and behavior.

Values, Attitude and Behavior

The study of human values has a long, if less than coherent, history. Since the early seventies, however,
interest in the subject has risen and a number of essays
and research studies have appeared. Extensive biblio-
graphies and reviews can be found in Becker and Connor
(1979), Connor and Becker (1975), and Rokeach (1979).

Exactly what is meant by the term, "values?" A reasonably clear consensus seems to be developing among social
scientists. Values are: "abstract ideals, positive or
negative, not tied to any specific object or situation,
representing a person's beliefs about modes of conduct and
ideal terminal modes... ." Values thus are global beliefs
that "transcendentally guide actions and judgments across
specific objects and situations" (Rokeach 1968, p. 160).

Values must be distinguished from attitudes, which do focus
on specific objects and situations: "An attitude is an
orientation toward certain objects (including persons -
others and oneself) or situations . . . An attitude results from the application of a general value to concrete
objects or situations." (Theodorson and Theodorson 1969,
p. 19). For consumer research, therefore, values are small
in number and thus a parsimonious unit of inquiry--partic-
ularly as compared to attitudes, which are virtually
infinite in number.

In brief, then, we take the Rokeachian position that values
may be thought of as global beliefs about desirable end-
states underlying attitudinal and behavioral processes.
Attitudes are cognitive and affective orientations toward
specific objects or situations. Behavior, finally, is a
manifestation of one's fundamental values and consequent
attitudes. The point of this paper is that store choice
may be no exception.

Literature Review

Only one author, Carman (1977), has developed a general
model that integrates values as a determinant of consumer
behavior. In Carman's formulation, values directly influence the individual's life style. Life style is composed of interests, time-use activities, and roles.
These variables, in turn, may significantly determine
the individual's shopping and consumption behavior.

As we suggested at the outset, few empirical studies have
explicitly examined relationships among values, attitudes
and consumer behavior. Most of these studies have focused
on the relationship between values and product/brand choice
(Carman's "consumption behavior"). Scott and Lamont
(1973), Henry (1976) and Vinson, et al. (1977) all found
variation in preferred automobile attributes and model/
brand choice to be related to differences in personal
values.

As to time-use activities and interests, Jackson (1979)
found that value orientation affected both the individual's
choice between work and leisure, and the selection among
alternative leisure activities. In a recent study, suggested by earlier work of Kassarjian (1965), Becker and
Connor (1981) found values strongly related to mass media
usage.

There is a large body of literature on the retail patronage
decision, absolutely immense compared to the nascent work
on values. This literature traditionally views the patronage decision as dependent upon attitudes plus other
variables exogenous to the consumer. Attitudes are then
typically related to the individual's past experience and
his or her personal characteristics. But this list of
personal characteristics has never included the most
fundamental element, the individual's values.

Monroe and Guiltinan (1975), have proposed a theoretical
model of the patronage decision process, in which store
choice is dependent upon attitude towards stores. Attitude, they suggest, is itself a function of perceived
store attributes and attribute importance. The importance
of store attributes, in turn, depends upon buyer characteristics - of the usual types.

What we are suggesting is a synthesis of Carman's model
with that of Monroe and Guiltinan. That is, we believe
that values affect store attribute importance (Carman);
in turn, attribute importance influences actual store
choice behavior (Monroe and Guiltinan).

METHOD

Information on personal values, price-sensitivity and
retail patronage behavior was collected as part of a
progammatic stream of research on values and consumer
choice behavior. A random sample of recent purchasers
of furniture was drawn from lists provided by the managers of two stores located in a small, Western city.
Individuals selected were then called on the telephone

to arrange for personal interviews. Personal interviews were necessitated by the length and complexity of the values instrument, and the wide range of other data collected. A total of 58 interviews were completed. Furniture stores were chosen as the focus for study because we believe that furniture is both an important purchase to most consumers as well as a difficult product for which to shop (see Davis et al. 1979).

Values were measured by means of the Rokeach Value Survey (RVS), Form D (Rokeach 1973). The RVS is a very popular structured values instrument, reflecting as it does the Rokeachian conceptualization of values referred to earlier. The RVS contains two sets of values: Terminal and Instrumental. Terminal values describe desirable conditions, states of the world (for example, "wisdom," "equality," "salvation"). Instrumental values describe desirable modes of conduct (for example, behaving in a manner that is "honest," "capable," "loving"). Each set consists of a list of 18 distinct values; within each set, the subject arranges the 18 values in order of their importance to him or her. Subjects thus report two sets of 18 rank-ordered values. Standard procedures were employed in the administration of the instrument; Form D uses moveable gummed labels, by which the subject arranges his or her values in the preferred priority ranking. Evidence on the validity, reliability and factorial structure of the RVS is available in Rokeach (1973).

FINDINGS

To examine the first of this study's research questions, whether personal values influence an individual's sensitivity to price, subjects were asked to evaluate the importance of six furniture store attributes. The attributes were scaled from 1 to 5, very unimportant to very important in furniture store patronage. Those who answered "5" to price were defined as "price-sensitive;" all others were defined as "price-insensitive." This definition provided 22 price-sensitive consumers and 36 price-insensitive consumers. The reader should note that we avoid the term "price-consciousness," which refers to a high importance attached to price in general. While our respondents may, indeed, be price-conscious, we have data only on their evaluation of this attribute with respect to furniture stores.

TABLE 1

PERSONAL VALUES OF PRICE-SENSITIVE AND PRICE
INSENSITIVE BUYERS OF FURNITURE

VALUES	PRICE INSENSITIVE (N=36)		PRICE SENSITIVE (N=22)	
	MEDIAN	RANK	MEDIAN	RANK
Terminal Values				
a comfortable life	11.0	(11)	9.3	(8.5)
an exciting life	10.3	(10)	11.3	(14)
a sense of accomplishment	7.3	(8)	7.0	(4)
a world at peace	11.4	(12)	10.0	(11.5)
a world of beauty	14.1	(15)	11.0	(13)**
equality	11.6	(13)	12.0	(15)
family security	5.3	(3)	3.4	(1)
freedom	4.9	(2)	8.0	(5)
happiness	7.4	(9)	4.3	(2)
inner harmony	6.7	(6)	10.0	(11.5)
mature love	6.6	(4)	18.3	(6)
national security	15.4	(18)	13.8	(16)
pleasure	13.8	(14)	15.3	(18)
salvation	15.0	(17)	9.0	(7)
self-respect	4.1	(1)	5.4	(3)*
social recognition	14.8	(16)	14.9	(17)
true friendship	6.6	(5)	9.8	(10)**
wisdom	7.0	(7)	9.3	(8.5)
Instrumental Values				
ambitious	11.0	(13.5)	9.4	(8)
broadminded	6.7	(5)	9.7	(9)*
capable	6.6	(4)	7.8	(4)
cheerful	10.6	(11)	8.3	(5.5)
clean	13.3	(16)	10.0	(10.5)
courageous	9.3	(7)	10.0	(10.5)
forgiving	10.9	(12)	10.3	(12)
helpful	9.8	(8)	9.0	(7)
honest	3.8	(1)	2.1	(1)
imaginative	12.3	(15)	15.0	(17.5)
independent	5.8	(3)	8.3	(5.5)
intellectual	10.3	(9.5)	11.8	(15)
logical	10.3	(9.5)	11.0	(13.5)
loving	7.9	(6)	6.3	(3)
obedient	17.5	(18)	15.0	(17.5)**
polite	13.4	(17)	11.0	(13.5)
responsible	5.3	(2)	5.7	(2)
self-controlled	11.0	(13.5)	13.0	(16)

* Median Test (χ^2): $p < 0.10$
** Median Test (χ^2): $p < 0.05$

Table 1 presents median scores, and rank orders for those medians, for the values of price sensitive as compared to price-insensitive furniture buyers. Medians are normally used in an analysis of RVS data, rather than means, because the instrument yields only ordinally scaled data. "Rank order" means the ranking of each value according to its median score; for example, the value with the lowest median score (most important), is ranked one - and so on through each set of 18.

Price-sensitive consumers ranked significantly higher the Terminal value "a world of beauty" and lower the Terminal values "self-respect" and "true friendship." Price sensitives ranked significantly higher the Instrumental value "obedient" and lower the Instrumental value "broad-minded."

Rokeach has identified several factors that logically group together various of the 36 values. Even though these factors do not account for a great deal of the overall variance in value systems, given the presumably independent nature of his 36 values, they do facilitate interpretation of the lengthy listing.

Both obedient and broad-minded are part of a factor Rokeach calls "self-constriction versus self-expansion." The price-sensitives evaluated higher three of the four self-constriction values: honest, obedient and polite. They ranked lower one of the two self-expansion values: broad-minded.

True friendship and self-respect are part of the "social versus personal orientation" factor. These two values comprise the personal orientation part of the factor, and are both ranked significantly lower by the price-sensitives. Conversely, two of the four social orientation values were ranked higher by the price-sensitives: a world at peace and national security.

There was a very clear distinction between the two groups on yet another value factor, "competence versus religious morality." The price-sensitives evaluate higher all the religious morality values: salvation, clean, forgiving, helpful. They ranked lower all the competence values: imaginative, independent, intellectual, logical.

Finally, price-sensitives are clearly more "other directed" than are non-price-sensitives. On Rokeach's "inner versus other-directedness" factor, the price sensitives ranked higher the single other-directed value, polite, and lower the two inner-directed values: courageous and independent.

In summary, price-sensitive furniture buyers appear to be self-constrictive rather than self-expansive. They are socially, rather than personally, oriented - which is consistent with their tendency to be other- rather than inner-directed. They also seem to be more involved with traditional religious values than are the non price-sensitive buyers, and less concerned with personal competence.

The connection between personal values and attitude (importance of price as a store attribute) has now been demonstrated. This, of course, is interesting in itself; no such connection has been previously demonstrated. However, also important is the second research question, whether values, operating through the intermediating effect of attitude, determine behavior. The question is fundamentally this: if certain values predispose individuals to be price-sensitive, is price-sensitivity in turn related to store choice?

The two stores from which customer lists were obtained were (purposely) different from one another. Store B is a traditional, full-line furniture store while Store C is simply and clearly a discount furniture store. The obvious null hypothesis is that no relationship exists between price-sensitivity and furniture store patronized.

TABLE 2

PRICE SENSITIVITY AND STORE CHOICE

	Store B	Store C	
Price-Sensitives	18%	82%	(n = 22)
Price-Insensitives	67%	33%	(n = 36)

$$x^2 = 10.9 \quad d.f. = 2 \quad p < 0.005$$

The results shown in Table 2 indicate that 82% of the price-sensitives shopped at store C, while 67% of the non price-sensitives shopped at store B. The difference is in the expected direction and significant at the 0.005 level. Put another way, 86% of the customers of store B are price-sensitive, while 60% of store C customers are price-insensitive.

The key findings, therefore, are that: (1) personal values do influence attitude towards price as a store attribute; and (2) this attitude, in turn, does influence store choice behavior.

DISCUSSION

In common with more traditional patronage studies, price-sensitivity was related to the usual demographic characteristics. Price-sensitivity was found to be unrelated to sex, to decrease slightly with higher levels of education, and to increase strongly with age. One could, then, infer that it is age or education that affect price-sensitivity. Such an inference, however, would miss the fundamental issue. Age, for example, does seem to affect price-sensitivity; but this is because people of different age levels possess different values (Rokeach 1973). That is, the values typically held by consumers age 40 and above are precisely those values that lead to price sensitivity. It is not education, or age, or whatever that determines one's attitudes and behavior. Rather, these are correlates of values possessed by individuals, values that actually underlie and condition their behavior.

We would argue, indeed, that numerous other studies that have correlated attribute importance and the patronage decision to "objective" variables have, in fact, found relationships that depend on differences in underlying values. In short, many researchers may have been investigating the influence of values when they thought they were investigating something else entirely.

CONCLUSION

Personal values are fundamental, parsimonious bases of both attitudes and behavior. The findings of this study specifically suggest that personal values influence individuals' price-sensitivity (attitude) and subsequent store choice (behavior).

Some interesting implications follow from this research. First, if a retail store can determine the salient attributes that attract its customers, then a promotional campaign can be developed to appeal to the specific values that cause people to evaluate highly those particular attributes. In the case of furniture stores, an appeal to price-sensitivity can be linked to the values of those to whom price is particularly important -- self-constriction, other-directedness, religious morality, and a social orientation. Furthermore, knowing something about customer values can assist in developing the entire ambience or image of the store.

Additionally, a connection can be made between the present findings and the research on values and attribute/brand preference cited earlier. In the ultimate, we suggest a segmentation scheme, based upon values-determined preference structures. That is, the manufacturer can look for retailers who cater to the segment characterized by a value system that leads to a preference for the attributes possessed by the manufacturer's brand/product. Further, if we can integrate the knowledge on media choice and values, an entire marketing strategy can be designed about values as the ultimate segmentation variable. The values of price-sensitive furniture purchasers turn out to be very similar to those of heavy television viewers with respect to religious morality, self-constriction, and other directedness (Becker and Connor 1981). Television, therefore, may be a particularly appropriate medium to reach price-sensitive furniture buyers.

This study, of course, is only an exploratory effort. The sample size is limited and the present findings deal only with furniture stores, and that in a limited geographic location. Nonetheless, to find many interesting and often statistically significant differences with a sample of modest size suggests that additional research is warranted.

There remain many challenging questions to investigate, such as the more general relationship between values and price-consciousness. Much remains to be done to answer the challenge posed by Nicosia and Glock in 1968.

REFERENCES

Becker, Boris W. and Patrick E. Connor (1981), "Differences in the Personal Values of the Heavy User of Mass Media," Journal of Advertising Research, 21 (October), 37-43.

__________ (1979), "On the Status and Promise of Values Research," Paper presented at annual meetings of Academy of Management, Atlanta, Georgia, August.

Carman, James (1977), "Values and Consumption Patterns: A Closed Loop," in Keith Hunt (ed.), Advances in Consumer Research, Vol. 5, Ann Arbor: Association for Consumer Research, 401-407.

Connor, Patrick E. and Boris W. Becker (1975), "Values and the Organization: Suggestions for Research," Academy of Management Journal, 18, 550-561.

Davis, Duane L., Joseph P. Guiltinan and Wesley H. Jones (1979), "Service Characteristics, Consumer Search, and the Classification of Retail Services," Journal of Retailing, 55 (Fall), 3-23.

Henry, Walter A. (1976), "Cultural Values do Correlate with Consumer Behavior," Journal of Marketing Research, 13 (May), 121-127.

Jackson, Royal G. (1973), "A Preliminary Bicultural Study of Value Orientations and Leisure Attitudes," Journal of Leisure Research, 5, 10-22.

Kassarjian, Harold H. (1965), "Social Character and Differential Preference for Mass Communication," Journal of Marketing Research, 2 (May), 146-153.

Monroe, Kent B. and Joseph B. Guiltinan (1975), "A Path Analytic Exploration of Retail Patronage Influences," Journal of Consumer Research, 2 (June), 19-28.

Nicosia, Francesco M. and Charles Y. Glock (1968), "Marketing and Affluence: A Research Prospectus," 1968 Fall Conference Proceedings, Chicago: American Marketing Association, 510-527.

Rokeach, Milton (1968), Belief, Attitude and Values. San Francisco: Jossey-Ball.

__________ (1973), The Nature of Human Values. New York: The Free Press.

__________ (1979), Understanding Human Values: Individual and Societal. New York: The Free Press.

Scott, Jerome E. and Lawrence M. Lamont (1973), "Relating Consumer Values to Consumer Behavior: A Model and Method for Investigation," Educators" Conference Proceedings, Chicago: American Marketing Association, 283-288.

Theodorson, George A. and Achilles G. Theodorson (1969), A Modern Dictionary of Sociology. New York: Thomas Y. Cromwill Company.

Vinson, Donald E., Jerome E. Scott, and Lawrence M. Lamont (1977), "The Role of Personal Values in Marketing and Consumer Behavior," Journal of Marketing, 41 (April), 44-50.

THE EFFECTS OF PERSONAL VALUES AND
USAGE SITUATIONS ON PRODUCT ATTRIBUTE IMPORTANCE[1]

Lorne Bozinoff, Bell Canada
Robert Cohen, Pennsylvania State University

ABSTRACT

Situational influences have not been considered in previous research investigating the effects of personal values on consumer behavior. However, there is considerable evidence that situational variables can influence consumer behavior. After briefly reviewing the consumer behavior literature concerning personal values and situational effects, a research approach combining both personal values and situational effects is suggested and investigated in an empirical study. The results indicate that product attribute importance is influenced by both personal values and usage situation.

INTRODUCTION

Previous research regarding the effects of personal values on consumer behavior has ignored situational influences. However, there is some evidence that consumer bevavior is influenced by both internal factors such as personal values and by external factors, such as situational variables. This paper will briefly review the consumer behavior literature regarding personal values and situational effects. A research approach combining both personal values and situational effects will be developed and empirically investigated.

Personal Values

The personal values research paradigm in consumer behavior essentially views consumer behavior as a function of certain latent variables or human values. These human values are conceptualized as forming belief systems which serve to guide behavior across situations. Human values include more than the individual's own needs. They also capture the effects of societal and institutional demands upon the person (Rokeach 1973). In doing so, values indirectly include some broad situational or external factors since societal and institutional demands are factors external to the individual.

Consumers who exhibit similar values should tend to use the same products because they have similar modes of behavior. Personal values have been found to be related to purchase intentions, purchase behavior and product attribute importance. For example Belch (1978) found that belief systems were related to purchase intentions for a number of products. Henry (1976) was able to relate cultural values to car choice. Several studies have linked personal values to product attribute importance and brand attitudes. (Scott and Lamont 1973, Lessig 1975, Vinson, Munson and Nakaniski 1977). However, these studies have ignored the influence of external factors on consumer behavior such as situational effects.

Situational Effects

The situational approach to consumer research views consumer behavior as being determined to a great extent by external or situational variables. There is considerable support for this approach in the consumer research litera-ture. Belk (1975) cites several studies which show a significant relationship between generic product choice and situations. For example, Belk (1974) has shown that the type of snack (e.g., popcorn) likely to be chosen depends upon the situation (e.g., watching T.V.). Miller and Ginter (1979) found that the choice of fast food outlets is significantly related to the situation. Other studies have linked situations to choice of beverage products, meat products, leisure activities, and motion pictures (Belk 1975). However, these studies have ignored the influence of internal factors on consumer behavior such as personal values.

Most studies of situational effects have looked only at frequently purchased consumer products. With such products, it is possible to purchase one product for one situation and another product for another situation. However, none of the advocates of the situational approach have discussed the purchase of infrequently bought durable goods. It is not immediately clear how a situational approach can be used for these purchases. For example, consider the purchase of an automobile. Many consumers cannot afford to buy several automobiles for use in different situations. Somehow a compromise must be reached so that the car most appropriate for the "average" situation can be purchased.

Fennell (1978) has suggested that the usage situation will determine the specific benefits sought in a product, which in turn will determine which attributes are important to the consumer. For example, a motorist who frequently faces situations involving fast-moving traffic will require a car with a lot of power and, hence, horse-power will become an important attribute for this motorist. A commuter who must park in crowded downtown situations will want a small car because of its ease of parking. For this consumer, size will be an important attribute. Srivastava, Shocker and Day (1978) have found some evidence that the usage situation does influence the choice of some frequently purchased products. It was found that the type of breath freshener used (e.g., toothpasts, mouthwashes, mints, etc.) was dependent upon the situation (e.g., at home, away from home).

A Combined Personal Values/Situational Approach to Consumer Behavior

Research examining the effects of internal factors such as personal values on consumer behavior is not in conflict with research examining the effects of external factors such as situational variables on consumer behavior. Instead, the two research streams are complimentary rather than competitive. It is suggested that consumer behavior is a function of both the situation and what the individual brings to the situation (i.e., personal values). Despite a considerable amount of consumer research utilizing the personal values and situational approaches, no study has attempted to merge these two research streams and look at consumer behavior from a combined personal values/situational viewpoint. It remains to be shown how the two approaches can be combined and exactly how much product choice variance can be explained by a combined personal values/situational approach.

[1] Support for this study was provided by the Margaret Brown-Byron Fund, University of Toronto and by the Center for Research, The Pennsylvania State University.

The study described below serves only as an initial investigation of the ideas discussed above. Specifically, there are two broad issues of major interest. First, how much consumer behavior variance can be explained with a combined approach? Within a combined approach, what are the relative contributions of personal values and situational effects in explaining consumer behavior? Second, can this combined approach be applied to consumer durables which must be purchased for use in the "average" situation?

METHODS

Subjects

Five hundred and twenty-two subjects were recruited from seven undergraduate marketing classes at three universities. During regular class time, students were asked to participate in the study. Participation was voluntary, although all of the students agreed to participate. A sample of students is defensible because as Kruglanski (1975) has argued, homogeneous samples (such as students) are appropriate for theory-oriented research where individual (i.e., demographic) differences are not of theoretical interest.

Measurement Instrument

The subjects were given questionnaires containing a series of personal values, usage situation frequency and attribute importance measures. The usage situation frequency and attribute importance measures were taken for three products - cars, stereo speakers and library services. Cars and stereo speakers were chosen because they are relevant to the sample and because they are durables. Durables were used so that the issue of situation effects in the purchase of durables could be examined. Library services were chosen to provide an illustration of the applicability of the research approach to a service as well as to products.

Personal values were operationalized by the Rokeach Value Survey (Rokeach 1973). The eighteen instrumental values (e.g., ambitious, boring, neat, careful) from Rokeach Value Survey were used instead of the terminal values because instrumental values are more closely linked to behavior. Instrumental values are specific modes of conduct (behaviors) while terminal values are end-states (behavioral outcomes). It is the specific modes of behavior which achieve the terminal values or end states. Personal values then was measured by the Rokeach instrumental values.

It was suggested earlier that durable goods are purchased according to how appropriate they are for the "average" usage situation since most consumers cannot afford to purchase more than one durable good at any one time. For example, often one car is bought for use in several different situations like travelling to work, going to parties, going on vacations and so forth. Many consumers cannot afford to buy one car for commuting to work, another car for travelling to social activities and another car for going on vacations. Rather, a compromise purchase is made and the car most appropriate for the "average" usage situation is bought (Berkowitz, Ginter and Talarzyk 1977).

This "average" usage situation was operationalized by relative usage situation frequency. Respondents were given 100 points in a constant sum scale to allocate among usage situations in terms of frequency of occurrence for cars (e.g., travelling to work, going to parties, racing, pulling a trailer), library services (e.g., casual reading, researching term papers) and stereo speakers (e.g., for music at parties, for listening to news reports). The list of usage situations for each product were developed from

focus group interviews conducted before the questionnaire was constructed. Situations then were measured by relative frequency.

As noted above, Fennell (1978) has advanced the view that the usage situation will determine which product attribute will be most important to the consumer. Such an approach suggests how the situational effects on durable good purchases can be analyzed. Rather than using durable good choice as the dependent variable, attribute importance can be examined directly. This preempts the problem of trying to account for durable good purchase choice based on "average" situations. Usage situation frequency will determine which attributes of a product are important and this in turn will impact upon choice through a multi-attribute decision-making model. The dependent variable, then was attribute importance and was operationalized by asking subjects to rate the importance of car features (e.g., horsepower, handling, appearance), library features (e.g., staff co-operation, ease of use, parking) and stereo speakers features (e.g., appearance, power rating, dispersion).

The combined personal values/situational approach to consumer behavior was operationalized by measuring the relationship between the two independent variables, instrumental values (personal values) and usage situation frequency (situation), and the dependent variable, attribute importance.

RESULTS

As an initial step, the reliability of the measures was assessed by again administering the questionnaire to a subsample of 46 subjects two weeks after the initial administration. The average reliability of the 18 instrumental values was .68. The average reliability of usage situation frequency ranged from .71 for cars to .65 for library services. The average reliability for the attribute importance measures ranged from .65 for car attribute importance to .595 for stereo speaker attribute importance.

For each product, three multiple regression analyses were conducted. First, the complete set of instrumental values for each respondent were regressed against each product attribute importance rating. This yielded one multiple correlation coefficient for each attribute. Second, the complete set of usage situation frequency ratings for each respondent were regressed against each product attribute importance rating. This also yielded one multiple correlation coefficient for each attribute. Third, the complete set of instrumental values and usage situation frequency ratings for each respondent were regressed against each product attribute importance rating. The first analysis provided a measure of the strength of the relationship between instrumental values and attribute importance (personal value approach). The second analysis provided a measure of the strength of the relationship between usage situation and attribute importance (situational approach). The third analysis provided a measure of the combined strength of the relationship among instrumental values, usage situation frequency and attribute importance (combined approach). By comparing the results on the first two analyses with the results of the third analysis, the incremental benefit of utilizing a combined personal values/situational approach in consumer research can be assessed.

Tables 1, 2 and 3 report the results of these analyses for each of the three products. The instrumental value results are typical of what has previously been found with studies utilizing a personal values approach. The multiple correlation coefficients between instrumental values and attribute importance ratings ranged from .17 to .27 for cars, from .15 to .25 for libraries and from .17 to .25

for stereo speakers. While all of these correlation coefficients are significant (p < .05), they represent an average explained variance of only 5% for cars and libraries and 4% for stereo speakers.

The usage situation results paralleled the instrumental value results. The multiple correlation coefficients between usage situation frequency and attribute importance ratings averaged from .12 to .40 for cars, from .03 to .36 for libraries and from .09 to .24 for stereo speakers. While most of these correlation coefficients are also significant (p < .05), they represent an average explained variance of only 4% for cars and libraries, and only 2% for stereo speakers. These results suggest that a personal values approach generally explains slightly more variance than a situational approach.

The results of combining both instrumental values and usage situation were significantly superior than either the instrument value or usage situation results when taken separately. The multiple correlation coefficients between both instrumental values and usage situation with attribute importance ratings ranged from .22 to .43 for cars, from .18 to .41 for libraries and from .22 to .32 for stereo speakers. All of these correlation coefficients were significant (p < .05) and represent an average explained variance of 9% for cars, 8% for libraries and 7% for stereo speakers.

A canonical correlation analysis was also undertaken in order to measure the magnitude of the relationship between the dependent and independent variables under the most optimal conditions. For this analysis, the personal values

TABLE 1

Comparison of Personal Value, Situational and Combined Approaches for Cars

| Feature Importance | Personal Value Approach | | Situational Approach | | Combined Approach | |
	Multiple Correlation Coefficient	Correlation Coefficient Squared	Multiple Correlation Coefficient	Correlation Coefficient Squared	Multiple Correlation Coefficient	Correlation Coefficient Squared
appearance	.27	.08	.27	.07	.37	.13
trade-in value	.17	.03	.16	.03	.24	.05
mileage	.17	.03	.22	.05	.26	.07
reliability	.29	.08	.20	.04	.36	.13
handling	.21	.04	.16	.03	.26	.07
comfort	.24	.06	.16	.03	.29	.09
service frequency	.18	.02	.13	.02	.22	.05
safety	.21	.05	.17	.03	.27	.07
price	.21	.05	.15	.02	.25	.06
emission control	.27	.07	.23	.05	.35	.12
horsepower	.23	.05	.40	.16	.43	.19
warranty	.19	.04	.12	.02	.22	.05
Average	.22	.05	.20	.04	.29	.09
Canonical Analysis	.38	.14	.44	.19	.50	.25

TABLE 2

Comparison of Personal Value, Situational and Combined Approaches for Libraries

| Feature Importance | Personal Values Approach | | Situational Approach | | Combined Approach | |
	Multiple Correlation Coefficient	Correlation Coefficient Squared	Multiple Correlation Coefficient	Correlation Coefficient Squared	Multiple Correlation Coefficient	Correlation Coefficient Squared
accessibility	.15	.02	.09	.01	.18	.03
ease of use	.21	.05	.20	.04	.28	.08
staff politeness	.18	.03	.06	.00	.20	.04
book selection	.22	.05	.25	.06	.32	.10
quiet	.23	.05	.36	.13	.41	.17
services	.21	.05	.26	.07	.33	.11
staff expertise	.25	.06	.11	.01	.27	.08
comfort	.21	.04	.29	.08	.33	.11
staff cooperation	.21	.04	.15	.02	.26	.07
shelf access	.25	.06	.10	.01	.27	.07
Average	.21	.05	.19	.04	.29	.08
Canonical Analysis	.31	.10	.43	.19	.47	.22

TABLE 3

Comparison of Personal Value, Situational and Combined Approaches for Stereo Speakers

Feature Importance	Personal Value Approach		Situational Approach		Combined Approach	
	Multiple Correlation Coefficient	Correlation Coefficient Squared	Multiple Correlation Coefficient	Correlation Coefficient Squared	Multiple Correlation Coefficient	Correlation Coefficient Squared
loudness	.25	.06	.19	.03	.32	.10
tone	.18	.03	.09	.00	.21	.04
treble	.19	.04	.21	.04	.28	.07
mid-range	.19	.03	.11	.01	.23	.05
bass	.17	.03	.13	.02	.22	.05
appearance	.24	.06	.21	.04	.31	.10
design	.24	.06	.09	.00	.25	.07
efficiency	.22	.05	.09	.00	.24	.06
warranty	.15	.02	.24	.06	.29	.08
price	.22	.05	.21	.04	.30	.09
dispersion	.20	.04	.15	.02	.26	.07
range	.18	.03	.15	.02	.26	.07
Average	.20	.04	.15	.02	.26	.07
Canonical Analysis	.35	.12	.45	.20	.48	.23

and situational variable sets were correlated with the set of attribute importance ratings for each product. Canonical correlation analysis seeks the linear combination of both dependent and independent variables which maximizes their correlation. Therefore, canonical correlation analysis will yield the strongest possible relationship among sets of variables and can be considered as an upper bound on the strength of the relationship between the sets of dependent and independent variables.

The instrumental values yielded canonical coefficients of .38 for cars, .31 for libraries and .35 for stereo speakers (using the first canonical correlation). In all cases the canonical correlation coefficients were significant ($p < .01$). The situational variables yielded (first) canonical coefficients of .44 for cars, .43 for libraries and .45 for stereo speakers. When combined, the instrumental values and usage situations yielded (first) canonical coefficients of .50 for cars, .47 for libraries and .48 for stereo speakers.

DISCUSSION

When taken separately, neither personal values nor the situational effects managed to explain, on the average, more than 5% of the variance. However, when the two influences were combined the variance explained was nearly doubled on the average to almost 10%. Thus the average variance explained using the combined approach tends to exceed the most variance explained using the personal values approach. For example, using a combined approach, it may be possible to explain 19% of the variance in automobile horsepower importance ratings. Similarly, with a combined approach it may be possible to explain 17% of the importance of a quiet environment in a library.

While the results are disappointing in terms of the still low amount of variance explained, the results do show that utilizing a combined approach does provide almost a doubling in the amount of variance explained. Indeed, the canonical correlation results suggested that a combined approach could explain as much as 25% of the variance. One conclusion based on this study is that a combined approach can add to predictive validity beyond that

possible with either a personal values usage approach. Furthermore, it appears that in general both personal values and usage situations contribute equally to explaining attribute importance variance. However, it also appears that the importance of some attributes is influenced more heavily by either personal values or usage situations. For example, the importance of quietness in a library depends upon the usage situation. On the other hand, the importance of car reliability appears to be more heavily dependent upon personal values rather than usage situation.

A second conclusion based on this study is that the effect of situations on durables can be assessed by looking at attribute importance. There is no doubt that attribute importance is significantly related to usage situation frequency. For example, the importance of horsepower is influenced by car usage situation frequency.

FUTURE RESEARCH DIRECTIONS

Epstein (1979, 1980) has shown that behavioral prediction based on internal factors can be greatly improved by taking multiple measures over time. As predicted by the Spearman-Brown formula, Epstein found that multiple measures increased the reliability of the measurement instrument. Because reliability puts an upper bound on predictive validity, an increase in the reliability of the measurement will invariably lead to an increase in predictive validity. For example, by increasing the length of the measurement instrument used in this study by a factor of twelve (which Epstein has shown is practical if multiple measures over time are used), the Spearman-Brown formula predicts that the reliability of the instrumental values, situation frequency and attribute importance measures would exceed .90 (Cronbach 1970). Such an increase in reliability would increase the average predictive validity of a combined approach to approximately .40. Therefore, by simply increasing the test length, a combined approach could double the average explained variance (Lord and Novick 1968).

A second avenue of future research concerns the usage situation measure. It was implied that the importance

of a situation is a function of the frequency of its occurrence. However, just because a product is used more
frequently in one situation does not mean that this is the
most important usage situation for the consumer. A consumer may very infrequently use a car for travelling to
social events. But, this may still be a very important
usage situation to the consumer. A better method of measuring usage situation effects may be to measure the importance _and_ frequency of usage situations. A frequently
occurring but relatively unimportant usage situation may
not have much of an influence on attribute importance.

In sum, a combined personal values/situational approach
does offer additional explanatory power beyond that offered by either the personal values or usage situation
approaches. Specifically, a combined approach can double
the explanatory power of the other approaches, although
from a practical point of view, the explanatory power of
a combined approach is still low. In any event the combined study of personal values and situational effects
does hold some potential for explaining consumer behavior,
although a considerable number of issues remain to be investigated.

REFERENCES

Belch, George E. (1978), "Belief Systems and the Differen-
tial Role of the Self-Concept," in _Advances in Consumer
Research_. Volume 5, Hunt, K. (ed.), Ann Arbor, MI:
Association for Consumer Research, 320-325.

Belk, Russell W. (1974), "An Exploratory Assessment of
Situational Effects in Buyer Behavior," _Journal of Marketing Research_, (May), 156-163.

_____________ (1975), "Situational Variables and Consumer
Behavior," _Journal of Consumer Research_, 2, 157-164.

Berkowitz, Eric N., James L. Ginter and W. Wayne Talarzyk
(1977), "An Investigation of the Effects of Specific
Usage Situations on the Prediction of Consumer Choice
Behavior," in _Contemporary Marketing Thought_, Greenberg,
B.A. and D. Bellenger, (eds.) Chicago, Ill.: American
Marketing Association.

Cronbach, L. (1970), _Essentials of Psychological Testing_,
New York: Harper and Row.

Epstein, S. (1979), "The Stability of the Behavior: I. On
Predicting Most of the People Much of the Time," _Journal
of Personality and Social Psychology_, 37, 1097-1126.

_____________ (1980), "The Stability of Behavior: II. Implications for Psychological Research," _American Psycho-
logist_, 35, 9, 790-806.

Fennell, Geraldine (1978), "Consumer's Perceptions of the
Product-Use Situation," _Journal of Marketing_, (April),
38-47.

Fornell, Claes and Robert A. Westbrook (1979), "An Exploratory Study of Assertiveness, Aggressiveness and Consumer
Complaining Behavior," in _Advances in Consumer Research_,
Wilkie, W. (ed.), Ann Arbor, MI: Association for Consumer Research, 105-110.

Henry, Walter A. (1976), "Cultural Values Do Correlate
with Consumer Behavior," _Journal of Marketing Research_,
8, 409-418.

Kruglanski, Arie (1975), "The Two Meanings of External
Validity," _Human Relations_, 28, 653-659.

Lessig, Parker V. (1975), "A Measurement of Dependencies
Between Values and Other Levels of the Consumer's Belief
Space," _Journal of Business Research,_ 3, 227-240.

Lord, Frederic M. and Melvin R. Novick (1968), _Statistical
Theories of Mental Test Scores_, Reading, MA: Addison-
Wesley.

Miller, Kenneth E. and James L. Ginter (1979), "An Investigation of Situational Variation in Brand Choice Behavior and Attitude," _Journal of Marketing Research_, 16
(February), 111-123.

Roeach, M. (1973), _The Nature of Human Values_, New York:
Free Press.

Scott, Jerome E. and Lawrence M. Lamont (1973), "Relating
Consumer Values to Consumer Behavior: A Model and Method
for Investigation," in _Increasing Marketing Productivity_,
Greer, T. V. (ed.), Chicago, IL: American Marketing
Association, 283-288.

Srivastava, Rajendra K., Allan D. Shocker, and George S.
Day (1978), "An Exploratory Study of the Influence of
Usage Situation on Perceptions of Product-Markets," in
Advances in Consumer Research, Volume 5, Hunt, K. (ed.),
Ann Arbor, MI: Association for Consumer Research, 32-
38.

Vinson, Donald E., Michael J. Munson and Masao Nakanishi
(1977), "An Investigation of the Rokeach Value Survey
for Consumer Research Applications," in _Advances in Consumer Research_, Volume 4, Perreault, W. (ed.), Atlanta,
GA: Association for Consumer Research, 247-253.

THE IMPACT OF EDUCATION ON THE RELATIVE EFFECTIVENESS
OF ONE-SIDED AND TWO-SIDED COMMUNICATIONS[1]

Mark I. Alpert, University of Texas at Austin
Linda L. Golden, University of Texas at Austin

ABSTRACT

This study investigates the relative effectiveness of one-sided and two-sided communication on a variety of communication and buyer behavior variables. The results indicate that the impact of alternative message strategies may interact with audience educational levels. Confirming hypotheses dating from forty years ago, two-sided messages may be relatively more effective with persons of higher education.

INTRODUCTION

The advertising prohibition against saying something negative about one's own brand is no longer strictly followed. Some advertisers (e.g., Avis, Volkswagen) have been "disclaiming" certain (often trivial) characteristics of their products in conjunction with positive claims. This paper will present theory underlying these phenomena, summarize historical and recent research, and present new findings regarding the effectiveness of two-sided communications and their potential interaction with educational level (which may be proxy for other receiver characteristics).

One-Sided and Two-Sided Communication Research

Two-sided arguments are typically used when a communicator takes into account both sides of an issue, but he is himself in favor of one side. Alternatively, a one-sided argument is an argument confined to one side of an issue (Hovland, 1954).

A series of studies starting from the 1940s, insightfully reviewed by McGuire (1964), seem to suggest that mention of opposing arguments should be handled with caution. The only groups that seem more positively affected by two-sided messages were those initially opposed to the conclusion and those of higher educational levels. However, two-sided messages can serve to "immunize" receivers against contradictory information in later messages (Hovland, Lumsdaine and Sheffield, 1949; Lumsdaine and Janis, 1953; McGuire, 1962, 1964 and 1969; McGuire and Papageorgis, 1961).

After a period of dormancy in the communications literature, studies of one-sided versus two-sided communication in an advertising context began to appear in the marketing literature. Sawyer (1973) found that repetition (over a short time period) of refutational appeals was more effective than repetition of supportive appeals for people who had never used the advertised brand. Settle and Golden (1974) found that attitudes tvoard important positive features may be improved by advertising that <u>disclaims</u> superiority for unimportant features, although overall product evaluation may not always be affected (Golden, 1977). Golden and Alpert (1978) found that copy believability, as well as perceptions of important product features, was higher for two-sided than for one-sided messages. Smith and Hunt (1978) found support for the conceptual arguments of the Settle and Golden (1974) and Golden and Alpert (1978) papers: that two-sided messages elicited respondent attributions that the positive claims were likely to be due to their validity, rather than the advertiser's desire to sell

[1] We gratefully acknowledge the support of the Department of Transportation program of University Research, Contract DOT-OS-30093.

the product (a more likely attribution with one-sided messages).

The effects that were noted in these studies were not strong, and in some cases, the one-sided messages were at least as effective in influencing purchase intentions. This lack of clear superiority for two-sided messages parallels the communications research studies, and to some extent may be due to countervailing impact on various audience segments. Sawyer (1973), for example, found no overall main effects, but did find two-sided messages to be relatively more effective for nonusers of the advertised brands. Given the literature and previous research, it is reasonable to suspect that educational level may have moderated the impact of the alternative strategies as well.

It has been argued that tolerance for ambiguity and avoidance of stereotyped thinking increase with education. Accordingly, one-sided (non-"mixed") messages should "work" better for lower-educated people, while the reverse should hold true for two-sided messages and persons of higher educational levels. The present study attempts to compare the relative effects of one-sided and two-sided communications over a set of advertising evaluations, belief measures, and purchase intentions, as well as test for interaction effects of communication strategy and education. Marketing researchers have not previously investigated the relative effectiveness of one- and two-sided messages for individuals of varying educational levels.

Hypotheses

Following from the theory and previous research results, the following hypotheses are advanced.

H_1: Two-sided messages will be more positively evaluated for general copy variables such as reading likelihood, believability, information quantity, information usefulness and affect and purchase intentions.

H_2: Two-sided messages will be more effective than one-sided messages for copy claim variables not disclaimed.

H_3: Advertisement type will interact positively with educational level such that two-sided advertisements will be more positively perceived for persons with a college degree or higher than for persons of lower educational levels.

METHODOLOGY

Presentation of both one- and two-sided experimental manipulations in a manner consistent with typical advertising's two-sided messages requires selection of both determinant and non-determinant attributes for the test product. In the two-sided manipulations, the ad does not claim that the product possesses the non-determinant attributes, but does claim possession of the determinant attributes. For deodorant, the frequently purchased and widely used product studied in this paper, a pilot study found five determinant attributes to be protection from odor, freedom from wetness, long-lasting, non-stain ingredient, and non-irritating to skin. The non-determinant attributes disclaimed in the two-sided treatment were:

beautiful package and five package sizes.

Another pilot study investigated three advertisement format alternatives and found the strongest manipulation for the use of check marks (√) beside attributes under columns labeled "Secure gives you" and "Secure doesn't give you." One-sided treatments consistently contained positive claims for all attributes.

After pretests and revisions, the final instrument contained the experimental manipulation printed on heavy glossy paper in order to simulate an advertisement. The treatment had a few sentences of copy and a column listing of attributes as described previously. A cover page told the respondent that the following page contained part of an advertisement and to please read it carefully. There was no illustration, simply straight copy.

The next section of the instrument contained five questions regarding the subject's reactions to the copy: likelihood of reading, believability, information quantity, information usefulness and affect toward the advertisement. Subjects were also asked to indicate to what extent they felt the product possessed each of the seven product attributes and purchase intentions. The questions are presented in Tables 1 and 2. The final section of the instrument obtained demographic information. A sample frame of 1500 individuals of a medium-sized Southwestern city was obtained from Cole's Directory. Potential respondents were contacted by telephone and mailed randomized versions of the questionnaire. Five hundred and sixty-eight usable surveys were returned, with the relevant sample for this study being two hundred and thirty-six subjects. Discriminant analysis revealed that subjects assigned to alternative treatments did not differ significantly on demographic dimensions (including education).

As a manipulation check, one-way analysis of variance (t-tests) was run between a control group and the treatment groups for each dependent variable regarding the product's possession of specific attributes. The control group mean ratings were lower than either the one- or two-sided treatments for each dependent variable for which a possession claim was made. The two-sided mean was lower for the disclaimed attributes. This pattern was consistent for all dependent variables. Thus, the manipulations "took."

Education was divided into two levels: some college and less, and college graduate and higher. Approximately fifty percent of the sample fell in each group. While the communication research conducted by Hovland, Lumsdaine and Sheffield (1949) during World War II had divided education at high school graduation, in the thirty-three years since those studies were published, the educational level of the general population has risen. Thus, it was considered appropriate to raise the educational level groupings to reflect the same relative population educational levels. The data were submitted to two-way analysis of variance for each dependent variable separately.

RESULTS

Table 1 presents the summary of analysis of variance for significant (α<.05) general copy variables and purchase intentions. There is a significant main effect of advertisement type for likelihood of reading, information quantity, information usefulness and affect. The two-sided treatment had a higher perceived likelihood of being read, higher perceived quantity of information, higher perceived usefulness of information and a more positive affect toward the ad than the one-sided copy treatment.

There was no significant main effect of education for any dependent copy variable; however, there was a significant interaction of education and copy type for believability, information usefulness and purchase intentions. Across all three dependent variables, the two-sided treatment for college graduate or higher subjects had the highest mean, followed by the two-sided treatment for some college or less and the one-sided treatment for some college or less, respectively. The one-sided treatment with college graduation and higher subjects was consistently the least effective interaction level. The differential effectiveness of the two-sided treatment was much stronger for persons having graduated from college than for persons who had not graduated from college.

Although not within a .05 level of alpha, there were marginally significant results following the above pattern. The alpha level for advertisement type on believability was .09, with the two-sided treatment being rated as more believable (mean of 4.14) than the one-sided treatment (mean of 3.25). The same pattern occurred for advertisement type on purchase intentions. The alpha level was .07 and the two-sided treatment elicited higher purchase intentions (mean of 1.96) than did the one-sided treatment (mean of 1.58).

The interaction of advertisement type and education for attitude toward the ad was also marginally significant with an alpha level of .07. Again, the previous pattern was seen. In decreasing order of affect, mean ratings were: two-sided with college grad or higher (3.28), two-sided with some college or less (2.83), one-sided with some college or less (2.32), and one-sided with college grad or higher (1.79).

Table 2 presents the summary of analysis of variance for significant copy claim variables. There was a significant main effect of advertisement type for all but one dependent variable.

Secure was perceived as possessing the attributes more for two-sided communications than for one-sided communications in non-disclaimer attribute situations (long-lasting, non-stain, freedom from wetness, and freedom from odor). For five package sizes and beautiful package, which were disclaimed in the two-sided treatment, the one-sided treatment received consistently higher mean ratings.

There were no main effects of education for any copy claim variables; however, the interaction of advertisement type and education was significant for protection from odor. Secure was perceived to provide more odor protection for two-sided communication with persons who have at least a college degree. The next two most effective interaction levels were one-sided communication with persons having some college or less and one-sided communication with persons having at least a college degree, respectively. The lowest perception occurs for the two-sided communication with persons having some college or less. These results contrast somewhat with those found for the advertisement copy variables. Two-sided communication was not more effective with both educational groups, as was true for the advertisement copy variables. For the attribute variable protection from odor, one-sided communication was more effective for persons having some college or less and two-sided communication was more effective for persons having a college degree or higher.

The interaction of advertisement type and education was marginally significant for two dependent variables. For non-irritating, the alpha level for the interaction was .07. The pattern of means was identical to that for protection from odor, indicating that the one-sided communication was more effective for persons having some college or less (mean of 2.3, vs. 2.07 for two-sided and less educated) and the two-sided communication was more effective for persons having a college degree or higher (mean of 2.76 vs. 2.2 for one-sided with high education level).

There was an alpha level of .06 for the interaction of advertisement type and education on freedom from wetness.

TABLE 1
SUMMARY OF ANALYSIS OF VARIANCE FOR SIGNIFICANT GENERAL COPY VARIABLES AND PURCHASE INTENTIONS

Treatment	MS	d.f.	F.	p	Mean[a]
Dependent variable: If you were to see the above copy in a magazine you were reading, how likely would you be to read all the copy?					
Ad Type	27.70	1	6.89	.01	
One-sided					2.37
Two-sided					2.99
Dependent variable: Overall, to what extent do you feel the statements made in the copy are true?					
Ad Type x Education	15.36	1	5.81	.02	
One-sided x some college or less					3.42
One-sided x college grad or higher					3.00
Two-sided x some college or less					3.93
Two-sided x college grad or higher					4.33
Dependent variable: How much information do you feel the copy provided?					
Ad Type	41.03	1	11.14	.00	
One-sided					3.26
Two-sided					3.90
Dependent variable: How useful do you feel the information in the copy is to you?					
Ad Type	21.42	1	7.28	.01	
One-sided					2.14
Two-sided					2.78
Ad Type x Education	13.76	1	4.68	.03	
One-sided x some college or less					2.37
One-sided x college grad or higher					1.81
Two-sided x some college or less					2.61
Two-sided x college grad or higher					2.95
Dependent variable: In general, to what extent do you like the copy:					
Ad Type	36.41	1	12.58	.00	
One-sided					2.10
Two-sided					3.08
Dependent variable: How likely is it that your next deodorant would be Secure if it is available at you favorite store?					
Ad Type x Education	10.09	1	4.71	.03	
One-sided x some college or less					1.86
One-sided x college grad or higher					1.19
Two-sided x some college or less					1.93
Two-sided x college grad or higher					1.97

[a]Ratings were elicited on a seven-point scale, with one representing the lowest rating and seven the highest rating.

TABLE 2
SUMMARY OF ANALYSIS OF VARIANCE FOR SIGNIFICANT COPY CLAIM VARIABLES

Treatment	MS	d.f.	F.	p	Mean[a]
Dependent variable: To what extent do you feel that Secure is long lasting?					
Ad Type	17.37	1	6.50	.01	
One-sided					2.31
Two-sided					2.89
Dependent variable: To what extent do you feel Secure gives you a non-stain ingredient?					
Ad Type	12.24	1	4.35	.04	
One-sided					2.66
Two-sided					2.74
Dependent variable: To what extent do you feel Secure gives you freedom from wetness?					
Ad Type	12.09	1	4.03	.05	
One-sided					2.45
Two-sided					2.97
Dependent variable: To what extent do you feel Secure protects you from odor?					
Ad Type	15.59	1	4.42	.04	
One-sided					3.12
Two-sided					3.64
Ad Type x Education	25.06	1	7.11	.01	
One-sided x some college or less					3.41
One-sided x college grad or higher					2.72
Two-sided x some college or less					3.31
Two-sided x college grad or higher					3.97
Dependent variable[b]: To what extent do you feel Secure has five package sizes?					
Ad Type	537.33	1	118	.00	
One-sided					4.88
Two-sided					1.75
Dependent variable[b]: To what extent do you feel Secure has a beautiful package?					
Ad Type	257.26	1	75.35	.00	
One-sided					3.89
Two-sided					1.71

[a]Mean ratings were elicited on a seven-point scale, with one representing the lowest rating and seven the highest rating.

[b]Attributes disclaimed in the two-sided treatment.

Consistent with all other results for this interaction, the highest perceptions occurred for the two-sided communication with persons having a college degree or higher (mean of 3.2). The lowest perceptions occurred for persons receiving the one-sided communication with a college degree or higher (mean of 2.28) For persons having some college or less, two-sided communication was more effective (mean of 2.7) than one-sided communication (mean of 2.58). These results were consistent with the pattern found for this interaction on the general copy variables: the two-sided communication was more effective for both educational groups; however, the one-sided communication did better for persons having some college or less than it did for persons having a college degree or higher.

The first hypothesis predicted that two-sided communications would be more effective than one-sided communications for general copy variables and purchase intentions. For five out of six of these dependent variables, there was a significant or marginally significant main effect of advertisement type supporting this hypothesis in the appropriate direction. Thus, hypothesis one is accepted.

The second hypothesis states that two-sided messages will be more effective than one-sided messages for copy claim variables which were not disclaimed. There was a significant main effect of advertisement type for four of the five non-disclaimed copy claim variables. Means were in the hypothesized direction and hypothesis two was supported by the data.

Hypothesis three predicts that advertisement type will interact with educational level such that two-sided communications will be more positively perceived by persons with a college degree or higher than for persons of a lower educational level. This hypothesis was consistently supported across copy claim variables and general copy variables as the interaction was significantly or marginally significant for seven of the thirteen dependent variables and in the hypothesized direction. However, this hypothesis was more strongly supported for general copy variables than for the copy claim variables.

CONCLUSIONS AND IMPLICATIONS

The conclusions and implications are restricted to the sample characteristics and methodology in this study. In addition, the specific product used was an unfamiliar brand of a frequently purchased, widely used product: deodorant. Future research is needed to determine whether these specific conclusions hold for other samples, methodologies (e.g., voluntary exposure, repetitions) and products.

An advertiser using a two-sided message might enhance readability, information quantity perceptions, information usefulness perceptions, affect, purchase intentions and the perceived probability that the product has the claimed characteristics. There were no significant differential effects of one-sided and two-sided communications for believability. However, believability was affected by the advertisement type when education was considered.

For general copy variables and purchase intentions, a one-sided message was more effective for persons who had not graduated from college than was a one-sided message for persons who had graduated from college. Thus, the impact of a one-sided message is likely to be relatively stronger at lower educational levels and a two-sided message appears to be genuinely stronger than a one-sided message at any level of education.

The conclusions are not as clear for copy claim variables (i.e., the extent to which the product possesses the attributes claimed). The consistent conclusion from above still holds: the most effective message is a two-sided message directed to persons having a college degree or higher. For copy claim variables, however, a one-sided message tends to be more effective for lower educational levels than is a two-sided message, although the results are mixed and there is some support for the previous conclusion that two-sided communications are more effective for both educational groups.

The implication for marketers is that two-sided communications can be a strong persuasive appeal for persons of any educational level. However, the effectiveness of a two-sided message will be enhanced with higher educational status persons (college graduate or higher) and a one-sided message may be more effective than a two-sided message for persons of lower educational levels for perceptions regarding the product's possession of some claimed attributes. Whether this is a function of less educated audience reaction to one-sided (vs. two-sided) messages, or to the specific types of attributes "better" perceived by this group when exposed to one-sided messages remains a topic for further conceptualization and empirical work.

Having found that the relative impact of one-sided and two-sided messages is conditional upon educational level, marketing managers and consumer researchers should share a common interest in extensions of the study. Future research might also extend the scope of this study to other communication strategies and their interaction with other audience variables, including race, sex, and prior attitude toward the advertised product.

REFERENCES

Golden, L. "Attribution Theory Implications for Advertisement Claim Credibility," Journal of Marketing Research, 1 (1977).

Golden, Linda L. and Mark I. Alpert. "The Relative Effectiveness of One-Sided and Two-Sided Communication for Mass Transit Advertising," in H. Keith Hunt, ed. Advances in Consumer Research, Vol. V., Ann Arbor: Association for Consumer Research (1978).

Hovland, C. "Effects of the Mass Media of Communication," in G. Lindzey, ed. Handbook of Social Psychology (vol. 2), Cambridge: Addison-Wesley, 1954.

Hovland, C., A. Lumsdaine, and F. Sheffield. Experiments in Mass Communication: Studies in Social Psychology in World War II (vol. 3), Princeton: Princeton University Press, 1949.

Klapper, J. The Effects of Mass Media. New York: Columbia University Bureau of Applied Social Research, 1949.

Lumsdaine, A., and I. Janis. "Resistance to 'Counterpropaganda' Produced by One-Sided and Two-Sided 'Propaganda' Presentations," Public Opinion Quarterly, 17 (1953).

McGuire, W. "The Nature of Attitudes and Attitude Change," in G. Lindzey, ed. Handbook of Social Psychology (vol. 3), Cambridge: Addison-Wesley, 1969.

McGuire, W. "Persistence of the Resistance to Persuasion Induced by Various Types of Prior Belief Defenses," Journal of Abnormal Social Psychology, 64 (1962).

McGuire, William J. "Inducing Resistance to Persuasion: Some Contemporary Approaches," in Leonard Berkowitz, ed., Advances in Experimental Social Psychology, Vol. I. New York: Academic Press (1964).

McGuire, W., and D. Papageorgis. "The Relative Efficacy of Various Types of Prior Belief--Defense in Producing Immunity Against Persuasion," Journal of Abnormal Social Psychology, 62 (1961).

Sawyer, Alan G. "The Effects of Repetition of Refutational and Supportive Advertising Appeals," Journal of Marketing Research, 10 (February 1973).

Schanck, R., and C. Goodman. "Reactions to Propaganda on Both Sides of a Controversial Issue," Public Opinion Quarterly, 3 (1939).

Settle, R., and L. Golden. "Attribution Theory and Advertiser Credibility," Journal of Marketing Research, 1 (1974).

Smith, Robert E. and Shelby D. Hunt. "Attributional Processes and Effects in Promotional Situations," Journal of Consumer Research, 5 (December 1978).

NEGATIVE INFORMATION: ASSET OR LIABILITY?

Jeffery M. Ferguson, University of Colorado, Colorado Springs
Donald W. Jackson, Jr., Arizona State University

ABSTRACT

The literature on negative information yields two conflicting hypotheses concerning its impact. The first, the
"negative information hypothesis," posits that negative
information will have a disproportionately negative effect
on the evaluation of a message. The second, based on
attribution theory predicts that there can be positive
outcomes from negative information. This paper reports on
a laboratory experiment designed to test these hypotheses.
The negative information hypothesis received strong support. Spokesperson did not have an effect upon the evaluation of the message nor did ordering of the messages.

INTRODUCTION

The marketing environment has increasingly been inundated
with negative information about products. Counter-adver-
tising, comparative advertising, and consumer-oriented
publications all have the potential to present negative
information about a particular product or service. A
number of theoretical and empirical analyses of the impact
of negative information have been offered. Examination of
these analyses reveals two opposing positions. The first
position suggests that negative information can counter-
balance a greater amount of positive information. The
second position stipulates that negative information can
produce positive results, that is, the inclusion of negative information in a message can actually increase the
message's effectiveness and believability. These opposing
hypotheses represent the focus of this paper. The theories underlying these hypotheses are discussed along with
a laboratory experiment which attempts to examine the
impact of negative information.

THE IMPACT OF NEGATIVE INFORMATION

Of the two positions outlined above, the notion that
negative information has a disproportionately negative
impact on a message has received the greatest support.
Several theoretical explanations have been offered to
defend this view. Feldman (1966) suggests that this phenomenon is due to the surprising nature of negative information. In a similar vein, Zajonc (1968) believes that
the less frequent use of negative information explains its
higher weighting. On the other hand, Kanouse and Hanson
(1971), argue against the surprise factor and frequency of
use as the causes of the inordinate impact of negative
information. They believe that since negative information
deviates from the norm, it tends to stand out in the
social environment. As a result, these uses attract more
attention and are more likely to be associated with the
stimulus object. Finally, Fiske (1980) argues that negative and extreme behavior provide more information about a
person's attributes. As a result, perceivers pay more
attention to these behaviors and weight them more heavily
in the final impression. The results of her study supported these contentions.

Besides these theoretical explanations there are numerous
studies which have demonstrated a negative information
effect. In an impression formation study, Anderson (1965)
found that highly negative adjectives had a disproportionate influence on the overall rating of a person. Highly
positive adjectives, on the other hand, showed no dispro-

portionate influence (Anderson 1965). A similar phenomenon occurred in a study by Feldman (1966) concerning the
modifying capabilities of adjectives. Subjects rated
adjectives alone and in pairs. The modifying capacity is
demonstrated by the ability of an adjective to pull the
overall rating to itself. And in this regard, the negative adjectives were the most powerful. Finally, the
generalizability of the negative information effect received support in a cross-cultural study (Gray-Little
1978) which found that Danes also give disproportionate
weight to negative information.

This brief summary gives an idea of the theoretical and
empirical support for the negative information effect.
For a more comprehensive review of the negative information literature see Weinberger, Allen, and Dillon (1981).

The positive effects of negative information are more
difficult to document. Some of the early studies on two-
sided messages showed some positive effects of negative
information. For example, Hovland, Lumsdaine, and Sheffield (1948) found that for those initially opposed to the
source's position and those with a higher level of education a two-sided message was more effective than a one-
sided message. In a different vein, Walster, Aronson, and
Abrahams (1966) found that sources were more believable
when arguing against their own best interests. Finally,
Settle and Golden (1974) varied the amount of negative
disclaimer information in experimental advertisements.
Their results suggest that negative information does not
inherently have a detrimental effect, but in some situations may enhance credibility. However, this study has
been criticized (Hansen and Scott 1976) for its conceptualization of theory and interpretation of the results.

Theoretical support for the idea that there can be positive results from negative information comes from attribution theory which looks at how subjects associate causes
with effect. While a complete review of attribution theory
is beyond the scope of this paper, several concepts seem
appropriate. According to attribution theory, if an advertisement represents positive information about a product this information may be discounted because of the
intent of the advertiser to influence the audience. According to Kelly (1973) "The role of a given cause in
producing a given effect is discounted if other plausible
causes are also present" (p. 113).

On the other hand, if an advertisement includes negative
information it may be more believable because of the augmentation principle which states that "when there are
known to be constraints, costs, sacrifices, or risks involved in taking an action, the action once taken is
attributed more to the actor than it would be otherwise"
(Kelley 1973, p. 114). Furthermore, the stronger the inhi-
bitory cause, the greater the tendency to make an internal
attribution. In terms of the advertisement this means
that the more negative the information in the advertisement, the higher the probability that the receiver will
believe it. This suggests that some negative aspects to
an advertisement may be beneficial.

Therefore, attribution theory suggests that discounting
may occur for the traditional, positive advertising messages making them less believable. While messages containing some negative information may follow the augmentation principle and be more believable.

Inoculation theory also provides support for the idea that there can be positive effects from negative information. According to this theory, exposing people to refuted counter-attitudinal arguments increases their resistance to such arguments in the future. Thus, by telling the other side of the story, the sender may reduce the likelihood that the audience will be persuaded by the arguments when encountered subsequently.

Although negative information may have positive results, its use is limited by practical considerations. Advertisers are not going to print or broadcast a message which is completely negative about their products or services. Thus, if negative information messages are to be of any value to advertisers, they must be negative enough so that the augmentation principle can take effect but not so negative that the customers develop a negative attitude about the advertised product/service. Two related factors to examining the effects of negative information are messages source and order of presenting the information.

Source Effects

Social psychologists and marketing researchers have long recognized that characteristics of the source of a persuasive communication are associated with the perceived believability of the message and ultimate acceptance by subjects (Hovland, Janis, and Kelley 1953; Engel, Kollat, and Blackwell 1973). The interaction between source and negative information has been summarized by Weinberger et al. (1981, p. 401).

> The empirical evidence indicates a clear interaction between negative information and message source. In the fear appeals area a credible source independent of the situation evokes the greatest effects. In a consumer context, the neutral spokesperson has been shown as a powerful source in several settings though with corrective advertising source effects research is more equivocal. In the case of comparative advertising where a competitor is the source, the impact of the unfavorable information is less powerful reflecting a potentially ineffective competitor source inherent in the comparative form of advertising.

While advertisements are marketer controlled sources, they may employ a variety of different spokespersons: a company representative, a consumer, or an independent observer. Each of these spokespersons may have a different effect upon the evaluation of a message.

Order Effects

The order in which the information is presented can also have a significant impact on the perception of a message. For this reason order effects are frequently controlled in experimental designs. An obvious question concerning negative information is where it should be located in the message. The literature on primacy and recency suggests that the middle of the message might be the appropriate location since information in this position tends to be overlooked. However, research by Mowen and Pollman (1982) indicates that a company was viewed more favorably when the worst possible outcome of a product defect was presented in the first press release and more moderate outcomes were indicated in subsequent releases. This finding is consistent with attribution theory since the company was viewed favorably when speaking against its best interests.

Thus, the impact of negative information may be affected by the source of the message and the order in which the information is presented.

HYPOTHESES

With this background in mind, three hypotheses may be examined. The first had to do with the impact of negative information on the evaluation of an advertisement. This hypothesis is as follows:

Hypothesis 1: There will be no difference in the attitude ratings of all positive versus mixed messages.

In this case mixed messages contain both positive and negative information.

The second hypothesis had to do with the nature of the spokesperson in the advertisement and examined three different spokespeople: a consumer, a representative manager of the company sponsoring the advertisement, and a consumer expert lawyer. Since the manager was supposedly more identified with the company it was predicted that he would have less impact than the other spokespeople. Specifically, the hypothesis states:

Hypothesis 2: Advertisements featuring a manager spokesperson will produce significantly lower attitude ratings than advertisements featuring other spokespersons.

Finally, the third hypothesis dealt with order effect due to the several competing hypotheses stated above. The hypothesis was stated in null form as follows:

Hypothesis 3: There will be no differences in the attitude ratings resulting from different orderings of messages.

Design

An experiment was conducted to test the hypotheses. The experimental design incorporated two manipulations of message content (all positive, and mixed positive and negative) and three types of sources (manager, consumer, and consumer expert). In addition, the negative information appeared in either the beginning, middle, or end of the message. The order of the positive attributes was also varied resulting in a 2x3x3 factorial between-subjects design.

Procedure

The eighteen message treatments which were prototype advertisements for a fictitious department store were combined with a "dummy" message which contained a different set of attributes about a different store. This additional message helped to disguise the true purpose of the study. The "dummy" message was presented first to give the subjects an opportunity to respond to an advertisement and practice on the dependent measures. The questionnaire booklets were randomly distributed to subjects. They were asked to carefully read the advertisements and then to answer the questions without referring back to the advertisements.

Subjects

The subjects were a convenience sample of 396 student volunteers from the Colorado Springs, Colorado area. They were randomly assigned to the eighteen treatments (22 per cell). It should be noted that these were not typical college students. The average age of the subjects was thirty-two and about two-thirds of them were married. While the sample does not represent a cross-section of the population, it was felt to be a reasonable sample because processing information about department stores is an appropriate task for them.

Attributes

The attributes used in constructing the messages were
selected in the following manner. A group of subjects was
asked to list all the characteristics considered when
selecting a department store. The importance of these
characteristics was then evaluated by another group on a
seven-point Likert-type scale. The mean score for each
characteristic was calculated. Two important characteristics (quality and assortment of merchandise) were then
selected which were rated significantly more important
($p<.001$) than the unimportant characteristic (gift wrapping). Determining the importance of the characteristics
in a pretest was necessary so that negative information
could be manipulated without making the message too negative. Therefore, negative information was provided for an
unimportant store attribute.

An example of an advertisement for People's Department
Store showing the manipulation of the negative information
is as follows:

> People's stocks only high quality brand name
> merchandise. While there have been quite a few
> complaints about the low quality and slow service
> of their gift wrapping department, steps are
> being taken to correct this problem. In addi-
> tion, there is a wide assortment of products to
> choose from.

Dependent Variables

Multiple dependent variables were used in the study.
Since there is no sound theoretical basis for selecting a
single criterion as as the "best" measure of advertising
effectiveness (Wind and Denny 1974), measures of each type
of attitude component (cognitive, affective, and conative)
were taken. A seven-point Likert-type scale (7 = most
positive) was used to measure each of these variables.
The specific questions are as follows:

1. How believable is the advertisement you just read?
    ("Not at all believable" to "Completely believable")

2. How knowledgeable is the spokesperson about depart-
    ment stores? ("Not at all knowledgeable" to "Com-
    pletely knowledgeable")

3. How likely is it that the contents of the preceding
    advertisement represent the spokesperson's true be-
    liefs about People's Department Store? ("Not at all
    likely" to "Completely likely")

4. What is your overall impression of People's Depart-
    ment Store? ("Highly unfavorable" to "Highly favor-
    able")

5. How do you feel People's Department Store compares
    with other department stores in which you would shop?
    ("Much worse than others" to "Much better than
    others")

6. What are the chances that you would shop at People's
    Department Store if it were located near you? ("No
    chance" to "Certain")

ANALYSIS AND RESULTS

Manipulation Checks

Before the data were analyzed a manipulation check was
performed to establish whether or not the manipulation of
the independent variable was perceived by the subjects
(Kerlinger 1973). In this experiment manipulation checks
were made of source, message content, and importance of
store characteristics. Measurements for determining the

effectiveness of the manipulations were obtained after the
subjects responded to the dependent measures so that the
manipulation checks would not influence the dependent
measures. Since it was hypothesized that subjects would
respond differently to different sources, a check was made
to determine if the subjects could recall who delivered
the message. The manager spokesperson condition was correctly identified in 83 percent of the cases; a similar
result was noted for the consumer expert condition in
which 82 percent of the subjects correctly identified the
lawyer as the spokesperson. Only 62 percent of the subjects, however, correctly identified the consumer spokesperson. The results of the consumer condition are less
likely to be due to the consumer spokesperson and must be
interpreted with caution.

The manipulation check for message content showed that
subjects were highly accurate in recalling the kind of
message presented in the advertisement. The subjects
correctly identified the positive messages and mixed messages in 86 percent and 87 percent of the cases, respectively. Thus, it appears that message content was manipulated successfully.

The manipulation check of the importance of the store
attributes showed this manipulation to be highly successful. Both assortment of merchandise and quality of merchandise were rated as more important ($p<.001$) than gift
wrapping.

Test of Hypotheses

Multivariate analysis of variance was used because the
dependent variables were components of the same attitude
measure. In addition, the responses were obtained from
the same subject. As a result, it cannot be assumed that
these measures are independent of one another.

Table 1 shows the results from the MANOVA program. Notice
that for message type the multivariate F statistic is
significant (F (4) = 3.190, $p<.013$) as well as the univariate F statistics for believability (F (1) = 3.927,
$p<.048$), favorability (F (1) = 3.818, $p<.051$), and compar-
ability (F (1) = 9.102, $p<.002$). This suggests that the
subjects did indeed react differently to the message
treatments. An examination of Table 2 shows that in all
cases the positive advertisement produced the most beneficial results. These findings are consistent with the
negative information hypothesis but inconsistent with the
attribution theory prediction.

In analyzing the source effects it can be seen from Table
1 that the manipulation of spokesperson yielded an insignificant multivariate F statistic as well as insignificant
univariate F statistics for all measures except comparabi-
lity. Since consecutive F-tests increase the Type 1 error, it is inappropriate to attach significance to a
univariate F statistic when the multivariate F statistic
is not significant (Hair Anderson, Tatham, and Grablowsky
1979). Therefore, there are no significant source effects.

Examination of Table 1 also shows no significant order
effects which is inconsistent with the findings of Mowen
and Pollman (1982).

DISCUSSION

This study produced strong support for the negative information hypothesis. Clearly the negative information
had an unfavorable impact. The mixed messages produced
not only less favorable attitude scores but also less
favorable believability scores. These things occurred
even though the negative information was about an unimportant store attribute. This could indicate a strong

halo effect or the subjects may have thought the advertiser was trying to deceive them.

TABLE 1
MULTIVARIATE ANALYSIS OF VARIANCE

Source of Variation	df	F	F significance
Multivariate			
Spokesperson (A)	8	1.629	.112
Message Type (B)	4	3.190	.013
Order (C)	8	1.524	.144
AxB	8	1.233	.276
AxC	16	1.284	.199
BxC	8	1.126	.342
AxBxC	16	1.162	.292
Univariate Believability			
Spokesperson (A)	2	2.053	.129
Message Type (B)	1	3.927	.048
Order (C)	2	.232	.793
AxB	2	2.899	.056
AxC	4	.934	.443
BxC	2	2.746	.065
AxBxC	4	1.646	.161
Univariate Favorability			
Spokesperson (A)	2	1.018	.361
Message Type (B)	1	3.818	.051
Order (C)	2	.105	.899
AxB	2	.977	.056
AxC	4	1.134	.340
BxC	2	2.432	.089
AxBxC	4	2.401	.049
Error	376		
Univariate Comparability			
Spokesperson (A)	2	3.357	.035
Message Type (B)	1	9.102	.002
Order (C)	2	1.387	.250
AxB	2	1.781	.169
AxC	4	.322	.862
BxC	2	.826	.438
AxBxC	4	1.665	.157
Error	354		
Univariate Intention			
Spokesperson (A)	2	2.309	.100
Message Type (B)	1	1.182	.277
Order (C)	2	.056	.945
AxB	2	1.046	.352
AxC	4	.953	.433
BxC	2	1.312	.270
AxBxC	4	2.381	.051
Error	354		

The study also showed no spokesperson effect nor any order effect. While the study did not support the presence of an order effect there are indications in the data that order effects are worthy of further study. For example, the univariate F statistic for the message type by order interaction approaches significance (F (2) = 2.746, p<.065). In addition, examination of believability and the underlying factors of trustworthiness and expertness as a function of message type and order shows two important things. First, when the negative information is presented first, the mixed message is always more favorably rated than the positive message. Second, presenting the negative information first yields the best ratings on the believability and trustworthiness scales and is second best on the expertness scale. These findings seem to suggest that there could be advantages to presenting the negative information first. This is especially true in light of the fact that the order manipulations in this experiment were contained within a single, short paragraph. More drastic differences in the order could possible produce significant effects. Moreover, the order manipulations in this study differed from those of Mowen & Pollman (1982) since this study manipulated the placement of the negative information within the advertisement while the other study manipulated whether the outcome of a defect increased or decreased in severity in subsequent press releases.

Overall, the findings indicate that negative information should probably be avoided. However, the effects of the order of presentation of the negative information needs further study to determine the extent to which positive results can be obtained. It may be that a more fruitful approach would be to concentrate on ways of minimizing the impact of negative information. Research in this vein would include studies of corrective advertising and warning labels since both of these areas represent situations in which negative information is unavoidable. Manipulating the degree of specificity of the negative information, and the order of presentation of the information as outlined above are manipulations to consider in future studies.

TABLE 2
MEANS AND STANDARD DEVIATIONS FOR BELIEVABILITY AND ATTITUDE MEASURES CLASSIFIED BY MESSAGE TYPE

	Message Type			
	Positive		Mixed	
Dependent Variable	$\underline{M}$	$\underline{SD}$	$\underline{M}$	$\underline{SD}$
Believability	4.459	1.702	4.121	1.562
Favorability	4.454	1.451	4.161	1.440
Comparability	4.542	1.189	4.151	1.277
Intention	4.420	1.298	4.252	1.824

REFERENCES

Anderson, N. H. (1965), "Averaging Versus Adding as a Stimulus -- Combination Rule in Impression Formation," _Journal of Experimental Psychology_, 70 (November), 1-9.

Engel, J. F., D. T. Kollat, and R. D. Blackwell (1973), _Consumer Behavior_ (2nd ed.), New York: Holt, Rinehart & Winston, Inc.

Feldman, S. (1966), "Motivational Aspects of Attitudinal Elements and Their Place in Cognitive Interaction," in S. Feldman (Ed.), _Cognitive Consistency_. New York: Academic Press.

Fiske, S. T. (1980), "Attention and Weight in Person Perception: The Impact of Negative & Extreme Behavior," _Journal of Personality and Social Psychology_, 38, (June), 889-906.

Gray-Little, B. (1973), "The Salience of Negative Information in Impression Formation Among Two Danish Samples," Journal of Cross-Cultural Psychology, 4, 193-
206.

Hair, J. F., Jr., R. E. Anderson, R. L. Tatham, and B. J.
Grablowsky (1979), Multivariate Data Analysis with
Readings. Tulsa, Oklahoma: Petroleum Publishing
Company.

Hansen, R. A. and C. A. Scott (1976), "Comments on 'Attribution Theory and Advertiser Credibility,'" Journal
of Marketing Research, 13 (May), 193-197.

Hovland, C. I., I. L. Janis, and H. H. Kelley (1953),
Communication and Persuasion. New Haven: Yale University Press.

Hovland, C. I., A. Lumsdaine, and F. Sheffield (1948),
Experiments on Mass Communication (Vol. 3). Princeton, New Jersey: Princeton University Press.

Kanouse, D. E. and L. R. Hanson, Jr. (1971), "Negativity
in Evaluating," in E. E. Jones et al. (Eds.) Attribution: Perceiving the Causes of Behavior. Morris-
town, New Jersey: General Learning Press.

Kelley, H. H. (1973), "The Process of Causal Attribution,"
American Psychologist, 28 (February), 107-128.

Kerlinger, F. N. (1973), Foundations of Behavioral Research (2nd ed.). New York: Holt, Rinehart and
Winston.

Mowen, J. C. and S. B. Pollman (1982), "An Exploratory
Study Investigating Order Effects in Reporting Negative Corporate Communications," Advances in Ch nsumer
Research, Vol. IX, (in press). Ann Arbor: Association for Consumer Research.

Settle, R. B. and L. L. Golden (1974). "Attribution
Theory and Advertiser Credibility," Journal of Marketing Research, 11 (May), 181-185.

Walster, E., E. Aronson, and D. Abrahams (1966), "On
Increasing the Persuasiveness of a Low Prestige Communicator," Journal of Experimental Social Psychology, 2 (July), 325-342.

Weinberger, M. C., C. T. Allen, and W. R. Dillon (1981),
"Negative Information: Perspectives and Research
Directions," in Proceedings of the Association for
Consumer Research, K. Monroe (Ed.), Ann Arbor: Asso-
ciation for Consumer Research.

Wind, Y. and J. Denny (1974), "Multivariate Analysis of
Variance in Research on the Effectiveness of TV Commercials," Journal of Marketing Research, 11 (May),
136-142.

Zajonc, R. B. (1968), "Attitudinal Effects of Mere Exposure," Journal of Personality and Social Psychology,
7 (August), 1-29.

TRUTH AND CONSEQUENCES: THE EFFECTS OF DISCLOSING
POSSIBLY HARMFUL RESULTS OF PRODUCT USE

Meryl P. Gardner, New York University
Rosalyn S. Levin, New York University

ABSTRACT

The effects of disclosing a possibly harmful result of product use are investigated with experimental and control advertisements for a hypothetical brand of tampons. A discussion of the risk of contracting toxic shock syndrome and the product's compensating benefits are included in the experimental advertisement and omitted from the otherwise identical control advertisement. Effects on beliefs and attitudes are assessed and analyzed. Results indicate less favorable attitudes toward the brand and toward buying/using the brand for subjects in the experimental condition than for those in the control condition. The paper concludes with a discussion of the attitude formation process for consumers exposed to an advertisement containing a product hazard disclosure.

INTRODUCTION

Using some products involves risking side effects. These hazards may vary in the likelihood of their occurrence and the severity of their consequences. If a product's side effects are prevalent and extremely serious, it may be withdrawn from the market by the manufacturer, either with or without government pressure. (For a more extensive discussion, see Weinstein 1978.)

If a product's adverse effects are rare or minor, the necessary course of action is not so clear cut. Its benefits may outweigh its expected costs. Under some circumstances, the government may require that a warning statement be included on each package and in each advertisement. For example, the government requires cigarette and diet soda manufacturers to include warning statements stating the possible side effects of using their products. Under other circumstances, the government may not require manufacturers to take any action. In such cases, manufacturers have a social responsibility to the public to openly state the product's side effects, as well as a corporate responsibility to their shareholders to present the reasons why the product is still a viable alternative. Armed with such information, consumers can then make their own choices.

Research Purpose

One industry currently grappling with the issue of side effects is the feminine protection industry. Tampon usage has been linked to a newly identified and sometimes fatal disease -- toxic shock syndrome (TSS). According to the Federal Center for Disease Control, the incidence of toxic shock is 10 cases out of every 100,000 women, with the fatality rate at approximately 13% (Chicago Tribune, May 3, 1981). Tampon manufacturers feel that women "have a bigger chance of being hit by a meteorite" than having a problem with tampons (Wall Street Journal, February 26, 1981). The risk of contracting toxic shock may be small; perfect substitutes for tampons do not exist. Thus, it is reasonable for the product to remain on the market.[1] The

---

[1] Only Rely, the brand associated with the vast majority of cases of TSS, was removed from the market.

government is in the process of discussing the possibility of requiring warning labels. In the interim, manufacturers have used package inserts to voluntarily inform consumers about TSS and about the product's compensating benefits.

As responsible marketers, tampon manufacturers may also consider including a message about the product's possible side effects and compensating benefits in their advertisements. The purpose of this study is to examine the effects of including such a message in an advertisement. How would it affect consumers' brand-related beliefs and attitudes?

Theoretical Perspectives

An ad containing a TSS disclosure would necessarily mention both positive and negative aspects of product use. Consequently, it might be expected to yield results analogous to those found with two-sided ads. This analogy would predict that exposure to an ad with the TSS disclosure would result in a more favorable brand attitude than exposure to an ad without the disclosure. Such optimism would be uncalled for in view of the mechanisms underlying the effectiveness of two-sided communications.

One reason for the success of some two-sided ads involves attribution theory. According to this perspective, the negative information in a two-sided ad is believed to enhance the advertiser's credibility. Consequently, attribution theory predicts that consumers would believe a two-sided ad more than a one-sided ad and therefore, form more favorable beliefs and attitudes about the brand after seeing a two-sided ad than after seeing a one-sided ad. The ads used to test this have always contained negative information about unimportant attributes.

For example, Settle & Golden (1974) tested two advertisements. One ad contained positive information about five product features of a blender. The other ad contained positive information about three of the product features and negative information about two of the features. The negative information concerned product characteristics which had been rated of least importance to the consumer. The authors concluded that in order to increase believability and credibility, it is better for the advertiser to disclaim at least one feature of _minor_ importance than to exclude it from the message entirely.

TSS, however, is not of _minor_ importance. Consumers may question the advertiser's motives for providing such devastating information. They may presume that an advertiser who says that his blender does not come in a variety of colors does so voluntarily. But, they may feel differently about an advertiser who says that his product may cause a disease which has resulted in several well-publicized fatalities. In the latter case, they may attribute the disclosure to government pressure or regulation. Consequently, an attribution framework would not predict that an ad containing the TSS disclosure would enhance brand evaluation.

Another reason for the success of some two-sided ads is that they may provide a way of refuting statements against a chosen brand. (Assael, p. 489) The ads used to test this idea have always selected the negative attributes to

be those which are least important. For example, Etgar and
Goodwin (1982) tested one-sided and two-sided comparative
advertisements. The one-sided ads contained positive information about all attributes of the sponsoring brand.
The two-sided ads contained negative information about some
unimportant attributes of the sponsoring brand. The authors found that the two-sided ads created more favorable
brand attitudes than the one-sided ads without differential
effects on attitudes toward the ad itself. Again, the analogy fails to hold for the tampon situation. TSS is a well-
publicized, serious disease; it is not a minor annoyance.
There is no material we can provide that is pro-TSS or that
can lessen its importance. It is unlikely that any message
can encourage people to think more about TSS in a way that
will result in more favorable attitudes.

Thus, although an ad which includes a TSS disclosure is
two-sided, it is unlikely to result in more favorable brand
attitudes than an ad which does not contain a TSS disclosure. In fact, there are several unfavorable possibilities
which may result from the inclusion of the TSS message.

One possibility is that including the negative information
may cause consumers to associate the disease with the advertised brand and so have a damaging effect on their
beliefs about that brand. Thus, consumers exposed to an
ad which mentions TSS may consider the advertised brand
more likely than other brands to cause TSS. The Fishbein
model postulates a link between a brand and its primary
attributes. (Fishbein and Ajzen 1975) The primary belief
"Is safe" may be associated with the supportive belief
"Does not cause TSS". Thus, the TSS message may link a
negatively evaluated attribute with the advertised brand.
(For a discussion of primary and supportive beliefs, see
Gardner, Mitchell and Staelin 1977).

A second possibility concerns the notion of availability
developed by Tversky and Kahneman (1973). Exposure to an
advertisement which mentions TSS may trigger beliefs about
the disease stored in memory. Rehearsing these ideas may
make them more easily retrieved in the future. If so, a
consumer's exposure to an ad which mentions TSS may increase her perception of the likelihood that she will get
TSS. The particular thoughts evoked by the message will
mediate this effect. If the message triggers the recall
of reports of TSS fatalities, it may even increase the
consumer's perception of the likelihood that she will
die of TSS.

A third possibility is analogous to the agenda-setting
role of the media in political elections (e.g., Cohen
1963). By drawing the consumer's attention to TSS, the
ad may cause her to think more about the attribute and to
use it in decision-making. The consumer may or may not
be consciously aware of this process. Its effect may be
strengthened by the fact that TSS is a negative attribute.
There is some evidence that negatively evaluated information may attract more attention and be more heavily
weighted than positively evaluated information (Fiske
1980). Thus, exposure to an ad which contains a TSS
message may change the consumer's evaluative criteria.

A fourth possibility is that the TSS message will change
the attitude formation process more fundamentally. Any
product whose use has resulted in some deaths will evoke
strong responses; reactions to toxic shock are not necessarily rational or based on fact. These reactions may
instead be "gut level" responses because the connection
between tampon use and death is fraught with all kinds of
emotions. Tampon use is a particularly sensitive, deli-
cate and highly charged issue due to societal taboos concerning menstruation, cleanliness and sexuality. Especially when TSS is mentioned, then, beliefs may not fully
mediate all of one's attitude toward an advertised brand.
It may be particularly important to look at an associative
view which predicts that the TSS message may result in

subjects associating the advertised brand with toxic shock
and death, thereby resulting in negative feelings. This
might encourage the use of emotional rather than cognitive
channels for brand evaluation. (These channels are analogous to the visual/emotional and verbal channels discussed
by Mitchell 1982.) In addition, because of the association
between TSS and death, a "halo effect" may occur (e.g.,
Nisbett and Wilson 1977). Exposure to an ad which includes a TSS message may make the consumer evaluate all
brand attributes less favorably.

HYPOTHESES

H_1: Subjects exposed to an ad which includes a TSS message
will have less favorable beliefs about the safety of
the advertised brand than subjects exposed to the same
advertisement without the TSS message.

H_2: Subjects exposed to an ad which includes a TSS message
will indicate a greater likelihood of getting TSS and
dying from the disease than subjects exposed to the
same advertisement without the TSS message.

H_3: Subjects exposed to an ad which includes a TSS message
will have less favorable overall evaluative beliefs,
attitudes toward the brand, toward buying/using the
brand and toward the ad itself than subjects exposed
to the same advertisement without the TSS message.

H_4: Subjects exposed to the different ad versions will
not use the same set of evaluative criteria.

METHOD

Subjects

Subjects were forty tampon users recruited from health
clubs, department stores, bus and subway stations, class-
rooms, jogging paths and offices. They ranged in age from
19 to 45 years old and varied widely in income, occupation,
education and marital status.

Over thirty women declined to participate in the project.
Of those, twenty-one declined because the subject matter
was too personal and nine declined because they were simply
not interested in participating. Nonresponse error may be
significant; there may be differences between women willing
to participate and those not willing to participate.

Procedure

A two group after-only design was used. Subjects were
assigned randomly to experimental and control conditions.
Those in the experimental or "TSS" group were exposed to
an advertisement which discussed the risk of contracting
toxic shock syndrome and the product's compensating benefits.[2] Those in the control or "No TSS" group were exposed to the same advertisement without that discussion.
A non-existent brand was used so that subjects' responses
would not be confounded by previously formed beliefs and
attitudes about the brand.

Each subject was run individually. Each was instructed to
read her advertisement and then to answer the questions
following without referring to the advertisement again.

____

[2] "Government statistics report that 10 out of every
100,000 women who use tampons get TSS. There are over
50 million women who regularly use tampons each month.
Their reasons -- Convenience, Absorbency, Comfort."

40

She was then debriefed. Each subject answered every question; all analyses involved twenty subjects per cell.

Dependent Variables

The questionnaire included measures of belief strengths (b_i), attribute evaluations (e_i), attitude toward the brand (A_o), attitude toward purchasing and using the brand (A_{act}) and attitude toward the advertisement (A_{ad}) (e.g., Fishbein and Ajzen 1975).

Belief strengths were measured on seven point scales anchored by how likely or unlikely it was that the advertised brand had the particular product characteristic that was mentioned. Evaluations of each attribute were taken on bipolar scales labeled good-bad (+3 to -3). Belief strengths and evaluations were assessed for the following attributes: comfort, safety, absorbency, price and scent.[3]

The mean score of three bipolar evaluative scales (good-bad, dislike very much-like very much, pleasant-unpleasant) was used as a measure of attitude toward the brand. Similarly, the mean score of four other bipolar evaluative scales (good-bad, foolish-wise, beneficial-harmful, safe-risky) was used as a measure of attitude toward purchasing and using the brand. Finally, the mean score of four other bipolar evaluative scales (good-bad, dislike-like, uninteresting-interesting, not irritating-irritating) was used as a measure of attitude toward the advertisement.[4]

Following Alpert's (1971) dual questioning procedure, subjects also evaluated the importance of each attribute and the perceived similarity of brands along each attribute. The importance of each attribute was taken on a five point scale ranging from "no importance" (scored 1) to "extremely important" (scored 5). The perceived similarity of brands along each attribute was taken on a five point scale ranging from "no difference" (scored 1) to "extreme differences" (scored 5). The dual questioning procedure uses the product of these self-report measures for an attribute to predict determinance.

Aided recall of the advertisement's content was assessed by simply asking whether or not the ad mentioned a given attribute. The subject's perceptions of the likelihood that she would get TSS and the likelihood that she would die from TSS were assessed with seven point scales ranging from "very unlikely" (scored 1) to "very likely" (scored 7).

RESULTS

Interpretation of Manipulation

Aided recall results indicate that all of the subjects exposed to the TSS ad recalled that TSS had been mentioned, while none of the subjects exposed to the No TSS ad falsely recalled that TSS had been mentioned. This difference was, of course, significant ($p < .0001$) when tested with a 1-tailed t-test.

Subjects exposed to the TSS ad version and those exposed to the No TSS ad version were almost equally likely to think the ad "said something about" safety. Contrary to experimentor expectations, the TSS message was not interpreted as a statement about the product's safety.

H_1 -- Subjects exposed to the TSS version of the ad believed it was slightly less likely ($\bar{x} = 3.90$) that the advertised brand was safe than those exposed to the No TSS version ($\bar{x} = 4.30$). This difference was not significant ($p > .05$) when tested with a 1-tailed t-test.

The contribution of an attribute to attitude in the Fishbein model is the evaluative belief about that attribute (b_ie_i) (Fishbein and Ajzen 1975). The evaluative belief for safety was slightly less positive for subjects exposed to the TSS ad ($\bar{x} = 10.50$) than for those exposed to the No TSS ad ($\bar{x} = 10.70$). This difference was not significant ($p > .05$) when tested with a 1-tailed t-test.

H_2 -- Subjects exposed to the TSS version of the advertisement indicated that they perceived a greater likelihood of getting TSS ($\bar{x} = 3.05$) than did subjects exposed to the No TSS version ($\bar{x} = 2.15$). This difference approached significance ($p < .07$) when tested with a 1-tailed t-test.

Subjects exposed to the TSS version of the advertisement indicated that they perceived a greater likelihood of dying from TSS ($\bar{x} = 2.10$) than did subjects exposed to the No TSS version ($\bar{x} = 1.55$). This difference approached significance ($p < .12$) when tested with a 1-tailed t-test.

H_3 -- Subjects exposed to the TSS version of the advertisement had less favorable overall evaluative beliefs[5] ($x = 28.30$) than subjects exposed to the No TSS version ($\bar{x} = 35.05$). This difference approached significance ($p < .11$) when tested with a 1-tailed t-test.

Subjects exposed to the TSS version had less favorable attitudes toward the advertised brand ($\bar{x} = 2.45$) than subjects exposed to the No TSS version ($\bar{x} = 2.83$). This difference approached significance ($p < .08$) when tested with a 1-tailed t-test.

Subjects exposed to the TSS version had less favorable attitudes toward buying/using the advertised brand ($\bar{x} = 2.47$) than subjects exposed to the No TSS version ($\bar{x} = 2.95$). This difference was significant ($p < .05$) when tested with a 1-tailed t-test.

Subjects exposed to the TSS version had less favorable attitudes toward the ad ($\bar{x} = 2.61$) than subjects exposed to the No TSS version ($\bar{x} = 2.76$). This difference was not significant ($p > .05$) when tested with a 1-tailed t-test.

H_4 -- Subjects exposed to either the TSS or the No TSS versions of the advertisement did not differ in their assessments of the importance of safety or their Alpert determinance scores. This equivalence applied to both their choice of feminine protection methods and their choice of tampon brands.

For subjects exposed to the TSS version, attitude toward the brand was not highly correlated with either attitude toward the ad (.35) or with overall evaluative beliefs (.23). Regression was used to account for both factors simultaneously ($R^2 = .16$). This model lacked statistical significance ($p > .05$).

For subjects exposed to the No TSS version, attitude toward the brand was highly correlated with both attitude toward the ad (.69) and with overall evaluative beliefs (.55). Regression was used to account for both factors simultaneously ($R^2 = .59$; $p < .001$). Both attitude toward the ad and overall evaluative beliefs were significant ($p < .005$ and $p < .001$, respectively).

---

[3] Measures for "scented" and "unscented" were assessed separately and combined.

[4] The Cronbach alpha measures for A_o, A_{act} and A_{ad} were 0.93, 0.94, 0.87, respectively.

[5] A subject's "overall evaluative belief" is defined as the sum of her evaluative beliefs, i.e. Σb_ie_i.

DISCUSSION

We had expected subjects to interpret the TSS message as a statement about the product's safety. They did not do so. Consequently, subjects exposed to different ad treatments had similar beliefs about the safety of the advertised brand. Moreover, subjects exposed to the TSS and No TSS versions did not differ in their assessment of the importance of safety or their Alpert determinance scores.

Although consumers failed to relate the TSS message to "safety", they did react to mention of the disease. This finding is consistent with the availability heuristic. The study was conducted in February, 1982. By then, TSS had received a great deal of publicity and had been strongly associated with tampons in the popular press. Therefore, many subjects had information about TSS stored in memory. The disclosure statement in the TSS version may have activated this knowledge. If so, the availability heuristic would predict our findings.

In addition, subjects exposed to the TSS version had less favorable overall evaluative beliefs, attitudes toward the brand and attitudes toward buying/using the brand than subjects exposed to the No TSS version.

It is conceivable that the TSS ad could have created unfavorable overall evaluative beliefs which, in turn, could have created negative attitudes. We note, however, that except for some positively evaluated attributes and the TSS warning, the ads were identical. The TSS information was not reflected in "safety" and was probably not interpreted as a component of any of the other attributes assessed, i.e., comfort, absorbency, price or scent. Thus, it seems unlikely that the assessed overall beliefs affected attitudes. It is more likely that attitudes affected assessments of overall evaluative beliefs by inducing halo effects.

We cannot attribute the observed brand attitude differences to a dislike of the TSS ad. Differential effects on attitude toward the advertisement were not observed.

For subjects exposed to the No TSS ad version, overall evaluative beliefs and attitude toward the ad explained a significant amount of the variance in attitude toward the brand (p < .001).

The same cannot be said for those subjects exposed to the TSS ad version. The low R^2 for that group may indicate that the equation was misspecified, i.e., that one or more of the variables needed to model attitude were omitted. The missing factor may be a cognitive attribute related to TSS, e.g., an evaluative belief concerning the likelihood that the brand will induce the disease. The omitted variable may also be a feeling, e.g., an emotional reaction to TSS which was not assessed by attitude toward the advertisement. The possibility that one or more of the missing factors may be affective is strengthened by the subjects' extremely emotional reactions to the product during their debriefing. They were unlikely to use the clinical euphemisms found in advertisements to describe brand attributes, but were inclined to use gestures and made-up words which described sensations of product use. The women seemed to have very strong feelings about tampons but seemed unable to express them articulately, perhaps because they are unaccustomed to thinking about the product.

Future research might well be directed at unraveling these cognitive and emotional aspects of tampon brand preference. In addition, research is needed to understand the effects of a disclosure on the entire product class -- with and without competitive reactions from alternative product forms, e.g., sanitary napkin manufacturers. Future studies might also investigate the long term effects of disclosing possibly harmful results of product use.

REFERENCES

Alpert, Mark (1971), "Identification of Determinant Attributes: A Comparison of Methods," _Journal of Marketing Research_, 8, 184-191.

Assael, Henry (1981), _Consumer Behavior and Marketing Action_, Boston, MA : Kent Publishing Company.

"A Monthly Gamble for 50 Million Women," _Chicago Tribune_, May 6, 1981, page 1.

Cohen, Bernard (1963), _The Press and Foreign Policy_, Princeton, NJ : Princeton University Press.

Etgar, Michael and Stephen Goodwin (1982), "Effectiveness of One-Sided and Two-Sided Comparative Message Appeals: An Inoculation Approach," _Journal of Consumer Research_, 9 (March).

Fishbein, Martin and I. Ajzen (1975), _Belief, Attitude, Intention and Behavior: An Introduction to Theory and Research_, Reading, MA : Addison - Wesley Publishing Co.

Fiske, Susan (1980), "Attention and Weight in Person Perception: The Impact of Negative and Extreme Behavior," _Journal of Personality and Social Psychology_, Vol. 38, No. 6, 889-906.

Gardner, Meryl, Andrew Mitchell and Richard Staelin (1977), "The Effects of Attacks and Inoculations in a Public Policy Context: A Cognitive Structure Approach," _Contemporary Marketing Thought_, ed. B. Greenberg and D. Bellenger, Chicago, IL : American Marketing Association, 292-7.

Mitchell, Andrew (1982), "Cognitive Processes Initiated by Exposure to Advertising," _Information Processing Research in Advertising_, ed. R. Harris, Hillsdale, NJ: Lawrence Erlbaum Associates.

Mitchell, Andrew and Jerry Olson (1981), "Are Product Attribute Beliefs the Only Mediator of Advertising Effects on Brand Attitudes," _Journal of Marketing Research_, 18.

Nisbett, Richard and Timothy Wilson (1977), "The Halo Effect: Evidence for Unconscious Alteration of Judgments," _Journal of Personality and Social Psychology_, Vol. 35, No. 4, 250-256.

Settle, Robert and Linda Golden (1974), "Attribution Theory and Advertiser Credibility," _Journal of Marketing Research_, 11, 181-5.

Tversky, Amos and Daniel Kahneman (1973), "Availability: A Heuristic for Judging Frequency and Probability," _Cognitive Psychology_, 5, 207-232.

"Tampon Industry is in the Throes of Change After Toxic Shock," _Wall Street Journal_, February 26, 1981, page 1.

Weinstein, Alvin (1978), "Product Safety: Dimensions for Consumer Policy," _Research for Consumer Policy_, ed. W.M. Denney and R.T. Lund, Cambridge, MA : Center for Policy Alternatives, 36-45.

THE EFFECT OF SEX ROLES ON FAMILY
FINANCE HANDLING AND DECISION INFLUENCE

Charles M. Schaninger, State University of New York at Albany
W. Christian Buss, State University of New York at Albany
Rajiv Grover, University of Massachusetts, Amherst

ABSTRACT

Sex roles of both husbands and wives were shown to significantly influence family finance handling and decision making. Sex-role modern families evidenced less wife, and greater joint and husband influence in areas traditionally assigned to the wife with the opposite in areas traditionally handled by the husband. This included deciding to buy, when to buy, and where to buy the last major durable purchased and the allocation of finance-handling tasks. Wives' sex-role norms had the greatest influence.

INTRODUCTION AND LITERATURE REVIEW

The norms for appropriate sex-role behavior for men and women have been changing rapidly, with a pronounced shift away from traditional norms of "man's work" and "woman's work" toward more egalitarian views (Araji 1977; Mason et al. 1976; Roper and Luboff 1977). Changing sex-role norms are a major social force impacting family formation, marital conflict, family dissolution, the workplace, the political system, and the marketplace.

Among the factors recognized as either contributing to or reflecting this shift in sex roles are: societal/economic evolution toward a more affluent post-industrial state, the abundance of labor saving products and services for activities traditionally performed by the wife, and the increasing occupational and educational attainment of women.

Although many researchers have examined sex roles, few empirical studies have attempted to link sex-role norms to family decision making or task allocation. Most of the literature has been either theoretical or conceptual (e.g. Pleck 1977; Scanzoni 1977) covering scale development or validation (e.g. Brogan and Kutner 1976, Osmond and Martin 1975, Scanzoni 1975), sex-role changes over time (Mason, Czajka, and Arber 1976; Thornton and Freedman 1979), or demographic links to sex-role attitudes (Albrecht, Bahr, and Chadwick 1977; Roper and Luboff 1977; Tomeh 1978).

A number of methodological problems recur in this literature. The vast majority of studies have attempted to measure sex roles for wives only. Several different types of scaling approaches have been developed, and most studies have utilized different scales, making generalization difficult. There is semantic confusion between sex-role norms as attitudes toward acceptable behavior and task-allocation perceptions, feministic beliefs, or masculine-feminine personality traits. Similar methodological and measurement problems apply to studies of family decision making and task allocation.

The principal purpose of this paper is to develop and empirically test a number of hypotheses linking sex-role norms to family finance handling and decision making. The remainder of this section first focuses on measurement of sex roles and of family decision making influence, finance handling, and task allocation. Next, a brief summary of the state of knowledge concerning areas traditionally dominated by the wife, the husband, or performed jointly is developed. That literature which ties sex-role norms to family decision making, finance handling, and task allocation is then summarized.

Measurement of Sex-Role Norms

Several different methodological approaches have been employed to examine sex-role norms. The first approach asks respondents to indicate who they feel should be responsible for various activities. Using this approach, Araji (1977) found that attitudes toward such roles were highly related to actual behavior in families. Albrecht, Bahr and Chadwick (1979) also utilized this approach and concluded that family life-cycle stage was not strongly related to sex-role beliefs. This approach limits the dimensions of sex-role norms only to task-allocation attitudes. A second approach has been the use of masculinity-femininity scales. However, this approach has been criticized as both too limiting, and as failing to make distinctions between underlying sex-role dimensions (Brogan and Kutner 1976, Kelly and Worrell 1977). This approach has recently been employed in the consumer behavior literature to relate self concept to product perceptions (Allison et al. 1980). A third approach used in the marketing literature has been Arnott's Autonomy Index (Green and Cunningham 1975, Venkatesh 1980). This scale was developed by selecting 10 Likert items from a 1930's feminism scale, and has been criticized by Brogan and Kutner (1976) as overly unidimensional and as inappropriate to administer to men.

The most recent and widely accepted approach has been the application of multi-item, Likert-scale batteries tapping a variety of dimensions. Various authors have used such an approach to develop one overall sum score (Brogan and Kutner 1976), to measure a priori determined dimensions (Osmond and Martin 1975), or in conjunction with principal components or factor analysis (Brown, Perry, and Harburg 1977; Scanzoni 1975). Although no one scale has become widely accepted as a standard, a number of common underlying dimensions emerge in various studies. Three common dimensions emerge in these studies:
1) Attitudes toward sex-based division of family tasks, and marital influence.
2) Traditional wife roles - "home, husband, children."
3) Attitudes towards a wife's career.
Scanzoni's study employed separate factor analyses with varimax rotations on samples of husbands' and wives' responses to two sets of items: 12 items for wife roles, and 9 items for husband roles. In both sets of factor analyses, comparable factors emerged for husbands' and wives' responses. However, all of the items characterized a priori as wife or husband roles may be performed by either spouse. A combined factor analysis on all items, run separately on the samples of husbands' and wives' responses, might have been more appropriate. Tomeh (1978) related simple-sum scores constructed on the basis of Scanzoni's factors to demographics for both women and men. Brown, Perry and Harburg (1977) employed principal components analysis to identify three factors emerging from 18 Likert items. All three studies utilized a number of items which were quite similar. Those studies generally conclude that each sex-role dimension (factor) should be examined separately when relating sex roles to other variables.

Measurement of Decision Influence and Task Allocation

Similar measurement techniques have been employed to measure task allocation ("Who does the dishes, cleaning, etc.?"), finance handling ("Who pays the bills?, "Who takes care of expenditures for food and beverages?, "insurance?," etc.), and family decision influence ("Who decides which brand to buy?, "When to buy?," etc.). Most studies employ three-point scales (husband, both, wife), although a number employ 5 to 7 point scales. A number of authors have examined the problem of incongruence between husband's and wife's responses (Douglas and Wind 1978; Granbois and Willett 1970; Sofilios-Rothschild 1970). Some of the incongruence appears to come from question ambiguity (e.g. asking "Who decides on clothing," rather than "Who decides on husband's or "on wife's clothing"). Most authors now agree that both spouses rather than just one should respond to the items. Other authors suggest the use of "semi-observational" techniques, examining some dimensions by self report or direct observation in contrived settings, while examining other dimensions by survey approaches. Examples of self observation include asking respondents the number of times they perform an activity, estimates of the portions of activities or decisions each partner performs, or estimates of the time spent performing each activity (Ericksen et al. 1979; Stafford et al. 1977).

Traditional Allocation of Tasks and Decision Influence

For such product areas as food and beverages, wife's and children's clothing, kitchenware, house furnishings, and furniture, wives typically have had a greater influence than husbands. Husbands have greater influence on deciding to buy, deciding which brand, and on deciding where to buy major durable purchases other than kitchen or laundry appliances or furniture. Wives traditionally play a greater role in such tasks as housecleaning, dishwashing, cooking, grocery shopping, laundry, and child care than do husbands. Husbands play a greater role in household repairs and automotive maintenance. Other tasks (e.g. paying bills) are typically handled autonomously by either spouse (Davis and Rigaux 1976; Douglas and Wind 1976; Stafford, Backman, and Dibona 1977).

Sex Roles and Family Decision Making

Although various authors have documented a shift toward more non-egalitarian sex-role attitudes, they have generally concluded that there is little behavioral evidence to indicate equal division of labor even among families with wives having sex-role modern attitudes (Araji 1977, Osmond and Martin 1975, Thornton and Freedman 1979). Scanzoni (1977), however, concluded that sex-role modern and younger families evidence greater joint and less husband or wife dominated decision making, as well as greater negotiation and bargaining. He states that bargaining and negotiation characterize families in which the wife becomes sex-role modern after several years of marriage. Green and Cunningham (1975) classified housewives as conservative, moderate, or liberal based upon Arnott's Autonomy (Feminism) Index. They found that husbands of liberal wives were perceived (by wives) as making fewer purchase decisions alone, both overall, and for major appliances, automobiles, and vacations, than husbands of conservative and moderate wives. They also found a marked shift from husband dominance toward joint or wife dominance in "How much to spend decisions" over-all, and for furniture, automobiles, housing, and how much to save, when liberal wives were compared to conservative ones. They concluded that the influence of sex roles may be product specific rather than general across product categories. This study, however, collected data only from wives and collected influence perceptions for products which may not have been recently purchased, and employed Arnott's previously criticized scale. Thus, both Cunningham and Green (1975) and Scanzoni (1977) suggest that sex-role norms do influence family decision making.

Thus, although a few studies have linked sex roles to family decision making, they typically have not done so by collecting data from both spouses or utilizing multiple dimension scales. Moreover, several alternative hypotheses concerning the effect of sex roles appear: 1) less husband and more wife influence overall, 2) product-specific changes in influence (Green and Cunningham 1975), and 3) more joint influence and less husband or wife dominance (Scanzoni 1977).

HYPOTHESES

Based upon the preceding literature review, three alternative hypotheses are presented. Sex-role modern families will demonstrate:
H1) Less husband influence overall across all product areas.
H2a) Less husband influence for product and finance-handling areas traditionally dominated by the husband (e.g. transportation, insurance).
H2b) Less wife influence in product and finance-handling areas traditionally dominated by the wife (e.g. food, home furnishings, paying bills).
H2c) The above influence shifts will be stronger among sex-role modern wives than among sex-role modern husbands.
H3) Greater joint and less husband or wife dominated decision making overall.

METHOD

The data set was gathered by the University of Illinois Survey Research Laboratory as part of a longitudinal consumption panel. Probalistic sampling methods were used to select 409 couples married during the summer of 1972 in Chicago. Only included were non-homeowning couples married for the first time, with the husband under age 30, and annual income of $5000 or more unless one spouse was a student. Data on a number of demographic, attitudinal, life-style, consumption and purchase variables were collected at approximately six-month time intervals. One section of each wave's data consisted of personal interviews of both spouses jointly, while a remaining section consisted of the interviewer supervising the completion of self-administered forms separately from husbands and wives.

To measure sex roles, 24 Likert-scale items were administered separately to both husbands and wives in Wave 8 (March 1977). The great majority (19) of these items were identical to those examined by Scanzoni (1975), although five additional items were added, and two of those employed by Scanzoni were not included. Joint (husband and wife together) responses were obtained on Wave 7 (November 1976) to the sixteen finance handling items presented in Table 2 of the results section. Couples were asked to indicate who handles expenditures for a variety of consumption areas on three-point scales (recoded to 1=husband, 2=both, 3=wife). Separately, husbands and wives were also asked to indicate who decided each of four aspects on the last major durable purchase: "Who made the initial decision to buy?," "Who decided how much to spend?," "Who decided when to buy?," and "Who decided where to buy?" Responses to these items collected in Wave 9 (September 1977) were also recoded to three-point scales.

RESULTS

Factor Analyses of Sex-Role Items

The results of factor analyses performed separately on husbands' and wives' response to all 24 sex-role items are presented in Table 1. Rather than split items a priori into two subsets as did Scanzoni (1975), we examine all items together, allowing the resulting factor structures to determine item assignment. Rao's canonical factoring was chosen because it is a scale-free procedure which tests the significance of the resulting factors. An oblique rotation of delta=0 was chosen to maintain the original, moderately correlated structure of factors.

Five factors with eigen values greater than one, accounting for 56% of the husbands' total variance and 60% of the wives' were found for both solutions. The first three factors were directly equivalent for the two samples, while the 4th wives' factor corresponded to the 5th husbands' factor. These four common factors accounted for 51 and 56 percent of the total variance for husbands and wives respectively. Table 1 presents the loadings, the percentages of variance explained, and the Cronbach's alpha of simple scores chosen to represent these four common factors. These four factors intercorrelated from .30 to .56 for the wive's solution, and from .15 to .42 for the husband's solution. Correlations are also presented between the husbands' and wives' loadings on each common factor.

TABLE 1

FACTOR ANALYSES RESULTS ON HUSBANDS' AND WIVES' SEX ROLES

	Husbands' Loadings	Wives' Loadings
Factor 1: Work and Family		
A married woman should work only if it does not interfere with her responsibilities as a homemaker.	.605	.765
A married woman should be able to work even if it involves some inconvenience for her family.	-.667	-.678
The fact that a woman enjoys working does not justify the costs and inconvenience it causes her family.	.603	.663
A married woman's most important task in life should be taking care of her husband and children.	.766	.729
A mother should realize that her greatest reward and satisfaction come through her children.	.789	.656
A wife should give up her job whenever it inconveniences her husband and children.	.826	.811
Chronbach's Alpha	.865	.875
Percentage of Variance Explained	31.1%	35.7%
Correlation of husbands' and wives' loadings	.971	
Factor 2: Share Responsibility		
If a married woman works, it is reasonable for her husband to do a greater share of the household tasks.	.502	.364
If his wife works, a husband should be just as willing as his wife to stay home from work and take care of a sick child.	.503	.570
If his wife works, he should share equally in household chores such as cooking, cleaning, and washing.	.742	.785
If a wife works, a husband should share equally in the responsibilities of child care.	.716	.801
Chronbach's Alpha	.696	.714
Percentage of Variance Explained	8.5%	8.7%
Correlation of husbands' and wives' loadings	.965	
Factor 3: Work With Young Children		
A woman who has young children should not work unless there is a serious financial need.	-.744	-.833
If a mother of young children works, it should be only while the family needs the money.	-.797	-.825
Chronbach's Alpha	.723	.826
Percentage of Variance Explained	6.0%	5.9%
Correlation of husbands' and wives' loadings	.963	
Factor 4: Wife's Career Importance		
A married woman's job should be just as important as encouraging her husband in his job.	.697	.573
A married woman who works should be able to make long range plans for her occupation, in the same way that her husband does for his.	.624	.833
If a wife makes more money than her husband, this should not bother him.	.344	.630
A married woman who works should not try to get ahead in the same way that a man does.	-.222	-.642
Chronbach's Alpha	.633	.756
Percentage of Variance Explained	4.7%	5.4%
Correlation of husbands' and wives' loadings	.927	

Four criteria were employed to select variables to construct simple sum scores to represent these four factors: substantial factor loadings, maximization of Cronbach's alpha, inclusion of an item on only one factor, and content relationship to other items on that factor. A straight summation (after recoding all items such that a high score represented sex-role modern) of variables was employed to allow equal weights on items for husbands and wives on the four resulting scales.

Sex Roles and Finance Handling

To permit examination of the combined effect of husbands' and wives' sex roles, the sample was split into halves for both husbands and wives on each scale, resulting in a 4 group assignment: (1) both traditional, (2) husband modern, wife traditional, (3) husband traditional, wife modern, and (4) both modern. This 4 group solution was chosen over a 9 group (3x3) one due to serious sparseness problems in the latter. In addition, a 3 group combined classification, in which groups 2 and 3 were combined as a mid group, was also examined as a test of equal husband and wife influence.

Crosstabulations were then run between the three-group, husband and wife classifications and the 3 and 4 group combined classifications with all 16 finance handling items. Chi-square's and Kendall Tau B's were examined for all 3-group classifications, while Chi-square's and Kendall Tau C's were examined for the four-group combined solution. The Kendall Tau's were examined to permit more powerful (than Chi-square) tests of our linear hypotheses (H1,H2a,H2b). With few exceptions, these Kendall Tau's demonstrated both more and stronger significant relationships than did the Chi-square's. For this reason, and to conserve table space, only the former are presented. Although all four sex-role scales demonstrated significant relationships with finance handling, Share Responsibility and Wife's Career Importance produced the most consistent and largest number of significant relationships, as examination of Table 2 reveals. Few significant relationships were observed on six of the finance handling items: getting cash, deciding how much cash to get, deciding on savings plans, recreational expenditures, insurance expenditures, and miscellaneous expenses. Although Work and Family and Work with Young Children produced weaker results overall, they produced stronger results on three items: food and beverages, gifts and contributions, and handling leftover money.

For Share Responsibility, 8 of the 16 finance handling items were significant for wives' scores, compared to 4 of 16 for husbands' scores, and 4 and 5 of the 16 for the three and four-group combined classifications. Hypotheses 2a, 2b, and 2c were generally supported, while H1 and H3 were not. Hypothesis 2b was supported for handling bills, food and beverages, housing, utilities, house furnishings, and clothing. Hypothesis 2a was supported for transportation expenditures, but not for insurance or savings plans. Hypothesis 3 was supported only for major appliance purchases, and to a lesser degree, clothing (as evidenced by examining the percentages of respondents answering "both").

Hypotheses 2a and 2b are generally supported for Wife's Career Importance, while H3 receives weak support and H1 and H2c are not supported. Six of the 16 items were significant for wives' scores, compared to 10 for husbands' scores, and 7 for both combined groupings. H2b is supported for paying bills, appliance purchases, and on expenditures for food and beverages, housing, utilities, house furnishings, and clothing. H2a is supported for transportation and recreation, and for husbands' scores on miscellaneous expenses and savings. H3 received some support on "who gets cash," (wife's Chi square), and on several variables for which H2a or H2b

TABLE 2
KENDALL TAU CORRELATIONS BETWEEN SEX ROLES AND FAMILY FINANCE HANDLING

	Work and Family		Combined		Share Responsibility		Combined		Work with Young Children		Combined		Wife's Career Importance		Combined	
	Wife	Husband	3grp	4grp	Wife	Husband	3grp	4grp	Wife	Husband	3grp	4grp	Wife	Husband	3grp	4grp
Who handles/decides:																
getting cash?	.036	.072	.086	.093[a]	-.033	-.016	-.008	-.005	.024	-.082	-.054	-.039	.080	-.045	.062	.074
how much cash to get?	.027	.109[a]	.062	.071	.014	.051	.101[a]	-.086[a]	-.053	-.007	-.033	-.025	-.011	-.118[b]	-.070	-.052
paying bills?	-.084	-.035	-.045	-.058	-.150[b]	-.058	-.073	-.111[a]	-.071	.023	-.176[c]	-.058	-.151[b]	-.102[a]	-.176[c]	-.172[c]
major appliance purchases?	-.062	.069	.003	.002	-.067	.131[b]	.130[b]	.049	-.066	-.070	.002	.016	.088	-.096[a]	.040	.040
savings plan?	-.059	.034	-.023	-.015	-.047	-.014	-.002	-.002	-.064	.080	-.004	-.028	-.074	-.092[a]	-.057	-.031
Who handles expenses for:																
food & beverages?	-.174[c]	-.126[b]	-.110[a]	-.093[a]	-.108[a]	-.066	-.071	-.070	-.130[b]	-.136[b]	-.113[a]	-.086[a]	-.117[b]	-.116[a]	-.104[a]	-.090[a]
housing?	-.053	.002	.001	-.014	-.134[b]	-.076	-.090	-.128[b]	-.033	.032	.016	.007	-.015	-.111[a]	-.116[a]	-.106[a]
utilities?	-.109[a]	-.032	-.061	-.078	-.198[c]	-.108[a]	-.131[b]	-.169[c]	-.097[a]	.008	-.046	-.072	-.098[a]	-.131[b]	-.177[c]	-.167[c]
furnishings?	.009	.041	.024	.023	-.119[b]	-.074	-.054	-.067	-.080	-.040	-.027	-.034	-.089[a]	-.100[a]	-.017	-.023
clothing?	-.100[a]	-.079	-.106[a]	-.079[a]	-.178[c]	-.008	-.127[b]	-.125[b]	-.203[c]	-.122[b]	-.196[c]	-.156[c]	-.115[a]	-.053	-.095[a]	-.088[a]
transportation?	.379[c]	.280[c]	.231[c]	.228[c]	.199[c]	.106[a]	.227[c]	.222[c]	.221[c]	.157[b]	.177[c]	.173[c]	.251[c]	.198[c]	.221[c]	.207[c]
recreation?	-.016	.061	-.001	.011	-.007	.012	-.011	-.003	.043	.057	.041	.017	-.057	.075	-.113[a]	.032
gifts and contributions?	-.136[b]	-.146[b]	-.114[a]	-.084[a]	-.088	-.050	-.056	-.069	-.177[c]	-.109[a]	-.113[a]	-.087[a]	-.057	-.035	-.072	-.066
insurance?	-.015	-.053	-.053	-.049	-.071	-.031	-.003	-.021	-.007	-.003	-.067	-.064	-.032	-.066	-.122[b]	-.109[a]
miscellaneous?	.008	.016	.003	.012	-.012	.015	-.022	-.010	.047	-.011	.048	.042	-.011	-.143[b]	-.054	-.027
use of surplus money?	-.071	-.152	-.077	-.025	-.040	-.079	-.033	-.003	-.044	-.122[a]	-.127[b]	-.085[a]	.001	.091	-.061	-.036

Note: Sample sizes varied from 168 to 154 due to missing data; sex-role scales were coded such that a higher score was more sex role modern; finance handling items were recoded to (1=husband) (2=both) (3=wife).

TABLE 3
KENDALL TAU CORRELATIONS BETWEEN SEX ROLES AND HUSBAND AND WIFE DECISION INFLUENCE RESPONSES

	Work and Family		Combined		Share Responsibility		Combined		Work with Young Children		Combined		Wife's Career Importance		Combined	
	Wife	Husband	3grp	4grp	Wife	Husband	3grp	4grp	Wife	Husband	3grp	4grp	Wife	Husband	3grp	4grp
Husband: Who decided:																
initially to buy?	.181[b]	.049	.203[b]	.220[c]	.099	.166[b]	.196[b]	.208[c]	.077	.055	.062	.040	.129[a]	.153[b]	.156[b]	.155[b]
when to buy?	.194[b]	.124[a]	.238[c]	.236[c]	.134[a]	.214[c]	.217[c]	.221[c]	.107	.153[b]	.083	.057	.101	.172[b]	.115[a]	.099
how much to spend?	-.100	-.049	-.011	-.027	-.208[b]	-.041	-.056	-.038	.013	-.027	-.088	-.093	-.073	.042	.035	.004
what to buy?	.186[b]	.055	.300[c]	.312[c]	.121[a]	-.017	.065	.117[a]	.098	.100	.079	.077	.104	.142[a]	.197[b]	.178[b]
Wife: Who decided:																
initially to buy?	.186[b]	.026	.144[b]	.193[b]	.113	.078	.126[a]	.112[a]	.060	.074	.103	.077	-.017	.103	.050	.060
when to buy?	.158[b]	.076	.150[b]	.180[b]	.133[a]	-.022	.093	.106[a]	.057	-.022	.079	.087	.052	.136[a]	.057	.075
how much to spend?	-.121	-.047	-.100	-.080	.047	-.146	.045	-.048	-.174[a]	-.028	.005	.007	-.096	.010	-.079	-.050
where to buy?	.117[a]	.049	.194[b]	.196[c]	.166[b]	.003	.096	.118[a]	-.029	.080	-.008	-.015	.143[b]	.196[b]	.125[a]	.115[a]

Note: Sample sizes for correlations on decision influence items other than "who decided how much to spend" ranged from a low of 96 on the combined groupings to highs of 113 for wives' sex roles and 112 on husbands' sex roles. Total sample sizes for "who decided how much to spend" was substantially smaller, ranging from 68 to 60, due to item nonresponse. Sex role scales were coded such that a high score represented sex-role modern. Decision influence items were recoded to (1=husband) (2=both) (3=wife).

[a] $p < .10$
[b] $p < .05$
[c] $p < .01$

are supported (house furnishings, clothing, transportation, and recreation).

As stated previously, the results for three items were stronger for <u>Work and Family</u> and <u>Work With Young Children</u> than for the two scales previously examined. H2b was supported on both scales for food and beverages, gifts and contributions, and for handling leftover money. Relationships on the remaining items were generally weaker, but consistent with previous results.

Although the actual magnitudes of many of the Kendall Tau correlations were small, the vast majority were consistent internally with those found for other scales; over husband, wife, and combined groupings; and with our hypotheses. The raw crosstabulations reveal this more sharply, although space considerations did not permit them to be presented as data displays. Examination of intervally scaled finance handling data by Pearson's product-moment correlations with raw sex-role scale scores might be expected to yield evidence of stronger and more substantial relationships.

Sex Roles and Decision Influence

Relationships between groupings based on the four sex-role scales and husbands' and wives' perceptions of purchase influence were also examined via crosstabulations, Chi-square's, and Kendall Tau's. The four aspects of the last major durable purchase examined were: "Who made the initial decision to buy?," "Who decided when to buy?," "Who decided how much to spend?," and "Who decided where to buy?" We attempted to break down these analyses further by the type of product purchased, but the resulting cell-size reductions made these analyses inappropriate. As with the finance

46

handling items, the Kendall Tau tests produced more and stronger significant findings than did the Chi squares. Thus, only the former are presented. The <u>Work and Family</u> scale produced the strongest results, followed by <u>Share Responsibility</u>, <u>Wife's Career Importance</u>, and <u>Work with Young Children</u>, as evidenced in Table 3.

Hypotheses 1, 2a, and 2c are supported for <u>Work and Family</u> and <u>Share Responsibility</u> on all decision aspects but "Who decides how much to spend?" The last result may be due to a high proportion of "not applicable" responses. Wives' sex roles clearly influence both husbands' and wives' perceptions of decision influence to a greater degree than husbands' perceptions as shown by significant Kendall Tau values for wives' and husbands' scores, and by the stronger results for the four-group over three-group tests. Basically similar, but weaker or less consistent patterns were found for <u>Wife's Career Importance</u>, while only 2 of 32 Kendall Tau's were significant for <u>Work with Young Children</u>.

SUMMARY AND CONCLUSIONS

Factor analyses of spouses' responses to 24 Likert-scale, sex-role items revealed four common factors equivalent to those found by other researchers in the marital and family relations discipline. Three of these scales: <u>Work and Family</u>, <u>Share Responsibility</u>, and <u>Wife's Career Importance</u> were related to inter-family differences in finance handling and in decision-making influence. For those areas traditionally handled by the wife autonomously (food and beverages, appliances, clothing, house furnishings, paying bills, housing expenditures, utilities, gifts and contributions, and leftover money), sex-role modern families showed less wife, but more joint and husband influence. For those areas traditionally dominated by the husband (transportation, recreation, and savings plans), less husband, but more joint and wife influence was observed among sex-role modern families. These three sex-role scales were also significantly related to both husbands' and wives' perceptions of influence on three aspects of the last major durable purchase: making the initial decision to buy, deciding when to buy, and deciding where to buy. Sex-role modern families showed less husband, and more joint and wife influence. Wives' sex roles are more strongly related to decision making influence than are husbands'. This conclusion also holds between <u>Share Responsibility</u> and finance handling, although the converse holds for <u>Wife's Career Importance</u>.

Although inappropriate to advance generalizations on the basis of only this study, the pattern of correlations which emerged was consistent internally and with our hypotheses. Moreover, this study examined both sex-role and decision-influence perceptions for both parties, rather than for wives only. This study also utilized scales which appear to measure most of the major dimensions recognized as underlying sex-role norms. Although separate perceptions of finance handling influence were not obtained for husband and wife, these influence ratings were obtained jointly from both partners. Unfortunately, the ordinal nature of the data collected (husband, both, wife) permitted only crosstabulations and Kendall Tau tests and did not permit a multivariate examination of the underlying relationships. Future research should use intervally scaled rating scales to examine decision influence, finance handling, or task allocation, with decision influence examined separately for different, recently purchased products.

The results of this paper show that sex-role norms clearly influence finance handling and family decision-making influence, and that traditional patterns of influence are changing. Sex-role modern families develop different consumption priorities and purchase patterns than traditional families. Further investiga-

tion of such influences should have major implications for strategic planning and market segmentation.

REFERENCES

Araji, S. (1977), "Husbands' and Wives' Attitude-Behavior Congruence in Family Roles," <u>Journal of Marriage and the Family</u>, <u>39</u>.2, 309-320.

Albrecht, S., M. Bahr, and J. Chadwick (1979), "Changing Family and Sex Roles: An Assessment of Age Differences," <u>Journal of Marriage and the Family</u>, <u>41</u>.1, 41-50.

Allison, N., L. Golden, G. Mullett, and D. Coogan (1979), "Sex-Typed Product Images: The Effects of Sex-Role, Self-Concept and Measurement Implications," in J. Olson (ed.), <u>Advances in Consumer Research</u>, <u>VII</u>, 604-609.

Brogan, D., and N. Kutner (1976), "Measuring Sex-Role Orientation: A Normative Approach," <u>Journal of Marriage and the Family</u>, <u>38</u>.1, 31-40.

Brown, P., L. Perry, E. Harburg (1977), "Sex-Role Attitudes and Psychological Outcomes for Black and White Women Experiencing Marital Dissolution," <u>Journal of Marriage and the Family</u>, <u>39</u>.3, 549-561.

Davis, H. (1976), "Decision Making Within the Household," <u>Journal of Consumer Research</u>, <u>2</u> (Mar.), 241-260.

__________, and D. Rigaux (1974), "Perception of Marital Roles in Decision Processes," <u>Journal of Consumer Research</u>, <u>1</u>.1, 51-61.

Douglas, S., and Y. Wind (1978), "Examining Family Role and Authority Patterns: Two Methodological Issues," <u>Journal of Marriage and the Family</u>, <u>40</u>.1, 35-47.

Eriksen, J., L. Yancey and E. Eriksen (1979), "The Division of Family Roles," <u>Journal of Marriage and the Family</u>, <u>41</u>.2, 301-312.

Granbois, D., and R. Willett (1970), "Equivalence of Family Role Measures Based on Husband and Wife Data," <u>Journal of Marriage and the Family</u>, <u>32</u>, 68-72.

Green, R., and I. Cunningham (1975), "Feminine Role Perception and Family Purchasing Decisions," <u>Journal of Marketing Research</u>, <u>12</u>, 325-332.

Kelly, J., and J. Worell (1977), "New Formulations of Sex Roles and Androgyny: A Critical Review," <u>Journal of Consulting and Clinical Psychology</u>, 45.6, 1101-15.

Mason, K., J. Czajka and S. Arber (1976), "Changes in U.S. Womens' Sex-Role Attitudes, 1964-1974, <u>American Sociological Review</u>, 41 (Aug.), 573-596.

Osmond, M. and P. Martin (1979), "Sex and Sexism: A Comparison of Male and Female Sex-Role Attitudes," <u>Journal of Marriage and the Family</u>, <u>37</u>, 744-758.

Pleck, J. (1977), "The Work-Family Role System." <u>Social Problems</u>, <u>24</u>, 417-427.

Roper, O. and E. Luboff (1977), "Sex Roles and Feminism Revisited: An Intergenerational Attitude Comparison," <u>Journal of Marriage and the Family</u>, <u>39</u>.1, 113-119.

Scanzoni, J. (1975), "Sex Roles, Economic Factors, and Marital Solidarity in Black and White Marriages," <u>Journal of Marriage and the Family</u>, <u>37</u>.1, 130-144.

__________ (1977), "Changing Sex Roles and Emerging Directions in Family Decision Making," <u>Journal of Consumer Research</u>, 4.3, 185-188.

Sofilios-Rothschild, C. (1970), "The Study of Family Power Structure," <u>Journal of Marriage and the Family</u>, (Nov.), 539-550.

Stafford, R., E. Backman and P. Dibona (1977), "Division of Labor Among Cohabitating and Married Adults," <u>Journal of Marriage and the Family</u>, <u>39</u>.1, 43-57.

Thornton, A. and D. Freedman (1979), "Changes in Sex-Role Attitudes of Women, 1962-1977: Evidence From a Panel Study," <u>American Sociological Review</u>, <u>44</u>(Oct.), 831-842.

Tomeh, A. (1970), "Sex-Role Orientation: An Analysis of Structural and Attitudinal Predictions," <u>Journal of Marriage and the Family</u>, 40.2, 341-350.

Venkatesh, A. (1980), "Changing Roles of Women - A Life Style Analysis," <u>Journal of Consumer Research</u>, <u>7</u>.2, 189-197.

FEMALE SHOPPERS: EXPLORING THE DIFFERENCES IN MARITAL STATUS
AND OCCUPATION FOR FASHION SHOPPING

James R. Lumpkin, North Texas State University, Denton
Gemmy S. Allen, North Texas State University, Denton
Barnett A. Greenberg, North Texas State University, Denton

ABSTRACT

Continuing shifts in the employment pattern of women from
housewives into the work-place and specifically into professional occupations create the need for a new look at market segmentation for women. This study focuses on the various aspects of the wearing apparel shopping behavior, psychographics, and demographics between single and married
females across occupational categories. Differences were
found to exist among the groups and distinct, viable segments identified although single working females are more
homogeneous than are married working females.

INTRODUCTION

Market segmentation, the identification of distinct subgroups of the total market, is a vital part of the strategic marketing process. It is an important aid in giving
direction to the marketing efforts of a firm. A useful
approach to segmentation is to group consumers based on
socioeconomic factors (Shaw, Semenik, and Williams 1981)
and then profile the groups with respect to variables of interest. One important socioeconomic factor is occupation.
Occupation is one of the most defining aspects of a person's
social identity. It is a clue to education, income, and
residence as well as buying behavior. Shifts in employment
patterns usually mean changes in buying patterns and require a new look at market segmentation. One such shift in
employment patterns affecting consumer goods purchasing is
the increasing number of employed females (Bartos 1977). In
1920, 23 percent of all women 20 to 60 years of age were
employed outside the home (Clayton 1979). In 1979, 50 percent of all women 16 years old and older were in the labor
force (U.S. Bureau of Census 1980). Of these, 60 percent
were married and 40 percent were single.

The majority of working women hold clerical jobs. Yet many
of the jobs created for women during the past decade were in
management and professional fields. Of the new jobs created
during the 1970's, 35 percent were in managerial and professional occupations, and women now hold over 22 percent of
these new jobs (Parks 1980). Women can no longer be thought
of as just housewives. Thus, working females may constitute
an important market segment that requires renewed study.

Previous studies of working women generally focus on demographic and socioeconomic changes (Hedges and Barnett 1972;
Lazer and Smallwood 1977; Grossman 1978, 1979; Johnson(1980).
Relatively little research has attempted to relate these
changes to market-place behavior, a prerequisite for effective segmentation (Douglas 1975; Bartos 1977; McCall 1977).

The previous research suggests that working women do differ
from housewives on some of their market-place behavior.
Douglas (1975) proposed that further research should examine occupational subsets of the working-nonworking groups.
This was done by Joyce and Guiltinan (1978) who compared
housewives, professional women and non-professional women
with respect to store attribute importance, shopping orientations and information search patterns for grocery shopping.

The previous research indicates that segmenting along occupational lines can be fruitful. The effect of "life situation" identified by Bartos suggests that research should
distinguish between married and single females as well as
across occupations (Golden 1979). One product category
that is likely to be effected by the changing role of
women is wearing apparel. Joyce and Guiltinan note that
because of the convenience nature of grocery products,
segmenting "may be even more appropriate for high-interest

products such as apparel, jewelry and home-furnishings."
Apparel, being highly visible, is indicative of social
position and role (Hirschman and Mills 1979). Thus, as
women are moving into the workforce and into higher status
occupations, the market-place behavior with respect to
apparel purchasing is hypothesized to differ from housewives and from women in lower status occupations. Due to
the importance of apparel as a product category and because of the desirability of studying market-place behavior
with respect to specific product categories, this research
focuses on wearing apparel.

The purpose of this study is to compare various aspects
of the wearing apparel shopping and purchasing behavior
and life style, shopping orientation, and demographic
patterns for single and married females in various occupational categories. Although little research has studied differences across both marital status and occupation, the limited research suggests that there are differences among these groups with respect to type of store
patronized, the source of information used when shopping,
the importance of various store and product related attributes, the amount and the price levels purchases, and
life styles, shopping orientations, and demographics.
To further define these differences for wearing apparel,
this study will develop profiles for each of these groups.
Specifically, the research will investigate the following question:

Do _married_ working females differ from _single_ working females with respect to store type patronized,
information sources used, attribute importances,
amount spent on apparel and usual price range, life
styles, shopping orientations, and demographics?

To further define the differences between housewives
and working females, and to profile single females, a
neglected group that is growing in size and importance,
other questions to be examined are:

Do _married_ females employed in _professional_ occupations differ from married females in _non-profes-
sional_ occupations and from _housewives_ on the above
variables?

and:

Do _single_ professional females differ from _single_
non-professional females on the above variables?

In this study "married" refers to those females living
with husbands, and "single" refers to females who are
divorced, separated, widowed, or never married. "Professional" refers to those who classified themselves as in
professional or managerial occupations while "non-professional" includes those in all other occupations.

By developing profiles of each of these potential segments
and determining where the differences occur, the understanding of how the changing role of women is effecting
behavior in the marketplace can be improved. Further,
the identification and description of these segments can
enhance the efforts of managers to assess the potential
of these groups and to select target markets. The manager can then match the needs of the most promising target markets with the proper marketing mix, thus allocating the resources of the firm efficiently.

METHODOLOGY

The data for this study was gathered as part of a national
survey conducted in the Fall of 1980. A self-administered
mail questionnaire, after a pretest, was sent to a sample of
2650 households drawn from the Market Facts Mail Panel. For
married households, both spouses were included, giving a total sample size of 4356. A total of 2854 completed questionnaires were obtained with 1728 being from females (71% response rate for females). Of the total, 1366 female respondents were usable for the purpose of this study. Unemployed
single females were not included in the analysis. Based on
census data available, the sample was generally representative of the U. S. population although slightly upscale in
terms of income. The questionnaire was constructed to obtain information regarding the respondent's lifestyle patterns, shopping orientations, demographic characteristics,
and patronage and purchasing behavior for wearing apparel.

The market-related data included the frequency of shopping
at various types of stores, the importance of store and
shopping related attributes, the importance of various information sources when shopping for apparel, the total dollar amount of apparel purchases over the last year as well
as for various apparel categories and the usual price range
of the purchases in the apparel categories. The apparel
categories and the price ranges for each category were chosen based on discussions with a number of apparel retailers
in a large Southwestern metropolitan city. They were chosen to reflect the categories of apparel and price ranges
usually carried by the various types of retailers investigated in this study.

The demographic and socioeconomic data included age, marital status, occupation, residence type, education, income,
and household size. The psychographic measures were obtained using a six-point, agree/disagree scale. Both general and fashion specific items were used. While some items
were developed specifically for this study, several appropriate items that have been used in previous research were
included (Darden and Aston 1974; Darden and Reynolds 1971;
Wells and Tigert 1971). The 132 psychographic statements
were factor analyzed using the _Statistical Analysis System_
(SAS) (Barr et al. 1976) principal axes factor program with
varimax rotation. A total of 27 factors were extracted
with the loadings on each factor required to be above .50
for inclusion. As a measure of reliability, Cronbach's
Alpha coefficient was calculated for each factor (Cronbach
1951). The large majority of the Alpha coefficients were
above .69 with only two scales having coefficients below
.60. In addition, the inter-item correlations were generally between .40 and .70. While the rule-of-thumb for the
optimal size of these measures varies among researchers, it
is believed that the scales have acceptable reliability for
this exploratory study.

To differentiate between the groups, discriminant analysis
is a useful technique. Discriminant analysis generates a
linear function based on the predictor variables that best
discriminates between the _a priori_ defined groups. With
discriminant analysis, the relative importance of each predictor variable in discriminating between groups, and whether there is a significant difference between the mean
predictor-variable profile for the groups can be determined.
In addition, the discriminant function developed can be
used to predict group membership. Since the actual group
membership is known, a table of correct and incorrect classifications can be created to check on the predictive ability of the model. Through this method, the dimensions on
which the groups differ can be determined and thus provide
a basis for effective market segmentation and development
of marketing strategies.

In order to determine which predictor variables best discriminate between the groups, the _Statistical Package for
the Social Sciences_ (SPSS) (Nie et al. 1975) stepwise discriminant analysis routine was utilized. A separate

discriminant analysis was performed for:
1. married _"working"_ females versus single _"working"_
   females;
2. _"married"_ females in professional occupations versus _"married"_ females in non-professional occupations versus housewives;
3. _"single"_ working females in professional occupations
   versus _"single"_ working females in non-professional
   occupations.

The discriminant function was validated by estimating the
function on half of the data for classification purposes
(Frank, Massey, and Morrison 1969). The classification
results presented reflect the application of the discriminant function to the hold out sample.

To evaluate differences between the "working" female and
"single" female groups on the dollar amount of apparel purchased in total and by apparel category, the price lines
usually bought for each apparel category, and the demographic and socioeconomic measure, the Kolmogrov-Smirnov
test was used. The Kolmogrov -Smirnov procedure compares
the two sample cumulative frequency distributions and determines whether the observed deviations indicate that
they have been drawn from two populations, one of which is
larger than the other. Because this procedure takes advantage of the ordinal properties of the data, it is more
powerful than the Chi-square test (Siegal 1956). For the
"Married" group, which has three categories, the Kruskal-
Wallis test was used. This test uses a one-way analysis
of variance by ranks to determine whether the samples are
from different populations (Siegal 1956). Both analyses
were performed using the _SPSS_ non-parametric routine (Hall
and Nie 1981).

RESULTS

Table 1, 2, and 3 present the standardized discriminant
coefficients, groups means, and significance level of the
F-test for difference in group means for the three discriminant analyses. Table 4 presents the cross-classification
matrices from the discriminant analyses. The cross-vali-
dated discriminant functions correctly classified the working females 58.7 percent of the time; the married females
44.5 percent of the time; and the single females 60.5 percent of the time. The analyses were at a level beyond
that due to chance (C proportional = 51.6 percent for working females; 33.4 percent for the married females; and 50.5
percent for the single females). The overall chi-square
results were significant at a level of .000 for all
analyses.

The cross-tabulation of the demographic/socioeconomic variable, total dollar spent by apparel category, and price
range usually purchased by apparel category respectively,
and the results of the Kolmogrov-Smirnov and Kruskal-
Wallis test of significance are summarized below but are
not shown in tabular form.

Working Females

The findings from this study reveal that there are differences between married working females and single working
females. Married working females were found to be in the
middle age categories, have less education, but have higher family incomes, and use credit less. Single females
seem to be more self-oriented versus the more traditional
family orientation of the married female (Table 1) as might
be expected.

Single working females may be an important segment to marketers as they were found to be more fashion innovators as
well as generalized and shopping opinion leaders. Because
of the relatively short span of time of an apparel fashion
season, establishing the identity of early buyers is important. The use of newspaper and catalog advertising should
be used to generate awareness of new fashions to this

segment, since they seem to be the best prospects for new
fashions. Advertising messages that reach both young and
older single females should be used.

Married working females would seem to be an important segment to marketers because their salaries represent 30 to 40
percent of the household incomes in families where both
husband and wife work (U. S. Bureau of Census 1980). The
results of this study found, however, that married females
actually spend _less_ on apparel than single females. The
married females _did_ tend to buy higher priced apparel overall, and for sportswear in particular. Both groups tend to
shop at department stores and the married females appear to
be a viable target for catalog shopping. Both groups rated
label/brand relatively lower than store reputation, high
quality, wide variety, and low price. Thus, individual retailers have an opportunity to reach these segments regardless of brand of apparel carried.

Married Females

When comparing housewives with professional and non-professional working females, some significant differences were
identified (Table 2). The professional female is well educated with her husband likely to also be a professional.
Consequently, this group has the highest income. Interestingly, professional females tend to be younger with housewives dominating the 55 and older category. This seems to
reflect the emergence of the professional female in recent
years. As McCall (1977) found, housewives seem to be more
home-centered while the professional female is more active
outside the home. They were found to be appearance conscious as McCall suggests but unlike McCall, the working
females and especially the professionals _were_ found to be
innovators and purchased slightly _higher_ priced apparel
than housewives. Both professionals and non-professionals
utilize friends as information sources. The working females
also spend more than housewives on apparel, with the professionals spending the most. This is consistent with their
clothing interest and needs and higher incomes. The professional females, who are sports enthusiasts, tend to purchase higher priced sportswear. This research found _no_
difference in where the groups shopped for apparel as all
three shop most often at department stores.

Single Females

Professional and non-professional single females were found
to be relatively homogeneous. However, some differences
were found (Table 3). The single professional has more
education, higher income, likes to shop for apparel and
likes to shop where she is known, In attracting this group,
retailers should emphasize the enjoyable attributes of
shopping and strive to create a personal relationship between the salesperson and the consumer. Professionals tend
to purchase more expensive dresses and coordinated separates
than non-professional, but no significant differences were
found in the total amount spent on apparel, where they shop,
the information sources used or the store or product attributes they consider important.

CONCLUSIONS

This study has developed profiles of the various segments
of the female wearing apparel market and implications for
retailers offered. Differences were found to exist between
married and single working females and between housewives
and working married females. Professional and non-professional females do appear to be distinct, viable segments
although the single working females seem more homogeneous
than married working females.

The single working females appear to be an important segment as they were found to be fashion innovators and would
be the best prospects for new fashions. Also important to
retailers would be that they were found to be generalized
and shopping opinion leaders influencing where their friends
shop. The professional female is an important segment as
they enjoy clothes and have the potential to account for a
substantial share of apparel purchases.

While very little research has gone beyond the working/house-
wife dichotomy in segmenting the female market, the results
from this study indicate more work in this area is needed.
Wearing apparel is a very broad topic and this exploratory
research has focused on wearing apparel in general. However,
additional insight could be gained and strategy implications
made more specific by developing profiles of females for
various apparel categories. Furthermore, other product
categories should be investigated in order to generalize
these findings. Further study of single females would seem
to be a particularily fruitful area.

REFERENCES

Barr, Anthony J. et al. (1976), _Statistical Analysis System
Users Guide_, Raleigh: SAS Institute.

Bartos, Rena (1977), "The Moving Target: The Impact of
Women's Employment on Consumer Behavior," _Journal of
Marketing_, 41(July), 31-37.

Clayton, Richard R. (1979), _The Family, Marriage, and Social
Change_. Lexington, Massachusetts: D. C. Heath and Co.

Cronbach, Lee J. (1951), "Coefficient Alpha and the Internal
Structure of Tests," _Psychometrika_, 16(September), 279-
334.

Darden, William R. and Fred Reynolds (1971), "Shopping
Orientations and Product Usage Rates," _Journal of Marketing Research_, 8(November), 505-508.

__________ and Dub Aston (1974), "Psychographic Profiles
of Patronage Groups," _Journal of Retailing_, 50(Winter),
99-112.

Douglas, Susan (1975), "Working Wife and Nonworking Wife
Families as a Basis for Market Segmentation," Marketing
Science Institute working paper report No. 75-114, Cam-
bridge, Mass.: Marketing Science Institute.

Frank, Ronald E., William F. Massey, and Donald G. Morrison
(1969), "Bias in Multiple Discriminant Analysis," _Journal
of Marketing Research_, 2(August), 250-258.

Golden, Linda L. (1979), "Research on Female Consumers:
We're Not There Yet," _Proceedings_, Southern Marketing
Association, 321-322.

Grossman, Allyson Sherman, (1978), "Divorced and Separated
Women in the Labor Force--An Update," _Monthly Labor Re-
view_, 101(October), 43-45.

__________ (1979), "Labor Force Patterns of Single Women,"
Monthly Labor Review, 102(August), 46-53.

Hedges, Janice Neipert and Jeanne K. Barnett (1972), "Working Women and the Division of Household Tasks," _Monthly
Labor Review_, 95(April), 9-14.

Hirschman, Elizabeth C. and Michael K. Mills (1979), "Women's Occupational Status, Innovations, Opinion Leadership and Innovative Communication," _Proceedings_, Southern Marketing Association, 270-273.

Hull, C. Hadlai and Norman H. Nie (1981), _SPSS Update_, New
York: McGraw-Hill Book Company.

Johnson, Beverly L. (1980), "Marital and Family Characteristics of the Labor Force," _Monthly Labor Review_,
103(April), 48-52.

Joyce, Mary, and Joseph Guiltinan (1978), "The Professional Woman: A Potential Market Segment for Retailers," Journal of Retailing, 54(Summer), 59-70.

Lazer, William, and John E. Smallwood (1977), "The Changing Demographics of Women," Journal of Marketing, 41(July).

McCall, Suzanne H. (1977), "Meet the 'Workwife'," Journal of Marketing, 41(July), 55-56.

Parks, Largent (1980), "Women: Roles Shifting with Decade," Dallas/Ft. Worth Business, (February 18), 12-13.

Suelzle, Marijean (1973), "Women in Labor," in Marriages and Families, Helena Z. Lopata, ed., New York: Van Nostrand.

Wells, William D. and Douglas Tigert (1971), "Activities, Interests, and Opinions," Journal of Advertising Research, 11(August), 17-35.

U. S. Bureau of the Census (1980), Statistical Abstract of the United States, Washington, D. C.

TABLE 1

DISCRIMINANT ANALYSIS RESULTS FOR MARRIED VERSUS SINGLE WORKING FEMALES

Variable[a]	Standardized Discriminant Coefficient	Prob.[b]	Group Means Married	Group Means Single
Frequency of Mail or Phone Order from Department Store	.327	.000	2.144	1.768
Radio as Important Information Source	.262	.069	1.796	1.623
High Quality Importance	.169	.653	4.207	4.114
Store Reputation Importance	.281	.099	3.777	3.587
Label or Brand Importance	-.309	.332	2.811	2.922
Shopping Ease Importance	-.203	.866	3.692	3.711
Community/Social Minded	.316	.771	3.023	3.054
"My Time" Orientation	-.164	.063	2.874	3.031
Generalized Opinion Leader	-.421	.002	3.520	3.811
Influenced by Opinion Leaders	.390	.004	3.187	2.969
Fine Art Enthusiast	-.244	.000	3.692	4.101
Inflation Conscious	.239	.098	4.272	4.082
Energy Conscious	-.357	.649	3.878	3.924
Shopping Opinion Leader	-.323	.085	4.192	4.340
Traditional Sex Role Orientation	.354	.066	4.227	4.032
Credit User	-.241	.072	3.305	3.561
Advertising Shopper	.293	.010	4.057	3.780
Personalizing Shopper	.191	.850	3.118	3.096
Clothing Conformist	.163	.158	2.840	2.737
Fashion Innovator	-.287	.010	2.791	3.035

[a] Includes only those variables entering the stepwise discriminant analysis.

[b] Probability of difference in group means with univariate F test.

TABLE 3

DISCRIMINANT ANALYSIS RESULTS FOR PROFESSIONAL VERSUS NON-PROFESSIONAL SINGLE FEMALES

Variables[a]	Standardized Discriminant Coefficients	Prob.[b]	Group Means Professional	Group Means Non-Professional
Frequency of Shopping at Specialty Stores	.261	.696	2.539	2.616
Frequency of Shopping at Department Stores	.239	.606	3.592	3.666
Importance of Magazines as Information Source	.399	.202	2.185	2.450
Importance of Catalogs as Information Source	-.528	.504	3.035	2.883
Importance of Television as Information Source	-.217	.278	2.159	1.993
Wide Variety Importance	-.557	.688	3.734	3.650
Store Personnel Importance	.688	.042	2.991	3.516
Financial Optimism	.276	.082	3.787	4.166
Dislike Housework	.433	.009	3.765	4.358
Time Manager	.199	.870	3.516	3.547
Dislike Discount Stores	-.356	.048	2.754	2.463
Shopping Opinion Leaders	.359	.031	4.252	4.533
Shopping Propensity	.172	.380	3.648	3.791
Personalizing Shopper	-.611	.053	3.192	2.819
Shopping Enjoyment	-.603	.047	3.844	3.575

[a] Includes only the variables entering the stepwise discriminant analysis.

[b] Probability of difference in group means with univariate F test.

TABLE 2

MULTIPLE DISCRIMINANT ANALYSIS RESULTS FOR HOUSEWIVES VERSUS PROFESSIONAL VERSUS NON-PROFESSIONAL MARRIED FEMALES

Variable [a]	Standardized Discriminant Coefficients	Prob.[b]	Group Means House-wives	Group Means Professional	Group Means Non-Professional
Frequency of Mail or Phone Order from Specialty Store	.270	.176	1.237	1.463	1.346
Importance of Newspaper as Information Source	.157	.592	3.082	3.158	2.948
Importance of Catalogs as Information Source	-.182	.776	3.010	2.878	2.987
Importance of Television as Information Source	-.225	.002	2.030	1.902	2.487
Importance of Friends as Information Source	.275	.096	2.711	2.890	3.128
Shopping Ease Importance	-.241	.544	3.701	3.536	3.717
Store Personnel Importance	.169	.271	3.206	3.512	3.358
Community/Social Minded	-.186	.000	3.123	3.176	2.560
"My Time" Orientation	-.338	.014	3.192	2.990	2.780
Influenced by Opinion Leaders	-.321	.812	3.082	3.054	2.974
Dieter	.371	.000	2.045	2.720	2.202
Dislike Housework	.485	.000	3.216	4.109	3.724
Time Manager	.213	.395	3.381	3.598	3.531
Fine Art Enthusiast	.065	.000	3.433	4.013	3.107
Sports Enthusiast	.237	.000	2.498	3.118	2.390
Shopping Opinion Leader	.414	.016	3.907	4.310	4.051
Advertising Special Shopper	-.259	.321	2.064	3.951	3.804
Fashion Innovator	.384	.064	2.470	2.777	2.705
Clothing Interest	.313	.005	2.358	2.826	2.666
Style Conscious	-.683	.515	3.588	3.403	3.496
Non-Style Conscious	.067	.021	3.378	3.265	3.787

[a] Includes only those variables entering the stepwise discriminant analysis.

[b] Probability of difference in group means with univariate F Test.

TABLE 4

DISCRIMINANT ANALYSIS CROSS-CLASSIFICATION TABLES FOR HOLD OUT SAMPLES [a]

TABLE 4a - Working Females

Actual	Predicted Married	Predicted Single	Sample Size
Married	70.4%	29.6%	277
Single	57.0%	43.0%	207

Percent correctly classified: Analysis Sample 68.5%
Hold Out Sample 58.7%

TABLE 4b - Married Females

Actual	Predicted Housewives	Predicted Professional	Predicted Non-Professional	Sample Size
Housewives	58.9%	20.0%	21.1%	90
Professional	36.7%	31.2%	32.1%	109
Non-Professional	33.0%	20.9%	46.2%	91

Percent correctly classified: Analysis Sample 64.2%
Hold Out Sample 44.5%

TABLE 4c - Single Females

Actual	Predicted Professional	Predicted Non-Professional	Sample Size
Professional	45.2%	54.8%	115
Non-Professional	23.9%	76.1%	113

Percent correctly classified: Analysis Sample 79.2%
Hold Out Sample 60.5%

[a] Overall chi-square results are significant at .000 level for all analyses.

PERCEPTIONS OF MODELS IN TELEVISION COMMERCIALS

Dean Sharits, Walt Disney Productions
H. Bruce Lammers, California State University, Northridge

ABSTRACT

In an adaptation of Schneider's (1978) person perception
approach, models from 128 randomly selected television
commercials were rated on a set of 13 social psychological
attributes. Contrary to traditional content analyses, it
was concluded that women are portrayed in a fashion that
is more positive than the way men are portrayed in today's
(1980) television commercials, especially in prime-time
airings.

INTRODUCTION

Critics have had a field day deprecating advertisers for
the manner in which women have been portrayed in television and print advertisements (Belkaoui & Belkaoui 1976;
Courtney & Lockeretz 1971; Courtney & Whipple 1974; Manstead & McCulloch 1981). According to these critics, women have often been underrepresented in working roles and
overrepresented in decorative and sex-object roles. (e.g.,
Belkaoui & Belkaoui 1976). Although recent studies have
reported that men too, are being increasingly cast in
decorative, sex-object roles in print advertisements
(Skelly & Lundstrom 1981; Wolheter & Lammers 1980), women
continue to express significantly greater dissatisfaction
than men with sex role portrayals in television advertisements (Lammers & Wilkinson 1980; Sciglimpaglia, Lundstrom,
& Vanier 1980).

The significance of the sex role portrayal issue to both
marketers and consumers, combined with some intriguing
reports of trends toward an improvement in role portrayals
(Kerin, Lundstrom, & Sciglimpaglia 1979; Scheibe 1979;
Schneider & Schneider 1979), prompted us to examine role
portrayals from a different perspective. Past content analyses of advertisements have traditionally focused on a
demographic approach to the analysis of roles played by
male and female models. The present study, however, followed Schneider's (1978) suggestion that a person perception approach rather than a demographic approach be used
to evaluate sex role portrayals.

In the person perception approach, subjects are exposed to
an advertisement and are asked to indicate the various
perceptions they have of the model in the advertisement by
rating the model on a set of social psychological attributes (e.g., "mature," "wise," "sociable"). In the demographic approach, several independent raters typically
categorize the model on such demographics as occupation,
sex and race. The former approach promises to provide a
richer understanding of consumers' reactions to the roles
portrayed by models.[1] The latter approach tends to be
merely descriptive and largely limited to conflicting interpretations (Schneider 1978; Skelly & Lundstrom 1981).

Conceptually, it is parsimonious to simply propose that
the formation of person perceptions involves the acquisition of information about the traits of an unknown person

____

[1]The person perception approach is also consistent with
Shimp's (1979) contention that social psychological representations in television advertising "may have a functionally equivalent impact on receivers as that which is
asserted directly" (p. 33).

(model). Primacy effects in impression formation research
suggest that the initial set of traits carry more weight
than information presented later (e.g., Anderson & Hubert
1963). In the present context of advertising, it is presumed that consumers generally process advertisements in
a low-involving manner (DeBruicker 1979) and that seldom
would more than the often-cited primacy effect be expected
to be operating. Thus, consumers' perceptions of models
in advertisements are likely to be based upon what may
appear to be a conclusion drawn from something less than a
full measure of attention. Despite the probability that
such perceptions may oftentimes be drawn with little
thought, there seems to be overwhelming evidence for the
notion that such perceptions once acquired, have a significant impact on the development of "expected" behavior (Jennings, Geis, & Brown 1980).

The major purpose of the present study was twofold: (a) to
examine current perceptions of how women and men are portrayed in television commercials, and (b) to demonstrate
that the person perception method is an informative and
useful approach to understanding sex role portrayals.

Finally, the present study also included an examination of
the extent to which the viewer's sex may affect perceptions of sex role portrayals, and of the extent to which
perceptions of the models portrayed in prime-time differ
from those portrayed in daytime television. These two
variables (viewer sex and time) were included primarily
for exploratory purposes and no a priori directional
hypotheses were generated.

METHOD

A total of 921 commercials were videotaped and edited from
43 hours of prime-time (7 p.m. to 11 p.m.) and 34 hours of
daytime programming which aired over the three major network affiliates in Minneapolis/St. Paul during February
and March, 1980. Of the 921 commercials, 493 commercials
contained a main character who had an on-camera appearance
of at least three seconds ($\overline{x}$ = 14.6 seconds, s = 7.3).
From this pool of 493 commercials, 128 were randomly selected via Fortran subroutine for use in the present study.
The distribution of the commercials broken down by Sex of
the Model (the main character or actor in the commercial),
Time of Airing (prime-time vs. daytime), and Product Class
is shown in Table 1.

Although the present study was concerned with generalized
rather than product perceptions of models, it is important
to describe the distribution of product categories represented in the randomly drawn samples of commercials. Thus,
two types of Chi Square analyses were performed on the
distribution shown in Table 1. The first type was a
Model's Sex $\underline{x}$ Product Class analysis within each Time
category. This analysis produced no significant differences within either the Daytime category or the Prime-
time category (both $\underline{p}$'s > .10). The second type was a
Time $\underline{x}$ Product Class within each Model's Sex category.
Here it was found that the types of products modeled by
males differed significantly from daytime to prime-time,
$\chi^2_{(7)}$ = 13.87, $\underline{p}$ < .054. As Table 1 shows, the most drastic difference was in the Household Cleaning Products
class, which accounted for 21% of the male-modeled ads on
daytime but for only 3% of the male-modeled ads from

prime-time. For female models, however, product class did not vary significantly as a function of the time of airing (p > .10).

TABLE 1

DISTRIBUTION OF COMMERCIAL BY

MODEL'S SEX, TIME, AND PRODUCT

| | Daytime | | Prime-Time | | |
Product	Male Models	Female Models	Male Models	Female Models	Total
Household Cleaning Products, Laundry Detergents Dish Soaps	20.7	20.6	3.1	9.1	13.3
Food, Nonalcoholic Beverages	41.4	26.5	31.3	15.2	28.1
Pet Foods	6.9	0.0	3.1	6.1	3.9
Drugs, Medicines, Alcoholic Beverages	10.3	8.8	21.9	15.2	14.1
Automobiles & Accessories	0.0	0.0	9.4	6.1	3.9
Personal Beauty & Hygiene	17.2	44.1	9.4	36.4	27.4
Finance & Real Estate	3.4	0.0	12.5	3.0	4.7
Household Furniture, Appliances	0.0	0.0	9.4	9.1	4.7
Base $\underline{n}$	29	34	32	33	128

Note: The figures above the base $\underline{n}$ represent column percentages.

Subjects

Thirty-two female and 32 male business school students from a large Midwestern university volunteered to participate in a "Study on Evaluation of Advertising." They received partial course credit for their participation.

It is recognized that the use of a "homogeneous" sample of university students may limit the generalizeability of the results. However, we were concerned primarily with the search for sources of differential perceptions that are not easily attributable to sample heterogeneity. Thus, our concern was primarily for internal validity at, unfortunately, the possible loss of some generalizeability (Sawyer, Worthing, & Sendak 1979). Still, it should also be pointed out that college students make up a large, often-aimed at target market. Their perceptions are well worth examination.

Procedure

A male graduate assistant served as the experimenter. After introducing himself, the experimenter explained to the subjects that they would be shown four separate sets of TV ads (32 ads per set) over four separate sessions. The sessions were approximately one hour long each and took place within a two-week period. The commercials shown in each set were randomly assigned to those sets. In addition, within each set, the order of presentation was randomly determined prior to the actual viewing of the commercials.

The subjects were given a booklet containing a set of 13 Semantic Differential-type scales for each commercial. The subjects were told to rate the main character in each commercial on the 13 scales. (The main character was explicitly identified in print on the top of each page of the questionnaire). For future comparison's sake, the 13 scales were adapted from Schneider (1978) and hereafter will be referred to as the RAM ("Ratings of the Attributes of the Model").[2] The scales in order of appearance on the questionnaire were:

* "Poor (1) - Rich (6)"

* "Bad Spouse (1) - Good Spouse (6)"

* "Foolish (1) - Wise (6)"

* "Unfriendly (1) - Friendly (6)"

* "Unattractive (1) - Good Looking (6)"

* "Unconcerned with the appearance of the home (1)- Concerned with the appearance of the home (6)"

* "Impulsive (1) - Logical (6)"

* "Dependent upon the opposite sex (1) - Independent of the opposite sex (6)"

* "Modern (1) - Traditional (6)"

* "Failure (1) - Successful (6)"

* "Bad Parent (1) - Good Parent (6)"

* "Immature (1) - Mature (6)"

* "Boring (1) - Interesting (6)"

Subsequent to the viewing of all four sets of T.V. commercials, the subjects were debriefed and thanked for their participation in the experiment.

RESULTS

Separate 2 x 2 x 2 mixed model univariate analyses of variance (ANOVAs) were performed on each of the variables. The independent variables for the ANOVAs were the between-subjects variable Viewer Sex (male vs. female), and the within-subjects variables of Model's Sex (male vs. female) and Time (prime-time vs. daytime). The data submitted to the ANOVAs were each subject's 13 mean responses to each of the four types of commercials (prime-time male model commercials, prime-time female model commercials, daytime-male model commercials, and daytime female model commercials).

Perceptions of Models as a Function of Model's Sex

Significant main effects of Model's Sex were found on all but two of the 13 RAM variables. The means for these main effects indicated that female models, relative to male models, were perceived to be better parents, better spouses, more mature, wiser, more logical, more concerned with the appearance of the home, more attractive, more sociable, more interesting, richer, and more modern. The

---

[2] A factor analysis of these scales yielded three significant factors. Subsequent analyses using aggregated factor scores produced results which were consistent with the disaggregated analyses reported here. Because of space limitations, those findings are not presented. They are available upon request from either author.

relevant $\underline{F}$s and $\underline{M}$s are presented in Table 2.

TABLE 2

MEANS OF THE PERCEIVED ATTRIBUTES OF MALE AND FEMALE MODELS

| | MODELS | | |
Responsible-Mature	Male	Female	F (1,62)
"Good Parent"	4.18	4.45	62.60***
"Good Spouse"	4.12	4.40	70.11***
"Mature"	4.00	4.23	6.38***
"Wise"	3.81	4.02	29.78***
"Logical"	3.64	3.73	3.31*
"Concerned with Appearance of Home"	3.59	4.43	189.97***
Social Image-Status			
"Good Looking"	3.54	4.17	155.25***
"Sociable"	4.36	4.58	73.55***
"Interesting"	3.30	3.49	6.57***
"Rich"	3.97	4.04	8.61**
"Successful"	4.24	4.26	0.19
Independence			
"Independent of Opposite Sex"	3.30	3.35	0.69
"Modern"	3.90	3.33	203.94***

*$\underline{p}$ < .10
**$\underline{p}$ < .05
***$\underline{p}$ < .0001

Perceptions of Models as a Function of Time of Airing

Significant main effects of Time were found on 10 of the 13 RAM items. Models in daytime commercials, relative to models in prime-time commercials, were perceived to be better parents, better spouses, more mature, more wise, more logical, more concerned with the appearance of the home, more attractive, more sociable, richer, and more successful. The relevant $\underline{F}$s and $\underline{M}$s are presented in Table 3.

TABLE 3

MEANS OF THE PERCEIVED ATTRIBUTES OF MODELS IN

DAYTIME AND PRIME-TIME COMMERCIALS

Responsible-Mature	Daytime	Prime-Time	F (1,62)
"Good Parent"	4.44	4.24	95.00***
"Good Spouse"	4.41	4.13	136.48***
"Mature"	4.27	3.97	22.73**
"Wise"	4.06	3.78	132.08***
"Logical"	3.79	3.59	66.63***
"Concerned with Appearance of Home"	4.21	3.86	196.18***
Social Image-Status			
"Good Looking"	3.97	3.77	11.10**
"Sociable"	4.55	4.41	35.04**
"Interesting"	3.46	3.34	2.56
"Rich"	3.99	4.03	8.05**
"Successful"	4.31	4.20	33.40**
Independence			
"Independent of Opposite Sex"	3.33	3.33	0.48
"Modern"	3.58	3.62	2.03

*$\underline{p}$ < .10
**$\underline{p}$ < .05
***$\underline{p}$ < .0001

Perceptions of Models as a Function of Viewer's Sex

As a main effect, Viewer's Sex affected only two of the 13 RAM variables. Female viewers ($\underline{M}$ = 3.83) perceived the models to be more logical than did the male viewers ($\underline{M}$ = 3.55, $\underline{F}$ (1,62) = 5.63, $\underline{p}$ < .01), but the male viewers ($\underline{M}$ = 3.47) perceived the models to be more independent of the opposite sex than did the female viewers ($\underline{M}$ = 3.19, $\underline{F}$ (1,62) = 7.52, $\underline{p}$ < .01).

Interaction Effects on Perceptions of Models

The Model's Sex $\underline{x}$ Time interaction was significant on the perceptions of "concerned with the appearance of the home," ($\underline{F}$ (1,62) = 29.22, $\underline{p}$ < .001, "good looking," $\underline{F}$ (1,62) = 38.84, $\underline{p}$ < .001, "successful," $\underline{F}$ (1,62) = 14.79, $\underline{p}$ < .01, and "modern," $\underline{F}$ (1,62) = 31.05, $\underline{p}$ < .001. Basically, the internal analyses of the interaction means (see Table 4) showed that male models, relative to female models, were perceived to be less concerned, less good looking, less successful, and less modern (more traditional) -- especially in prime-time commercials. No other interaction effects were significant.

TABLE 4

MEANS FOR SIGNIFICANT INTERACTION

EFFECTS OF MODEL'S SEX AND TIME

| | Time | |
Model's Sex	Daytime	Prime-Time
"Concerned with the Appearance of the Home"		
Male	3.84a	3.37b
Female	4.53c	4.33d
"Good Looking		
Male	3.74a	3.35b
Female	4.16c	4.18c
"Successful"		
Male	4.34a	4.14c
Female	4.27ab	4.24b
"Traditional"		
Male	3.81a	3.99b
Female	3.39c	3.27d

Note: For each dependent variable, means with no common subscripts differ at $\underline{p}$ < .05, Duncan's Multiple Range Tests.

DISCUSSION

The results demonstrated that women were portrayed in a more positive fashion than were men. Female models were perceived to be better parents, better spouses, more mature, wiser, more logical, more concerned with the appearance of the home, better looking, more sociable, more interesting, richer, and more modern than were male models. Although these findings contradict the conclusions of some earlier studies (e.g., Courtney & Lockeretz 1971), it is entirely in line with an extrapolation of the trends reported by Schneider and Schneider (1979) and, to a lesser degree, by Scheibe (1979). Moreover, to the extent that people attribute less favorable traits to models in sex-object roles than to models in other types of roles, the person perception results of the present study are consistent with recent reports that males have been increasingly portrayed in decorative, sex-object roles, while females have been portrayed in fewer such roles (cf. Skelly & Lundstrom 1981: Wolheter & Lammers 1980).

Another explanation for the unconventional findings may be that the present study, unlike some previous content analyses, went beyond a surface count of selected demo-

graphics. Instead, the present study focused on the social
psychological attributes perceived to be held by the models. Although such perceptions lend themselves to a great
deal of subjectivity, it is important to note that the
male and female viewers did not significantly differ from
one another in their perceptions of the models' attributes.
This finding underscores the convergent validity of the
person perception instrument used in the present study.

A second dominant theme running through the results of the
present study was that models in daytime commercials, relative to models in prime-time commercials, were perceived
to be portrayed in a more positive fashion. Perhaps these
perceptions were largely dictated by the products being
modeled. From Table 1 it can be recalled that the daytime
commercials were predominately pushing household cleaning
products, detergents, food, nonalcoholic beverages, beauty
care, and personal hygiene items. Thus, it should not be
altogether surprising that the models in daytime commercials were perceived to be, among other things, better
parents, better spouses, more concerned with the appearance of the home, more mature, and better looking.

A third theme was also displayed by the results. Several
scattered interactions suggested that the previously mentioned differences in perceptions of male and female models were greater in prime-time than in daytime commercials. More often than not, male models received less
favorable ratings on the attributes in prime-time than in
daytime, while female models were generally rated much the
same in prime-time as in daytime. One explanation is that
the commercials shown in daytime tend to be directed at a
female audience and may tend to make use of male models
who are mostly portrayed as "ideal" spouses, companions,
and parents. In prime-time, however, the commercials using the male models are aimed at a more heterogeneous audience. Thus, the use of a more heterogeneous and apparently less positive viewed pattern of role portrayals by
males occur.

With this line of reasoning, one would expect that perceptions of female roles ought to vary more than they were
observed to vary in the present study. However, this
limited variance in female role portrayals has also been
observed by others and is not unique to the present study
(cf. Jennings {Walstedt}, Geis, & Brown 1980). Perhaps
this simply reflects a reluctance on the part of advertisers to experiment as much with female role portrayals
as with male portrayals.

In conclusion, the results of the present study support
the contention that female models in television commercials are portrayed in a manner that is perceived to be
more favorable than the perceptions of how males are portrayed. Moreover, the discrepancy is greater in prime-
time than in daytime commercials. It is not clear, however, whether the differences can be ascribed to actual
shift in advertising strategy (a shift which had been detected in 1976 commercials), or whether Schneider's (1978)
person perception approach taken in the present study was
more sensitive than past demographic analysis approaches
in the detection of such differences. Regardless, the
present study is unique not only in its findings, but in
the approach taken. Unfortunately, the implications of
the unique findings are disquieting---especially if one
is a male.

REFERENCES

Anderson, N. H., & Hubert, S. (1963), "Effects of Concomitant Recall on Order Effects in Personality Impression Formation," Journal of Verbal Learning and Behavior, 2, 379-391.

Belkaoui, A., & Belkaoui, J. M. (1976), "A Comparative
Analysis of the Roles Portrayed by Women in Print
Advertisements: 1958, 1970, 1972," Journal of Marketing
Research, 13, 169-172.

Courtney, A. E., & Lockeretz, S. W. (1971), "A Women's
Place: An Analysis of the Roles Portrayed by Women in
Magazine Advertisements," Journal of Marketing Research,
8, 92-95.

Courtney, A. E., & Whipple, T. W. (1974), "Women in TV Commercials," Journal of Communications, 24, 110-118.

DeBruicker, F. Stewart (1979), "An Appraisal of Low-Involvement Consumer Information Processing," in R. J.
Lutz (Ed.) Contemporary Perspectives in Consumer Research.

Jennings {Walstedt}, J., Geis, F. L., & Brown, V. (1980),
"Influence of Television Commercials on Women's Self-
Confidence and Independent Judgment," Journal of Person-
ality and Social Psychology, 38, 203-210.

Kerin, Roger A., Lundstrom, William J., & Sciglimpaglia,
Donald (1979), "Women in Advertisements: Retrospect
and Prospect," Journal of Advertising, 8, 37-42.

Lammers, H. B., & Wilkinson, M. L. (1980), "Attitudes Toward Women and Satisfaction with Sex Roles in Advertisements," Psychological Reports, 46, 690.

Manstead, A. S. R., & McCulloch, C. (1981), "Sex-Role
Stereotyping in British Television Advertisements,"
British Journal of Social Psychology, 20, 171-180.

Sawyer, Alan G., Worthing, Parker M., & Sendak, Paul E.
(1979), "The Role of Laboratory Experiments to Test
Marketing Strategies," Journal of Marketing, 43, 60-67.

Schiebe, C. (1979), "Sex Roles in TV Commercials," Journal
of Advertising Research, 19, 23-27.

Schneider, K. C. (1978), "Sex Roles in Television Commercials: New Dimensions for Comparisons," Akron Business
and Economic Review, Fall, 20-24.

Schneider, K. C., & Schneider, S. B. (1979), "Trends in
Sex Roles in Television Commercials," Journal of Marketing, 43, 79-84.

Sciglimpaglia, D., Lundstrom, W. J., & Vanier, D. (1980),
"Psychographic Segmentation by Feminine Role Orienta-
tion," James H. Leigh & Claude R. Martin, Jr. (Eds.),
Current Issues and Research in Advertising, Ann Arbor:
University of Michigan.

Shimp, Terence A. (1979), "Social Psychological (Mis) Representations in Television Advertising," Journal of
Consumer Affairs, 13, 28-40.

Skelly, G. U., & Lundstrom, W. J. (1981), "Male Sex Roles
in Magazine Advertising, 1959-1979," Journal of Communication, 31, 52-57.

Wolheter, M., & Lammers, H. B., (1980), "An Analysis of
Male Roles in Print Advertisements over a 20-Year
Span," J. C. Olson (Ed.), Advances in Consumer Research,
7, Ann Arbor: Association for Consumer Research.

USE INNOVATIVENESS, VICARIOUS EXPLORATION AND PURCHASE EXPLORATION:
THREE FACETS OF CONSUMER VARIED BEHAVIOR

Linda L. Price, University of Texas at Austin
Nancy M. Ridgway, University of Texas at Austin*

ABSTRACT

A conceptual framework and empirical illustration is presented which describes the inter-relationships among four concepts relevant to exploratory behavior in consumers--optimal stimulation level, exploratory purchase behavior, vicarious exploratory behavior and variety seeking in product use (use innovativeness). Results of the study demonstrate the value of introducing use innovativeness in product use into the framework of exploratory behavior. Implications and directions for future research are discussed.

INTRODUCTION

A conceptual framework is presented which describes the interrelationships among four concepts relevant to exploration in consumers--optimal stimulation level, exploratory purchase behavior, vicarious exploratory behavior and use innovativeness. The focus is on the introduction of use innovativeness into the framework of exploratory behavior. First, each concept is discussed individually and background literature is noted. Next, these concepts are organized into a model to show the linkages among them and hypotheses are advanced. An empirical illustration which examines these hypotheses follows. In addition, a scale designed to tap use innovativeness is developed and tested. The conclusions suggest implications of the research and needed extensions in the area of consumer exploratory behavior.

OPTIMAL STIMULATION LEVEL

Considerable interest has recently been generated regarding those mechanisms which lead consumers to engage in variety seeking. Excellent review articles which illustrate consumer behavior perspectives on exploratory behavior are available (Venkatesan 1973, Faison 1977, Raju and Venkatesan 1980). Several probable sources of variety seeking co-exist (McAlister 1981, Pessemier 1981, Ridgway and Hoyer 1982), but one important source is the internal need for stimulation. The idea of a preferred level of stimulation and individual differences in that preference derives from a body of literature introduced in psychology first by Hebb (1955) and Leuba (1955). Since that time, variety seeking has become a major topic of research in the psychology literature (Dember and Earl 1957, Berlyne 1960, Fiske and Maddi 1961, Kish 1966). Although some differences between the various psychological theories exist, the common thesis is simply that as stimulation (complexity, arousal, etc.) falls below the ideal level, an individual will attempt to produce more stimulating input (through behaviors such as exploration and novelty seeking). As stimulation increases past the ideal level, an individual will attempt to reduce or simplify input. Although individuals are thought to differ in the amount of stimulation preferred, the optimal amount is thought to be at some intermediate level (Berlyne 1960, Fiske and Maddi 1961).

---

*The authors gratefully acknowledge comments from Robert A. Peterson and the anonymous reviewers.

EXPLORATORY BEHAVIOR IN THE CONSUMER CONTEXT

Exploration in the consumer behavior context can be divided into three main types: exploratory purchase behavior, vicarious exploratory behavior and use innovativeness (or variety in product use).

Exploratory Purchase Behavior

The first type, exploratory purchase behavior, is variety seeking that involves purchase and manifests itself in several different ways. Although the purchase behaviors can be thought of as a continuum, they have been organized into two types--innovating and brand switching--for convenience. A consumer may innovate--that is, buy a "new" product or buy a product category new to the individual consumer.[1] Examples of these behaviors are the buying of a microwave oven or home computer ("new" products) or buying a motorcycle or 35mm SLR camera for the first time (product category new to the individual consumer). The other type of exploratory purchase behavior is brand switching. Brand switching includes buying a previously untried brand for the first time or alternating between known brands simply for a change of pace. Examples of these behaviors would be buying Del Monte brand peas for the first time or alternating among Dr. Pepper, Coke and Pepsi on a regular basis to avoid boredom with any one soft drink. Both innovating and brand switching have been examined. Several researchers have invoked the optimal stimulation theory to explain the tendency to innovate (Mazis and Sweeney 1972, Mittelstaedt et al. 1976, Grossbart et al. 1976) and brand switching (Tucker 1964, McConnell 1968, Brickman and D'Amato 1975). The consensus conclusion of these researchers is that individuals with a high need for stimulation will be more likely to engage in exploratory purchase behavior than those with a low need for stimulation.

Vicarious Exploratory Behavior

The second type of exploratory behavior in the consumer context is vicarious exploratory behavior. This involves variety seeking by engaging in behaviors such as reading about, talking to others about, or shopping for new or unfamiliar products. Vicarious exploratory behavior differs from exploratory purchase behavior in that actual product purchase is not involved, although vicarious exploration could lead to eventual product purchase. Although the idea of vicarious stimulation is fairly new in the consumer context, Hirschman (1980) and Raju (1980) point out that vicarious variety seeking serves the purpose of gathering information about products for use in future decision making. It is expected that individuals with a high need for stimulation would be more likely to engage in vicarious exploratory behavior than those with a low need for stimulation.

Use Innovativeness

A major focus of this study is to examine the third major type of consumer exploratory behavior: use innovativeness.

---

[1]Although many definitions of innovating exist, Rogers (1962) and Rogers and Shoemaker (1971) stress the importance of perception of newness.

Use innovativeness was first introduced by Hirschman (1980). The term can be described by two levels of behavior. The first level is the use of a previously adopted product in a single novel way. An example of this would be the use of tin cans that previously held canned vegetables to hold nails in the workshop, rather than buying an organizer specifically designed to hold nails. Another example would be using an old garden hose to fashion a water hose for an automobile. The second level of use innovativeness is using a currently owned product in a wide variety of ways. For example, a consumer may own a home computer and either use it only to play electronic games or use it to play electronic games, keep personal finance records, do programming, interface with other computers, keep abreast of stock reports and learn a foreign language. In contrast to vicarious and exploratory <u>purchase</u> behavior, use innovativeness is a product <u>consumption</u> behavior. Still, the use innovativeness phenomenon has important implications for marketers. Old products may be given new life by redefining the type and number of uses of a product based on suggestions from consumers--i.e., Arm and Hammer baking soda. New products, with opportunities for use in a variety of ways (home computers, microwave ovens, SLR camers, video cassette recorders) could be promoted in terms of these opportunities to groups identified as use innovators--i.e., the Atari ads are now emphasizing that you can do more with their system than just play games. Operating features, accessory equipment, educational programs and product instructions could be geared to emphasize the variety of ways in which a product might be used. Individuals with a high need for stimulation would be expected to use currently owned products more creatively and in a wider variety of ways than individuals with a low need for stimulation.

INTERRELATIONSHIPS AMONG CONCEPTS AND HYPOTHESES

In general, high levels of stimulation needs should be correlated with all three types of consumer exploratory behavior--exploratory purchase behavior, vicarious exploratory behavior and use innovativeness. However, since the three types represent differing manifestations of high stimulation needs, some individuals may prefer one type over another. Variables that differentiate which type of exploratory behavior a consumer prefers might include: tolerance for risk (with a low risk individual preferring vicarious exploration over use or purchase exploration); skills (with skill in the marketplace associated with purchase exploration and creative or mechanical skill associated with use exploration); and values (with desire for materialism associated with vicarious and purchase exploration and desire for material simplicity and self-sufficiency associated with use exploration). Although individuals with high stimulation needs may prefer one type of exploration over another, the correlation between vicarious exploration and purchase exploration is expected to be positive (since both types are marketplace bound and since vicarious exploration can lead to eventual purchase).

Use innovativeness, however, is expected to be a separate phenomenon. First, in order to meet high stimulation needs, a consumer may purchase a product or instead choose not to purchase--stretching a currently owned product to additional uses. This decision to buy or not buy represents nearly dichotomous manifestations of high stimulation needs. Secondly, use innovativeness is dependent on certain skills that some consumers do not have. For example, in order to use products such as home computers, SLR cameras or hand calculators in a wide variety of ways, specialized skills and abilities are required. Likewise, to re-use products such as old appliance parts, mechanical skills are necessary. In fact, to use tin cans as nail holders, creativity is required (unless, of course, manu-

facturers tell consumers how to be creative with a product. Finally, as mentioned previously, values such as a desire for self-sufficiency or material simplicity might lead certain consumers to creative re-use rather than into the marketplace to solve a consumption problem. For the foregoing reasons, therefore, use innovativeness is not expected to be correlated with purchase exploration or vicarious exploration. These general hypotheses are tested in a more specific form in the empirical illustration. Figure 1 illustrates these expected relationships.

FIGURE 1

Relationships Between Optimal Stimulation
Level and Varied Behavior

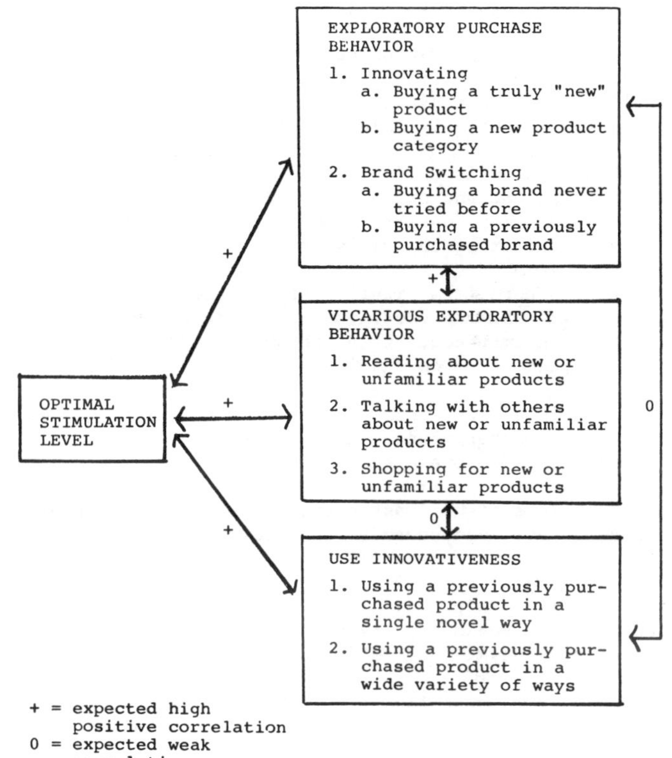

EMPIRICAL ILLUSTRATION

Background

Recent work by Raju (1980) has helped extend understanding of the construct of optimal stimulation level (OSL) and its relationship to exploratory consumer tendencies. Raju advances a 39-item scale to measure exploratory tendencies in a consumer context. The items are grouped into seven categories: repetitive behavior proneness, innovativeness, risk taking, exploration through shopping, interpersonal communication, brand switching and information seeking. Raju correlates his scale (a 7-point Likert-type scale) with a general scale that measures optimal stimulation level (Mehrabian and Russell 1974). The Mehrabian and Russell scale, called the Arousal Seeking Tendency scale, contains 40 items and measures individual preference for arousal caused by five major factors: arousal from change, arousal from unusual stimuli, arousal from risk,

arousal from sensuality and arousal from new environments.
Examples of items on the Arousal Seeking Tendency scale
are: "I seldom change the pictures on my walls," "It is
unpleasant seeing people in strange weird clothes," and
"I like to touch and feel sculpture."

In the current research, the Mehrabian and Russell scale
and the Raju scale were utilized to measure optimal stimulation level in both a general way and in the specific
forum of consumer behavior. In addition, a scale to measure individual differences in use innovativeness was developed and tested.

Specific Hypotheses

The following specific hypotheses, derived from the general relationships among the concepts diagrammed in
Figure 1, are advanced.

H1: There is a significant positive correlation between
optimal stimulation level (as measured by Mehrabian and
Russell scale) and exploratory behavior in the consumer
context (as measured by Raju scale).

    H1a: There is a significant positive correlation
    between OSL and exploratory purchase behavior in
    the consumer context (as measured by eighteen
    selected items on Raju's scale).

    H1b: There is a significant positive correlation
    between OSL and vicarious exploratory behavior in
    the consumer context (as measured by twenty-one
    selected items on Raju's scale).

H2: There is a significant positive correlation between
OSL and use innovativeness in the consumer context (as
measured by scale developed for this study).

H3: There is a significant positive correlation between
exploratory purchase behavior and vicarious exploratory
behavior.

H4: There is no significant correlation (either negative
or positive) between exploratory purchase behavior and
use innovativeness.

H5: There is no significant correlation (either negative
or positive) between vicarious exploratory behavior and
use innovativeness.

Scale Development

Items in Raju's scale were classified into two types,
exploratory purchase and vicarious exploratory behavior,
so that correlations between the types could be examined.
The method of categorization was to an extent subjective,
although independent judges' groupings, Raju's own seven
category scheme and principal components analysis on the
student data base described later were used as aids. The
exploratory purchase behavior category included eighteen
items, all of which related to specific purchase action.
Examples of these items are: "I get bored when buying
the same brands even if they are good," and "I enjoy
taking chances in buying unfamiliar brands just to get
some variety in my purchases." The vicarious exploratory
behavior category included twenty-one items, all of which
dealt with shopping for, reading about or talking about
new or unfamiliar products. Examples of these items are:
"I like to shop around and look at displays," "I often
read the information on the package of products just out
of curiosity," and "I don't like to talk to my friends
about my purchases."

In order to construct the use innovativeness scale tested
in this study, the researchers first developed a set of
eight items (using 7-point Likert-type response categor-

ies) based on personal interviews with a convenience sample of consumers (n=5). These interviews revealed that an
important inhibitor of use innovativeness is the fear of
misusing the product with resultant breakage, warranty
violation, personal physical hazard, etc. This deterrent
seemed particularly salient with expensive and/or technical products. On the other hand, an important trait which
seemed to be associated with creative use of products was
a high level of curiosity about how things work. Prior
to the analyses reported in this study, inter-item correlations were computed for the eight scale items. Based on
these correlations, three scale items were deleted from
further analyses. The five items retained for the use
innovativeness scale were:

    --When working on projects I'm afraid I will make a
      worse mess of them than if I had just left them
      alone.
    --As a child, I really enjoyed taking things apart
      and putting them back together again.
    --I am very curious about how things work.
    --When I try to do projects on my own, without exact
      directions, they usually work out really well.
    --I'm often uncomfortable using expensive products
      because I'm afraid of breaking or ruining them.

In order to validate the classification of the Raju items
as either purchase or vicarious exploration and to validate the use innovativeness items, two statistics were
calculated. The results are reported in Table 1. First,
item-total correlations within each category were obtained and then an average item-total correlation was calculated for each category. Second, Spearman-Brown reliability coefficients were calculated for each category as
a measure of internal consistency. As can be seen in the
table, the average item-total correlations and the Spearman-Brown coefficients are both quite adequate to support
the classification of items.

TABLE 1

Average Item-Total Correlation and Reliability for
Three Categories of Exploratory Consumer Behavior

CATEGORY	AVERAGE ITEM-TOTAL CORRELATION	SPEARMAN-BROWN RELIABILITY COEFFICIENT
Exploratory Purchase Behavior	.42	.78
Vicarious Exploratory Behavior	.52	.93
Use Innovativeness Behavior	.42	.74

Questionnaire Administration

A sample of college seniors (N=63) was used to test the
specific hypotheses. The students were presented with a
questionnaire consisting of the 39-item Raju scale, the
40-item Mehrabian and Russell scale, and the 8-item use
innovativeness scale.

Results

Table 2 presents the correlations of optimal stimulation
level with the overall Raju scale and with the item totals
for exploratory purchase behavior, vicarious exploratory
behavior and use innovativeness. As shown in the table,
all correlations were significant. The highest correlations with OSL were found for exploratory purchase behavior (r=.61) and use innovativeness (r=.50). The results
support hypotheses 1, 1a, 1b and 2. The high correlation
of use innovativeness with optimal stimulation level

TABLE 2

Correlation Coefficients of Optimal Stimulation
Level with Exploratory Behavior Categories

CATEGORY	CORRELATION COEFFICIENT	SIGNIFICANCE*
Raju Total Scale	.49**	.001
Exploratory Purchase Behavior	.61	.001
Vicarious Exploratory Behavior	.33	.01
Use Innovativeness	.50	.001

*one-tail test
**Raju reported a slightly higher correlation (.53)

suggests the importance of use innovativeness as one way
of obtaining optimal stimulation in the consumer context.
It is also noteworthy that the items in the vicarious
exploratory behavior scale (which with some variations
conform to the items in Raju's "exploration through shopping," "interpersonal communication," and "information
seeking" categories) had the lowest correlations with optimal stimulation level. This is consistent with Raju's
results (1980, p. 279).

Correlations between the three types of consumer exploratory behavior--exploratory purchase, vicarious exploratory and use innovativeness--are reported in Table 3.
Hypothesis 3 is confirmed. Exploratory purchase behavior
and vicarious exploratory behavior are correlated (r=.58).
Hypotheses 4 and 5 are also supported. Use innovativeness
appears to be a separate phenomenon. As shown in Table 3,
use innovativeness is not significantly correlated with
either exploratory purchase behavior or vicarious purchase
behavior.

TABLE 3

Item-Total Correlations

CATEGORY	Vicarious Exploratory	Use Innovativeness**
Exploratory Purchase	.58*	.20 (N.S.)
Vicarious Exploratory		.11 (N.S.)

*p < .001 (one-tail test)

**two-tail test

Use Innovativeness

Substantiation that use innovativeness is a separate and
important factor in variety seeking behavior is further
provided by correlations of use innovativeness with the
total Raju scale and with the seven categories provided
by Raju. Table 4 reports the results of this analysis.
A common element to both use innovativeness and Raju's
scale appears to be risk-taking, but given the low correlation (r=.24), further exploration is needed. As in
Raju's results, it is this risk-taking category which
correlates most highly with optimal stimulation level
(.622 in both this study and Raju's student sample, 1980,
p. 279).

IMPLICATIONS AND FUTURE RESEARCH

The conceptual framework and the results of the empirical

TABLE 4

Correlation Coefficients of Use Innovativeness
with Raju's Scale

CATEGORY	CORRELATION COEFFICIENT
Total Raju Scale	.01
A: Repetitive Behavior Proneness	.09
B: Innovativeness	.11
C: Risk Taking	.24*
D: Exploration Through Shopping	−.09
E: Interpersonal Communication	−.18
F: Brandswitching	.19
G: Information Seeking	−.09

*Significance at .05, two-tail test

illustration contribute to a fuller understanding of
variety seeking in consumer behavior. Three contributions are noteworthy: (1) An illustration of the importance and problems of use innovativeness as a possible
manifestation of high stimulation needs; (2) the conceptual differentiation between exploratory purchase behavior and vicarious exploratory behavior; and (3) a partial replication of Raju's study, providing additional
validation of his scale. Each of these contributions
and possible future research in each area is discussed
below.

First, it was found that individuals with high OSL's and
low OSL's differ with respect to their use innovativeness.
Relating use innovativeness to optimal stimulation level
is of direct importance to consumer behavior researchers.
Consumers fill the need for stimulation not only by buying a variety of products, but by using products in a
variety of ways. Marketers can work to fill this need by
providing opportunities for varied use of a product, and
by developing products and accessories which enable varied
use. Additional scale development is needed to expand
items on the use innovativeness measure. Furthermore, the
scale needs to be related to other types of variables
which may be of importance. Several variables, such as
risk, skill and values have already been discussed. Certainly, a linkage of use innovativeness to demographic
variables would be useful in helping marketers identify
individuals with high stimulation needs who meet that
need by engaging in use innovativeness. Finally, an important facet of this work should be the relationship of
an expanded scale of use innovativeness to specific behavioral variety in use. In this study, there is no real
way of knowing if the subjects really do engage in use
innovativeness or simply say they do. Research extensions
should move beyond the correlational level, represented
in this study, to experimental designs which group individuals by their need for stimulation, and measure their
responses to a variety of situations characteristic of
each of the three exploratory behaviors.

Several problems exist with the concept of use innovativeness. First, it can be argued that opportunities to engage in use innovativeness are not as frequent as opportunities to engage in either vicarious exploration or
purchase exploration. For example, a limited number of
products exist which can be used in a wide variety of
ways. Secondly, the consumer must desire to solve consumption problems by engaging in use innovativeness
(i.e., enjoyment of creative re-use, desire for material
self-sufficiency). A third problem is the requirement
of certain skills (mechanical, creative) in order to be

able to engage in use innovativeness.

The second major contribution of this study was to conceptually distinguish between exploratory purchase behavior and vicarious exploratory behavior. Results of this study demonstrated that exploratory purchase behavior is more closely related to stimulation needs than vicarious exploratory behavior. The study also found that the two areas are closely associated with each other. Extensions in this area might be directed toward distinguishing the two concepts empirically.

The third major contribution of this research was to partially replicate Raju's (1980) study. An important finding was that Raju's total scale, as well as various subcomponents of his scale, are related to stimulation needs. This reinforces Raju's finding that exploratory tendencies in the consumer context may be manifestations of the need for stimulation. Individuals with high stimulation needs also have greater exploratory tendencies in the consumer context.

The study of exploratory behavior offers a rich domain for the consumer behavior researcher. The extensions incorporated in this paper offer many opportunities for further research.

REFERENCES

Berlyne, D. E. (1960), Conflict, Arousal, and Curiosity. New York: McGraw-Hill Book Company.

Brickman, Philip and Barbara D'Amato (1975), "Exposure Effects in a Free-Choice Situation," Journal of Personality and Social Psychology, 32, 415-420.

Dember, William N. and Robert W. Earl (1957), "Analysis of Exploratory, Manipulating and Curoisity Behaviors," Psychological Review, 64, 91-96.

Faison, Edmond W. J. (1977), "The Neglected Variety Drive: A Useful Concept for Consumer Behavior," Journal of Consumer Research, 4, 172-5.

Fiske, D. W. and S. R. Maddi (1961), Functions of Varied Experience. Homewood, Ill.: Dorsey Press, Inc.

Grossbart, S. L., R. A. Mittelstaedt, and S. P. Devere (1976), "Customer Stimulation Needs and Innovating Shopping Behavior: The Case of Recycled Urban Places," Advances in Consumer Research, Beverlee B. Anderson, ed., Vol. 3, 30-35.

Hebb, D. O. (1955), "Drives and the C.N.S. (Conceptual Nervous System)," Psychological Review, 62, 243-254.

Hirschman, Elizabeth C. (1980), "Innovativeness, Novelty Seeking and Consumer Creativity," Journal of Consumer Research, 7 (December), 283-95.

Kish, G. B. (1966), "Studies of Sensory Reinforcement," in Operant Behavior: Areas of Research and Application, W. K. Honig, ed., New York: Appleton-Century-Crofts.

Leuba, C. (1955), "Toward Some Integration of Learning Theories: The Concept of Optimal Stimulation," Psychological Reports, 1, 27-33.

McAlister, Leigh (1979), "Choosing Multiple Items from a Product Class," Journal of Consumer Research, 6 (December), 213-224.

McConnell, J. Douglas (1968), "The Development of Brand Loyalty," Journal of Marketing Research, 5 (February), 13-19.

Mazis, Michael B. and Timothy S. Sweeney (1972), "Novelty and Personality with Risk as a Moderating Variable," AMA Combined Proceedings, Boris W. Becker and Helmut Becker (eds.), 406-11.

Mehrabian, Albert and James A. Russell (1974), An Approach to Environmental Psychology, Cambridge, Massachusetts: The MIT Press.

Mittelstaedt, R. A., S. L. Grossbart, W. W. Curtis and S. P. Devere (1976), "Optimal Stimulation Level and the Adoption Decision Process," Journal of Marketing Research, 3 (September), 84-94.

Pessemier, Edgar A. (1981), "Varied Consumer Behavior: Some Theory and Measurement Methods," Working Paper, Purdue University.

__________ and Leigh McAlister (1981), "Varied Consumer Behavior: Prior Work and Some Hypotheses," Working Paper, Purdue University.

Raju, P. S. (1980), "Optimum Stimulation Level: Its Relationships to Personality, Demographics, and Exploratory Behavior," Journal of Consumer Research, 7 (December), 272-282.

__________ and M. Venkatesan, "Exploratory Behavior in the Consumer Context: A State of the Art Review," Advances in Consumer Research, Vol. 3, 258-63.

Ridgway, Nancy M. and Wayne D. Hoyer (1982), "A Conceptual Framework for Exploratory Behavior in Consumer Behavior," Working Paper, The University of Texas at Austin.

Rogers, Everett (1962), Diffusion of Innovations, New York: The Free Press.

__________ and Floyd Shoemaker (1971), The Communication of Innovations, New York: The Free Press.

Tucker, W. T. (1964), "The Development of Brand Loyalty," Journal of Marketing Research (August), 32-35.

Venkatesan, M. (1974), "Cognitive Consistency and Novelty-Seeking," in Consumer Behavior: Theoretical Perspectives, Englewood Cliffs: Prentice-Hall.

Factors Associated with Changes In Evoked Set Among Purchasers of New Automobiles

David W. Stewart, Vanderbilt University
Girish Punj, University of Connecticut

ABSTRACT

Differences in the characteristics and behavior of individuals who purchased an automobile consistent with an initial evoked set and individuals who purchased an automobile outside of an initial evoked were examined. Changes in the price set were found to be associated with less certainty and confidence in the 'purchasers' own ability as a shopper. Individuals who manifested changes in their evoked sets of automobile makes were more likely to have spent greater amounts of time on various information search activities. Purchasers were most likely to buy products consistent with their initial evoked set of automobile makes and least likely to purchase products consistent with their initial evoked sets with respect to price range and size.

INTRODUCTION

Howard (1963) first introduced the concept of "evoked set" to the marketing literature to refer to those brands or products that the consumer actually considers in his/her purchase decision process. Since the introduction of the term it has become an important component of theories of consumer behavior (Howard and Sheth, 1969; Howard, 1977; Bettman, 1979) and it has been incorporated in at least one normative new product introduction model (Silik and Urban, 1978). Despite the wide-spread acceptance of the concept relatively little research has been directed toward the discovery of the determinants of consumers' evoked sets. Much of the research which has been done has sought to examine correlates of the size (width) of consumers' evoked sets (Belonax and Mittelstaedt, 1977; Bennett and Mandell, 1969; Campbell, 1969; Gronhaug, 1973-74; Jarvis and Wilcox, 1973; Maddox, Gronhaug, Homans, and May, 1977; May and Homans, 1977; Narayana and Markin, 1975; and Ostlund, 1973). Myers (1978) has questioned whether any research to date has provided an insight as to how evoked sets are formed over time within the individual consumer. Neither product-specific characteristics, such as risk and importance, nor person-specific factors, such as cognitive style, have been shown to be important determinants of evoked set size.

One reason for the lack of conclusive findings concerning the determinants of evoked sets may be the failure to consider an evoked set as a dynamic rather than a static concept. Myers (1978) has suggested the need for longitudinal analyses of evoked set formation rather than continued attention to cross-sectional analyses. Evoked set must change over time. Much of applied marketing is directed toward the task of changing the consumer's evoked set. Advertising, promotions, sales, and other elements of the marketing communication mix are designed to facilitate the entry of a brand into a consumer's evoked set or to reinforce the presence of an existing brand in the set. Much of the earlier work on evoked sets has sought to define

correlations of the size of an evoked set at an undefined point in the decision process. A more interesting and relevant issue is that of changes in the evoked set. It was toward this end that the present research was carried out.

Clearly one approach to the study of changes in evoked sets would involve monitoring behavior over time, perhaps using some type of panel. Constructing such a panel, particularly for infrequent purchases is difficult and expensive. Before such a project is undertaken some exploratory work on the dynamics of evoked sets is in order. An approach to this exploratory analysis would focus on reported changes in the evoked sets by a group of consumers. Individuals who purchase a product not in their initial reported evoked set should differ in some way or exhibit some differences in behavior not found among those who purchased a product consistent with their initial reported evoked set. The present research used this strategy to examine the characteristics of automobile purchasers who reported that their purchases were consistent with their initial evoked set versus purchasers who selected an automobile not included in the initial evoked set.

The initial evoked set of a consumer may be defined as that set of products to which the consumer would give consideration at the point of problem recognition. As the information search process proceeds products may enter or leave this evoked set. If relatively little information search takes place, there should be a low probability of changes in the initial evoked set. Determinants of information search should, therefore, be related to the probability of a change in the initial evoked set. A rather substantial literature on the determinants of information search is available. Sieber and Lanzetta (1964) and Hawkins and Lanzetta (1965) have found that the greater the initial uncertainty about a product class and the criteria for evaluating that class, the greater the information search. Product importance and the degree of risk associated with the product also increase search activity (Jacoby, Chestnut and Fisher 1978, Swan 1972, Wright 1975). It may be hypothesized that for a relatively expensive item such as an automobile, the probability of a change in an initial evoked set should be greater among individuals who express greater initial uncertainty about the product class and criteria for evaluating that class.

Task experience and product satisfaction (feedback) have also been shown to relate to information search. Numerous researchers have found that information search tends to be greater among individuals with moderate knowledge and experience than consumers with either high or low knowledge and experience (Bettman and Park 1980a/b, Staelin and Payne 1976, Jacoby, Chestnut, and Fisher 1978, Dover and Olson 1977, Edell and Mitchell 1977, Jacoby, Szybillo, and Busato-Schach 1977). Green, Mitchell and Staelin (1977), Chestnut and Jacoby (1976), and Lehman and Moore (1980) have demonstrated that the degree of information sought in later decisions is determined by the degree to which an acceptable set of alternatives is identified in early decisions and the degree to which some members of that set are better on an attribute for which feedback was received. The implications of the latter findings are that search activity should decrease with experience as long as the products considered in early decisions perform satisfactorily. Thus, there should be a general decrease in information search with experience unless all the products in an initial consideration set are unsatisfactory.

Closely related to this stream of research on experiential determinants of information search is a classic study by Bennett and Mandell (1969). Howard and Sheth (1973) argue that all experiences with a class of objects, whether positively or negatively reinforced, are important. Thus, as experience in buying and using the product class accumulates, the amount and intensity of search efforts decline. Bennett and Mandell (1969) failed to find support for the proposition that as product class experience increased, evidenced by the total purchases in the individual's history, the amount of effort expended on information search decreased. They did find support for the hypothesis that as the number of reinforced purchases of a brand increases, the amount of information seeking before the purchase of that brand decreased.

Maddox, May, and Homans (1977) attempted to replicate the Bennett and Mandell study and found some support for the earlier study among individuals with evoked sets of size one. For individuals with evoked sets of size one, Maddox, May, and Homans found total product class experience to be significantly related to information seeking. Further, Maddox, May, and Homans (1977) found no relationship between between reinforced experience and amount of information search among individuals with evoked sets of one and only directional support for such a relationship among individuals with evoked sets greater than one. Thus, variations in the size of the evoked set appear to influence the relationship between product experience and information search. This is consistent with the common assumption that the evoked set guides information search (Hawkins, Coney, and Best 1980, p. 432).

Ostlund (1973) found no relationship between overt search behavior and size of evoked set among automobile purchasers. His measure of search activity consisted of the number of weeks spent on the purchase task rather than the amount of time spent on the actual search. More recently, Maddox, Gronhaug, Homans, and May (1977) found relatively small and generally insignificant relationships between set width and such information search activity as advice seeking, dealer visits, reading ads, etc. in a group of U.S. automobile purchasers. However, these same authors report moderate and significant associations between set width and search behavior among a Norwegian sample. The measures of association for the Norwegian sample ranged from .62 for number of dealer visits, to .42 for number of test drives, to .13 for advice seeking. If evoked sets mediate the information process the nature of that mediation is not well understood.

One reason for the conflicting results of the studies cited above may lie in the operational definition used for evoked set. If evoked set is defined as the number of makes that the individual would consider at the time of problem recognition there may be little relation to amount of subsequent search. If evoked set is defined as all makes actually considered during the purchase process, including makes not in the evoked set at the time of problem recognition, then the amount of search may be related the size of this expanded set. Several of the previous studies fail to make this distinction.

A related issue is whether brand (make) should be the basis for defining the evoked set. Evoked sets are most frequently defined by brand (Campbell, 1973). Other characteristics, such as price, size, etc., make also serve to restrict the number and type of products considered. If evoked set is to be a useful construct it should demonstrate some degree of reliability over time. If consumers frequently make purchases outside of their evoked sets, the concept is not particularly useful as a means for explaining behavior. An important question, then, is whether brand, or other characteristics, really search to restrict the alternatives considered.

The present study seeks to provide clarification of the construct of evoked set by examining the frequency of change in the evoked sets of automobile purchasers from problem recognition to purchase event. The study will also examine differences between individuals whose actual purchase was consistent with their initial evoked set and individuals who purchased an automobile outside of the initial evoked set.

Method

<u>Data</u>   Data for the study were generated by consumers who had purchased a new automobile during the period of September to November, 1978, in the cities of Buffalo, Milwaukee, and Phoenix. All respondents were contacted by telephone and asked to participate in the study. Respondents received a questionnaire by mail. The questionnaire solicited information on variables associated with their automobile purchase. These variables were related to the decision process employed by consumers in making the selection of their new automobile. The questionnarie requested such information as the number of dealer visits, activities at each dealership visited, information search behavior such as talking to friends, reading magazines, etc., number and types of previous cars owned, satisfaction with car purchased, etc. Information was also requested concerning the automobile purchased, the dealer from which it was purchased, and the price paid for the automobile. Respondents were asked to indicate the initial price range, size (subcompact, full size, etc.) and make (Chevy, Olds, Ford, Mercury) of automobiles they had planned to consider prior to their actually beginning active shopping. The latter information provided the basis for examining respondents' evoked sets. Data was obtained from 2 weeks to 4 months after the purchase of the new automobile. The average elapsed time from purchase to receipt of the questionnaire was two months.

<u>Analysis and Results</u>   Each respondent's evoked set was initially defined by the price range, sizes, and makes the respondents indicated they were willing to consider prior to beginning active shopping. For example, an individual who stated that they were initially interested in intermediate and full-size automobiles, priced at more than $7000 but less than $10,000, and were interested in only two makes, Buick and Oldsmobile would have the following evoked set configuration:

Size	Price	Make
Intermediate	More than $7000	Buick
or	and	Oldsmobile
Full Size	Less than $10,000	

By this definition of evoked set 69% of the respondents purchased an automobile that fell outside of their initial evoked set. This clearly indicates that changes occurred in the evoked sets of consumers over the course of their shopping activity. To better understand the dynamics of this process each of the three components of the original definition was examined separately.

Initial price range proved the least restrictive constraint on the respondents purchase behavior. Only 37% of the respondents bought an automobile within the price range of their initial evoked set. Indeed, 50% of all respondents reported paying more for an automobile than they had originally planned. Thirteen percent paid less than they had planned. Table 1 provides a description of significant differences between those respondents purchasing within their initial price consideration set and those who did not. Table 2 provides a description of significant differences between those respondents who paid more than originally planned and those who paid an amount consistent with their initial price consideration set. Respondents who paid less than they had originally planned differed from those buying within their price consideration set on only one variable, the amount of time spent reading advertisements in newspapers and magazines. Respondents paying less than originally planned spent significantly more time in this activity.

The sizes of automobile respondents were willing to consider represented a greater constraint on purchase behavior than the initial price range. Nevertheless, 34% of all respondents purchased an automobile of a different size than was indicated in their initial consideration set. Table 3 provides a description of significant differences between those buying within their initial size consideration set and those outside of their initial set.

By far the greatest constraint on subsequent purchase behavior was the initial evoked set of makes. Only 71 of the 1056 respondents (6.7%) purchased an automobile that was not within their initial consideration set. Table 4 provides a description of the significant differences between those purchasing within their initial evoked set and those purchasing outside their consideration set.

Discussion

The present results clearly suggest that price is the least stable component of the evoked set of automobiles while make is the most stable. Individuals who changed their price consideration set were most likely to pay more, rather than less, for an automobile. Such individuals were characterized by greater initial uncertainty about automobiles, less experience with automobiles (as measured by the number of cars previously owned), and experienced less satisfaction with their previous automobile. In addition, these persons started their search process with a lower price range. They were likely to have spent less time driving to dealers and less time test driving automobiles. However, individuals who bought within their initial price set used the time of others to a lesser extent than those who purchased automobiles outside their initial price range. When only those persons who bought high are compared to those whose purchase was consistent with their initial price set several additional differences also emerge. Persons buying high expressed less confidence in their ability to judge automobiles, greater uncertainty about the deal they obtained, a

TABLE 1

SIGNIFICANT DIFFERENCES BETWEEN INDIVIDUALS BUYING
WITHIN PRICE SET AND THOSE BUYING OUTSIDE
OF PRICE SET
(By Tukey's HSD, P < .05)

	Bought Within Set (N = 391)	Bought Outside of Set (N = 665)
Satisfaction with Previous Car (1 = Totally Dissatisfied 7 = Totally Satisfied)	5.07	4.87
Number of Cars Previously Owned	4.37	3.96
Time Spent Driving to Dealers*	3.57	3.41
Initial Certainty relating to purchase (1 = Uncertain 7 = Certain)	4.95	5.02
Maximum Price Level of Price Set ($1000's)	7.11	6.24
Minimum Price Level of Price Set ($1000's)	5.49	5.08
Time Spent Test Driving Automobiles*	2.38	2.26
Number of Hours Others Spent for You*	2.19	2.58

*(1 = No Hours, 2 = up to 1/2 hr., 3 = 3/4-1 3/4 hrs., 4 = 2-4 3/4 hrs., 5 = 5-9 3/4 hrs., 6 = 10 or more hrs.)

TABLE 2

SIGNIFICANT DIFFERENCES BETWEEN THOSE BUYING
HIGHER THAN PRICE SET RANGE AND THOSE BUYING
WITHIN PRICE SET
(By Tukey's HSD, P < .05)

	Bought High (N = 528)	Bought Within Price Set (N = 391)
Initial Confidence in Ability to judge cars (1 = No Confidence; 5 = Total Confidence)	3.55	3.75
Initial Certainty Relating to an important purchase goal	4.92	5.12
Final Certainty Relating to an important purchase goal	5.77	5.94
Minimum Price Level of Price Set	4.99	5.51
Maximum Price Level of Price Set	6.09	7.09
Rating of Value of Car Bought Compared to What Expected When First Considered Buying a New Car (1 = Much Worse; 7 = Much Better)	4.80	4.51
Satisfaction with Previous car (1 = Totally Dissatisfied; 7 = Totally Satisfied)	4.82	5.07
Number of Cars Owned Previously	3.81	4.14
Overall Satisfaction with Car Bought (1 = Totally Dissatisfied 7 = Totally Satisfied)	5.44	5.52

TABLE 3

SIGNIFICANT DIFFERENCES BETWEEN INDIVIDUALS BUYING
WITHIN SIZE SET AND THOSE BUYING OUTSIDE SET
(By Tukey's HSD, P < .05)

	Bought Within Set (n = 697)	Bought Outside of Set (N = 359)
Satisfaction with Previous Car (1 = Totally Dissatisfied 7 = Totally Satisfied)	5.04	4.77
Number of Cars Previously Owned	4.30	3.74
Time Others Spent for You in Showroom	1.95	1.53
Time Others Spent for You Test Driving Automobiles	.69	.45

higher rating of the value of the deal they obtained compared to their expectations, and expressed less overall satisfaction with the car they bought. In the current inflationary economy, it is not surprising that persons buy outside of the initial price set. Information about price quickly becomes dated. Unless efforts are made to constantly update pricing information a consumer is likely to have an unrealistic price set. Purchasers who paid more for their automobile than originally planned appear to be generally less experienced and knowledgeable about automobiles and are more likely to rely on others for assistance in purchasing an automobile. The initial price range is also lower than that of others. This may reflect a pattern of disinterest in automobiles except during a particular purchase event and a pattern of not attending to pricing information between purchase events.

Individuals who purchased automobiles consistent with their initial size set manifested relatively few differences from those whose purchase was consistent with the initial size set. The number of cars previously owned, satisfaction with the previous automobile owned, and the involvement of others in touring showrooms and test driving automobiles were greater among those whose purchases were consistent with their initial size consideration set. This may suggest preferences for size tend to stabilize with product experience. Individuals with lesser experience with automobiles may be more inclined to experiment to determine their preferences. It may also reflect a lack of familiarity with the recent down-sizing of automobiles.

The most stable component of the initial evoked set was make. Less than seven percent of the respondents purchased outside of their initial set of makes. This may suggest that product features are not a particularly useful basis for defining an evoked set though it would be instructive to determine whether other features, color, size of engine, type of options, represented more stable determinants of purchase. It also raises the question of what information is carried by the name of the make. If the evoked set does guide information search and the ultimate purchase decision its influence is most profound only in the case where it is defined by brand (make), but it is not clear what direction this set gives behavior.

The present results are generally consistent with earlier findings that the amount of information search is related to the size of the evoked set. Persons purchasing automobiles not included in their initial evoked set report spending more time in a variety of information search activities ranging from total dealer visits, to reading ratings of automobiles in magazines and maufacturers' brochures, to talking with sales personnel. In addition, those individuals purchasing outside of their initial consideration set felt less satisfaction with their purchase and indicated that their initial expectations of value and performance were lower than persons purchasing within their set.

Information search behavior appeares to be associated with larger evoked sets of automobile makes. In addition, persons with larger sets were somewhat younger, better educated, less uncertain of the inability to obtain a good deal, and willing to pay a higher range of prices. Satisfaction with the previous automobile owned and the number of cars previously owned were not related to set size. This latter finding is consistent with the earlier findings of Ostlund (1973) and Maddox, May, and Homans (1977) but is contrary to the findings of Bennett and Mandell (1969).

Two hypotheses which might explain the change in make set were considered in the present study. One explanation for a change in evoked set would be that a consumer visited a dealer carrying several makes, one or more of which were not in the initial evoked set. Once on the lot the consumer may have been lead to examine and purchase a make not initially considered. Only 12 of the 71 cases were consistent with this hypothesis. A second hypothesis would hold that individuals who bought outside their initial consideration set did so because they were directed to a dealership on the basis of an acquaintence who worked at a dealership carrying makes other than those in the initial set. Only six of the 71 cases could be so explained.

The current findings suggest that the concept of an evoked set is still poorly understood. The make (or brand) of an automobile seems to represent the greatest constraint on purchase behavior. However, even in the case of automobile makes it is difficult to separate amount of search from the size of the consideration set and changes in the set. Such findings may suggest that the static examination of evoked sets is a less desirable approach to studying the consumer decision process than a more dynamic general information processing model. It may also suggest information search and evoked set size are involved in a feedback loop that can only be examined by dynamic analysis.

TABLE 4

SIGNIFICANT DIFFERENCES BETWEEN INDIVIDUALS WHO BOUGHT
WITHIN THEIR EVOKED SET OF MAKES AND THOSE
BUYING OUTSIDE OF THEIR SET
(By Tukey's HSD, P < .05)

Variable	$\bar{x}$ Bought Within Set (N = 985)	$\bar{x}$ Bought Outside of Set (N = 71)
Rating of value of Car Bought Compared to What Expected When First Considered Buying a New Car (1 = Much Worse; 7 = Much Better)	4.56	4.21
Total Visits to Dealers	5.21	6.44
Time Spent Reading Ratings of Cars in Magazines	2.18	2.75
Time Spent Reading Manufacturers' Brochures and Pamphlets	2.41	2.86
Time spent Driving to Dealers	3.45	3.8
Time Spent Talking to Salespersons	3.44	3.73
Time Spent Test Driving Automobiles	2.28	2.71
Rating of Performance of Car Bought Compared to Expectation Prior to Delivery (1 = Much Worse 7 = Much Better)	4.6	4.2
Rating of Overall Satisfaction with Automobile Purchased (1 = Totally Dissatisfied; 7 = Totally Satisfied)	5.55	5.02

REFERENCES

Belonax, J.A. and R.A. Mittelstaedt (1977), "Evoked Set Size as a Function of Choice Criteria and Information Variability," *Advances in Consumer Research*, Vol. 5.

Bettman, J.R. (1979), *An Information Processing Theory of Consumer Choice*, Reading, MA: Addison-Wesley Publishing Co.

Bettman, J.R. & Park, C.W. (1980a), "Effects of Prior Knowledge and Experience and Phase of the Choice Process on Consumer Decision Processess: A Protocol Analysis," Journal of Consumer Research, 7, 234-248.

Bettman, J.R. & Park, C.W. (1980b), "Implications of a Constructive View of Choice for Analysis of Protocol Data: A Coding Scheme for Elements of Choice Processes," in Advances in Consumer Research, Vol. 7, ed. J.C. Olson, An Arbor: Association for Consumer Research, 148-153.

Bennett, P.D. & R.D. Mandell (1969), " Prepurchase Information Seeking Behavior of New Car Purchasers - The Learning Hypothesis," Journal of Marketing Research, 6, (Nov.), 430-433.

Campbell, B.M. (1973), "The Existence of Evoked Set and Determinants of Its Magnitude in Brand Choice, in J. Howard and L. Ostlund (Eds.), Buyer Behavior: Theoretical and Empirical Foundations, New York: Alfred Knopf.

Chestnut, R.W. & Jacoby, J. (1977), "Consumer Information Processing: Emerging Theory and Findings, in A.G. Woodside, J.N. Sheth, and P.D. Bennett, (Eds.), Consumer and Industrial Buying Behavior, New York: Elsevier North-Holland.

Dover, P.A., & Olson, J.C. (1977), "Dynamic Changes in an Expectancy-Value Attitude Model as a Function of Multiple Exposures to Product Information," in Contemporary Marketing Thought, eds. B.A. Greenberg & D.N. Bellenger, Chicago: American Marketing Association, 455-460.

Edell, J.A. & Mitchell, A.A. (1978), "An Information Processing Approach to Cognitive Responses," in Research Frontiers in Marketing: Dialogues and Directions, ed. S.C. Jain, Chicago: American Marketing Association, 178-183.

Green, R., Mitchell, A.A., and Staelin, R. (1977), "Longitudinal Decision Studies Using a Process Approach: Some Results from a Preliminary Experiment," in Contemporary Marketing Association, 461-466.

Gronhaug, K. (1973/74), "Some Factors Influencing the Size of the Buyers Evoked set," European Journal of Marketing, 7, (Winter), 232-241.

Hawkins, D.I., K.A. Coney, and R.J. Best (1980), Consumer Behavior, Dallas: Business Publications.

Hawkins, C.K. and T. Lanzetta (1965), "Uncertainty, Importance, and Arousal as determinants of Pre-decisional Information Search," Psychological Reports, 17, 791-800.

Howard, J.A. (1963), Marketing Management: Analysis and Planning, Homewood, IL: Richard Irwin Co.

Howard, J.A. (1977), Consumer Behavior: Application of Theory, New York: McGraw-Hill.

Howard, J.A. & J.N. Sheth (1969), The Theory of Buyer Behavior, New York: Wiley.

Jacoby, J., Chestnut, R.W., & Fisher, W.A. (1978), "A Behavioral Process Approach to Information Acquisition in Nondurable Purchasing," Journal of Marketing Research, 15, 532-544.

Jacoby, J., Szybillo, G.J., & Busato-Schach, J., (1977), "Information Acquisition Behavior in Brand Choice Situations," Journal of Consumer Research, 3, 209-216.

Jarvis, L.P. and J.B. Wilcox (1973), "Evoked Set Size---Some Theoretical Foundations and Empirical Evidence," in T.V. Greer, ed., Combined Proceedings, Fall Conference of the American Marketing Association, No 35, 236-240.

Lehmann, D.R., & Moore, W.L. (1980), "Validity of Information Display Boards: An Assessment Using Longitudinal Data," Journal of Marketing Research, 17, 450-459.

Maddox, R.N., K. Gronhaug, R.E. Homans, and F.E. May (1977), "Correlates of Information Gathering and Evoked Set Size for New Automobile Purchasers in Norway and the U.S." Advances in Consumer Research, Vol. 4.

Maddox, R.N., F.E. May, & R.E. Homans (1977), "A Replication of Bennett and Mandell's Study of the Learning-Information Seeking Hypothesis," University of Missouri-St. Louis Working Paper.

May, F.E. & R.E. Homans (1977), "Evoked Set Size and the Level of Information Processing, Product Comprehension and Choice Criteria," in W.D. Perreault, Jr., ed., Advances in Consumer Research, Vol. 4, 172-175.

Myers, J.H. (1978), "Methodological Issues in Evoked Set Formation and Composition," Advances in Consumer Research, Vol. 6, 236-237.

Narayana, C.L. & R.J. Markin (1975), "Consumer Behavior and Product Performance: An Alternative Conceptualization," Journal of Marketing, 39, (October), 1-6.

Ostlund, L.E. (1973), "Evoked Set Size: Some Empirical Results," in T.V. Greer, ed., Combined Proceedings, Fall Conference of the American Marketing Association, 35, 226-230.

Sieber, J.E. & J.T. Lanzetta (1964), "Conflict and Conceptual Structure as Determinants of Decision-Making Behavior, "Journal of Personality, 32, 622-641.

Silk, A.J. & G.L. Urban (1978), "Pre-Test-Market Evaluation of New Packaged Goods: A Model and Measurement Methodology," Journal of Marketing Research, 15, 171-191.

Staelin, R., & Payne, J.W. (1976), "Studies of the Information Seeking Behavior of Consumers," in Cognition and Social Behavior, J. Carroll and J.W. Payne (Eds.), New York: Erlbaum Associates, 185-202.

Swan, J.E. (1972), "Search Behavior Related to Expectations Concerning Brand Performance," Journal of Applied Psychology, 56, 332-335.

Wright, P.L. (1975), "Consumer Choice Strategies: Simplifying vs. Optimizing," Journal of Marketing Research, 11, 60-67.

PREPURCHASE INFORMATION SEARCH AND POST PURCHASE SATISFACTION:
AN EMPIRICAL INVESTIGATION OF ALTERNATIVE THEORIES

Peter Thirkell, Victoria University of Wellington, New Zealand
Harrie Vredenburg, The University of Western Ontario

ABSTRACT

This paper empirically tests several published theories of
information search and satisfaction and extends the previous empirical work by investigating the effects of several information sources on satisfaction. Data were obtained from a national survey of recent Canadian purchasers of new automobiles. The research suggests that
none of the published theories adequately explains the relationship on either a global information search basis or
on a specific information source basis.

INTRODUCTION

Conventional wisdom has it that by doing a thorough
search of information on a product prior to purchase and
by doing careful comparison shopping, a consumer will make
a better purchase decision and thus be more satisfied with
the product purchased. The very purpose of consumer organizations such as the Consumers Union and the Consumers
Association of Canada rests on this premise (Consumer Reports 1982, Canadian Consumer 1982). Communications programs of business firms often encourage comparison shopping and further information search in the belief that
this will increase awareness and preference for their product and by inference, product satisfaction. Despite the
heavy reliance on this commonly held premise very few
empirical studies have been reported in the consumer
satisfaction literature exploring this link between prepurchase information search and post purchase product
satisfaction (Cardozo 1965, Hughes 1977, Westbrook 1979).
A better understanding of this relationship is useful not
only to business managers and consumer groups but especially to public policy makers charged with implementing effective consumer protection programs to minimize
consumer dissatisfaction with products and services.

This paper presents an exploratory investigation to assess
the impact of information consulted by consumers prior to
purchase on the ultimate satisfaction/dissatisfaction
with the product after purchase.

Theoretical and empirical articles dealing with the relationship between prepurchase information search and consumer satisfaction have all concentrated on the relative
amount of information sought by consumers rather than the
different types of information sources used and their
association with consumer satisfaction. The following
paragraphs review the contributions made by these writers.
Janis and Mann (1977) analyze the psychological dynamics
of decision making and postulate various orientations to
choice situations. These orientations are then related to
the ultimate level of satisfaction with the resulting
decision. The orientations are ostensibly based on
amount of pre-decisional information search. For example,
the highest information seeking orientation is termed
"vigilant information processing" and is theoretically
more likely to result in improved decisions as well as in-
sulating the decisionmaker from post decisional regret.
The other orientations based on lower levels of pre-deci-

sional information seeking are theoretically more likely
to result in decisional miscalculations, less satisfactory
choices, and more post-decisional regret for the decision-
maker. Careful search is seen to alert the decision-
maker to all the potential negative consequences of the
decision and prepare him mentally for their materiali-
zation. In other words, he is less likely to base his
decision on unrealistic expectations that cannot be fulfilled and may result in dissatisfaction. Janis and Mann
intend their theory to apply to all "consequential
choices", thus consumer decisions about durable products
ought to constitute appropriate situations in which to
test their theory.

From a different theoretical perspective Cardozo (1965)
reaches a similar prediction of effect of information
search. He hypothesizes that decisional effort moderates
the relationship between expectancy disconfirmation and
subsequent product evaluation. Accordingly, when consumers have invested high levels of decisional effort in
the form of prepurchase information search cognitive dissonance will occur when expectations are subsequently
negatively disconfirmed. Consumers will then reduce the
dissonance by raising their evaluation of the product.
Even when expectations are confirmed, evaluations will be
raised in order to be consonant with a high amount of
decisional effort expended. Cardozo's model, then, postulates that product evaluations are assimilated towards
expectations. His experimental investigation of the
model produced relationships that were in the directions
predicted but were not statistically significant.

Day's (1976) theoretical model of the psychological arrival at a judgment of product satisfaction/dissatis-
faction agrees with neither the Janis and Mann model nor
the Cardozo model of satisfaction with decision making.
Instead of prepurchase information seeking, he emphasizes
learning from previous consumption experiences. According to his model, consumers with previous ownership experience will have more realistic expectations of the
performance of the product and are thus less likely to
experience negative disconfirmation resulting in dissatisfaction. Consumers who do not have previous product ownership experience and must rely on external
sources of information are theoretized to have weaker,
less complete, and less stable expectations which are
more likely to be negatively disconfirmed resulting in
greater dissatisfaction.

Westbrook's (1979) paper is the only one which specifically addresses the empirical relationship between information search and post purchase satisfaction in a consumer decisionmaking setting. Although he mentions
Day's purchase experience theory of consumer satisfaction
as an alternate conceptualization, he does not incorporate it into his investigation. In a study of undergraduate college students he found that the impact of
prepurchase search on post purchase satisfaction varied
by product category. In the case of automobiles it was
found that search was related to satisfaction in an in-
verted U-fashion, suggesting that increased search improves subsequent satisfaction with the purchase only up
to a point, beyond which increased search is associated
with diminished satisfaction. In the case of recently
purchased footwear he found that search was only associated with post purchase satisfaction in the case where
expectations were negatively disconfirmed. Only where

____
[1] The authors thank Professors John R. Kennedy and Terry
Deutscher for their helpful comments on earlier drafts
of this paper.

the item fell below expectations was search associated
with satisfaction, and then in the negative direction.
The rationale he gives for the different results between
product categories is that automobile purchasers carry
out a rational search in order to choose wisely from among
various alternatives while fashion item purchasers search
for a predetermined item.

Hughes (1977), in a field study, measured information
search by the number of stores visited prior to purchase.
He reports only that prepurchase information search was
not the strongest of several independent variables measured in explaining consumer satisfaction. Neither strength
of relationship nor direction is reported. Clearly, further empirical research is needed to better understand the
relationship between prepurchase information search and
post purchase satisfaction.

PURPOSE OF THE STUDY

The primary objective of this study was to increase understanding of the relationship between prepurchase information search and levels of consumer satisfaction and dissatisfaction. Specifically the objectives were:
(1) To test Westbrook's (1979) and Cardozo's (1965) empirically derived theories.
(2) To test empirically Day's (1976) previous ownership
theory.
(3) To extend the research in the area by determining
how use of the various sources of prepurchase information
available to the consumer is associated with post purchase
product satisfaction.

RESEARCH DESIGN

The data for this study were obtained as part of a national survey research project undertaken to obtain information about consumer satisfaction and dissatisfaction in
Canada. Because consumer satisfaction research and conventional complaint statistics both have identified automobiles and major household appliances as products which
appear to be associated with a relatively high frequency
of post purchase problems, the questionnaire was mailed
in the spring of 1980 to 3,000 Canadian residents who had
purchased a new General Motors passenger car within the
previous eighteen months, and who still owned the car.
A quota sampling plan was employed such that respondents
would be drawn from various regions of the country (specifically British Columbia, Manitoba, Ontario, and Nova
Scotia) and would represent purchasers of four types of
car models (specifically Impala, Malibu, Camaro, and Chev-
ette). Time since car purchase was distributed from zero
to eighteen months and an urban/rural split within each
geographical region was ensured. Of the 3,000 questionnaires mailed, 982 or approximately one-third were returned. Non-response bias was tested in a telephone survey in southwestern Ontario and was not found to be significant.

Satisfaction was measured with a seven point Likert-type
scale anchored at opposite ends with "extremely satisfied"
and "extremely dissatisfied". Even though our sample was
large, the skewed distribution of the dependent variable
combined with the skewed distributions of most of the independent variables resulted in numerous very small cell
sizes. On average, more than 35 percent of the cells in
each table have expected cell frequencies of less than 5.
Because of these small cell-size problems when using the
complete seven point satisfaction scale, the scale was
recoded into a dichotomous satisfied/dissatisfied variable. Sixty-six respondents who indicated that they were
"neither satisfied nor dissatisfied" were excluded from
the sample, leaving an n of 916. The mode among all automobile owners was the "satisfied" response on the seven

point scale, and on the recoded dichotomous variable 90.7
percent of respondents fell into the satisfied classification.

Information search was measured by subjects' responses to
a series of questions about the number and types of information sources consulted. Following the classification
work of Andreasen (1968) and Markin (1972) subjects were
asked about use of marketer-dominated, consumer-dominated,
and neutral sources. Using four point Likert-type scales
subjects were asked to report on their use of television,
radio, newspaper, and magazine advertizing to assist them
in their purchase of their new car. Subjects were also
asked to report the number (if any) of dealers visited
from a list of nine North American and foreign automobile
manufacturers. Room was left for two "other" manufacturer's dealers visited. For neutral sources respondents
were asked to report how many (if any) of the following
sources they used:(a) Better Business Bureau (b) Consumer
Reports (c) Technical reports (d) Dealer brochures
(e) Mechanics and other car experts (f) Members of household (g) Friends and relatives.

It must be kept in mind that it has been argued (Newman
and Lockeman 1975) that survey based measures of information search may be subject to a downward bias as estimators of the actual degree of prepurchase search undertaken
by consumers. Although this will have a negative effect
on our estimates of importance of prepurchase search to
satisfaction with automobiles, it need not seriously
affect our identification of which types of information
sources impact on consumer satisfaction and in which direction.

RESEARCH FINDINGS

Total Information Research Effects

In order to avoid losing information by classifying information search within each category of information sources
into high, medium and low (Katona and Mueller 1955, Newman
and Staelin 1973, Westbrook 1979) and to facilitate comparison with specific information effects analyses, a
simple summated index score was constructed for total
information search. The sample was then split into quar-
tiles of the respondents using that number of information
sources. Analysis was then carried out using crosstabulation. Table 1 summarizes the relationship between total
number of information sources used and post purchase satisfaction.

TABLE 1
ASSOCIATION BETWEEN GLOBAL INFORMATION SEARCH INDEX
AND POST PURCHASE SATISFACTION
TOTAL NUMBER OF INFORMATION SOURCES USED

	Less than 9	9 to 11	12 to 16	Over 16	Total
Dissatisfied	16	15	27	85	
	6.8%	6.9%	11.1%	12.3%	9.3%
Satisfied	220	203	216	192	831
	93.2%	93.1%	88.9%	87.7%	90.7%
Total	236	218	243	219	916
	25.9%	23.8%	26.5%	23.9%	100%

(Kendall's Tau C = 0.052 Sig. 0.008)

Among consumers doing either no search or a moderate
amount of search satisfaction is quite high. About 93
percent of respondents were satisfied with their purchase.
The proportion of the sample that used more information
sources was overall less satisfied with their purchase.
Of those who reported use of 12 to 16 information sources,
88.9 percent were satisfied, while of those who reported
using more than 16 information sources, 87.7 percent were
satisfied with their purchase. It could be argued that

this negative correlation (Kendall's Tau C = 0.008) partially resembles Westbrook's curvilinear model. Certainly these results lend some support to his finding that
too much information search seems to lead to lower levels
of satisfaction. However, our results do not seem to
support his finding that low levels of search also lead
to lower levels of satisfaction. It seems that about
half the automobile buyers do no search or a moderate a-
mount of search and are relatively satisfied with their
purchase, while the other half do a more thorough search
and are subsequently less satisfied with their purchase.
These results directly contradict the Janis and Mann and
Cardozo theories of information search.

Previous Purchase Effects

Having found no support for the Janis and Mann and Cardozo theories and at best only partial support for the Westbrook theory, we tested Day's previous purchase theory.
It appears that in our national sample previous purchase
of a new or used automobile is not significantly related
to satisfaction with the present purchase. This finding,
based on an objective measure of whether a consumer did
or did not have previous purchasing experience, was validated with a more subjective measure in which respondents
were asked to rate their experience in purchasing new
cars. Of those rating their experience as "none", 91.5
percent were satisfied with their present purchase, 88.6
percent of those responding "hardly any" were satisfied,
while 90.8 percent and 91.8 percent of those responding
"some" and "substantial" respectively were satisfied.
These results suggest that the relationship is more a
matter of self perception rather than actual previous
purchase experience. Since Day's theory rested on the
premise that consumers who had previously purchased an
automobile would have more realistic expectations and
thus would not as likely be dissatisfied, our results do
not support his theory. Because of the lack of empirical
support for the Day hypothesis our subsequent analyses
have not controlled for previous ownership.

Specific Information Source Effects

In order to assess the relationship between the different
types of information sources used by consumers and their
post purchase satisfaction with the product, crosstabulation analysis was performed between differing levels of
utilization of an information source and post purchase
satisfaction/dissatisfaction. Tables 2 and 3 summarize
the relationships between various marketer-dominated information sources and post purchase satisfaction with the
new automobile.

TABLE 2

ASSOCIATION BETWEEN BROADCAST ADVERTISEMENTS USED AS
SOURCE OF PREPURCHASE INFORMATION SEARCH AND POST PURCHASE
SATISFACTION
BROADCAST ADVERTISEMENTS USED

	None		Just a few		Some or large no.		Total
	T.V.	Radio	T.V.	Radio	T.V.	Radio	
Dissatisfied	55	76	15	4	15	5	85
	8.0%	8.8%	10.5%	10.3%	17.6%	27.8%	9.3%
Satisfied	633	783	128	35	70	13	831
	92.0%	91.2%	89.5%	89.7%	82.4%	72.2%	90.7%
Total	688	859	143	39	85	18	916
	75.1%	93.8%	15.6%	4.3%	9.3%	2.0%	100%

(Kendall's Tau C = -0.043 Sig. 0.005 for television)
(Kendall's Tau C = -0.017 Sig. 0.035 for radio)

TABLE 3

ASSOCIATION BETWEEN PRINT ADVERTISEMENTS USED AS SOURCE OF
PREPURCHASE INFORMATION SEARCH & POST PURCHASE SATISFACTION
PRINT ADVERTISEMENTS USED

	None		Just a few		Some		Large No.		Total
	Paper	Mag.	Paper	Mag.	Paper	Mag.	Paper	Mag.	
Dissat-isfied	55	48	12	15	14	13	4	9	85
	8.6%	7.7%	8.5%	9.1%	13.5%	15.9	13.3%	20%	9.3%
Satis-fied	585	577	130	149	90	69	26	36	831
	91.4%	92.3%	91.5%	90.9%	86.5%	84.1%	86.7%	80.0%	90.7%
Total	640	625	142	164	104	82	30	45	916
	69.9%	68.2%	15.5%	17.9%	11.4%	9.0%	3.3%	4.9%	100%

(Kendall's Tau C = -0.024 Sig. 0.090 for newspaper)
(Kendall's Tau C = -0.053 Sig. 0.002 for magazine)

Higher usage of each of the four communication media commonly employed by marketers was found to be consistently
associated with higher incidence of post purchase dissatisfaction by consumers. Usage of magazine advertising as
a prepurchase information source had the strongest negative correlation with product satisfaction (Kendall's Tau
C = -0.053, Significance = 0.002), although usage of
each of the four media was statistically significantly
correlated with product dissatisfaction. These results
concerning specific information sources contradict the
Cardozo and Janis and Mann theoretical and empirical relationships reported in the literature based on a global
information search index.

A consistent direction of association was found with
dealer brochures as an information source. Although the
relationship is not a particularly strong one (Kendall's
Tau C = -0.031 Sig. 0.0649) there is a suggestion that
use of dealer brochures is negatively correlated with
post purchase satisfaction. The group with the largest
percentage of satisfied buyers was the one in which respondents reported that they did not use dealer brochures
as a prepurchase information source (92.3 percent). The
groups that did report use of dealer brochures ranged in
proportion satisfied from 80.6 percent to 91.6 percent.
This result, again,is inconsistent with reported results
based on a global prepurchase search index, while being
consistent with our results reported above on the relationship between other marketer-dominated information
sources and post purchase satisfaction.

Visits to other car dealers was also negatively correlated with post purchase satisfaction (Kendall's Tau C =
-0.039 Sig. 0.036 for American makes, Kendall's Tau C =
-0.028 Sig. 0.058 for foreign makes). This is consistent
with our other findings regarding relationships between
use of marketer-dominated sources and product satisfaction.

Use of several neutral sources of information was analyzed. Of the 2.4 percent who contacted a Better Business
Bureau prior to purchasing their last new car, 18.2 percent were subsequently dissatisfied with their purchase
as opposed to only 9.1 percent of those who did not (Kendall's Tau B = -0.048 Sig. 0.073). A negative relationship was also found between number of technical reports
used and dissatisfaction with the car purchased (Kendall's
Tau C = -0.033 Sig. 0.017). Technical reports were loosely defined and taken to include any written review of a
car in other than a consumer organization's publication.
Examples would be automobile magazine reports, AAA magazine reports, and newspaper new car reviews. A similar
relationship was tested for consumer reports and was not
found to be statistically significant. Both these relationships between specific neutral information sources
and satisfaction with the purchase contradict Westbrook's
(1979) findings using a global information search index
as the independent variable. These results also fail to
corroborate the Janis and Mann and Cardozo theories. Of
the remaining neutral information sources tested, only
members of the household approached conventional levels of

statistical significance (Kendall's Tau C = 0.024 Sig. 0.10) with respect to post purchase satisfaction. Consultation of mechanics and other car experts was positively correlated with satisfaction although the relationship did not attain significance at p<0.15. Consultation of friends and relatives also was not significantly related to satisfaction at p<0.15, but the weak relationship that was observed was in the negative direction.

DISCUSSION AND CONCLUSIONS

This study has found no evidence for the Janis and Mann and Cardozo theories that post purchase product satisfaction would tend to increase with amount of prepurchase information sought. At an aggregated prepurchase information search index level our data partially supported Westbrook's model. Although we did not find evidence of low levels of satisfaction at low levels of search, our data revealed a decreasing level of satisfaction as number of information sources used reached higher levels.

With regard to Day's previous purchase experience theory, we found no evidence that having previously purchased a new or used automobile was associated with satisfaction with the current new automobile. We found only a very weak relationship between perceived purchase experience and post purchase satisfaction but found this relationship to be somewhat weaker than relationships between prepurchase information search and post purchase satisfaction.

Testing the models using different information sources resulted in similarly negative findings. For impersonal marketer-dominated information sources (television, radio, newspapers, and magazines), the group which reported no use of the source had the greatest proportion of satisfied purchasers, while the proportion satisfied decreased with increased reported use of the medium as an information source. For personal marketer-dominated information sources (dealers visited, dealer brochures) we found a weak relationship with satisfaction parallelling our results with mass media sources. For impersonal neutral information sources (consumer reports, technical reports) we found very weak negative relationships. For personal neutral information sources (members of household, mechanics and other car experts, friends and relatives), we found no significant relationships with satisfaction. Only members of household approached significance at p< 0.10.

Overall, the results of this study indicate that the impact of prepurchase search on post purchase satisfaction is not as straightforward as previously believed. It is hoped that this research has shown other researchers that prepurchase search is a complex construct and that extant models appear to view the actual process of information seeking too simply. An alternative conceptualization might include the notion of risk or uncertainty. When entering the purchase process consumers decide how much uncertainty they have about the product class under consideration. All else being equal, the consumer with the greater amount of perceived uncertainty is more likely to experience post purchase dissatisfaction because he is more likely to make an inappropriate purchase decision. It is this uncertainty about the purchase, however, that induces the consumer to seek information. This information search then moderates the effect of the uncertainty on satisfaction. Some support for this conceptualization has been published in the psychological literature on uncertainty and decisionmaking based on laboratory experimentation (Driscoll and Lanzetta 1964, Hawkins and Lanzetta 1965, Driscoll and Lanzetta 1965, Driscoll, Tognoli and Lanzetta 1966). Information search may, thus, have a stronger effect on satisfaction than is suggested by the results of our study. Further research is needed if we are to understand the relationship between prepurchase information search and post purchase satisfaction. Fruitful directions for research would be to investigate the effect of uncertainty on satisfaction and how prepurchase search moderates this effect. Additionally, longitudinal designs and alternative data collection methods could be employed to overcome the shortcomings of the survey design used in this study to further investigate the effects of different information sources.

REFERENCES

Andreasen, A. R. (1968), "Attitudes and Customer Behavior: A Decision Model," in Perspectives in Consumer Behavior, H. H. Kassarjian and T. S. Robertson, eds., Glenview, Illinois: Scott, Foresman and Co.

Canadian Consumer (1982), Ottawa, Ontario: Consumers Association of Canada. (Stated purpose is: "...to provide consumers with information on matters relating to the expenditure of the family income")

Cardozo, R. (1965), "An Experimental Study of Consumer Effort, Expectations, and Satisfaction," Journal of Marketing Research, 2(August), 244-249.

Consumer Reports (1982), Mount Vernon, New York: Consumers Union of United States, Inc. (Stated purpose is: "...to provide consumers with information and counsel on consumer goods and services...")

Day, R. L. (1976), "Extending the Concept of Consumer Satisfaction," in Advances in Consumer Research 4, W. D. Perreault, ed., Atlanta, Georgia: Association for Consumer Research, 149-154.

Driscoll, J. M. and J. T. Lanzetta (1964), "Effects of Problem Uncertainty and Prior Arousal on Pre-Decisional Information Search," Psychological Reports, 14, 975-78.

Driscoll. J.M. and J.T. Lanzetta (1965), "Effects of Two Sources of Uncertainty and Decisionmaking," Psychological Reports, 17, 635-648.

Driscoll, J.M., J.J. Tognoli, and J.T. Lanzetta (1966), "Choice Conflict and Subjective Uncertainty in Decision Making," Psychological Reports, 18, 427-32.

Hawkins, C. K. and J. T. Lanzetta (1965), "Uncertainty, Importance, and Arousal as Determinants of Predecisional Information Search," Psychological Reports, 17, 791-800.

Hughes, D. (1977), "Consumer Dissatisfaction Related to Price Paid," in Consumer Satisfaction, Dissatisfaction and Complaining Behavior, R. L. Day, ed., Bloomington, Indiana: Indiana University, School of Business.

Janis, I., R. Mann (1977), Decision Making: A Psychological Analysis of Conflict, Choice and Decision, New York, New York: Free Press.

Katona, G. and E. Mueller (1955), "A Study of Purchase Decisions," in Consumer Behavior: The Dynamics of Consumer Reactions, L. H. Clark, ed., New York, New York: New York University Press.

Markin, R. J. (1972), Consumer Behavior: A Cognitive Orientation, New York, New York: MacMillan Publishing Inc.

Newman, J. W. and B. Lockeman (1975), "Measuring Prepurchase Information Seeking," Journal of Consumer Research 2, 216-222.

Newman, J.W. and R. Staelin (1972), "Prepurchase Information Seeking for New Cars and Major Household Appliances," Journal of Marketing Research 9, 249-257.

Westbrook, R. A., "Prepurchase Information Search and Post
   Purchase Product Satisfaction," in <u>Refining Concepts and
   Measures of Consumer Satisfaction and Complaining Beha-
   vior</u>, H. K. Hunt and R. L. Day, eds., Bloomington,
   Indiana: Indiana University, School of Business.

A SCRIPT THEORETIC ANALYSIS OF CONSUMER DECISION MAKING

Arno J. Rethans, The Pennsylvania State University
Jack L. Taylor, Jr., Portland State University

ABSTRACT

In this paper we employ script theory and consumer script
elicitation to provide some evidence for the "consumer decision making: fact or fiction" controversy. Specifically,
script elicitation is used as a new exploratory technique
to investigate the traditional five-step process model of
consumer decision making. The resulting scripts hint at
the validity of the five-step process as a conceptual model,
but at the same time suggest the usefulness of the adoption
of a contingency view of consumer decision making.

INTRODUCTION

In his presidential address to the Association for Consumer
Research, Kassarjian (1978) warned consumer researchers
against committing the error of anthropomorphism. He won-
dered whether consumer researchers did not project too much
onto the consumer. Because researchers care about information processing, prepurchase behaviors and choice rules,
they assume that the average consumer also cares.

Olshavsky and Granbois (1979) attempted to validate Kassarjian's position by examining empirical research for support
or lack of support for the "most persuasive and influential
assumption in consumer behavior" research namely that purchases are preceded by a decision process. They concluded
that a significant proportion of purchases may not be preceded by a decision process and furthermore that research
methodologies employed in the "positive-finding" studies
probably overstated the extent of prepurchase behaviors because of inherent bias. Their conclusions were quickly
challenged by Ursic (1980) who questioned Olshavsky and
Granbois' conceptualization of the consumer decision making
process, the evidence presented and the conclusions drawn.
In their rejoinder, the authors reiterated the purpose of
the original article to be the assessment of the degree to
which "available research did or did not seem to substantiate a five-step process" (1980, p. 333). They note that
the finding that research has found substantial evidence of
behavior apparently inconsistent with the prediction of a
five-step process (problem recognition, search, alternative
evaluation, choice and outcomes) suggests the need for new
exploratory research not biased by assumptions about the
nature of the process.

In this paper we follow Olshavsky and Granbois' suggestion
and explore consumer decision making by eliciting consumer
scripts for a variety of purchase situations. The elicitation and subsequent analysis of consumer scripts is in principle far less biased toward the five-step process than the
research techniques criticized by Olshavsky and Granbois.
Hence, the use of scripts to examine decision making behavior should form an interesting complementary research technique.

THEORETICAL FRAMEWORK

In 1976, Abelson proposed a theory which rested upon the
concept of a cognitive script. He defined script to mean
"a coherent sequence of events expected by the individual,
involving him either as a participant or as an observer"
(Abelson 1976, p. 33). He postulated that scripts which
have been stored in memory upon activation are used to direct behavior. This activation is believed to occur
automatically as a function of the situational context.
For example, upon entering a restaurant, a RESTAURANT
script would be activated and begin to guide behavior.
This script would contain a standard sequence of typical
activities in a restaurant from the point of view of the
customer. It may include such activities as talking to the
maitre d, being shown to a table, reading the menu, reading
the wine list and so forth. The script also includes
standard roles to be played, standard objects, ordinary
conditions for entering upon the activity, a standard sequence of scenes or actions wherein one action enables the
next, and some normal results from the performing of the
activity successfully (Abelson 1980). This information
contained in the script will enable the restaurant goer to
understand what is observed as well as aid the person to
plan and execute the conventional activities.

Empirical research on the nature of scripts is of rather
recent vintage. Bower, Black and Turner (1979) conducted a
series of studies on scripts involving the collection of
script norms, the investigation of script recall and the
relationship of scripts to schema memory. The significant
findings of these studies, for our purpose, are (a) script
norms do exist, i.e., when asked to describe familiar activities subjects agree on characters, props and actions,
and (b) subjects tended to agree on how to segment low-level
action sequences into constituent "scenes." Thus, scripts
of the same event sequence held by different subjects do
indeed overlap on at least the most salient aspects (Nottenburg and Shoben 1980).

The use of scripts in decision making was first suggested
by Abelson 1976 when he explained how script theory could
account Dawes' findings on graduated admission decision
making (1976) and Slovic, Fischhoff and Lichtenstein's
findings on risk decision making (1976). Yet, although
references to scripts have been made in the marketing literature (Bozinoff 1981; Calder 1978), no empirical use of
scripts in the study of consumer decision making has been
reported. The exploratory study reported below, then,
represents a first attempt at using script theory to examine
consumer decision making.

STUDY METHODOLOGY

Thirty consumers were asked to generate scripts for four
different consumer decision making situations. The situations were selected so as to be representative of the decision situations incorporated in Olshavsky and Granbois'
(1979, p. 6-8) review of the brand purchase literature.
They include the purchasing of groceries (Bettman 1970;
Wells and LoSciuto 1966), over-the-counter medicine (Wright
1979), a new automatic dishwasher (Newman and Staelin 1973,
Olshavsky 1973) and the purchase of a new automobile (Newman and Staelin 1972, Newman 1977). Thus, the scenarios
used differ along several dimensions.

The subjects were volunteers and members of civic groups in
an Eastern town. The group was predominantly female, married with children, median age in the 30-39 category with a
range of 21-83. The majority of subjects completed some
college and/or high school. Total household income was best
characterized as being in the $15,000-$25,000 category.

Each of the consumers was asked to generate a list of events
or actions involved in each of the four decision situations.
The specific instructions to the consumers for generating

the scripts were taken from Bower, Black and Turner (1979)
and read as follows:

> "Please write a list of actions describing
> what people generally do when they go grocery
> shopping. We are interested in the common ac-
> tions of a routine 'grocery shopping' stereotype.
> Start the list with 'enter the grocery store' and
> end it with 'put groceries in car.' Include
> about 20 actions or events and put them in the
> order in which they occur."

Subjects reported these instructions to be clear and found
the task to be easy, not too fatiguing, neither artificial
nor natural and a bit long. In addition, they considered
themselves to be familiar with the four decision making
processes.

STUDY FINDINGS AND DISCUSSION

The resulting scripts were edited and tabulated according
to the frequency of citation of specific events and actions. As might be expected, each consumer mentioned a
sample of very common actions or events along with some
less common ones, presumably reflecting his or her experiences. Indeed, across consumers there was a continuous
gradation of frequency of reporting of particular events.
As per Bower, Black and Turner (1979), we defined the
group's script to be those actions or events mentioned by
more than some criterion percentage of consumers. Specifically, we selected 25 percent mention as a criterion for
inclusion of an action in the consumer script.

Tables 1-4 report for each of the decision situations the
actions mentioned by at least one-fourth of the respondents.
Furthermore, the actions are listed in the serial order in
which they were usually reported. Each of the tables also
provides some further information about the percent-mention
distribution for each of the situations. The items in
italics were more popular, falling in the criterion of 40-
50 percent mention; actions in capital letters were most
popular, having been mentioned by more than 55-75 percent
of the consumers. Those actions mentioned by more than 75
percent of the consumers have been indicated in capital
letters followed by an asterisk. Finally, the split-half
reliability in the frequency which which the particular
actions of the respective scripts were mentioned, are reported.

TABLE 1: SCRIPT NORMS FOR GROCERY SHOPPING

ENTER STORE *

GET CART

CONSULT CHECKLIST

get out coupons

INSPECT AND GET VEGETABLES

INSPECT AND GET MEAT PRODUCTS

get dairy products

go up and down aisles

compare prices

decide on products

put products in cart

go to bakery

visit deli

GET IN CHECKOUT LINE*

UNLOAD GROCERIES ON BELT

give coupons

PAY CASHIER*

TAKE GROCERIES TO CAR*

PUT GROCERIES IN CAR*

Reliability: 0.836

TABLE 2: SCRIPT NORMS FOR PURCHASE OTC MEDICINE

ENTER STORE*

LOCATE APPROPRIATE SECTION

EXAMINE AVAILABLE REMEDIES

read labels

read ingredients

COMPARE PRICES

compare store-national brands

CONSULT PHARMACIST

MAKE SELECTION

GO TO CHASHIER

PAY CHASHIER*

leave store

get in car

GO HOME

read directions

TAKE REMEDY*

Reliability: 0.838

TABLE 3: SCRIPT NORMS FOR WASHER PURCHASE

DECIDE TO BUY NEW WASHER*

check consumer report/guide

talk to friends, relatives

decide on features

decide on dealer

VISIT STORE/DEALER

TALK TO SALESPERSON

discuss features

CHECK ON FEATURES

ask about prices

SELECT WASHER

talk to spouse

discuss/arrange financing

MAKE PAYMENT*

ARRANGE DELIVERY

ARRANGE INSTALLATION

WASHER INSTALLED

Reliability: 0.852

First of all, what is interesting about these data is the
degree of agreement in the "basic action" language that
consumers use to describe decision processes. We find a
high percent of the actions in capital letters indicating
that at least half the consumers perceive these as basic
script acts. This uniformity is further reflected in the
infrequency of unique actions or events. For example, in
the grocery shopping script out of the 599 actions mentioned
in total, there were no unique actions or events. So there
is at least someone who agrees with every action that any

TABLE 4: SCRIPT NORMS FOR AUTOMOBILE DECISION

DECIDE TO PURCHASE NEW CAR*

look at ads

talk to friends

discuss with family

discuss finances

observe cars in traffic/street

VISIT SHOWROOM/DEALER

talk to salespersons

check on color

check on mileage

get price estimates

TEST DRIVE

visit other dealers

decide on make-type

go to dealer

choose car

discuss trade-in

negotiate price

arrange financing

sign papers

pay dealer

DRIVE OUT CAR*

Reliability: 0.690

consumer writes into a script. Similarly, the ratio of
unique to total mention was 1/463 for the over-the-counter
medicine decision, 4/486 for the washer purchase and 1/540
for the automobile purchase decision script.

More importantly, these data provide clear evidence of at
least a limited amount of prepurchase processes. The
script data, thus, provide some corroborating evidence for
the conceptual model of a five-step process found in so
many of the textbooks (e.g., Engel, Blackwell and Kollat
1978).

More specifically, the grocery shopping script and the
over-the-counter medicine script seem to support Ursic's
(1980) contention that search and evaluation processes may
occur within the store. The grocery shopping script indicates a substantial amount of comparison shopping in the
aisles, while the OTC medicine script indicates a search
among available remedies coupled with an examination of
labels and consultation with the pharmacist. The washer
and automobile purchase scripts, on the other hand, seem to
reflect more closely the previous literature (Newman 1977).
These scripts indicate both out-of-store and in-store information seeking for buyers of these items (Newman and
Staelin 1972). Out of store information seeking involved
discussions with significant others, as well as consultation of published sources. In both scripts do we find the
importance of the salesperson as a source of information
for attribute information and price information. The percent-mention distribution of these sources seem to parallel
those obtained in survey and observation studies (Newman
1977).

Due to the varying dimensions underlying the decision situation stimuli employed in this study, the script data do
not allow a precise quantitative measure of the extent of
external information gathering and evaluation so as to confirm or disconfirm Olshavsky and Granbois' (1979) concern
for purchasing behavior "occurring in the absence of

external search and hence the non-decision behavior postulated by Kassarjian." However, a subjective analysis of
these data by the authors suggests the potential usefulness
of further exploring Olshavsky and Granbois' suggestion
that the consumer "has a repertoire of purchasing strategies" involving various levels and types of prepurchase
and decision processes. The type of purchasing strategy
employed in a specific situation may then be viewed as a
function of the specific characterstics and values of the
consumer and the task environment variables which characterize the particular purchase situation.

CONCLUSIONS AND RECOMMENDATIONS

We have attempted to employ script theory and script elicitation to partially fulfill Olshavsky and Granbois' (1980)
stated need for new exploratory research on the five-step
process model underlying much of the conceptualization of
consumer decision making. The research found some qualitative support for the five-step conceptual model in that
the model allows categorization of script actions and/or
events. At the same time, the scripts also corroborate
earlier findings on prepurchase activities and suggest that
some consumers in some purchase situations go through a
rather "shallow" decision making process. These findings
lead us to endorse Olshavsky and Granbois' call for the
adoption of a contingency view of consumer decision making.

As with so many exploratory attempts, this one too generated as many questions, both substantive and methodological, as it sought to answer. Our own future research
efforts will center on analyzing the relative efficacy of
script elicitation to assess consumer's internal processes.

REFERENCES

Abelson, Robert P. (1981), "Psychological Status of the
Script Concept," *American Psychologist*, 36, 7, 715-729.

__________ (1976), "Script Processing in Attitude Formation and Decision Making," in J. Carroll and J. Payne
(eds.), *Cognition and Social Behavior*, Hillsday, N.J.:
Erlbaum.

Bettman, James R. (1970), "Information Processing Models of
Consumer Behavior," *Journal of Marketing Research*, 7,
370-6.

Bower, Gordon H., John B. Black and Terrence J. Turner
(1975), "Scripts in Memory for Text," *Cognitive Psychology*, 11, 177-220.

Bozinoff, Lorne (1982), "A Script Theoretic Approach to Information Processing," in A. Mitchell (ed.), *Advances in
Consumer Research, Vol. 9*, Ann Arbor, MI: Association
for Consumer Research (forthcoming).

Calder, Boby J. (1978), "Cognitive Response, Imagery and
Scripts: What Is the Cognitive Basis of Attitude?", in
H. Keith Hunt (ed.), *Advances in Consumer Research, Vol.
5*, Ann Arbor, MI: Association for Consumer Research,
630-4.

Dawes, Robyn M. (1976), "Shallow Psychology," in J. S.
Carroll and J. W. Payne (eds.), *Cognition and Social Behavior*, Hillsdale, N.J.: L. Erlbaum Associates, 3-12.

Engel, James, Blackwell, Roger and Kollat, David (1978),
Consumer Behavior, 3rd ed., Hillsdale, IL: The Dryden
Press.

Gibbs, Raymond W. and Tenney, Yvette J. (1980), "The Concept of Scripts in Understanding Stories," *Journal of
Psycholinguistic Research*, 9, 3, 275-84.

Kassarjian, Harold H. (1978), "Antropomorphism and Parsimony," in H. Keith Hunt (ed.), Advances in Consumer Research, Vol. 5, Ann Arbor, MI: Association for Consumer
   Research, xii-iv.

Newman, Joseph W. (1977), "Consumer External Search:
   Amount and Determinants," in Arch G. Woodside et al.
   (eds.), Consumer and Industrial Buying Behavior, New
   York: North Holland Publishing Company.

__________ and Staelin, Richard (1972), "Prepurchase Information Seeking for New Cars and Major Household
   Appliances," Journal of Marketing Research, 9, 249-57.

Nottenburg, Gail and Shoben, Edward J. (1980), "Scripts as
   Linear Order," Journal of Experimental Social Psychology,
   16, 329-47.

Olshavsky, Richard W. and Granbois, Donald H. (1980), "Consumer Decision Making-Fast or Fiction: Rejoinder,"
   Journal of Consumer Research, 7, 3, 333-4.

__________ and __________ (1979), "Consumer Decision
   Making-Fact or Fiction?", Journal of Consumer Research,
   6, 2, 93-100.

__________ (1973), "Customer-Salesman Interaction in
   Appliance Retailing," Journal of Marketing Research, 10,
   208-12.

Slovic, Paul et al. (1976), "Cognitive Processes and Societal Risk Taking," in J. J. Carroll and J. W. Payne
   (eds.), Cognition and Social Behavior, Hillsdale, N.J.:
   L. Erlbaum Associates, 165-84.

Ursic, Michael (1980), "Consumer Decision Making-Fact or
   Fiction: A Comment," Journal of Consumer Research, 7, 3,
   331-3.

Wells, William and LoSciuto, Leonard A. (1966), "Direct Observation of Purchasing Behavior," Journal of Marketing
   Research, 3, 227-33.

Wright, Peter (1979), "Concrete Action Plans in T.V. Messages to Increase Reading of Drug Warnings," Journal of
   Consumer Research, 6, 3, 256-269.

AN EMPIRICAL INVESTIGATION OF THE SERIAL STRUCTURE OF SCRIPTS

George John, University of Wisconsin-Madison
John C. Whitney, University of Wisconsin-Madison

ABSTRACT

The present study serves to extend previous research in script processing. While considerable research in psychology indicates that the reliance upon schemata or scripts can significantly influence cognitive processes, a number of methodological issues remain. As an initial effort to assess the usefulness of scripts to marketers, the present study examined the cultural uniformity of events as well as the serial ordering of events within a script in a consumer context.

INTRODUCTION

In his 1978 Presidential address to the Association for Consumer Research, Kassarjian raised the possibility that researchers may be attributing choice processes to consumers when, in fact, no choice processes occur. Olshavsky and Granbois (1979) concurred with this belief by asserting that "the most pervasive and influential assumption in consumer behavior research is that purchases are preceded by a decision process" (p. 93). These authors further asserted that information processing as defined by consumer behavioralists is often performed with previously acquired and stored information, and that "prior decision making" occurs either when there is insufficient information stored in memory or with nonuse of relevant, stored information.

A mode of processing which is not inconsistent with this position is that of schematic processing. Although it has exhibited considerable influence in psychology, schematic processing has drawn little attention in marketing. This mode of processing suggests that perceptions, interpretations and inferences may be significantly affected by certain knowledge structures. The focus of this study will be upon "script processing," which is a type of schema, differentiated by the hierarchical or causal ordering of its elements.

Despite the popularity of the script concept in psychology, there has been no evidence of scripts in a consumer context. It is essential that the existence and homogeneity of scripts be established empirically before the marketer can utilize this body of knowledge strategically.

Bower, Black and Turner (1979) have demonstrated that it was possible to elicit scripts about a restaurant episode that exhibited high inter-subject agreement about the main events. However, they did not examine the degree of agreement regarding the sequencing of the listed events.

In the present study, we extend the Bower, Black and Turner approach to investigate the degree of inter-subject agreement relative to listed events and their hierarchical ordering. The paper is organized in three sections. First, the extant literature is reviewed to indicate the possible effects of schematic (and script) processing. The data collection, analysis and results are then presented, followed by a discussion of the implications of the study.

LITERATURE REVIEW

Scripts have evolved as a variation of schema theories which have exhibited considerable influence in cognitive psychology, social psychology, cognitive anthropology and artifical intelligence (e.g., Bartlett 1932; Bransford & Franks 1971; Mandler 1979; Minsky 1975; Rumelhart & Ortony 1977; Schank & Abelson 1977). These theories have been proposed as a means by which individuals deal with the redundancy of information in the environment. Rather than attending to all stimuli, computing time can be minimized and information search guided by the reliance upon stored, generic concepts, events, event-sequences, etc., in a "schema."

According to Taylor and Crocker (1981) a schema "is a cognitive structure which consists in part of a representation of some defined stimulus domain. The schema contains general knowledge about the domain, including the specification of the relationships among its attributes, as well as specific examples or instances of the stimulus domain" (p. 3). It is the basic premise of this research stream that abstract schematic conceptions of how the world works often determine a "hypothesis-driven" form of information processing by individuals. Neisser (1976) has referred to this as "schematic processing" and has made an analogy between it and computer programming. Like the format statement, which allows information to enter the system, a schema enables a person to take information in. Thus, we are unable to recognize a chair unless we have a conception or schema about what a chair is.

Rumelhart and Ortony (1977) have argued that all cognitive processes -- perception, comprehension and interpretation involve an interaction with existing cognitive representations as opposed to operating solely on objects in the environment. Thus, schemata are by no means static, but are the product of a continuous cognitive process which changes with experience.

Empirical evidence has been provided which suggests that individuals frequently draw upon different schemata for interpretative or understanding functions. These studies have shown that the recall of schema-relevant material is superior to the recall of schema-irrelevant material and that structure may be provided to ambiguous situations (Taylor, et al. 1978; Bransford & Johnson 1973; Dooling & Mullet 1973).

Once the understander has imputed meaning to a given stimulus configuration via the interpretive or understanding function of schemata, he is faced with the problem of how to use this meaning to solve problems, set goals, or select a behavior (Taylor & Crocker 1981). Schemata can also be utilized to accomplish these latter functions. This may be accomplished by relying upon schemata to fill in missing data for a stimulus configuration (Minsky 1975) or by providing direction for further information search (Garland, Hardy & Stephenson 1975). Other studies supporting this inferential function of schemata include Cohen (1977), Bower, Black and Turner (1979), Markus (1977), Fiske and Kinder (1978), Cantor and Mischel (1977), Snyder and Uranowitz (1978), and Loftus and Palmer (1974).

Finally, it should be recognized that the reliance upon schemata may lead to a bias during the encoding of information or its retrieval from memory. These biases result primarily from the stereotypical expectations associated with schemata (Snyder & Uranowitz 1978; Markus 1977).

Scripts (Abelson 1975, 1976, 1980; Schank & Abelson 1977) are considered to be a type of schema and may serve to accomplish the same functions. They include routine, well-practiced event-sequences or stories such as departmental meetings, cocktail parties, or going to a restaurant. According to Schank and Abelson, a script is "a structure that describes an appropriate sequence of events in a particular context. A script is made up of slots and requirements about what can fill those slots. The structure is an interconnected whole, and what is in one slot affects what can be in another" (1977, p. 41). In effect, scripts are a stereotyped sequence of actions in which the major distinction from schemata is their causal and often temporal nature. That is, early events in the sequence produce or at least enable the occurrence of later events (Nisbett & Ross 1980). Thus, a person may have a restaurant script which consists of 'entering,' 'being seated,' 'ordering,' 'eating,' 'paying' and 'exiting' scenes. Note that certain schemata, such as that of the "waiter" may represent significant components of the script and convey a great deal of information.

As with schemata, scripts may also serve to influence the inference function. In the restaurant script which contains expectations about ordering from the menu, eating, and leaving, the script can be viewed as governing a bundle of expectations. These expectations may serve to direct cognitive processing toward the appropriate influence (Abelson 1980). Thus, if someone involved in the restaurant script notes that he has forgotten his reading glasses, one may search through the restaurant script for events which involve reading. Finding the "reading the menu" event, one may infer that the individual will be unable to read the menu.

Evidence is also gathering which supports the structuring function of scripts. Anderson (1980) has obtained evidence that script arousal involves the simultaneous activation of a set of events (in the script). That is, the priming of one script event leads to faster recognition of another script event in the story. Bower, Black and Turner (1979) found substantial inter-subject agreement regarding the events in a script (see also Galambos and Rip 1979). In addition, they observed the tendency of subjects to "fill in the gaps" in incompletely presented scripts. During a recall test, subjects exhibited a strong tendency toward false recognition of non-mentioned, normative script events. This tendency is consistent with the notion that people's long-term memory of a scripted situation is by reference to the standard script, modified by tagging unusual events (Abelson 1980).

To further investigate the hierarchical organization of scripts, Bower, Black and Turner presented subjects with script-based stories with some events displaced from their usual sequential positions. When subjects tried to reconstruct the order of the events, they tended to recall them in the temporal order in which they logically occurred. There was also a tendency by subjects to falsely recall actions implied by the script but which were not a part of the original text.

Lastly, one should note that scripts can be expected to exert a strong influence upon behavior. The previously discussed research findings suggest an influence upon decision-making; however, we might also expect a more direct influence upon behavior. As noted by Taylor and Crocker (1981), a script represents a normative structure which can be used to generate schema-relative expectations. Expectations have been shown to exert a powerful influence upon emotions and behavior (Mette, Taylor & Friedman 1973; Martin 1977; Lawler 1973). Thus, for a given stimulus configuration, a perceiver may compare it to a script for evaluative purposes as when assessing one's satisfaction with an event, object or person. Alternatively, one may refer to a cocktail party script to determine what behavior should be undertaken upon arrival at the party.

The literature reviewed provides strong evidence of schemata (to include scripts) and their influence upon judgments and behavior. Knowledge of these cognitive structures and their consequences (i.e., "scripted" behavior) will offer the marketer strategic implications if he is able to influence the reliance upon these structures. Abelson has noted three conditions necessary for scripted behavior to occur. First, the individual must have a stable cognitive representation of the script. Second, an evoking context for the script must be presented. Marketing communications might be used for this purpose. Third, the individual must "enter" the script. This decision may be based upon relatively simple rules such as whether one is sufficiently hungry to go to a restaurant and may be subject to certain constraints such as financial resources (1980, p. 12). A fourth factor of importance to the marketer would be the homogeneity of the structure of a particular script.

However, in spite of this impressive number of studies that suggest the utility of these notions regarding scripts, there are some severe methodological issues that have to be resolved. For instance, there is no accepted way of measuring evoked scripts, especially with regard to characterizing it along relevant dimensions. In fact, it is not even certain whether scripts even exist for consumer situations. Even if their existence is presumed, they may be so idiosyncratic as to be useless to a marketer. In the present study, we will examine the cultural uniformity of events as well as the sequencing of events within a script in a consumer context. From a marketing perspective, "cultural uniformity" refers to the homogeneity of a script within a relevant market segment.

METHODOLOGY

Undergraduate students in the business school at a midwestern university were recruited to provide descriptions of a purchase episode at McDonalds. The choice of this purchase situation was prompted by several considerations. First, the restaurant script has been empirically investigated by Bower et al. (1979) which provides a basis for comparing results. Also, it was felt that undergraduate subjects would be more capable of providing scripts about this particular purchase situation because of their extensive familiarity with this restaurant.

Each student received a blank sheet with instructions at the top. These instructions were as follows:

> We are interested in knowing what kinds of experience people have when they stop at McDonalds. Write down a list of actions describing what you feel people generally do when they stop at McDonalds. Include about twenty actions and events. You can draw on your own experiences or on any other source of information. Please start with arriving at McDonalds, and end it with leaving. As far as possible, try and keep the events in the order that you would expect them to occur.

Fifty-six subjects provided these scripts in one session lasting about twenty minutes. They were also requested to complete some demographic, attitudinal and product usage questions following the generation of the scripts.

DATA ANALYSIS AND RESULTS

The subjects completed the script tasks without any difficulty. The responses were edited to delete all attitudinal statements or other unobservable events. The remaining action or event statements were coded for their frequency of mention and sequential order, after paraphrases and synonyms were lumped together.

76

The result of the editing left 40 separate actions or event statements that remained. The number of statements provided varied from eight to 37 with the large majority being around 20.

The first issue that was examined was whether people agree regarding the actions they mention. Obviously, the greatest disagreement occurs when each subject mentions events that are completely unique (i.e., 20 x 56 = 1120 events). However, the 40 events actually obtained indicates that there is considerable agreement regarding the actions and events in a McDonald's purchase episode.

Figure 1 indicates the frequency of mentioning of each statement. In computing these frequencies, multiple mentions of events by subjects were treated as equivalent to single mentions. It shows that in addition to the statements mentioned by the majority of the subjects, about 30% of the statements were mentioned only by a small minority (10%). Clearly, there is considerable agreement regarding the basic event structure of the script. However, some idiosyncratic variation was present as demonstrated by the 12 events mentioned less than 10% of the sample. These events included "cleaning the table before seating" (Event #22), "having a cigarette after eating" (Event #31) and "going to the bathroom" (Event #29) and may represent differences in personal experiences at McDonalds. The events mentioned in the elicited scripts would seem to constitute a common main-event conceptualization along with a number of idiosyncratic events.

In order to assess the degree of agreement regarding the ordering of the events, a paired comparison procedure was used. Each event was compared with all other events to assess whether the subjects agreed regarding their serial ordering. A high level of disagreement would be indicated by equal numbers of subjects reporting each event in a pair as the prior event. Obviously, this comparison is reasonable only if a sufficiently large number of people report both events in an event pair. Consequently, the comparisons are restricted to events mentioned by at least 40% of the subjects. This cut-off was chosen to correspond with the Bower et al. cut-off for high-frequency events. In case of multiple mentions of events by a subject, the net result of the multiple comparisons involving any specific pair are entered. Thus, for instance, if a subject mentioned Event #4 three times, and it appeared once before Event #5, and twice after #5, the net result was that Event #5 occurred after Event #4. In other words, only the net ordinal result was retained. It should be stressed that these multiple mention problems did not occur frequently enough to affect the results significantly.

The results of this procedure are reported in Figure 2. It is most readily interpreted by contrasting the entries in the lower diagonal half with corresponding entries in the upper diagonal for each event pair (i,j). High degrees of agreement are indicated if there is a highly unbalanced distribution of responses. In contrast, if the number of subjects with entries in the upper diagonal box (i,j) is roughly equal to the number in the lower diagonal box (j,i) this would suggest considerable variation between subjects regarding the sequence of that event pair.

The entries in Figure 2 indicate that there is virtually complete agreement among the subjects regarding the hierarchical ordering of the events elicited in the script. The greatest disagreement occurred regarding the event pair (15, 12). Twenty subjects reported that Event #12 ("wait for ordered items") occurred after Event #15 ("pay for ordered items") while seven subjects reported them in the reverse order. The only other event pair showing any significant disagreement was (5, 6). Here, nine subjects said that "they stood in line" and "observed the menu" in that order while six subjects reported these events in the reverse order. This may be explained in one of two ways.

First, it is possible that these actions may occur simultaneously. Alternatively, a subject may be drawing from memory a more general restaurant script upon which modifications are made to conform with the McDonalds experience. However, it is at this point that the individual may confuse certain events or event-sequences with their occurrence or ordering in other restaurants.

DISCUSSION

The results obtained here confirm the shared conceptualization of the main event structure of a script as reported by Bower, Black and Turner (1979). It also extends their results by addressing the issue of inter-subject agreement regarding the ordering of the events. A comparison of the common (at least 40% mention) events obtained from the two studies as shown in Figure 3, show some interesting contrasts. The McDonalds scripts shows a higher degree of mention of common events as evidenced by the larger proportion of capitalized events. This would be expected because the interaction during a purchase episode at McDonalds is a highly programmed sequence of events. In contrast, variations are more likely for restaurants, in general. We speculate that the Bower, Black and Turner data would also show greater disagreement regarding the serial structure of events for the same reasons.

The McDonalds scripts also show the differences between them and other types of restaurants. The present scripts do not include events such as "discuss menu" and "talk" found in the Bower et al. study as high-frequency items of their restaurant scripts. This difference suggests that the elicitation procedure used is sensitive enough to differentiate between scripts that belong in the same generic category. We are cautiously optimistic regarding the development of this methodology for eliciting other scripts at the brand level.

There are several methodological implications of the present study that need to be addressed in future research. While the present investigation revealed very high inter-subject agreement regarding the serial ordering of events, it is unlikely that this will occur in other instances. A pressing need is to develop a procedure for obtaining the "best" estimate of the serial order given some degree of disagreements. A promising approach in this regard is to view the paired comparison data as a dominance matrix and apply multidimensional scaling techniques. Another possibility is to use clustering algorithms to uncover the hierarchical or tree-structures in these data.

Another issue that has to be dealt with in future research is the reliability of the coding procedures used. In the present investigation, the Bower et al. results were available to guide the editing and coding of the elicited scripts. However, the establishment of inter-rater reliability is critical in other instances where no prior results are available.

Finally, it is essential to develop some procedure to describe elicited scripts along evaluative dimensions. Recall that the literature reviewed earlier indicated that script arousal affected attitudinal judgments and behavior. In order to assess these relationships empirically, it is necessary to be able to measure scripts along relevant dimensions (e.g., favorability toward object, a propensity to evoke script behavior in future situations). Presently, we are developing a scoring procedure along the lines of the analysis of cognitive response data. Subjects are requested to examine their elicited scripts and indicate their evaluation of each listed event during past instances of the interactions represented in the scripts. The relationship of these evaluations to attitudes and behavior can be systematically evaluated in experiments involving script arousal effects on these dependent variables.

FIGURE 1

DISTRIBUTION OF FREQUENCY OF MENTION OF SCRIPT EVENTS

Number of Events	Percentage Mention of Events
5	75–100%
5	50–75%
6	25–50%
12	10–25%
12	0–10%
Total 40 events	

FIGURE 2

PAIRED COMPARISONS OF SERIAL ORDERING OF
HIGH-FREQUENCY SCRIPT EVENTS

Event #

i_1 \ j_1	2	5	6	9	12	15	16	21	23	25	33	34	36
1	9	16	14	23	15	20	16	21	16	21	14	18	23
2		18	14	22	11	19	15	19	18	21	12	20	23
5			9	35	19	28	25	29	25	35	18	33	39
6		6*		26	18	24	19	25	21	27	16	26	29
9					30	39*	34	39	34	42	23	40	47
12						7	28	26	20	30	17	26	29
15					20*		34	37	32	40	23	37	43
16						2		30	27	36	19	33	35
21									30	39	23	27	41
23										33	21	37	37
25											24	43	44
33												25	27
34												1	42
36													

*Indicates cell entries included net results of multiple mentions of events.

The entries in cell (i,j) indicate the number of subjects who reported event i occurring _before_ event j. Unless indicated otherwise, entries in the lower diagonal are zero.

FIGURE 3

HIGH-FREQUENCY EVENTS IN ELICITED SCRIPTS

Events from Bower, Black and Turner	Event #	Events from Present Study
Enter	1	ARRIVE
Give reservation name	2	ENTER
BE SEATED	5	STAND IN LINE TO ORDER
Order drinks	6	OBSERVE MENU
Look at menu	9	ORDER ITEMS
Discuss menu	12	WAIT FOR ORDER
ORDER MEAL	15	PAY FOR ORDERED ITEMS
Talk	16	RECEIVE ORDER
Eat salad or soup	21	WALK TO TABLE
EAT FOOD	23	SIT DOWN
Order dessert	25	SET TABLE AND EAT
PAY BILL	33	CLEAR TABLE
Leave tip	34	DISPOSE OF TRASH
LEAVE	36	LEAVE
n=33		n=56

The events in capital letters were mentioned by 50% or more of the subjects. The events in small letters were mentioned by 40–50% of the subjects.

REFERENCES

Abelson, Robert P. (1975), "Concepts for Representing Mundane Reality in Plans," in _Representation and Understanding: Studies in Cognitive Sciences_, D. G. Bobrow and A. Collins, eds., New York: Academic Press.

__________ (1976), "Script Processing in Attitude Formation and Decision Making," _Cognition & Social Behavior_, in John S. Carroll and John W. Payne, eds., Hillsdale, NJ: Lawrence Erlbaum.

__________ (1980), "The Psychological Status of the Script Concept," Cognitive Science Technical Report #2, Yale University, Cognitive Science Program.

Bartlett, F. C. (1932), _Remembering_, Cambridge: Cambridge University Press.

Bower, Gordon H., John B. Black, and Terrence J. Turner (1979), "Scripts in Memory for Text," _Cognitive Psychology_, 11, 177–220.

Bransford, J. D., J. D. Barclay, and J. J. Franks (1972), "Sentence Memory: A Constructive vs. Interpretive Approach," _Cognitive Psychology_, 3, 193–209.

Bransford, J. D. and M. K. Johnson (1972), "Contextual Prerequisites for Understanding: Some Investigations of Comprehension and Recall," _Journal of Verbal Learning and Verbal Behavior_, 11, 717–726.

Cantor, Nancy and Walter Mischel (1977), "Traits as Prototypes: Effects on Recognition Memory," _Journal of Personality and Social Psychology_, 35, 38–48.

Cohen, C. E. (1977), "Cognitive Basis of Stereotyping," paper presented at the American Psychological Association Annual Meeting, San Francisco.

Dooling, D. J. and R. L. Mullet (1973), "Locus of Thematic Effects in Retention of Prose," _Journal of Experimental Psychology_, 97, 404–406.

Fiske, S. and D. Kinder (1978), "Schemas and Political Information Processing," paper presented at American Psychological Association, Toronto, Canada.

Lawler, E. (1973), _Motivation in Work Organizations_, Belmont, CA: Brooks-Cole.

Loftus, E. F. and J. C. Palmer (1974), "Reconstruction of Automobile Destruction: An Example of the Interaction Between Language and Memory," _Journal of Verbal Learning and Verbal Behavior_, 13, 585–589.

Mandler, J. M. (1978), "A Code in the Node," _Discourse Processes_, 1, 14–35.

Markus, Hazel (1977), "Self-Schemata and Processing Information About the Self," _Journal of Personality and Social Psychology_, 35, 63–78.

Martin, J. (1977), "When Prosperity Fails: Distributional Determinants of the Perception of Justice," unpublished doctoral dissertation, Harvard University.

Mettee, D. R., S. E. Taylor, and H. Freedman (1973), "Affect Conversion and the Gain-Loss Effects," _Sociometry_, 36, 494–513.

Minsky, M. (1975), "A Framework for Representing Knowledge," in The Psychology of Computer Vision, P. H. Winston (ed.), New York: McGraw-Hill.

Nisbett, Richard, and Lee Ross (1980), Human Inference:
Strategies and Shortcomings of Social Judgment, Englewood Cliffs, NJ: Prentice-Hall, Inc.

Olshavsky, Richard W. and Donald H. Granbois (1979), "Consumer Decision Making--Fact or Fiction?," Journal of
Consumer Research, 6, 93-100.

Rumelhart, D. E. and A. Ortony (1976), "The Representation
of Knowledge in Memory," in Schooling and the Acquisition of Knowledge, R. C. Anderson, R. J. Spiro, and W.
E. Montague (eds.), Hillsdale, NJ: Erlbaum.

Schank, Roger C. and Robert P. Abelson (1977), Scripts,
Plans, Goals, and Understanding: An Inquiry into Human
Knowledge Structures, Hillsdale, NJ: Lawrence Erlbaum.

Snyder, M. and S. W. Uranowitz (1978), "Reconstructing the
Past: Some Cognitive Consequences of Person Perception,"
Journal of Personality and Social Psychology, 36,
941-950.

Taylor, S. E. and Jennifer Crocker (1981), "Schematic
Bases of Social Information Processing," in The Ontario
Symposium on Personality and Social Psychology, E. T.
Higgins, P. Hermann, and M. P. Zanna, eds., Vol. 1,
Hillsdale, NJ: Lawrence Erlbaum.

Taylor, S. E., J. Crocker, and J. D'Agostino (1978),
"Schematic Bases of Social Problem Solving," 4, 447-451.

COGNITIVE STRUCTURE IN BUYING:
ITS GENERALITY IN ANOTHER CULTURE

Chin Tiong Tan, National University of Singapore
Hui Hoon Lim, Ngee Ann Polytechnic, Singapore

ABSTRACT

Evidence of the generality of congitive complexity in buying has been reported in the literature. This study
examines the same theoretical issue in a different culture.
Findings suggest that the construct is a rather consistent
mode of cognitive functioning across three product classes. A sex difference in generality was also found.

INTRODUCTION

In the last two decades, empirical research on consumer
behavior has flourished in the marketing literature. To
date, almost every theory from the social and behavioral
sciences has been borrowed and studied in the buying
domain. In general, most of the studies were conducted
in the Northern America, some in the Western Europe and
very little in the other parts of the world. Hence, it
is not unreasonable to criticize the discripline of
consumer behavior as having too narrow an empirical base
that is strongly rooted in the Western culture.

Among the new disciplines, a restrictive research domain
is often common. Consumer behavior is of no exception.
Being such a young subject it needs to take a while
before reaching maturity. However, researchers can help
its growth by adopting a broader empirical base in
research. In fact, the tradition to test concepts in new
domains and to replicate studies in different situations
is very much a part of the matured disciplines. For
example, sociology; economics; and psychology are definitely not lacking in empirical studies in different
situations and countries. Hence, for consumer behavior
to mature as a discipline, more research needs to be
conducted in different countries.

With this in mind, this study investigates a psychological
phenomenon reported in the U.S. in a different culture.
The objective is to examine whether the phenomenon is
cross-cultural in nature. The issue of interest here is
the generality of cognitive structure across different
product classes. More specifically, this research
examines the extent the generality of cognitive complexity
in buying is a cross-cultural phenomenon. The question of
whether a certain aspect of consumer behavior is a cross-
cultural phenomenon is important because it has practical
implications to international marketers planning marketing strategies in the foreign countries.

THEORY OF COGNITIVE COMPLEXITY

Treating a person's cognitive structure as a personality
attribute is not new in psychology. However, such an
approach is a relatively recent one in marketing.

The cognitive structure of a person is the hypothetical
link between stimulus inputs and judgemental outputs.
Psychologists have documented that differences in the
structure are instrumental in the persons' variation of
responses (Kelly 1955; Bieri 1971; and Schroder 1970).

It is suggested that cognitive structure is a system of
dimensions, elements or constructs. The relationships
among these elements determine the complexity of the
structure. In business and psychology several structural
characteristics such as the number of salient dimensions
(dimensionality), the articulation of dimensions
(discrimination), the extent dimensions are used in an
identical way (differentiation), and the ways dimensions
are related or organized (integration) have been
documented to mediate a wide range of behaviors (Schroder
1971; Bieri 1971). The label cognitive complexity has
been used loosely to denote the intensity of any one of
these characteristics.

In psychology, the empirical foundation of cognitive
complexity is rich. Since the interest here is strictly
differentiative complexity, only research on the
construct is examined. Researchers have found the
construct to affect a host of behaviors. For example, it
affects the accuracy of the prediction of another person's
behaviors (Bieri 1955), it is also related to attitude
change (Lundy and Berkowitz 1957), and information
processing behaviors (Petronko and Perrin 1970). Other
psychological constructs related to differentative
complexity include confidence (Tripodi and Bieri 1964),
probability preferences (Higgins 1959), and stereotyping
(Koening and King 1962).

In marketing, interests in cognitive complexity is recent.
Stiles (1974) found integrative complexity to be related
to information processing, and Park and Sheth (1975)
documented the effects of dimensional complexity on
usage of judgemental rules. Other researchers also found
dimensionality to be related to several personality
characteristics (Wilson and Tan 1977), and differentiative
complexity to be a moderating variable in usage of choice
models (Tan and Dolich 1980).

Cognitive Complexity as a Generalized Style

Although psychology theory has treated cognitive complexity
as a personality structure, the construct's generalized
characteristic is, however, empirically unresolved.
Adopting a rather similar orientation in differentiative
complexity, a group of psychologists found the construct
to correlate across different stimulus realms (Hall 1966;
Bieri and Blacker 1956; Allard and Carlson 1963) while
others like Scott (1963) and Signell (1966) argued that
it is less general and more like a domain specific
construct.

The generality issue was tested in the buying domain by
Tan and Dolich (1979). They found cognitive complexity to
be a rather consistent mode of cognitive functioning across
three product classes. In addition, they found psychologists' warning of a possible sex difference in generality
to have some support in marketing. In their research, the
male subjects exhibited slightly stronger generalized
relationship than the female subjects.

RESEARCH OBJECTIVE

Thus far, all the published empirical tests on the
generality of complexity have been conducted in the
Western culture. This study tested the same issue in a
different culture. Specifically, issues investigated in

the study by Tan and Dolich (1979) were examined in Singapore.

Singapore is an ideal site for cross-cultural research for the following reasons:

1 It is the second richest country in Asia after Japan. Hence, while all the features and characteristics of a developed western nation can be found there. The population, which is predominantly Chinese (75%), has a culture distinctly different from that of the west. Among its people, traditional values, closed family ties and the preachings of oriental philosophy are still highly treasured. Such an environment is a realistic one for cross-cultural research as it is not drastically different from or similar to the West. Finding any cross-cultural difference or similarity in research is therefore less obvious in this case.

2 English is one of the official languages in Singapore. It is widely used in schools, colleges, and businesses. Most people, especially the younger ones, know the language well. Conducting cross-cultural research there is therefore easy.

In this study, the following issues were examined:

1 Whether cognitive complexity is a generalized style in a different culture.

2 Whether males and females in a different culture differ on the generality of the construct.

RESEARCH METHODOLOGY

Respondents for this research were students attending the National University of Singapore. Since the research objective here is to test theoretical relationships using student subjects should not pose a serious problem.

Product Selection

A pre-test was conducted for product selection. Since college students were used as subjects, the products to be included in the study were selected from a list of products that they were familiar with. In order to study a range of product classes, three products of differential importance were needed. Furthermore, in order to adopt the Repertory Grid as a research method, product classes need to have multiple brands. The products in a decreasing order of importance were wrist watches; jeans; and soft drinks.

Research Instruments

The research instrument used to measure cognitive complexity was the modified Kelly's Repertory Grid Method (Kelly 1955). The original Repertory Grid was used in the clinical setting for elicitation of cognitive dimensions for ratings of stimulus objects. A completed grid was a matrix of ratings capturing a person's repertorie of cognitive evaluation.

In this study, the dimensions and brands for each product class were pre-determined from the pre-tests. Only the well-known brands and salient dimensions were included in the grid. The standardized Repertory Grid was found to be superior if not comparable to the original grid. It has replaced the original in many studies (Bieri 1970).

In each grid, 8 brands were provided horizontally and 8 dimensions all with positive and negative poles were listed vertically. Subjects were asked to treat each dimension like 6-point Likert type bi-polar scale ranging from +3, +2, +1, −1, −2, −3 to rate all the brands.

The 8 brands and 8 dimensions for the three products are as follows:

Brands

	Soft Drinks	Jeans	Wrist Watches
1	Coca-Cola	Wrangler	Seiko
2	Fanta	Levis	Pagol
3	Mirinda	Lee	Citizen
4	Pepsi-cola	Texwood	Titoni
5	7-Up	Peace & Joy (PJ)	Rolex
6	F & N	Rodeo	Tissot
7	Kickapoo	Roy	Timex
8	Wink	Amco	Omega

Dimensions

	Soft Drinks	Jeans	Wrist Watches
1	Good quality	Good quality	Durable
2	Popular brand	Nice cutting	Fashion
3	Refreshing	Popular brand	Well manufactured
4	Thirst quenching	Stylish	Not expensive
5	Right gassires	Wide color range	Prestigious brand
6	Right sweetness	Prestigious brand	Multiple functions
7	Nice Flavor	Not expensive	Dependable
8	Easily Available	Nice overall appearance	Large selection

In the present research, cognitive complexity is defined as the extent the dimensions are used in a differentiated manner when evaluating the product class (Bieri 1966). It is the same definition adopted in the study of Tan and Dolich (1979). Similarly, the matching of dimensions procedure as proposed by Bieri is adopted here (refer to Bieri et al. 1966, and Tan and Dolich 1979 for a detailed discussion of the method). Briefly, ratings on each dimensions were compared one at a time with ratings of all other dimensions for identical ratings. In a 8 x 8 matrix, a total of 28 combinations of comparisons was possible. If each exact match was counted as one point, a large total number of matches indicated that the dimensions were used identically or undifferentiated. A high score therefore denotes a simple cognitive structure.

ANALYSES AND FINDINGS

To analyze the generality of cognitive complexity, Pearson correlations were used to determine the strength of relationships across the three product classes (Bieri and Blacker 1956; Hall 1966; Tan and Dolich 1979). In Table One, inter-correlations of the subjects' cognitive complexity for all pairs of product classes are presented. Correlation analyses were also performed for each sex group. Results are presented in the same table.

TABLE 1: INTER-CORRELATIONS OF SUBJECTS'
COGNITIVE COMPLEXITY FOR ALL PAIRS OF
PRODUCT CLASSES

Products	Total (n=118)	Male (n=65)	Female (n=53)
Wrist watches/Jeans	.3366[a]	.4452[a]	.2021[c]
Wrist watches/Soft Drinks	.1802[b]	.2055[b]	.1845[c]
Jeans/Soft Drinks	.2649[a]	.3704[a]	.1813[c]

a < 0.01
b < 0.05
c < 0.10

It can be seen from Table One that correlations for the
total sample are all positive and statistically significant. Results can be taken to mean that persons who are
cognitively complex in their evaluation of one product
class tend to be more complex in their evaluation of the
other product classes as well. Tan and Dolich's finding
of generality of cognitive complexity in buying is therefore supported in a different culture. However, it must
be pointed out that like in their study, relationships
found here were not particularly strong. Hence, the
generally weak relationships in personality studies is
not unique to Western culture alone.

When each sex group was analyzed separately, results once
again supported psychologists' claim that sex difference
could be a factor in the functionings of cognition. In
this study, correlations for the male group were all
significant and stronger than those of the female group
or the total sample. Females exhibited weaker relationships and all three correlations failed the 0.05 level of
statistical significance. A t-test was conducted to
compare statistical difference between the two groups. It
was found to be significant at the 0.05 level. The findings therefore suggest that sex difference in generality
could even be more pronounced in oriental culture.

DISCUSSIONS

In psychology, empirical evidence on the generality of
cognitive complexity was documented. In the buying
domain, Tan and Dolich found the construct to be a rather
consistent mode of cognitive functioning across three
product classes. This study tested the same issue in a
different culture - Singapore, a predominantly Chinese
society.

Findings indicate that cognitive complexity is a fairly
consistent trait even in a non-western culture. This
finding has practical implications. It is obvious that if
functionings of cognitive structure can be treated as a
person's style that he manifests across product situations,
they can be used as market segmentation variables. Such
uses need not be restricted to the domestic market as the
results here indicate foreign consumers to exhibit a
similar generalized style in cognitive behavior.

The notion that cognitive complexity influences the way a
consumer evaluates; selects; and processes product information is well accepted in marketing. The cross-cultural
characteristic of the construct suggests the possibility of
segmenting world consumers into different style segments.
Each segment can then be dealt with using different
marketing approaches.

The second research issue of a sex difference in generality
is also supported in the oriental culture. In fact, the
sex factor was found to be more significant in this research than that reported in Tan and Dolich's study. One
explanation is that females have a tendency to be more
articulate and careful, and therefore more differentiative
in evaluating product classes that are salient to them.
In product classes that they are less involved with, they
consistently show simpler cognitive evaluations. However,
males are probably more stable in their cognitive functionings. Those who develop a differentiative cognition tend
to utilize it across product classes, while those who
prefer a simpler approach also remain so consistently.

Such a finding suggests different treatments for the two
groups. In the case of the male segment, treating
cognitive complexity as a personality trait, and adopting
one generalized measurement for the group is feasible.
Whereas, the female group requires measurements that are
product class or domain specific.

Cognitive structure as a personality style of a person
appears to exhibit evidence as a cross-cultural
phenomenon. Although results from a handful of empirical
research are not sufficient to justify such a generalization, the initial evidence we have thus far is encouraging. In general, if a psychological phenomenon found in
the U.S. is also found in the other cultures, it indicates
the universal character of the construct.

The attempt to replicate studies in different cultures
and to identify similarities or differences of behavior
is important in international marketing. It helps
marketers decide the extent international marketing
strategies can be standardized. With the growing
importance of international marketing, it is anticipated
that in the near future, more cross-cultural consumer
research will appear in the literature.

REFERENCES

Allard, M. and Carlson, E. R. (1963), "The Generality of
Cognitive Complexity," Journal of Social Psychology, 59.

Bannister, D. and Mair, J. M. (1968), The Evaluation of
Personal Constructs, London: Academic Press.

Bieri, J. (1955), "Cognitive Complexity-Simplicity and
Predictive Behavior," Journal of Abnormal and Social
Psychology, 51.

_______ (1971), "Cognitive Structures in Personality," in
H. M. Schroder and P. Suedfeld, (ed), Personality Theory
and Information Processing, New York: Ronald Press.

_______ and Blacker, E. (1956), "The Generality of
Cognitive Complexity in the Perception of People and
Inkblot,"Journal of Abnormal and Social Psychology, 52.

Caracena, P. F. and King, G. E. (1962), "Generality of
Individual Differences in Complexity," Journal of
Clinical Psychology, 18.

Hall, M. F. (1966), The Generality of Cognitive Complexity
-Simplicity. An unpublished PhD Dissertation, Department of Psychology, The Vanderbilt University.

Higgins, J. C. (1959), "Cognitive Complexity and Probability Preference," unpublished manuscript, Department of
Psychology, University of Chicago.

Kasulis, J. and Zaltman, G. (1976), "Message Reception
and Cognitive Complexity," in Perrault, W. (ed.)
Advances in Consumer Research, Vol. IV.

Kelly, G. A. (1955), Psychology of Personal Constructs,
New York: Norton Press.

Koening, F. W. and King, M. (1964), "Cognitive Simplicity
and Out-Group Sterotyping," Social Forces.

Lundy, R. and Berkowitz, L. (1957), "Cognitive Complexity
and Assimilative Projection in Attitude Change,"
Journal of Abnormal and Social Psychology, 55.

Menasco, M. (1976), "A Further Exploration of the
Moderating Effects of Cognitive Complexity Upon
Consumer Choice Behavior." Working Paper of the
Bureau of Business and Economic Research, University of
Iowa, July.

Mueller, Walter W. (1974). "Cognitive Complexity and
Salience of Dimensions in Person Perception"
Australian Journal of Psychology.

Park, W. and Sheth, J. (1975), "Impact of Prior Familiarity and Cognitive Complexity on Information Processing

Rules," <u>Communication Research,</u> Vol. 2, No. 3, July.

Petronko, M. and Perin, T. (1970), "A Consideration of Cognitive Complexity and Primacy-Recency Effects in Impression Formation," <u>Journal of Personality and Social Psychology</u>, 15.

Schroder, H. M. (1971), <u>Personality Theory and Information Processing</u>, New York: Ronald Press.

________, Driver, M., and Streufert, S. (1967), <u>Human Information Processing</u>, New York: Holt, Rinehart and Winston.

Scott, W. A. (1962), "Cognitive Complexity and Cognitive Flexibility," <u>Sociometry</u>, 25.

________ (1963), "Cognitive Complexity and Balance," <u>Sociometry</u>, 26.

Signell, K. A. (1966), "Cognitive Complexity in Person Perception and in Nation Perception: A Developmental Approach," <u>Journal of Personality</u>, 34.

Stiles, G. (1974), "Determinants of Industrial Buyer's Level of Information Processing: Organizations, Situations and Individual Differences," in D. Hughes and M. Ray (eds) <u>Buyer/Consumer Information Processing</u>, Chapel Hill, North Carolina: University of North Carolina Press.

Tan, C. T. and Dolich, I. (1979), "Cognitive Structure in Personality: An Investigation of Its Generality in Buying Behavior," in J. Olson (ed.) <u>Advances in Consumer Research</u>, Vol. 7.

________ and ________ (1980), "The Moderating Effects of Cognitive Complexity and Prior Product Familiarity on the Predictive Ability of Selected Multi-Attribute Choice Models for Three Consumer Products," in K. Monroe (ed.) <u>Advances in Consumer Research</u>, Vol. 8.

Tripodi, T. and Bieri, J. (1966) "Cognitive Complexity, Perceived Conflict, and Certainty," <u>Journal of Personality</u>, 31.

Vannoy, J. S. (1965), "Generality of Cognitive Complexity-Simplicity as a Personality Construct," <u>Journal of Personality and Social Psychology</u>, 2.

Wilson, D. T. and Tan C. T. (1977), "Dimensional Complexity of Cognitive Structure: A Personality Trait in Decision Making," in Stolen, J. D. and Conway, J. J. eds. <u>Proceedings of the American Institute of Decision Sciences Annual Meeting</u>.

AN EXAMINATION OF ETHNICITY AND CONSUMPTION USING FREE RESPONSE DATA

Elizabeth C. Hirschman, New York University

ABSTRACT

A brief framework for consumer ethnicity is presented which
is followed by an empirical examination of three exploratory hypotheses derived from this framework. These are tested and confirmed using the ethnic dimensions of race and
religion.

INTRODUCTION

This paper presents a brief framework for consumer ethnicity which is followed by an empirical examination of three
exploratory hypotheses derived from this framework. These
hypotheses will be tested using the ethnic dimensions of
race and religion. Two racial categories are studied:Amer-
ican Caucasian (white) and American Negro (black). Three
religious categories are examined: Catholic, Protestant,
and Jewish. The proposed relationships between ethnicity
and consumption are calculated on a bidimensional basis (i.
e., white Catholic, black Protestant, white Protestant, and
white Jewish).

Categorizing Ethnic Groups

Following from the work of Barth (1969) and Cohen (1978),
ethnicity is viewed as a subjective process of group identification in which people use ethnic labels to define
themselves and others. That is, an ethnic group exists
when a set of individuals assign to themselves a common
label. The ascription of an ethnic label to oneself and
to others provides a basis for the establishment of social
boundaries (Barth 1969). As such, the ethnic label may
act as a point of demarcation for consumption beliefs and
actions.

A Hierarchy of Ethnicity

An important extension to this reasoning is offered by
Vincent (1974) and Cohen (1978). They note the systemic
level at which ethnicity is subjectively perceived and used
as a basis for action "can be narrowed or broadened...in
relation to the specific needs of mobilization" (Cohen 1978,
p. 386). In other words, an individual may redefine his/
her ethnicity at more general or specific levels depending
upon the particular context of behavior.

Cohen (1978, p. 387) suggests that ethnicity is, therefore,
most appropriately viewed as "a series of nesting dichoto-
mizations of inclusiveness and exclusiveness...similar to
that of a social distance scale in which the greater the
number of diacritical (i.e., distinguishing) markers, the
closer one gets of a particular person and/or his kin group.
... The number of diacritics (i.e., distinguishing attributes) increases with the scale of exclusiveness." General
distinctions (e.g., black/white), which include the greatest number of people, are used to establish the outermost
boundaries of an ethnic group, while characteristics that
distinguish at more specific levels increase in salience
when more finely articulated groupings are required (e.g.,
Irish Catholic whites vs. Irish Protestant whites).

One predictive and descriptive value of this perspective of
ethnicity is that at increasing levels of specificity, increasing homogeneity of consumer belief and behavior
should be found. That is, all Catholics may possess some
common consumption traits, due to their religious homogeneity. However, all Catholics who are also Irish would be
expected to exhibit even more common consumption traits,
since they share both religious and national heritage.

HYPOTHESES

Three general hypotheses were advanced regarding ethnicity
and consumption. Because of prior findings, the first of
these could be extended to two, more specific sub-hypothesis. However, the latter two general hypotheses have not
been examined previously, and hence cannot be stated in a
specific manner.

H1: The average number of word associations provided to
product stimuli will vary across ethnic groups. This hypothesis is premised on the empirical observation that
ethnic groupings differ in their verbal fluency (Hirschman
1981, Jensen 1980). Based on prior studies two, more specific sub-hypotheses may be stated:

H1.a: White consumers will provide more word associations
to product stimuli, on average, than will black consumers
(Jensen 1980).

H1.b: Jewish consumers will provide more word associations to product stimuli, on average, than other ethnic
groups (Hirschman 1981).

A second, general hypotheses was:

H2: The relative salience of products will vary across
ethnic groups, where salience is measured as the number of
word associations provided for the product. This hypothesis
is premised on the general observation that group norms
often stress different aspects of the consumption environs
in different ethnic groups, for example, the emphasis upon
education among Jews and upon family relations among
Catholics (Greeley 1974). Such differing emphases may
lead to variation in product salience across ethnic groups.

A third, general hypothesis was:

H3: Operant ethnic boundaries for product meaning will
vary across products, where product meaning is measured as
the most frequent response given to a product stimulus.
This hypothesis is premised on the general observation
that products may have specific meanings within particular
ethnic groups. For example, music may evoke thoughts of
rock 'n roll among white Protestants, jazz among Jews,
and disco among blacks.

AN EXPLORATORY EXAMINATION

One valid way for assessing the cultural similarity of two
or more social groupings is by measuring the overlap of
semantic associations they have concerning the same stimulus (Triandis 1972). For example, to the extent that
members of two societies attribute the same meaning to the
same product, they possess the same subjective culture
(Triandis 1972). This position may be supported from two
perspectives. First, sociologists investigating the accu-
mulation of knowledge (e.g., Gurvitch 1971, Merton 1937)
propose that reality is inherently a social construction.
Gurvitch (1971), for example, discusses the cognitive systems created and maintained by social groups such as reli-
gions, states, and communities. Using this view, we may
examine ethnic groups as representing cognitive systems;
group members share beliefs based on a reality that is,
to some extent, unique or idiosyncratic to their group.

A second source of support is the view of cross-cultural
psychologists such as Triandis (1972) and Deese (Szaley
and Deese 1978). As Triandis (1972, p.4) states, "Subjec-

tive culture is a cultural groups' characteristic way of perceiving the man-made part of its environment." Deese (1963, 1965, 1975) has demonstrated that the free-response verbal associations characterizing individuals in various cultures and subcultures appear to reflect differences in their subjective perceptions of reality. Hence, to the extent that ethnic group members share cognitions unlike those possessed by nonmembers, they reside in a distinct culture.

<u>Sample</u>

Subjects for the research consisted of 138 students enrolled in undergraduate behavioral science and business courses at Georgia State University (Atlanta, Ga.), who were administered structured questionnaires in class. Ethnic group assignments were arrived at by the subjective self-assignment of an individual to both a religious and racial ethnic group. To measure their ethnicity, subjects responded to the following questions: (1) Do you have a religious affiliation: If so, please indicate your religious affiliation below. a. Catholic, b. Jewish, c. Protestant, d. Other, e. None, (2) Do you have an ethnic/racial affiliation? If so, please indicate the ethnic/racial group with which you primarily identify. a. Black, b. Hispanic, c. Japanese, d. Italian, e. Irish, f. Jewish, g. Chinese, h. Greek, i. Other, J. None.

Respondents who reported themselves as white[1] Catholics (n=20) were so classified for this research; similarly, respondents who reported themselves as white Protestants (n=66), black Protestants (n=24), and Jews[2] (n=28) were placed into these categories. Categorization was done on a bidimensional (religion-race) basis intitially, to aid in simplifying comparative analyses. Family income, age, marital status and personal education attainment displayed no significant differences (p=.20) across the four ethnic categories.

Despite the fact that no demographic differences were observed across the ethnic groups, the sample possesses several limitations as regards its external validity. First, the subjects were all undergraduate college students and, hence, their responses may differ from those in different age or educational cohorts. Second, the subjects were residing in an urban, Southeastern environment, which may cause them to differ from persons residing in rural or suburban settings or in other regions of the United States. Finally, the Southern locale of the study may interact with racial and/or religious ethnicity in unique ways. The reader is therefore urged to restrict generalizations from the study to similar subjects and settings.

<u>Stimulus Set</u>

The stimulus set consisted of 15 product names from four consumption domains: food, clothing, entertainment, and transportation. The product names (listed in Table 1) were drawn from varying levels of generality/specificity within each domain. After being verbally presented with a stimulus word, subjects were instructed to write down word associations during a timed, 60-second interval (Szalay and Deese 1978). This procedure continued until associations had been provided to all 15 product-name stimuli.

---

[1] Into the "white" category were placed Irish, Italian and self-labeled 'WASP', 'Caucasian', and 'white' respondents. There were no Hispanic, Chinese, Japanese, or Greek respondents.

[2] Respondents classified as Jews used that self-label in both the religious and ethnic/racial questions.

<u>Commonality of Associations</u>

The first observation is that the larger the sample size of the ethnic group, the more intersubject commonality, or overlap, occurred among responses to the product stimuli.[3] For example, the white Protestants (n=66) consistently produced more shared responses than did the white Catholics (n=20). This is probably a result of a greater central tendency operating for larger group sizes. The proportion of commonality in responses is given in Table 1 for each ethnic group. Kruskal-Wallis one-way analysis of variance by ranks indicated that commonality was related to ethnic group sample size at $p \leq .01$. Hence, it is inappropriate to compare proportionate commonality of responses across ethnic groups, because the distribution of commonality is tied to sample size and the independent effects of ethnicity on response commonality cannot be readily assessed.[4]

<u>Hypothesis One: Average Number of Associations</u>

The average number of words given in response to a particular stimulus is listed in Table 2 by ethnic group. As hypothesized all white ethnic groups provided more responses, on average, than the black Protestant ethnic group. The white Catholic average was 4.7, the Jewish average was 4.5, and the white Protestant average was 4.1; all of which were significantly greater than the black Protestant average of 2.8 ($p \leq .05$, Scheffé).

However, contrary to the second sub-hypothesis, Jewish consumers were not found higher than all other ethnic groups in number of word associations. While Jewish consumers ($\bar{x}=4.5$) significantly exceeded black consumers ($\bar{x}=2.8$) in this respect, they were insignificantly higher than white Protestant consumers ($\bar{x}=4.1$) and were insignificantly exceeded by white Catholic consumers ($\bar{x}=4.7$). The unexpectedly high verbal fluency among white Catholic consumers is perhaps due to the high proportion of persons of Irish descent in this sample (80%). As Greeley (1977) notes, Irish Catholics exhibit above average levels of achievement motivation, which is often linked to above average verbal fluency.

<u>Hypothesis Two: Variance in Product Salience</u>

To determine if there were variation in product salience within and across the four ethnic groups examined here, the data in Table 3 were prepared. These data are derived from the response averages given in Table 2. The average number of responses given per product was converted to an intraethnic ranking, because the previously noted variation in absolute response rates by the ethnic groups rendered direct mean-to-mean, cross-group comparisons invalid. Hence, the data were converted to ordinal rankings in order to make cross-group comparisons possible.

---

[3] A commonality index was computed for each product stimulus by dividing the number of different words given in response to the stimulus by the total number of responses. For example, if black Protestants named 25 different words in response to the product stimulus "entertainment", and provided a total of 50 responses to that stimulus, the commonality index is .5. The value of the index can range between 0 and 1. The closer to 1, the <u>lower</u> the commonality of responses given to a particular stimulus. Conversely, the closer to 0, the more respondents tended to give the same words for a given stimulus.

[4] A reviewer has suggested two ways to overcome this problem. First, respondents could be randomly deleted from the larger groups until equal sample sizes were obtained. Several replications of n=20 could provide good estimates of within-group commonalities. Alternatively, one could empirically obtain clusters in the sample which exhibit

These data exhibited an interesting correlative pattern, shown below. The highest congruence of product rank-order salience was found between white and black Protestant consumers (tau=.70). The members of these two ethnic groups share religious ethnicity, but not racial ethnicity. Conversely, for persons sharing racial ethnicity, but not religious ethnicity (e.g., Jewish and white Catholic subjects), the highest correlation was .60. This correlation significantly differed from the prior one at p $\leq$.10. This appears to suggest that for the subjects and products studied here, religious ethnicity may perhaps be more related to differences in product salience (measured as the number of word associations) than is racial ethnicity.

A second point suggesting religion may generate stronger subcultural differences for product salience than does race is that Jewish consumers exhibited the lowest correlation of product salience with the other three groups—all of which are Christian (J to WP = .60, J to WC = .53, J to BP = .52). In about half of these instances, the correlation was significantly lower for Jewish consumers than for those from the other ethnic groups (p $\leq$.10). Hence, drawing the ethnic boundary at the very general religious level of Christian/Jew, it is observed that there may be greater divergence of cultural patterns for product salience than when the ethnic boundary is drawn at the very general racial level of black/white.

Finally, the product salience rankings of the three minority ethnic groups (i.e., Jewish, white Catholic, black Protestant) exhibit a higher level of correlation with the majority ethnic group (e.g., white Protestant) than they do with each other. This may indicate that the pattern of cultural salience for products emanates primarily from the majority group. That is, patterns for the salience of products within the majority ethnic group may overlap those of the minority ethnic groups more than salience patterns from minority groups overlap with those of each other.

Hypothesis Three: Specific Product Associations

The third hypothesis examined the pattern of interethnic response differences found for each product.[5] The operant ethnic boundary for a given product was determined by comparing the <u>most frequently given response</u> across the four ethnic groups.[6] Using this procedure, some interesting exploratory observations may be derived. First, the most salient ethnic boundary for product associations, based upon the consumers and products studied here, appears to be the general racial dichotomy of black/white. Five (33%) of the products studied generated associational patterns whose most common response could best be partitioned racially: Entertainment, Movies, Pants, Shoes, and Ice Cream. This would seem to suggest that the cognitive associations made with products are more differentiated between racial categories of consumers than between religious categories.[7]

Also of interest is the fact that the general religious dichotomy, Christian/Jew, served as the basis for no associational distinctions. That is, in no instance did the three Christian groups (i.e., white Protestant, black Protestant, white Catholic) provide a most frequent common response that differed from that given most often by the Jewish consumers. Similar to this is the fact that the more specific religious typology of Protestant/Catholic/Jew did not serve as a relevant associational boundary for any products. Thus, in contrast to the findings concerning the ethnic salience of all products (Table 2) in which religion demonstrated more relevance as a discriminatory

device than did race; when specific word associations are being compared, race appears to be the more relevant discriminator.

The most frequent responses to three products—Food, Transportation, and Dairy Products—were common across all four ethnic groups. Thus, for these products, ethnic boundaries do not appear operative; the products are perceived similarly regardless of ethnicity. Conversely, the most frequent responses to two products—Clothing and Bicycles—were dissimilar across all four ethnic groups, suggesting high specificity of ethnic boundaries.

One product—Public Transportation—had the same most frequent response given by the three minority ethnic groups—white Catholic, black Protestant, and Jewish—in contrast to the association given most often by the majority ethnic group, white Protestant. Another product—Music—displayed associational commonality among white Christians (white Catholics, white Protestants), but was different for Jewish and black Protestant consumers. Finally, three products—Meat, Rock 'n' Roll, and Sneakers—displayed commonality of most frequent associations between two ethnic groups which were unrelated either racially or religiously.

SUMMARY AND CONCULSIONS

Keeping in mind the restricted nature of the sample, which may limit its external validity, several tentative generalizations may be suggested. First, ethnicity appears to be linked to consumer verbal fluency. White Catholic and Jewish consumers were found to provide more responses per product stimulus than white or black Protestants. Further, black Protestants consistently provided the fewest number of associations to the product stimuli. This suggests that there may be complex interactive relationships between religious and racial ethnicity and product word associational quantity.

Second, rank-order comparisons of product salience (measured as the average number of associations) revealed that salience patterns were more similar between white and black Protestant consumers and less similar between Jewish consumers and the other ethnic groups examined. This suggests that the general religious distinction of Christian/Jew perhaps may be the most discriminative subculture boundary for product salience patterns.

Third, the product salience rankings for the three minority ethnic groups (Jewish, white Catholic, black Protestant) displayed a higher level of correlation with the majority ethnic group (white Protestant) than they did with each other. This was interpreted as indicating that cultural norms concerning product salience may emanate from the dominant subculture.

Fourth, the pattern of most frequent responses for the fifteen stimulus products showed a complex interaction with ethnicity. Although most products generated most frequent responses that were more consistent within rather than across ethnic groupings, for three of the products examined the most common response was identical across ethnic categories. It appears that ethnic boundaries for product meaning are not operant in every instance. Further, for the products and respondents in the present research, it appears that race (black/white) is the primary ethnic dimension distinguishing between response content patterns.

---

[5]Complete listings of all responses provided to each product are available from the author.

[6]The most frequent response is generally considered to be the most reliable indicator of subcultural stimulus meaning (Szalay and Deese 1978).

[7]Recall that religion, however, was found to be more relevant for describing patterns of product <u>salience</u> (Table 3).

---

similar word associations and then crosstabulate them with the a priori ethnic typology. While these two options are excellent and appropriate, they are not used here due to time constraints on data re-analysis.

The present results illustrate, in an exploratory fashion,
the potential for ethnic influence in the perception of
products. However, the present data are limited in that
they are static; we have no knowledge of the factors that
may have influenced the respondents prior to their supply-
ing semantic association to the product stimuli. Future
research in this area should address issues not resolvable
given the present data, but which may enable us to understand better the influence of ethnicity on consumption.
First, the dynamic nature of ethnic identify could be
examined under varied environmental conditions. For example, does ethnicity exert a strong influence on consumption patterns in certain situations, while having no effect under other conditions? Second, the range of consumption areas in which ethnic influence is operational may
extend to many other activities relevant to marketing, such
as voting trends, fertility levels, product innovativeness,
and product information seeking (e.g., Hirschman 1981).
If future research demonstrates that the ethnic identity
of a consumer influences his/her behavior in areas such as
these, then ethnicity may emerge as one of the dominant
mechanisms for market segmentation.

	White Prot.	Jewish	White Cath.	Black Prot.
White Prot.	1	.60	.60	.70
Jewish		1	.53	.52
White Cath.			1	.58
Black Prot.				1

p <.005 in all instances (Kendall's tau)

Table 1

Proportion of Response Dissimilarity

	White Prot.	White Jewish	White Cath.	Black Prot.
Public Transportation	43	52	71	47
Music	56	58	88	76
Rock 'n' Roll	59	64	89	73
Movie	73	89	81	85
Meat	37	53	79	64
Shoes	56	76	91	81
Dairy Products	41	67	49	36
Transportation	39	47	61	49
Food	61	67	84	81
Clothing	58	70	88	62
Entertainment	41	52	63	57
Ice Cream	45	61	76	65
Bicycle	50	73	84	66
Pants	56	67	83	81
Sneakers	45	56	82	64
n=	66	28	20	24

Table 2

Average Number of Associations

	White Prot.	White Jewish	White Cath.	Black Prot.
	$\bar{x}$	$\bar{x}$	$\bar{x}$	$\bar{x}$
Public Transportation	3.9	4.6	4.1	2.6
Music	4.5	4.7	4.9	2.8
Rock 'n' Roll	4.0	3.8	4.9	2.0
Movie	2.7	3.4	4.1	1.5
Meat	3.8	5.1	5.1	2.3
Shoes	3.2	3.2	4.2	2.1
Dairy Products	3.3	2.8	5.0	2.8
Transportation	5.5	6.3	5.5	4.1
Food	4.9	6.8	5.9	4.2
Clothing	5.4	5.9	5.0	4.4
Ice Cream	4.9	4.1	4.7	3.1
Bicycle	4.0	3.9	4.4	2.6
Pants	3.4	3.2	3.9	2.3
Sneakers	2.6	3.2	3.1	1.6
Grand Mean	4.1	4.5	4.7	2.8
n=	66	28	20	24

REFERENCES

Barth, Frederick (1969), Ethnic Groups and Boundaries: The
Social Organization of Culture Difference, London: Allen
& Unwin.

Bell, Daniel (1975), "Ethnicity and Social Change, "in
Glazer, Nathan and Daniel P. Moynihan (Eds.), Ethnicity:
Theory and Experience, Cambridge, Mass.: Hargard Uni-
versity Press.

Cohen, Ronald (1978), "Ethnicity: Problem and Focus in
Anthropology," Annual Review of Anthropology, Palo Alto,
CA.: Annual Reviews., 7, 379-403.

Davidowicz, Lucy (1977), The Jewish Presence, New York:
Harcourt, Brace, Javonovich.

Deese, James (1975), "Mind and Metaphor: A Commentary,
"New Literary History, 6, 211-217.

___________ (1976), The Structure of Associations in
Language and Thought, Baltimore, MD.: Johns Hopkins
Press.

___________ (1963), "On the Structure of Associative
Meaning, "Psychological Review, 63, 161-175.

Ellis, John Tracy (1960), American Catholicism, Chicago,
IL: University of Chicago Press.

Ember, Carol R. (1970), "Cross-Cultural Cognitive Studies",
Annual Review of Anthropology, Palo Alto, CA.: Annual
Reviews, Inc., 6, 33-56.

Glazer, Nathan and Daniel P. Moynihan (Eds.), (1975),
Ethnicity: Theory and Experience, Cambridge, MASS.:
Harvard University Press.

Greeley, Andrew M. (1977), The American Catholic, New
York, Basic Books.

Gurvitch, George (1971), The Social Frameworks of Knowledge, New York: Harper & Row.

Hirschman, Elizabeth C. (1981), "American Jewish Eth-
nicity: Its Relationship to Some Selected Aspects of
Consumption Behavior, " Journal of Marketing, 45,
Summer, 111-119.

Hirschman, Elizabeth C. (1981), "Commonality and Idio-
syncracy in Popular Culture," in _Symbolic Consumer
Behavior_ , Elizabeth C. Hirschman and Morris
Holbrook (Eds.), Association for Consumer Research.

Jensen, A.R. (1980), _Bias in Mental Testing_, New York:
The Free Press.

Jorgensen, Joseph, G. (1979), "Cross-Cultural Comparisons,"
Annual Review of Anthropology, Palo Alto, Ca.: Annual
Reviews, Inc., 8:309-31.

Klobus-Edwards, Patricia, John N. Edwards, David L.
Klemmack (1978), "Differences in Social Participation:
Blacks and Whites," _Social Forces_, Vol. 56:4, June, 1035-
1052.

Merton, Robert K. (1937), "The Sociology of Knowledge,"
Isis, 75, 27, 3, 493-503.

Roof, Wade Clark (1979), "Socioeconomic Differentials
Among White Socioreligious Groups in the United States,"
Social Forces, Vol. 58:1, September, 280-289.

Szalay, Lorand B. and James Deese (1978), _Subjective Meaning and Culture_, New York: John Wiley & Sons.

Triandis, Harry C. (1972), _The Analysis of Subjective
Culture_, New York: John Wiley & Sons.

Vincent, J. (1974), "The Structuring of Ethnicity," _Human
Organization_, 33(4): 375-79.

TABLE 3

Intra-Ethnic Ranking of Product Salience
by Numner of Associations

	White Prot.	White Jewish	White Cath.	Black Prot.
Public Transport.*	9	7	13	9
Music	6	6	7	6.5
Rock 'n' Roll*	7	10	8	13
Movie	14	11	12	15
Meat*	10	5	4	10.5
Shoes	13	13.5	11	12
Dairy Products*	12	15	5.5	6.5
Transportation	2	2	3	3
Food	4	1	1	2
Clothing	1	3.5	2	4
Entertainment	3	3.5	5.5	1
Ice Cream	5	8	9	5
Bicycle	8	9	10	8
Pants	11	13.5	14	10.5
Sneakers	15	12	15	14

*Asterisk indicates more than 6 places difference in rank
separates at least two ethnic groups for that product.

TABLE 4

Operant Ethnic Boundaries*

A White/Black	B Christian/Jew	C Prot/Cath/Jew	D Majority/Minority
entertainment			
movie			
pants			
shoes			
ice cream			

E Common Culture	F WP/WC/J/BP	G White Chris. /Jew/Black	H Inter-ethnic Parings
food	clothing		meat
Transport.	bicycle	music	rock 'n' roll

* Based upon commonality of most frequent response.

CROSS-CULTURAL INFLUENCES ON BUYER BEHAVIOR:
THE IMPACT OF HISPANIC ETHNICITY

Wayne D. Hoyer, The University of Texas at Austin
Rohit Deshpande, The University of Texas at Austin

ABSTRACT

Although the Hispanic population is one of the fastest growing in the U.S., little research effort has been devoted to
examining the buyer behavior of these consumers, most particularly in the area of brand choice. The present study
investigated Hispanic buying behavior in the context of a
common convenience product. Results indicated that Hispanic consumers are more subject to family influence, more influenced by advertisements, more concerned with brand image,
and more receptive to ethnic advertising.

INTRODUCTION

Preliminary results from the recent 1980 census reveal that
a large proportion of the U.S. population (14.6 million or
6.4%) is of Hispanic heritage. The Census Bureau estimates
that by the year 2000, this segment will account for 20% of
the population and will overtake blacks as the largest minority. The domestic Spanish language market is therefore
substantial and, more importantly, one of the fastest growing.

Despite these demographic trends, consumer researchers have
thus far paid little attention to the needs and preferences
of Hispanic consumers (Cervantes, 1980; Hirschman, 1981).
In particular, the dynamics underlying consumer choice (e.g.,
use of evaluative criteria, choice rules employed) has been
a relatively unresearched area. In light of this void, the
purpose of the present study is threefold: (1) To develop
some empirical benchmarks in the general area of ethnic influence on consumer behavior; (2) To establish findings on
the choice criteria used by Hispanic-American consumers in
the context of a commonly purchased convenience product;(3)
To suggest implications for marketers interested in more effectively meeting the needs of Hispanic consumers.

Previous Literature Concerning Ethnic Influence on Consumer
Behavior

Consumer researchers are increasingly finding that ethnicity can have an important influence on consumer behavior.
According to Hirschman (1981), however, there have been
several major problems associated with this type of research.
First, much of the work has been atheoretical in nature.
Researchers have simply assigned consumers into ethnic categories and have identified group differences using post
hoc statistical analyses. Usually no attempt is made to
develop and test hypotheses which are based on meaningful
theoretical differences between the cultures.

Second, assignment to ethnic categories has many times been
determined by researchers' perceptions. Few attempts have
been based on how consumers perceive their own ethnic association.

Third, the majority of ethnic consumer behavior studies
have focused on black consumers. Little attention has been
devoted to other minority groups, most particularly Hispanics.

A goal of the present study is to somewhat account for these
problems by attempting to develop testable hypotheses based
on previous knowledge and research, by employing an individual-centered definition of ethnicity, and by focusing on
a subsegment of the Hispanic population--Mexican-Americans.

Research Findings on Hispanic Ethnicity as Related to Consumer Behavior

Most of the research related to Hispanic consumer behavior
has been carried out by practitioners (especially advertisers). Only a handful of academic studies can be located,
and the findings are generally scattered and unrelated
(i.e., not tied together by a meaningful theoretical framework). The major findings of these studies are: (1) Hispanic consumers are highly brand loyal and trust well-known
or familiar brands (Loudon & Della-Bitta, 1979; Watanabe,
1981); (2) The inability to understand English is an inhibiting factor in the purchase of new products (Loudon &
Della-Bitta, 1979); (3) Hispanic consumers tend to have
more negative attitudes toward marketing practices (including advertising) and government intervention in business
(Longman & Pruden, 1968; Pruden & Longman, 1972); (4) Hispanic consumers prefer fresh, staple items rather than fro-
zen, pre-prepared (and generally more expensive items)
(Berry & Solomon, 1971); (5) Hispanics are more price-
oriented and careful in their shopping, but express less
confidence in their shopping abilities than Anglo consumers
(Gillet & Scott, 1974); (6) Shopping at large supermarkets
rather than closer, smaller food stores is considered more
desirable (Berry & Solomon, 1971; Gillet & Scott, 1974).

In addition, a special report on Hispanic marketing in Advertising Age (April 6, 1981) summarizes some additional
features of the Hispanic market which have surfaced from
practical experience with these consumers. First, the family is of central importance in the Hispanic social structure and, thus, there is a desire to purchase what is 'best
for the family.' Second, Hispanics feel that is is very
important to sustain traditional values and 'ways of doing
things.' This leads to a greater resistance to trying new
products. Third, Hispanics possess a great deal of both
individual and family pride and this may influence product
preferences in the form of conspicuous consumption.
Fourth, Hispanic consumers are distrustful of non-brand
name products. Fifth, concern for high quality foods is
great.

Finally, a recent article in Marketing News (Dec. 25, 1981)
refutes an earlier finding that Hispanic consumers are a-
verse to coupon usage. Rather, most Hispanics are quite
receptive to using coupons once their purpose is fully understood.

Noticeably absent from this body of work is an examination
of ethnic influence on the more micro-level processes underlying brand choice. In other words, an important question concerns whether broad level cultural differences fil-
ter down to influence the types of choice strategies used
in a specific decision context. In light of this fact, the
present study examines differences between an Hispanic and
an Anglo population in the use of certain choice rules in
the purchase of a common consumer convenience product (i.e.,
laundry detergent). These choice tactics represent 'rules
of thumb' or choice criteria which are used to make a decision (Deshpande, Hoyer & Jeffries, 1982). For example, in
purchasing a common consumer product, consumers could use
the choice rules, "I'll buy the cheapest brand," "I'll buy
what my parents bought," or "I'll buy the brand for which I

have a coupon." Consumers may also use a combination of tactics (e.g., "I'll buy the cheapest _national_ brand"). Further, consumers vary in terms of how often they use a particular tactic (i.e., never use to always use). In other words, the same tactic may not always be used on every purchase occasion. The purpose of the present paper is to examine ethnic differences in the employment of these choice tactics.

Hypotheses

On the basis of the previously stated generalizations regarding Hispanic[1] consumers, the following hypotheses are offered:

H1: Hispanic consumers would be more likely than Anglo consumers to use the choice tactic, "I buy the brand my parents buy."

This hypothesis is proposed because of the central importance of the family in the Hispanic culture.

H2: Hispanics will be more likely to use a choice tactic, "Advertisements (on TV, in newspapers, and in magazines) help me decide which brand to buy."

Although studies have found that Hispanic consumers have negative attitudes toward advertising, they also possess a tendency to distrust unfamiliar brands. Since advertising would serve to increase familiarity with a brand, it may have a greater influence in the purchase.

H3: Hispanics will be more likely to use choice tactics which are related to price (e.g., "I buy the brand which costs the least," "I buy the brand for which I have a coupon," and "I buy the brand which is on sale.")

As mentioned previously, Gillet and Scott (1974) report that Hispanics are more price-oriented than Anglos.

H4: Hispanics will be more likely to employ the choice tactic, "I buy the brand that people think has the most prestige."

Hispanic pride may result in the desire for a more prestigious product (i.e., conspicuous consumption).

H5: Hispanics will be less likely to use the tactic, "I buy a generic brand."

Hispanics are concerned with high quality and, therefore, may not purchase generic brands, which may be perceived as lower in quality.

H6: Hispanic consumers will be more likely to employ the tactic, "I buy a brand which is advertised to my ethnic group."

Advertisers have reported that Hispanics are generally receptive to advertisements which are in Spanish.

RESEARCH DESIGN AND SAMPLE

Sample

The sample was randomly drawn from two separate voter registration lists of a central Texas county. One was composed entirely of Spanish surnames and the other of non-Spanish surnames. From each list, 1,000 names were randomly selected and questionnaires were sent to each of these households. In addition, a follow-up was sent 10 days after the initial mailing. In total, 529 questionnaires were returned for a

[1]Although the term "Hispanic" is used throughout this paper, the data have been collected for a specific subset of Hispanics, namely Mexican-Americans.

26.4% response rate (25.0% Hispanic and 27.9% non-Hispanic). Of this total, 171 or 32% considered themselves as Hispanic. Although non-respondent analysis was obviated due to the anonymity guaranteed respondents, a careful comparison of respondent sample demographics with county population demographics was conducted. This comparison revealed no significant differences.

Questionnaire Development

The first step in the development of the survey instrument involved the construction of the English version. This questionnaire contained two separate sections: (a) a set of choice tactics and (b) general demographics.

Choice Tactics

The first section of the questionnaire consisted of a series of choice tactics or simplified decision rules which consumers may use in making a choice for laundry detergent (see Table 1 for illustrations). Included in this set were the tactics relevant to experimental hypotheses and also, tactics which were included for exploratory interest and to disguise the true variables of interest. Consumers were asked to indicate the extent to which they use each of these choice rules on a 5-point scale ranging from 0 (never) to 4 (always).

Demographics

The second section contained general demographic questions regarding sex, marital status, education, income, household size, length of time living in the U.S., viewing, listening, and reading habits regarding Spanish media, and ethnicity.

Development of a Spanish Version Questionnaire

A Spanish version of the questionnaire was constructed in three steps. First, a research assistant fluent in both English and Spanish translated the questionnaire into Spanish. Second, two additional Spanish-speaking research assistants back-translated the questionnaire into English. Discrepancies between the versions were identified as trouble spots and these sections were reworded. Careful attention was devoted to ensuring that the language of both questionnaires was as simplistic and easy to understand as possible. Third, the questionnaire was pre-tested on a sample of Hispanic consumers by means of a personal interview. Personal interviews were conducted in order to collect first-hand feedback regarding unclear or culturally sensitive questions.

Survey Administration

Hispanic consumers were mailed both an English and a Spanish version of the questionnaire. They were told to use whichever form they felt most comfortable with. The non-Hispanic sample received only the English version.

FINDINGS

Classification of Ethnicity

Two hundred and fifty individuals with Spanish surnames returned questionnaires. Of this group, 171 or 68% considered themselves to be in the Hispanic ethnic group (which was defined to include Mexican-Americans and Chicanos). Thus, the criticalness of an individual-centered definition of ethnicity is evident.

Tests of Hypotheses

As indicated in Table 1, Hypotheses 1, 4, and 6 were strongly supported. That is, Hispanics were more likely than Anglos to buy what their parents bought (t= -3.79, p<.001), buy brands perceived to be more prestigious (t= -3.49, p<.001,), and buy brands advertised to their ethnic group (t= -3.06, p<.003). Additionally, Hypotheses 2 and 3 were partly supported since Hispanics were more likely to use T.V. and magazine advertising to assist brand choice (t= -2.46, p<.01) and (t= -2.13, p<.03), respectively, and buy brands which cost the least (t= -1.98, p<.05).

TABLE 1
Tests of Hypotheses

Choice Tactic	Anglo $\overline{X}$	Hispanic $\overline{X}$
1. "I buy the brand that my parents bought."	1.81[a]	2.29***
2. "TV advertisements help me decide which brand to buy."	1.53	1.74**
"Newspaper advertisements help me decide which brand to buy."	1.46	1.58
"Magazine advertisements help me decide which brand to buy."	1.40	1.55*
3. "I buy the brand for which I have a coupon."	2.26	2.19
"I buy the brand that is on sale."	2.56	2.64
"I buy the brand which costs the least."	2.26	2.52*
4. "I buy the brand that people think has the most prestige."	1.20	1.47***
5. "I buy a generic brand."	1.47	1.65
6. "I buy the brand that is advertised to my ethnic group."	1.14	1.36**

a The scale ranges from 0 (never) to 4 (always)

* = p<.05
** = p<.01
*** = p<.001

Other Analyses

Although none of the other choice tactics included for exploratory purposes exhibited any cultural differences, it was felt interesting to examine the collective influence of the variables and, also, the importance of each of these variables in distinguishing between the different ethnic groups. Consequently, a discriminant analysis was conducted in an attempt to differentiate between the two groups. Also, in order to provide additional discriminatory power, basic demographic variables were included in the analysis.

As shown in Table 2, these variables were somewhat successful in discriminating between the two groups (Wilks Λ = .7612, p<.0001). However, the step-wise table and group means point out that various demographic variables (e.g., education, household size, income, and sex) were more important than two decision tactics (e.g., "I buy the brand my parents bought" and "I buy the brand advertised to my ethnic group") in discriminating between the two groups. Although this finding is somewhat disappointing, it is still clear that parental influence and ethnic advertising are important factors in Hispanic consumer behavior.

CONCLUSIONS AND IMPLICATIONS

The major conclusion which can be drawn from the findings of the present study is that not only are there broad level cultural differences, but ethnic differences also exist in the specific criteria used to select a common convenience product. Thus, marketers should not assume that this minority group is identical to the total population and, in some cases, a marketing strategy tailored specifically to

TABLE 2
Discriminant Analysis

Function	Eigenvalue	Canonical Correlation	WilksΛ	df	p
1	.3137	.4887	.7612	6	.00001

Summary Table

Variable	WilksΛ	$\overline{X}$ Anglo	$\overline{X}$ Hispanic
1. Education	.8837***	6.74	5.64
2. Household Size	.8422***	2.79	3.66
3. Income	.8150***	5.86	5.07
4. Sex	.7926***	1.81	1.69
5. Parental Influence[1]	.7751***	1.81	2.29
6. Ethnic Advertising[1]	.7612***	1.14	1.36

*** = p<.00001

the smaller segment may be necessary. Although this study examined only one product category, the differences found suggest that future investigations across alternate product categories would be worthwhile.

A second important finding was that simply using Hispanic surnames was an inadequate sampling technique. Rather, one must focus on consumer perceptions (i.e., self-reported identification) of ethnicity.

Important implications can also be drawn from the specific findings of the study. First, it was found that Hispanic consumers were more subject to parental and family influence in their product choices. This finding is consistent with the tendency for a greater degree of Hispanic brand loyalty and greater resistance to the trial of a new product. The topic of family decision making is clearly critical to an understanding of Hispanic consumer behavior.

Second, Hispanic consumers were more likely to base decisions on the perceived prestige of the product. This may indicate that social factors are important in product purchases and that normative factors are essential in the development of a model of Hispanic consumer choice. Also, another concern appears to be the purchase of a brand which has the image of being of a quality product and, thus, brand image may be particularly important when trying to appeal to an Hispanic population.

In light of this fact, it was surprising to find that Hispanic consumers were not less likely to buy generic brands of laundry detergent. Generic brands are generally not considered prestigious, and one would think that generic brands would be purchased by those who value this criterion. One potential explanation is economic necessity. Although some Hispanics might prefer to purchase a more prestigious brand, financial considerations may necessitate buying a less expensive brand. This hypothesis receives some support from the finding that Hispanic consumers were slightly more likely to buy the brand which costs the least.

Finally, Hispanic consumers appear to be receptive to advertising which is directed specifically toward their ethnic group. This is an important finding for marketers who are interested in pursuing opportunities in this market and suggests that ethnic advertising is a worthwhile endeavor.

In summary, this study has provided data that there are meaningful cross-cultural differences in the choice criteria used in a specific decision context. However, this study is only an initial step and clearly points to the need for more refined and focused future research. In particular, two main areas are in need of investigation. First, a more representative sample needs to be employed in order to detect true ethnic differences. Hispanic populations in other areas of the country, such as the Puerto-Rican communities in New York, individuals of Cuban descent in Florida, and Mexican-American people in California need to be explored because each of these subsegments is quite different, and one cannot generalize from one of these subsegments to another (Cervantes, 1980). Finally, research is needed to pinpoint not only the refined aspects of Hispanic information processing, but also the direct causal antecedents of cultural differences.

REFERENCES

Berry, L. L. & P. J. Solomon (1971), "Generalizing About Low-Income Food Shoppers: A Word of Caution," _Journal of Retailing_, 47(2), 41-51.

Cervantes, F. J. (1980), "The Forgotten Consumers: The Mexican-Americans," _Proceedings, 1980 Marketing Educators Conference_, A.M.A., 180-183.

Deshpande, R., W. D. Hoyer, & S. Jeffries (1982), "Low Involvement Decision Processes: The Importance of Choice Tactics," to appear in _1982 AMA Theory Conference Proceedings_.

Gillet, P. L. & R. A. Scott (1975), "Shopping Opinions of Mexican-American Consumers: A Comparative Analysis," in R. C. Curhan (ed.), _1974 Combined Proceedings_, A.M.A., 135-141.

Hirschman, E. C. (1981), "American Jewish Ethnicity: Its Relationship to Some Selected Aspects of Consumer Behavior," _Journal of Marketing_, _45_ (3), 102-110.

"Hispanic Households Redeem Bilingual Cents-Off Coupons," _Marketing News_, _15_ (13), Dec. 25, 1981, 1.

"Hispanic Marketing: A Special Report," (1981), _Advertising Age_, April 6, A1-23.

Longman, D. S. & H. O. Pruden (1972), "Alienation from the Marketplace: A Study in Black, Brown, and White," in F. C. Allvine (ed.), _Combined Proceedings 1971 Spring and Fall Conferences_, A.M.A., 616-619.

Loudon, D. L. & Della Bitta, A. J. (1979), _Consumer Behavior: Concepts and Applications_, New York: McGraw-Hill.

Pruden, H. O. & Longman, D. O. (1972), "Race, Alienation, and Consumerism," _Journal of Marketing_, July 1972, 58-63.

ETHNIC VARIATION IN LEISURE ACTIVITIES AND MOTIVES

Elizabeth C. Hirschman, New York University

ABSTRACT

The present research extends an earlier study investigating the relationship of two forms of ethnicity--religion and nationality--to leisure activity preferences and motives. Exploratory hypotheses from the initial study were replicated with varying degrees of confirmation, and the mediating roles of imagery and sensation-seeking were explored and tentatively supported.

INTRODUCTION

A heightened level of recognition is being given to the important role that leisure activities play in the lifeof the consumer (Holbrook and Lehmann 1981). Two general trends in this leisure-research stream may be detected. First, researchers have begun to document the range of leisure activities that various types of consumers engage in; for example, college students, the elderly, religious groups (Havinghurst 1975; Hirschman 1982b; Szalai 1972). Second, investigators have examined the characteristics of consumers who participate in specific types of leisure activity; for example, theatre-goers, museum-goers, modern dance subscribers, and so forth (Sexton and Britney 1980; Andreasen and Belk 1980; Lapso 1981; Wachtel 1981). The present research is representative of the first trend, it is oriented toward an examination of the types of leisure activities engaged in by a priori defined groups of consumers. Hence, it has as its focus the various leisure behaviors of given consumers, rather than describing those who participate in a given leisure activity.

Despite this similarity to existing literature, the present study differs from earlier studies in two important respects. First, the a priori groups whose leisure activities it examines are defined ethnically. Two dimensions of ethnicity are used: religion and nationality. Prior leisure research has rarely used ethnicity as a means of differentiating consumers, yet there is ample evidence present in the social sciences that ethnic affiliation greatly affects life style (Jencks et al. 1979; Greeley 1977; Patai 1977). Thus, it is logical to assume that ethnicity will similarly affect leisure activity preferences and participation. Earlier research on this aspect of ethnicity and consumption (Hirschman 1982a) is extended in the present study.

Second, the present research differs from several prior studies by seeking to elicit consumers' motives for participating in leisure activities. Two individuals may not only participate in different leisure activities, they also may be motivated to do so by greatly different factors. Thus, to better comprehend consumers' participation in leisure activities generally, we must gain knowledge about the motivational factors that underlie participation.

CONCEPTUAL FRAMEWORK

The primary theoretical assumption made in the present research is that ethnic differences in preferences for certain leisure activities, as well as motives for participating in them, represent variation in subcultural norms governing such behavior. It is posited that by observing variations in leisure activity preferences and motives among ethnic subcultures, the operating norms may be deduced. Preferences and motives for leisure activi-

ties are therefore viewed as products of ethnic socialization. The present research utilizes ethnic groupings along the dimensions of religion and nationality. Three religious affiliations are studied: Catholicism, Judaism, and Protestantism; and six nationality affiliations are examined: Chinese, Hispanic, English, Irish, Italian, and Jewish.[1]

Earlier, exploratory research (Hirschman 1982a) revealed that both religious and national ethnic affiliations were related to leisure activity preferences and motives. However, the research was of unknown generalizability and lacked a set of mediating linkages between consumers' ethnicity and their leisure preferences. The present study replicates the earlier findings, extends them to some additional activities, and puts forward a preliminary set of mediating linkages. These are depicted in Exhibit One.

EXHIBIT ONE

GENERAL MODEL OF THE ETHNICITY-LEISURE ACTIVITY LINKAGE

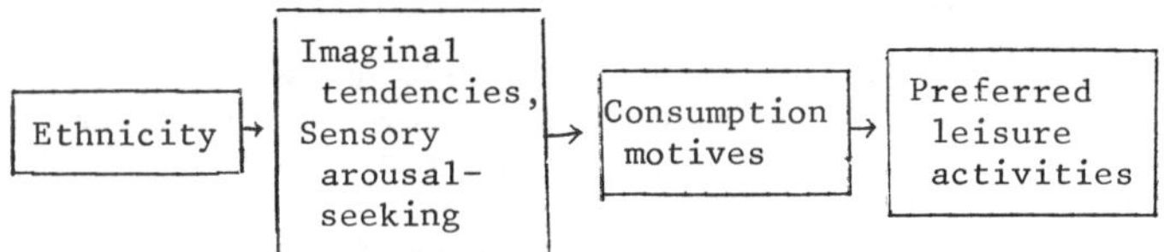

As shown, ethnicity is posited to contribute to the consumer's possession of two characteristics: imaginal tendencies and sensory arousal-seeking.[2] These are believed to enhance the development of certain consumption motives (e.g., fun/pleasure), which in turn lead to preferences for leisure activities. To provide consistency with the first study, the same set of consumption motives is used and the same types of leisure activities (favorite physical activities) are examined. The findings from the present study serve as a validity check on those generated earlier, and also provide some evidence of credibility for the suggested causal framework.

CONSTRUCT MEASUREMENT

Ethnicity

Ethnicity was measured using bi-dimensional scales developed in prior research (Hirschman 1981, 1982a, 1982b). These scales are emic in nature; that is, they permit the individual to ascribe religious and national identity to him/herself. Thus, ethnicity arises from the individual's subjective self-perceptions and not from the perceptions of the researcher, which may be biased by ethnocentrism. This method of measuring ethnicity is the approach deemed most appropriate by cross-cultural behavioral researchers, especially those in cultural anthropology and subcultural social psychology (Cohen 1978; Ember 1977; Jorgensen 1979).

---

[1] Judaism in the present study is defined along two discrete dimensions--religion and nationality. Although Judaism is a major religious tradition, Jews also constitute a nationality group in the Zionist sense.

[2] These are defined in detail later in this paper.

In the present study, two questions were used to assess
ethnicity. First, subjects were asked if there were any
religious group with which they identified. Five response categories were given: Catholic, Jewish, Protestant,
Other (specified), and None. Second, subjects were asked
if there were any nationality group with which they identified. Eleven response categories were given for this
question: Hispanic, Irish, Greek, Italian, Jewish,
Chinese, English, Japanese, Black, Other, and None. Thus,
ethnicity was measured bi-dimensionally for each individual; first as a religious identification and second as
a national affiliation.[3]

Sensory Arousal-Seeking

The construct of sensory arousal-seeking refers to tendencies to acquire sensory stimulation, even at the risk
of engaging in potentially dangerous activities (Zuckerman
1979). In the present study, this construct is measured
using the Sensation Seeking scale developed by Zuckerman
(1979). It is believed that ethnic norms to some extent
influence the level of sensory arousal sought by consumers.
Hence, sensation seeking is hypothesized to mediate
between ethnicity and certain consumption motives. Sensation seeking is measured using a 40-question, forced-
choice instrument, examples of which are given in
Appendix A. In the present study, the obtained distribution closely approximated a normal curve, having a mean
of 19.8 and a range of 5 to 35.

Imaginal Tendencies

This variable is the result of investigations conducted by
Hilgard (1970) and Swanson (1978) on imaginal involvement.
Imaginal tendencies concern the consumer's ability to construct imaginary sequences, to recall prior images, and to
alter his/her state of consciousness at will. Imaginal
tendencies are also believed to be influenced by ethnic
norms (Hirschman 1982a); thus, this variable was also
hypothesized to mediate between ethnic identity and consumption motives. In the present study, imaginal tendencies are termed Imagery, and were measured by an index
constructed by summing affirmative responses to five
indicators of this construct (Apprendix B) taken directly
from Hilgard (1970) and Swanson (1978). Internal consistency of the measure was .67.

Favorite Physical Activities and Motives

Replicating the earlier study (Hirschman 1982a), subjects
were asked to list their three favorite physical activities.[4] This was followed by a listing of nine consumption motives which could be selected as reasons why they
engaged in the activity. These were derived from Hilgard
(1970) and Swanson (1978) as being appropriate for physical activities, and are identical to those used in the
prior study. The operational measure of each is given
below:

---

[3]This measure of ethnicity is categorical in nature and
does not distinguish between high and low levels of ethnic
affiliation. A more accurate measure would utilize scaled
responses to assess strength of affiliation.

[4]Future research could usefully include nonphysical leisure activities as topics for investigation. Physical
activities were utilized in the present research to
provide consistency with the prior exploratory study and
the studies of Hilgard and Swanson.

I like to do this because it gives me lots of
pleasure; I enjoy it; it's fun to do; and I do it for
the pleasure it gives me at the moment. (Fun/Pleasure)

This activity takes a lot of physical stamina; I have
to give it everything I've got. It's the last ounce
of effort that really counts. (Stamina)

I enjoy this escape from the world of reality. When
I'm into this activity I feel as if I am in another
world, and I enjoy this feeling immensely. I really
lose myself in my enjoyment of this experience.
(Escape Reality)

I'm always striving to improve or perfect my performance in this activity. It takes a lot of effort
to do well, and the effort and improvement are very
satisfying to me. (Perfect Performance)

I get deeply involved in this activity; when I am
doing it I think of nothing else and throw myself
into it completely. (Involvement)

I have to be always alert, trying to figure out what
is going on around me; it takes a lot of concentration
and alertness to keep from making serious mistakes at
this activity. (Alert)

One reason I like to do this is because I can express
my feeling of competitiveness; really strive to win;
to be the best. I love to win. (Compete)

Doing this is an adventure. It's hard to say what
will happen next; things are always changing, new
challenges always arising; there is always a new
experience. (Adventure)

I like the excitement and feeling of power or thrill
of speed. The experience is really exhilarating.
(Excitement)

Each motive description was used as a single-item indicator of that motive. The score a given respondent
received for a particular motive could range from 0 to 3,
depending on how many of the three listed physical activities she/he indicated were undertaken to fulfill the
motive (Swanson 1978).

SAMPLE

The sample consisted of 532 adults (over age 19) who
responded to a structured, written questionnaire. Data
were gathered by administering questionnaires to graduate
and undergraduate students enrolled in behavioral science
classes at New York University. Students were required
to complete one questionnaire themselves and to have
four other individuals, who were not students, complete
questionnaires as well. Students were informed that the
data gathered would be used in class to construct models
of behavior. Instructors stressed the fact that accurate
completion of every questionnaire was essential, if the
data analyses were to be valid.

The students were enthusiastic about cooperating in the
project, since they viewed it as an opportunity to
discover more about themselves. The returned questionnaires were carefully checked for "nonsense" answers,
systematic response patterns, and other obvious signs
of deliberate falsification. In only eight instances
was suggestive evidence for discarding a questionnaire
encountered. Comparisons of students' responses (using
age, occupation, life cycle, and ethnic data) with those
of the non-students to whom they administered questionnaires revealed a pattern of administration to parents,
siblings, roommates, girl/boyfriends, employers, and
co-workers. The resulting sample possessed diversified

marital statuses, ages, and occupations. However, because the sample was generated from among college students and their social contacts, it is somewhat upscale in terms of socioeconomic status.

Because ethnicity may correlate or interact with various demographic factors, it was important to ensure that such factors did not distort the relationship of ethnicity to the leisure activities and motives examined here. Analysis of variance revealed that there were no significant differences among the ethnic groups examined on any major demographic variables (age, sex, education, job status, marital status) except one: father's occupational status. However, father's occupational status did not correlate with any of the leisure activity variables examined to a substantial degree ($r < .10$). Hence, this demographic difference should not affect the results reported.[5]

Within the sample were 166 Catholics, 172 religious Jews, and 80 Protestants, which constituted the religious groups examined. There were 26 Chinese, 46 English, 28 Hispanic, 42 Irish, 64 Italian, and 156 nationalist Jewish subjects, who constituted the nationality groups examined. The earlier study, with whose results the present research is being compared, contained 23 Greek subjects and no Hispanic subjects within the nationality groups (Hirschman 1982a).

Religious Group Hypotheses

Analysis of variance among Catholic, Jewish, and Protestant subjects in the first study revealed significant differences in the leisure activities and motives characterizing each group. An attempt was made to replicate these findings in the present study and, if they were supported, to then use them as the basis for deriving causal hypotheses. The findings which were successfully replicated from the prior study were:

1. Jewish, Catholic, and Protestant consumers were ordered as high, medium, and low in citing <u>making love</u> as a favorite physical activity ($p < .001$, t-test).

2. Jewish consumers exceeded their Protestant and Catholic counterparts in pursuit of the <u>fun/pleasure motive</u> for favorite physical activities ($p < .05$, Scheffé).

3. Jewish, Protestant, and Catholic consumers were found ordered as high, medium and low with regard to the <u>escape reality motive</u> ($p < .10$, Scheffé).

Further analyses revealed that six additional leisure activities and three additional motives exhibited significant differences among the religious groups. For four activities--<u>swimming</u>, <u>dancing</u>, <u>jogging</u>, and <u>biking</u>--Catholic and Protestant consumers displayed substantially more preference than did Jewish consumers ($p < .05$, t-test). All of these activities, except for dancing, are solitary athletic activities. In contrast, Jewish consumers displayed a marked preference for <u>basketball</u>--a team sport, and <u>eating</u>--a form of sensory stimulation ($p < .05$, t-test). Further, Jewish consumers were also found to be significantly higher in pursuit of the <u>excitement motive</u> than both Protestant and Catholic consumers ($p < .05$, Scheffé), and higher in pursuit of the <u>involvement</u> and <u>alertness motives</u> than Catholics ($p < .05$, Scheffé).

These findings, coupled with those replicating the prior study, led to the preliminary propositions:

1. Protestant and Catholic consumers exhibit stronger orientations toward solitary athletic activities as preferred physical leisure outlets than do Jewish consumers.

2. In contrast, Jewish consumers prefer leisure activities providing companionship and/or sensory stimulation (basketball, making love, eating).

3. Jewish consumers, as compared with Catholics and Protestants, are more prone to sensory arousal in choosing leisure activities, as evidenced by their pursuit of fun/pleasure, involvement, alertness, and excitement in engaging in these activities.

These propositions suggested the investigation of two potential mediating variables that may help to explain the linkage between ethnicity and leisure activity preferences: imagery and sensation seeking.[6] One-way ANOVA revealed strong ethnic differences in these two constructs, with Jewish subjects significantly exceeding Protestant and Catholic subjects in both characteristics ($p < .01$, Scheffé). The research hypothesis was formed that imagery and sensation seeking may serve as mediators between ethnicity and physical leisure activity motives. A causal rationale is next developed for their role in mediating between ethnicity and leisure motives, together with an empirical test of this hypothesis.

Imagery and Sensation Seeking as Mediators of Leisure Motives

As noted above, Jewish consumers were found to exceed their Catholic and Protestant counterparts in imagery and sensation seeking. This suggests that ethnic norms may predispose Jewish consumers to seek sensory and/or imaginal arousal in the leisure activities they pursue. This predisposition, it is posited, will lead to the development of motives such as fun/pleasure, excitement, alertness, and involvement.

The supposition that Jewish ethnicity may be characterized by norms favoring sensory/imaginal arousal is given credence by several studies summarized in Patai (1977). Jews appear to be higher in sensory awareness and predisposed toward sensory arousal because of parental emphasis on self-monitoring their children--especially to detect signs of illness or discomfort (Patai 1977). Further, a child reporting unusual sensory feelings is likely to receive a large measure of parental attention, reinforcing his/her monitoring process. Jewish parents have also been found to stress the importance of the child's feeling good sensorially and also tend to encourage over-eating (Patai 1977). Thus, the result of these early reinforcements may be a life-long orientation toward <u>sensory arousal-seeking</u>, with an emphasis on maximizing sensory pleasure.

---

[5]A limitation of the present data, however, is that they were all gathered in New York City--an ethnically-conscious, urban environment. Hence, representatives of the various religious and nationality groups sampled may not be congruent to their counterparts in rural or suburban settings or in other regions of the United States. Further, denominational differences among Protestants (e.g., Episcopalian, Presbyterian, Baptist) and Jews (e.g., Orthodox, Conservative, Reform) are not incorporated into the analysis.

---

[6]Although, as a reviewer notes, other constructs may mediate this linkage, only imagery and sensation seeking were investigated here.

The studies summarized by Patai (1977) also indicate
that Jews experience above-average levels of chronic
anxiety, largely as a result of real or perceived social
rejection. This may induce them to develop more active
imaginal/fantasy capacities in order to construct happy
subjective realities and to escape their anxieties
momentarily.

Hence, conceptual support can be generated for the proposition that Jewish ethnic norms may contribute to
observed above-average levels of imagery and sensation
seeking and, if these variables serve as mediators, to
the development of certain consumption motives. Satisfying these motives leads, in turn, to preference for
certain leisure activities.

This causal framework is shown in Exhibit 1. The Consumption Motives ⟶ Preferred Leisure Activities linkage is already documented by the fact that the motives
cited were given directly as reasons for participating
in the preferred activities. Hence, that relationship
is assumed valid and is not examined further. However,
it is useful to examine the Ethnicity ⟶ Imagery and
Sensation Seeking ⟶ Consumption Motive linkages. Since
we have already established the presence of a significant
relationship between ethnicity and certain consumption
motives, what remains to be determined is the relationship between the two mediating constructs and the consumption motives. If imagery and sensation seeking are
true mediators between ethnicity and consumption motives,
then we would expect to see a reduction in the amount of
variance accounted for by ethnicity when these two constructs are entered as covariates in an ANCOVA procedure.

To test this, an Analysis of Covariance procedure was
conducted on the consumption motives found related to
ethnicity, using imagery and sensation seeking as covariates and the three religious denominations--coded
as 0/1 dummy variables--as factors.[7] The covariates were
entered prior to the religious factors to ascertain if
any incremental variance was accounted for by religious
ethnicity, once effects of the covariates had been controlled. The findings with regard to each motive are
discussed in order: fun/pleasure, excitement, alertness, and involvement.

Fun/pleasure. Sensation seeking apparently is a significant mediator between religious ethnicity and the fun/
pleasure motive. This covariate was significant at the
$p < .001$ level, and acted to reduce the 8.45 original sum
of squares explained by ethnicity to 6.76 in the present
analysis. The significance of the main effect attributable to religious ethnicity was reduced from $p < .0094$
to $p < .052$, a substantial decline. Despite this, religious Judaism still exerted a significant effect on
the fun/pleasure motive ($p < .018$). The religious affiliation effect is thus weakened, but not eliminated.

Excitement. The covariates of sensation seeking and
imagery serve a moderate mediating role between religious
ethnicity and the excitement motive. Both were significant at the $p < .0001$ level, and their a priori inclusion
in the analysis reduced the sum of squares attributable
to ethnicity from 16.60 to 13.22 and the significance
level from $p < .0002$ to $p < .002$. Despite the decline in
its strength, religious Judaism still continued to exert
an influence on the excitement motive ($p < .012$).

Involvement. An analogous pattern was found for the
involvement motive, with the covariates of imagery and
sensation seeking playing a mediating role. Both are

____

[7]Tabular data from all analyses is available upon
request from the author.

significant at the $p < .0001$ level. Once these two
variables are controlled, the sum of squares attributable
to religious ethnicity declined from 3.13 to 2.51, with a
corresponding decline in significance from $p < .115$ to
$p < .325$.

Alertness. A very obvious instance of covariate mediation is found for the alertness motive. Imagery was
significantly related to this criterion ($p < .002$). Further, after its effects were removed, the sum of squares
explained by religious ethnicity fell from 4.69 to 2.37--
a decline in significance from $p < .06$ to $p < .402$. None
of the religious ethnicity factors continued to exert a
significant influence on the alertness motive, once the
covariates had been controlled.

In sum, therefore, we may conclude that the constructs of
imagery and sensation seeking intercede between religious
ethnicity and consumption motives to a significant degree
in these specific instances, as hypothesized.

NATIONALITY COMPARISONS

We now turn to a consideration of national ethnicity; an
analogous analytical procedure is adopted. First, the
validity of the first study's findings is examined;
second, significant extensions to the replicative findings are noted; third, the relationship of national
ethnicity to imagery and sensation seeking is tested; and
finally, the role of these two constructs in mediating
between national ethnicity and certain consumption motives
is examined.

The replicated first study/second study findings for the
nationality ethnic groups are summarized briefly below.

1. Jewish consumers were found to exceed other nation-
    ality groups in citations of making love as a
    favorite physical activity ($p < .00001$, t-test),
    with one exception: Hispanics were found equally
    as likely as Jews to name this activity. Recall
    that Hispanics were not included in the earlier
    study; thus, this finding does not contradict that
    found earlier.

2. English and Jewish consumers were found to exceed
    all other nationality groups in pursuing the fun/
    pleasure motive ($p < .10$, Scheffé); however,
    Italian consumers were not found lowest in this
    regard, as had been expected.

3. Chinese and Italian consumers were found to exceed
    all others in pursuit of the perfect performance
    motive in favorite physical activities. It was
    hypothesized that the Chinese would be highest in
    this regard; however, the Italians were found to
    be so, with the Chinese second ($p < .05$, Scheffé).

4. Finally, English consumers were found to be high-
    est and Chinese consumers were found to be lowest
    in pursuing the seek adventure motive, as antici-
    pated ($p < .05$, Scheffé).

Additional comparisons revealed six differences between
nationality groups not found in the earlier study. First,
all nationality groups, especially the Irish, exceeded
Jewish consumers in citations of dancing as a favorite
physical activity ($p = .0015$, t-test). This finding
parallels the pattern in the religious comparisons.
Further, as before, all nationality groups exceeded
Jewish consumers in citations of jogging ($p = .099$).
However, the pattern of Jewish non-participation in
solitary athletic activities did not hold for bicycle
riding and swimming and, hence, is apparently not as
distinct a phenomenon in the nationality contrasts as it
was in the religious comparisons.

96

Other strong similarities are present, however, between the religious comparisons and those for nationality groups. First, Jewish consumers were significantly higher in citing _eating_ as a favorite activity (p = .019, t-test) and Jewish consumers, together with Irish consumers, were significantly higher in citations of _basketball_ (p = .052, t-test). Further, Jewish consumers were once again higher in pursuing the _excitement motive_ (p < .05, Scheffé) than were the other nationality groups.[8]

Hence, we may formulate the following preliminary propositions regarding national ethnicity.

P1. Chinese and Italian consumers appear more oriented toward perfectionism in physical activities than most nationality groups examined here.

P2. Hispanic and Jewish consumers appear more oriented toward sensual behavior (e.g., making love) in leisure activity than the other nationality groups examined here.

P3. Jewish consumers, additionally, appear more disposed toward sensory gratification and arousal vis-a-vis other nationality groups, as evidenced by the types of leisure activities they prefer and their motives for engaging in these activities.

Construct Mediation for National Ethnicity

As before, the constructs of imagery and sensation seeking were found to be significantly related to ethnicity. Irish and Jewish consumers were both found to be significantly higher in imagery (p < .05, Scheffé) than the other nationalities, and Jewish consumers exceeded all other nationalities in sensation seeking (p < .05). Thus, the role of these two constructs as potential mediators between ethnicity and various consumption motives was again examined. Results are discussed in order below for fun/pleasure, excitement, perfection, and adventure.

Excitement. Both imagery and sensation seeking appear to play a modest mediating role between national ethnicity and pursuit of the excitement motive. Their entry as covariates reduced the sum of squares attributable to national ethnicity from 24.70 to 16.45. However, despite the entry of imagery and sensation seeking, the nationality categories of Jewish (p ≤ .049), English (p ≤ .035), and Italian (p ≤ .042) were still related to pursuit of the excitement motive. Thus, national ethnicity still exhibits a direct effect upon excitement, after controlling for the effects of imagery and sensation seeking as mediators.

Perfect performance. Imagery and sensation seeking also appear to possess a mediating function as regards the perfect performance motive. Both are significant positive correlates of this motive (p ≤ .003, p < .001). Further, their prior entry into the ANCOVA as covariates reduced the sum of squares attributable to national ethnicity from 19.95 to 13.21. Despite the entry of the covariates, however, three nationality categories still bear a significant relationship to the perfect performance motive: Italian (p ≤ .073), Chinese (p ≤ .074), and Spanish (p ≤ .091).

Adventure. Both covariates exhibited a statistically significant positive relationship to the adventure motive; the respective probability levels were: imagery,

p < .001 and sensation seeking, p < .007. Further, the mediating role these variables play between national ethnicity and pursuit of the adventure motive is evidenced by the decline in the sum of squares attributable to national ethnicity from 7.53 to 6.78, subsequent to their entry as covariates. Only Hispanic ethnicity continues to exhibit a significant relationship to the adventure motive in the latter analysis (p ≤ .014).

DISCUSSION

The findings, though certainly still at a tentative stage of development, have several implications of potential significance for marketing research. First, ethnicity appears to be linked directly and/or indirectly to leisure consumption patterns. This linkage is present for both in the types of leisure activities preferred and the reasons for engaging in them. This implies that consumers' ethnicity may serve as a potentially powerful predictor and determinant of leisure activity preferences. Second, it appears plausible that one cause of the observed variation in leisure behavior attributable to ethnicity may be ethnic differences in certain characteristics, such as sensation seeking.

This leads to a third implication: that consumer ethnicity--because it affects product choice and motivational values--may serve as a potent segmentation device for a wide range of consumption behaviors. As was suggested in an earlier study (Hirschman 1981), ethnicity may serve as a powerful categorization and prediction device for choice and purchase behaviors in such areas as media exposure, political elections, food preferences, and new product adoption, as well as the leisure activities investigated here. Comprehension of ethnic differences in consumer behavior could lead to effective marketing strategies based upon those differences, and deserves further investigation.

REFERENCES

Andreasen, Alan R., and Russell W. Belk (1980), "Predictors of Attendance at the Performing Arts, "_Journal of Consumer Research_, September, Vol. 7, 112-120.

Cohen, Ronald (1978), "Ethnicity: Problem and Focus in Anthropology" in _Annual Review of Anthropology_, Palo Alto, Ca.: Annual Reviews, Inc., Vol. 7, 379-403.

Ember, Carol R. (1977), "Cross-Cultural Cognitive Studies," in _Annual Review of Anthropology_, Palo Alto, Ca.: Annual Reviews, Inc., Vol. 6, 33-36.

Greeley, Andrew M. (1977), _The American Catholic_, New York: Basic Books.

Havinghurst, Robert J. (1975), "The Future Aged: The Use of Time and Money," _The Genrontologist_, Vol. 15, 10-15.

Hilgard, Josephine R. (1970), _Personality and Hypnosis: A Study of Imaginative Involvement_, Chicago: University of Chicago Press.

Hirschman, Elizabeth C. (1981), "American Jewish Ethnicity: Its Relationship to Some Selected Aspects of Consumer Behavior," _Journal of Marketing_, Vol. 45, Summer, 111-19.

__________ (1982a), "Ethnic Variation in Hedonic Behavior," _Journal of Social Psychology_, forthcoming.

__________ (1982b), "Religious Affiliation and Consumption Processes: An Initial Paradigm," in Jagdish N. Sheth ed., _Research in Marketing_, Vol. 6, forthcoming.

____
[8] Comparisons of group means indicated that nationalistic Jews were also highest in the involvement and alertness motives, as had been found in the religious comparisons. However, these differences were not statistically significant.

Holbrook, Morris B., and Donald Lehmann (1981), "Allocating of Discretionary Time: Complementarity among Activities," *Journal of Consumer Research*, Vol. 7 , March, 395-406.

Jencks, Christopher (1972), *Inequality: A Reassessment of the Effect of Family and Schooling in America*, London: Basic Books.

Jorgensen, Joseph G. (1979), "Cross-Cultural Comparisons," in *Annual Review of Anthropology*, Palo Alto, CA.: Annual Reviews, Inc., Vol. 8, 309-331.

Lapso, Russell, "Direct Marketing of Modern Dance," in Elizabeth C. Hirschman and Morris B. Holbrook, eds., *Symbolic Consumer Behavior*, Ann Arbor, Mich.: Association for Consumer Research, 90-91.

Patai, Rahael (1977), *The Jewish Mind*, New York: Charles Scribner.

Sexton, Donald E., and Kathryn Britney (1980), "A Behavioral Segmentation of the Arts Market," in Jerry Olson, ed., *Advances in Consumer Research*, Vol. 7, Ann Arbor, Mich.: Association for Consumer Research.

Swanson, Guy E. (1978), "Travels through Inner Space: Family Structure and Openness to Absorbing Experiences," *American Journal of Sociology*, Vol. 83, January, 890-919.

Szalai, Alexander (1972), ed., *The Use of Time*, Paris: Mouton.

Wachtel, George A. (1981), "Marketing Broadway: A Case Study in Audience Research, " in Elizabeth C. Hirschman and Morris B. Holbrook, eds., *Symbolic Consumer Behavior*, Ann Arbor, Mich.: Association for Consumer Research, 92-94.

APPENDIX A

Sensation Seeking*

A. I like "wild" uninhibited parties.
B. I prefer quiet parties with good conversation.

A. There are some movies I enjoy seeing a second or even a third time.
B. I can't stand watching a movie that I've seen before.

A. I often wish I could be a mountain climber.
B. I can't understand people who risk their necks climbing mountains.

A. I find that stimulants make me uncomfortable.
B. I often like to get high (drinking liquor or smoking marijuana).

A. I like to explore a strange city or section of town by myself, even if it means getting lost.
B. I prefer a guide when I am in a place I don't know well.

$$\overline{X} = 19.8; \; s.d. = 6.9$$

---

* These are sample items. The total sensation-seeking scale contains 40 pairs of items.

APPENDIX B

Imagery*

Have you ever had the experience of telling a story with elaborations to make it sound better, and then having the elaborations seem as real to you as the actual incidents?

________ 0. Yes
________ 1. No

Have you ever had the experience of recollecting a past experience in your life with such clarity and vitality that it was almost like living it again?

________ 0. Yes
________ 1. No

Have you ever focused at something so hard that you went into kind of benumbed state of consciousness? Or a state of extraordinary calm and serenity?

________ 0. Yes
________ 1. No

$$\overline{X} = 3.13; \; s.d. = 1.06$$

---

* Sample items: Scale contained 5 binary-coded items.

IT IS TIME TO LAY THE LOW-INVOLVEMENT
HIERARCHY TO REST

David W. Finn, Texas Christian University

ABSTRACT

This article argues that the Low-Involvement Hierarchy proposed by Ray (1973) is not a re-ordered learning hierarchy but is actually an incomplete learning hierarchy. Furthermore, it suggests that the term "low-involvement" places unnecessary restrictions on research in consumer behavior. If we eliminate the label "low-involvement hierarchy", explanations of the apparent Cognitive---->Conative---->Affective flow will come more easily.

INTRODUCTION

Interest in low-involvement consumer decision making has been increasing in recent years, and is perhaps best typified by Kassarjian's comment that "the simple concept of involvement offhandedly introduced by Krugman some years ago, may well qualify as one of the more important scientific ideas to emerge in consumer research in recent years" (Kassarjian 1981, p.33). Indeed, the volume of published articles in the area of low-involvement decision making that have appeared in the last few years lends credence to this statement. However, in researching and writing about this concept, we have sometimes demonstrated our confusion between the concepts of low-involvement learning (via passive information processing) and low-involvement choice behavior. Even in the Kassarjian piece referenced above, there is reference to low-involvement personalities, low-involvement products, and as part of a summary comment, reference to work in low-involvement information processing. This apparent assimilation of the terms demonstrates part of our confusion with the concept.

Low-involvement learning refers to Krugman's (1965, 1966, 1968) idea of passive information processing. The concept of low-involvement choice behavior, particularly when the term low-involvement product is introduced, does not seem to be related to the former construct -- choice by definition involves some type of active processing. I believe that we have been seeing imaginary connections between the two ideas, and this has been guiding our research.

LOW-INVOLVEMENT LEARNING

This idea was argued by Krugman (1965, 1966) and seems to refer, almost exclusively, to television advertising. Here we have a person sitting in front of a television screen when a commercial comes on. If the message is about a product category that is not currently causing problems with the viewer, we say that mere exposure to it (particularly with repetition) results in passive information processing and low-involvement learning. Cognitions are developed. The consumer becomes aware of the brand and/or of the claims of the brand, but since it has no particularly important meaning in his life at that time, no mental "connections" are made between the information and his needs. Later, a brand purchase opportunity triggers recognition, and the consumer may remember the advertised claims. Before the situational "trigger," the consumer could probably not verbalize much about the brand. The purchase opportunity brings the cognitions into prominence, and the consumer may or may not purchase the brand. One important thing to note here is that a purchase (or not) decision is made on the basis of cognitions alone -- no attitudinal mediator is present. Another important thing

to recognize (although not specifically mentioned by Krugman) is that the recognition trigger can only lead to purchase if the product has some meaning to the consumer (can we say that "connections" are made between the product and recognized needs?). For example, a consumer can learn a lot about new brands of beer through passive information processing, and a large display of an advertised brand will probably trigger recognition. However, no purchase will take place for a non-drinker, while a beer drinker might react differently. Both went through low-involvement learning, and the product is the same, but the triggered cognitions can influence only the involved consumer.

This first idea of low-involvement, then, refers to the amount of effort spent in processing unsearched-for information. A passive viewer of an active medium (television) has little choice but to sit through advertising information from beginning to end. Krugman (1966) compares this passive processing of television advertisements to the more active level of processing demanded of print advertisements, where we have a passive medium and an active audience. Here, the receiver of the information actively decides which particular messages he will "sit through" from beginning to end, and we have active information processing and high-involvement learning.

LOW-INVOLVEMENT CHOICE BEHAVIOR

The concept of low-involvement choice behavior relies on the assumption that some products are very trivial to consumers and have very little relation to their personal lives. They have little or no interest in them. Now the idea of unimportant product classes is, by itself, legitimate. It is only when we begin to link the behavioral outcomes of low-involvement products to low-involvement learning that we get into trouble.

Krugman's hypothesis was that low-involvement learning leads to behavior without attitude (or Affect), while high-involvement learning should reflect the more structured; Affect then Behavior, model. Krugman had argued that the low-involvement process follows the flow of Cognition (formed through repetition and triggered by a behavioral opportunity) to Conation, or "(b)ehavioral completion to release appropriate attitudes supportive and consistent with the shift in perceptual structure, i.e. if the brand is then purchased the new way of seeing it may then for the first time be expressed in words, for example, to 'explain' why it was selected" (Krugman, 1966 pg. 585;and 1968 pg. 224). In other words, Krugman postulates a Cognitive---->Conative---->Affective flow. In fact he implies (mistakenly I believe) that purchase leads to favorable attitudes. In a later part of this paper I'll explain why I believe this is in error.

Michael Ray (1973) took these behavioral outcomes of low- and high-involvement learning and offered them as hierarchies of behavior for low- and high-involvement products or topics. Specifically, Ray argued for a Cognitive---->Affective---->Conative model for high involvement products and labeled it the learning hierarchy, and for a Cognitive---->Conative---->Affective model called the low-involvement hierarchy (Figure 1). Furthermore, Ray suggested that this was just one possible permutation of the three components, implying that the labels "Cognitive," "Affective" and "Conative" in both models referred to the

THE LOW-INVOLVEMENT AND LEARNING HIERARCHIES
(From Ray 1973)

The Learning Hierarchy

```
COGNITION------------>AFFECT----------->CONATION
-Attention            -Interest         -Intention
-Awareness            -Evaluation       -Behavior
-Comprehension        -Attitude         -Action
-Learning             -Feeling
                      -Yielding
```


The Low-Involvement Hierarchy

```
COGNITION------------>CONATION--------->AFFECT
-Attention            -Intention        -Interest
-Awareness            -Behavior         -Evaluation
-Comprehension        -Action           -Attitude
-Learning                               -Feeling
                                        -Yielding
```

same concepts. I believe that, in this conceptualization, Ray has committed the same error as Krugman (mentioned above) and that these errors have gone relatively unnoticed in the literature.

THE PROBLEM

First, let's look at Krugman's suggestion that, with low-involvement learning, behavioral completion leads to attitudes "supportive and consistent with the shift in perceptual structure." This view is a statement that purchase (a favorable behavior) leads to favorable attitudes toward the brand. But what happens if the brand does not live up to expectations? The person should dislike the brand -- a negative attitude, and we would not expect a positive behavior (purchase) to lead to a positive attitude. In other words, there is no reason to expect a shift in attitude consistent with behavior change.

Similarly, if Ray's argument that the Learning- and Low-involvement hierarchies are permutations of the same concepts (1973, p.150) is correct, then these concepts should be similarly related to each other in both models. Specifically, if Conation is the same in both models, then the correlation of Conation and Affect should be the same in both models. But they're not! Ray (1973, p. 161) presents evidence that for "involved" individuals there is a positive relation between attitude (Affect) and purchase intention (Conation). This is the expected relation in the learning hierarchy. With the low-involvement hierarchy, there is no expectation of a relation of any kind between Conation and Affect: The only expectation is one of timing -- Conation is expected to precede Affect development. Positive purchase intention or actual purchase (by definition a positive Conation) can result in either positive or negative attitude, depending upon the outcome of usage experience. In the learning hierarchy we expect a consistent relation between Affect and Conation; in the low-involvement hierarchy no consistency is expected. What this leads to is the "revelation" that the Cognitive, Affective, and Conative components are not the same between models -- they are not merely permutations of the same three concepts. The problem lies with the "conative" variable. This variable (despite the language) is different in the two models, and to aid future research and discussion in consumer behavior we should label them differently.

By this point we have recognized two things. First, in the learning hierarchy Affect and Conation are expected to have a positive, directional relation. That is, a purchase (or not) decision comes about only after attitudes are formed. The consumer has used information from advertising and from other environmental sources to reach an attitudinal conclusion, and the attitude has a major impact on purchase behavior. Favorable attitude leads to purchase; unfavorable attitude leads to no purchase.

The second thing we have noted is that in the low-involvement hierarchy, Affect and Conation appear to be completely unrelated. However, product use is expected to have a rather large impact on attitude. Favorable usage experience with the brand will lead to positive attitudes, and unfavorable usage experience will lead to negative attitudes. In other words, the conation (purchase) is not causing attitude; attitude is formed from the information received through brand experience, and the purchase itself serves as a source of information (it helps form cognitions). This leads to the inevitable conclusion that there is only one hierarchy:

Cognition---->Affect---->Conation

In so-called "low-involvement" situations, first purchase is merely a source of information to aid in evaluation. I say "so-called" because involvement most likely has nothing to do with a consumer's willingness to collect information via trial. Either high- or low-involved consumers, it will be argued later, might find trial to be the best source of information. In so-called "high-involvement" situations, the use of sources of information other than trial is observed. The difference is in the evaluation method; if it is trial, we mislabel the observed sequence as Cognition---->Conation---->Affect; if it is some other method (resulting in positive Affect), we label it as Cognition---->Affect---->Conation. Smith and Swinyard (1980) recognized this and suggested the hierarchy of effects model as pictured in Figure 2.

FIGURE 2

THE SMITH AND SWINYARD MODEL

```
   (1)            (2)             (3)           (4)
Cognition------>Conation------>Affect------>Conation
               (Trial)                      (Commitment)
```

In Figure 2 the behavior associated with step #2 is expected, by Smith and Swinyard, to be information collection via trial for low risk products and extensive non-trial search for higher risk products. Step #4 is committed behavior, where the product is accepted as a legitimate purchase alternative for satisfying a particular need and parallels "Conation" in the learning hierarchy. A similar view of uncommitted behavior as being different than step #4 is offered by Robertson (1976) who argues that a low committed audience is passive and not seeking purchase information from the communication, "in fact most information seeking...will be based on trial of the product rather than on the use of evaluative symbolic sources" (Robertson, 1976, p. 21). Calder (1979) added to this by implying that attitude formation under low-involvement conditions is the same as under high-involvement conditions except in the source of the beliefs that lead to attitude. By allowing prior behavior (trial) to be a source of information, Calder also recognized the possibility of only one hierarchy. Unfortunately, his conclusions leave the implication that purchase-as-information is unique to low-involved consumers.

Looking back at Figure 1, it is clear that Ray's low-involvement hierarchy is simply the first three steps of the more complete hierarchy (Figure 2). Furthermore, Figure 2 represents a decision hierarchy that does not depend on the "involvement" of consumers. The Cognitive component (#1) includes awareness and comprehension-type activities; steps #2 and #3 cover the development of Affect via evaluation and interest-type activities; and the Conative component (#4) defines committed behavior -- the same three steps proposed by Ray (1973, p. 150). However, the label "conation" in both steps #2 and #4 may be confusing. As stated above, I believe that a re-labeling of the Conation variables to more closely define the type of behavior that takes place at each step will help bring the issue into focus. Figure 3 reflects a re-labeling and slight expansion of the Smith and Swinyard model.

FIGURE 3

THE SINGLE HIERARCHY MODEL

```
                  EVALUATION                  PURCHASE
COGNITION------->BEHAVIOR------->AFFECT------->DECISION
-Awareness        -Interest      -Attitude     -Intention
-Comprehension    -Evaluation    -Feeling      -Commitment
-Attention        -Existing      -Conviction   -Purchase
-Learning          Information   -Yielding     -Rejection
                  -Search
                    -Trial (Actual)
                    -Trial (Vicarious)
                    -Friends
                    -Etc.
```

As is indicated in Figure 3, Smith and Swinyard's second stage (the first Conation) has been re-labeled to define all evaluation activities, not only trial and external search. This allows for the possibility of total evaluation through information contained in the advertisement. These evaluation activities will result in an attitude toward the brand. Stage #4 of Figure 2 has been re-labeled "Purchase Decision" to reflect the fact that "Purchase" is not always the next step. This stage is a decision to purchase or not. The outcome will be positively related to Affect, and even non-purchase is thought of as a behavior.

The single hierarchy model of Figure 3 is obviously not new. In fact, it closely parallels Rogers and Shoemaker's (1971) paradigm of the innovation-decision process that also places heavy emphasis on trial as an evaluation activity. It is also a parallel of Lavidge & Steiner's (1961) hierarchy of effects, except that it does not rely exclusively on advertising's influence. Perhaps the most important contribution the single hierarchy approach makes follows from the elimination of the term "low-involvement hierarchy."

With the "low-involvement" label, research questions are constrained, or channeled into a low-involvement direction. An example of this is the temptation for some researchers to define low-involvement in terms of the hierarchy (if the consumer purchases without affect, he must be low-involved). Low-involvement explanations for purchase before evaluation tend to be forced, and no consistent answers are offered. However, by recognizing that there is no low-involvement hierarchy and that the reported "purchase without evaluation" may simply be part of an evaluation process, we can ask many more interesting questions -- unconstrained by any requirement to incorporate "involvement" explanations into our hypotheses.

To generate research from the decision model proposed in Figure 3, it is important to remember that this is a model based on new information. That is, Krugman (1965, 1966, 1968) was talking about information processing as a learning process about new brands or new brand claims; Ray (1973) presumed an Affect and Intention formation Process; and Figure 3 starts with first awareness and cognition formation in step #1. Since the only difference between this and the earlier models is the insertion of an evaluation stage that influences attitude formation, research questions should be centered there.

The most important question to ask about this stage is, "What are the conditions that effect different information collection strategies?" Granted, the search literature has asked this question before, but it has very seldom allowed for product trial as a possible source. This omission is highlighted in a study by Lutz and Reilly (1974) -- one of the few I found that included trial as a legitimate source of information. They found that when performance risk inherent in a product class was low, purchase (labeled "Go ahead and pick a brand") was the most favored information source. Similarly, Locander & Hermann (1979) found that the most favored information sources for paper towels, after shave/cologne, and electric toasters was "buying" and direct observation/experience (vicarious trial). These are all low performance risk products. However, with higher performance risk products and higher economic risk products like lawn mowers and stereos, non-personal independent sources (like Consumer Reports) were much more favored than buying. Perceived product risk, then, influences the importance of trial as an information source. It is questionable whether this is related to product involvement, although it is certainly a determinant of situational involvement (Houston and Rothschild; 1978).

Besides risk, another possible influencer of trial-as-search is "expected payoff." What I mean by this is, if this new product claim is true, can it solve a problem I have? I suspect that trial-as-search is positively related to this variable. Notice however, that top-of-mind recognition of an unsolved consumer problem defines a high "involved" individual, yet our observation of behavior would follow the old low-involvement hierarchy. For example, a person who has skin problems and just can't find a hand lotion that works for her (very involved with the product class) might try any brand that has promise. We observe the Cognition (awareness)---->Conation (purchase) sequence and find it hard to explain in the language of "involvement hierarchies," but easier to explain with the concept of "potential payoff". It may also be possible that "risk" and "payoff" as determinants of trial-as-search form a kind of ratio with each other. Specifically, the ratio of expected payoff to expected risk of trial (in terms of consequences of poor trial outcome perhaps?) may define the likelihood of trial in relation to other sources of information.

Another research area centers around the specific information needed for Affect development. Two examples are: whether the information sought is about an important attribute; and whether the information sought is capable of being collected through trial. On the first issue, Holbrook and Maier (1978) noticed a direct relation between the importance of a product attribute and the depth of search on that attribute in an information display board-type study; is this generally true? The second issue relates to the consumer's ability to evaluate via trial. This is similar to Rogers and Shoemaker's (1971) "trialability" characteristic of innovations. Whereas we would normally expect actual brand experience (trial) to be the most helpful kind of information in evaluating a brand (after all, the source of information then becomes "self," and who could be a better judge of how a brand will affect

me than me?), perhaps some kinds of information are simply
less suitable for evaluation via trial than other kinds of
information, and another source is needed. An example is
the difference in ability to evaluate "comfort" and
"durability" with trial. Comfort is easily evaluated, and
beliefs about comfort are easily formed through trial but a
mere trial use can never influence beliefs about durability. For information on durability, perhaps non-personal
independent sources (Consumer Reports, etc.) will be more
sought after. In instances where product trial is perceived to be the most "credible" source of information, it
may be preferred before other sources -- given that trial
is an affordable alternative.

As a further example, I would expect that people who are
very interested in the product class of toothpaste
(high-involvement) may vary in the importance they place on
the various attributes (as would Haley, 1968). One group
of people may feel that taste is the most important attribute. Taste is an easily recognized attribute, and we
would expect or predict low levels of external search activities in this high-involved group. On the other hand,
another group of people may perceive that decay prevention
is the most important attribute in this product, in which
case we would expect high levels of non-trial search
because decay prevention is a very difficult attribute to
evaluate -- it takes time and is not easily recognized.
This leads to other sources of information like the
American Dental Association, friends, dentist, etc., and
more likelihood of non-trial evaluation before purchase.
This is strongly related to the role of search in reducing
risk -- specifically the dimension of uncertainty in risk.
If trial use can lead to more certain beliefs about the
presence or absence of particular product attributes
without unduly increasing economic risk, it will probably
be chosen as a source of information. What are the determinants of "trialability"?

In summary, there are many potential research directions
evident with the single hierarchy approach (Figure 3). By
recognizing that there is no "low-involvement hierarchy" of
behavior we are free to explore different explanations for
the apparent Cognition---->Conation sequence identified by
Ray (1973), and come to accept that Conation, as defined by
Ray's low-involvement hierarchy, need not take the exclusive form of purchase. If it is all evaluation behavior,
we can explore beyond involvement to: (1) importance of
attributes, (2) risk of trial versus other information
collection strategies, (3) potential payoff of satisfactory
trial, (4) a payoff/risk ratio, and (5) type of information
to be evaluated. All these directions appear promising.

CONCLUSION

This paper has been an attempt to make two important
points. The first point is that low-involvement learning
is a separate concept from low-involvement behavior. The
theory of low-involvement learning postulates that repeated
exposure to television advertising at low levels of attention results in passive processing of the content of the
message, and it is learned without effort. Attempts to
develop a theory about low-involvement behavior center on
the assumption that it is represented by the Cognition---->
Conation---->Affect sequence of effects. The confusion
between the two theories stems from Krugman's speculation
about the behavioral outcome of low-involvement learning.

The second point of this paper is that the Cognition---->
Conation---->Affect sequence reported by Ray is not a reor-
dered learning hierarchy, but is actually an incomplete
learning hierarchy. The explanation is that first purchase
is often an evaluation activity performed in order to develop Affect. The concept of low- or high-involvement products is not needed to explain this trial-as-search; in
fact, much trial behavior may be conducted with high-

involvement products. It is not the purpose of this paper
to argue against the concept of low-involvement products;
they certainly exist. A purpose is, rather, to argue that
forcing the idea of low-involvement products to define a
set of behavioral outcomes is inefficient and misleading.
We would do better to first establish that a given behavioral situation exists, and then search for explanations.

A related point to be recognized, though not explicitly
mentioned in the body of this paper, flows from the
understanding that advertising is not always the cause of
the first step in the hierarchy: Awareness that a new
brand exists can come from many different sources. Perhaps
a common source of awareness is on-shelf availability ("Oh!
A new brand of________."), and cognitions are developed
from the label. In such a situation, regardless of the
level of interest in or importance of the product category,
low-involvement learning cannot influence behavior (it has
not occurred); yet a decision of whether to further evaluate the brand is made on the spot. The point is that,
even in the Krugman paradigm, the act of generating "connections" at the point of sale (the predicted behavioral
outcome of low-involvement learning),is not defined by low-
involvement learning: other causes are possible. It is
important, in both research areas, that we break the chains
that bind us to low-involvement explanations of behavior
that are as well explained with other concepts.

REFERENCES

Calder, Bobby J. (1979), "When Attitudes Follow Behavior -
    A Self-Perception/Dissonance Interpretation of Low
    Involvement," in J. C. Maloney and B. Silverman (eds.),
    Attitude Research Plays For High Stakes, Chicago:
    American Marketing Association, 25-36.

Haley, Russel I. (1968), "Benefit Segmentation: A
    Decision-oriented Research Tool," Journal of Marketing,
    32 (July), 30-35.

Holbrook, Morris B. and Karl A. Maier (1978), "A Study
    of the Interface Between Attitude Structure and
    Information Acquisition Using A Questionnaire-Based
    Information-Display Sheet," in H. K. Hunt (ed.),
    Advances in Consumer Research, Vol. 5, 93-98.

Houston, Michael J. and Michael L. Rothschild (1978),
    "Conceptual and Methodological Perspectives on
    Involvement," in S. C. Jain (ed.), Research
    Frontiers in Marketing: Dialogues and Directions,
    Chicago: American Marketing Association, 184-187.

Kassarjian, Harold H. (1981), "Low Involvement: A Second
    Look," in K. B. Monroe (ed.), Advances in Consumer
    Research, Vol. 8, 31-34.

Krugman, Herbert E. (1965), "The Impact of Television
    Advertising: Learning Without Involvement,"
    Public Opinion Quarterly, 29, 349-356.

___________ (1966), "The Measurement of Advertising
    Involvement," Public Opinion Quarterly, 30, 583-596.

___________ (1968), "The Learning of Consumer
    Likes, Preferences and Choices," in F. Bass, C. W.
    King, and E. A. Pessemier (eds.), Application of the
    Sciences in Marketing Management, New York: Wiley,
    207-225.

Lavidge, Robert J. and Gary A. Steiner (1961), "A Model For
    Predictive Measurements of Advertising Effectiveness,"
    Journal of Marketing, 25 (October), 59-62.

Locander, William B. and Peter W. Hermann (1979), "The
   Effect of Self-Confidence and Anxiety on Information
   Seeking in Consumer Risk Reduction," Journal of
   Marketing Research, 16, 268-274.

Lutz, Richard J. and Patrick J. Reilly (1974), "An
   Exploration of the Effects of Perceived Social and
   Performance Risk on Consumer Information Acquisition,"
   in S. Ward and P. Wright (eds.), Advances in Consumer
   Research Vol. 1, 393-405.

Ray, Michael L. (1973), "Marketing Communication and The
   Hierarchy-of-Effects," in Peter Clarke (ed.),
   New Models for Mass Communication, Beverly Hill: Sage
   Publications, 147-176.

Robertson, Thomas S. (1976), "Low-Committment Consumer
   Behavior," Journal of Advertising Research, 16 (#2),
   19-24.

Rogers, Everett M. and F. Floyd Shoemaker (1971),
   Communication of Innovations, New York: The Free
   Press.

Smith, Robert E. and William R. Swinyard (1980),
   "Involvement and the Hierarchy of Effects: An
   Integrated Framework," in G. B. Hafer (ed.), A Look
   Back, A Look Ahead, Chicago: American Marketing
   Association, 86-98.

CONSUMER INVOLVEMENT IN A LABORATORY SETTING

Daniel L. Sherrell, Louisiana State University, Baton Rouge
Terence A. Shimp, University of South Carolina, Columbia

ABSTRACT

Based on the premise that the amount of cognitive activity
can be used to indicate involvement states, three procedures were designed to test for differential effects between high and low involvement subjects. An experiment
manipulated involvement via the personality procedure.
Findings revealed that a decision time measure effectively
distinguished between high and low involvement groups,
while two verbally-oriented measures were ineffective. Implications and caveats are provided for future research.

INTRODUCTION

The concept of involvement is one of the most important
scientific units in consumer behavior; yet additions to
Krugman's (1965, 1967) explication of involvement have been
mostly by way of extended conceptualizations (e.g.,
DeBruicker 1979; Gardner, Mitchell, and Russo 1978; Houston
and Rothschild 1978; Leavitt, Greenwald, and Obermiller
1981; Mitchell 1979, 1981; Mitchell, Russo, and Gardner
1980). Empirical activity has not kept pace. Indeed,
this paucity of involvement research represents a serious
gap in the consumer behavior field (Assael 1981, p. 87).
Notable exceptions include the scale development research
by Bloch (1981), the experimental works by Mitchell and
colleagues (Gardner, Mitchell, and Russo 1978; Mitchell,
Russo, and Gardner 1980), and Tyebjee's (1979) response
time research.

The objective of the present research is to investigate the
process of involvement and to examine cognitive differences
in experimental subjects who have been induced with varying
degrees of task involvement. A laboratory setting was designed, and levels of consumer involvement were manipulated
for two product concepts. Three distinct measures were devised to investigate differences in cognitive activity between high and low involvement subjects.

INVOLVEMENT, ITS MANIPULATION, AND EFFECTS

The exact functioning of consumer involvement is not well
understood. More fundamentally, there is confusion over
precisely what involvement is. Perhaps the one common
perspective in the literature is that the amount of involvement influences the extensiveness of cognitive activity that consumers engage in when exposed to marketing
stimuli. Support for this cognitive activity perspective
is provided by Wright (1973), who proposes operationalizing
involvement in terms of the extensiveness of cognitive responses. Empirical justification is afforded by Petty and
Cacioppo (1979), who show that elevating subject involvement in an experimental task increases cognitive activity
in the form of more thought verbalizations.

A manipulation procedure that is consistent with this perspective is the personalization of the decision task approach (Apsler and Sears 1968; Petty and Cacioppo 1979,
1981). With this procedure both high and low involvement
subjects receive the same message or deal with the same
issue. However, high involvement subjects are given instructions designed to make them believe that their behavior in the situation will affect them personally, while low
involvement subjects are not led to believe that their actions will have personally relevant effects. The personalization of a decision situation is an attempt to increase
the importance or instrumentality of the stimulus information for achieving some goal of the subject. The goal
could be general (e.g., ego defense) or specifically manipulated by the involvement instructions (e.g., read and remember this material because you will have to discuss it
with another subject in front of an audience later).

Our research predicts that high involvement subjects will
engage in significantly greater cognitive activity. Three
alternative indicators of cognitive activity are tested.

The simplest and most conventional test involves responses
to "subjective state" scales. The underlying logic is that
the personalized manipulation given to high involvement
subjects will lead to greater thought, and that this will
be reflected on self report (subjective state) rating
scales that measure how involved in the experimental task
subjects consider themselves to be, how meaningful it is,
and so forth.

Another procedure for assessing differences between high
and low involvement subjects is a "self insight accuracy"
measure. The basic issue is whether high involved subjects
have greater self insight into their cognitive operations
than do low involvement subjects. The issue of self insight has been the focus of considerable debate (Nisbett
and Wilson 1977; Smith and Miller 1978; White 1979; Wright
and Rip 1981). However, the influence of involvement on
self insight has not been directly addressed nor manipulated in these prior studies. Indeed, one explanation for
the inconsistency of findings is that the degree of subject
involvement has varied across experiments. For example,
Nisbett and Wilson's (1977) experiments detected very low
levels of subject awareness, perhaps because the experiments
involved mundane, routine decision tasks. Wright and Rip
(1981), by comparison, detected moderately high levels of
self insight; their experiments employed a relatively high
involving task, however.

On the assumption that this "involvement differential" partially accounts for the inconsistencies in self insight
findings, it is hypothesized that self reports about decisions made under high involvement conditions will be more
accurate (i.e., reflect more self insight into cognitive
processes) than self reports under low involvement conditions. Because high involved subjects should devote more
attention to a cognitive task and utilize automatic processes less extensively, more accurate self reports should
result. Schneider and Shiffrins' (1977) work on the use of
attention indicates that the accuracy levels exhibited by
subjects under conditions encouraging automatic processing
remain unchanged under increased information loads. Subjects using non-automatic processing displayed decreased
accuracy levels under the same conditions, thereby suggesting that automatic processes operate independently of
attention.

The amount of time that subjects require to complete a decision task offers a third procedure for assessing cognitive
activity. Response time measures are especially appealing,
because they are less vulnerable to demand effects and other
biases. The logic underlying response time measures is that
high involvement manipulations should engender greater cognitive activity, thereby requiring greater amounts of time
to complete the same task required of low involved subjects.
Tyebjee's (1979) test of this notion obtained mixed results,
but the value of that otherwise excellent research as related to the present concern is limited, because involvement

was merely measured but was not experimentally manipulated.

Hypotheses

The foregoing discussion gives rise to three formal hypotheses.

H1: The subjective state (SS) scale ratings of high involved subjects will be significantly greater than those of low involved subjects.

H2: The self insight accuracy (SIA) of high involved subjects will be significantly greater than that of low involved subjects.

H3: The elapsed decision times (EDT) of high involved subjects will be significantly greater than those of low involved subjects.

METHODS

The hypotheses were tested by constructing an experiment that: manipulated levels of involvement; presented subjects with product attribute information; had them use this information to make product preference decisions; required them to self report the importance of each attribute on their decision; and then compared the self-reported importance scores against statistically estimated importance scores.

A convenience sample of 72 undergraduate students participated in the experiment. The experimental procedures required that the respondents return to the study site on five separate occasions, so a monetary incentive was used to help assure high completion rates. Of the 72 subjects who started the study, 65 completed all five sessions—results relate to these subjects only.

To create the correct setting for the decision tasks, subjects were given a cover story which informed them that they were participating in two product concept tests conducted by a national market research firm. One product concept was described as a low calorie candy bar containing a sugar substitute combined with conventional candy bar ingredients. The second product idea was a professional job placement service designed specifically for college seniors.[1] Subjects were told that both concepts were still in the design stage and that the client firms were interested in consumer's perceptions and opinions of different variations on each idea.

Subjects were assigned randomly to high or low involvement groups. Subjects in the high involvement condition were told that the city in which their university was located had been selected as a test market by the candy bar manufacturer, and that the firm was vitally interested in their perceptions of different versions of the low calorie candy bar. These subjects were also told that the firm developing the job placement service had selected their university as the test site for a professional job placement service and wanted to use their perceptions of different variations of the product concept to design the placement service. For both concepts a strong attempt was made to personalize the decision setting and make the high involvement subjects believe their decisions were important. Low involvement

subjects received the same information about the products, but the information was presented in an impersonal tone and no mention was made of the personal relevance or importance of the research. The involvement manipulation was administered prior to the first and third sessions only and not prior to the fifth so as to avoid biasing the self report involvement measure taken after the fifth session.

Product Concept Profiles

Multiple profiles were constructed for both product concepts by varying at high and low levels four attributes for each product. This amounted to a total of 16 (2^4) distinct profiles for each product concept. Extensive pre-testing was used to select attributes that were most relevant to each product category. The attributes manipulated for the candy bar included taste, size, endorsement by nutritionists, and procedures for promoting the candy bar. The four attributes chosen for the job placement service included company size, past placement record, personal qualities of the placement counselors, and name of the placement service.

In addition to these manipulated attributes, "normalizing" information was included in each product concept description to serve as a reference point for subjects to use in their evaluations of the different profiles. For example, subjects were told that traditional candy bars generally weigh 1.6 oz. This information was vital for subjects to meaningfully process size information, which was manipulated as either 1.8 oz. (high) or 1.2 (low). Similar normalizing information was provided for the job placement service.

Decision Tasks

The experiment consisted of five separate trials, each separated by one day. The intent was to create by the fifth trial a partially automated decision process corresponding to that characterizing the majority of consumer behavior decisions. At each of the five trials subjects were required to read through all 16 product profiles for the low calorie candy bar and rank the profiles in descending order of purchase likelihood. Subjects then read the 16 profiles for the job placement service and ranked these in terms of purchase likelihood.

Operationalizing the Cognitive Activity Measures

The subjective state, self insight accuracy, and elapsed decision time measures were operationalized in the following fashion.

Subjective State Measures. Two sets of items were administered to all subjects at the end of the fifth trial. Subjects indicated the degree to which their decisions were: interesting, important, difficult, and thought-provoking. Word pairs (e.g., interesting to me/not interesting to me) anchored 7-point scales. In addition, following Petty and Cacioppo's (1979) procedures, two 11-point scales were used to measure how much thought subjects estimated they put into their decisions and how involving they felt the decision tasks were.

Self Insight Accuracy Measures. Each subject's fifth-trial rank orderings of the two sets of 16 product concept profiles were input into individual-level conjoint models utilizing Kruskal's (1964) MONANOVA procedure.[2] The

---

[1] The two product concepts were designed to be conceptually different in their tendency to evoke involvement. Pretesting had indicated that the job placement service was more interesting to the sample of college juniors and seniors. It therefore was anticipated that the within product differences between involvement groups would be more pronounced for the job placement service.

---

[2] The fifth trial rankings were used on the assumption that subjects, having already made the same rank ordering decisions on four previous occasions, would make the fifth decision in a nearly automated fashion. Insight into the decision process should be most restricted under these conditions, thereby providing a stronger test of whether high involvement subjects would exhibit higher self insight accuracy.

absolute values of the part-worth utilities were used to indicate how much influence each of the manipulated attributes had on a subject's rank orderings. A constant sum scale was used by subjects to assign points to the manipulated attributes based on the relative importance that a subject believed each attribute had had on his/her ranking decision. Self insight accuracy was defined operationally as the degree of association between a subject's self-reported attribute importance and the statistical estimate of attribute importance.

Elasped Decision Time Measures. The elapsed decision times required to complete the two separate product profile rankings were recorded for each subject at each trial. The timing device was activated by the experimenter when subjects received the product profiles for each product concept. Subjects were instructed to deactivate their timer after they completed the 16 rankings. The elapsed time was recorded, the timer reset, and then reactivated when subjects received the set of profiles for the next product concept. Pains were taken to assure subjects that the elapsed times were not competitively based. Subjects were not informed of their times. Each subject wqs asked to specifically state the perceived purpose of the experiment. All subjects indicated perceptions consistent with the cover provided at the start of the study. In general, their comments indicated the personalization procedure was effective, with a number of the subjects wanting to know whether a sample of the candy bar was available or where the proposed job placement center was to be located.

RESULTS

Subjective State Results

Responses to the six subjective scales were factor analyzed to see if the scales were tapping into different dimensions of subject involvement. Results of the analysis are shown in Table 1. For each product concept, two factors accounted for the major portion of variation in the scale responses (65.4% for the low calorie candy bar and 63% for the job placement service). The first factor taps the degree of perceived task importance and subject interest, whereas the second factor concerns perceived task effort. One scale item ("difficulty of choice") switched factors from the candy bar to the job placement service, probably due to the increased complexity of the latter concept. All other items loaded on the same factor for both product concepts. Two additive scales were created: Scale 1 is the sum of each subject's responses to the items that loaded most heavily on factor 1, and Scale 2 contains the items loading heaviest on factor 2. Scale reliabilities (Cronbach alphas) are reported at the bottom of Table 1.

T-tests were performed to test the hypothesis (H1) that subjects assigned to the high involvement group would exhibit significantly higher mean responses than low involvement subjects. The bottom portion of Table 1 shows the scale means for high and low involvement groups as delineated by the two different combinations of scale items. For neither product category were there statistically significant differences between the high and low involvement subjects. These results thus fail to support the first hypothesis--the subjective state masure did not indicate greater cognitive activity for high involvement subjects.

Self Insight Accuracy Results

The Pearson Correlation between the statistical estimate of importance for a particular attribute (i.e., its part-worth utility score) and the self-reported importance of that attribute (as indicated by the constant sum points assigned to the attribute) represents the level of accuracy by a particular subject for a specific attribute. A positive coefficient represents some degree of self insight, while a negative coefficient indicates a notable absence

of insight.

TABLE 1

SUBJECTIVE STATE FINDINGS: FACTOR ANALYSIS
RESULTS, SCALE MEANS, AND (STANDARD DEVIATIONS)

Items	Factor Loadings	
	Factor 1	Factor 2
Low Calorie Candy Bar		
Interesting to Me	.23	.86
Important to Me	-.01	.90
Difficult to Choose	.53	-.10
Took a Lot of Thought	.75	.15
Task was Very Involving	.84	.23
Put a Lot of Thought into Choice	.68	.47
Job Placement Service		
Interesting to Me	.36	.71
Important to Me	.30	.73
Difficult to Choose	-.15	.55
Took a Lot of Thought	.84	.03
Task was Very Involving	.81	.15
Put a Lot of Thought into Choice	.89	.18

Scales[a]	Coefficient Alpha	High Involvement (n=33)	Low Involvement (n=32)
Low Calorie Candy Bar[b]			
Scale 1	.70	3.96(1.1)	3.55(1.1)
Scale 2	.76	4.29(1.7)	4.14(1.9)
Job Placement Service			
Scale 1	.67	4.75(1.0)	4.76(.08)
Scale 2	.69	6.09(1.1)	6.07(1.3)

[a]Scale means were adjusted for differences in the number of scale items.

[b]Low Calorie Candy Bar scale means were significantly lower (p < .05) than the comparable scales means for the Job Placement Service for both involvement categories.

Because the meaningfulness of this analysis rests heavily on the quality of the statistical estimates of attribute importance, an initial screening step was performed whereby subjects with poorly fitted data were removed from subsequent analysis. At a stress value cutoff point of 40 percent, which has been defined as poor by Kruskal (1964), 18 of the 65 subjects (28%) were excluded from the candy bar analysis; the average stress value for the remaining 47 subjects was an acceptable 9.6 percent. For the job placement concept, 54 subjects (83%) had stress values of less than 40 percent; the average stress value was 4.3 percent. The constant sum importance scores for the excluded subjects were compared via t-tests against the responses for the included subjects. No significant differences were found, thereby suggesting that the included subjects differed only in the degree of fit between their rankings and the conjoint model.

Candy Bar Results. The direction of influence shown in Table 2 for the accuracy scores between the different levels of involvement is exactly opposite of the predictions made in the research hypothesis (H2). Subjects in the low involvement condition consistently displayed higher levels of self insight than did the high involvement subjects. All of the coefficients in the low involvement condition were statistically significant at the .05 level or better. In the high involvement condition only one attribute was significant. Two other attributes were close to acceptable levels of significance, but the fourth attribute was actually slightly negative, indicating a notable lack of self awareness. This negative accuracy score, when compared to the corresponding accuracy score in the low involvement condition, produced the only high Z score. However, because the hypothesis is directional, the Z statistic of -2.71 is not significant. The hypothesis of higher self insight for high involvement subjects cannot be accepted on the basis of these results.

TABLE 2

SELF INSIGHT ACCURACY RESULTS

Low Calorie Candy Bar

Attribute	High Involvement (n=25)		Low Involvement (n=22)		Z-score[a]
	r	p	r	p	
Taste	.29	.17	.43	.05	-0.52
Size	.49	.01	.59	.00	-0.44
Endorsement	.30	.14	.55	.01	-0.99
Promotion	$-.03$	.89	.67	.00	-2.71

Job Placement Service

Attribute	High Involvement (n=24)		Low Involvement (n=30)		Z-score[a]
	r	p	r	p	
Company size	.18	.41	.42	.02	-1.13
Placement record	.15	.49	.46	.01	-1.21
Counselor qualities	$-.12$	.57	.48	.01	-2.22
Company name	.42	.04	.63	.00	-1.10

[a]The Z-scores represent tests of statistical difference between the high and low involvement correlation coefficients for each attribute. Fisher's r to z transformation was used to convert the correlation coefficients to Z-scores.

Job Placement Results. The scores in Table 2 (bottom portion) for the low involvement condition are all significant at the .05 level or better, while the only attribute to attain significance for the high involvement group was company name. The same pattern for the low calorie candy bar concept is apparent in these scores: Subjects in the low involvement condition, contrary to hypothesis, consistently displayed higher levels of introspective awareness than the more highly involved subjects.

Elapsed Decision Time Results

Low involvement subjects required 4.46 (SD = 1.76) and 4.66 (SD = 1.77) minutes, respectively, to rank order the candy bar and job placement profiles. High involvement subjects, by comparison, required 5.83 (SD = 1.70) and 5.55 (SD = 1.93) minutes, respectively, to rank order the profiles for the two product concepts. T-tests between the mean decision times for high and low involvement groups were performed for both product concepts. The T-value for candy bars was 3.18 (p < .01, 63 df, one-tailed), and for the

job placement service it was 1.93 (p < .1, 63 df, one-tailed). The fact that high involvement subjects took significantly more time supports the third hypothesis and suggests that the personalizing manipulation engaged greater cognitive activity.

DISCUSSION

Several reasons might account for the inability of the two verbal methods to yield hypothesized results. One possibility is that the personalization manipulation may be capable of initiating a high involvement state only under those restricted conditions where the experimental issue is truly meaningful. This may not have been the case for the two product concepts used in this research. However, the fact that the elapsed decision time method did detect significant differences between the high- and low-involvement groups, presumably because of differential levels of involvement, would seem to challenge this particular account.

A more plausible explanation is that the personalization manipulation did generate different degrees of cognitive activity in the high- and low-involvement groups, but that the two verbal methods were simply incapable of detecting this. Considering the subjective state method first, one possibility is that the impact of the manipulation eroded due to the gap between the time at which the personalization information was manipulated (at the 1st and 3rd trials) and the time at which the scales were administered (at the fifth trial). Thus, the subjective state scale items may not have been as sensitive in picking up differences between the two involvement groups as was the decision time measure, which, unlike verbal methods, is not subject to forgetting nor to bias. An important implication for future research is that the interval between inducing involvement states and administering this type of effect measure must be a short one to prevent impact erosion.

The self insight accuracy results are the most difficult to reconcile. One explanation for the inferior performance of the high-involvement subjects is that the high involvement manipulation did generate greater cognitive activity, but that this heightened activity imposed a greater burden on subjects' memories, thereby leading to lower self-report accuracy. In other words, it would be expected that the high-involved subjects would have been concerned about the outcome of their decisions as well as the process of making the decisions, but the low-involved subjects would have tended to store only the decision process, because this group probably perceived the decision task as rather inconsequential. It thus appears that self insight accuracy measurement procedures used here and similar to those previously used (Nisbett and Wilson 1977; Wright and Rip 1980) are "loaded" against high involvement subjects, such that lower self insight may actually be due to memory burden resulting from _greater_ cognitive activity.

Finally, these research results support the potential usefulness of decision time measures as a means of assessing involvement effects. However, the lack of consistent findings and the difficulty in interpreting results leads us to the unpleasant but realistic conclusion that any contributions from this research result more from the questions that may be stimulated than from the answers that are provided.

REFERENCES

Apsler, R., and D. Sears (1968), "Warning, Personal Involvement, and Attitude Change," _Journal of Personality and Social Psychology_, 9, 162-166.

Assael, Henry (1981), _Consumer Behavior_, Boston: Kent Publishing Company.

Bloch, Peter H. (1981), "An Exploration into the Scaling of Consumers' Involvement with a Product Class," in _Advances in Consumer Research_, Vol. 8, Kent Monroe, ed., Ann Arbor: Association for Consumer Research, 61-65.

DeBruicker, F. Stewart (1979), "An Appraisal of Low-Involvement Consumer Information Processing," in _Attitude Research Plays for High Stakes_, J.C. Maloney and B. Silverman, eds., Chicago: American Marketing Association, 112-130.

Gardner, Meryl P., Andrew A Mitchell, and J. Edward Russo (1978), "Chronometric Analysis: An Introduction and an Application to Low Involvement Perception of Advertisments," in _Advances in Consumer Research_, Vol. 5, H. Keith Hunt, ed., Ann Arbor: Association for Consumer Research, 581-89.

Houston, Michael J., and Michael J. Rothschild (1978), "Conceptual and Methodological Foundations on Involvement," in _Research Frontiers in Marketing: Dialogues and Directions_, Subhash C. Jain, ed., Chicago: American Marketing Association, 184-87.

Krugman, Herbert E. (1965), "The Impact of Television Advertising: Learning Without Involvement," _Public Opinion Quarterly_, 29, 349-56.

__________ (1967), "The Measurment of Advertising Involvement," _Public Opinion Quarterly_, 30, 583-96.

Kruskal, J.B. (1964), "Multidimensional Scaling by Optimizing Goodness of Fit to a Nonmetric Hypothesis," _Psychometrika_, 29, 1-27.

Leavitt, Clark, Anthony G. Greenwald, and Carl Obermiller (1981), "What Is Low Involvement Low In?," in _Advances in Consumer Research_, Vol. 8, Kent Monroe, ed., Ann Arbor: Association for Consumer Research, 15-19.

Mitchell, Andrew A. (1979), "Involvement: A Potentially Important Mediator of Consumer Behavior," in _Advances in Consumer Research_, Vol. 6, William Wilkie, ed., Ann Arbor: Association for Consumer Research, 191-96.

__________ (1981), "The Dimensions of Advertising Involvement," in _Advances in Consumer Research_, Vol. 8, Kent Monroe, ed., Ann Arbor: Association for Consumer Research, 25-30.

__________, J. Edward Russo, and Meryl Gardner (1980), "Strategy-Induced Low Involvement Processing of Advertising Messages," Carnegie-Mellon University manuscript (July).

Nisbett, Richard W., and Timothy DeCamp Wilson (1977), "Telling More Than We Can Know: Verbal Reports on Mental Processes," _Psychological Review_, 84 (May), 231-59.

Petty, Richard E, and John T. Cacioppo (1979), "Issue Involvement Can Increase or Decrease Persuasion by Enhancing Message-Relevant Cognitive Responses," _Journal of Personality and Social Psychology_, 37, 1915-26.

__________ (1981), "Issue Involvement As a Moderator of the Effects on Attitude of Advertising Content and Context," in _Advances in Consumer Research_, Vol. 8, Kent Monroe, ed., Ann Arbor: Association for Consumer Research, 20-24.

Schnieder, Walter, and Richard M. Shiffrin (1977), "Controlled and Automatic Human Information Processing: I. Detection, Search, and Attention," _Psychological Review_, 84 (January), 1-67.

Smith, Eliot R., and Frederick D. Miller (1978), "Limits on Perception of Cognitive Processes: A Reply to Nisbett and Wilson," _Psychological Review_, 85 (Summer), 355-62.

Tyebjee, Tyzoon T. (1979), "Response Time, Conflict, and Involvement in Brand Choice," _Journal of Consumer Research_, 6, 295-304.

White, Peter (1980), "Limitations on Verbal Reports of Internal Events: A Refutation of Nisbett and Wilson and of Bem," _Psychological Review_, 87, 105-112.

Wright, Peter (1973), "The Cognitive Processes Mediating Acceptance of Advertising," _Journal of Marketing Research_, 10 (February), 53-62.

__________ and Peter Rip (1981), "Retrospective Reports on the Causes of Decisions," _Journal of Personality and Social Psychology_, 40, 601-614.

STUDENTS AS CONSUMERS: PREDICTING SATISFACTION

Thomas E. Barry, Southern Methodist University, Dallas
Mary C. Gilly, Southern Methodist University, Dallas
William R. Schucany, Southern Methodist University, Dallas

ABSTRACT

This study reports the results of an investigation of predicting student satisfaction with performance on two examinations from their expectations of that performance versus the actual performance. A theoretical background in
the consumer satisfaction/dissatisfaction literature is
presented along with a brief discussion of existing research regarding student expectations. Results of the investigation are presented with a discussion and suggestions for further research.

INTRODUCTION

Marketing academics and practitioners have long been concerned about consumer satisfaction/dissatisfaction and a
considerable body of academic literature has been formed
around this topic. Consumer satisfaction is important in
that academics have long espoused the importance of the
marketing concept -- a concept that longevity in the business world of marketing is a function of consumer satisfaction with products and/or brands.

In the academic marketing sphere, a generally accepted
principle is that students are indeed consumers and,
therefore, the marketing concept should be practiced in
academic institutions. November (1981) has recently
studied student choice in a marketing principles course
and Murphy (1979) has advocated the use of consumer research for business schools in developing student (consumer) oriented curricula. Abell (1977) and Enis (1977)
have respectively argued for the implementation of the
marketing concept and the development of strategies for
mature products with respect to marketing education. Further, Dwyer (1977) has argued that marketing educators
must pay heed to diverse student segments in the principles course. If students are consumers, it may be that
the research methodologies and concepts which apply to the
"typical" consumer may be just as viable in academic settings.

Consumer Satisfaction/Dissatisfaction Literature

Four general theories permeate the dissatisfaction literature. Contrast theory predicts that when a difference exists between expectations and performance, consumers will
exaggerate the disparity (Spector, 1956). Dissonance theory (or assimilation) would predict the opposite effect
from contrast theory -- the consumer tends to minimize the
difference occurring between expectations and performance
(Festinger, 1957; Olshavsky and Miller, 1972). Generalized negativity theory predicts that any disparity in expectations and performance will result in less satisfaction than if expectations are met (Anderson, 1973). Finally assimilation-contrast theory predicts that small
differences in expectations and performance will be minimized while large differences will be exaggerated (Anderson, 1973).

The results of these four theories present a wide dispersion of conclusions. Miller (1977) has suggested that a
possible reason for the inconsistency in the literature
concerning expectations is that consumers have different
"types" of expectations they use as standards of comparison in performance evaluations. He contends that simply
asking someone what he or she "expects" can result in different interpretations by different people.

Within the context of consumer purchase behavior, Miller
offered a basic satisfaction model where an individual
brings a set of expectations to the purchase situation.
These expectations are a function of the individual's past
history and current situation. As performance is measured, the individual modifies and updates expectations
through processes such as dissonance reduction, rationali-
zation, or selective information gathering. Miller cites
evidence that expectations themselves influence the perception of outcomes. Thus, he contends that the system of
expectancies probably differs among consumers (on the
basis of experiences, traits, demographic characteristics,
etc.) as well as within the individual (changes due to recent experience, information, the situation, etc.).

Miller modified this basic model to recognize four potentially different types of expectations an individual might
have regarding anticipated performance levels. These are:
"Ideal," "Expected," "Minimum Tolerable," and "Deserved."
A brief explanation of each is warranted. The Ideal is
the "wished for" level, reflecting what the respondent
feels the performance of the product, service, or store
"can be." It is a function of prior experience, learning,
information, advertising, word-of-mouth, etc.

The Expected is thought of as having no affective dimension but as being the result of an objective calculation
of probability. Its bases are similar to the history, experience, and information inputs determining the level of
the Ideal. The Expected level reflects what the consumer
feels performance of the product probably "will be."

The Minimum Tolerable represents the least acceptable level, the minimum level the consumer feels performance
"must be." The inputs to this expectation level are similar to the Ideal and Expected levels.

The Deserved adds an affective dimension that may be most
critical in determining feelings of satisfaction or dissatisfaction. It may be the same as the Expected level,
but it includes other important factors. Unlike the other
expectation levels, the Deserved level is critically determined by the individual's evaluation of his/her "investment" in the purchase. This investment would include
all the costs associated with the time, money and effort
involved in purchasing the product. The Deserved level
reflects what the consumer feels performance "should be."

Conceptually, the Ideal would always represent the highest
expectation level and the Minimum Tolerable would always
represent the lowest level. The Deserved might be higher
than the Expected when the individual pays a premium price
or invests a great deal of time and effort. Alternatively, the Deserved may be lower than the Expected when the
product was "a steal," requiring little time or effort to
obtain.

While Miller was interested in the expectations of consumers buying products, these same expectation types and predictions about their relation to actual performance and
resultant satisfaction/dissatisfaction can be applied to
students' expectations about and satisfaction with their
performance on examinations. For example, the Ideal would
represent the best grade a student feels he/she could possibly get on a test. The Expected would reflect the

student's objective estimate of the grade. The Minimum Tolerable would be the worst possible grade the student thinks he/she could have gotten. Finally, the Deserved would reflect the grade the student feels he/she should get, given the amount of time and effort spent on studying for a test. The relation of the student's actual grade to these expectation types should result in the same satisfaction/dissatisfaction levels Miller discussed in the context of consumer purchase behavior.

Student Expectations

Educators have studied student expectations of grades, but mainly in relation to teacher and course evaluations rather than satisfaction. Marsh et al. (1976) examined undergraduate students' expectations of the grades they would receive and their evaluation of instructional quality. It was found that average responses to the overall instructor and course items, items most often used by administrators to obtain a summary impression, showed statistically significant correlations with average expected grades. However, factors most closely associated with teaching, such as instructor enthusiasm, breadth of coverage, interaction and organization, showed less significant relationships with expected grades.

Snyder and Clair (1976) further examined the relationship of student expectations and teacher evaluation. Their results indicated that the lower the expected grade or the higher the obtained grade, the more favorable the teacher evaluation. Similarly, Feldman (1976) found that students' anticipated or actual grades in class are positively related to their evaluation of courses and teachers.

The education literature does not address the issue of student expectations of grades and their resultant performance satisfaction.

If we truly believe that students are consumers, as suggested at the outset of this paper, it behooves us to be concerned about students' satisfaction with the performance of the "products" they buy. While standard course evaluations provide one measure of this, students' self-reported level of satisfaction with their own performance may be a more salient monitoring device.

THE STUDY

In the fall of 1981, students enrolled in two sections of an upper level marketing class in a major southwestern university served as subjects for the study. The sections were taught by the same professor. The students were required to take three tests during the semester and to write a term paper or participate in a group project. A questionnaire was distributed with each of the tests and students were asked to respond to expectation questions following completion of the test. For half of the questionnaires, relevant questions were reversed to minimize any order effect. As discussed earlier, it was possible for the Expected grade to be either higher or lower than the Deserved grade. When the tests were graded and returned to the student, he/she completed a questionnaire about his/her level of satisfaction with the grade. The basic research objective of the study is a comparison of the ability to predict student levels of satisfaction based upon their actual examination score versus the differences between their expectations of performance and their actual performance. The results follow.

Results

Due to the exploratory nature of this study, results were analyzed for only the first two examinations. Further, because the results of the analyses of both examinations were highly consistent and due to space limitations, most results presented are for examination two only. The level of student satisfaction (five levels ranging from very dissatisfied to very satisfied) was predicted from either the actual examination score or the various differences between expectations and actual examination performance. Differences are noted as follows:

D_1 = Ideal Score minus Actual Exam Score
D_2 = Deserved Score minus Actual Exam Score
D_3 = Expected Score minus Actual Exam Score
D_4 = Minimum Tolerable Score minus Actual Exam Score

For example, if a student's Expected Score is 84 and he/she actually scores 73, his/her D_3 score is 11. Hence, negative differences correspond to actual exam scores exceeding expectations.

Table 1 presents the average differences for all students by level of satisfaction. As can be seen, student satisfaction tends to be dispersed over the entire satisfaction spectrum (very dissatisfied to very satisfied). One-way analyses of variance confirm that the D_3 difference exhibits the greatest amount of variation across the five levels of satisfaction. This is the basis upon which it is selected first in the stepwise discriminant analysis procedure exhibited in Table 2. This procedure used the differences and actual exam score to construct the best classification rules for the five groups defined by the five levels of satisfaction.

Further inspection of Table 2 indicates that the actual exam score alone is a "better predictor" of satisfaction than D_3 while a linear best fit of all four differences $(D_1, \ldots, D_4)$ is the "best predictor" of student satisfaction with exam performance.

Table 1

Average Differences by Level of Satisfaction
(Examination 2)

Satisfaction Level	N	D_1 (Ideal)	D_2 (De-served)	D_3 (Ex-pected)	D_4 (Minimum Tolerable)
Very Dissatisfied	7	15	16	7	-15
Moderately Dissatisfied	13	9	13	3	-5
Neither	8	4	7	-3	-20
Moderately Satisfied	16	4	0	-3	-11
Very Satisfied	21	-6	-5	-13	-26
Combined	65	2.7	3.4	-4.0	-16.2
F-Ratio		14.1	13.0	14.4	4.0

[a]Average Differences for satisfaction levels are rounded to nearest whole number.

Table 2

Five Group Discriminant Analysis

Examination	N	Best Difference Found	F-Ratio	D_3	Actual Exam Score	$D_1, \ldots, D_4$ Combined
1	64	D_3	6.7*	45.3	48.4	51.6
2	65	D_3	14.4*	47.7	58.5	63.1
Pooled	129	D_3	26.4*	49.6	54.6	56.2

*$p < .01$

Continuing the analysis, Table 3 presents a comparison of the predictive performance of D_3 to that of the predictor based upon the actual score alone.

Table 3

Comparison of the Predictive Performance
of the Actual Exam Score Versus D_3
(Examination 2)

		D_3		
		Right	Wrong	Totals
Actual Exam Score	Right	20	18	38 (58.5%)
	Wrong	11	16	27
	Totals	31 (47.7%)	34	65

Recall that Table 2 suggests that, in terms of classification, the actual score alone is a better predictor of satisfaction than the D_3 score. The importance of this analysis is to ascertain whether this difference is significant. By inspecting Table 3, we can see the comparative performance of the two predictors. An analysis of this performance using the Sign test on the cases for which the two predictors were not in complete agreement, indicates that the differential performance of the test score alone versus D_3 is not statistically significant [$P(S_N < 11 \mid N = 29) = .1325$]. At this point one may conclude that satisfaction can be predicted as well by using a simple measure of performance (in this case a grade on an examination) _without_ using a measure of expectations of that performance. Recall, however, that Table 2 suggests that _some combination_ of expectations versus performance is a better predictor than either the single best difference (D_3) or the actual test score alone. Table 4 presents this analysis.

Table 4

Comparison of the Predictive Performance of
D_3 and a Combination of All Four Differences
(Examination 2)

		D_3		
		Right	Wrong	Totals
All Four Differences (D_1, D_2, D_3, D_4)	Right	27	14	41 (63.1%)
	Wrong	4	20	24
	Totals	31 (47.7%)	34	65

Table 4 contrasts the classification errors of a combination of all four differences to those of the single best predictor (D_3). This analysis, again using the Sign test, indicates that the best combination of all four difference scores significantly outperforms D_3 [$P(S_N < 4 \mid n = 18) = .0154$].

Discussion

While the results of this study cannot be generalized to student, much less consumer, populations, they provide some interesting implications and suggestions for further research. While some may argue that expectation measurement is unnecessary and the real test of satisfaction (students' or consumers') is some measure of performance, the findings suggest that expectations are relevant to ascertaining satisfaction. It is clear that differences between performance and expectations are useful for analyzing satisfaction.

What people "really expect" versus what they get (or how they perform) seems to be a fairly strong predictor of satisfaction levels. However, the evidence here is that the best predictor of satisfaction, at least for students, is some combination of the "subjective evaluations" students make versus their actual "performance distance" from these expectations. A key question is whether or not expectations make a difference on reported satisfaction levels. The consumer behavior literature indicates that they do. Miller (1977) suggests that several different expectation levels may interact. The results here, while tentative, seem to indicate that Miller is correct. However, further research is clearly necessary.

Because it is very difficult to measure consumers in the real world, it may be that students can provide marketers with a chance to get "real world" answers from a surrogate real world setting. Continued research in this area (which the authors have ongoing) suggests at least two additional inputs. First, further analysis of levels of satisfaction with additional performance measures (a final examination and a written paper project) and global levels of satisfaction seem imperative. Second, additional samples are planned which use a control not implemented in this study. The comparison of satisfaction levels for students whose expectations are measured with those whose expectations are not measured apppears warranted. These continued studies can perhaps shed more light on the predictive efficacy of expectations and performance toward levels of student and consumer satisfaction.

REFERENCES

Abell, Derek F. (1977), "Applying the Marketing Concept to Marketing Education," _Proceedings_, American Marketing Association, 141-144.

Anderson, Ralph E. (1973), "Consumer Dissatisfaction: The Effect of Disconfirmed Expectancy on Perceived Product Performance," _Journal of Marketing Research_, 10 (February), 38-44.

Dwyer, F. Robert (1977), "The Marketing Principles Course: Correspondence with Student Interests, Attendance to Diverse Segments," _Proceedings_, American Marketing Association, 149-154.

Enis, Ben M. (1977), "Marketing Education in the 1980's: Strategy Considerations for a Mature Product Line," _Proceedings_, American Marketing Association, 78-81.

Feldman, Kenneth A. (1976), "Grades and College Students' Evaluations of Their Courses and Teachers," _Research in Higher Education_, 4, 1, 69-111.

Festinger, Leon (1957), _A Theory of Cognitive Dissonance_, New York: Harper and Row.

Marsh, Herbert W., J. U. Overall and Christopher S. Thomas (1976), "The Relationship Between Students' Evaluations of Instruction and Expected Grades," paper presented at the Annual Meeting of the American Educational Research Association, San Francisco, California (April).

Miller, John A. (1977), "Studying Satisfaction: Modifying Models, Eliciting Expectations, Posing Problems, and Making Meaningful Measurement," in H. Keith Hunt, ed., _Conceptualization and Measurement of Consumer Satisfaction and Dissatisfaction_, Marketing Science Institute, 72-91.

Murphy, Patrick E. (1979), "The Need for Consumer Research in Higher Education," _Proceedings_, American Marketing Association, 110-115.

November, Peter John (1981), "Marketing Oriented Teaching
     Method Selection," <u>Proceedings</u>, American Marketing
     Association, 423-426.

Olshavsky, Richard W. and John C. Miller (1972), "Consumer
     Expectations, Product Performance and Perceived Prod-
     uct Quality," <u>Journal of Marketing Research</u>, 9 (Feb-
     ruary), 19-21.

Snyder, C. R. and Mark Clair (1976), "Effects of Expected
     and Obtained Grades on Teacher Evaluation and Attri-
     bution of Performance," <u>Journal of Educational Psy-
     chology</u>, 68, 1 (February), 75-82.

Spector, Aaron J. (1956), "Expectations, Fulfillment and
     Morale," <u>Journal of Abnormal and Social Psychology</u>,
     52 (January), 51-56.

THE TAKE-HOME/IN-CLASS EXAM
COMBO: AN EVALUATION

Marvin A. Jolson, University of Maryland, College Park

ABSTRACT

This paper presents a comparison of student grades on take-
home and in-class examinations covering the subject of
quantitative sales forecasting methods. The reasons for
the lack of grade correlation are discussed and student
responses disclose confidential behavior patterns during
and attitudes toward each exam type. The findings suggest
that the cited exam combination may be appropriate for
accomplishing the multiple objectives of testing.

INTRODUCTION

With the increasing use of case analysis, model building,
and other tools of management science in undergraduate
marketing courses, faculty members are attempting to
encourage student thinking beyond memory level. Accompanying this phenomenon has been a gradual decline of the
college classroom test in favor of out-of-class examinations (Marsh 1980). Indeed, as marketing and the decision
sciences become more compatible, both students and instructors may find that a frequent combination of take-home and
in-class testing may be a sound pedagogical approach.

The rationale for the use of take-home tests is that
reflective thinking, problem solving, and forms of analyzing information take more time than simply recalling or
recognizing principles or data (Svoboda 1971). It has also
been demonstrated that in many instances, anxieties introduced by timed classroom exams have a debilitating effect
upon some students (Sarasen 1961).

Additional Advantages of the Take-Home Exam

Once the take-home exam has been issued, the student will
have opportunities to ask for clarification of exam questions that remain unclear. Time pressures of the in-class
exam make this much more difficult to do. If one sub-
scribes to Marsh's (1980) notion that "failing a test for
which one can research the answers is almost unthinkable,"
fear and emotional blocking are surely reduced by the take-
home exam. The student can place less emphasis on memory
of facts and proceed, as marketing practitioners do, to
consult available resources and engage in reasoning and
the mastering of skills of finding and using information.
The final paper may be proofread and more neatly prepared
than the hastily written in-class exam which compels many
graders to be experts in interpreting chicken scratchings.

Finally, Svoboda (1971) suggests that when exams are written outside of class, more classroom time is made available
for instruction and/or analysis and discussion of student
test responses. Students can then benefit from discussion
of the whys of inappropriate answers to exam questions/
problems. Creative and divergent thinking can be explored
by citing varying approaches used in arriving at somewhat
different but defensible solutions.

Disadvantages of the Take-Home Exam

On the negative side, the out-of-class test provides the
student with a unique opportunity to submit answers which
do not represent his/her own efforts. For this reason,
the take-home exam may often function better as a learning
exercise rather than as an achievement test.

There is some evidence that the take-home test fails to
measure the student's proficiency on each of the six levels
of cognitive learning arrayed in Bloom's (1956) hierarchy
of learning, e.g., knowledge, comprehension, application,
analysis, synthesis, and evaluation. For example, a
student can merely copy or paraphrase materials from a
reference or handle the exam as a mechanical process of
following a resource as a cookbook, e.g., by substituting
numbers in the assigned problem for those cited by the
reference. Thus, little studying takes place and the
student acquires little or no knowledge and fails to progress along the hierarchy of learning. A frequent result
is that collaboration with others or the perfunctory use
of references may result in an undeserved good grade which
may mislead the student into believing that learning has
occurred.

PURPOSES OF THE STUDY

The preceding discussion identifies the major benefits and
shortcomings of the take-home exam as both a teaching and
evaluation alternative to the in-class exam when relatively
complex marketing exercises are involved. This includes
work in such areas as sales forecasting, consumer behavior
models, pricing models, case analysis, exercises in interpreting marketing research findings, and others.

While teaching the Sales Management course, the author has
recently begun to use a take-home exam early in the semester to cover material classified under the subject of
"quantitative sales forecasting methods." Later in the
semester, the mid-term in-class exam includes a section
covering the same material. A major intent is to realize
the advantages of both exam styles.

The primary purpose of this study is to evaluate the
potential of the take-home as an adjunct to conventional
in-class testing for selected marketing courses. A preliminary need is to determine and analyze the degree of
correlation between student grades on the material dealing
with sales forecasting on the two exams. It is then
important to elicit student responses to relevant issues
involving each exam type and the combination of the two.
Among the issues to be considered are:
-- students' perceptions of the impact of the cited
   exam combination upon their knowledge and comprehension of the subject
-- student behavior while taking the out-of-class exam
-- perceptions of the relative anxieties created by the
   two exams
-- perceived validity of the take-home grades
-- student perceptions of the reasons for variations in
   grades (if any) between the two exams
-- Students' thoughts as to the ideal examination program for maximizing the learning process.

METHOD

During the Fall 1980 and Fall 1981 semesters, undergraduate
students taking the Sales Management course at the University of Maryland were given a take-home examination covering the subject of quantitative sales forecasting methods.
Students were given 10 days to complete the exam which
required approximately 3 to 4 hours of concentrated work.
Students were given a four-year set of sales data (by

calendar quarter) and were first asked to deseasonalize the
data. They were asked to develop the equation of the trend
line and then submit forecasts for all quarters of 1980.
Two quarterly moving average forecasts were required as
were exponential smoothing forecasts using two different
values of alpha. Students were then required to compare
the accuracy of the five forecasts by use of the "mean
squared error" method. A summary exercise called for the
plotting of original data, deseasonalized data, and the
calculated trend line on graph paper. Finally, students
were asked to show how multiple regression analysis could
be used to forecast sales for a company selling residential
solar hot water heating systems. In order to do this,
students were required to name the relevant variables and
show how data would be gathered.

The unlimited use of written references was permitted.
However, collaboration with other students or faculty members was not allowed.

The take-home exam was graded promptly with numerous
detailed remarks inserted in red ink next to observed
errors. A step-by-step solution set was distributed with
the returned exams.

Approximately one week after the take-home exams were
returned to the class, the mid-term (in-class) examination
was given. This exam included multiple-choice problems
covering the identical areas that were tested by the take-
home exam. The student could earn a maximum of 10 points
for this section of the exam.

After the mid-term exam was graded and returned to the
class, 80 students completed a questionnaire which
addressed the issues described in the introductory section
of this paper plus several others.

RESULTS

Grade Correlation

Table 1 shows that although nearly 75% of the students
received A_S or B_S on the take-home exam, less than 30%
received comparative grades on the corresponding section
of the in-class examination. No significant correlation
was found between the two sets of exam grades ($r = -.055$).

Table 1

Distribution of Examination Grades

TAKE HOME EXAM GRADE	Percentage of Respondents						
	POINTS EARNED ON "SALES FORECASTING" SECTION OF IN-CLASS EXAM					Column	
	10	8	6	4	<2	Percentage Total	N
A	11.1	27.8	38.9	16.7	5.5	40.0	36
B	6.7	13.3	20.0	46.7	13.3	33.3	30
C	0	33.3	66.7	0	0	6.7	6
$\leq$D	11.1	11.1	55.6	22.2	0	20.0	18
Row Percentage Total	8.8	20.0	37.8	26.7	6.7	100.0	
N	8	18	34	24	6		

The McNemar test for the significance of changes shows
that an overwhelming percentage (81.8%) of students who
did very well on the take-home exam obtained mediocre or
poor scores on the in-class exam. Similarly, nearly half
(41.7%) of the average or poor performers on the take-home
exam did quite well on the in-class test. As shown in

Table 2, these findings are significant at the .0001 level.

TABLE 2

COMPARISON OF TAKE-HOME AND IN-CLASS EXAM GRADES

		POINTS EARNED ON IN-CLASS EXAM		
		$\leq$6	>6	N
Take-Home Grades	A or B	81.8%* (54)	18.2% (12)	66
	C, D, or F	58.3% (14)	41.7% (10)	24

*Read: Of the 66 students who earned a grade of A or B,
on the take-home exam, 81.8% earned 6 points or
less (out of a possible 10 points) on the sales
forecasting section of the in-class exam.

The McNemar test for the significance of changes yields
$p < .0001$.

An Explanation of Correlation Results

This obvious lack of correlation between grades on the two
exam types may be partially explained by the differences in
grading procedures for the two exams. The take-home exam
entails a more subjective procedure in terms of deciding
how well the student put together an answer. The in-class
test consists of forced choice responses which call for an
objective grading approach. Clearly subjective exams
appeal to some students and not to others. However, more
substantial explanations are found in the student responses
to the Likert-type statements shown in Table 3. The
Kolmogorov-Smirnov one-sample test was used to measure the
global significance of the distribution of responses to
each statement in this table. The chi-square test was used
to determine the differences in replies to statements (i)
through (r) among the three student groups: those who did
better on the in-class exam, those who did worse, and those
whose grades were about the same as on the take-home exam.

As shown by the answers to items (a) and (b), in Table 3,
a significant proportion of those who did better attributed their improvement to careful study of errors on the
take-home exam and the availability of the solution handout. Items (c) through (h) shed considerable light on
student perceptions as to why in-class grades were inferior to those on the take-home.

About two-thirds of the students whose grades on sales
forecasting materials dropped on the in-class exam
indicated that because of a decent take-home exam grade,
they felt they understood the subject and neglected to
study it in preparation for the midterm exam. As shown
by the responses to statement (g), about 47% of those
scoring lower on the in-class exam felt that they blacked
out due to time pressures and other anxieties. Although
a moderate number of students admitted to unauthorized
collaboration on the take-home exam, a significantly small
percentage attributed their grade differential to this
behavior. Similarly, few students associated their higher
grade on the take-home exam with the mechanical nature of
a take-home exam.

Responses to Selected Issues

On a global basis, there was no student consensus as to
whether the grades on the two exams should be highly
correlated. Interestingly, however, nearly 56% of those
who improved their grades felt that the grades should be
positively correlated. In contrast, about 38% of those
whose grades were about the same and none of the students
whose grades dropped felt this way.

Items a and b were completed by students who did better on the in-class exam than on the take-home exam (N = 18)	Agree 1	2	3	4	5	6	Disagree 7	Global Significance[1]	Significance of Differences in Responses among Groups[2]	Comparison of Group Responses[3] W	S	B
a. I studied my take-home errors very carefully to make sure I understood where I went wrong on the take-home exam.	44.4	0	22.2	0	11.1	11.1	11.1	D = 30.1; p < .01				
b. I found that the handout of solutions to the take-home exam enabled me to correct my weaknesses in the subject area.	11.1	33.3	11.1	11.1	22.2	11.1	0	D = 17.4; p < .05				
Items c through h were completed by students who did worse on the in-class exam (N = 36)												
c. My decent grade on the take-home exam convinced me I understood the subject so that further study was not necessary.	16.7	27.8	22.2	0	16.7	16.7	0	D = 23.8; p < .01				
d. I didn't study for the midterm exam since my decent grade on the take-home exam locked in 10% of my course grade.	5.9	5.9	5.9	11.8	11.8	35.2	23.5	D = 30.1; p < .01				
e. Since the take-home exam was a mechanical, cookbook-like exercise, I received a decent grade even though I didn't understand the subject.	0	11.8	5.7	11.8	17.7	35.4	17.4	D = 27.6; p < .01				
f. I did well on the take-home exam because I received help from fellow students.	0	0	5.9	0	0	35.3	58.8	D = 65.5; p < .001				
g. I blacked out on the midterm exam due to time pressures and other anxieties.	11.8	29.4	5.9	17.6	23.5	11.8	0	D = 16.9; p < .05				
h. I sacrificed the points on the midterm exam since I can never master quantitative materials.	0	0	0	5.9	5.9	17.7	70.5	D = 59.6; p < .0001				
Items i through s were completed by all students (N = 80).												
i. Without the take-home exam, I would know less about sales forecasting than I do now.	40.0	32.5	15.0	0	5.0	2.5	5.0	D = 44.6; p < .001	χ^2 = 17.4; p < .01	88.9	61.5	55.6
j. The in-class exam created much more anxiety than the take-home exam.	22.5	15.0	22.5	7.5	5.0	17.5	10.0	D = 17.1; p < .05	χ^2 = 21.9; p < .001	55.6	33.3	15.4
k. The take-home exam was a mechanical exercise in that I followed the text like a cookbook.	17.5	20.0	20.0	5.0	15.0	20.0	2.5	D = 14.6; N.S.	χ^2 = 1.9; N.S.			
l. To be honest, I required help with the take-home exam and so I collaborated with other students.	0	15.0	2.5	5.0	0	10.0	67.5	D = 53.2; p < .001	χ^2 = 9.5; p < .02	22.2	15.4	0
m. One or more fellow students needed assistance with the take-home exam, so I helped them.	2.5	15.0	7.5	5.0	0	5.0	65.0	D = 50.7; p < .001	χ^2 = 12.8; p < .02	27.8	15.4	0
n. Permitted collaboration on the take-home exam would benefit the learning process.	30.0	27.5	15.0	10.0	2.5	2.5	12.5	D = 29.6; p < .01	χ^2 = 20.5; p < .001	61.1	46.2	66.7
o. The take-home project should be graded but it shouldn't count as an exam.	22.5	5.0	0	15.0	7.5	27.5	22.5	D = 21.6; p < .01	χ^2 = 32.5 p < .0001	0	38.5	66.7
p. The handout of take-home solutions was not very helpful in furthering my knowledge.	15.0	17.5	7.5	15.0	12.5	22.5	10.0	D = 4.3; N.S.	χ^2 = 0; N.S.			
q. A student's performance on both exams should be positively correlated.	10.0	15.0	20.0	15.0	15.0	15.0	10.0	D = 4.8 N.S.	χ^2 = 24.0; p < .001	0	38.5	55.6
r. Grades given on the take-home exam are not indicative of a student's knowledge and comprehension of the subject.	12.5	20.0	10.0	10.0	7.5	35.0	5.0	D = 11.4; N.S.	χ^2 = 14.6; p < .02	22.2	23.1	66.7

	Take-home only	In-class only	Combination of both			
s. If I were teaching the sales management course and really wanted my students to learn as much as possible about quantitative forecasting methods, my examination preference would be:	30.0	12.5	57.5	D = 24.2; p < .01	χ^2 = 7.8; N.S.	

[1]Kolmogorov-Smirnov one-sample test.

[2]Chi-square test to compare responses of students who did worse on in-class exam (W), students whose grades were about the same on both exams (S), and students who did better on in-class exams (B). Because of several small cell frequencies, the following adjacent categories were combined: 1 and 2; 3, 4, and 5; 5 and 6 on Likert scale. Therefore, df = 4.

[3]This column shows percentages of students who showed relatively strong agreement with statement, e.g., responses 1 or 2 on Likert scale. For example, 88.9% of the W students, 61.5% of the S students, and 55.6% of the B students agreed with statement i.

A significant proportion of the students denied either
giving or accepting help on the take-home exam, but the
results indicate that approximately 35% either admitted
to collaboration or were less than adamant in claiming
innocence. As shown in Table 3 (1 and m), all students
who improved their grades vehemently denied that they
collaborated. In fact, the proportion of confessed collaborators varies significantly with the degree of negative grade deviation between the take-home and in-class
exams. More than 72% of the respondents agreed that collaboration should be permitted since cooperative effort
is a good way to learn. A significantly higher proportion
of the students who improved their grades favored author-
ized collaboration.

As shown by statement (r) in Table 3, when students were
asked whether grades given on the take-home exam are
indicative of a student's knowledge and comprehension of
the subject, the results were inconclusive. As might be
expected, two-thirds of those who improved their grades
rejected the take-home as an indicant of knowledge and
comprehension of sales forecasting. Yet the responses to
statement (o) shows that, on a global level, most students
felt the take-home should be counted as an exam. However,
the latter finding reflects the desires of 77.8% of the
students who did poorly on the in-class exam in comparison
to the take-home exam. Better than 66% of those who
improved their grades agreed that the take-home grades
shouldn't be counted.

Surprisingly, there was no significant support for the
helpfulness of the handout of solutions to the take-home
exam (statement (p)) either on a global basis or among
student groups. This is despite the previously reported
finding (statement b) that the cited handout enabled
several students to correct their weaknesses in the subject area.

A global majority (60%) of the students reported that the
in-class exam created more anxiety than the take-home exam
(p < .05). In contrast to other students, a significantly
larger proportion of students who faltered on the in-class
exam were of this opinion.

As shown in Table 3(i), better than 87% of the respondents
agreed that they wouldn't be as well informed on the subject of sales forecasting if the take-home exam had been
omitted. Students whose grades dropped on the in-class
exam tended to support statement (i) more than other
students.

Table 3(s) summarizes the responses to the question:
   If you were teaching in the sales management course
   and you really wanted your students to learn as much
   as possible about quantitative forecasting methods,
   what type of examination on the subject would you
   give?
The results indicate a significant preference for the
take-home/in-class combination (57.5%) followed by the
take-home exam only (30.0%). Only 12.5% of the students
preferred the in-class exam only.

SUMMARY AND CONCLUSIONS

This research has identified a lack of correlation between
student grades on a take-home examination and a section of
a subsequent in-class exam covering the same areas of
sales forecasting materials. Those whose grades improved
benefitted from the availability of a handout of solutions
to the take-home exam and the opportunity to study their
errors. Poorer performance on the in-class exam can be
attributed to lack of preparation due to overconfidence
created by good take-home grades, invalid take-home grades
due to cheating, and typical in-class exam anxieties.

In contrast to the in-class exam, one's grade on the take-
home exam may measure persistence of effort rather than
recall talents or quickness of intellect. Ebel (1972)
suggests that a composite of all of these factors provides
a more valid measure of achievement than any single factor.

Many students find it difficult to concentrate and thus
have poor study habits and are ill-prepared for in-class
exams that demand quick recall. But they succeed after
graduation since they are capable of performing assigned
tasks when they are not under time pressures and are free
to consult any resources at their disposal. Similarly, to
many students, the take-home exam represents the synthesis
level in Bloom's hierarchy, e.g., a process of locating
information, data, and methodologies and combining them to
form a completed project.

Although a take-home exam grade may be an invalid indicator
of a student's knowledge and comprehension of a subject,
students are almost in unanimous support of its effectiveness as a learning device. Marketing instructors consistently stress the need for diligent, thoughtful, and
scientific problem solving. Yet, for evaluation purposes,
our use of the in-class hour exam denies the student the
time to reflect, ponder, and investigate as successful
marketing problem solvers and decision makers often do.

Evidence provided by this research suggests that the in-
class test and the take-home exam are each somewhat inadequate in reporting student achievements. The results
suggest that by using the suggested combination of both
(for selected course segments), the effectiveness of the
examination mechanism as both an evaluative instrument and
learning device can be enhanced. Clearly, one instructor's
classes at a single university represent less than a
sufficient sample. Future investigations should consider
subject areas other than sales forecasting, including
those that require out-of-class preparations that are not
quantitative in nature.

REFERENCES

Bloom, Benjamin J., et al. (1956), Taxonomy of Educational
   Objectives, Handbook 1: Cognitive Domain, New York:
   David McKay Company.

Ebel, Robert L. (1972), Essentials of Educational Measurement, Englewood Cliffs, NJ: Prentice-Hall, Inc., 98.

Marsh, Robert (1980), "Should We Discontinue Classroom
   Tests: An Experimental Study?" High School Journal,
   63 (April), 288-92.

Sarasen, I. B. (1961), "Test Anxiety and the Intellectual
   Performance of College Students," Journal of Educational
   Psychology, 52 (May), 201-06.

Svoboda, William S. (1971), "A Case for Out-of-Class
   Exams," The Clearing House, 46 (December), 231-33.

ACKNOWLEDGEMENT

   The author wishes to acknowledge the very helpful
library research search conducted by graduate assistant,
Toby Axelrod of the University of Maryland.

BUSINESS STUDENT VIEWS ABOUT BUSINESS-ORIENTED SOCIAL ISSUES:
IMPLICATIONS FOR MARKETING EDUCATION

Paul Hensel, University of Kentucky, Lexington
Alan J. Dubinsky, University of Kentucky, Lexington
Thomas N. Ingram, University of Kentucky, Lexington

ABSTRACT

Previously published research and conventional business
wisdom suggest that business collegians are conservative in
their views. Are they conservative, however, on all major
issues? This paper reports the results of a study that
found that business students tend to be relatively liberal
toward business-oriented issues in relation to non-business-oriented issues. The findings of this study have direct implications for educators teaching marketing and social issues courses.

INTRODUCTION

Within the past decade the Vietnam War, Watergate caper,
ITT-Chilean affair, international business bribery, Ford
Pinto concealment, and nuclear power plant fiascoes have
undoubtedly left indelible impressions on many of the citizenry and, in some instances, generated strong responses
from them (such as their engaging in sit-ins, protest
marches and demonstrations, Congressional hearings, and
litigation). A key question facing business educators--especially in terms of curricula and pedagogical styles--is
how have the tumultuous seventies affected today's business
collegians' attitudes. Several comparative studies (e.g.,
Dubinsky and Rudelius 1980; Eitzen and Brouillette 1979;
Goodman and Crawford 1974; Hawkins and Cocanougher 1972;
Hurka 1980; Karvel and Grosz 1974; McFalls and Gallagher
1979; Shuptrine 1979; Thumin 1972) and conventional business wisdom indicate that contemporary business students
are: (1) basically conservative in their political views;
(2) against government intervention in the business arena;
and (3) insensitive to social issues.

Because of business students' attitudes, textbooks and
courses emphasizing social and moral issues have emerged to
"raise [students'] moral recognition vis-a-vis business decisions" (Barry 1979, p. xi). More specifically, social
and moral issues courses have been mandated by the American
Assembly of Collegiate Schools of Business. The purpose
of the mandate: to raise the social consciousness of business students and to help them deal with the reality of
government and special interest group demands upon the business community.

As the number of social issues courses has increased, much
of the responsibility for teaching these courses has been
shared by marketing faculties. Marketing professors have
either staffed "Business and Society" courses or offered
their own "Marketing and Society" electives. Marketing faculty involvement in social issues curricula has occurred
presumably because many of the visible, actionable, social
injustices of business can be traced to the marketing function (Stanton 1974, p. 24).

The perceived conservatism of business students has led to
curricula and pedagogical-style design and implementation
based upon the assumption that business students are conservative due to their self-selection into business courses,
enculturalization, and/or felt need to conform with expectations of business faculty and business people. Results
from published research that compared business students
with non-business students (Hurka 1980) and business students with salespeople (Dubinsky and Rudelius 1980) and
with non-sales personnel (Karvel and Grosz 1974) generally

support this assumption. Although business students appear
to be conservative, are they conservative, however, on all
major moral and social issues? For example, are their attitudes toward business issues more or less conservative
than their attitudes toward such social issues as civil
rights, employment discrimination, and government entitlements? If research revealed that business students' attitudes were inconsistent across social issue domains, then
such findings would have direct implications about how marketing professors should teach social and moral issues to
their students. No published research, however, has examined the relationship among business students' attitudes
toward business-oriented and non-business-oriented social
issues. Thus, a study was designed to focus on this topic.

Specifically, this paper compares business students' attitudes toward business- and non-business-related social issues. The remainder of this paper will suggest how student
attitudes may affect teaching style; describe the methodology; report the results; and discuss marketing education
implications.

STUDENT IDEOLOGY AND TEACHING STYLE

This study explored the relationship among business students' attitudes toward business-oriented and non-business-oriented social issues. If the assumption is valid that
business students are ideologically conservative and insensitive to business' societal role, then it is important to
know if this is a function of issue orientation or a consistency across issue domains.

From a teaching perspective, a marketing educator's pedagogical style (i.e., a forceful presentation of the liberal
view on business issues versus a general dissemination of
information about the issues) may hinge upon the strength
of students' generalized view of the world. And a students'
generalized view may take one of three stances: equally
conservative toward both business and non-business social
issues; more conservative toward business issues than non-business issues; and less conservative toward business issues than non-business issues.

Equally Conservative Toward Business and Non-Business Issues

If, in fact, business students are conservative, in general,
and conservative about business social issues, in particular, teaching methods that differentiate business issues
from other social issues might be used to fracture this
consistency. The teaching style would entail addressing
the more temporal issues of business separately and distinctly from those issues for which student attitudes may
be more culturally ingrained (e.g., racial equality or civil liberties).

More Conservative Toward Business Issues

If business students tend to be more conservative about
business issues than non-business issues, a teaching style
emphasizing the liberal position toward business--an advocacy of pro-liberal views--may be appropriate. This method
may engender a realignment of students' attitudes toward
business issues with those on other significant social issues. In a sense, this approach takes advantage of an individual's presumed need for attitude consistency and

represents the conventional wisdom of marketing and other
business educators.

Less Conservative Toward Business Issues

If business students' attitudes toward business social issues are less conservative than those towards non-business
social issues, a teaching style that is radically different
from that which is presently encouraged by prevailing educator assumptions may be appropriate. Any attempt on the
part of the marketing professor to invoke a pro-liberal advocate's role may reinforce students' current beliefs, but
fail to present issue conflicts in their realistic form.
Further, educators who assume that business students must
be "force-fed" moral and ethical philosophies may be greeted
with negative reactions from students who hold relatively
liberal views but view devil's advocate instructional techniques as non-traditional or inappropriate. In addition,
attempts to relate non-business social issues with business
social issues could produce a lowering of standards for the
business issues as students attempt to achieve ideological
consistency.

When business student attitudes toward business issues are
less conservative than non-business issue attitudes, a desirable pedagogical style would involve the instructor's
making a balanced, factual presentation of both conservative and liberal views. Students may need knowledge to become aware of specific issues and the nature of business
and societal conflicts. Emphasis could be placed on functional management of those conflicts, instead of attempting
to mold already existing attitudes vis-a-vis the propriety
of business behavior.

METHODOLOGY

Sample

The sample consisted of 301-day, undergraduate business
students enrolled in introductory marketing courses at a
major state university in the Southeast. The majority of
students were juniors who had just begun to specialize in
their business education. None of the students had taken a
"Social Issue in Marketing" course, nor had any been exposed to social issues in marketing in class prior to the
study's execution.

Questionnaire

A questionnaire containing 39 social issue items and demographic information (year in school, age, sex, and political ideology--conservative-liberal) was administered to respondents. Responses to the social issue items were recorded on a seven-point, Likert scale. Of the 39 social
issue questions, seven pertained to business-oriented social issues and 32 addressed non-business-oriented social
issues.

Developing the Non-Business Issue Items

The non-business issues were adapted from Nie, Verba, and
Petrocik (1977). They have analyzed consistency of the
American public concerning social issues. Their analysis
has examined survey responses from twelve surveys taken
during 1952 through 1973. The social issue items used for
the twelve separate surveys were developed and validated by
the Michigan Survey Research Center/Center for Political
Studies and National Opinion Research Center at the University of Chicago.

The statements in each survey were designed to represent
several social issue arenas. The specific wording of the
statements were modified each survey year to keep abreast
of language changes and to improve previous item wording
(e.g., "colored children" was reworded to "Black children").
Also, certain social issues covered in some survey years

were not addressed in subsequent surveys because of apparent non-existence or resolution of the issue (e.g., the
Viet Nam War).

By 1972 the majority of questions had been cast into a
seven-point, Likert framework representing a 20 to 35 item
scale, depending upon the number of social issues of interest to the researchers. The scales were validated and
shown to have high reliability with national random samples
of respondents. The version of the scale used in the <u>pre-
sent</u> study was determined by selecting <u>currently relevant</u>
items from each of six social issue domains: social welfare, social issues, Black welfare, size of government,
Cold War, and civil liberties (Nie, Verba, and Petrocik
1977).

Developing the Business Issue Items

The seven business-oriented social issue items were arrived
at from a review of relevant literature. For a business
issue statement to be included, it had to meet the following three criteria:

1. Because respondents were enrolled in their first marketing course, the issue had to be general and devoid
   of marketing-specific jargon.

2. As suggested by Churchill (1979, p. 227), the issue had
   to be controversial enough to elicit both agreement and
   disagreement from student respondents.

3. The issue had to be representative of those addressed
   in social issues and marketing texts.

With respect to the first criterion, each business issue
item was carefully reworded to ensure that more detailed
marketing terminology (such as price discrimination, channels of distribution, price fixing, and sales perquisites)
was replaced with a more common vernacular. The business
issues are specifically marketing oriented, but their terminology remains in the general business sphere.

To satisfy the second criterion, respondents were asked
their political ideology on a seven-point, conservative-
liberal, self-rating scale. Those respondents indicating
any degree of conservatism were compared with those exhibiting any degree of liberalism in terms of their responses
to the seven business issue items. A t-test for differences between conservative and liberal group means (after
summing each respondent's responses to the seven business
issues and dividing by seven) showed that the two groups
were indeed different (t = 2.72, p < .005).

The third criterion was satisfied by reviewing marketing
and social issues texts. Alder, Robinson, and Carlson
(1981) and Berenson and Eilbert (1973) have treated social
issues and marketing as a distinctive discipline. In both
texts, separate treatment is given to advertising regulation, environmental pollution through packaging decisions,
anti-trust and monopoly power, ethical practices in sales,
relationship between profit and corporate responsibility,
and competitive effects of merger policies. One question
related to each of these topics was included in the questionnaire. The wording of each statement, however, was
general because of criterion #1 (above). In addition to
these six specific business issue statements, a general
business issue item concerning the present trend toward
business deregulation was included. The seven business-
oriented social issues are presented in the appendix.

Principle components factor analysis (Hair et al. 1979) was
performed to ascertain the empirical distinctiveness of the
Business Issues Index. All thirty-nine items were loaded
and rotated to achieve maximum variance explanation. This
procedure generated seven factors having eigenvalues greater
than 1.0 and explaining 87.4 percent of the variance. For

an item to be classified within a particular factor, its factor loading had to exceed .30 and be associated with that factor more than any other factor. Although not all of the items fell where expected (for either the six Non-Business Social Issues Indices or the Business Issues Index), it is apparent that an identifiable structure emerged. The Business Issues Index is distinct within the structure. Five of the seven index items loaded into a factor that represents a multi-dimensional business issues conceptualization.

To ensure that the items were related to a liberal-conservative ideological dimension, respondents' recoded mean index scores for each of the seven social issues indices were correlated with their self-reported ideological position (1 = "very conservative" and 7 = "very liberal"). Table 1 reports the results of this correlational analysis. Each of the seven indices is positively correlated with the ideological position. This finding indicates that the liberal versus conservative direction of the indices was properly conceived.

TABLE 1

RELATIONSHIP BETWEEN STUDENTS' SELF-REPORTED IDEOLOGICAL POSITION
AND SOCIAL ISSUES INDICES

Index	Pearson Correlation Coefficient	Significance Level (p <)
Social Issues	.222	.001
Civil Liberties	.227	.001
Black Welfare	.316	.001
Business Issues	.200	.001
Size of Government	.116	.030
Cold War	.129	.020
Social Welfare	.270	.000

Finally, reliability analysis for the entire 39-item scale resulted in an alpha coefficient of .78. The alpha coefficient did not drop below .77 or go above .79 with the deletion of any single scale item.

Data Modification

During data preparation, student responses to the 39 issue items were recoded so that 1 = "strongly agree" on a liberal item and "strongly disagree" on a conservative item; 4 = "neutral"; and 7 = "strongly disagree" on a liberal item and "strongly agree" on a conservative item. The responses were then summed within each of the six Non-Business Social Issues and the sole Business Issues Index. After summation a mean index score was derived for each respondent by dividing the respective summed index by the number of items in the index. The higher mean index scores indicate more liberal respondent attitudes than lower mean index scores.

RESULTS

Because previous research has found that male and female college students are significantly different in their value orientations (Hurka 1980), it was necessary in the present study to determine whether disaggregation of the data by sex of respondent was required. Using respondents' self-rated ideological position, this analysis revealed that male business students rated themselves significantly _more_ conservative in ideology than did female college students (t = 2.60, p < .01). More specifically, males rated themselves slightly conservative, on average, and females rated themselves slightly liberal ($\bar{x}$ = 3.66 and 4.14, respectively, where 1 = "very conservative" and 7 = "very liberal").

Given the above findings, t-tests comparing male and female student index scores were performed. Table 2 presents mean scores, standard deviations, and t-values for each index by sex of respondent. Male and female student mean scores are not significantly different (p < .05) on the following indices: Social Issues, Civil Liberties, Size of Government, and Social Welfare. This finding suggests that business student men and women have relatively similar ideological views about the issues related to the above indices. Conversely, female mean scores are significantly higher than male mean scores on three of the seven indices: Cold War, Black Welfare, and Business Issues. Thus, female business students are _more liberal_ than male business students on issues associated with these three indices. Furthermore, contrary to conventional marketing education wisdom, the Business Issues Index mean scores of the two groups are in the _liberal_ direction (female mean = 5.40 and male mean = 5.11, where 1 = "very liberal" and 7 = "very conservative").

TABLE 2

COMPARISON OF MALE AND FEMALE INDEX SCORES

Index	Females (n = 140)		Males (n = 161)		
	Mean[a]	S.D.	Mean[a]	S.D.	t-value
Social Issues	4.27	.97	4.28	.91	-0.17
Civil Liberties	4.87	.91	4.72	.88	1.44
Black Welfare	4.46	1.30	4.18	1.25	1.96[b]
Business Issues	5.40	.78	5.11	.80	3.16[c]
Size of Government	4.16	.99	4.02	.97	1.25
Cold War	4.13	1.35	3.58	1.33	3.55[c]
Social Welfare	3.89	.94	3.76	.81	1.29

[a]Mean scores are based on a scale where 1 = "very liberal" and 7 = "very conservative."

[b]p < .05 (two-tailed t-test)

[c]p < .01 (two-tailed t-test)

Because of the significant difference between male and female mean scores on the Business Issues Index, t-tests using paired comparisons (Winkler and Hays 1975) between the Business Issues Index mean scores and the mean scores of the six Non-Business Issues Indices were performed separately by sex. Table 3 presents the results of this analysis. Without exception, _both_ male and female business students have significantly higher mean scores (p < .001) on the Business Issues Index than on any of the other indices. These results indicate that _both_ male and female students are significantly _more liberal_ in their attitudes toward business-oriented social issues than they are toward non-business-oriented social issues.

LIMITATIONS

The above results should be viewed in light of some limitations of the study. First, the majority of student respondents were from one class section. Consequently, a teacher bias may be operating. In addition, the geographic locale of the university (the Southeast) may not contain students whose attitudes are representative of college students in general. This may reduce the generalizability of the results.

Every effort was made during index construction to create Business Issues Index items that would appear equivalent (in nature) to the items used in the other six indices. No empirical evidence, however, exists to ensure conceptual equality of the statements in terms of either the agree-disagree or liberal-conservative dimensions.

Because the subject matter of the study could be considered sensitive to respondents, their scale ratings may not accurately reflect their true beliefs, but only socially desirable beliefs instead. In particular, the relatively more temporal nature of the items in the Business Issues Index may tend to deflate the scores on those index items relative to items in indices such as Black Welfare or Social Welfare which may be more likely to elicit untrue liberal ratings. Despite the above weaknesses, several implications for marketing education emerge from the findings of this investigation.

TABLE 3

PAIRED COMPARISONS OF MEAN BUSINESS INDEX SCORES
WITH ALL OTHER MEAN INDEX SCORES

Index	Females (n = 140)		Males (n = 161)	
	Difference in means[a]	t-value	Difference in means[a]	t-value
Social Issues	1.14	10.46[b]	.83	9.15[b]
Civil Liberties	.53	5.70[b]	.39	4.37[b]
Black Welfare	.94	8.22[b]	.94	9.42[b]
Size of Government	1.24	13.49[b]	1.09	13.51[b]
Cold War	1.27	10.27[b]	1.54	12.55[b]
Social Welfare	1.52	15.12[b]	1.36	17.70[b]
Male and Female Business Issues Means	5.40		5.11	

[a] Mean difference = the difference between the mean Business Issues Index score and the mean Non-Business Issues Index score of interest.

[b] $p < .001$ (two-tailed t-test)

DISCUSSION AND IMPLICATIONS

This study of business students enrolled in introductory marketing courses has found that female students are more liberal than their male counterparts. This finding is consistent with previous research (Hurka 1980) and conventional business/marketing education wisdom. More specifically, female students have more liberal attitudes than male students on issues related to the Cold War, Black Welfare, and business. Male business students, however, also have relatively liberal attitudes toward business issues (although they are less liberal than female students). This result contradicts conventional business/marketing education wisdom. Overall, both business student men and women have significantly more liberal attitudes toward business-oriented social issues than non-business-oriented social issues. Thus, business students may not be as conservative as prior research (noted earlier) and conventional wisdom suggest. These results have direct implications for marketing educators.

One implication pertains to what should be taught in a marketing-social issues course. Educators should teach in-depth, factual material that addresses temporally relevant business social issues (such as monopoly power, price fixing, deceptive advertising). Issues that are not under the direct purview of marketing and business (such as racial equality or civil liberties) should not be included in class discussions. Although non-business-oriented social issues are important and should be studied by students in college classes, they are beyond the scope of a marketing and social issues course. Given the time constraints placed on most courses, a marketing educator may be hard-pressed to cover the salient marketing issues during the academic term, let alone non-business issues.

A second implication is related to the pedagogical style the professor should adopt when teaching a marketing and society course. Because business students appear to be relatively liberal on business social issues, they may not need to be "force fed" a pro-liberal doctrine. Rather, a pedagogical approach that presents both conservative and liberal views (in a balanced, factual manner) is desirable. Special emphasis should be placed upon managing the situation of interest. That is, the marketing educator should identify the important temporal business issues for students and teach them how to deal with each situation as a marketer. This managerial orientation is in contrast to a traditional approach that devotes class time for the purpose of encouraging students' attitude formation, but not helping them solve the particular issues facing marketers.

A third implication concerns how a marketing and social issues course should be taught. The pedagogical style discussed above is especially amenable to a combination lecture-, readings-, and case-oriented course. Lectures and readings (articles and/or texts) help disseminate salient information to students. Case studies assist students with a resolution of relevant issue conflicts. Consequently, students' rewards (grades) are based upon the justification of their specific conflict resolution rather than whether they have adopted a socially desirable position. In other words, the professor places the emphasis on how students arrive at their position, not on the particular position they have assumed.

One final implication of the study is that the marketing professor should supplement the lecture, readings, and case materials with guest speakers. In particular, classroom debates between pro-business and pro-consumer groups could foster a meaningful dialogue and provide students with a "real world" perspective about marketing and social issues. Such debates should enhance the learning process and enjoyment of students.

In conclusion, a marketing and society course should be an important part of any college or university marketing curriculum. It provides marketing educators with one of the last opportunities with which to make students cognizant of critical business/marketing social issues. Hopefully, this paper will be of assistance to those marketing academicians currently teaching, or contemplating teaching, a marketing and society course.

REFERENCES

Adler, R. D., L. M. Robinson, and J. E. Carlson (1981), _Marketing and Society: Cases and Commentaries_, Englewood Cliffs, NJ: Prentice-Hall, Inc.

Barry, V. (1979), _Moral Issues in Business_, Belmont, CA: Wadsworth Publishing Company.

Berenson, C., and H. Eilbert (1973), _The Social Dynamics of Marketing_, New York: Random House.

Churchill, G. A. (1979), _Marketing Research: Methodological Foundations_, Hinsdale, IL: The Dryden Press.

Dubinsky, A. J., and W. Rudelius (1980), "Ethical Beliefs: How Students Compare with Industrial Salespeople," in _1980 Educators' Conference Proceedings_, R. P. Bagozzi et al., eds., Chicago: American Marketing Association.

Eitzen, D. S., and J. R. Brouillette (1979), "The Politicization of College Students," _Adolescence_, 14 (Spring), 123-134.

Goodman, C. S., and C. M. Crawford (1974), "Young Executives: A Source of New Ethics," _Personnel Journal_, 53 (March), 180-187.

Hair, J. F., R. E. Anderson, R. L. Tatham, and B. J. Grablowsky (1979), _Multivariate Data Analysis_, Tulsa, OK: Petroleum Publishing Company.

Hawkins, D. I., and A. B. Cocanougher (1972), "Student Evaluations of the Ethics of Marketing Practices: The Role of Marketing Education," *Journal of Marketing*, 36 (April), 61-64.

Hurka, S. J. (1980), "Business Administration Students in Five Canadian Universities: A Study of Values," *The Canadian Journal of Higher Education*, 10 (January), 83-93.

Karvel, J. M., and R. D. Grosz (1974), "Counterculture Businessmen: A Study of Values," *Journal of Counseling Psychology*, 21 (January), 81-83.

McFalls, J. A., and B. J. Gallagher (1979), "Political Orientation and Occupational Values of College Youth," *Adolescence*, 14 (Winter), 641-655.

Nie, N. H., S. Verba, and J. R. Petrocik (1977), *The Changing American Voter*, Cambridge, MA: Harvard University Press.

Shuptrine, F. K. (1979), "Evaluating the Ethics of Marketing Practices: Student Perceptions," in *1979 Educators' Conference Proceedings*, N. Beckwith et al., eds., Chicago: American Marketing Association.

Stanton, W. J. (1975), *Fundamentals of Marketing*, New York: McGraw-Hill Book Company.

Thumin, F. J. (1972), "The Relation of Liberalism to Sex, Age, Academic Field, and College Grades," *Journal of Clinical Psychology*, 28 (April), 160-164.

Winkler, R. L., and W. L. Hays (1975), *Statistics: Probability, Inference, and Decision*, New York: Holt, Rinehart, and Winston.

ACKNOWLEDGMENT

The authors gratefully acknowledge the data collection assistance provided by Professor James Donnelly (University of Kentucky).

AN EMPIRICAL TEST OF MICROCOMPUTER SIMULATION AS AN
ALTERNATIVE FOR THE TEACHING OF A MARKETING TOPIC

Dan L. Sherrell, Louisiana State University, Baton Rouge
Alvin C. Burns, Louisiana State University, Baton Rouge

ABSTRACT

The effectiveness of microcomputer simulation was investigated with the use of an equivalent-groups experiment comparing case study, experiential exercise, and a conventional approach. The student-involving pedagogies were
found to effect more positive attitudes but no greater
learning. The findings permit marketing educators to
seriously consider the microcomputer as a valuable teaching
facilitator and concurrently challenge them to discover
applications which will engender greater cognitive acquisition of marketing subject matter.

INTRODUCTION

The recent availability of microcomputer systems in the
price range of $500 to $1500 appears to have opened for
marketing educators the prospect of a highly potent teaching facilitator. In particular, it is possible for an
instructor to have a completely self-contained and interactive system with considerable memory capacity which is
compact, portable, and perhaps most important, independent
of "mainframe" aggravations such as slow turnaround, batch
processing, priorities, and constraints. Observation suggests, however, that marketing educators are at the onset
of the experience curve for this innovation as practically
no published articles exist in the marketing journals or
the proceedings of marketing-oriented conferences reporting
experiences with microcomputers. In fact, a tutorial workshop at the most recent ABSEL Conference (Jansen 1981,
Frazer 1981, Goosen 1981, and Schou 1981) lends credence
to this contention inasmuch as ABSEL members are supposedly current on computer technology applied to business education. While the advantages of microcomputers and their
attendant microsimulations seem intuitive, it is nonetheless necessary to design explicit comparisons to assess
the true impact and effectiveness of the pedagogy. Thus,
the primary intent of this paper is to report the results
of the use of microcomputer simulation compared to other
instructional alternatives currently in vogue. Implicit
to this intent, but dependent on the results, is the objective of appraising marketing educators of the relative
advantages of the microcomputer in the classroom.

Most empirical works on simulation fail to employ experimental designs and those with comparisons between pedagogical alternatives tend to focus on a single alternative
compared to the "conventional" approach (e.g., lecture
with individually assigned discussion questions from the
text). For example, Kulik, Kulik and Cohen (1980) report
a meta-analysis of over 500 studies in which they found
only 59 wherein computer based instruction was compared
with a conventional control group. A significant depar-
ture of the present study, however, is the attempt to
experimentally compare most representative alternative
approaches simultaneously. Thus, the microcomputer simulation approach was compared to the use of a case study,
an experiential exercise, and to the task of writing answers to questions similar to those found at the end of a
text chapter. Before continuing with a detailed description of the treatments, it is worthwhile to summarize the
general findings of previous comparative studies. With
respect to computer simulations, the aforementioned meta-
analysis concluded that the most pronounced advantage of
computer based instruction involved time savings for the
instructor, while more favorable student attitudes toward
the pedagogy and the subject matter emerged, and only
slight positive achievement differences were associated
with computer assisted instruction. Other studies and reviews have concluded that simulation tends to be most influential in the facilitation of satisfaction and involvement
with the learning experience (see Pierfy 1977, for example).
Dekkers and Donatti (1981) substantiate this conclusion
with their review article, although Bredimier and Greenblat (1981) have reported recent evidence that long-term
retention is enhanced. Cooke and Maronick (1977) have
also reported some increased learning of marketing concepts with the use of computer simulation.

Experiential exercises and case studies are sometimes confounded with one another in research, and it is difficult
to separate them in generalizations; consequently, both will
be combined here. Research results are very similar to
those for computer simulations: attitude, satisfaction,
and involvement are heightened while cognitive learning
shows no difference from lecture delivery (see, for example, Basuray and Scherling 1978, Brenenstul and Catalenello 1979, or Hoover and Whitchead 1979).

RESEARCH HYPOTHESES

Given the state of current pedagogical research findings
cited above, it seems premature to posit relative differences between the three nonconventional approaches. Instead, it seems more appropriate to expect that microsimulation will yield consistent results, at minimum. Thus,
   Hypothesis 1
      Microsimulation will yield attitude levels consistent
      with those effected by the case study and/or experi-
      tial exercise.
   Hypothesis 2
      The conventional approach will result in less posi-
      tive attitudes than will alternatives of micro-
      simulation, case study, or experiential exercise.
   Hypothesis 3
      No differences in cognitive learning will be exhib-
      ited between the various approaches.

METHOD

The experiment utilized a convenience sample of 85 undergraduate business students enrolled in 3 sections of an
introductory marketing principles course. Several factors
were considered in the selection of these students. An introductory marketing course was chosen to assure that the
subjects were relatively unfamiliar with the topic area of
the experiment (retail site location analysis). Care was
taken to locate sections of the course that were taught
close together during the day to minimize any differences
arising from the type of students who enroll in classes
at different times of the day (e.g., differences due to age,
experience, educational background). Finally, sections
were chosen that were all taught by the same instructor to
ensure that the students were all exposed to the same a-
mount and type of marketing principles material.

Administrative Procedures

The experiment was conducted in two sessions five days

apart. In the first session, subjects were given a fic-
ticious cover story stating that the authors were developing material for an instructor's manual of a text they
were writing. The subjects' help was requested in participating in several different exercises to determine the
appeal to students for inclusion in the instructor's manual.

All subjects were given a retailing text chapter on retail
site location analysis of 20 pages (Reidenbaugh 1976).
Each subject was asked to read the material with the
thought in mind that they would be asked to apply the information later. Upon completion of the material, subjects were randomly assigned to a treatment condition:
case study, microsimulation; experiential exercise,
or discussion question, and taken to four separate rooms
to continue the experiment. Three of the four groups were
randomly divided into groups of 3 subjects each and each
group was given the materials necessary for the treatment
to which they were assigned. The subjects assigned to the
discussion question condition were given questions on the
text material and asked to write answers individually,
approximating a normal or baseline classroom situation.

Subjects in the other groups were asked to read their
materials and to follow the enclosed instructions in preparing their responses. It was emphasized that an answer
was required only from the group, not from each individual.
The instructions were designed to be self-explanatory and
the administrator's interaction with the subjects was
limited to dispersal and collection of material to minimize demand characteristics.

Following completion of the treatment, each subject was
given an attitude scale constituting one dependent measure, and an objective test of 25 true-false questions was
administered in the next class meeting as the second dependent measure.

Stimulus Material

The hypotheses of this study required exercises which covered identical material but which differed in their demands and levels of involvement required of the subjects.
The exercises were designed with this objective in mind
and given to a group of 17 judges for evaluations of
similarity. MBA students enrolled in a graduate marketing
management course were given each set of materials in turn
and asked to evaluate each on a rating scale according to
the degree of emphasis placed on each of eight separate
elements of location analysis. The elements of interest
included information on: (1) geographical layout; (2)
population centers and growth trends; (3) demographics;
(4) competitors' locations; (5) competitor characteristics;
(6) local economic climate; (7) available sites and site
characteristics; and (8) potential effects of site location on marketing strategy. From these evaluations,
changes were made to make all the treatments as similar as
possible in content coverage.

Microsimulation

The microsimulation was designed and run using an ATARI
model 800 microcomputer (32K) and TV monitor and is described in a previous paper (authors, forthcoming). Using
the console, student groups were able to (1) activate the
programmed instruction for the rules of the game; (2)
enter the required decisions; and (3) receive the simulation results without the need for instructor intervention.
Teams were provided with the following information:
  1. <u>Objectives</u> - Teams were shown a map of an urban
      area on which alternative sites for a retail
      store were positioned. Teams were asked to select
      the most advantageous position for the particular
      environment in which they were competing.
  2. <u>Decision Environment</u> - Team stores and competitor's
      stores were of the same type. Convenience goods

were sold in all stores. The sites contained
specific sensitivity of response to the location
and the marketing decisions the team selected.
  3. <u>Environmental Data</u> - a) Teams were given informa-
      tion about the general retail trade area via a
      television monitor which depicted a map of the
      area. The map contained two major traffic ar-
      teries (north-south and east-west) and a river.
      b) The 25 major subdivisions were located on the
      map, each representing a randomly determined num-
      ber of houses. c) The competitors' locations
      were then overlayed on the map and teams were
      given information on their grid locations and
      approximate floor space (randomly varied between
      20,000-50,000 sq. ft.). d) Teams were told that
      the competitors were assumed to be in a relative-
      ly stable environment with no pronounced aggres-
      siveness on price or promotion. e) The possible
      alternative sites were sequentially displayed on
      the map, giving grid location, monthly rent, and
      square footage.
  4. <u>Decision Alternatives</u> - Based on the trade area in-
      formation, location of competitors, size of com-
      petitors stores, available retail sites and dis-
      tance from major clusters of subdivisions, teams
      were required to select the site they thought most
      advantageous. After the site selection decision,
      teams were asked to select the most effective
      level of price and promotion to effectively gen-
      erate sales from the location. The purpose was
      to illustrate the problems encountered in trying
      to overcome distance by lowering price or in-
      creasing promotion.
  5. <u>Decision Evaluation</u> - Once the decision was entered,
      teams received hypothetical results of competing
      with the other firms. The micrcomputer generated
      for the teams' store and the competitors: unit
      sales, total revenues, and profit levels.
  6. <u>Decision Refinement</u> - After receipt of the results
      of the first round of decisions, teams were al-
      lowed to make two additional rounds of promotion
      and price decisions. The location was fixed by
      the original decision, and through successive in-
      teractions, teams could determine the impacts of
      the other two decision variables. Competitors'
      actions were subject to random variation.

Case Study

Subject groups were provided with a four page report describing a small businessman interested in starting a
copying service in one of two towns located next to different universities. The write-up contained data on the
trade areas, possible sites, competitors locations and marketing strategies, population characteristics, and available site characteristics. The business man was described
weighing the alternative sites and associated information.
His choice of a site was described and the subjects in each
group were asked to evaluate his decision using the case
material and the information they had read in the chapter
on site location analysis.

Experiential Exercise

The experiential exercise asked students to imagine themselves as the owners of a successful stereo shop interested
in locating a second store in a nearby city. The profile
of the current customer base was given, two potential census tracts in the city of interest were located, and census data on population and retail business provided for
each area. In addition, one alternative site in tract A
and two sites in tract B were displayed on a map. Competitors' locations and operating characteristics (store size,
general marketing strategies) were noted as well as possible marketing strategy choices for the alternative sites.

Groups were asked to select a specific site, outline their general marketing strategy with respect to price and promotion, and justify their decisions with information from the descriptions and the chapter material.

Discussion Questions

Subjects in this group were given four discussion questions based on the text material read earlier and asked to write their answer to each. The questions asked the students to recall various elements of information from the text material similar to the areas covered in the other three methods. For example, students were asked to list factors which should be considered in a retailer's decision to locate a store on a specific site. The other questions were similar in nature and required recall of the chapter information.

Dependent Measures

Two separate measures were administered to the subjects. The first measure was a 43 item attitude scale administered at the end of the first session following exposure to the experimental treatment. The second instrument was a measure of cognitive learning and consisted of a 25 question true-false test administered during the second session of the experiment. The attitude scale items were measured on a 5 point Likert-type scale with 1 meaning "Strongly Disagree" and 5 indicating "Strongly Agree". Approximately 30 of the items were drawn from Greenblat's (1973) list of propositions on the pedagogical effects of simulations. An additional 13 items were derived specifically for the experiment and were designed to measure dimensions of interest, involvement, and perceived learning.

The objective test was developed from several test banks of questions from instructor's manuals for retailing text books. The questions were chosen for their coverage of the topic areas of location analysis mentioned in the rating scale used by the judges for the stimulus material evaluation. The questions were placed in a true-false format and combined to form the instrument.

RESULTS

The attitude scale was factor analyzed to determine the various dimensions tapped by the measure. Table 1 shows 5 factors accounting for almost 63% of the total variation in the data. Although there were a large number of items (45) relative to the number of subjects responding (85), the factor analysis was still undertaken to provide an approximation of the structure underlying the attitude scale. The findings discussed here should be interpreted with the limitation in mind along with the reminder that the study hypotheses relate to general attitudes toward the various teaching pedagogies.

The dimensions generally follow Greenblat's (1973) speculations on the different elements of opinions towards simulations. Factor 1 accounted for the majority of explained variance (41%) and can be best labeled as a Perceived Knowledge factor. The 9 items loading heaviest on Factor 1 all concern perceptions of information or understanding gained from participating in the different methods. Factor 2 concerns the level of interest or involvement and is labeled as the Enjoyment factor. A point to note in the interest of validation concerns the item "Exercise was boring", which had a negative correlation with the Enjoyment factor. Factor 3 concerns the Perceived Benefits of participation, while the items loading heaviest on Factor 4 involve perceptions of Student/Teacher Relations. Finally the fifth factor consisting of 3 items is related to Decision Skills. Note again, the negative loading on the item "Exercise was too-low level." Overall, the five factors breakout fairly diverse dimensions of students'

TABLE 1

ATTITUDE SCALE ITEM FACTOR ANALYSIS

Factors[a]

Factor 1 – Perceived Knowledge	Factor Loading
Gained insight into decision problem	.717
Increased awareness of difficulties involved	.708
Gained insight into pressures faced by decision makers	.699
Learned the procedures of location analysis	.693
Aided understanding of location decision elements	.684
Increased appreciation of problems faced	.683
Learned general principles involved	.665
Increased awareness of uncertainties faced	.636
Gained actual information from exercise	.609
Factor 2 – Enjoyment	
Exercise was interesting	.735
Exercise increased my interest	.770
Exercise was fun	.691
Exercise was enjoyable	.668
Exercise increased my enthusiasm to learn	.594
Exercise will make other coursework enjoyable	.532
Exercise was boring	-.522
Exercise increased my interest in course	.515
Exercise leads to more student independence	.513
Exercise leades to more relaxed exchange between students and teachers	.506
Factor 3 – Perceived Benefits	
Increased my sense of my personal abilities	.840
Increased my awareness of my own potential	.799
Helped increase my own self-awareness	.631
Would lead me to participate more in related class discussion	.551
Increased my interest in learning in general	.545
Factor 4 – Student/Teacher Relations	
Leads teachers to perceive students more positively in general	.779
Promotes better student/teacher relationships	.710
Leads to greater peer acceptance	.548
Helps students perceive teachers more positively	.537
Factor 5 – Decision Skills[b]	
Exercise was too low-level	-.687
Changed my perspective on some parts of marketing	.591
Gained better decision skills	.536

[a]Loadings derived using varimax rotation

[b]A total of 9 factors with eigenvalues ≥ 1.00 accounted for 75% of total variation. Factors 6 through 9 consisted of either single items or loadings below .50 and were eliminated from subsequent analysis. The 5 factors retained accounted for 63% of the total variance.

attitudes toward different teaching approaches.

The reliability scores (Cronbach's alpha) obtained for the total attitude scale as well as the subscales consisting of the items from each of the five factors were quite high. The total scale reliability score was .935. The Knowledge factor scale consisting of the 9 items shown in Table 1 produced an alpha of .921. The alpha coefficients for the Enjoyment, Perceived Benefit, and Student Relation scales were .837, .871, and .809 respectively. The final subscale, Decision Skills, consisting of only 3 items, had a reliability coefficient of -.725. The total scale and subscales displayed good levels of reliability, lending support for the construct validity of the attitude measure.

Table 2 presents the ANOVA results with method and class section as independent variables and the attitude and test scores as separate dependent measures. Composite attitude

TABLE 2

ANOVA RESULTS: TEST AND ATTITUDE
SCORES BY METHOD AND CLASS

Test Scores

Source	SS	DF	M.S.	F	$P \leq$
Main Effects	600.58	5	120.00	1.85	.116
Method	485.75	3	161.92	2.50	.068
Class	81.86	2	40.93	0.633	.535
Method X Class	183.20	6	30.533	0.472	.827
Error	3882.66	60	64.71		
Total	4666.43	71	65.72		

Attitude Scale Scores

Source	SS	DF	M.S.	F	$P \leq$
Main Effects	16034.25	5	3206.85	9.17	.0001
Method	14126.61	3	4709.87	13.47	.0001
Class	3150.43	2	1575.21	4.51	.014
Method X Class	3130.75	6	521.79	1.49	.193
Error	25168.43	72	349.56		
Total	44333.44	83	534.14		

and objective test scores exhibited a low correlation of
-.25 (p<.01). The total attitude scale showed significant
main effects for both method and class section, with the
method being the stronger influence. There were no significant interaction effects and post hoc tests of group
means (Scheffe's test) showed the attitude scores for the
microsimulation group were significantly greater (p<.05)
than those for the case study, experiential exercise, or
discussion questions. Attitude scores for those subjects
in the case study group were also significantly greater
(p<.05) than the scores for the discussion question group.
The test scores showed a significant (p<.10) main effect
for method, but none for class section. The post hoc contrasts showed no significant group differences. This par-
adox can be attributed to the fact that Scheffe's test is
fairly conservative and another technique would have
yielded siginificant results. It should be noted that the
group means show that the discussion question approach
was most effective in producing good test scores. The
group means for each method using the test and various
attitude scale scores are displayed in Table 3. The means

TABLE 3

MEANS OF TEST AND ATTITUDE SCALES
BY TEACHING METHOD

| | METHOD | | | | | |
Score	Micro Simulation	Case Study	Experiential Exercise	Discussion Questions	F-Ratio	$\hat{\omega}^2$
Test	n=20 .68 (.08)[f]	n=19 .67 (.06)	n=18 .72 (.07)	n=15 .73 (.09)	2.51[b]	.081
Attitude[c]	n=22 162.9 (12.7)	n-20 146.0 (13.5)	n=24 142.0 (26.6)	n=19 127.8 (21.4)	13.47[a]	.293
Subscales[d]						
Knowledge[c]	4.20 (3.65)	4.10 (4.04)	3.81 (8.22)	3.67 (5.89)	4.04[a]	.092
Enjoyment[c]	4.13 (2.92)	3.32 (4.97)	3.28 (6.86)	3.11 (7.26)	15.99[a]	.333
Perceived Benefits	3.46 (4.43)	3.32 (3.05)	3.18 (4.11)	2.53 (3.35)	6.45[a]	.161
Student/ Teacher Relations	3.86 (2.56)	3.09 (2.37)	3.12 (2.99)	2.28 (2.83)	17.04[a]	.400
Decision Skills	3.20 (1.01)	2.90 (1.38)	2.88 (1.63)	2.92 (1.63)	2.47[b]	.048

[a] p<.01

[b] p<.10

[c] Showed a significant main effect due to class section.

[d] Subscale scores were divided by the number of scale items to allow cross scale examination

[e] $\hat{\omega}$ 2 - represents contribution to total variation expressed in percent.

[f] numbers in parentheses are standard deviations

reflect the trends described thus far. The contribution
to explained variation ($\hat{\omega}^2$) indicates that certain attitude
components contributed strongly to the obtained main effects results.

DISCUSSION

The findings of this equivalent-groups experiment on the
effect of alternative pedagogies for the teaching of a
marketing topic substantiate findings reported in other
business disciplines. To be more specific, it has been
found that the more participative and more involving approaches, namely, experiential exercise, case study, and
microcomputer simulation engender more positive attitudes
than does a conventional method of requiring students to
write answers to questions at the end of a chapter. Also
as expected, the involving methods do not effect greater
learning than does the conventional approach. In fact,
slightly less cognitive learning was determined for the
case study and simulation than for the conventional
method. It seems reasonable to believe that the corroborative aspects of the findings lend a degree of external
validity to this study, while the unanticipated greater
learning result may point to a limitation of the study,
for the conventional treatment may well have allowed a
slight rehearsal effect to have entered into the results.

Nonetheless, the authors believe that there are some interesting nuances to this study's findings which warrant
discussion and speculative comment. In particular, the
attitude subscale dimension findings serve to reveal the
nature of differences between the conventional and the
student-involving pedagogies. Certainly the fact that
students perceive that they learn more with computer simulation and case study, specifically, when objective test
results show no differences is a significant finding. An
implication which comes to mind with this apparent contra-
diction is that is is possible that participative methods
foster students' self-confidence in their knowledge. In
short, they believe they have learned, and this belief
could conceivably underlie behavioral consequences at
later points in time. The precise nature of the resultant
behavior is unknown, but it does seem appropriate to
recommend the inclusion of a behavior component in subsequent research.

Another attitude subscale dimension, namely the perceived
enjoyment gained through participation in the teaching
method, serves to verify the intuitive reasons for adopting the less traditional teaching approaches. That is,
the interaction between student teams and a microcomputer
with a video monitor as well as the small group interaction
between students working on a case analysis problem are
apparently welcome diversions and obviously much more satisfactory activities than writing the answers to textbook
questions. The interesting point to make clear, however,
is the magnitude of this attitude component, for it is
not an all encompassing factor. True, its contribution to
the total effect is approximately one-third, but it does
not overwhelm other components.

Testimony for this statement comes from the student/teacher
relations subscale dimension finding where almost one-half
of the measured composite effect was revealed. This finding is not completely serendipitous, for Greenblatt (1973)
had differentiated classroom relations, cognitive learning,
motivation, and other components in her postulates on the
effects of computer simulations. In any case, the results
here speak loudly for the consideration of adoption of involving pedagogoes in the principles of marketing classes,
or, at the very least, it suggests strongly that those instructors concerned with student/teacher relationships
should become knowledgeable and perhaps proficient in
integrating student-involving pedagogical alternatives
in their courses.

Further comments could be addressed to specific subscale findings, but the authors prefer to progress to a more general level of speculative explanation of the overall findings. The logical and causal linkages between affect, cognition, and behavior have been debated for some time now in the behavior science literature, and those in the consumer behavior area of marketing are undoubtedly well acquainted with the various schools of thought. The authors suspect that similar phenomenona may well lurk within the teaching pedagogy area. In fact, the use of the term "involving" is entirely intentional and is meant to imply that a hierarchy of effect may well depend on the degree of participation - mental, sensory, and physical involvement - required by the pedagogy. Lowly involving experiences are essentially devoid of attitude change despite cognitive acquisition, while the more highly involving experiences foster affect and the belief of cognitive acquisition, even when no learning effect can be documented.

Regardless of the efficacy of this explanation, the most significant result of this study, in the eyes of the authors anyway, is the comparison of microcomputer simulation effects with the other two participative methods. The initial hope that the microcomputer alternative would perform at least as well as these approaches was not only substantiated, but it appears that the microsimulation performs even better in terms of perceived knowledge gained, enjoyment with the experience, and decision skills believed acquired. Consequently, we no longer hesitate to encourage the adoption of this device in the college classroom. At the same time, the findings issue a significant challenge to microcomputer simulation designers in the form of the need to discover approaches which will actually effect greater learning in our students.

REFERENCES

Basuray, Tom and Steven A. Scherling (1978), "Cognitive Complexity Development in Lecture versus Experiential Organizational Behavior Classes," Journal of Experiential Learning and Simulation,1 (Fall), 54-59.

Bredemier, Mary E. and Cathy Stein Greenblat (1981), "The Educational Effectiveness of Simulation Games: A Synthesis of Findings," Simulation and Games, 12 (Sept.), 307-33..

Brenensthul, Daniel C. and Ralph F. Catalenello (1979), "The Impact of Three Pedagogue Techniques of Learning," Journal of Experiential Learning and Simulation, 3 (June) 211-26.

Cooke, Ernest F. and Thomas J. Maronick (1977), "Simulations Do Increase Learning," in Contemporary Marketing Thought, 1977 Educator's Proceedings, Barnett A. Greenberg and Danny N. Bellenger, Eds., Chicago: American Marketing Association, 447-50.

Dekker, John and Steven Donatti (1981), "Integration of Research Studies on the Use of Simulation as an Instructional Strategy," Journal of Educational Research, 74 (July-Aug.), 424-27.

Frazer, J. Ronald (1981), "Microcomputers and Related Technology for Simulation Gaming," in Developments in Business Simulations and Experiential Exercises, William D. Biggs and David J. Fritzsche, Eds., Normal, Ill: ABSEL, 88.

Goosen, Kenneth R. (1981), "Microcomputers - A New Technology for Innovations in Business Simulation," in Developments in Business Simulations and Experiential Exercises, William D. Biggs and David J. Fritzsche, Eds,. Normal, Ill: ABSEL, 88.

Greenblat, Cathy S. (1973), "Teaching with Simulation Games," Teaching Sociology, 1 (October), 62-83.

Hoover, Duane J. and Carlton J. Whitehead (1979), "An Experimental Evaluation of a Cognitive-Experiential Leanrning Methodology in the Basic Management Course," Journal of Experiential Learning and Simulation, 2 (Jan.), 119-26.

Jensen, Ronald L. (1981), "Simulations and Microprocesors," in Developments in Business Simulations and Experiential Exercises, William D. Biggs and David J. Fritsche, Ed., Normal, Ill: ABSEL , 86.

Kulik, James A., Chen-Lin C. Kulik, and Peter A. Cohen (1980), "Effectiveness of Computer-Based College Teaching: A Meta-Analysis of Findings," Review of Educational Research, 50, (Winter), 525-44.

Pierfy, David A. (1977), "Comparative Simulation Game Research," Simulation and Games, 8 (May-June), 255-68.

Reidenbaugh, Larry D. (1976), Retailing Management: A Planning Approach, New York: McGraw-Hill, Inc., 149-67.

Schou, Corey D. (1981), "Microprocessor Controlled Interactive Video Simulation," in Developments in Business Simulations and Experiential Exercises, William D. Biggs and David J. Fritsche, Eds., Normal, Ill: ABSEL, 89.

AN ASSESSMENT OF THE IMPACT OF COMPUTER-ASSISTED
INSTRUCTION ON PERFORMANCE IN AND ATTITUDES
TOWARD THE INTRODUCTORY MARKETING COURSE

Steven J. Skinner, University of Kentucky, Lexington
Gary L. Sullivan, University of Cincinnati

ABSTRACT

Computer-assisted instruction has received minimal utilization as an instructional aid in the introductory marketing
course. The paucity of literature pertaining to the effectiveness of this pedagogical approach in marketing contributes to this low level of utilization. This paper reports the results of an empirical study which assessed the
effectiveness of a computer-assisted instruction program
which was used as an instructional aid in a large section
of an introductory marketing course. The results suggest
that use of typical computer-assisted instruction programs
does not produce significantly higher achievement levels
than more traditional instruction methods.

INTRODUCTION

Computer-assisted instruction (CAI) has been identified as
one alternative instructional method. The topic of CAI has
received more than adequate attention in the literature;
however, the issue of CAI's effectiveness has never been
resolved. The research discussed in this paper was undertaken to shed light on the unanswered question, does CAI
result in higher achievement on the part of students? The
population for this study was a class of basic marketing
students at the college level.

Most of the research which has been conducted relative to
the effectiveness of CAI pertains to elementary programs.
Edwards et al. (1974) attempted to answer questions dealing
with the effectiveness of CAI through an exhaustive review
of research on this topic. They concluded that increased
achievement results from the use of CAI as a supplement to
traditional instruction. Research has yielded conflicting
results for situations when CAI is substituted for traditional instruction. Edwards et al. cited studies in which
the CAI students did better than the non-CAI students while
they mentioned other studies that reported no differences.

While most of the reported studies dealt with drill and
practice in arithmetic, little research has been reported
on the use of CAI in marketing education; especially on the
college level. Fisk (1971) reported that CAI could be significant in achieving educational goals in marketing management development programs and in university marketing instruction. He concluded that CAI could be made a promising
technology for marketing education through the support of
marketing instructors. Scammon and Rice (1976) reviewed
some of the technical and human problems which could hinder
the implementation of CAI programs in marketing. For optimum use of CAI, they recommended coordination of the CAI
program with the course material and inclusion of CAI as an
integral part of the class activities. Grimm et al. (1979)
investigated student evaluation of a CAI program used in
the basic marketing course. They found students using CAI
were very positive toward CAI, thought the immediate feedback provided was beneficial, and found CAI very helpful in
studying for exams. Although these studies suggest CAI is
a feasible instructional aid for marketing education, they
did not address the issue of effectiveness.

The authors wish to thank Jon F. Bibb of Illinois State
University for making his undergraduate marketing class
available as the subject pool for this investigation and
for his invaluable assistance in monitoring the data collection process.

One study to date has attempted to evaluate the effectiveness of CAI when used in the introductory marketing course.
Skinner and Grimm (1979) examined the impact of CAI on examination scores for a large class of basic marketing students. They found that students using the CAI program
scored significantly higher on all exams than students using study guides and students using neither instructional
aid. Students were _not_ assigned randomly to user and non-
user groups, however, and the results were reported with
caution. Better students could have chosen to use the CAI
program and subsequently biased the results. The present
research was undertaken to more rigorously assess the issue
of effectiveness of CAI when used as an instructional aid
in the basic marketing course.

THE CAI PROGRAM

The program used for this study was coordinated with the
course material, as suggested by Scammon and Rice (1976).
Developed to accompany an introductory marketing text,
Tutorial Review of Marketing Principles (1977) or TRMP was
directly tied to the textbook used by students. TRMP was designed to allow a student to evaluate his or her understanding of the material in each textbook chapter. By following
simple instructions, the student has the option of obtaining
detailed instructions for using the program, chapter summaries, and objective questions. After the student responds
to a question, the program indicates whether the answer is
correct and gives a brief explanation and, in some cases,
refers the student to a page in the textbook. This type of
feedback encourages the student to review the textbook to
find out why a certain response was incorrect. TRMP also
reinforces the student with additional insights on the topic
when his or her response is correct. A sample question from
the TRMP program follows:

Question Number? 13

13. Selecting and analyzing a target market is a step in
    which process?

    1. Establishing marketing objectives
    2. Creating and maintaining satisfying marketing mixes.
    3. Organizing by types of customers.
    4. Implementing the marketing plan.
    5. Developing a marketing strategy

Answer Number? 2

No, you can't create a marketing mix if you haven't selected your target market.

Question Number? 13

Answer Number? 5

That's right! You win $50,000 and a Rolls Royce! Develop-
ing a marketing strategy consists of selecting and analyzing
a target market and then developing marketing mixes to satisfy the needs of the target market.

METHOD

A Posttest Only with Control Group design (Campbell and
Stanley, 1966) was employed to assess the effectiveness of
CAI as a learning aid in a range of classroom situations
commonly associated with the basic marketing course. The
treatment conditions were:

(1) Lectures and textbook (Control).
(2) Lectures, textbook, study guide for the textbook, and the CAI program (CAI/Study Guide).
(3) Lectures, textbook and study guide for the textbook (Study Guide).
(4) Lectures, textbook, and the CAI program (CAI).

Subjects using both CAI and study guides were provided with a personal copy of the study guide for the textbook and were given access to the computer system on which TRMP was stored. Study guide only subjects were also given copies of the study guide. CAI only subjects were provided access to TRMP. All subjects had equal exposure to lectures and purchase of the textbook was required of all students.

The subject pool for the study was a class of over one hundred undergraduate students enrolled in a principles of marketing course at a mid-western university. Prior to assignment to the treatment conditions, which was done on a careful, random basis, a battery of questions about past educational performance, prior coursework, customary study styles, prior computer exposure and preference for a variety of study formats was asked. These issues had been shown to be related to the issues currently under study in other research (Grimm et al. 1979). The rationale for gathering this background data was principally to determine if the randomization procedure was a complete success in producing equivalence between groups and, if not, to hold these items in reserve for more sophisticated data analysis in the event statistical control as well as manipulative (experimental) control was required (Winer 1971; Wildt and Ahtola 1978).

description of CAI, although they had not actually used TRMP. This enabled all students to respond to questions concerning CAI. Finally, a more objective performance measure was employed. Student's test scores, achieved on each of four objective-type examinations, were available for comparison to assess the efficacy of the treatments.

ANALYSIS AND DISCUSSION

Data from the preliminary instrument showed no significant between group differences (alpha = .05) for the following objective-type variables: sex, major, grade point average, hours to date in program, and prior coursework using CAI software. However, when the battery of more subjectively-oriented items was examined, fully five of these variables exhibited significant differences at this alpha level. Because of this finding, the one-way Analysis of Variance approach originally intended for this research was modified. Table 1 shows the premeasure items which exhibited significant differences and gives the cell means, by treatment groups, with corresponding cell sizes. The first item was measured on a six point importance scale (scored 1 = definitely unimportant to 6 = definitely important). The remaining four items exhibited in Table 1 were measured on six point Likert-type agreement scales (scored 1 = definitely disagree to 6 = definitely agree). See Table 1 for comparison purposes.

Because of the results reported in Table 1, it was necessary to revise the analysis procedure originally planned to include statistical control along with the manipulative control afforded by the true experimental design. The most

TABLE 1
PREMEASURE ITEMS SHOWING SIGNIFICANT DIFFERENCES*

| Item | Control | Cell Means: Importance | | | F |
		CAI and Study Guide	Study Guide	CAI	
(1) Opportunity to ask questions.	5.56 (n=27)	5.26 (n=23)	5.44 (n=25)	4.96 (n=24)	2.58
(2) I really don't see any need to go to class, I could accomplish the same amount of learning myself.	1.59 (n=27)	1.26 (n=23)	1.72 (n=25)	2.08 (n=24)	2.76
(3) Other than studying for exams, college courses don't entail much work outside of the classroom.	2.22 (n=27)	2.96 (n=23)	1.80 (n=25)	1.71 (n=24)	6.31
(4) I prefer a class in which the instructor lectures.	3.23 (n=26)	3.44 (n=23)	3.80 (n=25)	4.21 (n=24)	2.61
(5) Generally I study for a course which has multiple choice items with my friends.	2.44 (n=27)	3.04 (n=23)	2.48 (n=25)	1.75 (n=24)	3.82

* One-way Analysis of Variance, alpha = .05.

Participation in the experiment lasted for one full semester (approximately fifteen weeks). Several measures were taken during the semester to insure that all students were participating in the experiment in accordance with their group assignments. In addition to frequent encouragement from the instructor, students were asked to submit periodic assignments for evaluation. No evidence of any sort was detected to indicate confounding of the treatment conditions.

The posttest was administered during the final session of class. This consisted of a questionnaire which asked students specific questions about CAI programs plus several of the Likert-type attitudinal questions which were contained on the background questionnaire. All of the non-subjectively oriented items in the background instrument were deleted from the postmeasure. In order to properly test the effect of CAI, students in the control group and the study guide group (who were _not_ exposed previously to CAI) read a short scenario explaining what a CAI program is and how it is used. This provided them with an accurate

appropriate approach for analysis of metric dependent variables in light of these findings is a one-way Analysis of Covariance (Winer 1971; Wildt and Ahtola 1978). Using this statistical procedure permits the researcher to reduce the error component by adjusting statistically for specific sources of variation. This provides a more sensitive and rigorous test of treatment effects than would be obtained with Analysis of Variance alone. The influences under statistical control must be metric in character and are referred to as covariates. In this application, the variables in Table 1 will be used as covariates. Since the treatment groups were not equivalent on these premeasures, the contribution to error from these sources can be reduced by including them as covariates in the remaining analysis. The Statistical Package for the Social Sciences (SPSS) program for Analysis of Covariance was employed (Nie et al. 1975).

Results of the Analysis of Covariance performed on the test score data are presented in Table 2. Overall, the findings of this analysis suggest that no significant performance differences can be attributed to any of the course formats tested. With the exception of Exam I, which approached significance (alpha = .071) and in which the control group and CAI group were superior, performance when judged on a statistical basis was quite uniform. It is interesting to note, however, that the control group and CAI group were consistently superior to the CAI/study guide group and the study guide group.

The data were also analyzed to determine the impact of the treatment assignments on student's attitudes toward classroom practices. Analysis of Covariance was again used. It was run for each item in a twenty item inventory containing opinion statements which were rated using six point Likert-type scales (scored 1 = definitely disagree to 6 = definitely agree). These items were previously used by Grimm et al. (1979) in research on CAI. For organizational reasons, these results are presented in two parts. See Tables 3 and 4. The data in Table 3 show no significant differences (alpha = .05) in agreement levels across treatment groups for ten opinion items focusing on education-related issues. The remaining ten items in this opinion battery are presented in Table 4. Once again, no significant treatment effects were discovered.

Table 5 lists the results of Analysis of Covariance performed on ten items of an attitudinal nature which specifically address CAI. The reader will recall that the earlier opinion data was focused at a much more general level. It would be expected that these items, specifically tailored to tap feelings on issues associated with CAI, would have a higher likelihood of exhibiting treatment effects than the more general opinion measures. Looking at Table 5, it can be seen that the treatment effects on these CAI-specific issues were surprisingly modest. With the exceptions of items four and eight, the remaining ten issues had extremely small F values.

TABLE 2
MEANS AND SIGNIFICANCE TESTS
FOR GROUPS ON EXAMINATION SCORES*

| | Cell Means: | Test Scores | | |
	Control	CAI and Study Guide	Study Guide	CAI	F
**Exam I	72.00 (n=26)	68.64 (n=22)	65.12 (n=25)	73.42 (n=24)	2.43
Exam II	71.77 (n=26)	67.55 (n=22)	70.48 (n=25)	71.67 (n=24)	0.26
Exam III	73.77 (n=26)	68.64 (n=22)	68.72 (n=25)	73.58 (n=24)	1.24
Exam IV	69.27 (n=26)	63.36 (n=22)	65.16 (n=25)	68.75 (n=24)	1.27

* Analysis of Covariance with five covariates.
**Denotes nearly significant main effect due to treatment, alpha = 0.071.

TABLE 3
MEANS AND SIGNIFICANCE TESTS FOR GROUPS ON OPINION ITEMS (PART I)*

| Item | | Control | Cell Means: Agreement | | | |
			CAI and Study Guide	Study Guide	CAI	F
(1)	I prefer a class that primarily consists of lectures and a textbook.	3.73 (n=26)	4.09 (n=23)	4.08 (n=24)	4.22 (n=23)	0.24
(2)	I think instructional aids, such as study guides and case books are quite helpful in the learning process.	4.15 (n=26)	4.43 (n=23)	4.00 (n=24)	4.26 (n=23)	0.53
(3)	I really don't see any need to go to class; I could accomplish the same amount of learning myself.	1.88 (n=26)	1.74 (n=23)	1.79 (n=24)	1.87 (n=23)	0.32
(4)	If I had my choice, I would like a class that emphasized student involvement and interaction.	4.23 (n=26)	4.00 (n=23)	4.33 (n=24)	4.13 (n=23)	0.13
(5)	School is mostly busy work; when I complete a course, sometimes I find I really have not learned anything useful.	3.00 (n=26)	3.22 (n=23)	3.50 (n=24)	2.61 (n=23)	1.73
(6)	I think more emphasis should be placed on independent study outside of the classroom.	3.08 (n=25)	2.96 (n=23)	2.72 (n=25)	2.91 (n=23)	0.50
(7)	All in all, the system may have some problems, but I like the learning process as it exists today.	3.60 (n=25)	4.13 (n=23)	3.84 (n=25)	4.04 (n=23)	1.10
(8)	When I complete my degree, I feel I will be well prepared to go out into the "real world" with a career.	4.24 (n=25)	4.30 (n=23)	4.36 (n=25)	4.26 (n=23)	0.20
(9)	Other than studying for exams, college courses really don't entail that much work outside of the classroom.	2.32 (n=25)	2.30 (n=23)	2.28 (n=25)	2.43 (n=23)	0.82
(10)	Something needs to be changed; there seems to be something lacking in higher education today.	4.08 (n=25)	3.52 (n=23)	3.68 (n=25)	3.65 (n=23)	0.67

* Analyis of Covariance with five covariates.

TABLE 4

MEANS AND SIGNIFICANCE TESTS FOR GROUPS ON OPINION ITEMS (PART II)*

Item		Control	Cell Means: Agreement CAI and Study Guide	Study Guide	CAI	F
(1)	I prefer a class in which the instructor lectures from the assigned text.	3.40 (n=25)	4.04 (n=23)	3.92 (n=25)	4.17 (n=23)	1.20
(2)	I generally use workbooks in a course which has multiple choice exams.	2.96 (n=25)	3.26 (n=23)	2.96 (n=25)	2.65 (n=23)	0.60
(3)	Generally, I feel comfortable using the computer for class assignments.	3.40 (n=25)	3.26 (n=23)	2.88 (n=25)	3.13 (n=23)	0.46
(4)	Memorization is the major way I study for multiple choice exams.	3.48 (n=25)	3.78 (n=23)	3.80 (n=25)	3.17 (n=23)	1.13
(5)	Computer terminals are easy for me to use; I have few problems interacting with the computer.	3.80 (n=25)	3.52 (n=23)	3.80 (n=25)	3.91 (n=23)	0.58
(6)	Generally, I study for a course which has multiple choice exams with friends.	2.31 (n=26)	2.43 (n=23)	2.40 (n=25)	1.91 (n=23)	0.06
(7)	I enjoy courses with require some usage of the computer.	3.19 (n=26)	2.65 (n=23)	3.20 (n=25)	3.17 (n=23)	0.96
(8)	I feel confident that I can use the computer as a learning tool when required to in a course.	4.12 (n=26)	3.52 (n=23)	3.68 (n=25)	3.96 (n=23)	0.97
(9)	In classes in which I have used the computer, I feel it has helped my learning.	3.88 (n=26)	3.17 (n=23)	3.40 (n=25)	3.13 (n=23)	1.21
(10)	I prefer a class in which the instructor requires a text but lectures primarily on outside material.	3.04 (n=26)	2.91 (n=23)	3.00 (n=25)	3.22 (n=23)	0.71

* Analysis of Covariance with five covariates.

TABLE 5

MEANS AND SIGNIFICANCE TESTS FOR GROUPS' ATTITUDES TOWARD CAI*

Item		Control	Cell Means: Agreement CAI and Study Guide	Study Guide	CAI	F
(1)	CAI is difficult to use.	2.32 (n=25)	2.59 (n=22)	2.87 (n=23)	2.87 (n=23)	0.42
(2)	CAI is helpful in studying for exams.	3.72 (n=25)	3.73 (n=22)	3.65 (n=23)	3.13 (n=23)	0.21
(3)	CAI is a useful way to skip a class.	2.08 (n=25)	2.14 (n=22)	2.35 (n=23)	1.52 (n=23)	1.72
**(4)	CAI is a useful way to avoid reading the text.	2.04 (n=25)	2.41 (n=22)	2.48 (n=23)	1.52 (n=23)	2.40
(5)	CAI is convenient to use (location).	3.80 (n=25)	3.82 (n=22)	3.35 (n=23)	3.26 (n=23)	0.36
(6)	CAI supplements the text.	4.08 (n=24)	4.55 (n=22)	4.00 (n=23)	3.78 (n=23)	0.66
(7)	CAI is a complement to the lecture.	3.83 (n=24)	3.27 (n=22)	3.43 (n=23)	3.09 (n=23)	0.90
***(8)	CAI provides quick feedback on progress in the course.	3.96 (n=24)	3.50 (n=22)	4.39 (n=23)	3.65 (n=23)	2.17
(9)	CAI is an interesting way to learn.	4.00 (n=24)	4.00 (n=22)	3.91 (n=23)	3.70 (n=23)	0.04
(10)	CAI is an innovative way to learn.	4.08 (n=24)	4.18 (n=22)	4.22 (n=23)	4.09 (n=23)	0.17
(11)	Errors are (will be) problems with CAI.	3.19 (n=26)	3.73 (n=22)	3.57 (n=23)	3.35 (n=20)	1.16
(12)	There is a need for computer self-instructional assistance.	3.58 (n=26)	3.55 (n=22)	3.61 (n=23)	3.20 (n=20)	0.32

* Analysis of Covariance with five covariates.
** Denotes nearly significant main effect due to treatment, alpha = 0.074.
***Denotes nearly significant main effect due to treatment, alpha = 0.097.

Since items four and eight did not reach a standard level of statistical significance, no further analysis was performed to determine if significant differences between specific treatment conditions existed. However, for item four which reads "CAI is a useful way to avoid reading the text," it can be said that treatments 2 and 3 showed the smallest amount of disagreement. Treatment 2 contained CAI and a study guide, while treatment 3 added only the study guide. It is interesting to note that treatment 4, which added only the CAI program, showed the largest amount of disagreement with this statement.

Question eight which reads "CAI provides quick feedback on progress in the course" had highest agreement in treatments 1 and 3; the control group and the study guide only groups, respectively. This suggests, but does not prove, that actual experience with CAI does not live up to students' expectations as far as the basic marketing course is concerned.

CONCLUSIONS

The results of this research indicate that CAI, when used as a learning aid in a basic marketing course, did not have a positive effect on examination scores. Furthermore, students using CAI did not have significantly different attitudes toward computers at the end of the semester, as compared to the other groups. Finally, students who used the CAI program did not have a significantly different attitude toward CAI than students who did not have access to TRMP.

The results obtained in studies measuring effectiveness of learning aids are definitely influenced by randomization of treatment groups. Studies which have reported increased learning based on quasi-experimental designs should be viewed with extreme caution. Furthermore, CAI does not appear to be a feasible means of indoctrinating students to learning aids, as it did not have a significant impact on attitudes toward such learning aids.

For the purposes of this research, CAI was not used as a substitute for traditional instruction, but rather as a supplement. Furthermore, other important aspects of CAI were not explored, such as cost effectiveness, time utilities, and retention rates. Additionally, the teacher's evaluation of CAI was not measured. These issues are important, and they alone could warrant utilization of a CAI program.

Further research should be conducted concerning the use of instructional aids. Development of programs such as TRMP, and study guides, involve a large amount of time and money. The maximum benefit a student could receive from such instructional aids is increased learning. This study indicates that CAI did not increase learning, as measured by student performance on objective examinations.

REFERENCES

Campbell, Donald T., and Julian C. Stanley (1966), _Experimental and Quasi-Experimental Designs for Research_, Chicago: Rand-McNally.

Edwards, Judith, Shirley Norton, Sandra Taylor, Ralph Van Dusseldorp, and Martha Weiss (1974), "Is CAI Effective?" _AEDS Journal_, (Summer), 122-126.

Fisk, George (1971), "Computer-Aided Marketing Instruction," _Journal of Marketing_, 35 (January), 20-27.

Grimm, Jim L., Steven J. Skinner, and O. C. Ferrell (1979), "Computer-Assisted Instruction for the Basic Marketing Course: A Student Evaluation," _Journal of Marketing Education_, 1 (April), 63-70.

Nie, Norman H., C. Hadlai Hull, Jean G. Jenkins, Karin Steinbrenner, and Dale H. Bent (1975), _Statistical Package for the Social Sciences_, 2nd ed., New York: McGraw-Hill.

Scammon, Debra L., and William F. Rice (1976), "Computer-Aided Instruction in Marketing: Problems and Prospects," A paper presented at the Southwestern Marketing Association Meetings, San Antonio, Texas, (March), 1-15.

Skinner, Steven J. (1977), _Tutorial Review of Marketing Principles_, Boston: Houghton-Mifflin Company.

Skinner, Steven J., and Jim L. Grimm (1979), "Computer-Assisted Instruction Case Study: The Introductory Marketing Course," _Educational Technology_, 19 (July), 34-36.

Wildt, Albert R., and Olli T. Ahtola (1978), _Analysis of Covariance_, Vol. 12, Series: Quantitative Applications in Social Sciences, Beverly Hills, Calif.: Sage Publications.

Winer, B. J. (1971), _Statistical Principles in Experimental Design_, 2nd ed., New York: McGraw-Hill.

USING THEORY TO UNDERSTAND PRODUCT PRICING APPLICATIONS OF BREAK-EVEN ANALYSIS*

Jon M. Hawes, University of Akron
Michael F. d'Amico, University of Akron

ABSTRACT

Even though most marketing students develop the ability to work break-even problems, the full potential of break-even analysis as an aid in product pricing decisions is usually not realized. This paper describes a teaching technique which demonstrates how a simple variation of break-even analysis, when used in conjunction with demand analysis, can greatly enhance the ability to determine appropriate product prices.

INTRODUCTION

Virtually all texts designed for the Principles of Marketing course and most texts written for other marketing courses include a discussion of break-even analysis. Usually, this topic is included in the section of the text covering pricing strategy. While most marketing students master the elementary mathematical techniques of break-even analysis, most fail to understand the true significance of the concept as an aid in making marketing decisions. Indeed, the typical student in a marketing class does not comprehend how break-even analysis can be utilized in the pricing decision.

In fact, many students don't even understand why this topic is included in the section of the course covering product pricing. Many students and some professors question the relevance of studying break-even analysis in the Principles of Marketing course because students are exposed to break-even analysis in several of the other AACSB core courses. Perhaps one of the reasons that pricing decisions and break-even analysis have such an ambiguous relationship is the fact that break-even analysis is often included in other courses under the topic of "Cost/Volume/Profit" relationships. The absence of "Price" in this phrase is notable, and the discussions of break-even analysis in these classes often simply propose that price is "given".

Therefore, it is critical that the relevance and potential benefit of utilizing break-even analysis in product pricing decisions be recognized. This is not to suggest that the coverage of break-even analysis in the AACSB core be reserved for the Principles of Marketing course. Modifications in the way break-even concepts are presented, however, are needed. Professors in the business administration disciplines have often failed to adapt the presentation of break-even analysis to emphasize the applications of the concept that are most useful for that particular discipline.

Furthermore, even within particular disciplines, the variety of relevant applications of break-even analysis have not been presented with great clarity. For example, the topic is usually included in the pricing section of the Principles of Marketing course, but break-even analysis can also be useful in evaluating new product or retail store opportunities. Thus, while the application of break-even analysis in product pricing decisions is usually suboptimally realized, the approach is often ignored in other equally important potential marketing applications.

The teaching technique described in this paper was developed in an attempt to facilitate this process of demonstrating the relevance of break-even analysis in a particular topical area--product pricing decisions. The approach has been used in our Principles of Marketing classes at the University of Akron for several semesters and the results have been encouraging.

BASIC CONCEPTS OF BREAK-EVEN[1]

A basic assumption in break-even analysis is that all relevant costs can be categorized either as "Fixed" or as "Variable". Fixed costs are those which do not vary in total in relation to changes in quantity or output. (Output is used in a generic sense and may imply: production, quantity, sales, or some other end-result.) While Total Fixed Costs remain constant over the relevant range of output, the Fixed Cost per Unit would vary, of course, depending upon the level, or quantity of output under consideration.

Variable Costs per Unit, however, are costs that are capable of being efficaciously allocated to particular units of output. Variable Costs per Unit are assumed to remain constant over the relevant range of output. Total Variable Costs vary, however, in direct proportion to output. These relationships can by symbolically expressed as follows:

$$\text{Total Fixed Cost} \equiv \text{TFC} = f\ (\text{Time})$$
$$\text{Fixed Cost per Unit} \equiv \text{FC}_u = f\ (\text{Quantity})$$
$$\text{Total Variable Cost} \equiv \text{TVC} = f\ (\text{Quantity})$$
$$\text{Variable Cost per Unit} \equiv \text{VC}_u$$
$$\text{Selling Price per Unit} \equiv \text{SP}_u$$

Thus, some costs (TFC) are incurred regardless of the firm's level of output and are a function of the time frame under consideration. Some costs (TVC) vary in direct proportion to the firm's level of output. Furthermore, it is usually assumed that the selling price per unit (SP_u) charged by the firm is constant over the relevant range. This leads directly to the break-even formula:

$$BE_u = \frac{\text{TFC}}{\text{SP}_u - \text{VC}_u} \tag{1}$$

This may be effectively translated into words as follows:

"How many 'per unit gains' ($\text{SP}_u - \text{VC}_u$) are required in some time frame to cover some associated costs (TFC) which are a function (only) of time?"

STATIC AND DYNAMIC BREAK-EVEN ANALYSIS

Keep in mind that the goal of the discussion is to show the relevance of break-even analysis in product pricing decisions. It is useful at this point to discuss break-even in terms of its static and dynamic dimensions. A single calculation of the break-even point in units (or in dollars) that is based on a particular set of associated costs and a single, assumed selling price is static break-even analysis. The result of this calculation is useful information

---

*

The authors thank William R. Darden, University of Arkansas, and Allan D. Shocker, Vanderbilt University for their contributions to the literature which fostered some of the ideas presented in this paper.

[1] Readers familiar with the traditional approach to teaching break-even analysis can skip to the next section without loss of clarity.

for understanding how much output would be required so that
a firm would avoid losing money on a given project. Unfortunately, while an assumed selling price was a required
element in the determination of the break-even point, little
insight concerning the optimality of that particular assumed
price can be realized from this procedure.

Dynamic break-even analysis, on the other hand, is an iterative procedure in which a series of break even points are
calculated for a series of respective prices. By comparing
the change in break-even points in relation to the change
in price, the analyst is better able to understand the
relationships between these two factors. In addition, this
approach emphasizes the fact that price is a controllable
element of the marketing mix.

RELATING BREAK-EVEN ANALYSIS TO THE PRICING DECISION

It is with dynamic break-even analysis that the relevance
of the product pricing applications of break-even analysis
is best understood. Indeed, one can graphically show all
the possible combinations of selling prices and respective
break-even quantities. Shocker (1974) described a plot of
the combinations of selling price and quantity which resulted in equal profit (in this special case of zero profit)
as an "iso-profit curve".

Exhibit 1 graphically depicts such a curve. Notice that it
is convex to the origin and approaches the line representing the variable cost per unit (VC_u) as a horizontal asymp-
tote. The logic of this relationship is that as the selling price per unit approaches the variable cost per unit,
required volume increases in order to reach the break-even
point. Indeed, so long as the selling price per unit exceeds the variable cost per unit, theoretically there exists a possible break-even quantity. In reality, however,
the required volume becomes so large that it loses practical significance as the selling price per unit approaches
the variable cost per unit.

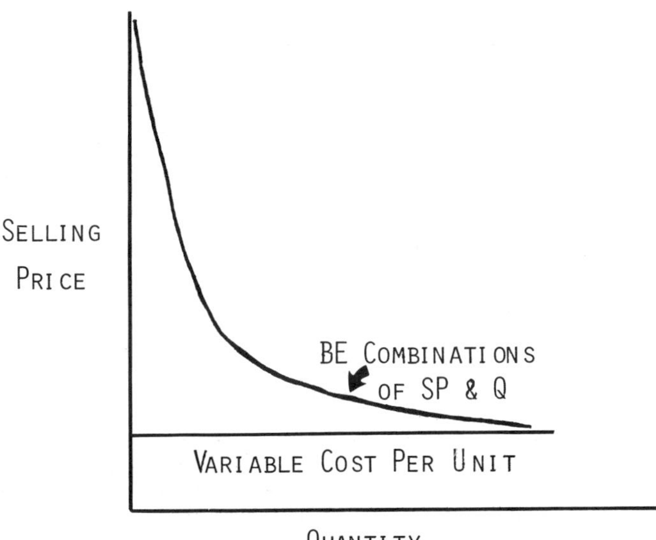

EXHIBIT 1

A PLOT OF SELLING PRICE AND QUANTITY
OVER ALL BREAK-EVEN COMBINATIONS

The zero level iso-profit curve is also asymptotic to the
vertical axis of the graph. As selling price increases the
required volume to reach the break-even point decreases.
As selling price reaches extremely high levels, the break-
even quantity becomes extremely low. Theoretically, at an
infinitely high selling price, the break-even quantity
would decrease without bound. In practice, however, some
reasonable range of prices and quantities must be established.

The range of prices worthy of consideration can easily be
determined by considering the relevant demand curve for the
product. While the exact parameters of the demand function
are never known, a number of authors (e.g., Darden 1968;
Kotler 1980, pp. 228-236; McCarthy 1971, pp. 655-660; or
Shocker 1974) have described methods for developing realistic estimates of demand.

An Example

Consider the data presented in Exhibit 2. Several combinations of selling price per unit and quantity which would
result in zero profit (break even) are provided. A plot of
the zero level iso-profit curve for the data presented in
Exhibit 2 is shown in Exhibit 3. Note that at any point on
the curve, break even would be achieved. Any combination
of price and quantity upward and/or to the right of the
zero level iso-profit curve would represent profitable combinations of price and quantity. Any combination of price
and quantity located below and/or to the left of the zero
level iso-profit curve would represent an unprofitable situation.

EXHIBIT 2

An Example Problem

Data: TFC = \$1,000 per year
           VC_u = \$ 40

BE_u	SP_u
250	44
200	45
100	50
50	60
33.33	70
25	80
20	90
16.67	100
14.29	110
12.5	120
11.11	130
10	140
9.09	150

The realm of possible levels of price and quantity which
the market demands, however, is represented by the demand
curve. Thus, in the absence of a shift in the location of
the demand curve, only those combinations of price and
quantity shown on the demand function (shown as D in Exhibit 3) would be achievable in the market place.

The demand curve intersects the zero level iso-profit curve
at two points, shown in Exhibit 3 as points A and B. These
would be the only two break-even combinations of price and
quantity that could be achieved in this market. All other
possible combinations of price and quantity would result
in either a profit, or a loss. The range of profitable
selling prices would be associated with a subset of the
demand curve which includes the line segment identified
as AB in Exhibit 3. Thus, any price within the range of
P_a to P_b in Exhibit 3 would represent a profitable price.
Any price higher than P_a (approximately \$85), or any price
lower than P_b (approximately \$55), however, would be to the

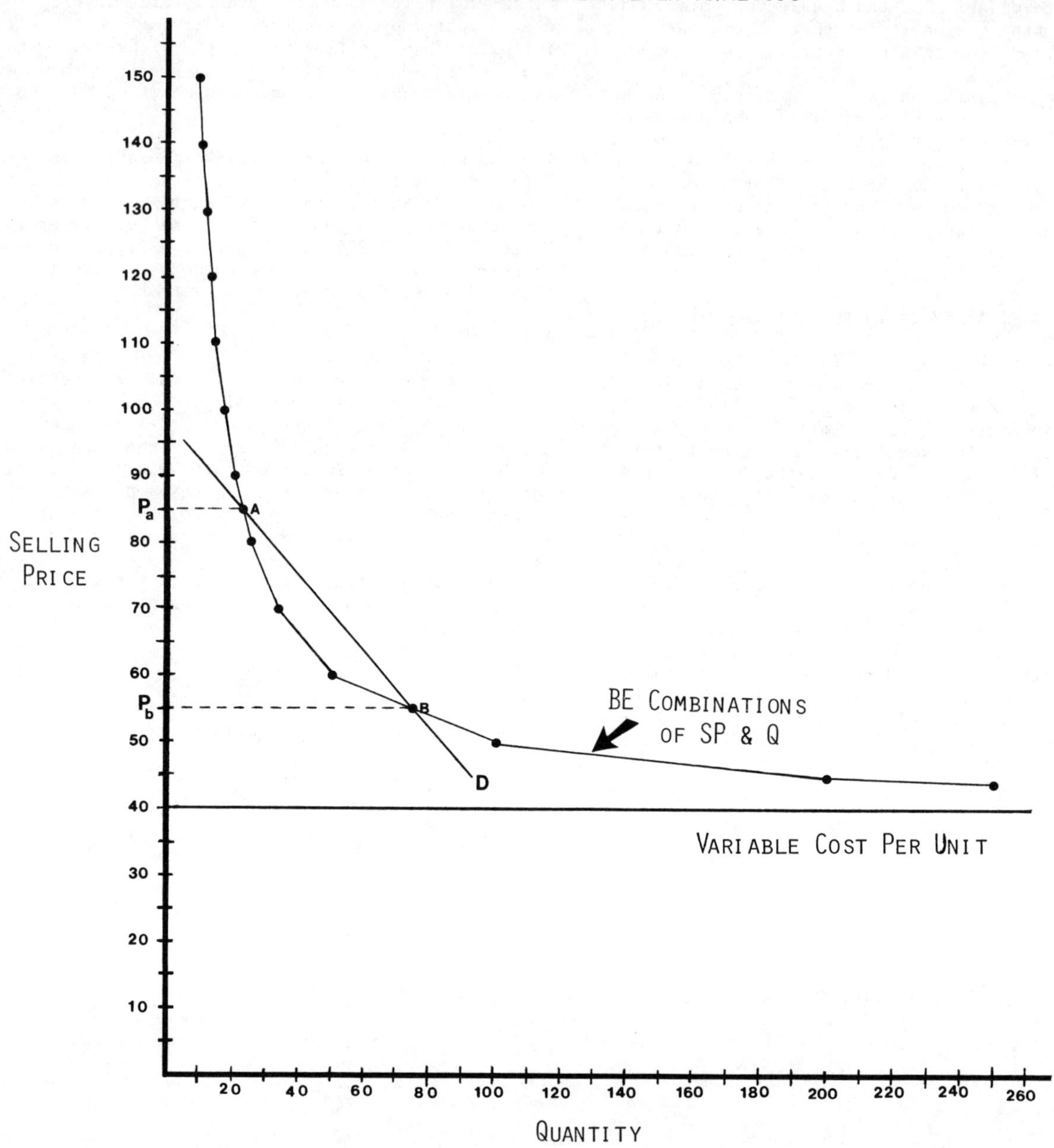

left of the zero level iso-profit curve and would therefore be a combination of price and quantity that would result in a loss.

This graphic presentation easily demonstrates the benefits of utilizing break-even in pricing decisions. The super-imposition of the demand curve on the graph of the zero level iso-profit curve permits the analyst to readily iden-tify the subset of profitable prices that are worthy of further consideration.

As proof of this understanding, the authors have found that at this point in the class discussion, one of the brighter students invariably asks "What is the most profit-able price?" An approximate solution can be found by iden-tifying the price associated with the point on the line segment AB of the demand curve that is the farthest hori-zontal distance from any point on the zero level iso-profit curve. An exact solution can be found by plotting iso-profit curves for increasingly positive levels of profit. The point of tangency between the demand function and the

highest iso-profit curve would exactly represent the most profitable price (Shocker 1974). An example of this is shown in exhibit 4. In this case the point of tangency occurs at the π_2 iso-profit curve. The most profitable price which is achievable in this market is therefore labeled P_2, and the corresponding quantity of demand is labeled Q_2.

SUMMARY

This paper has advanced a method for demonstrating the use of break-even analysis in determining a range of poten-tially profitable prices. The juxtaposition of an estima-ted demand curve with one or more iso-profit curves permits the identification of unprofitable as well as profitable prices, points of maximum profitability, and points of break-even that might be achieved in a given market. Com-bining these two essentially familiar concepts, that of break-even and that of demand, elucidates both. More

EXHIBIT 4

DETERMINATION OF MOST PROFITABLE PRICE

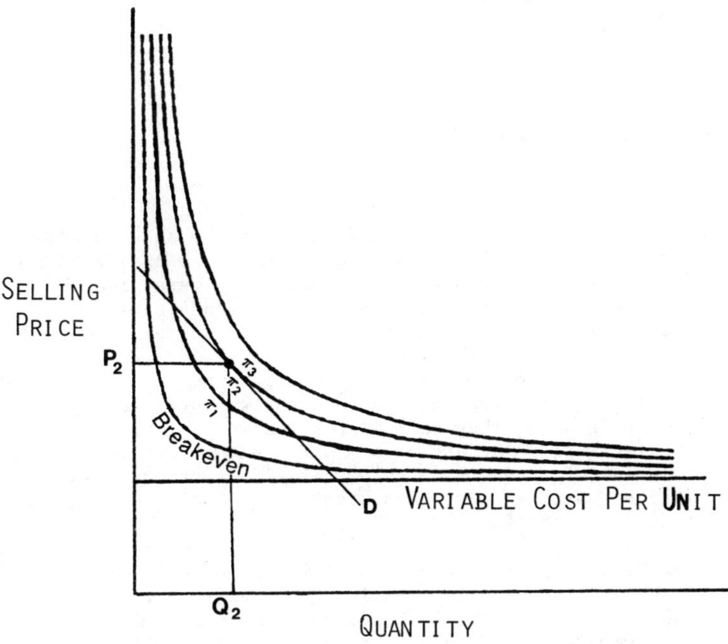

importantly, however, it demonstrates the fact that these
concepts have practical as well as theoretical integrity.
In addition, this approach to teaching break-even analysis
demonstrates to the student an application of the technique in product pricing decisions that may not be realized,
and which has certainly not been emphasized, in traditional
approaches to the topic.

REFERENCES

Darden, Bill R. (1968), "An Operational Approach to Product
  Pricing," Journal of Marketing, 32 (April), 29-33.

Kotler, Philip (1980), Marketing Management: Analysis,
  Planning, and Control, Fourth Edition, Englewood Cliffs,
  NJ: Prentice-Hall, Inc.

McCarthy, E. Jerome (1971), Basic Marketing: A Managerial
  Approach, Fourth Edition, Homewood, IL: Richard D.
  Irwin, Inc.

Shocker, Allan D. (1974), "Iso-Profit Analysis: A Useful
  Aid to Marketing Decision Making," Pittsburg Business
  Review, 44 (September-October), 2-10.

MASS LECTURE SETTINGS VERSUS TRADITIONAL LECTURE SETTINGS

Michael Smith, Temple University, Philadelphia
Rajan Chandran, Temple University, Philadelphia
James Talaga, Temple University, Philadelphia

ABSTRACT

A procedure is described for conducting a mass lecture format for introductory marketing. Topics included are: objectives, resources, planning, textbook/learning aid selection, outside materials, assignments, role of teaching
assistants and steps taken to remove dissonance. A methodology is described and analysis performed with regard to
the students' performance and evaluation of the mass lecture format as compared to students' performance and evaluation of a traditional single-section format. In essence,
the study indicates that the mass lecture format does not
have a significantly negative impact upon students' performance or perceptions of the course.

INTRODUCTION

The purpose of this article is to report on a change in the
method of teaching the undergraduate introductory marketing course at Temple University's School of Business. The
change involved moving away from small classes to mass lectures. The article discusses the inevitable movement to
mass lectures in most business schools. Next, the resources needed, the instructional methods used, and an assessment of the impact of a change to mass lectures on student
performance and attitudes towards the introductory marketing course are discussed. The report also provides
brief recommendations for others who might wish to use a
similar approach.

BACKGROUND

Many schools of business administration face a major dilemma today. On the one hand they are faced with increasing enrollments and demand for the required introductory
courses. On the other hand, they are faced with the prospect of:

(a) not enough supply of terminally qualified fac-
     ulty to teach the courses, and
(b) hiring freezes due to budget cuts and other
     factors.

In addition, schools of business must fulfill certain
AACSB requirements which mandate that a certain percentage
of courses be taught by terminally qualified faculty.
Given this situation, the movement to large lectures or
even TV/cassette methods of teaching in the future seems
likely.

The challenge in the mass lecture format is to make the
classes, despite the large size, a meaningful, personal
part of the students educational experience. Such classes
have to be taught with special techniques that will enable
large numbers of students to learn without sacrificing
learning quality.

PLANNING AND IMPLEMENTATION

Mass lectures require a different mix of faculty and assistants with a proportionately heavier emphasis on graduate assistants. Lectures were given by two qualified professors who lectured twice a week. They were aided by
three teaching assistants (recitation leaders) who met the
classes in smaller recitation groups of approximately 30
students once a week. The recitation leaders reemphasized
and highlighted the important concepts and answered student
questions about the lectures and assignments. Along with
the professors, they coordinated the work of the graders.
The recitation leaders also monitored the performance and
progress of students in the recitation sections. In addition, three graduate assistants were assigned to grading
and administration.

Teaching large sections calls for a great deal of preplanning and attention to detail. It is advisable to make an
exhaustive list of all the tasks to be preformed at least
one semester in advance to assure success. The tasks include, but are not limited to:

(a) Text book selection, along with appropriate sup-
     plemental materials such as workbooks, desk
     copies, instructor's manuals, transparencies,
     films, and slides.
(b) Preparation of an exhaustive syllabus which stip-
     ulates course objectives, policies, chapter ma-
     terial covered, assignments grading examinations
     and activities performed in lecture and recita-
     tion sections. (The syllabus for this course was
     17 pages.)
(c) Training of recitation leaders and graders along
     with establishing a means of coordinating the
     activities of the professors, recitation leaders
     and graders.

In addition to extensive preplanning there were weekly
meetings of the faculty, recitation leaders and graders.
These meetings served to:

(a) monitor the progress of the lectures during the
     week;
(b) provide guidelines for graders on weekly assign-
     ments to ensure uniformity across recitation
     sections;
(c) assess student feelings about the course.

Since more responsibility is placed upon the student in a
mass lecture setting, the text book and learning aids were
chosen carefully. Ease of readability was a major criterion in choosing a textbook. Due importance was also given
to the quality of learning aids accompanying the textbook -
student learning aid, exercises, transparencies, test bank
and the like. The text and the learning aids were chosen
in order to make the marketing concepts relevant to the
real world and thus, more interesting to the students.

Every effort was made to enliven and enrich the classes by
bringing in contemporary examples from the Wall Street
Journal, New York Times, Business Week, Fortune and others.
However, various other aids like films and guest speakers
were found to be impractical due to the time constraints
imposed by the mass lecture format.

The course was designed in such a way as to ensure continuous involvement of the students over the entire semester. Frequent exams and weekly work book assignments were given. The exams were given to ensure regular reading of the text and avoid the "drift and cram" approach. The assignments were given weekly so as to ensure that the student's were working constantly and also to get the students to demonstrate understanding of the concepts and principles through these assignments. Optional attendance review sessions were held before each examination to synthesize and review the material. More emphasis was placed on the activities discussed here because of the demands and/or limitations of the mass lecture setting.

The examinations were all of the multiple choice variety. Items for the examination were selected from the test bank and their suitability evaluated by the faculty and recitation leaders. To remove dissonance, with regards to the results, an item analysis was done on all the questions. Every question was discussed at the joint meeting of the faculty and recitation leaders. Each question and distribution of responses for each question was discussed openly in the recitation class and adjustments made where necessary. Finally students were permitted to make a written defense of their answers.

Every effort was made to keep lines of communication open. Among the things that were done to keep these lines open were:

(a) Telephone numbers (both home and office) of the professors and recitation leaders were made available. Students were encouraged to call in case of any difficulty.
(b) Ombudspersons were appointed. Students were encouraged to take up problems with the ombudspersons who would then contact the faculty if the students did not desire to meet with the faculty directly.
(c) Individual counselling was given to help students perform better.

The following sections will report on a methodology and analysis of the students' performance and evaluation of the mass lecture format as compared with students' performance and evaluation of a traditional single-section format.

METHODOLOGY

The mass lecture approach to the teaching of introductory marketing was established at both the main campus and an extension campus in the Fall of 1981. Policies described above were applied to both campuses. The mass lecture section on the main campus had a student enrollment of 240 while the mass lecture section on the extension campus had a student enrollment of 63. Two professors were involved in this project. One professor taught at the main campus while the other taught at the extension campus.

In order to facilitate the determination of the relative effectiveness of the mass lecture setting, a comparison group is required. The comparison group consists of a class of 24 students enrolled in an evening section of introductory marketing taught in a traditional format. One of the authors taught both the day mass lectures section and the evening section of introductory marketing at the extension campus thus, eliminating the biases inherent in class comparisons, within campuses, where different instructors are present. Similarities between the two class formats include: texts utilized, assignments, administrative policies, exams, grading and material covered. In each class format (mass lecture vs individual section), McCarthy's (1981) introductory marketing text was utilized as well as the McCarthy and Brogowicz (1981) Learning Aid, from which the assignments were drawn. Exams were developed from McCarthy's test bank. The same exams were given to all classes.

Differences between the class settings include the use of recitation leaders and student characteristics. In the mass lecture format, each student was required to attend a recitation section as described earlier. Graduate students were utilized as recitation section leaders. The evening section was not required to attend a recitation section. The evening students were exposed to a traditional single instructor format. With respect to student characteristics, the evening section students were much older (median age 30 vs 19) and more experienced with respect to actual business operations. The potential influence of student characteristics was one variable we were not able to control.

The measurement instrument which was utilized for the purpose of comparing the different class formats consisted of a 50 question comprehensive final examination and a set of 20 course/instructor evaluation questions. The course/instructor evaluation questions utilized were developed by Aleamani (1978). The validity and reliability of the 20 item evaluation scale has been established elsewhere (Aleamani, 1978). Students in each class format were given the same package of exam questions and course/instructor evaluation questions.

RESULTS

An analysis of variance (ANOVA) analysis was utilized to determine if any differences existed between the class formats with respect to exam scores and course/instructor evaluation. The results of this analysis along with a list of the evaluation questions are presented in Table 1. The first three questions of the course/instructor evaluation instrument are measured on a five point scale with values ranging from Very good (1) to Very poor (5). The remaining questions are measured on a four point scale with values ranging from Agree strongly (1) to Disagree strongly (4). It is interesting to note that there was a significant but small difference between group scores on the final comprehensive examination. The largest contrast (mass format, main campus versus mass format, extension campus) represents only a four percent difference in examination scores. This minor difference, though not alarming, may reflect differences between students across campuses as well as differences in teaching style across instructors. In light of these results, it is suggested that the mechanics of the mass lecture format did not inhibit the student's retention of the course material, as measured by the final examination.

With respect to the course/instructor evaluation questions, the only significicant between group differences dealt with worthwhileness of the course, instructor interest in students, student attentiveness, method of teaching and topic interest. In light of these differences, it is interesting to note that the students exposed to the mass lecture setting felt that the course was more interesting and that the instructor seemed to be more interested in the students as compared to the traditional setting format. On the negative side, the students exposed to the mass lecture format had more difficulty remaining attentive in class and would have preferred a different method of teaching the course. It is heartening to note that the mass lecture format did not negatively affect the student's perceptions of the course.

For many of the questions on the course/instructor evaluation instrument, no significant response differences were found between the groups. Some of the more noteworthy results indicate that the mass lecture students were in agreement with the traditional format students in that the course in general was rated "good", the material was not too difficult and that the course was taught quite well. It is heartening to note that the mass lecture setting did not negatively affect the student's perceptions of the course in general, instructor interest in students and

difficulty of material as one may have anticipated before
instituting a mass lecture format.

Universities and colleges vary with respect to what is
considered a "large" class. In this study, 63 students
were exposed to a mass lecture form of instruction. For
some schools, a class size of 63 may not be uncommon as
representing a traditional class setting. Therefore, the
mass lecture class of 63 was combined with the traditional
class of 24 and contrasted with the mass lecture class of
240 to reflect the variability in class size phenomenon.
This contrast also focuses upon inter-campus differences.
Student-t tests were conducted to analyze the differences
between these two groups. The results of this analysis
are presented in Table 2. The more significant results
suggest that the students exposed to the larger mass lecture class had more problems with remaining attentive in
class and would have preferred a different teaching method.
On an apriori basis, these results were expected in light
of the absolute class size and the expansive size of the
lecture hall.

In closing this section, it should be noted that the authors explored the relationship between student test score
and response to the course/instructor evaluation questions.
Table 3 presents the results of this analysis utilizing
Pearson correlation coefficients. As the results indicate,
in only six of the twenty items was a significant relation found and here, the correlation coefficients were
very weak. Therefore, it is suggested that student exam
scores did not bias students' responses to the course/in-
structor evaluation, which was expected in light of the
established validity and reliability of the evaluation
questions.

CONCLUSIONS

For those considering the institution of a mass lecture
format, it was found that successful implementation of
this type of format requires considerably more preplanning and attention to detail as well as control and coordination of the activities of the professors, teaching assistants and graders in contrast to the traditional format. In general, more management time as opposed to preparation time is required. Every effort must be made to
remove students' fears as to the perceived impersonality
of the mass lecture format. One way of achieving this
objective is to keep all direct and indirect lines of communication open to students at all times.

Given our methodology and the results of this research, it
is suggested that the mass lecture format is comparable to
the traditional single section/single instructor format.
In instituting the mass lecture format, we did not anticipate such a result. We were very satisfied to find that
the mass lecture format did not have a substantively negative impact upon student performance or perceptions of
the course. Such a result may be significant for those
wishing to consolidate introductory marketing sections into mass lectures as a means for dealing with the shortage
of qualified marketing professors, in response to increasing student enrollments or as a means of making available more time for faculty research.

As a final note, the results reported may reflect a novelty bias on the part of the professors. In other words,
a great deal of attention was given to the mass lecture
format to ensure its success in light of administration
attention focused upon this experiment. It remains to be
seen whether these results may be repeated in subsequent
semesters.

BIBLIOGRAPHY

Aleamoni, Lawrence M. (1978) _Arizona Course/Instructor
Evaluation Questionnaire (CIER). Results Interpreta-
tion Manual. Form 76_ (Tucson, AZ: Arizona University
Office of Instructional Research and Development).

McCarthy, E. Jerome (1981) _Basic Marketing_, 7th Ed. (Homewood, IL, Richard D. Irwin).

McCarthy, E. Jerome and Andrew A. Brogowicz (1981) _Learn-
ing Aid to Accompany Basic Marketing A Managerial Ap-
proach_, 7th Ed., (Homewood, IL, Richard D. Irwin).

Table 1

Differences Between Alternative Course Formats
Across Course/Instructor Evaluations and
Exam Scores

		Mass Lecture	Mass Lecture		
		Main Campus	Ext. Campus	Traditional	F
1.	The course content of Marketing 101 was:	1.95	1.82	2.13	.21
2.	The major instructor of my Marketing 101 was:	1.75	1.63	1.79	.36
3.	The course in general was:	2.26	2.05	2.29	.16
4.	This was a very worthwhile course:	1.99	1.79	2.21	3.7[a]
5.	The instructor seemed to be inter- ested in students as individuals:	1.68	1.98	2.21	10.6[b]
6.	The course material was too difficult:	2.90	2.92	3.1	.96
7.	Marketing is an important part of the study of business:	1.59	1.56	1.83	1.33
8.	It was easy to remain attentive in class:	2.46	2.02	2.12	7.1[b]
9.	I did not learn much by taking this course:	3.26	3.26	3.12	.75
10.	I would have preferred a different method of teaching in this course:	1.98	2.47	2.71	11.8[b]
11.	The course material in this course seemed worthwhile:	1.97	1.89	2.13	1.16
12.	Marketing as a subject is not part- icularly interesting:	3.1	3.13	2.63	3.9[a]
13.	This course was quite interesting:	2.2	2.03	2.23	1.56
14.	The instructor encouraged develop- ment of new viewpoints and approaches:	2.42	2.35	2.46	.203
15.	On the basis of this course I would want to major in marketing:	2.83	2.79	3.13	1.43
16.	This was one of my poorest courses:	3.14	3.1	2.92	1.31
17.	The course content was excellent:	2.33	2.22	2.54	1.72
18.	I think that the course was taught quite well:	1.90	2.03	1.92	1.23
19.	This course was quite boring:	3.09	3.06	2.86	1.51
20.	I would recommend taking this course to a friend:	2.25	2.05	2.42	2.27
21.	Exam Scores:	34.6	36.7	35.8	3.69[a]

a= $p < .05$, b= $p < .01$

Table 2

Differences Between Main Campus and
Extension Campus Classes

	Main Campus	Extension Campus	t Value
1. The course content of Marketing 101 was:	1.96	1.91	−.58
2. The major instructor of my Marketing 101 was:	1.75	1.67	−.97
3. The course in general was:	2.26	2.12	−1.44
4. This was a very worthwhile course:	2.0	1.91	−1.01
5. The instructor seemed to be interested in students as individuals:	1.68	2.05	3.96[b]
6. The course material was too difficult:	2.90	2.97	.84
7. Marketing is an important part of the study of business:	1.56	1.64	.57
8. It was easy to remain attentive in class:	2.45	2.06	−3.69[b]
9. I did not learn much by taking this course:	3.26	3.23	−.40
10. I would have preferred a different method of teaching in this course:	1.98	2.53	4.74[b]
11. The course material in this course seemed worthwhile:	1.97	1.95	−.21
12. Marketing as a subject is not particularly interesting:	3.09	2.96	−.97
13. This course was quite interesting:	2.2	2.1	−.98
14. The instructor encouraged development of new viewpoints and approaches:	2.42	2.38	−.33
15. On the basis of this course I would want to major in marketing:	2.82	2.88	.54
16. This was one of my poorest courses:	3.14	3.05	−1.12
17. The course content was excellent:	2.33	2.31	−.24
18. I think that the course was taught quite well:	1.90	2.0	1.16
19. This course was quite boring:	3.09	3.01	−.92
20. I would recommend taking this course to a friend:	2.25	2.15	−.94
21. Exam Scores:	34.6	36.6	2.88[b]

a= p < .05, b= p < .01

Table 3

Correlation Between Exam Scores and
Response to Course/Instructor Evaluation

	Exam Score with r
1. The course content of Marketing 101 was:	−.09
2. The major instructor of my Marketing 101 was:	−.06
3. The course in general was:	−.002
4. This was a very worthwhile course:	−.12[a]
5. The instructor seemed to be interested in students as individuals	−.05
6. The course material was too difficult:	.26[b]
7. Marketing is an important part of the study of business:	−.06
8. It was easy to remain attentive in class:	−.08
9. I did not learn much by taking this course:	−.10[a]
10. I would have preferred a different method of teaching in this course:	.09[a]
11. The course material in this course seemed worthwhile	−.004
12. Marketing as a subject is not particularly interesting:	.07
13. This course was quite interesting:	−.13[b]
14. The instructor encouraged development of new viewpoints and approaches:	.03
15. On the basis of this course I would want to major in marketing:	−.01
16. This was one of my poorest courses:	.23[b]
17. The course content was excellent:	−.06
18. I think that the course was taught quite well:	−.09
19. This course was quite boring:	−.08
20. I would recommend taking this course to a friend:	−.17[b]

a=p < .05, b=p < .01

EVALUATING MARKETING CASE COURSE PERFORMANCE:
ISSUES AND EMPIRICAL FINDINGS

Calvin P. Duncan, University of Colorado at Boulder
Phillip D. White, University of Colorado at Boulder

ABSTRACT

The marketing education literature is repleat with articles
on the purpose and objectives of case course instruction.
To this point in time, the vast majority of these articles
have approached the issue of educational effectiveness measurement in marketing case course settings on a strictly
qualitative basis. The objectives of this paper are two-
fold. The first is to argue that the case method warrants
more research attention than it has received to help explain why cases and case courses are effective learning
vehicles. The second and more specific objective is to
take a first step in identifying and empirically examining
some of the dimensions which may prove useful in evaluating
marketing case course performance.

INTRODUCTION

The effectiveness of a case course can be assessed in terms
of how well the course satisfies stated educational objectives. Case course objectives have been identified by
Bernhardt and Kinnear (1981), Corey, Lovelock and Ward
(1981), and McNair and Hansen (1949), among others. Typically, such goals are related to the impacts the instructor
wants the course to have on his students (Merry 1966).
While specific objectives will vary by instructor and by
level and subject matter of the course, two performance
areas are relevant for virtually all marketing case
courses--(1) knowledge acquisition/comprehension, and (2)
skill development. Progress in each of these goal areas,
in turn, can be evaluated from two perspectives. We may
judge the success of a case course in a "factual" sense by
focusing on measurable changes in students' command of marketing concepts, theories, and computational skills. Exams
are often used to assess such changes. In addition, we may
also be interested in changes in student perceptions.

Perceptions provide an important additional opportunity
for the evaluation of educational effectiveness. Of interest would be students' perceptions of the extent to
which the objectives of the course (i.e., learning in terms
of knowledge and skills) have been achieved. Additionally,
a common objective of case instruction is to instill within students an increased level of confidence in their own
ability to cope with complex business problems and to persuasively communicate their ideas. Measurements of self
perceptions and self perception changes in these areas
have substantial potential value for marketing educators.

It is clear that both evaluation perspectives (objective
or factual indicators of case performance and changes in
student perceptions as a result of case exposure) lend
themselves to empirical assessment. Yet, little attention
has been focused on the question of measuring the educational process and effectiveness of marketing case courses.
The benefit of adopting a more quantified approach extends
beyond encouraging instructors to identify measurable
course objectives and providing benchmarks for measuring
student progress and class effectiveness. Data can also
be collected which are designed to provide insights into
the questions of "why" and "how" case courses work. Feedback on how students perceive casework and their perceptions regarding the keys to success in a case course are
valuable to instructors who seek to improve their use of
marketing cases.

In order to demonstrate one approach for empirically measuring the performance of marketing case courses, an exploratory research project was undertaken. The findings
reported here are preliminary and constitute the first
step in a larger ongoing study being conducted by the
authors.

METHODOLOGY

Case Course Evaluation Statements

A set of forty five-point Likert type statements was
developed to examine students' beliefs about case and
case learning. The items were selected to elicit beliefs
in three categories related to case instruction: (1)
beliefs about how good decisions are made, (2) self perceptions of the student's own ability to analyze marketing
problems, and (3) beliefs about effective case teaching
and case course administration. The statement set is
shown in Table 1.

Procedure

Forty-six M.B.A. students responded to the statement set
by indicating their degree of agreement or disagreement
with each of the forty items. Subjects were enrolled in
a graduate level marketing management case course in the
Fall of 1981, and were surveyed during the last week of
the course. This class utilized the case method extensively, requiring both written and oral presentations.

RESULTS

The findings reported in this paper narrowly focus on
student responses to beliefs about "effective case
teaching and case course administration." Of the forty
statements examined, eleven fall into this category.
These items are designated "CT" in Table 1. For purposes of analysis and discussion, ten of these eleven
statements are clustered into three groups to distinguish
between student beliefs about: the value of the case
method, performance aspects of the case method, and the
instructor's role in case learning.

Value of Case Courses

The presumption among marketing instructors who use cases
has long been one which sees the marketing case course as
a valuable learning experience for students. However,
measurement of student beliefs on this point has not been
regular or rigorous. In most instances feedback has been
largely informal. In this study, students were asked to
respond to two statements which focused on the value of
studying marketing cases. The results are presented in
Table 2.

1. "Case Analyses Are Rewarding"
2. "Cases Are Effective For Learning"

In response to statement 1, a total of 80 percent agreed
or strongly agreed that case analyses were "rewarding."
A similar pattern exists for responses to statement 2
with 91 percent agreeing or strongly agreeing that cases
are "effective for learning."

These results do not contain much in the way of sur-
prises. Instructors who have used the case method are
likely to see these results as reconfirming their experiences and beliefs. However, acceptance of the argument that cases are rewarding and effective for
learning does not provide much insight into <u>why cases are
rewarding or how students react to various aspects of case
learning while concluding they are effective for learning.</u>

In view of the impressive positive ratings given to cases,
it is worthwhile to try to examine some aspects of performance in case courses as students see them. The next
section provides information about various aspects of
<u>performance</u> by examining responses to 7 different state-
ments. As a point of reference for the findings, a "normative position" is presented which is designed to represent one view of the "conventional wisdom" associated with
case method teaching. The discussions associated with the
7 "normative positions" represent an effort to formulate a
written statement which captures the essence of the assumptions made by instructors who use cases. The results of
student responses are then presented as a basis for comparison with the stated normative position. In spite of
the fact that these results are preliminary and have a
number of limitations, they provide some useful insights
and hopefully will spur further investigation into the
question of why and how case courses are successful.

Performance Aspects of Case Courses

3. "In Case Work, Success Is a Function of Time Expended"

<u>Normative position</u>: The view of most instructors is that
there is some merit in this statement, up to a point.
Case analyses do require a substantial amount of work.
However, expending excessive amounts of time does not
ensure high levels of performance. Successful case
analyses are time consuming but success is not exclusively a function of time expended.

<u>Findings</u>: Judging from the responses shown in Table 2, it
is clear that students have fairly clear cut beliefs about
this statement with only 11 percent marking NA. However,
the beliefs are substantially split with 39 percent on the
disagreement side while 50 percent either agree or strongly agree. Thus it appears that students believe success
is a function of time expended to a somewhat greater degree than some instructors might find desirable.

4. "In Case Work, The Amount Of Learning Is Directly
     Related To The Effort Invested"

<u>Normative position</u>: Effort invested is a somewhat
broader concept than time invested. Most instructors
would be more likely to agree with this statement by
reasoning that students could work very hard for relatively short periods of time. Such a pattern would represent a substantial investment in effort but would
involve a smaller time commitment.

<u>Findings</u>: Student responses appear to make a similar
distinction between "time" and "effort invested" with
nearly 83 percent agreeing or strongly agreeing with
this statement.

Statements 3 and 4 deal with "success" and the "amount of
learning" as a function of time expended and effort invested, respectively. A second aspect of performance
deals with the role that <u>marketing knowledge</u> plays in
successful performance in case courses. These issues
are examined in statements 5 and 6.

5. "Marketing Cases Are Easily Solved With The Applica-
     tion Of Knowledge Of Marketing Principles"

<u>Normative position</u>: This statement was included to focus

attention on the question of whether a "knowledge of marketing principles" makes it easier to solve marketing
cases. Many instructors would probably argue that at
least one objective of cases is to reemphasize the importance of key marketing principles as tools which can be
beneficially used to help solve a wide variety of marketing problems.

<u>Findings</u>: Student responses to this statement are not
clearcut. This could be attributed to the fact that
statement wording may not have been sufficiently precise
in focusing on the issue in question. Assuming that the
statement is adequate for measuring this concept, the fact
that 43 percent have no opinion and equal numbers agreed
and disagreed is not overly encouraging. If one objective
of the case method is to illustrate and reinforce key marketing principles, then these responses suggest that this
issue warrants more instructor attention.

6. "Students Who Are Successful In Marketing Case Work
     Are Those Who Have Previously Taken The Most Marketing
     Courses"

<u>Normative position</u>: It is argued here that most instruc-
tors would not agree with the statement for two reasons.
First, many other variables influence performance including work, analytical skills, experience and maturity.
Second, having had a number of marketing courses does not
ensure success as evidenced by the fact that many students
with a minimal background in marketing do very well. Conversely, many students with extensive marketing course
work do not excel in case courses.

<u>Findings</u>: The data reveal a split in opinion in the minds
of students involved in marketing case courses. The fact
that only 26 percent marked NA (indicating that they
"neither agree or disagree") clearly suggests that most
students have a belief about the extent to which performance is tied to the number of marketing courses taken.
The normative position receives relatively little support
as 54 percent agreed or strongly agreed with this statement. Only 19 percent marked the two disagreement alternatives. Interestingly, the number of students <u>strongly
disagreeing</u> outnumbered those <u>strongly agreeing</u> by a 7 to
1 margin. The high percentage of students who agree with
this statement suggests that instructors should evaluate
this issue more carefully.

In addition to looking at the "effort" and "knowledge"
aspects of performance, three other issues which are
related to performance in marketing case courses are
examined in statements 7, 8 and 9. The issues involve
frustration, discipline and the cumulative effect of
cases.

7. "Analyzing Cases Is Frustrating"

<u>Normative position</u>: It is difficult to state a normative
position on this issue. On the one hand, many instructors
would acknowledge that students often find cases frustrating, especially early in a case course. However, most
instructors would also argue that frustration subsides as
students become more experienced and comfortable with marketing cases. While student frustration is an aspect of
learning in case courses, the creation of such frustration
is presumably not an educational objective.

<u>Findings</u>: Responses to this statement suggest that cases
are rated highly in spite of the fact that "analyzing
cases is frustrating." Fifty-six percent of the students
responding agreed or strongly agreed with this statement.
Depending on one's expectations, these results may be
viewed differently, from "alarming" to "not all that bad."

While this is an interesting finding it is difficult to
explain why students view case analysis as frustrating or

whether their frustration changes during the conduct of the course. Assuming that instructors are not seeking to create frustration in case courses, then development of a better understanding of why frustration exists, how it changes during a case course, and how instructors can seek to manage it seems to be worthy of additional investigation.

8. "Discipline Is A Key To Successful Case Work"

<u>Normative position</u>: Most instructors would probably agree with the statement that discipline is a key to successful case work. Those instructors who emphasize the need for a systematic approach would be particularly likely to agree. Discipline is not meant to stifle creativity but rather to promote a systematic and comprehensive analysis of issues to ensure that problem solving efforts are focused on viable alternatives and is therefore more likely to produce workable results.

<u>Findings</u>: Students appear to agree that better performance is associated with a disciplined approach to cases. While 22 gave NA as a response, a total of nearly 70 percent agreed or strongly agreed with the statement.

9. "Because Every Case Is Different, Learning Is Not Cumulative"

<u>Normative position</u>: Case instructors would probably argue that there is a substantial amount of learning going on in any particular case course. However, learning can take place in terms of the acquisition of problem solving skills or factual marketing knowledge. In the latter case learning is not cumulative because of the wide variety of industries, companies and products in which cases are set. However, most instructors would be likely to strongly agree that learning related to methods of analyses, developing and evaluating alternatives, making a decision and making recommendations for implementation is cumulative.

<u>Findings</u>: The statement is written with a negative context "learning is not cumulative." Therefore if students disagree with this statement it would support the view that learning is cumulative. This is clearly the case with student responses indicating a total of 85 percent disagree or strongly disagree with the statement. Obviously there are some important aspects of case learning which students see as being cumulative in nature.

Role of the Instructor in Case Courses

10. "Student Learning In A Case Course Depends Heavily On The Instructor"

<u>Normative position</u>: Among those instructors who regularly teach marketing case courses there is a noticeable difference of opinion regarding the role that instructors play. Some view the instructor as an essential component of the case learning process while others view the instructor's role as one having little impact on student progress or performance.

<u>Findings</u>: The results suggest that students see the instructor as heavily influencing the quality of the learning experience. A total of 65 percent agreed or strongly agreed that student learning in a case course does depend heavily on the instructor. Regardless of which normative view is adopted, the views of students are very definitive in this regard. It should be noted that of the 10 sets of responses reported in Table 2, this statement received the highest number of <u>strongly agree</u> responses given for any statement.

In addition to the 10 statements discussed above dealing with the value of case courses, performance aspects of case courses and the role of the instructor, an eleventh state-

ment dealing with cases was included in Table 1 as statement 1, "Case courses adequately represent real world situations." This statement was included to determine the degree to which students regard cases as authentic and typical depictions of actual marketing decision settings. The findings presented in Table 3 indicate students do believe that cases are representative of "real world situations" with slightly more than 80 percent agreeing or strongly agreeing with this statement.

TABLE 1

CASE COURSE EVALUATION BELIEF STATEMENTS

1. Case studies adequately represent real world situations. (CT)

2. A problem well defined is half solved. (DM)

3. A systematic approach to problem solving is more valuable for inexperienced decision makers than for experienced ones. (DM)

4. I have a high degree of confidence in my ability to make decisions. (SP)

5. Case analyses are rewarding. (CT)

6. A single line of reasoning is sufficient to solve most business problems. (DM)

7. Students who are successful in marketing case work are those who have previously taken the most marketing courses. (CT)

8. I have a thorough knowledge of the most important marketing principles. (DM)

9. Substance is more essential than form in presenting solutions to marketing problems. (DM)

10. Every business problem requires a different analytical approach. (DM)

11. Good recommendations are specific. (DM)

12. Because every case is different, learning is not cumulative. (CT)

13. I have a high degree of confidence in my ability to make a thorough and well-reasoned written analyses of cases. (SP)

14. Theories are important in solving marketing problems. (DM)

15. Effective problem solving leaves little room for creativity. (DM)

16. Cases are effective for learning. (CT)

17. In case work, success in a function of time expended. (CT)

18. I have a low degree of confidence in my ability to approach decision making on a systematic basis. (SP)

19. A good case solution sells itself. (DM)

20. In case work, the amount of learning is directly related to effort invested. (CT)

21. Student learning in a case course depends heavily on the instructor. (CT)

22. Solving marketing problems is simply a matter of knowing the facts well. (DM)

23. I have a high degree of confidence in my ability to make reasonable assumptions and defend them in any subsequent analysis. (SP)

24. Business problems, when approached in a systematic way, take longer to solve. (DM)

25. The more data a decision maker has, the better the decision. (DM)

TABLE 2

SURVEY FINDINGS

VALUE OF CASE COURSES

		Number of Responses	Percentage
1. Case analyses are rewarding.	SD*	0	0.0
	D	1	2.17
	N	8	17.39
mean = 3.956	A	29	63.04
	SA	8	17.39
2. Case are effective for learning.	SD	0	0.0
	D	2	4.35
	N	2	4.35
mean = 4.09	A	32	69.56
	SA	10	21.74

PERFORMANCE ASPECTS OF CASE COURSES

		Number of Responses	Percentage
3. In case work, success is a function of time expended.	SD	4	8.69
	D	14	30.43
	N	5	10.87
	A	20	43.48
mean = 3.09	SA	3	6.52
4. In case work, the amount of learning is directly related to the effort invested.	SD	1	2.17
	D	3	6.52
	N	4	8.69
	A	27	58.69
	SA	11	23.91
mean = 3.96			
5. Marketing cases are easily solved with the application of knowledge of marketing principles.	SD	1	2.17
	D	13	28.26
	N	20	43.48
	A	13	28.26
	SA	0	
mean = 3.02			
6. Students who are successful in marketing case work are those who have previously taken the most marketing courses.	SD	7	15.22
	D	18	39.13
	N	12	26.09
	A	8	17.39
	SA	1	2.17
mean = 2.52			
7. Analyzing cases is frustrating.	SD	1	2.17
	D	8	17.39
	N	11	23.91
mean = 3.5	A	19	41.30
	SA	7	15.22
8. Discipline is a key to successful case work.	SD	1	2.17
	D	3	6.52
	N	10	21.74
mean = 3.67	A	25	54.35
	SA	7	15.22
9. Because every case is different, learning is not cumulative.	SD	11	23.91
	D	28	60.87
	N	4	8.69
	A	3	6.52
mean = 1.98	SA	0	

ROLE OF THE INSTRUCTOR IN CASE COURSES

		Number of Responses	Percentage
10. Student learning in a case course depends heavily on the instructor.	SD	1	2.17
	D	5	10.87
	N	10	21.74
	A	17	39.96
	SD	13	28.26
mean = 3.78			

*SD = strongly disagree; D = disagree; N = neither agree or disagree;
A = agree; SA = strongly agree

26. The goal of the marketing decision maker is to find
    the correct solution to the problem. (DM)

27. I have a low degree of confidence in my ability to
    make an effective presentation before a group. (SP)

28. There is no such thing as too much information. (DM)

29. Discipline is a key to successful case work. (CT)

30. I have a thorough knowledge of the important opera-
    tional differences between industrial and consumer
    markets. (DM)

31. Analyzing cases is frustrating. (CT)

32. All cases are solved in a similar way. (DM)

33. I have a low degree of confidence in my ability to
    organize material for an oral presentation before a
    group. (SP)

34. Decision makers should gather all available infor-
    mation before reaching a decision. (DM)

35. Most marketing problems are sales and profits
    problems. (DM)

36. I have a high degree of confidence in my ability to
    utilize important marketing principles in the
    analysis of business cases. (SP)

37. Marketing cases are easily solved with the applica-
    tion of knowledge of marketing principles. (CT)

38. I have a low degree of confidence in my ability to
    reason logically in business situations. (SP)

39. Business problem solving is an inductive process.
    (DM)

40. I have a high degree of confidence in my ability to
    conduct quantitative analyses in the solution of
    marketing problems. (SP)

Item Key: DM = beliefs about decision making; SP = self
           perceptions of case analysis ability: CT =
           beliefs about case instruction and case course
           administration.

TABLE 3

CASES AS REAL WORLD SITUATIONS

Case studies adequately	SD	0	0.0
represent real world	D	5	10.87
situations.	N	4	8.69
	A	27	58.69
mean = 3.91	SA	10	21.74

DISCUSSION

As emphasized earlier, the results presented in this paper
are preliminary. Nevertheless, it is hoped that these
findings will be viewed as sufficiently useful by marketing educators to prompt empirical investigation of these
issues in the context of their own courses. In reviewing
these findings, a number of questions were identified
which appear worthy of additional attention. For example,

1. a. How do the findings differ between undergraduates
      and graduate level students?
   b. How consistent are these results across levels of
      schools and geographic areas?

2. What other aspects of case learning experiences should
   be investigated? What research designs should be used
   to provide empirical evidence concerning these and
   other relevant dimensions?

3. How do student responses vary over time including:

   a. responses at different intervals during a course,
      as well as
   b. responses some specified time after the course
      was completed.

The third question dealing with changes in student responses during a particular course constitutes a potentially fruitful area for future research. To that end
a study is underway to examine that issue in more detail.

CONCLUSION

The findings reported here cannot be generalized with confidence. The obvious limitations of this early research
preclude any such widespread application. The purpose of
this paper was to argue that more attention needs to be
devoted to efforts to understand the issues which influence marketing case course effectiveness. It is argued
that this attention should be empirical. In an effort to
contribute to consideration of these issues, a framework
for thinking about the outcomes of marketing case courses
was introduced and a sample of forty Likert-type statements was identified. The second section of the paper
reports some preliminary results while the third section
suggests some additional areas of research interest.

REFERENCES

Bernhardt, Kenneth L. and Thomas C. Kinnear (1981), _Cases
    in Marketing Management_, Revised Edition, Plano, Texas:
    Business Publications, Inc.

Corey, E. Raymond, Christopher H. Lovelock and Scott Ward
    (1981), _Problems in Marketing_, Sixth Edition, New York:
    McGraw-Hill Book Company, Inc.

McNair, Malcolm P. and Harry L. Hansen (1949), _Problems
    in Marketing_, New York: McGraw-Hill Book Company, Inc.

Merry, Robert W. (1966), "Course Development," paper pre-
    sented at the Conference on the Case Method in Medical
    Care Teaching, December 28-30, Ann Arbor, Michigan.

AN ALTERNATIVE TO THE TRADITIONAL
CASE TEACHING TECHNIQUE

Charles S. Madden, Texas A&M University, College Station
Dan H. Robertson, Texas A&M University, College Station

ABSTRACT

A number of chronic problems with the traditional case
teaching method are raised. An alternative approach to presenting the case exercise is proposed. The use of video
tape recording of real or dramatized meetings with the prin-
cipals in a proposed case situation is suggested as the basis for the student's own notes which would form the nucle-
us of the exercise. The results of a preliminary experiment
compared this method with a parallel written case are presented.

INTRODUCTION

Over the past thirty years the case teaching method has
been incorporated into many aspects of marketing instruction, from the more obvious marketing strategy, sales
management and personal selling topics to consumer behavior
and marketing research. Many efforts have been made to increase "realism" in this instructional method. This paper
points out some of the areas of the traditional methods
that most need to be strengthened. One variation on the
traditional format of case instruction is suggested, with
a preliminary empirical comparison between that variation
and the more common case approach.

CASES AS A PEDAGOGICAL TOOL

While much of this discussion will appear critical of the
case teaching style for the purpose of showing the potential contribution of a case exercise innovation, the contribution of this time-honored classroom tool should not be
minimized. Its contribution to the teaching of marketing
courses has been very great. No pedagogical instrument,
however, should be accepted as being incapable of improvement. A number of efforts to accomplish such improvements
have been reported in marketing literature in recent years
(Doutt 1979; Richardson and Raveed 1980; Boewadt et. al.
1973)

Several criticisms have been leveled at the traditional
case teaching method. Among them are: (1) the learner does
not usually suspend disbelief and become "absorbed in the
case situation," (2) the learner does not have to develop
the listening skills that are needed to realistically com-
pile situation data from others in an organization, (3) the
learner is faced with a limited number of opportunities to
subjectively assess the value of case information thus leading to possible confusion as to whether statements represent
facts or opinions, (4) the learner does not have the benefit
of some kinds of exhibits that cannot be displayed on the
page of a book, such as a retail environment, (5) if the
case is long enough to thoroughly brief the student on the
situation, it may prove prohibitively long, (6) the point of
view of the case can be quite limited, such as with a single
narrator or as dialogue only.

AN INNOVATION IN CASE INSTRUCTION

No variation of the traditional method of case teaching
is likely to overcome all of the limitations listed above.
However, one such technique promises to minimize some of the
criticisms stated above.

Video tape recorders are usually available to most marketing educators today. If, instead of writing up a real
marketing problem into a case, the instructor simply asked
for the opportunity to tape interactions of the main characters in a case situation for editing into a "dramatized
case" much reality could be gained. The divergent points
of view presented are articulated by "real people" rather
than being attributed to mere "names on a page", If cooperation by the principles in a marketing organization could
not be gained, the services of students in theatre arts
programs can usually be obtained to dramatize the critical
meetings in the development of a case problem.

When the tapes have been made, the typical "exhibits" that
accompnay case materials must be added. This usually includes tabular material and other supporting data. Students
must then be fully briefed on the expectations of the
exercise before they view the taped material. Although
students are accustomed to taking classroom notes, they will
likely find taking notes from a live discussion of a situation a more complex and frustrating task. As in reality,
the student is only given one opportunity to record his
impressions of the tape (no instant replay!). In initial
experiences with this method, it may be helpful to the
student to be given a list of questions to direct their
case solving efforts.

Several potential advantages can be envisioned for
"dramatized" case presentations. Beyond the obvious increase in realism and increase in involvement, this methodological variation also offers to encourage the student to
be more integrative and take more initiative in solving the
case. By presenting different parts of a dramatized case,
different problems can be isolated. While the time required
to develop a case in this manner may be great, it may not
be greater than the time needed to develop a written case.
Students further develop their listening skills and learn to
trust their own impressions in a meeting using this method.
It is unlikely that an instructor would rely completely on
this style of case instruction, but it promises to enrich
the case teaching method. Also, a video taped case may
provide a stimulating break when used between a series of
written cases.

A number of disadvantages can also be cited. The production of any tape requires some technical expertise, which
may or may not be available. Not all case situations lend
themselves to this technique. Some companies that might
otherwise cooperate in the development of a case about their
firm will be reluctant to have their managers or other
employees taped. This technique may prove more costly than
alternative case instruction systems. Especially in the
initial efforts to use this method, much of the class discussion revolves around the facts of the case, as some
students listen better than others. Despite these drawbacks, this technique offers many advantages in the teaching of cases and appears to be of enough potential value to
test under classroom conditions. The next section reports
one such empirical test.

AN EXPERIMENT

To test the technique proposed above, an effort was made
to find an organization that would allow the researchers
to video tape record a live meeting that had been called to

discuss a marketing problem. The situation selected was a non-profit, multi-therapeutic, health care organization that was concerned about is public image in light of a planned capital fund drive to construct a new building. The board and staff of the organization met with one of the researchers to discuss their needs for marketing research information. The researcher served only as a moderator for the group and encouraged full participation of the twelve members in attendance. A single camera was used to tape the meeting in color. The meeting lasted approximately one hour and generated a list of research priorities that were tabulated and voted on by consensus.

To fairly test the use of video taped class material, the tape was then used to produce a matched written case. A packet of statistical material was added to the written version. Identical packets of statistical material were distributed to those using the video taped version.

A total of 67 students, 32 who watched the video taped form of the case and 35 who were assigned the written form of the case, took part in the experiment. Initially there were 35 students in each group, but three (3) were disqualified in the tabulation stage for reasons that will be discussed later. Because of the need to isolate the two treatment groups, random assignment was done at the course selection level. Two sections of marketing research at a southwestern university had an equal number of students as a third larger section. The halves were randomly assigned to each of the treatments. No obvious biases of student capability or interest were detected and all three sections were taught by the same instructor, who has taught the course many times before. Both groups were given essentially the same instructions and the same deadline for turning in written case solutions.

It was determined by the researchers that two types of measures were of interest in comparing the two methods of case instruction. First, student satisfaction/dissatisfaction measures would be helpful in assessing the acceptance and appreciation of the two systems. Second, an impartial and blind measure of the quality of the case work that was done by the students would have to be done also. When students turned in their written assignments they were asked to anonomously respond to questions listed in Table 1 on a five point Likert agreement scale. Statements in the list were presented in alternative positive and negative form and randomly assigned throughout both groups.

The completed written assignments were blind graded by two graders from a pool of four, using a scale of 1-12 for each item considered in Table 2. Graders were experienced in grading case work and did not know what treatment was assigned to any single paper. Three papers containing references to their treatment assignments were disqualified. The grading scale paralleled the letter grades D- to A+, including all minus and plus grades.

FINDINGS

The results of the student evaluation of the case exercise is best considered in light of a null hypothesis: There is no difference between the two samples, i.e., they are from the same population. The expectation was that for some items there would be some superiority shown for the video taped approach. As can be seen in Table 1, a test for statistical difference using Mann-Whitney U (Siegel 1956; pp. 116-127) revealed only two items that were statistically significant at the .05 level. Students rated the video taped case superior in "helping me learn much about planning a marketing research project" and "feeling very satisfied with my work on this case." Thus, students evaluated videotaped casework as equal to or superior to traditional casework.

Graders' evaluations reported in Table 2 show that problem identification, dealing with objectives, and considering a range of alternatives were significant at the .05 level or better using the Mann-Whitney U test. Additionally, problem identification and making reasonable assumptions were significant at the .10 level or better. Thus, the null hypothesis can be rejected for those items at their respective level of significance. In each case the video taped case treatment did better than the traditional case method.

CONCLUSIONS

This alternative approach to the traditional case method of teaching appears promising. Use of the video taped case resulted in student evaluations that were equal to or superior to traditional written cases.

Despite the positive results obtained in this experiment, generalization of these findings is hazardous. The authors propose as directions for further research replications involving students with varying levels of casework experience, use of profit making organizations (vs. the non-profit setting of this experiment), and cases focusing upon other marketing areas besides marketing research. Only by such additional research can this potentially promising approach be confirmed.

TABLE 1

Student Evaluations of Case Methods

	Mean Rank		*Significance
	Students Using[1] Written Case	Students Using[2] Videotaped Case	
This case helped me learn much about planning a marketing research project	29.59	37.92	.05
This case was very worthwhile	32.06	35.13	N.S.
This case was very relevant to this course.	34.47	32.40	N.S.
This case was relevant to my learning of marketing research.	32.64	34.47	N.S.
This case was very difficult for me to do.	33.96	32.98	N.S.
This case was very time consuming.	33.90	33.05	N.S.
This case was very challenging.	33.67	33.31	N.S.
This case was more enjoyable than most other cases I have done.	31.86	35.35	N.S.
This case was helpful to me in learning to do cases.	31.36	35.92	N.S.
This case provided me with a worthwhile learning experience.	32.87	34.21	N.S.
This case was helpful to me in understanding marketing problems.	34.67	32.18	N.S.
This case was very enjoyable for me to do.	33.46	33.55	N.S.
I feel very satisfied with my work on this case	29.80	37.68	.05

1. N = 35
2. N = 32
*1 tailed test Mann-Whitney U

TABLE 2

Grader Evaluations of Student Papers for Case Methods

| | Mean Rank | | *Signif-icance |
	Students Using[1] Written Case	Students Using[2] Videotaped Case	
Completeness	63.79	73.50	.10
Problem Identification	63.24	74.08	.05
Reasonableness of Assumption(s)	63.64	73.65	.10
Conciseness	67.25	69.83	N.S.
Suggested a Distinct Solution	66.31	70.82	N.S.
Dealt with Objectives	63.19	74.14	.05
Range of Considered Alternatives	63.00	74.33	.05
Rationale for Decision	64.79	72.43	N.S.
Imagination	64.84	72.39	N.S.
Organization	67.59	69.47	N.S.
Used All Relevant Information	65.38	71.81	N.S.
Overall Grade for Case	64.41	72.83	N.S.

1. N = 70 (2 graders per student)
2. N = 64 (2 graders per student)
*1 tailed test Mann-Whitney U

Doutt, Jeffrey, (1979) "Marketing Case-Study Analysis Using Videotape Simulation", Journal of Marketing Education, November, 78-81.

Boewadt, Robert J., Richard M. Durand, and Richard W. Mizerski, (1975) "An Experiment in Reality: A New Approach to Case Analysis", Proceedings in Southern Marketing Association, 493-498.

Richardson, Neil and Sion Raveed, (1980) "A Live-Case Program for Teaching Marketing Research", Journal of Marketing Education, April, 38-42.

Siegel, Sidney (1956) Nonparametric Statistics for the Behavioral Sciences, New York: McGraw Hill, Inc.

CRITICAL SKILLS METHODOLOGY: DEVELOPMENT AND IMPLEMENTATION

John H. Lindgren, Jr., McIntire School of Commerce, University of Virginia
Leonard L. Berry, Texas A&M University
William J. Kehoe, McIntire School of Commerce, University of Virginia

ABSTRACT

A critical skills methodology for use in marketing education curricula development is presented. The methodology
is operationalized using a sample of 725 financial services
marketing executives. Implications for marketing education
are discussed.

INTRODUCTION

This study investigates the educational needs of marketing
executives in commercial banks and thrift institutions,
i.e., savings and loan associations and savings banks.
Although limited to the financial services industry, the
results of the study seem to suggest implications for marketing education in general, especially services marketing
education.

The study has four major objectives. These are:
* to demonstrate a method of needs assessment for marketing education using the financial services industry as an example.

* to identify the skill/knowledge areas perceived most
   important in performing the financial services marketing function.

* to identify the skill/knowledge areas in which the
   respondents felt their peers had the greatest need
   for more education.

* to identify implications for marketing education.

BACKGROUND LITERATURE

The literature on important skill/knowledge areas for financial services marketers is non-empirical. Most of this
work discusses the specific skills or traits thought to be
most desirable for the financial services marketer.

Wright (1975) suggests the financial services marketer
should be creative, a persuasive communicator, personable,
analytic, a researcher, and a planner. Fillebrown (1975)
emphasizes the need for the financial services marketer to
know the financial services industry. Industry knowledge,
futuristic thinking, being an internal "educator," and
being a good risk manager are all noted as important skill/
knowledge areas for a person working in financial services
marketing. Dougherty (1973) calls for increased marketer
skills and knowledge in the area of automation, computer
applications and planning techniques. Phillips and Tyndall
(1980) stress the importance of planning skills; the understanding of strategic marketing; creativity/innovation
skills; the ability to conduct "good, solid, pragmatic
research;" an understanding of the essentials of product
development, pricing, promotion, and distribution; and the
ability to be a "team player."

In summary, the background literature is descriptive in
nature. Skills and knowledge in the areas of research and

The authors acknowledge the support received from the
Center for Financial Services Studies, McIntire School of
Commerce, University of Virginia.

planning, communications, creativity, and people are mentioned most often as necessary for financial services marketers.

RESEARCH APPROACH

The population for the study were members of the Bank Marketing Association (BMA) and the Savings Institutions Marketing Society of America (SIMSA). A systematic random
sample of 1000 was drawn from each of the BMA and SIMSA
membership rosters.

Data were collected by mail questionnaire. The questionnaire used was identical for the bank and thrift industry
respondents except for references to industry type, i.e.,
commercial bank versus thrift institution. In separate
questions, respondents evaluated a listing of 14 skill/
knowledge areas in terms of on-the-job importance, deficiency in the financial services marketing profession, and
desire for self-improvement. Likert-type scales were used.
The 14 skill/knowledge areas studied were identified in
earlier exploratory research employing open-ended questions. A variety of demographic data were also collected.

An initial and followup mailing resulted in a 37% response
from the SIMSA respondents (.n = 372) and a 35% response
from the BMA membership (n = 353). The total sample of
725 financial marketers represents an effective response
rate of 36%.

RESULTS

The Sample

The 372 SIMSA respondents were employed in thrift institutions an average of 11 years of which 6½ were spent in a
marketing capacity. The 353 BMA respondents had spent 12½
years in banks and had had one more year of marketing experience (7½ years) than did the SIMSA respondents. The average age of both groups was just over 40 years. In the BMA
sample, 84% were college graduates and 29% had advanced
degrees. In the SIMSA sample 58% were college graduates
and 25% held advanced degrees. Eighty-one percent of the
bankers and 78% of the thrift marketers were male.

Eighty-one percent of both groups held the position of
Director of Marketing. Almost 80% also held the title of
Vice President or above. In terms of institutional size,
44% of the banks and 20% of the thrifts were under $100
million in assets, 28% of the banks and 57% of the thrifts
were between $100-500 million, and 28% of the banks and 23%
of the thrifts were above $500 million in assets.

Important Skill/Knowledge Areas

The on-the-job skills and knowledge most important to financial services marketers were assessed by asking: "Which
particular skills or areas of knowledge are most important
to you in the performance of your marketing duties?" Respondents rated each of the 14 skill/knowledge areas on a
scale from "Not Important" (1) to "Very Important" (4).
Table I presents the mean results (and rankings) for the
BMA and SIMSA samples and for the combined sample.

The most important skill/knowledge area in the combined

TABLE I

SKILL/KNOWLEDGE IMPORTANCE[a]

SKILL/KNOWLEDGE AREAS	BANKS	THRIFTS	COMBINED SAMPLE
Group Presentation Skills	3.14 (4)	3.03 (7)	3.08 (6)
Interpersonal/Negotiating Skills	3.18 (3)	3.11 (5)	3.15 (4)
Analytical Skills	3.03**(7)	3.14 (4)	3.09 (5)
Supervisory Skills	2.90 (8)	2.95 (9)	2.92 (8)
Advertising/Promotion Skills	3.13* (5)	3.31 (2)	3.22 (3)
Lending Experience	1.87 (13)	1.93 (13)	1.90 (13)
Writing Skills	3.28 (2)	3.28 (3)	3.28 (2)
Marketing Research Skills	2.78* (9)	2.96 (8)	2.87 (9)
Planning Skills	3.48 (1)	3.51 (1)	3.50 (1)
Understanding of Economics	2.61* (11)	2.73 (10)	2.67 (10)
Banking (Thrift) Industry Experience	2.72* (10)	2.49 (12)	2.61 (11)
Personal Creativity	3.05 (6)	3.08 (6)	3.07 (7)
Computer Skills	1.72 (14)	1.66 (14)	1.69 (14)
College Education in Business	2.35 (12)	2.50 (11)	2.43 (12)
	n = 353	n = 372	n = 725

[a]Importance measured on a Likert-type scale from Not Important (1) to Very Important (4). Each number in the table is the mean value for a particular skill. Parentheses indicate rank order.

*Significant at p < .05

**Significant at p < .10

sample and in each individual sample was planning skills with a mean of 3.5 on a 4.0 scale. Second in importance for bank marketers was writing skills which rated third in importance for thrift marketers. Both samples rated computer skills lowest in terms of importance.

As can be seen in Table 1, advertising and promotion expertise, rated third in overall importance, was significantly more important for the thrift respondents as were marketing research skills. Other significant differences are shown in Table 1. The implications of these findings are discussed later in this paper.

Areas of Deficiency

Respondents were asked to assess the competency of their peers for each of the 14 skill/knowledge areas. The specific question asked was: "In which skill/knowledge areas are members of the bank (thrift industry) marketing profession typically most deficient?" Response alternatives ranged from "Not Deficient" (1) to "Very Deficient" (4).

Table II reports the data from this question. There are several noteworthy findings. First, the combined sample definitely perceives their colleagues in the profession to be more deficient in the "technical" skill/knowledge areas. The five highest ranked areas of deficiency are computer skills, lending skills, marketing research skills, understanding of economics, and planning skills. The five lowest ranked areas of deficiency are college education in business, advertising/promotion, group presentation skills, supervisory skills, and interpersonal/negotiating skills.

Second, there are a number of significant differences between the bank and thrift samples. Thrift respondents regarded the thrift marketing profession to be more deficient in the areas of marketing research, planning, and analytical skills. Bank marketers regarded their peers to be more deficient in the areas of computer skills, lending, and banking industry experience.

Areas of Desired Improvement

In addition to skill/knowledge importance and deficiency, preferred areas for self-improvement were also researched. Respondents were asked: "If you could improve your skill/

knowledge in any three areas, which ones would you choose? Select, only three and rank in order of importance from 1 to 3.

TABLE II

SKILL/KNOWLEDGE DEFICIENCY[a]

SKILL/KNOWLEDGE AREAS	BANKS	THRIFTS	COMBINED SAMPLE
Group Presentation Skills	1.72* (12)	1.93 (10)	1.83 (12)
Interpersonal/Negotiating Skills	1.97 (9)	1.95 (9)	1.96 (10)
Analytical Sills	2.02* (7)	2,26 (5)	2.14 (7)
Supervisory Skills	1.99* (8)	1.85 (11)	1.92 (11)
Advertising/Promotion Skills	1.60* (13)	1.93 (10)	1.77 (13)
Lending Experience	2.68* (2)	2.13 (6)	2.41 (2)
Writing Skills	1.88* (10)	2.06 (7)	1.97 (9)
Marketing Research Skills	2.03* (6)	2.51 (2)	2.36 (3)
Planning Skills	2.13* (5)	2.40 (3)	2.27 (5)
Understanding of Economics	2.37 (4)	2.31 (4)	2.34 (4)
Banking (Thrift) Industry Experience	2.39* (3)	1.98 (8)	2.18 (6)
Personal Creativity	1.80* (11)	2.13 (6)	1.97 (8)
Computer Skills	2.79* (1)	2.55 (1)	2.67 (1)
College Education in Business	1.57 (14)	1.71 (12)	1.64 (14)
	n = 353	n = 372	n = 725

[a]Deficiency measured on a Likert-type scale from Not Deficient (1) to Very Deficient (4). Each member in the table is a mean value for a particular skills. Parentheses indicate rank order.

*Significant at p < .05

Table III presents the frequencies with which each skill/knowledge area was ranked first, second and third by the bank and thrift samples. Totals and ranks for the combined sample are also presented.

By a large margin (324 total mentions), planning skills is the area in which financial services marketers would most like to improve. The next highest ranked areas for the combined sample are advertising/promotion skills, marketing research skills, interpersonal/negotiating skills, analytical skills, personal creativity skills, group presentation skills, and writing skills.

The areas in which respondents felt the least need for improvement were college education in business, lending, computer skills, banking industry experience (thrift industry experience) and supervisory skills.

DISCUSSION OF RESULTS

The results indicate that planning skills have become the most important skill/knowledge area for financial services marketers. Planning skills ranked first in both the "on-the-job importance" and "most like to improve" questions. The emphasis given to planning skills by the respondents undoubtedly reflects a mix of influences including the volatility of the financial institution environment and the increased attention to strategic planning in many financial institutions.

Another important finding is the weight given by sample members to writing, interpersonal/negotiating and group presentation skills which ranked second, fourth, and sixth respectively on the "importance" question. These results are consistent with the emphasis placed on planning skills given that plans have to be written and presented.

However, there are clearly other factors involved as well. The group presentation, interpersonal/negotiating, and writing skill areas can all be collapsed under the more general heading of "internal communication and persuasion." The emphasis given these areas by the respondents probably

TABLE III

AREAS OF DESIRED IMPROVEMENT

SKILL/KNOWLEDGE AREAS	NUMBER OF MENTIONS-BANKS				NUMBER OF MENTIONS-THRIFTS				NUMBER OF MENTIONS-COMBINED SAMPLE	
	First	Second	Third	Totals	First	Second	Third	Totals	Totals	Rank Order
Group Presentation Skills	28	34	29	91	29	21	30	80	171	7
Interpersonal/ Negotiating Skills	42	29	32	103	32	27	24	83	186	4
Analytical Skills	22	26	30	78	33	41	25	99	177	5
Supervisory Skills	8	19	24	51	7	19	15	41	92	10
Advertising/Promotion Skills	35	36	28	99	49	34	41	124	223	2
Lending Experience	3	8	10	21	7	9	5	20	41	13
Writing Skills	17	22	26	65	15	37	27	79	144	8
Marketing Research Skills	27	23	35	85	52	51	34	137	222	3
Planning Skills	62	64	36	162	66	42	54	162	324	1
Understanding of Economics	10	13	14	37	9	26	23	58	95	9
Banking (Thrift) Industry Experience	17	15	19	51	11	8	14	33	84	11
Personal Creativity	43	26	22	91	27	22	34	83	174	6
Computer Skills	8	9	14	31	5	8	18	31	62	12
College Education in Business	2	1	4	7	5	5	3	13	20	14
				n = 353				n = 372	n = 725	

relates to the realities of being in a staff rather than line job, marketing labor-intensive services rather than goods, and functioning in an industry that has traditionally viewed marketing in a narrow and peripheral way. Financial services marketers, more than toothpaste marketers, must find ways to win organizational support and cooperation for what has traditionally been a "tainted" function. Not surprisingly, in another section of the present study, lack of top management support and lack of interdepartmental cooperation were ranked first and second as the most frustrating aspects of the financial services marketing job (Lindgren, Berry and Kehoe, 1980).

Still another intriguing finding of the skills/knowledge research concerned advertising and promotion skills. This category ranked third on the "importance" question, second on the "improvement" question, but only thirteenth as an area of deficiency in the profession. One explanation is that advertising/promotion is an "old" skill area that remains important. In contrast, planning skills, a "newer" skill area, was highly rated on both the "importance" and "deficiency" questions.

One of the most interesting findings of the study is the lack of interest shown in computer skills. In contrast to other technical skill areas like planning, marketing research, and analytical skills, which were rated relatively high on both the "deficiency" and "improvement" questions, the computer skills area ranked high on the "deficiency" question but low on the "improvement" question. Given the growing business and marketing applications of micro computers, we predict financial services marketers will become more interested in developing computer knowledge and skills in the next several years.

IMPLICATIONS FOR MARKETING EDUCATION

On the "importance" question, the combined sample ranked college education in business twelfth. On the "improvement" question, it ranked last. To be sure, there are several plausible interpretations that can be made of these results. However, the overall data from this research suggest that one contributing factor is the uneven allignment between what business schools teach and what financial services marketers claim they need to know. Respondents indicate the significance in their work of technical skills and knowledge (planning, marketing research, analytical skills); internal communication and persuasion skills (writing, interpersonal/negotiating, group presentation skills); personal creativity, and marketing mix skill/knowledge areas like advertising/promotion.

Yet, studies of business school and marketing curricula would suggest that more emphasis is placed on the marketing mix and on technical skills than on internal communication/ persuasion skills and personal creativity skills (Murphy and Laczniak, 1980). Furthermore, responses to both the "improvement" and "deficiency" questions indicate that even more emphasis on technical skills - especially skills associated with planning - are probably warranted in most programs.

The findings of this study indicate that financial services marketers need to learn more than the "4 P's" when in school. In addition to the customary preparation in such areas as marketing management and marketing research, respondents in this study would seemingly benefit from college or post-college training in:
  * Strategic planning processes and tools.

  * Report writing, group presentation, and interpersonal skills.

  * Personal skills for developing and using creative approaches to problem solving.

Additional research is needed to determine the extent to which the findings from this study are generalizable to service marketers in other industries and to marketing executives in general. Our hypothesis would be that the skill/ knowledge needs of financial services marketers would be quite similar to the needs of marketers in many other industries, especially labor-intensive service industries.

CONCLUSION

This study has demonstrated a method of educational needs assessment and, through use of the methodology, identified the needs of a specific group of marketing executives; namely, financial services marketers. Research of this nature should be helpful in marketing curricula development at both collegiate and executive development levels.

150

REFERENCES

Dougherty, Daniel J., "Bringing Bank Marketing Up To Date,"
  United States Investor/Eastern Banker, September 10,
  1973, p. 15.

Fillebrown, T. Scott, Jr., "Marketing Personnel Need To
  Know Banking," American Banker, March 24, 1973, pp. 3
  and 22.

Lindgren, John H., Leonard L. Berry and William J. Kehoe
  (1980), "The Financial Institution Marketer," Journal
  of Retail Banking, 2 (September), pp. 39-45.

Murphy, Patrick E. and Eugene R. Laczniak (1980), Marketing
  Education: Current Status And A View For The 1980's,
  Chicago: American Marketing Association.

Phillips, Ronald A. and Marshall C. Tyndall, Jr., "What It
  Takes To Be A Winning Chief Marketing Officer In The
  80's," paper presented at the American Bankers Association National Marketing Conference, April 30, 1980.

Wright, Thomas L., "Management-Marketing: How To Enhance
  The Partnership," Northwestern Banker, June, 1975, pp.
  28-29 and 116.

THE UNDERGRADUATE MARKETING CORE, MARKETING ISSUES AND OTHER
EDUCATION-RELATED TOPICS OF THE 1980'S: VIEWS OF EDUCATORS AND PRACTITIONERS

Mary L. Wilson, University of the District of Columbia
William K. Darley, University of the District of Columbia

ABSTRACT

This paper presents the results of an empirical study of
the views of AACSB educators and national and local practitioners regarding the core of marketing courses that
should be required of all undergraduate marketing majors.
The suggested core includes a frequently unconsidered
course. Also included are the views of the above three
groups regarding the importance of selected educational
tools, training and preparation of the marketing graduate,
and pressing marketing issues of this decade.

INTRODUCTION

When endeavoring to develop or revise the undergraduate
marketing curriculum--in terms of marketing course offerings required, electives, etc.--one may become bewildered
by the myriad of choices and the abundance of advice as
to the appropriate inclusions that abound in the literature. Luck (1964) listed some forty different marketing
course titles in his study, and with the varying trends
that have occurred since then--consumerism, emphasis on
quantitative methods, computer usage, social and ethical
issues, broadened marketing, etc.--the number of possible
course titles has certainly increased.

At the same time, there is some disagreement as to what
three, four, five or more courses, in addition to the
basic course, constitute the group of courses that should
be required of every undergraduate marketing major. While
Tinsley (1980), and Bellenger and Bernhardt (1977) agree
on the core of required courses, results of studies performed by Loudenback (1973), Murphy and Laczniak (1980),
and Mulvihill (1981) suggest different cores.

There is, however, general agreement that the "ideal"
marketing curriculum would be one which is compatible
with the variety of publics whose needs it must satisfy
and upon which it draws--students, educators, and the
business community which hires marketing graduates.
This paper presents the results of an empirical investigation of two important publics--educators and national
and local practitioners--conducted by marketing educators
at one university to aid in the revision of its undergraduate marketing curriculum.

Previous studies have been conducted among educators
(Bellenger and Bernhardt, 1977; Murphy and Laczniak, 1980;
and Mulvihill, 1981); practitioners (Bellenger and Bernhardt, 1977); and graduates (Loudenback, 1973); and among
combinations of the above (Bellenger and Bernhardt, 1977).
However, no recent study has addressed educators and
national and local practitioners at once for the purposes
of determining the required core of marketing courses,
the importance of selected educational tools, the training and preparation expected of today's marketing graduate, and pressing marketing issues of this decade--which
are objectives of this paper.

This paper discusses the required core of marketing
courses in terms of six marketing courses that should
definitely be required of the undergraduate marketing
major. It should be stressed at this point that this
number was selected as it reflects the current state of
affairs at the authors' university. The results of this
study, as indicated in the conclusions and implications
section of this paper, are equally applicable in

instances where a smaller or greater number of specific
marketing courses comprise the required core.

METHODOLOGY

The Sample

During April, 1981, a questionnaire was mailed to marketing department heads at all AACSB accredited schools/
colleges of business. This survey group was chosen
because it was believed that department heads, if only
because of oversight responsibility, would be more
knowledgeable about curriculum development/revision than
a faculty member contacted by chance. Also, while AACSB
accredited schools represent a minority of the nation's
colleges/schools of business, they are widely accepted
as pacesetters in the business education process guided
by a common set of standards. Usable responses from
87 department heads (39% response rate) were returned
by the cut-off date.

Questionnaires were also mailed to the marketing vice
presidents of the top 200 firms of the Fortune 500,
which as the nation's largest corporations, hire a large
proportion of the nation's business and marketing graduates. Usable responses from 50 marketing vice presidents
(25% response rate) were returned by the cut-off date.

Finally, a third group of questionnaires was mailed to
the marketing vice presidents, or their equivalents, of
200 local firms from the Board of Trade and local Chamber
of Commerce listings in the metropolitan area of the
authors' university, as a large proportion of the university's marketing graduates are employed in that area.
Usable responses from 58 local firms (29% response rate)
were returned by the cut-off date.

While the above response rates compare favorably with
those from previous studies (Bellenger and Bernhardt,
1977; and Murphy and Laczniak, 1980), it is possible that
they could have been improved by follow-up contact(s).

The Instrument

The questionnaires mailed to the above three groups were
identical and included two questions pertaining to marketing courses--one requesting the respondents' indication
of courses considered appropriate for inclusion in the
undergraduate marketing curriculum, and analyzed via
paired comparisons of the Spearman rank correlation
coefficient; and the other requesting their selection and
ranking of the six courses that should definitely be
required, analyzed using Kendall's coefficient of concordance and interpretation of statistical significance.

A third question sought to determine the respondents'
views as to the rank-order importance of nine supplemental educational tools in the marketing education process, analyzed via paired comparisons of total mentions
for the top three ranks using the Spearman rank
correlation coefficient. Finally, two open questions
were included to gain the respondents' views of the
training and preparation required of the marketing graduate of the 1980's, and the pressing marketing issues
and/or problems of the 1980's, respectively; both
analyzed by use of the Chi-Square test for statistically
significant differences.

Questions pertaining to marketing courses considered appropriate or which should definitely be required included the phrase "other than the basic course," as the authors assumed the basic course in marketing to be a necessary requirement that was already well understood as such by respondents (Bellenger and Bernhardt, 1977; Murphy and Laczniak, 1980). Further, the authors assumed that a basic course in marketing is generally required of all business majors, and therefore, does not constitute a special additional requirement for the marketing major.

RESULTS

Table 1 shows the percentage of respondents from each of the three groups indicating that a particular marketing course, other than the basic course, is appropriate for inclusion in the undergraduate marketing curriculum. Various proportional mentions for the courses in the table show that the majority--70% or more--of:

    --the respondents in the three survey groups considered Marketing Research and Information Systems, Promotion/Advertising Management, and Marketing Strategy/Planning, appropriate for inclusion;

    --the educators and local respondents also considered Consumer Behavior appropriate; and

    --the educators and Fortune respondents also considered Sales Management appropriate.

Additionally, 70% or more of each of the respondent groups considered other and different courses appropriate--International Marketing, according to educators; Marketing New Products/Product Development and Management, Quantitative Methods in Marketing, and Pricing, according to Fortune respondents; and Principles of Selling, according to local respondents.

Conversely, while only a small minority of educators and Fortune respondents--22% or less--considered Procurement/Purchasing, Marketing in the Inner City/Urban Setting,

and Marketing to the Government, appropriate inclusions; greater proportions of the local respondents considered these courses appropriate, especially Marketing to the Government. This may be partially explained by the uniqueness of the local setting and raises the question of offering electives which specifically address local or regional needs.

Overall, while there were some differences, paired comparisons between the three groups resulted in a Spearman rank correlation coefficient of .67 (adjusted for tied ranks) for educators versus Fortune respondents; .65 (adjusted for tied ranks) for educators versus local; and .73 (adjusted for tied ranks) for Fortune versus local respondents--all statistically significant at the .01 level.

Table 2 shows the three groups' indication of the marketing courses that should be offered based on the number of mentions when respondents were asked to name and rank only six courses--where one was the first choice--which should definitely be required.

Although the table shows a few differences in the rankings assigned to courses by the three groups (especially the #3 ranking assigned to Principles of Selling by local practitioners), a comparison of the rankings resulted in a Kendall's coefficient of concordance of .87 (adjusted for tied ranks), which is statistically significant at the .001 level. Therefore, the rankings by the three groups are highly related. Based on Kendall's (Siegel, 1956) interpretation of a statistically significant coefficient of concordance, the three survey groups agree that the following six courses (Overall Ranking, Table 2) should definitely be required in rank order from one to six respectively:

1) Marketing Research and Information Systems,
2) Marketing Strategy/Planning,
3) Promotion/Advertising Management,
3) Consumer Behavior,
5) Marketing New Products/Product Development and Management, and
6) Sales Management.

TABLE 1
APPROPRIATE MARKETING COURSES FOR THE UNDERGRADUATE MARKETING CURRICULUM

	AACSB		Fortune		Local	
	Percent	Rank	Percent	Rank	Percent	Rank
Consumer Behavior	100.0*	1**	68.0*	8**	72.4*	3**
Marketing Research and Info Systems	96.6	2	92.0	2	82.8	1
Promotion/Advertising Management	90.8	3	70.0	3	72.4	3
Sales Management	87.4	4	70.0	3	53.4	8
Marketing Strategy/Planning	82.8	5	96.0	1	82.8	1
International Marketing	72.4	6	54.0	12	58.3	11
Marketing Channels	67.8	7	56.0	11	39.7	14
Retailing	66.7	8	50.0	15	53.4	8
Industrial Marketing	57.5	9	60.0	9	36.2	15
Physical Distribution	57.5	9	54.0	12	34.5	16
Mktg. New Prod./Product Dev. & Mgmt.	46.0	11	70.0	3	60.3	6
Quantitative Methods in Marketing	43.7	12	70.0	3	43.1	13
Marketing Problems	41.4	13	58.0	10	56.9	7
Principles of Selling	37.9	14	54.0	12	72.4	3
Marketing for Nonprofit Organizations	28.7	15	6.0	19	22.4	20
Pricing	23.0	16	70.0	3	50.0	10
Industrial Buyer Behavior	19.5	17	36.0	16	32.8	17
Procurement/Purchasing	16.1	18	22.0	17	32.8	17
Marketing to the Government	4.6	19	16.0	18	44.8	12
Marketing in the Inner City/Urban Setting	2.3	20	6.0	19	29.3	19
(Bases)	(87)		(50)		(58)	

    *Percentage of total respondents selecting the course.
    **Based on the Percentages.

TABLE 2
MARKETING COURSES THAT SHOULD DEFINITELY BE REQUIRED

	Overall Ranking	AACSB Percent	AACSB Rank	Fortune Percent	Fortune Rank	Local Percent	Local Rank
Marketing Research and Info Systems	1*	95.3**	1***	63.3**	2***	67.9**	2***
Marketing Strategy/Planning	2	58.1	4	79.6	1	73.6	1
Promotion/Advertising Management	3	69.8	3	44.9	4	52.8	4
Consumer Behavior	3	93.0	2	44.9	4	43.4	5
Mktg. New Prod./Product Dev. & Mgmt.	5	18.6	9	46.9	3	34.0	6
Sales Management	6	37.2	5	30.6	8	32.1	7
Marketing Problems	7	20.9	8	26.5	9	30.2	8
Marketing Channels	8	31.4	6	24.5	10	20.8	10
Quantitative Methods in Marketing	9	17.4	10	36.7	7	20.8	10
Principles of Selling	10	12.8	14	22.4	11	58.5	3
International Marketing	11	23.3	7	22.4	11	15.1	13
Retailing	12	14.0	13	22.4	11	28.3	9
Pricing	13	4.7	15	38.8	6	13.2	15
Industrial Marketing	14	16.3	11	20.4	14	17.0	12
Physical Distribution	15	16.3	11	14.3	15	9.4	17
Procurement/Purchasing	16	1.2	17	4.1	17	15.1	13
Marketing to the Government	17	1.2	17	6.1	16	13.2	15
Industrial Buyer Behavior	18	1.2	17	4.1	17	9.4	17
Marketing for Nonprofit Organizations	19	2.3	16	0.0	20	1.9	20
Marketing in the Inner City/Urban Setting	20	0.0	20	2.0	19	5.7	19

*Based on statistically significant Kendall's coefficient of concordance.

**Percentage of respondents ranking the course as one of six which should definitely be required.

***Based on the Percentages.

Table 3 shows the three groups' views as to the rank-order importance of nine supplemental educational tools in the marketing education process. It is based on the summary number of mentions of choices one, two and three, obtained from the question asking respondents to rank the objects from one to nine, where one was the first choice, etc.

The table shows that all three groups agree on the first and the last choices—case analysis and field trips, respectively. In ranks two through eight, however, there was considerable dissimilarity between practitioner groups versus educators, but considerable similarity between the two practitioner groups. Paired comparisons between the three groups resulted in a Spearman rank correlation coefficient of .28 for educators versus _Fortune_ respondents; and .25 for educators versus local; neither of which were statistically significant. The Spearman rank correlation coefficient for _Fortune_ versus local respondents was .97, statistically significant at the .001 level.

Table 4 shows the categorization of responses to the

question, "What kind(s) of training and preparation would you expect from a marketing graduate of the 1980's?" While all the groups had somewhat similar expectations of graduates, as shown by proportions in the table, there were significant differences between the groups in terms of:

1) Work Experience (internships, co-ops, work-study programs, etc.)--practitioners expect significantly more of this type of training than do educators;

2) Analytical/Problem-Solving/Decision-Making Skills--educators expect significantly more of this type of training and preparation to be required than do practitioners--possibly, practitioners were focusing on entry-level requirements and educators on managerial skills required at later levels;

3) Quantitative Skills--educators expect significantly more of this type of preparation than do practitioners; and

TABLE 3
RANK-ORDER IMPORTANCE OF NINE EDUCATIONAL TOOLS

	AACSB Percent	AACSB Rank	Fortune Percent	Fortune Rank	Local Percent	Local Rank
Case Analysis	85.0*	1**	56.8*	1**	60.0*	1**
Research and Consulting Projects	58.8	2	27.2	6	32.7	6
Guest Lecturers	42.5	3	27.2	6	25.5	7
Computer Simulation	40.0	4	13.6	8	7.3	8
Internships	27.5	5	50.0	2	58.2	2
Team Teaching (industry/academic)	16.3	6	40.9	3	36.4	4
Co-op Programs	11.3	7	34.1	5	36.4	4
Summer Work in Marketing	10.0	8	38.6	4	41.8	3
Field Trips	8.8	9	11.4	9	1.8	9
(Bases)	(80)		(44)		(55)	

*Percentage of respondents ranking the object one, two, or three.

**Based on Percentages.

TABLE 4
TRAINING AND PREPARATION
REQUIRED OF GRADUATES OF THE 1980'S

	AACSB	Fortune	Local
Analyt./Prob.-Solv./Dec.- Making Skills*	58.4%	39.5%	22.4%
Knowledge of Mktg. Concepts	55.8	55.8	63.3
Broad Business Background***	31.2	44.2	22.4
Oral and/or Written Skills	26.0	14.0	18.4
Quantitative Skills**	20.8	7.0	6.1
Research Skills	13.0	11.6	10.2
Behavioral Skills	9.1	7.0	6.1
International Mktg. Knowledge	5.2	2.3	2.0
General Ed. Background	3.9	4.7	2.0
Work Exp. (Internships, etc.)*	2.6	27.9	22.4
Other	19.5	9.3	14.3
(Bases)	(77)	(43)	(49)

*Significant at the .001 level.
**Significant at the .05 level.
***Significant at the .10 level.

4) Broad Business Background--all groups indicated
that this is an important aspect of undergraduate marketing training; however, the _Fortune_
group expressed somewhat higher expectations
in this area, mentioning most often such areas
as finance, accounting, legal training, and
computer usage.

TABLE 5
PRESSING MARKETING ISSUES/PROBLEMS OF THE 1980'S

	AACSB	Fortune	Local
Planning (Strategic, Careful, etc.)	31.0%	25.6%	20.0%
Inflation/Recession/Costs***	29.6	51.2	37.8
Resource Shortages**	23.9	9.3	8.9
Specific Marketing Mgmt. Concerns*	22.5	48.8	46.7
Internat'l. Mktg. Concerns	16.9	23.3	8.9
Regulatory Environment	12.7	7.0	11.1
Productivity	12.7	7.0	11.1
Technological Development	8.5	2.3	6.7
Other*	39.4	14.0	15.5
Soc. Resp./Societal	12.7	0	2.2
Public Sec./Non-prof.	9.9	0	2.2
(Bases)	(71)	(43)	(45)

*Significant at the .01 level.
**Significant at the .05 level.
***Significant at the .10 level.

Table 5 shows the categorization of responses to the
question, "In your opinion, what are the pressing marketing issues/problems of the 1980's?" While all groups
expressed concerns about productivity, regulations, inflation, resource shortages, etc., there were significant
differences between the groups in terms of:

1) Specific Marketing Management Concerns--the
practitioners had concerns for issues such as
competitive analysis, product planning, demand
analysis, product management, etc., and how to
best deal with these, to a greater extent than
did educators;

2) Resource Shortages--educators were significantly
more concerned about limitations of resources
than the practitioners;

3) Other (including social responsibility/societal
concerns, and public sector/nonprofit issues)--
educators were more concerned about these issues
than the practitioners; who perhaps see these
as non-crucial, having been supplanted by more
pressing issues related to the current economic
environment; and

4) Inflation/Recession/Costs--both groups of practitioners were concerned with such issues,
probably because they have to deal with such
problems as pricing and cost-cutting from day-
to-day, as opposed to educators, who while
recognizing such issues, are perhaps less
constrained by them.

CONCLUSIONS AND IMPLICATIONS

A major objective of this paper was to determine the six
courses, other than the basic course, which should form
the core of required marketing courses in the undergraduate marketing curriculum. The results of this study
reveal that these six courses, in rank order, should be:

1) Marketing Research and Information Systems,
2) Marketing Strategy/Planning
3) Promotion/Advertising Management
3) Consumer Behavior
5) Marketing New Products/Product Development and
   Management, and
6) Sales Management.

Schools/colleges not requiring six specific marketing
courses may benefit from this rank ordering of required
courses when selecting the three, four, or five that will
be required. Further, schools/colleges looking for possible additions to their elective course offerings may benefit from the overall ranking shown in Table 2.

A second objective of this study was to determine the
importance of selected supplemental educational tools to
the marketing education process. The results of this
study suggest that while educators and practitioners are
in total agreement as to the importance of case analysis
and the relative unimportance of field trips, there is
room for realignment of the educational process along the
lines expressed by the practitioners--more emphasis on
work experience training (internships, co-ops, summer
work), and on team teaching; and less emphasis on research
and consulting projects, and on guest lecturers.

A third objective of this study was to determine expectations regarding required preparation and training of
the marketing graduate of the 1980's. The results of
this study suggest that while educators and practitioners
are basically interested in a similar type of preparation
and training, some middle-ground approach should perhaps

be taken in the educational process. For example, the
relatively heavy emphasis on analytical/problem-solving/
decision-making skills, and on quantitative skills, should
perhaps be realigned somewhat to allow greater emphasis
on work experience training and a greater utilization of
general business concepts, etc., in the marketing education process.

A final objective of this study was to identify the pressing marketing issues and/or problems of this decade.
The results of this study suggest that educators and
practitioners have similar concerns in this area--the
greater necessity of strategic and careful planning, and
the impact of resource shortages and the economic,
technological and legal environments. Not unexpectedly,
however, practitioners tended to be less concerned with
the broader implications of the abovementioned, and more
concerned with the specific effects of these on their
own marketing management activities.

In sum, this paper has presented a suggested list of
required courses for marketing majors which may be used
by educators planning to develop or revise their undergraduate marketing curricula, and an overall ranking of
marketing courses that may be used by educators seeking
additional elective courses. A special consideration
for educators is the inclusion of a course in Marketing
New Products/Product Development and Management, a high
priority for practitioners and for educators participating
in a recent "future" workshop (Mulvihill, 1981), but one
not considered as such in other previous studies. Finally, while not purporting to advance new information as
to course content, philosophy or orientation, this paper--
by focusing on selected educational tools, required
training and preparation, and issues/problems of this
decade--discussed several interesting findings that may
become 'food for thought' in these areas.

REFERENCES

Bellenger, Danny N. and Kenneth L. Bernhardt (1977),
    "Revising the Undergraduate Marketing Curriculum:
    The Views of Practitioners and Educators" in
    Contemporary Marketing Thought: 1977 Educators
    Proceedings, Barnett A. Greenberg and Danny N.
    Bellenger, eds., Chicago: American Marketing
    Association.

Laczniak, Gene R. and Jon G. Udell (1979), "Dimensions
    of Future Marketing, MSU Business Topics, (Autumn),
    33-43.

Loudenback, Lynn J. (1973), "The Recent Graduate: A
    Source of Curriculum Evaluation," Collegiate News
    and Views, (Fall), 5-8.

Luck, David J. (1964), Marketing Education in the United
    States, Philadelphia: Marketing Science Institute.

Mulvihill, Donald F., ed. (1981), Marketing and the
    Future, Chicago: American Marketing Association.

Murphy, Patrick E. and Eugene R. Laczniak (1980), Market-
    ing Education: Current Status and a View for the
    1980's, Chicago: American Marketing Association.

Siegel, Sidney (1956), Nonparametric Statistics, New York:
    McGraw-Hill Book Company.

Tinsley, Dillard B. (1981), "Marketing Courses Required
    for Marketing Majors," Journal of Marketing
    Education, (Spring), 10-14.

IMPORTANT VOCATIONAL ATTRIBUTES:
DIFFERENCES BETWEEN MALE AND FEMALE MARKETING STUDENTS

Alan J. Dubinsky, University of Kentucky, Lexington
Thomas N. Ingram, University of Kentucky, Lexington

ABSTRACT

When recruiting college students for marketing positions,
recruiters must pay special concern to the recruitment of
college women. Afterall, such factors as government requirements and social action have engendered an increased
hiring of women in traditionally male-dominated occupations. One way for marketing recruiters to improve their
probabilities of hiring women is to identify the differences between male and female college students' preferred
vocational attributes and to tailor their recruitment messages based upon the preferred attributes. This paper reports the results of a study that examined college men's
and women's desired job characteristics. Implications for
marketing educators and practitioners are also discussed.

INTRODUCTION

Recruiting qualified personnel to fill marketing positions
has long been a major concern for organizations. Although
better training programs and improved supervisory and motivational techniques may enhance the productivity of a marketing department, an organization still needs a pool of
recruits from which to fill marketing positions that become
available through attrition, company expansion, or turnover.

One source of potential recruits is college students. Their
high level of education suggests they are trainable. In
addition, their relative youth makes it worthwhile for a
firm to expend resources training them, since ideally they
can provide the firm with several years of service. Consequently, it is not surprising that recruiters turn to college campuses every year as a source of potential marketing
recruits.

Of special concern to sales recruiters today should be the
recruitment of college women. Because of government requirements (such as the equal employment opportunity guidelines), social action (such as the Equal Rights Amendment
movement), the advent of women's employment in traditionally male-dominated occupations, and the opportunity costs of
not hiring women, business would be prudent to aggressively
seek women to fill marketing positions. There is evidence
that an increasing number of women are entering the field
of marketing (Boone and Kurtz 1977, p. 545; Kanuk 1978;
Scanlon 1973). These findings, however, also suggest that
marketing practitioners need to improve their recruitment
efforts directed at college women.

One approach to assist organizations in recruiting college
women is to identify the important vocational attributes of
both male and female students. This kind of investigation
would have implications for both academicians and practitioners. Academics, knowing which job characteristics are
important to college men and women, can assist students in
determining which marketing positions are likely to possess
the desired job attributes. From the practitioner's perspective, being cognizant of the salient vocational characteristics should suggest whether a different recruitment
program (vis-a-vis the important job characteristics)
should be directed at female students than that which is
directed at male students. The purpose of this paper is to
determine whether men and women have different vocational
attribute preferences and to suggest the implications of
these differences.

BACKGROUND LITERATURE

It is logical to assume that college men and women will
have different job characteristic preferences. Afterall,
previous research on various kinds of organizational members have found that male and female employees exhibit differences in their perceptions of, or preferences for, various
aspects of their jobs. For example, Busch and Bush (1978)
found that salesmen placed more importance than saleswomen
on promotion opportunities; saleswomen, however, gave more
emphasis than salesmen to having a positive feeling about
their customers. Schuler (1975) discovered that male employees in a manufacturing firm believed more strongly than
female employees that their job should provide the opportunity to direct others, influence important decisions, and
earn more money. In contrast, the female employees felt
that working with pleasant workers was more important than
did the male employees. Swan, Futrell, and Todd (1978) ascertained that salesmen were more interested than saleswomen in pay, promotion opportunities, and a secure future.
Saleswomen, however, were more interested than salesmen in
the opportunity to meet different people and to experience
independent thought and action.

Previous research has investigated differences between male
and female college students' preferred vocational attributes. For example, Wagman (1965) found that college men
and women differed significantly on two job characteristics: men desired esteem and women desired social service
opportunities.

Other researchers have determined that college men place a
greater emphasis than college women on various job characteristics including high salary (Gade and Peterson 1977;
Hales and Hartman 1978; Sampson, Stripling, and Loesch
1977; Singer 1974; Stake 1978); job security (Gade and
Peterson 1977; Sampson, Stripling, and Loesch 1977); fringe
benefits (Singer 1974); and power and prestige (Hales and
Hartman 1978; Singer 1974).

Conversely, female college students have been found to consider the following vocational attributes to be more important than do their male counterparts: the opportunity to
help others (Gade and Peterson 1977; Hales and Hartman
1978; Sampson, Stripling, and Loesch 1977); to accomplish
something worthwhile (Singer 1974); to learn new things
(Sampson, Stripling, and Loesch 1977; Singer 1974); and to
interact with people (Sampson, Stripling, and Loesch 1977).

In addition, Manhardt (1972) concluded that college men
rated characteristics related to long-range career success
significantly higher than did college women; the women,
however, evaluated attributes associated with the working
environment and interpersonal relations higher than the men
did. Also, Miner (1974) determined that college women had
lower levels of motivation to become managers than college
men had.

The above mentioned studies, then, suggest that college men
and women exhibit different preferences on certain vocational attributes. Bartol (1976), however, found that the
differences may not merely be a function of sex, but also
the educational discipline for which a student has matricu-
lated. That is, college men and women in business courses
were found to have relatively similar desired job characteristics; there were numerous significant differences,
however, between the desired vocational attributes of

business student males and psychology student females. Except for the Bartol study (1976), no previous research was found that controlled for a student's course of study when exploring preferred vocational attributes of college students. The present study sought to control for a student's discipline by examining only students enrolled in marketing classes.

METHODOLOGY

Sample

The sample consisted of 209 day-school students in marketing courses at a large, midwestern, state university located in a major metropolitan area. Although this sample is not representative of students at all colleges and universities, the students probably are reasonably representative of those attending large, public universities in major metropolitan areas. Of the 209 students, 110 are male and 99 are female.

Students enrolled only in marketing courses were selected for the sample for three reasons. First, it permitted us to control for a student's discipline and thus responds to Bartol's (1976) admonition. Second, although prior research has used marketing students exclusively when exploring their job attitudes (Bellenger, Bernhardt, and Wayman 1974), no previous published research has investigated marketing students' desired vocational attributes. Third, marketing students are likely to assume marketing positions after graduation. Consequently, it is important for academics and practitioners to be cognizant of marketing students' preferred job characteristics. Having this knowledge, academics and practitioners can then provide career information to students that indicates how various marketing positions can satisfy their salient vocational attributes.

Questionnaire

A self-administered questionnaire was distributed to students in class. The questionnaire focused on two kinds of data: (1) the importance of a set of 24 job attributes and (2) related demographic data (such as age, sex, and year in school). Respondents recorded their importance ratings on a Likert-type scale where 1 = "very unimportant" and 5 = "very important."

The 24 vocational attributes were arrived at from an examination of the sales and marketing management and industrial psychology literature (e.g., Burton 1976; Fretz 1972; Manhardt 1972; Ondrack 1973; Paul and Worthing 1970; Sales and Marketing Management 1962a, 1962b, 1962c; Singer 1974; Staunton 1958), as well as from a focus group interview with marketing students.

Data Analysis

The objective of the data analysis was to differentiate between male and female marketing students in terms of their preferred vocational attributes. Consequently, a stepwise discriminant analysis (BMDP-7M (Dixon 1977)) was performed. In addition, the jackknife validation technique (Crask and Perreault 1977) was utilized. The set of 24 job characteristics evaluated by students is found in the appendix.

RESULTS

Of the 24 vocational attributes examined in the investigation, nine entered a statistically significant discriminant function [Wilks' lambda = .86, $F(9,199) = 3.70$, $p < .01$]. Thus, the results suggest that college men and women in this study do differ in their preferences for certain job characteristics.

The nine attributes that entered the discriminant function are:

. excellent fringe benefits
. a feeling of accomplishment
. a good company reputation/image
. opportunity to perform a variety of tasks
. opportunity for rapid advancement/promotion
. dynamic/exciting job
. opportunity to travel
. complex/non-routine in nature
. much leisure time

More specifically, female marketing students believe that the following characteristics are more important than the male students believe: opportunity for rapid advancement/promotion; dynamic/exciting job; opportunity to travel; complex/non-routine in nature; and provides much leisure time. Conversely, male marketing students prefer these job characteristics more than the women do: excellent fringe benefits, a feeling of accomplishment, good company reputation/image, and perform a variety of tasks.

Table 1 depicts the classification matrix resulting from the analysis. As shown, 62.2 percent of male and female marketing students were correctly classified using the jackknife validation technique. The discriminant function performed substantially better than the C pro chance level discussed by Morrison (1974). Therefore, male and female college-level marketing students can be differentiated based upon their desired vocational attributes.

TABLE 1

DISCRIMINANT FUNCTION CLASSIFICATION MATRIX

Actual Group Sex	Predicted Group Sex[a]		
	Male	Female	Total
Male	74[b]	36	110
Female	43	56[b]	99
Total	117	92	209

[a]Proportion of total sample correctly classified using the jackknife statistic was 62.2 percent. The C pro value is 50.0 percent.

[b]Entries in the diagonal represent correct predictions.

DISCUSSION AND IMPLICATIONS

This exploratory study has found that even when controlling for a student's discipline--marketing in this case--male and female college students can be differentiated based upon their desired vocational attributes. More specifically, of twenty-four job characteristics rated by marketing students, nine tend to distinguish between male and female marketing students. That is, male marketing students are concerned about obtaining a job that provides excellent fringe benefits, a feeling of accomplishment, an opportunity to work for a firm with a good image or reputation, and a variety of tasks to perform. Female marketing students, however, prefer a job that provides an opportunity for rapid advancement or promotion, periodic travel, and much leisure time, as well as being complex/non-routine and dynamic/exciting. Given these somewhat disparate preferences, both marketing academics and practitioners have important roles in developing clear perceptions by students about what various entry-level and higher-level marketing jobs entail. Having a better understanding will hopefully assist students in seeing that their important vocational attributes can be found in a variety of marketing positions. Student perceptions can be clarified by various actions taken by academics and practitioners.

What Academics Can Do

Although marketing textbooks usually provide general descriptions about various marketing positions (e.g., sales or advertising jobs), their scope is usually limited. Consequently, academics should use class time to impart marketing job and career information to students, with particular emphasis given to how the various aspects of marketing jobs can satisfy male and female students' job criteria. In the introductory marketing class, a discussion of the panoply of marketing jobs is appropriate in order to familiarize students with, and to increase their interest in, the marketing domain. In more specialized courses (such as sales or advertising management), the discussion should focus exclusively on the vocational opportunities in that area of marketing specialization.

To supplement the professor-student discussion of marketing careers, guest speakers holding different marketing positions--both entry-level and higher-level positions--should be invited to class. The individual can describe various aspects of his or her job, placing special emphasis on the important job characteristics of male and female marketing students.

In addition, students could be assigned a class project that entails their interviewing personnel in various marketing jobs. The project not only will provide useful comparative information (assuming more than one person is interviewed), but also affords the student an opportunity to see the business person in his or her "natural" work environment.

Academics can also try to start (if one does not currently exist) a Pi Sigma Epsilon Sales and Marketing Fraternity or a student chapter of the American Marketing Association. If either of these associations presently exist on campus, an aggressive membership drive could be undertaken. Because these organizations provide business world exposure to marketing students, they could be very beneficial in demonstrating to marketing students how various aspects of marketing positions correspond to students' desired job characteristics.

Marketing professors could also establish marketing internships or a program that gives students an opportunity to spend at least a few days in the field observing marketing personnel execute their job tasks. Either approach would offer students sorely needed exposure to the marketing professions. In so doing, students could better determine which marketing jobs satisfy their job criteria.

What Practitioners Can Do

Several actions can also be taken by practicing marketers in an attempt to show students that marketing positions possess desirable vocational attributes. First, practitioners must be willing to provide marketing internships and guest speakers. An active business-academic partnership is needed so that students can acquire a familiarity with the field of marketing.

In addition, when practitioners are recruiting marketing students, they should consider the sex of the candidate when designing the recruitment message. The recruiter should emphasize how the job(s) under consideration can satisfy the requisite job characteristics of the male or female recruit. A short film, an anecdote, or an opportunity for the candidate to spend time in the field may help illustrate to the recruit the job's salient characteristics.

Also, when a marketing practitioner is speaking to a particular group of students (such as a business fraternity or a sorority), the message should focus on the particular job needs of the particular student group. That is, if the speaking engagement is with a group of college women, the discussion should emphasize how various marketing positions can meet the female students' job criteria. If the group consists of college men, the marketer should focus on how the jobs can satisfy the male students' job needs.

Practitioners could also establish a "Marketing Day." This could entail setting up booths on campus where marketing professionals are present to provide information about their companies and their marketing job opportunities. This is similar to a trade show except that rather than selling to purchasing personnel, the marketer is imparting important information to students.

And finally, marketers could establish advisory boards comprised of marketing students. The board could help a company monitor students' feelings about the company--and its marketing positions. This monitoring could then help a firm take corrective action (e.g., improve its image) if it finds that students have a negative impression of it.

CONCLUSION

In conclusion, attracting male and female marketing students to various marketing positions will continue to be an important concern for business. Both academics and practitioners have important roles to play in assisting students to see that marketing positions can possess students' desired job characteristics. Hopefully, the present study will be useful in increasing the "pool" of qualified candidates from which to fill marketing positions.

APPENDIX

Job Characteristics Evaluated by Students

1. The job provides a challenge.

2. The job provides job security.

3. The job makes a contribution to society.

4. The job permits me to use my creativity.

5. The job provides excellent benefits (e.g., life insurance, vacation, time, pension plans, etc.).

6. The job permits flexibility in my working hours (i.e., work at my own hours, within a given range).

7. The job provides a feeling of accomplishment.

8. The job permits me to use my college education.

9. The job entails working for a company that has a good reputation/image.

10. The job permits me to perform a variety of tasks.

11. The job provides an opportunity for rapid advancement/promotion within my firm.

12. The job does not require me to relocate.

13. The job is dynamic/exciting.

14. The job leads to interaction with intelligent, educated co-workers.

15. The job affords me the opportunity to travel periodically.

16. The job has much status/high prestige.

17. The job is complex/non-routine in nature (i.e., not boring or dull).

18. The job pays very well.

19. The job provides an intellectual reward.

20. The job permits me to be my own boss (i.e., management does not provide a large amount of supervisory control).

21. The job provides the opportunity to meet and interact with different people most of the time.

22. The job possesses a high degree of professionalism.

23. The job leads to interaction with co-workers who are similar to me.

24. The job provides me with mush leisure time.

REFERENCES

Bartol, K. M. (1976), "Relationship of Sex and Professional Training Area to Job Orientation," _Journal of Applied Psychology_, 61 (June), 368-370.

Bellenger, D. N., K. L. Bernhardt, and W. S. Wayman, Jr. (1974), "Student Attitudes Toward Selling As A Career: Implications for Marketing Education," in _1974 Combined Proceedings_, R. C. Curhan, ed., Chicago: American Marketing Association.

Boone, L. E. and D. L. Kurtz (1977), _Contemporary Marketing_, Hinsdale, IL: The Dryden Press.

Burton, G. E. (1976), "Job Values As Perceived by College Students, Their Employers, and Their Professors," _Marquette Business Review_, 20 (Summer), 90-94.

Busch, P. and R. F. Bush (1978), "Women Contrasted to Men in the Industrial Sales Force: Job Satisfaction, Values, Role Clarity, Performance, and Propensity to Leave," _Journal of Marketing Research_, 15 (August), 438-448.

Crask, M. R. and W. D. Perreault (1977), "Validation of Discriminant Analysis in Marketing Research," _Journal of Marketing Research_, 14 (February), 60-68.

Dixon, W. J. (1977), _Biomedical Computer Programs P-Series_, Berkeley, CA: University of California Press.

Fretz, B. R. (1972), "Occupational Values As Discriminants of Professional Student Groups," _Journal of Vocational Behavior_, 2 (July), 233-237.

Gade, E. M. and G. Peterson (1977), "Intrinsic and Extrinsic Work Values and the Vocational Maturity of Vocational-Technical Students," _Vocational Guidance Quarterly_, 26 (December), 125-130.

Hales, L. and T. Hartman (1978), "Personality, Sex, and Work Values," _Journal of Experimental Education_, 47 (Fall), 16-21.

Kanuk, L. (1978), "Women in Industrial Selling," _Journal of Marketing_, 42 (January), 87-91.

Manhardt, P. J. (1972), "Job Orientation of Male and Female College Graduates in Business," _Personnel Psychology_, 25 (Summer), 361-368.

Miner, J. B. (1974), "Motivation to Manage Among Women: Studies of College Students," _Journal of Vocational Behavior_, 5 (October) 241-250.

Morrison, D. G. (1966), "On the Interpretation of Discriminant Analysis," _Journal of Marketing Research_, 6 (May), 156-163.

Ondrack, D. A. (1973), "Emerging Occupational Values: A Review and Some Findings," _Academy of Management Journal_, 16 (September), 423-432.

Paul, G. W. and P. Worthing (1970), "A Student Assessment of Selling," _Southern Journal of Business_, 5 (July), 57-65.

Sales and Marketing Management (1962a), "Selling Is a Dirty Word," (October 5), 44-47.

Sales and Marketing Management (1962b), "People Shouldn't Be Forced to Buy," (October 19), 44-47.

Sales and Marketing Management (1962c), "Salesmen Are Prostitutes," (November 2), 46-54.

Sampson, J. P., R. O. Stripling, and L. G. Loesch (1977), "Male and Female Preferences in Selected Career Factors," _Journal of Employment Counseling_, 14 (September), 103-109.

Scanlon, S. (1973), "Ms. Is A Hit!" _Sales and Marketing Management_, (February 5), 22-30.

Schuler, R. S. (1975), "Sex, Organizational Level, and Outcome Importance: Where the Differences Are," _Personnel Psychology_, 28 (Autumn), 365-375.

Singer, J. N. (1974), "Sex Differences-Similarities in Job Preference Factors," _Journal of Vocational Behavior_, 5 (December), 357-365.

Stake, J. E. (1978), "Motives for Occupational Goal Setting Among Male and Female College Students," _Journal of Applied Psychology_, 63 (October), 617-622.

Staunton, D. J. (1958), "I Didn't Raise My Boy to Be a Salesman!" _Management Review_, 47 (March), 9-13, 72-79.

Swan, J. E., C. M. Futrell, and J. T. Todd (1978), "Same Job--Different Views: Women and Men in Industrial Sales," _Journal of Marketing_, 42 (January), 92-98.

Wagman, M. (1965), "Sex and Age Differences in Occupational Values," _Personnel and Guidance Journal_, 44 (November), 258-262.

INTERNATIONAL MARKETING NEGLECT STILL CONTINUES:
AN EXAMINATION OF TEACHING AND RESEARCH

Kyung-Il Ghymn, University of Nevada-Reno

ABSTRACT

Marketing today operates within a dynamic "global" environment (as opposed to "domestic" or "international").
However, the current marketing education still neglects
the importance of multinational marketing in both teaching
and research. This paper reports on the current academic
community's response to this ever increasing need for the
global business area. Results indicate that academic responses are still far behind the actual business
practices.

INTRODUCTION

One of the most significant developments in the world of
business since World War II is the emergence of multinational enterprises and their impact on the decision-making
of marketing managers, as well as on the lives of
consumers. Few would disagree with the fact that we are
now living in a "one-world-market" economy; and many would
agree with the statement that words such as "domestic marketing" or "international marketing" are no longer appropriate terms in describing the actual marketing world.
The proper term is now "global marketing."

In response to this trend the American Assembly of Collegiate Schools of Business (AACSB) formally changed its
accreditation standards in 1974 to stress the importance
of an international understanding through the business
curricula. In order to further emphasize the point the
AACSB sponsored a series of regional workshops on how to
implement these standards. As a result the assembly
issued a statement that if a business school dean, faculty, or curriculum committee recognizes the need to prepare
the students for the international environment, then every
student should have some minimum exposure to something
other than domestic oriented business courses (AACSB 1979).

Unfortunately, business curriculum in general and marketing education specifically (teaching materials, approaches
and research) appear to be far behind the actual marketing
business practices. Consequently, a majority of business
students leave school and enter the global marketing environment unprepared. Only a small segment of business
students, i.e., those who major in international business
(if there is a program available) or those who select several international courses as electives, seem to be getting some knowledge of this subject. Successful internationalization of the business curriculum requires a global
marketing orientation from research to courses to textbook
content.

The main objectives are to assess current academic practices with regard to their international perspective and
how the academic community has responded to this ever increasing need for strengthening the international marketing area. In order to accomplish this, the paper discusses the following subjects:

1. coverage of the subject in major academic marketing
    journals;

2. number of courses, number of business schools and
    number of students involved in the international mar-
    keting area; and

3. coverage and content structure of marketing textbooks
    regarding international marketing subjects.

In addition, a new approach for improvement was discussed
as to how international marketing education can be improved thereby resulting in business school graduates
being better prepared for the dynamic world of global marketing environment.

Current Marketing Environment and Multinational Business
Activities

A brief discussion on the importance of, and the need for
an integrated global marketing education seems to be in
order and this can be explained in terms of changing
structures of international economy.

A generation ago only the United States had emerged from
World War II with its economy intact and flourishing.
Today, however, Western Europe, Japan, the oil producers,
aspiring economic powers like Mexico, Brazil, and Korea,
and even the Communist nations have become major contend-
ers in the world economic arena. They have joined the
United States as major producers of the world's manufactured products and have emerged as more aggressive and
determined competitors. The United States can expect
even keener competition in the 1980's.

Another significant change is that communication and
transportation developments are making the world smaller
and smaller, thus moving the world closer to a one-market
economy. To illustrate:

> We are quite likely awakened in the morning by a
> clock radio made in Japan. We may sit at a breakfast
> table made in Denmark to eat a piece of Polish ham
> with stainless steel silverware made in Korea, sip
> juice from glass tumblers exported from Czechoslo-
> vakia, and drink coffee from cups made in Italy. And
> we are likely to sleep wearing pajamas made in Taiwan.

Not many Americans realize that products such as Bayer
asperin, Pepsodent toothpaste, Nestle's chocolate bars,
Kool cigarettes, Shell Oil, and Michelin tires are foreign
products. Familiar brands in the United States, such as
Norelco, Libby, and Honda are foreign owned and many
familiar United States companies are now foreign controlled: e.g. Motorola's Quasar, Paul Masson Wines,
Travellodge, Gimbles, Grand Union Department Stores,
Keebler cookies, etc., etc. Few Americans realize that
United States manufactured automobiles have thirty-one
materials imported from thirty-two countries; telephones
have forty-eight materials imported from eighteen countries, and daily newspapers are most likely printed on
imported newsprint (Ghymn 1979).

Despite the evidence of the one-market-world economy,
Americans, more than most peoples, are likely to underestimate the impact of international marketing on the
domestic economy and their own living standard. Even some
intellectuals may argue that the United States economy is
self-sufficient because export revenue is still below 10
percent of GNP as compared to other major countries whose
international trade accounts for more than 30 percent of
their GNP. Aggregate relationships, however, are often
deceiving; this is especially true in this instance. When
the dependence of the American economy on specific imports
as sources of supply and specific exports as outlets for
domestic production is examined, a better understanding of
the significance of international trade emerges.

Today there are only two metals (magnesium and molybdenum)
for which American industry is not wholly dependent on
foreign supplies. The United States industry is 100 percent dependent on imports of natural rubber, tin, coffee,
tea, bananas, and cocoa beans; industry imports 90 percent
or more of its consumption of nickel, bauxite, cobalt, and
chromite, just to name a few (Ghymn 1980).

International Marketing Reflected in Major Marketing
Journals

Academic journals are thought of as the barometer of contemporary thinking among acamedicians. Therefore it seems
reasonable to expect these journals would reflect the
growing influence of international marketing.

A content analysis of every issue of Journal of Marketing,
the Journal of Marketing Research, and the Journal of
Consumer Research from 1970 through 1980 was conducted.
Any major article that had a cross cultural or international aspect was included in the 'international'
category. Table 1 displays the total number of articles,
and the overall 12 year percent of international
orientation.

The Journal of Consumer Research had the lowest percent
(0.8) of international articles. Not only was there a
paucity of nondomestic articles, all of those counted for
in the analysis were published in one year! The Journal
of Marketing Research selected more of an international
flavor but still contained only 1.3 percent of an international orientation. The Journal of Marketing had the
greatest leaning toward the international subject with an
overall 6.0 percent. Furthermore, for every year included
in the content analysis at least one topical article
appeared.

International Marketing Courses Offered, Business Schools
and Student Participation

Results of the implementation of the 1974 AACSB standards
was measured by an increase in the number of courses offered and the number of business students enrolled in
these international courses. Data for this section were
obtained from the second and third International Business
Curriculum Surveys published by the Academy of International Business (Grosse and Perritt 1980; Daniels and
Radebaugh 1974).

Since 1974 the teaching of international business has
increased substantially. Tables 2, 3, and 4 clearly demonstrate this point. Each subsequent AIB survey has
become progressively more detailed therefore some information desirable for comparison is not available.

TABLE 1

INTERNATIONAL MARKETING ARTICLES APPEARED
IN MAJOR MARKETING JOURNALS
(1970-1981)

| | Journal of Marketing | | | Journal of Marketing Research | | | Journal of Consumer Research* | | |
Year	Total # of Articles	# of Int'l	%	Total # of Articles	% of Int'l	%	Total # of Articles	# of Int'l	%
1970	61	3	4.9	59	1	1.7			
1971	51	2	3.9	49	1	2.0			
1972	50	2	4.0	43	1	2.3			
1973	48	2	4.2	37	0	0			
1974	53	3	5.7	36	0	0	35	0	0
1975	48	3	6.3	39	1	2.6	31	0	0
1976	44	2	4.5	44	2	4.5	24	2	8.3
1977	51	4	7.8	69	0	0	25	0	0
1978	51	1	2.0	71	0	0	27	0	0
1979	36	1	2.8	68	0	0	36	0	0
1980**	45	12	26.6	61	1	1.6	37	0	0
1981	60	1	1.6	50	1	2.0	36	0	0
TOTAL	598	36	6.0	626	8	1.3	251	2	.8

* The Journal of Consumer Research began publication in 1974.

** The 1980 issues have 4, 1, 3, and 4 articles in Vol. 1, 2, 3, and 4,
respectively.

Table 2 is the least impressive of the three tables. We
see that the number of schools offering international
courses has only increased slightly. This leads us to believe the changes that have occurred are within those
schools already offering international courses in 1974.

TABLE 2

NUMBER OF SCHOOLS
OFFERING INTERNATIONAL MARKETING COURSES
(1974 and 1980)

Degree level	1974	1980
Undergraduate Only	56	67
Masters Only	28	16
Undergraduate and Masters Only	49	44
Undergraduate and Doctorate Only	NA	1
Masters and Doctorate Only	NA	3
Undergraduate, Masters and Doctorate	NA	7
TOTAL:	133	138

Source: John D. Daniels and Lee H. Radebaugh, International Business Curriculum Survey, Academy of
International Business, 1974; Robert E. Grosse
and G. W. Perritt, International Business
Curricula: A Global Survey, Academy of International Business, 1980.

Perhaps the important aspect of this table is that in 1980
only 43% of those schools responding to the survey offered
international courses. Given the stated importance of a
global orientation and Grosse and Perritt's conceptualization of international business as a 'maturing' product,
this 'acceptance rate' by schools would appear to be marginal and worthy of improvement.

TABLE 3

NUMBER OF INTERNATIONAL MARKETING
COURSES OFFERED
(1974 and 1980)

| | Undergraduate | | | Graduate | | |
Course Subject	1974	1980	%*	1974	1980	%*
International Marketing	124	282	127	77	77	0
International Trade	31	115	271	15	108	620
Export/Import	7	57	714	18	34	888
Comparative Marketing	7	56	700	7	22	214
TOTAL:	169	510	202	117	241	106

Source: Daniels and Radebaugh, Op. cit.; Grosse and
Perritt, Op. cit.

* Percent Increase

When one looks at the number of courses offered, the impact of the AACSB ruling is evident (see Table 3). This
dramatic increase may well be a result of a second contributing factor, student demand. The increase in the number
of courses offered has been phenomenal with a 202% increase at the undergraduate level and a 114% increase at
the graduate level.

Presenting 1980 figures only, Table 4 reflects the number
of students enrolled in international marketing courses.
Although this figure appears large, a closer look at the
percent of business students enrolled in international
courses is necessary. In 1977 approximately 200,000 business degrees were granted. In 1980, a total of 10,452
students participated in international marketing courses
(Ghymn, 1980). Without adjusting for an increase in the
number of dgrees granted in 1980, a maximum of only 5.2%
of graduating business students were exposed to international marketing courses.

TABLE 4

NUMBER OF STUDENT ENROLLED IN
INTERNATIONAL MARKETING COURSES
(1980)

Course Subject	Undergraduate	Masters	Doctorate
International Marketing	3,708	1,734	120
International Trade	2,390	1,161	163
Export/Import	773	885	35
Comparative Marketing	1,329	534	10
TOTAL:	5,810	4,314	328

Source: Grosse and Perrit, Op. cit.

One conclusion that can be drawn from the data presented in
these three tables is that only a small percentage of business students are exposed to the topic of international
marketing in any detail. This does not reflect the business environment's need for students well prepared for the
global influence.

Textbook Coverage of International Topics

A substantial number of marketing textbooks, both basic
marketing and marketing management, have allocated some
pages to international marketing subjects. For the purposes of this report only Basic Marketing and Marketing
Management texts were examined. An examination of Table 5
reveals that only 2.45% of the page content of basic texts
were devoted to an international orientation and a scarce
1.46% of the Marketing Management texts dealt with international influences on marketing.

TABLE 5

TEXTBOOK COVERAGE OF INTERNATIONAL
MARKETING TOPICS

Textbooks (# examined)	Total Pages	# of Int'l Pages	%
Basic Marketing (32)	20,788	509	2.45
Marketing Management (20)	11,575	169	1.46

Discussion: A New Approach

The importance of international marketing education in the
United States has not gone unnoticed. In 1967, some 95
international marketing courses were being offered (Baker
and Ryans 1975). The number has increased to 286 in 1974
and 751 in 1980 as shown in Table 3. In addition, 36 of
the 52 basic marketing and marketing management textbooks
examined have at least a chapter on international marketing
topics and several international marketing textbooks have
been published since 1967. Therefore, on the basis of this
coverage, one argued that marketing education is definitely
keeping pace with the current development of the global
marketing environment.

However, in terms of teaching the subject materials, marketing education appears to be far behind the actual practice of global marketing operations. Two interrelated
reasons can be cited for this less effective marketing
education in the multinational perspective. The primary
reason is that the textbook materials are not totally
integrated. Practically all basic marketing and marketing
management textbooks seem to treat "international marketing" as an independent subject which can be separated from
"domestic marketing." In practice they are inseparable in
today's global marketing environment.

The second reason, which is the result of the first, is
that, even in the colleges and universities where international marketing is taught, the professor's task is made
difficult by the lack of integrated course materials. As
a result, it is very difficult for the student to understand the field of international marketing and its interrelated functional areas as they apply to domestic marketing operation in terms of both practical and conceptual
aspects. The present teaching approach makes it difficult
to change the student's attitude toward international
marketing. The prevailing student attitude views international marketing only as a special course for those who are
majoring in international business or those who want to be
an international marketing manager. While there may be
several approaches, there appears one important solution to
this dilemma: A systematic integration of the basic teaching material in the marketing textbooks.

A systematic integration simply means that all major chapters of the textbook incorporate the multinational aspect
of marketing into the traditional marketing concepts. For
example: (1) Overseas market availability and its impact
on the product-life-cycle of domestic products should be
discussed in the Product Decisions and the Product Development Policy chapters; (2) The impact of import-export quantity, tariff and non-tariff barriers on price setting in
practice, and the multinational corporation's transfer
pricing should be included in the Pricing chapter; (3)
Development and implementation of promotional strategies
for overseas markets should be added to the Promotion
chapter. By so integrating, marketing education can effectively meet the challenge of the internationalization of
the marketing curriculum. More importantly, the marketing
student can better comprehend the complexity of the global
marketing environment, its problems as well as opportunities, at the same time he is studying general marketing
principles and marketing management practices.

Several marketing educators and practitioners have already
recognized the importance of and need for integrating an
international dimension into sections of the core marketing
course. Wortzel argues and emphasizes that two important
aspects of international products policy ought to be added
to the core course: (1) Motivation for taking products
abroad; and (2) The selection of products and countries
(Wortzel 1979). Weinstein argues that the advertising
chapter of a basic marketing course should have an international perspective in the area of advertising objectives,
budgets, media strategies, control, organization and agency
relationships (Weinstein). Reginal H. Jones, Chairman of
the General Electric Company, states that the era of international competition is already upon us, and we will have
to be sharp about internationalizing the curricula of the
business schools. There is no time to delay (1979).

Recently a former marketing student who took a job in a
procurement department of a large retail company visited
the author's office to get some reading materials of international marketing. He expressed his regret for not taking
international marketing courses while at school because he

was literally shocked to find how deeply this regionally
known domestic retail unit was involved in international
operations. More than sixty percent of the total merchandise sold was procured from 47 foreign countries.

Summary and Conclusion

The global marketing environment in which we live and operate requires a new approach. In order to effectively meet
the challenge of the internationalization of the marketing
curricula and in order to train future global-minded marketing managers, a totally integrated systematic organization and presentation of the basic teaching material is
suggested as an initial solution. Successful integration
does not mean an insertion of a chapter of a sporatic use
of examples regarding international marketing. It means
all major chapters of the textbook incorporate key aspects
of multinational marketing function into the general marketing concepts.

Also, there appears an urgent need for increasing both
quality and quantity of research articles published in
major marketing journals which would further stimulate the
current interest of international marketing.

REFERENCES

Background and Contents of the Plenary and Workshops for
the Internationalization of the Business School Curriculum, American Assembly of Collegiate Schools of Business,
St. Louis and Washington, D. C., March 1979.

Baker, James C. and John K. Ryans, Jr. (1975), Multinational Marketings; Dimensions in Strategy, Columbus, Ohio:
Grid Inc., Preface.

Daniels, John D. and Lee H. Radebaugh (1974), International
Business Curriculum Survey, Academy of International
Business, 154-166.

Ghymn, Kyung-Il (1979), "International Trade: How Impor-
tant is it to the U. S. Economy?" Working Paper Series
No. 79-11, Bureau of Business and Economic Research,
University of Nevada-Reno, 3.

_______________ (1980), "Internationalization of Business
Education: Marketing Courses," a paper presented at the
1980 Academy of International Business Conference, New
Orleans, Louisiana, 5.

Grosse, Robert E. and G. W. Perritt (1980), International
Business Curricular: A Global Survey, Academy of
International Business, 1980.

Jones, Reginal H. (1979), "Internationalizing the Cur-
ricula," The Internationalization of the Business School
Curriculum, American Assembly of Collegiate Schools of
Business, 2.

Weinstein, A. K. (1979), "Internationalizing the Advertising Management Section in the Basic Marketing Curriculum,"
Proceedings, American Marketing Association, 173-177.

Wortzel, Lawrence H. (1979), "Concepts and Sources for
Teaching International Aspects of Product Policy,"
Proceedings, American Marketing Association, 178-182.

ENRICHING THE INTERNATIONAL MARKETING COURSE:
CURRENT EVENTS NEGOTIATIONS SIMULATION

Russell M. Moore, Hofstra University, Hempstead, NY
Suresh B. Pradhan, Hofstra University, Hempstead, NY

ABSTRACT

This paper discusses the Current Events Negotiations
Simulation Technique as a component of the international
marketing course. The methodology enhances lectures,
case analyses, and term paper research by giving students
experience with the ambiguities involved in the personal
interactions of international marketing. Steps in preparing cases, conducting simulations, and evaluation are
suggested. Examples of elements in a negotiation are
provided. Areas of learning facilitated by the technique
and student evaluations are presented.

INTRODUCTION

It has become evident during the past 20 years that most
firms are operating within segments of markets which are
multinational in scope. Educators have responded to the
fact that the markets which comprise the world economy
are multinational by developing courses to teach the
functional areas of business from an international perspective. Courses in "international marketing" and
"multinational marketing" have been created at a large
percentage of schools offering rigorous undergraduate and
graduate programs in management education (Stein, Lamb,
and MacLachlan 1978). Students have elected to participate in these courses in increasing numbers. The
typical format for these courses has involved a mixture
of readings from textbooks and journals, case discussions,
and the preparation of term projects (Cateora 1981).
This paper reports on an additional methodology for
facilitating learning which has proven to be highly
effective in enriching educational experiences in courses
on international marketing: current events negotiations
simulation.

NEGOTIATIONS SIMULATION TECHNIQUE

The international negotiations simulation technique uses
cases which allow students to assume the roles of participants in negotiation processes. The roles typically
include different roles within the businesses or governmental organizations which are parties to a negotiation,
as well as different roles between the entities which are
negotiating on a particular issue. For example, the
negotiation might involve two firms which are attempting
to establish an international licensing agreement. The
negotiating "teams" would be comprised of "executives"
from each firm representing different areas such as
marketing, finance, legal, and public affairs. The
negotiators must work out intra-firm strategy and attempt
to establish inter-firm agreement. Cultural, political,
economic, and legal factors in the environment establish
parameters for the negotiating process, constraining the
personal and organizational capabilities of the negotiators.

Traditional Approaches to Negotiation Simulation

The use of negotiation simulation as a teaching technique
in international business has been pioneered by Ashok
Kapoor and John Fayerweather (1976). Their approach has
been to develop extensive and detailed case studies of
major business negotiations, largely focused on investment and disinvestment situations. Such cases have

proven to be extremely useful, but certain problems
exist for the instructor in using them over a period
of years. The cases require a great deal of firm-
specific data which is available only through research
based on privileged access to proprietary information.
The cases get stale as time goes on, and it is beyond
the resources of most students and instructors to
develop the information for updating the case. In
addition, the students are able to read at the outset
the outcome of the "real world" negotiation, which
distorts their own in-class negotiating process.

Current Events Negotiation Simulation

Current Events Negotiation Simulation (CENS) provide
a variation on the Kapoor and Fayerweather approach
which enhances the learning experience of negotiation
simulation and allows a case used over a period of many
years to remain fresh. The CENS cases focus on international marketing negotiations which are continuing
processes widely reported in the general press, trade
publications, government reports, and company publications. Case preparation involves extensive research
by the students which is open-ended, adding an important
new factor to the traditional benefits of negotiation
simulation. The students become involved in negotiation
situations based on information appearing in the media
daily. The constant appearance of fresh information
which the students must ferret out and integrate into
their negotiation approach imparts a sense of the
urgency of evolving events which is characteristic of
real-world international marketing. The search for
information to use in their negotiating tactics leads
the students to understand the reality, importance, and
interrelationship of concepts such as balance of payments, exchange rates, cartels, protectionism, and
business/government synergism which is difficult to
impart in a traditional lecture and discussion format.

The use of the CENS technique changes the classroom
environment completely. The instructor operates more
as a stage director than as a font of wisdom and
received knowledge. Intense one-to-one interactions
between student and instructor become the order of the
day as the instructor "stage manages" the negotiation
process without dominating it. The students become
highly involved with the subject matter, and committed
to absorbing it in order to perform effectively. Peer
learning is maximized, and the class becomes a coherent
social unit as all participants come to know each
other. Such social cohesion is characteristic of
business organizations, but is often difficult to create
in the classroom.

Current Events Negotiations Simulations cannot replicate
reality. Substantial elements of information will not
be available in the public domain which are important in
the actual negotiations being simulated. The deviation
from precise reality is not important from the standpoint of learning the process of negotiation. The
student negotiators operate in a world which starts from
actual information, but is then channeled by the
instructor and shaped by the students themselves. The
instructor will often be called upon to make simplifying
assumptions to adjust for lack of data. Nevertheless,
the outcome of negotiations will often be highly similar
to outcomes in the real world. The students typically

become intensely interested in comparing their outcomes with actual outcomes, and analyzing why the deviations occurred.

STRUCTURE OF A CURRENT EVENTS NEGOTIATION SIMULATION

Current Events Negotiation Simulations can be based on a variety of situations which receive press coverage over an extended period. Case studies have been used in the classroom on the following topics (Moore and Pradhan 1983):

Semi-Annual OPEC Interministerial Meetings
World Health Assembly Preparation of a Marketing Code for Infant Formula
Santa Fe International Acquisition by the Kuwait Petroleum Corporation
Japan/American Automotive Trade Negotiations
U.S./Canadian Automotive Trade Negotiations
International Advertising Policy for Apple Computer

The instructor can shape many situations into CENS cases, based on interest, data availability, and time constraints within the classroom. A case should include a basic introduction to the situation which outlines the roles involved and the matters at issue. A bibliography should be included for helping students to start their research. The instructor should be familiar with the facts of the situation being studied in order to fulfill the role of research consultant and negotiation stage manager. Case situations can be developed which are based on less accessible information when the instructor has a particular expertise based on research, consulting, or business experience. Exhibit 1 summarizes the steps involved in conducting a Current Events Negotiation Simulation.

Evaluating Negotiations Performance

A short (one to three page) statement of maximum and minimum objectives, and expected strategies and tactics, is required from each individual or team before the beginning of formal negotiations (between steps 6 and 7 on Exhibit 1). This report is confidential to the instructor and will not be referred to in newspaper articles. The report helps the instructor assess the preparation of the individual or team, and also provides a benchmark for assessing the achievement of objectives at the conclusion of the negotiation.

The instructor maintains a summary of discussions during the negotiations, noting who said what, and the sequence of comments. Note should also be kept concerning observations of informal negotiation interactions. The instructor should attempt to be unobtrusive to the group discussions, but can counsel individuals and teams if advice is requested. A tape recording of the plenary sessions can be made and, even better, the entire proceedings can be videotaped.

An evaluation form is completed for each student at the conclusion of the negotiation. A suggested evaluation format is included as Exhibit 2. These evaluations are based on the written statement of objectives and the observed performance during the negotiations. Negotiating performance often deviates substantially from performance on tests. Students who respond well to tests are often bewildered by the flexibility and indeterminate nature of the negotiating process, while students who are just "drifting through" become fired with enthusiasm and assume a leadership role. One way to develop a quantitative basis for evaluation is to count the total number of interventions made by each student in the formal negotiating sessions. Extra credit can be given for especially important comments such as new analytical

1. Background reading on the process of negotiation is assigned.

2. A case description outlining the situation and issues, and listing roles is distributed. A basic bibliography is included. An article, collection of clippings, or research paper can also be distributed as background.

3. Students are allowed to select their roles. Teams of students are often assigned to fulfill a given role. Clusters of roles with similar interests are often established (For example: several firms from one country negotiating as a body with several firms from another country).

4. A timetable for negotiation is established, allowing time for preparation, but imposing a time pressure as a parameter for negotiation.

5. The instructor counsels the students on their research problems.

6. A particular role is assigned the task of chairing or "hosting" the formal negotiations. This person or team must assume responsibility for establishing the ground rules for meetings, agendas, and decisionmaking. The physical layout of the room or rooms used for negotiation should also be established by this team. General guidelines can be established by the instructor, but it is important for students to struggle with format and procedural questions.

7. Formal negotiations commence after in-class and out-of-class preparations. Opening statements are made by all parties. The students must be aware that formal sessions can and should be interspersed with informal meetings. The pace, structure, and outcome of the negotiations should be only lightly controlled by the instructor. The students must be left to their own resources. Periods of frustration and lack of progress must be allowed to occur. The negotiations should be stopped at the pre-established time limit.

8. The instructor or a student(s) can perform the role of the press during the negotiation. The "press" interviews participants, publishes official press releases, and makes a "newspaper" available as the meetings proceed. This is often the most effective device for the instructor to use in guiding the negotiations.

9. The negotiations terminate with the issuance of a joint communique which describes the results of the negotiation. A formal contract or convention may be included. In case no agreement is reached and/or negotiations break off, separate communiques are required.

10. A debriefing is held during which the process of the negotiation is discussed by the participants and instructor.

---

insights or resolution of impasses. Peer evaluations can also be used, with the students using the same form as the instructor.

EXHIBIT 3

SAMPLE INITIAL OPEN NEWSLETTER

RIYAH MAIL

LTA, November 5, 1981. Reports have been coming
 around the world concerning the question of what
 on the agenda at the upcoming OPEC Interminis-
 meeting. Last week's agreement on price seems to
solved the price issue for the next eighteen
, at least on the surface. We are not so sure that
ed disunity will not exist as member countries
 to increase their income from oil exports. We
e that the issue of oil consumption and production
e next six months will be a lively item for debate.
 be possible to agree on acceptable output and
tion levels? Supposedly this can be easily
ned, but in reality no one ever seems to know
 how the market will perform.

uestions which are likely to come up for dis-
 are:

e establishment of a common price level for
tural gas.
e utility of the spot market to OPEC members.
e establishment of an automatic pricing formula
ied in with world economic indicators.
e continued use of the Dollar as the currency
r pricing oil.
 long-term strategy for avoiding the replacement
f petroleum as an energy source.
e development of better mechanisms for channeling
inancial resources to developing countries.
e development of more downstream control of
nergy marketing on the part of OPEC members.

r will be the site of the meeting. Reports from
indicate that preparations for negotiations are
complete.

---

rmal negotiations commence in the second session
e MBA students, and in the fourth session for the
raduates. The room is arranged similar to the UN
ty Council, and each country is expected to have an
fication sign. The meeting is called to order, and
ountry presents its opening statement. The chair-
 from the host country appoints a press committee
sue a press release after each session) and a
ary (to keep a running record of the proceedings).
ural and substantive decisionmaking processes are
ished, and subcommittees may be created. An agenda
ablished, and discussion proceeds (punctuated by
es when needed) for two periods in the graduate
nd three periods in the undergraduate class. At
clusion of the negotiations a formal communique
 prepared which is acceptable to all participants.
mportant that the negotiators be forced through
cess of negotiating the communique, because it is
 point that the students realize how important
t wording is for representing business relation-
 A post-mortem of the negotiation follows the
egotiating session. Exhibit 4 presents a sample
er article based on an "official" press release
e negotiators.

been found that the OPEC Simulation is effective
litating learning in the following areas:

tural Empathy -- The students study their coun-
es, attempt to adopt their perspective, and stay
rcely in role. Seeing the world as a "Libyan"
highly instructive.

EXHIBIT 4

SAMPLE OPEC PRESS RELEASE

BEAVER COUNTY TIMES (Beaver, Pa.)   11-17-81

UPI, QUITO, ECUADOR, November 13, 1981. The semi-annual
meeting of OPEC opened here today at the Quito Hilton,
with Ecuador serving as the host country. Their role is
to chair all formal negotiating sessions. Ecuador
stated the ground rules as far as voting throughout the
sessions: A) voting for procedural questions requires
a simple majority, and B) voting on OPEC issues (such
as price controls) will require a unanimous vote by all
member countries. Opening statements from the 10
member countries present and guest Mexico followed next,
the randomly picked order being Ecuador, Nigeria, Iran,
Saudi Arabia, Venezuela, Iraq, Indonesia, Kuwait,
Algeria, Libya, and Mexico. Some of the major points
or goals stated by the countries in their opening
statements included:

Ecuador - Seeks to better the foundation of the country, and will invest in Iraq. Nigeria - wants internal
funds for financing. Iran - interested in political
and economic aspects of oil. They protested against
Iraq. Saudi Arabia - seeks to keep oil as a long-term
energy source. Venezuela - looking to develop the
country as a whole, wants "reasonable" oil prices.
Iraq - concerned about the future, desires to get rid
of the Dollar as the currency. Indonesia - projects
to increase development, they seek $38 a barrel, with
a $3 premium. They want investment from fellow member
countries instead of from industrial countries.
Kuwait - seeking steady production levels, and will
follow Saudi Arabia. Algeria - seeks to keep prices
high at this point. Libya - wants to redistribute the
world's wealth, and OPEC unity through high stable
prices. Mexico - looking to establish a Third World
Petroleum Funding Organization by the Third World,
for the Third World.

In order to aid countries in their decision as to
whether to let Mexico vote at these sessions, a 10-
minute open question period followed to let Mexico state
their policies. The resulting vote was seven opposed
and two favoring a Mexican vote. (Kuwait passed.)

The agenda is to be discussed at the next meeting, and
the substantive negotiations will commence.

Country Analysis -- The students must utilize the
analytical tools they have learned in other segments
of the course related to market structures, socioeconomic trends, cultural analysis, balance of payments, and exchange rates, among other factors.

Demand Analysis -- The world energy market must be
studied, with projections made of future petroleum
supply/demand, and the nature of competition with
competing energy sources.

Pricing Strategy -- The elasticities of energy supply
and demand must be estimated, and the operation of an
international cartel understood.

Systematic Analysis -- The complex interactions
between politics and marketing, and between multinational corporations and petroleum exporters and
importers must be investigated.

Negotiation Tactics and Strategies -- The personal
and institutional factors which are important in a
negotiating process must be learned by going through
the motions of negotiating.

NAME: ____   NEGOTIATION TOPIC: ____________

EVALUATION FORM:
INTERNATIONAL NEGOTIATIONS SIMULATION

Mark an X in the Appropriate Slot for <u>All</u> Factors.

Comments are optional.

	Superior	Better Than Average	Average	B Av
Familiarity with the facts and supporting data on all sides.	______	______	______	______
Definition of objectives and strategy.	______	______	______	______
Communication and coordination with negotiating partners.	______	______	______	______
Communication with negotiation counterparts.	______	______	______	______
Manner of presenting self (behavior, body language, manner of speaking).	______	______	______	______
Use of negotiating tactics (timing, new proposals, firmness, flexibility, alliances, repetition, threats, agreement, compromise, haggling).	______	______	______	______
Achievement of objectives.	______	______	______	______
Overall assessment of effective negotiation.	______	______	______	______

GENERAL EXPLANATORY COMMENTS: ____________________________________

____

If videotape has been used, the students should be shown
excerpts from the tape, with commentary from the instructor on effective and ineffective performance. Videotaping is not necessary for the CENS to be effective.
Students are extremely responsive to analysis of their
performance through videotape playback.

OPEC NEGOTIATIONS SIMULATION

A case based on the "Semi-Annual OPEC Interministerial
Meetings" has been used extensively with graduate and
undergraduate classes, and provides an excellent example
of what can be done with current events negotiations
simulations. The "real world" meetings occur toward the
end of the Fall and Spring semesters, and occasion a
great deal of comment in the press. Students enthusiastically develop an in-depth knowledge of something that
had previously appeared quite exotic to them. The OPEC
CENS has been used with classes of 20 to 40 students, in
graduate courses meeting 14 times for 150-minute sessions,
and undergraduate classes meeting 28 times for 90-minute
sessions. The course work is structured as follows:

	Percent of Grade	
	Graduate	Undergraduate
Midterm	20	20
Final	20	20
Three Case Writeups	20*	20**
Term Project (Paper)	20	20
Negotiation Simulation	20	20
	100	100

 * From Keegan
** From Cateora and Hess

A complete coverage of basic internat
topics is accomplished before the CEN
simulation is run during three class
graduate course, and six class sessio
graduate course. The simulation take
diately after the midterms in each co
9-10-11 and 16-17-18-19-20-21, respec

The classes are divided into teams of
individuals, representing 10 to 13 of
depending on class size. A brief case
and the Interministerial meetings is
newspaper article is circulated which
topics for the agenda, and announces
host the meeting (the instructor selec
try with care, choosing a team which s
able to control the meeting, which may
rowdy in the heat of debate). Exhibit
sample of the initial newspaper articl
points for discussion. A directory of
with their country affiliation and tel
circulated to facilitate informal nego

In graduate courses the entire class m
library during the first period of the
the instructor meeting individually wi
teams to advise them on research, and
their country. The undergraduate clas
research sessions in the library. At
research period each team must present
Strategies for Negotiation" report. E
expected to meet for an additional 10
preparation outside of class. The prep
on the analysis of the politico-econom
country, petroleum policy, general econ
role of foreign investment, world energ
OPEC strategy, and relationships betwee
Editions of the newspaper reporting on
ments, rumors, and press releases are p
class period, and sometimes more often.

JAMAHI

UPI, M
in fro
will b
terial
have r
months
contin
attemp
are su
over t
Will i
consum
determ
exactl

Other
cussio

1. T
    n
2. T
3. T
    t
4. T
    f
5. A
    o
6. T
    f
7. T
    e

Ecuado
Quito
almost

The fo
for th
underg

NAME: _______________________________________   NEGOTIATION TOPIC: _______________________________________

EVALUATION FORM:
INTERNATIONAL NEGOTIATIONS SIMULATION

Mark an X in the Appropriate Slot for <u>All</u> Factors.

Comments are optional.

	Superior	Better Than Average	Average	Below Average	Poor
Familiarity with the facts and supporting data on all sides.	________	________	________	________	________
Definition of objectives and strategy.	________	________	________	________	________
Communication and coordination with negotiating partners.	________	________	________	________	________
Communication with negotiation counterparts.	________	________	________	________	________
Manner of presenting self (behavior, body language, manner of speaking).	________	________	________	________	________
Use of negotiating tactics (timing, new proposals, firmness, flexibility, alliances, repetition, threats, agreement, compromise, haggling).	________	________	________	________	________
Achievement of objectives.	________	________	________	________	________
Overall assessment of effective negotiation.	________	________	________	________	________

GENERAL EXPLANATORY COMMENTS: _______________________________________

____

If videotape has been used, the students should be shown excerpts from the tape, with commentary from the instructor on effective and ineffective performance. Videotaping is not necessary for the CENS to be effective. Students are extremely responsive to analysis of their performance through videotape playback.

OPEC NEGOTIATIONS SIMULATION

A case based on the "Semi-Annual OPEC Interministerial Meetings" has been used extensively with graduate and undergraduate classes, and provides an excellent example of what can be done with current events negotiations simulations. The "real world" meetings occur toward the end of the Fall and Spring semesters, and occasion a great deal of comment in the press. Students enthusiastically develop an in-depth knowledge of something that had previously appeared quite exotic to them. The OPEC CENS has been used with classes of 20 to 40 students, in graduate courses meeting 14 times for 150-minute sessions, and undergraduate classes meeting 28 times for 90-minute sessions. The course work is structured as follows:

	Percent of Grade	
	Graduate	Undergraduate
Midterm	20	20
Final	20	20
Three Case Writeups	20*	20**
Term Project (Paper)	20	20
Negotiation Simulation	20	20
	100	100

 * From Keegan
** From Cateora and Hess

A complete coverage of basic international marketing topics is accomplished before the CENS begins. The simulation is run during three class sessions in the graduate course, and six class sessions in the undergraduate course. The simulation takes place immediately after the midterms in each course (sessions 9-10-11 and 16-17-18-19-20-21, respectively).

The classes are divided into teams of two to four individuals, representing 10 to 13 of the OPEC countries, depending on class size. A brief case describing OPEC and the Interministerial meetings is distributed. A newspaper article is circulated which reviews the basic topics for the agenda, and announces which country will host the meeting (the instructor selects the host country with care, choosing a team which seems likely to be able to control the meeting, which may get somewhat rowdy in the heat of debate). Exhibit 3 presents a sample of the initial newspaper article which suggests points for discussion. A directory of all participants with their country affiliation and telephone number is circulated to facilitate informal negotiating contacts.

In graduate courses the entire class meets in the library during the first period of the negotiation, with the instructor meeting individually with each of the teams to advise them on research, and the stance of their country. The undergraduate classes meet for three research sessions in the library. At the end of the research period each team must present a "Goals and Strategies for Negotiation" report. Each team is expected to meet for an additional 10 to 20 hours of preparation outside of class. The preparation focuses on the analysis of the politico-economic stance of each country, petroleum policy, general economic policy, the role of foreign investment, world energy demand trends, OPEC strategy, and relationships between OPEC countries. Editions of the newspaper reporting on formal developments, rumors, and press releases are published for each class period, and sometimes more often.

SAMPLE INITIAL OPEN NEWSLETTER

JAMAHIRIYAH MAIL

UPI, MALTA, November 5, 1981. Reports have been coming
in from around the world concerning the question of what
will be on the agenda at the upcoming OPEC Interministerial meeting. Last week's agreement on price seems to
have resolved the price issue for the next eighteen
months, at least on the surface. We are not so sure that
continued disunity will not exist as member countries
attempt to increase their income from oil exports. We
are sure that the issue of oil consumption and production
over the next six months will be a lively item for debate.
Will it be possible to agree on acceptable output and
consumption levels? Supposedly this can be easily
determined, but in reality no one ever seems to know
exactly how the market will perform.

Other questions which are likely to come up for discussion are:

1. The establishment of a common price level for
    natural gas.
2. The utility of the spot market to OPEC members.
3. The establishment of an automatic pricing formula
    tied in with world economic indicators.
4. The continued use of the Dollar as the currency
    for pricing oil.
5. A long-term strategy for avoiding the replacement
    of petroleum as an energy source.
6. The development of better mechanisms for channeling
    financial resources to developing countries.
7. The development of more downstream control of
    energy marketing on the part of OPEC members.

Ecuador will be the site of the meeting. Reports from
Quito indicate that preparations for negotiations are
almost complete.

The formal negotiations commence in the second session
for the MBA students, and in the fourth session for the
undergraduates. The room is arranged similar to the UN
Security Council, and each country is expected to have an
identification sign. The meeting is called to order, and
each country presents its opening statement. The chair-
person from the host country appoints a press committee
(to issue a press release after each session) and a
secretary (to keep a running record of the proceedings).
Procedural and substantive decisionmaking processes are
established, and subcommittees may be created. An agenda
is established, and discussion proceeds (punctuated by
recesses when needed) for two periods in the graduate
class and three periods in the undergraduate class. At
the conclusion of the negotiations a formal communique
must be prepared which is acceptable to all participants.
It is important that the negotiators be forced through
the process of negotiating the communique, because it is
at this point that the students realize how important
contract wording is for representing business relationships. A post-mortem of the negotiation follows the
final negotiating session. Exhibit 4 presents a sample
newspaper article based on an "official" press release
from the negotiators.

It has been found that the OPEC Simulation is effective
at facilitating learning in the following areas:

   Cultural Empathy -- The students study their countries, attempt to adopt their perspective, and stay
   fiercely in role. Seeing the world as a "Libyan"
   is highly instructive.

SAMPLE OPEC PRESS RELEASE

BEAVER COUNTY TIMES (Beaver, Pa.)   11-17-81

UPI, QUITO, ECUADOR, November 13, 1981. The semi-annual
meeting of OPEC opened here today at the Quito Hilton,
with Ecuador serving as the host country. Their role is
to chair all formal negotiating sessions. Ecuador
stated the ground rules as far as voting throughout the
sessions: A) voting for procedural questions requires
a simple majority, and B) voting on OPEC issues (such
as price controls) will require a unanimous vote by all
member countries. Opening statements from the 10
member countries present and guest Mexico followed next,
the randomly picked order being Ecuador, Nigeria, Iran,
Saudi Arabia, Venezuela, Iraq, Indonesia, Kuwait,
Algeria, Libya, and Mexico. Some of the major points
or goals stated by the countries in their opening
statements included:

   Ecuador - Seeks to better the foundation of the country, and will invest in Iraq. Nigeria - wants internal
   funds for financing. Iran - interested in political
   and economic aspects of oil. They protested against
   Iraq. Saudi Arabia - seeks to keep oil as a long-term
   energy source. Venezuela - looking to develop the
   country as a whole, wants "reasonable" oil prices.
   Iraq - concerned about the future, desires to get rid
   of the Dollar as the currency. Indonesia - projects
   to increase development, they seek $38 a barrel, with
   a $3 premium. They want investment from fellow member
   countries instead of from industrial countries.
   Kuwait - seeking steady production levels, and will
   follow Saudi Arabia. Algeria - seeks to keep prices
   high at this point. Libya - wants to redistribute the
   world's wealth, and OPEC unity through high stable
   prices. Mexico - looking to establish a Third World
   Petroleum Funding Organization by the Third World,
   for the Third World.

In order to aid countries in their decision as to
whether to let Mexico vote at these sessions, a 10-
minute open question period followed to let Mexico state
their policies. The resulting vote was seven opposed
and two favoring a Mexican vote. (Kuwait passed.)

The agenda is to be discussed at the next meeting, and
the substantive negotiations will commence.

   Country Analysis -- The students must utilize the
   analytical tools they have learned in other segments
   of the course related to market structures, socioeconomic trends, cultural analysis, balance of payments, and exchange rates, among other factors.

   Demand Analysis -- The world energy market must be
   studied, with projections made of future petroleum
   supply/demand, and the nature of competition with
   competing energy sources.

   Pricing Strategy -- The elasticities of energy supply
   and demand must be estimated, and the operation of an
   international cartel understood.

   Systematic Analysis -- The complex interactions
   between politics and marketing, and between multinational corporations and petroleum exporters and
   importers must be investigated.

   Negotiation Tactics and Strategies -- The personal
   and institutional factors which are important in a
   negotiating process must be learned by going through
   the motions of negotiating.

The OPEC Simulation has been run for twelve semesters.
It is sometimes run concurrently with another class which
conducts an "International Energy Association" negotiation
which is interactive with the OPEC negotiation. Student
evaluations of the OPEC simulation have been uniformly
positive. Exhibit 5 presents some of the responses from
an undergraduate international marketing class in evaluating the exercise.

EXHIBIT 5

EVALUATIONS OF THE OPEC SIMULATION

Question: "What is your general evaluation of
the international negotiation simulation exercise?"

Note: This was the last of ten open-
ended questions requesting evaluation
of specific aspects of the simulation.

Respondent 1: In general it was a very good idea.
Overall, I think everybody learned
very much. In particular, I think
it is a very good manner to learn
about OPEC and also about how to
negotiate. This has been the best
experience I ever had in a class in
college.

Respondent 2: I really like the negotiations. Not
only did I learn from it, but everyone
was so involved that it was really
fun.

Respondent 3: It was a different way of learning,
instead of just classroom lectures.
You become more involved in what's
happening, and you become familiar
with everyone in the classroom.

Respondent 4: It was great. A nice change from
lecture and note taking. I think
the things I learned from the negotiation will stick. It isn't something
that I will have to go back and
memorize. The learning was easy.

Respondent 5: This is definitely the best exercise
I have had in all my years at the
University. I learned a lot about
OPEC and also about negotiation processes. I feel it also got the
students to know each other better,
and that is always a plus. There
were many humorous moments to lighten
up the seriousness of many of the
discussions, and the atmosphere was
good. Keep this up.

Respondent 6: Once you get involved you really get
into it. I kept researching and
checking current events to keep up
on the latest developments so I
would be prepared for negotiations.
In a lecture situation I don't think
I would have been so motivated. I
really enjoyed the simulations!

NOTE: Complete evaluations and additional information
is available on request.

SUMMARY AND CONCLUSIONS

Current Events Negotiations Simulations provide a means
for enriching international marketing courses along
several dimensions:

1) student motivation to learn and integrate
   material is heightened,
2) experience is gained in conducting international
   marketing research,
3) the importance of the personal interaction
   dimension of international marketing management
   is directly experienced, and
4) the dynamics of the classroom are radically
   altered to create greater group cohesion.

The instructor acts as facilitator for self-learning
and peer instruction, with a deemphasis on his or her
role as an authoritarian transmitter of information.
Students learn by doing rather than by concentrating
on the memorization of facts. A sense of immediacy and
relevance of the material is imparted. This technique
is an alternative to traditional means of instruction
in international marketing which reinforces and extends
other components of the course such as lectures, case
analysis, and term paper research. The methodology
can be based directly on the instructor's own research
and consulting activities. CENS has been used successfully with both graduate and undergraduate courses.
It is particularly useful as a means for engaging the
interest and enthusiasm of evening students who are
working full-time, and who are often skeptical of
purely academic approaches to marketing education.

REFERENCES

Cateora, Philip R. (1981), "The International Marketing
Course," unpublished lecture given at the AACSB
Workshop in Internationalizing the Business School
Curriculum, University of Colorado at Boulder.

Fayerweather, John and Ashok Kapoor (1976), Strategy
and Negotiation for the International Corporation:
Guidelines and Cases, Cambridge, MA: Ballinger
Publishing Company, Inc.

Moore, Russell M. and Suresh B. Pradhan (forthcoming
1983), International Marketing, New York: McGraw-
Hill Book Company, Inc.

Stem, Donald E. Jr., Charles W. Lamb Jr., and Douglas J.
MacLachlan (1978), "Curriculum and Enrollment Trends
in Various Marketing Subjects at AACSB Schools," in
Research Frontiers in Marketing: Dialogues and
Directions, Subhash C. Jain, ed., Chicago: American
Marketing Association, 427-31.

ISSUES IN MARKETING EDUCATION IN DEVELOPING COUNTRIES

Ronald McTavish, Concordia University, Montreal
Christopher A. Ross, Concordia University, Montreal

ABSTRACT

The continued growth of developing countries has led to an
increasing demand for marketing educators in these countries. However the teaching of marketing in the developing
world poses a series of special problems or issues. These
issues are summarized under the headings of societal, student derived, and university derived concerns. Because of
the problems, the marketing educator needs a different orientation and focus from his counterpart in the developed
country. The paper discusses the problems, and suggests
means whereby marketing educators might improve their effectiveness in the developing areas.

INTRODUCTION

The governments of many developing countries now readily
acknowledge that economic growth and development require
the efficient and effective management of available resources. They also recognise that the use of managerial
skills and competence is a necessary condition if the quality of life of their peoples is to be improved. This recognition has led to a growth in the demand for skilled personnel in the different functional areas of management.
These areas include accounting, personnel management, operations management, finance and marketing.

As a result of the increased demand for skilled managerial
personnel, there has been a phenomenal growth in the number of African, Asian and Latin American universities
which offer degree programs in management and business as
an integral part of their curricula. This growth is not
limited to the increase in the number of institutions offering degree programs. Also significant is the increase in
the number of students enrolled in the different institutions. Between 1970 and 1980, for example, the number of
students enrolled in the Department of Management Studies,
University of the West Indies, Jamaican Campus, has more
than doubled (U.W.I. 1980). An equivalent increase in
size also occurred at the Faculty of Business Administration, University of Nigeria, Enugu Campus. Interestingly
enough the number of eligible applicants increased five-
fold between 1970 and 1976 (Onah 1981).

Many of the programs that have been developed are modelled
after those found in the industrialized countries of the
Western world, especially the United States and Britain.
Thus textbooks and, in many instances, course content, are
similar to what is utilised in the developed countries.
Furthermore, there is heavy dependence on professors from
the developed countries. Where nationals hold professor-
ial positions, these nationals have often been trained
abroad. This lack of indigenous course content, course
materials, textbooks and professors gives rise to certain
pedagogical concerns and problems, especially in the marketing discipline.

These pedagogical concerns are important for marketing because the discipline is now an intrinsic part of the management and business programs in many developing countries.
Eastern Asia is probably the area where such countries
have recognized more fully than elsewhere the need for improving marketing technology, though several countries in
Africa and Latin America have developed a similar awareness (U.N.I.D.O. 1975). One should recognize, however,
that "developing" countries cover a wide spectrum in terms

of such things as infrastructure, standards of living, extent of industrialization, population characteristics, purchasing power and traditions. Some "least developed" countries are a long way from embracing modern marketing ideas.
Still, the observation that marketing education in these
countries receives almost no attention (Hunt 1974) is no
longer valid since there are many recorded instances of
developing countries seeking technical assistance in the
marketing field (U.N.I.D.O. 1975). The concerns of this
paper are also pressing because of the conspicuous nature
of the discipline and its susceptibility to public comment
and criticism. The rest of this paper illustrates these
problems and concerns and makes some recommendations for
their solutions.

THE CONCERNS

These pedagogical concerns stem from three sources. The
first set of concerns is related to certain socio-economic
characteristics of developing societies. Included here is
the question of applicability of the traditional marketing
framework, with its emphasis on the four p's, to economies
where government control of economic activity is pervasive.
These cornerstones of marketing strategy still have validity in a more constrained environment, of course, but the
impact of such an environment on them demands special
attention. Another aspect of this concern are questions
about the responsibility of the marketing educator in countries with low levels of per capita incomes. Other issues
relate to the contrast between the traditional focus of
marketing education on manufactured products, relatively
large businesses, and situations where supply exceeds demand; and the reality of many developing countries in the
form of dependence on the export of primary products,
agricultural marketing, small businesses, and the shortage
of many consumer products.

The second set of concerns has to do with the nature of
the typical undergraduate student. As Terpstra (1978)
points out, in some newly independent nations, for example
in Africa, the tribe [or the village] is the unit of social
identification and interaction. Resulting modes of thought
and behaviour become woven into the cultural and the socialization patterns of childhood. These patterns are themselves experienced in a rural environment. Students coming out of this milieu thus have difficulty grappling with
the course material, reflecting as it does, largely unfamiliar values. Formal education, prior to university, may
only have limited success in alleviating the situation.

The final set of concerns is connected with the "anti-bus-
iness anti-free enterprise" culture which the writers have
encountered among social scientists in some universities
of the developing world. It is difficult to say how widespread this attitude is. But perhaps it is ultimately a
reflection of the historical disrepute of private business,
because of the identification with either foreign interests
or ethnic or religious minorities (Robinson 1972).

Before turning to these concerns in more detail, it is important to make brief reference to an important background
factor: the relationship between marketing and economic
development.

Marketing and Economic Development

Any discussion of marketing education in third world countries demands an appreciation of the general conditions of
underdevelopment and its relationship to marketing. Much
has been written on this topic, although relatively little
has appeared in the standard marketing journals. In some
instances marketing is seen as an adaptive process in its
relationship to economic development (Bartels 1981). In
other cases it is seen as a propagator of economic development (Drucker 1958). The issue remains unresolved, although
the answer seems to lie at some point between the two extremes.

In more recent times, development has come to connote the
ability of developing societies to control their environment and to shape their societies in the way they see fit.
The connection between marketing and this conception of
development is a relationship for which there are no clear
guidelines and for which most of the existing frameworks
are seriously inadequate. However, at the very least the
marketing educator can expect to face some very searching
questions on the "relevance" of the discipline. The greater
his familiarity with economic growth literature, the better
it is.

An important aspect of economic development is the relationship between production and marketing, particularly in
light of the chronic shortage of many consumer products in
developing countries. In some instances, for example
Kenya, wide ranging cuts in imports from foreign countries
have been imposed by the government. A familiar problem is
the idea, referred to by different writers (Taylor 1965,
Kotler 1974, Onah 1979) that in a country of scarcity, production and not marketing is the problem. The issue which
faces the marketing educator because of these shortages is
the role of marketing management and of the marketing manager. To what extent should marketing management respond
to the dollar power of the highest bidder? Furthermore,
to what extent should the marketer be guided by the philosophy of maximising consumer satisfaction which in this situation means minimising consumer dissatisfaction or even
disappointment? The role of "managing demand" obviously
becomes prepotent in such situations and it may mean foregoing short term profits in the interest of serving the
total market with some semblance of equity. Kotler and
Levy (1971) outline some recommendations which may be useful during periods of shortage, notably their idea of "demarketing" at such times. Educators need to be willing to
modify their outlook and approach to suit such problems.

These are some of the background factors against which marketing education must be considered. The rest of this
paper focuses upon the three specific problem areas or concerns which are significant for teaching in developing
areas.

Societal Concerns

In their efforts to control their own destinies and to
stimulate the development of their societies, developing
countries have tended to institute a system of economic
planning with all its concomitant controls. Some countries,
for example Tanganika and Guinea, have deliberately set out
to build a society along socialist lines (Berg 1968).
Other examples are India, and Grenada in the Caribbean.
Other countries, such as Trinidad and the Philippines, without any attempt at labelling or promulgating a definite
ideological position, have simply instituted economic controls in the belief that development, justice and equity
would be better served. These economic arrangements have
a profound effect on the teaching of marketing management.

Marketing management traditionally uses a framework which
places the manager in a position of control over the four
key variables of product, distribution, promotion and price.
But in developing countries some of these variables may not

be at all controllable. Many consumer products, for example, are subject to price regulation. These products
include refrigerators, stoves, and basic food products such
as chickens, milk, canned sardines and corned beef. Even
cigarette manufacturers are not exempt from price restrictions. Key agricultural inputs such as fertilizers are
often also regulated. The presence of controls is even
more disconcerting when many of the examples in the marketing texts are drawn from consumer products - the products which are most subject to price control. This is not
to suggest that prices in the developed countries may not
be at times "regulated" in less direct ways, only that control is far more pervasive in many developing countries.

But price is not the only variable subject to governmental
control. Distribution is also subject to certain offic-
ially imposed rigidities. The distribution of basic agricultural cereals and commodities through the State Trading
Corporation in Jamaica is a good example. This corporation controls the importation of these products and subsequently distributes the commodities on the basis of government plans and direction. As a further example, up to
the middle of 1980, in Jamaica, canned fruits such as
peaches and pears, and cold cereals such as cornflakes were
restricted to those retail outlets which catered mainly to
tourists.

Product and promotion are less subject to controls but they
are not completely immune. Manufacturers, for example,
are sometimes forced to utilise local raw materials in the
development of products even if the imported raw material
produces a superior product and hence greater consumer satisfaction. The withholding of foreign exchange from the
manufacturer is an effective mechanism for the enforcement
of these controls. This mechanism can also be used to prevent the use of sales promotional materials emanating from
abroad, or the making of commercials in a foreign country.
In many instances, therefore, the nature of the society
and the dominant values and ideologies which exist force
the marketing professor to modify basic assumptions which
may not even be questioned by students in the industrialized countries of the world. These modifications sometimes require a substantial reorientation of the discipline
since the four key variables are still important for ensuring consumer satisfaction; but, ironically, these variables are not all controllable by the marketer.

The low level and highly uneven spread of per capita income also raise particularly important and haunting issues
for the marketing educator. How do we set prices, for example? Should we advocate a policy of charging what the
market will bear? Or should we price at a "reasonable"
level when we submit our prices to the government for
approval? Along the same lines are the questions which
relate to advertising. Should we really be promoting
apples to the citizens of tropical Africa when tropical
fruits lie rotting on the ground? And what of expensive
wines? To what extent should marketers be keepers of the
values and expectations of the citizenry? These questions
are of significance in the industrialized countries; in
developing societies they are of supreme importance.

Some typical characteristics of many developing countries
are their heavy reliance on a relatively large civil service (partly due to economic controls) to run their economies, their reliance on the production and export of primary products, both raw materials and agricultural, and the
the predominance of small enterprises - less than 50 employees - in the manufacturing sector of the economy. Some
of these characteristics may be found in the industrialized
countries, but their pervasiveness and intensity in developing
countries make them unique. Consequently much of our marketing frameworks and concepts are not geared specifically to
solving the problems associated with these characteristics.

A different focus is therefore required by the marketing
educator if the subject matter is to be relevant. Ques-

tions which deal with the problems of marketing by Government Boards and Agencies, and the marketing of agricultural products by the small peasant farmer become particularly pressing. And what of the problems faced by the small businessman? Small business management is a specialized field deserving specialized treatment. But armed with the technology and the textbooks of the developed world, the professor of marketing is relevant to only about 10% to 15% of the economy - the manufacturing sector - and then only to the relatively large firms within this sector. This is not to imply that marketing teachers are insensitive to problems of small business. Nevertheless, in the developing world, small-scale enterprise is pervasive thus making it central, not peripheral, to the knowledge required by marketing educators.

The problems outlined above concern the role of marketing education in the developing economies of the world. The intention is not to deny the importance of marketing, but rather to emphasize the need to rethink and reshape the approach to the subject. It is a plea for relevance and not an attempt to destroy or attack the discipline.

Student Derived Concerns

The bulk of the students in the universities of the developing world are the sons and daughters of middle-class families coming predominantly from rural societies. This rurality has many implications for their approach to the material in the marketing course, and for their reaction to different teaching methods. Also important for understanding the students' approach to the subject matter is the nature of the formal education received, prior to entering an institution of higher learning.

The rurality of the students is manifested in their basic unfamiliarity with the world of commerce (Onah 1981). The extent of their knowledge, in many instances, is limited to simple purchase transactions in retail outlets. Many students have never been inside a factory or inside the administrative office of a business; many have never seen a full scale department store. The majority of the developing countries do not have stock markets and the use of credit cards is severely limited. Mail Order is often non-existent. In some countries there is limited circulation of newspapers and no television. If there is only one manufacturer of a product, then the notion of choosing among brands is irrelevant. On entering the university, many students have only savings accounts. These accounts define the limit of their familiarity with banking transactions. Quite often check writing is perceived as the prerogative of the rich and privileged. One of the authors made this discovery when faced with the total disbelief of a senior Master's degree student in accounting on the occasion of writing a check in the student's presence. In contrast the student of the industrialized society usually has some familiarity with business transactions and marketing institutions. He has an "industrial mind".

The marketing educator in the Third World thus has to instruct students who possess a "non-industrial" mind. What are the consequences of this for the conventional marketing class? To answer this question we must add a final ingredient. This is the prevalent attitude in developing countries that most people have little impact on the environment anyway, so why bother to attempt change. This is reflected in the Latin American saying of "Que sera, sera!" (What will be, will be!). Such factors taken together produce the result that, typically, students do not recognise the need for urgency in business; they do not recognise the critical role of planning, and the importance of time and deadlines in the development of a marketing strategy. Faced with a formal exposure to decision-making and planning, many fail to see the merits of detailed steps, anticipation of possible problems and contingency planning. Such attitudes can actually operate as barriers to indus-

trialization in an economy (Terpstra 1978).

Those student characteristics pose special problems for the instructor utilizing case studies as an instructional vehicle. Because of the student's lack of familiarity with commerce, the marketing educator first has to interpret the case material before the class can begin the process of analysis. This observation holds even with the use of indigenous cases. This is so because typically the indigenous case deals with companies and situations which are very similar to those which exist in North America. Cases at the University of the West Indies, for example, deal with the problem of upgrading the image of a local perfume brand, or the problem of structuring the sales force by territory, product or customer. For consumer behaviour, a case may illustrate the process and forces which influence the consumer when buying a car or house. Thus, it is not unfair to say that for many "local" cases, the casewriter portrays the situation from an industrial country perspective. In a developing country, the industrial segment of the society is precisely the segment with which the student is least familiar.

In addition to the tremendous influence which society, as a whole, has on the student, the kind of formal pre-university education followed by the typical business student does little to prepare him for the process of decision-making. Educational systems in many developing countries are patterned largely after those which existed in Europe prior to the second World War. The emphasis, in these systems, is on the process of analysis, understanding, and the development of the whole man - an emphasis with real merit. However no attention is paid to decision-making. Nunes (1977), a faculty member at the University of the West Indies, describes this phenomenon well with the observation that this educational system produces analysts but no decision-makers, thinkers but no doers, those who understand the meaning but not the meaningfulness. The marketing educator, thus, confronts the situation where students analyse cases quite well, but the decision is poorly conceptualised.

University Derived Concerns

Marketing, as an academic discipline, is an area of business that is subject to much criticism by social scientists. This is evident in almost every society but it is more so in developing societies. Business faculties and schools are often criticized for transmitting "false" values and ideologies which are unsuited to the progress of developing countries. Marketing - particularly advertising - because it is the most conspicuous of the business activities, is especially vulnerable to this criticism. The marketing professor often faces the situation of having to defend marketing as a socially useful activity to fellow academics, such as economists, sociologists and political scientists, and to their students. What is the role of marketing in a socialist society is a question which both authors frequently faced in practice in the developing world. Since education is not value free, what of the values and ideologies which all educators, consciously or unconsciously, convey to their students? (Nunes 1978). Are those values compatible with those which one would desire in a developing society? Can one really use textbooks and materials from an industrialized country and not convey to the student the dominant values of these cultures? These are penetrating questions, but questions which, nevertheless, must be faced.

CONCLUSION

The concerns and questions raised in this paper are important to all those who currently teach marketing in the third world. They are also important to those who may one day find themselves teaching in that environment. With increasing emphasis on the training of skilled business and

marketing personnel, more and more professors will find
themselves in this position. Kirpalani (1975) suggests
that third world governments are very much interested in
academics from developed economies working in their countries. How should such educators deal with the concerns
raised in this paper?

To begin with, the teaching of marketing in a developing
country requires a different orientation and focus from
what one would adopt in a developed country. The basic orientation required is that marketing is fundamentally the
managing of demand, the managing of exchange, the maximi-
sation of customer satisfaction, or the minimization of
customer dissatisfaction, against a background of strong
State involvement, with the purpose of achieving whatever
objective the organisation sets for itself. This orientation requires that societal concerns be explicitly considered in all marketing decision-making - macro-marketing
takes an equal place alongside micro-marketing in developing countries. Any academic who feels uncomfortable dealing with macro-marketing issues such as decision-making in
an economy of scarcity, economic development goals, a
broader concept of humanity, government controls and economic and political instability (Kizilbash 1974) would be
less than credible in the developing world.

Also important is the need to inject a heavy dose of export marketing, agricultural marketing, and, especially
small business marketing into the basic marketing course.
It is true that the notions of consumer behaviour, the marketing mix, and environmental analysis can contribute to
the solution of small business problems. But standard
text-book principles, especially if couched in terms of
mix optimization and advertising modelling, cannot be applied to this area without serious modification. Yet there
is evidence that very little attention is being paid to
small business problems in college marketing curricult even
in the industrial countries (Brannen 1981). Accordingly,
the many students who find themselves as marketing advisors
to their government on small business, export marketing
and agricultural marketing may be ill-equipped to deal with
the special problems of these areas.

Important, as well, is the need to take cognisance of the
non-industrial mind of the typical undergraduate student.
Educators must teach basic business terminology in addition to marketing concepts and approaches. Field visits,
if these are possible, could serve a useful purpose. For
example, visits to government marketing agencies, business
development offices, and manufacturing concerns as well as
discussions with marketing personnel can be useful.

And finally, it behoves the marketing professor to be
familiar with alternative societal, economic and political
arrangements and the role of marketing in such arrangements. Examples include the role of price in a socialist
economy; the role of distribution for agricultural products
in an economy of chronic scarcity; the nature of marketing
research in a society which does not have a research ethic
and which views asking questions with suspicion (Hunt
1974). One of the authors had the experience of being tak-
en for a spy, by a local businessman, while doing research
in one country. It is also important to be able to operate
in a society where many small business people believe that
a disciplined scientific approach to marketing is not necessary for success.

Above all, it is vital to recognise that Western capital-
intensive mass-marketing technology may be ill suited to
serve low- and middle-income consumers in the third world.
There is an increasing awareness that marketing improvements are most likely to flow from adapting the traditional marketing systems of the developing country. This notion argues that educators be familiar with these systems
in the first place (Meissner 1981).

What this paper suggests is that marketing educators must,
like all good marketers, be sensitive to their environment
and to the needs of their students. A great deal of product adaptation is needed, especially because one cannot
afford to use only the yardstick of profitability to gauge
the marketing success of organisations. In present day
developing countries, social productivity is also critical.

REFERENCES

Bartels, Robert (1981), Global Development and Marketing,
Columbus, Ohio, Grid Publishing Inc.

Berg, Elliot J. (1968), "Socialist Ideology and Marketing
Policy in Africa," Markets and Marketing in Developing
Economies, Reed Moyer and Stanley C. Hollander, eds.,
Chicago, American Marketing Association, 24-27.

Brannen, William H. (1981), "Market for Training Students
in Small Business Marketing," Journal of Marketing
Education, (Spring), 24-26.

Drucker, Peter F. (1958), "Marketing and Economic Development," Journal of Marketing, Vol. 22 (January) 252-259.

Hunt, Lawrence, J. (1974), "Marketing Education in Developing Environments," Combined Proceedings, Ronald C. Curham,
ed., Chicago, American Marketing Association, 642-646.

Kirpalani, V.H. (1975), "Opportunities/Problems in the
International Transfer of Marketing Skills/Technology to
the Third World," Combined Proceedings, Edward M. Maaze,
ed., Chicago, American Marketing Association, 285-288.

Kizilbash, A.H. (1974), "New Perspectives on Training Man-
agers for Developing Countries," Combined Proceedings,
Ronald C. Curham, ed., Chicago, American Marketing
Association, 647-650.

Kotler, Philip (1974), "Marketing During Periods of Shortage," Journal of Marketing, Vol. 38 (July), 20-29.

____________, and Sydney J. Levy (1971), "Demarketing, Yes,
Demarketing," Harvard Business Review, Vol. 49 (November-
December 1971), 74-80.

Meissner, Frank (1981), "Capital-intensive Supermarket
Technology can't serve needs of poor in Third World or
U.S.," Marketing News, (November 27), 13.

Nunes, Frederick E. (1978), "Management Education and
Ideology: The Experience and Concerns at the University
of the West Indies," Proceedings, Second National Conference on the Third World, Omaha (November), 16-18.

____________ (1977), "Education Analysis and Indecision,"
in Handbook, Kingston, Jamaica: Department of Management
Studies, University of the West Indies.

Onah, J.O. (1981), "Teaching Marketing Management in a Developing Economy - The Nigerian Experience," Unpublished
Manuscript.

____________ (1979), "Education and Training," Marketing in
Nigeria, Julius O. Onah ed., London, Cassell Ltd., 204.

Robinson, Richard D. (1972), "The Developing Countries,
Development and the Multinational Corporation," The
Annals of the American Academy of Political and Social
Science, 403 (September), 39.

Taylor, Donald B. (1965), "Marketing in Brazil," Fall Conference Proceedings, Peter D. Bennett, ed., Chicago,
American Marketing Association, 110-115.

Terpstra, Vern (1978), The Cultural Environment of International Business, Cincinatti, Ohio, South-Western Publishing Co.

United Nations Industrial Development Organization (1975), Marketing Management and Strategy for the Developing World, New York, United Nations Publications.

University of the West Indies (1980), Departmental Reports, Kingston, Jamaica.

CONSUMER COMPLAINING: EXPLORING EXPECTED AND DESIRED RESPONSES

Robert R. Harmon, Portland State University
Alan J. Resnik, Portland State University

ABSTRACT

A study was conducted in order to explore consumer expectations regarding the complaint resolution process. Consumers were found to view complaints as legitimate, have definite perceptions concerning appropriate responses and were optimistic that their desires would be met. This optimism was supported by managers' responses to the complaint situations. The managerial implications are discussed.

INTRODUCTION

The evolution of the practice of marketing has brought an increasing emphasis on making the consumer the focal point of consideration in strategy formulation. Consumerism has exacerbated the need for even greater sensitivity to the consumer. One result of this heightened consumer awareness has been the growing interest by marketing scholars and practitioners in measuring consumer satisfaction and dissatisfaction.

One obvious measurement of consumer dissatisfaction is the number of complaints directed toward businesses. In fact, the volume of complaints has increased substantially in recent years. Andreason and Best (1977) found that about one in five consumer purchases results in dissatisfaction and of those about half result in voiced complaints. Although these findings represent averages across product categories and are susceptible to overstatement, the results indicate the pervasiveness of the complaint problem. Overt complaining behavior is not only important from a consumer standpoint, it also is significant from a business perspective. Complaints viewed by management serve as important feedback from the marketplace. They provide information about the level of dissatisfaction with company offerings and actions, and they offer an opportunity to reduce dissatisfaction. In complaining, consumers are providing valuable information to decision makers. Hence, from a consumer perspective, complaints represent an important form of communication. The responses received affect attitudes toward the company and toward business in general.

Research on consumers' complaints has been directed toward models of complaint activities (Landon 1976), the characteristics of complainants (Warland, Hermann and Willitts 1975; Mason and Himes 1975; Liefeld, Edgecomb and Wolfe 1975; Zaichkowsky and Liefeld 1977; Andreason and Best 1977; Diamond, Ward and Faber 1976; Hill 1971; Whitford and Kimball 1975), complaining behavior (Gaedeke 1972; Thomas and Shuptrine 1975), company response to complaints (Boschung 1976; Resnik, Gnauck and Aldridge 1977; Kendall and Russ 1975; Pearson 1976), and procedures for handling complaints (Blum, Stuart and Wheatly 1974; Gaedeke 1972; Andreason and Best 1977). Why consumers complain was the focus of Richins (1979) and Bearden, Crockett and Graham (1979). Other studies have investigated prepurchase expectations and postpurchase satisfaction/dissatisfaction (Anderson 1973; Andreason 1977) and satisfaction in the purchase decision process (Westbrook, Newman and Taylor 1978).

The purpose of this study is exploratory in nature. Although the primary focus of the paper is on the consumer, it will address the following questions that have implications for marketing managers:

1. Do consumers perceive complaints as legitimate?
2. What response would be necessary in order to achieve satisfaction?
3. What are consumers' expectations that they will receive the desired response?
4. Which company representative should respond?
5. Do managers give consumers what they want?

METHOD

A geographically-dispersed sample of consumers were personally interviewed after reading each of five complaint letters. Letters were selected from the complaint files of a _Fortune_ 500 company selling diversified lines of consumer goods. All letters dealt with familiar building materials used for new construction and remodeling, such as paneling and plywood. The letters were shown to a sample of consumers who were asked to assume the role of the complainant. In this role they were questioned about their expectations and requirements relative to company responses given the nature of the complaints contained in the letters. Managers at the company were shown the same letters and asked to give a detailed account of what they perceived to be an appropriate response. Part of the study contained a comparison of consumer expectations and desires with the managers' responses.

Sample

The consumer sample was drawn from four cities in the United States: Chicago, Atlanta, Los Angeles and Portland, Oregon. The sample consisted of 122 homeowners (approximately 30 from each city) which provided a broadly-based sample with geographic and cultural diversification. Middle to upper-middle class homeowners were chosen because the results of Warland, Hermann and Willitts (1975) indicate this segment is the most likely to write complaint letters thus facilitating playing the requested role. This market segment was also heavily targeted for the home improvement products that were the subject of the selected complaint letters. Exhibit 1 contains a brief profile of the subjects.

EXHIBIT 1
CONSUMER PROFILE

Sex	Percent	Ever Written to Complain	Percent
Male	51.2	Yes	76.7
Female	48.8	No	23.3
	100.0		100.0

Age	Percent	Income/Family Income	Percent
18-24	9.1	Less than $10,000	7.3
25-35	39.7	$10,001 - $15,000	8.3
36-49	40.5	$15,001 - $25,000	24.8
50-64	9.9	$25,0001 - $35,000	45.0
65 & Over	.8	Greater than $35,000	14.6
	100.0		100.0

The managers' sample was chosen from among the branch managers belonging to the company division to which the complaint letters were addressed. A branch manager has profit and loss responsibility for up to 40 million dollars in a specified geographic area and receives training in complaint handling. Forty managers were asked to participate in the study by the divisional vice-president. All agreed to provide the necessary information. Despite the obvious involvement in the project, all managers were assured of the researchers' independence and of the anonymity of their responses.

Procedure

Consumer subjects were asked to read each of five letters and respond to a series of questions during an interview in their homes. The letters were all chosen from company files with the removal of company and complainant names the only alteration. After reading each complaint letter, the same series of questions was asked. The questionnaire alternated between five complaint letters and five questionnaires with a single series of demographic questions at the end. The order of complaint letters was varied to avoid any order bias. Although fabrication of the letters at first seemed desirable in order to control for extraneous variables, the authors ultimately decided that using genuine letters would add realism to the study. Two of the letters had relatively obvious solutions while solutions to two other letters were far from obvious. The final letter included a highly inflated request from the company. Letters and corresponding questions were pretested on a small group of subjects with characteristics similiar to those in the actual study.

Accompanying each letter was an evaluation report. These reports presented objective information about the substance of the complaint and were derived from on-site inspections. Subjects were asked to play the role of the person writing the letter and respond to the questions in that role. Role playing permitted the researchers to place subjects in a precisely defined situation without committing company resources or compromising recognized standards for ethical research. By placing the subject in a familiar situation many of the disadvantages of role playing can be minimized (Spencer 1978). The authors believe sample and product selection accomplished this minimization. The role playing format of Bem (1967) and Kogan and Wallach (1964) was used.

After reading each letter and corresponding report and completing the series of questionnaires, subjects were thanked for their participation and given a gift which was promised in advance (valued at about $10).[1]

The managers were administered their questions via mail. They were sent a set of instructions underscoring the need to respond as if it meant actual commitment of company resources. The letters and inspection reports were identical to the ones evaluated by the consumers. After each letter, managers were required to enumerate what the appropriate response to each complaint situation would be.

RESULTS

In order to assess whether the respondents were reacting to a general complaining situation or to the specific situation presented in each letter, responses by letter were evaluated. If the consumers did perceive differences in the letters and responded to them differentially, this finding would lend support to the effectiveness of the role-playing inductions. Table 1 shows that consumers did perceive differences in the legitimacy of complaints by letter (χ^2=310.1, d.f.=4, p <.001). Therefore, the subjects

---

[1]The total interview took about 45 minutes.

did perceive differences in the letters and apparently responded accordingly.

TABLE 1

CONSUMERS' PERCEPTIONS OF LEGITIMACY OF COMPLAINT BY LETTER

Complaint Legitimate?	Letter* 1	2	3	4	5	Total
Yes	114 (95.0)	20 (16.5)	115 (95.8)	50 (41.7)	19 (15.7)	318 (52.8)
No or Undecided	6 (5.0)	101 (83.5)	5 (4.2)	70 (58.3)	102 (84.3)	284 (47.2)
n =	120	121	120	120	121	602
% =	(19.9)	(20.1)	(19.9)	(19.9)	(20.1)	(100.0)

χ^2= 310.1, d.f.=4, p <.001

*Letters 1 and 3 had obvious solutions. Letters 2 and 4 did not suggest obvious solutions. Letter 5 contained the inflated request.

The consumers were asked if they believed that a response was necessary for each letter. Table 2 shows that consumers overwhelmingly expressed the necessity for the company to respond to each letter. Over 60% thought that a response was necessary for even the inflated request letter. It appears that when dissatisfaction is manifested in the form of a complaint letter, consumers believe that a response from the company is necessary.

TABLE 2

NECESSITY OF RESPONSE BY LETTER

Response Necessary?	Letter* 1	2	3	4	5	Total
Yes	112 (91.8)	100 (83.3)	110 (93.2)	98 (82.4)	73 (60.8)	493 (83.2)
No	10 (8.2)	20 (16.7)	8 (6.8)	21 (17.6)	47 (39.2)	106 (17.7)
n =	122	120	118	119	120	599
% =	(20.4)	(20.0)	(19.7)	(19.9)	(20.0)	(100.0)

χ^2= 38.2, d.f.=4, p <.001

*Letters 1 and 3 had obvious solutions. Letters 2 and 4 did not suggest obvious solutions. Letter 5 contained the inflated request.

Consumers were asked to specify the responses that they would need in order to satisfy the complaint. They were also asked to indicate the type of response they thought the company would most likely provide. These data are summarized in Table 3. The consumers in most cases were optimistic that the company would indeed respond in the manner desired.

TABLE 3

RESPONSES DESIRED BY CONSUMERS AND EXPECTED FROM COMPANY
(n=599 cases)

Method of Contact/ Emphasis of Response	Response Needed by Consumers	Response Expected from Company
Method of Contact		
Personal Contact	34.1%	38.6%
Contact by Letter	65.9	61.4
	100.0%	100.0%
Emphasis of Response		
Explanation	34.5	31.1
Apology	12.4	7.9
Replacement	18.5	13.0
Repair	3.7	6.4
Refund	12.2	5.4
Suggestion	13.8	6.1
Other	16.9	12.8
No Response	1.2	16.1

To further analyze the optimism or pessimism of the consumers, a comparison between desires and expected company response was made using the criteria in Table 3. The results of this comparison are presented in Table 4. The results confirm a general level of optimism. Over 60% expected to receive what they desired or more from the company. When the solution was relatively apparent (letters 1 and 3) subjects were more positive about their desires being met. When the solutions were less apparent (letters 2 and 4), however, or the request inflated (letter 5), there was considerably less optimism.

TABLE 4
CONSUMER DESIRES VS. EXPECTED COMPANY RESPONSE

Letter

	1	2	3	4	5	Total
Wrong Emphasis	15 16.0[a]	6 7.6	7 7.9	6 7.7	6 10.5	40 10.1
Less Than Desired	12 12.8	27 34.2	26 29.2	27 34.6	16 28.1	108 27.2
What They Desired	36 38.2	39 49.4	28 31.5	34 43.6	26 45.6	163 41.1
Greater Than Desired	31 33.0	7 8.8	28 31.5	11 14.1	9 15.8	86 21.6
n =	94	79	89	78	57	397
% =	23.7[b]	19.9	22.4	19.6	14.4	100.0

[a]Column percentages
[b]Row percentages

Another important question from a managerial perspective deals with who should respond to consumer complaints. As can be seen in Table 5, consumers do not have strong preferences concerning which corporate employee responds. This finding may be the result of a lack of knowledge of corporate structure on the part of the consumer or perhaps it may indicate that consumers do not care who responds as long as someone does.

TABLE 5
APPROPRIATE PERSON FOR RESPONSE
(n=599 cases)

Who Should Respond	Percent
Top Executive	11.9
Sales Representative	10.0
Manager	20.4
Customer Service	10.8
No Preference	46.9
	100.0

In order to investigate whether consumers' desires were in line with what managers would be willing to give, company managers were asked to evaluate the complaint letters and indicate appropriate responses for each. Comparisons of consumer desires and manager responses were then made for each consumer-letter-manager triad using the criteria in Table 3. This analysis quantitatively compared consumer desires with manager responses. The results are presented in Table 6. There appeared to be considerable agreement between consumers and managers concerning the emphasis of responses. Only 10.9% of the cases resulted in the manager giving the wrong response. They were somewhat more likely to make a wrong response when the solutions were not obvious (letters 2 and 4) or the request was inflated (letter 5).

There was a strong tendency for managers to give consumers what they wanted or more. This occurred in 65.5% of the cases. This was true even for the inflated request case. This liberal response pattern by managers is supportive of the overall level of consumer optimism about receiving a

TABLE 6
MANAGERIAL RESPONSES COMPARED WITH CONSUMER DESIRES
Letter

	1	2	3	4	5	Total
Manager's response has wrong emphasis	295 (7.3)*	334 (10.0)	341 (8.6)	532 (15.9)	386 (14.4)	1,888 (10.9)
Manager gave less than required	549 (13.6)	930 (27.8)	750 (18.9)	1,303 (39.0)	564 (21.0)	4,096 (23.6)
Manager gave what was required	714 (17.7)	1,271 (38.0)	256 (6.4)	1,061 (31.7)	1,324 (49.4)	4,626 (26.7)
Manager gave more than required	2,482 (61.4)	809 (24.2)	2,631 (66.1)	448 (13.4)	406 (15.1)	6,776 (38.8)
n =	4,040	3,344	3,978	3,344	2,680	17,386
% =	(2.32)**	(19.2)	(22.9)	(19.2)	(15.5)	(100.0)

* Column percentages
**Row percentages

satisfactory response. It may be that the act of writing and sending a complaint letter to a company represents a strong commitment on the part of the consumer to obtain satisfaction. Or, they feel that their complaint is reasonable and will be perceived similiarly and acted upon favorably by managers.

On the other hand, managers may find it easier to satisfy their personal goals by giving a liberal response designed to make sure the consumer is satisfied, rather than risk consumer dissatisfaction and face possible review by top management when the irate consumer presses the case.

SUMMARY AND DISCUSSION

The study has some important implications for managers who must deal with complaint situations. A major finding is that consumers who have made the effort to write a complaint letter expect a response, regardless of the relative merits of the case. The consumers are generally confident and optimistic that the complaint will be resolved satisfactorily. This finding may be an outcome of the consumerist movement that has encouraged consumers to demand their rights in the marketplace and to aggressively seek redress of grievances.

Consumers in this study had no clear preferences for who should respond to their complaints. It appeared that the actual response was more important than who responded.

Another important finding is the existence of considerable variability among consumers regarding the type of response necessary in order to satisfy a complaint. Standardized responses by management would not appear to be appropriate for all consumers. Managers were, however, able to minimize the incidence of incorrect responses as evidenced by the low (10.9%) wrong response rate.

It appears that consumer optimism concerning a satisfactory response to a complaint is justified by managerial action. Managers in over 65% of the cases gave the consumer what they wanted or more.

Company response or non-response to consumer complaints affects consumer confidence and satisfaction. A sincere effort by the company to rectify the consumer's complaint increases the consumer's confidence that the firm has a concern for his welfare, stimulates patronage and triggers favorable word-of-mouth. A non-response, on the other hand, undoubtedly deflates consumer optimism about the company's sincerity, magnifies the animosity the consumer already has toward the firm, tarnishes the company's image and acts to stimulate the spread of negative information via word-of-mouth.

In addition to improving its relationship with existing customers by responding to consumer complaints, the firm can benefit in other ways by being attentive to these unsolicited sources of information. The spacial separation of producer and consumer decreases the likelihood that difficulties with the actual use of a product will be detected rapidly. Complaints may also concern problems customers are having with dealers, services or parts, warranty and availability. Geographically dispersed markets may cause serious difficulties in these areas to go undetected for long periods of time. The orderly recording and handling of complaints can be an important means of discovering previously undiagnosed problems thereby alerting the firm to potentially dangerous market share declines.

The study underscores the importance of input from the complainant for effective complaint handling. A response, in and of itself, is a necessary but perhaps not a sufficient condition to satisfy a consumer's needs if the consumer perceives the response to be insincere, inadequate or contrary to his reasonable expectations. The study indicates the necessity for two-way communication to meet consumer desires and avoid excessive commitments of company resources for complaint resolution. The variability of desires and expectations emphasizes the importance of this type of system.

For many years American firms, having recognized the importance of consumer input in retaining old and attracting new buyers, have been training their sales people in the art of listening. These same listening skills must be developed with regard to mass markets. Consumer complaints are communication from customers which not only offer a firm the opportunity to alleviate dissatisfaction but provide managers with potentially valuable information. Clarifying policy regarding complaint handling has the dual benefit of insuring a more satisfied consumer and furthering corporate objectives.

REFERENCES

Anderson, R.E. (1973), "Consumer Dissatisfaction: The Effect of Disconfirmed Expectancy on Perceived Product Performance," Journal of Marketing Research, 10, 38-44.

Andreason, A.R. (1977), "Consumer Dissatisfaction and Market Performance," in Jagdish Sheth and Paul Leonardi (eds.), Proceedings of the Fourth International Research Seminar in Marketing. Senague-Abbey, Cordes, France: French Foundation for Management Education, 1-15.

___________ and Best, A. (1977), "Consumers Complain-- Does Business Respond?" Harvard Business Review, 56 (4), 93-101.

Bearden, W.O., Crockett, M. and Graham, S. (1979), "Consumers Propensity-to-Complain and Dissatisfaction with Automobile Repairs," in H. Keith Hunt and Ralph L. Day (eds.), Refining Concepts and Measures of Consumer Satisfaction and Complaining Behavior, Indiana University, 35-43.

Bem, D.J. (1967), "Self-Perception: An Alternative Interpretation of Cognitive Dissonance Phenomena," Psychological Review, 74, 183-200.

Blum, M.L., Steward, J.B. and Wheatley, E.W. (1974), "Consumer Affairs: Viability of the Corporate Response," Journal of Marketing, 38, 13-19.

Boschung, M.D. (1976), "Manufacturer's Response to Consumer Complaints on Guaranteed Products," Journal of Consumer Affairs, 10, 86-90.

Diamond, S.L., Ward, S. and Faber, R. (1976), "Consumerism: Analysis of Calls to a Consumer Hot Line," Journal of Marketing, 40 (1), 58-62.

Gaedeke, R.M. (1972), "Filing and Disposition of Consumer Complaints: Some Empirical Evidence," The Journal of Consumer Affairs, 6, 45-56.

Hill, L.B. (1971), "Socio-Psychological Dimensions of Complaints to Ombudsmen: A New Zealand Analysis," paper presented at the 6th Meeting of the American Political Science Association, Chicago, Il.: 100-109.

Kendall, C.L. and Russ, F.A. (1975), "Warranty and Complaint Policies: An Opportunity for Marketing Management," Journal of Marketing, 39, 36-43.

Kogan, N. and Wallach, M.A. (1964), Risk Taking: A Study in Cognition and Personality, New York: Holt.

Landon, E.L., Jr. (1976), "Consumer Satisfaction Research Orientation Differences Between Industry and Government," in H. Keith Hunt (ed.), The Conceptualization of Consumer Satisfaction and Dissatisfaction, Cambridge, Mass.: Marketing Science Institute.

Liefeld, J.B., Edgecomb, F.H. and Wolfe, L. (1975), "Demographic Characteristics of Canadian Consumer Complainers," Journal of Consumer Affairs, 9, 73-80.

Mason, J.B. and Himes, S.H., Jr. (1976), "An Exploratory Behavioral and Socio-Economic Profile of Consumer Action About Dissatisfaction With Selected Household Appliances," Journal of Consumer Affairs, 7, 121-127.

Pearson, N.M. (1976), "A Note on Business Responses to Consumer Letters of Praise and Complaint," Journal of Business Research, 61-68.

Resnik, A., Gnauck, B. and Aldrich, R. (1977), "Corporate Responsiveness to Consumer Complaints," in Ralph E. Day (ed.), Consumer Satisfaction, Dissatisfaction and Complaining Behavior, Indiana University, 148-152.

Richins, M.L., "Consumer Perceptions of Costs and Benefits Associated with Complaining," in H. Keith Hunt and Ralph L. Day (eds.), Refining Concepts and Measures of Consumer Satisfaction and Complaining Behavior, Indiana University, 50-53.

Spencer, C. (1978), "Two Types of Role Playing: Threats to Internal and External Validity," American Psychologist, 33 (3), 265-268.

Thomas, W.R. and Shuptrine, F.K. (1975), "The Consumer Complaint Process: Communication and Resolution," Business and Economic Review, 21, 13-22.

Warland, R.J., Hermann, R.O. and Willitts, J. (1975), "Dissatisfied Consumers: Who Gets Upset and What They Do About It," Journal of Consumer Affairs, 9, 152-162.

Westbrook, R.A., Newman, J.W. and Taylor, J.R. (1978), "Satisfaction/Dissatisfaction in the Purchase Decision Process," Journal of Marketing, 42 (4), 54-60.

Whitford, W.C. and Kimball, S.L. (1974), "Why Process Consumer Complaints? A Case Study of the Office of the Commission of Insurance of Wisconsin," Wisconsin Law Review, 613-690.

Zaichkowsky, J. and Liefeld, J. (1977), "Personality Profiles of Consumer Complaint Letter Writers," in Ralph L. Day (ed.), Consumer Satisfaction, Dissatisfaction and Complaining Behavior, Indiana University, 124-129.

INTERVENING VARIABLES BETWEEN SATISFACTION/DISSATISFACTION
AND RETAIL REPATRONAGE INTENTION[1]

James M. Stearns, Miami University
Lynette S. Unger, Miami University
Jack A. Lesser, Miami University

ABSTRACT

The evolution of the retail satisfaction/dissatisfaction literature has produced an empirically supported model which indicates a direct relationship between customer satisfaction and repatronage intention. This paper contends that other variables intervene in this seemingly axiomatic relationship. Specifically, this study focused on the four major reasons subjects indicated were sources of retail dissatisfaction and hypothesized that they may have varying effects on repatronage intention. Customers dissatisfied as a result of stock-out or price were shown to have significantly lower repatronage intentions than satisfied customers. Conversely, repatronage intentions of customers dissatisfied as a result of selection or employee service did not differ significantly from satisfied customers.

INTRODUCTION

The evolution of consumer satisfaction/dissatisfaction (CS/D) conceptualization and measurement has led to a recent emphasis on retail satisfaction. Early CS/D research focused on satisfaction correlates (for example, Mason and Hines 1973; Hughes 1977) and theoretical models explaining product satisfaction (Oliver 1977, 1979, 1980a, 1980b; Swan & Coombs 1976; Swan 1977; for reviews see Oliver 1980a and Westbrook 1981). Because the retailer is the contact point with the consumer, researchers have recognized the importance of studying retail satisfaction (Oliver 1981). Indeed, the entire Fall, 1981 issue of the <u>Journal of Retailing</u> was devoted to retail satisfaction, dissatisfaction, and complaining behavior.

BACKGROUND

This recent emphasis has resulted in several significant advancements in and expansion of the understanding of retail satisfaction. Oliver (1981) described a multiphase satisfaction program based upon the major components of the satisfaction process and discussed the latest developments in measurement including implications for retail satisfaction. Westbrook (1981) developed a conceptualization which included the identification and estimation of importance of components of retail satisfaction. Westbrook concluded that for a department store, components could be identified and importance weights estimated.

Particularly relevant for this research was a longitudinal study by Swan and Trawick (1981a) which investigated the applicability of the general disconfirmation model (Oliver 1980a) to the retailing area and extended previous research by Swan (1977). The basic model tested was (see Swan & Trawick 1981a for definitions of terms and a discussion of the model):

expectations
inferred disconfirmation→perceived disconfirmation→satisfaction→intentions

The Swan and Trawick research was significant because it tested and found support for the basic disconfirmation model in a retail service setting. The authors assert that "the expectation-disconfirmation model may apply over a wide domain of consumer satisfaction occurrences" (Swan & Trawick 1981a, p. 61). Additionally, the Swan and Trawick (1981b) study provides evidence for "the commonsense idea that satisfaction increases as the customer's expectations are fulfilled, that as satisfaction increases so do the customer's intentions to repatronize the establishment" (p. 140).

Although a direct relationship between satisfaction/dissatisfaction and intentions to repatronize may appear axiomatic, this paper provides evidence that when retail consumers are dissatisfied (negative disconfirmation), the source of dissatisfaction may intervene between satisfaction/dissatisfaction and intentions. In other words, in the most critical situation to retailers, namely when consumers have been negatively disconfirmed, whether intention to repatronize is significantly altered (lowered) may be dependent upon the primary store attribute that caused the dissatisfaction. The managerial implications of identifying the most frequent sources of dissatisfaction for a retailer and the sources that significantly affect repatronage intentions are obvious.

Additionally, this research provides some information about the "cost" of dissatisfaction in terms of dollar expenditures. Etzel and Silverman (1981) raise several questions that relate to this issue: 1) Should retailers attempt to satisfy all customers? 2) Is the cost of a dissatisfied customer significant? 3) Is an attempt to reduce the number of dissatisfied customers worth the effort? Although this research does not completely answer these questions, the results do provide information in one retail setting about the cost of dissatisfaction in terms of patron dollars expended.

HYPOTHESES

In this study six hypotheses are tested. H_1 explores the difference between satisfied and dissatisfied consumers in dollars expended on the store visit. H_2 examines the relationship of satisfied and dissatisfied consumers and repatronage intent. Rejection of H_2 would substantiate the last phase of the disconfirmation model discussed above. H_3 through H_6 examine the impact of source of dissatisfaction on intent to repatronize.

H_1: No difference in expenditures per store visit exists between satisfied and dissatisfied retail patrons.

[1] The authors wish to thank Bert C. McCammon, Jr. for the use of data collected by the Distribution Research Center at the University of Oklahoma.

H2: No difference in repatronage intent exists between satisfied and dissatisfied retail patrons across all product categories.

H3: No difference in repatronage intent exists between satisfied and dissatisfied retail patrons when stock-out is the source of dissatisfaction.

H4: No difference in repatronage intent exists between satisfied and dissatisfied retail patrons when selection is the source of dissatisfaction.

H5: No difference in repatronage intent exists between satisfied and dissatisfied retail patrons when service is the source of dissatisfaction.

H6: No difference in repatronage intent exists between satisfied and dissatisfied retail patrons when price is the source of dissatisfaction.

METHOD

As part of a larger study, 5895 shoppers of a leading discount department store chain were interviewed as they left nine representative stores. These stores were chosen to provide a typical cross-section of both large metropolitan outlets and stores in smaller cities. Oliver (1981, p. 27) suggested that an exit interview is particularly appropriate for satisfaction measurement, since it does not allow time for satisfaction to decay into attitude.

Customers were asked to indicate how satisfied they were with their visit to the store on a 5-point scale. The scale used was typical of single-item rating scales used previously in measuring consumer satisfaction (Westbrook 1980; Westbrook & Oliver 1981). Patrons who indicated they were moderately or very dissatisfied were grouped categorically as "dissatisfied" (n_1=285). Those who indicated they were very or moderately satisfied or neutral/indifferent were grouped as "satisfied" (n_2=5610). While operationalized differently, such categorical groupings have precedent in previous satisfaction research (Ash & Quelch 1980; Duhaime & Ash 1980).

Dissatisfied shoppers were further asked to provide the main reason for their dissatisfaction. Content analysis of this open-ended question revealed that the bulk of responses (88%) fell into four groupings: stock-out, inadequate selection, bad employee service or price too high. Distribution of these responses is shown in Table 1. Other response categories were provided, but did not have sufficient number of responses to be included in this paper. These four reasons for dissatisfaction correspond with major retail decision areas (Davidson, Doody, & Sweeney 1975) and with other empirical work on instore attributes (Krishnan & Mills 1979; Westbrook 1981), confirming their face validity.

Respondents were further asked to indicate total amount of purchase. Finally, subjects indicated the likelihood of making a purchase at the store (repatronizing) on a 10-point scale ranging from "would never buy" to "would always buy" across 27 product categories. These categories are listed in Table 3. Scales of this type are commonly used to measure future purchase intent (Engel, Blackwell, & Kollat 1978, p. 402).

TABLE 1

DISTRIBUTION OF REASONS FOR DISSATISFACTION

Reason	# of Respondents	% of Respondents	Average Purchase Amt.
Stock-out	127	44.6%	$3.08
Selection	86	30.2%	$1.98
Service	50	17.5%	$5.82
Price	22	7.7%	$1.41
	285	100.0%	

FINDINGS

To test the first hypothesis, a two-tailed t-test was used to compare expenditures between dissatisfied and satisfied patrons. As Table 2 indicates, the hypothesis was rejected. The dissatisfied group spent an average $3.10 per store visit, while the satisfied patrons' mean expenditure was significantly higher ($p < .01$) at $8.11.

TABLE 2

AVERAGE PURCHASE AMOUNT FOR SATISFIED AND DISSATISFIED PATRONS

	Dissatisfied (n_1=285)	Satisfied (n_2=5610)	Two-Tailed T-Test Probability
Average Purchase Amt.	$3.10	$8.11	< .01

The second null hypothesis was tested by using Hotelling's T^2 statistic to compare the mean repatronage likelihood scores of the dissatisfied and satisfied groups across all 27 product categories. As shown in the first column in Table 3, the T^2 statistic (T^2 = 40.8, d.f. 27, 5867) was significant at $p < .06$. While this level of significance is somewhat marginal, the finding supports the relationship between satisfaction and repatronage intent proposed and supported in the Swan & Trawick research: dissatisfied customers indicated lower product-general repatronage likelihood than satisfied customers. Two-tailed t-tests were further used to compare repatronage likelihood means between dissatisfied and satisfied customers within the 27 product-specific categories. In 16 of these categories, repatronage intent was significantly different for the two groups in the anticipated direction at $p < .05$.

To test the last four null hypotheses, dissatisfied customers were grouped according to their reason for dissatisfaction (stock-out, selection, employee service or price). Hotelling's T^2 statistic was again used to compare product-general mean repatronage likelihood scores of the dissatisfied patrons in each reason group versus the satisfied customers. The results are shown in Table 3. The third hypothesis was rejected, as the T^2 statistic comparing the repatronage intent of satisfied customers with dissatisfied patrons who cited stock-out as their reason for dissatisfaction was significant in the anticipated direction (T^2 = 48.5; d.f. 27, 5709; $p < .01$). Moreover, t-tests conducted for the individual product categories indicated satisfied consumers showed significantly greater repatronage intent than customers dissatisfied as a result of stock-out in 24 of the 27 product-specific categories.

The fourth and fifth hypotheses could not be rejected. Customers who expressed dissatisfaction as a result of selection did not display significantly different product-general repatronage intent in comparison to satisfied customers (T^2 = 36.0; d.f. 27, 5668; $p < .15$). Similarly, customers who expressed dissatisfaction as a result of ser-

vice were also not found to have different product-general
repatronage intent than their satisfied counterparts (T^2 =
27.3; d.f. 27, 5632; p < .51). By specific product category, patrons dissatisfied because of selection were found
to differ from satisfied customers on intent in 15 of the
27 product categories. Patrons who cited service as their
reason for dissatisfaction differed significantly from satisfied consumers in only 3 product categories.

Finally, Hypothesis 6 was rejected marginally (T^2 = 40.0;
d.f. 27, 5604; p < .07). Customers dissatisfied as a result of high prices were found to have lower repatronage
intent across all product categories than satisfied customers. In some 22 of the 27 product-specific categories,
dissatisfied patrons demonstrated lower repatronage intent
than satisfied customers.

TABLE 3

COMPARISON OF DISSATISFIED AND SATISFIED CUSTOMERS
ON LIKELIHOOD OF STORE REPATRONAGE

Product-specific (T-tests)	Total Dissatisfied (n=285)	Dissatisfied Grouped by Reason for Dissatisfaction			
		Stock-out (n=127)	Selection (n=86)	Service (n=50)	Price (n=22)
Small appliances	a[1]	a	b	-	a
Automotive supplies	b[2]	a	-	-	a
Candy	a	a	a	a	a
Boys' clothing	a	a	a	-	a
Girls' clothing	a	a	a	-	a
Infants' clothing	b	a	b	-	a
Men's clothing	a	a	a	-	a
Women's hosiery	a	a	a	-	b
Women's accessories	b	a	b	b	a
Costume jewelry	a	a	a	-	a
Women's clothing	b	a	b	-	a
Domestic goods	a	a	b	a	a
Decorative & gift items	b	a	-	b	a
Electronics	-	a	-	-	-
Fabrics	a	a	a	a	a
Footwear	a	a	a	-	a
Unfinished furniture	-	-	-	-	a
Hardware, plumbing & paint supplies	a	a	a	-	a
Kitchen accessories	-	b	-	-	a
Lawn & garden	b	a	b	-	a
Pets & pet supplies	b	b	a	-	b
House plants	a	a	a	-	b
Records & tapes	a	a	a	-	a
Sporting goods	a	a	a	b	b
Stationery	b	a	-	-	a
Craft & hobby supplies	a	a	a	b	a
Toys	a	a	a	b	a
Product-general (Hotelling's T^2)	40.8	48.5	36.0	27.3	40.0
	p < .06	p < .01	p < .15	p < .51	p < .07

[1]"a" indicates dissatisfied customers had significantly lower purchase intent
than satisfied (p < .05), based on a two-tailed t-test.

[2]"b" indicates dissatisfied customers had significantly lower purchase intent
than satisfied (p < .10), based on a two-tailed t-test.

LIMITATIONS

This research was conducted as part of a larger retail image and satisfaction study. The measurements, therefore,
were not optimum for all variables. Specifically, given
recent evidence about satisfaction scales (Westbrook 1980;
Westbrook & Oliver 1981), the five point satisfaction
scale may not have been ideal. The classification of satisfied
and dissatisfied consumers, although not without precedent,
was by necessity arbitrary. Although this research expands
the settings in which retail satisfaction has been conducted, measurements from only one type of store were presented. A wider cross section of retail types would have improved the generalizability of the research.

CONCLUSIONS AND IMPLICATIONS

The findings of this study suggest several major conclusions and implications. Although satisfied and dissatisfied consumers had different overall repatronage intentions, the source of dissatisfaction apparently intervened
between dissatisfaction and intention. This finding does
not contradict existing expectation-disconfirmation theory
and evidence, but does suggest a modification to the model
by pointing out the need to identify the source of dissatisfaction to determine the degree of impact on intention.
Stated differently, although there is the axiomatic direct
relationship between satisfaction and intention, that relationship may not be as simple as previous research has described.

In this research, stock-out and price as sources of dissatisfaction had significant impact on repatronage intention.
Conversely, consumers dissatisfied because of selection and
employee service did not have significantly lower repatronage intention than satisfied customers. The significant
sources of dissatisfaction appear consistent with the nature
of the retail stores used in this research. Subjects apparently were willing to be dissatisfied with bad employee
service and inadequate selection in a discount store setting. Unavailable merchandise and prices that were too
high were less acceptable in this setting. This finding is
intuitively appealing when one considers that this discount
store is a mass merchandiser that emphasizes low prices.
These findings, however, cannot be generalized beyond discount stores. Research is needed that identifies critical
dissatisfaction sources across a wide range of retail store
types. For example, one might expect that employee service
dissatisfaction may significantly affect repatronage intention for department stores.

This study has several significant managerial implications.
Because repatronage is the sine qua non of retailing, retailers need to know store attributes that are most likely
to significantly reduce intentions if customers' expectations are not met. A retail information system that carefully monitors customers' perceptions of determinant dissatisfaction sources could serve as a warning device for
declines in repatronage intentions. Also, by better understanding the importance of dissatisfaction sources, retail
managers will have better information upon which to base
decisions when scarce resources force tradeoffs among store
attributes.

Another significant managerial implication of this research
is the "cost" of dissatisfaction evidence. Dissatisfied
customers did differ significantly from satisfied patrons
in amount spent for the store visit. Retailers could combine this type of data with their proportion of dissatisfied customers to develop an expected value of total satisfaction. For example, if the retailer knows that 10% of
his customers are dissatisfied and the cost of a dissatisfied customer is $5.00 per store visit, he could easily
calculate the maximum possible sales increase if all

patrons are satisfied. This value would place a ceiling on expenditures to gain satisfaction much the same as the expected value of perfect information limits expenditures on marketing research. Also, this data partially answers the often-raised managerial question: How beneficial is resolved dissatisfaction (see Etzel & Silverman 1981, p. 128)?

This research presents evidence for a slight modification of the most commonly accepted retail satisfaction/dissatisfaction model and points out several significant managerial implications. As with most previous retail satisfaction studies, the research was limited in scope by the inclusion of only one type of retail store. The role of the retail setting and the associated implications for theory and practice remain questions for further research.

REFERENCES

Ash, Stephen B. and John A. Quelch (1980), "Consumer Satisfaction, Dissatisfaction and Complaining Behavior: A Comprehensive Study of Rentals, Public Transportation and Utilities," in Refining Concepts and Measures of Consumer Satisfaction and Complaining Behavior, H. Keith Hunt and Ralph L. Day, eds., Bloomington, Indiana: Indiana Univeristy, Division of Research, 120-131.

Davidson, William, Alton Doody, and Daniel Sweeney (1975), Retailing Management, 4th ed., New York: The Ronald Press.

Duhaime, Carole and Stephen B. Ash (1980), "Satisfaction, Dissatisfaction and Complaining Behavior: A Comparison of Male and Female Consumers," in Refining Concepts and Measures of Consumer Satisfaction and Complaining Behavior, H. Keith Hunt and Ralph L. Day, eds., Bloomington, Indiana: Indiana University, Division of Research, 102-111.

Engel, James F., Roger D. Blackwell, and David T. Kollat (1978), Consumer Behavior, 3rd ed., Hinsdale, Illinois: Dryden.

Etzel, Michael J. and Bernard I. Silverman (1982), "A Managerial Perspective on Directions for Retail Customer Dissatisfaction Research," Journal of Retailing, 57 (Fall), 124-136.

Krishnan, S. and Michael K. Mills (1979), "Dissatisfaction with Retail Stores and Repatronage Behavior," in New Dimensions of Consumer Satisfaction and Complaining Behavior, Ralph L. Day and H. Keith Hunt, eds., Bloomington, Indiana: Indiana University, Division of Research, 124-128.

Mason, J. Barry and S.H. Hines, Jr. (1973), "An Exploratory Behavioral and Socio-Economic Profile of Consumer Action about Dissatisfaction with Selected Household Appliances," Journal of Consumer Affairs, 7, 121-127.

Oliver, Richard L. (1977), "Effect of Expectation and Disconfirmation on Post-exposure Product Evaluations: An Alternative Interpretation," Journal of Applied Psychology, 62 (August), 480-486.

Oliver, Richard L. (1979), "Product Satisfaction as a Function of Prior Expectation and Subsequent Disconfirmation: New Evidence," in New Dimensions of Consumer Satisfaction and Complaining Behavior, Ralph L. Day and H. Keith Hunt, eds., Bloomington, Indiana: Indiana University, Division of Research, 66-71.

Oliver, Richard L. (1980a), "Conceptualization and Measurement of Disconfirmation Perceptions in the Prediction of Consumer Satisfaction," in Refining Concepts and Measures of Consumer Satisfaction and Complaining Behavior, H. Keith Hunt and Ralph L. Day, eds., Bloomington, Indiana: Indiana University, Division of Research, 2-6.

Oliver, Richard L. (1980b), "Theoretical Bases of Consumer Satisfaction Research: Review, Critique, and Future Direction," in Theoretical Developments in Marketing, Charles W. Lamb, Jr. and Patrick M. Dunne, eds., Chicago: American Marketing Association, 206-210.

Oliver, Richard L. (1981), "Measurement and Evaluation of Satisfaction Processes in Retail Settings," Journal of Retailing, 57 (Fall), 25-48.

Swan, John and Linda J. Coombs (1976), "Consumer Satisfaction and Product Performance: A New Concept," Journal of Marketing, 40 (April), 25-33.

Swan, John (1977), "Consumer Satisfaction with a Retail Store Related to the Fulfillment of Expectations on an Initial Shopping Trip," in Consumer Satisfaction, Dissatisfaction and Complaining Behavior, Ralph L. Day, ed., Bloomington, Indiana: Division of Research, 10-17.

Swan, John and I. Frederick Trawick (1981a), "Disconfirmation of Expectations and Satisfaction with a Retail Service," Journal of Retailing, 57 (Fall), 49-67.

Swan, John and I. Frederick Trawick (1981b), "Executive Summaries," Journal of Retailing, 57 (Fall), 137-145.

Westbrook, Robert A. (1980), "A Rating Scale for Measuring Product/Service Satisfaction," Journal of Marketing, 44 (Fall), 68-72.

Westbrook, Robert A. (1981), "Sources of Consumer Satisfaction with Retail Outlets," Journal of Retailing, 57 (Fall), 68-85.

Westbrook, Robert A. and Richard L. Oliver (1981), "Developing Better Measures of Consumer Satisfaction: Some Preliminary Results," in Advances in Consumer Research, Vol. 8, Kent B. Monroe, ed., Ann Arbor, Mich.: Association for Consumer Research, 94-99.

SOCIO-PERSONALITY AND DEMOGRAPHIC INFLUENCES
ON DEVIANT CONSUMER BEHAVIOR IN RETAIL STORES

Michael K. Mills, University of Southern California

ABSTRACT

This study examined the relationship between individual consumers' demographic characteristics, levels of trust, honesty, locus of control, and the incidence of five deviant acts in retail stores. The results show a significant relationship between each of these variables (excepting locus of control) and the incidence of deviant occurrences. Marketing implications are also discussed.

INTRODUCTION

Deviant consumer behavior is defined here as behavior in a retail store that society considers in conflict with previously accepted societal norms. Examples include shoplifting, price altering, destroying or damaging merchandise, marring in-store fixtures or restrooms, and fraud by consumers. Such behavior is rampant and is on the increase, and involves a substantial cost to merchants. FBI figures show that the cost of recovered merchandise alone from arrested shoplifters was approximately twenty-two million dollars in 1975 (Uniform Crime Reports 1975). FBI figures also show that the total estimated cost of shoplifting-related expenses totaled three billion dollars in 1959. A conservative estimate for 1982 would place this figure closer to twenty-five billion dollars.

Not only are the economic costs of deviant consumer behavior enormous, but given the tremendous involvement of all sectors of the economy in these acts, such deviant consumer behavior must also be classified as a rising social problem (Mills and Bonoma 1979).

Thus deviant consumer behavior is deserving of much marketing attention. Yet, there has been relatively little research done in this area. (Cameron 1964; Robin 1963; Cohen and Stark 1974; Wilkes 1978; Jolson 1974). Especially needed is research which contributes greater knowledge of the particular motivation underlying deviant consumer acts. It was the intent of the present study to address these issues.

METHODOLOGY

Retail shoppers were intercepted at mall locations in the Greater Pittsburgh SMSA. A total of 153 retail shoppers responded to a written survey instrument which utilized several demographic and socio-personality measures in an attempt to determine the specific relationship between these variables and the incidence of deviant acts. The specific measures of interest used in the study included Scott's (1965) Personal Value Scale on honesty, the Chun and Campbell (1974) short form of the Rotter (1971) Interpersonal Trust Scale, the Rotter (1967) I-E Scale, and seven demographic measures.

For purposes of the analysis, "deviant" consumers (n=74) were operationally defined as those who self-reported committing at least one of five retail-related deviant consumer offenses at least once. The five acts included destroying or damaging merchandise, the making of fraudulent returns, shoplifting, vandalism, and the making of fraudulent complaints. "Nondeviants," (n=79), based on the self-report measure, had never committed any of the deviant consumer offenses listed in the study.

Hypotheses

Two substantive hypotheses were addressed in the study:

Hypothesis One: In general, deviant consumers will not differ significantly from nondeviant consumers with respect to traditional demographic and personality measures.

Hypothesis Two: There will be a significant relationship between the occurrence of specific deviant consumer acts and certain of the investigated demographic and psychological measures.

RESULTS

Hypothesis One

The statisical test of this hypothesis was accomplished by means of a univariate analysis of variance performed on the means for the two groups (deviants-nondeviants) on the ten measures used in the study.

Table 1 shows the means and univariate F-ratios computed for each of the ten personality and demographic measures. As seen in Table 1, none of the calculated F-ratio values computed for the ten measures was significant. Thus, the statistical null hypothesis of equality of group means could not be rejected.

Hypothesis Two

To test this hypothesis, a series of chi-square analyses was made between each personality and demographic variable and variables representing the incidence of each of the listed deviant consumer acts. Because of low expected cell frequencies on the occurrence side, as well as for greater interpretability, these chi-square analyses utilized collapsed breakdowns on nearly all tests. The results are shown in Table 2 and will now be further discussed.

I-E. As shown in Table 2, the results of the chi-square analyses for I-E showed that there was a nonsignificant relationship between the I-E score and the occurrence of each of the five deviant consumer acts.

Trust. The second row of Table 2 shows the trust score to be significantly related to the occurrence of each of

TABLE 1

Social-Personality and Demographic
Comparisons for Deviant and Nondeviant Consumers
(Means)

Variable	Deviant	Nondeviant	Univariate F-Ratio (1,151 d.f.)
I-E	10.5270	11.4557	1.9935
Trust	31.8243	30.8101	1.2513
Honesty	8.1081	8.9367	1.3623
Sex	1.3919	1.4430	0.4065
Age	5.7162	5.5823	0.1391
Race	7.0946	7.7722	2.0657
Income	10.4189	10.2911	0.0508
Education	14.0946	14.3797	0.4119
Marital Status	1.9595	1.7342	1.6800
Occupation	6.6486	6.5190	0.0264

the deviant consumer offenses with the exception of shoplifting. Specifically, the computed chi-square tables showed that those with a high score on the trust scale were overrepresented with respect to destroying or damaging merchandise, committing fraudulent returns, and for the occurrence of vandalism and fraudulent complaints.

Thus, the relationship between trust and occurrences of deviant consumer acts was a significant one. Though interpretation of the relationship between "high trusters" and deviance is somewhat difficult, previous research has shown that high trusters often exhibit nonrational decision-making styles, perhaps partially accounting for these results (Bonoma and Johnston 1979).

Honesty. As Table 2 shows, the score on the honesty measure was significantly related to the occurrence of each of the deviant consumer acts, with the exception of fraudulent returns. Examination of each of the computed chi-square tables showed that, in each case, persons scoring in the low category on the honesty measure accounted for disproportionate percentages of these deviant occurrences.

Sex. Table 2 reveals that sex of respondent and occurrence of the listed deviant consumer offenses were related, except in the case of shoplifting, which had a nonsignificant relationship. More detailed examination of the specific chi-square table computed for each of these relationships showed that for each of the offenses of destroying or damaging merchandise, the making of fraudulent returns and complaints, and vandalism, males accounted for a greater percentage of deviant acts than did females. Sex of respondent was then, for the most part, significantly related to the occurrence of the listed deviant consumer offenses.

TABLE 2

Chi-Square Analyses (Social-Personality
Variables and Deviant Acts)

Soc.-Pers. Variables	Destroy/ Damage Merchandise	Fraudulent Returns	Shoplifting	Vandalism	Fraudulent Complaints
I-E	$x^2=4.270$ 2df(.1182)	$x^2=.091$ 2df(.9554)	$x^2=1.670$ 2df(.4337)	$x^2=4.362$ 2df(.1129)	$x^2=2.041$ 2df(.3606)
Trust	$x^2=9.839$ 2df(.0073)	$x^2=9.435$ 2df(.0089)	$x^2=4.743$ 2df(.0933)	$x^2=13.759$ 2df(.0010)	$x^2=8.743$ 2df(.0126)
Honesty	$x^2=20.153$ 2df(.0001)	$x^2=2.504$ 2df(.2589)	$x^2=20.529$ 2df(.0001)	$x^2=17.378$ 2df(.0002)	$x^2=8.049$ 2df(.0179)
Sex	$x^2=9.179$ 1df(.0024)	$x^2=10.154$ 1df(.0014)	$x^2=.718$ 1df(.3969)	$x^2=5.646$ 1df(.0175)	$x^2=8.274$ 1df(.0040)
Age	$x^2=33.717$ 6df(.0001)	$x^2=12.209$ 6df(.0575)	$x^2=23.104$ 6df(.0008)	$x^2=37.740$ 6df(.0001)	$x^2=12.927$ 6df(.0442)
Race	$x^2=31.011$ 2df(.0001)	$x^2=11.967$ 2df(.0025)	$x^2=15.152$ 2df(.0005)	$x^2=32.426$ 2df(.0001)	$x^2_1=.892$ 2df(.0043)
Income	$x^2=1.046$ 2df(.5925)	$x^2=5.476$ 2df(.0647)	$x^2=2.202$ 2df(.3325)	$x^2=3.238$ 2df(.1981)	$x^2=1.795$ 2df(.4074)
Education	$x^2=10.219$ 2df(.0060)	$x^2=.842$ 2df(.6564)	$x^2=13.995$ 2df(.0009)	$x^2=9.318$ 2df(.0095)	$x^2=.521$ 2df(.7704)
Marital Status	$x^2=8.049$ 3df(.0450)	$x^2=1.563$ 3df(.6676)	$x^2=14.088$ 3df(.0028)	$x^2=14.313$ 3df(.0025)	$x^2=4.880$ 3df(.1801)
Occupation	$x^2=24.472$ 7df(.0009)	$x^2=8.096$ 7df(.3242)	$x^2=15.256$ 7df(.0328)	$x^2=25.950$ 7df(.0005)	$x^2=9.921$ 7df(.1930)

Age. As shown in Table 2, age was significantly related
to the occurrence of each of the five deviant acts. More
detailed analyses revealed that in every case, those
under 20 years of age accounted for a greater percentage
of deviant acts than other age groups (though the
offenses of making fraudulent returns and complaints
showed nearly equal participation by those in the 45-49
year age group). The chi-square analyses thus tended to
support previous findings regarding the involvement of
the young age group in deviant consumer acts, although
the data have also shown the involvement of older members
in these acts, a factor not detailed in previous studies.

Race. As shown in Table 2, the race variable was significantly related to the occurrence of all of the listed
deviant acts. For the offense of destroying or damaging
merchandise, two groups (blacks and other nonwhites) were
disproportionately involved. Similar findings were also
revealed for the occurrence of fraudulent returns, while
shoplifting occurrences were significantly related to
black offenders. Additionally, members of the white
racial classification admitted to only small involvement
in vandalism occurrences, compared to high percentages
for blacks and other nonwhites. Blacks and other nonwhites also showed high involvement in the making of
fraudulent complaints. Thus, much of the stereotypic
findings of previous studies with respect to the race
variable were evidenced here as well.

Income. As shown in Table 2, subject income was significantly related to only one deviant consumer offense,
that of the making of fraudulent returns. Further
analysis of this relationship showed that the making of
fraudulent returns was significantly related to those in
the high income category. Fifty percent of the respondents in the $25,000-or-over category admitted to making
fraudulent returns at least once, compared to only 24.1
percent and 28.9 percent in the low- and medium-income
categories. Thus, this offense was disproportionately
engaged in by more affluent offenders.

Education. As Table 2 shows, level of education was
significantly related to the occurrence of three deviant
consumer acts--destroying or damaging merchandise, shoplifting, and vandalism. Conversely, level of education
was not significantly related to the occurrence of
fraudulent returns or the making of fraudulent complaints.

More detailed examination of each of the significant
relationships showed the following: for each of these
offenses (destroying or damaging merchandise, shoplifting, vandalism), respondents with a high school
education or less accounted for a greater percentage of
self-reported deviance than did respondents having higher
levels of education. Thus, the impact of education (or
lack of it) was seen in these results.

Marital Status. Examination of Table 2 reveals that
respondents' marital status was significantly related to
the occurrence of three deviant consumer acts--destroying
or damaging merchandise, shoplifting, and vandalism.
Conversely, respondents' marital status was not significantly related to the occurrence of fraudulent returns
or the making of fraudulent complaints.

An examination of the specific chi-square tables for each
of the significant relationships was conducted, and
showed that divorced respondents, as compared to other
groups, were disproportionately involved in these offenses. Thus, respondents' marital status was seen to
be related to the occurrence of vandalism, as well as to
destroying or damaging merchandise and shoplifting
offenses.

Occupation. The chi-square analyses aimed at discovering
the relationship between respondents' occupation and the
occurrence of the listed deviant consumer offenses used a
collapsed breakdown for both the occupation variables as
well as the deviant occurrences variables, due to low
expected cell frequencies in some cells. For the occupation variables, eight classifications were utilized.
These were (1) professional and technical workers, (2)
managers and administrators, (3) sales and service
workers, (4) clerical and similar workers, (5) craftsmen,
foremen, or similar workers, (6) operators and laborers,
(7) students, and (8) housewives, and unemployed or not
otherwise in the work force. The two-group breakdown for
the incidence of deviant acts was (1) never and (2) once
or greater than once. The last row of Table 2 lists the
computed chi-square values, degrees of freedom, and
significance levels for each of the examined relationships. As shown in Table 2, the respondents' occupation
was significantly related to the occurrence of destroying
or damaging merchandise, shoplifing, and vandalism, and
was not significantly related to the making of fraudulent complaints, or to the occurrence of fraudulent
returns.

An examination of the chi-square tables for each of the
significant relationships was undertaken, and revealed
that students admitted to a large percentage of deviant
acts. For example, with respect to vandalism, 41.7
percent of those in the student occupational class
admitted to vandalizing stores, compared to only minor cr
nonexisting percentages for other occupational groups.
For shoplifting, a similar set of findings was true. Ten
of 24 students (41.7) percent admitted to shoplifting, as
did 32 percent of unemployed individuals (8 of 24 individuals), compared to smaller percentages for other
occupational groups. Students and craftsmen also had a
high percentage of representation with respect to
destroying or damaging merchandise. Thus, the stereotypic findings of past studies utilizing apprehended
offenders are similar to these results, which showed
students to be actively involved in several deviant acts.

CONCLUSIONS

Given the enormity of the deviant consumer behavior
problem, it is imperative that a better understanding of
the motivational and correlational aspects underlying the
behavior be obtained. This study has addressed the
relationship between ten potential socio-personality and
demographic influences and deviant consumer behavior in
retail contexts. The study results have shown a significant relationship to occur between nine of the ten
variables and the occurrence of five deviant consumer
acts (the exception being the locus of control variable).

It is clear, then, that certain socio-personality and
demographic variables do influence the incidence of
deviant consumer acts. While previous studies have
pointed to the general nature of several of these relationships, this study has extended this preliminary work
by elaborating on the specific relationship between each
of these variables and five specific deviant consumer
acts.

The implications for improved understanding of this
behavior are clear. Further attention must be given to
the impact of these measures on consumer deviance, and
on strategies for better dealing with the needs and
motivations of consumers possessing these socio-
psychological traits.

REFERENCES

Bonoma, T. V. and W. J. Johnston (1979), "Locus of Control, Trust, and Decision-Making," _Decision Science_, 10, 39-56.

Cameron, M. O. (1964), _The Booster and the Snitch_, New York: Free Press.

Chun, K. T. and J. B. Campbell (1974), Dimensionality of the Rotter Interpersonal Trust Scale," _Psychological Reports_, 35, 1059-1970.

Cohen, L. and R. Stark, (1974), "Discriminatory Labeling and the Five-Finger Discount," _Journal of Research in Crime and Delinquency_, 2 (1), 25-39.

Jolson, M. A. (1974), "Consumers as Offenders," _Journal of Business Research_, 42 (January), 89-98.

Mills, M. K. and T. V. Bonoma (1979), "Deviant Consumer Behavior: New Challenge for Marketing Research," _Proceedings_, American Marketing Association Annual Conference.

Robin G. (1963), "Patterns of Department Store Shoplifting," _Crime and Delinquency_, 9, 1963-172.

Rotter, J. B. (1967), "A New Scale for the Measurement of Interpersonal Trust," _Journal of Personality_, 35, 651-665.

Rotter, J. B. (1966), "Generalized Expectancies for Internal Versus External Control of Reinforcement," _Psychological Monographs_, 80, (1 whole no. 609).

Scott, W. (1965), _Values and Organizations: A Study of Fraternities and Sororities_, Chicago: Rand-McNally.

Uniform Crime Reports (1975), Washington: Federal Bureau of Investigation.

Wilkes, R. (1978), "Fraudulent Behavior by Consumers," _Journal of Marketing_, 42, 67-75.

A CROSS-CHANNEL COMPARISON OF RETAILERS'
PERCEPTIONS OF DISTRIBUTION CHANNEL POWER*

James R. Brown, University of Nebraska, Lincoln
Edward F. Fern, Virginia Polytechnic Institute and State University, Blacksburg
Glenn T. Stoops, State University of New York, Buffalo

ABSTRACT

For marketing channel systems to compete more effectively with each other, it is becoming increasingly important for channel leaders to better utilize the sources of power available to them. An exploratory study of retailers' perceptions of channel leaders' sources of power found that leaders in more centrally coordinated channels utilized their power sources more effectively than those in less centrally coordinated ones.

INTRODUCTION

It is widely recognized that power is a critical element in the effective management of marketing channels (Heskett, Stern, and Beier 1970; Bowerson et al. 1980). Power in the distribution channel is defined here as the ability of one channel member to affect the decisions of other channel members (Robicheaux and El-Ansary 1975, Bowerson et al. 1980). To the extent that one channel member can successfully influence other channel members to work in a concerted manner, the benefits of scale economies and increased efficiencies can accrue to the channel system as a whole (Etgar 1978a). Thus, the effective use of power can lead to higher levels of performance for the channel system, as well as for the individual channel members.

Since some evidence indicates that more centrally coordinated channel systems achieve greater efficiencies than do less centrally coordinated ones (Etgar 1976a), channel leaders in the former systems may more effectively use their power than those in the latter systems.[1] To test this notion, an exploratory study was conducted to examine how retailers' perceptions of marketing channel power varied according to the different types of channel arrangements. Prior to presenting the results of that study, the different types of marketing channels will be briefly discussed. A review of the relevant literature will provide the overall hypothesis which guided the research design. After the results are presented, their implications for future research and managerial practice will be discussed.

TYPES OF MARKETING CHANNELS

Marketing channels may be classified in many different ways (Bowersox et al. 1980). A particularly useful scheme for categorizing these interfirm relations is according to their degree of centralized coordination (McCammon 1970). Marketing channels can be characterized as conventional, administered, contractual, and corporate channels where conventional channels are the least centrally coordinated and corporate are the most.

A conventional marketing channel is composed of independently owned and operated distributive institutions which have little concern about the overall marketing of the product or service (Stern and El-Ansary 1977). Independent channel members, whose marketing activities are coordinated through marketing programs developed by one or a small number of firms, are said to belong to administered channel systems (McCammon 1970). Contractual marketing channels occur where legal agreements or contracts are used to coordinate the efforts of independent channel members (Stern and El-Ansary 1977). Corporate marketing systems are those which combine "... successive stages of production and distribution under a single ownership" (McCammon 1970, p. 45).

POWER IN MAREKTING CHANNELS

Power in marketing channels has been the subject of an increasing amount of empirical research (Reve and Stern 1979). Researchers have utilized two complementary theoretical frameworks in their investigations: (1) the power-dependence approach first posited by Emerson (1962) and (2) the sources of power approach developed by French and Raven (1959). In the former perspective, power is a function of dependence where the dependence of channel member i upon channel member j is based upon j's ability to satisfy i's goals and i's ability to find a satisfactory substitute for j (Heskett, Beier, and Stern 1970). In the sources of power view, a channel member's power is determined by the means which he uses to gain power (Beier and Stern 1969). These means or sources of power have been classified as reward, coercive, legitimate, referent, and expert power (French and Raven 1959). Reward power is the ability of one channel member to mediate rewards for another while coercive power refers to the ability of one channel member to mediate punishments over another (Hunt and Nevin 1974). Power which results from one channel member believing that another has the legitimate right to influence him is termed legitimate power (Beier and Stern 1969). Referent power occurs when one channel member has a feeling of oneness with or wishes to identify with another (Hunt and Nevin 1974). Finally, expert power is based on one channel member's perception that another possesses some special knowledge or expertise (Heskett, Stern, and Beier 1970).

El-Ansary and Stern (1972), in a study of marketing channels for heating and cooling equipment, utilized both the power-dependence and the power sources approaches. Unfortunately, because power was apparently diffused in these channels, no significant relationships between power and dependence or between power and its sources were found. In a study of fast-food franchisees and franchisors, Hunt and Nevin (1974) found that the

---

*The authors wish to thank Arun Thangaraj for his valuable assistance in the design and execution of the data collection phase of this research.

[1] When channel leaders are able to increase other channel members' reliance upon leader-provided operational and marketing strategy assistances, the channel leaders are said to more effectively utilize their power.

franchisors' coercive power sources explained more of their power over their franchisees than did their noncoercive sources, i.e. reward, legitimate, referent, and expert power. Etgar (1976b) examined power relations between insurance companies and their agents. He found that insurers' power was positively related to the insurers' power sources and the agents' dependence, and that it was inversely related to the agents' power sources. In another study, Etgar (1978a) examined the relationship between channel leaders' power sources and retailers' perceptions of the channel leaders' power. His results indicated that economic power sources (reward and coercion) contributed more strongly to these perceptions of power than did noneconomic power sources (legitimate, referent, and expert). Finally, Etgar (1978b) investigated the sources of power used by leaders in conventional and contractual channels. He found that in conventional channels, channel leaders relied primarily upon product support power sources while those in contractual channels relied mainly upon their retail management assistances power sources.

The empirical study to be described herein is an extension of Etgar's (1978b) research in that a third type of channel arrangement, corporate channels, was also investigated. In addition, this study will take the sources of power perspective; therefore, the subsequent discussion will focus upon that view of power within marketing channels.

As mentioned earlier, the effective use of power in marketing channels is an important determinant of successful channel performance. More centrally coordinated channels appear to be more efficient than less centrally coordinated ones (Etgar 1976a). A plausible reason for this is that leaders in centrally controlled channels have more power sources available to them to effectively cooridnate their channels' activities. On the other hand, because channel leaders have more power sources available and have been able to effectively use them, they have been able to centralize the marketing programming of the distribution channel (Stern and Reve 1980).

Regardless of the direction of causality, it seems clear that channel leaders in more centrally coordinated distribution systems more effectively use their sources of power than those in less centrally coordinated ones. Accordingly, this is the overall hypothesis guiding the exploratory empirical study to be discussed.

AN EXPORATORY STUDY

To test the overall hypothesis developed above, an exploratory study was designed. A survey of 104 managers and assistant managers of retail outlets located in a large eastern metropolitan area was undertaken. Extensive pre-testing indicated that the sample should contain retailers which carried either cosmetics, stereos, cameras, furniture, fast foods, or shoes in order to insure that participants in conventional, contractual, and corporate channels were represented in the study. Pretesting also revealed that the retailers were not the channel leaders.

Trained interviewers, using a structured questionnaire, attempted to gather retailers' perceptions as to the power sources used by their major suppliers. The major supplier was defined as the supplier of the brand which accounted for the highest proportion of sales of a prespecified product class. The product class was chosen from the six listed above. Thus, the major supplier served as the reference point for the retailers' perceptions about their channel leaders' use of various power sources.

The items reflecting these power sources were generated from a review of the relevant literature and from pre-testing with retailers representative of the final sample (Exhibit). Responses were obtained on seven-point scales ranging from "1" (strongly agree) to "7" (strongly disagree). In addition to these fourteen power source items, an additional question was included to determine the type of channel which described the relationship between the retailer and his major supplier: "What type of an agreement regulates your relationship with the supplier of your leading brand?" Where the response to this question was "no agreement" or "informal agreement" with the supplier, the relationship was classified as a conventional channel. Where the response was "franchise contract" or "contract other than franchise," the relationship was considered contractual. Where "corporate policy" regulated the channel relationship, the channel was categorized as a corporate channel.

ANALYSIS

The various channel types were arrayed from conventional to contractual and, finally, to corporate channels and were assigned values of "1", "2", and "3", respectively. These three groups were used as the criterion and the 14 power perception items were used as the predictor variables in a discriminant analysis test of the overall hypothesis.

Because of incomplete data in some of the questionnaires, the final sample size included 55 retailers. A single discriminant function, accounting for approximately 71% of the total variance, was extracted (Wilks' Lambda = .285; Approx. F (28, 78) = 2.434; p <.01). This result along with the group centroids (see Exhibit) may indicate that there are significant differences in the use of the power sources across channel types. It appears that suppliers in corporate channels use their power sources to a greater degree than do those in contractual or conventional channels.

To further explore this finding, the standardized discriminant coefficients were examined. These coefficients indicate the unique effects of the various power perception items relative to each other (Morrison 1969) and are tested for statistical significance by the univariate F-ratio. As can be seen from the Exhibit, eight of the standardized discriminant coefficients were significant at the 0.05 level. These univariate F-ratios also indicated that the means for eight of the power perception items were significantly different across the various channel types.

Perrault, Behrman, and Armstrong (1979) caution, however, that the standardized discriminant coefficients may be misleading, particularly when there is some intercorrelation among the predictor variables. In such cases, Perrault et al. recommend using discriminant loadings which are analogous to factor loadings and testing the significance of the variables by using the stepdown F-ratio; both of these procedures control for the intercorrelation among the predictor variables.

Since a mild degree of intercorrelation was uncovered among the predictor variables in this study, the Perrault et al. (1979) procedure was followed. The size of the discriminant loadings indicate the strength of the relationship of the predictor variables with the discriminant function. The signs of the loadings in the Exhibit indicate that greater use of all of the 14 power sources is associated with more centrally coordinated marketing channels. As shown in the Exhibit, the number of power sources which significantly varied across the three channel types was reduced from eight to four when the stepdown F-ratio was used.

To examine the sources of these four significant differences, Tukey's HSD method of testing a posteriori analysis of variance contrasts was used (Winer 1971). The results indicate that retailers belonging to corporate channels felt that their suppliers' financial support for advertising was more essential to them than did those belonging to conventional channels (p <.05). Retailers belonging to corporate channels relied more heavily (p <.05) on their suppliers for management assistances than those belonging to either conventional or contractual channels. Retailers belonging to corporate channels felt more strongly (p <.05) than those belonging to either conventional or contractual channels that the supplier has the right to determine how the major brand is sold. Finally, retailers belonging to conventional and contractual channels relied less heavily (p <.05) on their suppliers for equipment and fixtures than did those belonging to corporate channels. None of the other possible contrasts was significant at the 0.05 level.

In general, suppliers (i.e. channel leaders) in more centrally coordinated marketing channels were seen as more effectively utilizing their sources of power than were those belonging to less centrally coordinated ones. In other words, retailers in centrally coordinated systems relied more heavily upon their channel leaders for such things as financial support for advertising, retail management assistances, and fixtures and equipment. These results, then, generally fail to reject the overall hypothesis underlying this exploratory research.

IMPLICATIONS

Although the above results are not conclusive, some tentative managerial prescriptions may be provided. First, if leaders wish to achieve the benefits of centralized channel programming, they must more effectively use the power sources they have available to them. By offering various incentives (e.g., retail management assistances, financial support for advertising) to retailers, suppliers may be able to enlist their cooperation in developing centrally coordinated marketing programs. In addition, channel members in centrally coordinated channels may expect certain incentives to be provided by the channel leader; if they are not provided, channel conflict may result.

Some limitations of this study should be overcome in future research so that more conclusive implications can be provided. First of all, the sample can be improved upon to include more products, a larger number of retailers, and retailers representative of other geographic areas. In addition, measures of the power sources can be improved upon to more appropriately reflect French and Raven's (1959) conceptualization. Finally, other constructs such as performance should be included to examine how the use of power sources can enhance marketing channel performance.

SUMMARY

An exploratory study was designed to test the notion that channel leaders in more centrally coordinated channel systems more effectively use their sources of power than those in less centrally coordinated ones. A discriminant analysis of retailers' power perceptions failed to reject this notion. Retailers in corporate channels relied more heavily upon their suppliers for retail management assistance, and equipment and fixtures than did those in either conventional or contractual channels. They also relied more heavily upon the suppliers' financial support for advertising than did those in conventional channels. Finally, retailers in corporate channels felt that the supplier had the legitimate right to determine how the product is sold compared with retailers in conventional and contractual channels.

The implications of these results and the limitations of this study were discussed. Future research should improve upon the weaknesses of this investigation so that a better understanding of marketing channel relations may be obtained.

REFERENCES

Beier, Frederick J. and Louis W. Stern (1969), "Power in the Channel of Distribution," in Distribution Channels: Behavioral Dimensions, Louis W. Stern (ed.), (Boston: Houghton Mifflin), 92–116.

Bowersox, Donald J., M. Bixby Cooper, Douglas M. Lambert, and Donald A. Taylor (1980), Management in Marketing Channels, New York: McGraw-Hill.

El-Ansary, Adel I. and Louis W. Stern (1972), "Power Measurement in the Distribution Channel," Journal of Marketing Research, 9(February), 47–52.

Emerson, Richard M. (1962), "Power-Dependence Relations," American Sociological Review, 27(February), 31–41.

Etgar, Michael (1976a), "Effects of Administrative Control on Efficiency of Vertical Marketing Systems," Journal of Marketing Research, 13(February), 12–24.

__________ (1976b), "Channel Domination and Countervailing Power in Distributive Channels," Journal of Marketing Research, 13 (August), 254–262.

__________ (1978a), "Selection of an Effective Channel Control Mix," Journal of Marketing, 42(July), 53–57.

__________ (1978b), "Differences in the Use of Manufacturer Power in Conventional and Contractual Channels," Journal of Retailing, 54(Winter), 49–62.

French, John R. P., Jr. and Bertram Raven (1959), "The Bases of Social Power," in Studies in Social Power, Dorwin Cartwright (ed.), (Ann Arbor, MI: Institute for Social Research, University of Michigan), 150–167.

Heskett, J. L., Louis W. Stern, and Frederick J. Beier (1970), "Bases and Uses of Power in Interorganizational Relations," in Vertical Marketing Systems, Louis P. Bucklin (ed.), (Glenview, IL: Scott, Foresman), 75–93.

Hunt, Shelby D. and John R. Nevin (1974), "Power in a Channel of Distribution: Sources and Consequences," Journal of Marketing Research, 11(May), 186–193.

McCammon, Bert C., Jr. (1970), "Perspectives for Distribution Programming," in Vertical Marketing Systems, Louis P. Buckliln (ed.), (Glenview, IL: Scott, Foresman), 32–51.

Morrison, Donald F. (1969), "On the Interpretation of Discriminant Analysis," Journal of Marketing Research, 6(May), 156–163.

Perrault, William D., Jr., Douglas N. Behrman, and Gary M. Armstrong (1979), "Alternative Approaches for Interpretation of Multiple Discriminant Analysis in Marketing Research," Journal of Business Research, 7: 151–173.

Reve, Torger and Louis W. Stern (1979), "Interorganizational Relations in Marketing Channels," Academy of Management Review, 4(July), 405–416.

Robicheaux, Robert A. and Adel I. El-Ansary (1975), "A
General Model for Understanding Channel Member Behavior,"
Journal of Retailing, 52(Winter), 13-20, 93-94.

Stern, Louis W. and Adel I. El-Ansary (1977), Marketing
Channels, Englewood Cliffs, N.J.: Prentice-Hall.

Stern, Louis W. and Torger Reve (1980), "Distribution
Channels as Political Economies: A Framework for Comparative Analysis," Journal of Marketing, 44(Summer), 52-
64.

Winer, B. J. (1971), Statistical Principles in Experimental
Design, 2nd ed., New York: McGraw-Hill.

EXHIBIT
Discriminant Analysis Results

Power Perception Item	Standardized Discriminant Coefficient	Discriminant Loading	Group Means			Univariate F-Ratio	Stepdown F-Ratio
			Conventional Channels	Contractual Channels	Corporate Channels		
Your supplier's financial support is essential for your advertising.	-.058	-.356	4.063	3.020	1.853	4.995[b]	4.995[b]
Your supplier insists that in order to purchase a desirable item you have to purchase additional items.	.076	-.256	6.460	6.240	5.399	2.213	0.748
Your supplier extends liberal credit for purchase of merchandise.	-.032	-.204	4.350	3.479	2.888	1.934	0.670
You rely a great deal on your supplier for assistance in bookkeeping, management and payroll procedures, training, etc.	-.159	-.580	6.607	5.818	3.615	11.479[a]	6.368[c]
Co-operative advertising with your major supplier has been greatly beneficial to your sales.	-.575	-.430	4.600	4.065	1.978	6.228[a]	1.079
Sales training provided by your supplier is of great help to you and/or your sales men in selling the product.	.169	-.230	3.765	4.348	2.589	2.470	1.592
The supplier has the right to determine how your major brand is sold.	-.417	-.478	6.300	5.045	3.231	8.487[a]	3.952[d]
The management assistance provided by your supplier has tremendously increased the efficiency of your operations.	-.077	-.339	5.465	4.858	3.462	3.987[b]	0.824
The product information provided by your supplier is of immense help to you in selling the product.	-.039	-.174	3.150	2.364	2.077	1.774	1.709
You have to sell a certain minimum number of units in order to retain your major supplier.	.234	-.049	6.455	5.873	6.040	0.647	0.453
Your supplier's reputation is an important factor in helping you sell your merchandise.	.074	-.382	3.250	3.500	1.077	5.332[a]	1.900
You rely a great deal on product information provided by your supplier.	.332	-.138	3.550	2.318	2.462	2.683	2.422
Your supplier provides most of the equipment and fixtures in your business establishment.	-.630	-.766	6.504	5.871	2.538	19.729[a]	3.827[e]
It is important for you to be associated with your major supplier because of his reputation.	-.218	-.290	3.049	3.545	1.768	3.640[b]	0.406
Group Centroid			-0.837	-0.395	1.957		

[a] p <.01 ; df = 2, 52

[b] p <.05 ; df = 2, 52

[c] p <.01 ; df = 2, 49

[d] p <.05 ; df = 2, 46

[e] p <.05 ; df = 2, 40

COORDINATION IN MARKETING CHANNELS: DETERMINANTS AND MECHANISMS

Dov Izraeli, Tel Aviv University, Israel
Michael Etgar, New York University, New York and The Hebrew University, Israel

ABSTRACT

A process model for selection of intrachannel coordinative
mechanisms is developed. It proposes that the structure
of intrachannel task interdependency shapes the coordination requisites which in turn determine the selection of
channel coordination mechanism. Characteristics of the
task environment moderate the relationship between type of
inter-dependency and the rigidity with which coordinative
mechanisms are applied.

BACKGROUND

Marketing channels behave as interorganizational systems
comprised of interdependent units or subsystems (McCammon
and Bates, 1965; Stern and El Ansary, 1981). Their interdependence makes coordination among units a necessary prerequisite for the continued operation and goal achievement
of the system as a whole, as well as of its parts. Coordination, "principally concerns the relationships between
tasks or activities which must fit in both form and time
into an integrated accomplishment of some overall goal or
purpose" (Litterer, 1965).

The problem of coordination in marketing channels has been
researched from a number of different perspectives although not explicitly conceptualized in terms of coordination. A number of studies focused on conflict among members of the marketing channel (Mallen, 1963; Lusch, 1976).
Other studied use of power and influence (Hunt and Nevin,
1974; Heskett et al. 1970; Etgar, 1976b, 1978) and of
hierarchies to coordinate channels (Etgar, 1976a; Stern
and Reve, 1980). Several studies examined the effects and
relative effectiveness of various institutional arrangements among channel members (Izraeli, 1972; Bucklin and
Carman, 1976).

No effort however has been made so far to present the
actual intrachannel coordination mechanisms. The purpose
of this paper is to present such mechanisms and discuss a
decision model for their selection which is based on an
approach developed by Thompson (1967).

THE MODEL

Figure 1 presents a process model for selection of coordination mechanisms by a channel member. The steps in
the process are: definition of tasks to be coordinated,
determination of intrachannel interdependence, and of
resulting coordination requisites. Those in turn lead to
selection of coordination mechanisms while the levels of
certainty, stability, and uniformity of the task environment moderate the scope of application of the coordination
mechanisms. The implementation of coordination mechanisms
results in performance outcomes which in turn supply the
feedback for future decisions.

Defining the Tasks

The term 'task' refers to any activity which is related to
the functioning of the channel. It may be used in a narrow
sense, referring to a basic activity (a simplex task), or
in a broader sense referring to a number of inter-related
activities (complex task). The most complex tasks are
those of the total channel system. Channel members responsible for similar, related or parallel tasks are linked
horizontally, vertically and/or diagonally with indivi-

FIGURE 1
MODEL OF INTRACHANNEL COORDINATION

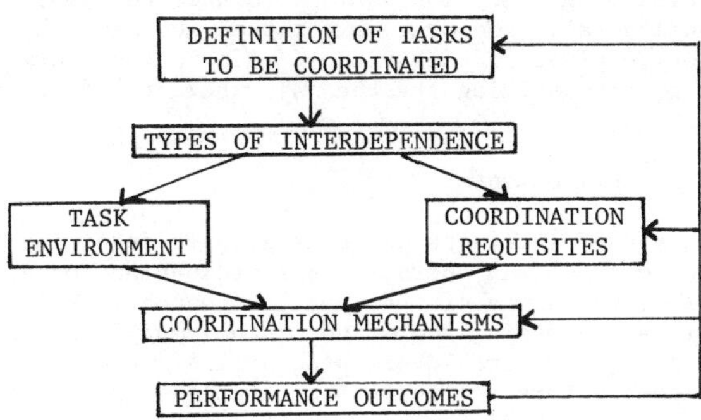

duals or groups in other organizations in the marketing
channel.

Types of Interdependence

The analytical framework developed by Thompson (1967) provides a useful basis for the classification of three types
of intrachannel dependencies: pooled, sequential and
reciprocal.

Pooled interdependence exists where the activities of each
member of the system affect the general welfare of other
or all participants, although no direct interaction necessarily occurs among them. In marketing channels, it is
essentially a 'horizontal' phenomenon, such as among retail units who well an identical product or product line.
Whether they are independent entities, or branches in a
retailing chain, successful or unsuccessful marketing of
one affects the success of others.

Sequential interdependence exists when there is a sequential link between task performers and the output of one
serves as the input for another. Sequential interdependence in marketing channels is essentially a 'vertical'
phenomenon prevalent in national brands channels where
producers 'feed' products to distributors without prior
orders.

In reciprocal interdependence the relationship between
units is symmetrical and two or more channel members 'feed'
each other, whereby the output of one serves as the direct
input for the task performance of the other. Reciprocal
interdependence exists for example, when a distributor and
manufacturer undertake to introduce a private brand, prepare a custom made product or service or undertake a joint
promotional campaign.

Coordination Requisites

The type of interdependence among tasks determines the
coordination requisites for their effective performance.
Under pooled interdependence, coordination is required
mainly for achieving economies of scale, derived from a
group of channel units operating as one system. This
allows the introduction of advanced technologies reducing
costs of transportation, warehousing, storage and data
collection and processing. Channel members can also benefit from lower promotion costs (per exposure) in the mass
media and from the advantages of a uniform product/brand
image (Etgar, 1976a).

Under sequential interdependence, coordination is required primarily to speed up intrachannel flows and reduce duplication. Channel flows may operate at a low level of efficiency because of inappropriate arrangements for making payments, filing reports and scheduling deliveries. Duplication of effort and resource investment appears due to desire of independence by channel members. For example, overstocking as a measure to cope with uncertainty is a frequent occurrence. Retailers overstock to secure supplies; wholesalers and manufacturers to be able to respond to sudden shifts in demand by retailers. Under reciprocal interdependence, coordination is required to facilitate and speed joint decision making. Since the members cannot act unilaterally and must make mutual adjustments of their respective plans and activities, information sharing and joint problem solving are the major targets of coordination.

The Task Environment

While type of interdependence is a major determinant in the selection of an appropriate coordination mechanism, degree of certainty of the task environment, influences decisions concerning the scope of their application, and the degree of desirable pre-programming. According to Lawrence and Lorsch (1967), each organizational subsystem interacts with a different segment of the environment which may differ radically in level of certainty and stability from that of other subsystems of the organization. Izraeli (1969) defined task environment as that segment of the environment with which channel units interact in the performance of simplex or complex tasks.

The characteristics of the task environment influence the level of flexibility required in the process of coordinating among tasks (Emery and Trist, 1965). Where the levels of certainty, stability, and/or uniformity are high, some mechanisms may be applied to a wide range of units and/or issues. Conversely, where stability and uniformity are low, the application of coordination mechanisms is constrained by the need for preserving discretion and authority to meet with contingencies as they arise.

SELECTION AND APPLICATION OF COORDINATION MECHANISMS

Each type of interdependence thus generates a different kind of a coordination requisite and calls for a different coordination mechanism. The conceptual framework for applying this approach to intrachannel coordination is presented in Figure 2. According to it, pooled interdependence requires coordination through standardization, that is, "establishing standard decisions, rules, and procedures." In sequential interdependence, coordination is achieved by planning, while under conditions of reciprocal interdependence it is derived by mutual adjustment.

FIGURE 2
SELECTING THE COORDINATION MECHANISM

TYPES OF INTERDEPENDENCE	COORDINATION REQUISITES	COORDINATION MECHANISM
Pooled	- Economies of scale	Standardization - Operational - Performance
Sequential	- Speeding flows - Reduction of duplication	Planning - Routinization - Formalization - Orchestration
Reciprocal	- Improved decision making	Mutual Adjustment - Direct contact - Liaison roles - Task forces - Integrating units

Standardization

In cases of pooled interdependencies, channel effectiveness can be greatly enhanced through economies of scale. Economies of scale are achieved through the introduction of standards which may apply to the mode of operation (process) of channel members or to their performance (outcome).

Operational standards refer to specified practices and procedures with which channel members are expected to conform. These may apply to a wide range of different tasks including merchandise display, product mix, promotion, transhipment formats, size of packages, number of units to a batch or physical decor of retail units (such as is prevalent in franchising organizations). The imposition of standards are necessary for achieving a uniform product/brand image, and organizational goodwill, while uniformity in preparation and packaging of products is necessary for economies of scale in handling, transporting and storing of products.

An underlying assumption in operational standardization is that the situations in which standard practices and procedures are applied, are relatively stable, repetitive and predictable, as well as uniformly so for all the units affected. Where this assumption does not apply, standardization may be counter productive. For example, consider a voluntary chain operating branches in areas with markedly different clientele. The imposition of standards on product mix, promotional campaigns (e.g. in terms of symbols projected) or price structure, may fit the demands of some customer segments but not others. In such cases, greater flexibility is required and less uniform standards.

Planning

Where tasks are sequentially interdependent, planning is the dominant coordination mechanism for increasing flow efficiency. Planning first of all involves routinization whereby intrachannel flows between channel members receive a repetitive and predictable form. Deliveries, sales, flows of information are routinized through specification of the day and hour of deliveries, the terms of sales, timing, content and format of reports, etc.

Second, planning requires formalization -- use of written procedures and directives in place of informal and ad hoc arrangements to increase the level of certainty in the interactions between channel members and permit more efficient use of resources.

Finally, planning requires orchestration of channel flows -- the overall coordination of one dyad arrangements with those in other dyads in the particular channel. Thus, to ensure channel wise efficient delivery scheduling, timing of deliveries by one distributor to his retailers must be coordinated with deliveries of other distributors. Similarly, a manufacturer who markets new products must orchestrate the appearance of his products in the various outlets.

The extent to which tasks may be routinized and formalized and plans programmed is influenced again by the task environment. When the environment of a task for one unit differs from that for another or it is changing and uncertain, greater flexibility must be retained and plans must be devised to permit adaptation to changing contingencies. For example, in a highly certain environment, planning delivery schedules may be accomplished through a computerized transportation model, designed at headquarters and detailing routes, time schedules and so forth. Where the environment is uncertain, the transportation plan must reserve discretion for the area manager and even for the truck drivers so that they may adapt to the changing contingencies.

Mutual Adjustment

Under conditions of pooled and sequential interdependence, information is primarily concentrated at a single point in the flow, permitting greater contralization of the coordination process. Under reciprocal interdependence, where each party to the interaction is a continuous source of needed information for the other(s) and where discretion is dispersed. Cordination is achieved through mechanisms of mutual adjustment, and joint decision making. Such mechanisms may be classified in terms of the degree of resource commitment required by channel members.

Direct contact between managers of separate channel units who jointly resolve a common problem is the simplest mechanism of mutual adjustment. It engages the resources of only two people who meet on an ad hoc basis as problems arise. When the volume of required contacts between two channel members increases, it becomes economical to set up a specialized position of liaison coordinators. Channel members may then assign employees from their own organizations to that task. An example of liaison roles is that of missionary salesmen employed in the insurance, pharmaceutical and the health and beauty aids industries (Stern and El-Ansary, 1981).

For channels composed of many organizations, the above mechanisms may be insufficient. Then task forces are set up. The task force is a temporary group established to handle a specific problem and operating only for the duration of the problem. When a solution is reached, the task force is dissolved. As certain problems consistently arise, task forces initially set up temporarily, become permanent. These groups are labelled teams.

Finally, coordination issues may be solved by creating a new role in the channel -- an integrating role or unit, with a formal (or legal) designation. Integrating units may be voluntary, established by channel members such as trade associations, chambers of commerce and industry lobbying offices (Assael, 1968), or government sponsored and endowed with statutory powers such as marketing committees or Advisory Boards in the U.S. or Marketing Boards in other countries (Izraeli et al., 1977).

Outcomes

The final stage of the model is that of evaluation of outcomes resulting from the use of coordination mechanisms. For each condition of interdependence, outcomes are assessed in terms of the extent to which they meet coordination requisites associated with it. The feedback requires a review whether the channel tasks have been properly defined, the appropriate mechanisms selected, and the constraints of the task environment well taken into account.

CONCLUSION

The division of labor and the dependencies that it generates, make coordination among tasks a crucial issue for marketing channels where the units involved are not subsumed under a single ownership and/or source of authority. This paper presents a model for intrachannel coordination based on the view of the channel as an intraorganizational system. The model does not consider the issue of which channel member(s) should be responsible for selecting and implementing coordination mechanisms. It suggests however, that their 'fit' with the requirements of the type of interdependence and task environment is a major factor in determining channel success. Not all coordinative mechanisms are suitable or optimal under all channel conditions; rather the model proposes that particular channel coordination requisites lead to selection of specific coordinative mechanisms. Selection of inappropriate mechanisms are very likely to have a detrimental effect on channel performance.

The paper, furthermore, does not distinguish among conventional, contractual or corporate channels. Intrachannel interdependence exists in all three types and all type of coordination requisites may be found in each.

REFERENCES

Assael, Henry (1968), "The Political Role of Trade Associations in Distributive Conflict Resolution," *Journal of Marketing*, 32, 21-28.

Bucklin, Louis P. and James Carman (1974), "Vertical Market Structure Theory and the Health Care Delivery System," in *Marketing Analysis of Societal Problems*, J. N. Sheth and P. L. Wright eds., Urbana-Champaign, Ill., Bureau of Economic and Business Research, 7-41.

Emery, F. and E. Trist (1965), "The Causal Texture of Organizational Environment," *Human Relations*, 18 (February), 21-32.

Etgar, M. (1976a) "Effects of Administrative Control on Efficiency of Vertical Marketing Systems," *Journal of Marketing Research*, 13 (February), 12-24.

__________ (1976b) "Channel Domination and Countervailing Power in Distributive Channels," *Journal of Marketing Research*, 13 (August), 254-262.

__________ (1978) "Difference in the Use of Manufacturer Power in Conventional and Contractual Channels," *Journal of Retailing*, 54, 49.52.

Hesket, J., L. Stern and F. Silver (1970) "Bases and Uses of Power in Interorganizational Relations," in *Vertical Marketing Systems*, L. P. Bucklin, ed., Glenview, Ill., Scott Foresman, 75-93.

Hunt, S. D. and J. R. Nevin (1974), "Power in a Channel of Distribution: Sources and Consequences," *Journal of Marketing Research*, 11 (May), 186-193.

Izraeli, Dov (1969) *Aspects of Integration in Marketing Channels*, unpublished doctoral dissertation, Manchester Business School, University of Manchester, England.

__________ (1972) *Franchising and the Total Distribution System*, London, G. B. Longman Group Limited, 147-163.

__________, D. N. Izraeli and J. Zif (1977) "Integrative Processes in Agricultural Marketing Channels," *Journal of the Academy of Marketing Science*, 5 (Summer), 203-219.

Lawrence, P. R. and J. W. Lorsch (1967) "Differentiation and Integration in Complex Organizations," *Administrative Science Quarterly*, 12 (June), 1-47.

Litterer, Joseph A. (1965) *The Analysis of Organization*, New York, John Wiley & Sons, 215.

Lusch, Robert E. (1976) "Sources of Power: Their Impact on Intrachannel Conflict," *Journal of Marketing Research*, 13, 382-390.

Mallen, Bruce (1963), "A Theory of Retailer-Supplier Conflict, Control and Cooperation," *Journal of Retailing*, (Summer) 24-33 and 51.

McCammon, B. C., Jr. and A. D. Bates (1965), "The Emergence and Growth of Contractually Integrated Channels in the American Economy," in *Economic Growth, Competition, and World Markets*, P. D. Bennett, ed., Chicago: American Marketing Association, 496-515.

Stern, Louis and Torger Reve (1980) "Distribution Channels as Political Economies: A Framework for Comparative Analysis," *Journal of Marketing*, 44:3, 52-64.

__________ and Adel El-Ansary (1981) *Marketing Channels*, Englewood Cliffs, N.J.: Prentice-Hall, Inc.

Thompson, James (1967) *Organizations in Action*, McGraw Hill.

POWER AND DEPENDENCY IN THE MARKETING CHANNEL: A METHODOLOGICAL NOTE

Robert H. Ross, Wichita State University, Wichita
Robert F. Lusch, University of Oklahoma, Norman
James R. Brown, University of Nebraska, Lincoln

ABSTRACT

This study examines the relationship between food brokers'
self perceived and attributed power and their corresponding
food wholesalers' dependence. In addition, the relationship between power and dependence in settings of both
agreed-upon and discrepant perceptions of power is investigated. This research indicates that significant relationships between power and dependence are present in both of
these situations.

INTRODUCTION

From both a managerial and theoretical standpoint, the concept of power has significant importance within a marketing
channel. Because of recognition of this importance, a number of empirical studies have been conducted over the past
fifteen years, dealing with the power-based behavioral interactions within a channel. These studies, summarized in
Reve and Stern (1979), have principally focused on mechanisms for developing a channel power structure, as well as
on ways of effectively utilizing power in achieving integration of channel effort.

As the subject of the study at hand, power will be defined
in the manner originally suggested by Stern (1965, p. 655)
as: "The ability of one member of a marketing channel for
a given product (or brand) to stipulate marketing policies
to other channel members." In terms of the mechanisms
through which one channel member may achieve power over
others, two primary thrusts are evident in the literature.
The first assumes that power is derived from a firm's
sources of power. This position, first discussed in a channel setting by Beier (1969), was based on a theoretical
conceptualization initially offered by French and Raven
(1969). The second assumes that power is a function of dependence; the theoretical basis of this notion was first developed by Emerson (1962). The power-dependence relationship will be the focus of this research.

The first empirical study to investigate the relationship
between power and dependence within a marketing channel was
that of El-Ansary and Stern (1972). Because of its importance as a foundation for further empirical work within the
channel, and as a source of a description of dependence for
the study at hand, a summary of some of the components of
El-Ansary and Stern's methodology, and some of their conclusions is in order.

Based on a procedure suggested by Lippitt et al. (1952),
El-Ansary and Stern (1972) argued that the presence of
agreed-upon perceptions of power within a channel can be
ascertained through a comparison of a channel member's attributed and self-perceived power. If attributions and
self-perceptions were equal or similar then power was
agreed-upon in the channel, otherwise there would exist discrepant perceptions of power.[1] El-Ansary and Stern then
adopt Emerson's description of the dependence of entity $\underline{P}$
on entity $\underline{O}$ as "(1) directly proportional to P's motivational investment in goals mediated by O, and (2) inversely

____

[1]El-Ansary and Stern (1972) refer to agreed-upon power
in the channel as "well-defined power" and discrepant perceptions of power as "diffused power".

proportional to the availability of those goals outside of
the O-P relationship" (Emerson 1962, pp. 31-32). Consequently, the authors hypothesize that if there are agreed-
upon perceptions of power within a channel, a negative relationship should exist "between a channel members' self-
perceived power over another member and the latter's perception of the former's dependence on him" (El-Ansary and
Stern 1972, p. 50).

El-Ansary and Stern's results indicated that there was an
absence of agreement between attributed and self-perceived
power. In their words, "...power was diffused in the channel: no power structure existed" (El-Ansary and Stern
1972, p. 50). Predictably, therefore, they were unable to
demonstrate a relationship between power and dependence,
assumedly because of discrepant perceptions of power within
the channel studied.

Two issues from El-Ansary and Stern's (1972) pioneering research emerge. First, is the additional expense involved
in obtaining power perceptions from both sides of a marketing channel dyad justified? In other words, do different
channel members have different perceptions of power and
dependence within the channel? Secondly, can the relationship between power and dependence be observed in situations
where there exist discrepant perceptions of power within
the channel? The objective of this research is to explore
answers to these two issues.

SELF-PERCEIVED AND ATTRIBUTED POWER

There are a variety of approaches to the measurement of
power relationships within an organizational setting. One
which has been applied in channel studies is the reputational approach, which consists of asking people "where the
power lies in organizations" (Pfeffer 1981, p. 54). To
strengthen the reputational approach, El-Ansary and Stern
added a measure of self-perceived power to the attributed
power measure. This approach operates on the premise that
while attributed power indicates the readiness of channel
member B to accept control from channel member A within a
specific area (i.e., the dependence of B upon A), unless
channel member A realizes that it has this control, it will
not be utilized (Lippitt et al. 1952).

Although this methodology is intuitively pleasing, a careful reading of Lippitt et al.'s original study causes one
to consider whether the use of the two measures is necessary. Lippitt's results indicate that (1952, p. 631) "An
analysis of the degree of correspondence of self-rankings
and attributed rankings of power...reveals a significant
positive relationship (p=.001)...." In general, the (subjects) who had power attributed to them perceived that
"power does not refer to the objective ability of one individual or group to control or influence the behavior of
another, but rather to the potential ability...as perceived
by the controlee or influencee" (Hunt and Nevin 1974, p.
188).

If the results suggested by Lippitt et al. (1952) are demonstrable in channel settings, channel members' evaluations of the power-dependence structure within the channel
would be similar. In a two firm channel, this situation
would preclude the need for obtaining measurements from
both sides of a channel dyad to ascertain the presence of a
power-dependence structure within the channel.

DEPENDENCY AND DISCREPANT PERCEPTIONS OF POWER

Traditionally, research into isolation of power structures
within a channel has focused on finding one "all powerful"
channel member who would control all or most policy areas.
This was the approach, for example, of authors such as
Ridgway (1957), Wilemon (1972), El-Ansary and Stern (1972),
Bucklin (1973), and Hunt and Nevin (1974).

Earlier in this paper, it was suggested that dependence was
a source of power and that dependence is created through
the capacity of one (powerful) channel member to exclusively mediate (or control) another channel member's ability to
achieve what the latter perceives to be important goals.
El-Ansary and Stern (1972) suggest that when there are discrepant perceptions of power, i.e., where power is diffused
within a channel, it will be impossible to demonstrate a
relationship between power and dependence. This conclusion
is predicated on the belief that if there is no single
agreed-upon powerful member of a channel, there can be no
strong dependency relationships found.

On the other hand, when channel members' perceptions as to
the distribution of power in a channel are in agreement,
the relationship between power and dependency should hold.
Thus far, this outcome has not been demonstrated empirically.

HYPOTHESES

Based on the previous theoretical development, a series of
hypotheses dealing with a specific channel dyad were generated to test the issues raised earlier.

H1. There is an inverse relation between the power channel
member B perceives or attributes itself to have over
channel member W, and B's perceived dependence on W.

H2. There is an inverse relation between the power channel
member W perceives or attributes itself to have over
channel member B, and W's perceived dependence on B.

H3. When there are agreed-upon perceptions of power in a
marketing channel dyad, there will be an inverse relation between the power channel member B perceives or
attributes itself to have over channel member W, and
B's perceived dependence on W.

H4. When there are agreed-upon perceptions of power in a
marketing channel dyad, there will be an inverse relation between the power channel member W perceives or
attributes itself to have over channel member B, and
W's perceived dependence on B.

H5. When there are discrepant perceptions of power in a
marketing channel dyad, there will be no relationship
between the power which channel member B perceives or
attributes itself to have over channel member W, and
B's perceived dependence on W.

H6. When there are discrepant perceptions of power in a
marketing channel dyad, there will be no relationship
between the power which channel member W perceives or
attributes itself to have over channel member B, and
W's perceived dependence on B.

RESEARCH DESIGN

Data and Sampling

The research hypotheses were tested with data gathered during a nation-wide study of the channel relations between
food wholesalers and food brokers.

A random sample of 100 matched wholesaler-broker pairs was
chosen from a national list of wholesalers and brokers
dealing in general grocery products. Selection criteria
assured that the participants dealt in the general grocery
trade, and that the members of each dyad did business with
each other. Of the 100 dyads contacted, usable questionnaires were received from both members of 54 dyads.

Measurement

Power was defined for purposes of this study as "the ability of one member of a marketing channel for a given product
(or brand) to stipulate marketing policies to other channel
members" (Stern 1965, p. 655). To measure the ability of a
food broker to "stipulate" marketing policy to wholesalers,
both parties were asked to evaluate the extent of the broker's influence over the wholesaler's decision making in
nine marketing policy areas. The term "influence" was
utilized in the questionnaire rather than "stipulate",
since the researchers felt that "influence" was more representative of the concept of power (Simon 1953, p. 503).

The nine policy areas, chosen from the literature as well
as from discussions with representatives of the dyads under
study, were: depth of inventory maintained; size of inventory maintained; price level; amount of sales promotion
undertaken by the wholesaler; product mix stocked by the
wholesaler; decisions regarding the wholesaler's addition
of new products; the size of orders placed by the wholesaler; decisions to delete products; and choice of transportation mode to be utilized on incoming shipments.

A five point rating scale was used to measure power (influence) on each of these nine areas. Broker's perception
of power was measured through use of a rating scale which
ran from "wholesaler has considerably more influence than
I" (rated a "1") to "I have considerably more influence
than the wholesaler" (rated a "5"). The wholesaler's perception of power was measured through use of a similar
rating scale which ran from "I have considerably more influence than the broker" (rated a "5") to "broker has considerably more influence than I" (rated a "1"). It is important to note that these power scales are hybrid--they
each contain self-perceived and attributed power. For
instance, "I have considerably more influence than the
broker" depicts a self-perception of power by the wholesaler; whereas, "Broker has considerably more influence
than I" depicts the wholesaler attributing power to the
broker.

Measurement for the presence of agreed-upon and discrepant
perceptions of power was undertaken in each of the marketing policy areas previously identified. This measurement
consisted of comparing the broker's and the wholesaler's
perception of the power (influence) held by the broker in
each of the nine areas. The results of this comparison are
included in Table 1. Agreed-upon power was found in five
of the areas: Depth of inventory maintained; size of inventory maintained; amount of sales promotion undertaken;
decision to add new products and choice of inbound transportation mode.

In the other four areas, there was no agreement regarding
the relative power enjoyed by the broker versus the wholesaler. These areas were: price level to be charged for
goods; decisions regarding the product mix the wholesaler
would keep; decisions regarding the size of order to be
placed by the wholesaler, and decisions by the wholesaler
to delete a product.

Dependence was described as being created by the ability to
exercise exclusive control over another channel member's
goal attainment. In the study at hand, broker dependence
was measured by averaging each broker's responses to the
following three items: (1) As an overall source of business to you, this (specific) wholesaler is: (responses
ranged from "not important" rated a "1" to "very important"
rated a "9"); (2) In case of a discontinued relationship

TABLE 1

A Comparison Of Broker's vs. Wholesaler's Perceptions
Of Power
(Using Wilcoxon's Matched Pairs Tests)

Wholesaler's Marketing Policy Decision Variable	Minus Ranks	Mean Minus Ranks	Plus Ranks	Mean Plus Ranks	Z	Significance Level
In Bound Transportation Mode	25	19.54	15	22.10	-1.055	.291
Depth of Inventory	14	17.86	22	18.91	-1.304	.192
Size of Inventory	13	19.85	24	18.54	-1.411	.158
Amount of Sales Promotion	16	19.03	25	22.26	-1.633	.103
New Product Additions	13	20.88	27	20.31	-1.862	.063
Price Level	8	15.25	23	16.26	-2.469	.014*
Product Mix	10	14.70	26	19.96	-2.922	.003*
Order Size	9	16.50	29	20.43	-3.220	.001*
Product Deletion	7	16.14	33	21.42	-3.992	.000*

*Significant difference between power perceptions at the .05 level or better.

with this wholesaler and the outlets he represents, the difficulty you would face in replacing his volume with one equally acceptable to you would be: (responses ranged from "easy" rated a "1" to "difficult" rated a "9"); and (3) In the event of a discontinuance discussed above, the negative effect on your profits would be: (responses ranged from "low" rated a "1" to "high" rated a "9"). A high value on this measure depicts high broker dependence on the wholesaler.

Wholesaler dependence on the broker was measured by averaging each wholesaler's responses to three similar items: (1) As an overall source of supply to you, this broker is: (responses ranged from "not important" rated a "1" to "important" rated a "9"); (2) In case of a discontinued relationship with this broker and the lines he represents, the difficulty you would face in replacing his lines with others equally acceptable to you (and your customers) would be: (responses ranged from "easy" rated a "1" to "difficult" rated a "9"); and (3) In the event of the discontinuance discussed above, the negative effect on your profits would be: (responses ranged from "low" rated a "1" to "high" rated a "9"). A high value on this measure depicts high wholesaler dependence on the broker.

RESULTS

Each of the six hypotheses was tested through use of a regression between type of power and the related dependence measure. The results of these regressions are reported in Tables 2 through 4, with each table reporting the results of the broker and the wholesaler's independent evaluation of the operative power-dependence relation.

The first pair of hypotheses investigated the relationship between power and dependence across all nine of the policy areas. This is the traditional, over-all relationship, which El-Ansary and Stern (1972) attempted to demonstrate. Although the coefficients of determination (Table 2) are fairly low in both situations, each of the regressions are significant, thus, supporting these two hypotheses, H1 and H2.

The second pair of hypotheses dealt with the power-dependence relationship in situations where agreed-upon perceptions of power exist in the dyad. The regressions in this case covered those areas upon which there was agreement between the broker and the wholesaler with respect to the relative power held by each. As might be expected in situations where there is a mutually agreeable division of power, Table 3 indicates that significant relationships were demonstrated between power and dependence. Thus, support was found for this pair of hypotheses (H3 and H4) although once again the R^2 in each regression equation is low.

The third pair of hypotheses indicated that there should be no significant relationship between power and dependence in situations where there are discrepant perceptions of power within the dyad. The regressions in this case covered those areas upon which there was no agreement between the broker and the wholesaler with respect to the relative power held by each. Interestingly, the regressions in both cases were again significant, thus forcing rejection of H5 and H6.

DISCUSSION

The results of this investigation are interesting and, for the most part, consistent. It appears possible, at least in channel settings where the participants might be expected to have the type of close working relationship demonstrated by many food brokers and wholesalers, that both sides of a channel dyad will evaluate the power-dependence relation similarly. This is evidenced in the present research by the existence of similar B_1 (slope) coefficients for each of the pairs of regressions (see Tables 2-4). In Table 2, the coefficient for the broker's evaluation of his power is -.233, while the wholesaler's evaluation in the same setting is -.249. In Table 3, the coefficient for the broker's evaluation of his power is -.137, while the wholesaler's evaluation in the same setting is -.158. Finally, in Table 4, the coefficient for the broker's evaluation is -.096, while the coefficient for the wholesaler's evaluation is -.091.

TABLE 2

AGGREGATE POWER AS A FUNCTION OF DEPENDENCY*

$\sum\limits_{i=1}^{9} P_{bwi} = B_o + B_1 D_{bw}$					$\sum\limits_{i=1}^{9} P_{wbi} = B_o + B_1 D_{wb}$			
B_o	B_1	t	R^2		B_o	B_1	t	R^2
38.204	−.233 (.083)	2.80	.138		41.480	−.249	2.41	.106

*P_{bwi} = Broker's perceived power over wholesaler on decision i.

P_{wbi} = Wholesaler's perceived power over broker on decision i.

D_{bw} = Broker's perceived dependency on wholesaler.

D_{wb} = Wholesaler's perceived dependency on broker.

TABLE 3

AGREED-UPON POWER AS A FUNCTION OF DEPENDENCY

$\sum\limits_{i=1}^{5} P_{bwi} = B_o + B_1 D_{bw}$					$\sum\limits_{i=1}^{5} P_{wbi} = B_o + B_1 D_{wb}$			
B_o	B_1	t	R^2		B_o	B_1	t	R^2
21.265	−.137 (.051)	2.66	.126		22.286	−.158 (.068)	2.33	.100

TABLE 4

DISCREPANT POWER PERCEPTIONS AS A FUNCTION OF DEPENDENCY

$\sum\limits_{i=6}^{9} P_{bwi} = B_o + B_1 D_{bw}$					$\sum\limits_{i=6}^{9} P_{wbi} = B_o + B_1 D_{wb}$			
B_o	B_1	t	R^2		B_o	B_1	t	R^2
16.939	−.096 (.042)	2.27	.095		19.194	−.091 (.045)	2.04	.078

The relationship between dependence and power in the areas
where agreed-upon perceptions of power exist in the channel
was found to be consistent with the hypotheses. Logically,
for dependence to be created, there should be mutual recognition of the ability to control. If this is not the
case, conflict and possibly dissolution of the channel may
be the result. The demonstration of a dependency-power
relationship in the dyad as a whole might be explained by
the existence of an agreed to distribution of power in
five of the nine policy areas. The development of agreed-
upon perceptions of power in a majority of the policy
areas was sufficient to create strong dependency relationships in the dyad as a whole.

Although weaker than the other findings, the result which
is inconsistent and difficult to explain is the existence
of a power-dependency relation in situations where there
are discrepant perceptions of power. In fact, this result
runs counter to El-Ansary and Stern's (1972) explanation of
their results, as well as to logic based on behavioral
theory. One possible explanation would suggest that even
in those policy areas where there is disagreement regarding the relative amount of power held by each member of
the broker-wholesaler dyad, the relationship between these
channel members is clearly enough perceived by both parties
that the balance of dependency is known. Another plausible
explanation for this result is that in each regression one
channel member's perceptions of power were regressed on
his perceptions of dependence. Although there may be disagreement across channel members as to the distribution of
power, a statistically significant relationship between
one channel member's perceptions of power and his perceptions of dependence might be expected. Thus, the second
reason for this finding is that it may be due to the unit
of analysis chosen. Clearly, this is an area in need of
further empirical investigation.

SUMMARY AND CONCLUSIONS

To researchers the results of this study suggest several
things. In channels research it may only be necessary to
examine one side of the dyad to determine the nature of
power and dependence relations within that channel. The
benefit of studying only one side of the dyad is the savings in time and money that would accrue to the researcher.
Power and dependence were, for the first time, empirically
found to be related as hypothesized in a situation of
agreed-upon perceptions of power. Thus, this research may
have provided the stepping-stone for future studies in
this area. Finally, this investigation has also presented
several opportunities for future research including: (1)
the generalizability of the findings to other channel settings, (2) the nature of the power and dependence relationship when there are discrepant perceptions of power, and
(3) the direction of causality between the constructs of
power and dependence.

For managers, the implications of this research are limited
as the objectives of the study were aimed at more basic
rather than applied findings. However, the interrelationship between power and dependence is one which should not
be ignored. The results indicate that channel members can
improve their power positions vis-a-vis other channel members by increasing the others' dependence upon them. The
reverse may also be true although it was not explicitly
tested in this research.

To summarize, the major objective of this study was to investigate the relationship between power and dependence in
channel settings with both agreed-upon and discrepant perceptions of power. In both settings we found a significant
relationship between power and dependence.

REFERENCES

Beier, Frederick J. (1969), "Power in the Channel of Distribution: An Interdisciplinary Approach," unpublished Ph.D.
thesis, The Ohio State University.

Bucklin, Louis P. (1973), "A Theory of Channel Control,"
Journal of Marketing , 37 (January), 39-47.

El-Ansary, Adel I. and Robert A. Robicheaux, Jr. (1974), "A
Theory of Channel Control Revisited," Journal of Marketing, 38 (January), 2-7.

El-Ansary, Adel I. and Louis W. Stern (1972), "Power Measurement in the Distribution Channel," Journal of Marketing Research, 9 (February), 47-52.

Emerson, Richard M. (1962), "Power Dependence Relations,"
American Sociological Review, 27 (February), 31-41.

French, John R.P. and Bertram Raven (1959), "The Bases of
Social Power," in Studies in Social Power, Darwin Cartwright, ed., Ann Arbor, MI: University of Michigan Press,
150-167.

Hunt, Shelby D. and John R. Nevin (1974), "Power in a Channel of Distribution: Sources and Consequences," Journal
of Marketing Research, 11 (May), 186-193.

Lippitt, Ronald N., N. Polansky, F. Redl, and S. Rosen
(1952), "The Dynamics of Power: A Field Study of Social
Influence in Groups of Children," in Readings in Social
Psychology, George Swanson, T.N. Newcomb, and E.L.
Hartley, eds., New York: Henry Holt, 622-636.

Pfeffer, Jeffrey (1981), Power in Organizations, Marsh-
field, MA: Pitman Publishing Company.

Reve, Torger and Louis W. Stern (1979), "Interorganizational Relations in Marketing Channels," Academy of Management Review, 4 (July), 405-416.

Ridgway, Valentine F. (1957), "Administration of Manufac-
turer-Dealer Systems," Administrative Science Quarterly,
1 (March), 464-477.

Simon, Herbert (1953), "Notes on the Observation and Measurement of Power," Journal of Politics, 15 (November),
500-518.

Stern, Louis W. (1965), "Channel Control and Inter-Organi-
zation Management," in Marketing and Economic Development, Peter D. Bennet, ed., Chicago: The American Marketing Association, 655-665.

Wilemon, David L. (1972), "Power and Negotiating Strategies
in Marketing Channels," Southern Journal of Business, 7
(February), 71-82.

FASHION LIFESTYLE AND CONSUMER INFORMATION USAGE:
FORMULATING EFFECTIVE MARKETING COMMUNICATIONS

Jonathan Gutman, University of Southern California
Michael K. Mills, University of Southern California

ABSTRACT

The research presented in this paper used a new theoretical framework and a behavior-specific conceptualization of lifestyle in examining the link between fashion lifestyle and consumer uses of information. The study results indicate that shoppers possessing different fashion orientations exhibit different usage and have different preferences in marketing communication. The findings of the study suggest that fashion lifestyle characteristics can be effectively used to reveal shoppers' needs for differing forms of marketing communications and to design more effective promotional strategies for reaching those groups.

INTRODUCTION

A growing amount of research has recently dramatized the usefulness of consumer lifestyles and shopping orientations as effective segmentation bases and as focal points for retail strategy formulation (e.g., Darden and Ashton 1974; Bearden, Teel, and Durand 1978; Moschis 1976; King and Ring 1980). Such studies have shown the importance of lifestyle in a variety of shopping contexts (including the fashion area), and have suggested the viability of the relationship between lifestyles and product usage (Reynolds and Darden 1971), store loyalties (Gutman and Mills 1981), and store image dimensions (King and Ring 1980).

Comparatively less attention, however, has been focused on the important area dealing with the usage of information by these lifestyle groups, or on the effective design of promotional campaigns aimed at these segments once they are identified (e.g., Moschis 1976). Yet this is a crucial area for research, as several studies (e.g., Bearden, Teel, and Durand 1978; Harris and Mills 1980; Hirschman and Mills 1979; Kassarjian 1965; Moschis 1976; Wilding and Bauer 1968) have suggested that consumers' differential use of various forms of marketing information may be related to their shopping orientations and behavior. It was the intent of the present study to investigate these relationships within the communication-dynamic area of consumer fashion behavior. Specifically, the study, which was approved by the Los Angeles Times and some of their major retail accounts, examined the relationship between consumers' fashion lifestyle and the specific sources of information used in learning about fashions and fashion promotions, consumer preferences for specific types of information, and their media usage habits.

METHODOLOGY

Sampling Procedure

Following an extensive pilot investigation in which the basic methodological issues of questionnaire construction,

item reliability, and response rate were pretested, a 28-page questionnaire was developed with retailer input and mailed to potential female respondents in eleven major geographic areas of greater Los Angeles. Selection of the areas to be sampled was done to approximate the major trading areas of the retail sponsors of the survey. Names of potential participants were randomly selected from zip codes in these trading areas. Subjects in each area were offered a $10 gift certificate redeemable at participating stores as an inducement for completing the survey. In all, 20,000 questionnaires were mailed out and 6261 were returned for a response rate of 30.5% (excluding 1,657 non-deliverables). Need for the data and an upcoming Christmas season prevented follow-up mailings. The low response rate as well as the geographic location of the study hurt the generalizability of the results somewhat, but any bias toward more fashion-involved respondents provides retailers with a group with which they have the utmost interest.

The Instrument

The instrument was composed of several sections, three of which are pertinent to the present study. These sections included a fashion-lifestyle battery, a fashion information usage inventory, and a general classificatory section.

Lifestyle Battery. The first section employed 67 clothing fashion lifestyle items, pretested in the pilot phase of the investigation, which served as input to the development of the lifestyle cluster groupings. Specifically, lifestyle, as defined in the study, referred to attitudes, interests, opinions, and behaviors of consumers as they relate to the acquisition of fashion merchandise. Thus, the concept of fashion-lifestyle used in this study was specifically grounded in shopping characteristics. Development was guided by a broad conceptual lifestyle framework put forth by Yang (1979), as well as by previous fashion research (King and Sproles, in press; King, Tigert, and Ring 1975; Tigert and Bourgeous 1975).

The lifestyle portion of the instrument was composed of two broad types of items--"General Shopping Behavior" and "Fashion Orientation." "Fashion Orientation" was to be the primary focus of the retail fashion spectrum along which respondents were to be clustered. The "Shopping Behavior" items were to serve the function of broadening out the dimensionality and profile completeness of the various retail fashion segments (only the Fashion Orientation terms will be discussed in this paper).

Fashion Information Usage Inventory. Respondents also were asked to indicate their exposure to various forms of fashion information (broadcast and/or print media, friends, in-store displays and so on), as well as how important they felt each of these information sources was to them in (1) determining the availability of fashion items they might wish to purchase, (2) as a source of fashion information useful <u>in learning about sales</u> or other promotions, and (3) in helping them <u>keep up with current fashion trends</u>.

<u>Demographics and Other Classificatory Data</u>. The final section of the instrument dealt with a number of demographic and other classification variables.

DATA ANALYSIS

A major aspect of the analysis was the development of clothing fashion lifestyle segments based on a limited number of items that could be easily employed in subsequent surveys.

Selecting the Appropriate Items

The model discussed above provided clear guidelines regarding the types of items desired for clustering respondents into clothing fashion lifestyle segments. Nonetheless, a factor analysis was carried out to provide a detailed view of the respondent's patterns of response to the items. The results of the factor analysis were treated as one input, along with the dictates of the model in determining desirable types of items.

As all the items were not to be used in future studies, the calculation of factor scores based on all the items was rejected as a course of action. Instead, following Gorsuch (1974, p. 238), each variable was examined to determine the factor upon which it had its highest loading. Each variable was then used to measure only one factor. In all, ten factors (item-groups) were developed as having relevance to either fashion or shopping orientation. The Fashion Orientation dimension important to this paper included four factors--leadership, interest, social importance, and anti-fashion attitude.

Developing Clothing Lifestyle Segments

Two criteria dominated the search for clothing fashion lifestyle clusters: reproducibility and interpretability. Accordingly, six subsamples of 150 each were selected from the total sample. Separate cluster analyses were run on each subsample using the SAS cluster program (SAS, 1979) with the standardized scores for each respondent on the four fashion-orientation factors as input data. The resulting clusters in each subsample were searched for reoccurring patterns. And, the patterns which did reoccur were checked to see if they could be logically related to one another in one coherent overall pattern (e.g., the fashion spectrum). Seven cluster profiles met these criteria and were used as target profiles in the SAS Fastclus program.

RESULTS

Explanation of Clothing Fashion Lifestyle Segments

Table 1 show the target profiles along with the resulting profile scores for these segments on the fashion-orientation factors. A review of the talbes makes it evident that for all segments, the acutal profiles (discussed below) were practically identical to the initial target profiles (the largest divergence occurred with respect to the followers group).

TABLE 1
STANDARDIZED SCORES ON FOUR FACTORS FOR CLOTHING-FASHION LIFE-STYLE TARGET PROFILES AND RESULTING CLUSTERS

Segment	Percent (6261)	Fashion Leadership	Fashion Interest	Fashion Importance	Anti-Fashion Attitude
Leaders	14.0				
Target		1.50	1.50	0.80	-0.75
Actual		1.36	1.32	0.76	-0.74
Followers	8.3				
Target		-0.35	1.00	0.80	-1.50
Actual		0.02	0.50	0.75	-1.34
Independents	10.4				
Target		1.50	1.00	0.75	1.25
Actual		1.13	0.90	0.75	0.91
Neutrals	23.6				
Target		0.00	0.00	-0.40	-0.30
Actual		0.14	0.14	-0.30	-0.33
Uninvolveds	8.7				
Target		-1.00	-1.00	-1.25	-0.90
Actual		-0.98	-0.94	-1.10	-0.90
Negatives	21.8				
Target		-0.60	-0.60	0.30	0.70
Actual		-0.57	-0.58	0.44	0.67
Rejectors	13.2				
Target		-1.00	-1.00	-1.30	0.85
Actual		-0.97	-1.07	-1.35	0.96

As shown in the table, the actual fashion segments which emerged (and their interpretation) included the following seven profiles:

<u>Leaders</u>: As shown in Table 1, leaders scored high on fashion leadership, interest, and importance, and scored low on anti-fashion attitudes.

<u>Followers</u>: The followers exhibited a similar profile to the leaders but obviously had a lower score on the leadership dimension. This group emulates the leaders need these followers--it's no fun being a leader without a following).

<u>Independents</u>: A review of Table 1 shows that independents also are fashion-aware but differ from the above two groups in that they hold strong anti-fashion attitudes. Independents are interested in fashion but resent the "fashion establishment" dictating tests to them.

<u>Neutrals</u>: Table 1 shows that the neutrals are true to their label--they scored in the neutral range on all the fashion orientation factors. This group does not regard fashion as particularly important, but neither do they hold anti-fashion attitudes.

<u>Uninvolveds</u>: The uninvolveds do not invest any affect in fashion. Their scores showed no desire for leadership, as well as little interest in fashion. This group neither feels fashion is important nor holds anti-fashion attitudes.

Negatives: The negatives (see Table 1) have no desire for leadership nor any interest in fashion. They do feel it is moderately important to be well dressed. But, perhaps this stems more from the feeling that it is important to be "neat and clean" than "fashionably clothed."

Rejectors: The rejectors were the mirror image of the leaders. Their profile is similar to that of the negatives, excepting that they do not attach any importance to fashion even to the point of being unconcerned with what they wear.

Segment Sizes

Table 1 shows the number of respondents in each segment. As shown in Table 1, the leaders, followers, and independents, who constitute the fashion-involved part of the fashion spectrum, represented 32.7% of total respondents. Almost a quarter (23.6%) of the respondents were classified as neutrals, while the remaining 43.7% of respondents represented the less fashion-involved of the fashion spectrum.

Demographic Characteristics of Clothing-Fashion Lifestyle Segments

A demographic breakdown of the fashion lifestyle segments was also carried out, with the results showing some minor although statistically significant demographic differences between segments. In general, the sample was up-scale compared to the population from which it was drawn (although up-scale areas were sampled). This was partly a result of the length of the questionnaire and its impact on the response is to (30.5%). With respect to age, the leaders had the largest percentage in the 18- to 24-year-old group, (χ^2 = 173; p < .0001). However, the median ages of respondents were essentially equal (about 29 years) with the exception of the uninvolveds, who were older.

Although income figures, overall, were higher than the median incomes in the Los Angeles SMSA, the negatives and rejectors reported lower incomes than the other segments (about $20,000 each, as compared to annual incomes of about $30,000 for the other five groups (χ^2 = 118; p < .0001). This suggests that their disaffection with fashion may stem, in part, from a lack of financial ability to "keep up with the game." Educational differences were minimal, although, as previously mentioned, overall education levels were quite high (median about 14 years) pointing to the somewhat up-scale nature of the sample (χ^2 = 139.8; p < .0001).

The largest demographic differences between segments, not surprisingly, were seen with respect to marital status. Leaders were more likely to be single (45.5% vs. 33.2% overall); those on the low-involvement end of the fashion spectrum were much more likely to be married (χ^2 = 165.2; p < .0001). The rejectors and the uninvolveds were more likely to be unemployed (χ^2 = 89.4; p < .0001).

Fashion Lifestyle Segments and Media Importance

An analysis of the perceived importance of various media for three fashion-related purposes--learning about (1) clothing sales, (2) the availability of clothing, and (3) in keeping up with current fashion trends--as these might vary by the seven lifestyle groups, was also undertaken. Each of several potential sources of fashion information was evaluated as to its importance on a four-point scale ranging from (1) very important to (4) not important for each of the fashion-related purposes listed above. The resulting analysis, broken down by fashion lifestyle segment, are shown in Table 2.

The table lists the mean importance ratings of each information source by lifestyle segment as well as the grand mean. In each instance a one-way analysis of variance was performed for each use-by-media combination, with the resulting F values, in every case, significant at the .01 level. Since the focus of the analysis was to arrive at managerially meaningful differences, if any, between the perceived importance of the media by those highly involved in the fashion purchase acquisition process as opposed to those who were not so involved, further analysis involved a posteriori contrasts between the mean responses of three groups of respondents--the highly fashion-involved (Fashion Leaders, Followers, and Independents), those not fashion-involved (Uninvolveds, Negatives, and Rejectors) and a middle group (the Neutrals).

Obtaining Information About Sales

The three most important means for obtaining information about sales were newspaper ads, direct mail, and friends (see Table 2). Print media do have an advantage in that the scanning of the announcement is under the control of the reader.

In most cases, the importance ratings for fashion-involved, neutral and anti-fashion groups were significantly different. In all but one instance, the non-significant differences which did occur were between the fashion-involved and the neutral group. The general finding from this table is that the fashion-involved group of respondents feels that all media are more important than does the anti-fashion group. And, the more effort involved in using the source (magazine and newspaper articles), the more likely there is a significant difference in importance rating between all three groups.

The largest difference in importance ratings between the three groups was for newspaper articles as a source of information about clothing sales. Finding such information obviously requires reading these articles--which high involvement consumers are more apt to do. It also suggests that, along with "friends," nonmarketer-controlled sources are important, especially for the highly involved fashion-conscious shopper.

Determining the Availability of Clothing

Again, newspaper ads, direct mail and friends were seen as the most important sources. In almost all cases, the more involved respondents were with fashion, the more important they felt the sources were.

The biggest difference between groups, for determining the availability of clothing, was the use of magazine articles and ads and newspapers articles. Again, use of such sources requires that women actively scan these media.

Keeping Up With Current Fashion Trends

With exception of TV ads and radio ads, all sources were rated as important ways to keep up with current fashion trends. In almost all cases, each fashion involvement group differed significantly from the others on the rated importance of the sources. The differences between the means are larger here than for the other two media uses

TABLE 2
IMPORTANCE OF FASHION INFORMATION SOURCES

Obtaining Information About Clothing Sales	Leaders (860)	Followers (511)	Independents (640)	Neutrals (1441)	Uninvolveds (530)	Negatives (1340)	Rejectors (806)	Totals (6128)
TV Ad	2.30	2.38	2.30	2.30 *	2.44	2.56	2.56	2.41
Magazine Ad	2.45	2.66	2.53	2.61	2.87	2.89	2.99	2.72
Magazine Article	2.67	2.90	2.72	2.87	3.07	3.15	3.23	2.95
Newspaper Ad	1.40	1.40	1.44	1.50	1.61	1.53	1.63	1.50
Newspaper Article	2.12	2.20	2.18	2.28	2.41	2.45	2.50	2.32
Radio Ad	2.42	2.46	2.45	2.45	2.55	2.62	2.74	2.53
Direct Mail	1.54	1.52	1.56	1.56	1.68	1.63	1.69	1.60
Friends	1.68	1.73	1.73	1.77	1.86	1.87	1.95	1.80

Keeping Up With Current Fashion Trends

	Leaders	Followers	Independents	Neutrals	Uninvolveds	Negatives	Rejectors	Totals
TV Ad	2.47	2.52	2.55	2.58 *	2.77	2.85	3.03	2.69
Magazine Ad	1.58	1.75	1.81	2.04	2.45	2.42	2.71	2.13
Magazine Article	1.71	1.89	1.92	2.17	2.57	2.57	2.81	2.26
Newspaper Ad	1.81	1.86	1.93	2.07	2.34	2.25	2.53	2.12
Newspaper Article	2.01	2.10	2.13	2.29	2.54	2.51	2.79	2.35
Radio Ad	3.00	3.09	3.03	3.06 *	3.20	3.29	3.36	3.15
Direct Mail	1.78	1.88	1.83	1.95	2.27	2.15	2.39	7.04
In-Store Display	1.47	1.53	1.54	1.66	1.95	1.84	2.10	1.73
Friends	1.84	1.90	1.89	1.99	2.28	2.19	2.34	2.06

Determining the Availability of Clothing

	Leaders	Followers	Independents	Neutrals	Uninvolveds	Negatives	Rejectors	Totals
TV Ad	2.83	2.95	2.92	2.92 *	3.06	3.16	3.20	3.01
Magazine Ad	1.95	2.26	2.24	2.46	2.82	2.79	2.98	2.52
Magazine Article	2.20	2.56	2.40	2.67	3.00	3.01	3.15	2.73
Newspaper Ad	1.84	1.79	1.84	1.93	2.07	1.92	2.15	1.93
Newspaper Article	2.26	2.40	2.37	2.54	2.67	2.67	2.83	2.55
Radio Ad	3.00	3.05	3.08	3.06	3.16	3.20	3.25	3.12
Direct Mail	1.94	1.98	2.06	2.03	2.17	2.11	2.19	2.07
Friends	1.96	1.97	1.99	2.06	2.17	2.18	2.22	2.09

*Difference not significant using Scheffe Test at .01 level.

202

(sales and clothing availability) indicating that as the effort involved increases, the difference in rated importance of the sources increases as those less involved downgrade the importance of "effortful sources."

Here, magazine ads take on special importance, particularly for fashion leaders. This is a strong indication that this group is actively involved in the fashion acquisition process. Obviously, the graphic aspect of ads in communicating fashion looks, contributes to their importance. Other fashion involvement groups either don't make this effort or find the process too abstract in comparison with actually seeing the garment in an in-store situation.

CONCLUSION

This study has explored the relationship between a retail customer's fashion lifestyle and his or her preferences, need for, and use of various forms of marketing communications. A main hypothesis of this investigation was that customers exhibiting different fashion lifestyle orientations would demonstrate significant differences with respect to their use of information, suggesting more effective promotional strategies for reaching these market segments.

The study results appear to support the investigated relationship. Retail shoppers representing different dimensions along the fashion spectrum exhibit different patterns of information usage. More specifically, those more involved with the fashion purchase acquisition process (and particularly fashion leaders) exhibit patterns of media usage that reflect the greater information gathering effort expended by the groups. This finding broadens out previous efforts by Engel, Blackwell, and Keggerreis (1970), and King (1975), which have shown that innovators are active information gatherers.

The study results have significant implications for directing those concerned with more effective marketing communications towards these fashion market segments. The results provide a methodology for more specific identification and profiling of segments along the fashion spectrum. This profiling can serve in obtaining more useful information about consumers' communication needs and preferences for certain types and forms of information and media and about how the contents can be more effectively presented. Fashion markets of various types can use this information in a more effective channelling of time, money, and other resources into fashion promotional efforts.

REFERENCES

Bearden, William O., Jesse E. Teel, Jr., and Richard M. Durand (1978), "Media Usage, Psychographic and Demographic Dimensions of Retail Shoppers," _Journal of Retailing_, 54 (Spring), 65-74.

Darden, William R., and Dub Ashton (1974), "Psychographic Profiles of Patronage Preference Groups," _Journal of Retailing_, 50 (Winter), 99-112.

Engel, James F., Roger D. Blackwell, and Robert J. Kegerreis (1970), "How Information is Used to Adopt an Innovation," _Journal of Advertising Research_, 9, 4, 3-8.

Gorsuch, Richard L. (1974), _Factor Analysis_, Philadelphia: W. B. Saunders Company, 236-239.

Gutman, Jonathan, and Michael K. Mills (1981), "Fashion Life-Style and Store Patronage: A Different Approach," in _Retail/Patronage Theory Workshop Proceedings_, Robert F. Lusch and William R. Dorden (eds.), Norman, Oklahoma: Center for Economic and Management Research, School of Business Administration, The University of Oklahoma, 155-160.

Harris, Brian F., and Michael K. Mills (1982), "The Impact of Item Price Removal in Scanner Supermarkets: A Los Angeles-Based Study," _Journal of Consumer Affairs_ (forthcoming).

Hirschman, Elizabeth, and Michael K. Mills (1979), "Women's Occupational Status, Innovativeness, Opinion Leadership, and Innovative Communication," _Proceedings_, Southern Marketing Association Annual Conferences, 270-275.

Kassarjian, Harold (1965), "Social Character and Preference for Mass Communication," _Journal of Marketing Research_, 2 (May), 146-153.

King, Charles W. (1965), "Communicating With the Innovator in the Fashion Adoption Process," in _Marketing and Economic Development_, Peter D. Bennett (ed.), Chicago: American Marketing Association, 429.

King, Charles W., and Lawrence J. Ring (1980), "Market Positioning Across Retail Fashion Institutions: A Comparative Analysis of Store Types," _Journal of Retailing_, 56 (Spring), 37-58.

King, Charles W., Douglas J. Tigert, and Lawrence J. Ring (1975), "Contemporary Fashion Theory and Retail Shopping Behavior: A Segmentation Analysis," _Combined Proceedings of the American Marketing Association_, Chicago.

Moschis, George P. (1976), "Shopping Orientations and Consumer Uses of Information," _Journal of Retailing_, 52 (Summer), 61-70.

Reynolds, Fred D., and William R. Darden (1972), "Intermarket Patronage: A Psychographic Study of Consumer Outshoppers," _Journal of Marketing_ (October), 50-54.

SAS User's Guide (1979), Raleigh, North Carolina: SAS Institute.

Tigert, D. J., and T. C. Bourgeous (1975), "Retail Fashion Segmentation: A Lifestyle Application," paper presented at the annual meetings of the Marketing Division of the Canadian Association of Administrative Sciences at the University of Alberta, Edmonton, Alberta.

Wilding, John, and Raymond A. Bauer (1968), "Consumer Goals and Reactions to a Communication Source," _Journal of Marketing Research_, 5 (February), 73-77.

Yang, C. E. (1979), "Lifestyle: A Conceptualization and Measurement," Unpublished manuscript, University of Southern California.

NON-STORE RETAILING AND PERCEIVED PRODUCT RISK

Pradeep K. Korgaonkar, Wayne State University, Detroit

ABSTRACT

Over the last few years non-store retailing has become an important and integral part of the American retailing scene. However, very little published research exists regarding these new methods of retailing.

This study examines the role of level _and_ type of perceived product risk on consumers' purchase intentions towards seven non-store retailers. The results indicate that type and level of perceived risk and type of non-store retailers, have a significant influence on consumers' purchase intentions. The managerial implications are discussed.

INTRODUCTION

In a period characterized by profound economic and technological changes, increasing attention has centered on understanding the impact of these changes on retail institutions. Some studies have focused on: understanding retailing of services (Upah 1980), changes in gasoline retailing (Mitchell 1980), effects of optical scanning technology (Pommer, Berkowitz and Walton 1980), while others have considered the impact of these changes, on consumers life styles and demographics (Bellenger and Korgaonkar 1980; Berry 1979; May 1979). More importantly, several recent articles in retailing literature have identified non-store retailing, sometimes called direct marketing, as the shape of the future for an increasing share of the retail dollar (Rosenberg and Hirschman 1980; May and McNair 1978).

A decade of impressive growth has convinced numerous retailers and analysts that the growth of non-store retailing in the years ahead is virtually unlimited. Not only would the various forms of direct marketing in existence continue to increase from three to five times faster than those of traditional store outlets; the application of such new marketing technologies as interactive cable television would add more support to their current spectacular growth rate (Rosenberg and Hirschman 1980). All these developments demonstrate growing interests in understanding the underlying determinations of non-store retail patronage.

In spite of this impressive growth of non-store retailing, very little empirical research exists regarding the correlates of non-store retailing patronage--of why and what type of consumers buy from these sources. The need for academic research about this new form of distribution method has already been suggested by retailing practitioners and academicians (Davidson and Rodgers 1979; Hirschman 1981). The purpose of this study is to fill this void in the existing retailing literature.

The term non-store retailing encompasses six modes of distribution: mail order selling, telephone selling, catalog showrooms, interactive cable television, door-to-door selling, and vending machines. For the purpose of this study vending machines and interactive cable television systems are not included. Vending machine method is omitted because it is not in-home, an attribute which is an important dimension of non-store retailing (May 1979). ICT system is excluded because recent studies indicate that many consumers disagree that television would be of material assistance in their shopping (Davidson and Rodgers 1979; Quelch and Takeuchi 1981). Thus, this study is geared towards understanding shoppers' intentions of purchasing certain products from the following non-store sources:

a. mail or telephone ordering from a catalog of a department store;
b. mail or telephone ordering from a catalog of a discount chain store;
c. mail or telephone ordering from a catalog of a catalog showroom merchandiser;
d. mail or telephone ordering based on the direct mail solicitations by the manufacturer of the product;
e. mail or telephone ordering based on the direct mail solicitations by the distributor of the product;
f. from a door-to-door salesperson;
g. mail or telephone ordering based on the direct mail solicitations by the credit card companies, such as American Express.

Due to lack of published research about the topic, the specific hypotheses are derived from past literature on "perceived risk."

HYPOTHESES

Since Bauer's (1960) seminal statement, several researchers have utilized the construct of perceived risk in investigating various aspects of consumer behavior. Bauer postulated that purchasing a product/service involves risk since it produces social and economic consequences that the consumer cannot anticipate with certainty. Thus, purchase decisions involve different types (social and economic) and levels of risk (high and low) associated with making an incorrect choice. The past research on store patronage suggests that the perceived risk of a product is transferable to the "outlet" that sells the product (Hisrich, Dornoff, and Kernan 1972; Prasad 1975; Dash, Schiffman, and Berenson 1976; Gillett 1976). Thus the store itself becomes vulnerable to the same kind of risk handling mechanism typically accorded to products.

However, except for Prasad's study (1975), most of the prior research in retailing has dealt with the influence of level of risk. Prasad (1975) investigated the influence of level _and_ type of perceived risk on consumers' patronage preference of discount store. Past studies in perceived risk literature suggest that in addition to level of risk, type of risk (social, economic) can have significant influence on consumers' decision strategies and store preferences (Perry and Hamm 1969; Peter and Tarpey 1975; Prasad 1975). Thus, in this study we have incorporated level (high, low) as well as type (social, economic) of risk associated with purchase of a product.

Though several factors such as consumer lifestyles, demographics, and economic conditions indicate that non-store retailing will prosper in future years, it can be argued that not all products will be amenable to this new mode of distribution. Specifically, we feel that consumers perceive greater risk in the act of buying from a non-store retailer than in buying from a store. The uncertainty generated by an inability to examine items of high-economic or high-social risk may be sufficiently great to cause many consumers to avoid buying such high risk items from non-store retailers. Hence, we hypothesize that:

H_1: Consumers purchasing products of high economic risk will have significantly lower patronage intentions than intentions of purchasing products of low economic risk; independent of the level of social risk.

H_2: Consumers purchasing products of high social risk will have significantly lower patronage intentions than intentions of purchasing products of low social risk; independent of the level of economic risk.

Though, all the seven modes are classified as non-store retailers, substantial variations exist in their methods of operation, merchandise selection, pricing and promotional methods. For example, store based catalog operations, typically use non-store method to build in-store traffic and business (Pennington 1979). Most, of the catalog showrooms offer phone and mail ordering, but the proportion of sales recorded via phone or mail is reported to be something less than 10 percent (May 1979).

On the other hand, many manufacturers or distributors rely solely upon non-store retailing methods to distribute their items. This has given an impetus to what are called "specialty" catalogs. These specialty catalogs typically carry such items as sporting goods, outdoor equipment, gift items, and garden equipment. Additionally many manufacturers rely exclusively upon: (i) a door-to-door selling method, for example Avon products, Fuller Brush; (ii) solicitations from the credit card holders of American Express and Chemical Bank; (iii) "800" phone numbers for soliciting telephone orders from their customers, examples of such products are costume jewelry, cookware, record albums, etc.

These variations in different modes of non-store retailers and the variations in the products they sell suggest that:

H_3: Consumers' intentions of purchasing products from non-store retailers will be significantly related to specific mode of non-store operation.

METHODOLOGY

The methodology entailed: (a) selection of a set of products differing in types and levels of perceived risk, and (b) data collection of patronage intentions toward each of the seven non-store shopping modes for purchases of the selected products from the retail shoppers.

Data for the study were collected via mail questionnaires sent to a randomly selected sample of 500 households in the SMSA of a large midwestern city. The person responsible for the majority of non-food purchases of the household was asked to complete a questionnaire and to return it in a stamped envelope provided for that purpose. This procedure yielded 207 usable responses, on which the analysis is based. The demographic profile of the respondents showed them to be slightly older and higher in income than the population of the area from which they were selected.

The procedures used to classify the products were similar to the ones used in previous studies (Perry and Hamm 1969; Mazis and Sweeney 1973; Prasad 1975). The respondents were asked to rate social and economic risk of sixteen products based on the following descriptions:

<u>Economic Significance</u> refers to how the purchase decision will affect the individual's ability to make other purchases. Thus, economic significance varies with the financial considerations of price in relation to factors such as the individual's income, ability to pay, and alternate uses of the money.

<u>Social Significance</u> refers to how the purchase decision will affect the opinions other people hold of the individual. Thus, social significance varies with such factors as a product's social importance and its social conspicuousness.

Next, the subjects were asked to (separately) rate each product purchase decision according to social and economic significance on a five-point scale ranging from "very low significance" to "very high significance". A product was categorized as high (low) in social (economic) risk if more than two-thirds of the subjects rated the purchase decision as high or very high (low or very low). The order of presentation of the sixteen products was randomized to avoid response bias. The sixteen products were selected from advertisements and catalogs of non-store retailers in the city. The classification of the products based on the subjects ratings is shown in Figure 1.

FIGURE 1

PRODUCT RISK CATEGORIES

Economic Risk

		Low	High
Low		Pen Holder	Electronic Calculator
		Umbrella	Typewriter
		Cookbook	Vacuum Cleaner
		Cookware	Encyclopedia
Social Risk		Perfume/Cologne	Leather Briefcase
		Wallpaper	Stereo Hi-fi
		Costume Jewelry	Wall Clock
High		Pair of Dress Shoes	Color Television

The subjects were asked also to indicate their intentions of purchasing each of the sixteen products from each of the seven non-store retailers, if they were shopping for it, on a scale of (0%) "definitely would not buy" to (100%) "definitely would buy". The measurement of purchase intention was in line with prior studies in the area (Banks 1950; Katona 1960; Douglas and Wind 1970). The order of presentation of the products and shopping modes were randomized to avoid response bias.

ANALYSIS

The first step in the analysis was aimed at estimating the reliability of the purchase probability scale. The patronage probability scores of the four products in each of the four risk categories were summated to calculate the reliability and to operationalize the dependent variable. The coefficients of reliability alpha of the scale were in the range of 0.77 to 0.81, often suggested adequate in the initial stages of research (Nunnaly 1967).

The means and standard deviations of the purchase intention scale for each of the four perceived risk classification and each of the non-store types are shown in Table 1. The research hypotheses were tested by utilizing the ANOVA method. The results are shown in Table 2. The results indicate that consumer purchase intentions are significantly related to: perceived economic risk ($p < .000$), type of non-store retailer ($p < .000$), interactions between perceived social risk and type of non-store retailer ($p < .000$), interactions between perceived economic risk and type of non-store ($p < .000$), three-way interactions between perceived economic risk, perceived social risk and type of non-store retailer ($p < .05$).

The results are supportive of the research hypotheses suggesting that type and level of perceived risk and type of non-store are significantly related to consumers' purchase intentions. Specifically, Hypotheses 1 and 3 were supported, as evidenced via the ANOVA analysis. Hypothesis 2 was not supported. Thus consumers' purchase intentions were not significantly related to level of social risk of the selected products. However, the level of economic risk and type of non-store "outlets" were significantly related to consumers' purchase intentions.

TABLE 1

MEANS AND STANDARD DEVIATIONS OF CONSUMER PURCHASE
INTENTIONS SCORES (n=207)

Type of Non-Store Retailer	Low Social Risk		High Social Risk	
	Low Economic Risk	High Economic Risk	Low Economic Risk	High Economic Risk
A Department Store Based Operation	72.0 (23.71)	23.76 (21.33)	83.34 (29.73)	31.26 (23.23)
A Discount Store Based Operation	66.1 (25.74)	20.0 (18.42)	72.0 (36.94)	26.26 (21.77)
A Catalog Showroom Based Operation	83.6 (35.66)	68.76 (54.79)	65.34 (27.99)	41.26 (31.99)
Directly From a Manufacturer	53.6 (22.89)	23.76 (22.19)	46.26 (26.69)	25.0 (24.17)
Directly From a Distributor	50.0 (26.52)	15.30 (21.06)	47.50 (26.25)	24.0 (21.41)
A Door-to-Door Salesperson	16.26 (12.0)	24.92 (6.11)	25.0 (29.93)	8.0 (12.93)

TABLE 2

ANOVA OF CONSUMER PURCHASE INTENTION SCORES

Variable	Sum of Squares	D.F.	M.S.	F Ratio
Main Effects	53998.664	8	6749.832	104.793[a]
Social Risk	0.017	1	0.017	0.987
Economic Risk	23677.559	1	23677.559	367.559[a]
Non-Store Type	30843.887	6	5140.645	79.810[a]
2-Way Interactions	11596.891	13	892.068	13.850[a]
Social Risk x Economic Risk	80.312	1	80.312	1.247
Social Risk x Non-Store Type	3820.650	6	636.775	9.886[a]
Economic Risk x Non-Store Type	7615.723	6	1269.287	19.706[a]
3-Way Interactions	1046.645	6	174.441	2.708[b]
Social Risk x Economic Risk x Non-Store Type	1046.645	6	174.441	2.708[b]
EXPLAINED	68715.875	27	2511.699	38.995[a]
RESIDUAL	371522.648	5768	64.411	
Total	439338.523	5795		

[a]Significant at 0.00   [b]Significant at 0.05

DISCUSSION

A closer examination of the results in Table 1 indicate that: (a) consumers express higher probabilities of purchasing products of low economic risk than products of high economic risk; irrespective of the level of social risk, (b) overall, the consumers express higher probabilities of purchasing products from a catalog showroom and a department store based catalog operation, than purchasing products from the other five non-store retailers, (c) overall, the consumers express low probabilities of purchasing products from a direct mail solicitations of credit card companies and from a door-to-door salesperson. Thus, the results of the study indicate that in spite of the rapid growth in non-store retailing, significant variations exist between types of operations and types of products.

Overall, store based operations such as catalog showrooms, department and discount stores seem to have been successful in gaining consumers' acceptance of this form of retailing method as evidenced in this study. The store based non-retailers offer the following advantages to the consumer: (i) Physical proximity: makes returning an item easy and inexpensive, (ii) consumers may have formed positive attitudes towards these stores based on their past in-store purchases, (iii) if desired, consumers have an opportunity to physically inspect the product before purchasing it through mail/telephone order. This could probably account for consumers' favorable responses to buying products from store based operations. However, even within these types of institutions, variations based on product differences are evident. Catalog showrooms seem to be preferred mainly for purchasing products of low social risk, whereas, department store based operations are preferred for purchasing products of low economic risk.

Door-to-door method seems to be more acceptable for low social-high economic risk products and high social risk-low economic risk products. This is not surprising since many manufacturers of such types of products (cosmetics, vacuum cleaners, etc.) rely upon door-to-door method to sell their products.

The remaining three methods of retailing: directly from a manufacturer/distributor and solicitors of credit card companies, seem to be suitable mainly for low-economic risk products. This could be partly related to the "newness" of these forms of retailing compared to the other non-store methods. Consumers seem to have high reluctance in purchasing products of high social-high economic risk, from all of these "outlets". Thus suggesting that this method of retailing is probably not amenable for all kinds of products. The significant two-way interactions between non-store retail types and risk perceptions are shown in Figures 2 and 3.

The results of this study should be of value to retail management in formulating the appropriate merchandising and promotional policies. The results indicated here suggest that significant interactions exist between product and type of non-store retailing. The reluctance of the consumers to purchase products of high economic-high social risk could be overcome by implementing: (a) a liberal returns policy, (b) a policy of stocking well known national brands of such products, (c) a policy of offering a significant price advantage to consumers, and (d) a promotional policy stressing the opinions of "significant others" or well known celebrities to reduce consumers' social risk perceptions.

Thus, the results of this study indicate that type and level of perceived risk may predict which types of products will or will not be bought from different non-store retailers. However, the past research in retailing indicates that perceived risk is not necessarily the only determinant of the patronage decisions; shopping orientations, psychographics, demographics also interact to influence the patronage decision. Future research may attempt to understand the influence of these factors in the context of non-store retailing.

To sum up, this study reveals that consumer acceptance of "non-store" shopping will be forthcoming. Consumers have expressed favorable intentions of purchasing "packaged" (low economic risk) products from these outlets. On the other hand, consumers seem to be hesitant in purchasing products of "high economic" risk from these outlets. Perceived risk concept utilized in this study can aid retail management in alleviating consumers' risk perceptions.

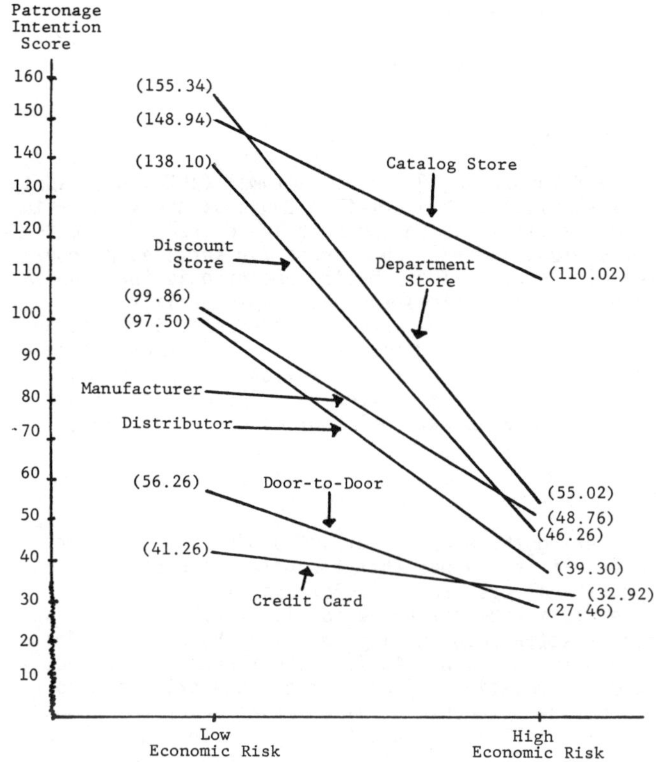

FIGURE 2

INTERACTION EFFECT
(Economic Risk x Non-Store Type)

Figure 3

INTERACTION EFFECT
(Store Risk x Non-Store Type)

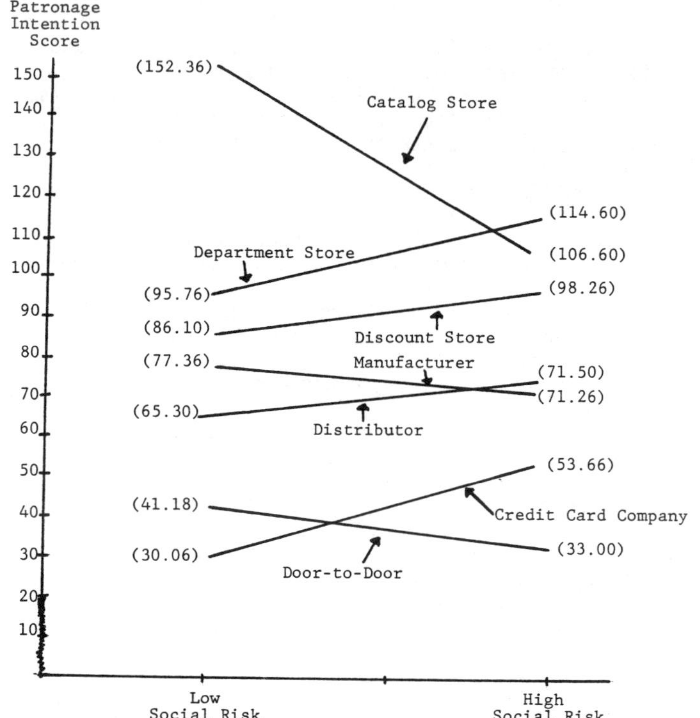

REFERENCES

Banks, Seymour (1950), "The Relationship Between Preference and Purchase of Brands," _Journal of Marketing_, 15 (October), 145-157.

Bauer, Raymond A. (1960), "Consumer Behavior as Risk Taking," in _Dynamic Marketing for a Changing World_, Robert S. Hancock, ed; Chicago: American Marketing Association, 389-398.

Bellenger, Danny N. and Pradeep K. Korgaonkar (1980), "Profiling the Recreational Shopper," _Journal of Retailing_, 56 (Fall), 77-92.

Berry, Leonard L. (1979), "The Time-Buying Consumer," _Journal of Retailing_, 55 (Winter), 58-69.

Coe, Barbara J. and Benjamin Lipstein (1979), "The Impact of Expanding Non-Store Retailing on Major National Brand Strategies," in _The Growth of Non-Store Retailing: Implications for Retailers, Manufacturers and Public Policy Makers_, The Institute of Retail Management, New York University, 35-44.

Dash, Joseph F., Leon G. Schiffman, and Conrad Berenson (1976), "Risk- and Personality-Related Dimensions of Store Choice," _Journal of Marketing_, 40 (January), 32-39.

Davidson, William R. and Alice Rodgers (1979), "Non-Store Retailing: Its Importance to and the Impact on Merchandise Supplies and Competitive Channels," in _The Growth of Non-Store Retailing: Implications for Retailers, Manufacturers and Public Policy Makers_, The Institute of Retail Management, New York University, 22-29.

Doody, Allen F. and William R. Davidson (1967), "Next Revolution in Retailing," _Harvard Business Review_, (May-June), 4.

Douglas, Susan P. and Yoram Wind (1971), "Intentions to Buy as Predictors of Buying Behavior," paper presented at the _Association of Consumer Research Conference_.

Gillett, Peter L. (1976), "In-Home Shoppers--An Overview," _Journal of Marketing_, 40 (October), 81-88.

Hirschman, Elizabeth C. (1980), "From the Editor," _Journal of Retailing_, 56 (Winter), 4.

Hisrich, Robert D., Ronald J. Dornoff, and Jerome B. Kernan (1972), "Perceived Risk in Store Selection," _Journal of Marketing Research_, 9 (November), 453-459.

Katona, George (1960), _The Powerful Consumer_, New York: McGraw-Hill Book Company, 145-157.

May, Eleanor A. and Malcolm P. McNair (1978), "The Next Revolution of the Retailing Wheel," _Harvard Business Review_, (September-October), 8.

May, Eleanor A. (1979), "The Outlook for Non-Store Retailing," in _The Growth of Non-Store Retailing: Implications for Retailers, Manufacturers and Public Policy Makers_, The Institute of Retail Management, New York University, 6-18.

Mazis, Michael B. and Timothy W. Sweeney (1973), "Novelty and Personality with Risk as a Moderating Variable," in _Marketing Education and the Real World and Dynamic Marketing in a Changing World_, Boris W. Becker and Helmut Becker eds., Chicago: American Marketing Association, 406-411.

Mitchell, Edward J. (1980), "Recent Changes in Gasoline Retailing: An Economic Interpretation," _Journal of Retailing_, 56 (Winter), 5-22.

Nunnaly, Jim C. (1967), _Psychometric Theory_, New York: McGraw-Hill.

Pennington, Allan L. (1979), "Discussion," in _The Growth of Non-Store Retailing: Implications for Retailers, Manufacturers and Public Policy Makers_, The Institute of Retail Management, New York University, 30-34.

Perry, Michael and B. Curtis Hamm (1969), "Cannonical Analysis of Relations Between Socio-Economic Risk and Personal Influence in Purchase Decisions," _Journal of Marketing Research_, 6 (August), 351-354.

Peter, J.P. and L.X. Tarpey (1975), "A Comparative Analysis of Three Consumer Decision Strategies," _Journal of Consumer Research_, 2, 29-37.

Pommer, Michael D., Eric N. Berkowitz, and John R. Walton (1980), "UPC Scanning: An Assessment of Shopper Response to Technological Change," _Journal of Retailing_, 56 (Summer), 25-44.

Prasad, Kanti V. (1975), "Socioeconomic Product Risk and Patronage Preferences of Retail Shoppers," _Journal of Marketing_, 39 (July), 42-47.

Quelch, John A. and Hirotaka Takeuchi (1981), "Nonstore Marketing: Fast Track or Slow?" _Harvard Business Review_, #4, 75.

Rosenberg, Larry J. and Elizabeth C. Hirschman (1980), "Retailing Without Stores," Harvard Business Review, (July-August), 103-112.

Upah, Gregory D. (1980), "Mass Marketing in Service Retailing: A Review and Synthesis of Major Methods," _Journal of Retailing_, 56 (Fall), 56-76.

DIFFERENCES BETWEEN GOODS AND SERVICES:
AN EMPIRICAL ANALYSIS OF INFORMATION SOURCE IMPORTANCE

Joseph L. Orsini, Loyola Marymount University/UCLA, Los Angeles

ABSTRACT

Marketing differences between goods and services is receiving increasing consideration. This exploratory study empirically supports the contention of significant differences, based on the importance of consumer information sources.

INTRODUCTION

Recently, both educators and practitioners have expressed an increasing interest in the distinctive differences between the marketing of goods and the marketing of services. Recent editions of marketing textbooks include a chapter devoted to the marketing of services, articles on the subject and appear in journals, and the American Marketing Association recently sponsored a special symposium on services marketing, and plans to sponsor another one in 1982.

Despite this apparent trend toward acceptance of the marketing of services as being different from the marketing of goods, substantial doubt exists, on the part of many marketers, as to the importance of the differences. These doubts are probably best expressed in a recent article by Enis and Roering (1981). They note that, while marketing taxonomies may be useful for descriptive purposes, the goods/services classification "is sufficiently inadequate to be confusing to those contemplating strategy formulation." (p. 1).

The purpose of this paper is to select a variety of goods and services and examine them empirically for distinctive differences between goods and services. The particular item of distinctiveness selected is the importance of different sources of information. This is relevant to consumer behavior, while also being pertinent for formulating marketing strategy. In addition, other possible causes of information source information will be examined simultaneously to determine the unique contribution of the goods/services taxonomy, over and above that explained by other variables.

OPERATIONALIZATION AND HYPOTHESES

Information Sources

Classification of the variety of sources of information available to consumers can be performed in several ways, but the approach devised by Andreasen (1968) appears to be useful. The first source he identifies is derived from the consumer's own experience, such as using the product or seeing it in a showroom. Other sources for acquiring information are external in nature. His five categories of sources of consumer information are:
- direct observation or experience (examining or using the product)
- impersonal advocate (advertisements)
- impersonal independent (professional articles, radio or televsiion programs not controlled by the marketer)
- personal advocate (salespersons, clerks)
- personal independent (friends, family, associates)

Combining two of the external sources of information, personal independent and impersonal independent, constitutes the definition of "guidance sources," a term used in the hypotheses developed below.

Goods and Services

Eiglier and Langeard (1977) and Zeithmal (1981) address the issue of services and information sources; however, neither is very explicit as to the relative degree of importance of various information sources for services as contrasted with goods. Their basic reasoning is that the intangibility of services reduces inspectability and causes consumers to seek external sources of information not under the control of the marketer. Consumers therefore rely less on personal observation or experience, and marketer controlled sources, and increase the importance of the unbiased external sources of information, i.e., "guidance sources".

Price

In considering the wide variety of products a consumer purchases, it is obvious that the price of various types of products differs greatly. For example, a roll of paper towels may be purchased for less than a dollar, while a video cassette recorder may cost many hundreds of dollars. Unfortunately, no studies were found which directly examined the relationship between product price and sources of information, supporting the observation by Westbrook and Fornell (1979) that surprisingly little research has been done on information sources in general. However, several studies, which looked at a variety of products, tangentially pertain to the information source, either by implication or by inspection of their tabular results.

Jacoby and Kaplan (1972) concluded that there was a price-related component of overall perceived risk over and above subjective financial risk. If higher priced products lead to greater search efforts for all types of information (Newman 1977), it also seems reasonable to expect that greater importance would be placed on the experience and expertise of guidance sources for higher priced rather than lower priced products. This expectation is supported by examination of the tabular results of studies by Lutz and Reilly (1973) and Locander and Herman (1979).

Evaluation Difficulty

A recent paper by Zeithaml (1981) looked at the goods/services issue in the framework of the consumer evaluation difficulty concept proposed by economists Nelson (1970) and Darby and Karni (1973). Under this concept, products are categorized by both the timing and the ability of consumers to evaluate the product attributes. Three categories are proposed: search, experience and credence.

Search products are those which the consumer usually is able to evaluate in the normal course of shopping prior to actually making the purchase; clothing is an example. Experience products are those which the consumer is unable to evaluate until purchase and use; an example would be canned tuna fish. Credence products are those which the consumer is usually unable to fully evaluate even after purchase and consumption; an example would be motor oil.

Only the original work of Nelson (1970) specifically addresses the relationship between the evaluation difficulty categories and information sources. Based on his findings, the hypothesis for this paper is that guidance sources are most important for credence products, and least important for search products.

Purchase Frequency

It should be noted that Nelson (1970) used product purchase frequency as an independent variable in his hypothesis, in addition to his product categorization, holding that increasing purchase frequency should decrease use of guidance sources (p. 321). This stems from his reasoning that consumers use purchase and utilization of the product class as a source of information, thereby decreasing their necessity to utilize other external sources (p. 317). The following hypotheses are proposed:

H1: Guidance sources are more important for services than for goods.

H2: Guidance sources are more important for high price type of products than for low price type of products.

H3: Guidance sources are most important for products of high evaluation difficulty (credence products more important than experience products) and least important for products of low evaluation difficulty (search products less important than experience products).

H4: Guidance sources are more important for infrequently purchased products than frequently purchased products.

METHOLOGY

Subjects

The subjects used were convenience samples of a total of 57 MBA students attending two universities, both located in Southern California. While constituting a group of adults (one-third of the subjects were over 30 years of age) approximately evenly divided between the sexes, other characteristics of these subjects (e.g., education) make tenuous the generalizability of the results obtained.

Product Selection and Variable Measure

Subjects were asked to consider a new brand for each of several types of product. Each product has the importance of each of the five information source categories measured on a 7 point scale. End points of the scale were labeled "extremely important" and "not at all important".

Product selection for inclusion in the study was made on a priori basis according to several criteria: familiarity; variance in purchase frequency; and at least one product in each of the categories of the variables considered in the hypothesis. Purchase frequency was included as an item in a questionnaire, goods and services were readily determined by inspection, and a price of $25 was selected a priori as the dividing point for high price and low price products.

As anticipated, the classification of products by evaluation difficulty into search, experience and credence categories proved to be the most difficult. A random sample of 15 subjects from the pool of subjects available were selected to act as judges. In order for a product to be included in the analysis, 2/3 or more of the judges had to agree on the classification into one of the three categories. As indicated in Table I, only 17 of the 26 products met this criteria. As only three products were classified as credence, the credence category was dropped from the analysis.

Design

The research approach used in this study was generally similar to that of Lutz and Reilly (1973) and Locander and Hermann (1979). A variety of products were selected for study, a questionnaire designed to measure the dependent variable and various independent variables, subjects selected, and the questionnaire administered. While having each subject make observations on several products is efficient design, in the sense of acquiring a high level of information per subject, there is the potential problem of violation of one of the assumptions of the linear regression model: autocorrelation. Standardization of the dependent variable within subjects was used to reduce these effects, but a Durbin-Watson test still indicated a mild degree of autocorrelation. With autocorrelation the parameter estimates may remain unbiased, but the analysis is more likely to indicate a higher level of significance than is actually the case (Lewis-Beck 1980, p. 28). In order to account for this, the .01 probability level was adopted as the appropriate level of significance rather than the more usual .05 level.

TABLE 1

CLASSIFICATION OF PRODUCTS

| | Low Price | | High Price | |
	Goods	Services	Goods	Services
Search	(1)FLOWERS LAMPSHADE FRESH FRUIT SLIPPERS (2)scissors under- garments		OUTDOOR FURNITURE	
Experience	COFFEE BATH SOAP	DRY CLEANERS (3)LAWN TRIMMERS	VACUUM CLEANER VIDEO CASS- ETTE RECORDER	MOVING & STORAGE (3) DAY CARE PEST CONTROL
Credence (4)	Pick proof lock	assembly candidate senate candidate	PERSIAN RUG antique vase	ATTORNEY TV REPAIR auto repair auto insurance

(1) UPPER CASE = products used in analysis
(2) lower case = products not used in analysis due to lack of conclusive classification as Search/Experience/Credence
(3) initially proposed as Search Classification; judges categorized as Experience
(4) Credence category not used in analysis; see text

Analysis

Results of the analysis indicate that all the guidance source importance levels are as hypothesized. Table 2 shows the average relative importance of guidance sources of information for the products in each of the categories. The larger the number in absolute value, the further the importance is from the average importance of all products; the sign of the number indicates whether the importance is greater (a positive sign) or less (a negative sign) than the average importance. Thus guidance information sources are least important for low price search goods, and most important for high price experience services.

TABLE 2
TABLE OF CELL MEANS
IMPORTANCE OF GUIDANCE SOURCES
EXPRESSED IN STANDARD DEVIATIONS

| | Low Price | | High Price | |
	Goods	Services	Goods	Services
Search	-0.67* (138)**		0.14 (57)	
Experience	-0.18 (98)	0.19 (114)	0.47 (73)	0.54 (48)

 * minus sign indicates less than average importance numbers
** numbers in parentheses are the number of observations
   used in the regression analysis

Table 3 shows the significance of each of the variables,
using the $p \leq$ .01 level of significance. It indicates the
significance of the contribution of each of these variables
independent of the other variables, i.e., the unique contribution to explanation of changes in the guidance source
importance dependent variable. Purchase frequency is not
significant, nor are any interactions significant.

TABLE 3
REGRESSION RESULTS
IMPORTANCE OF GUIDANCE SOURCES

Variable	B	Beta	F
Goods/Services	0.28	0.13	8.76 (a)
Search/Experience	0.47	0.24	26.47 (b)
High/Low Price	0.56	0.28	38.20 (b)
Purchase Frequency	0.35	0.07	2.39

** no significant higher order interactions

r^2 (main effects only)= 0.21
a = $p \leq$ 0.01   b = $p \leq$ 0.001

Discussion

The most important result is the support of Hypothesis regarding goods and services, particularly with respect to
the potential usefulness of the goods/services taxonomy.
With respect to the lack of significance of purchase frequency, it may well be that the instruction to the subjects
to evaluate a new brand of the product class obviates the
effect of experience with purchases of the product class.

With respect to the generalizability of these findings,
two comparisons are noteworthy. First is the similarity
of the unstandardized information importance scores of this
study (not shown) with those found by Lutz and Reilly (1973)
and Locander and Hermann (1979). They used undergraduates
and civic club members as subjects, respectively, thereby
supporting generalizability by age, time and geography.
Second is the corroborative finding of significance of the
Nelson (1970) hypothesis, particularly since his analysis
used a completely different methodology and was based on
actual sales data.

Limitations

The purpose of exploratory research is to investigate an
area with the intent of determing whether or not more detailed study is warranted. To that end, this study appears to have served its purpose. However, due to shortcomings with respect to subject selection, measure of importance, design, and product selection, any findings produced are tentative.

CONCLUSIONS

Several previous studies have cited the mangerially-re-
lated differences in marketing between goods and services,
primarily related to the simultaneous production and consumption of services. This study provides empirical evidence of one type of significant difference from the consumer's perspective of services: the perceived importance
of product information from family, friends and associates,
and from unbiased experts. While the question of the importance of the marketing differences between goods and
services is one of a difference in degree vs. a difference
in kind, the results of this study lend evidence to support the continued study of services marketing as distinct
from goods marketing.

While this study analyzed the guidance information sources
as a group, due to existing theory, some insights can be
gleaned from inspection of each of the five information
source categories as proposed by Andreasen (1969). Examination of raw score means (not shown due to space limitations)
duplicates the tabular findings of previous research by
Lutz and Reilly (1973) and Locander and Hermann (1979): personal observation/experience is the most important information source over all products, followed by personal independent (word of mouth) sources, with the other three information source categories being similar to each other and
and lowest in importance. Similarly all sources of information were more important for high price products than for
low price products, a reasonable expectation in light of
previous findings on the extent of information search, e.g.,
Newman (1977).

The greater variety of products used in this study as compared to previous studies allows additional conjecture. In
particular, with reference to the main thrust of the hypotheses herein, word of mouth communication for services
(not shown) was perceived as the most important source of
information; this holds for all goods vs. all services as
well as for just experience goods vs. experiences services.

Confirmation of this finding by more focused research would
indicate important strategic implications for marketing
managers of services, effecting such areas as product development and advertising. With respect to product development, the greater variability of services production
(Eiglier and Langeard 1977), combined with higher word of
mouth importance, indicates greater marketer concern with
consumer satisfaction is warranted. The satisifed consumer may not only be a repeat purchase, but the generator
of additional customers. Methods for obtaining rapid feedback information on satisfaction should be developed, and
production personnel should possess the capability and authority to make field changes in service production.

Services advertising has previously been addressed by Shos-
tock (1977) who admonishes the use of highly tangible portrayals of intangible services. The results of this study
would indicate the wisdom of greater use of advertising for
services which follows the advice of Dichter (1966) to simulate and stimulate word of mouth communication. Examples
of this might be the television advertisement showing one
"housewife" extolling the virtues of a new cleaning service
to another "housewife", or a "tell your friends" promotional effort.

Directions for Future Research

The necessity for more confirmatory research was discussed
in the findings section of this paper: a greater variety

of subjects, alternative measures of information source importance, a greater variety of products, and more conclusive research designs. Additionally, with increasing interest in public sector marketing, public services should be included in future studies.

Other aspects of the goods/services taxonomy warrant study. One is the effect on consumer behavior of the degree to which any given marketing offering is composed of goods and services. That is, since most products are bundles of goods and services, it is not known if the consumer makes a clear distinction between the categories, and behaves accordingly. Another is if the observability of the results of the service by someone not present at the service creation makes a difference with respect to information source importance, e.g., a haircut vs. a live concert.

More broadly, other aspects of consumer behavior should be included in the investigation of services as well as goods. The literature on information search should also be re-evaluated, as even recent studies do not give a good overview of the breadth of consumer search behavior indicated in this study. For example, some studies, e.g., Beales, et. al., (1981) do not even include word of mouth communication as being a worthy source of information for study.

Tangentially, the results of this study indicate other areas for research. The search/experience/credence taxonomy appears to have promise, particularly as a segmenting variable at the individual level. The effect of the general price of the product class may also have important ramifications on many aspects of consumer behavior.

REFERENCES

Andreasen, A. R. (1968), "Attitudes and Consumer Behavior: A Decision Model" in Kassarjian and Roberson, eds. Perspectives in Consumer Behavior, Glenview: Scott, Foresman & Co.

Beales, H., Magis, M., Scalop, S. and Stalin, R. (1981), "Consumer Search and Public Policy", Journal of Consumer Research, 8 (June) 11-21.

Darby, Michael R. and Karni, Edi (1973), "Free Competition and The Optimal Amount of Fraud", Journal of Law and Economics, 16, 67-88.

Eiglier, Pierre and Langeard, Eric (1977), "A New Approach to Service Marketing" in P. Eiglier, et. al., eds., Marketing Consumer Services: New Insights. Cambridge: Marketing Science Institute.

Enis, Ben M. and Roering, Kenneth J. (1981), "Services Marketing: Different Products, Similar Strategy", Marketing of Services, J. Donnelly and W. George, eds., Chicago: American Marketing Association, 1-4.

Jacoby, Jacob and Kaplan, Leon (1972), "The Components of Perceived Risk: in M. Vanketesan ed., Proceedings of the Third Annual Conference, Association for Consumer Research, 382-393.

Lewis-Beck, Michael S. (1980), Applied Regression, Beverly Hills: Sage Publications.

Locander, William B. and Hermann, Peter W. (1979), "The effect of Self-Confidence and Anxiety on Information Seeking in Consumer Risk Reduction", Journal of Marketing Research, 16, 268-274.

Lutz, R. J. and Reilly, P. J. (1973), "An Exploration of the Effects Perceived Social and Performance Risk on Consumer Information Acquisition", in Advances in Consumer Research, Vol. 1, S. Ward and P. Wright eds., Urbana: Association for Consumer Research, 393-405.

Nelson, Philip (1970), "Information & Consumer Behavior", Journal of Political Economy, 28, 311-329.

Newman, Joseph W. (1977), "Consumer External Search: Amount and Determinants", in A. G. Woodside, and P. D. Bennett, eds., Consumers and Industrial Buying Behavior, New York: North-Holland.

Westbrook, Robert A. and Fornell, Claes (1979), "Patterns of Information Source Useage Among Durable Goods Buyers", Journal of Marketing Research, 16 (August), 303-312.

Zeithaml, Valarie A. (1981), "How Consumer Evaluation Processes Differ Between Goods and Services", Marketing of Services, J. Donnelly and W. George, eds., Chicago: American Marketing Association, 186-190.

A GAME THEORETIC APPROACH TO RETAIL LOCATION STRATEGY

Avijit Ghosh, New York University
C. Samuel Craig, New York University

ABSTRACT

The store location choice is one of the most important strategic decisions for retail firms. This paper develops a game theoretic approach to store location decisions in a dynamic competitive environment. An iterative procedure is developed to determine the maximin strategies for a firm desiring to locate multiple stores in an area where changes in the level of competitive activity are expected in the future. The model helps identify robust locations which protect a firm's market share against competitive encroachment.

INTRODUCTION

Firms are increasingly relying on strategic planning to ensure long run viability. In attempting to design strategies to achieve success, firms must take into account not only the marketing environment which confronts them today, but also to anticipate possible changes in the environment. Such changes often occur due to actions taken by competitors attempting to improve their own performance and seeking their own preferred strategies (Kotler, 1971). Moreover, strategy changes by any one firm might lead to reactive changes by competitors attempting to protect their own performance. Successful strategic planning procedures, therefore, must take into consideration possible future actions by competitors in response to actions contemplated by a given firm.

In retailing the need for such dynamic strategic planning is critical in decisions to locate new stores. Store location is an important determinant of overall success in retailing. While other marketing mix elements may be easily changed in response to a changing environment, store locations represent long term investments that can be changed only at considerable cost.

Given that locational decisions are not readily reversible, various models for determining optimal store location have been proposed (see Huff, 1962 and Applebaum, 1968 for representative approaches). For the most part, however, models of retail site selection tend to treat competition as a static factor. They examine existing competitive locations, but do not try to anticipate likely competitive changes. Thus, a desirable location may become undesirable as competition locates additional stores.

Existing models tend also to evaluate sites for the addition of a single store only. In practice, however, retail chains increasingly pursue multiple location strategies and eventually establish a network of stores in an area. A site selected as optimal when the firm is considering only one store, may not be optimal when more stores are eventually located (Scott, 1975).

Thus, the basic problem becomes, what happens to the desirability of retail locations as the firm locates multiple outlets and the competition does likewise. To deal with the problem a procedure for locational decisions in a dynamic environment has been developed. This procedure involves three components: 1) an algorithm for assessing site desirability, 2) a criterion for selecting among alternatives, and 3) an heuristic to facilitate the computational procedures. The key element is the use of game theoretic concepts to provide the best strategies under a variety of competitive reactions.

The paper is divided into two major sections. First, the game theory model is developed along with its applicability to retail location decisions. In this section the Multiplicative Competitive Interaction (MCI) formulation for assessing site desirability is discussed along with the vertex substitution heuristic which makes the procedure for determining desirable strategies computationally feasible. These procedures are used in an iterative algorithm developed to determine the equilibrium solution to the game formulation. In the second section the model is applied to a retail location problem to illustrate its use.

THE GAME THEORY MODEL

Game theory has been applied to a number of competitive marketing situations (Baligh and Richartz, 1967; Krishnan and Gupta, 1967; Barcun and Jeming, 1973) with varying degrees of success. Game thoery presents a particularly appealing framework to view competitive retail site selection processes. All competitors have equivalent knowledge about the environment from census data and observation of the physical surroundings. Each feasible site offers similar market potential to each competitor. It is truly competitive, in that locating an outlet forecloses that location to competition. Also, a deficiency common to other applications of game theory in a marketing context does not hold. Dutta and King (1980) maintain that the most serious limitation in the use of game theory is the assumption that market share is proportional to the firm's share of industry marketing effort. However, with locational decisions the relationship between a chosen strategy and market share is well documented (Hansen and Weinberg, 1979). Finally, since store location decisions represent major fixed investments, it is reasonable to assume that all parties behave in an economically rational manner --a critical assumption of all game theoretic models.

The strategic decisions of two retailers attempting to improve their share of a market can be modeled as a zero-sum noncooperative game between two players.[1] In a two person zero-sum game, the amount that one player wins is precisely the amount that the other player loses (since the total market share is always the same). The basic game theory framework applies to situations where competitive retail stores impact each others profits. The game theoretic solution to such problems is the maximin strategy in which the players choose the strategy which maximizes the minimum possible pay-off from that strategy (Rapoport , 1973). When a competitor's reaction to a particular strategic choice is unknown, a player evaluates any strategy in terms of the worst case scenario--the pay-off received if the competitor chose the best reactive strategy. The pay-off under the worst case scenario represents a guaranteed level of performance for that strategy irrespective of the competitor's future actions. A player should, therefore, choose the strategy that performs best under the worst case scenario.

---

[1] When there is more than one competitor, the competition may be considered to be a single entity as long as there is no collusion among them. While the addition of competition increases the computational burden, since the number of possible strategies increases, the methodology remains unchanged.

Site Evaluation Model

Central to any store location model is the estimation of the relationship between store characteristics and the expected performance of stores. A popular approach to modeling such a relationship is to use the Multiplicative Competitive Interaction (MCI) model (Nakanishi and Cooper, 1974; Jain and Mahajan, 1979; Hansen and Weinberg, 1979). Based on Huff's gravity model of spatial behavior (Huff, 1962) and belonging to the general class of market share attraction models, the MCI model states that the probability p_{ij} of any person at residential zone i shopping at store j is given by:

$$p_{ij} = \prod_{k=1}^{K} A_{ijk}^{\alpha_k} / \sum_{j \in N} \prod_{k=1}^{K} A_{ijk}^{\alpha_k} \qquad (1)$$

where, A_{ijk} = k^{th} of the K attributes of a store j (j=1, 2,...,N) as viewed by individuals at zone i (i=1,2,...,M)

α_k = empirically determined parameters reflecting the effect of the kth attribute on store choice probabilities.

Given equation (1) the expected market share of store j is given by $\sum_{i=1}^{M} a_i p_{ij}$ where a_i is zone i's share of total retail expenditure.

The MCI model can be used to simulate the effect of changes in store configuration on the market share of different stores in the area. Similarly, for a new store(s) entering the area the model can be used to choose the strategy that maximizes the expected market share. For a retail chain the optimal strategy is one which maximizes the total share of all outlets belonging to the chain--both existing and new. The optimal network of multiple stores must be selected simultaneously to minimize the cannibalizing effect of any one store on the performance of other stores belonging to the same chain. Moreover, in a competitive situation the chosen configurations must also be robust against competitive encroachment.

Consider a study area where N stores are operated by two retail chains. Chain A, which operates r of the n existing stores, plans to locate p new facilities in the area. During the same period the competitor is also expected to locate q new facilities in the area. How should Chain A determine the optimal configurations for its new stores?

Let $Y_p = (y_1, y_2, \ldots, y_p)$ be a particular configuration for the p new stores. Similarly, let $Z_q = (z_1, z_2, \ldots, z_q)$ be the set of store configurations for the competitive facilities. Both Y_p and Z_q are chosen from the set of feasible configurations F. Define $S(Y_p(Z_q)/N)$ as the expected dollar market share of stores belonging to Chain A. To find the set Y_p^* which maximizes the market share of stores belonging to Chain A, we solve the following combinatorial problem:

$$\text{Max } S(Y_p(Z_q)/N) = \text{Max } \sum_{\substack{j \in r \\ j \in F}} \sum_{i=1}^{m} a_i p_{ij} x_j$$

Subject to $\sum_{j \in F} x_j = p$ \qquad (2)

$x_j \leq 1$ for $j \in F$; $x_j = 1$ for all $j \in Z_q$, $j \in N$.

$$p_{ij} = (\prod_{k=1}^{K} A_{ijk}^{\alpha_k} x_j) / \sum_{j \in F} \sum_{j \in N} \sum_{j \in Z_q} (\prod_{k=1}^{K} A_{ijk} x_j)$$

$$x_j = \begin{cases} 1 & \text{if store configuration j is selected} \\ 0 & \text{otherwise} \end{cases}$$

Maximin Objective Function

The objective function of problem (2) is to maximize the total market share of the set of existing (r) and new (p) stores belonging to the firm. The constraints dictate that only p new facilities can be opened and that each store has a unique configuration. Since location is one component of store configuration, this implies that two stores cannot be located at the same site. Solution to problem (2) provides the best configurations for the p new stores given the set of existing stores and the particular configuration, Z_q, of the set of new competitive stores.

It is reasonable to assume that the competitor engages in a similar decision making procedure to determine the optimal configuration of its own stores. The optimal store configurations for the competitor would, however, be different from Y_p^* since the configuration of the existing stores belonging to the two chains could be very different and this would affect the ideal configurations of the new stores. This is because the model tries to maximize the total market share of the chain rather than looking at the new stores in isolation. The competitor's choice of the best configuration for its stores, for a particular Y_p, is given by $(Y_p(Z_q^*)/N)$. To determine Z_q^* the competitor solves a problem similar to (2) with the objective $\text{Min}_{Z_q} S(Y_p(Z_q)/N)$.

Since Z_q^* represents the best strategy for the competitor given a choice Y_p, the best strategy for Chain A is to choose the maximin configuration:

$$S(Y_p^*(Z_q^*)/N) = \underset{Y_p}{\text{Max}} \ \underset{Z_q(Y_p)}{\text{Min}} \ S(Y_p(Z_q)/N).$$

The expected market share of this maximin strategy represents a guaranteed performance level for the chain irrespective of the choice of configurations by the competitor.

When a large number of alternatives are available to the firms determining the maximin location is a difficult task. Combinatorial programming and analytical procedures are difficult to implement because of the complex form of the function relating market share with store characteristics. To find the maximin solutions to the store configuration problem we develop an iterative procedure based on the metagame analysis methods suggested by Dutta and King (1980). In this section we explain this procedure with the help of the hypothetical scenario shown in Table 1. In this scenario each firm has eight alternative options. The matrix entries indicate firm A's market share for each possible scenario.

TABLE 1

ILLUSTRATION OF ITERATIVE PROCEDURE FOR FINDING MAXIMIN SOLUTION

Market Share for A

A Adopts Strategy	B Adopts Strategy							
	B1	B2	B3	B4	B5	B6	B7	B8
A1	56.0	56.1	53.2	56.0	53.9	56.2	61.8	57.5
A2	55.3	53.7	52.7	56.3	53.9	55.5	61.0	56.5
A3	53.9	56.0	51.0	54.5	53.8	55.1	60.3	58.6
A4	57.8	59.0	58.0	56.5	56.0	57.1	62.1	57.1
A5	50.9	52.3	50.1	56.2	50.1	51.7	57.1	55.1
A6	59.2	60.1	58.0	57.0	63.7	57.7	64.9	61.1
A7	54.8	56.1	54.2	53.4	58.9	54.0	64.0	55.0
A8	49.1	50.4	48.3	48.2	53.7	48.3	49.2	48.8

[a]Roman numerals incidate iteration number.

213

The iterative procedure is initiated by specifying an initial strategy for Firm A (assume A1). The next step is to determine the most desirable strategy for B, given A's initial choice. In our example B should clearly choose strategy B3 in response to A1. The next step is one of considering countermoves by A to B's preceding choice. In other words what is A's best response to strategy B3. At this step the algorithm chooses strategy A4 as A's optimal response. The algorithm continues through the iterations by choosing a firm's optimal response to its competitor's move in the previous iteration. In Table 1 the strategy path of the first five iterations are shown:
(A1, B3)⟶(A4, B3)⟶(A4, B5)⟶(A6, B5)⟶(A6, B4).

At the end of iteration five, there is no strategy that guarantees A an improvement over its present choice of A6. At the same time strategy B4 represents B's optimal response to A6. Thus, neither firm can improve its position by a unilateral move. The strategy combination (A6, B4) represents an equilibrium combination for the two firms as long as no collusion or cooperation is permissible.

The Vertex Substitution Heuristic

The procedure outlined above allows the determination of the equilibrium strategies in an iterative fashion providing an analytically tractable method for finding the maximin strategy. Adapting this procedures to the store location model involves solving the multiple store location model (2) at each step of the algorithm. The large amount of computer time necessary to arrive at optimal solutions for large combinatorial problems of this type has lead to the popularity of a number of heuristic procedures for solving multiple location problems. Of these the vertex substitution algorithm of Tietz and Bart (1968), has been found to be the most efficient and robust and is used in this model.

In order to determine the best location for p stores the Tietz and Bart algorithm starts with any arbitrarily chosen p locations and attempts to improve the solution by substituting locations that are in the solution with those that are not. Every time a substitution is made the market share performance of the resulting store configuration is calculated from the site evaluation model. Whenever the performance is improved, an interchange is made by substituting the new one. The cycle is repeated by comparing each location in the solution with those feasible sites not included in the solution. The algorithm terminates when no further improvement in the solution can be obtained by the substitution procedure. Since the final solution may be sensitive to the choice of the p starting solutions, multiple runs of each problem reported in the next section were performed with different starting solutions. In all cases the problems converged to the same equilibrium.

To summarize, the sequence of steps necessary to implement the model are as follows:

(1) Conduct a consumer survey to calibrate the site attraction model, equation (1). Note that while we use the MCI model, any formulation that models the relationship between store characteristics such as location, store size, image, service characteristics, etc., and store performance can be utilized.

(2) Divide the study area into a number of zones and determine the consumer expenditure level in each zone.

(3) Determine the set of feasible alternatives for each firm.

(4) For a given value of p and q, initiate the maximin algorithm by arbitrarily selecting p locations for A.

(5) Use the vertex substitution algorithm to find firm B's best reaction to A's choice. Similarly find A's best countermove.

(6) Repeat step 5 until the equilibrium configuration is found.

In the next section the application of this procedure is illustrated.

APPLICATION OF THE MODEL

Description of Market Area

To illustrate the use of the model, data were collected from a mid-western town of about 50,000 people. The area has four existing grocery stores, operated by two supermarket chains (A and B). An earlier study (Ghosh and McLafferty, 1981) had found relative store size and the distance separating the consumer from a store to be the determinants of store market share. The study area (see Figure) was divided into 48 customer zones (i) and the market share distributions across all the stores from each of these zones were collected through a trip origin survey.

FIGURE
MAP OF MARKET AREA

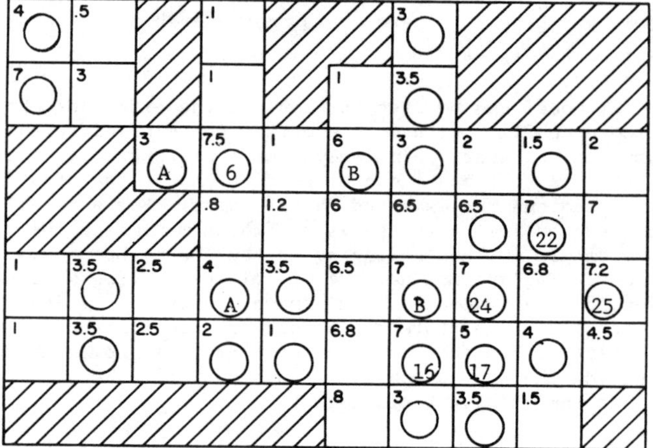

NOTE: Numbers in upper left hand corner of cells indicate zone attractiveness (higher numbers indicate greater attractiveness). Circles indicate a feasible site and capital letters, A or B, indicate existing store locations.

The size of each store was obtained by direct inspection. The distance separating a customer from a store was found from a city map using a city block metric. The log transformed procedure developed by Nakanishi and Cooper (1974) was then used to estimate the parameters. The values obtained were 1.418 and -2.5071 for store size and distance respectively.

Now consider the following scenario. Management of Chain A, which presently operates two stores, has decided to strengthen its position in the market by locating new stores. It is expected, however, that firm B will also locate new stores in response to A's expansion. Twenty-one feasible sites for new store locations for the two chains were identified on the basis of land availability and zoning regulations. To simplify the presentation of the results (Table 2) we consider the addition of up to three new stores by the firms and that all stores are of equal size.[2]

Firm A begins with 2 outlets and a 42.6 percent share of the market. Firm B also has two stores and the remaining 57.4 percent of the market. A evaluates its three loca-

---

[2]The equal store size assumption is made to facilitate presentation of results. The application of the model is not dependent on such an assumption.

tional strategies (locating one, two or three stores)
against the three possible strategies of B. Both are assumed to have the same knowledge of the environment and to make locational choices according to the MCI formulation. What differs is A's use of the planning model. This enables A to systematically evaluate multiple locations in terms of maximizing its likely gain relative to any counter move by its competitor.

TABLE 2
STORE LOCATION AND DOLLAR MARKET SHARE

	Number of Stores Located by A					
	1		2		3	
	$\underline{\underline{A}}$[a] 17	$\underline{B}$ 22	$\underline{A}$ 16,22	$\underline{B}$ 25	$\underline{A}$ 16,22,24	$\underline{B}$ 25
Number of Stores Located by B 1	(44.57)[b]	(56.43)	(56.40)	(43.60)	(62.83)	(37.17)
2	17 (37.90)	22,10 (62.10)	16,24 (47.77)	17,22 (55.23)	16,22,17 (55.29)	25,24 (44.71)
3	16 (31.89)	10,17,6 (68.11)	16,24 (41.51)	17,22,6 (58.49)	16,22,17 (49.71)	6,24,25 (50.29)

[a] Optimal location for firm, see Figure.
[b] Figures in parentheses indicate dollar market share.

Optional Location Strategy

Developing a successful locational strategy for Firm A requires an answer to two questions: 1) where to locate, and 2) how many to locate. The best locational strategies for Firm A for up to three additional outlets can be obtained from inspection of Table 2. Certain locations (see Figure for map identities) are particularly robust and are prominent in many of A's possible strategies. Others are not only robust but also preemptive in that they also figure prominently in B's possible strategies (e.g. 17). The diagonal entries of Table 2 provide some indication of how the model enhances the locational choices of the firm employing it. At the outset B enjoyed a 14.8 point market share advantage. That advantage gradually erodes until with three additional outlets for each the shares have become virtually identical.

An essential component of any locational decision is the number of stores that a firm should operate in a given market area. One useful approach to this decision is to compare the cost of the incremental outlet with the gain in revenue resulting from the increased market share. Lilien and Rao (1979) suggest that the relationship between market share and the share of outlets can be represented by an S-curve. They further suggest that the data to fit this curve can be obtained by observing the relative shares in different market areas. Calibrating the S-curve from empirical observations has its perils in that the actual locations may not represent the optimal sites for the firm.

The current model allows a determination to be made of the growth in share with additional outlets as a planning tool. Table 3 shows the effect on market share of Firm A going from 3 to 8 total stores holding B constant at three stores. The number of outlets to locate can be gotten by knowing the cost of locating the incremental outlet and the likely gain in market share. Obviously, the result depends on the number of stores B locates. In a complete application of the model a range of likely responses by B would have to be evaluated.

CONCLUSION

In a dynamic retail environment a firm must take into account the state of the entire system, not only as it currently exists, but also as it will be in the future. In general terms retailers must find locations that are both economically viable as well as possessing strong defensive properties. Thus, they must take into account not only their existing stores and those of competition, but also the impact that future locational choices will have on their

TABLE 3
RELATIONSHIP BETWEEN NUMBER OF OUTLETS AND
MARKET SHARE FOR FIRM A

Total Number of Stores	Number of Additional Stores	Market Share[a]	Increase in Market Share
2	0	29.09	--
3	1	44.57	15.48
4	2	56.40	11.83
5	3	62.83	6.43
6	4	66.94	4.11
7	5	69.29	2.35
8	6	71.10	1.81

[a] Dollar market share for A with 3 stores for B.

operating success. To do this effectively a retailer must be able to treat the locational decision for multiple stores as a simultaneous rather than sequential process.

The model we have developed can guide retail location decisions. It provides managers with a means to simultaneously evaluate their own locational decisions relative to possible competitive moves. The game theory framework employed in the model allows the retailer to select the locational strategy that will maximize his gain in market share relative to competition. Thus, it provides the retailer with a valuable planning tool for making locational decisions.

REFERENCES

Applebaum, W. (1968) *Guide to Store Location Research with Emphasis on Supermarkets*. Reading, MA: Addison-Wesley.

Baligh, H. H. and L. E. Richartz (1967), "Variable-sum Game Models of Marketing Problems," *Journal of Marketing Research, 4*, 173-85.

Barcun, S. C. and P. Jeming (1973) "Airline Seat Share: A Study in False Optimization," *Management Science, 20*, 146-53.

Dutta, B. K. and W. R. King (1980) "Metagame Analysis of Competitive Strategy," *Strategic Management Journal, 1*, 357-369.

Ghosh, A. and S. L. McLafferty (1981) "Strategic Location Models for Retail Chains," New York University, Graduate School of Business Administration, Working Paper.

Hansen, M. H. and C. B. Weinberg (1979) "Retail Market Share in a Competitive Environment," *Journal of Retailing, 55*, 37-46.

Huff, D. L. (1962) "Determination of Intra-Urban Retail Trade Areas," Real Estate Research Program, Los Angeles, CA: University of California.

Jain, A. K. and V. Mahajan (1979) "Evaluating the Competitive Environment in Retailing Using Multiplicative Competitive Interactive Model," in J. Sheth (ed.), *Research in Marketing, 2*, 217-235.

Kotler, P. (1971) *Marketing Decision Making: A Model Building Approach*, New York: Holt, Rinehart and Winston.

Krishnan, K. S. and S. K. Gupta (1967) "Mathematical Models for a Duopolistic Market," *Management Science, 13*, 568-83.

Lilien, G. L. and A. G. Rao (1979) "Emerging Approaches to Retail Outlet Management," *Sloan Management Review, 6*, 27-35.

Nakanishi, M. and L. G. Cooper (1974) "Parameter Estimate for Multiplicative Interactive Choice Model-Least Squares Approach," *Journal of Marketing Research, 11*, 303-311.

Rapoport, A. (1973) *Two Person Game Theory*, Ann Arbor, MI: University of Michigan Press.

Scott, A. J. (1975) "Discrete Dynamic Locational Systems: Notes on a Structural Framework," in A. Karlquist, L. Lungquist and F. Snickards (eds.) *Dynamic Allocation in Urban Space*, Lexington, MA: Saxon House.

Teitz, M. B. and P. Bart (1968) "Heuristic Models for Estimating the Generalized Vertex Median of a Weighted Graph," *Operations Research, 16*, 955-961.

CMROI: A NEW VIEW OF PLANNING AND MEASURING MERCHANDISING PERFORMANCE

Charles A. Ingene, The University of Texas at Dallas, Dallas
Michael Levy, Southern Methodist University, Dallas

ABSTRACT

A return on investment measure for planning merchandising decisions and for measuring the efficacy of those
decisions is developed in this paper. The model is an extension of the familiar gross margin return on investment
(GMROI) criterion. The new view, CMROI, is argued to be
more meaningful in today's volatile business climate. In
particular, it is of value in (1) planning merchandise investment, (2) evaluating departmental performance, and
(3) comparing the relative performance of two or more departments. For both evaluation and comparison, CMROI may
aid senior management in determining when and where policy
changes should be implemented.

INTRODUCTION

This paper reviews and refines the relationship between
merchandising decisions and return on inventory investment. Improvements are suggested in a currently employed
managerial tool, gross margin return on inventory investment (GMROI). The modified model, termed contribution
margin return on inventory investment (CMROI), requires
more data to implement than does GMROI. However, it provides a superior picture of merchandise performance, one
which is more closely related to the overall financial
performance of a business organization.

In this paper, CMROI is discussed and illustrated at the
departmental level of a retail store for a planning horizon of one evaluation period, that is, a season or a year.
CMROI is also applicable for larger or smaller units of
analysis (stores, merchandise items) and for larger planning horizons. To ease the exposition, only the single
period, departmental case is discussed. The major theme
of this paper is that with CMROI, managers can utilize the
expected return on inventory investment to plan their merchandising portfolio and can also employ the actual (ex
post) return to evaluate the efficacy of their actions.

GMROI: THE TRADITIONAL VIEW

A global measure of a retailer's financial performance is
return on assets (ROA = net profit after taxes/total assets). While merchandising and other marketing activities
should be utilized to enhance ROA, ROA itself is an inappropriate aid for merchandise planning or evaluation for
two reasons. First, several aspects of costs and of assets are independent of any merchandising decisions. Attempts to assign overhead costs or common assets tend to
be arbitrary and to distort managerial impressions of what
is occurring (Kirplani and Shapiro 1973). Second, in
larger retail organizations, merchandising decisions are
decentralized. The decision makers (merchandise managers
or buyers) should make decisions and be evaluated on the
basis of variables under their control, within the constraints imposed by senior management (Sweeney 1973). Return on inventory investment has been offered as a solution to these problems, provided that the funds available
for inventory investment are the primary constraints faced
by merchandise managers and buyers.

Several authors have proposed GMROI as an appropriate return on investment tool for planning and evaluating merchandise decisions (Sweeney 1973, Robicheaux 1979, 1981;
Ahern and Romano 1979). GMROI is currently used, often

under a proprietary title, by some of America's largest
retailers (e.g., Sears and Federated Department Stores)
and is reported in publications of the National Retail
Merchants Association (1979) and Price Waterhouse (1981).
Sweeney has catalogued five reasons for using GMROI.
First, it is a meaningful measure of managerial
performance. Second, the desired GMROI may be established
by senior management to be consistent with overall corporate financial goals. Third, GMROI may be used for merchandise planning. Fourth, it is a meaningful measure of
merchandise performance. Fifth, its data needs are readily available.

The standard measure of GMROI is:

$$\frac{Gross\ Margin}{Net\ Sales} \times \frac{Net\ Sales}{Average\ Inventory\ At\ Cost} = \frac{Gross\ Margin}{Average\ Inventory\ At\ Cost} \quad (1)$$

Planning decisions may be made on the basis of expected
gross margin percent and expected turnover. Evaluation
focuses on the deviation of the actual from the expected
gross margin percent and turnover, and the reasons for the
deviation. Although all five points listed above for using GMROI are valid, in the next section it is argued that
GMROI may not be sufficiently comprehensive in today's
business environment to be judged adequate on the first
four points.

CMROI: AN IMPROVEMENT OVER GMROI

This section starts with the definition of contribution
margin return on inventory investment. Each element of
CMROI is then explained in some detail, including an explanation of how each modification improves upon GMROI.
Two points need to be stressed. (1) GMROI is not wrong;
but, it is not as comprehensive as the authors of this paper believe is necessary. (2) The explanation of CMROI
presented here is written rather broadly to cover as many
situations as possible. Not all retailers would (or
should) want to utilize the CMROI model presented here because the expense of so doing could exceed the benefits.
Further, some of the components of CMROI are not relevant
to every level of analysis nor to all time horizons.

A definition of CMROI is:

$$CMROI = \frac{(GM-IE-SE-OAE)}{Net\ Sales} \times \frac{Net\ Sales}{\{\$INV\}} \quad (2)$$

where: GM   = gross margin dollars
       IE   = interest expense of maintaining and
           selling inventory
      SE   = spatial expense of storing and displaying
           inventory
     OAE   = other allocable expenses associated with
           the merchandise
   {\$INV} = average dollars invested in inventory.

The term (GM-IE-SE-OAE) is referred to as the contribution
margin. (GM-IE-SE-OAE)/(Net Sales) is the contribution
margin percent (CM%), while (Net Sales/{\$INV}) is the rate
of (financially measured) inventory turnover. The average
dollars invested in inventory, {\$INV} is discussed prior

to an exploration of the components of contribution margin.[1]

Average Dollar Investment in Inventory, {$INV}

The traditional accounting definition of average inventory includes the physical inventory when it is purchased. However, this does not reflect the true investment. The dollar investment in inventory begins when merchandise is paid for by the store. The investment terminates when the store collects for the merchandise. An accurate measure of inventory investment then includes a reduction in inventory investment by the amount of accounts payable on that merchandise and an increase in inventory investment by the amount of accounts receivable for merchandise sold on credit. This relationship is expressed on a daily basis as:

$$I_i = (DVI_i - AP_i + AR_i) \tag{3}$$

where: DVI_i = dollar value of inventory (at cost) on day i, this is the definition of inventory used in the GMROI model,

AP_i = accounts payable on day i for this merchandise,

AR_i = accounts receivable at cost on day i for this merchandise.

Average inventory would be expressed as:

$$(\$INV) = \sum_{i=1}^{n} I_i \div n \tag{4}$$

where: n = number of days in the time period under consideration.

Terms of Purchase (AP_i). It is typical for retailers to pay after delivery. Financial terms of sale such as 2/10/net 30 are common.[2] However, any combination of discount and payment dates is possible. The cash discount is included in retailers' gross margin calculation[3] but the discount period is neglected. The effect on financial performance can be profound since a longer period reduces inventory investment; in fact, its effect is equivalent to a loan. The inclusion of accounts payable into CMROI improves the accuracy of the return on investment measure and therefore the accuracy of management decisions. In essence, buyers ought to be encouraged to seek improved terms of purchase from various vendors and should be evaluated on their ability to do so successfully.

Consumer Credit (AR_i). Retailers' investment in inventory ceases when collection is made for items sold. Since most retailers grant consumer credit of some kind, this is not always coterminous with the date of sale. Indeed, only for cash payment does financial investment and physical relinquishment occur simultaneously. If payment is made by bank credit card, by check, or if the retailer sells his accounts receivable to a factor, the lag between sale and collection is small.[4] If the retailer maintains his own credit system, the time lag between sale and collection, and the inventory investment, will be greater.

Note that accounts receivable should be evaluated here at the merchandise cost rather than at the retail value.

---

[1]Some of the concepts discussed in this section were first developed by Mullins (1972).

[2]2/10/net 30 means that a 2% discount is offered if paid within 10 days of invoice date; otherwise, the full invoice amount is due on the 30th day.

[3]Gross margin dollars equals net sales plus cash discounts minus workroom expenses minus cost of goods sold.

[4]The factoring fee is deducted from gross margin. It is part of other allocable expenses (OAE).

Consider a simple example of a single item which costs $10. It is sold on credit for $19. Suppose further that the retailer has already paid for the merchandise. Then immediately prior to the sale, DVI = $10. After the sale DVI drops to zero because the item is no longer in inventory. The relevant accounts receivable figure is still $10 because that is all the retailer has invested in the item. The additional $9 is included in the contribution margin and is discussed below.

The effect of consumer credit on merchandising decisions may appear somewhat elusive on the surface. The credit cost to the retailer is identical across product categories and departments. However, certain products are more apt to be bought on credit than others, e.g., furniture, men's suits and other large expenditures. These "credit-prone" products adversely affect dollar inventory investment. Thus, departments which are "credit prone" have a larger inventory investment than is indicated by the GMROI formulation. Correspondingly, they contribute less to the financial performance of the organization.

A Negative Inventory Investment. Examination of (4) reveals that I_i can be negative on any given day! Suppose a shipment of merchandise is received with terms of net thirty. If the merchandise is sold for cash, and is sold out by the twentieth day, then the retailer has, in effect, received an interest free loan from the vendor. This "loan" is equal to the total dollar value of the shipment for days 21 to 30, and is equal to a lesser amount on the preceding days. For illustrative purposes, suppose the shipment were 20 units with a cost of $10 each. Further assume that the daily selling rate is one unit per day. The "loan" would then be $10 on day 2, $20 on day 3, ... and $200 on days 21 to 30. This phenomenon is not uncommon for retailers with relatively rapid turnover and adequate terms from vendors (e.g., restaurants). A department which has, on average, a negative inventory investment should not plan or be judged on the basis of CMROI since a negative denominator results in a misleading measure. In these cases, the numerator, contribution margin, appears to be the appropriate criterion.

Contribution Margin

As noted previously, gross margin is the earnings ratio in the traditional GMROI formula. Gross margin does not capture all the important components necessary for merchandising decisions. The necessary adjustments to gross margin which are reflected in contribution margin are now considered.

IE: Interest Expense of Maintaining and Selling Inventory. In today's economy, the interest expense of maintaining inventory is more significant than in the past. Therefore, proper consideration of interest expense is more critical. The cost of maintaining an inventory investment is the product of the daily interest rate (r), the magnitude of the investment, and the duration of the investment. Thus, the period of time associated with the terms of sale and the terms of purchase, in conjunction with the daily interest rate, affect the interest expense. Mathematically, interest expense of maintaining inventory is:

$$IMI = r \sum_{i=1}^{n} I_i \tag{5}$$

for whatever duration of time is chosen for investigation.

The interest expense of selling (as opposed to maintaining) inventory is related to the markup when an item is sold on credit. Specifically, the difference between the markup and its discounted present value is this interest expense (ISI). Delayed collection causes the discounted present value of the markup to be less than the markup itself. It is larger when (a) interest rates are higher, (b) the time between sale and collection is longer and

(c) the markup is larger. Note that the interest charged
the consumer on the credit sale (if any) is already added
into gross margin.

The interest expense of maintaining and selling inventory
is:

$$IE = IMI + ISI \tag{6}$$

<u>SE: Spatial Expenses of Storing and Displaying Inventory.</u>
The cost of displaying and storing merchandise is rarely
inconsequential. There is a direct rental expense for the
space occupied. A maintenance expense may also be incurred. Even when space is owned there is an opportunity
cost in foregone revenues from renting the space to
others. It must be emphasized that it is not always ad-
vantageous to trace spatial expenses. Such data should be
collected when the value of the knowledge gained exceeds
the gathering cost and when the unit of analysis and the
planning horizon are appropriate. In particular, spatial
expenses are probably useful for comparing the performance
of stores for a middle to long term planning horizon of
greater than one year. However, it would probably be too
difficult, expensive and managerially unjustifiable to determine spatial expenses for specific merchandise items.
The space occupied by specific items fluctuates drastically in the short run. Further, buyers and merchandise managers often have little control over space allocations.
The level at which it is worthwhile to compute spatial expense will vary by retailer.

Assuming it is worthwhile to include SE in CMROI, it is
calculated as the value of a square foot of space per day
(COST) times the average square footage (SPACE). COST is
determined by a number of factors. In general, the location of a store determines the average value of space.
The value of space in a prime location in a major shopping
center is greater than in an average strip shopping center. Within the store, the locations of some departments
are more desirable than others. In one major retail department store chain the value of space is based upon the
amount of traffic past each department. (Personal communication, Gary Milleson, Vice President of Finance, Sanger
Harris Department Stores.) High traffic locations are expected to outperform low traffic locations. Cost is an
attempt to consider the opportunity cost of the location.
By including SE in CMROI, retailers are able to explicitly
evaluate the productivity of merchandise with different
space requirements.

<u>OAE: Other Allocable Expenses.</u> Finally, expenses which
are directly associated with merchandise could often be
incorporated into CMROI. Examples include, but are not
restricted to, commissions paid to salespersonnel, direct
promotional expenses, the department manager's salary, and
some of the maintenance costs associated with holding inventory. (See LaLonde and Lambert (1977) for a full discussion of inventory carrying costs).

<u>Comment.</u> One might wonder why the denominator of CMROI
does not include the value of assets, like space and
equipment, which are necessary for the sale of the merchandise. The CMROI model described in this paper is
designed to assist senior management in planning and evaluating merchandise inventory decisions at the departmental
level. Space and equipment are fixed assets which are
present independent of merchandising decisions. The flow
of their services is charged against the numerator of
CMROI. Fixed assets should only be included in a return
on investment denominator when decisions are being made on
the allocation of those assets.

CMROI IN USE

There are three uses for CMROI at the departmental level.
They are (1) planning a merchandise assortment, (2) evaluating the financial performance of a department during a
review period, and (3) comparing the performance of two or
more departments.

Planning

Merchandise managers determine a target CMROI for their
buyer's departments given a budget for inventory investment. Buyers would examine the components of CMROI to
plan their inventory investments for specific merchandise
items. CMROI is dependent upon the inventory investment
for two reasons. First, the larger the inventory of a
brand, the greater will be ($INV) and the interest expense
of holding inventory. Both of these factors will lower
CMROI. Second, a larger inventory will also yield a larger gross margin, raising CMROI. However, these two factors cannot be expected to offset each other: a larger
inventory can be anticipated to take longer to sell and to
be more likely to lead to markdowns than a smaller inventory. Therefore, as the inventory of any brand rises,
gross margin should rise at a decreasing rate while interest expense rises at an increasing rate. There must be a
point beyond which CMROI declines with additional inventory. It follows that by adjusting the inventory of each
brand, the buyer can program the merchandise mix to attain
the targeted level of CMROI. Such an analysis may also
aid the buyer in bargaining for better terms of purchase.

Note that if managers are charged with maximizing return
on inventory investment, they will have an incentive to
avoid some profitable investments which would lower the
average CMROI (Solomons 1965, Dearden 1969). Thus, it is
essential that planning and evaluation occur relative to a
<u>target</u> CMROI which will generally not be the maximum at-
tainable CMROI.

Evaluation

At the end of a review period, buyers and their merchandise manager will evaluate why the realized CMROI deviated
from the targeted CMROI. For example, CMROI may be lower
than expected because contribution margin is low, because
inventory investment is high, or both. This inferior
CMROI may, however, be beyond the buyers' control. By examining the CMROI components along with current economic
and competitive factors, the merchandise manager can determine if the buyers reacted to the environment in the
most appropriate manner.

Comparison

CMROI provides senior management with information for comparing the financial performance of departments. In order
to maximize overall profitability, return on investment,
or other financial goals of the firm, it may be necessary
to shift inventory funds between departments in response
to buyer and merchandise manager talents, changing environmental conditions, or alterations in supply factors.
CMROI summarizes the relevant financial information relevant for these decisions. In addition, CMROI can be used
as a basis for making spatial decisions. CMROI can indicate when the amount of space, or the charge per square
foot of space, needs to be changed. While CMROI cannot
prescribe specific actions, it can indicate a need for
more detailed investigation. The following section provides an illustration of how GMROI and CMROI are used for
comparing the performance of departments.

CMROI VS. GMROI: A SYNTHETIC EXAMPLE

Table I presents a synthetic example of the operating results in two different departments. The data in column A
approximates a woman's sportswear department, while the
columns labeled B approximate a furniture department.
B(60) represents 60 day terms from the source, B(45) rep-

218

resents the effect of a reduction in the maximum payment
period to 45 days. Accounts payable (AP) are computed on
the basis of turnover, with terms of net 10 days, net 60
days and net 45 days for departments A, B(45) and B(60),
respectively. Accounts receivable assumes that all of A's
sales are for cash or check, while 90% of B's sales are on
credit and that it takes consumers 45 days to pay their
accounts. Although the differences are pronounced, they
represent a typical A purchase of low dollar value and
typical B purchase of high dollar value. Interest expense
reflects a .05% daily interest rate (20% annual rate).
Spatial expense indicates A occupying less space but at a
higher per square foot charge due to greater traffic
flow.

TABLE 1

SYNTHETIC OPERATING CHARACTERISTICS FOR TWO DEPARTMENTS

	A	B(60)	B(45)
Sales	$1,000,000	$1,000,000	$1,000,000
Gross Margin	400,000	500,000	500,000
Dollar Value of Inventory (DVI)	150,000	250,000	250,000
Inventory Turnover	4	2	2
Accounts Payable	16,438	82,192	61,644
Accounts Receivable	0	55,479	55,479
Total Interest Expense	26,734	55,798	59,911
Interest Expense of Maintaining Inventory	26,734	44,693	48,806
Interest Expense of Selling Inventory	0	11,105	11,105
Total Spatial Expense	35,000	20,000	20,000
cost/sq.ft./yr.	4	2	2
space (sq.ft.)	8,750	10,000	10,000
Other Allocable Expenses	25,000	20,000	20,000
Contribution Margin	313,266	394,202	390,089
Average Dollars Invested in Inventory ($INV)	123,266	223,287	243,835
GMROI	267%	200%	200%
CMROI	254%	177%	160%

Three phenomena are immediately apparent from Table I.
First, for department A, CMROI and GMROI are almost identical because the modifications suggested in this paper
are essentially self-cancelling. For such departments,
use of CMROI rather than GMROI offers few benefits. Second, for department B (60 day terms), the modifications
show an 11.5% reduction in return on investment ((200-
177)÷200), a significant decrease which might well alter
senior management's opinion of a department manager's performance. (It should be noted that one can create an example in which CMROI exceeds GMROI.) Third, CMROI is
quite sensitive to changes in terms of purchase, as shown
in the third column of Table I: this is a 20% reduction
from GMROI and a 9.5% reduction from the CMROI with 60 day
terms.

A retailer currently employing GMROI would have to augment
his information processing in order to obtain the type of
data described above. However, provided the retailer has
participated in the "electronic revolution" (Mason and
Mayer 1980, Broeren 1981) by acquiring computer linked
cash registers with U.P.C. or O.C.R. capabilities, the raw
data needed to implement CMROI are available. Specifically, firms which already use GMROI have knowledge about
gross margin, turnover, and the dollar value of inventory.
Spatial expense and other allocable expenses are either
known or can easily be obtained. Accounts payable data
are obtained through accounting records. Accounts receivable must be tracked on a departmental basis. This represents a feasible extension of current practice. When combined with the firm's current capital costs the interest
expense of maintaining inventory is derived. The interest

expense of selling inventory and of accounts receivable
can be captured at the time of purchase.

CONCLUSION

Planning merchandising assortments, evaluating merchandising performance, and comparing various departments'
contribution to an organization's financial goals are activities which have become increasingly important to marketers. Contribution Margin Return on Investment (CMROI)
has been introduced as a comprehensive tool which would be
useful to buyers and merchandise managers for planning and
evaluation and to senior management for comparison. In
many situations, CMROI is a more useful and a more accurate return on investment measure than the more traditional GMROI. CMROI considers the spatial expense of storing
and displaying merchandise, the interest expense of maintaining and selling inventory, and other allocable expenses associated with selling inventory. In addition,
CMROI considers the terms of purchase by the retailer as
well as its terms of sale to the customer; thus, it more
accurately measures inventory investment. The use of
CMROI, combined with an analysis of why any particular
CMROI level is achieved, should provide insight into some
of the dynamics of merchandising which have been unobtain-
able in the past.

REFERENCES

Ahern, John T., Jr. and Patrick L. Romano (1979), "Managing Inventories and Profits Through GMROI," _Management
Accounting_ (August), 22-6.

Broeren, Mary Ann (1981), "Perspectives on Profit," _Re-
tailing Update_, Price Waterhouse and Co. (April), 1-3.

Dearden, John (1969), "The Case Against ROI Control," _Har-
vard Business Review_ (May-June), 124-35.

Lalonde, Bernard J. and Douglas M. Lambert (1977), "A
Methodology for Calculating Inventory Carrying Costs,"
International Journal of Physical Distribution 7 (No.4),
195-231.

Mason, J. B. and M. Mayer (1980), "Retail Merchandise Information Systems for the 1980's," _Journal of Retailing_
(Spring) 56-76.

_Merchandising and Operating Results of Department and
Specialty Stores_ (1979) New York: National Retail Merchants Association.

Mullins, Peter L. (1972), "Integrating Marketing and Financial Concepts in Product Line Evaluations," _Finan-
cial Executive_, (May), 32-6.

Robicheaux, Robert A. (1979), "Comprehensive Wholesale Inventory Management," _Proceedings: Southern Marketing
Association_, 414-17.

__________ (1981), "GMROI/Share Product Portfolio Analysis," in K. Bernhardt, et al. (eds.), _The Changing Marketing Environment: New Theories and Applications_,
Chicago: American Marketing Association, 47: 31-34.

Solomons, David (1965), _Divisional Performance: Measurement and Control_, Richard D. Irwin.

Sweeney, Daniel J. (1973), "Improving the Profitability of
Retail Merchandising Decisions," _Journal of Marketing_
37 (January), 60-8.

AN ANALYSIS OF MARKET STRATEGY AND
STORE PROFITABILITY BY AREA COMPETITION

L. Lynn Judd, Western Illinois University
Bobby C. Vaught, Southwest Missouri State University

ABSTRACT

This study evaluates the perceived importance of several
retailing strategy variables in the grocery industry and
their relationship to store profitability. The perceived
competitive situation of the researched stores was also
entered into these relationships. The six selected strategy variables are price (in comparison to competition),
customer service, advertising and store promotion, store
location and physical plant, product assortment, and store
personnel.

INTRODUCTION

Effective merchandising has sometimes been defined as having the right goods at the right place, at the right time,
and at the right price and quality to satisfy consumer
wants (Mason and Mayer 1981). Ideally, the consumer's
wants and needs will match the merchandising strategies of
the retailer.

However, no store can be all things to all people (Hartley
1980). Thus, one set of strategies will not appeal to all
potential consumers in the same way. Therefore, for the
purpose of success, retailers typically seek to develop
strategies for reaching aggregates of people. This strategy is known as market segmentation (Mason and Mayer 1981).
As formulated, the strategy includes two distinct and yet
interrelated parts. The first part consists of the selection of one or more target markets to which the marketer
will attempt to sell his products or services. The second
part of the strategy is the creation of a marketing variable mix which the marketer will combine to conform to the
want satisfaction needs of the target consumers. Marketing
broadly defines these marketing variables as product, place,
promotion, and price (McCarthy 1981).

Leading authorities in the field of retailing have theoriz-
ed various combinations of variables as the retailing mix
(Lazer and Kelley 1979). For example, Robert F. Hartley
(1980) considers the retailing mix to be composed of the
following variables: 1) convenience of shopping (time,
place, effort), 2) merchandise assortment--breadth and
depth, 3) quality and fashion level of merchandise, 4)
price, 5) services, and 6) store excitement. Further,
Ronald Gist (1971) considers the retailing mix as a unique
combination of location, store layout, organization, promotion, pricing, service, merchandise assortment, and buying. On the other hand, William H. Bolen (1978) considers
the retailing mix to be composed of the basic product,
place, promotion, price and personality variables.

The major thrust of this study is to evaluate the perceived
importance of several retailing strategies in the grocery
industry and their relationship to store profitability.
For the purposes of the study, the perceived competitive
situation of the researched stores was also entered into
these relationships.

Six basic retailing mix variables were selected as the independent variables of the study. The retail variables
were price (in comparison to competition), customer service,
advertising and store promotion, store location and physical plant, product assortment, and store personnel. These
variables are similar to the factors utilized by Engle,
Blackwell, and Kollat (1978) within their Store-Choice

Processes model which illustrates consumer evaluative criteria and perceived characteristics (image) of stores.

SAMPLE AND METHODOLOGY

Five retailing indices of success were utilized as the dependent variables of the study. These primary indices are
percent gross profit margin (GPM), percent net profit margin (NPM), gross margin return on inventory investment
(GMROI), net profit return on inventory investment (NPROI),
and stockturn rate per year. Gross profit margin is defined as sales minus cost of goods sold and net profit margin is defined as gross profit margin minus operating expenses. The stockturn rate is the number of times the
average inventory is sold annually. Gross margin return on
inventory investment (GMROI) is a single comprehensive
ratio which allows retail management to review inventory
results from a return on investment perspective (Sweeney
1973). GMROI can be obtained via gross profit margin multiplied by the stockturn rate. Accordingly, net profit return on inventory investment (NPROI) would be a logical extension of this retail productivity ratio. Thus, NPROI
equals net profit margin multiplied by the stockturn rate.
This ratio reflects the same basic components of the classic
du Pont system of return on investment (Kline & Hessler 1952).

For this study, the members of a selected grocery retailer-
cooperative in Texas supplied the primary research data.
The retailer-cooperative is composed of multi-type retail
grocery establishments who jointly own and operate a wholesale grocery corporation. Even though the retailer-cooperative is operated by professional managers, the member
stores operate as individually owned independent merchants.
Since each member store employs a unique retail mix strategy, the subject members of the retailer-cooperative are
considered appropriate for the research study.

Data collection from the retailer-cooperative subjects was
accomplished via a pretested mail questionnaire. In the
questionnaire, the owner/managers were asked to rank the
six selected retailing strategies in their order of perceived importance. In addition, each owner/manager was
asked to indicate their perceived competitive situation
(weak or below average, moderate, strong or vigorous). The
questionnaire also obtained each retail establishment's
average gross profit margin, percent operating expenses,
stock turnover rate per year, store type, and dollar sales
volume for the previous calendar or fiscal year. Two mailings resulted in a 60 percent return (N = 379) from the
selected universe. These cases were analyzed by SPSS Subprogram Frequencies and Subprogram Spearman Correlation
(Norman Nie et al. 1975).

FREQUENCIES ANALYSIS

As noted, each retailer was requested to rank the relative
importance of the six retailing strategy variables in terms
of their perceived impact on strategic marketing decisions.
In addition, each retailer was asked to indicate the competitive situation of his retail establishment. Therefore,
for the purposes of the study, the respondents are classified into the following three competitive situation categories: 1) weak or below average, 2) moderate, 3) strong
or vigorous. Table I reflects the strategy rating results
of the study by each competitive situation category.

TABLE I

PERCEIVED IMPORTANCE OF SELECTED RETAILING MIX VARIABLES
BY COMPETITIVE SITUATION

Retailers Perceived Competitive Situation	Customer Service	Price (In Comparison to Competition)	Quality of Store Personnel	Store Location	Product Assortment	Advertising and Store Promotion
Weak or Below Average (N=47)						
Rank	1*	2	3	4	5	6**
Actual	2.18	2.67	3.30	3.34	4.00	4.43
Moderate (N=75)						
Rank	1*	5	2	3	4	6**
Actual	2.15	3.74	2.54	3.35	3.65	5.02
Strong or Vigorous (N=253)						
Rank	1*	3	2	4	6**	5
Actual	2.17	3.07	2.96	3.64	4.38	3.95

*1 = Most Important
**6 = Least Important

TABLE II

MEANS OF SUCCESS VARIABLES BY PERCEIVED COMPETITIVE SITUATION

Retailers by Perceived Competitive Situation	N	Percent GPM	Percent NPM	Stockturn Rate	Percent GMROI	Percent NPROI
Indice Means of all Retailer Respondents	379	22.5	5.6	15.561	337.9	79.2
Weak or Below Average	47	22.9	7.1	13.780	314.3	86.4
Moderate	75	23.7	6.1	16.034	353.2	75.0
Strong or Vigorous	253	22.1	5.1	15.783	338.7	79.0

The table indicates that the respondents for all three categories ranked customer service as number one in perceived importance. In addition, quality of store personnel was ranked either second or third in importance by all three categories. The reflected low rankings of the product assortment variable and the advertising/promotion variable were most unusual. These variables are generally the most utilized factors for store differentiation purposes.

Table II reflects the frequency results of the dependent variables of the study. The table indicates that the average retailer respondent had a GPM of 22.5 percent and a NPM of 5.6 percent. The average inventory stockturn was 15.561. This figure compares favorably with the 15.4 stockturn rate for grocery stores reported by Dun and Bradstreet, Inc., in 1979. Table II further indicates that the average GMROI is 337.9 percent and the average NPROI is 79.2 percent. The profit margin figures reported are operating profit margins and do not include depreciation, state taxes, and Federal taxes.

The data indicates that the moderate competition category had the highest GPM percentage of 23.7. However, the high NPM percentage of 7.1 was obtained by the weak competition category. The moderate competition category had a stockturn rate of 16.034 while the weak competition category had the low stockturn rate of 13.780.

Two major profit paths for retailers are either through "healthy" profit margins or good inventory turnover rates. However, for a much better "bottom line" view of potential store profitability, one must consider GMROI and NPROI

TABLE III

CORRELATION ANALYSES BETWEEN RETAILING STRATEGIES
AND FIVE INDICES OF RETAILING SUCCESS

Retailers by Perceived Competitive Situation	Customer Service	Price (In Comparison to Competition)	Quality of Store Personnel	Store Location	Product Assortment	Advertising and Store Promotion
Weak or Below Average (N=47						
Stockturn Rate	NS	.26*	-.29*	NS	NS	NS
GPM	NS	.24*	NS	NS	NS	NS
NPM	NS	NS	NS	-.24*	NS	.41**
GMROI	NS	.28*	NS	-.26*	NS	NS
NPROI	NS	NS	NS	-.31*	NS	.31*
Moderate (N=75)						
Stockturn Rate	-.35**	NS	NS	NS	NS	NS
GPM	NS	.48**	-.20*	-.33**	-.27*	.34**
NPM	.24*	NS	NS	NS	NS	NS
GMROI	-.27*	.28*	NS	NS	NS	.31*
NPROI	NS	NS	NS	NS	NS	NS
Strong or Vigorous (N=253)						
Stockturn Rate	-.18**	NS	NS	.22**	NS	NS
GPM	NS	.21**	-.15*	-.11*	-.18**	.26**
NPM	NS	.11*	-.18**	NS	-.22**	.26**
GMROI	-.18**	.17**	-.13*	.14*	-.16*	NS
NPROI	NS	.11*	-.17**	NS	-.30**	.18**

*P <.05
**P <.01

which combine both profit margin and stockturn rate. The data indicates that although the moderate competition category reflects the highest average GMROI percentage, this category reflects the lowest NPROI percentage. In like manner, the weak category indicates the lowest GMROI but the highest NPROI percentage. These figures not only reflect the combination of the turnover and margin variables but also some of the faults of averaging. Since Table II only indicates the mean of each indice by category, further analysis is necessary to obtain meaningful success relationships.

CORRELATION ANALYSIS

Significant Spearman correlation relationships between each retailing mix variable and the five retailing success criteria are indicated in Table III. Positive and negative coefficients are significant at the .05 level.

Because of the rating system utilized in the questionnaire, an inverse relationship is reflected in the significant relationships in the table. For example, a positive significant relationship between a strategy variable rated high in importance by respondents and store success indicators (stockturn rate, GPM, NPM, GMROI, and NPROI) reflects less successful store performance. In like manner, a negative significant relationship indicates that respondents who rated a given variable as having a high priority tend to have more successful store performance.

In the weak or below average competition category, Table III reflects significant positive relationships between retailing mix variables (price and advertising/promotion) and two or more retail success indicators. These positive relationships indicate that less successful retail establishments in this category emphasize these strategy variables. The table also indicates significant negative relationships between retail mix variables (store personnel and store location) and one or more retail success indices. These negative relationships indicate that more successful retailers in this category emphasize quality of store personnel and store location within their retailing strategy mix.

For the moderate competitive situation category, Table III reflects significant correlations for all six variables. The data analysis indicates significant positive relationships between retailing mix variables (price and advertising/promotion) and retail success indices--GPM and GMROI. The data analysis also indicates significant negative relationships between retailing mix variables (store personnel, store location, and product assortment) and GPM. Mixed positive/negative significant relationships exist for the customer service variable in the moderate category. Even though the NPM indice reflects a positive relationship, the customer service variable reflects negative significant relationships with retail indices--stockturn rate and GMROI. These two "bottom line" relationships indicate that more successful retailers in this category emphasize the customer service variable within their retailing strategy.

For the strong or vigorous competitive category, Table III shows a number of positive and negative coefficients. The table indicates significant positive relationships between retailing mix variables (price and advertising/promotion) and three or more retail success indicators. Significant negative relationships exist between retail variables (customer service, store personnel, and product assortment) and two or more retail success indices. Table III also reflects a mixed positive/negative success variable for the strong or vigorous category. Although a negative significant relationship is indicated between the store location variable and GPM, two significant positive relationships are indicated for this retailing variable. The statistics indicate that less successful retailers in this category emphasize the location variable within their retailing strategy.

SUMMARY AND CONCLUSIONS

A study was conducted to determine the relationship between several retailing variables and store success. An analysis of 379 grocery stores located in the state of Texas revealed some interesting findings in regard to store profitability by competitive situation. Specifically, the following results were reported:

1. Customer service/price/quality of store personnel was ranked first, second, or third by stores operating in a weak or strong competitive situation.

2. Store location/product assortment/advertising--promotion was ranked fourth, fifth, or sixth by stores operating in a weak or strong competitive situation.

3. Customer service/quality of store personnel/store location was ranked first, second, and third by stores operating in a moderate competitive situation.

4. The highest average GPM and GMROI was reported by stores operating in a moderate competitive situation.

5. The highest average NPM and NPROI was reported by stores operating in a weak competitive situation.

6. The highest average stockturn rate was reported by stores operating in a moderate competitive situation.

7. Stores that emphasize quality of store personnel and product assortment tend to be more successful when operating in a strong or vigorous competitive situation.

8. Stores that emphasize customer service tend to be more successful when operating in a moderate to strong or vigorous competitive situation.

9. Stores that emphasize store location tend to be more successful when operating in a weak or below average competitive situation.

10. Stores that emphasize price or advertising/promotion tend to be less successful regardless of competitive situation.

Thus, it appears that the competitive environment in which a store operates does affect its profitability and stockturn rate. However, the perceived importance of the selected marketing mix variables varied very little from one retailer to the next by competitive situation. The price variable seemed to be the only exception. Price was ranked fifth in perceived importance by the retailers within the moderate competitive category. This low rating seems to reflect the competitive pricing strategy of pricing at the market. When utilizing this strategy, competition is not largely based on price (above or below) but more on the basis of other marketing mix variables such as location, products carried, services offered, etc. (Mason and Mayer 1981).

The correlation analysis between store success and marketing strategy was affected very little by competitive situation. However, notable exceptions were indicated by the data analysis. In the strong to vigorous competitive category, stores who emphasize marketing mix variables, store personnel and product assortment, seem to enjoy greater "bottom line" success. In the weak or below average competitive category, stores who emphasize the store location variable seem to enjoy greater "bottom line" success. In addition, the correlation analysis indicates a negative effect on profitability for all stores who emphasize the price or advertising/promotion variables.

The results of the study reinforce the statement that "no store can be all things to all people" (Hartley 1980). Thus, the formulation and application of an appropriate retailing strategy would seem essential for store success. The study findings support the need for more intensive research of selected marketing strategies within various competitive environments. Since a variety of retailers are increasingly relying on retail strategy variables for competitive or differential advantage, it appears that significant benefits may be derived from generating more empirical data on the subject for grocery or other types of retailers.

REFERENCES

Berman, Barry and Joel R. Evans (1979), _Retail Management A Strategic Approach_, New York, Macmillan Publishing Co., Inc.

Bolen, William H. (1978), _Contemporary Retailing_, Englewood Cliffs, New Jersey, Prentice-Hall, Inc.

Dun's Review (October 1979), copyright 1979, Dun and Bradstreet Publications, Inc.

Engel, James F., Roger D. Blackwell, and David T. Kollat (1978), _Consumer Behavior_, 3rd ed., Hinsdale, Illinois, The Dryden Press.

Gist, Ronald R. (1971), _Basic Retailing: Text and Cases_, New York, John Wiley and Sons.

Hartley, Robert F. (1980), _Retailing Challenge and Opportunity_, 2nd. ed., Boston, Houghton Mifflin Company.

Kline, C. A., Jr., and Howard L. Hessler (1952), "The du Pont Chart System for Appraising Operating Performance," _N.A.C.A. Bulletin_, No. 33 (August), 1595-1619.

Lazer, William and Eugene J. Kelley (1961), "The Retailing Mix: Planning and Management," _Journal of Retailing_, 37 (Spring), 34-41.

Mason, J. Barry and Morris L. Mayer (1978), _Modern Retailing Theory and Practice_, Dallas, Texas, Business Publications, Inc.

__________ (1981), _Modern Retailing Theory and Practice_, Revised Edition, Plano, Texas, Business Publications, Inc.

McCarthy, E. Jerome (1981), _Basic Marketing A Managerial Approach_, 7th ed., Homewood, IL, Richard D. Irwin, Inc.

Nie, Norman H., Hadlai Hull, Jean G. Jenkins, Karin Steinbrenner, and Dale H. Bent (1975), _SPSS: Statistical Package for the Social Sciences_, 2nd ed., New York, McGraw-Hill Book Company.

Sweeney, Daniel J. (1973), "Improving the Profitability of Retail Merchandising Decisions," _Journal of Marketing_, vol. 37 (January), 60-68.

A FACTOR-ANALYTIC STUDY OF CRITERIA EXAMINED
IN THE FIRST-LINE SALES MANAGER PROMOTION PROCESS

Alan J. Dubinsky, University of Kentucky, Lexington
Thomas N. Ingram, University of Kentucky, Lexington

ABSTRACT

Although much anecdotal "evidence" exists, little is known empirically about what promotion criteria sales executives consider when deciding whom to promote to a first-line sales management position. Such information is important because of the integral, multi-faceted role first-line sales managers play in sales organizations. This paper reports the results of a study that examined first-line sales management promotion criteria. Several implications for sales practitioners and academicians are also discussed.

INTRODUCTION

When selecting personnel to become first-line sales managers (FLSMs), what qualifications must candidates possess? That is, what criteria do sales executives examine when assessing the potential of an FLSM candidate? Answers are vague, or nonexistent.

FLSMs are integral members of a sales organization. Their roles generally include planning, organizing, and controlling the activities of their sales subordinates (Futrell 1981); maintaining personal account responsibilities (Jolson 1977); and serving as intermediaries between their salespeople and organizational members within and without the FLSMs' companies (Still, Cundiff, and Govoni 1976; Stanton and Buskirk 1978).

The process of identifying potential FLSMs and promoting them into those positions is a critical task of sales executives. It is important because correct promotion decisions should result in selecting FLSMs who execute their managerial duties and responsibilities effectively, thus assisting the firm to achieve its sales department, marketing department, and organizational objectives. Incorrect promotion decisions, however, can become expensive sunk costs--and opportunity costs. Consequences of bad promotion decisions may include FLSMs' recruiting inept salespeople, inadequately developing sales subordinates, improperly evaluating sales personnel performance, or generating customer ill-will.

Despite the import of identifying viable FLSM candidates, minimal published research has been performed to assist sales executives in this process. Several writers have suggested what qualifications or characteristics of general-type (non-sales) managers are (e.g., Ghiselli 1971; Heisler 1978; Koontz and O'Donnell 1976; Mahoney 1961; Miner 1973). Qualifications of general-type managers, however, may be different from those of FLSMs. This issue has not been extensively researched. In fact, a review of relevant literature revealed only one relatively recent study that explored the FLSM promotion process. Spencer (1972) surveyed personnel at four organizational levels to determine important qualifications of FLSMs. He found that FLSMs' superiors and home office sales management rated "sales performance" as the most important criterion for becoming an FLSM. FLSMs and sales personnel judged "leadership" to be the most critical determinant. A weakness that limits the generalizability of these results, however, is that the investigation involved only one firm.

Given the dearth of previously published research concerning FLSM qualifications, an exploratory study was conducted to examine important criteria sales executives consider when promoting personnel to FLSM positions. Because of the potentially large number of factors that could be examined by sales executives, the purpose of the research was to ascertain an underlying structure (if one exists) that conceptualizes FLSM promotion criteria. If an underlying structure can be identified, the number of criteria examined may be reduced to a far more manageable number, thus facilitating the FLSM promotion process.

The remainder of this paper will describe the methodology, report the results, discuss the limitations, and present the conclusions of the study.

METHODOLOGY

Sample

Data were collected from a national survey of 1,000 randomly selected senior-level sales executives. Names and addresses of these executives were provided by a commercial mailing list firm. Of the 1,000 executives, 190 returned usable questionnaires for a response rate of 19 percent. This response rate is consistent with similarly published research that has used commercial populations (e.g., Childers, Pride, and Ferrell 1980; Dubinsky, Barry, and Kerin 1981; Hansen 1980).

The field sales forces of respondent companies sell such products as machine tools, textiles, chemicals, office products, and hardware supplies, and such services as data processing, advertising, transportation, and insurance. Respondent company annual sales are between $1 million and $5 billion; approximately 70 percent of the firms have annual sales of $85 million or less. Seventy-seven percent of the organizations promote their FLSMs directly from the sales force. In addition, newly-appointed FLSMs in this study are typically 36 years old with six years or less of sales experience. Also, the median span of control for FLSMs in respondent organizations is seven salespeople.

Questionnaire

A self-administered questionnaire was sent to respondents. The survey instrument sought two kinds of information: (1) respondents' perceived importance of 44 promotion criteria and (2) related demographic information (such as annual company sales). The 44 criteria were arrived at from an examination of relevant sales management, personnel management, and industrial psychology literature (Behling and Schriesheim 1976; Campbell et al. 1970; Futrell 1981; Ghiselli 1971; Heisler 1978; Koontz and O'Donnell 1976; Lipsett and Gebhardt 1966; Mahoney 1961; Miner 1973; Rawls, Rawls, and Radosevich 1975; Spencer 1972; Stanton and Buskirk 1978; Still, Cundiff, and Govoni 1976). Although not an exhaustive list, the 44 criteria are reasonably representative of criteria available to sales executives and address a wide range of areas.

To determine the perceived importance of each criteria, respondents were asked the following question: "In your company, how important are the following criteria when deciding which personnel will be promoted to first-line sales management positions?" Respondents recorded their answers on a five-point, Likert-type scale where 1 = "very unimportant" and 5 = "very important."

Data Analysis

Because the purpose of the study was to identify an underlying structure that conceptualizes FLSM promotion criteria, factor analysis (Hair et al. 1979) was used. Varimax rotation was utilized to improve the interpretability of the factors. Factors were maintained with eigenvalues greater than 1.0. In assigning variables (promotion criteria) to factors, a factor loading cutoff point of .30 was employed. The results of this analysis are discussed below.

RESULTS

Factor analysis generated an eight-factor solution that explains 83.6 percent of the variance. Table 1 presents the 44 promotion criteria, identifies and labels the factors, and summarizes important factor loadings. The eight factors have been labeled "sales performance dimensions," "traditional salesperson traits," "ideal manager dimensions," "observable dimensions," "political power dimensions," "managerial orientation dimensions," "education di-

mensions," and "miscellaneous." Thus, sales executives may be examining at least these eight kinds of criteria when assessing a candidate's capability to assume an FLSM position.

Factor 1 ("sales performance dimensions") contains items that are purely sales job evaluation criteria (e.g., sales volume performance) and are generated from a candidate's track record. "Traditional salesperson traits" (factor 2) refers to qualifications that sales management and personal selling conventional wisdom posits as being desirable characteristics of sales personnel (e.g., persistent, creative, self-confident). Factor 3 ("ideal manager dimensions") includes qualifications that traditionally have been considered ones that any effective supervisor should possess (e.g., integrity, dependability, emotional maturity). "Observable dimensions" (factor 4) consists of criteria that generally can be acquired directly, either by observing the candidate (i.e., physical appearance) or by perusing his or her employment application (e.g., parents' occupations).

Factor 5 ("political power dimensions") is comprised of

TABLE 1

FACTORS AND FACTOR LOADAINGS OF FORTY-FOUR PROMOTION
CRITERIA[a, b, c]

Factor 1 (Sales Performance Dimensions)		Factor 4 (Observable Dimensions)	
• Sales Volume Performance	.696	• Being Married	.678
• Percent of Quota Performance	.768	• Being Single	.721
• Gross Margin Performance	.758	• General Business Experience	.429
• Net Profit Performance	.655	• Parents' Occupations	.391
• Expense/Sales Ratio Performance	.535	• Physical Appearance	.404
• Customer Relations	.418		
		Factor 5 (Political Power Dimensions)	
Factor 2 (Traditional Salesperson Traits)		• Works for Successful Supervisor	.745
• Creativity	.493	• Has Upper Management Sponsor	.717
• Good Judgement	.478	• Length of Service in Company	.308
• Self-Confidence	.467	• Political Instincts	.311
• Persuasiveness	.611		
• Persistence	.546	**Factor 6 (Managerial Orientation Dimensions)**	
• Aggressiveness (A Take-Charge Attitude)	.420	• High Regard for Authority and Company Policy	.565
• Outspokenness	.341	• Has Colleagues' Respect	.548
• Extrovertedness	.331	• Exhibits Strong Desire to be Promoted	.532
		• Time Management Ability	.308
Factor 3 (Ideal Manager Dimensions)			
• Integrity	.509	**Factor 7 (Education Dimensions)**	
• Dependability	.563	• Having a College Degree	.760
• Emotional Maturity	.409	• Having an Advanced (graduate) Degree	.798
• Cooperativeness	.343		
• Overall Intelligence	.321	**Factor 8 (Miscellaneous)**	
• Overall Job Knowledge	.462	• Well-Adjusted Home Life	.420
		• Willingness to Relocate	.488
		• Civic Mindedness	.671

[a] Factors were maintained with an eigenvalue greater than 1.0.

[b] In assigning variables (promotion criteria) to factors, a factor loading cutoff point of .30 was used.

[c] Thirty-eight of the forty-four criteria loaded on some factor. The six criteria that did not load on any factor are positive attitude, self-motivation, technical background, oral communication skills, written communication skills, and being a "workaholic."

items that pertain to candidates' abilities to be promoted
because of whom they know (e.g., an upper management sponsor), political savvy, or job tenure, rather than because
of their inherent skills and abilities. "Managerial orientation dimensions" (factor 6) contains characteristics
which suggest that a candidate has the appropriate ethos to
be an FLSM (e.g., has colleagues' respect and a desire to
be promoted). Factor 7 ("education dimensions") refers
to the educational (college-level) background of an individual. "Miscellaneous" (factor 8) consists of a miscellany
of criteria (i.e., home life, relocation willingness, civic
mindedness).

LIMITATIONS

The results of this investigation should be viewed in light
of at least two important limitations. First, the nature
and number of the criteria examined were limited. Although
generated from relevant literature, and addressing a number
of different areas, the 44 items do not constitute an exhaustive list of FLSM candidate criteria. Future research
should examine additional criteria not explored here.

Second, the data were analyzed in the aggregate and did not
control for variables that may be related to FLSM promotion
criteria. Perhaps factors such as nature of the firm's
product mix (complex versus non-complex), industry practices, degree of organizational decentralization, company
philosophy about promotion (e.g., promote from within or
without), or FLSM span of control affect which criteria are
scrutinized during the FLSM promotion process. Insufficient
cell sizes prevented this kind of analysis here, but future
research should perform such an analysis. Despite these
limitations, the study still is of importance to sales
practitioners and academicians.

CONCLUSIONS

This survey of 190 senior-level sales executives has found
that when determining whom to promote to FLSM positions,
sales executives may be considering several different kinds
of criteria. More specifically, based upon respondents'
perceived importance ratings, 44 promotion criteria were
reduced to eight broad categories. These eight general
classes of criteria include: measures of a candidate's
sales job performance; dimensions of an "ideal" salesperson
and supervisor; objective, background information of an
FLSM candidate; political aspects of an individual; managerial ethos of a candidate; educational background of an
individual; and a miscellany of characteristics (e.g., civic
mindedness) about the potential candidate. Based on the
study results, several conclusions emerge.

Little is known (except for primarily anecdotal "evidence")
about whether the FLSM promotion process is executed in a
haphazard, ad hoc manner, or whether it is a highly formalized, carefully implemented procedure. The results of the
present investigation, however, suggest that, at least in
terms of promotion criteria sales executives may be considering, there is some underlying structure--and, therefore,
some implicit formalization--in part of the FLSM promotion
process. That is, sales executives may be focusing on certain key criteria when identifying and selecting potential
FLSMs. Thus, the FLSM promotion process seems to be characterized by some degree of organization as opposed to its
being a perfunctory sales management activity.

This research effort has identified 44 promotion criteria--
which subsequently were reduced to eight general criteria--
that sales executives might review when determining whom to
promote to FLSM positions. These dimensions can serve as
guides to sales executives who are designing (or redesigning) company FLSM promotion processes. The criteria suggest, at a minimum, what might be examined when assaying a
potential FLSM's capabilities.

Sales managers with responsibility for personnel who conceivably could become FLSMs can also make use of the list
of criteria. To increase the probabilities of their personnel being promoted into FLSM positions, sales managers
could assist in the development of their potential FLSM
candidates. Developmental activities might pay particular
attention to promotion criteria examined here. In other
words, sales managers should seek to develop their subordinates so that they will possess the requisite FLSM qualifications when the time is ripe for promotion.

The findings of this study should also be of benefit to
marketing educators. Because the present study has revealed
basic FLSM promotion criteria, marketing educators can impart this information to their marketing students. Such
information should have a two-fold impact on students.
First, possessing this knowledge should help students acquire a greater understanding and appreciation than they
presently have for the FLSM position. That is, the broad
list of criteria should indicate to students that sales
managers must be more than mere "hucksters." Previous research (e.g., Bellenger, Bernhardt, and Wayman 1974; Dubinsky 1980; Paul and Worthing 1970) has found that students
have negative attitudes toward sales jobs. Acquiring a
greater appreciation for FLSMs may reduce student negati-
vism toward selling and, concomitantly, make selling and
sales management appear as viable career opportunities.

The list of criteria also suggests to students what qualifications potential FLSMs might need. The second effect of
having this information is that students assuming sales
jobs upon graduation can begin to prepare themselves for
FLSM positions early in their careers. That is, they can
engage in a program of self-development that focuses on
critical FLSM promotion criteria.

Finally, additional research should explore the FLSM promotion process in general, and FLSM promotion criteria, in
particular. The present investigation sought to identify
an underlying structure of FLSM promotion criteria (based
upon respondents' perceived importance assessments). Future
research should examine which promotion criteria actually
make for (or predict) _effective_ FLSMs. In addition, as
previously mentioned, research should examine more and different criteria than were investigated here, as well as determine whether certain variables (such as span of control)
are related to criteria sales executives employ in making
an FLSM promotion decision. Such research--like the present study--should be of value to those concerned with improving the FLSM promotion process and the overall productivity of sales organizations.

REFERENCES

Behling, O. and C. Schriesheim (1976), _Organizational Behavior: Theory, Research, and Practice_, Boston: Allyn
and Bacon, Inc.

Bellenger, D. N., K. L. Bernhardt, and W. S. Wayman (1974),
"Student Attitudes toward Selling as a Career: Implications for Marketing Education," in _1974 Combined Proceed-
ings_, R. C. Curhan, ed., Chicago: American Marketing
Association.

Campbell, J. P., M. D. Dunnette, E. E. Lawler, and K. E.
Weick (1970), _Managerial Behavior, Performance, and Ef-
fectiveness_, New York: McGraw-Hill Book Company, Inc.

Dubinsky, A. J. (1980), "Recruiting College Students for
the Salesforce," _Industrial Marketing Management_, 9 (February), 37-45.

____________, T. E. Barry, and R. A. Kerin (1981), "The
Sales-Advertising Interface," _Journal of Advertising_, 10
(Number 3), 35-41.

Childers, T. L., W. M. Pride, and O. C. Ferrell (1980), "A Reassessment of the Effects of Appeals on Response to Mail Surveys," Journal of Marketing Research, 17 (August), 365-370.

Futrell, C. (1981), Sales Management: Behavior, Practices, and Cases, Hinsdale, IL: The Dryden Press.

Ghiselli, E. E. (1971), Explorations in Managerial Talent, Pacific Palisades, CA: Goodyear Publishing Company, Inc.

Hair, J. E., R. E. Anderson, R. L. Tatham, and B. J. Grablowsky (1979), Multivariate Data Analysis, Tulsa: The Petroleum Publishing Company

Hansen, R. (1980), "A Self-Perception Interpretation of the Effect of Monetary and Nonmonetary Incentives on Mail Survey Respondent Behavior," Journal of Marketing Research, 17 (February), 77-83.

Heisler, W. J. (1978), "Promotion: What Does It Take to Get Ahead?" Business Horizons, 21 (April), 57-63.

Jolson. M. A. (1977), Sales Management: A Tactical Approach, New York: Petrocelli/Charter.

Koontz, H. and C. O'Donnell (1976), Management: A Systems and Contingency Analysis of Managerial Functions, New York: McGraw-Hill Book Company, Inc.

Lipsett, L. and M. Gebhardt (1966), "Identifying Managers," Personnel Journal, 45 (April), 205-208ff.

Mahoney, T. A. (1961), Building the Executive Team, Englewood Cliffs, NJ: Prentice-Hall, Inc.

Miner, J. B. (1973), "The Real Crunch in Managerial Power," Harvard Business Review, 51 (November-December), 146-158.

Paul, G. W. and P. Worthing (1970), "A Student Assessment of Selling ," Southern Journal of Business, 5 (July), 57-65.

Rawls, J. R., D. J. Rawls, and R. Radosevich (1975), "Identifying Strategic Managers," Business Horizons, 18 (December), 74-78.

Spencer, H. (1972), "Salesmen and Sales Managers Look at the District Manager," California Management Review, 15 (Fall), 98-105.

Stanton, W. J. and R. H. Buskirk (1978), Management of the Sales Force, Homewood, IL: Richard D. Irwin, Inc.

Still, R. R., E. W. Cundiff, and N. A. P. Govoni (1976), Sales Management: Decisions, Policies, and Cases, Englewood Cliffs, NJ: Prentice-Hall, Inc.

ACKNOWLEDGMENT

The authors gratefully acknowledge the financial support provided by the University of Kentucky Research Foundation.

COMBINING THE EQUITY/INEQUITY MODEL AND THE EXPECTANCY-VALENCE
MODEL FOR PREDICTING SALESPERSON MOTIVATION AND PERFORMANCE

Pradeep K. Tyagi, San Diego State University

ABSTRACT

This paper examines how (in)equity theory can be used to
assess the components of expectancy-valence model more
meaningfully. It is argued that both the equity model and
the expectancy-valence model can be combined to provide a
more meaningful measure of salesperson motivation and prediction of performance. An attempt has been made to
examine the relationships between equity theory and expectancy theory particularly from a perspective of sales
environment.

INTRODUCTION

In recent sales management studies there have been many
attempts to study salesperson motivation within the framework of expectancy valence theory (Churchill, Ford, Walker
1979; Oliver 1974, 1979; Teas 1981; Tyagi 1980, 1982;
Walker, Ford, Churchill 1977). Expectancy-valence theory
is classified as a "process" theory - in contrast to content theories (e.g., need and drive theories, two factor
theory) - primarily because it attempts to identify relationships among variables in a dynamic state as they affect
individual behavior (Oliver 1974). This system orientation is in direct contrast to the content theories which
have attempted largely to specify correlates of motivated
behavior (Campbell et al. 1970). Drawing heavily on the
work of Lewin (1935, 1938), Toleman (1932, 1959), and
Peak (1955), the expectancy model is also viewed as a cognitive theory of motivation where individuals are viewed
as thinking, reasoning beings who have beliefs and anticipation concerning future events in their lives (Steers and
Porter 1979).

Equity theory of motivation (Adams 1963, 1965; Weick 1964)
is also a "process" theory and posits that the major
determinant of job performance and satisfaction is the
degree of equity, or inequity, that an individual perceives in a work situation. Like expectancy-valence
theory, this theory focuses on an understanding of the
process by which behavior is prompted and sustained. It
is thus an equally dynamic and potent approach to the
study of motivationally relevant variables in a sales
management situation.

The main objective of this paper is to examine how these
two powerful theories can be combined to explain salesperson motivation and performance more meaningfully. The
major focus has been placed on how perceptions of equity/
inequity, and inequity resolution strategies might influence various components of the expectancy-valence model.
It is argued that stronger predictions can be made about
salesperson behavior and satisfaction when expectancy
theory is used in association with the equity/inequity
model as compared to the expectancy-valence model alone.

Expectancy Theory

Expectancy theory maintains that the motivation to perform
a given act is a function of the strength of the expectancy that the act will be followed by a given outcome
(reward or goal) and the value of that outcome to the
individual (Lawler 1968; Vroom 1964). In its widely discussed version, two levels of outcomes are considered
(Galbraith and Cummings 1967; Lawler 1970; Lawler and
Porter 1967). The first-level outcomes are the ones that
the investigator is interested in predicting (e.g., job
performance). The second-level outcomes (e.g., monetary
rewards, recognition, promotion) are expected to result
from first-level outcomes. The resulting model is
generally expressed in the following terms:

$$M = f[E_j \times \sum_{k=1}^{n} (V_k \times I_{jk})] \tag{1}$$

where:

 j = the performance level
 k = the outcome as a result of the performance level j
 n = total number of outcomes
 E_j = the salesperson's subjective estimate that his
   efforts will lead to the performance level j
 I_{jk} = the instrumentality (belief) that the performance
   level j will lead to the attainment of second-level
   outcome k
 V_k = the valence of second-level outcome k

Though there are a number of competing theories of motivation (e.g., need theory, reinforcement theory, motivation-
hygiene theory), expectancy theory is regarded as more
meaningful because of its ability to explain the cognitive
process by which behavior is initiated, directed, and sustained (Campbell et al. 1970). The cognitive process
identifies relationships among variables in a dynamic state
as they affect individual behavior. Individuals are viewed
as thinking, reasoning beings who have beliefs and antici-
pations concerning future events in their lives (Steers
and Porter 1979). The expectancy-valence model is particularly appealing because of its pragmatic usefulness.
Multiplicative composites as well as individual V, I, and
E components have successfully predicted work behavior in
sales management (Oliver 1974, 1979) and in other job situations (Galbraith and Cummings 1967; Hackman and Porter
1968; Lawler and Suttle 1973; Leon 1981; Maturi, Okada,
and Mizuguchi 1981; Mitchell and Nabekar 1973; Peters 1977;
Pritchard and Sanders 1973; Stahl and Harrel 1981; Schwab,
Olian-Gottlieb, Heneman 1979; and Vroom 1964). The model
also provides enough information to present some clear and
useful implications for sales managers concerned with the
question of how to motivate their salespersons. The implications include the design of pay and reward systems, the
design of jobs and roles, the importance of group structures, the sales manager's role, measuring motivation, and
individualizing organizations.

Equity Theory

Social comparison process is a pervasive phenomenon in
sales organizations (Andrews and Henery 1963). In such a
process the salesperson compares his/her rewards (outcomes)
to a reference point in order to evaluate the rewards in
question. Equity theory attempts to explain the process by
which people compare and evaluate outcomes. Adams (1965)
defined (in)equity as follows:

The author wishes to thank M. J. Sirgy of Virginia Tech
and two anonymous reviewers for their insightful comments.

(In)equity exists for a Person whenever he perceives
that the ratio of his outcomes (Op) to inputs (Ip)
and the ratio of Other's outcomes (Oa) to Other's
inputs (Ia) are (un)equal. This may happen either
(a) when he and Other are in a direct exchange relationship or (b) when both are in an exchange relationship with a third party and Person compares
himself to Other [p. 280].

A condition of equity exists when:

$$\frac{Op}{Ip} = \frac{Oa}{Ia} \tag{2}$$

where $O = \Sigma_{oi}$, $I = \Sigma_{oi}$, and p and a are subscripts denot-
ing Person and Other.

Inequity is experiences when either

$$\frac{Op}{Ip} < \frac{Oa}{Ia} \tag{3}$$

or

$$\frac{Op}{Ip} > \frac{Oa}{Ia} \tag{4}$$

For a salesperson, outcomes in the job situation include
such things as pay, fringe benefits, status, and feelings
of accomplishment. Inputs include such things as how hard
the person works, his educational level, and his general
qualification for the job. Equity theory stresses that
the pressure of inequity will motivate an individual to
achieve equity or to reduce inequity. Adams (1965) stated
that the strength of the motivation to reduce the inequity
will vary directly with the perceived magnitude of the
imbalance experienced between inputs and outcomes. Adams
also suggested a variety of ways which individuals may use
to reduce feelings of inequity. For example, changes in
productivity and work quality are considered to be two of
the important ways subjects use to reduce feelings of pay
inequity.

A critical examination of equity model can be particularly
meaningful in the assessment of what determines which
inequity-reduction mode a person will choose (Weick 1964,
1965), how perceived inequity influences the valence or
attractiveness of rewards and expectancy beliefs (Lawler
1968; Mowday 1979), if and how the equity model can be
combined with expectancy model to measure the individual's
motivation more accurately (Goodman and Friedman 1971;
Lawler 1973). These issues play an important role in
examining salesperson motivation because of the pervasiveness of both equity/inequity and expectancy cognitions in
sales environments. In the following section, an attempt
has been made to address the above issues and examine how
the equity/inequity model can be used along with the expectancy model to explain and measure salesperson motivation more meaningfully.

Combining the Equity Model and the Expectancy Model to
Predict Salesperson Behavior

The relationship between the equity model and the expectancy model appears to be complimentary than competitive.
Equity theory, for example, puts more emphasis on the
"desire to achieve justice" (Adams 1968). If rewards are
perceived as unjust, then relative deprivation will occur
and produce adverse influence on satisfaction and motivation to perform. The major thrust of expectancy theory,
on the other hand, is that the individual's desire to
maximize outcomes is a powerful determinant of behavior.
That is, the more attractive are the rewards associated
with a performance level then the greater will be the
motivation to perform at the level. As shown in Figure 1,
expectancy theory and equity theory attempt to explain

two distinct but related steps in the motivational process.
In the first stage, salespersons tend to evaluate whether
or not rewards are equitable and in the following stage
they examine the desirability/undesirability of available
rewards. In a sense then equity model can be considered
as an additional tool to be used along with expectancy
model for understanding the motivational phenomenon among
salespersons and predicting behavior. The "ratio inconsistency" between an individual's output/input ratio and
the other's output/input ratio (i.e., Op/Ip - Oa/Ia) inversely influences the VIE components of the expectancy
model. Algebraically, this can be shown in the following
manner:

$$M = f\left[\frac{1}{\dfrac{Op}{Ip} - \dfrac{Oa}{Ia}} \cdot \left(E_j \sum_{k=1}^{n} V_k I_{jk}\right)\right] \tag{5}$$

All of the terms in the above model have been specified in
earlier equations (1) through (4). The specific nature of
the influence between "ratio inconsistency" and VIE components of the expectancy model will be discussed in the
following paragraphs.

(In)equity and Valence of Job Outcomes

The major aspect of the relationships between expectancy
theory and equity theory involves how perceived equity/
inequity might influence the attractiveness or valence of
the rewards resulting from performance. When salespersons
receive rewards that are perceived to be inequitable, it
is possible that they may attach low importance to these
rewards in order to reduce the tension caused by inequity
feelings. In personal selling situations, it is not uncommon for some salespersons to earn exceedingly high sums
of money not because of any extra effort but because of a
good territory (i.e., territory with little competition,
established customers, compact design requiring little
travel). It is likely that salespersons will regard such
incomes as inequitable and thus assign lower valence to
money and other rewards resulting from similar situations.
Vroom (1964) has suggested that ". . . the valence of a
given level of wages to a worker is dependent not only on
its amount but on the extent to which it is believed to be
deserved. Explaining [equity] findings in terms of the
[expectancy] model requires the additional assumption that
[individual(s)] prefer equitable payment and tend to perform at a level which maximizes the equity of their wages"
(p. 260). In organizational psychology studies, there is
empirical evidence that under a commission system an overpayment may lead employees to perceive rewards as inequitable and thus lower their valence (Adams 1963; Adams and
Jacobson 1964).

In an early study, Adams (1963) found that overpaid
workers under a commission system performed less well
possibly because of inequitable perceptions about the rewards and hence a lower valence was attached to money.
Adams stressed this point in describing the results of his
study when he stated that "the results also suggest that
the need to establish (reward) equity was a more potent
motivation than the motivation to maximize economic gains
(rewards)." In other words, the subjects were not producing, despite the fact that there appeared to be high probability it would lead to a valued reward (money). Presumably, the lower valence for money was brought about because the subjects felt unjustified in receiving such high
rewards in return for their job performance. Adams and
Jacobsen (1964) have stated, "simple motivations is . . .
subordinate to the motivation to achieve consonance between
perceived inputs and outcomes." Basically, then, the above
arguments follow that increasingly large quantities of
a given reward will not have increasingly higher valence
for the salesperson if the reward is not perceived as
equitable. Perceived equity/inequity should, therefore,
be considered as one of the major factors that influences

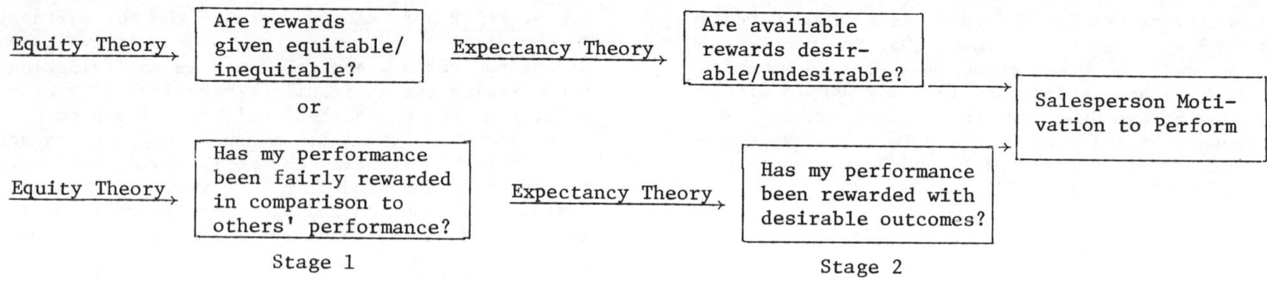

Figure 1

A Two-Stage Explanation of the Motivational Process

the attractiveness of pay, such that too large amounts of pay will have less valence than will smaller but more equitable amounts of pay.

(In)equity and the Instrumentality Component

Perceptions of (in)equity can also influence the instrumentality component of the expectancy-valence model. When a salesperson feels that his efforts are inequitably rewarded and are not in line with the performance level, his instrumentality belief that performance will be appropriately rewarded will decline. This is particularly true when no well defined performance evaluation criteria (e.g., quota systems) are used. In the abscence of appropriate performance measurement systems sales managers may adapt subjective criteria and reward performance inequitably. Such a performance → reward situation would likely induce feelings of inequity among salespersons and lower instrumentality beliefs that rewards are tied to sales performance. Litwin and Stringer (1968) in a series of sales management experiments were able to demonstrate a similar relationship. When rewards are consistently <u>not</u> based on performance, the risk of being compensated inequitably increases causing a corresponding decline in the instrumentality component of the expectancy model.

(In) equity and the Expectancy Component

Equity theory can also be used to explain the effect of perceived inequity on the expectancy component under the conditions of job (in) security. When salespersons perceive insecurity in their jobs under perceived inequitable situations, their expectancy beliefs tend to decline. Job insecurity forces people to place a greater emphasis on quality in work rather than quantity because they feel that producing the quality work is a better way to protect jobs. New salespersons, operating on a salary plus commission basis would be more concerned about the customer goodwill they can generate along with sales. Customer goodwill is generally seen as a key to longterm job success and hence a secure job. As a result, they will spend more time in customer servicing, handling customer complaints as opposed to generating pure sales. Once the job is secured, they may be able to relax their emphasis on work quality and focus more on quantity. Adams (1964) presented the data which showed when employees were paid at greater than normally expected levels (an inequitable situation) and were induced with the feelings of job insecurity, they felt that the best way to protect their jobs was to produce a little very high quality work. This is likely to happen in sales situations, as a significant part of the salesperson's compensation is based on a commission system. Pure commission plans tend to introduce feelings of job insecurity among salespersons (Churchill, Ford, Walker 1981; Stanton and Buskirk 1979). Consequently, salespersons may resort to the strategy of focussing on quality work by restricting productivity. In short, such a situation may adversely effect the expectancy beliefs that efforts will lead to greater performance. Of

course, such problems can be ractified by using security assurance strategies. The research in personal selling environments aimed at investigating the above issues can be very useful in making the expectancy theory predictions of salesperson behavior more accurate.

Situations Where Expectancy Theory is Unable to Predict Performance

The usefulness of (in) equity theory is also evident in situations where expectancy theory is unable to predict the relationships between salesperson performance and valued rewards. For example, expectancy theory which focuses primarily on the perceived performance-reward relationships, would not predict increased performance for overpaid salespersons in a straight (fixed) salary situation because performance is not related to pay. Salespersons working on straight salary are not likely to be motivated to expand extra effort on the job because of a lack of belief that additional performance will be rewarded. However, the inequity model is able to provide performance predictions in such situations. For example, in a straight salary arrangement, if a salesperson perceives his performance to be inadequate as compared to that of others, the following condition of inequity will result:

$$\frac{O_p}{I_p} < \frac{O_a}{I_a}$$

This in turn, will likely create the psychological tension and induce the salesperson to expand a greater effort on the job.

Organizational Climate and the Equity-Expectancy Models

Another potentially useful area of investigation, with respect to the relationships between equity theory and expectancy theory, is to examine how organizational climate may interact with perceptions of equity/inequity to form salespersons' cognitive maps (containing perceptual information about organizational conditions) that may be used to formulate their expectancy beliefs (Tyagi 1982). It has been suggested that organizational climate variables (e.g., leadership behavior, work-group relationships, management concern and awareness) are used by employees to develop their cognitive maps. As shown in figure 2, these maps in turn serve as the major source of situational information to form expectancies and instrumentalities (James et al. 1977; Lawler 1970; Porter and Lawler 1968).

It is also likely that perceived organizational climate would influence equity/inequity perceptions. Open versus secret pay policies, for example, have been reported to influence salespersons' feelings of equity/inequity. When secret compensation policies are used, salespersons tend to guess the salaries of fellow workers. Such a guess work often results in the perceptions of inequity

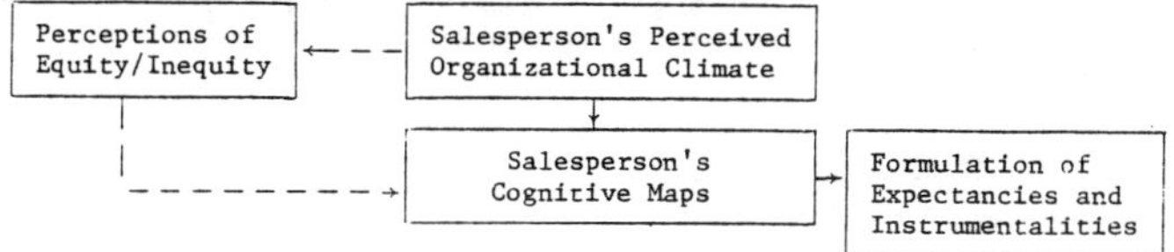

Figure 2

Organizational Climate-(In)equity-
Expectancy Relationships

(Lawler 1973). These inequity perceptions, in turn,
effect salespersons' cognitive maps which determine their
beliefs about performance-reward relationships. Frequent
work-group interactions and communications between the
sales manager and salespersons can offset salespersons
feelings whether their rewards are equitable or not and
such a perception can then be used to develop cognitive
maps. This is another avenue of research which can help
identify the antecedents and the process of formation of
expectancy beliefs.

Selection of Rewards

Another contribution of the equity model is making expectancy theory predictions more meaningful is in the area of
interchangeability of salespersons' rewards. This kind of
research can assist sales managers in identifying the
types of rewards that have an additive effect on other
rewards, and which rewards can be substituted for others.
Penner (1967) in a salary satisfaction study found that
workers tended to substitute certain rewards for pay, and
rewards like freedom had an additive effect on monetary
rewards. In personal selling situation, it is possible
that many perceived inequitable rewards may not be substituted for each other and therefore their effect on performance may not be predictable from the expectancy model.
Equity theory research on reward outcomes suggest that
achieving balance between input and outcome is an important factor in influencing the attractiveness or valence
of various rewards. The way salespersons use rewards to
balance their input-output ratios may help identify their
preferences and selection of rewards available in the
organization and thus strengthening the predictability of
the expectancy model.

SUMMARY AND CONCLUSIONS

Both expectancy-valence theory and equity/inequity theory
are powerful process theories for measuring salesperson
motivation. The preceeding analysis indicates that the
equity model can be used to assess the components of the
expectancy model more meaningfully and that the concepts
of two theories can be combined to provide a better prediction of salesperson behavior. The combined use of two
theories is particularly meaningful in situations where
predictions about individual behavior are difficult to
incorporate into one theory. In view of the complexity of
the motivational phenomenon, taking such a perspective may
enhance our understanding of the process of salesperson
motivation. Systematic empirical research is recommended
to substantiate and clarify the combined role of the equity
and the expectancy model in explaining salesperson motivation and behavior.

REFERENCES

Adams, J. S. (1963), "Towards an Understanding of Inequity," Journal of Abnormal and Social Psychology, 67,
422-436.

Adams, J. S. (1965), "Injustice in Social Exchange," in
L. Berkowitz (ed.), Advances in Experimental Social
Psychology, Volume 2, New York: Academic Press.

___________ (1968), "Effects of Overpayment: Two comments on Lawler's paper," Journal of Personality and
Social Psychology, 10 (November), 315-316.

___________ and P. Jacobsen (1964), "Effects of Wage
Inequities on Work Quality," Journal of Abnormal and
Social Psychology, 69, 19-25.

Andrews, I. R. and M. M. Henery (1963), "Management Attitudes Toward Pay," Industrial Relations, 3 (October),
29-39.

Campbell, S. P., M. D. Dunnette, E. E. Lawler, III, and
W. S. Weick, Jr. (1970), Managerial Behavior, Performance and Effectiveness, New York: McGraw-Hill.

Churchill, G. A., Jr., N. M. Ford, and O. C. Walker, Jr.
(1979), "Personal Characteristics of Salespeople and
the attractiveness of Alternative Rewards," Journal of
Business Research, 7 (April), 25-49.

___________, ___________, ___________ (1981), Sales-
force Management: Planning, Implementation and Control,
Homewood, Illinois: Richard D. Irwin.

Galbraith, J. and L. L. Cummings (1967), "An Empirical Investigation of the Motivational Determinants of Task
Performance: Interactive Effects Between Instrumental-
ity-Valence and Motivation-Ability," Organizational
Behavior and Human Performance, 2 (August), 237-57.

Goodman, P. S. and A. Friedman (1971), "An Examination of
Adam's Theory of Inequity," Administrative Science
Quarterly, 16, 271-288.

Hackman, J. R. and L. W. Porter (1968), "Expectancy Theory
Predictions of Work Effectiveness," Organizational
Behavior and Human Performance, 3 (February), 417-426.

James, L. R., A. Hartman, M. W. Stebbins, and A. P. Jones
(1977), "Relationships Between Psychological Climate
and a VIE Model for Work Motivation," Personnel Psychology, 30 (Summer), 229-254.

Lawler, E. E., III (1968), "Equity Theory as a Predictor of
Productivity and Work Quality," Psychological Bulletin,
70 (December), 506-610.

___________ (1970), "Job Attitudes and Employee Motivation: Theory, Research and Practice," Personnel
Psychology, 23 (Summer), 223-237.

___________ (1970), Pay and Organizational Effectiveness,
New York: McGraw-Hill.

___________ (1973), Motivation in Work Organizations,
Monetary, California: Brooks/Cole Publishing Company.

___________, and L. W. Porter (1967), "Antecedent Atti-
tudes of Effective Managerial Performance," Organizational Behavior and Human Performance, 2, 122-142.

___________, and J. L. Suttle (1973), "Expectancy Theory
and Job Behavior," Organizational Behavior and Human
Performance, 9 (June), 482-503.

Leon, F.R. (1981), "The Role of Positive and Negative Outcomes in Causation of Motivational Force," _Journal of Applied Psychology_, 66 (February), 45-53.

Lewin, K. (1935), _A Dynamic Theory of Personality_, New York: McGraw Hill.

__________. (1938), _The Conceptual Representation and the Measurement of Psychological Forces_, Durham, North Carolina: Duke University Press.

Matsui, T., A. Okada, and R. Mizuguchi (1981), "Expectancy Theory Predictions of the Goal Theory Postulate: The Higher the Goals, the Higher the Performance," _Journal of Applied Psychology_, 66 (February), 54-58.

Mitchell, T.R. and D.M. Nebekar (1973), "Expectancy Theory Predictions of Academic Effort and Performance," _Journal of Applied Psychology_, 57 (February), 61-67.

Mowday, R.T. (1979), "Equity Theory Predictions of Behavior in Organizations," in R.M. Steers and L.W. Porter (ed.), _Motivation and Work Behavior_, New York: McGraw-Hill, 124-146.

Nadler, D.A. and E.E. Lawler, III (1977), "Motivation: A Diagnostic Approach," in J.R. Hackman, E.E. Lawler and L.W. Porter (ed.), _Perspectives of Behavior in Organizations_, New York: McGraw-Hill, 26-36.

Oliver, R.L. (1974), "Expectancy Theory Predictions of Salesmen's Performance," _Journal of Marketing Research_, 11 (August), 243-253.

__________. (1979), "Alternative Conceptions of Motivational Components in Expectancy Theory," in _Sales Management: New Developments from Behavioral and Decision Model Research_, R. P. Bagozzi (ed.) Massachusetts: Marketing Science Institute.

Peak, H. (1955), "Attitude and Motivation," in _Nebraska Symposium on Motivation_, M.R. Jones (ed.), Lincoln: University of Nebraska Press.

Penner, D. (1967), _A Study of Causes and Consequences of Salary Satisfaction_, Crontonville, New York: General Electric Behavioral Research Service.

Peters, L.H. (1977), "Cognitive Models of Motivation, Expectancy Theory and Effort: An Analysis and Empirical Test," _Organizational Behavior and Human Performance_, 20 (October), 129-148.

Porter, L.W. and E.E. Lawler, III (1968), _Management Attitudes and Performance_, Homewood, Illinois: Richard D. Irwin.

Pritchard, R.D. and M.S. Sanders (1973), "The Influence of Valence, Instrumentality and Expectancy on Effort and Performance," _Journal of Applied Psychology_, 57 (February), 55-60.

Schwab, D.P., J.D. Olian-Gottlieb, and H.G. Heneman, III (1979), "Between Subject Expectancy Theory Research: A Statistical Review of Studies Predicting Effort and Performance," _Psychological Bulletin_, (January), 139-147.

Stahl, M.J. and A.M. Harrel (1981), "Modeling Effort Decisions with Behavioral Decision Theory: Towards an Individual Differences Model of Expectancy Theory," _Organizational Behavior and Human Performance_, 27 (June), 303-325.

Stanton, W.J. and R.H. Buskirk (1979), _Management of Salesforce_, Sixth edition, Homewood, Illinois: Richard D. Irwin.

Steers, R.M. and L.W. Porter (1979), _Motivation and Work Behavior_, New York: McGraw-Hill.

Teas, R.K. (1981), "An Empirical Test of Models of Salespersons' Job Expectancy and Instrumentality Perceptions," _Journal of Marketing Research_, 18 (May), 209-26.

Tolman, E.C. (1932), _Purposive Behavior in Animals and Men_, New York: Appleton-Century-Crafts.

__________. (1959), "Principles of Purposive Behavior," in S. Koch (Ed.), _Psychology: A Study of a Science_, Volume 2, New York: McGraw-Hill, 92-157.

Tyagi, P.K. (1980), "Influence of Organizational Climate on Salespersons' Valence for Intrinsic and Extrinsic Job Outcomes," _Marketing in the 80's_, AMA Educators' Conference, 46, 234-37.

__________. (1982), "Perceived Organizational Climate and the Process of Salesperson Motivation," _Journal of Marketing Research_ (May).

Vroom, V.H. (1964), _Work and Motivation_, New York: Wiley.

Walker, O.C., Jr., G.A. Churchill, Jr., and N.M. Ford (1977), "Motivation and Performance in Industrial Selling: Present Knowledge and Needed Research," _Journal of Marketing Research_, 14 (May), 156-168.

Weick, K.E. (1964), "Reduction of Cognitive Dissonance Through Task Enhancement and Effort Expenditure," _Journal of Abnormal and Social Psychology_, 68, 533-39.

__________. (1966), "The Concept of Equity in the Perception of Pay," _Administrative Science Quarterly_, 11, 414-439.

SALESFORCE PERFORMANCE AND SATISFACTION:
CONTEMPORANEOUS RELATIONSHIPS AND SELECTED ANTECEDENTS

George R. Franke, University of North Carolina, Chapel Hill
Douglas N. Behrman, Florida State University, Tallahassee
William D. Perreault, Jr., University of North Carolina, Chapel Hill

ABSTRACT

A model of hypothesized relationships between salesforce job performance and satisfaction and certain individual-difference and work-related factors is presented. Drawing data from an industrial sales organization, the model is tested using ordinary least squares and two-stage least squares procedures. Salesforce satisfaction and performance are found to be negatively related to role conflict and ambiguity, but little evidence is found of a contemporaneous satisfaction-performance relationship.

INTRODUCTION

The saying that "nothing happens till the sale is made" is perhaps an oversimplification, but it is certainly the case that organizational marketers require effective salesforce performance to achieve sales, profits and growth. Similarly, salesforce satisfaction is a concern to managers both because of the relationship between job satisfaction and worker behavior and because of a humanistic concern for employees (Bagozzi 1978).

Following in the tradition of recent research concern in these related areas, the objective of this study is to (1) examine the influence of a select set of individual characteristics and work-related variables on salesforce satisfaction and performance, and (2) to test the contemporaneous satisfaction-performance relationship. Toward these objectives, the variables of concern in this study are discussed, and a model of their hypothesized relationships is presented. Then, the data collection and analysis procedures are described and the results of the analysis are given. Finally, implications of these results, as well as some limitations of the study, are discussed.

BACKGROUND

The Performance/Satisfaction Relationship

While salesforce performance and satisfaction are both important in their own right, research on the relationship between the two is not unequivocal. Greene (1972) argues that there is no empirical evidence of satisfaction causing performance, and only moderate support for performance causing satisfaction. He concludes that current performance causes rewards which lead to future performance. The issue is far from settled, however, so the model presented here includes reciprocal, contemporaneous causation between satisfaction and performance (see Bagozzi (1980) for selected work in this area).

Influencers of Performance and Satisfaction

Two hypothesized causes of reduced performance and satisfaction are role conflict and role ambiguity. Role ambiguity occurs when the salesperson is uncertain about what is expected, or how best to perform the job (Walker, Churchill and Ford 1975). Role conflict, which concerns the extent to which an individual faces incompatible demands in the performance of his or her job, may take several forms (Miles and Perreault 1976). For example, intersender conflict occurs when customers, managers, family, and other members of the sales representative's

role set make competing demands. Moreover, competing or inconsistent demands may come from a single individual, producing intrasender conflict. Salespeople may also experience person-role conflict if they face job expectations that disagree with their personal values or orientations. Finally, work overload may result when, as is often the case, the salesperson is expected to accomplish more than is possible given available time and resources. Though previous marketing research has focused on intersender conflict (e.g., Walker, Churchill and Ford 1975), the present research taps all four types in measuring role conflict and thus broadens the study of the salesforce role-stress/job outcomes relationship.

Several characteristics of the salesperson's position tend to bring about role conflict and ambiguity (Walker, Churchill and Ford 1975). The salesperson's boundary spanning activities between the organization and its publics, the often-inadequate availability of information concerning customers' needs, physical and psychological separation from the parent company, and the innovativeness required of the salesperson are all factors conducive to conflict and ambiguity (Donnelly and Ivancevich 1975; Teas, Wacker and Hughes 1979).

Although conflict and ambiguity may in part develop from the same sources, they are typically treated as independent constructs (perhaps due to the influence of Rizzo, House and Lirtzman (1970)). Yet, conflict may also affect ambiguity directly. It is logical to expect that conflicting demands on the salesperson would lead to ambiguity about which demands to satisfy. This hypothesis is tested in the current study.

The same "objective" level of ambiguity may be perceived differentially depending on the salesperson's need for clarity. Thus, need for clarity is expected to affect satisfaction and performance through its influence on perceived ambiguity (cf. Ivancevich and Donnelly 1974). Specifically, it is hypothesized that a sales representative with a high need for clarity seeks reductions in ambiguity through actions to clarify the expectations of others.

A person's perception of causality determines his locus of control (Rotter 1966). "Internal" people believe that they have greater control over the events affecting their lives than do "externals". With the uncertainty and relative autonomy of the salesperson's position, it is predicted that internal salespeople will be more satisfied than external ones. There is scant evidence concerning the effect that locus of control might have on performance, however. The research of Behrman et al. (1981) suggests that if such a relationship does exist, it may be nonlinear. Thus, no (linear) relationship between locus of control and performance is predicted here.

Three other variables which are relevant, but of less direct interest here, are included to facilitate estimation of the performance-satisfaction and satisfaction-performance relationships. Job experience (the number of years in this and similar selling positions) and the number of hours worked per week are assumed (perhaps heroically) to be positively related to job performance without being influenced by it and without influencing satisfaction except through other variables included in the model. Spending nights away from home while traveling on company

business is predicted to have personal disutility without
contributing systematically to performance; for the purposes of the model, working nights is assumed to negatively influence satisfaction without any reciprocal causation and with no relationship to unmeasured causes of
performance. These assumptions derive from the use of
these variables in developing decontaminated estimates of
performance and satisfaction in the two-stage least
squares analysis used to test the overall model.

THE MODEL

The predicted relationships discussed above are shown in
Figure 1. The structural equations for the variables to
be explained by the model are:

$$A = K_A + B_{AC}C + B_{ANc}Nc + U_A \qquad (1)$$

$$P = K_P + B_{PC}C + B_{PE}E + B_{PH}H + B_{PA}A + B_{PS}S + U_P \qquad (2)$$

$$S = K_S + B_{SC}C + B_{SN}N + B_{SI}I + B_{SA}A + B_{SP}P + U_S \qquad (3)$$

where the Ks stand for constants, the Bs are structural
equation coefficients, the Us are disturbance terms, and
the other letters stand for the variables in Table 1. The
subscripts follow the path analysis convention of putting
the symbol for the criterion variable first. Standardiz-
ing the equations converts the structural coefficients to
path coefficients and removes the constants.

FIGURE 1

MODEL OF ANTECEDENTS AND INTERRELATIONSHIP
OF SALESFORCE PERFORMANCE AND SATISFACTION

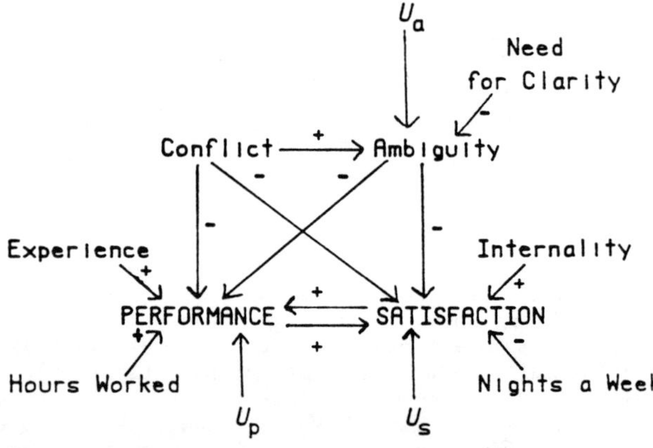

To estimate unique parameters for the model, the structural equations must be identified. The model in Figure 1
satisfies the order condition of identifiability (Bass and
Parson 1975) and is in fact overidentified (there are more
instrumental variables than are strictly necessary).

METHOD

Data Collection

Data from an industrial manufacturer's sales organization
are used in the study. The sales reps were responsible
for technical, creative selling of component parts (fluid
drive systems) to original-equipment manufacturers and
replacement-parts distributors. Self-administered questionnaires were returned by 71 of 75 salespeople, who participated in the study at the request of management. Of
these, 69 questionnaires were complete and useable in this
study, yielding an effective response rate of 91%. The
salespeople were assured that their responses would be
confidential.

General role ambiguity and role conflict were measured by
modifications of scales developed by Rizzo, House and
Lirtzman (1970). The ambiguity scale consisted of 3
Likert-type items (alpha=.80) and the conflict scale of 18
items tapping the four different types of conflict
(alpha=.85). A modified Rotter (1966) scale with 20
forced-choice items was used to assess subjects' perception of causality (alpha=.78). Questions on four Likert-
type items indicated subjects' need for clarity
(alpha=.79) (Lyons 1971; Miles and Petty 1975). A 95-item
scale developed by Churchill, Ford and Walker (1974) was
used to assess overall job satisfaction (alpha=.96). A
31-item scale developed by Behrman and Perreault (1982)
asked the sales representatives to rate different aspects
of their sales performance relative to other salespeople
in similar situations (alpha=.94). Finally, questions
were asked concerning the salespeople's years of selling
experience and the number of hours and nights they worked
per week.

Data Analysis

Correlations among the variables and the possible and
observed ranges of scale responses are presented in Table
1. The average salesperson worked 52 hours and travelled
1.6 nights per week, and had 12 years of selling experience. The sales representatives tended to have an internal perception of causality and a high need for clarity.
Average conflict and ambiguity were both moderate. The
salespeople were generally satisfied with their jobs, and
almost all of them rated their performance at or above the
midpoint of the scale.

The path analysis model employs least squares regression
to estimate the strengths of the relationships between
variables. In addition to the usual regression assumptions, the system is assumed to have been in equilibrium
when the data were collected (Kenny 1979, p. 51). Ordinary least squares (OLS) analysis is used for the one-way
relationships but is not appropriate for the relationships
in the model which involve reciprocal causation. Therefore, two-stage least squares (2SLS) analysis is used to
estimate the structural equation coefficients and their
significance levels for the nonrecursive relationships.

Estimation of structural coefficients for a nonrecursive
relationship from cross-sectional data requires the availability of instrumental variables for each variable in the
relationship (Heise 1975). Such instrumental variables
make it possible to partially control for spurious relationships between variables in the nonrecursive relationship (James and Singh 1978). The variable X can be an
instrument for the Y to Z relationship (where Y and Z
cause each other) if: (1) X does not affect Z directly,
(2) X affects or is at least correlated with Y, (3)
neither Y nor Z affects X directly or indirectly, and (4)
X is not coordinated with disturbances in Z (cf. Heise
1975, p. 160-1). Though 2SLS works as a one-step process,
conceptually it involves using OLS with the instrumental
variables to generate an "uncontaminated" estimate of one
of the variables in the nonrecursive relationship. This
estimate is then used as a predictor of the other variable
in another round of OLS regression.

RESULTS

The results of the analysis are given in Table 2. The
unstandardized coefficients are useful for comparison with
results of studies using the same measures on other populations. The path coefficients are based on the underlying population distribution rather than being metric-de-
pendent, giving a better view of the structural
relationships.

TABLE 1

CORRELATION MATRIX AND DESCRIPTIVE STATISTICS

	(A) Ambiguity	(C) Conflict	(E) Experience	(H) Hrs. per Week	(I) Internality	(Nc) Need for Clarity	(N) Nights per Week	(P) Performance	(S) Satisfaction	Mean	Std. Dev.	Possible Range	Observed Range
A	1.000									2.40	.53	1-5	1.00-3.75
C	.582[a]	1.000								2.81	.49	1-5	2.00-4.00
E	-.209	.062	1.000							12.12	8.17	NA	1.00-33.00
H	-.131	-.150	.004	1.000						51.94	8.50	NA	24.00-75.00
I	-.413[a]	-.409[a]	-.017	.079	1.000					4.86	3.49	0-20	0.00-13.00
Nc	-.246[b]	-.043	.070	.186	-.092	1.000				15.32	3.67	4-20	6.00-20.00
N	.213	.179	.302[b]	.064	-.277[b]	-.090	1.000			1.58	1.23	NA	0.00-6.00
P	-.488[a]	-.113	.409[a]	.160	.276[b]	.107	.014	1.000		165.90	21.75	31-217	119.00-209.00
S	-.626[a]	-.628[a]	-.117	.102	.550[a]	.191	-.387[a]	.250[b]	1.000	3.56	.39	1-5	2.57-4.74

Note: N = 69.

[a] $p < .001$

[b] $p < .05$

TABLE 2

OLS AND 2SLS REGRESSION RESULTS
FOR ORIGINAL AND REVISED MODELS

Dependent Variable and R Squared[a]	Predictors	Path Coefficients	Structural Equation Coefficients	$p \leq t$
Ambiguity[b] [$R^2 = .39$]	Conflict	.573	.623	.0001
	Need for Clarity	-.221	-.032	.0249
	Intercept		1.147	.0032
Performance[c] [$R^2 = .38$]	Satisfaction	.351	19.463	.2940
	Ambiguity	-.375	-15.310	.0560
	Conflict	.325	14.422	.0743
	Experience	.318	.846	.0053
	Hours Worked	.125	.321	.2264
	Intercept		66.058	.5065
Satisfaction[c] [$R^2 = .61$]	Performance	-.345	-.006	.2848
	Ambiguity	-.523	-.385	.0317
	Conflict	-.235	-.188	.0929
	Internality	.242	.027	.0202
	Nights Worked	-.161	-.051	.1102
	Intercept		6.255	.0001
Performance[d] [$R^2 = .34$]	Ambiguity	-.421	-17.186	.0001
	Experience	.321	.855	.0026
	Intercept		196.856	.0001
Satisfaction[d] [$R^2 = .60$]	Ambiguity	-.297	-.218	.0045
	Conflict	-.323	-.257	.0021
	Internality	.240	.027	.0107
	Nights Worked	-.200	-.064	.0190
	Intercept		5.036	.0001

[a] N=69 and p <.0001 for all regressions

[b] The ambiguity results are the same for the original and the revised models.

[c] The original model.

[d] The revised model.

About 39% of the variation in ambiguity scores is explained by perceived conflict and need for clarity (p < .001). The path coefficients for both predictors are significant (p < .025) and in the predicted directions, with the coefficient for the conflict-ambiguity relationship being over twice that of the need for clarity-ambiguity relationship (.57 vs. -.22).

The two-stage regression of performance on ambiguity, hours worked per week, experience, and the decontaminated satisfaction variable results in an R-squared of .38. The path coefficient for the decontaminated satisfaction variable is .35, which is in the predicted direction but not significant (p < .30). The number of hours worked per week does not have a significant impact on performance, and perceived conflict (p < .08) and ambiguity (p < .06) do not quite reach significance. The path coefficient for the number of years worked (.32) suggests that selling experience has a positive, significant (p < .01) impact on self-rated performance.

A significant portion (61%) of the variation in the salespeoples' satisfaction is explained by the variables in the model. An internal locus of control is positively related and ambiguity is negatively related to satisfaction. None of the other predictors are significant at p < .05. The coefficient for the decontaminated performance variable is negative, contrary to the predicted relationship, but is not significant (p < .29).

A Trimmed Model

It may be argued that a "relationship should not be eliminated from a model if the coefficient indicates that the magnitude of the effect is comparable to other effects being considered, even if a statistical test suggests that the coefficient is not 'significantly' different from zero" (Heise 1975, p. 195). By this rule probably the only variables that might justifiably be dropped from the model are the number of hours and nights worked per week. However, a simpler model may be developed which performs nearly as well as the original model in terms of explained variance (Figure 2).

The regression results for this model are also given in Table 2. The conflict-ambiguity and need for clarity-ambiguity relationships are unchanged. When performance is regressed on just selling experience and perceived ambiguity, R-squared drops (nonsignificantly) to .34 and the coefficients appear more reliable (p < .01 for both). When the performance-satisfaction relationship is dropped from the original model, all the remaining predictors of satisfaction are significant at p < .02 and R-squared drops only slightly, to .60.

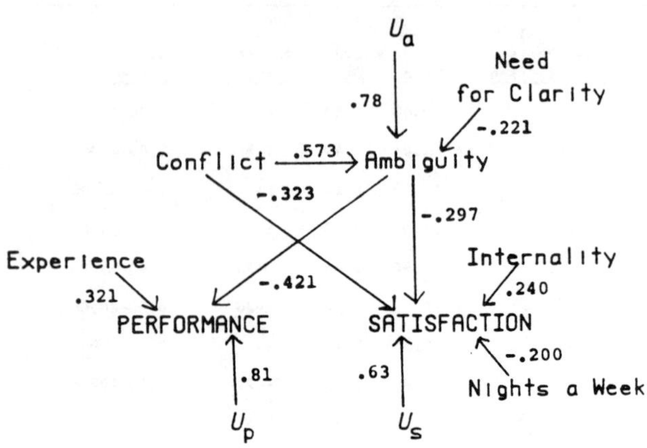

Note: All path coefficients significant at p < .02.

DISCUSSION

Several limitations to the study should be taken into consideration in drawing conclusions from the results presented here. First, the use of salespeople from a single company at a single time period may have led to sampling artifacts and ignores the temporal dynamics of the system. Inconsistencies between the data and the original model may be due to these limitations, to weaknesses in the model and the instrumental variables chosen, to errors of measurement in the dependent and independent variables, to violations of the traditional least squares computational assumptions, or to some combination of all of these.

Another limitation of the study is that salespeople's perceptions were measured rather than "actual" levels of conflict, ambiguity, performance, and so on. Development of procedures to provide objective measures of conflict, ambiguity and performance would add an important dimension to this study and more generally to research in this area. From a substantive perspective, such an improvement has the potential to provide a better basis for management prescriptions, and from a methodological perspective would reduce potential bias from method variance.

With these limitations in mind, it is useful to briefly summarize the key results and implications of the study. First and perhaps foremost, the results of this research provide little evidence for a contemporaneous relationship between salesforce satisfaction and performance. While salesforce satisfaction is important in its own right, managers and researchers should keep in mind that organizational climate and other variables which are related to higher levels of satisfaction are not necessarily related to improved performance.

This study is different from much previous salesforce research in that it uses a broader conceptual definition of role conflict. An operational measure is used which assesses intrasender, person-role, and overload conflict as well as intersender conflict. When this measure is used, a negative relationship between conflict and satisfaction is revealed. The path analysis results also suggest that such conflict aggravates problems of role ambiguity. Given the negative relationship between ambiguity and both performance and satisfaction, the results indicate the importance of managing conflict and reducing ambiguity.

The simple model developed here represents an effort to specify and test some of the causal forces which may affect salesforce performance and satisfaction. Clearly, this effort is limited in that many aspects of the overall sales role have not been considered, measured, or analyzed. Such broader efforts in this area reflect an important challenge for future research.

REFERENCES

Bagozzi, Richard P. (1978), "Salesforce Performance and Satisfaction as a Function of Individual Difference, Interpersonal, and Situational Factors", _Journal of Marketing Research_, 15 (November), 517-31.

__________ (1980), "Performance and Satisfaction in an Industrial Sales Force: An Examination of Their Antecedents and Simultaneity", _Journal of Marketing_, 44 (Spring), 65-77.

Bass, Frank M. and Leonard J. Parsons (1975), "Regression Methods with Simultaneous Equations", in _Handbook of Marketing Research_, R. Ferber, ed., New York: McGraw Hill, 427-41.

Behrman, Douglas N., William J. Bigoness and William D. Perreault, Jr. (1981), "Sources of Job Related Ambiguity and Their Consequences Upon Salesperson's Job Satisfaction and Performance", _Management Science_, 27 (November), 1246-60.

__________ and William D. Perreault, Jr. (1982), "Measuring the Performance of Industrial Salespersons", _Journal of Business Research_.

Churchill, Gilbert A. Jr., Neil M. Ford and Orville C. Walker, Jr. (1976), "Measuring the Job Satisfaction of Industrial Salesmen", _Journal of Marketing Research_, 11 (August), 254-260.

__________, __________, and __________ (1976), "Organizational Climate and Job Satisfaction in the Salesforce", _Journal of Marketing Research_, 13 (November), 323-32.

Donnelly, James H. Jr. and John M. Ivancevich (1975), "Role Clarity and the Salesman", _Journal of Marketing_, 39 (January), 71-74.

Greene, Charles N. (1972), "The Satisfaction-Performance Controversy", _Business Horizons_, (October), 31-41.

Heise, David R. (1975), _Causal Analysis_, New York: John Wiley & Sons.

Ivancevich, John M. and James H. Donnelly, Jr. (1974), "A Study of Role Clarity and Need for Clarity for Three Occupational Groups", _Academy of Management Journal_, 17 (March), 28-36.

James, Lawrence R. and B. Krishna Singh (1978), "An Introduction to the Logic, Assumptions, and Basic Analytic Procedures of Two-Stage Least Squares", _Psychological Bulletin_, 85 (September), 1104-22.

Kenny, David A. (1979), _Correlation and Causality_, New York: John Wiley & Sons.

Lyons, T. F. (1971), "Role Clarity, Need for Clarity, Satisfaction, Tension, and Withdrawal", _Organizational Behavior and Human Performance_, 6, 99-110.

Miles, Robert H. and William D. Perreault, Jr. (1976), "Organizational Role Conflict: Its Antecedents and Consequences", _Organizational Behavior and Human Performance_, 17 (October), 19-44.

__________ and M. M. Petty (1975), "Relationship Between Role Clarity, Need for Clarity, and Job Tension and Satisfaction for Supervisory and Nonsupervisory Roles", _Academy of Management Journal_, 18 (December), 877-83.

Rizzo, J. R., R. J. House, and S. E. Lirtzman (1970), "Role Conflict and Ambiguity in Complex Organizations", _Administrative Science Quarterly_, 15 (June), 150-63.

Rotter, J. B. (1966), "Generalized Expectancies for Internal Versus External Control of Reinforcement", _Psychological Monographs_, 80, no. 1, Whole No. 609.

Teas, R. Kenneth, John G. Wacker and R. Eugene Hughes (1979), "A Path Analysis of Causes and Consequences of Salespeople's Perceptions of Role Clarity", _Journal of Marketing Research_, 16 (August), 355-69.

Walker, Orville C. Jr., Gilbert A. Churchill and Neil M. Ford (1975), "Organizational Determinants of the Industrial Salesman's Role Conflict and Ambiguity", _Journal of Marketing_, 39 (January), 32-9.

PROBLEM SITUATIONS EVOKING THE PRODUCT ELIMINATION
DECISION IN THE INDUSTRIAL MARKET

by

George J. Avlonitis, University of Strathclyde

ABSTRACT

This paper reports a part of the results of a major exploratory investigation into the product elimination decision in the U.K. engineering industry. The findings reported in this paper indicate that there is a wide variety of problem situations under which a product may be eliminated in the industrial field and that the frequency of occurrence of these problem situations is a function of the company's certain contextual organisational and environmental conditions. The theoretical implications of the findings are explored and suggestions for new research directions are made.

INTRODUCTION

There is little doubt that the current harsh economic environment in the industrialised world has shifted the product elimination decision from an important to a critical position in corporate strategy. Yet, product elimination is one of the key remaining "gaps" in the marketing literature. Most contributions to this area have been theoretical in nature (e.g. Berenson 1963; Alexander 1964; Kotler 1965; Hamelman and Mazze 1972), while little research has been undertaken to test the theory and to provide a thorough understanding of the rudiments of the product elimination decision-making process. Indeed, to date, very little is known not only about the way in which companies make and implement the elimination decision, but also about the problem situations which evoke the elimination decision in the first place. To assume, as the bulk of the pertinent literature does, that the elimination decision arises only when a product reaches the maturity and decline stage of its life cycle and is not performing satisfactorily with respect to company's sales, profit and/or market share objectives, is no doubt an oversimplification. Not all "poor old heavyweights" are ready for elimination, nor are elimination candidates only those which have been around for a long time and show signs of low profitability and declining sales. The various factors which result in the elimination decision are not always clear to detect and in a number of cases a company may be dependent on outside forces to form the "lead" in its elimination decision. These issues were fully investigated in an extensive study of product elimination decision-making behaviour recently conducted by the author within selected sectors of the U.K. engineering industry (Avlonitis 1980). Specifically, the study attempted, among other things, to:

(a) identify the problem situations which evoke the product elimination decision in the industrial field and their relative importance;[1] and

(b) examine whether the relative importance of these problem situations is a function of the company's size, product/market diversity, operations technology, technological and competitive environment.

METHODOLOGY

The study involved two main stages; twenty in-depth company interviews ranging from two days to one week duration each and ninety-four completed mailed questionnaires constituting a thirty-one per cent response rate from the sample contacted.

The twenty in-depth company interviews were made with those companies who agreed to collaborate on the basis of a judgmental sample of thirty-five companies drawn from a population of fifty-two companies operating in the West of Scotland area, employing more than one hundred people, and engaged in the manufacture of mechanical, instrument and/or electrical engineering products. Judgment was used to select a cross-section of companies exhibiting variation in terms of size, product/market diversity and industry (engineering) sector. The interviews were conducted with the organisational equivalents of the Managing Director, the Senior Marketing Executive, the Financial Director and the Technical/Engineering Executive utilising two somewhat different interview schedules. The purpose of this initial phase of the study was to discover the behaviour of the engineering companies vis-a-vis the product elimination process.

The testing and quantification of the results of the personal interviews was the main purpose of a mail survey conducted by a self-administered questionnaire designed to measure not only the behavioural aspects of interest in this study, but also certain aspects of the company's environment (internal/external) to enable us to examine whether the reported behaviour was a function of the company's internal and external setting. The questionnaire was mailed to 300 companies in the U.K. drawn from a population of 550 engineering companies listed in the 1977 edition of Kompass Directory and in the 1977/78 edition of the Dun and Bradstreet Key to British Enterprises Directory and stratified by size (small = 100-499; medium = 500-999; and large = over 1,000 employees) and industry/engineering sector (machine tools SIC 332; pumps valves compressors SIC 333; other machinery including textile SIX 335 and 339; scientific instruments and systems SIC 354; electrical machinery SIC 361). A census (complete coverage) was undertaken within the medium and large size strata, while only a portion (40%) of the companies in the small size strata was selected using a random sampling procedure.

The ninety-four usable questionnaires received were all answered by chief executives within the respondent companies, and all responses were received during Spring 1978. Analysis of the response revealed no significant difference between the type of respondents and the population from which they were drawn.[2]

ANALYSIS AND RESULTS

Problem Situations

Analysis of the descriptions of 107 elimination decisions made by the twenty sample interview companies over a five-year period (1972/3 - 1976/7) revealed eight kinds of problem situations under which a product may be eliminated in the industrial field: (a) Government policies and regulations; (b) Parent organisation decisions and policies; (c) Changes in the third party specifications; (d) Decline in market potential; (4) Poor product performance (financial, commercial and/or technical despite a generally viable market); (f) Development of a new and improved product; (g) Rationalisation due to mergers and acquisitions; (h) Development of a variety reduction policy. Table 1 illustrates the distributio of the 107 elimination decisions among the eight classes of problem situations identified in the twenty interviews.

Table 1. Classification of 107 Product Elimination Decisions by the Problem Situation that Evoked them: Sample of 20 Interview Companies

CLASS	PROBLEM SITUATION DESCRIPTION	OBSERVED FREQUENCY
I	Government Policies & Regulations	4
II	Parent Organisation Decisions & Policies	7
III	Changes in the Third Party Specifications	4
IV	Decline in Market Potential	18
V	Poor Product Performance (Despite a Genearlly Viable Market)	27
VI	Development of a New Product	34
VII	Rationalisation brought about by Mergers & Acquisitions	5
VIII	Development of a Variety Reduction Policy	8

It is obvious that the management of a company is not always "independent" in making an elimination decision. There are situations under which management has little or no control of the subject matter or the scheduling of the elimination process. Indeed, the situations described by classes I, II and III present problems which are unanticipated by management in terms of content (the type of products affected) and time of arrival. These problems are often accompanied by severe limitations with respect to time in which management has to define and choose its action and this becomes apparent in the follwoing specific cases.

Class I- Government Policies and Regulations - A Small company engaged in the manufacture of mixers and pumps for process plants was manufacturing and marketing a range of metric pumps under licence from a company in the U.S.A. The licence was exclusive to the U.K. The licensor in the U.S.A. had also granted a licence to a French company to manufacture and market the same range in the Common Market on an exclusive basis. When Britain joined the E.E.C. in January 1973 it became illegal according to the Treaty of Rome to have two exclusive licencees serving the Common Market. Under these circumstances the management of the subject company decided to terminate the licence agreement and drop the product.

Class II - Parent Organisation Decisions and Policies - A medium sized subsidiary of a large international group engaged in the manufacture and marketing of a wide range of electronic communication test measurement equipment, discontinued certain product types from its data transmission measurement equipment line as a result of a business policy decision made by the parent group board.

Class III - Changes in the Third Party Specifications - A manufacturer of a range of standard motor control gear and distribution equipment included in its range a line of starters which were designed to comply with the BS (British Standards) and I.E.C. (International Electrotechnical Commission) specifications. A change in the I.E.C. specifications, which was introduced in order to reduce technical barriers between countries, accounted for about one-third of the items in the line being dropped and new ones being introduced.

In contrast to the aforementioned problem situations, there is a distinctly lower level of urgency vis-a-vis the elimination decision under the problem situations described by Classes IV, V, VI, VII and VIII. These problem situations are either identified (Classes IV and V) and/or created (Classes VI, VII and VIII) to a large extent by management itself as a part of its product planning process. Furthermore, the products eliminated under these situations are most frequently of the management's choosing. The following specific cases exemplify these points.

Class IV - Decline in Market Potential - A company engaged in the scientific instrumentation field was manufacturing among other products a range of portable battery driven voltage censors serving the need of users of electrical installations to test alternating voltages. However, due to technological developments in this field, this particular product became less useful in its application and its sales declined for a consecutive number of years leading to uneconomic production batches and consequently to increased costs. The product was eventually eliminated and such elimination may be viewed as a natural consequence of the decline in its market potential due to technological obsolescence.

Class V - Poor Product Performance - A large company manufacturing a wide range of domestic heating and appliance automatic controls developed a product to meet the needs of a specific segment of the central heating and hot water controls market. However, the design of the product proved to be unsatisfactory and the company experienced a series of complaints from the customers. Attempts to improve the product's design tended to push the costs up and led to the establishment of an uncompetitive price. Eventually the product was eliminated from the range, almost five years after it was first introduced.

Class VI - Development of a New Product - A medium sized company manufacturing a wide range of hermetic compressors and condensing units mainly for the appliance industry and commercial market, developed through its internal R & D a new range of low pressure hermetic compressors. The new range caused an area of overlap with the existing range and as a result of this the older range was making less profit and was eventually eliminated. In this case the elimination decision was a natural consequence of the development of a new product.

Class VII - Rationalisation brought about by Mergers and Acquisitions - A manufacturer of industrial laundry machinery, including washer extractors and ironing machines merged with another company specialising in the manufacturing and marketing of ironing machines. Since some of the newly acquired models of ironing machines were closely related to the subject company's product offerings, the management of the company faced the problem of harmonising the expanded range. After an analysis of the interrelationships between all models in the range, management decided to drop those models wich it believed were less promising.

Class VIII - Development of a Variety Reduction Policy - A small privately-owned company manufacturing two broad ranges of refrigerator display cases found that it was producing too many variations of specifications and quality within one of its ranges and decided that it should rationalise this particular range. The driving forces behind the decision to develop a variety reduction policy was the declining profitability and the high levels of stock and work-in-progress. The variety reduction policy developed led to the discontinuation of certain products (items) from the range.

An inspection of Table 1 reveals that the majority of the elimination decisions reported were made under problem situations which were either identified and/or created by management itself. The "Development of a new product" and the "Poor product performance" problem situations accounted for about 60 per cent of the elimination decisions reported. Only fifteen per cent of the reported decisions were made under problem situations which were beyond the management's control, e.g. those which were created by Government policies and regulations, parent organisation decisions and policies, and changes in the third party specifications.

These indications regarding the relative importance of the different kinds of problem situations in evoking the deletion decision were tested and quantified in the mail survey. The respondents were firstly asked to state the number of products that had been eliminated in their companies over the last five-year period (1973-78). This number ranged in the sample from 3 to 500 (Mean = 34, Median = 8, Standard Deviation 95; see Avlonitis 1980, pp. 380-381). They were then asked to write against each of the problem situations listed in the questionnaire the number of products that had been eliminated due to this particular situation. Their responses are summarised in Table 2. Notice the striking differences between the eight problem situations as to their effects on the number of products being dropped. For instance, whilst there was a considerably greater number of companies who cited "poor product performance" than those who cited "changes in the third party specifications" as a problem situation evoking the deletion decision, the number of products dropped due to "poor product performance" was only slightly greater than the number dropped due to "changes in the third party specifications." It was felt, therefore, that a more accurate measure of the relative importance of each problem situation evoking the deletion decision would be derived by using as a basis for analysis the individual company rather than the product. Besides, the use of the individual company as a basis for analysis facilitates a comparison of the relative importance of problem situations experienced by individual companies with certain characteristics of their respective environments, which is one of the main objectives of this study (and is discussed in the next section.)

Table 2. Problem Situations Evoking the Product Elimination Decision

	Number(Percentage) of Companies Citing N = 92*	Number(Percentage) of Products Dropped N = 3.167
1. Government Policies & Regulations	6 (7)	11 (0.03)
2. Parent Organisation Decisions & Policies	15 (16)	62 (1.9)
3. Changes in the Third Party Specifications	9 (10)	136 (4.3)
4. Decline in Market Potential	54 (59)	254 (8.0)
5. Poor Product Performance (despite a generally viable market)	45 (49)	159 (5.0)
6. Development of a new product	63 (68)	787 (24.8)
7. Rationalisation brought about by Mergers & Acquisitions	13 (14)	98 (3.1)
8. Development of a Variety Reduction Policy	39 (42)	1660 (52.4)

Consequently, the following approach was employed. Based on the responses summarised in Table 2, we allocated, per company in the sample, <u>100 points</u> among the eight problem situations according to the percentage of dropped products that they accounted for. For instance, if a company had eliminated a total of 5 products and one of them (20% of the total) had been eliminated due to "Government policies and regulations," two (40% of the total) due to "poor product performance" and the remaining two (40% of the total) due to "new product development" then we allocated 10, 40 and 40 points to these problem situations respectively. The resulting frequency distribution of the points allocated to each problem situation (exhibited in Table 3) indicates its relative importance in evoking the deletion decision in the industrial market.

It is interesting to note that the findings of the mail survey show a high degree of agreement with the findings of the interview survey, especially at the extremes. In both phases of the study it was found that the "Development of a new product" and the "Government policies and regulations" account for the largest and the smallest proportion of the elimination decisions made in the engineering industry respectively. However, in the best of circumstances these results must be treated with caution. The assignment of a product elimination decision to any of these eight kinds of problem situations is not a straightforward task mainly for two reasons: Firstly, there might be an overlap between the problem situations under which a product may be eliminated. For instance, the development of a new product leading to the elimina-

Table 3. Relative Importance of Problem Situations Evoking the <u>Elimination Decision N = 92</u>

PROBLEM SITUATIONS	FREQUENCY DISTRIBUTION OF POINTS ALLOCATED				MEAN	DEVIATION
	Pts. 0-20	21-40	41-60	Over 60		
1. Government Policies & Regulations	89*	2	1	-	2.0	7.8
2. Parent Organisation Decisions & Policies	87	3	1	1	3.6	11.0
3. Changes in the Third Party Specifications	85	4	2	1	3.0	11.1
4. Decline in Market Potential	52	23	8	9	26.1	27.8
5. Poor Product Performance	63	14	22	4	16.6	22.9
6. Development of a New Product	44	24	25	9	28.8	25.8
7. Rationalisation brought about by Mergers & Acquisitions	87	2	4	-	3.6	10.3
8. Development of a Variety Reduction Policy	62	16	8	6	16.3	23.8
			Total Points		100.0	

*To be Read: In 89 companies the "Government Policies & Regulations" problem situation was allocated points ranging from 0 to 20 (on a scale running from 0 to 100) on the basis of the percentage of dropped products that it accounted for.

tion of the existing one may be the natural consequence of the "poor" performance of the existing product. Secondly, more than one problem situaton may evoke the elimination decision at the same time. For instance, a product considered for elimination because of its poor financial and market performance may be eventually dropped because of changes in the third party specifications. These problems notwithstanding the findings are indicative of the character, mix and magnitude of the problem situations under which products may be eliminated in the industrial field.

Environmental Influences

An attempt was also made in the mail survey phase of the study to examine, as has already been mentioned, whether the relative importance of the different kinds of problem situations varies with certain characteristics of the company's environment. The Spearman-rank correlation model was used to compute the rank correlation between measures of the importance of the four most prominent problem situations namely "Development of a new product," "Poor product performance," "Decline in market potential" and "Variety reduction policy" and measures of company size, product/market diversity, operations technology, rate of technological change and market competition in this study.[3] As Table 4 indicates, of the twenty-four correlations, as many as nine are significant at the ten per cent level and seven at the five per cent level. The proportion of the correlations that are statistically significant is much larger than what we should expect from purely random relationships. The high proportion also suggests that the investigaton of the problem situations evoking the elimination decision in terms of response to the task environment is theoretically and empirically a very rich area, all the more because it has been hardly explored.

Table 4. Spearman Rank-order correlation coefficients of the importance of <u>various problem situations with contextual variables. N = 92</u>

CONTEXTUAL VARIABLE / PROBLEM SITUATIONS	SIZE (SALES) TURNOVER)	PRODUCT DIVERSITY	OPERATIONS TECHNOLOGY (MASS OUTPUT ORIENTATION)	TECHNO- LOGICAL CHANGE	MARKET COMPETITION	MARKET DIVERSITY
Development of a new product	-0.07	-0.13	-0.01	0.32***	0.02	-0.11
Poor product performance	0.12	-0.05	-0.06	0.10	-0.21**	0.13
Decline in market potential	-0.23**	-0.07	-0.11	-0.06	-0.23**	0.18**
Development of a variety reduction policy	0.05	0.19**	0.16*	-0.17	0.18**	-0.12

***Significant at the 1 per cent level
**Significant at the 5 per cent level
*Significant at the 10 per cent level

It seems as though the importance of the "Development of a new product" as a problem situation evoking the elimination decision is enhanced by technological change while the importance of the "Decline in market potential" is decreased by size, market competition and market diversity.[4] Also, whereas the importance of the "Poor product performance" problem situation is decreased by market competition, the importance of the "Variety reduction policy" is enhanced by this particular factor as well as by operations technology (mass output orientation) and product diversity; and it is decreased by technological change.

It is easy to see the rationale for many of these relationships. To the extent that technological change threatens a company with the obsolescence of its products we should expect the company to place a priority on the new product development activity resulting in the replacement (elimination) of the existing products. To the extent that market competition poses complex financial contingencies to a company we should expect the company to be keen to examine every possible avenue for costs savings including that of variety reduction, particularly if it manufactures a wide range of products employing primarily batch (as opposed to unit) production technology. This is so because the most important economic effects of variety reduction stem from the reduction in the stock levels held and the consequent increases in batch size.

The lack of competition, on the other hand, may allow a company to carry in its range (even for a short while) products which although they have reached their decline stage, they may still produce sales receipts above out-of-pocket costs and thus making contribution to overheads. The lack of competition also provides no great incentive to the company to use sophisticated management techniques to scan all product proposals with great care and to make sure that only products that market research and forecasting reveal are likely to compete successfully are allowed to be produced and marketed. As a result, a company experiencing low competitive pressures may carry more weak or obsolete products in its range than does a company facing strong market competition (which forces it into continual enhancement of existing products in terms of features, increased performance, and greater economies); and therefore, the former is likely to face the "Decline in market potential" and "Poor product performance" problem situations more often than does the latter.

Finally, given the derived demand characteristic of the industrial market a company's sales and market potential of its products tend to be more severely affected by changes taking place in any one of its customers' industries when it has a narrow market spread than when it enjoys a broad market coverage. Naturally, therefore, a company with a low degree of market diversity faces the "Decline in market potential" problem situation more often than does a company serving multiple market segments.

DISCUSSION

Despite the limitations in extendibility and methodology the data reported in this paper highlights two areas of specific concern to which workers in this field should turn their attention, if a useful body of product elimination theory is to be developed.

One area of concern is the problem situation that evokes the elimination decision. Indeed, the existence of different kinds of problem situations under which a product may be eliminated implies thatthere are different types of product elimination decisions, each necessitating a different kind of approach. In fact, evidence from our study reported elsewhere (Avlonitis and James, 1982) suggests that the decision variables and procedures utilised in the product elimination process tend to vary even within a given organisation, depending, among other things, on the problem situation that evoked such a process. The different problem situations, therefore, can provide a useful starting base for the development of a typology of the product elimination decisions made by a business organisation and their associated processes. Consequently, in-depth field studies would be required to uncover the decision variables and procedures utilised by companies under specific product elimination situations. Pletcher's (1973) research effort designed to determine the decision variables utilised by the American small-appliance companies in their elimination processes initiated by the "Poor product performance" problem situation may be seen as a step in the right direction.

The second area of concern in the contextual environment of the product elimination decision. Indeed, one of the major shortcomings of the existing product elimination theory is the lack of consideration of a number of variables describing the environment to which theory is to apply. However, as the findings reportedin this paper suggest, the product elimination situations experienced (and consequently, the elimination approaches adopted) by a particular company is a function of its internal and external setting.

In summing up, we believe that advances in our knowledge of product elimination decision-making behaviour depend very much on future research efforts designed to determine the product elimination process as it is being conducted by management in particular organisational settings and for particular product circumstances. Indeed, there is a need for a "micro" rather than a "macro" approach to the product elimination problem.

FOOTNOTES

1. By 'importance' we mean the amplitude and frequency of occurrence of each problem situation.
2. A fuller account of choice of sample frame, selection of the sample, and company characteristics at each phase of the study as well as details of the research methodology may be found in Avlonitis, (1980, Vol. 1, pp. 272-316).
3. A full discussion of the operationalisation and measurement of all these contextual variables is to be found in Avlonitis (1980, Vol. 2, pp. 349-362).
4. The positive sign of the correlation is due to the manner in which the market diversity variable was measured in this study; the higher the company's market diversity score, the lower its market diversity.

REFERENCES

Alexander, R.S. (1964), "The Death and Burial of Sick Products," Journal of Marketing, 28 (April), 1-7.

Avlonitis, G.J. (1980), "An Exploratory Investigation of the Product Elimination Decision Making Process in the U.K. Engineering Industry." Unpublished Ph.D Thesis, University of Strathclyde.

Avlonitis, G.J. and B.G.S. James (1982), "Some Dangerous Axioms of Product Elimination Decision-Making," European Journal of Marketing, 16, (forthcoming).

Berenson, C. (1963), "Pruning the Product-Line," Business Horizons, 6 (Summer), 63-70.

Hemelman, P.H. and E.M. Mazze, (1972), "Improving Product Abandonment Decisions," Journal of Marketing, 36 (April), 20-26.

Kotler, Philip (1965), "Phasing-Out Weak Products," Harvard Business Review, 43 (March-April), 108-118.

Pletcher, B.A. (1973), "The Product Elimination Process in the Small Home Appliance Industry: An Empirical Study," Unpublished DBA Dissertation, Kent State University.

BEHAVIORAL EFFECTS OF BOUNDARY SPANNING ON THE PRODUCT MANAGER

Steven J. Lysonski, University of Rhode Island, Kingston

ABSTRACT

Boundary spanning theory and role theory are used to examine the product manager's role in consumer industries. A research model depicting associations between boundary spanning, role conflict and ambiguity, and job satisfaction, tension and performance is developed and tested. The results suggest that boundary spanning leads to role conflict but not role ambiguity; and role conflict and ambiguity result in dissatisfaction, tension and lowered performance. Suggestions to mitigate these outcomes are provided.

INTRODUCTION

Although the product management system was instituted over a half century ago by Procter and Gamble, behavioral studies of the product management institution are sparse. This apparent lack of research is especially surprising given that almost 85% of consumer packaged goods firms use the product management system (Buell 1975). Even though behavioral aspects of the product management system have been largely ignored, research has progressed in other disciplines contributing behavioral concepts and insights germane to product management. Such research, for example, deals with the general concept of boundary role theory applied to sales people, project managers, R & D engineers, and a host of others.

There are several characteristics of the product manager's role within an organization which make it important and somewhat unique. First, it is a "boundary role" at the interface between the firm and the market environment. Moreover, as a boundary role, the product manager must also function along the various departmental boundaries within the firm. As the product manager moves in and out and across departments he finds himself entangled in a web of conflicting pressures and influences. He can identify an array of social exchanges, many of which are formal, routine and associated with the official business he must conduct. Frequently, however, many of these exchanges are informal. Hence the product manager must deal with role expectations and demands not only from persons in other departments, such as Finance, Engineering, Production, but also from individuals outside the firm, such as the trade, consultants and advertising agencies.

Second, the product manager's role is of central importance in determining the success of his company's profit making activities. When environmental uncertainty is high, he is faced with the task of adapting the marketing mix of his product line to this uncertainty. The product manager's performance, therefore, has a direct and major impact on the success or failure of his assigned product responsibility. Since the product manager needs the cooperation of supporting departments such as manufacturing, sales and research and development to administer his product line, he engages in boundary activities to establish many different role relationships to solicit this cooperation. In effect, his boundary spanning links resources together to optimize product line performance. Ultimately, the success of his product influences a large number of related positions, whose occupants have a vested interested in attempting to influence and control the product manager's behavior.

Third, the product manager's role is subject to countless pressures in the form of conflict and ambiguity. As the product manager interfaces with internal-external and formal-informal sources, he is exposed to a vast number of demands and parochial interests. When these pressures reach heightened proportions, the product manager's performance, satisfaction and feeling of control may be affected.

These unique characteristics of the product manager's role not only make it critical to the success of the firm's marketing efforts, but they also produce an unusually high potential for conflict, ambiguity, tension and job dissatisfaction. In recognition of the product manager's importance and the potential for many organizational problems, several researchers have begun to describe and study the social organizational and behavioral dimensions of the product manager's role (Clewett and Stasch 1974, Venkatesh and Wilemon 1976), but these studies have not yet examined its boundary spanning implications.

BOUNDARY SPANNING CONCEPT

One of the most potentially rewarding areas for research concerning the product manager's role is to examine his boundary activities, since communication and integration are essential ingredients for his effective performance. Leifer and Delbecq (1978) note that "Persons who operate at the periphery or boundary of an organization performing organizational relevant tasks, relating the organization with elements outside it are called boundary spanners". Product managers can be characterized as boundary spanning agents when they function as communication linkages between the external environment and the internal operating environment. The product manager facilitates the transmission of information from the environment into the firm and vice versa. Boundary spanning also applies to linkages between the subunits within the firm.

PROBLEM STATEMENT AND MODEL ANALYSIS

The purpose of this study is to examine the relationships of several crucial behavioral variables relating to the boundary role of product managers. To gain a better perspective of the forces operating on the product manager, an exploratory model was developed as presented in Figure 1.

FIGURE 1

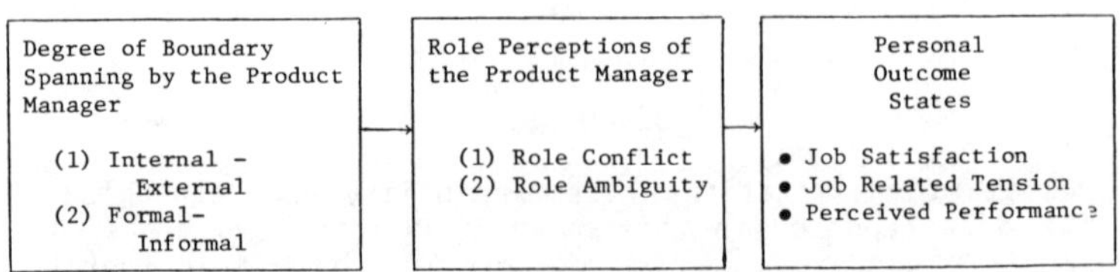

Basically, the model suggests that high levels of boundary spanning by the product manager lead to role conflict and ambiguity. This conflict and ambiguity then create lower satisfaction, high tension and reduced perceived performance for the product manager. Each bivariate relationship in the model is tested. Finally, the managerial implications of the findings are explored and actions which might lead to the improvement in the product manager's performance are discussed.

The model conceptualizes the current theoretical views surrounding the variables examined and reflect the unique characteristics of the product manager's role. The proposed linkages in the model are consistent with the current perspectives on the constructs examined. It is important to note that the model does not propose to provide a complete explanation of the forces operating on the product manager. The model does, however, capture parsimoniously the state of knowledge on the relationships among the variables.

VARIABLES AND HYPOTHESES

The variables in the study can be divided into 3 categories: 1) boundary spanning; 2) role perceptions; and 3) personal outcome states. Although the focus of this study is exploratory and emphasizes the discovery of relationships, a number of prior hypotheses can be stated, based on previous research. The discussion of each set or relationships (linkages) implied by the model will result in the statement of the hypotheses tested.

<u>Boundary Spanning and Role Perceptions of Conflict and Ambiguity</u>

The product manager's role is characterized by diverse expectations and frequent interactions with others--both internal and external to the firm. Role conflict is generally defined as the incompatibility of expectations associated with a role. Several types of role conflict, identified by Kahn <u>et al</u>. (1964), are explored: intrasender, intersender, role overload and person role conflict. Although many studies have attempted to assess the impact of boundary spanning on the degree of role conflict, none has focused on the product manager. Several studies, however, have illustrated that boundary spanning can have a negative impact on the individual by generating role conflict (Kahn <u>et al</u>. 1964, Organ 1971).

Role ambiguity refers to the lack of clarity regarding what an individual is required to do on his job and how his performance will be evaluated. Because the product manager's responsibilities are often incommensurate with his authority, role ambiguity is likely to arise. Research on other types of personnel has shown an association between role ambiguity and boundary spanning (Keller and Holland 1975).

On the basis of the arguments above, the following hypotheses are proposed:

H_1: There is a positive relationship between the product manager's boundary spanning and his role conflict.

H_2: There is a positive relationship between the product manager's boundary spanning and role ambiguity.

<u>Role Conflict and Personal Outcome States (of satisfaction, tension and performance)</u>

Role conflict can subject the product manager to high levels of anxiety and emotional turmoil as it does for workers in other settings. The product manager may ultimately conclude that regardless of his activity and performance, someone will be discontented with him. Not the least important result may be disillusionment with the job. Kahn <u>et al</u>. (1964) were among the first theorists to suggest that role conflict is a cause of job related tension, dissatisfaction and lower levels of trust, liking and respect for role senders. Research by organization theorists over the last 15 years has tended to confirm the existence of relationships among role conflict, dissatisfactions, anxiety, and performance (Miles 1976, Miles

and Perrault 1976). In particular, Miles (1975) used crossed lagged and dynamic correlated techniques in a recent study to provide additional support for the theory that role conflict causes job tension and dissatisfaction. Several marketing studies, for example, have found a negative relationship between role conflict and job satisfaction and between role conflict and performance for salesmen (Bagozzi 1978, Churchill <u>et al</u>. 1974). Nonetheless, one would expect the relationships to apply to product managers given the pressures they experience.

Thus the following hypotheses are proposed:

H_3: There is an inverse relationship between role conflict and performance. The greater the perceived role conflict, the lower the perceived job performance.

H_4: There is an inverse relationship between role conflict and job satisfaction. The greater the perceived role conflict, the lower the job satisfaction.

H_5: There is a positive relationship between role conflict and job tension. The greater the perceived role conflict, the greater the job tension.

<u>Role Ambiguity and Personal Outcome States (of satisfaction, tension and performance)</u>

When the product manager feels that he has insufficient information to perform his job adequately, when he is unclear about what his role partners expect of him, and when he is unclear about how his performance will be evaluated, role ambiguity occurs. The literature on role ambiguity for other professionals in both organizational behavior and marketing provides evidence that this factor is positively related to feelings of tension, turnover, a sense of futility, dissatisfaction, physical symptoms, and negative attitudes towards role senders (Rizzo <u>et al</u>., 1970, House and Rizzo 1972, Keller 1975). Miles (1975) discovered that role ambiguity causes a decrease in job satisfaction. Therefore, one would suspect that a product manager who experiences a high degree of role ambiguity would be less satisfied with his job, and that this high role ambiguity is likely to adversely affect his performance as well as increase his job related tension. In light of previous research and these arguments, the following hypotheses are proposed:

H_6: There is an inverse relationship between role ambiguity and performance. The greater the perceived role ambiguity, the lower the perceived job performance.

H_7: There is an inverse relationship between role ambiguity and job satisfaction. The greater the perceived role ambiguity, the lower the job satisfaction.

H_8: There is a positive relationship between role ambiguity and job tension. The greater the perceived role ambiguity, the greater the job tension.

METHOD

<u>The Sample</u>

The foregoing hypotheses were tested with data obtained by mail questionnaires from a sample of 449 product managers in consumer packaged goods industries drawn from the <u>Fortune 500</u>. Letters were sent to senior level executives in marketing departments (identified in <u>Advertising Age</u> and <u>Standard Directory of Advertising</u>) asking them to provide names of 4 or 5 product managers who would participate in the study. Via this approach, 293 senior executives were identified and sent requests resulting in a return rate of roughly 25%, providing names of 171 product

243

managers. In addition, names of 278 product managers were identified in <u>Advertising Age</u> and the <u>Standard Directory of Advertising</u>, making the total sample size 449. When the 449 product managers were sent questionnaires, 224 were returned of which 170 were usable.

Prior to the collection of data, interviews were conducted with group product managers and product managers. These interviews led to the design and selection of the instruments in the study. The questionnaire was pretested on product managers and marketing managers in the Syracuse, New York area. For this pretest, the alpha coefficients on all the instruments exceeded .6.

Data Collection Instruments

Boundary spanning defined as communication beyond the product manager's boundary was measured by refining and expanding an instrument developed by Aiken and Hage (1972) and used by Leifer (1975). Moreover, the development of the instrument benefited from the role diversity instrument developed by Snoek (1966), the boundary instruments used by Keller and Holland (1975) and the dimensions of boundary spanning as identified by Miles (1975). The instrument measured verbal and written communication in terms of: (1) formal-informal, (2) within the firm and outside the firm, and (3) other selected aspects.

Role conflict, defined as the degree of incongruity or incompatibility of expectations associated with a role, was measured by 10 items rated on a 6 point Likert scale. The specific types of role conflict measured were: <u>Intrasender</u>: Incompatible expectations from a single role sender; <u>Intersender</u>: Expectations from one role sender which are incompatible with those of another role sender; <u>Person Role</u>: Incompatibility between the expectations of the product manager and the expectations otherwise associated with his role; <u>Role Overload</u>: The product manager's responsibilities exceed the amount of time and resources available for their accomplishment.

Role ambiguity, defined as a lack of clarity in terms of how one will be evaluated and what is expected was measured with 6 items on a Likert scale. Both of these scales were developed and validated by Rizzo, House and Lirtzman (1970). Several researchers have reported the psychometric soundness of these scales (Schuler, Aldag and Brief 1977). Job satisfaction was measured with five items using Likert scales. A scale of this type was successfully used in a number of other settings (Beehr, Walsh and Taber 1976). Job tension was determined by eleven items employing Likert scales, incorporating measures of work related worry, relief when leaving work, items from the Taylor Manifest Anxiety Scale (1953) and dimensions from a study by House and Rizzo (1972). Perceived performance was measured by asking the product manager how he would rate himself in terms of his overall performance and coordinating activities for his product line. A 10 point scale was used with the endpoints of just satisfactory and clear excellence. This method was shown to have high validity when developed by Pym and Auld (1967) and to be related to actual job performance of industrial salesmen in a study reported by Pruden and Reese (1972).

RESULTS

Boundary Spanning, Role Conflict, Role Ambiguity

The findings presented in Table 1 support H_1 in that the product manager's boundary spanning is positively associated with role conflict (r = .31, p $\leq$ .001). However, the measures of boundary spanning were found to be unrelated to role ambiguity (r = .02) except for internal boundary spanning. Hence H_2 was not upheld.

In a careful investigation of H_1, the analysis of various types of role conflict demonstrated that role conflict as experienced by the product manager cannot be viewed simply as a global variable. For example, intersender conflict which relates to the role conflict the product manager experiences from two or more sources, was consistently strongly related to the various measures of boundary spanning with the highest association of (r = .35, p < .001) unlike role overload conflict which was not associated with any of the measures of boundary spanning. The absence of an association of boundary spanning with role ambiguity suggests that boundary spanning does not create a situation where the product manager is uncertain how he will be evaluated or what is expected from him in his boundary spanning.

TABLE 1: BOUNDARY SPANNING AND ROLE PERCEPTIONS

Role Perceptions

Measures of BOUNDARY SPANNING	ROLE CONFLICT	Person-Role Conflict	Intersender Conflict	Intrasender Conflict	Role-Overload Conflict	ROLE AMBIGUITY
Aggregate Boundary Spanning	.31***	.21**	.35***	.18**	.11	.02
Informal Boundary Spanning	.23**	.18**	.26***	.15*	.08	.06
Formal Boundary Spanning	.27***	.14*	.25***	.21**	.10	.02
Internal Organizational Boundary Spanning	.25***	.12*	.23***	.18***	.12	.12*
External Organizational Boundary Spanning	.19**	.08	.22**	.16*	.08	-.02

*p$\leq$0.05; **p$\leq$0.01; ***p$\leq$0.001

Role Perceptions and Personal Outcome States

Table 2 presents the correlations in testing hypotheses H_3 to H_8. The results clearly support the contention that the product manager's role conflict is associated with low job satisfaction (r = -.24, p $\leq$ .001), high job related tension (r = .31, p $\leq$ .001), and low perceived performance (r = -.18, p $\leq$ .01). Moreover, the results support H_6, H_7, and H_8 in showing that the product manager's role ambiguity is related to low job satisfaction (r = -.26, p $\leq$ .001), job related tension (r = .15, p $\leq$ .05), and low perceived performance (r = -.32, p $\leq$ .001). Therefore, all correlations were in the predicted direction. The role overload

TABLE 2: ROLE PERCEPTIONS AND PERSONAL OUTCOMES

ROLE PERCEPTIONS	JOB SATISFACTION	JOB RELATED TENSION	PERCEIVED PERFORMANCE
ROLE CONFLICT	-.24***	.31***	-.18**
Person-role Conflict	-.32***	.20**	-.07
Intersender Conflict	-.17***	.31***	-.15*
Intrasender Conflict	-.28***	.28***	-.23***
Role Overload Conflict	-.03	.18*	-.04
ROLE AMBIGUITY	-.26***	.15*	-.32***

*p<0.05; **p<0.01; ***p<0.001

conflict experienced by the product manager was not associated with job satisfaction (r = .03) or with perceived performance (r = .04). Most of the other forms of role conflict, however, were associated with the personal outcome state as Table 2 reflects.

IMPLICATIONS

The implications should be of interest to product managers, managers of product managers, and organizational theorists. The findings illustrate that boundary spanning was directly associated with role conflict experienced by the product manager but not with role ambiguity. This role conflict was found to be associated with lower satisfaction, lower performance and higher tension for the product manager. Similarly, role ambiguity was found to be related to the same dysfunctional personal outcomes. What this suggests is that these forces should be kept at manageable levels for the product manager. Suboptimal product line performance is likely if role conflict and ambiguity peristently impact on the product manager. According to Kahn et al. (1964), role conflict and ambiguity in extreme states are "identity destroying" and have effects on the physical and psychological well being of the individual. Since the product manager must interact with others in a boundary spanning capacity, role conflict may be inevitable. Therefore, the issue may not be the total elimination of role conflict and ambiguity from the product manager's role; it is the management of this conflict to levels that are not destructive to the product manager's well being.

Though managers may be unable to moderate the product manager's perceptions of ambiguity and conflict, they may be able to influence the way product managers cope with and attempt to resolve these interpersonal outcomes. Supportive senior management and appropriate training programs, for example, might help reduce the product manager's anxiety over ambiguity and conflict and the resulting dissatisfaction that results. Development of coping skills would benefit the product manager.

These findings suggest that if management wants to enhance job satisfaction, reduce tension and increase performance, steps should be taken to reduce role conflict and ambiguity. Several approaches can be used to achieve this reduction. First, via a meticulous screening selection process, management can attempt to choose personnel who will be better able to cope with tension and strain. Since role conflict is likely to emerge from boundary spanning, specific skills are required by the product manager. Trained interviewers, role playing, and psychological testing are fruitful procedures to realize this process. Second, management can be more alert to the structure of the work situation to diminish the opportunity for interpersonal conflicts to occur. Hence, modifications which can be developed are: adjustment of the product manager - group product manager relationship, streamlining rules and procedures, better coordinating departments to achieve an overall goal, moving personnel and so on. Explicitly communicating the expectations of senior management and other departments to the product manager could also reduce the potential for role conflict and ambiguity. At a minimum, management must examine its product management system to assess the degree and where exactly conflict occurs.

SUMMARY

In sum, this study has not only reinforced existing knowledge about individuals who span organizational boundaries, but has provided a different approach in examining the product management system. Many more issues, however, need to be examined. As was stated initially, the model is realistic from a theoretical standpoint. Future research should be directed at analyzing the realism of the model via causal analysis or path analysis. Moreover, the impact of environmental uncertainty on boundary spanning and the influence of moderating variables such as the product manager's need for affiliation and years of experience should be investigated. Since the product management system has been responsible for significant gains in administering complex product lines, this research illuminates many areas of concern.

REFERENCES

Adams, J. Stacey (1976), "The Structure and Dynamics of Behavior in Organizational Boundary Roles," M. Dunnette (Ed.), Handbook of Organizational and Industrial Psychology, Chicago: Rand-McNally.

Aiken, Michael and Hage, Jerald (1972), "Organizational Permeability, Boundary Spanners, and Organizational Structure," paper presented at the American Sociological Association, New Orleans (August).

Bagozzi, Richard P. (1978), "Sales Force Performance and Satisfaction as a Function of Individual Difference, Interpersonal, and Situational Factors," Journal of Marketing Research (November), pp. 517-531.

Beehr, Terry A.; Walsh, Jeffrey T.; and Taber, Thomas D. (1976), "Relationship of Stress to Individual and Organizationally Valued States: Higher Order of Needs as a Moderator," Journal of Applied Psychology, pp. 41-47.

Buell, Victor P. (1975), "The Changing Role of the Product Manager in Consumer Goods Companies," Journal of Marketing (July), pp. 3-11.

Churchill, Gilbert A.; Ford, Neil M.; and Walker, Orville C. (1974), "Measuring the Job Satisfaction of Industrial Salesmen," Journal of Marketing Research (August), pp. 254-260.

Clewett, Richard M. and Stasch, Stanley F. (1974), "Shifting Role of the Product Manager," Harvard Business Review (January-February).

House, Robert and Rizzo, John (1972), "Role Conflict and Ambiguity as Critical Variables in a Model of Organizational Behavior," Organizational Behavior and Human Performance, pp. 467-505.

Kahn, Robert L.; Wolfe, D. M.; Quinn, R. P.; Snock, J. D.; and Rosenthal, R. A. (1964), Organizational Stress, New York: John Wiley & Sons, Inc.

Keller, Robert T. (1975), "Role Conflict and Ambiguity: Correlates with Job Satisfaction and Values," Personnel Psychology, pp. 57-64.

Leifer, Richard Paul, and Delbecq, Andre (1978), "Organization/Environment Interchange: A Model of Boundary Spanning Activity," Academy of Management Review (January), pp. 40-50.

Miles, Robert H. (1975), "Role Requirements as Sources of Stress in R & D Organizations," Proceedings of the Thirty-Fifth Meeting of the Academy of Management, pp. 191-193.

Organ, Dennis W. (1971), "Some Variables Affecting Boundary Role Behavior," Sociometry, pp. 524-537.

Pym, D. L. A. and Auld, H. D. (1967), "The Self-Rating as a Measure of Employee Satisfactoriness," Occupational Psychology, pp. 103-113.

Quinn, R. P. and Shepard, L. J. (1974); "The 1972-1973
    Quality of Employment Survey: Descriptive Statistics
    with Comparison Data from the 1969-1970 Survey of Work-
    ing Conditions," Ann Arbor, Michigan: The Institute
    for Social Research.

Rizzo, John; House, Robert; and Lirtzman, Sidney (1970);
    "Role Conflict and Ambiguity in Complex Organizations,
    Administrative Science Quarterly, pp. 150-163.

Schuler, Randall S.; Aldag, Ramon J. and Brief, Arthur P.
    (1977); "Role Conflict and Ambiguity: A Scale Analysis,"
    Organizational Behavior and Human Performance, pp. 111-
    128.

Sheridan, J. E. and Slocum, J. (1974), "The Direction of
    the Causal Relationship Between Job Satisfaction and
    Work Performance," Organizational Behavior and Human
    Performance, October, pp. 159-72.

Snoek, J. Diedrick (1966), "Role Strain in Diversified
    Role Sets," The American Journal of Sociology, January,
    pp. 363-372.

Taylor, J. A. (1953), "A Personality Scale of Manifest
    Anxiety," Journal of Abnormal Social Psychology, pp.
    285-290.

Venkatesh, Alladi and Wilemon, David L. (1976), "Inter-
    personal Influence in Product Management," Journal of
    Marketing, October, pp. 33-40.

AN ORGANIZATION DESIGN APPROACH TO
IMPROVING THE EFFECTIVENESS OF NEW PRODUCT INTRODUCTIONS

James H. Myers, Claremont Graduate School, Claremont

ABSTRACT

There has been almost no change in the structure of the
marketing function within the firm since the Marketing
Concept was introduced over 25 years ago. It is likely
that some changes are needed due to major differences in
the business environment during the intervening years,
plus changes in marketing techniques and practices. This
paper suggests an organization design change intended to
make the marketing function within the firm more effective in the difficult task of bringing new products and
services to the market.

INTRODUCTION

The organizational structure of marketing within the firm
has undergone almost no changes since the concept of marketing gained widespread acceptance in the 1950's. The
latest textbooks show the organizational design of "typical" marketing departments almost exactly the same as did
texts 20-25 years ago. Yet marketing today is very different in some ways from those days, and some of these
differences are large enough to suggest that a re-evalua-
tion of the organizational structure of marketing is
needed.

One difference is that the current business climate is
more complex in most ways than in the 1950's. For one
thing, there are now greater competitive pressures (both
intra- and international); as a result, the general pace
of planning and execution within the firm is much faster
than before. Also, generally unstable and often unfavorable environmental conditions have become endemic. Recent developments in management theory have stressed the
importance of adapting the organizational design of business firms to fit the environments in which they operate.
This is the structural-contingency theory, in which organizations are viewed as open systems subject to environmental and technological conditions (Thompson [17]; Katz
& Kahn [7]; Lawrence & Lorsch [9]; Pennings [14]). Such
writers as Drucker and Toffler have discussed the problems of operating business firms in a "turbulent" environment (Drucker [4]; Toffler [16]).

There have also been some major changes in marketing
planning and operating practices within the firm. While
the basic marketing tasks have remained the same over the
years, the general level of sophistication in carrying
out these tasks has increased greatly in the past two
decades. In particular, marketing practitioners now have
a much wider variety of sophisticated research designs and
technologies (Green & Tull [6]; Myers & Tauber [11]). The
output from these can be used directly by many types of
marketing planners within the firm, greatly extending
their ability to understand the structure and needs of the
market and to develop more actionable plans. However, the
actual usage of these technologies is probably limited to
a relatively small number of the largest consumer products
and services firms (Market Facts [10]). This may be due
in large part to the lack of both researchers and planners
within the firm who understand these technologies and who
have the time necessary to utilize them effectively.

These, as well as other developments and changes within
the past two decades (e.g., new strategic planning tools
and concepts, consumerism, social responsibilities and

other public policy issues), suggest that marketing is in
some ways operating within a "new ball game", the parameters of which are constantly changing in ways that are
not always clearly defined. And this in turn suggests
the need to reappraise the current structure of marketing
within business firms. The purpose of this paper is not
to undertake a comprehensive review of the organization
design of marketing; this would require more than a single
manuscript. Instead, it will present a proposal for one
type of organization change aimed at improving the effectiveness of business firms in one especially important
area: the planning and introduction of new products/
services.

There are several reasons for this choice: 1) American
business firms in general have not been very successful
in introducing new products (Crawford [3]), and there is
evidence that the success rate has declined considerably
during the past 20 years, particularly for consumer packaged goods firms (Nielsen [12]); 2) while there has been
extensive coverage in the marketing literature of ways to
improve the effectiveness of new product introductions,
nearly all of the scholarly work has been devoted to new
research designs and tools. Very little of it has discussed organizational aspects of new product planning
(Grayson [5]), and no one seems to have proposed ways of
improving the effectiveness of innovation efforts by newer
types of organization designs; 3) it is generally agreed
that at least some of the current U.S. economic malaise
can be traced to our lack of success in competing with
foreign products by innovating in a number of important
types of product categories. Thus, the new product/ser-
vice aspect of marketing may be a particularly fruitful
and relevant area within which to consider new organization design options.

Vice-President: New Products Marketing

The purpose of this paper is to propose a new position at
a high management level within the firm: Vice-President,
New Products Marketing. The rank of this position would
be equal to that of the current vice-presidents of both
marketing and R&D. It is argued that this high level is
necessary for several reasons; it would: (1) reflect
the importance the firm places on preparing for future
markets, (2) provide the required expertise and leverage
at the upper management level, and (3) allow for the considerable amount of time required for planning and coordinating all efforts of the firm toward the successful
introduction of new products.

FUNCTIONS OF NEW PRODUCTS MARKETING

Functions which would be assigned to the Vice-President,
New Products Marketing are shown in Exhibit 1; these include some micro-organizational forms that are designed
especially to overcome the internal obstacles that plague
new product planning efforts in nearly every company.
Specific responsibilities of this new position would lie
in four major areas: (1) monitoring and forecasting, (2)
screening and planning specific new products/services, (3)
executing marketing introduction programs and (4) developing and utilizing advanced market research technologies
to support all functions of this department. These functions are currently scattered in many firms, often resulting in such problems as empire building and protection,

247

NIH (Not Invented Here), and general internecine warfare.
The net effect is the erection of barriers that inhibit
the effective, rapid, and orderly flow of new products/
services to marketplace.

EXHIBIT 1

FUNCTIONAL RESPONSIBILITIES
PROPOSED FOR NEW PRODUCTS MARKETING

MONITORING THE ENVIRONMENT

    Social and cultural forces
    Technological state-of-the-art
    Changes in competitive structures and forces
    Legal and regulatory climate
    Ecological factors and pressure group activities
    Delphi and other scenario-building techniques

PLANNING NEW PRODUCTS/SERVICES

    Development of entirely new product/service concepts
    "Innovative imitation" in growth categories
    Major modifications of present products
    Major line extensions
    Marketing aspects of mergers, acquisitions
    Planning marketing mixes for new products

EXECUTING NEW PRODUCT/SERVICE MARKETING

    Line functions for promotion and distribution
    Venture divisions
    Venture teams (internal and external)
    Entrepreneurial marketing
    Outside consultants and services

ADVANCED MARKET RESEARCH TECHNOLOGIES

    MDS and related technologies
    Early predicting of market share models
    Conjoint analysis
    Market Structure Studies and Benefit Structure
      Analysis
    Multivariate segmentation analyses
    Techniques for identifying product-market
      boundaries

Monitoring Changes in the Business Environment

While the literature on monitoring and forecasting techniques is vast, discussion of their organizational aspects
is quite limited. Experience suggests that formal forecasting efforts are most often carried out within either
Strategic Planning or Present Marketing operations in most
large, well-run business firms today. This often results
in forecasts that are tailored more to the needs of these
specific units than to the needs of other parts of the
firm. For example, Strategic Planning is more interested
in macro-economic factors that will shape the business
climate in the future, such as GNP, interest rates and
the money supply, labor availability, and consumer spending for very broad categories of goods (e.g., durables,
non-durables, services). For many companies, forecasting
such broad components of GNP is of little help in understanding trends and changes in the social fabric and in
consumers' individual life styles, values and micro-spend-
ing patterns. On the other hand, forecasting efforts by
today's marketing departments concentrate more on the
latter types of factors and less on macroeconomic considerations. Only a few firms tie these together well.

Consolidation of all types of forecasting activities and
personnel within New Products Marketing should result in
improving the quality of these efforts and their usefulness throughout the firm. But more importantly, they
would exert a strong force toward making sure that any and
all new product/service planning efforts are based on
current and probable future trends in the market and in
the environment in which the firm must operate. It is
often the case today that new product ideas come from company technological personnel whose interest lies more in
improving the "state of the art" than in closely and carefully monitoring the environment and customer needs and
then responding to these needs (Kotler, 1980).

Very large business firms would probably elect to use specialized personnel in the forecasting group. A full complement of professionals would include one or more persons
from each of the disciplines of economics, political science, psychology/sociology, international relations, quantitative business models, and one or more representatives
from the engineering/technological portions of the company.
Not all of these would need to be assigned full-time to
the forecasting group, of course; such services might even
be obtained from outside consultants as needed.

Planning New Products/Services

The systematic, market-oriented planning of new product/
service offerings is a task that is vastly underestimated
in many large, otherwise well-run business firms. It requires a far greater quantity of funds and personnel that
are commonly committed. (Many firms find that 100 or more
ideas are required in order to get a single successful new
product.) The evidence clearly shows that business firms
that have formal new product planning departments or staffs
are normally much more effective in introducing new pro-
ducts/services than firms which do not (Grayson [5]). The
role and function of new product planning has been discussed at length elsewhere and need not be pursued here. Since
most large, well-managed business firms already have some
form of new product planning within the Present Marketing
department, they would merely have to move these functions
into New Products Marketing. Other firms would have to
establish such a group.

A corollary problem is the matter of what to do with pro-
ducts/services that are not doing well. Should they be
revitalized in some way, or discontinued? Such decisions
involve the consideration of many factors: portfolio management techniques, product life cycles, the PIMS data
base, strength of competition, company resources, and the
changing environment. Several writers have pointed out
how difficult decisions of this type are and how poorly
they are done in many companies (Alexander [1]; Berenson
[2]). Robert Townsend, in his book Up the Organization,
observed that even the most unprofitable products can often be dropped only by someone at a very high level within
the firm (he proposed a Vice-President of Killing!).
(Townsend [18]).

All of the above planning, for individual products as well
as the firm's entire portfolio, requires a considerable
amount of time and attention by knowledgeable professionals. It is highly doubtful that this can be done carefully and thoroughly within the Present Marketing organization. All such planning there must be subordinate to
the primary responsibilities of Present Marketing person-
nel--maintaining growth, market share, and profitability
for existing product offerings. New product planning and
strategic portfolio management are given no more attention
than a foster child in many companies.

Advanced Market Research Technologies

The past 15-20 years have witnessed the development of a
remarkable body of quantitative techniques which provide
a much more solid foundation for marketing planning than
anything previously available. These techniques include,
but are not limited to the following: 1) MDS and related

technologies, 2) conjoint analysis, 3) multivariate segmentation techniques, 4) Market Structure Studies, 5) Benefit Structure Analysis, 6) market partitioning models,
7) market share prediction models. Continuous professional application of these technologies can provide very useful information for marketing planning purposes; it can
also prevent some of the strategic planning blunders found
in many business firms today.

Yet the overall impact of these techniques on marketing
planning has been marginal, even in the largest and best-
run business firms, according to a recent study/(Market
Facts, Inc. [10]). There are probably several reasons for
this: 1) most of these tools require advanced training in
quantitative methods, and few market researchers have had
this kind of training; 2) at best, most techniques are
much more difficult to explain to line management personnel, who are often looking for simple and understandable
information for their own immediate needs (which focus
groups, for example, appear to provide); 3) marketing
planners and researchers now utilize a wide variety of conventional research tools and syndicated data services,
which require many years to master even for well-trained
research personnel; it is asking too much of most researchers to master both the old and new technologies.

As a consequence, the newer research techniques have not
for the most part entered the mainstream of marketing planning for any but a few firms that are much more sophisticated in their marketing efforts. And even in these firms,
their use has often been spotty and discontinuous. It is
simply unreasonable to expect today's journeyman marketing
researcher to stop his/her regular work long enough to acquire the considerable amount of expertise necessary to
become facile with most of the newer research technologies.
Indeed, many researchers who are quite competent in the
conventional research methods and tools simply lack the
intellectual aptitude for sophisticated quantitative methods.

Executing New Product/Service Marketing

Several writers have discussed the severe problems of moving even good new product ideas through the organizational
pipeline. These problems stem from the necessity of involving so many people and functions within the firm in the
screening, development, testing and commercialization
stages of new product/service introduction. Each functional area has its own legitimate requirements and points
of view, and each presents its own particular types of
"obstacles" within the pipeline. Stefflre [15] observed:

   "It is my belief that the majority of new product failures are due to the selection of possible alternatives
   for evaluation, and the evaluation of alternatives
   selected, on the basis of the ability of these alternatives to satisfy individual and organizational goals
   unrelated to the nominal project goal of successful and
   profitable introduction of a new product ... and that
   successful new product introduction is not the major
   goal of the segments of the organization connected with
   the development process."

It is precisely these kinds of "people" problems that have
prompted business firms to explore alternative approaches
to new product organization and staffing. Some of these
alternatives include venture divisions, internal venture
teams, internal entrepreneurship, and outside consulting
firms (and, of course, acquisitions and mergers). For
example, the spirits division of Heublein, Inc., at one
time established a Venture Marketing Group within the company to integrate all marketing functions involved in new
product development under a single administrative office.
This group was responsible for all aspects from the creation of new product ideas, to in-home testing and test
marketing, and on to national roll-out of new products.

The division even had its own sales force, based on the
belief that the present sales force would not, and even
could not, spend the amount of selling time required for
the successful launch of an entirely new type of distilled
spirits product. Several products were introduced in this
manner, the most successful of which was Malcolm Hereford's
Cows, which continues to be a strong seller to this day.

Internal venture teams have been used in one form or another for decades, but they have probably received their
widest usage at 3M, which has utilized them extensively
to launch new products and product modification of all
types. Such teams provide a degree of centralized coordination and thrust that usually cannot be duplicated in the
normal new product process, which involves moving the product idea through several functional areas of the firm.
Each of these areas is always more interested in its own
current problems and goals than in new ventures that often
have a great deal of uncertainty.

These and other options have been useful in different ways
for various companies, but each has presented its own
special kinds of problems. Perhaps the biggest problem is
that none of these is really integrated into normal company organization and operation. Each represents an ad hoc
approach of a temporary nature, without a clear home within
the firm and without nominal, high-level supervision. Of
course, the proposed New Products Marketing Division would
be free to utilize any or all of these approaches within
its more conventional organization framework.

THEORETICAL ORGANIZATION DESIGN CONSIDERATIONS

Modern organization theory gives little guidance as to
whether or not there should be a place for New Products
Marketing within the present organization structure of
large business firms. A few writers have at least formally recognized the need for the general type of function represented by New Products Marketing. Within the
context of organizational systems theory, Parsons [13] has
identified the institutional, managerial, and technical
subsystems of the organization. Katz and Kahn [7] expanded on these by postulating three additional subsystems:
adaptive, maintenance and production supportive. The adaptive subsystem, in particular, seeks to "adapt the organization to new processes and products"; it includes such
functions as research and development, organization and
methods, market research, operations research, and the
like.

It seems clear that New Products Marketing would be a part
of the adaptive subsystem of the firm; it would even be a
major part of this subsystem since it and research and
development are the primary functions within the firm that
look outward toward satisfying future customer needs and
providing new products/services to sell.

Beyond the general notion of the adaptive subsystem, however, organization theory offers little guidance as to
whether or how New Products Marketing would fit within the
firm. Khandwalla [8] observed that many new organizational practices precede theory that is based upon professional and systematic research. "For example, the so-called
matrix organization, with its highly flexible structure,
began to be practiced widely in the sophisticated aerospace industry before theories appeared attempting to explain its use." The same kind of comment could be made
for the entire marketing department within a firm.

The same writer discussed the effects of "turbulence" in
the external environment (i.e., dynamic, unpredictable,
expanding, fluctuating) and concluded that "the more turbulent the external environment, the more strategically
important to management are uncertainty absorption and
avoidance mechanisms like market research, forecasting,

advertising . . . .". (p. 124) Few business executives
would argue the notion that the environment in which they
operate has become increasingly turbulent in recent years
and will probably be even more so in the future, lending
further support to the need for New Products Marketing.

From a structural standpoint, the overall effect of New
Products Marketing on the organization of the firm would be
minimal. It would simply amount to the addition of one
position at the vice-president level, as shown in Exhibit
2, but it would also require additional professional
staffing of various kinds, as indicated earlier.

Relationship to Present Marketing

It was observed earlier that the marketing department in
most companies today is concerned primarily with carrying
out line operations for present products/services and with
the staff support for these operations. All of this type
of activity would continue to be included within the
Present Marketing department. In general, any functions
or personnel assigned to planning, promoting, or distribu-
ting the company's present product/service lines on an ongoing basis, plus the staff support for this work, would
be assigned to present marketing. This would even include
such "new" products/services as relatively minor line extensions and product modifications (e.g., slight variations
in product formulations, container sizes or designs; new
package forms,   new uses or markets for present pro-
ducts/services).

Separating the planning of present products from that for
future products would insure much greater attention to
each. Present products would not be neglected in favor of
planning and introducing newer products, and vice versa.
Thus, the proposed split should result in greater concentration of efforts on both present and future lines. And
perhaps more importantly, each of these types of offerings
may require very different types of planners. For example,
most present products are in the maturity or decline stages
of their life cycles, and this ordinarily suggests the need
for more conservative, financially-oriented types of managers. Conversely, new offerings are by definition in the
introductory or growth stages and would usually benefit
more from aggressive, entrepreneurial types of managers
who are builders and conquerors. This consideration may
help explain why at least some of the new products introduced by/through present product managers fail.

While the proposed organization structure has not been
fully implemented in any U.S. company, to the writer's
knowledge, a few firms have recently given high corporate
status to the new product planning function. The John
Deere Company (farm machinery & equipment) has a Senior
Vice President, New Product Planning. The Mead Corporation
(Alka Seltzer) has a Vice President, Growth and Development. As discussed earlier, the Spirits Division of Heublein at one time had a Venture Products Division, headed
by a vice president (who later was put in charge of all
marketing operations and consolidated the two groups).

Crown Zellerback currently separates its Consumer Products
Division marketing operations into two groups: Established Brands and New Enterprise. The latter contains product
managers who guide introduction of new products within the
Division. A product brought out under New Enterprise will
be shifted to Established Brands after 6-12 months; it will
usually be assigned to a product manager responsible for
introduction, who will often remain with the product after
it has become established successfully.

The Nestle Company for many years followed the practice of
inter-changing the incumbents of two positions at the
senior vice president level: R&D and marketing. Both were
technically trained well enough to handle the R&D function,
and both became knowledgeable about marketing operations.
The company was pleased with this practice, since it
tended to integrate the two functional areas to a degree
rarely found in any business firm.

The J. C. Penney Company now has a Vice President/Corpor-
ate Planning who heads up three important departments:
planning/research, domestic/international development, and
strategic research. The latter department conducts the
"far-out" types of research that serve as forecasting inputs for the other groups in corporate planning. They, in
turn, can provide more specific plans for operational
implementation than is the case with most corporate long-
range planning departments.

This and other evidence suggests that U.S. business firms
are now giving much more attention to assessing the most
probable environments in which they will be operating in
the future and to moving more consumer-based new product
ideas through the many bureaucratic obstacles within the

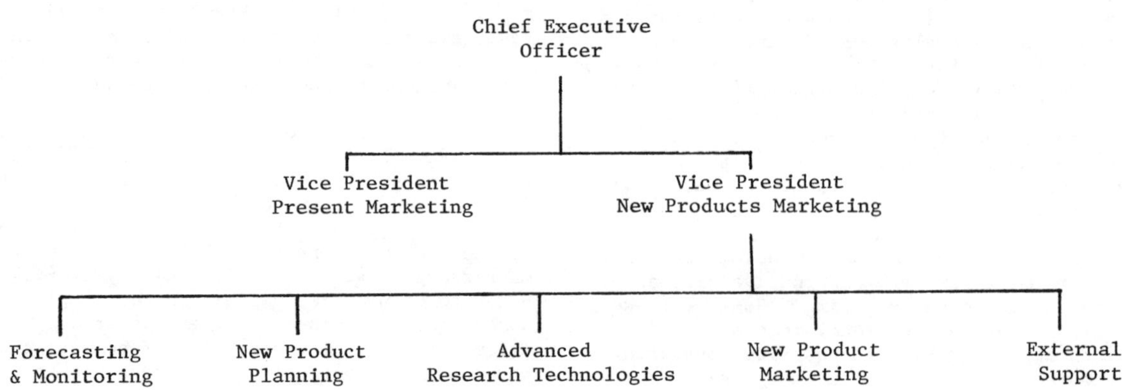

EXHIBIT 2

firm.

Implementation is the Key

Thus, the emphasis in some business firms today is on
improved forecasting and monitoring of the external environment, to provide better inputs for today's decisions
and tomorrow's plans. But the full utilization of this
type of information will be limited by the ability and
time of busy executives to follow through on the implications of this information and to implement plans designed
to exploit these implications. This would be especially
true in the matter of introducing new products and services. The proposed organization would help to insure a
more complete utilization of future planning scenarios,
for the purpose of introducing new products/services that
are in tune with the expected environment and are not
simply the laboratory-generated "good ideas" that have
plagued top management in the past in so many firms.

The new organization will not be at all easy to implement.
Neither was the Marketing Concept when it was introduced
30 years ago. But the time has come to take the next step
in developing the implications of this Concept, by making
marketing even more responsive to the rapidly changing
needs of consumers and of other business firms.

REFERENCES

1. Alexander, R. S. (1964), "The Death and Burial of
    'Sick' Products," Journal of Marketing, Vol. 28
    (April), pp. 1-7.

2. Berenson, Conrad, (1963), "Product Abandonment: A
    Forgotten Step In Innovation," Proceedings of the
    46th National Conference, Chicago: American
    Marketing Association, pp. 619-629.

3. Crawford, C. Merle, "Marketing Research and the New
    Product Failure Rate", Journal of Marketing, April,
    1977, pp. 51-61.

4. Drucker, Peter F., (1980), Managing in Turbulent
    Times, New York: Harper and Row.

5. Grayson, Robert A., (1969), "If You Want New Products
    You Better Organize to Get Them," in Marketing in
    a Changing World, Proceedings of the June Confer-
    ence, Chicago: American Marketing Association,
    pp. 75-79.

6. Green, Paul E. and Donald S. Tull (1975), Research
    For Marketing Decisions, New Jersey: Prentice-Hall.

7. Katz, Daniel and Robert L. Kahn, (1966), The Social
    Psychology of Organizations, New York: John Wiley
    and Sons, pp. 19-26.

8. Khandwalla, Pradip N., (1977), The Design of Organi-
    zations, New York: Harcourt Brace Janovich, p. 18.

9. Lawrence, Paul R. and Jay W. Lorsch, Organization and
    Environment: Managing Differentiation and Integra-
    tion, Boston: Graduate School of Business Adminis-
    tration, Harvard University, 1967.

10. Market Facts, Inc., A Study of Market Research Usage
    Patterns and Attitudes--Among the Major Manufactur-
    ers, 1978.

11. Myers, James H. and Edward M. Tauber (1977), Market
    Structure Analysis, Chicago: American Marketing
    Association.

12. Nielsen Researcher, The, New York: The A.C. Neilsen
    Co., No. 5, 1971 and No. 1, 1979.

13. Parsons, Talcott, (1960), The Structure and Process
    in Modern Societies, New York: The Free Press,
    pp. 63-4.

14. Pennings, Johannes N., "The Relevance of the
    Structural-Contingency Model for Organizational
    Effectiveness", Administrative Science Quarterly,
    20 (September, 1975), pp. 393-407.

15. Stefflre, Volney, (1968), New Products and New
    Enterprises: An Experiment in the Applied Social
    Sciences, Social Sciences Division, University
    of California at Irvine, pg. 17.

16. Toffler, Alvin, (1970), Future Shock, New York:
    Random House.

17. Thompson, James D., Organizations in Action, New
    York: McGraw Hill, 1967.

18. Townsend, Robert J., (1970), Up the Organization,
    New York: Alfred A. Knopf, pg. 93.

AN APPROACH FOR IMPLEMENTING SALESFORCE DECISION MODELS

Raymond W. LaForge, Oklahoma State University
David W. Cravens, Texas Christian University

ABSTRACT

Achieving implementation has been a major problem in
salesforce decision model research. Both the costs of
implementation and distrust of complex models by managers
and salespeople have contributed to limited use of size
and deployment models. This paper presents an operational
approach for implementating model results utilizing a
sampling procedure, and a simplified scheme for transfer-
ring model results from the sample to the entire sales
organization. An application is presented which tests
the approach and illustrates how it can be used to achieve
cost-effective results from model applications and to
encourage acceptance by management and salespeople.

THE IMPLEMENTATION PROBLEM

The need to increase sales productivity has led to renewed
interest in salesforce decision modeling during recent
years (Cravens 1979; LaForge 1980; Zoltners and Gardner
1980). Salesforce decision models can lead to increased
sales productivity by helping sales managers improve their
salesforce size and deployment decisions. The models
have consistently indicated sales productivity improvements of 10% or more by changing the level of selling
effort and/or redeploying sales resources (Lambert and
Kniffin 1970; Lodish 1971, 1975; Beswick and Cravens 1977;
Parasuraman and Day 1977; LaForge and Cravens 1980).

Despite the obvious value of salesforce decision models,
few firms appear to be using the models on a large scale
basis. Reported model applications typically include
only small, unrepresentative portions of a sales organization (LaForge 1980). One reason for the apparent lack
of model usage is that model development and implementation require the collection and processing of large a-
mounts of empirical or judgmental data. The process can
be extremely complex and time consuming.

Consider, for example, a relatively small organization
which employs 34 salespeople who call on some 4000 retail
accounts. For the firm to develop and implement a salesforce decision model, sales management must obtain and
process either measures of several variables, or response
estimates at several levels, for each of the 4000 accounts. This information is needed to develop sales response relationships as a basis for determining the optimal allocation of selling effort. This would be an enormous undertaking for this small organization, and the
problems are greatly magnified for the many firms with
much larger salesforces.

Our objective is to present a cost-effective approach
for sales managers and salespeople to implement salesforce
decision model results across their entire selling situation. The approach consists of using a salesforce decision model to determine sales call levels to segments
of planning and control units (PCU) that are similar in
response to different levels of selling effort. Once
the segments have been identified and appropriate call
levels determined, the approach can be expanded quite
easily to cover all of the PCU's served by the sales organization. We discuss each step in the procedure and
then provide an application example to illustrate the
usefulness of the approach.

THE IMPLEMENTATION APPROACH

Our approach for implementing salesforce decision models
is presented in Figure 1. The procedure consists of the
following steps:

• Determine the planning and control unit to be used

• Select a representative sample of PCU's

• Develop and apply a salesforce decision model to PCU's
  in sample

• Develop sales call matrix

• Classify PCU's in sample and determine sales call levels
  to segments of the matrix

• Expand the classification to include all PCU's in the
  sales organization to determine recommended call levels.

Each step in the approach is discussed in more detail
below.

FIGURE 1
IMPLEMENTATION APPROACH FOR SALESFORCE DECISION MODELS

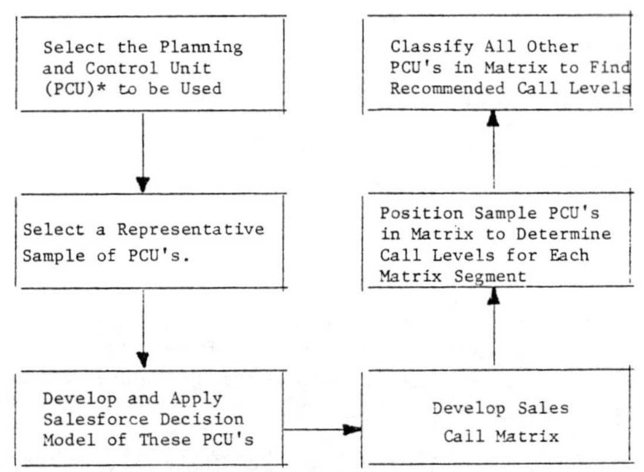

* A PCU may be an account, group of similar accounts, trading
  area, or other appropriate unit for size and/or deployment
  analysis.

Select Planning and Control Unit

A planning and control unit (PCU) may be an account, group
of similar accounts, geographical trading area, sales
territory, or any other unit that is considered appropriate for salesforce size and/or deployment analysis. The
more disaggregate the unit of analysis, the more sensitive
the resulting analysis. The use of very small PCU's such
as individual customers (or product categories within
customers) increases the data requirements, particularly
if an entire sales organization receives a comprehensive
analysis. One of the features of the implementation approach shown in Figure 1 is that by using a sampling procedure for model development and determination of deployment guidelines, total data requirements are greatly reduced. Thus, disaggregate PCU's can be used on a cost-
effective basis.

Selection of Sample Accounts

A probability sampling procedure can be used to select
a small number of PCU's that represent the major sources
of market response variation existing in a selling situation (LaForge and Cravens 1980). A sampling approach
will lead to model applications that approximate full
scale coverage, but substantially reduce data collection
and processing costs.

The sampling procedure must be designed to ensure that
the selected PCU's encompass the variation in market response relationships that would be encountered if all
PCU's were included in the model application. This requires an analysis of the specific selling situation to
identify the important factors that determine PCU response
and vary across PCU's. Several conceptual frameworks
are available to assist in properly analyzing a selling
situation (Cravens, Woodruff, and Stamper 1972; Walker,
Churchill, and Ford 1978; Ryans and Weinberg 1979; LaForge
and Cravens 1982).

Salesforce Decision Model Application

The next step is to develop an empirical salesforce decision model using the sampled PCU's and to use the model
to determine the optimal number of sales calls to each
PCU in the sample. Several model development methodologies have been reported (Beswick and Cravens 1977; Ryans
and Weinberg 1979; LaForge and Cravens 1980). In general,
these procedures consist of:

1. Identifying important determinant variables

2. Obtaining measures of these variables for each account
    during the previous period

3. Developing a market response function using multiple
    regression on the logarithmically transformed vari-
    ables and converting the results to form a multiplica-
    tive power function

4. Using the response function and a search procedure
    to determine the optimal number of sales calls to
    each account in the sample

Develop Sales Call Matrix

Once optimal call allocations to each PCU in the sample
have been determined, a sales call matrix is developed.
The purpose of the sales call matrix is to classify PCU's
into segments such that all PCU's in a particular segment
exhibit similar response to changes in selling effort.
The basic task is to determine how many segments to use
and what criteria should be used to define each segment.

The approach we suggest is to develop a four segment sales
call matrix defined by two criteria: a PCU attractiveness
criterion and a business position criterion. The PCU
attractiveness criterion provides an evaluation of the
total opportunity available from a PCU, while the business
position criterion assesses the ability of the sales organization to take advantage of the opportunity offered
by the PCU. This approach is similar to the
product/business portfolio analysis used in strategic
market planning (Abell and Hammond 1979). We are classifying each PCU according to attractiveness and business
position criteria in order to determine the appropriate
level of sales calls to make to each PCU in a particular
segment.

A four cell sales call matrix is presented in Figure 2.
Each segment in the matrix represents a different market
situation and requires a different sales call strategy.
For example, Segment 1 PCU's offer future opportunity
and the firm is in a strong position to take advantage
of this opportunity. This is a very favorable market

situation and the firm should respond with a heavy investment of sales calls to capitalize on its strong position
and the future opportunity available from the PCU. The
market situations and sales call strategies for the other
segments are described in Figure 2.

FIGURE 2
SALES CALL MATRIX

<table>
<tr><td></td><td>Segment 1

Situation: PCU's offer future opportu-
nity and firm has strong
business position

Sales Call
Strategy: Heavy investment of sales
calls to maintain/improve
business position and take
advantage of future oppor-
tunities</td><td>Segment 2

Situation: PCU's offer future op-
portunity, but firm has
weak business position

Sales Call
Strategy: Substantial sales call
investment to strengthen
business position and
take advantage of future
opportunities. An al-
ternative is to drop the
PCU, shifting the avail-
able effort to Segment 1</td></tr>
<tr><td></td><td>Segment 3

Situation: PCU's where firm has
strong business position,
but future opportunities
are limited

Sales Call
Strategy: Sufficient sales call in-
vestment to maintain cur-
rent business position</td><td>Segment 4

Situation: PCU's offer limited op-
portunity and firm has
weak business position

Sales Call
Strategy: Minimize sales call in-
vestment and selectively
eliminate salesperson
coverage</td></tr>
</table>

The vertical axis is labeled PCU Attractiveness (High at top, Low at bottom). The horizontal axis is labeled Business Position (Strong at left, Weak at right).

Determine Segment Call Levels

The procedure for calculating segment sales call levels
consists of classifying all sample PCU's according to
the sales call matrix and then determining the number
of sales calls for PCU's in each segment using model results. Once the PCU's are grouped into the appropriate
segments, the average number of sales calls and average
predicted sales for the PCU's in each segment are calculated from salesforce decision model results. It is then
possible to compare actual calls and sales with model
predictions to assess potential sales improvement from
redeployment. For example, suppose there were 50 accounts
in Segment 1 and salespeople were currently making an
average of 30 sales calls per year to obtain an average
of $120,000 sales. For these same accounts, model re-
sults indicate that an average of 35 sales calls should
be made with predicted annual sales of $150,000. Thus,
model results indicate a potential $1.5 million sales
increase through an increase of 250 sales calls to Segment
1 accounts. This example suggests a 25% sales improvement
from redeployment. Complete analysis of all segments
would indicate whether the extra sales calls should be
obtained by reducing calls to accounts in other segments
and/or increasing the total level of selling effort.

The underlying assumption is that by increasing call activity in some segments and reducing activity in others,
sales will be increased for the existing total amount
of available selling effort. We are able to verify this
premise by comparing PCU call patterns determined by the
empirical model to segment position on the matrix. We
are also assuming that substantial shifts in current
levels of selling effort will be indicated by the deployment analysis. If selling effort is already optimally
deployed across all or most of the PCU's, then all segment
positions would indicate maintaining current levels of
calls. Of course, we would expect much higher average
call levels in the more attractive segments, if the empirical model and matrix are consistent. Our approach

is to use the optimal call allocations calculated by the empirical salesforce decision model as a basis for determining the specific number of sales calls to be made to each PCU in each segment.

Expand Call Allocations to All Accounts

Once segment call levels are established, it is quite easy to incorporate all of the remaining PCU's served by the firm. Each PCU is classified in the sales call matrix according to its attractiveness and business position evaluation and assigned the number of sales calls determined by the salesforce decision model for its segment. Total call levels and expected sales can be calculated for each segment and compared to actual results to assess the expected benefits from redeployment of sales calls.

Although this implementation approach does not apply a salesforce decision model to all of the PCU's served by a firm, it does provide a procedure to expand model results from a representative sample of PCU's to all PCU's. The approach should be operationally feasible for most sales organizations and should lead to improved sales productivity in most cases. The results from using the approach in a specific selling situation are presented to illustrate the value of the approach.

AN IMPLEMENTATION EXAMPLE

The implementation approach was applied to the 34-member sales organization of a marketer of low-priced consumer grocery products. The salespeople call on approximately 4000 retail accounts. Although the firm is quite small relative to its major competitors, it does have a strong market position in some geographical areas. Personal selling is the major promotional tool used by the firm, although some advertising and sales promotion are also employed. The individual retail account was selected as the planning and control unit for deployment analysis.

Selection of Sample Accounts

We used a conceptual model of market response as a framework for analyzing the firm's selling situation (LaForge and Cravens 1982). Discussions with management indicated that the important sources of market response variation differed by geographic area. Since the firm's sales territories were geographically defined, we stratified the accounts served by the firm according to the sales territory location of the account. This stratification ensures that all geographic areas and all salespeople are represented in the sample of selected accounts. A secondary stratification was used to classify accounts as to whether they were major accounts or other accounts. This stratification ensures that the most important accounts are not underrepresented in the final sample.

Our approach was to categorize the 4000 retail accounts served by the firm into the above strata and then select a systematic random sample of 6 accounts from each stratum. This resulted in a total sample of 408 retail accounts. This sample was then systematically subdivided into samples of 204 accounts. Sample 1 was used to develop and apply the empirical salesforce decision model, while Sample 2 was used to illustrate how the implementation approach can be expanded to include accounts not used in model development.

Salesforce Decision Model Application

An empirical salesforce decision model was developed and used to determine optimal call allocations to each account in Sample 1. A detailed discussion of the entire model development and application is available elsewhere (LaForge and Cravens 1980). Of particular importance to this discussion was the use of a retail outlet attrac-

tiveness and a business position variable in the sales response function. Both variables were found to be important determinants of account response in this selling situation. This provides strong evidence for using attractiveness and business position as criteria for defining segments of accounts that respond similarly to changes in selling effort.

Develop Sales Call Matrix

Retail account attractiveness and business position were both evaluated on a 7 point scale. These scale values were used to determine the segments indicated in Figure 3. The figure indicates the number of Sample 1 accounts in each segment and the average number of actual sales calls and the average actual sales (in cases) for each segment. It does not appear that the firm is using the sales call strategies discussed earlier for each segment. For example, one would expect more sales calls would be made to Segment 2 accounts than to those accounts in Segment 3. The opposite is the case in this situation. Note also the wide variation in average sales between each segment, but limited variation in average sales call levels between segments.

FIGURE 3
SALES CALL MATRIX EXAMPLE

Retail Account Attractiveness	SEGMENT 1	SEGMENT 2
High 7	$N_1 = 97$	$N_2 = 15$
6	Actual Calls – 27.27 Actual Sales – 2437.79	Actual Calls – 21.40 Actual Sales – 1247.67
5	Model Calls – 35.70 Model Sales – 2662.92	Model Calls – 21.40 Model Sales – 1327.87
4	SEGMENT 3	SEGMENT 4
3	$N_3 = 26$	$N_4 = 66$
2	Actual Calls – 23.00 Actual Sales – 1016.92	Actual Calls – 16.91 Actual Sales – 402.21
Low 1	Model Calls – 16.19 Model Sales – 1001.81	Model Calls – 7.24 Model Sales – 366.67

	7	6	5	4	3	2	1
	Strong						Weak

Business Position

Determine Segment Call Levels

Figure 3 also shows the average number of sales calls and average expected sales to accounts in each segment based on the salesforce decision model results. As indicated, model results suggest decreasing sales calls to Segment 3 and Segment 4 accounts, while increasing sales calls to Segment 1 accounts. The firm appears to be making the appropriate number of calls to Segment 2 accounts. Model results are consistent with the appropriate sales call strategies for each segment (see Figure 2).

A comparison of actual results to model generated results is presented in Table 1. Model results indicate a 6.7% improvement in sales by changing sales call allocations across the different segments. Sales calls to accounts in Segment 1 are substantially increased. These increases are accompanied by a large decrease in calls to Segment 4 accounts and a moderate decrease in calls to Segment 3 accounts. Sales productivity is increased from an average of 65.8 cases/sales call to the 70.2 cases/sales call expected from model generated redeployment. Since model results promise a substantial increase in sales productivity, model results can now be expanded to include all accounts served by the firm.

TABLE 1
ACTUAL RESULTS VS. MODEL RESULTS FOR SAMPLE 1 ACCOUNTS

SEGMENT	NUMBER OF ACCOUNTS	TOTAL ACTUAL CALLS	TOTAL ACTUAL SALES	TOTAL MODEL CALLS	TOTAL MODEL SALES
1	97	2645.19	236,465.63	3462.90	258,303.24
2	15	321.00	18,715.05	321.00	19,918.05
3	26	598.00	26,439.92	420.94	26,047.06
4	66	1116.06	26,545.86	477.84	24,200.22
	204	4680.25	308,166.46	4682.68	328,468.57

Expand Call Allocations to All Accounts

Although the implementation results could be expanded to any number of accounts, our example illustrates the approach by implementing the results for the 204 accounts in Sample 2. Table 2 presents the comparison of actual results and model results for Sample 2 accounts. This comparison indicates that a 13.5% increase in selling effort is needed to properly cover the accounts, while model derived call allocations are expected to increase sales by 16.6%. Model results are again consistent with the expected sales call strategies for each segment, since sales calls are increased to Segments 1 and 2 and decreased for Segments 3 and 4. A sales productivity improvement from 68.1 cases/sales call to 69.9 cases/sales call is also expected from implementing the model results.

TABLE 2
ACTUAL RESULTS VS. MODEL RESULTS FOR SAMPLE 2 ACCOUNTS

SEGMENT	NUMBER OF ACCOUNTS	TOTAL ACTUAL CALLS	TOTAL ACTUAL SALES	TOTAL MODEL CALLS	TOTAL MODEL SALES
1	95	2306.60	204,443.80	3391.50	252,977.40
2	32	593.92	25,583.04	684.80	42,491.84
3	20	463.00	34,380.00	323.80	20,036.20
4	57	877.23	24,168.00	412.68	20,900.19
	204	4240.75	288,574.84	4812.78	336,405.63

This example illustrates an operational approach for implementing the results of a salesforce decision model application to all of the accounts served by the firm. Increases in sales productivity are expected from the changes in call allocations indicated by the model for both Sample 1 accounts (used in model development) and Sample 2 accounts (not included in model application). The approach is applicable to any type of selling situation and can be of substantial value to large sales organizations where full scale model implementation is often prohibitive due to data requirements and difficulties in communicating the underlying logic of deployment models. The simple, yet powerful, logic of the sales call matrix is easily communicated to sales management and salespeople.

DISCUSSION

We have developed and applied an approach for implementing the results of a salesforce decision model across all of the accounts served by a sales organization. The approach is based on developing and applying a salesforce decision model for a representative sample of PCU's. A sales call matrix is developed to classify all PCU's into segments according to their attractiveness and business position evaluations. Model results are then used to determine sales call levels for each segment and all PCU's in the same segment are assigned the same level of sales calls. Actual results can be compared to model derived results to assess expected sales productivity improvement from redeployment. The approach can be applied to any type of selling situation and can be used by salesforces of any size.

In order to make the approach operational, we lose the ability to determine exact optimal call allocations to all accounts as might be determined from a full scale salesforce decision model application. Nevertheless, the example application presented earlier indicates that the approach can lead toward optimal allocations. It is likely that any move toward optimal allocation of sales resources will result in substantial sales productivity improvements for most sales organizations.

The current approach could be improved in at least two ways through future research. First, we used a four-cell sales call matrix similar to the BCG approach in portfolio analysis (Abell and Hammond 1979). Since call levels are derived from average levels determined by a salesforce decision model for each segment, one would expect better sales call guidelines from matrices with more segments. Future research should investigate the value of using larger matrices to determine if expected benefits from the additional analyses are sufficient to cover the increased costs.

Second, there is a need for future research to investigate different approaches for evaluating the attractiveness and business position of accounts. The 7-point scale used in our approach is easy to use, but other methods might provide better criteria for segmenting accounts.

In sum, our implementation approach promises to be a means for improving call allocations to all of the accounts served by a firm. Future research is needed to apply the approach in different selling situations and to investigate the suggested producedure improvements.

REFERENCES

Abell, D. F. and J. S. Hammond (1979), *Strategic Market Planning: Problems and Analytical Approaches*, Englewood Cliffs, New Jersey: Prentice-Hall Inc.

Beswick, C. A., and D. W. Cravens (1977), "A Multistage Decision Model for Salesforce Management," *Journal of Marketing Research*, 14 (May), 135-144.

Cravens, D. W. (1979), "Salesforce Decision Models: A Comparative Assessment," in *Sales Management: New Developments from Behavioral and Decision Model Research*, R. P. Bagozzi, ed., Cambridge, MA: Marketing Science Institute, 310-324.

________, R. B. Woodruff, and J. C. Stamper (1972), "An Analytical Approach for Evaluating Sales Territory Performance," *Journal of Marketing*, 36 (January), 31-37.

LaForge, R. W. (1980), "Salesforce Decision Models: Trends in the 1970s, Directions for the 1980s," in *Evolving Marketing Thought for 1980*, J. H. Summey and R. B. Taylor, eds., Carbondale, IL: Southern Marketing Association, 41-45.

________ and D. W. Cravens (1980), "Comparative Testing of Empirical and Judgement-Based Salesforce Decision Models," Working Paper #6, M. J. Neeley School of Business, Texas Christian University.

________ and D. W. Cravens (1982), "A Market Response Model for Sales Management Decision Making," *Journal of Personal Selling and Sales Management* (forthcoming).

Lambert, Z. V., and F. W. Kniffin (1970), "Response Functions and Their Application in Sales Force Management," *Southern Journal of Business*, 5 (January), 1-11.

Lodish, L. M. (1971), "CALLPLAN: An Interactive Salesman's Call Planning System," *Management Science*, 18 Part II (December), 25-40.

________ (1975), "Sales Territory Alignment to Maximize Profit," *Journal of Marketing Research*, 12 (February), 30-36.

Parasuraman, A., and R. L. Day (1977), "A Management-Oriented Model for Allocating Sales Effort," *Journal of Marketing Research*, 14 (February) 22-33.

Ryans, A. B., and C. B. Weinberg (1979), "Territory Sales Response," *Journal of Marketing Research*, 16 (November), 453-465.

Walker, O. C., G. A. Churchill, and N. M. Ford (1978), "Where Do We Go From Here?--Selected Conceptual and Empirical Issues Concerning the Motivation and Performance of the Industrial Salesforce." Paper presented at the Sales Management Workshop, American Institute for Decision Sciences, St. Louis, Missouri, October.

Zoltners, A. A., and K. Gardner (1980), "A Review of Salesforce Decision Models," working paper, Northwestern University.

TRAINING SALES MANAGERS: AN ORGANIZATIONAL PERSPECTIVE

W. Austin Spivey, The University of Texas at San Antonio
David F. Caldwell, The University of Santa Clara
Raydel Tullous, Multivariate Research Associates

ABSTRACT

Assessing the effectiveness of sales training is a complex problem. This paper delineates a conceptual model designed to help researchers and practitioners interested in sales training. In addition, an illustrative example is presented. The intent of the illustration is twofold: 1) to high light the usefulness of the model as a guide to properly assessing sales training; 2) to demonstrate the importance of properly operationalizing the various constructs incorporated within the conceptual model.

INTRODUCTION

Even a cursory glance at the sales management literature reveals the importance of training; many sales managers feel that training is the single most important task for which they are responsible (Robertson and Bellenger 1980). Stanton and Buskirk (1973) offer a partial explanation for these feelings. They note that the number of proven sales people is so scant that few firms can afford to ignore training as a vehicle for insuring an adequate supply of able representatives. Xerox (Xerox Sales Training Marketing Case History 1976) has proven to its satisfaction that training is cost effective and offers a better return on investment than advertising. Consequently, many companies spend more on sales training than they do on advertising (Stroh 1978).

A significant part of the money is spent on training sales managers themselves. Since they control a level of sales and profits that far exceed the output of any one salesperson (Jolson 1977), their training is perhaps even more influential than that for individual salespeople. This belief is reinforced by recent research which has shown the impact of field sales supervision on territory sales response (Ryans and Weinberg 1979).

Even though most companies recognize its importance (Shapiro 1977), sales training is not well-understood. Indeed, sales training is conspicuously absent in the summary of salesforce research presented by Ryans and Weinberg (1979). While they mention research in the basic areas of deployment, motivation, and evaluation, there is no reference to sales training, in general, or its effectiveness, in particular.

The purpose of this paper is to present a model of sales training and to demonstrate its usefulness in an empirical context. Specifically, the potential effectiveness of training sales managers is discussed in view of the complexities surrounding both the training process and the sales management job itself.

A CONCEPTUAL MODEL OF SALES TRAINING

Perhaps the most significant reason for the lack of research about sales training relates to the differing philosophies of training assessment. Randall (1960) identifies holders of three different philosophies: negativists, positivists, and frustrates. Negativists see evaluation of training as either impossible or unnecessary. In general, they see training outcomes either as unamenable to quantitative analysis or as so patently

obvious that only the most cursory examination is necessary. Their preconceived idea is that someone undergoes training and becomes a more effective salesperson or sales manager regardless of organizational or individual makeup. For example, to the negativists, there would be no question that the 250 percent increase in sales to chain accounts reported by Armour-Dial (Business Week January 6, 1973) was a direct result of recent training for its salespeople. Positivists, on the other hand, believe that a scientific evaluation of training is the only possible course. Without rigorous experimental design and control, pretesting, and random assignment, positivists believe any evaluation is essentially useless. The positivist's preconceived ideas demand skepticism about seemingly indisputable results. The third group, frustrates, hold somewhat of a middle ground. They see training evaluation as an important and necessary function, but express concern about the possibility of carrying out the positivists' rigorously designed experimental studies in an organization environment. Thus the frustrate is often in a situation of desiring careful evaluation of training, yet not having the time or resources to conduct the type of evaluation demanded by the positivist.

If one adopts an organizational perspective, a potential solution to the frustrate's dilemma exists. This solution requires the development of a conceptual model which delineates the complex environment within which one must assess the impact of sales training. Figure 1 shows a diagram of the major parameters within such a model. It is an integration of variables related to both the individual and the organization.

As suggested by Hinrichs (1975), two types of inputs are used to conceptualize sales training. Both signal inputs and maintenance inputs impact the outcomes achieved by a trainee (either a salesperson or a sales manager). Maintenance inputs are more or less "givens"; that is, they are variables which are likely to influence the particularities of skill acquisition. Present multiplicative models of performance (Churchill, Ford and Walker 1979) suggest that at least four such variables be included: ability, skill level, motivation and role perception. In addition, the recent efforts of Ryans and Weinberg (1979) have shown the impact on sales performance of maintenance variables related to the territory to which an individual is assigned. Such territorial variables are typified by: field supervision, potential, concentration of potential, geographic dispersion, and workload. The training process itself is conceptualized as a set of signal inputs. Two broad types of signal inputs exist. One is the content of the sales training. The other is the methodology used to present the content; for example, the number of hours of training, the number of days of training, the pedagogy used, etc.

As a result of the inputs, two types of output may be observed. One is a change in individual need satisfaction which generally manifests itself via changes in employee attitudes toward the company, subordinates, etc. These changes may be grouped into two categories: a sense of personal growth and a sense of personal competence (Hinrichs 1975). The second type of output is formal achievement which manifests itself via changed performance.

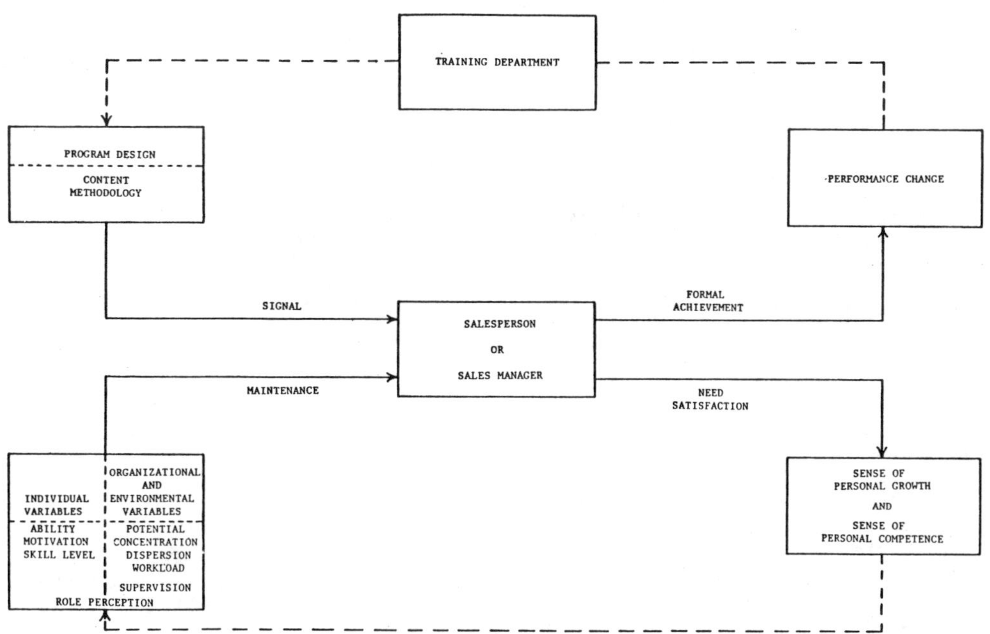

While a conceptual model of training is useful, more effective analytical techniques are needed before the frustrate's concerns can be assuaged. By using multivariate statistics as a post hoc tool, rather than relying solely on a priori experimental design, meaningful analysis of sales training can be undertaken.

AN ILLUSTRATION FROM AN ORGANIZATIONAL PERSPECTIVE

The Training Program

To demonstrate the usefulness of these ideas to an organization, an illustrative example has been created based upon information obtained from a sales management training program in a large, national firm. The example will focus on determining the effectiveness of different amounts of sales training (a methodological input).

The company's program was made up of a number of discrete modules, including a basic program, a follow-up program and a series of advanced specialized programs. The focus of every module was on the application of behavior modification (Hamner and Hamner 1976) to organizational problems.

Sample Parameters

To test the effectiveness of this training program, 87 sales managers were studied. Data from corporate records and from a survey of the individuals were obtained. Data about these employees were collected regarding maintenance inputs (background about the individual), signal inputs (the nature of the training), need satisfaction outcomes (individual perceptions and affect) and formal achievement outcomes (measures of individual/organizational results).

Both individual variables and organizational/environmental variables may influence training outcomes; therefore, both types were collected. Data were obtained regarding job position, company tenure, territory (Ryans and Weinberg 1979), age, race, and education. Personality data were unnecessary because the company used a proprietary selection model based on Cattell's 16PF (Cattell 1957) as an integral part of the selection process for sales managers.

No significant deviations between the individual sales managers studied and the selection profile were observed. In addition, all the sales managers studies were male.

The independent variable of interest was the amount of training an individual received. Four training levels were defined: no training, basic training, follow-up training, and advanced training. The number of sales managers in each group was about the same. For need satisfaction, the cell sizes were 23, 12, 17, and 15, respectively. For formal achievement, the corresponding cell sizes were 23, 10, 20, and 12.

Separate distributions were necessary for analyzing need satisfaction and formal achievement outcomes. Formal achievement data were collected from company records and need satisfaction data from questionnaires; therefore, data were incomplete for some employees. Also since there was a time lag for formal achievement measures, it was necessary to change group assignments depending upon the outcomes being analyzed and the timing of an individual's training.

Measures of individual perceptions and affect were obtained via questionnaire. Subjects completed a set of semantic differentials including: my subordinates, communication skills, myself, and stroking/reinforcement (the label given to the basic concepts underlying all training).

Subjects also completed the Job Characteristics Index (Sims, Szilagyi and Keller 1976) and the Job Descriptive Index (Smith, Kendell and Hulin 1969). The JCI measures individual perceptions of the degree of skill variety, autonomy, feedback and task identity in the job. The JDI measures satisfaction with pay, promotion, co-workers, supervision and the work itself.

Three measures of formal achievement were obtained: sales, profit, and inventory management. Both sales and profit were measured in dollars. Inventory management was measured by calculating the amount of inventory unaccounted for as a percent of sales. Data were available for each of four fiscal years (fiscal 1976 through fiscal 1979).

Hypotheses

A single global hypothesis about the effectiveness of
sales management training was formulated to demonstrate
the usefulness of the conceptual model and analytical
technique. Specifically, it was hypothesized that the
amount of training impacts both formal achievement and
need satisfaction.

Analytical Technique

In order to analyze the effectiveness of sales training,
multivariate analysis of variance (MANCOVA, Harris 1978)
was used.

MANCOVA was used to determine the overall impact of sales
training on outputs controlling for the effects of maintenance inputs. Recall that MANCOVA allows for simultaneous testing of dependent variables and considers the
various interrelationships among them (Hair, Anderson,
Tatham, Grablowsky 1979). The use of covariates serves
to measure and partial out the effect of confounding predictor variables. MANCOVA, therefore, is a potentially
simple solution to the problems of interrelationship between sets of outputs and inputs, and it acts as a partial substitute for experimental control. In this study,
training levels could not be matched for both output
types; therefore, the outcome vector was split into separate achievement and need satisfaction vectors. Further,
according to the conceptual model being used, the need
satisfaction measures could, a priori, be viewed as measures of two separate dimensions: growth and competence.
Consequently, three separate MANCOVA's were planned.

Data Reduction via Factor Analysis

Initially, however, factor analysis was completed for the
Need Satisfaction outputs. A separate factor analysis
was computed for each of the concepts measured by semantic differential scales. Scales with high loadings on
the evaluative factor were retained as a measure of individual attitude toward the concept (Fishbein and Ajzen
1975). Next, all nineteen Need Satisfaction measures
(10 semantic-differential, evaluative factors; 4 JCI
scales; 5 JDI scales) were analyzed together to determine
any underlying dimensions and possibilities for variable
reduction. Since these variables were regarded as a
sample of other possible affective or perceptual variables which may or may not be independent, Alpha factoring (Kim 1975) was used.

Two need-satisfaction vectors were created: personal-
competenence and personal-growth. The personal-compete-
nence vector included only five variables: four JDI
scales and "JCI Skill Variety." The semantic differentials loading highly with these variables were eliminated primarily because they were considered less reliable
than the JDI and JCI scales. The personal-growth vector
included only four high-loading semantic differentials:
"my subordinates, SUBORD," "communication skills,
COMSKILL," "myself, MYSELF," and "stroking/reinforcement,
S/R." The other variables were eliminated because of
their low loadings.

Testing the Effects of Training via MANCOVA

The MANCOVA results for need satisfaction are summarized
in Tables 1 and 2. Significance levels were derived by
using the greatest characteristic root (GCR, Morrison
1967). Note also that the "eta squared" statistic is
reported for training level. Statistically, the percentage shown pertains to the specific linear combination
of the vector variables derived by the GCR algorithm.
Conceptually, this percentage gives an indication of the
amount of variance in the response vector accounted for
by differences in the amount of training an individual

received.

TABLE 1
MANCOVA RESULTS FOR PERSONAL COMPETENCE
(JDIWORK, JDIPAY, JDIPROM, JDISUPER, JDICOWOR, JCISKILL)

Source	Significance Level (GCR)
Covariates	
Age	.55
Education	.85
Job Position	.50
Race	.35
Tenure	.80
Territory	.75
Training	.75

Characteristic Root Tested: irrelevant, since none significant

TABLE 2
MANCOVA RESULTS FOR PERSONAL GROWTH
(MYSELF, COMSKILL, SUBORD AND S/R)

Source	Significance Level (GCR)
Covariates	
Age	.15
Education	.50
Job Position	.65
Race	.60
Tenure	.20
Territory	.55
Training	.05

Eta-squared for Training equals 0.25

Characteristic Root Tested (90% variance explained): 110*S/R + 50*COMSKILL
+37*SUBORD + 4*MYSELF

For personal competenence, the results are quite clear in
this example: training has no impact, nor do there appear
to be any systematic differences in satisfaction arising
from any of the maintenance variables.

Just the opposite picture emerges from a study of Table 2:
training does appear to affect personal growth, and there
are systematic differences associated with both age and
tenure with the company. Differences in training level
alone account for about 25 percent of the variance in response. The impact of training is concentrated primarily
on attitudes toward S/R. The first characteristic vector,
which accounts for 90 percent of the variance, implies
that S/R is about twice as important as the next most important variable (COMSKILL) in leading to a rejection of
the null hypothesis at the 0.05 level of significance.

At first glance, the conclusion about age and tenure may
seem a bit presumptuous given the relatively "low" significance levels (.15 and .20). However, the selection of
a significance level is an arbitrary matter; the decision
depends upon how much risk there is in incorrectly rejecting a true null hypothesis. From the organization's perspective, incorrectly rejecting the null hypothesis of no
difference is potentially far less damaging than failing
to reject the null when it is indeed false. In statistical parlance, the cost to the organization of a Type I
error is much more than the cost of a Type II error.
Since the sales training efforts of the company are

clearly directed toward the tenets of behavior modification, a myopic reliance on "traditional" significance levels could seriously impede the adoption of these ideas. There is evidence from these results that, for the company being studied, older and longer-tenured employees have less positive feelings about both their communication skills and positive reinforcement. Consciously addressing these feelings costs little compared to the potential costs of ignoring them.

The MANCOVA for formal achievement (Table 3) also shows the significant impact of covariates. Job position affects output. On the one hand, it may be that the significance of job position is an artifact of the data: that is, both sales and profit would 'naturally' be aggregated by district and region. Generally, however, the data were not collected that way. Furthermore, the GCR tested for the significance of job position involved only inventory management - and it was non-dimensionalized for sales level. On the other hand, therefore, the impact of job position seems related to the closeness of supervision: district managers by the very nature of their job have tighter supervisory control than do regional managers who must attempt to control results almost "third" hand by working through both the district managers and the sales people.

TABLE 3
MANCOVA RESULTS FOR FORMAL ACHIEVEMENT
(SALES, PROFIT AND INVENTORY MANAGEMENT)

Source	Significance Level (GCR)
Covariates	
Age	.60
Education	.45
Job Position	.005
Race	.50
Tenure	.70
Territory	.30
Training	.20

Eta-squared for Training equals 0.20

Characteristic Root Tested (95% of variance explained):
100*INVENTORY MANAGEMENT + 10*PROFIT + 5*SALES

The implied impact of training on formal achievement is misleading. According to Table 3, there is only a 20 percent chance that training level actually affects performance. However, the true, positive impact of training on formal achievement is obscured because changes in managerial behavior cannot affect all the measures used to operationalize the vector.

In this paper, a key error has been intentionally integrated: formal achievement is improperly operationalized. That is, the measures used to operationalize formal achievement capture more than a sales manager's performance; they also capture factors over which a sales manager has no control. As emphasized by previous authors (Campbell, Dunette, Arvey, and Hellervik 1973) neither sales nor profits is a measure of performance. Instead, both are summary indices of the organizational outcomes for which an individual is only partially responsible. Of the three measures of formal achievement outputs, inventory management comes closest to being a measure of performance; that is, an individual behavior that has been measured with respect to its contribution to the goals of the organization. Therefore, if inventory management were analyzed within an ANCOVA framework, one would find higher levels of statistical significance. And one would conclude that sales training without a doubt has a positive impact on formal achievement.

In conclusion, the implications of the illustrative example are clear. Field sales supervision can affect organizational results, and sales training can improve the performance of field supervisors. The results, however, emphasize the importance of properly operationalizing formal achievement. If "results," rather than "performance," are used to index formal achievement, the true impact of training may be obscured. And this possibility cannot be overcome merely by using highly sophisticated analytical techniques. As always, the quality of the research effort depends primarily upon whether or not the "right" tool has been applied to solve the "right" problem. In the case of sales training, the "right" problem requires one to explicitly recognize the complexity surrounding any study of sales training, especially regarding the job the employee performs. For future research about salespeople, the job should be conceptualized as having at least three dimensions: direct sales, customer service, and organizational communications (Lamont and Lundstrum 1975). Proper evaluation of the effectiveness of training requires a performance measure for each of these dimendions: for example, direct sales could be measured as percent attainment of sales quota while both customer service and organizational communications could be measured via a BARS system as described by (Cocanougher and Ivancevich 1978).

As these results indicate, assessing the impact of sales training is a complex task. And careful statistical analysis cannot substitute for clearly-designed, properly-controlled, longitudinal studies. However, by using a systematic model of sales training to guide the analysis, it is possible to use a post hoc procedure to answer some of the pragmatic questions about sales training which an organization might ask. In a sense, this marriage of a conceptual model and multivariate statistics provides a partial answer to the frustrates' dilemma; that is, how can sales training be meaningfully assessed taking into account the complexities of organizational life.

The appropriateness of the method of assessing training is a function of the type of question being asked. If the questions to be addressed are intra-individual, careful pretesting, random assignment and experimental control are likely to be of high concern. On the other hand, if one desires to assess the impact of an ongoing sales training program on organizational outcomes, using careful modeling of the sales training process and statistical control provides a meaningful set of conclusions within the constraints of time and resources.

REFERENCES

Campbell, J., Dunnette, M. Arvey, R., and Hellervik, L. (1973), "The Development and Evaluation of Behaviorally Based Rating Scales," *Journal of Applied Psychology*, 57, 15-22. Campbell, J., Dunnette, M., Lawler, E. and Weick, K. (1970), *Managerial Behavior, Performance and Effectiveness*. New York: McGraw-Hill.

Cattell, R. (1957), *Personality Motivation Structure and Measurement*. New York: Harcourt, Brace and World.

Churchill, G.A., Ford, M.M. and Walker, O.C., Jr. (1979), "Predicting a Salesperson's Job Effort and Performance: Theoretical, Empirical and Methodological Considerations," in *Sales Management: New Developments from Behaviroal and Decision Model Research*, ed. Richard P. Bagozzi, Cambridge, Mass.: Marketing Science Institute.

Cocanougher, A. Benton and Ivancevich, John M. (1978), "BARS Performance Rating for Sales Force Personnel," *Journal of Marketing*, 42 (July), 87-95.

Fishbein, M. and Ajzen, I. (1975), _Belief, Attitude, Intention and Behavior_. Reading, Mass.: Addison-Wesley.

Hair, J., Anderson, R., Tatham, R., Grablowsky, B. (1979). _Multivariate Data Analysis with Readings_. Tulsa, Okla.: Petroleum Publishing.

Hamner, W.C., Hamner, E.P. (1976). "Behavior Modification and the Bottom Line," _Organizational Dynamics_, Spring, 2-21. Luthans, F. and Krietmer, R. (1975), _Organizational Behavior Modification_, Scott Foresman and Co., Glenview, Ill.

Harris, Richard J. (1978), _A Primer of Multivariate Statistics_, New York: Academic Press.

Hinrichs, J. (1975), Personnel Training, in _Handbook of Industrial and Organizational Psychology_, Marvin Dunnette (ed.) Chicago: Rand McNally.

Jolson, Marvin A. (1977). _Sales Management: A Tactical Approach_. New York: Petrocelli/Charter.

Kim, J. (1975). "Factor Analysis," in Nie, N., Hull, C., Jenkins, J., Steinbrenner, K., and Bent, D. _Statistical Package for the Social Sciences_. New York: McGraw-Hill.

Lamont, Lawrence M. and Lundstrom, William G. (1975). "Defining Industrial Sales Behavior: A Factor Analytic Study" in _1974 Combined Proceedings_, Series 36, ed. Ronald C. Curhan, American Marketing Association.

Morrison, D. (1967), _Multivariate Statistical Methods_. New York: McGraw-Hill.

Randall, L. (1960), "Evaluation: A Training Dilemma," _Journal of the American Society of Training Directors_, 14, 29-35.

Robertson, Dan H. and Bellenger, Danny N. (1980), _Sales Management: Decision Making for Improved Profitability_. New York. Macmillan Publishing Company, Inc.

Ryans, A.B. and Weinberg, C.B. (1979), "Territory Sales Response," _Journal of Marketing Research_, 16 (November), 453-65.

Shapiro, Benson P. (1977), _Sales Program Management: Formulation and Implementation_. New York: McGraw-Hill. Hartley, Robert F. (1979), _Sales Management_. Boston, Mass.: Houghton Mifflin Company.

Sims, H., Szilagyi, A. and Keller, R. (1976). "The Measurement of Job Characteristics," _Academy of Management Journal_, 19 2-21.

Smith, P., Kendell L. and Hulin C. (1969), _The Measurement of Satisfaction in Work and Retirement_. Chicago: Rand McNally.

Stanton, W.J. and Buskirk, R.H. (1973), _Management of the Sales Force_, Homewood, Illinois: Richard D. Irwin, Inc.

Stroh, T.F. (1978), _Managing the Sales Function_. New York: McGraw-Hill.

Xerox Sales Training Marketing Case History (1976), Intercollegiate Video Clearing House, Miami, Florida.

CLOSE ENCOUNTERS OF THE SALESPERSON-CUSTOMER KIND AS INFLUENCED BY FAMILY CONSTELLATION

David R. Rink, Northern Illinois University, DeKalb

ABSTRACT

This paper presents a composite variable (called family constellation) and a model from the social sciences that when extended will isolate the determinants of successful salesperson-customer interactions, thereby permitting more sophisticated analysis of this dyad.

DEVELOPMENT OF PROBLEM

Salesperson selection studies have traditionally concentrated on forecasting performance in terms of the salesperson's personality attributes (Mayer and Greenberg 1964; Scheibelhot and Albaum 1973), socioeconomic and demographic characteristics (Baehr and Williams 1968; Tanofsky, Shepps, and O'Neill 1969), and interest and ability factors.[1] Several scholars have noted such research fails "to take explicit account of who the (salesperson) interacts with in attempting to make a sale" (Cotham 1968; Cotham 1969; Davis and Silk 1971). Acknowledgement of this theoretical gap has propelled recent researchers in the direction of investigating the salesperson-customer interaction (Capon, Holbrook, and Hulbert 1977).

Although several conceptualizations of salesperson-customer association exist (Bearden 1969; Willett and Pennington 1966), all share three commonalities that differentiate them from the traditional approach. First, sales outcomes--positive or negative--are a function of the dyadic interaction of a customer and salesperson, not of the individual qualities of either alone (Evans 1963). Second, the nature and attributes of the interaction as well as the roles portrayed by salesperson and customer are examined. Finally, more complex variables and relations are employed to discriminate the determinants of successful interactions (Engel, Kollat, and Blackwell 1973).

Several marketing researchers have empirically examined transaction characteristics, interaction determinants of transaction outcomes, salesperson-customer interaction, and salesperson-customer similarity.[2] In this paper, the author will concentrate on the latter two areas--interaction and similarity between salesperson and customer. Furthermore, of the intervening variables that influence customer and salesperson characteristics, family will be the locus of attention.

The purpose of this paper is to present another complex variable that will be useful in isolating the determinants of successful salesperson-customer relationships. This composite variable will also permit more sophisticated investigation of the roles portrayed by the salesperson and customer in a dyadic exchange. This variable is labelled family constellation. It includes such components as family size, birth order, sex, and spacing of children. Finally, instead of concentrating on either similarity or dissimilarity of personality characteristics between dyad participants, the author will discuss a model that incorporates both viewpoints.

____

[1]For an excellent review of this literature, refer to Cotham (1970).

[2]For excellent reviews of research conducted in these areas, refer to Engel, Kollat, and Blackwell (1973) as well as Capon, Holbrook, and Hulbert (1977).

SELECTED LITERATURE REVIEW

Interpersonal Relations: Similarity and Dissimilarity

The phenomenon of interpersonal (or dyadic) relations has been extensively investigated by social scientists at both the theoretical and empirical levels. A question commonly addressed by these researchers concerns what determines a successful association between individuals. One school of inquiry, which is supported by a relatively large body of evidence, maintains a successful association is partially a function of how "similar" the participants are in terms of opinions, values, etc. Several marketing researchers have found empirical support for this notion (Brock 1965; Evans 1963; Gadel 1964; Lombard 1955; Tosi 1966). However, another philosophy, which is substantiated by some research (Ktsanes 1955; Winch 1955a; Winch 1955b) purports "dissimilarity" between individuals tends to result in a favorable interaction. Only a few marketing studies have substantiated the "dissimilarity" (or complementary) hypothesis (Burck 1956; Stafford and Greer 1965; Zuckerman and Grosz 1958).[3]

Family Constellation

Individuals tend to perceive new situations in terms of historically similar instances. Their experiences and attitudes are generalized from the past to present situations.

> Since family contexts are among an individual's oldest, . . . longest-lasting contexts stemming from the individual's earliest years, . . . generalizations and transferences from them to new social situations are likely to have . . . influenced the perception and . . . shaping of contemporary life contexts more strongly than those life contexts . . . experienced only later in . . . life (Toman 1976, p. 77). (underlining added)

Hence, the types of individuals one has lived with most closely and longest will partially dictate the types of individuals selected as future friends, companions, etc. New associations, therefore, tend to duplicate old ones.[4] In general, "the more complete the duplication, the greater the chance that the relationship will last and be happy" (Toman 1970, p. 45).

One way for ascertaining when a new relationship is similar to an earlier relationship is to examine the

____

[3]For excellent reviews of theory and research in both areas, refer to Heider (1961), Homans (1961), Berscheid and Walster (1969), and Thibaut and Kelley (1959).

[4]When Toman speaks of duplication, he is referring to the degree of "dissimilarity" (or complementarity) between the individuals' personality characteristics.

position that each partner in the association had in his/ her original family.[5] This position can be characterized by the individual's age rank among his/her siblings and by the sex distribution among them (Toman 1976). Toman (1970) maintains it is possible to describe a person's major personality characteristics and those of his/her friends, the likelihood of stability in marriage, what he/she is like at work, and his/her philosophy on the basis of <u>only</u> <u>two</u> <u>facts</u>: sex and age rankings of siblings in the person's family. Systematic research of more than 3,000 families has not only confirmed this predictive ability but has also lead to the development of 10 portraits of basic sex and sibling positions (Toman 1976).

By cross-tabulating these sibling positions according to sex and age ranks, Toman (1976) arrived at 16 types of parental couples, which are depicted in Figure 1. For convenience purposes, he did not include "onlys" in this treatment but did comment briefly on their impact (Toman 1976, pp. 229-232). The expected degree of favorability of each relationship is a function of possible age rank and/or sex conflicts between the participants. In an age rank conflict, "the partners . . . have had similar or identical age ranks in their respective original families." Since neither individual is used to the age rank of the other, they will demand that age rank for themselves in their association. With a sex conflict, "a partner has had no siblings of the opposite sex in his original family." Such an individual will have difficulty getting used to a partner of the opposite sex in any interaction. "Rank conflicts as well as sex conflicts are examples of non-complementary relationships" (Toman 1976, p. 85). While space limitations preclude a detailed discussion of all 16 parental couples, four will be highlighted.

<u>Oldest Brother of Sisters (OBS) and Youngest Sister of Brothers (YSB)</u>. This is usually a good relationship, because there are no age rank and no sex conflicts. A good understanding exists. Quarreling is rare. Father sets the tone of the relationship; he is friendly and tolerant. Mother is submissive.

<u>Youngest Brother of Brothers (YBB) and Oldest Sister of Sisters (OSS)</u>. This relationship is only moderately good, because a rank or sex conflict exists. Neither has experienced a sibling of the opposite sex in their original family. According to age ranks among siblings, they should be compatible. The wife is the responsible leader in all matters, and the husband submits to her command. But this relationship is not a relaxed or contented one, because the husband secretly opposes his wife's strict rule, demand for order, and achievements.

<u>Oldest Brother of Sisters (OBS) and Oldest Sister of Sisters (OSS)</u>. This is an unfavorable relationship, because rank and partial sex conflicts exist. As both parents were oldest siblings in their original families, there may be a fight for family dominance. Although mother has not experienced an opposite sex sibling in her original family, father has, and he offers advice. But mother lets her

---

[5]One group of researchers has investigated this area using birth order as their primary variable. Although they have found significant personality differences between first-born and later-born individuals, the influences of family size, sex and age spacing of children, etc., have been considered only on an implicit basis as intervening or confounding variables. For excellent reviews of research in this area, refer to Sampson (1965) and Saiyadain (1974). Other researchers, however, have explicitly incorporated some of these family constellation variables into their theories. This results in a more objective, systematic, and sophisticated analysis of family relationships (Forer 1969; Sutton-Smith and Rosenberg 1970; Toman 1976).

FIGURE 1

Toman's Sixteen Parental Couples[a,b]

		Mother			
		OSB	OSS	YSB	YSS
Father	OBB	Rank & Partial Sex Conf Rel Unf Relation	Rank & Sex Conf Unf Relation	Partial Sex Conf Rel Fav Relation	Rank or Sex Conf Mod Fav Relation
	OBS	Rank or Sex Conf Mod Fav Relation	Rank & Partial Sex Conf Unf Relation	No Rank & No Sex Conf Good Relation	Partial Sex Conf Rel Good Relation
	YBB	Partial Sex Conf Rel Good Relation	Rank or Sex Conf Mod Good Relation	Rank & Partial Sex Conf Unf Relation	Rank & Sex Conf Unf Relation
	YBS	No Rank & No Sex Conf Good Relation	Partial Sex Conf Rel Good Relation	Rank or Sex Conf Mod Good Relation	Rank & Partial Sex Conf Unf Relation

[a]To conserve space, the following codes have been employed: Conf = conflict; Rel = relatively; Unf = unfavorable; Relation = relationship; Fav = favorable; and Mod = moderately. Also, OBB = oldest brother of brothers; YBB = youngest brother of brothers; OBS = oldest brother of sisters; YBS = youngest brother of sisters; OSS = oldest sister of sisters; YSS = youngest sister of sisters; OSB = oldest sister of brothers; YSB = youngest sister of brothers.

[b]Adapted from Toman (1976).

pride, independence, and obedience to her father get in the way. She is strict and rigid while her husband is sympathetic and tolerant.

<u>Youngest Brother of Brothers (YBB) and Youngest Sister of Sisters (YSS)</u>. This is an unfavorable relationship, because both rank and sex conflicts exist. Neither has had experience with a peer of the opposite sex. Both have the same age rank; they are juniors. Both are accustomed to being taken care of and guided by their families. They are somewhat at a loss with each other. Both are looking for a third person, who is willing to help, guide, and understand them.

SALESPERSON-CUSTOMER DYADS BY SEX AND AGE RANKS

Most retail selling involves a single salesperson-customer encounter. Toman's model would probably not apply to such brief, one-time exchanges. Industrial selling, on the other hand, is "developmental in nature, requiring a period of months or even years to culminate in a firm order" (Capon, Holbrook, and Hulbert 1977, p. 329). In this situation, where a relatively long-term relationship similar to marriage is maintained, the major aspects of Toman's theory would most likely generalize to industrial selling. Like marriage, industrial selling requires a commitment from both parties if the relationship is to endure. Both must work hard at it. Compromise is the rule rather than the exception. A lot of time and patience are required

Cross-Classification of Customer and Salesperson Sibling Positions[a,b]

Salesperson \ Customer	OBB	OBS	YBB	YBS	OSB	OSS	YSB	YSS	OM	OF
OBB	Sim Unf	Sim Unf	Com Mof	Com Mof	Sim Unf	Sim Unf	Com Fav	Com Mof	Com Mof	Com Mof
OBS	Sim Unf	Sim Unf	Com Mof	Com Mof	Sim Unf	Sim Unf	Com Fav	Com Fav	Com Mof	Com Mof
YBB	Com Mof	Com Mof	Sim Unf	Sim Unf	Com Fav	Com Mof	Sim Unf	Sim Unf	Sim Unf	Sim Unf
YBS	Com Mof	Com Mof	Sim Unf	Sim Unf	Com Fav	Com Fav	Sim Unf	Sim Unf	Sim Unf	Sim Unf
OSB	Sim Unf	Sim Unf	Com Fav	Com Fav	Sim Unf	Sim Unf	Com Mof	Com Mof	Com Mof	Com Mof
OSS	Sim Unf	Sim Unf	Com Mof	Com Fav	Sim Unf	Sim Unf	Com Mof	Com Mof	Com Mof	Com Mof
YSB	Com Fav	Com Fav	Sim Unf	Sim Unf	Com Mof	Com Mof	Sim Unf	Sim Unf	Sim Unf	Sim Unf
YSS	Com Mof	Com Fav	Sim Unf	Sim Unf	Com Mof	Com Mof	Sim Unf	Sim Unf	Sim Unf	Sim Unf
OM	Com Mof	Com Mof	Sim Unf	Sim Unf	Com Mof	Com Mof	Sim Unf	Sim Unf	Sim Unf	Sim Unf
OF	Com Mof	Com Mof	Sim Unf	Sim Unf	Com Mof	Com Mof	Sim Unf	Sim Unf	Sim Unf	Sim Unf

[a]Every combination of salesperson and customer is coded relative to similarity/dissimilarity (or complementarity) of personality characteristics and degree of favorability of the relationship. Specifically, in terms of personality attributes, Sim = similar and Com = complementary. Regarding degree of favorability, Unf = unfavorable, Fav = favorable, and Mof = moderately favorable. Also, OM = only male; OF = only female.

[b]Contrary to Toman's model in Figure 1, two dyads (OBS–OSB and YBS–YSB) were switched from moderately favorable to unfavorable interactions, because the age rank conflicts are substantial.

if the relationship is to grow.

Before applying Toman's model, several adjustments are necessary. First, salespersons can be either male or female. Therefore, sibling positions corresponding to the "female" and "male" categories in Figure 1 must be aggregated to form one salesperson dimension. Second, customers can be either male or female. Hence, the sibling positions corresponding to salespersons are duplicated for customers. Finally, "onlys" in terms of male and female are added to each dimension. The end result is a 10 x 10 matrix that cross-classifies customer sibling positions with salesperson sibling positions (Figure 2).

Degrees of Favorability

As in Toman's model (Figure 1), there are three different degrees of favorability of salesperson-customer interaction in the author's extended model (Figure 2): favorable, moderately favorable, and unfavorable. Favorable associations are characterized by no sex and no rank conflicts as well as partial sex conflicts. Moderately favorable rela-

tionships consist of either a rank or sex conflict, not both. In terms of their psychological significance, favorable and moderately favorable interactions may be perceived as complementary relationships. Unfavorable interactions, on the other hand, are symbolized either by a rank and partial sex conflict or by both rank and sex conflicts. Hence, these associations may be viewed as noncomplementary (or similar) (Toman 1976). Space limitations preclude a detailed discussion of all three degrees of favorability. However, the "favorable" interactions will be highlighted.

Favorable Interactions. Generalizing Toman's work, the following six salesperson-customer dyads should result in relatively good or complementary relationships, because the individuals complement one another: OBS-YSB, OBS-YSS, OBB-YSB, YBS-OSB, YBS-OSS, and YBB-OSB (Figure 2). In all six cases, mutual understanding generally exists between the parties. However, in the first three cases, the salesperson sets the tone of the relationship, because he was the "older" sibling in his original family. As a result, the salesperson can be friendly and tolerant while

the customer is submissive (OBS-YSB). Or, he may be tough
and self-righteous, but the customer is used to this and
can usually tone the salesman down (OBB-YSB). In another
instance, the salesperson will have to inconspicuously establish the tone of the interaction. If he does not, the
customer will become stubborn, insistent, and oppose him.
Fortunately, such a potential dilemma will not last long
(OBS-YSS).

With the last three dyads (YBS-OSB, YBS-OSS, and YBB-OSB),
the customer assumes the leadership position in the interaction, because she was the "oldest" sibling in her original family. The salesman, acting out his role of the
"younger" sibling, generally submits to the customer's will
(YBS-OSB). In another case, the salesman may not like the
customer's highly authoritarian behavior, but he does not
contest the customer's leadership (YBS-OSS). Also, the
customer may treat the salesman in a motherly way, but he
accepts this guardianship and nurturance since it is tolerant and friendly rather than possessive (YBB-OSB).

By switching the order of the members of each dyad from
salesperson-customer to customer-salesperson, the corresponding symmetrical interactions are obtained (Figure 2).
While this exchange does not affect the favorability of
these interactions, the results of each dyad are reversed.
For example, with the three customer-salesperson dyads of
YBS-OSB, YBS-OSS, and YBB-OSB, the saleswoman sets the
leadership and authoritative tone of the relationship, and
the customer generally consents. In fact, he seeks the
advice, understanding and encouragement of the saleswoman
in a motherly fashion. This complementary association occurs because of the saleswoman and customer's indoctrina-
tions as "older" and "younger" siblings in their respective family experiences. However, in the cases of OBS-YSB,
OBS-YSS, and OBB-YSB, the saleswoman is subservient to the
customer's domineering and authoritative personality.

LIMITATIONS

Before discussing the marketing implications of Toman's
theory and the author's extension, several limitations
merit attention. First, and foremost, it is questionable
whether an industrial selling relationship between salesperson and customer approximates a marriage association.
Most industrial selling situations are not likely to exist
as two individuals living together day-to-day in close
physical proximity (e.g., sharing several meals daily in
the confines of their home). Nor is the commitment explicitly written down in the form of a marriage certificate
or a ceremony performed by a religious person. It is hard
to imagine what the "offspring" from an industrial selling
relationship would look like. Also, the expected duration
of any selling relationship is probably a function of the
selling task required and the technical sophistication of
the product involved (Dodge 1973). Given an extensive
selling task and a highly technical product, it is likely
that a "close" relationship would evolve between salesperson and customer.

The 10 portraits developed by Toman are most applicable to
highly industrialized nations, urban populations, and societies where the family represents the primary early educational medium. Also, it is presumed that one parent financially supports the family while the other stays home
and takes care of the children, parents have an average
distance between each other themselves, and no unusual circumstances arise (e.g., early death of one parent, divorce,
etc.) (Toman 1976). A change in one or several of these
variables is likely to have a significant impact on the
model.

The 16 types of parental couples as well as the 10 portraits were derived from extensive research of over 3,000
German families. Although Germany and the United States
are highly industrialized countries, the fact that the two

cultures differ may hamper the generalization of Toman's
theory to American families. The portraits do not distinguish between an individual who has several siblings of
the same sex and an individual who has only one sibling of
that sex. However, Toman mentions his characterizations
do apply up to cases where an individual has three siblings of the same sex. Although he focuses on only two
siblings per portrait, Toman (1976) does present several
guidelines for interpreting multiple and middle sibling
positions.

Finally, Toman's model concentrates on only age rank and
sex distribution of the family. While several variables
are addressed implicitly (e.g., family size and age spacing of children), family constellation researchers generally ignore such important confounding variables as socioeconomic status, education level attained, religion, nationality, geography, climate, and sibling positions of
the parents.

MARKETING IMPLICATIONS

Although many marketing implications probably exist concerning Toman's model and the author's extended model,
these seem the most relevant to industrial selling.

Market Segmentation and Salesperson Selection

Regardless of whether the firm embraces the "similarity"
or "dissimilarity" (or complementarity) hypothesis, it can
apply this notion to market segmentation, thereby leading
to more effective salesperson selection (Engel, Kollat,
and Blackwell 1973). The firm will first measure various
characteristics (including family constellation) of the
customers--individuals, not firms--in its target markets.
After determining which attributes best segregate its market into homogeneous groupings (and assuming family constellation is one of these characteristics), the firm can
then ascertain the sibling position that represents the
majority of the customers in its specific segments. Finally, depending on which theory is followed, the firm can
use Figure 2 as a guideline for selecting the most appropriate salesperson type to recruit. Some degree of lati-
tude exists in this process, because each possible customer sibling position corresponds to at least four suggested salesperson types. For example, under the "complementarity" theory, if the customer is an OSS, then
Figure 2 recommends that one of these six salespersons be
selected and recruited: YBB, YBS, YSB, YSS, OM, or OF.

Allocation of Salespersons

The initial allocation of salespersons will adhere closely
to the market segmentation scheme formulated in the previous section. However, continual feedback concerning
customer changes is required if favorability is to be
maintained within the salesperson-customer relationship.
That is, if an OBB customer replaces a YBB customer, then
the proper adjustment for the firm that is employing the
"complementarity" theory is to substitute the "older" sibling salesperson (e.g., OBB, OBS, OSB, or OSS) with either
a "younger" sibling (e.g., YBB, YBS, YSB, or YSS) or
"only" child (e.g., OM or OF) salesperson. In this way,
the firm will avert sex and/or age rank conflicts that
characterize interactions involving two "older," "younger,"
or "only" children.

SUMMARY AND CONCLUSIONS

Any social science theory that incorporates the "similarity" and "dissimilarity" hypotheses concerning the personalities of dyadic members is important for marketers to
examine. This is especially true in areas involving interpersonal relations, such as industrial selling. One
such theory labelled family constellation, which was

developed by Toman from his research of marriages, was presented and extended by the author. By determining the extent of complementarity of participants' personalities, the
marketer can predict the degree of success of any interaction. While Toman's theory is based upon research, the
author's extension is hypothetical. Hence, research must
be conducted to empirically test the validity of this extension.

REFERENCES

Baehr, M. and G. Williams (1968), "Determined Dimensions of
Personal Background Data," _Journal of Applied Psychology_,
52, 98–103.

Bearden, James (1969), "Decision Processes in Personal
Selling," _Southern Journal of Business_, 4 (April), 189–
199.

Berscheid, Ellen and Elaine Walster (1969), _Interpersonal
Attraction_, Reading, MA: Addison-Wesley Publishing Company.

Brock, Timothy (1965), "Communicator-Recipient Similarity
and Decision Change," _Journal of Personality and Social
Psychology_, 1 (June), 650–654.

Burck, Gilbert (1956), "What Makes Women Buy?" _Fortune_,
(August) 93–94, 174–194.

Capon, Noel, Morris Holbrook, and James Hulbert (1977),
"Selling Processes and Buyer Behavior: Theoretical Im-
plications of Recent Research," in _Consumer and Indus-
trial Buying Behavior_, Arch Woodside, Jagdish Sheth, and
Peter Bennett, eds., New York: Elsevier North-Holland,
Inc., 323–332.

Cotham, James (1968), "Job Attitudes and Sales Performance
of Major Appliance Salesmen," _Journal of Marketing Re-
search_, 5 (November), 370–375.

__________ (1969), "Predicting Salesmen's Performance by
Multiple Discriminant Analysis," _Southern Journal of
Business_, 4 (January), 25–34.

__________ (1970), "Selecting Salesmen: Approaches and
Problems," _MSU Business Topics_, 18 (Winter), 64–72.

Davis, Harry and Alvin Silk (1971), _Behavioral Research on
Personal Selling: A Review of Some Recent Studies of In-
teraction and Influence Processes in Sales Situations_,
Cambridge, MA: Marketing Science Institute.

Dodge, H. Robert (1973), _Field Sales Management_, Dallas,
TX: Business Publications, Inc.

Engel, James, David Kollat, and Roger Blackwell (1973),
Consumer Behavior, 2nd edition, New York: Holt, Rinehart and Winston, Inc.

Evans, Franklin (1963), "Selling as a Dyadic Relationship--
A New Approach," _American Behavioral Scientist_, 6 (May),
76–79.

Forer, Lucille (1969), _Birth Order and Life Roles_, Springfield, IL: Charles C. Thomas.

Gadel, M. (1964), "Concentration by Salesman on Congenial
Prospects," _Journal of Marketing_, 28 (April), 64–66.

Heider, Fritz (1961), _The Psychology of Interpersonal Re-
lations_, New York: John Wiley & Sons, Inc.

Homans, George (1961), _Social Behavior: Its Elementary
Forms_, New York: Harcourt.

Ktsanes, T. (1955), "Mate Selection on the Basis of Personality Type: A Study Utilizing an Empirical Typology
of Personality," _American Sociological Review_, 20,
547–551.

Lombard, George (1955), _Behavior in a Selling Group_, Boston: Harvard University.

Mayer, D. and H. Greenberg (1964), "What Makes a Good
Salesman," _Harvard Business Review_, 42, 119–125.

Saiyadain, Mirza (1974), "Birth Order: A Literature Review," _Indian Educational Review_, 9 (January), 115–139.

Sampson, Edward (1965), "The Study of Ordinal Position:
Antecedents and Outcomes," in _Progress in Experimental
Personality Research_, Vol. 2, Maher, ed., New York:
Academic Press, 175–228.

Scheibelhot, J. and G. Albaum (1973), "Self-Other Orientations Among Salesmen and Non-Salesmen," _Journal of Marketing Research_, 10, 97–99.

Stafford, James and Thomas Greer (1965), "Consume Prefer-
ence for Types of Salesmen: A Study of Independence-
Dependence Characteristics," _Journal of Retailing_,
(Summer), 27–33.

Sutton-Smith, B. and B. Rosenberg (1970), _The Sibling_,
New York: Holt, Rinehard and Winston.

Tanofsky, R., R. Shepps, and P. O'Neill (1969), "Pattern
Analysis of Biographical Predictors of Success as an
Insurance Salesman," _Journal of Applied Psychology_, 53,
136–139.

Thibaut, John and Harold Kelley (1959), _The Social Psychology of Groups_, New York: John Wiley & Sons, Inc.

Toman, Walter (1970), "Never Mind Your Horoscope, Birth
Order Rules All," _Psychology Today_, 4 (December), 45–49,
68–69.

__________ (1976), _Family Constellation_, 3rd edition,
New York: Springer Publishing Company.

Tosi, Henry (1966), "The Effects of Expectation Levels and
Role Consensus on the Buyer-Seller Dyad," _Journal of
Business_, 39 (October), 516–529.

Willett, Ronald and Allan Pennington (1966), "Customer and
Salesman: The Anatomy of Choice and Influence in a Retail Setting," in _Science, Technology and Marketing_, R.
Haas, ed., Chicago: American Marketing Association,
598–616.

Winch, R. (1955a), "The Theory of Complementary Needs in
Mate-Selection: A Test of One Kind of Complementari-
ness," _American Sociological Review_, 20, 52–56.

__________ (1955b), "The Theory of Complementary Needs in
Mate-Selection: Final Results on the Test of the General Hypothesis," _American Sociological Review_, 20,
552–555.

Zuckerman, M. and H. Grosz (1958), "Suggestibility and
Dependency," _Journal of Consulting Psychology_, 26
(October), 32–38.

STRATEGIC PIGGYBACKING: A SELF-SUBSIDIZATION STRATEGY FOR BOTH
NONPROFIT AND BUSINESS INSTITUTIONS

Richard P. Nielsen, Boston College

ABSTRACT

Strategic Piggybacking is a self-subsidization strategy
of investing in and/or developing a new(for the institution)business that generates good cash flow, is
relatively safe, but that is also relatively unrelated
to the institution's primary mission. The new(for the
institution)business is sufficiently compatible with
market opportunities so that it can generate revenues
to help subsidize in the long run (for nonprofit
institutions) or short run (for both business and nonprofit institutions) the primary mission activities that
are less compatible with market opportunities. A case
is made for considering strategic piggybacking as a
synthesis of specialization and diversified portfolio
strategies.

INTRODUCTION

Different strategies can be more or less consistent with
institutional mission vs. market opportunities. More
specifically and the focus of this article, market
opportunities might favor a diversified portfolio
strategy more than a specialization strategy, but the
specialization strategy might be more consistent with
the institution's mission than the diversified portfolio
strategy. Thus, how to resolve such a conflict among
mission, market opportunities, and alternative strategies
becomes somewhat of a dilemma. A strategy that is
different from and a synthesis of diversified portfolio
and specialization strategies that can help address and
resolve this dilemma is "strategic piggybacking".
Strategic piggybacking is investing in and/or developing
a new for the institution business that is relatively
unrelated to the institution's primary mission, but
that is sufficiently compatible with current market
opportunities so that it can generate revenues to help
support in the short term (for both business and nonprofit institutions) or long term (for nonprofit
institutions) the primary mission activities that are
less compatible with current market opportunities. A
case is made for considering strategic piggybacking as a
syntheses of diversified portfolio and specialization
strategies.

This article explains the conceptual foundations for the
strategic piggybacking strategy, illustrates what the
strategy is, discusses how the strategic piggybacking
strategy is a syntheses of the specialization and
diversified portfolio strategies, and considers the
reasons and conditions under which a decision to adopt
the strategy might reasonably be made by business and
nonprofit institutions. Throughout this article,
references are made to three cases: one corporation, one
nonprofit institution, and one corporation where an
acquisition could be used as either a diversified portfolio or strategic piggybacking strategy.

The Three Case Studies

Case 1 is the Boston Symphony Orchestra. Its primary
mission concerns the performance of classical symphonic
music. Ninety years ago, ten years after its own
founding, the BSO established the Boston Pops which
plays established popular music befor a large audience
that eats and drinks liquor and wine in something of a
cabaret atmosphere. The surpluses generated from the

food, wine, liquor and ticket sales help support the
primary mission concerning the performance of classical
symphonic music (Boston Symphony Orchestra 1975-1980).

Case 2 is the American Natural Resources corporation.
Its primary mission concerns natural gas distribution.
It bought five regional trucking (non-gas) companies.
These highly profitable trucking companies were bought
in order to provide the revenues required to develop
the natural gas pipeline and distribution primary
mission activities needed during a period of relatively
low profitability in the natural gas areas (Business
Week 1979).

Case 3 is United States Steel Corporation. It acquired
Marathon Oil Corporation. It could use the profits
from the oil area to help finance the extensive
modernization of its steel manufacturing plants if it
considers steel still to be its primary mission, or it
could use its oil revenues to help finance further
portfolio diversification if it defines its primary
mission as more in the nature of a diversified
conglomerate than as a specialist in the steel area. It
is not yet clear whether the acquisition of Marathon
Oil was more of a diversified portfolio or a strategic
piggybacking strategy (Kirkland 1982; Business Week 1981).

Conceptual Foundations For Strategic Piggybacking

In Alfred D. Chandler's 1962 book Strategy and Structure:
Chapters In The History Of The American Industrial
Enterprise it is revealed that there have been generalized
expansion strategies successfully adopted in different
circumstances primarily in response to external market
conditions. The generalized strategies are geographic
expansion, verticle integration (i.e., a move into a
new for the institution function such as extraction,
processing, marketing, etc.), horizontal combination,
specialization, and diversification.

In Chandler's 1977 Pulitzer and Bancroft prize winning
book The Visible Hand: The Managerial Revolution In
American Business it is also revealed that another
factor, the professional manager's definition of
institutional mission, had a large and important role
in defining and deciding strategies for realizing
mission. External market conditions and management
definition of mission interact in influencing selection
and decision among alternative strategies.

Definitions of strategic management have come to
recognize the important interaction between market
opportunities and definition of institutional mission in
selecting among alternative strategies (Uyterhoeven,
Ackerman, Rosenblum 1977, p. 7; Newman and Logan 1971,
p. 70; Steiner and Miner 1977, p. 19).

As suggested above, there can be a conflict among
institutional mission, market opportunities, and
strategies. Ideas and case experiences from the general
strategic management, adoption of innovation, product
life cycle, specialization, and diversified portfolio
strategy analysis areas help provide the conceptual
foundations for a solution to this dilemma.

The French sociologist Gabriel Tarde (1903) was one of
the first to suggest that the adoption of a new idea
follows a normal S shaped distribution over time. The
first and also largest empirical research tradition
concerning the adoption of innovation S curve is in rural
sociology which was begun during the 1920's and 1930's
in the midwestern United States. For example, in the
1920's and 1930's the Iowa Extension Service and commercial seed companies cooperated in using the adoption of
innovation S curve concept to introduce hybrid seed
corn (Rogers 1971; Wilson 1927; Gross 1942; Ryan and
Gross 1943).

Despite these early origins, the concept of product life
cycle management was not explicitly introduced into the
management literature until Theodore Levitt's (1965)
Harvard Business Review article "Exploit The Product
Life Cycle."

Since that time Bruce D. Henderson and the Boston
Consulting Group extended and integrated the concepts of
adoption of innovation curve and product life cycle with
the diversification strategy into their "Portfolio
Matrix" approach to diversified strategic planning
(Henderson 1970; Day 1977; Abell and Hammond 1979; Abell
1980).

Uyterhoeven, Ackerman, and Rosenblum (1977, p. 55)
explain the classical diversification alternative as
follows.
     "Of all the strategic alternatives, diversification
     is undoubtedly the most glamorous. Admittedly this
     glamour has paled somewhat as several well-known
     conglomerates have come upon hard times...Diversifi-
     cation is an alternate way of committing one's
     resources. The strategist may decide that his
     existing business does not hold sufficient potential.
     He may wish to cut back or even liquidate it and
     commit his resources elsewhere. Alternatively,
     he may keep his existing activities at current
     levels or exploit their growth to their full
     potential but seek additional growth elsewhere.
     Thus growth through diversification may not always
     be a better spreading of business risks or at
     achieving a growth rate which cannot be accomplished
     within a company's original given field of endeavor."

There are of course different levels of specialization
and diversification (Chandler 1962; Uyterhoeven,
Ackerman, Rosenblum 1977). An institution could
diversify into related and unrelated areas. For example,
Coca Cola could diversify into an unrelated area such
as the acquisition of a film company such as Columbia, or
it could diversify into a related area such as the
acquisition of a fruit juice company. Similarly, a
classical symphony orchestra company might develop a
classical chamber orchestra that is very much related to
classical symphonic music or it could organize rock
concerts.

The generalized portfolio strategy recommended by
Henderson and the Boston Consulting Group is based on the
product life cycle and diversification concepts. An
institution develops a balance of businesses such that
there is a dynamic where an investment is made to enter a
product/market segment in its introductory (question mark)
stage, then gain market share and profitability in its
growth (star) stage, then generate high cash flow in its
maturity (cash cow) stage to be used for financing new
potential "stars", and then gradually lose market share
and profitability in its decline (dog) stage (Henderson
1970; Day 1977; Abell and Hammond 1979; Abell 1980).

Diversified Portfolio Vs. Strategic Piggybacking

While the strategic piggybacking strategy is related
to the diversified portfolio strategy, it is also
different in two important ways, the intention of the
strategy and the dynamic of the investment flow.

1. Intention Differences. The intention of the
strategic piggybacking strategy is to help subsidize an
historical primary mission that in the short run (for
both business and nonprofit institutions) and/or the
long run (for nonprofit institutions) is not very
compatible with market opportunities. The intention of
a diversified portfolio strategy is to spread
financial risks and to help finance the development of
new potential "stars".

The Boston Symphony Orchestra established the Boston
Pops in order to help subsidize its primary mission
concerning the performance of classical symphonic
music which it did and does not expect to be able to
support itself. For ninety years since its establishment, the Boston Pops through food, wine, liquor, and
ticket sales has produced surpluses which have helped
subsidize the deficits the BSO has incurred in every
one of its 100 years. Instead, if, for example, the
intention had been to establish new, likely profitable
classical or popular music businesses for their own
sakes, then the strategy could be considered more in the
generalized diversified portfolio than strategic
piggybacking mode.

American Natural Resources bought its five regional
trucking businesses with the intention of generating
profits to improve its natural gas operations with the
expectation that in the long run its primary mission
concerning natural gas would be very profitable.
Instead, if, for example, the intention had been to
establish a profitable trucking business to be a "star"
rather than a vehicle for subsidizing its primary
mission, then the strategy might be considered more
diversified portfolio than piggybacking.

In the U.S. Steel acquisition of Marathon Oil case, it
is not yet clear what U.S. Steel's intention was. If
U.S. Steel based its investment decision in acquiring
Marathon Oil on the intention of moving away from the
depressed steel industry or of generating profits
for a new "star" industry, then the strategy could be
considered diversified portfolio. However, if U.S. Steel
purchased Marathon Oil more with the intention of
using oil profits to modernize its steel business,
then the strategy could be considered more one of
piggybacking.

2. Dynamic Investment Flow Differences. In the
strategic piggybacking strategy, the institution invests
in new for the institution and relatively safe cash flow
surplus producing, moderate or low growth, advanced
life cycle "cash cow" activities in order to support
its subsidization needing primary mission. In contrast,
the investment flow dynamic of the generalized diversification portfolio strategy suggests that an institution
should use older "cash cow" business profits from
businesses it is already in to take relatively
greater financial risks in newer, earlier life cycle
high growth potential activities since the institution
should be interested in the development of potential
new "stars". In strategic piggybacking, the institution
invests to acquire/develop a "cash cow" to support a
primary mission. In the diversified portfolio strategy,
the institution takes profits from "cash cow" businesses
it already owns in order to finance new potential
"stars".

Ninety years later it is difficult to assess how financially risky the establishment of the Boston Pops by the BSO was then. However, ninety years of uninterupted surpluses that have helped subsidize the BSO suggest that the Boston Pops has been a very safe "cash cow". The idea of performing and listening to established popular music forms while eating and drinking wine and liquor is generally accepted by the public and advanced in its life cycle. If the BSO had instead decided to establish, for example, a business for the purpose of concentrating on the performance of newly composed symphonic music or new popular music for their own sakes and which had the potential of becoming "stars", then such a strategy could have been considered more diversified portfolio than piggybacking.

When ANR purchased its regional trucking companies, such businesses were neither new nor very risky. They generated substantial amounts of cash to finance the natural gas mission and trucking was relatively advanced in its life cycle. Instead, if ANR had, for example, invested in a synthetic fuel business that had the potential of becoming a "star", then such a strategy could be considered more in the dynamic of the diversified portfolio stragegy than the piggybacking strategy.

The adquisition of Marathon Oil by U.S. Steel did not represent the acquisition of a business new in its life cycle. The oil business was well advanced. In addition, the oil reserves of Marathon were well known. Marathon is more of a "cash cow" than a potential "star" for U.S. Steel. Instead, if, for example, U.S. Steel had adquired a synthetic fuel company or a company with a new advanced methodology for manufacturing steel, then it could be considered more in the dynamic of the diversified portfolio strategy than a strategic piggybacking strategy.

Specialization Vs. Strategic Piggybacking

Strategic piggybacking is similar to a specialization strategy in that they both share a concern for a specialized mission. They are different in that strategic piggybacking invests in different businesses in order to subsidize the specialized mission while specialization would call for investment within the specialized mission.

The Boston Symphony Orchestra is concerned with a specialized mission, the performance of classical symphonic music. However, instead of investing its capital in the orchestra, it invested its resources in a different business, established popular music with food, wine, and liquor to help subsidize its specialized mission.

ANR is concerned with a specialized mission in natural gas activities. However, it invested in five regional trucking companies not related to natural gas in order to help finance its specialized mission.

It is not yet clear how U.S. Steel is defining its mission. Perhaps it has a specialized mission concerning steel and is using Marathon Oil as a piggybacking mechanism to further modernization of steel production and its specialized mission in steel. Or, perhaps U.S. Steel has changed its mission more in the direction of a diversified conglomerate and away from a specialization strategy.

Strategic Piggybacking As Synthesis Of Diversified Portfolio And Specialization Strategies

Strategic piggybacking combines the specialized mission emphasis of the specialization strategy with the diversified investment activity of the diversified portfolio strategy. While combining elements from both strategies, it is also different from both specialization and diversified portfolio strategies. It is different than specialization in that it invests resources in relatively unrelated areas. It is different than the diversified portfolio strategy in that its intention is to subsidize a specialized primary mission while diversified portfolio strategies intend more to develop other businesses on their own merits. It is also different than the diversified portfolio strategy in that its investment flow dynamic is to seek new for the institution, safe, relatively advanced life cycle "cash cow" businesses rather than using "cash cow" businesses it already owns to help finance relatively more risky high growth potential "star" businesses.

For example, The Boston Symphony Orchestra is concerned with a specialized mission concerning classical symphonic music, but it invests in relatively unrelated advanced "cash cow" established popular music, food, wine, liquor activities to help subsidize its specialized primary mission.

ANR is concerned with a specialized mission concerning natural gas, but it invests in relatively unrelated advanced life cycle "cash cow" businesses in trucking to help subsidize its specialized natural gas mission activities.

U.S. Steel may have either a specialized mission concerning steel production or a diversified portfolio mission. Its acquisition of Marathon could be a piggybacking strategy for helping modernize its steel operations or it could be used to help finance portfolio diversification. Time may tell.

Conditions Appropriate For A Strategic Piggybacking Strategy

For a business institution, strategic piggybacking is an appropriate strategy when the primary mission is temporarily not being favored by the market and/or resources are needed to make the specialized mission more compatible with market opportunities. For example, in the ANR situation, it was correctly judged that the 1970's would not be boom years for natural gas activities relative to the potential of the 1980's. In the meantime, the trucking activities helped subsidize and develop the specialized natural gas mission capabilities for very good potential benefits in the 1980's. U.S. Steel is in a position with the acquisition of Marathon to either improve its specialized mission in steel through financing modernization or to adopt a diversified portfolio strategy for a modified mission.

While for the business institutions, the piggybacking strategy was adopted primarily to help support a specialized primary mission in temporarily difficult markets, for the nonprofit institution, the strategic piggybacking strategy can also be used to help offset structural long term dificits and permit the nonprofit institution help self-subsidize specialized missions over the longer term. For ninety years the food, wine, and liquor activities of the Boston Pops have helped support the continuous deficits of the BSO's specialized mission.

While a nonprofit institution may wish to use a strategic piggybacking strategy for long term self-subsidization, it would probably make more sense for a business institution to change its specialized mission if that mission could not be profitable in the long term rather than subsidize a long term unprofitable specialized mission.

There is also an important caution that should be considered in evaluating whether either a business or a nonprofit institution should adopt a strategic piggybacking

strategy. Does the institution have the capability of
managing effectively relatively unrelated businesses? An
unrelated business activety may have actual or potential
high and stable "cash cow" benefits, but if the parent
institution does not have the experience required to
manage such an unrelated activity, it could lose money
for both the new for the institution "cash cow" as
well as the parent specialized mission activities and
capabilities.

CONCLUSION

This article explained the conceptual foundations for
the strategic piggybacking strategy from the general
strategic management, adoption of innovation, product
life cycle, specialization, and diversified portfolio
strategy literatures. The strategic piggybacking
strategy is compared and contrasted with the diversified
portfolio and specialization strategies. Intention,
dynamic investment flow, short vs. long term, and mission
similarities and differences are addressed. A case is
made for considering strategic piggybacking as a
synthesis of the specialization and diversified portfolio
strategies. The conditions appropriate for adoption
consideration of a strategic piggybacking strategy are
also discussed. For business and nonprofit institutions
with specialized missions that are not being favored
by market opportunities in the short run (for both
business and nonprofit institutions) and the long run
(for nonprofit institutions), and who wish to retain
their specialized missions, then strategic piggybacking
should be a strategy worthy of serious consideration.

REFERENCES

Abell, Derek F. (1980), Defining The Business: The
  Starting Point of Strategic Planning, Englewood
  Cliffs, New Jersey: Prentice-Hall.

Abell, Derek F. and John S. Hammond (1979), Strategic
  Market Planning, Englewood Cliffs, N.J.: Prentice
  Hall.

Boston Symphony Orchestra, Annual Reports, (1975-1981).

Business Week (February 5, 1979), "Corporate Strategies:
  American Natural Resources - A Pipeliner Turns
  Trucker," 90-91.

Business Week (December 7, 1981), "Is Big Steel Abandoning
  Steel?" 34-45.

Chandler, Alfred D. (1962), Strategy and Structure:
  Chapters In The History of the American Industrial
  Enterprise, Cambridge: MIT Press.

Chandler, Alfred D. (1977), The Visible Hand: The
  Managerial Revolution In American Business,
  Cambridge: Harvard University Press.

Day, George S. (1977), "Diagnosing the Product Portfolio,"
  Journal of Marketing, 41 (April), 29-38.

Gross, Neal C. (1942), The Diffusion of a Culture Trait
  In Two Iowa Townships, M.S. Thesis, Ames: Iowa
  State University.

Henderson, Bruce D. (1970), The Product Portfolio, Boston:
  The Boston Consulting Group, Inc.

Levitt, Theodore (1965), "Exploit The Product Life Cycle,"
  Harvard Business Review 43 (November-December),
  81-94.

Newman, W.H. and L.P. Logan (1971), Strategy,
  Policy, and Central Management, Cincinnati:
  South-Western Publishing.

Rogers, Everett M. with F. Floyd Shoemaker (1971),
  Communication of Innovation: A Cross-Cultural
  Approach, New York: The Free Press.

Ryan, Bryce and Neal C. Gross (1943), "The Diffusion
  of Hybrid Seed Corn in Two Iowa Communities,"
  Rural Sociology, 8, 15-24.

Steiner, G.A. and J.B. Miner (1977), Management Policy
  and Strategy, New York: Macmillan.

Tarde, Gabriel (1903), The Laws of Imitation, New York:
  Holt (translated by Elsie Clews Parsons).

Uyterhoeven, Hugo E.R., Ackerman, Robert W. and John W.
  Rosenblum, Strategy and Organization, Homewood,
  Illinois: Richard D. Irwin.

Wilson, Meredit C. (1927), "Influence of Bulletins,
  News Stories, and Circular Letters upon Farm
  Practice Adoption with Particular Reference to
  Methods of Bulletin Distribution," Federal Extension
  Service Circular 495, Washington, D.C.: U.S.D.A.

PRODUCT POSITIONING IN A COMPETITIVE MARKET

Kishore Pasumarty, Georgia Institute of Technology, Atlanta

ABSTRACT

Existing models for positioning products in attribute space ignore competitive factors. This paper uses the Similarity Adjusted model (Pasumarty, 1980) to determine the location of brands with foresight - i.e., this analysis accounts for the location rules that subsequent entrants into the market will use. Market shares obtained using the proposed analysis are higher than when competitor reaction is ignored.

INTRODUCTION

Various models have been proposed to determine the ideal location of a product in joint space (eg., Shocker and Srinivasan, 1974; Albers and Brockhoff, 1977; Urban, 1975). The implicit reasoning in all these models is that one can do well by meeting customer needs and demands. But this argument ignores some competitive factors which can be very crucial. As Oxenfeldt and Moore (1978) point out, marketing decisions and plans give far too light weight to competitive factors, and marketing planners fail to deal with them in the most effective ways. 'Competitor' orientation suggests that the attainment of most goals - sales, profits, and growth - must usually come at the competitor's expense.

Joint space maps present information not only about consumer needs but also about the competitive situation. The ideal point is the consumer's preferred combination of attributes. Therefore, the primary strategy should be to locate as close to as many ideal points as possible. At the same time, relative positions of other brands should be taken into consideration. Moving too close to competitors may hurt the market share. The overall strategy should account for the existing positions of other brands and the location of potential entrants expected into the market.

This paper shows how competitive factors can be introduced in determining the 'optimum' location for a product. The results apply to industries in which there is product differentiation (i.e., there is imperfect competition). Each firm is assumed to choose a market share maximizing position based on the ideal points of consumers and the observed choice of firms already located. In addition, this firm also takes into account the location rules that subsequent, equally rational potential entrants will use. Thus, each firm takes into consideration the effect of its location decision upon the ultimate configuration of the industry.

The first part of this paper presents a choice model and explains its application for product positioning. The second part extends this application and presents a heuristic method for determining the optimal product location after incorporating competitive reactions.

BACKGROUND

The analysis is based on the Similarity-Adjusted (SA) model proposed by Pasumarty (1980). If $P(X;S)$ denotes the probability of choosing brand x from the set S, then the model states that

$$P(x;S) = \frac{e^{-nD_x} \left(\sum_i D_{xi} \right)^z}{c} \qquad (1)$$

where

c = normalizing constant such that the total market share for all brands equal 1

$\sum_i D_{xi}$ = Sum of distance from brand x to all other brands

D_x = distance of brand x from the ideal point

$$= \left\{ \sum_i w_i (I_i - X_i)^k \right\}^{1/k}$$

where

w_i = 'importance" or weight of dimension i

I_i = location of the ideal point on dimension i

X_i = location of brand x on dimension i

and k (>0) determines the metric chosen; eg., k=1 (city block and k=2 (Euclidian).

There are three parameters - k, n and z - which have to be determined empirically. Actual market shares of brands are known. Parameters k, n and z are found such that the fit between the model predictions and market shares is 'optimum'. Values of n and z, which are specific to each market, determine the relative influence of distance from the ideal point (D_x) vs. interbrand distances $(\sum_i D_{xi})$ in predicting preferences in that particular market. The first term is a measure of utility while the second term measures similarity.

The SA model is an extension of an <u>operationalization</u> of Luce's (1959) Choice Axiom which does not have the second term of the numerator (i.e., $\sum_i D_{xi}$) in equation (1). This term was introduced as a measure of similarity and it improved predictions significantly in a study using purchase recall data and rank order preference data on paper towels.

FINDING THE IDEAL LOCATION

Overall attitude towards a brand has been considered to be a combinaton of beliefs as to the 'amount' of certain attributes given objects posess, weighted by the importance of each attribute to the individual. Since marketing managers have some control over physical characteristics and consumer perceptions, the SA model (equation 1) can be used as a guide by management to help relocated old products or introduce new ones. This can be done by changing the physical attributes of the product, or changing the consumer's perception of the product, or combination of both. The purpose is to relocate the product. The question now arises as to what will be the ideal location of the new product.

In the short run, the firm is assumed to be interested in obtaining the maximum possible market share subject to a budget constraint. The goal of trying to maximize market share makes sense since it is one of the main correlates of business profitability. In their project, involving 57 companies, on the profit impact of market strategies, Buzzell, Gale, and Sultan (1975) found that, on the average, a difference of 10 percentage points in market share is accompanied by a difference of about 5 points in pretax return on investment (ROI).

Suppose the objective function to be maximized is the total market share of a firm which has existing products in
the relevant product market. Let A be the set of the
firm's existing brands and let S represent the set of all
brands in the product market (A is a subset of S). The
intention is to position a new product such that this firm
has the maximum market share possible (i.e., sum of market
share for all brands, including the new one, is maximized).
If X is a new product, then the probability of choosing
the firm's product is

$$P = \frac{\text{Prob. of choosing X + Prob. of choosing set A}}{\text{Prob. of choosing X + Prob. of choosing set S}}$$

Substitution of the terms of the Similarity Adjusted Model
gives

$$P = \frac{e^{-nD_x}(\Sigma D_{xj})^z + \sum_{i \in A} e^{-nD_i}(\Sigma_j D_{ij})^z}{e^{-nD_x}(\Sigma_i D_{xj})^z + \Sigma_{i \in S} e^{-nD_i}(\Sigma_j D_{ij})^z} \qquad (2)$$

where

D_x = distance of brand x from the ideal point, and

$\Sigma_j D_{ij}$ = sum of distance of brand i from all other brands.

Equation (2) accounts for potential cannibalization of the
firm's existing brands by introduction of the new product.
The function, P, can be maximized using gradient methods
of non-linear programming (Hadley, 1964), or a search procedure using grids. While the gradient methods would generally require less computation time, the heuristic search
procedures are more flexible in that they can readily incorporate different distance metrics, cost functions,
choice models, search boundaries, etc. A search procedure
using grids was employed in this paper because it offered
a simpler solution and the computation involved was not
much.

Luce's Location vs. SA's Location

To appreciate the usefulness of the SA model, suppose that
Luce's model is believed to hold by every firm in all situations, i.e., brand similarity can be ignored while determining probability of choice. If all firms are trying to
maximize brand share, they will all position their products
at the same spot since that position will maximize share
for all brands. Consider Figure 1. A,B,C,D, and E are existing brands. Luce's model will predict that the next
brand should be positioned at X. If another brand enters
the market, the 'optimum' position will again be X. And
the same for any new brand. Since it has been shown that
brand similarity affects market share, we clearly need a-
nother model. On the other hand, the SA model predicts
that the first entering brand be positioned at Y_1 and the
next one at Y_2 (given that a brand exists at Y_1). Of
course, it is understood that profit would be positive at
all these points. Similarly, we obtain points Y_3 and Y_4.

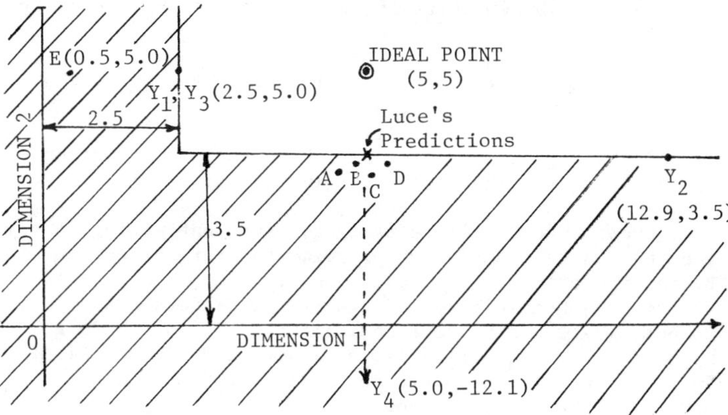

Figure 1

LUCE AND 'SA' PRODUCT POSITIONS

Y_1,Y_2,Y_3,Y_4: Locations of entrants 1,2,3,4, respectively
A,B,C,D,E : Existing Brands
NUMBERS IN PARENTHESES DENOTE COORDINATES
Shaded area represents region of technological feasibility.

COMPETITION

Determining points Y_1 and Y_2 (Figure 1) advance can have
important strategic implications. Assume that the competition has recourse to similar optimizing models. Suppose
we are at Y_1 and expect a new entrant. If the strategy is
to maximize our share of the market (at the expense of the
new entrant), one possible move would be to pre-empt the
competitor and reposition an existing brand near or at Y_2.
Even if we do not assume that others use similar models,
the implication remain the same. (However, we still need
to assume that the predictions of the SA model are correct). If the competitor uses some other model (which
does not give the same predictions) then he will position
the product at some point other than Y_2. This point is
not the 'optimum' for him (because Y_2 is the 'optimum').
Thus, the opportunity lost for the competitor is at the
expense of all other brands. This is discussed in detail
later.

Once the first new entrant (called 1) is established at
Y_1, a new entrant (called 2) searches the complete attribute space and positions the product at Y_2. Now that 2
is established at Y_2, does 1 have the maximum possible
market share? The first entrant came to Y_1 when 2 did not
exist. With 2 at Y_2, the market share function changes
and it is possible that 1 will be better off at some other
point (say P_1) in Figure 2.

Figure 2

HYPOTHETICAL EXAMPLE TO ILLUSTRATE
PRODUCT POSITIONING WITH FORESIGHT

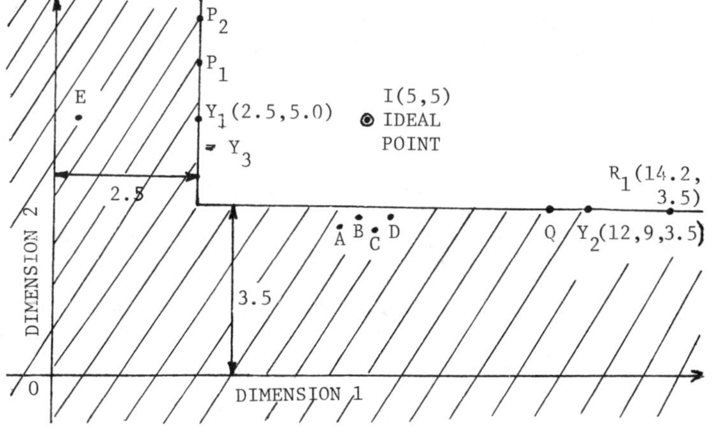

But, if 1 was positioned at P_1 (instead of Y_1), then 2 <u>may</u> have found Q to be the 'optimum' position. If 2 is at Q, then 1 may find P_2 to be the 'optimum', and so on. We need an equilibrium solution that satisfies the following conditions:

1. 1's market share is the maximum possible, given that 2 is also in the market, and

2. At the same time 2's market share is the maximum possible, given that 1 is also in the market.

If 1 knows that 2 will be using the same optimizing model, then he can take advantage of being the earlier entrant. By incorporating 2's reaction function into his objective function, a Stackelberg solution (eg., Henderson and Quandt, 1971) can be obtained which would assure him a higher market share than if he had ignored 2's reaction. In this context, the approach to find such a solution numerically can be outlined as:

1. Divide the joint space into a grid (say 100 points). Either 1 or 2 can potentially locate at any of these points.

2. Locate 1 at any point.

3. Search the space and locate 2 at a certain point which maximizes his market share given 1's location. Note the corresponding market shares.

4. Locate 1 at all the grid points and go through step (3) each time.

5. Locate 1 at the point that maximizes his market share.

This will always give an optimum solution but there may be computational problems with this method. In this particular case $(100)^2$ points will need to be searched. This search increases with an increase in the number of dimensions. In addition, the amount of computation increases expontially with the number of entrants. For n brands, $(100)^n$ points will have to be looked at. Of course, efficient algorithms could be written to reduce search, but still the problem is serious. The next part of this paper presents a heuristic method which may not provide optimal solutions all the time but is computationally feasible and very simple to understand.

Heuristic Solution

Briefly, the heuristic involves the following steps (for two entrants, 1 and 2):

1. Locate 1 at Y_1 to maximize his market share.

2. Locate 2 at Y_2 to maximize his market share.

3. Search the space to see if Y_1 still gives 1 the maximum market share now that 2 has entered the market. If yes, then the solution has been reached. If not, then relocate 1 to obtain the maximum market share.

4. Search the space to see if Y_2 still gives 2 the maximum market share now that 1 has moved. If yes, then the solution has been reached. If not, then relocate 2 to obtain the maximum market share.

5. Go through steps (3) and (4) till an equilibrium solution is obtained.

With respect to the example in Figure 2, Y_1 was determined using a fine grid. Given Y_1, 2 is located at Y_2 (12.9,3.5) as shown. Given that 2 is at Y_2, it was seen that 1 did have the highest possible market share at Y_1. At these positions, entrant 1 has 17.98% and 2 has 15.6% of the market share.

The following two possibilities were considered:

a. The expression for market share always finds points which are not only 'ideal' but also sequentially 'ideal' (at least, once removed). In other words, the model determines Y_1 and Y_2 such that market shares for 1 and 2 are maximized given the other's location. It may hold for more entrants too, but at the moment we are concerned only with two new entrants. Or

b. The configuration in this particular case is such that the market shares for 1 and 2 are maximized without any iteration. With different functions, brands, or constraints we might, in general, need several iterations to find the equilibrium solution.

To resolve this indeterminacy, a new entrant (3) was introduced. Suppose 1 is part of the existing brands like A, B, C, D, and E. Given A,B,C,D,E,1 entrant 2 (the first entrant) locates at Y_2 (after searching the space). Given A, B,C,D,E,1,2 entrant 3 (the second entrant) locates at Y_3 to maximize his market share. But given that 3 is at Y_3, Y_2 is not the optimum position for 2. It is at R_1 (coordinates: 14.2,3.5). Thus, we conclude that possibility (b) is true i.e., that, in general, we may have to resort to iterations to find equilibrium (if there is any).

In this particular case we do not have to resort to many iterations. Given that 2 is at R_1, we find (after searching through the space) that Y_3 is the 'optimum' position for 3. Therefore, entrant 2 at R_1 and entrant 3 at Y_3 is the equilibrium solution.

There will be finite costs involved in moving brands around in the attribute space. The above analysis should not be interpreted as the trace of the movement of the competitors. Entrant 1 will have to evaluate (through theoretical analysis before entering the market) where to locate. All 2 has to do is to maximize his market share given the position of 1, assuming that there are no more entrants.

Three Entrants

Now extend the analysis to the situation where 3 entrants can enter the market. When entrant 1 positions himself, he has to plan for the moves of entrants 2 and 3. It seems that positions Y_1 for entrant 1, R_1 for entrant 2, and Y_3 for entrant 3 give the equilibrium solution for this case. No further computation is required to evaluate this. Let's start with entrant 1's case. Given that 2 and 3 are R_1 and Y_3, respectively, 1 maximizes his share at Y_1 (since Y_1 and Y_3 are coincident, and Y_3 is obtained by maximizing share when positions Y_1 and R_1 are occupied). Given that 1 and 3 are at Y_1 and Y_3, respectively, 2 maximizes his share at R_1 (as seen in the previous paragraph - two entrant case). And given that 1 and 2 are at Y_1 and R_1, respectively, 3 maximizes his share at Y_3 (as seen in the previous paragraph). Although at first look it seems so, it is not the optimum equilibrium solution given that entrant 1 locates before the other two. A look at Table 1a will help clarify the argument.

Table 1a

MARKET SHARES AND COORDINATES OF ALL BRANDS

Brands	Market Share (%)	Coordinates
A	10.95	4.8,3.3
B	11.74	4.9,3.4
C	13.06	5.0,3.5
D	11.89	5.1,3.3
E	12.45	0.5,5.0
1	12.64	2.5,5.0
2	14.62	14.2,3.5
3	12.64	2.5,5.0

Table 1b

EFFECT OF MARKET SHARE USING FORESIGHT

Brand	Share Without Foresight	Share With Foresight
1	12.75% (2.5,5.0)	14.62% (14.2,3.5)
2	14.59% (12.9,3.5)	12.64% (2.5,5.0)
3	12.75% (2.5,5.0)	12.64% (2.5,5.0)

NUMBERS IN PARENTHESIS DENOTE COORDINATES

This table gives the coordinates of all brands and corresponding market shares. Coordinates of brands A, B, C, D, and E are fixed. Locations of entrants 1, 2, and 3 are as determined earlier. At the positions specified, entrant 2 has a larger share than entrant 1. Since entrant 1 comes before 2, he can choose to locate at R_1 (14.2,3.5). If 1 is at R_1, then it can be shown (by searching the space using a grid) that 2 will locate at Y_1 and 3 at Y_3. Thus, the equilibrium map has 1 at R_1, 2 at Y_1, and 3 at Y_3.

Effect of Foresight

It will be instructive to compare the market shares of the three entrants obtained by the two different methods considered. The first method did not employ the concept of sequential foresight, while the second one did. The results are displayed in Table 1b where the figures in parenthesis denote coordinates. It is apparent that with foresight, the first entrant gains 1.87% more of the market, which can be a large amount in dollar terms.

CONCLUSION

The hypothetical example considered in the text was two-dimensional because it is easy to represent it pictorially. The above analysis is the same for higher dimensional space. However, it has been found that in most situations, two or three dimensions are sufficient to represent the choice process.

In this example a particular form of the preference function is assumed, as determined by the values of parameters n and z. As mentioned earlier, these paramters are determined empircially, and their values depend on the market being studied.

Since only one ideal point was considered, the concept of region of technological feasibility is absolutely necessary. Otherwise, the problem of finding the optimal location becomes trivial - the ideal point is always the best location and that brand will capture the complete market. With more ideal points, the problem is not so straightforward.

BIBLIOGRAPHY

Albers, S. and K. Brockhoff, "A Procedure For New Product Positioning in an Attribute Space," European Journal Operations Research 1(1977)230-238.

Buzzell, Robert D., Bradley T. Gale, Ralph M. Sultan, "Market Share a Key to Profitability," Harvard Business Review, (Jan.-Feb., 1975), 98-106.

Hadley, G., Non-linear and Dynamic Programming, Addison-Wesley, Reading, Mass., 1964.

Henderson, James M. and Richard E. Quandt, Microeconomic Theory: A Mathematical Approach, McGraw-Hill Book Company, 1971.

Luce, R. D. (1959), Individual Choice Behavior: A Theoretical Analysis, New York: Wiley.

Oxenfeldt, Alfred R. and William L. Moore, "Customer or Competitor: Which Guideline For Marketing?" Management Review (August 1978), 43-48.

Pasumarty, Kishore R., "Extending Luce's Choice Axiom to Account For Brand Similarity," Working Paper, Graduate School of Business, Columbia University (1980).

Shocker, Allan D., and V. Srinivasan, "A Consumer Based Methodology for the Identification of New Product Ideas," Management Science, 20(February 1974), 921-37.

Urban, Glen L., "Perceptor: A Model for Product Positioning," Management Science, 21(April 1975), 858-871.

MARKET SHARE STRATEGY IMPLICATIONS OF
THE CONCEPT OF SUSTAINABLE GROWTH

Poondi Varadarajan, Texas A&M University, College Station

ABSTRACT

Market share objectives constitute a key element of a
firm's corporate strategy. Market share strategy deci-
sions--to build, maintain, or harvest share--are generally
based on a careful consideration of the long-term and short-
term profitability and cash flow implications of such decisions. The product sales growth rate and capacity expansion implications of share building strategies, the sustainability of implied sales growth targets and its consistency
with the firm's established financial policies and objectives are the subject of this report.

INTRODUCTION

Portfolio strategies are generally expressed in terms of
of market share objectives to be achieved in each of the N
strategic business units (SBUs) that constitute a firm's
portfolio of businesses. The increasing importance
assigned to achieving market share objectives as a key
element of a firm's corporate strategy can be attributed in
part to the emerging body of literature relating to two
contemporary approaches to strategic market planning. The
notion that market share is a major determinant of profitability has been empirically demonstrated in a number of
PIMS (Profit Impact of Market Strategy) studies (see,
Schoffler, Buzzel and Heany 1974; Buzzel, Gale and Sultan
1975). Also, the conceptual and empirical works of the
Boston Consulting Group (BCG) relating to "experience
effects" and the resulting relationship of market growth
and market share to profitability lend further credence to
the proposed relationship between market share and profitability (Boston Consulting Group 1972).

Besides the steady state market share-profit relationship, the short-term and long-term cash flow and profit
implications of share building, maintenance, and harvesting
strategies is another major area of concern. The cash flow
implications of share building, maintenance and harvesting
strategies in high, moderate and low growth markets have
been addressed in Gale and Branch (1981). Further, from the
standpoint of financial feasibility of share building objectives, it has been pointed out that for a firm wanting
to maintain a target payout ratio and capital structure
without issuing new equity, and that also wants to increase
sales at a rapid rate, the firm's growth rate is not an
independent variable, but rather is only one of several
variables in an interdependent system (Babcock 1970;
Robinson 1979).

The focus of this paper is on share building strategies. The product sales growth rate and product sales
(capacity expansion) implications of stated market share
building strategies are explored in this paper. In addition,
the issues of the sustainability and consistency of the
stated market share building objectives with the established
financial policies of the firm are addressed. Towards this
end a theoretical framework is first presented which constitutes the basis for subsequent discussion.

THE FRAMEWORK

Let S_o equal the market size expressed in standard
units (tons, pounds, units, etc.) for a given product during
the base time period (t=0), and G (>0) represent the projected market growth rate over the time horizon t = 1, 2,...
T. Let i = 1, 2,...N represent the competing businesses
and $s_{1,t}$, $s_{2,t}$,...$s_{N,t}$ their respective market shares
during any time period "t". Quite generally, it can be expected that competing firms would experience differential
growth rates. Let g_1 g_2,...g_N (≥ 0) represent the volumetric
sales growth rates of the competing businesses i = 1,2,...N.

Assumptions. In regard to S, G, g_i and $s_{i,t}$ the following
assumptions are made:
1. The market size is assumed to be exogenous. That is,
   the effect of the marketing effort of any single firm
   on industry demand (the total sales of the firm and its
   competitors) is assumed to be negligible.
2. The market growth rate "G" and the product growth rates
   (g_i) are assumed to be constant during the time horizon
   considered.
3. Both the market growth rate "G" and product growth
   rates "g_i" refer to product (volumetric) growth rates
   and not dollar sales (proceeds) growth rates. Further,
   all growth rates are expressed in decimals. For example, g_i = 0.10 is equivalent to a growth rate of 10%.
4. The market shares of competing businesses are assumed
   to be determined on the basis of number of units sold
   (volumetric) and not on the basis of dollar sales.
5. The market share of each firm individually and all
   firms collectively are assumed to satisfy the bound
   and sum constraints, respectively. That is $0 \leq s_{i,t} \leq$
   1.0 (the bound constraint) and $\sum_{i=1}^{N} s_{i,t} = 1.0$ (the sum
   constraint) for all "i" and "t".

Given S_o and G, the market size S_t during any future time
period can be expressed as

$$S_t = S_o(1+G)^t \tag{1}$$

The unit sales $d_{i,t}$ of business "i" during time period "t"
can be expressed in terms of S_t and $s_{i,t}$ as

$$d_{i,t} = s_{i,t} S_t = s_{i,t} S_o (1+G)^t \text{ or alternatively,}$$

$$d_{i,t} = d_{i,o}(1+g_i)^t = s_{i,o} S_o (1+g_i)^t \tag{2}$$

$$s_{i,t} = \frac{d_{i,t}}{S_t} = \frac{s_{i,o} S_o(1+g_i)^t}{S_o(1+G)^t} = s_{i,o}\frac{(1+g_i)^t}{(1+G)^t}$$

$$\text{or}$$

$$\frac{s_{i,t}}{s_{i,o}} = \frac{(1+g_i)^t}{(1+G)^t} = k \tag{3}$$

DISCUSSION

From the above set of equations which constitute the
basis for the remainder of this discussion it follows that,
in a growth market (G>0) for all t>0:

i) if g_i > G, the $\dfrac{(1+g_i)^t}{(1+G)^t}$ > 1 and $s_{i,t} > s_{i,o}$ → (implies)

   market share build-up;

ii) if g_i = G, then $\dfrac{(1+g_i)^t}{(1+G)^t}$ = 1 and $s_{i,t} = s_{i,o}$ →

   market share maintenance; and

iii) if $g_i < G$, then $\dfrac{(1+g_i)^t}{(1+G)^t} < 1$ and $s_{i,t} < s_{i,o} \rightarrow$

    market share decline or harvest.

As noted earlier the focus of this paper is on share building strategies. Quite generally, the share building strategy of a firm can be expressed as the percentage increase in market share to be achieved during the planning horizon "t". (For example, a 14% increase in market share (Δs_i) from the present level of 18% ($s_{i,o}$) to 32% ($s_{i,t}$) over a three year time period (t = 3). Stated as a ratio, this is equivalent to expressing the market share objective as a "k" fold increase in the market share (see, equation (3): $s_{i,t} = k\, s_{i,o}$) in reference to the base period (t=0) market share over a time period "t". (For the case illustrated $k = \dfrac{s_{i,3}}{s_{i,o}} = \dfrac{32\%}{18\%} = 1.78$). Before embarking on such a share building strategy, from a marketing perspective a number of issues need to be addressed. These include: what strategy will help achieve such a share gain? From which competitors will the share come? What competitive reactions can be expected? (Abell and Hammond 1979). What will be the magnitude of marketing investment required to realize the stated market share objectives during the planning horizon and maintain the share at that level during the post planning period? (Larreche and Srinivasan 1981).

More importantly, from a corporate perspective, a number of issues need to be addressed. These include:
1. For a given industry growth rate G, what is the rate (g_i) at which the firm's unit sales would have to grow in order to realize the stated market share increase objectives in the prescribed time frame?
2. What are the manufacturing capacity expansion and incremental product sales implications of the stated share building strategy?
3. Can the implied product sales growth rate be sustained consistent with the firm's established financial policies?
4. If not, what steps can be taken to resolve the inconsistency between targeted growth rate and sustainable growth rate?

These issues are addressed next:
1. Product Sales Growth Rate Implications
   From equation (3) it follows that

$$(1+g_i)^t = k\,(1+G)^t \text{ or}$$
$$1+g_i = k^{1/t}\,(1+G). \text{ Therefore,} \qquad (4)$$
$$g_i = k^{1/t}\,(1+G) - 1$$

For a given projected market growth rate, equation (4) provides a pro forma projection of the product growth rate required to realize the stated market share objectives in a given time frame. Table 1 provides an illustration of the product sales growth rate implications for various values of "k" and "t" for a projected market growth rate of 10% (G = 0.10). The interpretation of cell entries "g_i" in Table 1 is as follows. Given the firm's present market share $s_{i,o}$, the targeted market share $s_{i,t}$ ($=ks_{i,o}$), time frame within which the market share objective is to be achieved "t", and the projected annual market growth rate "G", then for the firm to realize its market share objective, its product sales will have to grow at an annual rate of "g_i". Similar figures can be generated for any projected market growth rate and various values of "k" and "t".

2. Incremental Product Sales (Capacity Expansion) Implications
   As noted in equation (2)

$$d_{i,t} = d_{i,o}(1+g_i)^t.$$
$$d_{i,t} - d_{i,o} = d_{i,o}\{(1+g_i)^t - 1\} \text{ or } \frac{d_{i,t} - d_{i,o}}{d_{i,o}} = (1+g_i)^t - 1.$$

Substituting $k(1+G)^t$ for $(1+g_i)^t$ results in

$$g^*_i = \frac{d_{i,t} - d_{i,o}}{d_{i,o}} = k(1+G)^t - 1 \qquad (5)$$

The numerator in (5) refers to the additional product sales (capacity expansion) implied by the stated market share objective. Table 2 provides an insight of the percentage increase (g^*_i) in product sales (and capacity) in comparison to the present sales level that would be required to realize a k-fold increase in market share over a time frame of "t" years for a projected market growth rate of 10% (G=0.10).

TABLE 1

PRODUCT SALES (CAPACITY) GROWTH RATE IMPLICATIONS
OF STATED MARKET SHARE OBJECTIVES[A]

T: PLANNING HORIZON IN YEARS

K \ T →	1	2	3	4	5
1.1	.21	.15	.14	.13	.12
1.2	.32	.20	.17	.15	.14
1.3	.43	.25	.20 [B]	.17	.16
1.4	.54	.30	.23	.20	.18
1.5	.65	.35	.26	.22	.19
1.6	.76	.39	.29	.24	.21
1.7	.87	.43	.31	.26	.22
1.8	.98	.48	.34	.27	.24
1.9	1.09	.52	.36	.29	.25
2.0	1.20	.56	.39	.31	.26

K: SHARE MULTIPLICATION FACTOR

A - Cell entries are computed for a projected market growth rate of 10% (G = 0.1).

B - Interpretation of cell entries: The firm's product sales (and capacity) would have to grow at an annual rate of 20% for the firm to realize its stated market share objectives (VIZ: (K)$S_{I,O}$ = 1.3 times the present share by the end of year 3), with the market projected to grow at an annual rate of 10%.

The pro forma projections presented in Tables 1 and 2 provide certain insights into the feasibility and desirability of stated objectives. For example, in order to realize a doubling of market share (k=2) over a four year time span, a business will have to grow at an annual rate of 31% or over three times the projected market growth rate of 10% (see, Table 1). Further as evidenced in Table 2, this would call for an increase in capacity of almost 200 percent. More importantly, there is a need to evaluate whether the stated market share objectives are consistent with the firm's established financial policies. Unrealistic market share aspirations might possibly call for capital commitment quite out of proportion to the capital generating ability of the firm (Fruhan 1972). The sustainable growth concept discussed next provides an insight of the interdependency between growth objectives and financial policies.

TABLE 2

PRODUCT SALES (CAPACITY EXPANSION) IMPLICATIONS
OF STATED MARKET SHARE OBJECTIVES[A]

T: PLANNING HORIZON IN YEARS

K: SHARE MULTIPLICATION FACTOR \ T →	1	2	3	4	5
1.1	.21	.33	.46	.61	.77
1.2	.32	.45	.60	.76	.93
1.3	.43	.57	.73	.90	1.10
1.4	.54	.69	.86	1.10	1.25
1.5	.65	.82	1.00	1.20	1.42
1.6	.76	.94	1.13	1.34	1.58
1.7	.87	1.06	1.26	1.49	1.74
1.8	.98	1.18	1.40[B]	1.64	1.90
1.9	1.09	1.30	1.53	1.78	2.06
2.0	1.20	1.42	1.66	1.93	2.22

A – Cell entries are computed for a projected market growth rate of 10% (G = 0.1).

B – Interpretation of cell entries: Given the projected market growth rate to be 10%, for the firm to realize its market share objective (1.8 times its present share by the end of year 3), total sales (and capacity) will have to grow by 140% by the end of year 3.

3. <u>Sustainability of Implied Product Sales Growth Rate</u>
The concept of sustainable growth rate and its myriad characteristics and nuances have been addressed in a number of sources (Babcock 1970; Zakon 1971; Fruhan 1972, 1979; Higgins 1977; Abell and Hammond 1979; Robinson 1979). Alternative computational methods for determining the maximum sustainable long-term assets growth rate, product sales (volumetric) growth rate and/or dollar sales (proceeds) growth rate are detailed in these sources. While a complete discussion of this topic is beyond the scope of this paper, some of the salient issues are addressed.

a) The factors governing the maximum sustainable long-term product sales growth rate are predominantly financial in character (return on assets, debt-equity ratio, cost of debt, total assets to net sales, to list a few). For a firm wanting to maintain a target payout ratio and capital structure without issuing new equity, sustainable growth would be the annual percentage increase in sales that can be supported consistent with the firm's established financial policies. A rate of growth higher than this figure can be sustained only at the expense of compromising in regard to one or more financial objectives of the company. This in turn could possibly affect the financial soundness of the company. At a lower sales growth rate a firm will be in a position to increase its dividends, reduce its leverage or build up liquid assets (Higgins 1977).

b) An estimate of the sustainable annual growth rate can be obtained by equating annual capital requirements and capital generation potential as detailed below.

Let, $S_{i,o}$ – current level of sales (in dollars)

ΔS_i – increase in annual sales

P_i – After tax profit margin on sales (profits per dollar of sales)

E – Earnings retention ratio (= 1 – target dividend payout ratio)
L = Target debt equity ratio
T_i – Total assets to sales ratio

Profit after taxes = $P_i (S_{i,o} + \Delta S_i)$

Dividend payout = $P_i (S_{i,o} + \Delta S_i) (1-E)$

Earnings retention = $P_i (S_{i,o} + \Delta S_i) E$

Debt potential at target debt equity

$$\text{ratio} = P_i (S_{i,o} + \Delta S_i) EL$$

Total capital generation potential =

$$P_i (S_{i,o} + \Delta S_i) E (1 + L) \qquad (6)$$

Total capital required to support incremental sales = $T_i(\Delta S_i)$ $\qquad (7)$

Equating capital requirements and capital generation potential and solving for $\dfrac{\Delta S_i}{S_{i,o}}$:

sustainable annual dollar sales growth rate

$$g_S = \frac{\Delta S_i}{S_{i,o}} = \frac{P_i E (1+L)}{T_i - P_i E(1+L)} \qquad (8)$$

The sustainable growth model outlined is based on certain restrictive assumptions, chief among them being:
i) The after tax profit margin on current sales and incremental sales are assumed to be the same
ii) The total assets to net sales ratio is assumed to be constant
iii) The depreciation provision (reinvested in the business) is just sufficient to maintain the value of existing assets.
iv) Inflation induced increases in working capital requirements (inventory and accounts receivables) are offset by corresponding increases in accounts payable and higher nominal profits.

In light of these restrictive assumptions, the general model of sustainable growth while serving to highlight the interdependency between sales growth objectives and established financial policies of the firm, fails to provide a realistic estimate of sustainable growth. More realistic models of sustainable growth which take into consideration factors such as differential profit margins on new and existing sales, changing assets to sales ratio, inadequacy of depreciation provision to maintain the value of existing assets, changes in total assets to sales ratio and the impact of inflation are discussed elsewhere (Higgins 1977, 1981; Johnson 1981).

c) It appears to be an accepted practice to employ the maximum sustainable long-term asset growth rate as a surrogate for maximum sustainable long-term product sales growth rate (Abell and Hammond 1979, p. 182). However, this might be appropriate only if the total assets to sales ratio can be assumed to be constant for the current and new level of sales as detailed below.

Assuming $\dfrac{T_{i,o}}{S_{i,o}} = \dfrac{T_{i,1}}{S_{i,o} + \Delta S_i} = C$ (9)

$$T_{i,1} = C (S_{i,o} + \Delta S_i)$$

$$T_{i,o} = C\, S_{i,o}$$

$$\frac{T_{i,1} - T_{i,o}}{T_{i,o}} = \frac{C(S_{i,o} + \Delta S_i - S_{i,o})}{C\, S_{i,o}}$$

$$\frac{T_{i,1} - T_{i,o}}{T_{i,o}} = \frac{\Delta S_i}{S_{i,o}} \qquad (10)$$

or

Assets growth rate 'g'$_A$ = Sales growth rate 'g'$_S$ (11)

However, if the rate of increase in net assets per dollar of sales volume is "j",

then $(1+g_A) = (1+j)(1+g_S)$ or

$$g_S = \frac{g_A - j}{(1+j)} \qquad (12)$$

Hence, "g_A" and "g_S" will only coincidentally be identical (when j = 0). If net assets necessary to support a given volume of sales are increasing (j>0) due to cost inflation or other reasons, volume will increase more slowly than net assets. Conversely, if the net assets required to support a given volume are decreasing (j<0), volume will increase more rapidly than net assets. In this regard, it has been noted that at a time of technological improvements, increasing scale of activity and falling selling prices, even a modest growth in net assets can support a high product (volume) sales growth rate. On the other hand, when plant and equipment costs and selling prices are on the increase, possibly necessitated by increased environmental and safety requirements or other considerations, even modest product sales growth rates would require high asset growth rates and additional cash infusion even when profitability is high (Robinson 1979).

4. Resolving Inconsistency

Finally, we address the question of major options open to a firm when its growth targets are inconsistent with the maximum sustainable growth rate. Among the feasible options are: a) sell new equity shares, b) lower the dividend payout ratio, c) increase the leverage, d) improve operating performance in various functional areas, and e) revise growth targets.

The desirability and implications of options 1 to 4 are discussed in other sources (see, Higgins 1977; Robinson 1979). From a marketing perspective, Figure 1 serves to summarize options for revising growth targets consistent with sustainable growth rate. As is evidenced in Figure 1, the targeted share increase ($s_x - s_o$) and time frame "t" within which the objective is to be achieved together determine the speed with which a strategy has to be implemented (the required growth rate) and hence, the cost of implementing the strategy. In regard to case 2 in Figure 1 ($s_{targeted} = s_x$, time frame = T) it is evident that the required growth rate is higher than the sustainable growth rate. If options 1 to 4 noted earlier were to be ruled out as either infeasible or undesirable, under these conditions the only feasible options consistent with the sustainable growth rate are: a) lowering share objective to s_x' holding T constant, b) extending the time horizon to T' holding s_x at the original level, and c) lowering share objective to s_x'' and extending time horizon to T".

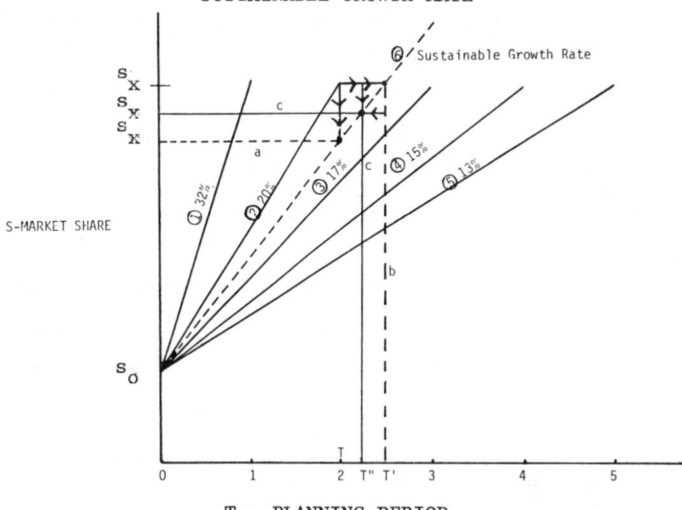

FIGURE 1

REVISING GROWTH TARGETS FOR CONSISTENCY WITH SUSTAINABLE GROWTH RATE

T – PLANNING PERIOD

1 to 5 – Product sales growth rate required to achieve market share objective (from present level of s_o to s_x) in time frames of one, two, three, four, and five years, respectively. (Growth rate computation shown in Figure are for a projected G of 10% and $\dfrac{s_x}{s} = k = 1.2$.

6   – maximum sustainable product sales growth rate determined on the basis of the firm's financial considerations.

s_x', s_x'', T', T" – Revisions in growth targets (in reference to $s = s_x$ and t = T) consistent with maximum sustainable growth rate.

CONCLUSION

The market share objectives to be achieved by the different business units in a firm's portfolio constitute a key aspect of the firm's corporate strategy. Needless to say, it is important that market share strategies--designed to build, maintain, or harvest share--are to be based on a careful consideration of the short-term and long-term cash flow and profit implications as well as the sustainability and consistency of targeted sales growth rate with a firm's established financial policies and objectives. This paper attempts to explore the product sales growth rate (g_i) and capacity expansion implications of share building strategies under conditions of real market growth (G>0). In addition, the issues of the sustainability of targeted sales growth rate and its consistency with the firm's established financial policies and objectives are addressed.

In conclusion, it might be appropriate to point to some of the implications of the assumptions made in regard to market growth rate and the product sales growth rate. Market size and market growth rate are assumed to be exogenous and hence, beyond the influence and control of any single firm. This can be viewed as a realistic assumption in regard to most competitive marketing environments. However, generalization might be erroneous in light of reported case histories which seem to attest to the fact that under certain conditions the marketing actions of individual firms can positively influence industry demand. Case histories such as Black and Decker's expansion in the hand held electric tool market and Texas Instrument's dominance in the electronic pocket calculator market serve to illustrate this point. By reducing prices as costs fell or in anticipation of declining costs with experience, these firms not only realized substantial market share increases but also increased primary demand, and, hence, higher market growth rate (Abell and Hammond 1979). Also, to the extent that a firm is successful in promoting a new use for its present products (for example: Arm & Hammer brand baking soda as a refrigerator deodorizer; Lysol brand deodorant as a disinfectant, deodorant and air/room freshener) the firm's marketing policies influence primary demand. The impact of Kodak's entry into the instant camera market on market size and market growth rate points to a third variant of the basic problem. The pooled marketing effort of Polaroid and Kodak coupled with Polaroid's increased level of marketing effort as a defensive measure are reported to have led to almost a doubling of the annual demand for instant cameras. The Kodak-Polaroid case history also serves to highlight the inherent problems in assuming "G" to be constant over the time frame considered in light of the potential impact of the entry or exit of one or more dominant firms on market size and market growth rate.

As stated earlier and evidenced in Figure 1, the product sales growth rate "g_i" is assumed to be constant over the time frame considered. This in effect implies that the market share evolution is uniform over the entire planning period. However, it is quite conceivable that the bulk of the market share change is accomplished in only a fraction of the total planning period (see, Larreche and Srinivasan 1980). Scenarios 1 and 3 in Figure 2 are illustrative of situations where neither market share evolution is uniform nor the product sales growth rate

FIGURE 2

MARKET SHARE EVOLUTION

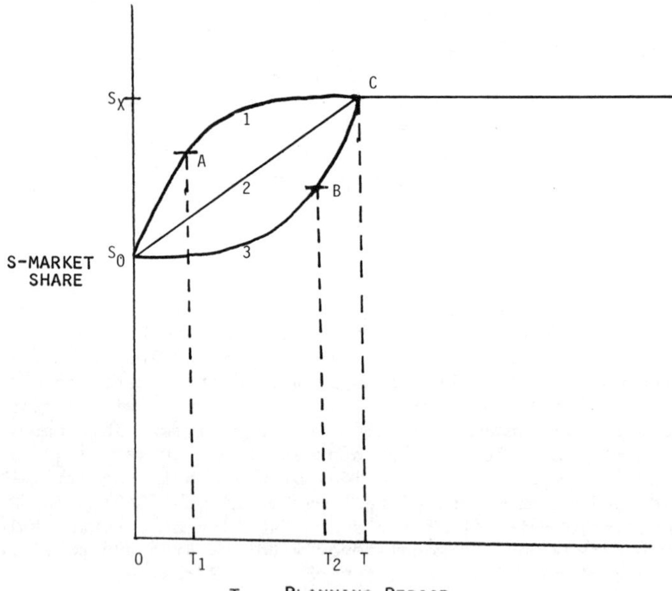

1, 2, 3 - ALTERNATE SCENARIOS OF MARKET SHARE EVOLUTION

constant over the planning period. In reference to scenario 1 in Figure 2, it is evident that a substantial part of the market share change occurs during the time period 0 to T, and the product sales growth rate is highest during this period. Under market share evolutionary patterns similar to 1 and 3 a relevant issue that needs to be resolved is: "which of the two growth rates--the average product sales growth for the entire planning period or the highest product sales growth rate during some part of the planning period (region s_0A under scenario 1 and region BC under scenario 3)--should be evaluated from the standpoint of maximum sustainable growth?" Problems relating to 'efficient capacity increments' point to another related area of concern.

Finally, it might be appropriate to point that in its current form, the framework presented and the issues outlined are largely relevant only in the context of single product businesses. In the case of large corporations with a portfolio of businesses, different strategic roles are assigned to the various strategic business units based on a number of considerations. Thus, positive cash flows from certain businesses are used to finance the growth of certain other businesses. Such actions facilitate the growth of the latter class of businesses at higher rates than would be feasible if they were required to be self-reliant for financing growth, and therefore, are not constrained by the relationships described here. However, there is still a need to compare the weighted average corporate dollar sales growth rate implied by the strategic roles assigned to the individual SBU's with the maximum sustainable long-term sales growth rate for consistency.

REFERENCES

Abell, Derek F., and John S. Hammond (1979), <u>Strategic Market Planning</u>, New Jersey: Prentice-Hall, Inc.

Babcock, Guilford C. (1970), "The Concept of Sustainable Growth", <u>Financial Analysts Journal</u> (May-June), 108-114.

Boston Consulting Group (1972), <u>Perspectives on Experience</u>, Boston.

Buzzell, Robert D., Bradley T. Gale, and Ralph G. M. Sultan (1975), "Market Share: A Key to Profitability", <u>Harvard Business Review</u> (January-February), 97-106.

Fruhan, Jr. William E. (1972), "Pyrrhic Victories in Fights for Market Share," <u>Harvard Business Review</u> (September-October), 100-107.

__________ (1979), <u>Financial Strategy</u>, Homewood, Illinois: R. D. Irwin, Inc.

Gale, Bradley T., and Ben Branch (1981), "Cash Flow Analysis: More Important than Ever", <u>Harvard Business Review</u> (July-August), 131-136.

Higgins, Robert C. (1977), "How Much Growth Can a Firm Afford", <u>Financial Management</u> (Fall), 7-16.

__________ (1981), "Sustainable Growth Under Inflation", <u>Financial Management</u> (Autumn), 36-40.

Johnson, Dana A. (1981) "The Behavior of Financial Structure and Sustainable Growth in an Inflationary Environment", <u>Financial Management</u> (Autumn), 30-35.

Larreche, Jean-Claude, and V. Srinivasan (1981), "STRATPORT: A Decision Support System for Strategic Planning", <u>Journal of Marketing</u> (Fall), 39-52.

Robinson, S. J. Q(1979), "What Growth Rate Can You Achieve?" <u>Long Range Planning</u> (August), 7-12.

Schoeffler, Sidney, Robert D. Buzzell and Donald F. Heany (1974), "Impact of Strategic Planning on Profit Performance", <u>Harvard Business Review</u> (March-April), 137-145.

Zakon, Alan (1971), "Growth and Financial Strategies", Boston: The Boston Consulting Group.

IDENTIFYING RATIONALE FOR MEMBERSHIP TERMINATION
IN A NONPROFIT SERVICE ORGANIZATION

Alan J. Dubinsky, University of Kentucky, Lexington
Paul J. Hensel, University of Kentucky, Lexington

ABSTRACT

There is an abundance of previously published research that
has explored various facets of marketing in nonprofit organizations. One area not yet examined is _why_ patrons of a
nonprofit _service_ organization terminate their memberships.
This topic should be of special interest to nonprofit service organization administrators because it may be less
costly to retain current members than it is to obtain new
ones. This paper reports the results of a study that investigated reasons for membership nonrenewal in a nonprofit
service organization. Implications for nonprofit service
organizations are also discussed.

INTRODUCTION

Since the seminal article by Kotler and Levy (1969), marketing principles and practices have been introduced into,
and adopted by, an increasing number of non-business entities (Kotler 1979). Collateral with this movement has been
an abundance of research examining the employment of marketing by non-traditional users. In other words, research
has investigated what Hunt (1976) labels nonprofit-macro
sector and nonprofit-micro sector issues. For example,
nonprofit-macro sector studies have explored topics such as
the effects of political advertising on voters (Rothschild
1978); reasons for consumers' hesitancy to practice energy
conservation (Milstein 1977); equity considerations in the
distribution of public services (Crompton and Lamb 1981);
evaluation of the federal government's consumer protection
policy (Duyck and Rosenberg 1979); and reinforcement and
the rate of consumer littering (Kohlenberg and Phillips
1973). Nonprofit-micro sector investigations have explored
areas such as problems of using marketing communications in
nonprofit organizations (Rothschild 1979); management of
the performing arts (Raymond and Greyser 1978; Weinberg
1977; Weinberg and Shachmut 1978); improvement of televised
public service messages by nonprofit health institutions
(Moore, Gombeski, and Ramirez 1979); determination of people's attitudes toward donating time to a worthy endeavor
(Yavas and Riecken 1981); and segmentation of charitable
givers (Craig, Deutscher, and McCann 1977).

Within the _nonprofit-micro_ sector, a topic not explored in
previously published research is _why_ patrons/users/consum-
ers of a nonprofit service organization terminate patronage, as well as how terminators might be classified (à la
market segmentation). Although prior investigations have
examined _how_ to attract patrons (e.g., Flexner and Berkowitz 1979; Geltzer and Ries 1976; Houston 1981; Morison and
Fliehr 1968; Ryans and Weinberg 1978), a void in the literature exists regarding member termination. This topic
should be of special concern to nonprofit organization administrators for at least one major reason: It is probably
less costly to retain current patrons than to attract new
ones (_Retailing Today_ 1979). Thus, in this day of rampant
inflation, debilitating recession, and astronomical interest rates, a nonprofit organization administrator should
develop a marketing program that will foster a high retention rate of existing patrons.

In seeking means to retain current members, administrators
could puruse the substantial body of consumer behavior literature that focuses on the concepts of consumer brand loyalty (e.g., Jacoby and Kryner 1973; Jacoby and Chestnut
1978; Jarvis and Wilcox 1976; Lutz and Winn 1974; Srini-

vasan and Kesavan 1976) and consumer satisfaction/dissatis-
faction (e.g., Day 1977; Hunt 1977; Swan and Combs 1976;
Swan and Trawick 1981; Warland, Herrman, and Willits 1975).
The preponderance of this research, however, is product-
oriented. Because there is a stream of literature that
suggests product marketing is different from service marketing (e.g., Bateson 1977; Johnson 1969; Lovelock 1981;
Sasser, Olsen and Wyckoff 1978; Shostack 1977), it may be
imprudent for nonprofit organization administrators to employ the findings from brand loyalty and satisfaction/dis-
satisfaction research. In other words, determining why
members drop from a nonprofit service organization appears
to warrant special research attention. Thus, a study was
directed toward examining this issue.

Specifically, an investigation was undertaken to ascertain
why members of a nonprofit service organization--The Better
Business Bureau (BBB)--terminate membership. Three reasons
for membership termination were hypothesized: financial
difficulties of a member, failure to receive benefits from
membership, and failure of member expectations to be realized. Each of these reasons will be briefly described below.

Members of the BBB that are facing financial difficulties
may terminate their membership to conserve cash. Given
that present-day economic conditions are generally adverse,
many organizations are likely to experience setbacks.
Facing such situations, organizations are likely to curtail
their expenditures for nonessential goods or services (Kotler 1980; Stanton 1981). Because the BBB can generally be
considered a nonessential service for most organizations,
it is likely that some members may not renew their memberships when trying to conserve precious funds.

A second reason for terminating organization membership was
hypothesized in terms of Assmus' (1975) purchase triers.
In this context, an organization may join the BBB as a
"trier." After "trying" membership for a year or two, the
organization may realize no net benefits from being a member. By not receiving any benefits, the member becomes a
"skeptical trier" and terminates membership.

Related to the failure to obtain any benefit is the third
reason for membership termination. While the BBB may be
perceived as offering some benefits to potential members
upon joining, these members' expectations may not be realized. That is, members may not renew memberships because
their subjective expectations are not met. These terminators, then, would feel that the costs of membership are
greater than the received benefits, and they would be dissatisfied with the BBB service offerings. While strong
theoretical and empirical support for this contention
exists in the product arena (e.g., Engel, Kollat, and
Blackwell 1978; Howard and Sheth 1969; Nicosia 1966; Swan
and Combs 1976), no previously published research has examined services having long-term commitments (such as a one-
year membership).

METHODOLOGY

Sample

The target population consisted of all businesses that
failed to renew their BBB membership during a thirteen-

month period. The BBB of interest in this study is located
in a major metropolitan area in the Southwest. BBB was
chosen as the host organization because it satisfies the
definition for a nonprofit service organization and because
it maintains information about membership terminators.

A systematic random sample of membership terminators was
drawn from the target population. The actual eligible sample was comprised of 257 businesses. Sixty businesses refused to participate in the study. In addition, 94 (with
working telephone numbers) could not be contacted within
three attempts made during business hours over a two-week
period. One-hundred-three of the 257 businesses provided
usable questionnaires (for a response rate of 40.1 percent).
An examination of potential differences between respondents
and the target population was performed. This analysis indicated that there are no statistically significant differences between these two groups with respect to the following variables: membership longevity, company location
(metropolitan versus nonmetropolitan area), average yearly
dues, type of business, and company size (number of employees).

Questionnaire

The survey instrument was administered over the telephone
by trained researchers. The questionnaire contained both
open-ended and closed-ended questions. The questionnaire
focused on four key areas: (1) respondent reasons for
joining BBB and for terminating membership; (2) respondent
general attitudes toward BBB (such as satisfaction with offerings); (3) respondent degree of expected (prior to joining) benefit to be derived from each of thirteen potential
benefits; and (4) respondent degree of benefit received
(after joining) from each of thirteen potential benefits.
Respondents reported their responses to the first two areas
in both open- and closed-ended formats. They reported
their responses to the latter two issues on a Likert-type
scale, where high value = "very beneficial" and low value =
"not at all beneficial." The items in the questionnaire
were arrived at from a focus group of several BBB managers
and were refined with the assistance of the host bureau's
management.

RESULTS

The results of the study will be presented in relation to
the three a priori reasons posited for membership termination: financial difficulties, failure to receive benefits,
and failure for expectations to be realized. The findings
are discussed below.

Termination Because of Financial Difficulties

Table 1 presents reasons for respondent nonrenewal. (Results in Table 1 are based on responses to an open-ended
question pertaining to the primary reason for member termination.) The major reason for nonrenewal appears to be
that the BBB was not useful/provided no benefits. Closer
examination of the table, however, reveals that 28 percent
dropped their membership for some monetary reason (financial problems, scarce dollars, or prohibitive membership
cost), while 72 percent did not renew for some nonmonetary
rationale (such as BBB's providing too few benefits or
failing to do an adequate job). Thus, these findings suggest that some BBB terminators did so because of financial-
related reasons, as was hypothesized earlier.

Given that two groups of terminators were identified--those
dropping for financial reasons and those dropping for nonfinancial reasons--an analysis (using chi-square tests) was
performed to determine whether there were differences between the two groups' attitudes toward the service organization. Several interesting findings emerged from this analysis. In relation to nonfinancial terminators, financial
terminators are significantly more likely:

- to be very satisfied with BBB services (see Table 2)
- to feel that membership benefits exceed costs (see Table
  3)
- to feel that they had a very good relationship with BBB
  (see Table 4)
- to have been members for more than one year (see Table 5)
- to rejoin BBB (see Table 6)

Termination Because of Failure to Receive Benefits

As posited earlier, some BBB members may have terminated
their memberships because they felt they were receiving no
benefits. Such members could be viewed as those willing to
pay dues to determine whether membership would be beneficial; if not, membership would be terminated. This contention received some support. Analyses revealed that, of
those terminating membership because they received no benefit, 83 percent were members for only one year. In addition, 77 percent of one-year members did not renew membership specifically because BBB provided no benefit. Only
forty-three percent of all BBB terminators did so because
no benefits accrued to them.

Further examination of the data indicated that some respondents who dropped out of BBB because of failure to receive
any benefit did not even expect to derive any benefit by
joining. That is, when asked how much benefit they expected
(prior to joining) to derive from thirteen potential BBB
benefits, 13 percent did not expect to receive a benefit
from any of the thirteen benefits. In fact, as shown in
Table 7, a substantial number of respondents did not expect
to receive any benefit from the thirteen potential BBB benefits. For only the Bulletin Service, Look-Out List, and
Donor's Guide did more than one-half of the respondents expect to receive any benefit. Thus, the above results suggest the possibility that some respondents dropped out because membership provided no benefit upon "trial."

Termination Because of Failure to Realize Expectations

The third hypothesis was that BBB members may terminate because the benefits they received were less than the benefits they expected (prior to membership) to receive. To
make this analysis, the data were modified. For each respondent the degree of expected benefit from the thirteen
potential benefits was summed, as was the degree of benefit
received from the thirteen benefits. The sum of the benefits expected score was then subtracted from the sum of
benefits received score for each respondent. A positive
difference was recoded to indicate the respondent received
more than expected; a zero difference, the respondent received the same as expected; a negative difference, the respondent received less than expected.

The above modification subsequently revealed that over the
thirteen benefits, 54 percent of respondents received less
than they had expected; only 18 percent received more than
they had expected. In addition, 37 percent who had had an
expectation on any of the thirteen benefits said that they
received less than they had expected.

Additional analysis showed that those respondents who had
received more than they had expected were more likely to be
very satisfied with BBB services (see Table 8) and to feel
that they had a very good relationship with BBB (see Table
9) than those who received less than they had expected.
Also, in relation to nonfinancial terminators, financial
terminators were more likely to feel that they received
more than they had expected (see Table 10).

A more detailed look at respondent benefit expectations and
benefit receipts is presented in Table 11. The table exhibits the number of respondents that expected some benefit
from each potential benefit, as well as the percent of this
group that received less than they had expected. Except
for the tax advantage, which is out of the BBB's control,
between 42 percent and 63 percent of relevant respondents

received less than they had expected. Simply put, the BBB is failing to satisfy many of the respondents on the thirteen potential BBB benefits examined here.

LIMITATIONS

The results of this study should be viewed in light of some important limitations. First, the size of the total sample (n = 103), in general, and the financial and nonfinancial subsamples (n = 28 and 75, respectively), in particular, was small. This serves to reduce the generalizability of these findings. This sample, however, is representative of the overall population of BBB terminators in the city studied, representing over 40 percent of such businesses.

Second, the results may not be generalizable to service organization memberships in other cities. In particular, the geographic locale of the host organization (the Southwest)--and the business philosophy in that area--as well as the size of the host city (in excess of one million people) may be related to respondent answers. Additional research needs to explore if such relationships exist.

Third, the potential BBB benefit list was derived from BBB managers, not from BBB membership or, more specifically, from BBB terminators, as suggested by Fishbein and Ajzen (1975). Therefore, it is possible that some benefits that are important to members were not included here. This is relatively unlikely, however, because respondents were asked (prior to specific benefit questions) to provide their own primary benefit for joining BBB. There were no elicited benefits which could not readily be subsumed by the benefit list used.

And fourth, respondents' ability to recall their expectations prior to joining an organization may have been hampered. While there was no substantial number of "don't know" or "can't remember" answers to survey questions, the demand characteristics of this study are unmeasured. Despite the above weaknesses, the investigation still has important implications for academics and practitioners.

DISCUSSION AND CONCLUSIONS

This survey of former BBB members has provided a modicum of support for the three a priori reasons posited for nonprofit service organization membership termination. Twenty-eight percent of the respondents did not renew their memberships because of financial reasons. In relation to nonfinancial terminators, financial terminators were more likely to be satisfied with the BBB; to feel that their relationship with BBB had been good; to perceive that membership benefits exceed its costs; to have been members for more than one year; and to have intentions of rejoining BBB. Thus, financial terminators appear to have relatively positive attitudes toward the organization.

Also, the findings indicate that some terminators--particularly first year members--dropped their memberships because they received no benefits, even if they expected none prior to joining. Furthermore, a substantial percentage of respondents did not have their benefit expectations realized after joining BBB. This failure to meet expectations is generalized across twelve of the thirteen potential BBB benefits examined. Failure to have expectations met, then, may imply that some BBB terminators did so because of dissatisfaction with BBB offerings.

Given that financial terminators tend to have positive impressions of BBB, action should be taken by management to retain them as members. Special programs could be designed that address potential financial terminators' monetary concerns. Managerial actions could include offering these members a reduced membership dues, installment dues-payment plan, deferred dues-payment plan, or even short-term dues-

free membership. The intent of these plans is to retain currently satisfied members who might provide favorable word-of-mouth communication about the organization. The end result may be the attraction of new members via financial terminators' communications.

Managers should also direct their attention toward potential nonfinancial terminators. In dealing with this group, a three-pronged approach is required. First, when members initially join a nonprofit service organization, they should be queried about their reasons for joining, as well as their expectations about membership. Second, approximately half-way into their first-year membership, an audit of their membership satisfaction should be undertaken. And third, results of the audit should be compared with the initial investigation about member reasons for, and expectations of, membership benefits. Where adverse discrepancies between benefits expected and benefits received exist, corrective action should be taken. Focus should be on assisting potential terminators to realize benefits they expected, but are not receiving. Moreover, if management identifies, via the audit, certain terminators who did not expect to receive anything from joining and are not receiving any benefit, attention should focus on providing them with a benefit--or illustrating to them that such a benefit is available. Failure to do so could lead to the potential terminator's nonrenewal.

One other managerial implication is that management should periodically survey its membership to ascertain what changes in offerings are desired. By monitoring member needs, programs can be designed that are attuned to membership needs. The end result should be an increased number of satisfied current members and, hopefully, an increased number of new members who see membership offerings as being attractive.

Finally, additional research pertaining to why nonprofit service organization members terminate their association should be performed. Within the BBB itself, examinations should investigate whether such variables as BBB locale, size of city in which it resides, type of business, size of business, business location, and sales tactics used are related to why members terminate. In addition, future studies should extend the present research effort by focusing on other kinds of nonprofit service organizations (e.g., Chamber of Commerce, Rotary International) and their problems of member termination. Such investigations, like the present one, should aid nonprofit service organization administrators interested in designing effective marketing programs and service offerings.

TABLES

TABLE 1

PRIMARY REASONS FOR TERMINATING BBB MEMBERSHIP

Primary Reason	Number of Respondents	Percent
·Membership was not useful/provides no benefit[a]	36	35.0%
·Other (nonmonetary reason)[a]	16	15.5
·Membership was too expensive[b]	14	13.6
·Membership was no longer needed[a]	9	8.7
·Membership didn't do the job[a]	9	8.7
·Company funds were scarce[b]	8	7.8
·Company faced financial difficulties[b]	6	5.8
·Membership didn't provide enough benefits[a]	5	4.9
Total	103	100.0%

[a]This reason for membership termination was classified as a "nonfinancial" reason.

[b]This reason for membership termination was classified as a "financial" reason.

TABLE 2

RELATIONSHIP BETWEEN REASON FOR MEMBERSHIP TERMINATION
AND SATISFACTION WITH BBB SERVICES[a]

| | Degree of Satisfaction with BBB Services | | | |
| | Very Satisfied | | Less Than Very Satisfied | |
Reason Membership Terminated	Percent	Number	Percent	Number
Financial	62.5	15	20.6	13
Nonfinancial	37.5	9	79.4	50

[a]Corrected chi-square = 12.104, df = 1, p = .0005.

TABLE 3

RELATIONSHIP BETWEEN REASON FOR MEMBERSHIP TERMINATION AND MEMBER ASSESSMENT
OF COST VERSUS BENEFIT OF BBB MEMBERSHIP[a]

| | Member Assessment | | | |
| | Benefits Exceed Costs | | Costs Exceed Benefits | |
Reason Membership Terminated	Percent	Number	Percent	Number
Financial	30.4	7	10.7	6
Nonfinancial	69.6	16	89.3	50

[a]Corrected chi-square = 3.289, df = 1, p = .0697.

TABLE 4

RELATIONSHIP BETWEEN REASON FOR MEMBERSHIP TERMINATION AND MEMBER ASSESSMENT
OF RELATIONSHIP WITH BBB[a]

| | Member Assessment | | | |
| | Very Good Relationship | | Less Than Very Good Relationship | |
Reason Membership Terminated	Percent	Number	Percent	Number
Financial	45.0	18	22.2	10
Nonfinancial	55.0	22	77.8	35

[a]Corrected chi-square = 3.996, df = 1, p = .0456.

TABLE 5

RELATIONSHIP BETWEEN REASON FOR MEMBERSHIP TERMINATION
AND LENGTH OF MEMBERSHIP[a]

| | Length of Membership | | | |
| | One Year | | More Than One Year | |
Reason Membership Terminated	Percent	Number	Percent	Number
Financial	22.2	14	58.3	14
Nonfinancial	77.8	49	41.7	10

[a]Corrected chi-square = 8.795, df = 1, p = .003.

TABLE 6

RELATIONSHIP BETWEEN REASON FOR MEMBERSHIP TERMINATION
AND MEMBER INTENTION TO REJOIN BBB[a]

| | Member Intention | | | |
| | Will Rejoin | | Will Not Rejoin | |
Reason Membership Terminated	Percent	Number	Percent	Number
Financial	59.4	19	8.8	3
Nonfinancial	40.6	13	91.2	31

[a]Corrected chi-square = 16.750, df = 1, p < .001.

TABLE 7

NUMBER AND PERCENT OF RESPONDENTS NOT EXPECTING ANY BENEFIT
FROM THIRTEEN POTENTIAL BBB BENEFITS

Potential Benefit	Number	Percent
·Employee Benefit Program	81	78.6%
·Tax Advantage	70	68.0
·Advertising Assistance	67	65.0
·Referral Program	65	63.1
·Executive Information Service	64	62.1
·Hot-Line Service	63	61.2
·Increased Sales	62	60.2
·Public Relations	55	53.4
·Complaint-Handling Service	53	51.5
·Prestige	52	50.5
·Donor's Guide	43	41.7
·Look-Out List	38	36.9
·Bulletin Service	28	27.2

TABLE 8

RELATIONSHIP BETWEEN SATISFACTION WITH BBB SERVICES AND MEMBER ASSESSMENT
OF BENEFITS RECEIVED LESS BENEFITS EXPECTED[a]

| | Member Assessment | | | | | |
| | Received Less Than Expected | | Received Same As Expected | | Received More Than Expected | |
Level of Satisfaction	Percent	Number	Percent	Number	Percent	Number
Very Satisfied	26.8	15	14.3	4	47.4	9
Less Than Very Satisfied	73.2	41	85.7	24	52.6	10

[a]Corrected chi-square = 6.268, df = 2, p = .0435.

TABLE 9

RELATIONSHIP BETWEEN MEMBER ASSESSMENT OF RELATIONSHIP WITH BBB AND MEMBER ASSESSMENT
OF BENEFITS RECEIVED LESS BENEFITS EXPECTED[a]

| | Member Assessment | | | | | |
| | Received Less Than Expected | | Received Same as Expected | | Received More Than Expected | |
Relationship With BBB	Percent	Number	Percent	Number	Percent	Number
Very Good	41.8	23	37.0	10	68.4	13
Less Than Very Good	58.2	32	63.0	17	31.6	6

[a]Corrected chi-square = 5.105, df = 2, p = .078.

TABLE 10

RELATIONSHIP BETWEEN REASON FOR MEMBERSHIP TERMINATION AND MEMBER ASSESSMENT
OF BENEFITS RECEIVED LESS BENEFITS EXPECTED[a]

| | Member Assessment | | | |
| | Received Less Than Or Same As Expected | | Received More Than Expected | |
Reason Membership Terminated	Percent	Number	Percent	Number
Financial	27.8	20	53.3	8
Nonfinancial	72.2	52	46.7	7

[a]Corrected chi-square = 2.636, df = 1, p = .105.

TABLE 11

NUMBER OF RESPONDENTS EXPECTING TO RECEIVE A POTENTIAL BBB BENEFIT
AND PERCENTAGE OF THAT NUMBER THAT DID NOT RECEIVE
BENEFIT AS EXPECTED[a]

Potential Benefit	Number of Respondents Expecting To Receive Benefit	Percentage Of Those Expecting To Receive Benefit That Did Not Receive Benefit
Hot-Line Service	40	63%
Employee Benefit Program	22	55
Sales Increase	41	53
Complaint-Handling Service	50	52
Referral Program	38	50
Bulletin Service	75	49
Advertising Assistance	36	47
Prestige	51	47
Executive Information Service	39	46
Look-Out List	65	45
Donor's List	60	43
Public Relations	48	42
Tax Advantage	33	28

[a]Read table as follows: 40 of the 103 respondents expected to receive a benefit from the Hot-Line Service; 63% of those 40 respondents received no benefit from the Hot-Line Service.

REFERENCES

Assmus, G. (1975), "NEWPROD: The Design and Implementation of a New Product Model," Journal of Marketing, 39 (January), 16-23.

Bateson, J. (1977), "Do We Need Service Marketing," in Marketing Consumer Services, P. Eiglier et al., eds., Cambridge, MA: Marketing Science Institute, 1-30.

Craig, S., T. Deutscher, and J. McCann (1977), "Segmenting Charitable Givers: An Application of Tobit," in 1977 AMA Educators' Conference Proceedings, Chicago: American Marketing Association, 34-38.

Crompton, J.L., and C.W. Lamb (1981), "Equity Considerations in the Distribution of Public Services," in Marketing of Services, J.H. Donnelly and W.R. George, eds., Chicago: American Marketing Association, 122-125.

Day, R.L. (1977), "Extending the Concept of Consumer Satisfaction," in Advances in Consumer Research, W.D. Perreault, ed., Atlanta: Association for Consumer Research, 149-154.

Duyck, R., and L.J. Rosenberg (1979), "Evaluating Governmental Consumer Protection Policy: Product Safety in the U.S. and Europe," in 1979 AMA Educators' Conference Proceedings, N. Beckwith et al., eds., Chicago: American Marketing Association, 530-534.

Engel, J.F., R.D. Blackwell, and D.T. Kollat (1978), Consumer Behavior: Theory and Application, Hinsdale, IL: The Dryden Press.

Fishbein, M., and I. Ajzen (1975), Belief, Attitude Intention and Behavior: An Introduction to Theory and Research, Reading, PA: Addison-Wesley.

Flexner, W.A., and E.N. Berkowitz (1979), "In Search of New Hospital Markets: An Analysis of the 'Have No Physician' Segment," in 1979 AMA Educators' Conference Proceedings, N. Beckwith et al., eds., Chicago: American Marketing Association, 609-613.

Geltzer, H., and A. Ries (1976), "The Positioning Era: A Marketing Strategy for College Admissions in the 1980s," in A Role for Marketing in College Admissions, New York: College Entrance Examination Board, 73-85.

Houston, M.J. (1981), "The Marketing of Higher Education: A Multimarket, Multiservice Approach," in Marketing of Services, J.H. Donnelly and W.R. George, eds., Chicago: American Marketing Association, 138-140.

Howard, J.A., and J.N. Sheth (1969), The Theory of Buyer Behavior, New York: John Wiley and Sons.

Hunt, H.K. (1977), "CS/D Bits and Pieces," in Consumer Satisfaction, Dissatisfaction, and Complaining Behavior, R.L. Day, ed., Bloomington, IN: Indiana University, School of Business.

Hunt, S.D. (1976), "The Nature and Scope of Marketing," Journal of Marketing, 40 (July), 17-28.

Jacoby, J., and D.B. Kryner (1973), "Brand Loyalty vs. Repeat Purchasing Behavior," Journal of Marketing Research, 10 (February), 1-19.

________, and R.W. Chestnut (1978), Brand Loyalty: Measurement and Management, New York: John Wiley and Sons.

Jarvis, L.P., and J.B. Wilcox (1976), "Repeat Purchasing Behavior and Attitudinal Brand Loyalty: Additional Evidence," in 1976 AMA Educators' Conference Proceedings, K. Bernhardt, ed., Chicago: American Marketing Association, 151-152.

Johnson, E.M. (1969), "Are Goods and Services Different: An Exercise in Marketing Theory," St. Louis, MO: Unpublished Ph.D. Dissertation, Washington University.

Kohlenberg, R., and T. Phillips (1973), "Reinforcement and Rate of Litter Deposit," Journal of Applied Behavioral Analysis, 6 (Fall), 391-396.

Kotler, P., and S.J. Levy (1969), "Broadening the Concept of Marketing," Journal of Marketing, 33 (January), 10-15.

________ (1979), "Strategies for Introducing Marketing into Nonprofit Organizations," Journal of Marketing, 43 (January), 37-44.

________ (1980), Marketing Management: Analysis, Planning, and Control, Englewood Cliffs, NJ: Prentice-Hall, Inc.

Lovelock, C.H. (1981), "Why Marketing Management Needs to be Different for Services," in Marketing of Services, J.H. Donnelly and W.R. George, eds., Chicago: American Marketing Association, 5-9.

Lutz, R.J., and P.R. Winn (1974), "Developing a Bayesian Measure of Brand Loyalty: A Preliminary Report," in 1974 AMA Educators' Conference Proceedings, R.C. Curhan, ed., Chicago: American Marketing Association, 104-108.

Milstein, J.S. (1977), "Consumer Behavior and Energy Conservation," in Advances in Consumer Research, W.D. Perreault, ed., Atlanta: Association for Consumer Research, 315-321.

Moore, T.J., W.R. Gombeski, and A.G. Ramirez (1981), "Use of Television Public Service Messages by Nonprofit Health Institutions: Improving Their Effectiveness," in Marketing of Services, J.H. Donnelly and W.R. George, eds., Chicago: American Marketing Association, 117-121.

Morison, B.G., and K. Fliehr (1968), In Search of an Audience, New York: Pitman Publishing Corp.

Nicosia, F.M. (1966), Consumer Decision Processes, Englewood Cliffs, NJ: Prentice-Hall, Inc.

Raymond, T.J.C., and S.A. Greyser (1978), "The Business of Managing the Arts," Harvard Business Review, 56 (July-August), 123-132.

Retailing Today (1979), "Why Does Management Allow Incompetents to Handle Complaints?" (April).

Rothschild, M.L. (1978), "Political Advertising: A Neglected Policy Issue in Marketing," Journal of Marketing Research, 15 (February), 58-71.

________ (1979), "Marketing Communications in Nonbusiness Situations or Why It's So Hard to Sell Brotherhood Like Soap," Journal of Marketing, 43 (Spring), 11-20.

Ryans, A. B., and C. B. Weinberg (1978), "Consumer Dynamics in Nonprofit Organizations," Journal of Consumer Research, 5 (September), 89-95.

Sasser, E.W., R.P. Olsen, and D.D. Wyckoff (1978), Management of Service Operations: Texts, Cases, and Readings, Boston: Allyn and Bacon, Inc.

Shostack, L. (1977), "Breaking Free from Product Marketing," Journal of Marketing," 41 (April), 73-80.

Srinivasan, V., and R. Kesavan (1976), "An Alternate Interpretation of the Linear Learning Model of Brand Choice," Journal of Consumer Research, 3 (September), 76-83.

Stanton, W.J. (1981), Fundamentals of Marketing, New York: McGraw-Hill Book Company.

Swan, J.E., and L. Combs (1976), "Product Performance and Consumer Satisfaction: A New Concept," Journal of Marketing, 40 (April), 25-33.

________, and I.F. Trawick (1981), "Satisfaction Explained by Desired vs. Predictive Expectations," in 1981 AMA Educators' Conference Proceedings, K. Bernhardt et al., eds., Chicago: American Marketing Association, 170-173.

Warland, R.H., R.O. Herrman, and J. Willits (1975), "Dissatisfied Consumers: Who Gets Upset and Who Takes Action," Journal of Consumer Affairs, 9 (Winter), 148-163.

Weinberg, C.B. (1977), "Building a Marketing Plan for the Performing Arts," Bulletin (May), 1-7.

________, and K.M. Shachmut (1978), "ARTS PLAN: A Model Based System for Use in Planning a Performing Arts Series," Management Science, 24 (February), 654-664.

Yavas, U., and G. Riecken (1981), "Volunteer Recruitment: A Marketing Approach," in 1981 AMA Educators' Conference Proceedings, K.L. Bernhardt et al., eds., Chicago: American Marketing Association, 77-80.

ACKNOWLEDGMENT

The authors gratefully acknowledge the valuable assistance provided throughout this project by Professor E. Laird Landon (University of Houston).

THE PREDICTION AND EXPLANATION OF VOTING BEHAVIOR

Bruce I. Newman, University of Wisconsin-Milwaukee

ABSTRACT

This paper examines voting behavior in the 1980 presidential primary in Illinois. A comparative study is carried out to determine the predictive and explanatory power of political-demographic and psychographic variables. The results clearly indicate that psychographic variables are more useful for predicting and explaining voting behavior.

INTRODUCTION

The application of consumer behavior concepts to the study of voting behavior has been advanced by several researchers: (Sherrod 1971); (Palda 1973, 1980); (Fishbein 1974); (Shama 1974); (Nygren and Jones 1977); (Rothschild 1978); (Shikiar 1979); and (Crosby et al. 1981). The results of these studies reinforce the proposition that a voter can be analyzed as a consumer of a service. The limited amount of empirical research done in this area has been very encouraging.

The most recent study which looked at actual voting behavior in a presidential primary race was carried out by (Newman 1981). The point is made that with the advent of political marketing, it is no longer sufficient for the candidate to rely on percentages attached to standard demographic breakdowns in an effort to predict who is in favor of certain issues, or who will vote for a candidate at a specific point in time. The candidates want to know more about voter opinions on a number of different subjects, and then utilize the knowledge to develop marketing strategies to either change or reinforce voter attitudes and perceptions.

METHODOLOGY

A sample of approximately 2,000 respondents' names were chosen from the records of the March, 1978 Illinois congressional primary held in Champaign-Urbana. It was assumed that a respondent who voted in the congressional primary would be very likely to vote in the next presidential primary.

A PPS (probabilities proportionate to size) design was chosen to develop the sample. The desired sample size was determined by the number of democratic and republican candidates to be surveyed. Three republican candidates (John Anderson, George Bush, and Ronald Reagan) and two democratic candidates (Jimmy Carter and Edward Kennedy) were chosen as the subjects of analysis. Therefore, the final desired sample size was 450 and 300 for the republicans and democrats respectively (or 150 respondents for each candidate). To arrive at that final sample size, both the democrats and republicans were oversampled in the initial stage of gathering names from the registration lists.

In order to survey voters intending to vote in either the democratic or the republican party, it was necessary to develop two separate questionnaires. This was due to the fact that voting criteria varied according to the party as well as the individual candidates in each party. Both questionnaires were structured identically. The questionnaires covered three major areas. The first area covered the political background of the respondent. The questions

in this area were developed in part from standard questions used as background information in the classic studies carried out in political science by (Campbell et al. 1960).

TABLE 1

SAMPLING FRAMES

Democrats	List Size	Sample Desired	Fixed Interval
Champaign	2,534	400	6
Urbana	1,161	400	3
Republicans			
Champaign	7,544	600	13
Urbana	2,733	600	4

The second area covered the psychographics, which included voters' opinions on a broad range of topics. Several sources were used to generate these items. First of all, a survey of the literature was done on major news magazines, major and local newspapers, campaign literature and television news and analysis programs over a five month period beginning in November, 1979. Secondly, qualitative research was done on fifty respondents who intended on voting in the primary. For each of the five candidates, ten respondents were identified on the basis of their intention to vote for that candidate. This was done six weeks before the election in order to get as accurate an indication of the respondent's intention as possible. These interviews were conducted over the telephone to residents living in Champaign and Urbana. Finally, the last area covered standard demographics about the voters, which was developed in part from the studies carried out in sociology by (Berelson et al. 1954) and (Lazarsfeld et al. 1968).

Each questionnaire was pretested to detect either conceptual or operational flaws. Approximately ten respondents were chosen at random in a local shopping mall to participate in the pretest. The respondents represented a cross-section of the electorate. Very few changes were made as a result of the pretest.

The method of data collection chosen was a mail survey. The choice of a mail survey over a telephone survey or personal interview was based on the following criteria:

1. A method was needed to enable data collection to be carried out over a period of one week for approximately 800 respondents.

2. Due to the personal nature of the topic, as little interaction as possible was called for.

3. By allowing the respondent time to fill out the survey in privacy and at their leisure, a minimum amount of contamination would be incurred.

Six stages were needed to carry out the data collection. The first stage involved the identification of phone numbers for the approximately 2,000 names. Approximately

66% of the names were identified in the phone directory. The second stage involved a telephone screening process during which voters were classified according to their intention to vote in the primary. Only those respondents indicating an intention to vote in the primary were asked to participate. The screening process was done three weeks prior to the primary in order to maximize the number of respondents who had formed an intention to vote for a specific candidate.

The third stage involved the mailing of a postcard nine days before the primary to alert the respondents to the fact that they would be receiving their questionnaire in the next few days. The fourth stage covered the execution of the mail survey. The questionnaires were mailed six days before the primary. The fifth stage involved the mailing of a second postcard four days before the election to remind the respondents to return their questionnaires before they voted. Only those questionnaires that were postmarked before the primary were used.

TABLE 2

RESPONSE RATE ON MAIL SURVEY
(n=845)

Good Returns	655	(78%)
Post Office Returns	6	(1%)
Not Usable	26	(3%)
Total Responses		(82%)

The final stage involved the determination of the respondents' actual voting behavior. In order not to contaminate the data, a different interviewer telephoned those respondents who returned their questionnaire(s) within two weeks after the primary. The interviewer said she was studying the phenomenon of "crossover voting" for one of her classes at the university, and was therefore interested in how the respondent voted. The results of respondents' voting intentions and actual behavior are compared with voting results in the cities of Champaign and Urbana in Table 3.

TABLE 3

VOTING RESULTS
Crosstabulation of Intention with
Actual Voting Behavior

	Intention	Behavior			
		Carter	Kennedy	Anderson	
Dem.	Carter	103	1	21	125(65.4%)
	Kennedy	1	36	9	46(24.1%)
	Anderson	2	1	17	20(10.5%)
		106(55.5%)	38(19.9%)	47(24.6%)	191(100%)
Cities Results		2661(63%)	1464(35%)	*	4230(100%)

		Anderson	Bush	Reagan	
Rep.	Anderson	99	3	4	106(44.7%)
	Bush	2	44	8	54(22.8%)
	Reagan	3	1	73	77(32.5%)
		104(43.9%)	48(20.3%)	85(35.9%)	237(100%)
Cities Results		7672(55%)	2056(15%)	4212(30%)	4230(100%)

*There is no information on the number of democrats who voted for Anderson because the results were listed according to the candidate's declared party, which was republican for Anderson. Therefore, the results for Anderson include both the democratic and republican voters' ballots.

FINDINGS

To test the effectiveness of the political-demographic and psychographic variables, two stepwise discriminant analyses were carried out in each party on the stated intentions of respondents, since this is the only information we have prior to the election.[1] In the democratic party, Carter and Kennedy were used; and in the republican party, Anderson and Reagan were used.[2] Each model was then validated using the respondents' actual voting behavior. In other words, the prediction for each voter generated from the discriminant analysis based on voter intentions will be compared with the actual voting behavior of the respondents.

If one were only interested in prediction without explanation, the most parsimonious variable would be a stated intention to vote for a candidate. The results from this study indicate that 81% of the democratic voters and 91% of the republican voters actually voted as they intended. While these results are impressive, they do not supply the candidate with the necessary information to develop his marketing strategy on.

Political-Demographic Variables

The following seven variables were chosen to run in the discriminant analyses in both the democratic and republican parties: education, occupation, age, socioeconomic status, party affiliation, parents' party affiliation, and political ideology. The independent variables are specified as follows:

* Education includes: grade school, high school or trade school, some college, college degree, and masters or doctorate.

* Occupation included: retired, homemaker, student, laborer, service worker, craftsman or foreman or machine operator, sales or clerical, executive or manager, and professional or technical or proprietor.

* Age included all those respondents over the age of 18.

* Socioeconomic status included: lower class, lower middle class, middle class, upper middle class, and upper class. This was a self-report measure.

* Party affiliation was measured on a 7-point bipolar scale going from very likely to very unlikely that the respondent would vote in the primary according to his party preference.

* Parents' party affiliation included three responses: both parents were democrats, both parents were republicans, and parents had no consistent partisanship.

* Political ideology included three possible responses: conservative, moderate, and liberal.

The dependent variable was based on a measure of intention which was simply stated by asking whom the respondent intended on voting for in the Illinois primary on March 18.

---

[1] In each party, pairwise T-tests were run to screen out the most significant psychographic variables.

[2] Bush was not used in the republican discriminant analysis due to insignificant T-test results.

A review of Table 4 indicates that education, age, party
affiliation and political ideology all entered into both
analyses, while occupation entered into only the republican analysis. Among those variables that entered, political ideology was the most discriminating variable in both
analyses, as it had the largest coefficient (Appendix 1).
In the republican analysis, education had the second
largest coefficient. In the democratic party, age had the
second largest coefficient. When these two discriminant
models are validated, prediction rates only go as high as
81% for the republicans, and only 63% for the democrats
(Table 6).

TABLE 4

POLITICAL-DEMOGRAPHIC VARIABLES
Stepwise Discriminant Analysis
Significant Variables

Variable Description	Republicans Anderson/Reagan	Democrats Carter/Kennedy
1. Education	+	+
2. Occupation	+	−
3. Age	+	+
4. Socioeconomic Status	−	−
5. Party Affiliation	+	+
6. Parents' Party Affiliation	−	−
7. Political Ideology	+	+

+ Entered into the discriminant analysis
− Not entered into the discriminant analysis

Psychographic Variables

Seven different areas were covered in this section. Each
area is operationalized by developing a listing of statements which are used to measure voter opinions. The
following areas will be specified by a description of the
type of opinion statements that were used to describe each
one. (Due to the large number of statements listed for
each area, only a sample will be presented here. The
number of statements in the democratic and republican
questionnaires is listed below.)

* Issues and policies included a series of statements
covering four areas: economy, leadership, foreign policy,
and social issues. Each statement (e.g.: I believe my
candidate will cut taxes for individuals, etc.) was
measured on a binary scale (agree:disagree). Total number
of statements: democrat (22); republican (24).

* Social groups included a listing of groups of people who
are likely to be supportive of the candidates. A binary
scale (most likely:least likely) was used to measure
whether the respondent thought that group was likely to
vote for his candidate. (The groups mentioned included:
conservatives, independents, veterans, students, and
environmentalists, among others.) Total number of statements: democrat (14); republican (14).

* Feelings towards the candidate were measured on a binary
scale (yes:no) by listing a series of feelings (e.g.:
patriotic, hopeful, excited, responsible, etc.). An indication was made as to whether these feelings were e-
licited by voting for their candidate. Total number of
statements: democrat (9); republican (9).

* Candidate characteristics included several personality
traits (e.g.: articulate, compassionate, charismatic,
stable, etc.) which were measured on a binary scale (yes:
no). A statement about the belief that a candidate possesses each of the characteristics was surveyed. Total
number of statements: democrat (17); republican (15).

* Current events (domestic and international) were measured
on a binary scale (yes:no) with respect to the belief that
any of the following situations (e.g.: If we get to a
point where we are on the brink of war, etc.) would influence a voter to switch to another candidate. Total
number of statements: democrat (9); republican (8).

* Events about the candidate were measured on a binary
scale (yes:no) with respect to the belief that any of the
following hypothetical situations (e.g.: Had lied to the
press, etc.) would influence the voter to switch to another
candidate if they knew they had occurred. Total number of
statements: democrat (11); republican (9).

* Nonspecific issues about the candidate included a series
of statements (e.g.: I am voting for my candidate because
of his performance in one of the prior debates, etc.) about
the specifics of that election which might trigger the
curiosity of the voter. Each issue was measured on a binary scale (yes:no). Total number of statements: democrat
(8); republican (9).

A review of Table 5 suggests that in both the democratic
and republican analyses, the issues and policies and social
groups areas dominated as the discriminating variables.
However, in the democratic analysis, two additional areas
(candidate characteristics and nonspecific issues) entered
into the discriminant run. In the republican analyses, one
additional area (events about the candidates) also entered
into the discriminant run.

A most interesting result is the fact that the most discriminating variable in the democratic analysis (Appendix
2) is the desire for a change in the present administration. This is voiced by the Kennedy voters. The second
most discriminating variable as voiced by Carter voters is
the reinstatement of the draft. In the republican analysis, the most discriminating variable centered on the influence of students on behalf of Anderson. The next most
discriminating variable was the influence of conservatives
on behalf of Reagan. However, issues that concerned voters
dealt with inflation, defense spending, and E.R.A.

A review of Table 6 indicates a marked improvement in the
rate of prediction for both the republicans and democrats.
The prediction rate for the republicans and democrats was
93% and 97% respectively. Carter voters were predicted
with 99% accuracy. This is clearly a definite improvement
over the political-demographic variables.

SUMMARY

The modern day voter has a whole host of opinions, which
makes understanding him very difficult. The broad range
of opinions identified in this study creates a situation
for the candidate which makes it almost impossible for him
to create a campaign platform that reflects all of them.
In effect, the candidate can be identified in consumer behavior terms as a single brand in the market. Therefore,
his appeal should be geared toward that segment(s) of
voters whom he considers to be his target market. It is
possible for the candidate to appeal to several market
segments, each with a different set of opinions. Of
course, the risk he runs is that he may attract one segment and alienate another.

The results in this study indicate that the traditional
approach of identifying political-demographic profiles to
study voting behavior does in fact have room for improvement. The use of psychographic variables allows the candidate to get a better understanding behind the voter's
choice. The major advantage of studying the voter as a
consumer in the "political marketplace" is that the candidate is in a position to utilize a sophisticated marketing
orientation that has been successful in the "commercial

marketplace". In this way candidate platforms and images can be developed to appeal to a chosen base of voters.

TABLE 5

PSYCHOGRAPHIC VARIABLES
Stepwise Discriminant Analysis
Significant Variables

	Variable Description	Republicans Anderson/Reagan
1.	Reduce inflation	+
2.	Cut taxes	−
3.	Develop a strong intelligence community	−
4.	Build up our military	+
5.	Reject Salt II	+
6.	Reinstate the draft	−
7.	Build more nuclear plants	−
8.	Cut social programs	−
9.	Fight for ERA	+
10.	Conservatives	+
11.	Rich people	+
12.	Independents	+
13.	Liberal republicans	−
14.	Farmers	−
15.	Veterans	−
16.	Businessmen	−
17.	Students	+
18.	Environmentalists	−
19.	Had no chance of winning rep. nomination	+

	Variable Description	Democrats Carter/Kennedy
1.	Reduce inflation	−
2.	Impose gas rationing	−
3.	Lower interest rates	−
4.	Increase defense spending	−
5.	Reinstate the draft	+
6.	Build more nuclear plants	+
7.	Institute a Nat'l Health Program	+
8.	The Silent Majority	+
9.	Traditional democrats	+
10.	Chicago politicians	+
11.	Students	+
12.	Liberals	−
13.	Downstate voters	+
14.	Environmentalists	−
15.	Charismatic	+
16.	Innovative in implementing policies	+
17.	Able to get things done	+
18.	I want change in present administration	+

+ Entered into the discriminant analysis
− Not entered into the discriminant analysis

TABLE 6

COMPARATIVE RESULTS

Political-Demographic Variables

Democrats

		Predicted C	Predicted K	
Actual	C	64 (61.5%)	40 (38.5%)	104
	K	11 (29.7%)	26 (70.3%)	37

63.8% correctly classified

Republicans

		Predicted A	Predicted R	
Act.	A	84 (82.3%)	18 (17.7%)	102
	R	15 (19.4%)	62 (80.6%)	77

81.5% correctly classified

Psychographic Variables

Democrats

		Predicted C	Predicted K	
Actual	C	103 (99%)	1 (1%)	104
	K	3 (8%)	34 (92%)	37

97% correctly classified

Republicans

		Predicted A	Predicted R	
Act.	A	94 (92.2%)	8 (7.8%)	102
	R	4 (5.2%)	73 (94.8%)	77

93% correctly classified

APPENDIX 1

POLITICAL-DEMOGRAPHIC VARIABLES
Stepwise Discriminant Analysis

	Variable Description	Coefficients Rep. A/R	Coefficients Dem. C/K	Means A	Means R	Means C	Means K
1.	Education	.38	.48	4.05	3.32	3.96	3.84
2.	Occupation	−.13		6.37	5.76	5.59	5.84
3.	Age	−.25	.65	46.78	54.33	48.55	43.88
4.	Socioeconomic Status			3.38	3.44	3.26	3.24
5.	Party Affiliation	−.13	−.35	4.27	5.87	5.16	5.43
6.	Political Ideology	.81	−.69	2.16	1.36	2.00	2.21

	Analysis	Group Means A	Group Means R	Group Means C	Group Means K
A.	Anderson/Reagan	.69	−.93		
B.	Carter/Kennedy			.11	−.36

	Analysis	Eigen-value	Wilks Lambda	Chi-Squared	DF	Significance
A.	A/R	.65	.60	115.44	5	p < .00
B.	C/K	.04	.95	9.55	4	p < .04

APPENDIX 2

PSYCHOGRAPHIC VARIABLES
Stepwise Discriminant Analysis

Republicans

	Variable Description	Coefficients Anderson/Reagan	Means Anderson	Means Reagan
1.	Reduce inflation	.24	.79	.16
2.	Build up our military	−.12	.34	.87
3.	Reject Salt II	−.13	.24	.70
4.	Fight for ERA	.24	.83	.20
5.	Conservatives	−.34	.19	.95
6.	Rich people	−.19	.24	.73
7.	Independents	.12	.95	.54
8.	Students	.54	.91	.11
9.	Had no chance of winning rep. nom.	−.17	.21	.50

Group Means	
1.65	−2.23

Eigenvalue	Wilks Lambda	Chi-Squared	DF	Significance
3.74	.21	355.70	9	p < .00

Democrats

	Variable Description	Coefficients Carter/Kennedy	Means Carter	Means Kennedy
1.	Reinstate draft	−.38	.72	.10
2.	Build more nuc. plants	−.16	.67	.14
3.	Institute nat'l health program	.16	.44	.95
4.	Silent Majority	−.23	.80	.26
5.	Traditional democrats	−.18	.90	.51
6.	Chicago politicians	.26	.32	.83
7.	Students	.22	.28	.89
8.	Downstate voters	−.10	.71	.21
9.	Charismatic	.11	.30	.75
10.	Innovative in implementing policies	.16	.36	.85
11.	Able to get things done	.21	.49	.96
12.	I want change in present admn.	.64	.09	.92

Group Means	
−1.19	3.60

Eigenvalue	Wilks Lambda	Chi-Squared	DF	Significance
4.35	.18	370.87	12	p < .00

REFERENCES

Berelson, Bernard, Paul F. Lazarsfeld, and William N. McPhee (1954), Voting: A Study of Opinion Formation in a Presidential Campaign, Chicago: The University of Chicago Press, Chapters 10, 13.

Campbell, Angus, Gerald Gurin, and Warren E. Miller (1954), The Voter Decides, New York: Row, Peterson and Company.

Campbell, Angus et al. (1960), The American Voter, New York: John Wiley and Sons, Inc., Chapters 2, 4.

Crosby, Lawrence A., James D. Gill, and James R. Taylor (1981), "Consumer/voter Behavior in the Passage of the Michigan Container Law," Journal of Marketing, Vol. 45, 19-32.

Fishbein, Martin and Fred S. Coombs (1974), "Basis for Decision: An Analysis of Voting Behavior," Journal of Applied Social Psychology, Vol. 4, 95-124.

Lazarsfeld, Paul, Bernard Berelson, and Hazel Gaudet (1968), The Peoples Choice: How the Voter Makes Up His Mind in a Presidential Campaign, New York: Columbia University Press.

Newman, B. I. (1981), "The Explanation and Prediction of Voting Intentions and Actual Voting Behavior in a Presidential Primary Race," unpublished doctoral dissertation, University of Illinois.

Nygren, Thomas E. and Lawrence E. Jones (1977), "Individual Differences in Perceptions and Preferences for Political Candidates," Journal of Experimental Social Psychology, Vol. 13, 182-197.

Palda, Kristian S. (1973), "The Marketing of Political Candidates: An Econometric Exploration of Two Quebec Elections," in T. V. Greer, ed., American Marketing Association Combined Conference Proceedings, Chicago: American Marketing Association, 421-423.

_____________ (1980), "The Effect of Campaign Expenditures on Voting: Evidence from Canadian Provincial Elections," in American Marketing Association Combined Conference Proceedings, Chicago: American Marketing Association, 452-455.

Rothschild, Michael L. (1978), "Political Advertising: A Neglected Policy Issue in Marketing," Journal of Marketing Research, Vol. 15, 58-71.

Shama, Avraham (1974), "Political Marketing: A Study of Voter Decision-making Process and Candidate Marketing Strategy," in Proceedings of the AMA, 381-385.

Sherrod, Drury R. (1974), "Selective Perceptions of Political Candidates," Public Opinion Quarterly, Vol. 35, 554-562.

Sheth, Jagdish N. and Bruce I. Newman (1981), "Determinants of Intention-behavior Discrepancy in the 1980 National Elections," 1981 American Psychologial Association Meetings, Los Angeles: American Psychological Association.

Shikiar, Richard (1979), "The Perception of Politicians and Political Issues: A Multidimensional Scaling Approach," Multivariate Behavioral Research, 447-461.

BENEFIT SEGMENTATION STRATEGIES FOR THE PERFORMING ARTS

Margery Steinberg, University of Hartford, Hartford
George Miaoulis, University of Hartford, Hartford
David Lloyd, Boston University, Boston

ABSTRACT

The purpose of this paper is to demonstrate the linkage
between benefit-oriented market segmentation and the
development of marketing strategies for the performing
arts. Research performed in rural New Hampshire and
Dayton, Ohio provides the basis for identification of
seven benefit segments, as well as recommendations to
enhance the achievement of four main objectives of arts
organizations.

INTRODUCTION

In recent years the performing arts have been using
marketing research without receiving all of its potential
benefits. (Di Maggio, Useem, and Brown, 1977) This
paper will describe the application of benefit segmentation as a useful tool for 1) identifying markets and
2) designing marketing strategies consistent with the
goals of performing arts organizations.

Although the use of market research by performing arts
organizations has increased sharply in recent years,
many of the studies limit their definitions of arts
audiences to attendance patterns or demographic characteristics. Early work was done in a nation-wide performing arts study by Baumol and Bowen (1966), segmenting audiences at various types of performances by
attendance pattern. The next important piece of research,
Americans and the Arts (1975), used four performance
types as a basis for market segmentation. A study conducted by Nielson, McQueen and Nielson (1977) determined market segments based on experiential information
identifying segments by type of program. More recent
market research for the performing arts has studied
audiences according to their attendance patterns and
demographic characteristics (Semenik and Young, 1979;
Robbins and Robbins, 1979; Sexton and Britney, 1979).
Behavior patterns over time and at different stages of
arts subscription were utilized as a basis for segmentation by Ryans and Weinberg (1978). Miaoulis and
Lloyd (1979) and Nevin and Cavusgil (1981) combined
audience attendance factors with demographics in
categorically identifying market segments for the performing arts. Market segmentation research examining
consumer dynamics has been conducted by Andreasen and
Belk (1980) on life-style, attitudinal and experiential
variables, and by Bamossy and Semenik (1981) on tangible
and intangible motivators of art attendence.

Benefit segmentation, (Haley, 1968) an approach to
identifying markets based on similarities among consumers
with respect to purchase motives and preference patterns,
has potential as a tool for designing effective marketing strategies and positioning for artistic programs.
Combining a benefit-oriented analysis of segments with
demographic and utilization data can give the arts
administrator a more complete picture of target audiences
for understanding arts consumption behavior and making
artistic programming decisions. Laczniak and Murphy
(1977) suggest that artists often seek unquestioned
acceptance of their "new products" by audiences, but
fail to adequately consider the reasons why individuals
might attend their performances. Benefit segmentation
responds directly to the underlying purpose for conducting

marketing research, to assist the arts community in the
design and delivery of marketing programs which consider
the needs and wants of various groups, by identifying
benefits sought. (Miaoulis and Lloyd, 1979)

Consistent with the belief that arts organizations can
enhance the success of their program offerings and
marketing and promotion activities through an understanding of the benefits sought by arts attenders and
non-attenders alike, two contributions are made by this
paper. First, the study conducted provides a segmentation and analysis of actual and potential arts audiences
based on the benefits sought. Second, utilizing the
research conducted, recommendations are made which
illustrate the development of marketing strategies and
programming positions based on benefit segments. Application of this approach can assist arts administrators
in developing the marketing mix, and in more effectively
determining and achieving their marketing objectives.

BENEFIT SEGMENTATION RESEARCH

Research Methodology

The research process employed to identify benefit segments
paralleled the methodology developed by Haley (1968)
and extended by Miaoulis, Haley and Sims (1978). Four
hundred in-depth interviews were conducted with performing arts attenders and non-attenders (defined as during
a given one-year period), adult men and women, in the
Dayton, Ohio SMSA and the Monadnock Region of Southwestern New Hampshire. This sample design provided the
opportunity to identify the(leisure time-related)
benefits sought by a diverse actual and potential performing arts audience. (Estimation of segment size was
not a goal of this research effort.) The sample was
selected as follows:

TABLE 1

Sample Selection

	Dayton		Monadnock		Totals
	Men	Women	Men	Women	
Arts Attenders	47	53	46	54	200
Non-Attenders	48	52	47	53	200
Totals	95	105	93	107	400

The in-depth interviews, each approximately one-half hour
in length, were conducted over a one-month period by two
teams of marketing graduate students. The teams then met
with the authors employing a modified nominal group technique
(Claxton, Ritchie, Zaichkowsky, 1980) to identify benefit
segments. Seven benefit-oriented market segments were
identified: three segments among performing arts attenders and four among the non-attenders. The benefits sought
by each segment are summarized in Table 2. Tables 3 and
4 present a detailed accounting of both the benefits
sought and descriptive factors for each of the seven identified benefit segments.

TABLE 2

Seven Benefit Segments

          Segment Name   Benefits Sought

Arts Attenders

1. Cultural Aspirant   Cultural and intellectual
                              expansion

2. Temporary Diversionist   Passive entertainment-relax-
                              ation

3. Peak Aesthetic
   Experience   Emotional and intellectual
                              stimulation

Arts Non-Attenders

1. Security Seeker   Relaxation and peer approval

2. Hedonist   Action-oriented entertainment,
                              excitement

3. Pragmatist   Diversions with productivity
                              and excitement

4. Child-Oriented   Education and upward mobility
                              for children

Benefit Segments

Each individual segment is identified according to the
specific benefits sought by its members. The integrity of
each benefit segment is provided through the unique pattern
of benefits sought by each audience group, indicating
different motives, preferences and expectations. This,
in turn, provides the basis for differentiated marketing
strategies. The segmenting benefits provide the basis
for program positioning, and descriptive factors provide
the basis for consumer access.

The "Cultural Aspirant", Segment 1, represents the most
frequent arts attender, among the several attender segments.
Members seek intellectual expansion, are socially active,
are rather sophisticated in their interests, and are, in
the earlier stages of their professional careers. They
are "ladder climbers" and tend to view leisure time
activities as a way of further enhancing their social
and/or professional life. Members of this segment find
fulfillment of their needs in terms of reference group
acceptance. For example, they may select leisure time
activities according to such criteria as those which will
make them visible among selective groups or enable them
to make impressive cocktail party conversation. The
understanding of benefits sought can assist the arts administrator in responding appropriately to the under-·
lying reasons for this group's attendance patterns.

Although clearly separate from Segment 1, members of
Segment 3 exhibit some close similarities. Members of
the "Peak Aesthetic Experience" segment participate in
the arts for intellectual involvement and stimulation.
They are socially active, sophisticated and well-
educated, but unlike the other-directed "Cultural Aspirants", this segment is inner-directed and seeks
"serious" arts performances. Members seem to attend
programs almost exclusively for the merit of the performance rather than for an evening out. The research
conducted tends to suggest that members of Segment 3
receive a great deal of pleasure and personal satisfaction from being present at an outstanding arts performance, and exhibit strong feelings of agreement or
disagreement with the reviews of arts commentators.
For example, some may even fancy themselves as being
astute critics of the arts.

Identification of these two large groups of arts participants extends the research of Ryans and Weinberg
(1978) relating the benefits sought by arts subscribers
to component characteristics of the subscription itself (i.e.: price, priority seating and ease of ordering) through identification and analysis of the personal
motivations stimulating arts attendance.

Segment 2 of the arts attender category consists of
those seeking "Temporary Diversion". This group is
comprised of consumers with somewhat lower socioeconomic characteristics than the previous two segments,
yet is equally socially active in a different way from
the other two groups. Arts performances appear to be
viewed as an opportunity to relax among family and
friends, and seem to provide more intellectual stimulation than any of the other leisure time interests
identified by segment members. Consistent with seeking
the benefit of a pleasant, effortless, trouble-free
evening out, this group will respond well to convenience,
moderate pricing and entertaining programming. Of the
three arts attender segments revealed, this one seems
to offer the most growth potential. The concentration
of marketing resources, designing appropriate communications channels and careful programming, as recommended
by Laczniak and Murphy (1977), in the light of the
identified benefits sought, the "Temporary Diversion"
segment could become more frequent arts participants.

A question often raised by arts administrators is, "Can
we attract non-attenders?" Benefit segmentation provides
some guidance. From study findings, arts non-attenders
have been segmented into four groups. Most significant
for the question raised is Segment 4, those identified
as being centrally concerned with their children's
developmental processes, or, "Child-Oriented". Through
analysis of the benefits sought by this group, opportunities are suggested for converting this segment into
arts attenders. Segment members seek the benefit of
upward mobility and educational and social experiences
for their children. They tend to be moderately too
highly involved in activities outside of the home, and
have personality traits which include practicality and
a family-orientation. Study results indicate that many
activities which are educationally and/or socially beneficial to their children will be of interest to the
"Child-Oriented" segment. With this insight arts
administrators can begin to design benefit-oriented
strategies to transform members of this group into
arts attenders.

The remaining three non-attending segments, although
seeking diverse benefits from leisure time activities,
hold similar central beliefs about the arts; that arts
performances are designed for groups other than theirs,
for snobbish, sophisticated people. Non-attender
segments 1, 2 and 3 appear to seek weekend and holiday

TABLE 3

SEGMENTATION GRID FOR ARTS ATTENDERS

Name of the segment	Segment #1 Cultural Aspirants	Segment #2 Temporary Diversion	Segment #3 Peak Aesthetic Experience
Benefits sought	Enlightenment – Cultural Exposure Intellectual Expansion Identification with the "Cognoscenti".	Passive Entertainment- Relaxation Non-cognitive Diversion A Social Medium An evening out	Emotional and Intellectual involvement/stimulation. Professional excellence; creativity and beauty
Category Beliefs	Arts attendance helps provide the intellectual sophistication of the "cognoscenti" with whom I identify.	Arts performances should offer entertainment and diversion; a relaxing atmosphere while enjoying the company of friends and family.	Arts performances should offer a high level of artistic excellence, and permit complete emotional and intellectual involvement.
Preferred Leisure Activities	Reading, Crafts, Antiquing "Serious" arts performances felt to be attended by segment #3.	Dining out, movies; skiing, biking, sightseeing. Lighter arts performances	Crafts, sailing, reading, skiing, etc. "Professional" arts performances of particular merit.
Participation	Frequent	Infrequent to Moderate	Moderate to Frequent
Occasions of Participation	Evenings, weekends – whenever programs offered	Predominantly Weekends	Evenings, weekends – performances and activities of special interest
Media Habits	Printed Media: Local/National newspapers Posters, mailers, handbills.	Printed Media: Local newspapers, posters and handbills. Broadcast Media: Moderate T.V. and radio	Printed Media: Local/National newspapers Posters, mailers, handbills Broadcast Media: Light T.V. and radio
Personality/life Style	Other directed Impressionable	Other oriented and socially active	Sophisticated and well educated – Inner directed Socially active
Demographics	Age: Younger, 21-35 College education Beginning professional career	Age: 25-49 High School or some college education. Income: $10-15,000	Sophisticates of all ages College educated. Professional Income: $15,000 and over.

TABLE 4

SEGMENTATION GRID FOR ARTS NON-ATTENDERS

Name of the segment	Segment #1 Security Seeker	Segment #2 Hedonist	Segment #3 Pragmatist	Segment #4 Children-Oriented
Benefits sought	Relaxation. Security of family and friends Peer approval To feel at ease.	Entertainment Excitement Action	Convenience Diversion Feeling of productivity and involvement	Upward mobility for children; well-rounded education for children.
Category Beliefs	Arts are designed for more sophisticated group. Would feel insecure, uncomfortable and out of place.	Arts are too formal, serious and passive.	Arts are for snobbish, non-active people. Don't understand or relate to arts. Find them boring, uninteresting	Children should have the educational and social opportunities needed for a successful life.
Preferred Leisure Activities	Television, dining out, family outings. Peer and family – oriented activities	Hunting, fishing, Boating, sports, etc. Action-oriented activities	Gardening, hunting, woodworking, sewing Productive activities	Family activities: outings, camping, sports, etc. Scouting, school clubs encouraged.
Volume of Activity involvement	Low to moderate	High	Moderate to high	Moderate to high
Occasions of Leisure activity involvement	Weekends, holidays, vacations	Evenings, weekends, whenever possible.	Evenings, weekends, vacations	Encouraged to become involved frequently
Media Habits	Local newspapers Heavy radio and T.V.	Local/national newspapers. Moderate radio and T.V. Special interest mags. Posters	Local newspapers Low to moderate T.V. Special interest mags. Posters, mailers	Local newspapers Mailers Moderate radio and T.V.
Personality/life Style	Reticent, insecure, conforming. Oriented toward family and friends.	Outgoing, active; Fast-paced lifestyle	Practical, organized. Family and work – oriented.	Conservative, practical, hard-working. Family – oriented
Demographics	Age: 25-64; unskilled or semi-skilled. Educ.: High school or less Income: Below average	Age: 25-49; technician, white collar. or Educ. High school / college Income: Above average	Age: 35-64; tradesman Educ.: High school or technical school. Income: Above average	Age: 35-49; semi-skilled or clerical. Educ. High school Income: Average

entertainment, lead otherwise fairly sedetary lives, and are oriented toward family and friends. The benefit segmentation analysis suggests that arts administrators focus on those segments with the greatest response potential: "Temporary Diversionists" and "Child-Oriented". Efficient use of marketing resources would argue against attempting to convert arts non-attenders segments 1, 2 and 3 to arts attenders.

MARKETING STRATEGY IMPLICATIONS

The fundamental marketing goal of any arts organization is to make its offerings more responsive to the needs of the various publics it serves (Miaoulis and Lloyd, 1979). Benefit segmentation assists in developing fine-tuned strategies which relate the limited available marketing resources to potential audiences. Attendance patterns, subscription purchases and contribution behaviors can all be related to benefits sought (Ryans and Weinberg, 1978).

Four main objectives should be considered in the application of benefit segmentation to the development of marketing strategies for arts organizations. Table 5 identifies each of the objectives as it relates to the arts attenders and arts non-attenders segments. These objectives are:

1. To increase awareness of arts programs and the potential benefits they offer to the community.

2. To clarify misconceptions about the arts, particularly on the part of non-attenders, and induce trial attendance.

3. To increase overall attendance at arts programs.

4. To increase support of current funding sources and attract new contributors.

In order to achieve these objectives, arts administrators should approach the task with an understanding of the benefits people seek from participation in the arts. Arts organizations should seek to increase the variety of backgrounds represented in their audiences (Newmann 1977) in order to increase both the attendance at performances as well as the amount of dollars contributed. Research by Ryans and Weinberg (1978) indicates that arts supporters must become subscribers or frequent attenders before they will become contributors. Relating the seven benefit-oriented segments to the four main objectives cited (Table 5) leads to specific recommendations for strategy design in marketing the arts.

TABLE 5

Analysis of Benefit Segments and Arts Marketing Objectives

Benefit Segments	Arts Marketing Objectives			
	Increase awareness of arts programs & potential benefits offered	Clarify misconceptions about the arts & induce trial attendance	Increase attendance at arts programs	Increase support of current funding sources & attract new contributors
Arts Attenders				
1. Cultural Aspirant			L	H
2. Temporary Diversionist	M		H	
3. Peak Aesthetic Experience			H	H
Arts Non-Attenders				
1. Security Seeker	L*	L*	L*	
2. Hedonist	L*	L*	L*	
3. Pragmatist	L*	L*	L*	
4. Child-Oriented	H	H	H	

H = High Priority   M = Moderate Priority   L = Low Priority

* Limited resources will typically exclude these segments from being the target of aggressive marketing, hence, they are given a low priority in terms of marketing objectives.

Strategies to Increase Awareness

Benefit segmentation enhances the ability of arts administrators to achieve the first objective, increased awareness of arts programs. Our research points out that different benefit-oriented segments relate to the arts in different ways. For example, the benefits sought by the "Child-Oriented" segment make it the most likely target for achievement of this first objective. Information about leisure time activities is most often sought by this group in local newspapers. The "Child-Oriented" segment values the arts as part of the overall education of their children. This is not inconsistent with a family and outdoor orientation.

Combining knowledge of the benefits sought by the "Child-Oriented" segment with information about their beliefs, attitudes and values allows us to develop elements of the marketing mix. In particular, the product, promotion and place elements should be addressed. Artistic performances positioned to appeal to this segment should be family-oriented rather than heavily sophisticated in nature. Promotion in newspapers and direct mail, as well as some local radio and television advertising should portray the event as an enjoyable family activity as well as one which will enhance the personal growth of the children. The outdoor orientation of this segment can be addressed through creative programming. By bringing performances to the people in parks, community centers and other public areas, arts organizations can attract some reluctant non-attenders to a familiar environment.

Clarifying Misconceptions and Inducing Trial

Knowledge of the benefits sought can also assist in the achievement of the second objective - clarifying misconceptions about the arts. Analysis of the

"Security Seeker" segment can exemplify marketing
strategy development for this objective. The benefits
sought by this group are relaxation, security of family
and friends, and peer approval, yet its members view the
arts as being designed for other more sophisticated
people. Since, according to our research, this segment
seeks peer and family-oriented activities, marketing mix
elements should be designed to emphasize the low cost,
informal atmosphere, and family enjoyment, rather than
the high level and traditional intellectual appeal of
arts programs. The location of performances in less
formal atmospheres as well as low-risk invitation type
of advertisements can help allay the fears and misconceptions of the "Security Seeker". Once they try an
arts performance, members of this segment may realize the
benefits consistent with those they seek in leisure time
activities.

Strategies to Increase Attendance

An analysis of the benefits sought, particularly by arts
attenders, enhances opportunities for achieving the third
objective, increasing attendance at arts programs. The
"Temporary Diversion" segment, for example, seeks passive
entertainment, relaxation and a social evening out.
Marketing strategy design can respond to these identified
benefits sought by including elements such as offering
promotional packages for an "evening out" (dinner and
performance), selecting "hassle-free" locations with
easy access and ample parking, and making available
season subscription discounts. Direct mail brochures
and letters should address the broader appeal of diversion and social benefits sought as well as the traditionally used cultural and intellectual focus on the
product - the arts performance.

Increasing Funding Support

Although not central to the primary focus of this research,
the fourth objective, that of enhancing funding sources,
is a logical extension of the overall benefit segmentation strategy design. Appeals based on identified
benefits sought can make fund-raising programs more
attractive to specific target groups. For example,
"Cultural Aspirants" seek enlightenment, intellectual
expansion and identification with the "cognoscenti". Our
research points out that this group is interested in
serious arts performances, and is also characteristically
other-directed, impressionable, and socially active.
"Cultural Aspirants" can be the target of active campaigns for funds as well as for fund-raising assistance
through their employers by appealing to the contributors' interest in enhancing the quality of arts
programs.

CONCLUSION

The marketing concept suggests that the arts, as with
any other product or service, must be responsive to the
needs and wants of its target customers. The application of benefit segmentation analysis to marketing
strategy development is an effective means for guiding
responsive efforts on the part of arts administrators.
Benefit segmentation provides a basis for motivational
assessment of the behavioral patterns of arts attender
categories, and also provides similar insights into the
relevant behavioral patterns of non-attenders. Further
examination of the arts attender and non-attender
segments offers arts administrators useful descriptive
information, such as demographics, usage patterns and
media habits upon which to build effective marketing
communications programs. More importantly, benefit
segmentation contributes to effective targeting and
differentiation in the development of marketing strategy
and programming positions.

REFERENCES

Andreason, Alan R. and Belk, Russell W. (1980),
  "Predictors of Attendance at the Performing Arts,"
  Journal of Consumer Research, September 1980.

Bamossey, Gary and Semenik, Richard J. (1981), "Tangible
  and Intangible Motivators of Performing Arts Patronage,"
  AMA Educators Conference Proceedings.

Baumol, William J., and Bowen, William G. (1966),
  Performing Arts -- The Economic Dilemma, New York:
  Twentieth Century Fund.

Claxton, John D., Ritchie, J.R. Brent and Zaichkowsky,
  Judy (1980), "The Nominal Group Technique: Its
  Potential for Consumer Research," Journal of Consumer
  Research, December 1980.

DiMaggio, Paul, Useem, Michael and Brown, Paul (1978),
  Audience Studies of the Performing Arts and Museums:
  A Critical Review, Washington, D.C.: National
  Endowment for the Arts.

Haley, Russell I. (1968), "Benefit Segmentation: A
  Decision-Oriented Research Tool," Journal of Marketing, July 1968.

Laczniak, Gene R., and Murphy, Patrick E. (1977),
  "Marketing the Performing Arts," Atlantic Economic
  Review, November-December 1977.

Miaoulis, George and Lloyd, David (1979), Marketing the
  Arts in a Rural Environment, Wright State University,
  1979.

__________, Haley, Russell I., and Sims, J. Taylor
  (1978), "An Experimental Exercise in Product Benefit
  Segmentation," Proceedings of the Association of
  Business Simulation and Experiential Learning. (April)

National Research Center for the Arts, Inc. and
  Associated Councils of the Arts (1975), Americans and
  the Arts: A Survey of Public Opinion, New York:
  American Council for the Arts.

Nielsen, Richard P., McQueen, Charles and Nielsen,
  Angela B. (1977), "Performing Arts Audience Segments,"
  Marketing Update, Berkman, Fenyo, Hertz, Ryans, eds.,
  Dubuque, IA: Kendall/Hunt Publishing Company.

Nevin, John R., and Cavusgil, S. Tamer (1981),
  "Audience Segments for the Performing Arts," AMA
  Services Marketing Conference Proceedings, 1981.

Newmann, Danny, Subscribe Now! (1977), Theatre Com-
  Munications Group, Inc., 1977.

Robbins, John E., and Robbins, Stephanie S. (1979),
  "Segmentation for 'Fine Arts' Marketing: Is King
  Tut Classless As Well As Ageless?" AMA Educators
  Conference Proceedings.

Ryans, Adrian B. and Weinberg, Charles (1978), "Consumer
  Dynamics in Nonprofit Organizations," Journal of
  Consumer Research, September 1978.

Semenik, Richard J. and Young, Clifford E. (1979),
  "Market Segmentation in Arts Organizations," AMA
  Educators Conference Proceedings.

Sexton, Donald E. and Britney, Kathryn (1979), "A
  Behavioral Segmentation of the Arts Market," Advances
  in Consumer Research, VII.

EXPLORING INDUSTRIAL EXPORT STRATEGIES

Kjell Grønhaug, The Norwegian School of Economics and Business Administration
Tore Lorentzen, The Norwegian Fund for Market and Distribution Research

ABSTRACT

The present paper forcuses on export strategies among a
sample of 40 Norwegian industrial firms. As hypothesized
positive overlaps were observed between organizational
size and internal organization of export activities; between organizational resources and the application of resource requiring export strategies; and between relative
importance of exports and resources devoted to such activities and the export strategies applied. The majority of
the exporting firms were found to concentrate most of
their exports to a limited number of markets - in most
cases organized through sole importeres - making them
vulnerable to external changes.

INTRODUCTION

Exports are considered important by most countries facing
open economies, foreign competition and international division of labor. This is reflected in an increasing literature on exports and international marketing, in governmental involvement, and through various activites conducted
by the exporting firms (cf. Cavusgil & Nevin 1981, Grønhaug
& Lorentzen 1982, McGuinness & Little 1981, Piercy 1981).

From the literature on internationalization of firms and
international marketing the reader is often left with the
impression that export is the domain of the large, successful industrial companies only, which partly is due to the
focus on this subset of firms in earlier research (cf.
Carlson 1979; Kindleberger 1969). However, also to small
and medium-sized industrial firms export may be important
(cf. Hackett 1979). In Norway for instance, 26% of all
industrial firms had at least some export in 1978. The
industry in this country is characterized by a very large
fraction of small firms. The fact that almost 80% of the
exporting firms has less than 100 employees, demonstrates
that small - as well as large and medium - sized firms -
are confronted with export decisions. Due to the importance
of small firms in this economy, and the usually assumed
relationships between organizational size and resources (cf.
Needham 1978), and between resources and strategy (cf.
Pfeffer & Salancik 1978; Porter 1980), the impact of resources on the firm's export strategy is of particular
interest in the present case.

THEORETICAL FRAMEWORK

Organizations may be viewed as open systems continuously
interacting with their unstable environments (cf. Katz &
Kahn 1980). In order to survive the organizational output
must be exchanged to get input for continued survival (cf.
Thompson 1967). Business firms may be viewed as a subset
of organizations, characterized by great dependence on the
market. In order to export the firm has to establish exchange relationships _outside_ the domestic market. Viewed
in an exchange perspective export requires:

- _identification_ of exchange partners;

- _establishment_ of, and

- _maintaining_ exchange relationships.

A variety of activities such as market research, product
development, sales visits abroad, advertising, participation in exhibitions and symposiums etc. may be conducted
to establish and maintain such exchange relationships. Such
activities are goal directed and require resources to
be performed. Figure 1 shows the conceptual framework
underlying the present piece of research.

FIGURE 1

Conceptual framework

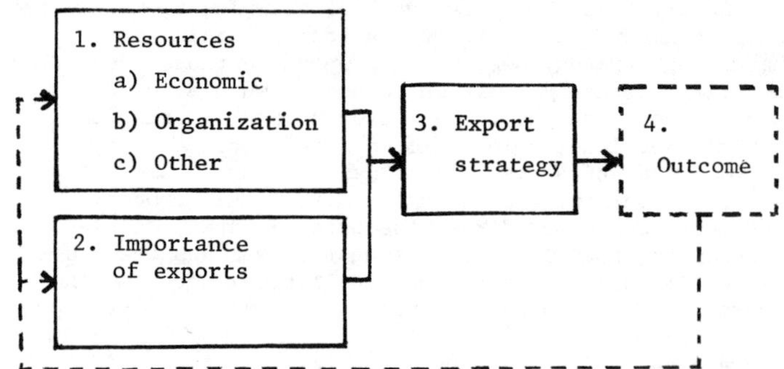

The firm possesses certain _resources_ (cf. box 1) necessary
to run the day to day operations. As noted by Pfeffer &
Salancik (1978) the activities of the firm are directed towards acquiring and maintaining resources. From the firm's
point of view exports may thus be seen as activities conducted in order to survice and strengthen its competitive
basis. Resources may be grouped in various ways. Here a
distinction has been made between economic resources,
organizational, and "other" resources. Economic (as well as
other) resources are needed to overcome certain _barriers_.
More specifically, the exporting firm may be confronted
with economic barriers imposed by new or modified products,
by the establishment of a new sales force etc. necessary to
enter a new market and/or to maintain such relations.

Also the internal _organization_ may be considered as an
important resource. The way the export marketing activities is organized may definitely influence the outcome of
such activities, and thus the ability of the firm to acquire and maintain resources.

The _importance of exports_ (cf. box 2) may vary across
firms. The resource base and the importance of exports may
exert influence on the internal organization of the export
activities (cf. box 1), as well as on the _export strate-
gies_ applied (cf. box 3), and on the outcome of the export
activities (cf. box 4).

The feedback-lines indicate that the outcome of the export
activities may influence the resource base, importance of
export, and choice of export strategies. Here the focus
will be on boxes 1-3, and their direct relationships (from
left to right).

H 1: The larger the organization the more people involved
     in exports (H 1a); and the larger the organization,
     the higher the degree of labor specialization, and
     thus, the higher the probability of having a separate
     export department (H 1b).

     The first part of the hypothesis (H 1a) implies noth-
     ing else than large compared to small firms are higher
     in exports, and thus, more people are assigned to
     export activities in such firms. The second part of
     the hypothesis (H 1b) implies both increasing degree
     of labor specialization, and more specialized depart-
     ments with organizational size.

H 2: The higher the firm is in resources, the higher the
     probability of applying resource requiring strategies.

     Export activities require resources. The various ac-
     tivities, do not, however, require the same type and
     amount of resources. Here it is assumed that firms
     high in resources more than firms low in resources
     are able to apply resource requiring strategies.
     Cavusgil & Nevin (1981) reported positive overlaps
     between "resources" (as measured in terms of techn-
     ology intensiveness and sales) and export marketing
     behavior, which are in concordance with the stated
     hypothesis.

H 3: Positive overlap is assumed between relative impor-
     tance of export and the fraction of resources directed
     towards export activities.

     The internal resources are scarce, and intuitively the
     fraction of resources devoted to a specific task will
     covary with the importance of this task. Observations
     regarding export-behavior and internationalization of
     firms as reported by Carlson (1979), Kindlerberger
     (1969), Johansen & Vahlne (1971), and Welch & Wieders-
     heim - Paul (1980), support the proposed hypothesis.

METHODOLOGY

Data from a research project conducted in order to evaluate
the impact of governmental export subsidies were used to
explore the indicative hypotheses raised above.

Sample

The present piece of research is based on cross-sectional
data gathered among a sample of 40 Norwegian industrial
firms. The sampling prosedure was as follows: In 1978 4.8%
of all Norwegian industrial firms applied for governmental
export subsidies. A stratified sample of 44 firms were
drawn among these firms. Data were obtained from 40 of the
44 firms. The remaining four firms did not receive export
subsidies, and these firms were not contacted due to the
prime purpose of the research project.

Data

A questionnaire adressing various questions related to products, markets, sales costs and export activities performed,
was mailed to the firms. In addition long, semi-structured
interviews were conducted with top management in each firm
emphasizing the export behavior and - strategy followed by
the firms studied.

Measurement

The operational definitions of the basic variables are reported below:

Economic resources: measured in terms of sales and number
of employees. These measures may be questioned due to the
global character of the size concept (cf. Kimberly 1976
for thorough discussion). However, these were the most
relevant resource indicators available in the data-base
applied. A very high correlation between the two indicators
was observed (r = .97, p <.001).

Internal organization of exports was mapped by the following indicators:

-   Whether or not the firm had an export department
    (1 = yes, 0 = no).

-   Number of persons assigned to export activities
    (0, 1, ...).

-   The involvement of top-management in the export
    activities, as measured by mapping the time used
    for such activities (% of working hours per week).

Importance of exports was measured as exports in percentage
of total sales.

Export strategy was mapped by the following indicators:

-   Number of foreign countries the firm is
    exporting to (1, 2,...).

-   The most important foreign market (i.e. country)
    for the firm (share of exports).

-   Channel of distributions for the most important
    export market (i.e. sole importer, wholesalers/
    retailers, own distribution office).

Number of foreign countries entered indicate division of
market risk and degree of country specialization. The most
important foreign market is useful in order to map geographical and cultural distance from the domestic market.
The third indicator, i.e. channel of distribution indicates
linkage to foreign markets and commitment to exports.

FINDINGS

The main findings are reported below:

The indicators

Table 1 reports means and ranges (in paranthesis) for the
various interval- and ratio-scaled and percentages for the
nominal-scaled indicators applied.

TABLE 1

The indicators - means/ranges and percentages

1.	Sales (mill \$)[1] -	16,9 (144)
2.	Employment (no. of persons)	330.2 (3.496)
3.	Export department: yes / no	48% / 52%
4.	No. of people assigned to exports	3,5 (9,0)

(cont.)

5.	Top-mgmt. involvement (% of working hours)	35% (98%)
6.	Importance of exports	40% (96%)
7.	No. of foreign markets entered (average)	5,7 (7,0)
8.	Most important market: Scandinavia Europe outsides other countries	58% 30% 12%
9.	Channnel of distribution: sole importer wholesaler/retailer own distr. other arrangements	60% 10% 12% 18%

(n = 40)

The ranges for size and employment, i.e. the economic indicators reflect great variations, indicating that large as well as small firms may act as exporters. 48% of the firms studied had a separate <u>export department</u>. Great variations were observed for the <u>number of people</u> assigned to the export activities. It should also be noted that 42% of the firms studied had <u>no</u> full-time personel assigned to such activities. These findings clearly indicate that the resources devoted to exports may vary across firms. Exports seem to be a <u>top-management</u> task in the firms studied. However, as seen from Table 1, the time devoted to exports varies considerably across the firms studied.

The mean value for the <u>importance</u> measure indicates that exports generally are highly important for the firms. The range, however, clearly reflects great variations in the relative importance of exports for the firms studied.

The data on <u>export strategies</u> are interesting in several ways. As noted from Table 1 the mean <u>number of foreign markets</u> (countries) is 5.7. Two of the firms marketed their products to nine (or more) countries, while three of the firms involved in the study restricted their export activities to three or fewer foreign markets.

An interesting observation is that 58% of the firms reported another <u>Scandinavian</u> country to be their most important foreign market. This finding reflects that the search for new markets takes place <u>close</u> to the home market.

The fact that 60% of the firms, in the sample, are connected to their most important foreign market by <u>sole importers</u> is striking. This finding combined with the modest number of foreign markets entered indicate high <u>dependence</u> as well as high <u>risk</u> for reductions in the export operations.

---

1   Sales were reported in N kr. Here the currency rate 1$ = 6 N kr has been applied.

Below are shown the correlation matrix for the interval- and ratio-scaled variables reported in Table 1.

TABLE 2

Bivariate results(r)

	(1)	(2)	(3)	(4)	(5)	(6)	(7)
1. Sales	X	.97[a]	.24[c]	.54[a]	.07	-.01	.05
2. Employment		X	.29[b]	.58[a]	.04	.15	.15
3. Exp. department			X	.29[b]	.13	.16	.39[a]
4. No. of people ass. to exports				X	-.17	.31[b]	.61[a]
5. Top-mgmt. involvement					X	.56[a]	.16
6. Importance of exports						X	.53[a]
7. No. of foreign markets							X

a) $p < .01$, b) $p < .05$, c) $p < .10$.

The numbers on the top of the correlation matrix correspond to the variables listed at the left hand side.

<u>H 1</u>: Table 2 contains three indicators related to the internal organization of exports, i.e. (3) – export department (4) – number of people assigned to export activities, and (5) – top-management involvement. Significant positive overlaps are observed between the two size-indicators, and number of people preoccupied with export (r = .54, p <.01 and r = .58, p < .01), and the existence of an export department (r =.24, p < .10 and r =.29, p <05). These observations are in concordance with our initial hypotheses H 1a–H 1b.

<u>H 2</u>: No significant correlations are observed between the two size indicators and the strategy indicator, – number of foreign markets (r = .05, n.s.; r = .15, n.s.). In other words, the assumed overlap between resources (economic) and export activities is not supported by the findings (cf. H2).

However, when inspecting the relationship between internal organization of exports and number of foreign markets, the following is found: Positive significant overlap between number of foreign markets and the existence of an export department (r = .39, p < .01), and strong positive overlap between number of foreign markets and number of people involved in exports (r = .61, p <.01). In considering the existence of an export department and number of people involved in exports, these findings may be interpreted as being in concordance with the stated resource-hypothesis (H 2).

<u>H 3</u>: When looking at the correlations between importance and internal organization of exports, the following is observed. A significant positive overlap between importance of exports and number of people involved (r = .31, p <.05). There is also a strong positive correlation between importance and top-management involvement (r = .56, p <.01), which is in accordance with our initial stated hypotheses H 3. In assuming positive overlap between resources devoted to exports and number of markets entered, the positive correlation between importance and strategy, i.e. number of foreign markets (r = .53, p <.01) may also be interpreted as being in concordance with the stated hypothesis.

Closer inspection of Table 2 reveals that there is <u>no</u> significant overlap between size and importance of exports (r = 1-.01, n.s. and r = .15, n.s.), indicating – as

stressed previously – that exports may be of importance
to small as well as to large firms.

In order to get a better perspective on the bivariate results presented above, the following display may be useful:

FIGURE 2

Display of bivariate results

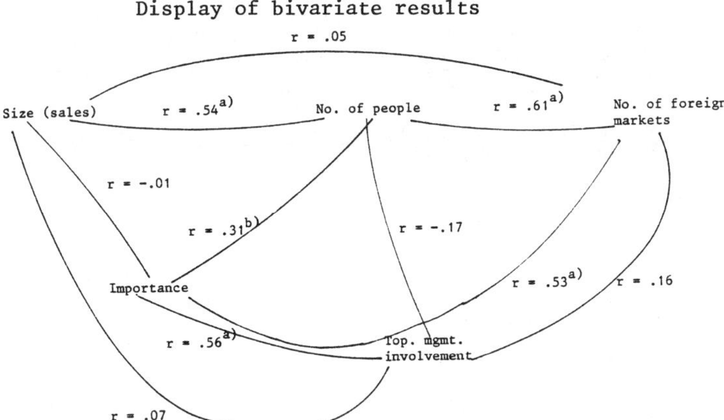

It should be stressed that Figure 2 displays the bivariate
correlation coefficients (and not the path-coefficients).
Only one size indicator (sales) is presented in Figure 2.
The export-department indicator has also been left out in
order to ease the presentation.

Figure 2 reveals some very interesting patterns. Size as
such seems to have <u>no</u> direct impact on the choice of export
strategy, i.e., on the number of foreign markets entered,
but does exert influence on the people involved in exports.
As seen from Figure 2 also a strong positive correlation
between number of people involved in exports and number
of foreign markets is observed ($r = .61$, $p < .01$).

When calculating the partial correlation between people
involved and number of markets controlling for size, the
following is found:

$$r_{PM.S} = .67 (p<.01);$$

where P = people, M = markets, S = size. This high degree
of overlap may be interpreted in the following way: A minimum level of manpower is required to serve a new export
market, and as new markets are entered new people are hired.
The modest number of people assigned to exports (cf. Table
1) do also indicate that manpower/market-ratio is low.

Possible interpretations of this high degree of overlap
may be that new people are assigned to new markets, and/or
a minimum level of manpower is required to serve a new
market, and that this minimum is kept low (cf. the modest
number of people assigned to export activities).

The high positive correlation between importance and top
management involvement is also noteworthy ($r = .56$, $p <
.01$). An intuitive interpretation is that the top-manage-
ment allocates its attention and time to the tasks perceived to be the most important to the firm. When calculating the partial correlation between top management involvement and number of people involved in exports controlling for importance, a strong negative correlation is
observed,

$$r_{TP.I} = -.47 (p <.01)$$

(where T = top mgmt., P = people involved, I = importance),
indicating that when exports are important to the firm lack
of collaborators within the firm has to be substituted with
top management involvement.

As demonstrated above high correlations are observed between some of the indicators applied in this study. Focusing
on top-management involvement (i.e., using this indicator
as the dependant variable), when running a multiple regression analysis, importance was found to be the most powerful
variable. Together with size, number of foreign markets and
export department, importance counted for 38% of the explained variance of top-management involvement ($R^2 = .38$,
$p < .01$). Due to multicollinearity the regression coefficients should be interpreted with care (and thus are not
shown here).

When running an additional multiple regression analysis,
importance of export was found to be the most powerful
variable in explaining number of foreign markets. Together
with size, export department and top management involvement, this variable explained 23% of the variance ($R^2 =
.23, .01$).

CONCLUSIONS AND IMPLICATIONS

The results presented above are interesting in several
ways. First, the hypothesized relationships were supported,
indicating that this type of theory (cf. the discussion of
hypotheses) possesses descriptive and predictive power. It
has also been demonstrated that several of the results are
in concordance with observations made in other cultures
(cf. the studies quoted in the hypotheses-section), indicating that previous studies possess external validity and
to some extent can be generalized.

Some of the findings ought also to be discusses in some
detail:

(1) It has been clearly demonstrated in the present study,
     that exports may be of crucial importance both to
     small and large firms as stressed by some authors (cf.
     Hackett 1979) contrary to the impression conveyed in
     much of the previous literature (cf. Carlson 1979;
     Kindelberger 1969).

(2) Other Scandinavian countries were found to represent
     the most important market for 58% of the firms in-
     volved in the study. This finding is definitely in
     concordance with the commonly held assumption of a
     gradual internationalization process, starting with
     modest pre-export activities and export activities
     directed towards foreign countries close to the
     domestic market (cf. Johanson & Vahlne 1977; Cavusgil
     1980; Czinkota & Johnston 1981). At a more general
     level this observation does also coincide with the
     search theory as proposed by Cyert & March (1963),
     i.e. search for new alternatives starts in the
     immediate surroundings of the present ones.

(3) The relative few foreign markets entered combined
     with the frequent dependence on only one importer,
     definitely indicate that the exporting firm may be
     <u>vulnerable</u> to various external threats. This is also
     reflected in the following observation: In comparing
     export sales for the preceeding and the present year,
     43% of the firms studied reported an increase and
     30% an decrease in exports. Such observations are in
     concordance with previous findings as reported by
     Welch & Wiedersheim – Paul (1980).

(4) The relatively modest fraction of internal resources
     devoted to exports (cf. number of people assigned)
     in spite of the importance of this activity (cf. Table
     1), may indicate that resource allocation to exports

297

is inappropriate, which may be due unclear and biased
mapping of the relationship between marketing and outcomes
of such activities.[2]

(5) The modest ratio for number of people assigned/no. of
     markets does also indicate that foreign markets in
     most cases only are extensively exploited. This
     may be relevant in som cases, but not always. Where
     entrance of new markets requires recognition, demon-
     stration of resources and commitment (which often
     will be the case), the extensive exploitation -
     strategy should be questionned.

(6) From the firm's point of view the findings reported
     call for a more serious and professional treatment
     of the export-activities. Increased attention to
     export marketing, better education, may in turn lead
     to more appropriate resource allocation and improved
     export-marketing.

(7) The high fraction of small exporting firms should
     also be noted. For one thing the "myth of the large
     exporting firm" need to be corrected. Small firms
     are lower in economic resources and knowledge, which
     is of crucial importance to become successful ex-
     porters (cf. Johansen & Vahlne 1977). Thus increased
     attention by educational institutions to export
     education is needed. Attention should also be paid
     to how to increase co-operations between exporting
     firms and how to improve the governmental export
     policies (cf. Grønhaug & Lorentzen 1982).[3]

REFERENCES

Carlson, S. (1979), Swedish Industry Goes Abroad, Lund,
     Studentlitteratur.

Cavusgil, S.T. (1980), "On the Internationalization Pro-
     cess of Firms", European Research, Vol 8, No 6,
     (November), 273-281.

___________, & Nevin, J.R. (1981), "Internal Determinants
     of Export Marketing Behavior: An Emperical Investi-
     gation", Journal of Marketing Research, Vol. XVIII,
     (February), 114-119.

Cyert, R.M. & March, J.G. (1963), A Behavioral Theory of
     The Firm, N.J., Prentice-Hall.

Czinkota, M.R. & Johnston, W.J. (1981), "Segmenting U.S.
     Firms for Export Development", Journal of Business
     Research, Vol. 9, No 4, (December), 353-365.

Grønhaug, K. & Lorentzen, T. (1982), "Exploring the Impact
     of Governmental Export Subsidies", European Journal
     of Marketing, (forthcoming).

Hackett, D.W. (1979), "Penetrating International Markets:
     Key Considerations for Smaller Firms", in H.W. Beck-
     man & I.R. Vernon (eds.), Contemporary Perspectives
     in International Business, Chicago, Rand McNally.

Johansen, J. & Vahlne, J. (1977), "The Internationaliza-
     tion Process of the Firm: A Model of Knowledge
     Development and Increasing Foreign Commitments",
     Journal of International Business Studies, Spring/
     Summer, 23-32.

Katz, E. & Kahn, R.K. (1980), The Social Psychology of
     Organizations, N.Y., John Wiley & Sons. (2nd. ed.)

Kimberly, J.R. (1976), "Organizational Size and the
     Structuralist Perspective: A Review, Critique, and
     Proposal", Adm. Science Quarterly, Vol. 21,
     (December), 571-604.

Kindleberger, C. (1969), American Business Abroad, New
     Haven, Yale University Press.

Lave, C.A. & March, J.G. (1975), An Introduction to models
     in the Social Sciences, New York, Harper & Row.

McGuinness, N.W. & Little, B. (1981), "The Influence of
     Product Characteristics on the Export Performance of
     New Industrial Products", Journal of Marketing,
     Vol. 45, No 2, (Spring), 110-122.

Needham, D. (1978), The Economics of Industrial Structure
     Conduct and performance, London, Holt, Reinehart and
     Winston.

NOU (1978), Eksportfremmende tiltak, NOU 1978:53, Oslo,
     Universitetsforlaget.

Pfeffer, J. & Salancik, G.R. (1978), The External Control
     of Organizations, N.Y., Harper & Row.

Piercy, N. (1981), "How Some Industrial Firms Select
     Foreign Markets and Set Export Prices", Industrial
     Marketing Management, Vol. 10, (October), 287-297.

Porter, M.E. (1980), Competitive Strategy, New York,
     The Free Press.

Thompson, J.D. (1967), Organizations in Action, N.Y.,
     McGraw-Hill.

Welch, L.S. & Widersheim-Paul, F. (1980), "Initial
     Exports - A Marketing Failure", Journal of Management
     Studies, vol 17, No 3, (October), 333-344.

____

2   For a thorough and interesting discussion of biased
     "models of the world" see Lave & March (1975).

3   Such questions have recently been raised by several
     countries depending extensively on exports, also in
     the country where this piece of research was con-
     ducted (cf. NOU 1978).

COMMERCIALLY SUCCESSFUL PROJECT UNSHELVINGS AMONG
INDUSTRIAL FIRMS

Timothy L. Wilson, Indiana University of Pennsylvania
James D. Hlavacek, Case Western Reserve University

ABSTRACT

A study has been made of projects that produced commercially successful products after a enforced lapse, or
period of inactivity, on the project. A survey of 216
research directors participating in nine industries
indicated project unshelving is a recognizable activity
and five distinct patterns could be accessed from the
responses. These patterns were associated with (1)
changes in perceived payoffs, (2) real shifts in basic
demand, technology, economics or politics, (3) evolution
of licensing opportunities, (4) appearance of a project
champion, or (5) customer mandated shelving. The decision
to unshelve projects is apparently complex and many factors affect this decision. Changes in marketing factors
appeared to be most important in the decision to unshelve
projects, followed by technology/technical factors and
management vision. Lapses in activity were relatively
long; the average was about 5 years, although peak activity in unshelving occurred in the 2-3 year period
after shelving.

INTRODUCTION

Only infrequently does progress on projects proceed as
planned. Success is not assured, not only because of
human failings, but because of the unpredictable state of
the marketing environment. Marketers recognize this situation and thus recognize that new product development is
inherently a risky business. Despite precautions taken,
many ideas and much effort go into the production mill for
each successful new product launched (Booz, Allen and
Hamilton, 1968). Among practitioners, it is common to
talk about reaching a stage where a project is "shelved".
That is, a stalemate in progress is reached. There is
neither adequate incentive nor sufficient progress to warrant proceeding with the project and it is therefore effectively terminated. Reekie, for instance, (1970) published an account of 53 new product developments that were
shelved for nontechnical reasons. Likewise Myers and
Sweezy in their study of 200 unsuccessful projects used
shelving as one of three categories to describe projects
stoppage -- there was no ongoing activity on the project,
but neither could the project be considered terminated
(1970). The firm was still interested in the project,
but only if it could be determined that further work would
lead to a commercial success.

Attention was attracted to these projects during a review
of literature concerned with project initiation. That
is, despite the number of projects that must be sitting
"on the shelf", no references were found that directly
dealt with unshelving projects. Further, discussions with
knowledgeable colleagues produced no references that suggested this approach to initiating successful innovations.
Surely, this was an oversight. Unshelvings do occur. In
the Reekie study referred to previously, six projects (11%)
were successfully unshelved within the brief two years that
he was conducting his study.

Exploratory research was thus initiated to determine patterns of occurrence in commercially successful, unshelved
projects. This research was initiated because it was
felt
- project unshelving certainly has been overlooked
  in project management.
- project unshelving is probably overlooked within
  the firm as a source of successful projects.
- project unshelving may be important in successfully
  growing a business from internal sources.

As a consequence of the exploratory research essentials
were determined concerning the process of unshelving projects. Insight was gained into how the process occurs in
the firm, especially the organizational features that seem
important. More was learned about why unshelving occurs,
i.e., the factors that contribute to a situation conducive
for unshelving (Wilson, 1981, Wilson and Hlavacek, 1982).
Little was learned, however, about the frequency with
which unshelving occurred or the breadth of practice across
industry. This validation study was thus undertaken to
investigate the generality of the practice. The results
should be important to marketers because of the appreciation the study lends to understanding the complexity of
the product development process and the role these projects
have in internally growing businesses.

PROCEDURE

The exploratory phase of this research placed it in a position in which modelers frequently find themselves. A model
had been developed which described project unshelving in
business development. Of concern were the model's applicability, meaning and generality. Naylor has suggested that
strict validity is impossible to demonstrate in this situation (1971). A degree of confirmation is possible, however, if the model appears rational, is based on facts and
is capable of positive predictions. This approach has been
used to evaluate computer simulations by a form of a
"Turing Test" as discussed by Van Horn (1969). In this
approach, unidentified results are exposed to experts in a
field and their reactions are queried. Positive responses
indicate a degree of generality of the model. As a second
step in this approach, comments and criticisms from the
panel of experts are used to make the model more realistic.
Although this process is most frequently used with numerical simulations, its applicability is not limited to computer output. In fact, it has been suggested that this
confirmation process should find greater applicability
(Naylor and Finger, 1971).

This confirmation procedure was adapted to the present study
in the following manner. A composite case was compiled and
a brief description was written covering its essential
features. The essential features, of course, were project
initiation, activity prior to shelving, time on the shelf,
the unshelving, and project success. This description was
progressively distilled until it could be written on one
page in neutral terms. The intent was to capture the

essence of the exploratory results without biasing the description toward any particular case or groups of cases. This description included the phases found in the exploratory research, and the case, as presented, is shown in Table I.

Table I - Case Description Used in Validation Study

Case Description

To respond to our study, we ask that you read the following case and refer to it as you answer inquiries on the enclosed questionnaire. The case is a composite description of shelving and unshelving resulting from a series of hypotheses that were made. This proportion of your response will permit us to validate our results and add conceptual depth to our understanding. In particular, we are interested in refinements, improvements and additions that you might add from your experience.

Project Generation and Early Effort

A staff member at company A had an idea that, if pursued, could bring benefit to the company. The more he thought about it, the better the idea seemed. He did some preliminary work on the idea that served to substantiate his feelings. He presented the results to his immediate supervisor and after some further work, the supervisor also became a supporter of the idea. Subsequently, other groups in the company were informed of the project. Work spread in the organization, and progress continued.

Project Termination

One day the unexpected occurred. A barrier to commercialization was discovered by one of the cooperating groups. At first, attempts were made to surmount the hurdle. The project was given even higher priority and work became more intense. The barrier was a legitimate one, however, and there was eventual agreement that the project could not be successful. Work on the project was thus terminated and effort of the groups involved was redirected.

Period of Inactivity

Life at company A continued. Personnel were reassigned to other projects and became engrossed in other work. Ongoing activity continued as usual and the project was almost forgotten.

Unshelving the Project

As sometimes occurs, the barrier to commercialization of the original idea disappeared. This fact was recognized and it appeared that it would be possible to commercialize the project. There was some skepticism, but preliminary studies removed these hurdles. Work was therefore reinitiated, and this time the project was successful.

Please go to page one of the questionnaire.

A questionnaire was developed to accompany the case description. The questionnaire contained four questions designed to confirm aspects of both the face and external validity of the original research. The first question was open ended and probed the applicability of the model to general observations. This question was in accord with the general procedure described by Van Horn. Its intent was to not only provide respondents with the opportunity to signal general recognition of unshelving, but also to add their personal modifications to the model. The second question dealt with specific findings of the exploratory research;respondents were asked to pick a case and relate to us its gap time and the factors important in unshelving the project. The "factors" were arranged in categories

consistent with the Reekie, Myers and Sweezy, and the original study. Importance was determined by ranking on a five-point Likert scale. The assumption was made that these results would be in accord with the exploratory findings, and thus the model would have some generality. The question also required that respondent to be specific about the general case and therefore could help in gaining response to question 1. The third question asked the nature and size of the business; the intent of adding this question was to demonstrate generality beyond the original 20 firms in three business areas in the exploratory research. The listing used in the questionnaire was an adaptation of the listing used in Business Week quarterly financial reports. The fourth question was an open ended question that encouraged the respondent to comment generally on project unshelving and their knowledge of factors contributing to unshelving.

A cover letter explained the intent of the research, gave a preliminary definition of unshelving, indicated how the respondent had been selected, and requested a response. It also requested, in the event that the addressee felt disinclined to respond, that the letter be forwarded in the organization. A telephone number was included in the event the respondent had questions. This package, in a preliminary form, was tested on executives of four Fortune 500 companies before being sent to the survey sample. Comments from this preliminary test were incorporated in the final instruments.

A research design was selected in which a mailing was made to research directors in the United States. This group was selected on the basis of the exploratory results that indicated research directors well understood the unshelving process. In fact, they frequently were our first contacts in obtaining cases among companies in the field research. These individuals not only identified cases, but key personnel as well. Thus, they formed a suitable audience for the confirmation phase of the research. Actual names, titles and addresses were obtained from Cattell's publication, "Industrial Research Laboratories in the United States." A sample of 216 directors was drawn from this population on the basis of an association listing of research organizations. The private listing included both consumer and industrial firms, as does Cattell, and suggested a high propensity to cooperate in the research.

About a 40% response was expected from the mailing. This response rate would place the results in the "expected, but not spectacular" category referred to by Lambert (1979). The main factor responsible in such a response is overuse of the sample. Two of the four executives in the survey's test indicated, however, that ours was better than most and required far less detail than some. It was hoped that the relative novelty of the approach would improve the rate, and a response rate in the 40% range was thought usable for validation purposes.

RESULTS AND DISCUSSION

The response to the questionnaire was in line with the expectations of about 40% return. Of the 216 letters mailed, the returns were as shown in Table II.

Table II - Response to Questionnaire Mailing

Response	n	%
Complete, including citation of case.	75	
No case cited, but questionnaire completed.	17	
Special Letter written, detailing case.	7	
Elected not to participate, letter written.	8	
Mailing returned; no forwarding addresss.	4	
Questionnaires accounted for	111	51.4
Questionnaires unaccounted for	105	48.6
Total	216	100.0

The results cited in this chapter thus come from the 99 usable returns from the mailing. This portion constituted a 46% usable response and the results are thought applicable to the special task of validation. The "special task" in this situation is determining if research managers recognize and practice unshelving, as defined. The concern, of course, is that nonrespondents do not recognize the practice. As shown in Table III, there was a fairly constant response to the questionnaire across industries. Adjusted R^2 between response and mailing was 0.9. Therefore, at least on the basis of response rate, there appeared to be no special bias in the sample.

Table III - Model's Fit with Experience
by Industry Response*

	Yes	No	Sent Out	% Response
Aerospace	2	1	5	60
Chemical, Chemical Products and Petroleum Products	35	6	61	67
Consumer Durables	3	2	10	50
Consumer Nondurables and Personal Care Products	7	6	22	59
Drugs	5	2	19	37
Electrical and Electronic Products	5	3	20	40
Industrial Components, Materials and Packaging	9	3	33	36
Industrial Equipment and Machinery	3	2	19	26
Primary Materials, including Pulp and Paper	13	5	27	67
Other	2	0		
No Indication	1	0		
Total	80	26	216	

*Note: Total is greater than total number of cases because of multi-industry participation of firms.

Among the respondents to the questionnaire there was a high degree of recognition of "unshelving" as a business development practice. It thus was concluded that unshelving has wide recognition among practitioners in industry and the concepts described in this research capture its essential features. Aside from the roles that key people must play, most of the comments related to complexities that were generally stripped away in formulating a general description. In response to the first inquiry on the questionnaire,

"Does this model agree with your experience in unshelving?"

75% replied positively. Agreement was greatest among respondents who supplied cases where 86% agreed the description fit their general experience or perception. Results are shown in Table IV.

Table IV - Does Model Fit Experience?

	Yes	No	Total
Questionnaires with citations	64	10	74
Special Letters	2	5	7
Questionnaires without cases	8	10	18
Totals	74	25	99
%	75	25	100

The high degree of agreement did not mean that comments were not made indicating they were not entirely typical of experience. Essentially, our results paralleled those of Van Horn, whose panel objected to the lack of "noise" in his model (1969). This feedback is one of the advantages of this approach.

Generally, the case was recognized as a simplification.

Typical among respondents that agreed with the description was,

"(agrees) relatively well although obviously oversimplified", or

"The model is basically the definition of unshelving. It is idealistic, but reasonable."

Some respondents, however, may have thought it grossly over simplified. One respondent wrote,

"It is a fantasy. This is a highly unlikely sequence of events."

Most respondents agreed, however, that the case described unshelving, and that there was some basis in experience. Further, these comments, because they were volunteered, provide unusual insight into project unshelving.

The comments on the project termination phase indicated that barriers were, or could be, anticipated and that termination could be a lingering process. Thus, it might be more proper to address barriers as known, although undesired, possibilities that accompany projects undertaken under uncertain outcomes.

Some respondents wrote that it is not proper to suggest that all activity stops in the inactivity period. This insight is at variance with field interview reports that indicated work did stop. Further, persistence and clandestine activity were suggested to completely describe this period. The comments on the unshelving were among the richest received. Respondents not only inserted the roles that people must play in unshelving projects within a formal organization, they contributed to the variety of factors that must be considered in unshelving projects. New ideas and new technologies received heavy mention as well as volunteer championship and sponsorship. In addition, it was suggested that success, even the second time through, was not as easy as the case suggested.

Additional value came from these comments because they appeared to suggest various patterns occur among cases. Whatever exceptions may exist for unshelving as an industry practice, respondents urged us not to be too specific in conceptualizing unshelving. Comments such as "covers one type of unshelving", or "covers 50% of cases" were common in the free response section of question 1. The types of unshelving that seemed to appear for survey firms, and also in retrospect were observed in the field study, are shown in Table V. Also in Table V are estimates of occurrence frequencies; these estimates derive from respondents' reactions to the "sterile" case in Table I. These reactions are comparable , we believe, to Van Horn's panel comments on lack of noise.

Table V - Types of Unshelving Patterns
Suggested by Respondents
(The figures in parentheses are author estimates of occurrence.)

Type 1. The Vulnerable Barrier (35 - 40%) - a barrier existed, which could again be attacked because the expected payoff increased.

Type 2. A Significant Shift (35 - 40%) - basic demand, technology, economics, or politics changed, so the project could again be reconsidered, perhaps with different goals.

Type 3. Licensing Opportunities (10 - 15%) - although the original project was not worth pursuing as an internal development, commercialization could be pursued through licensing.

Type 4. Championship Cases (10 - 15%) - a champion appeared saying, "Give me a chance. I'm stronger and have a better idea."

Type 5. Forced Shelving (5%) - after the customer, or an
         intermediary, had evaluated results, the ball
         came back again to the firm's court.

This portion of the research thus confirmed that successful project unshelving is a fairly general occurrence in
project development. Cases tend to have their own
peculiarities, but a finite set of patterns in cases
seemed to emerge. Recognition of these patterns should
not only be beneficial to project management in general,
they should also prove useful to the particular phase of
project unshelving or "re-initiation". It is our concern
that far too little attention is paid to the inventory of
shelved projects that exist within each firm.

Some assistance is afforded to project managers from the
second portion of this study in determining a climate
suitable for an unshelving. The importance of a range of
factors was ascertained from Likert scaling in the response to the second question about the "specific case."
In general, it was found that casual factors suggested
from the field of study were equally important among
questionnaire respondents. In fact, because there was
an average of eight-plus factors rated per case, one
would conclude that each of these factors played some
role in the decision to unshelve the project. Aggregate
results are shown in Figure 1.

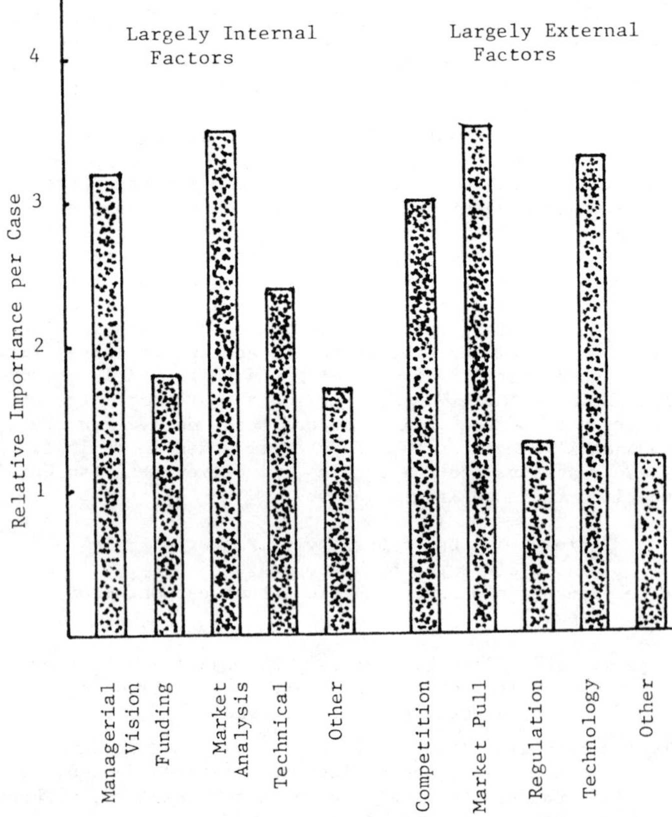

Figure 1 - Contributing Factors in Unshelving Projects

These results somewhat distort observations in individual
cases where usually two factors would be very important
(4 or 5 on the scale) and other factors would be only
moderately important (1 to 3 on the scale). Averaging
tends to make virtually all factors appear moderately
important. There was no doubt, however, that marketing
factors appeared most important. In some cases "pull"
was very evident - potential customers inquired about
development possibilities or even suggested possibilities.
In other cases, timing, as ascertained from internal study,
simply appeared more suitable for the development. These
two together overwhelm any other factors.

These results are consistent with the field interview
observation that these projects were originally technology
driven. That is, the firms were attempting to take a
substantial step in product innovation. Thus, it was
conceivably easy to decide that the innovation was unnecessary, or development was impossible in terms of the state
of art at that time. Eventually, however, the marketing
environment shifted so as to make the original idea more
attractive.

This initial technology-drive of projects also explains
the importance attributed to technology (the external
state) and technical (the firm's internal capability to
use technology). In many cases changes in these factors
permitted progress to go forward. In this regard it is
interesting that in 14 of the original 20 field cases,
"lack of a viable product" was attributed as being a
main reason for shelving the project. Note, however, here
that progress has ostensibly proceeded without direct project expense to the firm. That is, progress has occurred
without, or little, project expense. By definition, the
project has been shelved during the time project occurred;
it has been inactive. Thus, _shelving_ projects should also
appear more attractive from these results _if_ it is done
properly.

The other factor that appeared very important in unshelving
was management vision - the ability to assess the environment and sense the change required for the firm. On this
particular factor research directors varied with some
consistency from the field respondents. This factor was
ranked most important in the original portion of the study.
There are various explanations that could be used to
rationalize this result - one very attractive one, however,
is that it may be the research director that necessarily
carries the load in supporting these projects. Thus, when
they respond there may be a certain cynicism for the vision
of top managers. The engineers and marketers in the
original sample, however, may only have responded that
some top manager, i.e. a director, had vision.

In all, there was reasonable agreement in ranking among the
two sets of data.   The data produced a Spearman rank coefficient of 0.50, which for eight degrees of freedom
indicates a 15% chance that the order of factors was random. Beside the management factor referred to above, funding also fell out of order in the second set of data; it
was last (by a considerable margin) in the original study.
On the basis of the original select sample, it is very
easy to see how funding would be much more important in
the more general cases.

The final item we attempted to determine in the survey was
the timing required before unshelving because both attractive and feasible. Gap times supplied from survey results
varied from 0.5 to 15 years with a mean of 4.6 years (n=70)
and a sample standard deviation of 3.5 years. The histogram of these times is shown in Figure 2a. Within the
levels of usual statistical significance (p=.05), this
mean for the field study gap lies within the envelope
permitted in a one tail test from the 5.5 year mean
determined in the field study.

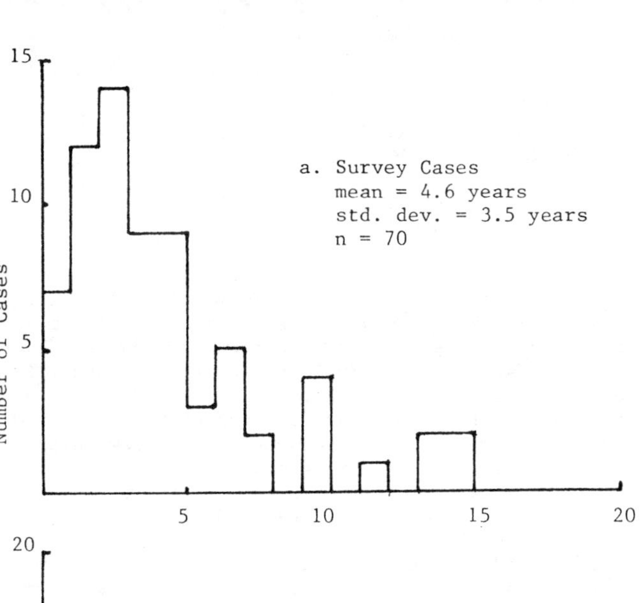

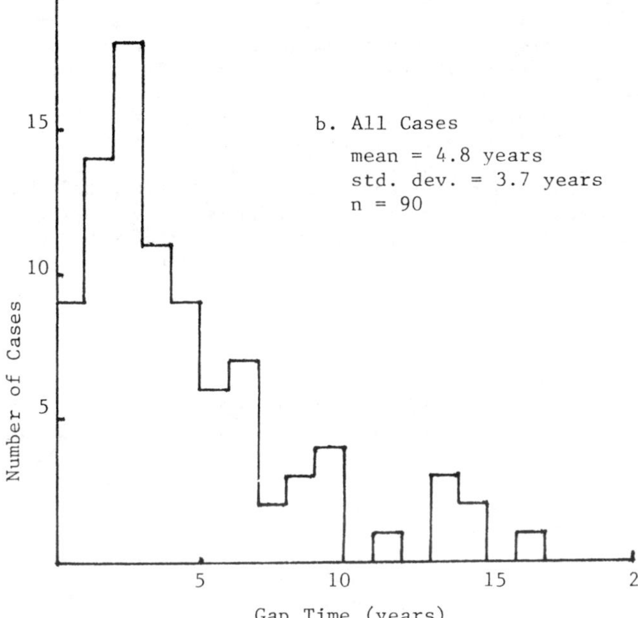

Figure 2 - Histograms of Cases

The mean value for the survey of 4.6 years was on the low side of expected results. This observation might be anticipated because both higher technology and more marketing directed industries were added among questionnaire respondents to the field study sample of materials, components and capital equipment firms. Within the framework of this study, however, selecting data for only these industries to calculate a "survey" mean for the three industries did not appreciably produce results different from the all-survey mean of 4.6 years. Although the field study indicated some tendency to consistently underestimate gap times, the most reasonable interpretation of these observations is simply to accept that the histogram of all cases is skewed left, e.g., most projects are shelved for relatively short times. Thus, extending the sample size as was done here has the tendency to lower the mean determined in the original study. If it is accepted that both the field and survey results are typical of the same universe, then results for the two samples may be added together to produce the more general histogram shown in Figure 2b. An appropriate suggestion for managers from this figure is to be very cognizant about projects shelved for less than five years; the 2-3 year period seems to be

a period of highest activity.

CONCLUSIONS

Length limitations preclude a complete discussion of results, but some comparison is appropriate between this study and relatively recent observations on industrial innovation. The study relates to Cooper's observations on dimensions of new product success and failure (1979). At least eight of the eleven factors he found important in discriminate analysis would find support in this study. Certainly unique, superior products and market knowledge appear synonomous with success. It might be noted, however, that this study leads to some concern for research that compares "successes" with "failures" as was the situation in the Cooper study. All the cases found in this study were probably considered failures at one time. Thus, timely analysis of perception appears important. This study also relates indirectly to von Hippel's observations on external sources, i.e., customers for new product ideas (1978). This research suggests an internal source that may be overlooked; firms may have a stock of viable new products that are waiting to be unshelved.

The managerial implications of the research should also be covered. Shelved projects have been found to be a viable source of successful new product developments across a range of industries. Thus, this source of product successes should be aggressively pursued. Projects may need several years to match a suitable marketing window, and a large number of cases appear to take 2-3 years. In ascertaining appropriate action, market developments, along with evolution of technology, appear to be key in making strategic decisions on these projects.

REFERENCES

Booz, Allen & Hamilton (1968), _Management of New Products_, New York: Booz, Allen & Hamilton, Inc.

Cooper, R. G. (1979), "The Dimensions of Industrial New Product Success and Failure," _Journal of Marketing_, 43 (Summer), 93-104.

Lambert, D. R. (1979), "Transfer Pricing and Interdivisional Conflict," _California Management Review_, (Summer), 70.

Myers, S. and E. E. Sweezy (1976), "Why Innovations Falter and Fail: A Study of 200 Cases," _Report PB - 259-208_, National Technical Information Service, Springfield, VA.

Naylor, T. H. and J. M. Finger (1971), "Validation" in _Computer Simulation Experiments with Models of Economic Systems_, T. H. Naylor, ed. New York: Wiley.

Reekie, W. D. (1970), _On the Shelf_, London: Centre for the Study of Industrial Innovation.

Van Horn, R. (1969), "Validation" in _The Design of Computer Simulation Experiments_, T. H. Naylor, ed. Durham, NC: Duke University Press.

Von Hippel, E. (1978), "Successful Industrial Products From Customer Ideas," _Journal of Marketing_, 42 (Jan.), 39-42.

Wilson, T. L. (1982), "Patterns of Successful Project Unshelving in Industrial Business Development," Ph.D. Dissertation, Case WRU, Cleveland, OH.

ACKNOWLEDGEMENTS

The authors wish to acknowledge the contributions of Professor Luis Dominguez who originally proposed this phase of the work and recommended the approach used. We are also indebted to one of the anonymous reviewers who recommended certain additions in content for completeness.

MARKETING EXECUTIVES' PERCEPTIONS OF THE RELATIVE IMPORTANCE
OF SALARY INCREASE DETERMINANTS: AN EXPLORATORY INVESTIGATION

Poondi Varadarajan, Texas A&M University, College Station
Charles M. Futrell, Texas A&M University, College Station

ABSTRACT

Marketing executives' perceptions of the relative importance of factors influencing salary increase decisions is
the subject of this report. A factor analytic study of pertinent data suggests that marketing executives as a group
seem to perceive the performance dimension and its manifest variables to be the major determinants of salary increase decisions. Further, while there exist differences
in the meaning or significance attached to a salary increase, there appears to be a measure of consistency in the
factors utilized by groups of marketing executives in
reaching composite perceptions of salary increase determiners.

INTRODUCTION

Various authors have addressed the issue of executive
compensation with varying degrees of orientation and generality (Lawler and Porter 1963; Andrews and Henry 1963;
Hinrichs 1969; Giles and Barrett 1971; Schuster and
Colletti 1973; Futrell and Schul 1980). An important topic
in the area of executive compensation is determination of
salary increases. In this regard, it has been noted that
an organization's pay practices and policies are expressed
most demonstrably as changes in pay and that salary increases are generally viewed as an important form of organizational reward at all levels (Hinrichs 1969). It has
also been pointed out that executives tend to view salary
increases as a more salient reward than their present
salary (Haire, Ghiselli and Porter 1963).

Typically, organizations base their salary decisions
on a number of criteria. Quite generally, these relate
to an individual's performance, nature of job, level within the organizational hierarchy, education, training and
experience, and economic considerations, to list a few.
Further, it is common practice to use multiple measures
of most of these criteria.

In motivating executives to maximize their performance,
it is desirable for organizations to facilitate information
dissemination designed to promote better understanding
among executives of criteria employed by the organization
for determining salary increases. Also, it would be appropriate for the organization to investigate the executive's
perceptions of the relative importance of salary increase
determinant criteria. Such information could be helpful
to the organization in formulating action programs designed
to diminish any ambiguity that might exist regarding
salary increase procedures and minimize problems that
might possibly arise due to perceived inequity.

PRIOR RESEARCH

Among the major issues that have been addressed in the
area of executive's perceptions of salary increase decisions are: a) the concept of reward threshold--the smallest
meaningful pay increase (SMPI)--and individual differences
in reward thresholds; b) the meaning or significance of
salary increases to executives; and c) executives' perceptions of the relative importance of determinants of salary
increases.

The notion that certain levels of salary increases

may be perceived as too small to be meaningful by employees
and that this threshold varies among individuals in a way
which may be related to their current pay levels and other
organizational and individual characteristics underlies
a number of studies relating to SMPI (see, Zedeck and Smith
1968; Hinrichs 1969). Salary increases are considered
important for a variety of reasons. Some view salary increases as a form of organizational recognition while
others view monetary considerations as the rationale
underlying salary increases. Based on a survey of marketing executives, Futrell and Schul (1979) reported that 82%
of the respondents viewed salary increases as a sign of
organizational recognition while 16% of the respondents
viewed monetary considerations as the primary reason
underlying salary increases. Significant differences in
group membership across different age groups and years of
supervisory experience were also observed. Krefting and
Mahoney (1977) note that, for individuals who view salary
increases as a form of organizational recognition, SMPI is
a function of expected pay increase and anticipated changes
in the cost of living, while for the monetary considerations group, SMPI is reportedly a function of expected
changes in the cost of living, last pay increases, and pay
satisfaction.

A number of studies have focused on the effects of
selected organizational and individual characteristics of
executives on the perceived importance of various criteria
employed by organizations for determining salary increases.
Significant differences relating to the perceived importance of salary increase determinant criteria have been
reported with respect to age, sex, education, income,
experience, and level within the organizational hierarchy
(see, Schuster and Clark 1970; Futrell and Schul 1979).

The works of Schuster and Clark are characteristic of
studies conducted along these lines. In this study, the
perceived relative importance of twelve salary increase
determinant criteria were investigated. A rating scale
with scale positions ranging from "not important" to "very
important" was used for this purpose. Schuster and Clark
note that respondents rated as good performers by their
superiors, perceived supervisor, work quality, productivity, job responsibility and pressure, and effort extended
as the most important determiners (in the order stated) of
salary increases. Lower rated performers, on the other
hand, viewed skills scarcity and economic factors as the
first and second most important determiners of salary
increases. The following results are illustrative of the
nature of other findings reported in this study.

Respondent Group	Perceived Importance of Salary Determinant Criteria (in order of importance)		
	1	2	3
Better educated	Skills scarcity	Starting salary	Economic factors
Less educated	Work quality	Productivity	Effort expended
Higher paid	Supervisor	Work quality	Job responsibility
Lower paid	Economic factors	Starting salary	Technical knowledge
Older	Work quality	Productivity	Education, training and experience
Younger	Starting salary	Economic factors	Length of service

In a recent study based on a survey of marketing executives, it has been reported that marketing executives as
a class generally tend to perceive performance related factors as major determinants of salary increases. Productivity, work quality, job responsibility and pressure, experience, effort expended and administrative skills were
perceived as the relatively more important determinants of
salary increases. Further investigation of the effects of
selected organizational and individual characteristics
revealed significant differences in the perceived importance of salary increase determinant criteria (Futrell and
Schul 1979). In summary, it might be stated that the observed differences in the perceived relative importance
of determinants of salary increases have been attributed
in part to: (1) different sets of criteria being employed
by organizations for determining appropriate salary increases for marketing personnel at various levels within
the organization (Opshal and Dunnette 1966); (2) organizational and individual characteristics (Schuster and
Clark 1964; Futrell and Schul 1979); and (3) possible lack
of clarity on the part of executives about the salary
increase determinant criteria and their relative importance
(Futrell and Schul 1979).

RESEARCH PURPOSE

In light of the previously described and other reported differences on the perceived relative importance of
salary increase determinant criteria, the issue of consistency in factors utilized by various groups in reaching
their composite perceptions assumes considerable importance.
That is, is there a measure of consistency in the factors
utilized by the two groups, namely, the organizational
recognition group and the monetary considerations group
in reaching their composite perceptions of pay increase
determiners?

Expectancy theory hypothesizes that motivation to perform
depends on three types of perceptions - valence, instrumentality and expectancy (Porter and Lawler 1968). In
using expectancy theory to predict the motivational consequences of salary increases, it can be expected that salary
increases would motivate employees to perform better when:
  - Salary increases are perceived as positively valent.
  - Salary increases are perceived as dependent upon
    higher levels of performance as opposed to lower
    levels of performance
  - Effort is perceived to lead to high performance.
    (Heneman and Schwab 1975). To the extent that salary
increases are perceived as positively valent and
salary increases are perceived as dependent on
performance by a majority of the respondents, it can
be expected that a cross sectional sample of marketing executives (despite differences in their organizational affiliations, product offerings, served
markets, market and competitive structure) would
demonstrate a common factor structure for the determinants of salary increases. Further, it can be
expected that the factor underlying the performance
dimension would be the dominant factor.

The dimensions underlying the marketing executives'
perceptions of salary increase determinant criteria, the
commonality of factors underlying the perceptions for the
organizational recognition and monetary consideration
groups, and the similarity/dissimilarity of factor structures for the two groups are explored in this paper. Data
pertaining to the marketing executives' perceptions of the
relative importance of fifteen criteria generally used for
determining salary increases in organizations are analyzed.

METHODOLOGY

The results of the study reported here are based on a
national survey of marketing executives affiliated with
organizations of various sizes involved in varied domains
of activity. The survey was conducted in the spring of
1978. An eleven page questionnaire addressing a wide range
of issues relating to the marketing executives' perception
of various aspects of their job such as leadership, organizational climate, job satisfaction, etc. was mailed to
1,637 marketing executives whose names and addresses were
selected from the 1977 edition of the Standard and Poor's
directory. The initial mailing and follow-up efforts resulted in 460 usable responses. The position held by the
top 86% of the respondents range from president to district
sales manager with the remaining 14% accounted for by sales
representatives.

As a part of the larger study, the respondents' perceptions of the relative importance of fifteen salary increase determinant criteria listed in Table 1 were elicited.
More specifically, the resondents were asked to indicate
(on a seven point scale with scale positions ranging from
1 to 7--"not important" to "extremely important") their
perception of the extent to which each of the fifteen
salary increase determinant criteria were influential in
determining their salary increase.

Additionally, respondents were provided with a select
list of five possible reasons and a sixth open option and
were requested to indicate the one single most important
reason why a pay raise was important to them. This list
was composed of three organizational recognition factors
(reward for past performance, sign of improvement in work,
sign of progress in the company or career), and two monetary incentive factors (keeping up with changes in the cost
of living, improving the standard of living). Classification data relating to the respondents' age, sex, position
within the organization, salary, education, etc. were also
obtained.

The analysis was performed in two stages. First, in an
attempt to identify the underlying constructs, the entire
data set of 460 observations relating to the 15 pay increase
determinant variables was factor analyzed using the principal components method. The second phase of the analysis
focusing on commonality of factors and factor structure
similarity involved factor analysis of subgroups of the
total data set. Towards this end the original data were
divided into two groups--respondents who viewed organizational recognition as the prime criterion underlying salary
increases and those who viewed monetary considerations
as the primary rationale underlying salary increases. The
number of observations in the two groups were 317 and 62,
respectively.

ANALYSIS AND DISCUSSION

Summary statistics in the form of mean scores for each
criterion and the perceived rank order of importance of the
various determinants of salary increase are reported in
Table 1 for the two groups as well as the total data set.
Also reported are the results of univariate tests of
equality of group means. Understandably, a certain degree
of caution needs to be exercised in drawing inferences
based on the results reported in Table 1 for obvious reasons. As noted earlier, ordinal rating scales with scale
positions ranging from "1" representing "not important" to
"7" representing "extremely important" have been used in
this study. In computing unweighted mean scores and rank
order of importance, however, the ratings are treated as
if they were measured using an interval scale.

The matrix of correlation coefficients is presented in Table
2. An examination of these coefficients points to a high
degree of correlation between the subset of variables V1 to
V8. Also, as might be noted from Table 1, the mean perceived importance rating for these variables is higher than
for the other variables.

TABLE 1

PERCEIVED IMPORTANCE OF DETERMINANTS OF SALARY INCREASE: SUMMARY STATISTICS

Variable Number	Variable Label	Total Sample	Organizational Recognition Group	Monetary Considerations Group	Univariate Test of Equality of Group Means
V1	Training	4.59 (7)[c]	4.67 (7)	4.20 (7)	S[b]
V2	Experience	5.52 (4)	5.58 (4)	5.24 (4)	-
V3	Administrative skills	5.44 (5)	5.52 (5)	5.01 (6)	S[b]
V4	Technical knowledge	4.56 (8)	4.59 (8)	4.43 (7)	-
V5	Job responsibility and pressure	5.67 (3)	5.75 (3)	5.28 (3)	S[b]
V6	Work quality	6.02 (2)	6.13 (2)	5.52 (2)	S[a]
V7	Productivity	6.13 (1)	6.21 (1)	5.69 (1)	S[b]
V8	Effort expended	5.35 (6)	5.40 (6)	5.07 (5)	-
V9	Economic factors	4.30 (9)	4.29 (9)	4.31 (8)	-
V10	Education	3.66 (11)	3.75 (11)	3.17 (13)	-
V11	College training	3.44 (13)	3.49 (13)	3.19 (12)	-
V12	Boss	4.22 (10)	4.26 (10)	4.00 (10)	-
V13	Starting salary	2.96 (14)	2.95 (14)	3.06 (14)	-
V14	Luck	2.27 (15)	2.28 (15)	2.26 (15)	-
V15	Skills scarcity	3.47 (12)	3.42 (12)	3.70 (11)	S[b]

a - Denotes significant differences in group means at the $p < .01$ level
b - Denotes significant differences in group means at the $p < .05$ level
c - Entries in brackets denote perceived rank order of importance of criteria

In the first phase of factor analysis, the principal components method was employed to analyze the total data set. A total of six factors were extracted and rotated using the varimax rotation method. The number of factors extracted is, in part, based upon researchers' judgement. A common rule of thumb is to include as many factors as there are principal components with eigen values greater than one. Most authorities in the field, however, recommend using the roots > 1.0 criterion in conjunction with the scree test to determine the number of factors to extract (Cattell 1978; Gorsuch 1974; Harman 1976). Further, there are no objective prohibitions on electing to use fewer or more factors in the interests of plausible, interpretable structures. Although principal components analysis resulted in only three factors with eigen values greater than one, a six factor solution (consistent with the use of the roots criterion and the scree test) resulted in a more interpretable structure than solutions with fewer factors. (In both cases--the three factor and six factor solutions--variables V1 to V8 tend to correlate more substantially with the first factor, and variables V10 and V11 correlate higher with the second factor. With a three factor solution variables V9 and V12 to V15 load high on F3; with a six factor solution, V9 and V12 to V15 get to be distributed between factors F4 and F5, and F6 (see Tables 3 and 4). However, F3 is not easily interpretable with a three factor solution.)

TABLE 2

Correlation Matrix - Salary Increase Determinant Criteria*

Variable Number	V1	V2	V3	V4	V5	V6	V7	V8	V9	V10	V11	V12	V13	V14	V15
V1	1.00														
V2	.71	1.00													
V3	.56	.73	1.00												
V4	.53	.60	.58	1.00											
V5	.55	.71	.77	.56	1.00										
V6	.55	.69	.78	.57	.81	1.00									
V7	.54	.71	.73	.54	.79	.89	1.00								
V8	.52	.63	.65	.67	.70	.76	.72	1.00							
V9	.29	.41	.47	.46	.52	.50	.47	.54	1.00						
V10	.55	.43	.36	.43	.35	.36	.35	.35	.25	1.00					
V11	.38	.25	.22	.34	.20	.21	.18	.28	.22	.64	1.00				
V12	.22	.25	.27	.25	.30	.30	.23	.36	.41	.19	.27	1.00			
V13	.22	.19	.16	.30	.22	.18	.15	.25	.36	.26	.27	.30	1.00		
V14	-.06	-.17	-.16	-.05	-.19	-.22	-.22	-.13	.09	.01	.25	.28	.24	1.00	
V15	.32	.32	.32	.31	.35	.32	.32	.28	.32	.31	.16	.21	.27	.02	1.00

*See Table 1 for a description of variable numbers.

The factor loadings resulting from a six factor varimax solution are summarized in Table 3. Together, these factors account for over 80% of the variance contained in the data matrix. To facilitate ease of interpretation, the variables have been grouped together on the basis of their

TABLE 3

Factor Loadings: Six Factor Varimax Solution*

Variable Number	Variable Label	F1	F2	F3	F4	F5	F6	Communality
V1	Training	.707**	.416					.798
V2	Experience	.867						.814
V3	Administrative skills	.854						.769
V4	Technical knowledge	.634	.306		.341			.631
V5	Job responsibility and pressure	.843						.800
V6	Work quality	.867						.857
V7	Productivity	.864						.814
V8	Effort expended	.746		.351				.759
V10	Education	.304	.847					.828
V11	College training		.878					.843
V9	Economic factors	.417		.612				.711
V12	Boss			.710		.426		.761
V13	Starting salary				.898			.897
V14	Luck					.871		.860
V15	Skills scarcity						.947	.988

*The eigen values and percent variance extracted for the first six unrotated factors are:

Factors	F1	F2	F3	F4	F5	F6
Eigen Value	6.84	1.89	1.26	0.85	0.70	0.60
Variance Extracted (%)	45.6	12.6	8.4	5.7	4.6	4.0

**Only factor loadings greater than .30 are reproduced here

TABLE 4

VARIMAX ROTATED FACTOR LOADINGS: TOTAL SAMPLE AND SUBGROUPS*

Variable Number	Variable Label	The Total Sample F1	F2	F3	Organizational Recognition Group F1	F2	F3	Monetary Considerations Group F1	F2	F3
V1	Training	.59	.57	-	.48	-	.63	.52	.49	-
V2	Experience	.80	.31	-	.68	-	.35	.77	.46	-
V3	Administrative skills	.84	-	-	.77	-	-	.78	.35	-
V4	Technical knowledge	.64	.35	-	.48	-	.35	.71	-	.39
V5	Job responsibility and pressure	.88	-	-	.82	-	-	.85	-	-
V6	Work quality	.91	-	-	.88	-	-	.76	.32	-
V7	Productivity	.89	-	-	.83	-	-	.80	.36	-
V8	Effort expended	.79	-	-	.68	.34	-	.86	-	-
V10	Education	-	.84	-	-	-	.88	.32	.74	-
V11	College training	-	.82	-	-	-	.81	-	.56	.56
V9	Economic factors	.54	-	.57	.32	.72	-	.71	-	-
V12	Boss	-	-	.70	-	.70	-	-	-	.67
V13	Starting salary	-	-	.66	-	.63	-	-	-	.43
V14	Luck	.38	-	.66	-	.63	-	-	-	.76
V15	Skills scarcity	.37	-	.37	-	.38	-	-	.72	-

*Only factor loadings greater than .30 are reported here.
Total Variance Extracted: The two groups combined: 66%
Organizational recognition group: 59%
Monetary considerations group: 65%

loadings. That is, variables loading high on the first factor are grouped together and listed first, followed by variables loading high on the second factor and so on.

The variance contained in each of the salary increase determinant variables is fairly well represented by the six factors as reflected in their communalities which range from a high of 0.988 (V15) to a low of 0.631 (V4).

The first factor seems to involve the elements of performance (work quality, productivity, effort expended), potential for performance (training, experience, administrative skills, technical knowledge) and the nature of the job (job responsibility and pressure). Hence, the first factor may be appropriately labeled as the "performance-job characteristics" dimension, or more simply as the performance dimension. Education appears to be the construct underlying the second factor. The third factor includes the concepts of economic factors and supervisor's evaluation while the fifth factor includes the concepts of supervisor's evaluation and luck.

Starting salary and skills scarcity appear to be essentially unidimensional concepts (in this analysis) as evidenced
in the fact that they load heavily only on one factor each,
the fourth and sixth factors, respectively.

Interestingly, it might be noted that in the works of Hinrichs (1969) and others it has been reported that average
perceptions of salary increases follow a relatively consistent pattern that is largely a function of an individual's current absolute level of earnings. Further, it has
been noted that some variability exists around the average
which is generally associated with an individual's background, particular situation, and other factors.

In summary, the results reported in Table 3 seem to suggest
that marketing executives as a group seem to perceive the
performance dimension and its manifest variables as the
major determinants of salary increase decisions.

As stated earlier, in the second phase of the analysis our
interest is centered on the distribution of the original
set of variables on various factors for the two groups.
If there is a measure of consistency in the factors utilized by various groups in reaching their composite perceptions, then the underlying factors should be the same
for the organizational recognition and monetary considerations groups. Further, if marketing executives as a group
were to have fairly stable perceptions regarding the relative importance of salary increase determinant criteria,
hopefully, this would be reflected in the similarity of
factor structures for the two groups.

The data subsets were once again analyzed using the principal components method and varimax rotation techniques were
employed. The rotated factor loadings resulting from a
three factor solution for the two groups and the total
data set are summarized in Table 4. The columns of data in
Table 4 list the factor loadings (based on a three factor
varimax rotation solution) for the total sample, the
organizational recognition group and the monetary considerations group. An examination of Table 4 reveals that
the underlying dimensions are essentially the same for the
organizational recognition group and the monetary considerations group. (Note that there is a reversal in the
order of extraction of F2 and F3 for the two groups.) The
composite of variables underlying the performance dimension
appear to be very similar for the two groups.

The loadings associated with variables V2 to V8 are all
higher on the first factor in both cases. For both groups,
variables V1 (training) and V2 (experience) are substantially correlated with the performance dimension as well as
the education and training dimension. However, the degree
of similarity evidenced in the pattern of loadings on the
performance dimension for the two groups is not reflected
to a comparable extent in the other two factors. An examination of the factor laodings for variables V3, V4 and V6
to V11 for the two groups point to certain visible differences. In spite of these differences, the analysis suggests that the factors underlying the perceptions of salary
increases for the two groups are the same. Further, the
results indicate substantial similarity in the pattern of
loadings along the performance dimension for the two groups.

CONCLUSION

The study reported suggests that marketing executives as a
group tend to perceive the performance dimension and its
manifest variables to be the major determinants of salary
increase decisions. Notwithstanding organizational and
individual differences, the perceived salience of the performance dimension appears to be fairly widespread. Further, while marketing executives seem to have different

orientations regarding the primary criterion underlying
salary increases--organizational recognition and monetary
considerations--there appears to be a measure of consistency
in the factors utilized by the two groups in reaching
composite perceptions of salary increase determiners. A
comparison of executive responses based on other characteristics such as level of managerial position (top,
middle, operations), age, etc. might provide further
insight. Failure to consider the impact of the perceptions
of nonrespondents on the reported findings is a major
limitation of this study.

Given current indications that top management is often
critical of the marketing function (Webster 1981), it seems
that more effort is needed in understanding how marketers
perceive their functions and the rewards which follow from
their performance. In this regard, to the extent that
organizations seek to use salary increases to achieve improved performance, greater satisfaction and lower voluntary employee turnover among its marketing executives, it
is important that pay increases are perceived as dependent
upon higher levels of performance. Further, all of this
requires an effective system of performance measurement
and appraisal. In the absence of such a system, it is unlikely that executives will be able to perceive the effort-
performance and performance-outcome relationships accurately.

REFERENCES

Andrews, J. R. and Mildred M. Henry (1963), "Management
Attitudes Toward Pay", Industrial Relations, (October),
41-49.

Cattell, R. B. (1978), The Scientific Use of Factor Analysis
in the Behavioral and Life Sciences, New York: Plenum Press.

Futrell, Charles M. and Patrick L. Schul (1979), "Salary
Increases for the Marketing Executive", Industrial Marketing Management, 8, 318-324.

__________, and __________ (1980), "Marketing Executives'
Perceptions of a Salary Increase", California Management
Review, (Spring), 87-93.

Giles, Brian A. and Gerald V. Barrett (1971), "Utility of
Merit Increases", Journal of Applied Psychology, 55 (No.2),
103-109.

Gorsuch, R. L. (1974), Factor Analysis, Philadelphia: W. B.
Saunders Company.

Haire, Mason, Edwin E. Ghiselli, and Lyman W. Porter (1963),
"Psychological Research on Pay: An Overview", Industrial
Relations, III (October), 3-8.

Harman, H. H. (1976), Modern Factor Analysis, Chicago:
University of Chicago Press.

Heneman, G. Herbert and Donald P. Schwab (1975), "Work and
Rewards Theory", in Motivation and Commitment, Dale Yoder
and Herbert G. Heneman, eds., Washington, D.C.: The Bureau
of National Affairs, Inc.

Hinrichs, J. R. (1969), "Correlates of Employee Evaluations
of Pay Increases", Journal of Applied Psychology, 53 (No.
6), 481-489.

Krefting, Linda A. and Thomas A. Mahoney (1977), "Determining the Size of a Meaningful Pay Increase", Industrial
Relations, 16 (No. 1), 83-93.

Lawler III, Edward E. and Lyman W. Porter (1963), "Perceptions Regarding Management Compensation", Industrial
Relations, 3, 41-49.

Opshal, Robert L. and Marvin D. Dunnette (1966), "The Role
of Financial Compensation in Industrial Motivation",
Psychological Bulletin, (February), 94-118.

Porter, Lyman W. and Edward E. Lawler (1968), Managerial
Attitudes and Performance, Homewood, Illinois: R. D.
Irwin, Inc.

Schuster, Jay R. and Barbara Clark (1970) "Individual
Differences Related to Feelings Toward Pay", Personnel
Psychology, 23, 591-604.

__________, and Jerome A. Colletti (1973), "The Relation-
ship Between Perceptions Concerning Magnitudes of Pay and
the Perceived Utility of Pay: Public and Private Organizations Compared", Organizational Behavior and Human
Performance, 9, 110-119.

Webster, Jr. Fredrick E. (1981), "Top Management's Concerns
about Marketing: Issues for the 1980's", Journal of
Marketing, (Summer), 9-16.

Zedeck, Sheldon and Patricia C. Smith (1968), "A Psychological Determination of Equitable Payment", Journal of
Applied Psychology, (October), 343-347.

SUCCESS FACTORS IN EXPORT MARKETING:
AN EMPIRICAL ANALYSIS

S. Tamer Cavusgil, University of Wisconsin-Whitewater
Erdener Kaynak, Mount Saint Vincent University

ABSTRACT

In contrast to a large number of studies on exporting
which examine firm and decision-maker characteristics
associated with exporting activity, this paper focuses on
marketing decision variables. The purpose is to: delineate underlying marketing factors perceived to influence
success in export marketing and understand to what extent
key marketing mix variables require modification for
export markets. The results of the empirical analysis with
the data obtained from a sample of North American firms
suggest that marketing-related success factors can be
expressed in four independent dimensions.

INTRODUCTION

Much of export marketing research has focused on the
characteristics of exporters and nonexporters, perceived
obstacles to exporting, the initiation of export activity,
and public policy towards exporting. (For a review of the
literature on export marketing refer to Bilkey 1978 or
Cavusgil and Nevin 1981). Surprisingly few studies have
deliberately examined marketing decision variables and how
they affect the firm's export performance. Rather, a pre-
occupation with structural characteristics (i.e., firm and
industry-related) and, to a limited degree, with individual
characteristics (i.e., decision-maker related) has pre-
vailed.

This paper attempts to identify principal marketing variables associated with success in exporting. Based on data
gathered from a mail survey of export managers, it addresses the following issues: What are the major marketing
decision variables which account for success in export
markets? Can these variables be reduced to a few underlying dimensions? To what extent do various marketing mix
variables undergo adaptation for foreign markets?

A SURVEY OF THE LITERATURE

Among the studies which directly dealt with the key
ingredients of successful exporting, two British investigations are notable. The first study, conducted by Hunt,
Froggatt and Hovell (1967), examined pricing, advertising,
distribution, credit, technical and service policies in
40 companies in the machinery industry. The authors
provided valuable insights as to how these elements of the
export marketing mix are handled by the firms, but avoided
a discussion of their relative importance in the total
marketing mix. The other study by Cunningham and Spigel
(1971) focused on those companies who had received the
Queen's Award to Industry for export achievements in recent
years in an attempt to ascertain the factors for their
success. Cunningham and Spigel noted: There is general
agreement amongst almost all successful firms that the most
important factor to be considered for successful exporting
is the personal visit of company executives to their overseas markets. This plays a key part throughout the
planning, implementation and follow-up stages of marketing
abroad, and is the main source of marketing information.
Thereafter the larger firms favour the establishment of
overseas distribution facilities and the use of agents,
whereas the smaller firms name agents as the next most
important factors.

When all the companies retrospectively analyzed the reasons
for their own success there is an insistence that attention
to product design and quality comes first. The larger
companies believe that the adoption of an international
marketing outlook for the firm is the most vital stage in
management policy formulation and forward planning from
which stems other plans for the export marketing mix such
as pricing, sales organization, and customer service. The
smaller companies rely on the "feel" of the overseas
markets gained by personal visits to these countries as
substitutes for more sophisticated and formalized plans
adopted by the larger firms. This provides them with the
means for decision-making in exporting companies. As one
might expect, there are no "best" ways to exporting."
(p. 11)

Weinrauch and Rao (1974) analyzed the changing nature of
the marketing mix among a group of Arkansas exporters.
Their study revealed that some modifications are necessary
in the export marketing mix. Pricing and credit were
found to be the most important ingredients requiring modification. Promotion and packaging, on the other hand, were
assessed by the respondents as requiring least modification
in exporting.

In their study of a number of export-intensive industries,
Czinkota and LaLonde (1980) were able to assess the significance of critical marketing variables for firms at
varying stages of internationalization (see Cavusgil 1980,
for the internationalization hypothesis). They found that
the firms in earlier stages of internationalization
emphasized communication and sales effort while firms in
the higher stages identified customer service as critical
variables.

A recent study by Kirpalani and Macintosh (1980) related a
series of marketing variables to the firms' success in
export marketing. Success was expressed as a function of
export sales growth and the level of export activity
relative to competition. The authors concluded that
pricing and promotion were significantly associated with
the firms' export performance. The pricing variable
reflected the firm policies concerning prices, discounts,
and credits--relative to competition. Surprisingly,
distribution (quality and compensation of dealers and
adequacy of stocks and parts) did not have a significant
relationship with success.

While these and other studies have provided insights into
the nature of export marketing mix--and, in fact, served
as a basis for formulating the data collection instrument
used in our study--none of them considered a comprehensive
set of marketing decision variables and attempted to
examine the interrelationships among them in the context
of export marketing. The present analysis differs from the
other studies in that it searches for principal factors
contributing to export marketing success on the basis of
self-reported assessments.

METHOD

Sample

Data used in this paper are derived from a mail-survey of
manufacturing firms in an Eastern province of Canada. The
broader study investigated the characteristics of exporting

and nonexporting firms; perceived difficulties in exporting; geographical orientation of exporters; and other
issues. The data collection phase of the study was
completed in early 1981.

The sampling frame for the survey was a comprehensive list
of exporting firms reported in the latest edition of the
Directory of Manufacturers in the province. A total of
325 exporting firms listed in the _Directory_ were first
contacted through an introductory letter. The letter
identified the sponsor of the study--a well-known university in the province,--described the objective of the
survey, and requested their cooperation. A questionnaire
was later mailed to the firms, along with a postage-free
reply envelope. All correspondence was addressed to the
owner/president of the firm. They were instructed to
either complete the questionnaire themselves or forward it
to the person within the organization primarily responsible
for export activity.

The data collection instrument was a five-page questionnaire which minimized the use of open-ended responses.
Typically, the respondent was required to respond to a
question on a five-point or seven-point scale. The
questionnaire sought background information on the firm;
the nature and scope of exporting activities; manager's
perceptions about company weaknesses and strengths; the
importance of marketing mix elements in export markets;
geographical distribution of exports and other issues.
This questionnaire was the revised version of an earlier
one which was pretested among a small, convenience sample
of firms.

After two mailings, the survey generated 104 usable
responses, representing a net return rate of 32 percent.
A follow-up investigation of nonrespondents was not
attempted. It was felt, however, that the nonrespondents
do not differ from respondents in any significant manner
other than lacking an interest in export marketing.

A Brief Profile of Responding Firms

Forty-three percent of the responding firms had annual
sales of less than $1 million, and another 23 percent
ranged between $1 and $5 million. Major industries represented by the exports of these companies included metal
fabricating, paper and allied products, chemical products,
textiles, leather, plastics, and food processing equipment.
Approximately one-half of the responding firms classified
their export products as primarily consumer goods.

This is a high proportion compared to the make-up of
exports from other Canadian provinces and American states.

For slightly more than one-third of the exporting firms,
export sales account for less than 10 percent of total
sales. Forty-one percent of the firms export between 10
and 50 percent, while another twenty-four percent export
more then 50 percent of their sales. Compared to other
studies conducted in North America, this sample represents
a relatively active group of exporters.

Parallelling findings elsewhere, unsolicited orders from
foreign customers were primarily responsible for the
export start. The majority of the respondents reported
that they maintained their export involvement as a response
to problems experienced in the domestic market. Growing
competition, saturated market, and unfavorable economic
climate are examples of these problems. Approximately
40 percent of the firms, on the other hand, maintain their
involvement in foreign markets simply because they perceive better opportunities for their products.

Measures of Marketing Variables

Eighteen marketing decision variables directly related to
the firm's offering were included in this study. Examples
are product quality, delivery, warranty, promotion, prices,
after sales service, and other determinants of demand. A
complete listing appears in Table 1. The relevance of
these variables in export marketing is evident from the
studies reviewed above as well as others. We asked the
responding managers in our sample to rate the importance
of each variable for export success on a five-point
ordinal scale where "1 = No Importance" and "5 = Very
Important."

Data Analysis

A principal components analysis was performed on the
respondents' assessments of the significance of each
marketing variable. This analysis produced four factors
as presented in Table 1. Factor IV, although it has an
eigen value of less than unity, was retained in the
analysis since it identified a dimension of export
marketing mix which has been found to be very critical by
previous studies.

In the view of the possibility that a sample size of 104
with 18 original items may generate spurious results,
several additional runs were made with randomly chosen
subsamples equaling 60 percent of the original sample.
These runs did cause varying orderings of the four factors;
but three of the four factors in Table 1 emerged in every
run. Therefore, it was concluded that the particular
interrelationships reflected in the four dimensions were
relatively stable.

TABLE 1

PRINCIPAL COMPONENTS ANALYSIS OF MARKETING VARIABLES[a]

	FACTOR I	FACTOR II	FACTOR III	FACTOR IV
Overall reputation of company	.69			
After sales service	.66	.39		
Consistent quality	.65			
Personal visits to foreign markets	.44			.44
Unique features of offering	.40		.37	
Meeting delivery dates	.30			
Special discounts to distributors		.74		
Motivation of distributors/agents		.65		
Promotion directed at distributors or end users		.56	.55	
Contacts at trade shows/fairs		.49	.49	
Negotiation skills	.38	.46		
Advanced technology		.38	.33	
Combination of related products			.73	
Word of mouth among customers			.49	
Competitive price				.67
Extension of credit				.67
Special warranties				.52
Matching customer specifications				.42
Sum of squares	4.14	2.06	1.27	0.72
Percent of variance	50.60	25.20	15.50	8.80

[a]Varimax rotated. For simplicity, only those factor loadings in excess of
0.30 are shown.

DISCUSSION

The four factors in Table 1 lend themselves to relatively
straightforward interpretation. Factor I appears to

represent the "basic" company offering: quality products, after sales service, and company image. Apparently the respondents perceive the dimension reflected by these variables as a key factor in successful exporting. The relatively high loading for company reputation may be explained by the fact that, in export marketing, communication between the buyer and the seller is hindered by physical as well as psychological distance. A visit by the prospective customer to manufacturer's facilities, although useful for gaining an impression about the company, is not always feasible. Therefore, reputation of the manufacturer serves as valuable cue--an assurance of a satisfactory business relationship.

Factor II reflects the critical role foreign distributors/ agents play in export marketing. In that sense, it identifies the contactual component of the export marketing mix. Distributors/agents are an extension of the manufacturer in foreign markets, performing a contactual function for them. The majority of exporting firms prefer to utilize this channel rather than establishing their own sales/service branches overseas (see e.g., Cavusgil 1982). This is due to many reasons including: (a) limited potential of a foreign market; (b) cost savings; and (c) foreign distributor's natural advantage in better identifying with the local market.

Motivating foreign distributors/agents through financial (such as discounting) and nonfinancial incentives is apparently very helpful in export marketing. Indeed, recent research on manufacturer-distributor relationships confirms this finding (Rosson and Ford 1980, Ford 1979). Sales promotion as well as attendance at international trade shows/fairs seem to be a part of the contactual function as well.

Factor III appears to be related to the promotion function in export marketing. Promotion directed at distributors or end users, participation in trade shows/fairs, and word of mouth are all part of this dimension. The association of the "combination of related products" with this dimension is not immediately apparent. One plausible explanation may be that promotion in foreign markets is made easier when the manufacturer has a line of related products to offer rather than a single item. It would make more sense for the manufacturer to advertise in the former case. Relatively high loading for "unique features of offering" on this dimension can also be explained in a similar manner. When the manufacturer has a unique/differentiated offering as opposed to a standardized product, he should be more willing to advertise in export markets.

The importance of promotion function has also been domonstrated in the export literature. One particularly helpful form of promotion in export marketing is participation in trade shows/fairs. (It is, in a way, surprising that this item did not have a higher loading in this factor).

Such participation allows the manufacturer to: (a) better assess the potential for his products; (b) demonstrate the equipment; and (c) provide face-to-face contact with potential distributors/end users, and even result in immediate sales (Turnbull 1979). There are, indeed, excellent international shows/fairs in various regions of the world which provide the producers exposure to other participants in a given industry [Geddes 1981].

Factor IV is associated with the pricing/terms of sale component of the marketing mix. Having a competitive price in export markets, extending credit to foreign buyers, offering special warranties are all part of this dimension which is perceived to be a distinct determinant of success in export marketing. It is interesting to find "personal visits to foreign markets" to be moderately associated with this dimension. One possible implication

is that such visits and face-to-face contacts are essential in finalizing the terms of sale including prices, warranty, and credit.

The importance of prices has been elaborated in detail in the export marketing literature (see e.g., Kirpalani and Macintosh 1980). Therefore, it is surprising that the eigen value for this dimension is less than one, and the percent of variance explained is less than 10 percent. The relative importance of pricing depends, of course, on the interrelationships with other elements in the marketing mix. It is reasonable to expect that consistent quality, unique products, promotional support, etc. will tend to downplay the relative importance of pricing in export marketing. One should also be reminded of the fact that foreign buyers often have less than perfect information about the availability and prices of competing products, which may also help explain the weak association of pricing with export success.

The above discussion attempted to provide insights into the nature of independent marketing dimensions perceived to be related to success in export marketing. An additional issue of interest in this investigation was to assess the importance of various adaptations/adjustments in the marketing mix for exporting. For this purpose, we asked the managers in our sample to indicate the extent of modification each element of the marketing mix would undergo in preparation for export markets. The results are shown in Table 2.

TABLE 2

EXPORT MARKETING ADAPTATIONS AND ADJUSTMENTS AS INDICATED BY EXPORTERS (Percent of Total Responses)

Marketing Variables	Major Modification	Slight Modification	No Change
Credit	25%	32%	43%
Promotion	24	32	44
Channels of Distribution	19	31	49
Pricing	11	51	38
Physical Product	10	41	49
Packaging	9	36	55

The results are in line with previous research, except with respect to the relative rank of "promotion." Weinrauch and Rao (1974), for example, categorized promotion as an element which requires little adaptation. It is possible that the make-up of the firms has an effect; whether or not the sample is dominated by industrial versus consumer goods producers will create a difference. In addition, one may expect differential responses between producers of standardized versus specialized products.

As in other studies, credit policy stands out as the key marketing variable in need of modification when a company sells abroad. A distinguishing feature of export marketing is that the transactions take place over a longer period of time which makes long-term financing imperative. Just how the costs of financing will be shared between the buyer and the manufacturer is subject to negotiations. Indeed, a very valuable competitive advantage of an exporter is the ability to offer attractive credit terms to the foreign customer--much more relaxed than what he is accustomed to practice in domestic business.

CONCLUSIONS

This investigation has shown that success factors in
export marketing can be reduced to four independent
dimensions. The first dimension seems to identify the
basic company offering: quality, service, and image.
The second dimension identified the contactual linkage
with foreign distributors/agents. The third factor was
associated with promotion. Finally, the fourth dimension
was labeled pricing/terms of sale component. Export
managers in our sample appear to attribute success in
exporting to these underlying marketing dimensions.

Beyond this, it was found that the marketing mix variables
which required most modification to be suitable for
foreign markets were, in order of importance, credit,
promotion, and channels of distribution. The variables
which needed least adaptation, on the other hand, were
packaging, physical product, and pricing.

The findings reported in this investigation should be
considered tentative since the firms included in the
sample came from only one region of North America. The
authors did not encounter any other study of similar
nature; it would seem desirable to replicate the research
design with samples of firms representing varying regions
and industries. Future investigators may perhaps expand
the original list of marketing variables on the basis
of the findings reported here, and then identify underlying success factors through a data reduction technique.
One can make a distinction, for example, between
"promotion directed at distributors" and "promotion
directed at final customers."

REFERENCES

Bilkey, Warren J. (1978), "An Attempted Integration of
   the Literature on the Export Behavior of Firms,"
   Journal of International Business Studies, vol. 9, no.
   1 (Spring/Summer), 33-46.

Cavusgil, S. Tamer (1980), "On the Internationalization
   Process of Firms," European Research, 8, 6 (November),
   273-281.

Cavusgil, S. Tamer (1982), Foreign Market Potential
   Analysis: A Study of Current Practices Among Wisconsin
   Firms, unpublished manuscript, University of Wisconsin,
   Whitewater.

Cavusgil, S. Tamer and John Nevin (1981), "State-of-the-
   Art in International Marketing," in Review of Marketing
   1981, Ben M. Enis and Kenneth J. Roering, editors,
   American Marketing Association, 195-216.

Cunningham, M. T. and R. I. Spigel (1971), "A Study in
   Successful Exporting," British Journal of Marketing 5
   (Spring), 2-12.

Czinkota, Michael and Bernard J. LaLonde (1980), "An
   Analysis of Export Development Strategies in Selected
   U.S. Industries," Working Paper No: 80-17, Ohio State
   University.

Hunt, H. G., J. D. Froggatt, and P. J. Hovell (1967),
   "The Management of Export Marketing in Engineering
   Industries," British Journal of Marketing, Vol. 1,
   10-24.

Ford, David (1979), "Developing Buyer-Seller Relationships in Export Marketing," Organisation: Marknad Och
   Samhalle, Vol. 16, No. 5, 291-307.

Geddes, John M. (1981), "Small U.S. Firms Use European
   Trade Fairs As An Inexpensive Way to Tap New Markets,"
   Wall Street Journal (November 12), 27.

Kirpalani, V. H. and N. B. Macintosh (1980), "International Marketing Effectiveness of Technology-Oriented
   Small Firms," Journal of International Business Studies,
   11, 3 (Winter), 81-90.

Rosson, Philip & I. David Ford (1980), "Some Aspects of
   Manufacturer-Distributor Relationships in Exporting,"
   Paper presented at the Academy of International
   Business Conference October, 1980.

Turnbull, Peter W. (1979), "Roles of Personal Contacts in
   Industrial Export Marketing," Organisation: Marknad Och
   Samhalle, Vol. 16, No. 5, 325-337.

Weinrauch, J. Donald and C. P. Rao (1974), "The Export
   Marketing Mix: An Examination of Company Experiences
   and Perceptions," Journal of Business Research, 2
   (October), 447-52.

THE MARKETING OF HIGH TECHNOLOGY PRODUCTS IN FOREIGN MARKETS

Michael G. Harvey, Southern Methodist University, Dallas
James T. Rothe, Southern Methodist University, Dallas

ABSTRACT

The marketing of high technology products by United States firms in foreign markets has not been extensively explored in the marketing literature. A vast preponderance of the recent international articles address the difficulties of marketing consumer goods and service abroad. This article develops an analysis format for the marketing of high technology products (i.e., state of the art applications of science to industrial management, for example, satellite telecommunications, fiber optics, three-dimensional seismic readings for hydrocarbon exploration, lazer sites for defense and the like) to economies of varying levels of economic development.

INTRODUCTION

Economic growth and prosperity have traditionally been identified as hallmarks of the United States economy. A great deal of the economic growth and prosperity in the domestic economy has been attributed to the rate of technological development in the United States following the Second World War. The marketing of high technology products throughout the world has also become of increasing interest to United States based organizations (Green, 1980). There are many obstacles to the marketing of high technology in foreign markets: (1) increased economic and political tensions between Third World countries and industrialized economies; (2) lack of government (United States) incentive to market high technology products; (3) increase in restrictions by foreign governments; (4) growth of Third World multinational corporations; and (5) a lack of adequate decision criteria by United States organizations on how to market and/or transfer high technology products in foreign markets.

There are numerous additional factors which make the international marketing functions of non-consumer, high technology products significantly different from other consumer and industrial products. Some of these factors include:

1. High technology products often have very specific and limited uses, and adaptations to different market segments, e.g., countries, may not be possible or possible only at great cost;

2. High technology products are usually capital intensive and require a high level of financing;

3. The technological sophistication of the products has implications for any relationship with institutions and/or partners in a prospective host country;

4. High technology products often require sophisticated support systems that must be installed and maintained to allow optimum utilization;

5. These products may, and usually do, play an important role in the national economic development plans of any given country; and

6. The marketing functions, e.g.,especially pricing, distribution and advertising/promotion vary by country as a function of economic development.

This paper examines some of the key factors involved in the international marketing of high technology products and suggests marketing differences that might be expected in various countries based upon levels of economic development. An awareness of these differences will help to place potential marketing opportunities into a more realistic decision framework. The key factors analyzed are:

(1) Relevant market segments (by end-user); (2) the nature of the legal/organizational/ownership format that must exist between the multinational corporation and the host country; (3) product characteristics; (4) pricing; (5) advertising/promotion; and (6) distribution options. To help segment the various potential markets for high technology products, the United Nations standard classification system of levels of economic development are used i.e., less developed country - LDC, developing country - DC, industrial country - I, and post-industrial country - PI., (see Exhibit One).

I. ANALYSIS OF RELEVANT MARKET SEGMENTS

The end-user market for high technology products in any country may be broadly segmented into two major groups; public and private sectors. Regardless of a country's level of economic development, the public sector will normally constitute at least some portion of the total market. Frequently, defense related applications and countrywide communications networks are the most important public sector markets for high technology products. To a certain extent, public sector market size is inversely related to a country's level of economic development and its existing industrial base, i.e., the higher the level of economic development, the lower the size of the public sector market (with the possible exception of defense). In LDC's and DC's most, if not all, of the funds for investment in high technology products and systems come from public sector budget allocations that are related to national economic development plans and priorities. As a country develops and establishes an industrial base, requiring additional technological systems and products, private sector involvement in the market increases.

A. <u>LDC</u>: The public sector most likely will constitute 100% of the market. It is quite possible that all sales will be to the government or one of its semi-autonomous agencies. Market opportunities will be a function of the priority given to technology in the government's yearly budgets as well as the longer term, e.g., five year development plans. In many cases much of the technology desired may relate to the establishment of communications networks. In 1978, for example, the Saudi Arabian government awarded a $3.1 billion contract to two European firms to build a nationwide communications network (Saudis,

Exhibit One
Market Function/Economic Development Matrix

MARKET/ FUNCTION	LDC	DC	Industrial	Post-Industrial
1. End-User Market Segments	100% public sector	Majority public sector some private sector related to development of industrial base	Increasing importance of private sector; R&D financing from public	Increasing regulation by public sector; private sector heavily involved
2. Legal/ Organization/ Ownership Format	High involvement; subsidiary or joint venture with local government participation (Example: Turnkey Op)	High involvement; tripartite ventures (Example: Tripartite Ventures) Management/Ownership Requirements	High involvement Joint ventures; foreign and local private investors (Example: Tech. Royalty) Few ownership requirements	High involvement (Example: Technology Transfer)
3. Product Strategy	Complete transfer of product and system; No adaptation	Adapt existing levels of facilities and technical capabilities to your product and systems	Adaptation of your product and systems to existing network; compliance of your product with international specifications and standards	
4. Pricing Strategy	Sensitivity to real needs including ancillary services and training; services priced on basis of local costs	<--------------- Competitive Bidding Procedure --------------> Awareness of the existence of "buy local" policies		
5. Advertising/Promotion	Education of public sector officials; Personal promotion and contact	Educate public sector officials and potential private sector partners; some technical journal ads	Promotion focuses on attributes & services to key public sector and many private sector individuals; ads in technical journals	Promotion focuses on contributions to social welfare; ads in technical journals
6. Distribution/ Servicing	Highly centralized; Company responsible for initial distribution and servicing	Centralized distribution; servicing somewhat decentralized (company's responsibility)	Decentralization of both distribution and servicing; Delegation of both responsibilities to local agencies	

1977). Penetration into LDC marketing would involve a combination of several factors, including:

(1) Ability to deal with a different culture that may have major philosophical and business differences compared to the U.S.;

(2) Ability to adapt business practices to allow competition with non-U.S. firms from other industrial and post-industrial countries;

(3) Ability (and patience) to deal with a morass of bureaucratic red tape; and

(4) Ability to respond to a low or non-existent level of technical expertise.

These factors will have important implications for the company's level of involvement in the country (discussed in Section II).

B. DC: With the expansion of an industrial base, the size of the public sector market while still high (as a percentage of the total market), will begin to decrease. High technology products and systems may have to be specialized to meet the needs and standards imposed by an existing system. In Brazil, for example, special microwave equipment is being supplied by Rockwell International to service the newly formed private power utilities companies (Brazil 1978). Also, in DC's, technological systems may begin to play a role in the defense budgets as these countries try to strengthen and upgrade their existing capabilities.

C. Industrial: In an industrialized economy the rapid expansion of the industrial base and growth in the size and strength of the private sector will make it an increasingly important market segment to United States' sale of high technology products. Technologies will have to be customized to local markets and specific applications of various target segments.

The public sector, however, may provide levels of research and development financing with the objective of developing indigenous technologies, e.g., the United States in the late 1950s and 1960s. In addition, it is probable that an increasing portion of the national budget will be allocated to defense and its related technologies.

D. Post-Industrial: While public sector financing may not be as high as under the three previous categories, its involvement through regulation may be quite intense. Of major concern will be that no technology introduced has an adverse impact on the country's environment or health of its people. Companies penetrating even the private sector market will be confronted with government regulation that may require considerable adaptation of their present technology.

In this phase of economic development, the actual public sector market may consist mainly of allocations for defense and information technologies. In both industrial and post-industrial societies, significant portions of the public sector budget may be devoted to the acquisition of sophisticated communications and weapons technology for defense purposes, e.g., the United States, Germany, Great Britain and, increasingly, Japan.

II. LEGAL/ORGANIZATIONAL/OWNERSHIP FORMAT

Conceptually, it is not difficult to understand that the lower a country's level of economic development, the

higher will be the required degree of involvement and the
resulting organizational commitment, i.e., staff, investment, managerial expertise in the country on the part of
the United States company attempting to penetrate the market. The introduction of high technology products and
systems normally requires a high level of support, including; sophisticated maintenance and repair capabilities,
spare parts inventory and, perhaps, support industries, in
addition to technically qualified personnel to operate,
maintain and repair systems. The lower a country's level
of development, the less likely it is that these requirements will be met from internal sources.

A. LDC: In an LDC, it is unlikely that there will be any
existing support infrastructure or technically qualified
personnel available. This lack of technical infrastructure suggests the need for a high level of involvement in
which the company, in addition to installing the product
and related systems, must develop an elaborate support
system to operate, maintain and repair their high technology products. The expected relationship will probably be
a "turnkey" operation or a corporate subsidiary with government participation.

Increasingly, LDC governments are imposing ownership and
management restrictions on private foreign investors.
These restrictions, in addition to requiring majority local ownership (usually by the public sector since only it
has sufficient resources to participate) make it mandatory
for the foreign investor to train local technicians and
managers, phasing out expatriates over a specified time
period. The risk of nationalization or the imposition of
restrictive measures making it difficult or impossible for
a business to survive are greatest in this type of relationship since seldom are indigenous private sector interests involved. Once again, reference may be made to the
Saudi experience. Corporate subsidiaries with joint ownership with local governments (25% Saudi government participation in ownership) in priority development areas are
encouraged. These companies are given tax holidays for a
period of five years and other incentives to make the
joint venture option an attractive one (Doing, 1979).

B. DC: Once an industrial base has begun to form, it is
likely that low level technologies will have been adopted.
There probably will be some support facilities available
and personnel already will have received some technical
training. The task of a company penetrating the DC market
will be to build upon the already existing capacity, allowing for maximum utilization of indigenous facilities
and personnel.

With the development of a private sector, it is not uncommon for tripartite joint ventures to be established in
which the foreign investor has a minority participation
with the remaining majority split between the government
and local private investors. The management and ownership
restrictions imposed by LDCs are maintained, but some of
the risks (e.g., nationalization) are decreased by having
a broader degree of participation. Venezuela is a good
example of this strategy. It is seeking to form a tripartite joint venture for the maintenance and repair of electronic avionics equipment. Brazil, too, has given recent
emphasis to the formation of such ventures and they are
becoming increasingly popular (Brazil, 1978).

Often, in both DC's and LDC's, contributions to the joint
venture made by the foreign investor (the United States
firm) must be in the form of capital and/or plant and
equipment. Local contributions, however, may be in the
form of services or a donation of land. In this sense, of
course, the foreign investor would probably suffer disproportionately in the event of nationalization or any other
unforeseen termination of the relationship.

C. Industrial and Post-Industrial: A logical extension
of the preceding analysis suggests that the level of

development in both industrial and post-industrial countries would allow for a lower level of involvement, e.g.,
the establishment of a licensing or export relationship.
In these countries, support facilities are usually available and technically qualified personnel can be found or
easily trained.

However, these countries often have developed their own
technological products and systems and competition for
market share is keen. Because of the nature of the product, and common pricing and promotion strategies (discussed in sections IV and V), it is very difficult to capture a share of the market without a rather high level of
involvement via a joint venture or subsidiary. Among
others, this is one of the chief problems currently facing
many United States based MNC's attempting to further penetrate industrial markets in Japan (Suzuki, 1979).

Unlike LDC's and DC's, Industrial and Post-Industrial categories frequently impose no ownership or management requirements. Because of the keen competition and different
business practices among countries, however, it is usually
a wise strategy to penetrate the market with participation
of local investors. These local investors usually have a
much better understanding of the dynamics of the market
and are more acceptable to business and government leaders.

III. PRODUCT ANALYSIS

High technology products often require the installation of
sophisticated support systems. The product strategy must
be adapted to the extent that such technologies and systems are already in place in the country. This will determine the extent to which the product must be modified
to be compatible with and easily integrated into any existing system.

A. LDC: In an LDC that has a complete lack of technological products and systems, it may be quite possible for a
company to simply transfer its products and systems without the need to make any modifications or adaptations. Of
course, a company's ability to be successful with this
strategy will depend upon local needs and concerns, e.g.,
price competitiveness, versatility of the equipment,
adaptability to neighboring countries' systems, and ease
of integration with other systems worldwide. This was
precisely Rockwell's strategy in Saudi Arabia when it won
a $100 million contract from Western Electric to install
microwave equipment for long distance communications in
that country (The Saudis, 1978).

B. DC: In most DC's, with a developing industrial base,
there will be a need for some degree of adaptation necessary in products and systems sold. One strategy would be
to determine how best to utilize existing facilities and
technical capabilities and integrate them into the products and systems of the company. This would minimize the
need for adaptation while simultaneously recognizing that
a certain level of local development and expertise does
exist. In the Venezuelian project mentioned earlier, the
company took great pains to assure that their final proposal to Venezuela recognizes the fact that there was a
certain level of facilities and expertise in-country
(Brazil, 1978).

C. Industrial and Post-Industrial: Because these countries usually already have a certain level of technological sophistication, a company's success in market penetration will depend upon its ability to adapt its products
and systems to allow the fullest level of integration into
the existing systems.

In addition, industrial and post-industrial countries usually are concerned about the extent to which their

systems comply with specifications established by international commissions and agencies. The purpose of such international specifications is to facilitate worldwide standardization in important technological areas, e.g., satellite communications.

IV. PRICING ANALYSIS

The selection of an appropriate pricing strategy is a function of the country's level of development, the conditions under which the product is to be offered, and expectations regarding the future potential of that particular market. Unlike consumer product pricing, competitive bidding procedures are frequently used as one means of assuring the best possible cost/quality mix.

It is not uncommon for bid and proposal (B&P) costs to run into the hundreds of thousands and even millions of dollars on large, complex projects. In a major telecommunications project for Saudi Arabia, previously mentioned for example, ITT spent $8.0 million on its B&P and lost the contract to a European consortium (The Saudis, 1978). A company can ill-afford to submit many B&Ps without being awarded contracts on a good percentage of those submissions. In view of the costs, it is important that a company be aware of several factors prior to undertaking a B&P effort on a given project. Some of the factors are listed here and discussed in more detail as they relate to a country's level of development:

    1. A keen awareness of and sensitivity to the real needs of the country (not always articulated in the bid documents);

    2. Strategic importance to the company of establishing a presence in this particular country and potential for future market growth;

    3. The likelihood that loss of this contract will eliminate the company from penetrating this country or region in the foreseeable future and its impact; and

    4. Strategic importance of this country's market, or this particular project to the company's principal competitor.

A. _LDC and DC_: Often, it is in these countries that a sensitivity to real needs of the economy and of the government must be the keenest. In addition to the costs of the hardware (and software, if applicable), transportation and installation, particular attention must be devoted to needed ancillary services. These services might include maintenance and repair for a specified period, training for local personnel and a sufficient inventory of spare parts. The pricing of these services might be based on local rather than United States costs.

While an LDC or DC may not have the existing capacity to operate and maintain any system, many do have some technically qualified personnel that could be hired and, with additional training, be fully operational on the system at a much lower cost than a United States expatriate technician. Alternatively, a joint ownership plan might be proposed that would minimize capital costs to the host country and establish the United States based company in the country. While there are numerous plans that could be developed, the point is that not only would the United States organization lower the bid price, but would also make for a better proposal, indicating a sensitivity to the existing environment, and the host country's desire to transfer technology. Rockwell recently lost a contract in Honduras to a Japanese firm for this very reason. In its B&P, Rockwell quoted engineering services at U.S. rates. Not only did this greatly increase the bid, but it also indicated to the Hondurans that Rockwell not only did not

feel that Honduras had any engineers, but also could not train any (The Breakdown, 1976).

Other innovations might be included in the proposal depending upon the strategic importance of winning the contract not only for the company, but also for the company's competitor. For example, if the contract is highly important to the company, the bid and proposal might include a plan that provides a warranty on the system and related servicing, or free spare parts over a specified time period. On the other hand, if it is known that the contract is of great importance to the competitor, it is important to understand how that competitor is likely to bid, e.g., the competitor might be subsidized by its government, giving it a competitive advantage.

B. _Industrial and Post-Industrial_: In addition to being aware of the above factors, it is important to recognize that in these countries, local companies (and many will have companies capable of providing the needed products and systems) often will have the competitive advantage on any contract. A "buy local" policy, whether overt or covert, may effectively eliminate the company from competition regardless of the cost and/or responsiveness of the bid. Considerable expense may be avoided if this is the case and it is recognized at an early stage. This has long been the policy in Japan's telecommunications industry and this whole area is one of the prime sources of tension in the multilateral trade negotiations (A Survey, 1978).

V. ADVERTISING/PROMOTION ANALYSIS

In analyzing the nature of the advertising/promotion that should be undertaken for high technology products, there are several factors to be considered:

    1. In any country (depending upon size and level of development), there are usually a limited number of buyers, many of whom are in the public sector;

    2. Product costs are high, and sophisticated servicing and maintenance is often required; and

    3. It is often difficult to differentiate one product/ system from another.

In general terms, these factors suggest that success may depend upon a company's ability to make a name and generate a brand loyalty. This requires a high level of personal promotion and selling. Personal contact with potential customers is critical. It is only after this loyalty is established and maintained that the product will stand a chance of being pulled through the distribution channels. Even then, because of the rapid change in technology, it is important that close contact be maintained to assure the customer that the company and its products keep pace with new technological developments.

In all cases, a good relationship with the host country government is imperative. The public sector will constitute a certain percentage of the overall market in every country. Also, in competitive bidding for public sector financed projects, firms wishing to submit B&Ps often must be prequalified in order to participate. Convincing public sector officials of the capabilities of the firm is an important promotional activity required in almost all countries.

While this is the overall strategy, its implementation will differ by country as a function of economic development.

A. <u>LDC</u>: In an LDC, the primary purpose of the advertis-
ing/promotion will be to educate public sector officials.
Since the media are usually undeveloped and the public
sector generally constitutes almost one hundred percent of
the market, a high level of personal interaction will be
required to educate public officials vis-a-vis the attributes of the company's products and the reasons it is superior to those of competitors.

B. <u>DC</u>: The same type of interpersonal strategy will apply to a DC, but it must be carried further. With an emphasis on tripartite joint venture development in DCs, the
education process must be taken to the private sector.
Local private investors must also be convinced of the value of the technology. In some developing nations, a few
technical journals are published. Advertising in these
publications will likely reach everyone in the potential
private sector market. The message should be designed to
further educate members of that market.

C. <u>Industrial</u>: In these countries the message must focus
on the attributes of the product/system, the distinctive
services it will perform, and the qualities that differentiate it from competitors' products. Emphasis in the public sector should be focused directly on potential end-
users, e.g., Ministries of Defense and Communications. In
the private sector, prospective business partners should
be sought out and further educated. A wealth of technical
journals are normally available from which to select. Efforts should concentrate on those that are most likely to
reach public sector end-users and potential partners.

Other public sector officials must also be informed (especially in regulatory agencies) since frequently government regulation has an impact on the potential sales of
the product/system in a particular country.

D. <u>Post-Industrial</u>: In post-industrial countries, the
promotion/advertising activities are similar to industrial
countries, but the message should include an elaboration
of additional benefits that will serve to improve social
welfare, e.g., non-polluting nature of the technology, low
and efficient user of natural resources (especially energy).

VI. DISTRIBUTION/SERVICING ANALYSIS

Distribution and servicing strategies/problems associated
with high technology products/systems are somewhat unique
in that initial distribution is only one small part of the
overall problem. Characteristic of these products/systems
is that they frequently require maintenance and servicing.
Any distribution system must also fulfill this need.

A. <u>LDC</u>: The distribution system in an LDC will most
likely be highly centralized and the responsibility for it
probably will rest with the company. Because of the lack
of infrastructure, low level of internal technical expertise and small number or absence of medium sized satellite
cities, it is highly probable that initial distribution as
well as the follow-up distribution of maintenance services
will have to be handled by the company from a central location, i.e., the capital city. It may be the only place
where infrastructure needed not only for initial distribution, but also for adequate servicing, is available.

B. <u>DC</u>: Developing countries often have some internal
capabilities and infrastructure along with a small number
of satellite cities with needed facilities, i.e., energy.
While initial distribution still may be centralized, indigenous services may be strengthened and utilized. Servicing may be somewhat decentralized at a few locations --
i.e., satellite cities.

C. <u>Industrial and Post-Industrial</u>: Needless to say, indigenous capacity, infrastructure and satellite cities

should present few, if any, problems and initial distribution as well as servicing may be highly decentralized and
immediately, or within a relatively short period of time,
delegated to local agents. The problem in these countries
often is selecting the appropriate agent.

REFERENCES

Abernathy, William S. and Balaji S. Chakravarthy (1978),
"Government Intervention and Innovation in Industry: A
Policy Framework," <u>Sloan Management Review</u>, (Spring),
3-18.

<u>A Survey of U.S. Exporting Opportunities: Japan</u> (1978),
U.S. Department of Commerce, Industry and Trade Administration, U.S. Government Printing Office, (August),
252-255.

"Brazil Business Guide" (1978), <u>Nation's Business</u>, (December), 6-8.

Control of Restrictive Practices in Transfer of Technology
(1978), (New York UNCTAD document TD/AC. 1/17), 12-18.

Crawford, Merle C. and Gerard J. Tellis (1981), "The Technology Innovation Controversy," <u>Business Horizons</u>,
(July-August), 76-88.

Davidow, J. (1977), "The United States Developing Countries and the Issue of Intra-Enterprise Agreements,"
<u>Georgia Journal of International and Comparative Law</u>,
Vol. 7, 502-508.

David, Edward E., (1977), U. S. Innovation and World Leadership: Facts and Fallacies," <u>Research Management</u>,
(November), 7-10.

Dean, Robert (1978), "Technical Innovation in U.S.A.,"
<u>Mechanical Engineering</u>, (November), 23-32.

Hill, John and Richard Still (1980), "Cultural Effects of
Technology Transfer by Multinational Corporations in
Less Developed Countries," <u>Columbia Journal of World
Business</u>, XV (Summer) 40-51.

Irwing, Robert R. (1978), "Why America's Technology Is In
Trouble and What Can Be Done About It," <u>Iron Age</u>,
(July 31), 79-71.

"Saudis Pick Ericson and Philips" (1977), <u>Financial Times</u>,
(December 15), 12.

Suzuki, Ryohei (1979), "Worldwide Expansion of U.S.
Exports-A Japanese View," <u>Sloan Management Review</u>,
(Spring), 67-70.

Quinn, Jerry B. (1979), "Technological Innovation, Entrepreneurship, and Strategy," <u>Sloan Management Review</u>,
(Spring), 19-30.

"The Breakdown of U.S. Innovation" (1976), <u>Business Week</u>,
(February 16), 56-68.

"The Saudis Say 'Wrong Numbers' to the U.S." (1978),
<u>Business Week</u>, (January 7), 51.

Von Othegraven, Rainer (1979), "German Export Success-A
Model for the U.S.?" <u>Sloan Management Review</u>, (Spring),
71-76.

Walter, Ingo and Kent A. Jones (1981), "The Battle Over
Protectionism: How Industry Adjusts to Competitive
Shocks," <u>The Journal of Business Strategy</u>, 2, No.2,
(Fall), 37-46.

GREASING THE FOREIGN CHANNEL MECHANISM

Stan Reid, Syracuse University
James McGoldrick, Syracuse University

ABSTRACT

A substantial portion of expenditures in foreign business
is devoted to greasing distribution channels. Many of
these payments are, however, necessary and most firms have
no explicit policies to help managers to cope with them.
This paper suggests some reasons why greasing payments are
pervasive and offers some approaches that can help firms
recognize the strategic importance of such transactions
and accommodate them in their market entry strategy.

INTRODUCTION

Legislative responses to the issue of questionable payments by U.S. businesses to facilitate conducting of foreign operations can be queried on two grounds. Firstly,
they ignore the fact that such activities have had a long
tradition and are regarded as a normal course of business
activity. Secondly, by invoking legal penalties for
broadly described behavior, they can be a major inhibitor
to the firm conducting foreign business where such payments can confer strategic competitive advantages.

Since 1977 the number of voluntary disclosures of questionable payments to the Securities and Exchange Commission
and incidence of such reports in the press suggests that
the activity is widespread and is not confined to U.S.
firms (Basche 1977) nor to foreign activities (Coe 1977,
Kennedy and Simon 1978). The Abscam undercover operation
was an extension of this discovery and indeed provided
additional confirmatory evidence that questionable payments as a lubricant for business activity are more pervasive than usually acknowledged (Hougan 1978, Clinard and
Yeager 1980, pp. 135-199).

While the Foreign Corrupt Practice Act (FCPA) excludes
some specific payments which facilitate business activity
abroad, a strictly legalistic interpretation of the regulations is likely to force management to deal with such
payments on a case by case basis (Kaikati 1981). As a
result, firms are not encouraged to develop policies which
would allow for quicker resolution of the problems involved in such payment activities. Studies of such payments
indicate that very few firms have explicit guidelines to
help their managers even though a great majority of them
acknowledged that they either encounter demand for them or
that they may be necessary in certain countries (Baasche
1976).

This paper explores the issues associated with facilitating payments in order to assist managers and policy makers
in planning for the explicit costs of such activity. This
will lead to closer identification of the circumstances
under which such payments should be regarded as 'normal
operational items' and enable minimization of "channel
greasing" costs in the long run. Knowledge of potential
market areas in which questionable payments may be encountered can assist the firm in developing alternative strategies such as those recommended by Kaikati and Jabel
(1980).

BRIBE VS. FACILITATING PAYMENTS

For purposes of this study, facilitating payments are distinguished from the large-scale bribing activity which has
received substantial attention in recent years from both
the SEC and the FTC. A bribe is a voluntarily-offered
payment made in order to induce an official to do or omit
doing something in violation of his lawful duty, or to
exercise official discretion in favor of the payor's request. Since 1974, corporations have admitted to making
over $300 million in illegal payments in order to secure
long term contracts and influence legislation (Baasche
1976, Kaikati and Jabel 1980). Similar behavior is often
condoned in the U.S.A. under the guise of lobbying or
political donations.

Facilitating payments, on the other hand, usually take
the form of relatively small sums of cash or gifts to low
and middle level government officials. Such payments are
often expressly or implicitly permitted in various countries and are meant to expedite flows of goods or express
"appreciation" for normal performance of a ministerial or
procedural duty by the official.

The bribery provision of the Foreign Corrupt Practices
Act states that "a firm is prohibited from making or
authorizing payments, offers, promises or gifts for the
purpose of 'corruptly' influencing action by governments
or their officials in order to obtain or retain business
for a company." The act, however, expressly exempts payments made in order to expedite nondiscretionary official
actions (Hurd 1979).

In 1978, the SEC recognized a difference between payments
made to government officials to "procure special and unjustified" favors and those made to low and middle level
officials to perform functions that they are obliged to
perform as part of their governmental responsibilities.
Facilitating payments usually fall into the SEC-sanction-
ed category. Due to the broad scope of the definition,
however, there are many instances in which payments are
made which cannot be neatly categorized. Such definition-
al problems are, however, inconsequential to the development and conclusions of this study.

NATURE OF CHANNEL GREASING PAYMENTS

The fact that payments may be a necessary part of economic activity, even though in conflict with prevailing
social norms, has long been recognized as a major characteristic of extra-market operations. Analysts view them
as strategies for circumventing market imperfections,
encouraging channel reciprocity and thus achieve organizational aims (Walker 1943, Bucklin 1973). Foreign business for the small firm is usually conducted in situations where channel intermediaries, if used, have more
likelihood of having the potential to exercise reward and
coercive power. The lack of knowledge of the market, its
remoteness and, in some cases, different value systems,
place the interested firm in a relatively dependent situation on foreign retailers and foreign agencies (Rosson
and Ford 1980).

Greasing payments are predominantly associated with those
functions and agencies which facilitate the movement of
goods in export channels. Custom officials, for example,
have considerable power in appraising import values, dis-
allowing importation of goods and slowing down the documentation process (Crowe 1979, Gould 1980). Civil ser-
vants and other state functionaries may be vested with
considerable discretionary power to grant or withhold
authorization for many private sector activities (Jacoby,
Nehemkis and Eells 1977). Foreign firms that refuse to

provide such facilitating payments may eventually find themselves unable to operate (Nehemkis 1975).

In many cases, government officials conduct such activities with the implicit approval of the State which may be systemically corrupt (Nye 1967; Gould 1980). A World Bank report (1979) on (Zaire) is enlightening in this regard. It concludes,

> "Yet in nearly all agencies absences from work are silently sanctioned out of recognition of the need for most people to pursue other activities in order to afford working for the Government."

Most channel "grease" payments are made to such state officials as customer officers, port employees, railroad employees and others whose actions or failure to act can threaten to harm an exporting firm's marketing efforts. Generally, individual payments can help in expediting the flow of goods through distribution channels and may also be made to other third parties as, for example, customers, political organizations, and union officials who have the ability to interrupt normal business activity (Kennedy and Simon 1978).

In addition to these types of payments, firms often indir-indirectly grease channel mechanisms through the use of foreign agents. These agents provide access to important government officials and company representatives, help the firm with its market entry strategy, give advice on shaping bids and represent intelligence sources as to particular government needs. Such agents, through use of their market knowledge, contacts, and well placed "gifts" can substantially eliminate bureaucratic red tape and shorten the time span between initial market appraisal and actual product sales (Morgan 1980). The contractual function which such intermediaries serve is critical for information gathering and operating knowledge in foreign countries irrespective of whether they actually produce business (McGarry 1951).

FORECASTING GREASING SCENARIOS

If greasing payments are viewed as functional, acting as "lubrication' devices to remove impediments in the way of market access and expansion of overseas sales activity, they can be more objectively regarded as part of the market transaction costs. Such expenses of doing business can then be viewed as institutionalized payments customary to specific markets which can be anticipated in planning exporting strategies and in estimating part of the logistics costs.

There seem to be three basic factors which facilitate the growth of quasi- channel payments. These are (1) the existing level of regulated market activity; (2) the type of final buyer; and (3) the nature of the product being sold (see Exhibit I). Regulated markets provide both the opportunity and the means for inducing extra-channel costs, particularly where these are accompanies by shortages in trained personnel to supervise and administer laws.

An inadequacy of administrative resources along with a variety of regulations promote bureaucratic red tape and encourage delay in market transactions. The procedures for importing specific goods may be cumbersome and extremely detailed, involving several branches of the state bureaucracy and in some instances may result in a particular channel activity being subject to territorial conflict between institutions.Because the exercise of formal discretion is maximized in such situations, they present the greatest potential for incurring greasing payments. In addition, the presence of lax supervision or control encourages subordinates to use their offices for private gain (Nye 1967; Morgan 1980).

Large purchases may often involve a number of different institutions each representing different elements of the purchasing decision. Authorization for the actual purchase, decision as to type of product, terms of payment and user specification are activities that can involve several different institutions and institutional layers. The search for and access to key decision-makers by the prospective seller in such situations can be prohibitive in costs and use of managerial time. It is here that the agent or middleman exercising his contractual function with its consequential expenses is likely to be most visible (Scenario 1, 2, 5, 6).

EXHIBIT I

MATRIX OF RELATIVE CHANNEL GREASING POTENTIAL

Scenario	Extent of regulated market[1]		Market structure Final Buyer Concentration[2]		Product Value[3]		Greasing Potential
	High	Low	High	Low	High	Low	
1	√		√		√		High
2	√		√			√	Medium
3	√			√	√		Low
4	√			√		√	Low
5		√	√		√		High
6		√	√			√	Medium
7		√		√	√		Low
8		√		√		√	Low

1. Presence of extensive government red tape and legal requirements.

2. Concentration of buyers as a result of extensive state participation, and state monopolies.

3. Product unit value or aggregate contract size.

Should the State be also a major institutional trader in a highly regulated environment, the opportunities for channel blockage become even more apparent. In some cases the Government may be acting as both monopolist and monopsonist, having commercial trading relationships with specific firms which act as institutionalized barriers to entry for prospective entrants. In addition there is likely to be significant overlap in kinship ties, occupational roles and economic interests between the private sector and the state apparatus (Reid 1980). The existence of commercial family elites strategically placed in the decision-making process is a persistent feature in many modern states (Tokman 1973; Zeitlin, Eiven and Ratcliff 1974; Reid 1977).

What the above suggests is that those countries having governments as a major economic actor in highly regulated markets are likely to impose on foreign business an operating climate where access to crucial decision-makers, knowledge of terms of trade, securing market entry and facilitating logistics flows become strategic issues of the utmost importance. Analysts of market behavior have long held that the resolution of channel conflicts depends upon the relative ability of channel participants to exercise reward and coercive power inside a distribution system (Beier and Stern 1969, Bucklin 1973). The presence of monopsonic market structures and highly bureaucratic economies in foreign markets puts the foreign firm at a negotiation disadvantage. This dependency on foreign agents is enhanced if the firm produces products that have high unit value (Scenario 1 and 5).

According to a recent study (Jacoby, Nehemkis and Eell 1977) the highest frequency of questionable payments among American firms in foreign markets occurred in the aerospace, chemical, oil and gas drilling, rubber

fabrication and tobacco industries . These sectors have
common characteristics of high value products or disproportionately large contract arrangements, extensive state
participation and a relatively high degree of Government
regulation. In contrast the insurance, food retailing,
apparel and automobile parts sectors showed the lowest
cited frequency of questionable payments (Scenarios 3, 4,
7, 8). These industries tend to involve less costly products and are in relatively competitive markets in most
countries (Jacoby, Nehemkis and Eell 1977).

Physical perishability represents another aspect of product risk which, in contrast to the characteristics noted
above, can make the firm particularly vulnerable to petty
facilitating payments. Where products are subject to perishability because of logistics delays, firms may use payments to facilitate movement of the product. While the
alternative channel scenarios presented in Exhibit I summarizes the particular contingencies which suggest maximum
opportunity for greasing payments, it must be borne in
mind that the prevailing ethos and code of public conduct
circumscribes the extent to which such activities occur.
Although countries differ in the extent to which they
subscribe to and define ethical business practices (Frank
1980), this paper argues that the potential for extra-market payments is structurally determined.

CORPORATE LUBRICATION STRATEGIES

While individual facilitating payments are usually insignificant in terms of an item's final market value, their
aggregate value in a particular distribution channel can
be a significant factor in the final selling price. On
average such costs amounted to nearly 2% of gross revenues
in companies cited by the Jacoby et. al study (1977).
Should firms not manage to "grease" payments effectively,
additional inventory carrying costs will invariably be
borne as a result of bottlenecks in the distribution pipeline. The amount of goods lost to theft and vandalism
also increase as a function of the time they spend on
docks and in warehouses at ports of entry (Crowe 1979).
In addition, losses due to obsolescence and spoilage will
be experienced by firms in industries such as apparel and
food products in which timely distribution is critical to
the marketing effort.

Currently most managers are forced to make decisions as to
where and what extent "grease" payments are to be made on
the basis of sketchy market information. Often the necessity for making facilitating payments in a given country
is not recognized until the exporter finds himself in a
compromised position. Effective planning could eliminate
unnecessary "grease" by allowing the exporting firm to
design distribution channels which require various degrees
of facilitating payments. In addition, the firm could
develop a "channel greasing" strategy in advance of market
entry which would pinpoint key officials requiring payment
as well as channel links where payment pressure could be
avoided or even ignored.

Information on greasing costs may be secured from non-com-
peting firms which export to common markets. In addition,
commercial agencies such as banks, which deal extensively
with countries in which "greasing" is pervasive, are a
likely source for this type of marketing intelligence.
Naturally such knowledge is gathered informally. Individual firms can arrive at proxies for these distribution
costs through knowledge of channel intermediary margins
and the final selling price of the product.

For the small firm this type of research need not be prohibitive. It could, for example, use such unobtrusive
research techniques as securing quotations on similar pro-
products from a variety of sources including original suppliers, channel intermediaries and simple observation of
the market place. This provides some grounds for

comparison where channel greasing costs are recovered
from within the markets in which they occur.

In situations where such information cannot be obtained,
managers should avoid involvement and entry into markets
with high greasing potential and sell on the basis of
minimum channel responsibility. This is not to suggest
that these markets are not opportune for business expansion but more to underline the difficulty in assessing
the relative profitability of entry.

CONCLUSION

This analysis suggests that extra-market transactions are
a pervasive form of business activity which can vary in
intensity across foreign markets and should be formally
acknowledged in planning expansion strategies for the
firm. Pinpointing the costs of greasing channels can
provide the manager with critical market information
necessary to plan selling and channel entry strategies in
the foreign market.

The initial costs of obtaining the needed information
should be viewed as a marketing expenditure necessary to
reduce distribution costs in the long run. Firms that
recognize this are more likely to be sensitive to situations which may be proscribed by U.S. law and are in a
position to set operating guidelines which can help their
managers in making decision as to both the extent and
type of discretionary payment that the firm is willing
and can support.

The article quite deliberately avoids the ethical issues
which some readers are bound to suggest are present in
such situations. It recognizes that bribes, inducements,
favors, and greasing payments are defined in the context
of value systems which vary from country to country and
are all situationally proscribed. Furthermore, these
activities are regarded as functional properties specific
to certain market structures and products. From this
perspective, those firms which do not want to engage in
such behavior at least have some heuristics which can
allow them to pinpoint avoidable markets.

References

Baasche, J. (1977). "Questionable payments and the
regulation of multinational corporations." Journal of
Contemporary Business, Vol. 6, 4, 165-178.

_________ (1976). Unusual foreign payments. A survey of
the policies and practices of U.S. Companies (New York,
N.Y., Conference Board).

Beier, F.J. and L. Stern (1969). "Power in the channel
of distribution." Distribution channels: Behavioral
Dimensions, (ed.) L. Stern, Boston: Houghton Mifflin
Company, 92-116.

Bucklin, L.P. (1973), "A theory of channel control,"
Journal of Marketing, (January), 39-47.

Clinard, M. and P. Yeager (1980) Corporate Crime. New
York, N.Y.: The Free Publishers.

Coe, B.J. (1977), "The questionable foreign payments
controversy: Dimensions of the problem," Contemporary
Marketing Thought, (eds.) B. Greenberg and D. Bellenger,
Chicago: American Marketing Association, 473-476.

Crowe, D. (1979), "Growing trade markets demand flawless
paperwork," Canadian Transportation and Distribution
Management, Vol. 82, 3, 39-40.

Frank, I. (1980). Foreign enterprise in developing
countries. Baltimore, Maryland: The John Hopkins Press.

Gould, D. (1980). Bureaucratic corruption and underdevelopment in the Third World - The Case of Zaire.
Elmsford, New York: Pergamon Press.

Hougan, Jim (1978). "The business of buying friends."
Crime at the Top, (eds.) J. Johnson and J. Douglas. New
York, N.Y.: J.P. Lippincott Company, 196-226.

Hurd, Baruch (1979). "The foreign Corrupt Practices
Act." Harvard Business Review, (January-February),
32-38.

Jacoby, N.H., P. Nehemkis and R. Eells (1977). Bribery
and Extortion in World Business. New York, N.Y.:
McMillan Publishing Company, Inc..

Kaikati, J.G. and W. Jabel (1980). "American Bribery
Legislation: An obstacle to international marketing.
Journal of Marketing, Fall, 38-43.

Kaikati, J.G. (1981). "The anti-export policy of the
U.S." California Management Review, Vol. 23, 3, 5-19.

Kennedy, Tom and Charles Simon (1978). An examination of
questionable payments and practices. New York, N.Y.:
Praeger Special Studies.

McGarry, E. (1951). "The contractual function in marketing." Journal of Business, (April), 96-113.

Morgan, D. (1980). Merchants of Grain, New York, N.Y.:
Penguin Books.

Nehemkis, Peter (1975). "Business payoffs abroad:
Rhetoric and reality," California Management Review,
Winter, 5-20.

Nye, J.S. (1967). "Corruption and political development:
A cost benefit analysis," The American Political Science
Review, Vol. 2 (June), 417-427.

Reid, S.D. (1980). "Economic elites - A study in monis-
tic influences," Anthropologica, Vol. 22, 1, 25-34.

_________ (1977). "An introductory approach to the concentration of power in the Jamaican corporate economy."
Essays on Power and Change in Jamaica, (eds.) C. Stone
and A. Brown, Kingston, Jamaica: Jamaica Publishing
House, 15-44.

Rosson, P. and I. Ford (1980). "Stake, conflict and
performance in export marketing channels," Management
International Review, Vol. 20, 4, 31-37.

Tokman, V. (1973). "Concentration of economic power in
Argentina," World Development, Vol. 1, 10, (October),
33-41.

Walker, Ronald (1943). From economic theory to policy,
(Chicago, Ill.: University of Chicago Press), 100-141.

World Bank Report (1979). Zaire Economic Memorandum:
The Zairean economy: Current situation and constraints.
Report nos. 2518LR, Washington, D.C.: World Bank.

Zietlin, M., L. Eiven and R. Ratcliff (1974). "New
princes for old? The large corporation and the capital-
ist class in Chile."" American Journal of Sociology,
Vol. 80, 1 (July), 87-123.

THE EFFECTS OF PERSONAL SELLING:
AN INDUSTRIAL ORGANIZATION ECONOMICS APPROACH

William Gaidis, University of Wisconsin-Madison
Michael Levas, University of Wisconsin-Madison
George John, University of Wisconsin-Madison

ABSTRACT

This paper examines the effects of personal selling on market structure and profitability within an industrial organization economics framework. Received models from this approach are modified to incorporate the personal selling variable. The results indicate that personal selling affects profitability while it does not affect market concentration significantly. The strategic implications of these results are examined and contrasted with the corresponding results for advertising.

INTRODUCTION

There has been a recent trend toward empirical investigations of marketing strategy issues in contrast to earlier nonempirical work. Two approaches seem to predominate in this new literature. One can be considered an inductive attempt to discover the determinants of firm profitability and its relationship to strategy-related variables (e.g., Buzzell, Gale, & Sultan, 1975; Schoeffler, 1977). The other approach has attempted to use models deduced from theories of industrial organization economics to examine strategic issues (e.g., Porter & Spence, 1978; Newman, 1978; Porter, 1979). While the first approach has provided some useful insight into the effects of important strategic variables on firm profitability, its lack of a theoretical framework has hampered interpretation of sometimes contradictory findings. For example, Buzzell, et al. (1975) suggested there was a positive relationship between market share and firm profitability. However, Porter (1979) demonstrated that this relationship is strong, weak, or even reversed depending on the type of industries comprising the sample. It is difficult to reconcile or interpret such findings without some theoretical framework to organize the results.

In contrast, the industrial organization approach is based on well-founded theoretical models but suffers from the drawback that the models studied have tended to omit managerially important variables. Consequently, the strategic implications drawn from this work have generally not been supported by direct empirical evidence.

Clearly, an improved understanding of strategy-related issues depends on being able to overcome the shortcomings identified in each of these approaches. A promising approach in this regard are studies that utilize the theoretical models derived from industrial organization (IO) economics, but which incorporate managerially important variables. In this paper, we will use such an approach to examine the strategic implications of an important promotional variable, personal selling.

The paper is organized in four sections. First, the relevant theoretical models are presented followed by a discussion of the data collection and model estimation procedures. The strategy implications relating to the personal selling variable are then examined, and are contrasted with the corresponding implications relating to the other major promotional variable, advertising. Finally, the limitations of the present study are discussed.

MODELS

The models that are presented here are based closely on the specifications proposed by Strickland and Weiss (1976), Martin (1979) and Hirschey (1981). The discussion relating to the specification of the equations and the variables is necessarily brief, and the interested reader is referred to the above sources for a complete discussion of the issues involved. Before the individual equations are presented, a discussion of the general nature of personal selling is warranted.

Advertising, sales promotion efforts, personal selling and publicity are generally considered to be the four promotion variables that are available to a firm. While each variable is more or less effective in varying circumstances, personal selling constitutes a large component of total promotional expenditures across a variety of industries. Indeed, annual expenditures on personal selling exceed those of advertising. For example, in 1976 American firms spent approximately $100 billion on personal selling compared with $33 billion spent on advertising (Kotler, 1980). The importance of personal selling is undoubtedly due to the versatility of the sales representative. Sales representatives can perform a wide variety of tasks for their employer. The sales representative is a highly versatile component in the manufacturer's arsenal of promotional weapons.

Marketing thought suggests that in industrial markets the promotional mix should heavily stress personal selling; in consumer durables a more equivocal allocation between personal selling and advertising is used and in consumer nondurables, advertising is heavily emphasized. However, in a survey of executives of 336 industrial, 52 consumer durable and 88 consumer non-durable goods producers, personal selling was seen as most important (vs. the other promotional tools) in all three types of firms (Udell, 1972).

Two points seem obvious. First, the sales representative can play a critical role in a firm's marketing efforts across a variety of settings. Secondly, tremendous amounts of funds are invested in this component of the promotional mix. It would appear reasonable, then, to consider relationships between such expenditures and profitability. However, these issues have been virtually ignored in the extant literature on personal selling.

The early studies in the area (e.g., Magee, 1953; Brown et al., 1956; Ward et al., 1956) were concerned with issues such as the analysis of market sales potential, sales force size allocation and break-even analysis. In later studies (Talley, 1961; Buzzell, 1964; Cloonan, 1964), some pioneering attempts were made to identify the sales response function to personal selling expenditures. More recently, attempts have been made to develop quantitative models useful for determining optimum sales force size and allocating selling effort between territories. For example, Beswick and Cravens (1977) developed a market response model which used individual sales territories as the primary unit of analysis. Likewise, Lilien (1979) developed a model useful in making promotional allocation decisions for industrial products using the product as the primary unit of analysis.

In sum, efforts in the marketing literature have been made toward modeling sales force size and territory allocation decisions. But, we know little about the impact of personal selling expenditures upon profitability. Further, the explanations for the presumed effects of personal selling on profitability (e.g., product differentiation effects, economies of scale effects, entry barrier effects) have not been empirically examined.

Personal selling expenditures and their effects have also not been considered in the classic investigations of market structure and industry performance that have appeared in the economics literature. Bain (1956) suggested that profitability would be influenced by entry conditions and seller concentration. Others proposed that profitability could be explained by advertising intensity or concentration (e.g., Comanor and Wilson, 1967; Ornstein, Weston and Intriligator, 1973). More recently, Strickland and Weiss (1976) investigated the determinants of industry concentration, advertising intensity, and industry profitability via a three-equation system from which a personal selling variable was conspicuously absent. Martin (1979) respecified the Strickland and Weiss model in his investigation of the market structure industry performance relationship. None of these studies included personal selling expenditures as an explanatory variable.

The present paper attempts to provide some insight regarding these issues. Specifically, it examines the effects of personal selling expenditures upon market structure and industry profitability. Briefly, IO models of market concentration and profitability are extended to include personal selling.

INDUSTRY PROFITABILITY MODEL

Industry profitability will be examined as a function of market structure, conduct, and demand conditions.

Industry Profitability = f(ease of collusion, barriers to entry, scale of operations and demand conditions)

This specification follows the general form used in IO studies. Phillips (1976) and Strickland and Weiss (1976) discuss this specification in detail. The variables used to measure each of the constructs are discussed below.

Industry Profitability

The measure of industry profitability used here will be the widely used price-cost margin (M) based on census data. While this measure is unfamiliar to most marketers, (i.e., value added minus payroll divided by value of shipments) it avoids many of the accounting problems associated with using other profit data and can be precisely obtained at the four-digit S.I.C. level. As this measure implicitly includes the cost of capital, an essential independent variable is some measure of industry capital intensity (Hirschey, 1981; Strickland & Weiss, 1976). The coefficient estimated for this variable reflects required rates of return on invested capital and may be a source of lower costs to an established firm. In the present study, capital intensity (K/S) will be defined as the gross fixed value of assets divided by the value of shipments.

Ease of Collusion

The variables that indicate ease of collusion are the four-firm concentration ratio (CR4) and the geographical dispersion (GD) of the industry. The CR4 variable is suggested by various theories of oligopoly. Virtually all of them posit an increase in the effectiveness of collusion as industry concentration rises, with an attendant rise in price-cost margins. Hirschey and Wichern (1981) and Martin (1979) provide empirical support for this notion. The measure used here is the share of industry shipments accounted for by the four largest firms in the industry.

The geographical dispersion (GD) variable is suggested by the models presented by Strickland and Weiss (1976) and Martin (1979). It captures the regional or local nature of markets where the national concentration ratios do not adequately characterize extant concentration. Weiss' (1972) measure of GD (distance radius in miles where 90% of industry shipments are made) is the measure used here.

Barriers to Entry

Economic theory suggests that the attainable profits of effectively colluding firms can be expected to rise with increased barriers to entry. These barriers insulate existing firms from potential entrants and also constitute mobility barriers within industries, thus reducing the intensity of intra-industry rivalry. The variables included in this set relate to product differentiation variables and scale requirements.

The first indicator of product differentiation is advertising intensity (AD/S) which is measured by advertising expenditures as a fraction of sales. This has been used as the sole indicator of product differentiation in the bulk of the previous studies in this area. In the present study, we have supplemented this with the personal selling variable (PS). It measures the intensity of personal selling as a fraction of sales. We expect that product differentiation can be achieved by the use of both advertising and personal selling, and that the relative levels of each of these variables represent managerial responses to particular environments. The inclusion of both of these variables was felt to constitute a more realistic characterization of product differentiation efforts, and would enable us to examine the presumed effects of these managerially relevant variables in a theoretically rigorous fashion. These variables were expected to relate positively to the profitability measure.

Scale of Operations

There are two variables used to characterize scale-related effects on profitability. The first variable is the minimum efficient scale of plant (MES) suggested by Weiss (1963). It is defined as the estimated output of the plant size found at the midpoint of an industry's output size distribution, expressed as a percentage of total industry output. The bulk of previous studies have utilized this variable as an indicator of scale effects. This variable is supplemented by the cost disadvantage ratio (CDR) proposed by Caves et al. (1975) which captures the disadvantage of operating small plants below MES levels. It is defined as the value added per employee in smaller plants producing the bottom 50% of industry output divided by value added per employee in plants producing the top 50% of output. Both of these variables are expected to be positively related to profitability because such scale effects also constitute barriers to entry.

Demand Conditions

There are two variables included here to characterize the variations in demand conditions that can affect profitability. The first variable is the industry growth measure (GR) and is simply the value of industry shipments in 1967 divided by the value of industry shipments in 1963. As Strickland and Weiss (1976) note, this variable can be expected to relate positively to profitability as it captures unanticipated increases in demand or unanticipated decreases in costs.

The other variable relating to demand conditions is a measure of the fraction of industry output going to final consumer demand (CDS). Martin (1979) suggests that this variable will relate positively to profitability because the potential for successful product differentiation is higher when the output is sold to final consumers rather than producers.

INDUSTRY CONCENTRATION MODEL

An industry concentration model was developed because of the importance of this structural variable. As Porter (1980) indicates, market structure has a strong impact on the effectiveness of marketing strategy. It is, therefore, important to understand how managerial efforts to differentiate a product via personal selling affect industry structure.

The model of concentration proposed here is derived from Strickland and Weiss (1976) and Martin (1979) and it proposes that the degree of concentration in an industry can be described as:

Industry Concentration = f(scale of operations, barriers to entry, demand conditions)

Scale of Operations

There are two variables that relate to the scale of operations factor. First, the presence of large economies of scale relative to the size of the market will dictate that only a few firms will exist. These economies of scale are characterized by the MES variable. This measure has been discussed previously.

A second variable relating to scale effects on concentration is the cost disadvantage ratio (CDR) described earlier. This variable describes the intensity of the disadvantages suffered by small producers relative to large producers, and as this increases, extant industry concentration increases correspondingly.

Barriers to Entry

Entry barriers constitute an important cause of concentration, as economic theory posits that it is the existence of entry barriers that cause high concentration levels to be achieved and maintained even if there are no compelling production-related economies of scale.

The first variable included was the intensity of advertising variable (AD/S). Higher levels of advertising and consequent product differentiation may insulate existing products from potential entrants. Further, it has been argued elsewhere that there are economies of scale in advertising (e.g., Comanor & Wilson, 1967) that favor large firms. These economies would tend to increase concentration levels.

The second variable associated with entry conditions was the intensity of personal selling variable (PS). While it might be argued that this variable would have the same effect on concentration as the advertising variable, there are some crucial differences. Undoubtedly, personal selling enhances product differentiation, but marketers generally consider that personal selling can be effective regardless of the scale and size of the firm. Also, it does not tend to have the long-term carry-over effects attributed to advertising, and thus would not constitute a barrier to new firms entering an industry. In fact, new firms entering an industry on a small scale may be able to compete successfully because personal selling efforts can be focused on a small market segment to carve out a profitable niche. For these reasons, we hypothesize that personal selling, unlike advertising, will not have an effect on concentration.

Demand Conditions

The first variable in the demand conditions category is the fraction of industry sales going to final consumers (CDS). The potential for product differentiation may be higher in the case of buyers who are final consumers compared to buyers who are producers themselves. Consequently, it may be more difficult to enter industries as the value of CDS increases, hence we would expect concentration levels to relate positively to this variable.

The second variable included here is the industry growth (GR) variable. It is expected that a rapidly growing industry poses fewer problems for a potential entrant because of unmet consumer needs and unoccupied market niches. For these reasons, this variable is expected to relate negatively to industry concentration.

DATA

The primary source of data was the 1967 <u>Census of Manufacturers</u>. 355 four-digit S.I.C. industries constituted the estimation sample. Industries classified as "Miscellaneous" and "Not Elsewhere Classified" were omitted to reduce measurement problems. Most of the variables were constructed directly from the census figures, but some variables were derived from other sources.

The advertising intensity variable (AD/S) was obtained from Ornstein (1977) with the 1967 input-output table of the U.S. Economy as the original source. Twenty-eight industries not accounted for by Ornstein came directly from the input-output tables. The fraction of industry output going to final consumers (CDS) was also obtained from the input-output tables. The <u>Annual Survey of Manufacturers</u>, 1968, was used to calculate the capital intensity variable (K/S). The geographical dispersion variable (GD) was obtained from the Appendix of Weiss (1972).[1]

The personal selling variable (PS) used here is obtained from the industry-level selling expenses as a fraction of sales as reported in the 1972 survey of selling costs reported in <u>Sales Management</u>. However, these data are reported at a more aggregate level than the four-digit S.I.C. level. Consequently, a dummy variable was coded equal to one if an industry exhibits relatively intense sales expenses, and zero otherwise on the basis of the obtained data which was at the two and three-digit S.I.C. level. The midpoint of the reported range (i.e., 4%) was used as the cutoff for coding purposes. This parallels the method used by Hirschey (1981) with regard to R&D expenditures. As these data are from a later year, we examined their stability over a four-year span (1972-1976). A McNemar test showed no significant change.

The two equations for profitability and concentration were estimated by the OLS procedure. Examination of the correlation matrix indicated that multicollinearity was not a problem here. Table 1 provides the estimates of the parameters and associated statistics.

RESULTS AND IMPLICATIONS

The profitability equation indicates that capital intensity, personal selling, advertising intensity and the four-firm concentration ratio had a significant positive impact on profitability. Geographical dispersion, minimum efficient scale, cost disadvantage ratio, fraction of sales to final consumers and industry growth were insignificantly related to profitability.

----

[1] We would like to thank Mark Hirschey for making the above data available to us.

In the concentration equation, minimum efficient scale, advertising intensity, fraction of sales to final consumers and the cost disadvantage ratio are significantly related to concentration. The personal selling and industry growth variables are insignificant.

The results obtained here are similar to those obtained in previous studies. The insignificant coefficients of minimum efficient scale, cost disadvantage ratio, and fraction of sales to final consumers in the profit equation is probably due to the fact that these variables affect concentration which, in turn, affects profitability in a significant way. The major motivation for the study was to examine the effect of the personal selling variable, and with regard to these effects, the results indicate that it enhances profitability significantly while it does not increase industry concentration levels. In contrast, the intensity of advertising variable increases both profitability and concentration.

These results have some interesting strategic implications. Clearly, product differentiation via personal selling and/or advertising is possible across a broad variety of industries. Without subsample analysis, it is difficult to know the relative efficacy of each of these promotional variables in different settings. However, there is an important general difference between personal selling and advertising. It appears that personal selling does not confer any size advantages to larger firms or pose difficulties for potential entrants as evidenced by its insignificant coefficient in the concentration equation. In contrast, the expected economies of scale effect and barrier effect is evident for the advertising variable.

Porter (1979, 1980) and Newman (1978) provide a framework for devising firm-level strategy implications from the present results. In their analysis of strategy effects on firm profitability from an IO perspective, they invoke notions regarding mobility barriers and strategic groups within industries to explain the wide variations in intra-industry profits. Briefly, mobility barriers inhibit the range of profitable strategic moves available to firms. As for strategic groups, the benefits flowing from industry barriers to entry are unequally distributed to members in different groups. The following discussion regarding firm strategy is developed from this perspective.

In terms of marketing strategy, this suggests that personal selling may constitute a very useful promotional device for small market share firms that are attempting to fashion a viable competitive strategy. It provides direct empirical evidence of the viability of a "focus" strategy that Porter (1980) presents in his analysis of competitive strategy. Such a strategy involves trading off an emphasis on market dominance through size advantages for a strategy of focusing on a relatively narrow segment. Porter (1979) suggests that this is one reason why firms with small market shares are sometimes more profitable than large share firms.

The results pertaining to the advertising variable offer some different strategy implications. From a competitive strategy perspective, it appears that promotional efforts via advertising would favor relatively larger firms. Within the framework presented by Porter (1980), it indicates that advertising efforts are an important component of a "dominance" strategy where firms capitalize on one or more size advantages to achieve higher profits.

LIMITATIONS

The limitations of the present study are those endemic to industrial organization investigations, and are primarily data-related problems. Reliance on secondary data is unavoidable, and the limitations of the present data are self-evident. A very useful direction for future studies would be to assess the psychometric adequacy of these measures. Such assessments are virtually absent from the literature.

From a substantive perspective, studies examining these kinds of relationships in various types of industry groups would help to uncover the nature of changes and variations in the effects, and to provide more precise strategic guidelines for managers.

TABLE 1
OLS ESTIMATES OF THE TWO EQUATIONS
(t-ratios in parentheses)

	Dependent Variables	
	CR4	M
Constant	23.91	15.91
CR4		.05* (2.26)
GD		−.0002 (.328)
MES	3.415* (11.08)	.2111 (1.46)
AD/S	1.184* (2.673)	1.66* (9.22)
CD/S	−1.042* (3.26)	−.012 (.84)
K/S		.1019* (6.22)
PS	.508 (.088)	5.599* (7.167)
GR	7.068 (.57)	2.892 (.578)
CDR	2.863 (1.89)	−.134 (.217)
R^2	.402	.389

*Sig. @ .01 level

REFERENCES

Bagozzi, R. (1980), "Performance and Satisfaction in an Industrial Salesforce: An Examination of their Antecedents and Simultaneity," _Journal of Marketing_, 44 (Spring), 65-77.

Bain, J. (1956), _Barriers to New Competition_, Cambridge: Harvard University Press.

Beswick, C. A. and D. Cravens (1977), "A Multistage Decision Model for Salesforce Management," _Journal of Marketing Research_, 14 (May), 135-144.

Brown, A., F. Hulswit, and J. Kettelle (1956), "A Study of Sales Operations," _Operations Research_, 4 (June), 269-308.

Buzzell, R. (1964), _Mathematical Models and Marketing Management_, Boston: Harvard University Graduate School of Business Administration.

Buzzell, R., B. T. Gale, and R. G. M. Sultan (1975), "Market Share--A Key to Profitability," _Harvard Business Review_, 53 (January/February), 97-107.

Caves, R. E., J. Khalilzadeh-Shiraz, and M. E. Porter (1975), "Scale Economies in Statistical Analyses of Market Power," *Review of Economics and Statistics*, 57 (May), 133-140.

Cloonan, J. (1966), "A Heuristic Approach to Some Sales Territory Problems," Proceedings of the IFORS Conference, (September), 284-292.

Comanor, W. S. and T. A. Wilson (1967), "Advertising, Market Structure, and Performance," *Review of Economics and Statistics*, 47 (November), 423-440.

Cravens, D. (1979), "Sales Force Decision Models" in *Critical Issues in Sales Management: State of the Art and Future Research Needs*, G. Albaum and G. A. Churchill eds., Eugene, Oregon: Division of Research, College of Business Administration, University of Oregon.

Greer, D. F. (1971), "Advertising and Market Concentration," *Southern Economic Journal*, 38 (July), 19-32.

Hirschey, M. (1981), "The Effect of Advertising on Industrial Mobility, 1947-72," *Journal of Business*, 54 (April), 329-339.

___________, "Economies of Scale in Advertising," *Managerial and Decision Economics*, forthcoming, in 1981.

___________ (1978), "Television Advertising and Profitability," *Economics Letters*, 12, North-Holland Publishing Company, 259-264.

Hirschey, M. and Dean Wichern (1981), "Indicators and Causes of Size Advantages in Industry," Wisconsin Working Paper.

Kotler, P. (1980), *Marketing Management, Analysis, Planning and Control*, 4th 3d., New Jersey: Prentice-Hall, Inc.

Lilien, G. L. (1979), "Advisor 2: Modeling the Marketing Mix Decision for Industrial Products," *Management Science*, Vol. 25, No. 2 (February), 191-204.

Magee, J. F. (1953), "The Effect of Promotional Effort," *Operations Research*, 1 (February), 64-74.

Martin, S. (1979), "Advertising Concentration and Profitability: The Simultaneity Problem," *The Bell Journal of Economics*, 639-647.

Newman, H. H. (1978), "Strategic Groups and the Structure-Performance Relationship," *Review of Economics and Statistics*, (August), 417-427.

Ornstein, S. I., J. F. Weston, and M. D. Intriligator (1973), "Determinants of Market Structure," *Southern Economic Journal*, 39 (April), 612-625.

Porter, Michael E. (1976), "Interbrand Choice, Media Mix and Market Performance," *American Economic Review*, (Proceedings), 66 (May), 398-406.

___________ (1979), "The Structure Within Industries and Companies' Performance," *Review of Economies and Statistics*, (May), 214-227.

___________ (1981), *Competitive Strategy*, New York: The Free Press.

Porter, M. E. and M. Spence (1978), "Capacity Expansion in A Growing Oligopoly: The Case of Wet Corn Milling," Discussion Paper, Harvard Graduate School of Business Administration.

Schoeffler, S. (1975), "Cross-Sectional Study of Strategy, Structure and Performance: Aspects of the PIMS Program," in *Strategy Plus Structure Equals Performance*, H. B. Thorelli, ed., Bloomington: Indiana University Press.

Strickland, A. D. and L. W. Weiss (1976), "Advertising, Concentration, and Price Cost Margins," *Journal of Political Economy*, 84 (October), 1109-1121.

Talley, W. (1961), "How to Design Sales Territories," *Journal of Marketing*, 25 (January), 7-13.

Udell, J. G. (1972), "Successful Marketing Strategies in American Marketing," Madison, Wis.: Mimir Publishers, Inc., 47.

Ward, C., D. Clark, and R. Ackoff (1956), "Allocation of Sales Effort in the Lamp Division of the General Electric Company," *Operations Research*, 4 (December), 629-647.

Weiss, L. W. (1972), "Factors in Changing Concentration," *Review of Economics and Statistics*, 54 (August), 245-257.

MARKETING STRATEGY AND FINANCE THEORY

Adam Finn, University of Illinois, Urbana-Champaign
Roy Howell, Texas Tech University, Lubbock

ABSTRACT

Marketing strategy decisions can be viewed as investment decisions. Normative criteria for such decisions have evolved through five stages. The most recent employs the finance theory concept of systematic risk, the covariance between the expected return on an investment and the return on a portfolio of all assets. Here it is argued that such covariance originates within the marketing manager's domain, in the changing responsiveness of consumers to a marketing mix as the environment changes, and in the updating of the firm's marketing mix as the environment changes. Decision rules based on systematic risk have not considered this complication.

INTRODUCTION

Marketing theory and finance theory have developed quite independently. But recently, Anderson (1979) suggested that contemporary finance theory offers a new and preferable basis for marketing investment decisions. This paper examines the evolution of marketing investment decision criteria, and then reviews the Capital Asset Pricing Model approach raised by Anderson. It is argued that the processes underlying systematic risk are logically and traditionally processes investigated by marketers. An attempt is made to specify their nature and suggestions are made for further study of these issues.

MARKETING STRATEGY DECISIONS AS INVESTMENT DECISIONS

Virtually any change in marketing strategy requires management make investment decisions. Examples of such decisions include initiating an advertising campaign, adding a new product, starting a second salesforce, switching from wholesalers to direct distribution, or expanding into another international market. Five stages can be identified in the evolution of normative decision criteria for such marketing investment decisions.

1. **Deterministic individual project stage.** This approach, reflecting the marginal analysis of the classical economic theory of the firm, dominated marketing until about 1960. The firm was assumed to be able to specify the returns which would be produced by a marketing investment. Then, using a universal cost of capital, the investment could be evaluated on its return on the marketing investment, or in more sophisticated firms, on net present value using discounted cash flows.

2. **Deterministic multiple project stage.** The simple single project approach appeared inadequate when multi-product and multiple activity firms increasingly dominated western economies. Marketing and business synergy were used to explain diversification (Ansoff 1965), necessitating the simultaneous evaluation of multiple projects using contribution theory still advocated in a recent marketing and finance text (Mossman et al. 1977). The distinction between shareholder and managerial control was first explored by organizational behaviorists. Power seeking, satisficing, and survival strategy biases were called upon to account for the observed discrepancies between the prior normative and actual behavior of firms (Cyert and March 1963). A number of areas of marketing theory remain at this stage. Examples include market segmentation (Winter 1979) and the more general product design optimization models (Green et al. 1981).

3. **Risk individual project stage.** Risk was incorporated into marketing decision theory through Bayesian analysis in the sixties (see Green 1962). An assumption of risk aversion produced the view that the cost of capital should be dependent on the variance in expected returns on an investment. Marketing investment decisions required risk adjusted discount rates or hurdle rates of return. As a result it was possible to postulate a risk-return frontier in a graphical representation of the investment decision criteria (see Kotler 1971, p. 265).

4. **Risk multiple project stage.** The seventies brought consideration of portfolio theory initially proposed by Markowitz (1952). For example Wind (1974) suggested treating a firm as a portfolio of products or of projects, so that investment would depend on the contribution of one project to the total variance in returns for the firm. Sophisticated models appeared necessary to optimize a firm's product portfolio, given the complex pattern of correlations between cash flows produced by a set of products (see Fabozzi 1978).

5. **Systematic risk stage.** Modern finance theory suggests the Capital Asset Pricing Model (CAPM) is the appropriate tool for marketing investment decisions (Anderson 1979). It proposes that the cost of capital for an investment is determined by its systematic risk—the covariance between its expected returns and a portfolio of all assets, normally approximated by a stock market index. This approach has yet to be digested in marketing.

THE CAPITAL ASSET PRICING MODEL

The CAPM has become the dominant theme in normative theories of investment. Developed by Sharpe (1964) and Lintner (1965) from the portfolio theory of Markowitz (1959), the CAPM is:

$$E(R_j) = R_f + (E(R_m) - R_f)\beta_j \tag{1}$$

where $E(R_j)$ expected single period rate of return on asset j

R_f rate of return on a risk free asset

$E(R_m)$ expected single period rate of return on a market portfolio of all assets

β_j beta coefficient for asset j, the covariance between returns on asset j and the market portfolio m divided by the variance of the market portfolio

This model, shown in Figure 1, holds for a hypothetical world where investigators are risk averse maximizing price takers with homogeneous expectations about a frictionless market for perfectly divisible assets, information is costless, there are no taxes or market regulations, and unlimited borrowing and lending is possible at a risk free rate. Under these conditions the expected return on every asset would lie exactly on the security market line (see Figure 1). Normatively, the CAPM advises "acceptance of a

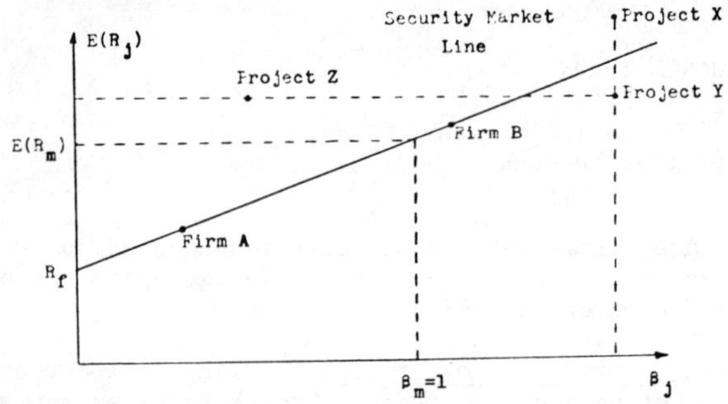

project only if its expected rate of return exceeds the appropriate risk-adjusted discount rate for the project: this discount rate is equal to the expected rate of return on a security with the same risk (β) as the project." (Rubinstein 1973).

In Figure 1, both firms A and B would accept projects X and Z and reject project Y because of their positions relative to the security market line.

Application of the Capital Asset Pricing Model

While the real world is not the hypothetical world of Figure 1, the CAPM has been accepted as a practical aid in investment decisions. Ex post return data is used to estimate the future values of $E(R_m)$ and β_j. The rate of return on government treasury bills and on a broad stock market index are used for R_f and $E(R_m)$ respectively.

Projects are not traded on stock markets, so even past values are not usually available for a project's beta. Anderson (1979) follows finance theory in recommending the use of the past average value of beta for traded firms operating in the industry in which the project lies as a surrogate.

Thus beta is treated as an industry characteristic (Rosenberg and Marathe 1975). This approach fails to discriminate between projects within an industry, even though, a priori, there appears to be no reason why all such projects should have the same systematic risk. This failing reflects the lack of consideration of the processes that produce systematic risk and beta.

Within the finance literature a limited number of factors have been considered in trying to explain the values of beta for traded firms.

1. Capital structure: Increasing financial leverage (debt to equity) is expected to increase beta when other things are held constant. Hamada (1972) found that leverage accounted for about twenty percent of the observed variance in beta for stocks within an industry.

2. Operating leverage: Lev (1974) found that higher ratios of fixed to variable operating costs were associated with higher values of beta in a three industry study.

While useful these factors leave some important questions unanswered. What accounts for the remaining variances in the values of beta for firms within an industry, and what accounts for the differences between betas for different industries?

Modifications to the Capital Asset Pricing Model

Breedon (1979) presents a theoretical argument for a Consumption Asset Pricing Model that is readily viewed as a modification to the CAPM. In the consumption model:

$$R_j = R_f + (R_{ic} - R_f)\beta_{icj} \tag{2}$$

where R_{ic} rate of change of instantaneous aggregate consumption

β_{icj} beta coefficient for asset j, the covariance between the return on asset j and the instantaneous aggregate consumption, divided by the variance in instantaneous consumption.

Thus the consumption model has the virtue that systematic risk is clearly conceptualized in terms of aggregate consumer behavior. It would appear to be easier for marketers to think about marketing investments in terms of their covariance with total consumption than in terms of their covariance with stock market indices.

MARKETING MANAGEMENT AND SYSTEMATIC RISK

A basic representation of the marketing process is shown in Figure 2. It consists of two elements--the marketing organization (firm) and the market (consumers) in the spirit of marketing as exchange (Bagozzi 1975). The goal of the firm is marketing mix optimization. So taking, purely for convenience, the four P classification of marketing decision variables, the firm has a market response function:

$$Q = f(P,A,D,R) \tag{3}$$

where Q quantity of product demanded by the market

P price

A promotion (advertising)

D place (distribution)

R product

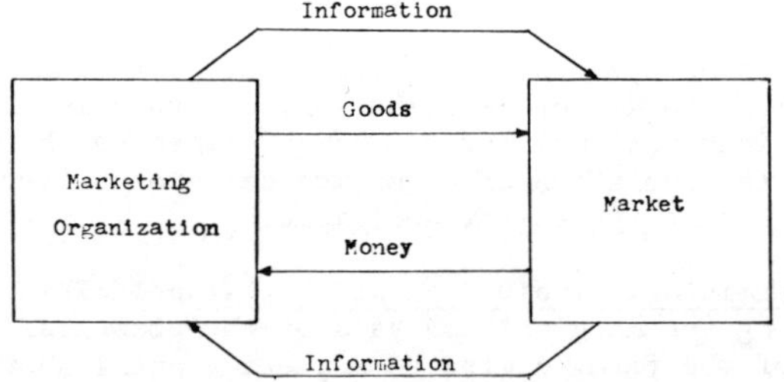

Further, if the firm has a cost function able to be expressed in terms of the same variables, then necessary conditions for optimizing the firm's marketing mix can be determined. Details can be found in Kotler (1971, Ch. 3) who then generalized the optimization for competitive firms, carryover effects, multiple markets, multiple products, joint costs, and multiple goals (1971, Ch. 4 to 9). However a more general representation of marketing is shown in Figure 3. It is a three element system: the marketing organization and the market as before, but adding the environment standing for the economic, social, political, and technological forces which act on the marketing organization and the market.

In this systems view, the firm has a response function which includes environmental state variables:

$$Q_t = f(P_t,A_t,D_t,R_t,E_{1t},E_{2t}, ..., E_{kt}) \tag{4}$$

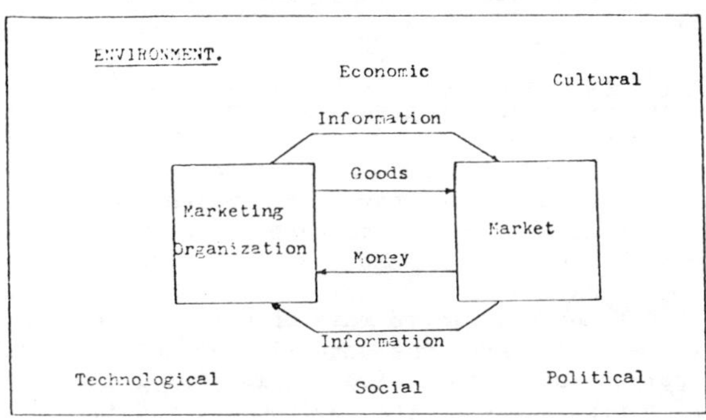

where E_{it} vector of environmental variables for period t,
        and

P_t, A_t, D_t, R_t marketing mix variables for period t.

Once again, if the firm has costs which can be expressed as a function of the same variables, a similar 'cash flow' response can be established:

$$CF_t = f(P_t, A_t, D_t, R_t, E_{1t}, E_{2t}, \ldots, E_{kt}) \qquad (5)$$

where CF_t cash flow for the period t.

However, the firm must decide its marketing mix for time period t (the budgeting process) during, and based on information available to it during the time period t-1. For example, a firm might set its promotional budget as a constant fraction of its sales revenue in the prior period:

$$A_t = a(P_{t-1}Q_{t-1}) \qquad (6)$$

where A_t promotional budget for time period t

P_{t-1} price of the product during time period t-1

Q_{t-1} quantity of the product sold during time
        period t-1

More generally the budgeting process can be viewed as an updating process, so that:

$$M_{jt} = f(M_{jt-1}, E_{it-1}) \qquad (7)$$

where M_{jt} vector of marketing mix variables for period t

M_{jt-1} vector of marketing variables for period t-1

E_{it-1} vector of environmental variables for period
        t-1

Equations (5) and (7) specify the marketing system as an economet ric model. If it were possible to assume linear functions, a consistent updating policy over time, and stochastic errors, it would be possible to test and estimate the parameters of such models using a combination of firm and macroeconomic and environmental data (see Parsons and Schultz 1976).

So long as the firm follows a consistent updating policy in its marketing mix decisions, its 'cash flow' function is:

$$CF_t = f(M_{jt-1}, E_{it-1}, E_{it}) \qquad (8)$$

Given (8), the return on the investment for the period will be:

$$R_{jt} = f'(M_{jt-1}, E_{it-1}, E_{it}) \qquad (9)$$

But from (1) and (2):

$$R_j = R_f + (R_m - R_f)\beta_j \quad \text{or} \quad R_j = R_f + (R_{ic} - R_f)\beta_{icj}$$

Therefore the systematic risk parameters used in the finance literature (β_j or β_{icj}) must capture two marketing effects. First there must be an effect of the relative change in consumer response to a particular marketing mix as the environment changes. Secondly there must be an effect of continuing or changing the policy for updating the marketing mix as the environment changes.

For example, if the economy turned from expansion towards recession, varying changes in consumer response to a constant marketing mix across a series of products would appear as varying betas across the series of products. Similarly, varying modifications in inventory carrying policies across a series of products would appear as varying betas across the series of products.

Because of the second effect there is circularity in basing marketing mix investment decisions on the cost of capital given by the beta for the marketing investment. The significance of the circularity will depend on the relative magnitude of the two effects.

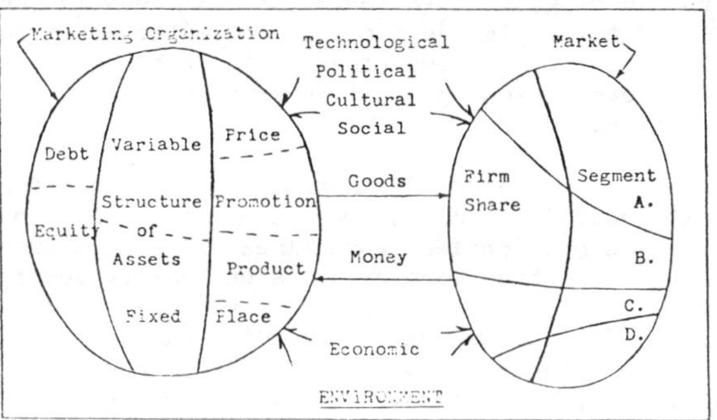

This sytem is represented in Figure 4. It shows a market consisting of a number of segments. The size of the market and of its component segments depends on the environment and the marketing mix of the firm. The firm determines its marketing mix based on its knowledge of consumer needs and environmental conditions in the prior period, to obtain its current share of each segment. Its chosen marketing mix gives the firm a structure of fixed to variable costs and of debt to equity. Note that different marketing mixes can give the same cost and equity structure.

DIRECTIONS FOR FURTHER INVESTIGATION

The fact that systematic risk is determined by two effects complicates further development of the theory of marketing investment decisions. First make the simplification to a firm whose marketing mix policy is not updated at all. Assume the firm is considering a marketing investment such as the addition of a new product. The return on the new product investment depends on the cash flow it produces and the change in the disposal value of the investment. The cash flow component is:

Cash Flow = Sales Revenue - Variable Costs - Fixed Costs

or briefly, CF = SR - VC - FC. Therefore the systematic risk of the new product investment can originate in a number of covariances with instantaneous aggregate con-

sumption (or stock market index) IAC. That is the cash
flow covariance can partitioned:

$$Cov(CF,IAC) = Cov(SR-VC-FC,IAC)$$

$$= Cov(SR,IAC) - Cov(VC,IAC) - Cov(FC,IAC) \quad (10)$$

Therefore sources of systematic risk include:

1. covariance between total product class demand and IAC,
   with the new product obtaining a fixed market share.

2. covariance between the new product's market share and
   IAC, with total product class sales volume remaining
   constant.

3. covariance between the price obtained in a sale and
   IAC, with the product's sales volume remaining constant.

4. covariance between production costs for the new product
   and IAC, with sales revenue remaining constant.

5. covariance between such marketing costs as selling
   costs and IAC, with sales revenue remaining constant.

6. covariance between fixed costs such as product manager's salary and expenses and IAC, with other costs
   and revenue constant.

No discussion of these covariances can be found in the marketing literature. In addition the net effect of a number
of simultaneous covariances presents interesting analytical
problems. However some practitioners have generated their
own conventional wisdom.

Both the movie and record industries have been considered
relatively recession proof because consumers are supposed
to turn to cheap diversions when times are tough. Others
assume consumers place more emphasis on quality during re-
cessions. Segment effects include very high income groups
remaining unaffected by the economic fluctuations of the
seventies, and blue collar workers bearing the brunt of
those fluctuations. As a result, top and bottom of the
line retailers have reportedly experienced less covariance
than those aiming at the mass middle market.

Little has been reported on the effect of specific marketing mix elements on covariance with the environment.
Yawitz et al. (1978) showed that if the cash flow from an
investment in an advertising campaign was a function of
exposures obtained, and if that exposure covaried with
macro-economic conditions, then optimal advertising expenditure depends on the covariance of the exposure and
the market index. They ignored the possibility of covariance in consumer response to the exposures and the market
index, so their model was limited to consideration of cost
covariance contributions to systematic risk.

In the absence of other data in this area, the following
effects are postulated to illustrate possible implications
and stimulate research:

1. Distribution: A firm with its own distribution system
is postulated to have a greater systematic risk than the
same firm using outside wholesalers and retailers.

2. Salesforce: A firm with its own salesforce is postulated to have a greater systematic risk than the same firm
using agents or selling on commission.

3. New products: Addition of a new product line is postulated to increase the systematic risk of a firm. Wensley
(1981) has suggested that new product ventures may involve
higher systematic risks than line extension projects for
established products.

4. Price: The greater the emphasis on price in the marketing mix of a firm, the greater the systematic risk of
the firm.

5. Advertising: A firm with an advertising level above
the norm is postulated to have systematic risk above the
norm. Perhaps supporting this is the Reilly et al. (1977)
finding that a portfolio made up of stocks of the top 100
national advertisers outperformed the market between 1965
and 1972 with an average annual rate of return of 0.11
compared with 0.05.

Recall that these postulated main effects will be complicated by the fact that firms actually revise their marketing mix policy rather than simply maintaining a constant
marketing mix policy when the environment changes. Therefore, we add to the above:

6. Mix policy updating frequency: A firm which updates
its marketing mix policy will be postulated to have a lower
systematic risk than a firm which simply maintained a particular marketing mix policy. The Reilly et al. (1977)
study also found that a portfolio of the companies that
were most consistent in their advertising expenditures
achieved an annual rate of return of 0.15 compared with
only 0.07 for the portfolio of companies that were least
consistent (presumably revising their marketing mix policy)
in their advertising.

CONCLUSION

As noted by Anderson (1979) modern finance theory offers a
new normative approach to marketing investment decisions.
It suggests that the fundamental characteristic of any
security, asset, or marketing investment is its systematic
risk--the covariance of its expected returns with environmental conditions. But that covariance is only partially
accounted for by the factors considered in the finance
literature--financial structure and the ratio of fixed to
variable costs.

The fundamental processes that underlie systematic risk are
processes that must be managed by marketing managers. Here
it has been argued that they are the changing responsiveness of consumers to a particular marketing mix with changing environmental conditions, and the updating of the marketing mix policy of a firm with changing environmental
conditions. As a result it is necessary to go back to the
fundamental relations between marketing policies and environmental conditions when considering systematic risk of
marketing investments.

REFERENCES

Anderson, Paul F. (1979), "The Marketing Management/Finance
    Interface," in Neil Beckwith et al., eds., 1979 Educators
    Conference Proceedings, 44, Chicago: American Marketing
    Association.

Ansoff, H. Igor (1965), Corporate Strategy, New York:
    McGraw-Hill.

Bagozzi, Richard P. (1975), "Marketing as Exchange,"
    Journal of Marketing (October), 32-39.

Breedon, Douglas T. (1979), "An Intertemporal Asset Pricing
    Model with Stochastic Consumption and Investment Oppor-
    tunities," Journal of Financial Economics, 7, 265-296.

Cyert, Richard M. and James G. March (1963), A Behavioral
    Theory of the Firm, Englewood Cliffs, N.J.: Prentice-
    Hall.

Fabozzi, Frank J. (1978), "A Portfolio Approach to Capital
Budgeting: An Application to the Expansion to Addi-
tional Product Lines," _Journal of the Operations Research
Society_, Vol. 29, No. 3, 245-249.

Green, Paul E. (1962), "Bayesian Decision Theory in Advertising," _Journal of Advertising Research_, 2 (December),
33-41.

__________, J. Douglas Carroll, and Stephen M. Goldberg
(1981), "A General Approach to Product Design Optimization via Conjoint Analysis," _Journal of Marketing_, Vol.
45, No. 3 (Summer), 17-37.

Hamada, R. (1972), "The Effects of the Firm's Capital
Structure on the Systematic Risk of Common Stocks,"
Journal of Finance (May), 435-452.

Kotler, Philip (1971), _Marketing Decision Making_, New York:
Holt, Rinehart and Winston.

Lev, Baruch (1974), _Financial Statement Analysis_, Englewood
Cliffs, N.J.: Prentice-Hall.

Lintner, John (1965), "Security Prices, Risk and Maximal
Gains from Diversification," _Journal of Finance_, 20
(December), 587-615.

Markowitz, Harry M. (1952), "Portfolio Selection," _Journal
of Finance_, 7 (March), 77-91.

__________ (1959), _Portfolio Selection: Efficient Diversification of Investments_, New York: John Wiley.

Mossman, Frank H., W. J. E. Crissy, and Paul M. Fischer
(1978), _Financial Dimensions of Marketing Management_,
New York: John Wiley.

Parsons, Leonard J. and Randall L. Schultz (1976), _Market-
ing Models and Econometric Research_, New York: North-
Holland.

Reilly, Frank K., Anthony F. McGann, and Raymond A.
Marquardt (1977), "Advertising Decisions and Stockholders
Wealth," _Journal of Advertising Research_, Vol. 17, No. 4
(August), 49-56.

Rosenberg, Barr and Vinay Marathe (1975), "The Prediction
of Investment Risk: Systematic and Residual Risk," in
Proceedings: Seminar on the Analysis of Security Prices,
Graduate School of Business, University of Chicago.

Rubinstein, Mark E. (1973), "A Mean Variance Synthesis of
Corporate Financial Theory," _Journal of Finance_, 28
(March), 167-181.

Sharpe, William F. (1964), "Capital Asset Prices: A Theory
of Market Equilibrium Under Conditions of Risk," _Journal
of Finance_, 19 (September), 425-442.

Wensley, Robin (1981), "Strategic Marketing: Betas, Boxes,
or Basics," _Journal of Marketing_, Vol. 45, No. 3
(Summer), 173-182.

Wind, Yoram (1974), "Product Portfolio Analysis: A New
Approach to the Product Mix Decision," in Ronald C.
Curhan, ed., _1974 Combined Proceedings_, 36, Chicago:
American Marketing Association.

Winter, Frederick W. (1979), "A Cost Benefit Approach to
Market Segmentation," _Journal of Marketing_, Vol. 43,
No. 4 (Fall), 103-111.

Yawitz, Jess B., Francis J. Connelly, and William J.
Marshall (1978), "Advertising and Value Maximization:
An Integrative Approach," _Decision Sciences_, 9, 196-205.

PRODUCT/MARKET ELEMENTS, PRODUCT MANAGERS, AND PRODUCT PERFORMANCE

John E. Young, University of Colorado, Denver
James E. Nelson, University of Colorado, Denver

ABSTRACT

Locations of product/market elements in a product/market matrix make differing demands on operating product managers. Such varying demands imply that successful product managers might possess different skills and psychological characteristics across matrix cells. This article suggests that product performance be measured differently across cells. Based on locations, skills, psychological characteristics, and performance measurements, five propositions about products and product managers can be stated.

INTRODUCTION

Product/market elements, which constitute specific and distinct products or services interfacing with well-defined markets, represent the basic component upon which marketing strategy is based (Abell 1978; Lorange 1980). As fundamental components of marketing strategy, product/market elements are typically distinguishable from and essentially independent of other product/market combinations. Product managers, responsible for product/market elements, oversee planning, coordination, and control activities for one or more products in one or more markets (Buell 1975; Kotler 1980). As a result of differences in the nature of product/market elements, product managers might possess different skills and psychological characteristics across cells in a product/market matrix. Product performance evidences the results of product management decisions. Also because of differences in the nature of product/market elements, product performance might be measured different ways across cells in a product/market matrix.

Figure 1 shows operating product management decisions influencing product performance inside two environments, product/market and organizational. The diagram indicates that dimensions of the product/market element--growth rate and market share--affect product management decisions and product performance. Also shown are the dimensions of organizational goals, basic strategic alternatives, decisions in functional areas other than marketing (finance, production, personnel, research and development), decisions in other marketing areas (advertising, distribution, public relations, sales, marketing research), and the ever-present externalities of competitors, technology, laws, ethics, politics, customers, and other factors. In summary, Figure 1 shows that dimensions of the organizational and product/market environments moderate the relationship between operating product management decisions and product performance.

PRODUCT/MARKET ELEMENTS

Several authors have set forth helpful guidelines for identifying and distinguishing unique strategic product/market elements (Abell 1978; Ansoff 1965; Day & Shocker 1976; Lorange 1980). Essentially, a strategic product/market element can be defined in terms of (a) specific products serving a single market, (b) a specific product serving several markets, (c) a single market served by several products or (d) a specific group of related products or markets. According to Lorange (1980), criteria that determine when a strategic product/market element

can be identified as such revolve around the following issues:

    (1) the degree of strategic independence of the products and markets,

    (2) the degree of dependence of the overall organization upon the products and markets,

    (3) the strategic intent of company management for the products and markets, and

FIGURE 1

A MODEL OF PRODUCT PERFORMANCE

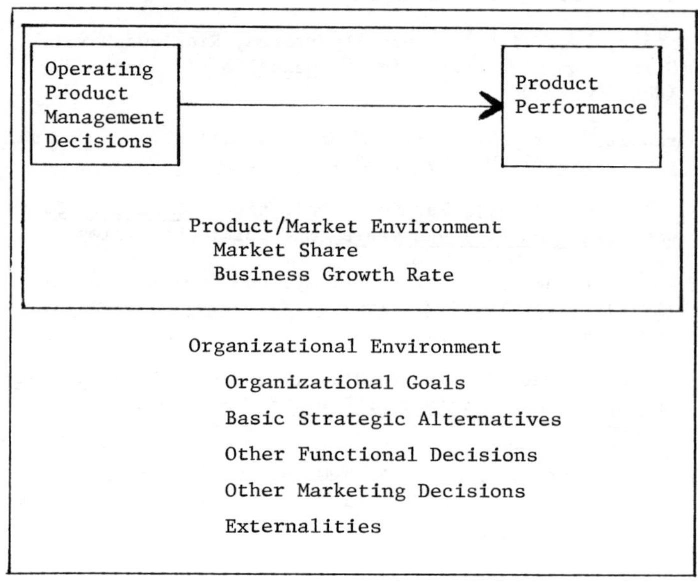

    (4) the depth of the potential managerial talent for adequately developing a product/market element.

Top corporate marketing executives (typically, vice presidents of marketing) are responsible not only for maximizing operating revenues and profits for the company's current products, but also for the strategic planning of future product portfolios to assure the company's long-term viability. When considering this latter responsibility, top marketing executives find it useful to group and coordinate strategic product/market elements based on each element's rate of growth and its market share. Corporate examples of strategic product/market elements include General Electric's forty to fifty strategic business units (SBUs), Texas Instruments' "strategies," and General Foods' meal-oriented SBUs. Figure 2 illustrates the conventional visual arrangement, called a product/market matrix (Hedley 1977).

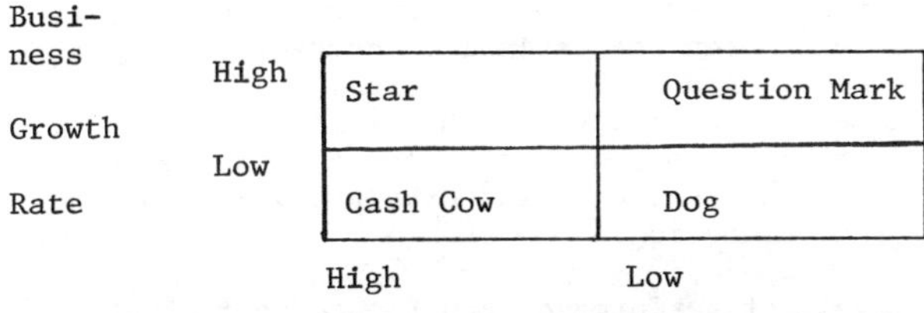

Top marketing executives also make staffing decisions to determine which managers will have operating responsibility for strategic product/market elements. Specifically, top marketing executives must hire, train, direct, and evaluate operating product managers. Finally, top marketing executives are responsible for evaluating and controlling marketing strategies in general and product strategies in particular, in each strategic product/market element.

PRODUCT MANAGERS

Product managers report to top corporate marketing executives in consumer and industrial goods manufacturing organizations. A typical organization chart appears in Figure 3, showing relationships between product and other operating marketing managers. Figure 3 depicts a typical operating organizational structure as opposed to a strategic structure (e.g., Anthony 1965; Springer & Hofer 1978; Vancil 1972, etc.).

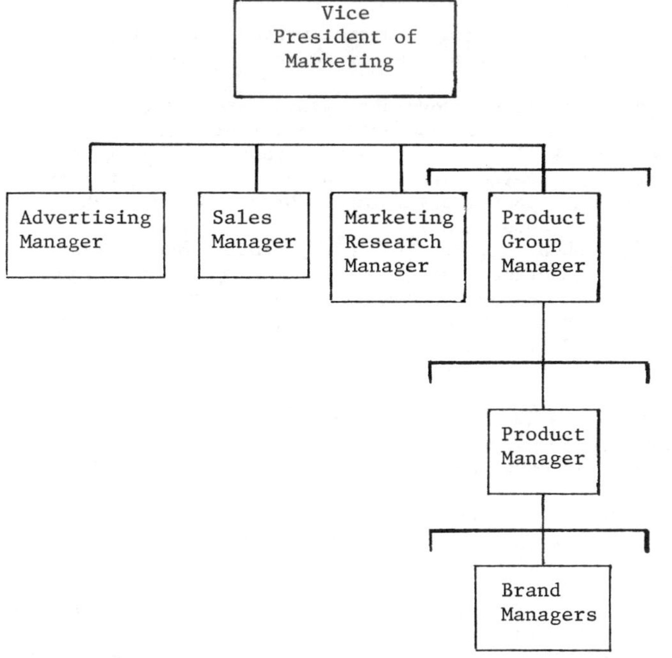

Product managers occupy three levels in a typical operating structure. At the lowest level, a brand manager will have primarily planning, scheduling, coordinating, and controlling responsibilities for one or a few assigned brands. Responsibilities for product advertising, pricing, and design are typically located in other operating departments (e.g., advertising, sales, and market research departments). At the middle level, a product manager will have more influence on advertising, pricing, and design decisions, but not to the point of direct line authority. At the highest level, a product group manager will have even greater responsibility for making entrepreneurial recommendations for a large number of products, but again seldom to the point of actual line authority (Dietz 1973). In short, while product managers may participate in advertising, sales, marketing research, pricing, and product design decisions, they typically do so without formal decision-making authority (Hise & Kelly 1978). Nearly 90 percent of all consumer packaged goods manufacturers and over 50 percent of all industrial goods manufacturers employ product managers at one or more of these levels (Association of National Advertisers 1974).

Skills

Apart from communication, coordination, negotiation, and technical marketing skills, Sands (1979) identifies four managerial skills as critical for product (and division) success:

(1) Investigative skills - identify factors having the greatest influence on results and give these factors priority attention. Investigative skills also aid in recognizing when the priority of a factor needs to be changed.

(2) Innovative skills - innovate within the bounds of corporate policy. Innovative skills include being open to suggestions and encouraging others to innovate. Innovators depart from traditional practices when practices are no longer adequate.

(3) Interpersonal skills - encourage and communicate high standards for selection, training, and performance. Good interpersonal skills mean balanced appraisals of subordinates, not just criticisms.

(4) Implementation skills - react to a problem without overreacting. Implementation skills help avoid creating a new problem in the process of solving an existing one.

Reference to Figure 2 suggests that some of these skills would be more important than others, depending on location in a product/market matrix. For example, investigative skills would seem more important for product managers of stars and question marks, to move question marks to stars and stars to cash cows. Interpersonal skills would seem important for product managers in any cell, but especially so for those managing stars and cash cows, where high group standards and distinct goals can be stated. Implementation skills would seem important for managers of question marks and dogs, to avoid creating additional problems, equal in number to the multitude they already face.

Beyond these four operational skills, Lorange (1980) describes two types of planning skills - adaptive and integrative - that a product manager should possess depending on matrix location. Adaptive skills describe a product manager's ability to change in response to new and unique environmental situations (e.g., to develop more effective competitive strategies, to reposition with respect to new consumer tastes, to expand to new geographic markets, etc.). Integrative skills describe the ability to develop plans for efficient production and distribution, scheduling, and product design, and effective coordination between the various functional areas of the firm. Product managers of stars and question marks should be strong adaptive planners; product managers of stars and cash cows should be strong integrative planners.

Personality Traits

Successful product managers in each matrix quadrant might
also possess different personality traits. The Edwards
Personal Preference Schedule measures fifteen psychological needs or traits, six of which might describe significant differences between product managers:
    (1) Achievement - the need to do one's best, to
        accomplish something of great significance.
    (2) Aggression - the need to attack contrary points
        of view, to get revenge for insults.
    (3) Change - the need to do new and different things,
        to participate in new fads and fashions.
    (4) Dominance - the need to be a leader in the groups
        to which one belongs, to tell others how to do
        their jobs.
    (5) Endurance - the need to stay with a job until
        finished, to keep at a problem until finished,
        to keep at a problem until solved.
    (6) Order - the need to have organized work, to have
        things arranged to run smoothly (Cohen 1980).
A seventh trait, risk, or the tolerance of financial and
social uncertainty might also distinguish product managers (Lorange 1980).

Specifically, product managers of question marks and stars
might show high needs for achievement, aggression, and
change along with high and medium risk tolerances, respectively. Product managers of stars might show further a
high need for dominance. Product managers of cash cows
might show high needs for dominance and order, while product managers of dogs might show the need for order. Finally, managers of dogs and question marks might show high
needs for endurance.

PRODUCT PERFORMANCE

Product performance can be evaluated on five basic dimensions. Within each, several variables (apart from market
share) exist on which top marketing executives take measurements. Dimensions and variables are:
    (1) Consumer related - trial rate, repeat purchase
        rate, brand awareness, beliefs, satisfaction.
    (2) Distribution related - distribution coverage,
        shelf facings, stockouts.
    (3) Profit related - profits or contribution margins
        in absolute terms or as percentages of assets,
        investment, owner's equity, sales.
    (4) Volume related - sales revenues, unit sales,
        cost of sales.
    (5) Warranty related - warranty costs, defective and
        return rates, service record.

Many of the product performance variables are more appropriate for high growth product/market elements and, thus,
are better suited for measuring new product rather than
old product performance. All of the consumer related
performance variables fall into this category as do distribution coverage, shelf facings, unit sales, and the
product's defective and return rates. The performance of
low growth product/market elements would be more appropriately measured by consumer beliefs and satisfaction,
shelf facings and stockouts, all profit related variables, all volume related variables, and the product's warranty costs and service record.

However, the appropriateness of any product performance
measurement variable depends on the basic strategic alternative chosen for the product/market element. For example, if the basic strategy is to adopt an aggressive
posture and build market share, most of the consumer,
distribution, volume, and warranty related variables will
produce more meaningful measurements. On the other hand,
if the basic strategy chosen is to harvest a product/mar-
ket element, the profit related variables are more relevant.

Finally, all five product performance dimensions may be
measured using three different procedures:
    (1) Absolute level - the magnitude of the variable's
        current value is measured.
    (2) Deviation level - the magnitude of the differ-
        ence between the variables' current value and
        some planned value is measured.
    (3) Rate of change level - the variable's value for
        a previous period is subtracted from its current
        value and is then divided by the value for the
        previous period.

Absolute levels of performance constitute appropriate
measurement procedure for any product/market element.
However, deviation levels of performance require reasonably stable and well understood markets to calculate
planned values and, thus, are more appropriate for low
growth product/market elements. In contrast, because of
the uncertainty associated with high growth markets and
because product managers desire products to move from
question marks to stars to cash cows, rate of change procedures are more appropriate in these quadrants.

Figure 4 summarizes the preceding discussion on product
manager skills and personality traits, product performance measurement, and product/market elements.

PROPOSITIONS AND SUMMARY

Propositions

Some propositions about product managers and product performance may now be stated. When dimensions of the organizational environment are held constant, variations in
skills and personality traits of product managers influence product management decisions and, hence, product performance. Thus, the first proposition is:
   P_1: Within a quadrant of a product/market matrix,
       higher product performance will occur when pro-
       duct managers' skills and personality traits
       are consistent with those required by the qua-
       drant.
The proposition should hold true whether product managers
have responsibility for one or several products.

When product managers oversee several products, all contained within single quadrants consistent with managers'
respective skills and personality traits, managers should
perform more proficiently. Because proficiency and satisfaction are positively related (Bass & Barrett 1981),
the second proposition is:
   P_2: When skills, personality traits, and matrix
       quadrants are all consistent, product managers
       will experience greater satisfaction.
The proposition implies that the nature of skills training and product management responsibilities should vary
over a product manager's career.

When products in a product group are homogeneous with
respect to location in a matrix quadrant, their product
managers (in management teams or other integrated organizational units) do not face diverse product/markets and
performance measurements. Therefore:
   P_3: Work groups responsible for product groups of
       greater homogeneity will show greater cohesive-
       ness, satisfaction, and productivity than work
       groups responsible for product groups of less
       homogeneity.
This proposition indicates the desirability of management
team members possessing similar operational and planning
skills and similar personalities.

Also when product groups are homogeneous with respect to
matrix quadrant, management processes within assigned organizational units will exhibit greater consistency.

FIGURE 4

CHARACTERISTICS, SKILLS, AND PERFORMANCE MEASUREMENTS FOR PRODUCT/MARKET ELEMENTS

	High — Relative Market Share — Low
High Busi- ness Growth Rate **Low**	(see quadrants below)

Star

Skills

- Investigative
- Innovative
- Interpersonal
- Adaptive planning
- Integrative planning

Personality Traits

- Achievement
- Aggression
- Change
- Risk (medium)
- Dominance

Performance Variables

- All consumer related
- Distribution related
  - coverage
  - shelf facings
- Volume related
  - unit sales
- Warranty related
  - defective and return rates

Measurement Procedures

- Absolute level
- Rate of change

Question Mark

Skills

- Investigative
- Innovative
- Implementation
- Adaptive planning

Personality Traits

- Achievement
- Aggression
- Change
- Risk (high)
- Endurance

Performance Variables

- All consumer related
- Distribution related
  - coverage
  - shelf facings
- Volume related
  - unit sales
- Warranty related
  - defective and return rates

Measurement Procedures

- Absolute level
- Rate of change

Cash Cow

Skills

- Interpersonal
- Integrative planning

Personality Traits

- Dominance
- Order

Performance Variables

- Consumer related
  - beliefs
  - satisfaction
- Distribution related
  - shelf facings
  - stockouts
- All profit related
- All volume related
- Warranty related
  - warranty costs
  - service record

Measurement Procedures

- Absolute level
- Deviation level

Dog

Skills

- Implementation

Personality Traits

- Endurance
- Order

Performance Variables

- Consumer related
  - beliefs
  - satisfaction
- Distribution related
  - shelf facings
  - stock outs
- All profit related
- All volume related
- Warranty related
  - warranty costs
  - service record

Measurement Procudures

- Absolute level
- Deviation level

Relative Market Share: High ... Low

Hence:

    P_4: More homogeneous product groups will show more
products achieving specified organizational
goals than will less homogeneous product groups.

This proposition addresses the goal of uniform product
performances in firms whose product portfolios are large.

Finally, because the identity of suitable product performance measures varies by matrix quadrant, the fifth proposition is:

    P_5: Product managers whose assigned products are
appropriately measured will experience greater
satisfaction and productivity than managers
whose products are inappropriately measured.

This proposition implies that firms with diverse product
portfolios should employ diverse measures of product performance.

If one or more of these propositions finds strong empirical support, top marketing executives might modify procedures to hire, train, direct, and evaluate operating product managers. However, executives need not, and perhaps should not, assign managers to one best suited matrix (based on skills and personality traits) permanently. Such practice would considerably narrow the product management experience and lead to inferior career path development. Such a practice also would quite likely produce inferior organizational performance. Thus, top marketing executives might best use empirically supported propositions to enlarge their understandings of each product manager's performance and how it might be improved.

Summary

This article presents a normative framework that aligns quadrants in a product/market matrix with product manager skills and personality traits, performance measures, and measurement procedures. The next step would consist of developing operational definitions and testable hypotheses for empirical research. Such research must take care to control for moderating effects of the organizational environment as well as issues associated with measurement and sampling.

REFERENCES

Abell, D. F. (1978), "Strategic Windows," _Journal of Marketing_ 42, No. 3, 21-26.

Ansoff, H. I. (1965), _Corporate Strategy_, New York: McGraw-Hill.

Anthony, R. N. (1965), _Planning and Control Systems: A Framework for Analysis_, Cambridge, Mass.: Harvard Business School.

Association of National Advertisers (1974), _Current Advertising Practices: Opinions as to Future Trends_, New York: The Association.

Bass, B. M. & Barrett, G. V. (1981), _People, Work and Organizations_, 2nd edition, Boston: Allyn and Bacon.

Buell, V. P. (1975) "The Changing Role of the Product Manager in Consumer Goods Companies," _Journal of Marketing_, 39, No. 3, 3-11.

Cohen, D. (1981) _Consumer Behavior_, New York: Random House.

Day, G. S. & Shocker, A. D. (1976), _Identifying Competitive Product - Market Boundaries: Strategic and Analytical Issues_, Cambridge, Mass.: Marketing Science Institute.

Dietz, S. (1973), "Get More Out of Your Brand Management," _Harvard Business Review_, 51 (July - August), 127-136.

Hedley, B. (1977), "Strategy and the Business Portfolio," _Long Range Planning_, No. 2 (February), 9-15.

Hise, R. T. & Kelly, J. P. (1978), "Product Management On Trial," _Journal of Marketing_, 42, No. 4, 28-33.

Kotler, P. (1980), _Marketing Management_, 4th edition, Englewood Cliffs, N. J.: Prentice-Hall.

Lorange, P. (1980), _Corporate Planning: An Executive Viewpoint_, Englewood Cliffs, N. J.: Prentice-Hall.

Sands, S. (1979), "Is the Product Manager Obsolete?," _The Business Quarterly_, Autumn.

Springer, C. & Hofer, C. (1980), "General Electric's Evolving Management System," in _Strategic Management: A Casebook in Business Policy and Planning_, C. Hofer, E. Murray, Jr., R. Charan, & R. A. Pitts, St. Paul, Minn.: West.

Vancil, R. F. (1977), "Texas Instruments, Incorporated," in _Strategic Planning Systems_, P. Lorange & R. F. Vancil, Englewood Cliffs, N. J.: Prentice-Hall.

DEREGULATION'S CHALLENGES FOR MARKETERS

Paul N. Bloom, University of Maryland, College Park

ABSTRACT

The current government deregulation effort could have a significant impact on marketers. This article contains several propositions about how deregulation might challenge the members of the marketing profession.

INTRODUCTION

After several decades of ever-increasing government regulatory activity, the business community in the United States is heaving a collective sigh of relief as the Reagan Administration pushes forward with its deregulation program. While the ultimate effects of the current deregulation efforts remain to be seen, it appears that, at least for the next few years, business managers will not need to function continuously with a wary eye toward the government. This new freedom should extend to managers in the marketing area, as less government regulation of advertising content, pricing methods, distribution arrangements, and product features should be forthcoming. Marketers should be able to give less weight to how the FTC or Consumer Product Safety Commission will react to their strategies, and can instead concentrate on how consumers and competitors will react.

But marketers should not be tempted to luxuriate in their new-found freedom for too long. For although deregulation may remove one set of worries for marketers, it will surely bring a new assortment of challenges that require prompt, serious attention. Deregulation should change the "rules" of the marketing "game" for both business firms and consumers, creating a new -- and potentially more difficult and unpredictable -- marketplace in which marketers must function. To a degree, marketing will be put on "trial" and given the chance to show what it can do, in an unrestrained form, for stakeholders of business firms and the general public.

This article contains an examination of the challenges that deregulation presents to the marketing profession. It provides a look into the future and, consequently, does not contain definitive conclusions about the effects of various deregulation initiatives. Rather, it offers several propositions or hypotheses about the future effects of deregulation for the purpose of stimulating thinking, research, and discussion. Propositions are offered about how deregulation might affect the ability of marketers to (1) monitor and understand their external environments, (2) formulate and implement marketing strategies, and (3) improve the public image of marketing. These propositions are presented after first providing some clarification of the meaning and scope of the concept of deregulation.

DEREGULATION DEFINED

The term "deregulation" was used until the mid-1970s to refer primarily to the process of freeing the so-called "regulated" industries (e.g., transportation, communications, banking, liquor) from strict regulatory control and allowing them to become more like unregulated, "competitive" industries. However, through the efforts of President Reagan and regulatory reform advocates from places like the American Enterprise Institute and Washington University's Center for the Study of American Business, the term "deregulation" has gradually taken on a broader meaning. Deregulation has come to be associated with the curtailment of all types of government regulatory practices and programs. Thus, the concept of deregulation -- as being implemented by President Reagan -- now encompasses such elements as:

- a reduction in how strictly and vigorously the antitrust laws are enforced -- including a more permissive policy toward mergers.

- the elimination or severe modification of price controls and price-approval systems for gasoline, natural gas, airline, and other industries.

- a reduction in how vigorously deceptive advertising and selling are policed.

This "broad" defintion of deregulation has been adopted in this article.

In trying to understand the implications for the marketing profession of a broad deregulation effort, one must keep in mind two additional features of deregulation. First, deregulation is taking on significantly different forms in different industries. For example, in the learned professions such as law and dentistry, deregulation has brought the removal of restrictions against advertising and competitive bidding. On the other hand, in the banking and airline industries, deregulation has brought major changes in the services firms are permitted to offer and in the prices they are permitted to charge for those services.

A second feature to keep in mind is that deregulation is having equal, if not greater, impact on managers who do not have marketing responsibilities. Marketers are not alone in having to cope with deregulation, and in many industries marketers are being confronted with less changes than their colleagues in finance, accounting, personnel, and production. In fact -- as discussed later -- marketers may see the regulatory activities of government agencies essentially replaced, as thorns in their sides, by an upsurge in legal actions by competitors and consumers.

In spite of the highly diverse and often minor regulatory changes in store for many marketers, it is possible to identify a set of general problems or challenges that are likely to have a significant overall impact on marketing as deregulation progresses. These challenges are enumerated in the remainder of this article.

ENVIRONMENTAL SCANNING CHALLENGES

The turbulent political and social conditions of the past few decades have taught marketers the importance of continuously scanning and studying the external environments of their organizations. Careful environmental scanning can provide marketers with an early warning about potential threats and opportunities, allowing them to formulate appropriate defensive or offensive strategies for coping with changed environments. But obtaining early warnings about impending changes by competitors, consumers, regulators, or other external forces should become more difficult under deregulation. Three propositions that express this viewpoint are presented and discussed below.

Monitoring Competitors

The first proposition relates to the problem of predicting the behavior of competitors. It states:

- Deregulation will make it more difficult to predict the strategies and counterstrategies of competitors.

The experience thus far with deregulation clearly indicates that the removal of regulations stimulates the use of many new, previously-avoided, hard-to-predict marketing strategies. What has happened is not unlike what would happen in a game theory experiment if the payoff matrix were suddenly changed from a "Prisonser's Dilemma" array -- that encourages players to make conservative choices -- to an array that encouraged the choice of more aggressive moves. In a sense, business firms in many industries are being freed from a "Prisoner's Dilemma" and are pursuing aggressive strategies that in the past would have brought a high probability of negative payoffs in the form of regulatory sanctions or antitrust difficulties.

Hence, we are seeing deregulation produce developments such as the following:

- Aggressive fare cutting and promotional programs in the airline industry.

- Aggressive promotion and new product development programs in the banking industry.

- The formulation of heavy-advertising legal clinics and dental care franchises.

- The removal of item-marking on groceries, and concurrent lowering of prices, by Giant Foods--the Washington, D.C. area's largest food retailer and a firm that has been viewed as a champion of consumer rights.

- The offering of "guaranteed" maximum prices, prior to pick-up and delivery, by household movers.

Firms are finding that strategies that would have previously been labeled as predatory, collusive, unethical, anti-competitive, cutthroat, anti-consumer, or bad for small businesses are being viewed by regulatory officials and others as pro-competitive, pro-productivity, and pro-consumer.

To use an analogy from the sport of boxing, the "gloves" have been taken off and the "referees" seem to be letting all the contestants battle it out. And these fights can be expected to become more intense and unpredictable as the "referees" allow numerous new competitors to enter or merge into industries that were previously illegal or overly risky to enter. The new small airlines entering the airline industry, the movement of Merrill Lynch into the banking industry (with its "cash management" accounts), and the proposed movement of AT&T into markets of the communication industry provide examples of the kinds of changes in the competitive structure of many industries that could occur as deregulation proceeds.

Needless to say, the highly turbulent competitive environments that are emerging under deregulation should increase the importance of having strong marketing intelligence systems. Further, it might prove valuable for firms to do more basic behavioral research on seller or marketer decision-making, just as they have been doing for years on buyer decision-making.

Monitoring Consumers

Partly as a consequence of having more turbulent competitive environments, the behavior of consumer and organizational buyers should become difficult to understand as deregulation proceeds. This notion is expressed in the following proposition:

- <u>Deregulation will make it more difficult to predict buyer behavior.</u>

The increased competitive fervor of many industries can be expected to provide buyers with a huge and possibly bewildering, array of new choices and information. Old shopping and buying habits will be challenged, as buyers will be continuously provided with new products and services, new pricing schemes, and new forms of promotion. Buyers should become interested in attributes of products or services they never before considered--such as whether a dentist takes credit cards--and they should become less inclined to stay loyal to certain brands for long periods of time. Moreover, many buyers could begin to suffer from information "overload"--as have many travel agents following airline deregulation--and this could make their behavior even more unpredictable.

As a result of deregulation, marketers may find it wise to shift significant amounts of marketing research toward more explanatory or causal research. Mathematical models that forecast market share or brand loyalty rates may simply lose much of their predictive validity in deregulated environments, suggesting a need for research that seeks to understand buyer behavior on a more basic level.

Monitoring the Legal and Social Environment

The next proposition has to do with problems associated with scanning the legal and social environment:

- <u>Deregulation will make it more difficult to predict the timing, intensity, and sources of legal and social challenges to marketers.</u>

In the past, the federal government could be the focus of a substantial portion of many marketers' efforts to scan their legal and social environments. But the impending cutback in federal government regulatory activity will probably lead to several developments that will make the legal and social environment of marketers more varied and unpredictable. First, the federal regulatory cutback should produce a large assortment of lawsuits filed by public interest groups, small businesses, and other parties who would not only like to challenge the legality of certain deregulation initiatives, but who would also like to see if they can win court judgments against business firms by themselves under old antitrust and consumer protection laws (<u>Business Week</u> 1981). Growth in the number of private lawsuits could also be accelerated by a hunger for work on the part of the huge cadre of Washington-based lawyers who specialize in regulatory matters. This hunger for work was highlighted in a recent article by former FTC official Robert Reich (1981), who has labeled these lawyers and their associated experts and lobbyists as the "intermediaries" between business and government.

The cutback in federal regulatory activity should also have an impact on the media, providing them with an opportunity to diversify their coverage of business and consumer matters. It would not be surprising to see many newspapers, magazines, and television news program begin to do more of their own "60-Minutes" type investigative reports on business abuses and consumer problems. Such reports would be hard to predict in advance and would probably be more difficult for attacked firms to counter than many of the carefully worded government reports or press releases of the past. To an extent, deregulation may lead to the replacement of the reasonably open, controlled investigations of agencies like the FTC by the relatively secretive, unregulated investigations of the Press and the consumer groups with whom they might become associated.

Finally, the federal regulatory cutback might also contribute to an already existing trend of fragmentation among consumer groups (Bloom and Greyser 1980). A lack of federal activity and monies in the consumer protection area could hurt the ability of Ralph Nader and national consumer organizations to mobilize support for national issues, providing an opportunity for more special-interest and local groups to arouse support for less traditional issues. A more fragmented--both geographically and issue-wise--consumer movement should be less predictable and harder to monitor. Consumerist challenges could begin to come from all over the place and from people of all

political persuasions. The campaign currently underway by
"The Moral Majority" to pressure major advertisers to
help reduce sex and violence on television may be the
first of many new and different consumer challenges to
marketers.

Among other things, the impending changes in the legal and
social environment suggest that marketers might find it
worthwhile to shift resources presently being devoted toward monitoring the activities of the federal government
toward mechanisms for monitoring the activities of the
courts (at all levels), the media, and consumer groups.

STRATEGY FORMULATION CHALLENGES

The increased turbulence in the external environment of
business firms should require marketers to give serious
consideration to their marketing strategies and programs.
In formulating strategies, the propositions discussed
below might deserve considerable attention. The first of
these is:

● <u>Conservative marketing approaches will be unsuccessful.</u>

Marketers should find that "doing things by the book" or
"the way they have always been done around here" will be
highly risky. The new, agressive behavior of competitors
in many industries will make the use of bold, innovative
marketing strategies advisable and even necessary. Sudden
price cuts, big promotional campaigns, unconventional
advertising appeals, major product reformulations, new
segmentation and positioning approaches, and innovative
delivery systems will appear with greater frequency
in many industries, forcing many marketers to make one
bold move after another. Marketers may find themselves
feeling much like military officers during times of war,
as they find it necessary to develop contingency plans
and attack and counter-attack maneuvers. In fact, many
marketers may find it valuable to think seriously about
their problems in military terms, as Kotler and Singh
(1981) recommended in a recent article titled "Marketing
Warfare in the 1980s." In this article, they discuss
several attack (e.g., frontal, flanking, encirclement,
bypass, and guerilla) and defense (e.g., position, mobile,
perceptive, flank-positioning, counteroffensive, and
hedgehog) strategies that deserve consideration from
marketers who find themselves in war-like situations.

A second proposition about strategy is:

● <u>Conducting consumer education and information programs
will be profitable for business firms.</u>

Consumers should welcome efforts by business firms to provide them with assistance on how to cope with the turbulent, confusing marketplaces created by deregulation.
The offering of consumer education courses or pamphlets
on how to buy and use products and services should be
well-received by consumers and could, perhaps, provide
firms with a competitive advantage. For example, it
appears that Shell has benefited from its "Look to Shell
for Answers" campaign. And one can envision consumers
responding positively to objective, non-self-serving
materials provided by banks, travel agents, or movers on
how to buy or use their services. One can also envision
a favorable consumer reaction to advertising that projects an educational and helpful quality. Moreover, the
effectiveness of business-generated consumer education
and information programs could be even greater if government programs of this type are cut back as part of the
deregulation effort.

A third strategy is:

● <u>Carefully formulated corporate communications programs</u>
<u>will become a necessary venture for many business firms.</u>

A growing interest among marketers in the area of "corporate communications" has been identified by Greyser (1980).
More and more business firms have been mounting large-
scale efforts designed to communicate to employees, stockholders, and the general public information about (1) the
trustworthy character and socially beneficial activities
of the firms and (2) the positions of the firms on public
issues. This is being done with corporate advertising,
employee training, press releases, and other communication vehicles. Sears, AT&T, and General Electric are but
a few of the firms that have undertaken major efforts of
this type.

The importance of having a sound corporate communications
program should grow stronger if, as predicted earlier,
the media begins to do more investigative reporting of
business abuses and consumer problems. Corporate communications provide a mechanism for countering bad publicity.
Further, corporate communications could also serve the
interests of a firm by helping to reassure confused
consumers that they are buying from a trustworthy company.

A final strategy proposition is:

● <u>"Numbers" will require more attention when formulating
marketing strategies.</u>

Deregulation should make it more important than it has
been previously for marketers to do careful financial
analyses when developing strategies. The more heated competition in many industries should make prices for supplies, transportation, and other factors less stable and
more difficult to project. This should have more opportunities for errors to be made in the financial analyses
that are typically done before rolling out new products,
pricing a product line, choosing distribution channels,
and so on. Marketing planners will need to spend more
time studying the cost dynamics of their own and connected
industries, and they will need to devote more effort toward doing sensitivity analyses to understand how financial projections are affected by changes in their assumptions.

THE CHALLENGE OF IMPROVING MARKETING'S IMAGE

Marketing has always had image problems. Historically,
marketing has been seen by many social critics as being
wasteful, manipulative, unethical, and so forth. Recently, marketing has even had image problems within the
executive ranks of large corporations. As Webster (1980)
concluded in a recent report, chief executive officers
are generally satisfied with marketers, but to some
officers:

Marketers are seen to be risk-avoiders, short-term in
their orientation, and lacking in innovative and entrepreneurial outlook. There is concern about the impact of
inflation on marketing costs and the erosion of productivity in marketing expenditures. The marketing function is
criticized for inadequate attention to the financial
dimensions of marketing decisions (Webster 1980, p. 27).

However, the future may have marketing seen in a different
light. As the following proposition states:

● <u>Deregulation will provide marketers with numerous
opportunities to improve marketing's image among social
critics, chief executive officers, and others.</u>

These opportunities will vary bsed on the type of industry. In industries that have had very restricted forms
of marketing in the past -- such as the learned professions
-- there is a chance to demonstrate to social critics

that marketing can contribute to lower prices, better service, higher quality, and, overall, higher levels of consumer satisfaction. If marketers working in these fields
avoid the use of deceptive or misleading promotional techniques and, instead, emphasize the use of financially prudent, consumer-oriented marketing, then there is a good
chance that marketing's image would be enhanced. In fact,
marketing scholars might want to conduct studies of the
effects of introducing marketing into professions such as
law and dentistry in order to provide the public with
evidence about marketing's social value (Bloom 1981).

As for industries that have had considerable past experience with marketing, but are seeing deregulation produce
a surge of aggressive competition with more varied forms
of marketing, an opportunity exists to show how bold,
carefully formulated marketing strategies can bring substantial returns to business firms. Competitive pressures
should put many firms in the position of having to rely
on good marketing to defend themselves against inroads by
aggressive new competitors. Marketing budgets and autonomy
for marketers should therefore grow -- at least for a time
-- in many firms. Marketers can use the larger budgets
and greater autonomy to develop sound, research-based,
financially prudent marketing approaches, while avoiding
wasteful, overly intuitive, quick-hitting approaches that
could make non-marketing executives develop even greater
skepticism toward marketing.

Finally, marketers in all industries have an opportunity
to show social critics and the general public that marketing is not something that requires constant government
monitoring and regulation to be ethical and honest. To a
degree, deregulation is putting marketers "on their honor,"
and by showing they deserve this trust, marketers can do
much to enhance their public image. But if too many
marketers violate this trust by using deceptive and unfair
selling practices, then a strong public backlash against
marketing -- and stricter regulation than has been seen in
the past -- could result.

RESEARCH IMPLICATIONS

Marketing academicians who are interested in helping marketing practitioners meet these proposed challenges could
do so by conducting the following types of research:

1. Econometric and structural equation studies, using
    archival data (such as the PIMS data base), of the
    effects of different competitive marketing strate-
    gies. Studies of the effects of severe price cutting,
    very intensive advertising, etc. would fit this des-
    cription.

2. Experimental studies of consumer brand loyalty and
    brand switching behavior following the introduction
    of new offerings to a market, where the offerings
    have been brought out by major firms with established
    reputations from very different markets.

3. Studies seeking to explain and predict the evolution
    of the consumer movement (see Bloom 1982).

4. Studies seeking to evaluate the effects of corporate
    consumer education and information programs.

5. Studies (like Webster's) on how marketing is viewed
    by top management and other key people in our society.

CONCLUSION

The emerging era of deregulation will be a trying time
for members of the marketing profession. While challenges
from regulatory officials should subside, challenges

stemming from other forces in the external environments of
business firms should become more frequent and threaten-
ing. In particular, many marketers will be challenged to
develop approaches to cope with the effects of having
several new, aggressive competitors in their industries.
By being bold, doing careful financial analysis, and
remaining sensitive to the problems deregulation can cause
consumers, marketers will improve their chances of reap-
ing positive monetary returns from deregulation. Bold-
ness, financial prudence, and consumer sensitivity should
also help marketers enhance the image of marketing.

REFERENCES

Bloom, Paul N. (1982), "Research on Consumerism: Opportunities and Challenges," in Andrew Mitchell, ed., _Advances
in Consumer Research: Vol. 9_, Ann Arbor, MI: Association
for Consumer Rsearch, in press.

___________ (1981), "What Marketers Need to Know About
the Marketing of Professional Services," in J.H.
Donnelly and W.R. George, eds., _Marketing of Services_,
Chicago, IL: American Marketing Association, 1981,
86-87.

___________, and Stephen A. Greyser (1981), "The Matur-
ing of Consumerism," _Harvard Business Review_, November-
December, 130-139.

Business Week (1981), "Deregulation: A Fast Start for
the Reagan Strategy," (March 9), 62-67.

Greyser, Stephen A. (1980), "Marketing Issues," _Journal of
Marketing_, 44 (Winter), 89-92.

Kotler, Philip and Ravi Singh (1981), "Marketing Warfare
in the 1980s," _Journal of Business Strategy_, 1 (Winter),
30-41.

Reich, Robert B. (1981), "Regulation by Confrontation or
Negotiation," _Harvard Business Review_ (May-June), 82-93.

Webster, Frederick E., Jr. (1980), "Top Management Views
the Marketing Function," Report No. 80-108, Marketing
Science Institute, Cambridge, Mass.

THE ECONOMIES OF SCALE IN ADVERTISING:
THE MYTH, THE CONCEPT, THE FACTS

Johan Arndt, University of California, Berkeley

ABSTRACT

This paper reviews important empirical evidence relating
to suggested economies of scale in advertising. For the
issues of advertising effectiveness of large vs. small
firms, multibrand economies, and "stay-out advertising"
the conclusion is the same: economies of scale have not
been unequivocally documented. Indeed, the paper argues
that it is even meaningless to use the economies of scale
concept with regard to advertising or any other single input factor.

INTRODUCTION

The general issue to be discussed in this review paper is:
Does the advertising cost per dollar of sales increase as
increases in total advertising expenditures occur?* Stated
in this fashion, however, the question of economies of
scale and increasing returns to advertising is vague and
equivocal. The difficulty of formulating the question in
a rigorous enough fashion is the root cause of much of the
controversy and confusion about the efficiency of advertising at various levels of advertising expenditures or other
forms of advertising input.

Regardless of the formidable theoretical and methodological problems involved, the economies of scale in advertising remain an important issue. More often than not, antitrust measures and public regulation of the marketplace
are based on (or legitimized by) assumptions of substantial scale economies enabling established large corporations
to maintain market power keeping competitors our and price
up.

The purpose of this paper is to critically review the most
important empirical evidence relating to economies of scale
in advertising. The article is organized as follows:

> Economies of scale vs. the response function of adver-
> tising.
>
> The shape of the advertising response function.
>
> Sources of economies of scale in advertising.
>
> The problems of conceptualizing economies of scale.
>
> Studies using the A/S ratio.
>
> Advertising and prices.
>
> Cost advantages due to media rate structures.
>
> Dynamic barrier effects-"stay-out advertising".
>
> Future studies regarding economies of scale in adver-
> tising.

ECONOMIES OF SCALE VS. THE RESPONSE FUNCTION OF ADVERTISING

In the literature as well as in the public debate, the notion of economies of scale in advertising is often confused with the advertising response function.

The advertising response function refers to the relationship between sales, or some other effect indicator, and
advertising input, holding other inputs constant. Formally

---

*This article is an expansion of an earlier paper with
 Julian L. Simon as co-author.

the advertising response function may be expressed in terms
of the advertising elastisity, defined as the proportionate
rate of change in sales (S) with respect to advertising (A):

$$\frac{\partial S}{\partial A}\ \frac{A}{S}$$

While the advertising response function is concerned with
the <u>short term</u> relationship between sales and advertising,
the economies of scale concept refers to the relationship
between sales and advertising or other inputs in the <u>long
run</u>, when the individual firm has complete flexibility in
determining the character of the productive process (Koch
1980, Chapter 6). Generally, the concept of economies of
scale refers to the case when the proportions of all productive inputs remain the same as the scale or size of the
firm changes. In formal terms, economies of scale may be
expressed by the so-called <u>passus coefficient</u> which in this
case is defined as the elasticity of sales with respect to
advertising when advertising and all other factors are varied proportionately (Frisch 1971, pp. 78-80):

$$\frac{d^{pr}S}{d^{pr}A}\ \frac{A}{S}$$

where $d^{pr}A$ denotes the infinitesimal <u>proportionate</u> change
in advertising (the relative magnitude of advertising to
other input factors remains the same), and $d^{pr}S$ denotes the
corresponding change in sales.

This paper focuses on the latter concept, economies of scale in advertising. First, however, a few words on the evidence relating to the advertising response function would
seem in order.

THE SHAPE OF THE ADVERTISING RESPONSE FUNCTION

Many theoreticans and practioners of marketing believe that
there is a threshold effect in that the advertising response curve is S-shaped, which implies initial increasing returns. Advertising campaigns involving high degrees of domination, concentration, and repetition would be unlikely if
there was not widespread belief in some kind of S-shaped
curve.

To evaluate the empirical evidence, the present author,
together with Julian Simon, recently conducted a comprehensive review of the literature (Simon and Arndt 1980).
The studies reviewed covered a wide range of designs, from
laboratory and field experiments to econometric analyses
of cross-sectional or time-series data. The independent
variable, advertising input, was measured by advertising
expenditures as well as by quantity in terms of size (size
of print advertisements, length of TV commercials, etc.)
or number of repetitions. The dependent variable indicators
included sales and "intermediate" effect measures such as
intentions to buy, attitudes, or awareness.

After a critical review of both the substantive findings
and the methodologies, only <u>one</u> study was found to present
clear evidence of initial returns to scale to advertising,
McNiven's (1969) field experiment concerning Du Pont's
Teflon product.

But even if the advertising response function is downward-
concave, advertising could give an advantage to the big
spender over the smaller spender. This could happen if
there is an interaction between the various levels of ad-

vertising and various other factors of production, for example in a multiplicative way. This is the issue which is explored in this paper.

SOURCES OF ECONOMIES OF SCALE IN ADVERTISING

In general, economies of scale may be traced to two broad classes of factors, "real" factors and "pecuniary" factors. "Real" economies of scale refer to higher efficiency because larger firms may benefit from specialization and division of labor, indivisibilities of input factors (less excess capacity as the scale increases), better administration, and less uncertainty. Larger firms may also be able to take the advantage of "pecuniary" economies by utilizing monopoly or monopsony power to squeeze customers or suppliers (Koch 1980, pp. 109-123).

Though there are ideological issues involved and the empirical evidence is somewhat mixed, it is fair to conclude that the literature has convincingly documented the existence of economies of scale, at least at the lower end of the scale. Similarly, at the high end, there are diseconomies owing to the difficulties of managing very large enterprises (Koch 1980, Chapter 6).

The issue of interest in this paper, however, is not whether there are general returns to scale, but whether there are advantages of size in advertising. Writers such as Chamberlin (1962, pp. 133-134), Comanor and Wilson (1974, pp. 49-53), and Ferguson (1974, pp. 73-75) suggest that advertising economies of scale result from media advertising rates (which tend to increase less than proportionately with audience size - large advertisers can then use national media with lower contact costs per customer), special volume discounts, better organization of advertising expenditures, and indivisibilities (large advertisers may use high grade copy and art work).

THE PROBLEMS OF CONCEPTUALIZING ECONOMIES OF SCALE

At first look, the notion of economies of scale appears deceptively simple. However, when it comes to research, it is difficult to make sense out of the concept of economies of scale with respect to advertising - or with respect to any other single input factor, for that manner. The difficulty is that, as earlier pointed out, the concept of economies of scale refers to differences in just that, the scale of the enterprise with all factors taken together, including their interaction. As the economies of scale concept assumes that all inputs in the productive process are variable in nature, it would seem to be empirically and conceptually meaningless to attempt to isolate the role of advertising. The concept was not designed to throw light on the operation of a single factor alone. Hence the criticism below of empirical research on scale economies in advertising really applies also to the research in the economic literature on other input factors (Koch 1980, Chapter 6).

True economies of scale would be shown if a firm that has been operating in one market moves into a second identical market, uses the same amounts of inputs in the second market that it did in the first market, and obtains more than double the total sales.

Within a given market, it is clear that the larger firm will not employ all factors in the same proportion as the smaller firms. And geographic expansions of the sort demanded for a pure test of economies of scale are seldom, if ever, available. But even if such a test were available in practice, it would not tell anything definite about advertising's role in economies of scale. One would never know whether it is advertising that has a role in the interactive combination of factors that leads to the economies of scale, whether advertising operates independently or whether

it even exerts a drag effect. So it is impossible in principle to know that advertising is responsible for economies **of scale, given that there are not increasing return**s to advertising when other factors are held constant - as the empirical evidence shows (Simon and Arndt 1980).

Another way of looking at economies of scale is to ask whether twice as much output can be produced with twice as much of some inputs and less than twice as much of other inputs. But because a larger firm in a given market usually does not employ factors in the same proportions as the smaller firm, empirically it is customary to consider the results achieved by firms of different total size; that is, "bigger" and "smaller" are now one-dimensional concepts for which the total inputs are reduced to a common dimension - money. Such a study then considers physical output as a function of a total expenditure. Such an investigation is commonly referred to as a study of "economies of scale" e.g. Stigler (1958), though it would be clearer to speak of "economies of size". Furthermore, such studies usually measure the total assets rather than expenditures, but this last deviation from theory (unlike the others) is not serious.

The difficulty of empirically pinning down the concept of economies of scale is illuminated by the study by Peles (1971), in which he estimated regression equations for beer that are variants of the following:

$$\text{Market Share}_t = a_1 \text{Advertising Share}_t +$$
$$a_2 \text{Advertising Share}_{t-1} +$$
$$a_3 \text{Advertising Share}_{t-2} +$$
$$a_4 \text{National or local firm}$$

Peles found negative coefficient for a_4, a dummy variable equal to one for local firms and zero for national firms, which may be considered a proxy for size of firm. And Peles concluded: "The minus sign means that a dollar spent for advertising will increase the demand for the product of a big firm more than of a small firm. In other words, it is plausible to interpret the above finding as evidence of economies of scale in the advertising of the beer industry ..." (Peles 1971, p. 35).

A more valid interpretation of Peles' linear regression, however, is simply that a national firm obtains more sales than a local firm, perhaps because of its distribution network and without regarding to advertising. The additive linear form does not permit a test of the interaction between advertising and size. Morever, to get closer to showing that advertising is more effective for large firms, a slope dummy rather than an intercept dummy should have been used.

Lambin's (1976) ambitious and exhaustive study may be considered the centerpiece investigation of the advertising-sales relationship. His sample covered 107 brands of 16 product classes in 8 European countries. First, in his time-series analysis, each individual response function was best described by a concave-downward diminishing returns equation.

Second, Lambin examined the relationship of each brand's advertising share to its market share. The results showed that brands with relatively small market shares had advertising shares larger than their market shares. This Lambin interpreted as indicating that there is a threshold for advertising effectiveness below which advertising expenditures have no effect. Such a threshold constitutes an inflection point, the lower boundary of a region of increasing returns. In the words of Lambin: "Therefore, to reach the level of communication effectiveness, small brands have to keep their advertising shares higher than their market shares" (Lambin 1976, p. 128).

These data need not indicate a threshold, however, as will be explained below. In essence, the data involve a comparison of the response functions from one brand to another

with <u>nothing held constant</u>. The first set of findings, however, showed the returns to advertising with all other (empirically controllable) factors <u>held constant</u>. That is, it
is reasonable and likely that a larger firm has a much more
extensive distribution network and a larger sales force
than a smaller one. That would explain <u>both</u> why the larger
firm has a higher response function <u>and</u> why it advertises
more in total than does its smaller competitor.

Many of the economies-of-scale studies focusing on advertising have used the advertising-to-sales (A/S) ratio as
a central variable. In a sense, the A/S ratio may be viewed as a rough indicator of the unit cost of advertising.

STUDIES USING THE A/S RATIO

Like the other data reviewed above, A/S ratio data by themselves are flawed for the purpose of examining the role of
advertising in economies of scale because that there are
many other policies and strategies that may be systematically different between larger and smaller firms.

Many economists have found evidence that higher output levels are associated with lower unit advertising costs (lower A/S ratios). Therefore, the argument is that smaller
firms, including most potential entrants, are placed at a
substantial disadvantage. For instance, in the automotive
industry in the 1950's, the two smaller firms - Studebaker
and American Motors - spent more than twice as much on advertising per car than did General Mortors and Ford. This
fact has been interpreted as evidence of a threshold volume
for advertising out of reach for the smaller firms (Comanor
and Wilson 1974, pp. 52-53).

Several studies have linked the A/S ratio to differences
in profitability among firms and industries. Imel and Helmberger (1971) related the profitability of food processing
firms to the A/S ratio (allowing for concentration ratio,
R&D expenditures, assets, and other variables) and found
a positive relationship. Similar results were reported by
Vernon and Nourse (1973) who added that "the association
should be interpreted as advertising barriers causing high
profits". But the sensible firm will increase its advertising well into the region of diminishing returns, the pro-
fit-maximizing criterion being that advertising expenditures should be increased to the point where marginal revenue equals marginal cost. Hence no conclusions about <u>in-
creasing</u> returns can be drawn from such a relationship,
even if it exists, and it may imply diminishing returns.

Comanor and Wilson (1974) have studied at book length the
dependence of profits and optimal firm size on the A/S ratio and firm size in cross-sections of industries and size-
classes of firms within industries. They concluded flatly
that, "The findings provide empirical support for the view
that there are advantages to size that are related to the
level of advertising intensity in an industry" (p. 234).

The main warrant for this conclusion is that there is a positive relationship between the profit rate and an interactive term (assets per size-class of firms x industry ad-
vertising/sales ratio), whereas the asset term by itself
had no principal effect (p. 220). Additionally, they found
that "advertising outlays interact with scale economies at
the plant level to influence the minimum size of an efficient firm. Particularly where scale economies are small in
relation to the market, heavy advertising outlays may increase the minimum share of the market accounted for by an
efficient firm" (p. 228).

It would require an entire article to consider the Comanor-
Wilson method and findings in satisfactory detail. It is
fair to say in brief that whatever they do show, the Comanor-Wilson findings do not throw light on whether any particular seller of a given product has an advantage over another seller of the same product by virtue of using more

advertising than the other firm. A long chain of logic
would be needed to connect the behavior of competing sellers of a given specific product and the Comanor-Wilson
findings. One would need to assume that larger and smaller
firms in various industries have the same product mix; this
is most unlikely, and the product mix is likely to be related to the extent to which the various specific products
are advertised, which would invalidate the Comanor-Wilson
conclusion. Furthermore, if smaller sellers of a given product do choose a different marketing strategy than do larger sellers, emphasizing low price rather than heavy advertising - because smaller firms can cut prices more flexibly
than can large firms - this also would invalidate the conclusion of Comanor and Wilson.

Comanor and Wilson's results would seem to tell more about
the <u>structure of markets</u>, such as which size class of firms
choose products which they then advertise heavily, and
which size classes of firms emphasize advertising rather
than price within the marketing mix, than they do about
economies of scale related to advertising.

Porter (1976b) reported that the A/S ratio had a positive
effect on profits for "convenience goods" industries, but
not in the "shopping goods" industries. These well-documen-
ted findings suggest that the relationship between profitability and advertising intensity is not homogeneous
across industry groups or even across firms. It implies
that there are dangers of uncritical pooling of observations across potentially heterogenous firm and industry
groups. The issue of homogeneity has also been addressed
by Bass and his associates (Bass 1974; Bass, Cattin, and
Wittink 1978). They found that when firms were clustered
into homogeneous groups, the relationship between profits
and advertising evaporated in some cases. This suggests
again that effects of advertising in ordinary cross-sectional studies may be confounded with effects of structural
variables.

In brief, studies of the relationship between size or profitability and the A/S ratio may be useful as evidence on
the role of the <u>structure</u> of markets, but tell little or
nothing about <u>economies of scale</u> related to advertising.

The review so far leads to the conclusion that it has been
convincingly demonstrated that large firms may be more efficient than smaller firms. On the other hand, it has not
been possible to relate the higher efficiency to <u>advertis-
ing</u>.

Though it appears that a total and <u>direct</u> test of economies of scale in advertising is futile and meaningless, the
matter may be approached by partial, indirect tests. Below
the following indirect tests of the scale issue will be
briefly addressed: advertising and prices, cost advantages due to media rates, multibrand economies, and dynamic
barrier effects-"stay-out-out advertising".

ADVERTISING AND PRICES

Economies of scale might be involved if large advertisers
were found to have lower prices than their smaller competitors (though the relationship could also be explained by
other factors).

In the formulation of Farris and Albion (1980), there appears to be two main schools of thought among economists
concerned with the advertising-prices issue. The first
school adheres to the Advertising = Market Power model and
maintains that advertising results in weakened competition
and higher prices. The contrast, the Advertising = Information school argues that advertising strengthens competition and decreases industry prices.

Instead of reviewing the many studies here in detail, I
will build on the review of Farris and Albion (1980). Not

343

surprisingly, Farris and Albion concluded that the evidence
connecting manufacturer advertising and prices was neither
complete nor definitive (p. 30). However, as far as the data went there were two strong tendencies. At the factory
level advertising was found in most cases to decrease price
sensitivity and to increase relative manufacturer prices.
However, at the retail (consumer) level there was an opposite relationship as advertising was found to increase
price sensitivity and to lower absolute prices. In this
way, Farris and Albion called a draw for the two opposing
schools of thought. The two effects appeared to neutralize
one another. Hence, unfortunately the main issue remains
unresolved.

COST ADVANTAGES DUE TO MEDIA RATE STRUCTURES

Increasing returns to advertising expenditure may result
from volume discounts in media rates structures. It has
been suggested that such discounts are important in national magazines, network radio, and specially network television (Ferguson, 1974, pp. 74-75). Comanor and Wilson (1974,
pp. 53-61) who investigated price structure for the three
American networks, reported that the principal source of
cost advantages to large-scale advertisers was quantity discounts on individual programs (but not on aggregate firm
purchases from the network).

Another potential advantage of large advertisers is the
access to essentially indivisible nation-wide media such
as television networks. Though the evidence is mixed, such
economies have been pointed out. For instance, Porter
(1976a) found that network rates ranged from approximately
10 to 70 per cent of the sum of the individual station
(spot) rates, with the discount varying by time of day and
season. Moreover, in regression estimates of profit rates
across 39 consumer goods industries, significantly positive
results were obtained for variable relating to network advertising as per cent of sales. However, a newer analysis
using improved methodology showed that the difference between network and spot rates in television was much smaller
than the range suggested by Porter (Peterman 1979).

In conclusion, the evidence available is suggestive rather
than conclusive. Obviously more work is needed before firm
conclusions may be made regarding the cost advantages due
to media rates. However, as far as the results go, there
appears to be some scale economies relating to network television.

THE TRICKY ISSUE OF MULTIBRAND ECONOMIES

Multibrand economies of size stemming from advertising are
logically similar to geographical economies. One might speculate that a merger of two related-product brands, of the
development of a related-product brand by a going firm,
might produce both volume discounts in advertising and communication economies such as the use of a common trademark.
And the increase in the number of advertised brands in a
majority of consumer categories (Simon 1970 pp. 232-234) is
consistent with this speculation. (This also represents les-
sened industrial concentration at the brand level, by the
way, an important phenomenon in its own right.)

But a trend toward a larger number of brands sold per firm
might also stem from economies of distribution, production,
and purchasing (e.g., packing materials). Hence, this is
certainly not strong evidence for multibrand economies of
size flowing from advertising. Nor is there other relevant
evidence. And it is difficult to think of a sound design
to test for this effect.

DYNAMIC BARRIER EFFECTS - "STAY-OUT ADVERTISING"

Advertising might be used as a barrier against potential
entrants into the market, just as "stay-out pricing" might
be used. The latter has been discussed under the title of
"limit pricing", analyzed in a static manner by Bain (1956),
Modigliani (1958), and Sylos-Labini (1962), and in more dynamic content by Gaskins (1971).

It appears that the dynamic theory of advertising barriers
effects has yet to be spelled out in a rigorous enough fashion. Cubbin (1981) argues persuasively that the positive
associations often found between advertising intensity and
profitability do   not mean that advertising acts as an entry barrier. The relationship may be a spurious one, as the
studies have not controlled for the monopoly power effect.

It is not immediately obvious how one would formalize for
a mature market the ideas vaguely expressed by the literary
concept. For a new product, it seems rather straightforward
that a firm making high profits from an innovation might
buy advertising beyond what a monopolist would, in order
to bind customers more closely for the future. And in this
way, as well as by simply lowering the prospective profits
because of advertising expenditures, a firm with a new product might render entry less attractive. That is, more advertising in period t might mean fewer sales in period t+1
for a potential entrant with given levels of price and
advertising.

Why would one set up a barrier with advertising instead of
price? It may be that advertising is a better barrier because advertising in t results in a real change in the entry conditions in t+1, whereas a stayout price in t is only
a signal of intentions about behavior in t+1 and can be
interpreted only as a bluff.

Working in the other direction is advertising's role as a
competitive tool that makes it easier for potential entrants to actually enter successfully. If one could not advertise, it would be much harder for a potential entrant
with a product improvement - a ball-point pen or a rotary
engine - or even a potential entrant without a product improvement, to enter the market. In this way advertising has
a procompetitive dynamic effect.

Unfortunately, no body of empirical work could be found to
determine whether the net outcome of advertising is to increase or decrease the rate of market entrance. And it will
not be an easy task to design sound research to answer this
question. One research possibility is to investigate changes in industrial structure in countries that have banned
advertising for a product group such as tobacco, alcoholic
beverages, etc.

This question must be distinguished from the advertising-
and-competition question that has so much interested economists in recent years. In practice, the latter has reduced
to the question whether industries that, for one reason or
other, spend a relatively high proportion of sales on advertising also have a relatively high concentration ratio. But
the logical links between this question and questions about
the effects of more or less advertising, whether or not in
conjunction with controlled changes in other variables, are
tenuous indeed.

FUTURE STUDIES REGARDING ECONOMIES OF SCALE IN ADVERTISING

Where does this situation point us? It points apparently
towards explicit studies of the returns to a combination
of advertising and one or more other factors. An experimental study that holds all other factors constant but increases expenditures on advertising by 20%, could reveal something about advertising's role in bigness. Studies of joint
advertising and price effects, or joint advertising and
distribution effects, might also be illuminating. Of course,

such studies would be complex, because a change in total
sales as a result of changes in advertising and price would
bring about changes in production expenditures.

An economies-of-size question of the following sort might
be asked by a firm: We are a regional brewer (say). Will
we improve our market strength and profitability by merg-
ing with other regional brewers to the point that we can
employ national advertising media at lower national rate
costs per exposure? The answer to this question in principle is "yes" if - not a small "if" - offsetting costs of
increased organizational size do not offset the reduced
cost of advertising (and any other cost reductions). The
growth of national brands of beer and many other consumer
goods is consistent with such an economies-of-size effect
indeed being at work. But there are also other important
cost reductions that accompany "going national", most especially the reduced costs of capital that accompany increased
size (Shepherd 1970, pp. 98-99, and 174-176). So without
close study, it is not possible to know from this sort of
evidence how important are advertising discounts in the
geographic combination of firms. And the relevant research
has not been done.

Another sort of economies-of-size question arises if a national seller of, say beer, wonders whether the firm might
gain an advantage over its competitors by increasing its
advertising level together with changes in another input
such as store distribution or price. It is possible that
some interaction between the advertising and the other
jointly manipulated variables might increase total sales and
profits with a less-than-propotional increase in total expenditures. But there is little evidence that illuminates
the matter. One of the few studies of interactions of this
kind was reported by Eskin (1975) who found that advertising
had less effect the higher the price.

REFERENCES

Bain, Joe S. (1956), _Barriers to New Competition_. Cambridge:
Harvard University Press.

Bass, Frank M. (1974), "Profit and the A/S Ratio", _Journal
of Advertising Research_, XIV (December), 9-19.

___________, Phillippe Cattin, and Dick R. Wittink (1978),
"Firm Effects and Industry Effects in the Analysis of
Market Structure and Profitability," _Journal of Mar-
keting Research_, XV (February), 3-10.

Chamberlin, Edward H. (1962), _The Theory of Monopolistic
Competition_. Cambridge: Harvard University Press.

Comanor, William S. and Thomas A. Wilson (1974), _Adverti-
sing and Market Power_. Cambridge: Harvard University
Press.

Cubbin, John (1981), "Advertising and the Theory of Entry
Barriers," _Economica_, XL, 289-98.

Eskin, Gerald J. (1975), "A Case for Test Marketing Experiments", _Journal of Advertising Research_, XV (April),
27-33.

Farris, Paul W. and Mark S. Albion (1980), "The Impact of
Advertising on the Price of Consumer Products", _Jour-
nal of Marketing_, XLIV (Summer), 17-35.

Ferguson, James M. (1974), _Advertising and Competition:
Theory, Measurement, Fact_. Cambridge: Ballinger.

Frisch, Ragnar (1971), _Innledning til produksjonsteorien_.
Oslo: Universitetsforlaget.

Gaskins, Darius W., Jr. (1971), "Dynamic Limit Pricing:
Optimal Pricing under Threat of Entry," _Journal of
Economic Theory_, III (September), 306-22.

Imel, J. Blake and Peter G. Helmberger (1971), "Estimation
of Structure-Profit Relationships with Application to
the Food Processing Sector," _American Economic Review_,
LXI (September), 614-27.

Koch, James V. (1980), _Industrial Organization and Prices_,
2nd ed. Englewood Cliffs, New Jersey: Prentice-Hall.

Lambin, Jean-Jacques (1976), _Advertising, Competition and
Market Conduct in Oligopoly over Time_. Amsterdam:
North-Holland.

McNiven, Malcolm, ed. (1969), _How Much to Spend for Adver-
tising_? New York: Association of National Advertisers.

Modigliani, Franco (1958), "New Developments on the Oligopoly Front," _Journal of Political Economy_, LXVI (June),
215-32.

Peles, Yoram (1971), "Economies of Scale in Advertising
Beer and Cigarettes", _Journal of Business_, XLIV, 32-7.

Peterman, John L. (1979), "Differences between the Levels
of Spot and Network Television Advertising Rates",
Journal of Business, LII (October), 549-61.

Porter, Michael E. (1976a)," Interbrand Choice, Media Mix
and Market Performance," _American Economic Review_,
LXVI (May), 398-406.

___________ (1976b), _Interbrand Choice, Strategy and Bilateral Market Power_. Cambridge: Harvard University
Press.

Shepherd, William G. (1970), _Market Power and Economic Wel-
fare_. New York: Random House.

Simon, Julian L. (1970), _Issues in the Economics of Adver-
tising_. Urbana, Illinois: University of Illinois Press.

___________ and Johan Arndt (1980), "The Shape of the
Advertising Response Function", _Journal of Advertising Research_, XX (August), 11-28.

Stigler, George J. (1958), The Economies of Scale," _Journal
of Law and Economics_, 1 (October), 54-71.

Sylos-Labini, Paolo (1962), _Oligopoly and Technical Progress_.
Cambridge: Harvard University Press.

Vernon, John M. and Robert E.M. Nourse (1973), "Profit Rates and Market Structure of Advertising Intensive
Firms," _Journal of Industrial Economics_, XXII (September), 1-20.

GOVERNMENT REGULATION OF ADVERTISING: A QUESTION OF BALANCE

Debra L. Scammon, University of Utah
Kenneth D. Bahn, University of Utah

ABSTRACT

Government regulation can play an important role in the coordination of the multiple individual and social goals in
our market economy. This paper discusses the potential
need for government regulation of advertising practices to
balance the sometimes conflicting goals of consumers and
business. It illustrates the problems inherent in identifying situations where regulation might improve the operation of the marketplace and in procedures for assessing the
impacts of government regulation. Finally, some suggestions are offered for the improvement of policy decision-
making regarding the regulation of advertising practices.

INTRODUCTION

The economic impact of government regulation of advertising
practices is of concern to policy makers but accurate assessment of the impacts of regulation is difficult. Recent
regulatory reform bills have both mandated (FTC Improvement
Act 1980) and inferred (Executive Order 12044, 1978) that
cost/benefit analysis is required in rule-making proceedings. To properly assess the impact of government intervention in advertising practices, the intended benefits of
a regulation must be articulated and the likely impact on
consumers, businesses and society identified. The identification of the specific sectors of the economy affected
and the estimation of the magnitude of the effects of
government regulation are not easy tasks.

The purposes of this paper are to: (1) briefly discuss one
rationale for government regulation of advertising practices; (2) outline some of the costs and benefits potentially associated with the regulation of advertising; (3)
explore some of the difficulties inherent in making reasonably accurate estimates of the effects of regulation of advertising; and (4) propose some tentative suggestions for
improving regulatory decision making.

The focus of this paper on the regulation of advertising
practices is particularly important in light of the attention given this area by the Reagan Administration via the
new Chairman of the Federal Trade Commission. Chairman
Miller's perspective on the cost and value of existing advertising regulations appears to be somewhat different from
the perspective which has guided the FTC's policies over
the last decade.

A RATIONALE FOR THE REGULATION OF ADVERTISING

Economic regulation, that is, regulation of business practices that affect the economy, is often restrictive in nature and thus may impose some costs on those regulated.
But it also encourages and stimulates some "socially desirable" business practices thus contributing to the overall
benefit of society. The regulation of advertising practices offers an example of just such a situation. The economic rationale for advertising is its provision of information to the marketplace. The "public interest" theory of
regulation (Posner 1972; Stigler 1971) would suggest that
regulation of advertising practices would be necessary (and
desirable) only to the extent that insufficient or inaccurate information is available to consumers. Thus, to correct the problem of inaccurate information, regulation may
constrain what the advertiser can say, and to deal with the
problem of insufficient information, regulation may mandate

what an advertiser must say. Both of these actions would
very likely impose costs on the advertiser. But these
costs would presumably be accompanied by benefits to the
"public." The goal of these regulations would be to foster
an environment of complete and accurate information enabling consumers to make "better" decisions which would lead
to greater economic efficiency as well as greater individual and societal well being.

INFORMATION CONTENT OF ADVERTISING

Advertisers and consumers have different motivations for
using advertising. Sellers not only want to communicate
facts about their brands, they also want to communicate
those facts in such a way as to influence consumers' perceptions of the desirability of their brands compared to competitors' brands. Advertising offers sellers a means of
differentiating their brands. Sellers' shares of a market,
and in fact, at the extreme, an entire market may be based
on how successfully they communicate the advantages of
their brands. Thus, the information which advertisers want
to include in advertising is that which will portray their
brands as unique.

Consumers desire information that will help them to choose
among competing brands. Although the strategy of product
differentiation can be overdone, advertising which informs
consumers about the advantages of a brand may help them decide which brand is best. For example, an advertisement
which compares the EPA estimated mileage of two automobiles,
portraying one as more fuel efficient than the other, may
help consumers decide which car to purchase. Thus, often
seller and buyer information needs coincide. Both advertisers and consumers want information included in advertising that will differentiate brands.

Advertisers and consumers may disagree on what information
is useful for distinguishing brands, however. In their
zeal to communicate a differential advantage for their
brands, advertisers may be tempted to make untruthful, exaggerated, or unsubstantiated claims about their products.
In their search for the "best" brand, consumers may relie
on such inaccurate information. This may be a problem in
instances where the information contained in advertising is
the only information available to consumers or, at least,
is the only information consulted by consumers prior to
making purchase decisions.

Consumers frequently purchase products whose benefits are
hard to confirm (e.g., energy consumption of a refrigerator)
or which may have hidden costs (e.g., adverse side effects
of a drug) (Scammon, McNeil and Preston 1980). In such
cases, what advertisers tell consumers may be all they will
know about these products before making a purchase. Infrequent purchases of durable goods are likely to be made
without consideration of all available alternatives and
even without cognizance of important decision criteria
(Westbrook and Fornell 1979). Again, in these cases, consumers' knowledge comes to a large extent from advertising.

If consumer decisions are based on imperfect information,
then their choices can lead to misallocation of resources
by both the producer (less long run profits) and the consumer (less derived utility from consumption) (Scammon,
McNeil and Preston 1980).

The availability of accurate and complete information is a
necessary condition for consumers to make informed choices

which facilitate the effective and efficient functioning of the marketplace. Advertising regulation should help foster such an environment. Whether any particular regulation is necessary and/or justified depends upon how effective it is in rectifying an imperfection in the marketplace and the cost incurred in implementing and administering the regulation.

HOW MUCH AND WHAT TYPE OF REGULATION?

Most marketplace imperfections can be remedied to a greater or lesser degree by alternative actions or forms of intervention. Each alternative will have its own advantages (e.g., probability of success in correcting the problem; type, magnitude, and distribution of benefits) and its own costs (e.g., implementation, administration). Policy makers need a way of determining which regulatory proposals will be the best, in balance, for all concerned.

The regulation of advertising by the FTC in the past decade has focused on ensuring that the information in advertising is accurate and that "purchase relevant" information is available to consumers. This has led to requirements for substantiation of claims made in advertising (e.g., tests supporting comparative performance claims) and affirmative disclosure of important facts (e.g., the Surgeon General's warning in cigarette advertising). The underlying theory has been that consumers need this information in order to make informed purchase decisions and that sellers are the appropriate ones to supply this information.

The new leadership at the Commission has given early attention to some of the Commission's existing programs, questioning their effectiveness. Chairman Miller has suggested that consumers are not as gullible as they have been portrayed and thus some of the regulations of advertising currently being enforced may not be needed. He feels that unnecessary regulations may be contributing to higher prices paid by consumers (Miller 1981).

The counterpoint of philosophies illustrates the desirability of developing methods for determining the costs and benefits of regulations. Such techniques are vitally needed if effective policy decisions are to be made. These will not be easy analyses however, since many of the costs and benefits of regulations are likely to be indirect, delayed, and difficult to predict. In fact, there is not always agreement as to whether a particular impact should be considered a cost or a benefit nor whether, in balance, the benefits of a regulation outweigh the costs.

The following discussion attempts to identify some of the types of costs and benefits which might be important in policy decisions regarding the appropriateness of regulation of advertising. It focuses on ad substantiation and affirmative disclosure in order to provide concrete examples. The discussion by no means includes an inventory of the possible impacts. Consideration is given to some of the problems frequently hampering accurate evaluation of the extent of the impacts of regulation.

Costs

The most obvious costs associated with any regulation are the direct costs to the industries affected by it. In the case of ad substantiation, these costs may include capital costs (e.g., engaging in testing to substantiate claims made in advertising), operating costs (e.g., inclusion of more expensive materials in products as a means of differentiating a company's brand so that claims can be substantiated), maintenance costs (e.g., more frequent inspections of manufacturing systems to ensure consistent product quality), and administrative costs (e.g., increased paper-work involved in filing compliance reports). Estimation of these sorts of costs may be fairly straight-

forward, and these costs are likely to be significant. But policy decisions must also include consideration of a regulation's indirect effects. These consequences are necessarily quite hypothetical and the estimation of their magnitude depends substantially upon the underlying assumptions which are incorporated into the analyses.

A complete cost analysis should include estimates of both social (aggregate) and private (individual) costs. For ad substantiation, social costs may include, among others, opportunity costs (e.g., resources devoted to an ad substantiation program cannot be spent in other programs; expenditures by a firm to meet substantiation requirements pull resources away from other activities such as new product development), redistributive effects (e.g., producers must bear the cost of providing product information rather than relying on consumers to seek it out), and costs of policing compliance and processing compliance reports (e.g., reviewing the volumes of data submitted to the FTC by some companies to substantiate their advertising claims).

Private costs borne by consumers relate to consumers' choice opportunities. Regulation may impact the prices paid by consumers. For example, the costs of conducting exacting research to back performance claims may be passed on from the producer to the consumer in the form of higher prices to the consumer.

It is often difficult to attribute costs solely to a regulation. For example, some production or marketing practices that are initiated by regulation may become incorporated over time as part of normal industry practice and would be continued even if the regulation were repealed. The required disclosure of tar and nicotine content of cigarettes is an example of such a situation. Although this disclosure was originally mandated by a regulation, cigarette manufacturers soon discovered there was a market for low tar and nicotine cigarettes and these attributes became the basis for effective product differentiation strategies.

It is also often difficult to separate out the costs of redesign that are in response to changing market demand (e.g., retooling by automobile manufacturers to meet the market demand for smaller, more fuel efficient cars) from those due exclusively to regulation (e.g., substantiation of mileage claims with EPA tests and disclosure of the test results). Similarly, it is difficult to sort out the costs of a particular regulation when an industry (or firm) is redesigning to meet other regulatory requirements simultaneously (e.g., emission limitations for automobiles).

Another factor that should be considered when estimating the costs of a regulation is that compliance costs may decrease over time. The first time a firm conducts a study to substantiate its performance claims research costs may be high but as such testing becomes routine procedure, costs may be significantly reduced. The extent of this "learning curve" effect is extremely difficult to estimate, yet it may be substantial.

The regulation of advertising may affect the availability of products by stimulating or stifling innovation. If the profitability of the introduction of new products is affected by a regulation, product development activities may decrease (e.g., a new brand may be withheld from the market because it is too costly to develop support for the claimed advantages/differences of the brand). Regulation thus may slow the rate of innovation in an industry resulting in fewer alternatives from which consumers can choose. On the other hand, regulation may encourage innovation. For example, the requirement that cigarette manufacturers disclose the level of tar and nicotine in their brands led to a battle to differentiate brands on those dimensions and new "low tar and low nicotine" brands were introduced to the market. Similarily, the disclosure of EPA mileage estimates by automobile manufacturers contributed to increased competition among producers on that dimension.

Even when costs can be identified, it is often difficult to establish a cause and effect relationship between the regulation and the costs. If, for example, the promulgation of a regulation is preceded by the establishment of a more general public policy, it may be difficult to determine whether costs can legitimately be considered costs of the regulation or whether they are more precisely the result of the social policy. To illustrate, the requirement that advertisers substantiate their claims was only one rule following from a policy adopted by the Commission to help foster a more complete information environment for consumers. Costs incurred by firms to substantiate their claims could be considered costs of the regulation, or alternatively, costs of the broader Commission policy.

Unfortunately, it seems that the better job analysts do of identifying all of the types of costs which might be associated with a regulation, the more difficult the task of valuing those costs becomes. It is also true that the more indirect the costs are, the weaker is the link between regulation and the cost and the more dependent estimates of the costs are on the assumptions made by the analysts.

Benefits

The objectives of the regulation of advertising, and thus the benefits expected from regulation, are diverse. Some regulations have broad goals (e.g., prevent unfair and deceptive advertising); others are very specific (e.g., advertisers must have a "reasonable basis" for claims made in advertising). The benefits of regulation may be viewed as intermediate outputs (e.g., misleading and deceptive information removed from the marketplace) to the ultimate objective (e.g., increase the opportunity for consumers to make informed decisions). Benefits may also be categorized as direct (only truthful information is allowed in advertising) or indirect (product quality may increase because claims regarding product benefits can then be effectively substantiated). Benefits may accrue to primary beneficiaries (e.g., consumers who can have more confidence in ad claims that have been substantiated), as well as to secondary beneficiaries (e.g., members of an industry required to substantiate ad claims may face more honest competition).

An example illustrating the complexity of assessing the benefits of regulation is offered by the FTC's Used Car Trade Regulation Rule (FTC 1982). The rule requires dealers to post window stickers, called "Buyers Guides," on all used cars. These stickers must contain a description of the terms of any warranties offered, whether the car is being sold "as is," and any mechanical defects known to the dealer. The benefits can be direct -- providing the car buyer with more information upon which to decide how much he/she is willing to pay for a particular car. They can be indirect -- fewer defective cars will be offered for sale since there may be an incentive for the dealer to repair defects prior to sale. The benefits may accrue to buyers, that is, they will be better able to evaluate the "worth" to them of a particular car. They may also accrue to the used car dealers who now will be able to charge what a car is really worth because "better" cars will be distinguishable from "lemons."

The magnitude of the benefits actually received from any regulation depends not only upon the standards set by the regulation but also upon the attitude of those being regulated and their methods of compliance, the vigor with which the regulations are enforced, the severity of any penalties for violations, and so on. Elements beyond the control of the regulators can have a significant impact upon the benefits received from a regulation.

Many of the benefits of a regulation are difficult to value in monetary terms. However, some estimate of their magnitude must be made in order to determine whether a regulation is cost-effective. The problems of accurately assessing the benefits of a regulation revolve around the difficulties in foreseeing consequences and appraising their social value. Because regulations frequently function in precisely those markets where prices either do not exist or fail to reflect social values, no clear market price exists to appraise the social contributions of many regulatory programs. Many of the desired outcomes from regulatory actions thus defy traditional economic valuation. Assigning a quantitative value to such things as consumer confidence or informed decisions is necessarily subjective and to some extent arbitrary.

One of the most uncomfortable problems is that even with the difficulties in accurately assessing benefits, it is very common to find an unjustified level of confidence being placed on the crude projections. The assessment of benefits is laced with critical assumptions and frequently omits entirely important but immeasurable consequences, such as reduction in psychological suffering, improvement in aesthetics or equity. The Used Car Rule (FTC 1982) illustrates this problem. The disclosure of known mechanical defects and warranty terms on used cars is expected to benefit consumers in a variety of ways. One expected benefit is that used cars will be priced more in line with their value. Thus, the price paid for a used car after passage of the rule would provide an easy estimate of the impact of the rule. However, other more intangible benefits may also result, such as increased consumer confidence or decreased consumer reliance on seller-dominated information. The magnitude of these sorts of benefits is not easy to estimate, nor is it easy to attach a value to such benefits.

Despite the fact that the benefits of regulation are likely to be indirect and not immediately obvious and are likely not to be easily valued in traditional monetary terms, it is important to consider them in as much depth and with as much rigor as possible. If the key impacts of a regulation--both costs and benefits--can be outlined, then decisions regarding whether a particular regulation is necessary and beneficial can be made by explicitly balancing all the considerations.

CONCLUSION

Government regulation of advertising practices may sometimes be necessary to ensure the efficient operation of the marketplace. The goal of an efficiently functioning marketplace is not a simple goal, however. The achievement of many goals simultaneously, some of which may even be contrary to one another, is the real challenge for successful government regulation.

It is not difficult to see that the impacts of a regulation, or the aggregate of regulations, will at once be beneficial and costly to society. If public policy decision-making is to be rational, then some balancing of costs and benefits is required in determining whether government regulation is necessary in a particular instance and, if it is, what sort of intervention would be the most effective for achieving the desired goals. This paper has discussed some of the types of costs and benefits which might be important in such analyses and has presented some of the problems likely to impede accurate assessment of them. Dealing with these issues successfully will pay off by facilitating the striking of an appropriate balance between government intervention and non-intervention in advertising practices. Some conclusions and suggestions for improving decision-making regarding advertising regulation follow:

1. The question of whether government regulation is
    necessary rarely has a simple yes or no answer.
    Rather, the question is how much and what kind

of intervention would be the most cost-effective.
The solutions to marketplace failures thus must be
simultaneously judged along two dimensions: cost
and effectiveness. The choice among alternative
solutions to the problem requires understanding the
factors contributing to the problem. Solutions can
then be assessed with regard to their impact on the
causes of the problem rather than their impact merely upon the problem's symptoms. When the problem is
well-defined, the benefits of eliminating or minimizing the problem become more obvious.

2. It is critical to develop data bases that include
    data on actual experiences whenever possible. Often
    data are available on various aspects of a situation
    prior to any government intervention. Once a regu-
    lation has been implemented, comparable data should
    be analyzed in order to assess any changes that have
    occurred. Currently, this sort of before-after
    analysis of regulations of advertising is the res-
    ponsibility of the Impact Evaluation staff at the
    FTC (personal conversation, various dates). Rarely
    can cause and effect conclusions relating the ob-
    served changes to the imposition of the regulation
    be drawn. However, the actual impacts experienced
    can be compared to the estimates of impacts derived
    prior to implementation. Future estimates can then
    be refined, incorporating this new information.

3. Whenever possible, attempts should be made to quan-
    tify costs and benefits. A basic difficulty with
    many benefits estimates is that regulation is seek-
    ing to achieve ends for which the marketplace sim-
    ply provides no readily comparable value. However,
    it is critical that benefits which cannot be relia-
    bly quantified not be ignored. An attempt must be
    made to identify the nature of such benefits and
    estimate their magnitude and distribution. Subjec-
    tive analyses must be included since the difficult
    to measure impacts of a regulation are often the
    most significant ones.

4. It is essential to continue working on developing
    methodologies for estimating costs and benefits and
    for isolating causal relationships between regula-
    tions and their impacts. However, it is also criti-
    cal for policy makers to recognize that if strong
    cost/benefit analyses are required in regulatory
    rule-making proceedings, no rules will be promul-
    gated until there is a break through in evaluation
    methodology. In this way, requiring strict cost/
    benefit analyses can be an indirect method of elim-
    inating or severly curtailing rule making (annon.
    1982).

Determination of an appropriate balance between government
intervention and non-intervention in advertising practices
must be made in light of the many goals of society, its
citizens and its businesses. Policy makers must set priorities for correction of marketplace failures. Government
regulation is not a panacea for all market problems. Thus,
once policy makers have identified an objective for regulations, cost-effectiveness analysis should be used to determine the extent to which a rule can achieve that objective.

REFERENCES

Annon. (1982), Comments from anonymous reviewer, American
Marketing Association Educator's Conference paper competition.

Executive Order 12044 (1978), Improving Government Regulations, 43 FR 12661, March 24.

Federal Trade Commission (1980), Improvements Act of 1980,
P.L. No. 96-2532.

FTC Trade Regulation Rule (1981), Used Motor Vehicles, 16
CFR 455 (FR Aug. 14).

Miller, James C. (1981), Remarks before the Association of
National Advertisers, San Francisco, California, November 10.

Personal conversation (various dates), Federal Trade Commission staff members, Washington, D.C.

Posner, Richard A. (1972), "Theories of Economic Regulation," Bell Journal of Economics, Feb. 5, 335-355.

Ross, Richard B., (1979), "Some Difficulties in Measuring
the Costs and Benefits of Regulation," in The Dialogue
That Happened, G. David Hughes and E. Cameron Williams
(eds.). Boston: Marketing Science Institute, 56-70.

Scammon, Debra L., Dennis L. McNeil, and Ivan L. Preston
(1980), "The FTC's Emerging Theory of Consumer Protection Via Increased Information," in Proceedings of the
Second American Marketing Association Theory Conference.

Stigler, George J. (1981), "The Theory of Economic Regulation," Bell Journal of Economics and Management Science,
Spring.

Westbrook Robert A. and Claes Fornell (1979), "Patterns
of Information Source Usage Among Durable Goods Buyers,"
Journal of Marketing Research, 16 (August), 303-312.

THE PROBLEM OF ECONOMIC VALUATION IN SOCIAL MARKETING

Michael Morris, Virginia Polytechnic Institute and State University

ABSTRACT

This paper urges caution in efforts to extend the boundaries of the marketing discipline into the social marketing
arena. It is argued that a fundamental lack of fit exists
between techniques marketers have developed to be effective in the free market and the selling of ideas. The
marketing concept as a philosophy does not apply in a
social marketing context. Moreover, no objective means
exist for attributing value to an issue, idea, or concept.
This is because there is not a marketplace for ideas in
the same sense as for goods and services. Social marketers may actually distort whatever semblance of a market
does exist.

INTRODUCTION

A number of questions have been raised in recent years concerning the ethical implications of various marketing
activities (Galbraith, 1967; Levitt, 1970; Moyer and Hutt,
1978; Tuerk, 1978; DeGeorge and Pichler, 1978; Beauchamp
and Bowie, 1979). At the same time, a number of authors
have argued for the application of such marketing techniques in non-business situations, including the provision
of public goods (Shapiro, 1973; Kotler, 1975; Lovelock and
Weinberg, 1977; Montana, 1978; Rothschild, 1979; Weinberg,
1980; Mokwa, Dawson, and Prieve, 1981). A somewhat widely
discussed concept is that of "social marketing", which has
been explained as "the design, implementation and control
of programs calculated to influence the acceptability of
social ideas, and involving considerations of product
planning, pricing, communication, distribution, and marketing research" (Kotler, Zaltman, 1971, p. 5). This is
generally legitimized by viewing the selling of social
issues, ideas, and causes as a social exchange process, and
marketing as a facilitator of exchange. Social marketing
is thus assumed to provide a potential source of efficiency
and effectiveness in the distribution of ideas and issues.
This paper will question both the efficacy and the ethic
involved in utilizing marketing techniques in the dissemination of ideas and behavioral changes supported by government, nonprofit organizations, and commercial firms.

Social Marketing - Background

In their famous "broadening" article Kotler and Levy (1969)
exhort marketers to move beyond their narrow, private
sector, managerially-oriented conceptions of the discipline.
This was followed by a debate in the literature, which was
concluded, if not resolved, with Kotler's generic concept,
which indicates that marketing is involved any time two
social actors exchange value in a transaction. Under the
generic concept, marketing is involved when a person
watches television, gives to the United Way, visits an art
gallery, or listens to an appeal that he/she stop smoking.

In an attempt to define the scope of the marketing discipline, both Hunt (1976) and Fine (1981) have presented
multidimensional typologies for classifying marketing
phenomena. Hunt's dimensions include micro/macro, positive/
normative, and profit/nonprofit perspectives in the discipline, and allow for analysis generating normative decision rules as well as that aimed at positivist questions
concerning the explanation and understanding of phenomena.
Fine's typology explicitly deals with ideas and social
issues. The two dimensions he uses are profit/nonprofit
and product tangibility. Tangibility is broken down into

four groups: a tangible product, a service, an idea, and
an issue or cause. Fine's is not a typology in the
strictest sense, in that groups are not mutually exclusive,
and all possibilities for study in marketing do not logically fit this model. Rather, it is an attempt to rationally show that idea or concept marketing fits within the
bounds of the discipline.

This broadened perspective has led Fox and Kotler (1980) to
point out some confusion in the literature regarding terms.
They distinguish between marketing the goods and services
of organizations not seeking a profit (nonprofit organization marketing), the social responsibility of marketers
and the social impact of marketing activities (societal or
macro marketing), and the marketing of social issues and
ideas (social marketing). This third area is the concern
in this paper.

The principle theoretical efforts in this area have been
provided by Bagozzi (1974, 1975, 1979, 1980). He speaks
(1975) of an exchange paradigm, and the study of exchange
as a distinct subject matter marketers should adopt as
their raison d'etre. The key to this view of marketing is
that exchange is not the sole focus, but also "the underlying processes and dynamics of the exchange relationship."
(Bagozzi, 1974, p. 87). There are, in his (1975) view,
potentially three types of exchange involved in any transaction: utilitarian, symbolic, and mixed. Utilitarian exchange involves the transfer of goods or services for some
tangible quid pro quo. Symbolic exchange involves the more
intangible psychological and social costs or benefits trans-
ferred between the parties to the exchange, and focuses on
meaning rather than utility. Mixed exchange is characterized by both utilitarian and symbolic aspects. Bagozzi
(1975) also distinguishes between restricted, generalized,
and complex exchange. Restricted exchange includes just
two actors, where each gives to and receives from the other,
in tangible terms, and each attempts to maintain equality.
Generalized exchange involves three or more actors who benefit each other, but only indirectly. Complex exchange also
involves at least three actors, but each engages in both
direct mutual exchanges and indirect exchange.

Social marketing would thus appear to focus upon the creation and resolution of exchanges in social relationships.
These might often be generalized or complex exchanges involving both tangible and intangible consideration. An example of such intangible return might be the social insurance society receives in return for responding to
campaigns urging its members to "support your local police",
"stop littering", and "fluoridate your water". These
efforts represent attempts to attribute value to ideas, and
so, to win support for them.

The Efficacy of Social Marketing

Kotler and Zaltman (1971) present a social marketing planning system which links product, price, promotion, and
distribution strategies to primary, secondary, and tertiary
target markets, and which incorporates environmental influences. This model is general, however, and ignores
problems in specifically applying marketing technology to
ideas, issues, and concepts. A very applied perspective
is provided by Rothschild (1979), where he presents a set
of five hypotheses regarding barriers to success in social
marketing communications. For example, such communications
will have less success in prompting behavior changes where
they concern ideas or concepts with low perceived personal

value to the individual. The same is thought to be true
for ideas with low latent or preexisting demand, ideas
that are more complex, ideas with which the individual has little past involvement, and ideas that require
greater levels of participation by the individual in
adopting them.

Bloom and Novelli (in Fox and Kotler, 1980, p. 31) present
a number of other difficulties in designing and implementing campaigns. Some of these include receiving funding
for market research and actually performing such research,
political difficulties in aiming campaigns at specific
target audiences rather than the entire market, limited
control over price and distribution variables, a lack of
much marketing expertise in organizations doing such work,
and difficulty in measuring the impact or effectiveness of
such campaigns.

Problems also arise when considering the nature of what is
being sold. Levitt (1981, p. 94) states that "everybody
sells intangibles in the marketplace, no matter what is
produced in the factory". What is actually being sold is
a set of promises regarding some bundle of attributes,
such as performance, durability, freshness, or taste. It
is his contention that intangible aspects of goods and
services must be tangibilized. For example, an insurance
company might provide customers with their policies bound
in an expensive leather binder in order to emphasize the
dependability, quality, and importance of their insurance.
The notion that consumers purchase attributes as opposed
to products per se has been well developed by such researchers as Fishbein (1975), Lancaster (1966), and Haley
(1968). From a social marketing perspective, problems
arise both in trying to tangibilize ideas or concepts, and
in specifying attributes/benefits to be garnered from ideas
or concepts. It is not that either is not possible, but
that the challenge is greater than in marketing goods or
services. Inferences that you (or society) will somehow
be better off if you stop smoking, vote, and respect the
rights of the elderly may not be as meaningful as the
gas mileage of an automobile or the accuracy of a C.P.A.'s
services.

Underlying these and other specific hurdles to effective
social marketing is a very fundamental issue: Can the
marketing strategies and tactics of the profit-seeking
manager be extracted from the private sector and made to
fit applications in the sector for ideas. There is no
question that this has taken place, albeit in a piecemeal
fashion for the most part. However, the fragmented approach social marketers take to their task may simply be
due to a fundamental lack of fit between the tools and
techniques marketers have developed to be effective in the
free market, and the selling of ideas. To pursue this
issue, the role played by the marketing concept requires
review.

From a philosophical perspective, the marketing concept is
meant to guide all marketing activities in a free enterprise economy. Basically, the concept has three major
elements: 1) satisfaction of consumer needs lies at the
center of all marketing decisions, for such satisfaction
is the "economic and social justification for a company's
existence"; 2) all of the organizational functions and
activities must be integrated and coordinated around a
customer orientation, and 3) such an orientation is the
means by which profits can be best generated, especially
from a long-run perspective. Formalized statements of the
concept originated in the marketing literature during the
1950's, at which time some large firms indicated that they
were adopting such a philosophy (Sachs and Benson, 1978;
Bell and Emory, 1971). The degree to which firms generally have implemented the philosophy in the ensuing years
is not clear, nor are the effects of such implementation.
Nonetheless, theorists would relate concept adoption to
sales, profitability, innovativeness, and so forth.

The marketing concept is analogous to the economist's
notion of consumer sovereignty. It is an outgrowth of
the neoclassical economic tradition wherein the theory of
the firm was developed. Neoclassical economics is based
upon the assertion that society is best served by each
individual and each individual firm behaving so as to
maximize self-interest. So long as ample competition
exists among the many and varied interests, societal welfare should also be maximized. The firm is encouraged to
take advantage of its various environments so as to best
serve its own constituency. This leads Dixon (1978, p. 51)
to refer to "the manipulative context of the marketing
concept".

It is not immediately apparent that this concept applies
in the social marketing arena. Fine (1981) supports the
adoption of the concept by social marketers, explaining
that it begins with ascertaining consumers' felt needs and
wants. However, social marketing represents an attempt to
convince consumers that certain beliefs or behavioral
changes are in their best interests, rather than responding
to expressed needs or wants of consumers who are pursuing
their own self-interests. Further, the term "social" would
seem to imply that society is best served by such beliefs
or behaviors. The reason for the lack of fit between the
marketing concept and social marketing lies in the difference between the role played by the goods and services
marketer and that played by the idea marketer. The goods
and services marketer is motivated by self-interest, and
fits within the neoclassical economic paradigm. The idea
marketer, in the majority of instances, is motivated by
some perception of social welfare. This is another way
of saying that the "manipulative context of the marketing
concept" is at odds with the societal orientation of many
social marketers.

The Ethical Issue

Laczniak, et al (1979), have addressed some of the broader
ethical issues posed by social marketing in a survey of
social psychologists, marketing practitioners, economic
historians, and professors of ethics. They found support
for the use of marketing tools in a social context, but
encountered some concern that accountability be ensured.
Further, they found that respondents had difficulty
separating the ethics involved in using marketing techniques from those involved in the idea or issue being marketed. The ethical concerns centered around the potential
to manipulate public opinion as well as to communicate
socially harmful ideas. Further, questions were raised
about the potential dominance of the ideas or positions
held by those with the most economic or political power.
Let us pursue these concerns in a bit more detail.

Kotler has recently acknowledged that social marketing is
used, at times, to promote ideas which have adverse consequences. He is willing, however, to make the following
assumption: "We have to assume that all ideas enter a
marketplace where consumers of ideas are exposed to multiple claims and counterclaims and in the end are intelligent
enough to know which ideas best serve their interests"
(Foreword to Fine, 1981, p. v). This gives rise to the
following three interrelated questions:

(1) Is there any difference between marketing products and
     marketing ideas?;
(2) Is there a free marketplace for ideas?; and
(3) Is social marketing a means of social control?

The first question concerns whether or not marketing
directed at prompting a consumer to make a cognitive decision to engage in purchase behavior is synonymous with
marketing aimed at convincing the consumer that a certain
idea or issue is acceptable. For example, is it the same
to persuade consumers to buy laundry detergent as it is to
get them to accept a message concerning birth control or,

in an earlier era, prohibition? A person answering in the affirmative might claim that the idea of buying the product is what is actually being marketed, and so, in both cases an idea or issue is the focus. However, the difference is not a practical one, for the manner in which marketing tools and techniques are applied is sufficiently similar in both instances. A more suitable basis for distinguishing product or service marketing from social marketing centers around an ethical issue. The consumer has no objective measure for judging the value of the socially marketed idea or issue. Certainly, he/she can attribute some value based on subjective estimates of source credibility, message credibility, or reference group influences. This is insufficient, for what is required is an environment which provides for competing claims. Thus, the question arises concerning the existence or lack of a free marketplace.

The marketplace provides a measure of objectivity for goods and services from both the profit and nonprofit sectors of the economy. Lazer (1969, p. 9) has indicated that "perhaps nowhere is the inner self of the populace more openly demonstrated than in the marketplace; for the marketplace is an arena where actions are the proof of words and transactions represent values, both physical and moral". In the earlier quote from Kotler, he speaks in terms of a free market for ideas. It is important that the requisite assumptions be laid out for such a free market.

The economic model of pure competition assumes consumer sovereignty, a very large number of competing sources of supply, a homogeneous product, perfect mobility of resources, perfect information and information processing, profit maximizing behavior, and rational economic man. Although none of these are typically present in the real world, the less they are present, the less the market mechanism works as efficiently and effectively as it might. It is difficult to apply such a framework to ideas, issues and concepts. While there is competition among viewpoints and ideas, there is no price mechanism which assigns values to ideas, and efficiently allocates them. This is not to say there is no price involved with ideas. Fine (1981) speaks of a social price in consumer adoption of ideas. Specifically, he notes an intangible cost to consumers in the form of time, effort, lifestyle changes, and psychological demands. The difficulties in measuring such dimensions of price, combined with the very subjective nature of such "costs" as changes in lifestyle or psychological demands on one's self-esteem further discredit the private marketplace analogy. This social price does not have the capability of matching the supply of ideas with the demand for them. It presents a weak criterion for establishing the value of an idea. Major strides must be made on measurement issues in consumer psychology.

Even if it is granted that consumers purchase ideas or concepts, or that there is some sort of demand curve for an idea which is a function primarily of the social price discussed above, the supply side of the equation raises some interesting issues. For example, are ideas produced as a function of that same social price mechanism? Do ideas directly compete with one another for the limited resources of consumers? Can any two ideas be compared with one another in the same way as any two products? Given the intangible nature of what the idea producer is receiving in return for his/her productive effort, what is the motivation for generating ideas or concepts? These issues are raised here to point out problems in conceptualizing a marketplace for ideas. Marketing activities are often justified on the basis of the role they fulfill in the market. The lack of such a market raises concerns about the impact of social marketing.

Marketing can be viewed as a fundamental part of the free market approach to economics (Alderson, 1958). Marketing provides communication in a world of imperfect information, and adds time, place, possession, and form utilities

to products through product development, pricing, promotion, and distribution. One might question whether marketing adds utility to an idea or issue, and whether it adds efficiency to the dissemination of such ideas or issues. In both cases, the answer is probably in the affirmative. Marketing technology can help get the right message to the right target audience while minimizing the cost. The impact of social marketing goes beyond this, though, which raises the issue concerning the degree to which social marketing can be construed as a potential means of social control.

Marketing is a fundamental social process which facilitates exchange between production and consumption units in society. Brien, et al, (1972, p. 23) assert that "marketing is the preeminent social force today in the United States to such an extent that the nation may accurately be called The Marketing Society". Lazer (1969, p. 8) has indicated that "marketing is truly an institution of social control in a relatively abundant society, in the same sense as the school and the home ... It is a very formative force in our culture". Others (Feldman, 1971; Shapiro, 1978) attribute marketing with the ability to move society from a production to a consumption orientation, and from consumption to a conservation orientation.

If marketing has this kind of impact in the presence of a competitive marketplace, what are the implications for its application to ideas, where no true marketplace exists? Fine (1981, p. 17) claims that the marketer of concepts is to social change what the pharmacist is to health. The social marketer is, in a sense, the dispenser of pharmaceuticals to remedy societal ills and improve societal health. An appropriate means to label this process might rest with the psychological theories of behavior modification. Nord and Peter (1980) emphasize that behavior modification techniques work better in the controlled laboratory than in the marketplace, but that they clearly have some applicability. Rothschild and Gaidis (1981) agree that behavioral learning techniques work most effectively when one party controls the situation. They indicate (1981, p. 72) that "this implies a lack of competition, an imbalance of power, and a closed system". The greater the competitiveness of the environment, the less effective are such techniques, and the more they require continuous reinforcement schedules. Thus, it would seem behavior modification has a more pronounced potential in the marketing of ideas and concepts than in the area of products and services. Rothschild and Gaidis see the greatest potential in the promotional area, which is the primary marketing tool used in the concept area. The key role played by extensive reinforcement schedules in behavioral learning would indicate that when social marketing is dominated by the economically powerful, then all the more social control is likely.

Ethics is fundamentally concerned with the question of what is good or bad in human conduct. Some (Moore, in Albert, et al, 1975, p. 309) prefer to drop the conduct limitation and speak more broadly of "what is good". Unfortunately, "good" is a fairly indefinable term, and connotes a value judgement. One means of addressing this problem is to establish some societal role for the institutions engaged in social marketing, and then examine whether the effects of such marketing are consistent with that role. There is an emerging concept sector consisting of government, nonprofit organizations, and commercial firms. It appears that government, with advertising expenditures projected at close to $.5 billion in the year 2000, is the dominant social marketer, and so will receive the primary focus here (Fine, 1981, p. 45).

In the case of commercial firms, the ethical issue can be addressed by looking for any conflicts between the role of business in society, and the involvement of business in social marketing. This is a potential pandora's box in that it raises the whole spectre of the corporate social

responsibility debate. For example, should manufacturers
of alcoholic beverages promote campaigns for responsible
drinking? One argument (Friedman, 1962) holds that the
sole purpose of business is profit maximization in the
interests of stockholders. Another position (Steiner, 1975)
is that business, like all institutions, is engaged in a
"social contract", wherein firms are granted certain rights
(e.g., profit-making, limited liability) in return for fulfilling certain functions and responsibilities in society
(e.g., employment or production of goods and services).
Beauchamp and Bowie (1979, p. 27) would seem to support
this functionalist perspective that "businesses are
chartered for the public good", but question the meaning
of the public good. This is not to say that business can
legitimately engage in any activity so long as it serves
the public good. The possibility that social marketing is
done in the interest of the public good is not enough to
make it a legitimate pursuit of business. Rather, it is
necessary to investigate the extent to which social marketing activities help or hinder the business sector's ability
to perform its basic function in society. This requires
some consensus on the nature of that basic function.

Establishing the role of government is potentially a
larger Pandora's box. It would seem that a distinction
should be drawn between behavior that is of a private
nature and that which legitimately concerns the public
interest. A rationale for government regulation of citizen
behavior relates to a principle espoused by John Stuart
Mill where "no adult member of a civilized community can be
rightfully compelled to perform or to desist from performing an act, unless the action or the failure to perform it
is likely to produce harm or evil to others" (Nagel, 1968,
p. 22). However, support also exists for two other doctrines of relevance here, those of legal moralism and legal
paternalism. That is, respectively, the use of law to enforce positive morality, and the use of law to protect
people against themselves (Nagel, 1968, p. 23). Of course,
laws directed at enforcing certain moralities (e.g., the
prohibition against marijuana smoking) can be interpreted
as paternalistic.

Many of the activities performed by modern government go
well beyond Mill's rationale. Examples include helmet laws
for motorcycles, rules against swimming at public beaches
without lifeguards, laws against suicide, homosexuality,
and dueling, as well as prohibitions against women performing certain kinds of jobs. It requires some stretch of the
imagination to interpret these as having directly negative
effects on those in society other than the perpetrator.
The same is true for the ideas and issues that are pushed
in social marketing campaigns. Such campaigns involve the
implicit assumption that the person being solicited may not
adopt the idea unless solicited, but should. The social
marketer has determined that the idea or concept is "good"
for the consumer, but that this is not readily apparent to
the consumer. Thus, the idea needs an extra push not given
to competing ideas. The social marketer has attributed
value to the idea based on non-market criteria (which are
not clear), and is trying to achieve a consensus about that
value through promotional efforts.

The government, as social marketer, is using a moralistic
and/or paternalistic rational for its activities. To the
extent that the social campaigns are a means of social
control, they have an impact not all that different from
actual legislation governing human activity. Legislation,
of course, requires a vote by some popularly elected representation of the citizenry. Thus it involves a somewhat
objective application of value to the issue being voted
upon. Admittedly, there is some competition among varied
interests for budgetary allocations in the legislative
chambers of federal, state, and local governments, including the budgets for social campaigns. At the same time,
the assumption that the value of any idea or issue can be
directly associated with the amount of money awarded it is
questionable, given the realities of legislative compromise, log-rolling, special interest influences, and
porkbarrel politics. No clear market-based valuation of
ideas would seem to be achieved. Moreover, marketing
techniques can be used to generate support on controversial issues such as abortion, unpopular issues such as the
Vietnam War, or special interest issues such as trade
protectionism. While each of these potentially has
significant negative consequences for society, extensive
social marketing campaigns can help ensure societal
acceptance or adoption of the position supported by the
social marketer. The fundamental issue, then, becomes one
of value. Specifically, how is value applied to ideas,
concepts, and social issues. The position taken here is
that social marketing represents a distortion of whatever
semblance of a market exists for ideas, in that it places
greater weight on certain ideas without ensuring that
competing ideas receive proper consideration.

SUMMARY AND CONCLUSIONS

Marketing is much more than a technology of the firm, as
it involves a social process. The reason that social
marketing should not be accepted with open arms is a
philosophical one. There is something more dangerous
about bad ideas as opposed to bad products. No objective
means exist by which to judge the propriety of a social
idea.

Underlying marketing in a free enterprise economy is the
marketing concept, which emphasizes consumer satisfaction
as the key to producer satisfaction. Not only does the
marketing concept fail as a philosophy to explain the
selling of ideas, but it is a mistake to assume the
existence of a free marketplace for ideas which functions
anything like the marketplace for soap. The interplay
of competing sources of supply with competing sources of
demand provides an objective means of evaluating products.
The price mechanism does not efficiently determine the
production and allocation of ideas or concepts. The more
extensive the social marketing campaign, the more it only
serves to distort the consumer's ability to objectively
apply value to ideas. For these reasons, social marketing
does not represent a logical broadening of the discipline.
Rather, it represents uncharted and very foreign territory
with uncertain consequences.

REFERENCES

Albert, E., Denise, T., and Peterfreund, S., (1975),
Great Traditions in Ethics, Third Edition, D. Van
Nostrand Co., New York.

Alderson, W., (1957), Marketing Behavior and Executive
Action, Richard D. Irwin, Homewood, Illinois.

Bagozzi, R., (1974), "Marketing as an Organized Behavioral
System of Exchange", Journal of Marketing, Vol. 38,
(October), pp. 77-81.

___________ (1975), "Marketing as Exchange", Journal of
Marketing, Vol. 39, (October), pp. 7-14.

___________ (1979), "Towards a Formal Theory of Marketing
Exchanges" in Conceptual and Theoretical Developments in
Marketing, American Marketing Association, pp. 431-447.

___________ (1980), Causal Models in Marketing, John Wiley
and Sons, New York, 1980.

Beauchamp, T., and Bowie, N., (1979), Ethical Theory and
Business, Prentice-Hall, Inc., Englewood Cliffs, New
Jersey.

Bell, M., and Emory, C.W., (1971), "The Faltering Marketing Concept", _Journal of Marketing_, Vol. 35, (October), pp. 37-42.

Brien, R., Gelb, B., and Trammell, W., (1972), "The Challenge to Marketing Dominance", _Business Horizons_, (February), pp. 23-30.

DeGeorge, R., and Pichler, J., eds., (1978), _Ethics, Free Enterprise, and Public Policy_, Oxford University Press, New York.

Dixon, D., (1978), "The Poverty of Social Marketing," in _MSU Business Topics_, (Summer), pp. 50-56.

Etgar, M., and Ratchford, B., (1975), "Marketing Management and the Marketing Concept: Their Conflict in Nonprofit Organizations", in Ronald Curhen, ed., _1974 Combined Proceedings_, Series #36, American Marketing Association, pp. 258-260.

Feldman, L., (1971), "Societal Adaption: A New Challenge for Marketing", _Journal of Marketing_, Vol. 35, (July), pp. 54-60.

Fine, S., (1981), _The Marketing of Ideas and Social Issues_, Praeger Publishers, New York.

Fishbein, M., (1975), "Attitude, Attitude Change, and Behavior: A Theoretical Overview", in Philip Levine, ed., _Attitude Research Bridges the Atlantic_, American Marketing Assn., Chicago, pp. 3-16.

Flew, A., (1972), "Indoctrination and Doctrines", in Snork, I.A., editor, _Concepts of Indoctrination_, Routledge and Kegan Paul, London, pp. 67-93.

Fox, K., and Kotler, P., (1980), "The Marketing of Social Causes: The First Ten Years", _Journal of Marketing_, Vol. 44, (Fall), pp. 24-33.

Friedman, M., (1970), "The Social Responsibility of Business is to Increase Its Profits", _The New York Times Magazine_, pp. 33, 122-26.

Galbraith, J.K., (1967), _The New Industrial State_, Houghton Mifflin Company, London.

Glueck, W., (1980), _Business Policy and Strategic Management_, Third Edition, McGraw Hill, New York.

Haley, R., (1968), "Benefit Segmentation: A Decision-Oriented Research Tool", _Journal of Marketing_, Vol. 32, pp. 30-35.

Hunt, S., (1976), "The Nature and Scope of Marketing", _Journal of Marketing_, Vol. 40, (July), pp. 17-28.

Kotler, P., (1975), _Marketing for Nonprofit Organizations_, Prentice-Hall, Inc., Englewood Cliffs, New Jersey.

__________ (1972), "A Generic Concept of Marketing", _Journal of Marketing_, (April), pp. 46-54.

__________, and Levy, S., (1969), "Broadening the Concept of Marketing", _Journal of Marketing_, Vol. 33, (January) pp. 10-15.

__________, and Zaltman, G., (1971), "Social Marketing: An Approach to Planned Social Change", _Journal of Marketing_, Vol. 35, (July), pp. 3-12.

Laczniak, G., Lusch, R., and Murphy, P., (1979), "Social Marketing: It's Ethical Dimensions", _Journal of Marketing_, Vol. 43, (Spring), pp. 29-36.

Lancaster, K., (1966), "A New Approach to Consumer Theory", _Journal of Political Economy_, Vol. 74, pp. 132-57.

Lazer, W., (1969), "Marketing's Changing Social Relationships", _Journal of Marketing_, Vol. 33, (January), pp. 3-9.

Levitt, T., (1970), "The Morality of Advertising", _Harvard Business Review_, Vol. 48, (July-August), pp. 84-92.

__________ (1981), "Marketing Intangible Products and Product Intangibles", _Harvard Business Review_, Vol. 59, No. 3, (May-June), pp. 94-102.

Lovelock, C., and Weinberg, C., (1975), "Contrasting Private and Public Sector Marketing", in Ronald Curhan, editor, _1974 Combined Proceedings_, Series #36, American Marketing Association, Chicago, pp. 242-6.

Mokwa, M., Dawson, W., and Prieve, E., editors (1981), _Marketing the Arts_, Praeger Publishing, New York.

Montana, J., ed., (1978), _Marketing in Nonprofit Organizations_, AMACOM, New York.

Moore, G.E., (1975), "The Indefinability of Good", in Albert, E., Denise, T., and Peterfreund, S., editors, _Great Traditions in Ethics_, Third Edition, D. Van Nostrand Co., New York, pp. 304-323.

Moyer, R., and Hutt, M., (1978), _Macro Marketing_, Second Edition, John Wiley and Sons, New York.

Nagel, E., (1968), "The Enforcement of Morals", _The Humanist_, Vol. 28, No. 3, (May/June), pp. 20-27.

Nord, W. and Peter, J.P., (1980), "A Behavior Modification Perspective on Marketing", _Journal of Marketing_, Vol. 44, (Spring), pp. 36-47.

Rothschild, M., (1979), "Marketing Communication in Non-Business Situations", _Journal of Marketing_, Vol. 43, (Spring), pp. 11-20.

__________, and Gaidis, W., (1981), "Behavioral Learning Theory: Its Relevance to Marketing and Promotions", _Journal of Marketing_, Vol. 45, (Spring), pp. 70-78.

Sachs, W., and Benson, G., (1978), "Is it Time to Discard the Marketing Concept", _Business Horizons_, Vol. 21, (August), pp. 68-74.

Shapiro, S., (1978), "Marketing in a Conserver Society", _Business Horizons_, Vol. 21, (April), pp. 3-13.

Steiner, G., (1975), _Business and Society_, Random House, New York.

Sweeney, D., (1972), "Marketing: Management Technology or Social Process?", _Journal of Marketing_, Vol. 36, (October), pp. 3-10.

Tuerk, D., editor, (1978), _Issues in Advertising_, American Enterprise Institute for Public Policy Research, Washington, D.C.

Weinberg, C., (1980), "Marketing Mix Decisions Rules for Non-Profit Organizations", in Sheth, ed., Research in Marketing: _A Research Annual_, Vol. 3, JAI Press, Inc., Greenwich, Connecticut, pp. 191-234.

PARENTAL DIFFUSION ROLES AND CHILDREN'S RESPONSES TO NUTRITION EDUCATION

Sanford Grossbart, University of Nebraska, Lincoln
Lawrence A. Crosby, University of Nebraska, Lincoln
Joyce Robb, University of Nebraska, Lincoln

ABSTRACT

This study examines the cognitive, affective and behavioral consequences of nutrition education for children. Effects on children are analyzed in relation to parental diffusion roles. Theoretical and strategic implications are discussed from a diffusion of innovations and social marketing perspective.

INTRODUCTION

Ironic circumstances have stimulated marketing interest in nutrition education for children (Baird and Shutz 1976; Ward 1978; Fox and Kotler 1980; Fleming and Brown 1981). The quality of their diets belies the affluent environment in which they live. While few may be starving, many are victims of malnutrition. Mineral and vitamin deficiencies in children's diets have reached alarming proportions and excessive caloric consumption is widespread (Sims 1971; Caliendo and Sanjur 1978; Federal Trade Commission 1978). From a developmental standpoint, the results may be devestating. Poor nutrition impairs physical and mental health and development and forms a basis for harmful eating habits lasting through adulthood (Deutsch 1976; Grotkowski and Sims 1978).

Poverty is clearly a factor but not the major reason for poor nutrition. Changing lifestyles have reduced food preparation and consumption time while fast food items and "junk foods" have replaced more nutritious dietary components. The most prevalent factor may be parents' lack of knowledge, which has been found to have a significant impact on childrens' diets (Eppright et al. 1970; Caliendo and Sanjur 1978). Research has revealed that many mothers cannot describe a balanced meal, answer questions about healthful eating habits or use available nutrition information (Bauman 1973; White 1976; Jacoby et al. 1977; Richmond 1977).

RESEARCH FOCUS

Concern over these matters has prompted governmental action, including federal funding for state development of nutrition education in the schools. This paper deals with the effects of one such project, consisting of a set of psychometrically developed modules designed to change children's nutrition orientation and eating behavior. Children were provided with classroom discussions, food tasting experiences, and information on family food preparation and consumption activities. Federal regulations required the use of student surveys to evaluate the program (Abt Associates 1980). While results appeared positive, it was recognized that survey information had two important defects. First, students may have treated surveys as tests and provided answers which did not reflect their views or behavior. Second, long term effects were likely to depend on family interactions. Consequently, this study was conducted to focus on the relation between parental influence and the effects of nutrition education as observed within the family. The underlying conceptualization for this research is provided by a social marketing and diffusion of innovations perspective. Definition and empirical classification of parental diffusion roles are based on an adaptation of a theoretical typology developed by Midgley (1976). Program effects are gauged by comparing responses gathered from a control group and three treatment groups, categorized in terms of parental diffusion roles.

NUTRITION AS AN INNOVATION

Ideas, practices and objects which people view as being new are innovations (Rogers and Shoemaker 1971). While nutritional ideas and practices are hardly new in an objective sense, they possess considerable perceived newness for persons unfamiliar with principles of sound diets and nutritional requirements for children's growth and development (Fox and Kotler 1980). Viewed in this light, it is possible to understand the factors which may have restricted the adoption and diffusion of proper nutrition practices for children by reviewing their innovative characteristics.

Innovations with high perceived relative advantage, compatibility with existing values and behavior, low complexity, high trialability and observability normally have accelerated diffusion rates (Rogers and Shoemaker 1971). Limited family time and budgets and apparent inconvenience may diminish the perceived relative advantage of providing a proper diet for children. Nutritional concepts may also be incompatible with the lifestyles, experiences and usual food planning behaviors of parents who never learned about dietary require- ments. The perceived complexity of these requirements may even have been enhanced by conflicting governmental suggestions on nutrition over the last thirty years (Fox and Kotler 1980). Even the trialability of necessary practices may be hampered by parents' and children's reluctance to try new foods or dietary regimens because of the effort, conflict or costs involved. Finally, many of the benefits of children's nutrition are not immediately observable. Many factors influence physical and mental develoment (e.g. exercise, heredity) and results are often not apparent until later years.

In combination, these inhibiting factors prevent the rapid diffusion of nutrition practices. Isolated educational attempts to only improve children's cognitive grasp of related issues seem doomed to fail. Fostering widespread understanding and beneficial consumption behavior requires differentiated social marketing programs which impact on both children and parents (Kotler and Zaltman 1971; Fox and Kotler 1980; Fine 1980). The diffusion perspective provides a useful basis for the preliminary delineation of segments, based on parental roles.

Parental Diffusion Roles

Interpersonal influence is a critical factor in the diffusion process. Midgely (1976) extended understanding of the nature of this influence by identifying different interpersonal diffusion roles, including 1) active adoptors, who communicate favorable innovation experience 2) passives, who do not provide indications of their evaluations to others and 3) active rejectors, who relate unfavorable experiences to others. This study employs a modified version of this typology. The relevant social system is defined as the family, since this is the behavioral unit in which children's adoption behavior unfolds. A three-fold categorization of parental influence is used, i.e. _actives_ who accept and reinforce the concepts in the nutrition education program, _passives_ who accept but fail to reinforce the concepts and _rejectors_, who do not accept the concepts or provide reinforcement to their children.

HYPOTHESES

Employment of this typology suggests the following hypotheses:

H1: Children of active parents will evidence greater cognitive, affective and behavioral responses to nutrition education than children of passives, rejectors or the control group.

H2: Children of passive parents will evidence greater cognitive and affective response to nutrition education than children of rejectors or the control group.

These expectations are based on the presumption that positive parent-child interaction provides a necessary basis for children's adoption of nutrition concepts. Without parental acceptance and reinforcement, nutrition education should have no significant effect, i.e. the responses of rejector versus control groups should be similar. Parental acceptance should provide a basis for children's enhanced understanding of nutrition concepts and positive attitudes toward nutrition. When parents do not verbally reinforce program content, their nonverbal actions and lack of overt criticism should provide a minimally positive or neutral atmosphere which does not impede and may even foster cognitive and attitudinal effects. Without parental reinforcement, however, there should be no difference in behavioral effects among passive, rejector and control groups. Verbal reinforcement is likely to lead to changes in the child's behavior because a) it is apt to occur in a behavioral context, i.e. when the parent responds to the child's food choices, requests, etc. and b) parental reinforcement serves to legitimize new concepts learned in school (Rogers and Shoemaker 1971). Therefore, given acceptance and reinforcement, as found in the active group, greater cognitive and attitudinal effects should provide a basis for significant behavioral consequences.

METHOD

After a year of implementation, questionnaires were completed by parents of children (grades 1-3) in one of eleven schools participating in the Experience Nutrition project. Schools were randomly assigned to test and control groups and represented a cross-section of rural and urban communities. The 349 returned questionnaires constituted a fifty percent response rate.

Parents in the test group were classified according to the extent to which they agreed with the ideas presented in the program and reminded their children about them. This was accomplished by dividing four-point agreement and reinforcement scales at their mid-point and cross-classifying responses (see Table 1). Estimated program effects were based on parental reports (on four-point scales) of changes in children's nutritional knowledge, attitude and behavior over the past academic year. Attitude was measured in terms of the importance of nutrition and a balanced diet to the child. Cognitition and behavior were reflected in additive indices. Two cognitive items dealt with the child's general knowledge about nutrition and different foods. Four eating behavior items covered the child's willingness to eat new foods, fruits and vegetables as snacks and at meals and lunches served at school.

Mean scores on the attitudinal scale and the multiple item cognitive and behavior scales served as dependent measures. Responses for the four groups (actives, passives, rejector and control) were analyzed by means of MANOVA profile analysis. Following a preliminary inspection for parallelism (Morrison 1976), Roy-Bargman (1958) step-down analysis and Sheffe contrasts were used to test for group response differences.

RESULTS

Classification of parents in the treatment group, based on acceptance and reinforcement of the program ideas, is presented in Table 1. Over ninety-nine percent of the cases were categorized as actives (51.7 percent), passives (36.6 percent) or rejectors (11.0 percent). These results indicate that while there was a high level of program acceptance among parents, reinforcement occurred in only slightly more than half of the cases.

Information on reliabilities and magnitudes of response is presented in Table 2. For each type of response, mean levels for the treatment group are greater than those for the control group. As might be anticipated, given a cognitive-affective-behavioral heirarchy, these differences were smaller at successive hierarchical levels. A comparison of responses for

TABLE 1

CATEGORIZATION OF PARENTAL DIFFUSION ROLES

REJECTORS (n=24) PASSIVES (n=80) ACTIVES (n=113)

Acceptance

Reinforcement	Agree Not At All		Agree A Little		Agree Some		Agree A Lot	
	Number	%	Number	%	Number	%	Number	%
Remind Not At All	8	3.7	3	1.4	4	1.8	1	0.5
Remind A Little	0	0.0	13	5.9	49	22.4	26	11.9
Remind Some	0	0.0	1	0.5	33	15.1	61	27.9
Remind A Lot	1	0.5	0	0.0	3	1.4	16	7.3

TABLE 2

CHILDREN'S RESPONSES FOR ENTIRE SAMPLE, CONTROL AND TREATMENT GROUPS

Response	Number of Items	Coefficient Alpha	Sample (n=349)		Control (n=130)		Treatment (n=217)	
			Mean	Standard Deviation	Mean	Standard Deviation	Mean	Standard Deviation
Cognitive change	2	.840	2.991	0.784	2.627	0.753	3.210	0.719
Attitudinal change	1	----	2.591	0.909	2.269	0.905	2.784	0.857
Behavioral change	4	.821	2.789	0.726	2.650	0.757	2.872	0.696

Note: Two cases were not classified as actives, passives or rejectors and were not included in the analysis.

control, rejector, passive and active groups is presented in Table 3. As expected, children of actives evidenced the highest level of response while children of passives exhibited greater response than those of rejector or control groups.

The test for parallel group response profiles revealed significant group by response interaction ($F=3.11$, $p<.01$). Equality of group effects were therefore tested by step-down analysis. In this procedure the test statistic for the first dependent variable, cognitive change, was the the univariate F-statistic. To avoid overlooking possible correlations among dependent variables, successive F-values for the remaining variables were computed only after eliminating the effects of the previous dependent variables. Thus cognitive change served as a covariate for tests involving attitudinal change and both of these variables serve as covariates when change in eating behavior was examined.

Step-down results and significant Sheffe contrasts are presented in Table 4. Significant differences were found for each dependent variable. As predicted by the first hypothesis, children of parents with an active diffusion role had the highest levels of cognitive, attitudinal and behavioral response. While all mean response levels were in the expected order, as indicated in Table 3, there was only partial support for the second hypothesis. Children of passives exhibited significantly greater cognitive and affective responses than those from the control group but, possibly due to rejector sample size limitations, significant differences between passive and rejector groups were not present. As anticipated, no significant differences were obtained for rejector versus control groups.

DISCUSSION

These results indicate the potential utility of dealing with children's nutrition education from a parental diffusion role perspective. Future research is needed to validate findings in other states, gauge responses for children in higher grades, and measure effects on a longitudinal basis. Parents' responses may reflect their views on nutrition education rather than actual program effects on children. Therefore, it would also be useful to cross-validate results by comparing parents' observations with self-reports from children. The authors are now involved in such efforts.

Diffusion of nutrition concepts and practices involves a collective innovation decision by parents and children (Rogers and Shoemaker 1971). These findings underscore the importance of parental legitimization in these processes. Significant psychological differences between treatment and control groups were observed for actives and passives while behavioral differences were evidenced only for children of actives. Thus it appears that producing changes in children's eating behavior will require tactics that precipitate parental acceptance and reinforcement. This makes it essential to monitor parents' and children's responses and initially treat actives as the primary audience for nutrition education. Social marketing strategies can then be used to a) accelerate adoption by actives, b) generate interaction among actives, passives and rejectors and c) re-position programs to make them more acceptable to passives and rejectors. Monitoring responses and fostering interaction will help to identify bases of parental rejection and passivity and suggest ways to increase the perceived simplicity and compatibility of nutrition concepts.

The trialability of the nutrition practices can also be increased by modified distribution techniques which bring parents into more direct contact with the program -- e.g., by developing joint parent-child participation in activities at school. Such forums may stimulate diffusion by providing opportunities for actives to relate possible benefits to passives and rejectors. For example, pricing information could be used to demonstrate the financially feasibility or relative advantage of providing necessary nutrition to children. Non-monetary aspects of relative advantage could also be discussed, e.g. how to introduce new foods to children with less effort and conflict. As implied earlier, a segmented audience strategy for promotional efforts is likely to be

TABLE 3

CHILDRENS' RESPONSES FOR CONTROL GROUP AND TREATMENT GROUPS WITH DIFFERENT DIFFUSION ROLES

Response	Control (n=130)		Rejectors (n=24)		Passives (n=80)		Actives (n=113)	
	Mean	Standard Deviation	Mean	Standard Deviation	Mean	Standard Deviation	Mean	Standard Deviation
Cognitive change	2.627	0.753	2.667	0.778	3.069	0.688	3.425	0.645
Attitudinal change	2.269	0.905	2.125	0.947	2.575	0.759	3.071	0.787
Behavioral change	2.650	0.757	2.333	0.779	2.716	0.684	3.097	0.590

TABLE 4

MANOVA RESULTS AND SIGNIFICANT CONTRASTS

Response	Step-down F-Statistic	df	Scheffe Test[d]
Cognitive change	27.754[a]	3,343	4>3[b], 4>2[b], 4>1[b], 3>1[c]
Attitudinal change	3.197[b]	3,342	4>3[b], 4>2[b], 4>1[b], 3>1[c]
Behavioral change	2.507[a]	3,341	4>3[b], 4>2[b], 4>1[b]

[a] $p < .01$; [b] $p < .05$; [c] $p < .10$

[d] Groups are defined as: 4 = Actives, 3 = Passives, 2 = Rejectors and 1 = Control.

needed. The salient benefits of the program are apt to differ for actives versus passives and rejectors. This provides an opportunity to emphasize different benefits to other groups once adoption by actives is obtained. Low cost media, including handouts to be taken home, school and local newspapers, and inserts in school mailings to parents may be used. Timing may be a crucial factor since actives are likely to be the earliest adopters and passives and rejectors may require more message repetition. While it seems unrealistic to expect the vast majority of parents to legitimize a nutrition education program to their children in the early stages, carefully timed social marketing efforts aimed at different audiences should lead to more success over time (Richmond 1977; Celendar, Sloan and Tanis 1978).

Future research can help guide these activities There is a need to determine the demographic and psychosocial antecedents of parental diffusion roles. Profiles of socioeconomic characteristics and child-rearing styles, for example, would facilitate the formulation of segmented social marketing programs. The effects on parents of children's consumer education also require investigation. Parental knowledge, attitudes, and purchasing decisions and meal planning behaviors may be influenced by these programs. Food marketers have a vested interest in understanding these effects (Ward 1978). Finally, there is a need to study the diffusion of nutrition behavior among households. Actives and their children may prove to be influential in later adoption decisions by passives and rejectors, even when special forums are not employed. Hopefully, this paper will stimulate interest in these important social marketing issues.

REFERENCES

Abt Associates (1980), "The Feasibility of Using the School Lunchroom as a Nutrition Education Classroom," unpublished report to the Nebraska Department of Education, Abt Associates, Cambridge, MA.

Baird, Pamela C. and Howard G. Shutz (1976), "The Marketing Concept Applied to 'Selling' Good Nutrition," Journal of Nutrition Education, 8 (1), 13-17.

Bauman, Howard E. (1973), "What Does the Consumer Know About Nutrition?," Journal of the American Medical Association, 225 (1), 61-2.

Caliendo, Mary Alice and Diva Sanjur (1978), "The Dietary Status of Preschool Children: An Ecological Approach," Journal of Nutrition Education, 10 (2), 69-72.

Celender, Ivy M., A. Elizabeth Sloan and Beverly H. Tanis (1978), "What Are The Needs of Nutrition Educators?," Journal of Nutrition Education, 10 (2), 82.

Deutsch, Ronald M. (1976), Realities of Nutrition, Palo Alto, California: Bull Publishing Co.

Eppright, Ercel S., Hazel M. Fox, Beth A. Fryer, Glenna H. Lamkin, and Virginia M. Vivian (1970), "Nutrition Knowledge and Attitudes of Mothers," Journal of Home Economics, 62 (5), 327-332.

Federal Trade Commission (1978), "Staff Report on Television Advertising to Children," Federal Trade Commission, Washington, D.C.

Fine, S. H. (1980), "Toward a Theory of Segmentation by Objectives in Social Marketing," Journal of Consumer Research, 7 (June), 1-13.

Fleming, Phyllis L. and Judith E. Brown (1981), "Using Market Research Approaches in Nutrition Education" Journal of Nutrition Education, 13 (1), 4-5.

Fox, Karen F. A., and Philip Kotler (1980), "The Marketing of Social Causes: The First 10 Years," Journal of Marketing, 44, 24-33.

Grotkowski, Myrna L. and Laura S. Sims (1978), "Nutritional Knowledge, Attitudes, and Dietary Practices of the Elderly," Journal of the American Dietetic Assocation, 72 (May), 499-506.

Jacoby, Jacob, Robert W. Chestnut, and William Silberman (1977), "Consumer Use and Comprehension of Nutrition Information," Journal of Consumer Research, 4 (September), 119-28.

Kotler, Phillip, and Gerald Zaltman (1971), "Social Marketing: An Approach to Planned Social Change," Journal of Marketing, 35 (July), 3-12.

Midgely, David F. (1976), "A Simple Mathematical Theory of Innovative Behavior," Journal of Consumer Research, 3 (1), 31-41.

Morrison, Donald F. (1976), Multivariate Statistical Methods, New York: McGraw-Hill.

Richmond, Frederick W. (1977), "The Role of the Federal Government In Nutrition Education," Journal of Nutrition Education, 9 (4), 150-51.

Rogers, Everett M. and F. Floyd Shoemaker (1971), Communication of Innovations, New York: The Free Press.

Roy, J., and R. E. Bargman (1958), " Tests of Multiple Independence and the Associated Confidence Bounds," Annals of Mathematical Statistics, 29, 491-503.

Sims, Laura S. (1971), "Nutritional Status of Preschool Children in Relation to Selected Factors Characterizing the Family Environment: An Ecological Approach," unpublished thesis, Michigan State University.

Ward, Scott (1978), "Compromise in Commercials for Children," Harvard Business Review, 56 (6), 128-36.

White, Philip L. (1976), "Why All The Fuss Over Nutrition Education?," Journal of Nutrition Education, 8 (2), 54.

ENERGY CONSERVATION IN RETAILING:
ATTITUDES, PRACTICES, AND REACTIONS TO GOVERNMENT REGULATIONS

Joseph A. Bellizzi, Colorado State University
Robert F. Hoel, Colorado State University
William D. McCarty, Tele-Communications, Inc.

ABSTRACT

This article reports the results of a physical audit of
temperature and lighting levels in retail stores at a time
when the temperature restrictions were legally binding,
and lighting restrictions were voluntary. Retailer attitudes toward energy conservation and to the government
programs then in effect are also reported. The study
strongly suggests that changes in public policy may be
necessary should the federal government once again attempt
to reduce energy consumption through programs similar to
the ones investigated in this study.

INTRODUCTION

Retailing is a major consumer of energy. For example, a
study sponsored by the National Science Foundation (1975)
reported that the commercial sector of the economy
accounted for 14.4 percent of total U.S. energy consumption in the mid-1970's and the Federal Energy Administration (1977) estimated that the largest portion of the
commercial sector's demand for energy was by retailers.
As energy reserves decrease and energy costs increase,
retailers and government policy makers have become more
concerned about retail energy consumption levels and potential conservation methods. The government's policy has
vascilated between voluntary and mandatory energy usage
restrictions. The federal government first issued voluntary temperature guidelines for retailers, later made them
mandatory, and then in 1981 a new President cancelled the
program. The guidelines for store lighting standards
always have been advisory and never mandatory.

The purpose of this article is to examine retailer compliance with government temperature and lighting standards
and to analyze retailer energy conservation practices and
attitudes. The findings suggest that changes in public
policy are warranted should the federal government attempt
in the future to again reduce energy consumption through
programs similar to the ones investigated in this study.

RELATED LITERATURE

Significant reductions in retailers' energy consumption
are possible. It has recently been reported that
retailers can save 15-20 percent of their energy bill at
little or no cost by simply trimming energy wastes (Chain
Store Age Executive 1978; Department of Energy 1978). The
American Retail Federation (undated) and others (Chain
Store Age Executive 1977) have suggested that even more
could be saved, perhaps from 20 to 40 percent, by implementing higher cost approaches. The American Retail
Federation (undated) has published a list of energy saving
recommendations.

When required, retailers have dramatically reduced energy
consumption. During the 1973-1974 oil embargo, according
to the Federal Energy Administration (1975), the City of
Los Angeles reduced energy consumption in the retail sector by 28 percent. Merchants in Los Angeles agreed that
this cutback was achieved without suffering lost sales or
customer discomfort. These reductions were in response to
a city ordinance which required commercial, industrial,
and retail concerns in Los Angeles to reduce consumption

by at least 20 percent. Even after the ordinance expired
electrical consumption in Los Angeles remained 14 percent
below the previous year level.

The Massachusetts Public Interest Group (1975), conducted
a study to measure compliance with the Federal Energy
Administration's voluntary temperature guideline (no more
than 68°F in cold weather). The study reported that 75
percent of the retail stores measured were in excess of
the guideline. The study also found 52 percent of the
stores were not complying with the voluntary lighting
guideline of the Federal Energy Administration. Recently
the Massachusetts study has been criticized for using a
small and nonprobability sample which, of course, should
limit the generalizability of the findings (McCarty 1975).

In 1977, a study was completed during warm weather months
to verify the compliance with the Federal Energy Administration's warm weather temperature guideline (no lower than
78°F) and lighting level guidelines (Roberts et al. 1977;
Roberts 1980). The study was conducted in Florida where
mid-day temperatures easily reach 100°F. Fifty-one percent
of the stores audited were not in compliance with the temperature guideline, and 43 percent were not in compliance
with the lighting level guideline. The study further
found that retailers have a strong willingness to conserve
energy; however, they appeared to lack energy conservation
information (Roberts and Redfering 1979). Retailers
reported taking various energy saving steps such as reducing exterior and interior lights, but they expressed concern about the cost effectiveness of conservation programs
and concern for customer discomfort which could result in
a sales decline. The study also found that 66 percent of
the retail managers interviewed were not aware of the federal temperature guidelines, and 91 percent were not aware
of the federal lighting guidelines.

In 1979, the Congress of the United States approved the
Energy Policy and Conservation Act (Public Law 94-163)
which gave the President the power to implement the program
in the case of severe energy supply interruptions. The
President exercised his power under the law and placed the
act into operation in July of 1979. Under the law, the
Emergency Building Temperature Restriction Program (EBTR)
was created and temperature restrictions became mandatory.
The EBTR program was due to expire in January of 1981, but
the program was extended during the final days of the
Carter Administration but only to be curtailed by incoming
President Reagan. However, in the event of future energy
shortages, conservation measures may again become mandatory.

The EBTR program made the voluntary temperature guidelines
(no less than 78°F for cooling and no more than 65°F for
heating) mandatory. Water temperature regulations were
also specified, but lighting levels remained voluntary.
The program was directed at all non-residential buildings
except for guest rooms in hotels and other commercial
lodges, hospitals and other health care facilities, elementary schools, nursery schools, and day care centers.
The law provides for fines of up to $10,000 per day for
violations. Although audits of compliance have been
limited, the Deputy Secretary of Energy, John C. Sawhill
said in 1979 that spot checks had determined that the
national rate of compliance was over 80 percent (Rocky
Mountain News 1980). While actual compliance may or may
not be as high as 80 percent, it is very clear that the

EBTR program is controversial (Business Week 1979; French
1979; Mahoney 1979). Much of the criticism centers on the
inflexibility of the program, i.e., all buildings are
treated as the same and all energy savings are derived
essentially in the same way, through temperature restrictions, even though there are many other ways to conserve
energy. The purpose of the present study was to investigate energy practices of retailers during the time that
the EBTR program was in effect and to measure retail
management attitudes toward the program and to examine the
broader issue of retail energy utilization and conservation.

THE STUDY

In order to measure energy practices and attitudes of
retailers, physical temperature and lighting audits and
self-administered questionnaires were used. The study was
conducted in a medium-sized SMSA (Fort Collins, Colorado).
Temperature and lighting levels were measured in 111 stores
and questionnaires were mailed to 353 stores in the area.
A follow-up mailing was conducted three weeks after the
first mailing to improve the response rate. The final
response rate for the questionnaire was 58% or 221 completed questionnaires. The respondent stores represent
six general Standard Industrial Classifications (SIC).
Respondent stores were from the following categories: eating, food, general merchandise, building materials,
apparel, and furniture.

The 111 stores in the area selected for the physical audit
were also in the six general classifications listed above.
Almost all the stores in the general merchandise category
were audited because of the size of these stores and
because this group had the fewest number of stores. Therefore, in order to analyze the stores in the general merchandise category separately, it was decided to audit 16
out of 19 general merchandise stores. All other stores
were selected at random in quotas which were based on
approximate population proportion.

Temperature readings were taken in the front, back, and
middle of each store, and these three readings were averaged to obtain an overall store temperature. Light readings were taken to measure the incidence of light on ten
displays in each store. Incidence light is the amount of
light striking an object on a display shelf. Two readings
were taken around the middle of each display, and two
readings were taken at the top and bottom of the display.
The four readings for the ten displays were averaged to
obtain an overall score for each store. The researcher
was careful to stay away from light coming through store
windows which would bias the data.

A General Electric light meter (Model 214) was used to
measure light readings and an Electro-Therm digital, dry
thermometer (Model T-C-100) was used to measure store
temperatures. It was particularly important to this study
to measure store temperatures on days when the heating
system was in use. The physical audit was conducted in
January which is the peak winter energy consumption month
in the area where the study was conducted. Outside temperature (daily high temperature) during the audit period
ranged from 48°F to 3°F. It is believed that store heating equipment was in use under these climatic conditions.

RESULTS AND DISCUSSION

The results of the temperature audit (found in Table 1)
reveal that 82 percent of the retailers were not complying
with the EBTR requirement. This high rate of noncompliance
is in sharp contrast to the 80 percent compliance estimated
by the Deputy Secretary of Energy in 1979. However, the
results are similar to the 1975 study which found 75 percent noncompliance. Two differences between this study
and the 1975 study are that in 1975 thermostat settings

TABLE 1

Compliance with EBTR
Temperature Restrictions
by Retail Store Type

	Compliers	Noncompliers	Totals
Restaurants	18.5% n=5	81.5% n=22	100% n=27
Food Stores	50% n=7	50% n=7	100% n=14
Gen. Merch.	12.5% n=2	87.5% n=14	100% n=16
Build. Mat.	14.3% n=2	85.7% n=12	100% n=14
Apparel	7.7% n=2	92.3% n=24	100% n=26
Furn. & Equip.	14.3% n=2	85.7% n=12	100% n=14
Totals	18% n=20	82% n=91	100% n=111

χ^2 = 12.1, significant at .03;
Maximum Likelihood χ^2 = 10.3, significant at .07

were voluntary, and during this study they were legally
required; and the maximum temperature guideline in 1975
was 68°F and the EBTR program set the limit at 65°F which
was in effect during this study. Compliance rates, however, have not improved.

Store temperatures ranged from 58°F to 77°F with a standard deviation of 3.57° and a mean of 68.7°F. The range
and the standard deviation suggest wide variability in
store temperature readings. Analysis by store type found
a significant relationship between store type and temperature compliance. The compliance and noncompliance rate of
the six store categories were tested using a maximum likelihood chi-square test. The maximum likelihood test was
used because the expected cell frequency is less than five
in more than 20 percent of the cells (Churchill 1976).
Although Snedecor and Cochran (1967) have suggested that
the standard chi-square is accurate enough, the more conservative maximum likelihood test was run anyway. The
test was significant at the .07 level. More food stores
appear to comply while the other categories appear to have
fewer compliers.

Just over half the stores audited (51.4 percent) were in
compliance with the federal government's voluntary lighting levels which call for lighting between 40 and 60 foot-
candles. Data on lighting compliance is in Table 2.
Analysis by retail store type again indicates differences
in compliance among various store categories. A chi-
square test of differences among stores was significant at
the .01 level.

Restaurants were generally in compliance with recommended
lighting levels, but it must be noted that restaurants are
often dimly lit for the purpose of creating an atmosphere
associated with pleasant dining. Furniture stores, also
high compliers, registered a 71.4 percent compliance rate
while food stores, general merchandise, building and material, and apparel stores all were low in compliance.

The questionnaire which was mailed to retail managers,
asked respondents whether their store was adhering to the
65°F or lower temperature restrictions and whether the
management of the store was aware of the voluntary lighting program. Seventy-four percent of the respondents said
that their store was complying with the temperature
restrictions, but only 41 percent of the store managers
said they were adequately informed about the voluntary

TABLE 2

Compliance with Federal Energy
Office Voluntary Lighting Guidelines
by Retail Store Type

	Compliers	Noncompliers	Totals
Restaurants	88.9% n=24	11.1% n=3	100% n=27
Food Stores	21.4% n=3	78.6% n=11	100% n=14
Gen. Merch.	37.5% n=6	62.5% n=10	100% n=16
Build. Mat.	28.6% n=4	71.4% n=10	100% n=14
Apparel	38.5% n=10	61.5% n=16	100% n=26
Furn. & Equip.	71.4% n=10	28.6% n=4	100% n=14
Totals	51.4% n=57	48.6% n=54	100% n=111

χ^2 = 27.0, significant at .01

lighting program. The low level of awareness of the
lighting program may be a prime reason for the low level
of compliance to the lighting guidelines. The same
cannot be said for the low temperature compliance. Many
retailers said they are complying, but the actual store
audit indicates widespread noncompliance. Based on the
data generated in this study, it is not possible to determine if (1) retail managers knew they were not complying
but were unwilling to admit their noncompliance, (2) retail
managers believe they were complying but were unaware of
the actual 65°F limitation, or (3) retail managers incorrectly believed that their stores were satisfying the specific 65°F limitation.

Some explanations for noncompliance can be found in retail
managers' attitudes toward and perceptions of the federal
programs and their possible effects on store operation as
found in Tables 3 and 4. While many managers (48 percent)
stated that the temperature restrictions are an effective
way of reducing energy consumption, many (41.8 percent)
felt that the program discriminates against some types of
retailers. Over 53 percent thought that reducing temperatures to 65°F would not decrease sales volume, but the
respondents were equally divided on whether the reduced
temperatures lead to customer complaints. Approximately
44 percent said customers complain when temperatures are
65°F while about 45 percent said customers do not complain.
Many respondents (54.8 percent) also indicated that they
felt that a 65°F store temperature would not lower employee
productivity. In general, the EBTR program was viewed by
the respondents as an effective program for reducing energy
consumption although it might discriminate against some
retailers. In the eyes of the respondents, the program
may not lead to sales declines or reductions in employee
productivity but could spark customer complaints.

Many store managers surveyed (43.8 percent) stated that
reducing light levels to conform to the government's guidelines is an effective means of retail energy conservation.
In addition, many managers (36.8 percent) believed that
reducing lighting to the government guideline would not
reduce sales volume. However, it should be noted that many
respondents (37.7 percent and 39.3 percent respectively)
were undecided about the energy conservation effectiveness
and the sales effect of reducing store lighting to meet
government guidelines.

TABLE 3

Attitudes Toward Federal Temperature Restrictions[a]

1. The federal government's mandatory
   "Emergency Building Temperature
   Restriction Program" is an effective
   program for reducing energy consumption by retail stores.

Strongly Agree	Agree	Undecided	Disagree	Strongly Disagree
11.0%	37.0%	22.4%	22.4%	7.3%

* * * * * * * * * * * * * *

2. The "Emergency Building Temperature
   Restriction Program" discriminates
   against some type of retailers.

Strongly Agree	Agree	Undecided	Disagree	Strongly Disagree
8.3%	33.5%	36.7%	19.7%	1.8%

* * * * * * * * * * * * * *

3. Reducing the temperature level to 65°
   decreases sales volume in retail stores.

Strongly Agree	Agree	Undecided	Disagree	Strongly Disagree
5.0%	16.9%	24.7%	42.5%	11.0%

* * * * * * * * * * * * * *

4. Customers complain when the temperature
   is 65° in retail stores.

Strongly Agree	Agree	Undecided	Disagree	Strongly Disagree
13.2%	31.1%	10.5%	39.7%	5.5%

* * * * * * * * * * * * * *

5. Keeping the store temperature at 65°
   lowers productivity of employees in
   retail stores.

Strongly Agree	Agree	Undecided	Disagree	Strongly Disagree
8.7%	17.8%	18.7%	44.3%	10.5%

* * * * * * * * * * * * * *

[a]After eliminating the uncertain responses, each statement
for Tables 3 and 4 was subjected to a two-tailed z test.
The hypothesis tested was that P = .5, where the observed
proportion was computed as the ratio of the sum of
"strongly agree" and "agree" responses to the reduced
sample size. In Table 3 only statement 4 is not significant at the .01 level; n = 219 except for statement 4
where n = 218.

A more detailed analysis of the reaction to the EBTR program was accomplished by reviewing and cross-tabulating
various questionnaire data with temperature audit data. A
total of 67 retail stores which were audited also returned
questionnaires. The results of this analysis indicated
that compliance was significantly related to (1) attitudes
of overall EBTR program, (2) attitudes toward the possible
discriminatory effects of the EBTR program, (3) attitudes

TABLE 4

Attitudes Toward the Voluntary Lighting Guidelines[a]

6. Reducing the amount of light to the
   federal government's guidelines of 40
   to 60 foot candles on the sales floor
   is an effective way for retailers to
   conserve energy.

Strongly Agree	Agree	Undecided	Disagree	Strongly Disagree
7.3%	36.5%	37.7%	15.5%	2.7%

* * * * * * * * * * * * * *

7. Reducing the amount of light to the
   federal government's guidelines of
   40 to 60 foot candles on the sales
   floor decreases sales volume.

Strongly Agree	Agree	Undecided	Disagree	Strongly Disagree
5.5%	18.3%	39.3%	31.3%	5.5%

* * * * * * * * * * * * * *

[a]Statements 6 and 7 are significant at the .01 level (see
footnote a, Table 3); n = 219

about customer complaints, and (4) attitudes toward
employee productivity. Chi-square test probabilities
ranged from .03 to .10. Most of the noncompliers (58.2
percent) said they were generally not in favor of the EBTR
program while most of the compliers (80.0 percent) were in
favor of the program. Many noncompliers (44.6 percent)
stated that the EBTR program discriminates against some
types of retailers while few compliers (20 percent) felt
the program discriminates. A majority of the noncompliers
(54.4 percent) believed that customers complain when the
store is at 65°F while fewer compliers (30.0 percent) said
customers complain. Over 31 percent of the noncompliers
said that 65°F store temperatures reduces employee productivity while only 10 percent of the compliers agreed that
the temperature requirement reduces productivity. Chi-
square tests failed to show a relationship between compliance and the belief that there is an energy crisis in
the U.S. or between compliance and retailer attitudes on
the sales effects of the EBTR program.

CONCLUSIONS

The data (82 percent noncompliance) suggest that the mandatory EBTR program has not been highly successful. Not only
did many stores fail to comply, but almost half of the
stores audited (45.9 percent) had store temperatures in
excess of 70°F and 61.2 percent had temperatures in excess
of 68°F. Perhaps retailers in other parts of the country
are complying more than the retailers in this sample. However, even a compliance rate closer to 50 percent might
still be less than what most energy conservation advocates
would consider sufficient to call the EBTR a clear-cut
success.

One reason for the lack of conformance to the 65°F temperature restriction may be the lack of enforcement. To date,
not one retailer has been fined for not complying. Furthermore, the amount of money offered to the state governments to enforce the program was insufficient according to
many state officials (Business Week 1979). The American
Society of Heating, Refrigeration, and Air-Conditioning
Engineers argues that 100,000 to 300,000 buildings would
have to be inspected per year in order to achieve a 65 percent compliance rate (Air-Conditioning, Heating and

Refrigeration News 1980). The Department of Energy had
only ten inspectors assigned to enforce the program in
the summer of 1979 which is very inadequate for proper
enforcement (Rocky Mountain News 1980).

Food stores were most likely to comply to EBTR standards
because supermarkets have the most to gain from an energy
conservation program. They consume more energy per square
foot than any other type of store (Chain Store Age Executive 1979). It is interesting that this study found the
food stores to have the highest rate of compliance concerning the winter temperature restrictions; but the West
Florida study found that the food stores were the worst
offenders of the 78°F temperature restrictions in the
summer months, 71 percent were cooler than the guideline
recommendations (Roberts et al. 1977). Perhaps food stores
were cooler because of the amount of refrigeration utilized.

Apparel stores were found to be the worst violators in the
present study with only 7.7 percent complying to temperature restrictions. Apparel store managers could be keeping their stores at a higher temperature because they feel
that customers will not try on clothes if the temperature
of the store is too cold.

The fact that there is a relationship between compliance
and the type of retail store demonstrates that efforts to
enforce the EBTR program could be more efficiently executed
by focusing efforts on the types of stores that tend to not
comply. These offenders might be able to save more energy
by implementing other conservation efforts that do not
involve temperature restrictions and lend themselves more
readily to their types of businesses.

Attitudes were related to the likelihood of compliance. A
store that complies is also apt to have a store manager who
(1) has an overall favorable attitude toward the program,
(2) is either uncertain about or disagrees that the EBTR
program is discriminatory, (3) feels that customers do not
complain about the store temperature, and (4) believes that
employee productivity does not decline with lower temperatures. On the other hand, noncomplying stores tend to have
managers that have unfavorable attitudes toward the program
and feel that the program discriminates against some types
of retailer, that customers complain, and that employee
productivity is lowered by the 65°F temperature.

While energy conservation may be a means of reducing energy
consumption and energy dependence, this study shows that
the retail sector has not been particularly receptive to
two programs adopted by the federal government. While
these programs are no longer in effect, this study suggests
that retailer attitudes may need to be changed and that
these government programs may need modification if they are
to be adopted to meet future energy shortages. There are
many ways to conserve energy. Perhaps retailers should be
given more flexibility in selecting energy conservation
practices which are most appropriate for their operations.
Saving energy, rather than reducing temperature or light
levels, should be the objective.

It must be remembered that attitudes and practices may be
difficult to change and that short-run reactions may not be
indicative of long-run adjustments. Prolonged energy supply problems may result in more positive attitudes toward
energy conservation. While some retailers may believe that
customers complain when the store is too cold, after prolonged energy supply problems, retailers may be criticized
for keeping their stores too warm. A long-term seriousness
associated with energy supplies may change not only the
attitudes of retailers but shoppers alike resulting in a
greater concern for energy conservation by whatever means
are available.

REFERENCES

Air-Conditioning, Heating and Refrigeration News (1980),
  "DOE Standby Energy Plan Would Curtail Heating, Cooling
  Levels," 149(February 25), 1, 38.

American Retail Federation (undated), Energy Cost Reduction in Retailing, Washington, D.C.

Business Week (1979), "Why Carter's Temperature Rule May Not
  Work," (August 13), 92-94.

Chain Store Age Executive (1979), "Groping for a Way Out
  of the Energy Maze," 55 (August), 156-159.

Chain Store Age Executive (1978), "New Energy for Conservation," 54 (August), 138-140.

Chain Store Age Executive (1977), "Grapling with Energy:
  Are Chains Doing Enough?" 53 (August), 21-28.

Churchill, Gilbert A. Jr., (1976), Marketing Research:
  Methodological Foundations, Hinsdale, IL: The Dryden
  Press.

Department of Energy (1978), Energy Audit Workbook for
  Retail Stores, publication number DOE/CS - 0041/11
  (September), Washington, D.C.

Federal Energy Administration (1977), Energy Consumption
  in Commercial Industries by Census Division - 1974,
  publication number PB - 268-851 (March), Washington, D.C.

Federal Energy Administration (1975), How Business in Los
  Angeles Cut Energy Use by 20 Percent, publication number
  WN - 8866, Washington, D.C.

French, Vernick O. (1979), "From Washington - A Better
  Energy Plan: Simply Percentage Reductions in Any
  Standard Energy Unit," Stores, 61 (May), 47.

Mahoney, Thomas A. (1979), "Engineer Blasts DOE Building
  Temperature Rule as Unjust," Air-Conditioning, Heating
  and Refrigeration News, 147 (June 25), 1-2.

Massachusetts Public Interest Group (1975), Commercial
  Energy Waste: An Extravagance No One Can Afford, Boston.

McCarty, William D. (1980), "Energy Conservation and
  Retailing: Attitudes, Practices, and Government Guide-
  lines," unpublished Master's Thesis, Department of
  Marketing, Colorado State University.

National Science Foundation (1975), Energy Conservation,
  A Technical Guide, (March), Washington, D.C.

Roberts, Ralph M. (1980), "Energy Conservation in the
  Retail Sector," Journal of the Academy of Marketing
  Science, 8 (Fall), 405-415.

__________, et al. (1977), Potential Energy Conservation
  in the Commercial Sector, publication grant number -
  STAR - 76 - 002 (December), Pensacola: The University of
  West Florida.

__________, and David L. Redfering, (1979), "Retailers
  and Energy Conservation - Problems and Promotions."
  Developments in Marketing Science, Vol. 2, Howard S.
  Gitlow and Edward W. Wheatley, eds., Miami: Academy of
  Marketing Science, 62-65.

Rocky Mountain News (1980), "Temperature Controls
  Extended," (April 16), 15.

Snedecor, George W. and William G. Cochran (1967), Statistical Methods, 6th ed., Ames, IA: The Iowa State University Press.

THE EFFECT OF ECOLOGICAL CONCERN ON PRODUCT ATTRIBUTE UTILITY

David J. Fritzsche, Illinois State University
Ronald Duehr, Country Companies

ABSTRACT

The relative utility provided by the product attribute
possessing an environmental dimension was investigated.
The magnitude of this utility was then examined for differences between consumers who were environmentally concerned and those who were not concerned.

INTRODUCTION

The effect which consumer ecological concern has upon
consumer purchasing behavior began to receive serious
study in the early 1970's. The questions asked were:
Do consumers who possess a concern for the environment
exhibit different consumption behavior than consumers who
do not evidence such concern? If so, is ecological concern a variable which should be included in the strategic
marketing plan? In addition, if ecological concern is a
discriminating variable, public policy makers might be
able to influence consumers' ecological concern in such
a way as to encourage the consumption of ecologically
positive products at the expense of ecologically negative
products currently on the market.

To date, the studies reported in the marketing literature
have tended to focus upon the characteristics of the consumer who evidences an ecological concern (Peters 1973,
Kinnear and Taylor 1973, 1974, Webster 1975, Cox et al.
1975), and upon environmental aspects of the purchase
activities of consumers (Kassarjian 1971, Henion 1972,
Fritzsche 1974). Two studies have focused upon specific
product attributes. Kerin and Peterson (1974) examined
the effect which environmental consciousness had upon
the preference for product attribute combinations. Henion, et al. (1980) investigated the trade-offs in product
attribute levels which consumers were willing to make in
the purchase of products which are environmentally benign.

The present study examines product attributes with respect to their relative importance to the purchase decision. Specifically, the paper addresses the following
questions: (1) Given a set of product attributes for a
product which incorporates a significant perceived environmental impact, how important to the purchase decision
is the attribute possessing environmental consequences
relative to the remaining attributes? (2) Does the importance of the environmentally related attribute differ
for the ecologically concerned consumer compared to the
unconcerned consumer?

METHODOLOGY

In order to investigate the above questions, a product
was sought which possessed a significant environmental
impact that was generally recognized by consumers. In
addition, it must be possible for the consumer to alter
the environmental impact by selecting alternative offerings of the product. There is a temporal quality to
products with these characteristics as demonstrated by
three products which were popular in past studies: laundry detergent, unleaded gasoline, and paper towels. Many
states and municipalities have banned the sale of detergents containing phosphates or have set low maximum levels of phosphates which are allowed in detergents. Most
automobiles built after 1974 require unleaded gas. Paper
towels made of recycled paper are no longer available in

most stores. Thus, for these three products most consumers no longer have a choice of brands which have a differential impact upon the environment.

When the study design was being formulated, a public discussion was taking place concerning the impact which aerosol sprays containing fluorocarbons have on the environment, a discussion which is still open to debate. Thus
a decision was made to use a product which was available
in both aerosol and nonaerosol containers as a representative product for the study. Deodorants were selected
because they are used by most people and met the above
criteria.

Since the time the data were collected, aerosols containing fluorocarbons have been removed from the market.
Thus the particular deodorant the consumer selects no
longer has a perceived differential impact upon the environment. However, by interpreting the data as representing an example of how consumers respond to the environmental attributes of a product, insight may be gained into future purchase behavior regarding products which possess a significant perceived environmental impact.

Two hypotheses were developed focusing upon the above
questions. The assumption was made that consumers tend
to be somewhat brand loyal in their deodorant purchases
and that brand would be the most important attribute in
the choice of a deodorant offer. The deodorant's scent
was considered to be the attribute of second importance
because the scent stays with consumers throughout the day.
The container providing the method of application was believed to be less important than scent as the consumers'
contact with the container is for a much shorter period
of time than the scent. Thus,

Hypothesis 1: The container attribute is less important
to the consumer than either the brand or the scent attribute of deodorants.

The environmental dimension of deodorants consists of the
container attribute. According to current scientific beliefs, an aerosol container possessing a fluorocarbon
propellant is a significant threat to the environment.
Thus consumers who are ecologically concerned would be
expected to avoid aerosol containers when possible. It
was assumed that the container attribute would take on a
greater level of importance for ecologically concerned
consumers than for unconcerned consumers. Secondly, it
was thought that concerned consumers would place a much
lower value on the aerosol container than the unconcerned
consumer. The second hypothesis, in two parts, focuses
upon these two aspects of the container attribute.

Hypothesis 2a: Ecologically concerned consumers consider
the container attribute to be more important than unconcerned consumers.
              2b: Ecologically concerned consumers place a
lower utility on the aerosol container than unconcerned
consumers.

The sample consisted of 449 college students who were
enrolled at a medium-sized Midwestern university. Students were used since there was no reason to believe
that their deodorant consumption patterns differed from
the consumption patterns of the total adult population.
The sample was drawn to include a series of classes from
the social science, the physical science and the business

disciplines.

After the study was completed, a comparison was made between the proportion of students who reported using various deodorant containers and the market share each of the container types held as reported by the Simmons Market Research Bureau.

	Population	Students
Aerosol	30.6%	18.4
Pump spray	5.2	9.4
Roll on	44.3	50.3
Stick	19.8	21.9

The students tended to use a higher proportion of pump spray and roll on containers than the general public. However, some of this difference may be explained by the sex composition of the two groups. There is a definite difference in the aerosol share for the two groups. This suggests that student ecological attitudes and behavior may differ from the general population. Thus one should use care in generalizing from the findings of this study to the total adult population.

The procedure used to collect the data consisted of administering self-report instruments to the respondents in group settings. The initial data collected included a preference ranking of a series of 18 deodorant offerings currently on the market. The offerings represented all possible combinations of the three product attributes--brand, scent, and container. The brand attribute was represented by three levels: Arrid, Ban, and Right Guard. The scent attribute was represented as either scented or unscented. The container attribute was represented at three levels: roll-on, aerosol, and pump spray. The specific levels of these product attributes were selected on the basis of their shelf space captured in the city surrounding the university.

Each of the offers was presented to the respondent on a card in pictorial form in black and white. Each card contained a photograph of an actual deodorant with the words "scented" or "unscented" printed at the bottom. None of the aerosol containers was shown with the label containing the message "contains no fluorocarbons" which had begun to appear on some deodorants at the time the data were collected. The respondents were asked to rank the card deck in the order of their preference for the individual offers using the standard three stack sort routine.

After the respondents had recorded their preferences for the deodorant offers and the cards were retrieved, they responded to a series of questions which required them to rank the levels of the individual product attributes on the basis of their preference for the attribute levels. Following the ranking of each attribute, they were asked why they ranked their number one level most preferred with the response being open ended. Their justification for the container attribute became the basis for determining whether a respondent was environmentally concerned. Respondents who ranked a container other than an aerosol as number one and who provided an ecological reason for ranking their preferred container number one were classified as environmentally concerned. All others were classified as unconcerned. It should be noted that the individual attribute rankings was a separate task from the product preference rankings using cards. The respondents were asked to rank the brand attributes first with the container attributes being ranked second and the scent attributes ranked third. No indication was provided as to the purpose of the attribute rankings.

After responding to a series of additional questions not related to this paper, the data collection ended with the respondents providing a set of ratings for deodorant offerings shown in color on slides. The subjects were instructed to assume that they had just run out of deodorant. They were asked to rate each of the slides using a nine point scale anchored by the phrases "definitely would consider" and "definitely would not consider". The slides contained the eighteen deodorant offers previously ranked using cards. Three of the eighteen slides, selected at random, were duplicated. The duplicate slides were rated prior to rating the set of eighteen slides in order to familiarize the respondents with the rating exercise. The data from the three duplicate slides were not included in the analysis.

RESULTS

Ranked Data

In addition to the data collection discussed above, a second set of deodorant preference rankings was collected from a subset of the respondents for use in testing the data's reliability and validity as suggested by Green and Srinivasan (1978). The second data collection effort took place three and one half months from the time the first data collection activity was completed. It used the same full factorial set of deodorant offers which were used in the initial collection effort. It is believed that the time interval between the two collection activities was long enough to prevent the occurrence of any testing effect.

To obtain a measure of the reliability of the respondents' judgments, the preference rankings of the deodorants from the first data collected were correlated with the rankings from the second collection using the Spearman rank correlation procedure. The mean rho coefficient was .63 and the median coefficient was .68. The values ranged from 1.0 to .01 for the respondents as shown in Table 1.

TABLE 1

SPEARMAN CORRELATION OF DEODORANT PREFERENCE RANKINGS
COLLECTED THREE AND ONE HALF MONTHS APART

Correlation Coefficient	Frequency	Cumulative Frequency	Percent
.9 - 1.0	4	4	15
.8 - .89	4	8	15
.7 - .79	5	13	19
.6 - .69	2	15	7
.5 - .59	5	20	19
.4 - .49	4	24	15
.2 - .29	2	26	7
.0 - .09	1	27	3
			100%

Mean   .63
Median .68

The preference data for the deodorant offerings were analyzed using Johnson's nonmetric regression program (Johnson, 1975). The internal validity of the data was then examined by correlating the respondents' input rankings with the predicted rankings supplied by the nonmetric regression program. The Spearman's rho mean value was .84 with a range of 1.0 to .27. The data collected for the above reliability test were used to conduct a cross-validation of the data (see Table 2). First the predictions from the first rankings were correlated with the second set of rankings collected. This yielded a mean Spearman rho of .55 with a range of 1.0 to .16. Next the first set of rankings was correlated with the predictions obtained from the second set of rankings using the Johnson program. The mean rho value for this test was .60 with a range of 1.0 to -.26.

TABLE 2

CROSS-VALIDATION OF PREDICTIONS AND RANKINGS

Correlation Coefficients	First Predictions & Second Rankings	%	Second Predictions & First Rankings	%
.9 - 1.0	3	11	4	15
.8 - .89	3	11	1	4
.7 - .79	3	11	4	15
.6 - .69	3	11	7	26
.5 - .59	2	7	4	15
.4 - .49	7	26	2	7
.3 - .39	2	7	1	4
.2 - .29	2	7	2	7
.1 - .19				
.0 -(-.09)			1	4
-.1 -(-.19)	1	4		
-.2-(-.29)	1	4	1	4
	Mean .55		Mean .60	
	Median .55		Median .68	

To provide a further test of the validity of the ranked data, data indicating the actual deodorant products used by the respondents were collected in a session which took place at least one month after the original ranked data were collected. In a series of three questions the respondents were asked to specify the brand, scent, and container of the deodorant they were currently using. The position of the product currently used within the respondent's ranked preferences was then determined. A frequency tabulation of the individual rank of the deodorant the subjects used was then completed as shown in Table 3. Over half of the respondents were currently using the product they had ranked number one, and three quarters of the respondents were using their first or second ranked choice. It should be noted that there are several reasons why people might not be using the deodorant which they ranked number one. Through use experience with their present product they may have decided that they would prefer another offer which they would likely rank number one. Also, some of the individuals may have been using deodorant which someone else had purchased for them. Thus they may have been given (quite likely with students) or have purchased through an agent an offer which was not their personal first choice. Of course some of the respondents may have run out of deodorant between the time of the first and second data collection. They then may have purchased their number one choice.

TABLE 3

RANK OF DEODORANT CURRENTLY USED

Rank	Number	Percent	Cumulative Percent[a]
1	49	57	57
2	16	19	76
3	2	2	78
4	3	4	82
5	2	2	84
6	6	7	91
7	2	2	93
8	1	1	94
9	1	1	95
10	1	1	96
12	1	1	97
13	1	1	98
18	1	1	99

[a]Does not total 100% due to rounding error.

In order to test the first hypothesis concerning the relative importance of the environmental dimension of deodorants, in this case represented by the container attribute, the partworths derived from the Johnson program were converted into importance weights using the following formula (Jain et al. 1979).

$$w_i = \{\max_j (\alpha_{ij}) - \min_j (\alpha_{ij})\}, \text{ for each } i$$

where α_{ij} = the partworth for the ith attribute at the jth level.

$$w_i = \text{importance weight for attribute } i.$$

The partworths were normalized prior to calculating the importance weights so that the partworths and weights would be comparable across respondents. The weights for the three attributes were as follows:

	Brand	Scent	Container
Mean Importance Weights (rankings)	1.62	1.02	2.25

The container attribute was found to be significantly
more important than either the brand or the scent attributes, {t(448) = 6.54, p = .000 and t(448) = 14.37,
p = .000}. Thus this hypothesis was not supported. It
should be noted, however, that while the container attribute was found to be the most important to the respondents, the attribute was likely to be important to
many of the respondents for reasons which were not environmental in nature. Of the 449 people participating
in the exercise, only 96 or 21 percent of the respondents were concerned with the environmental aspects of
the container attribute, such concern being previously
defined as indicating an environmental reason for not
preferring aerosol containers.

Part "a" of the second hypothesis concerning the relative importance of the container attribute was tested
by subjecting the mean importance weight of the container attribute to a t-test across the two groups of consumers. The importance weight for the concerned consumers was 2.51. The unconcerned consumers' weight was
2.17. The difference between these two weights was significant at the .01 level; thus part "a" of the hypothesis was supported.

Part "b" of Hypothesis 2 concerning the differential
utility derived from the different container types was
examined by comparing the mean partworths using a t-test.
The means of the partworths for each group are shown below:

	Roll-on	Aerosol	Spray
Concerned	.54	−1.10	.16
Unconcerned	.13	− .30	−.21

In all cases the means were significantly different at
the .00 level. The aerosol containers provided the lowest mean utility for both groups. However, the aerosol
partworths for the concerned respondents were much lower than for the unconcerned respondents. Thus part "b"
of the hypothesis is also supported. As one would expect, the concerned consumers tended to value the roll-
on and spray containers more highly than the unconcerned
respondents. It is interesting to note that the roll-on
container appeared to be valued more highly than the
spray by both groups.

Rating Data

The rating data were collected in order to provide another measure of the reliability of the ranked data.
Corroboration of the ranking data with the rating data
would increase one's confidence in the findings. The
preference data obtained by the rating technique were
analyzed using ordinary least squares regression (OLS).
As with the ranked data, a second set of ratings was
collected from a subset of the respondents from the
first collection exercise. No respondents provided both
a second set of ratings and second set of rankings. The
second set of ratings was collected from two groups with
the first collection taking place one and a half months
after the initial collection, and the second taking
place three months after the initial data collection.
As with the ranked data, the second set of ratings was
collected using the same technique as used in the first
collection activity.

A measure of the reliability of the respondents' judgments was obtained by correlating the ratings obtained
from the first collection with the ratings obtained
from the second collection using the Pearson correlation
technique. The mean correlation coefficient was .56,
and the median coefficient was .67. It can be seen from

Table 4 that the three negative coefficients had a significant effect on the coefficient mean. If the three
negative coefficients were discarded as outliers, the
mean coefficient would rise to .64 which is slightly
higher than the mean rank coefficient.

TABLE 4

PEARSON CORRELATION OF DEODORANT PREFERENCE RATINGS

Correlation Coefficient	Frequency	Cumulative Frequency	Percent
.9 − 1.0	4	4	10
.8 − .89	8	12	20
.7 − .79	6	18	15
.6 − .69	7	25	17
.5 − .59	3	28	7
.4 − .49	3	31	7
.3 − .39	3	34	7
.2 − .29	2	36	5
.1 − .19	1	37	2
.0 − .09	1	38	2
−.01− (−.09)	1	39	2
−.3 − (−.39)	1	40	2
−.9 − (−1.0)	1	41	2

Mean   .56
Median .67

The internal validity of the rating data was examined by
creating a set of predictions for each respondent using
the partworths obtained using OLS. The predictions were
correlated with the ratings for each respondent. The
mean r value was .87 with a range of 1.0 to .38. The
data collected to test the reliability of the rating data
were used to cross-validate the data. The predictions
generated from the first set of ratings were correlated
with the second set of ratings yielding a mean r of .55
with a range of .96 to −.93. The first set of ratings
were then correlated with the predictions generated from
the second set of ratings to yield an r of .57 with a
range of .96 to −.95.

As with the ranked data, a further test of the validity
of the rating data was conducted by comparing the product the respondents were currently using with the rating
they gave that particular product. Table 5 shows the
ratings of the deodorants the respondents were using.
Sixty-four percent of the subjects ranked their current
deodorant at least as high as the other seventeen offers.
Eighty percent ranked their deodorant no lower than one
rating point above their highest rated product.

The relative importance of the environmental dimension
derived from the ratings, a test of the first hypothesis,
was examined using importance weights in a manner similar to that used for the ranked data. The weights cal-

culated from the normalized partworths derived from the ratings are shown below:

	Brand	Scent	Container
Mean Importance Weights (ratings)	1.92	.92	2.35

The container attribute again comes out being the dominant attribute in deodorants. The mean container importance weight was significantly different from the other two attributes at the .00 level. {t(448) = 4.69, p = .000 for brand and t(448) = 19.87, p = .000 for scent}.

TABLE 5

RATING OF DEODORANT CURRENTLY USED

Rating	Number	Percent	Cumulative Percent[a]
1	54	64	64
2	13	16	80
3	3	4	84
4	7	8	92
6	3	4	96
7	1	1	67
9	3	4	111

[a]Does not equal 100 due to rounding error.

The importance weight for the container attribute was examined for differences between respondents who were environmentally concerned vs. respondents who were not environmentally concerned, as previously defined. The mean weight for the concerned group was 2.59 compared to 2.17 for the unconcerned group. These differences were significant at the .01 level. Thus additional support is provided for Hypothesis 2a.

The partworths for the container attribute were examined to determine whether the aerosol container was of less value to the concerned respondents as Hypothesis 2b predicted. The normalized partworths are shown below:

	Roll-on	Aerosol	Spray
Concerned	.70	−.97	.27
Unconcerned	.26	−.25	−.01

The partworths were significantly different across consumers at the .01 level. Again as with the rank data, the aerosol appears to be the least valued container by both groups; however, the concerned consumers tend to attach significantly less value to the aerosol than do the unconcerned respondents. The concerned respondents seem to place a much higher value on the roll-on and, to a lesser extent, on the spray container.

DISCUSSION

Several limitations of the current study must be considered when interpreting the data. First, there was no attempt to draw a random sample from the adult population. Thus the specific results may not be generalizable to the U.S. population. Second, while none of the sample population mentioned the legislation removing fluorocarbons from aerosol containers in any individual discussions or questions, it is possible that a few of the subjects were aware of the bill and this could have influenced their responses. Third, several of the reliability and validity tests gave conflicting signals.

In spite of the low scores, the partworths derived from the ranked and the rating data showed remarkable agreement. Given that the agreement among the two types of data collection is the stronger measure of reliability, it is concluded that the data possess at least a satisfactory level of reliability.

The internal validity of the data proved to be moderate. However, the cross-validation test of the data again proved to be somewhat disappointing. The predictive validity of the data proved to be quite high when the input data were compared with the deodorant offers the respondents were currently using. Thus the quality of the data was quite good from the standpoint of being able to predict actual usage from the data collected.

The product attribute yielding the greatest utility to the respondents was the container. While the container attribute provided the environmental dimension of the deodorant product, it also provided the means of application for the user. However, consumers may prefer one container over another for reasons which have no environmental aspects such as ease of application and convenience of transport. For example, an individual who travels by air frequently may opt for a non-aerosol container out of concern that the aerosol could possibly fail at the lower atmospheric pressures experienced at altitude. The fact remains, though, that the product attribute possessing environmental dimensions was found to be the most important attribute of the three studied.

Given that there may be a number of reasons for selecting a container which has environmentally positive characteristics, some quite removed from a concern for the environment, the question becomes: How many of the consumers preferring environmentally positive containers do so for ecological reasons? The data indicate that just over 20 percent of the respondents indicated that they preferred non-aerosol containers for reasons which were environmental in nature. This finding is consistent with Henion's (1976) claim that ecologically concerned consumers comprise a substantial market segment.

Upon examining the utility provided by the levels of the container attribute, it became clear that the utility derived by the ecologically concerned from the three containers was significantly different from the utility derived by the unconcerned respondents. Not only did the ecologically concerned consumers derive more utility from non-aerosol containers both in an absolute and relative sense, but the concerned consumers preferred a nonspray container, presumably because they perceive a spray of any type to be less beneficial to the atmosphere. It is interesting to note that, for the sample studied at least, the aerosol container appeared to yield the least utility of the three containers studied.

The implications for management, at least for deodorants, appears to be clear. There is a significant segment of the market out there that is concerned and will tend to buy deodorants which they believe are environmentally benign. In terms of current practice, the aerosols which were regarded as damaging to the environment are now banned from the market. However, it may be possible to capitalize upon the perceived benefits of nonspray applicators when attempting to penetrate the concerned consumer market.

From the standpoint of the public policy maker, this study confirms what other recent studies concerning environmentally concerned consumers have found. There is a segment of concerned consumers in the market. They tend to purchase certain products which are environmentally positive. However, the study also found that the environmental attribute of a product may be a very important part of the bundle of attributes which comprise a product. The problem becomes one of whether unconcerned consumers can be converted to concerned consumers or whether public policy makers will be required to enact legislation requiring specific behavior which is environmentally positive. The latter path was chosen in the deodorant case with the passage of the legislation banning the use of fluorocarbons for propellants. Kinnear and Taylor (1974) tend to take a more pessimistic view while Henion (1976) seems to believe that much can be accomplished through consumer education.

Given the current administration's apparent attitude toward environmental issues, it is unlikely that any effort will be made to either convert or force consumers to become more environmentally positive in their consumption behavior in the near future. Thus any movement in this direction will have to be created in the private sector through education programs and through the marketing of ecologically positive products.

There are several areas offering opportunities for future research. First, the importance of the environmental dimension of additional products should be examined. One would expect that the nature of the product plus the popularity of the environmental impact of the product would affect the relative importance of the environmental dimension. Second, it would be interesting to examine the importance that a person places upon the environmental dimension of a series of products. There may be certain segments of the market which place a high value upon the environmental dimension of all products they purchase. A more likely situation is that the environmental dimension is quite important for some products and less important for other products with the relative importance for individual products differing by segments of the market (Fritzsche, 1974). Thus there may be certain market segments which respond to environmental appeals for one product which may be unresponsive to environmental appeals for other products. Third, research needs to be conducted concerning the linkage between the importance of the environmental attribute of the product and actual consumer purchase behavior. Fourth, more work needs to be done to determine satisfactory reliability and validity levels.

REFERENCES

Burnett, Stephen C. (1978), "Assessing the Impact of Increased Product Safety on Consumer Utility," Advances in Consumer Research, 5, H. Keith Hunt (ed.) Proceedings of the eighth annual conference of the Association for Consumer Research, 186-193.

Cox, Eli P. III, W. Thomas Anderson, Jr., and Karl E. Henion, (1975), "Differentiating Ecologically Concerned Consumers: Strategic Implication," Paper presented at the Southern Marketing Association Conference.

Fritzsche, David J. (1974), "The Environmental Consistency of Consumer Purchases," American Marketing Association Combined Proceedings, (Spring & Fall), 312-315.

Green, Paul E. and V. Srinivasan (1978), "Conjoint Analysis in Consumer Research: Issues and Outlook," Journal of Consumer Research, 5 (September), 103-123.

Henion, Karl E., Russell Gregory, and Mona A. Clee (1980), "Trade-Offs in Attribute Levels Made By Ecologically Concerned and Unconcerned Consumers When Buying Detergents," Advances in Consumer Research, 8, Kent Monroe (ed.) Proceedings of the eleventh annual conference of the Association for Consumer Research, 624-629.

Henion, Karl E. (1976), Ecological Marketing. Columbus, Ohio: Grid, Inc.

____________ (1972), "Effect of Ecologically Relevant Information on Detergent Sales," Journal of Marketing Research, 9 (February), 10-14.

Jain, Arun K., Franklin Acito, Naresh K. Malhotra, and Vijay Mahajan (1979), "A Comparison of the Internal Validity of Alternative Parameter Estimation Methods in Decompositional Multiattribute Preference Models," Journal of Marketing Research, 16 (August), 313-22.

Johnson, Richard M. (1975), "A Simple Method for Pairwise Monotone Regression, Psychometrika, 40 (June), 163-8.

Kassarjian, Harold H. (1971), "Incorporating Ecology into Marketing Strategy: The Case of Air Pollution," Journal of Marketing, 35 (July), 61-5.

Kerin, Roger A. and Robert A. Peterson (1974), "Selected Insights Into the Dynamics of Ecologically Responsible Behavior," American Institute for Decision Science Proceedings, Manfred Hopfe (ed.), p. 33.

Kinnear, Thomas C., James R. Taylor, and Sadrudin A. Ahmed (1974), "Ecologically Concerned Consumers: Who Are They?" Journal of Marketing, 38 (April), 20-24.

Kinnear, Thomas C. and James. R. Taylor (1973), "The Effect of Ecological Concern on Brand Perceptions," Journal of Marketing Research, 10 (May), 191-197.

Parker, Barnett R. and V. Srinivasan (1976), "A Consumer Preference Approach to the Planning of Rural Primary Health-Care Facilities," Operations Research, 24 (September - October), 991-1025.

Peters, William H. (1973), "Who Cooperates in Voluntary Recycling Efforts?" American Marketing Association Combined Proceedings, (Spring & Fall), 505-508.

Webster, Frederick E., Jr. (1975), "Determining the Characteristics of the Socially Conscious Consumer," Journal of Consumer Research, 2 (December) 188-196.

A PROACTIVE APPROACH TO THE IDENTIFICATION
OF POTENTIAL CONSUMER SAFETY HAZARDS IN
ALTERNATIVE SOURCES OF HEATING

Richard F. Beltramini, Arizona State University, Tempe
Kenneth R. Evans, Arizona State University, Tempe

ABSTRACT

This paper offers a technique for developing a proactive approach toward identifying the hazard potential associated with the direct consumption of alternative sources of heating. Specifically, coal and wood-burning stoves are examined in this study due to the increasing rate of consumer injuries associated with these products, and the anticipation of accelerated consumer demand for these alternative heating sources. The perception of naive consumers are statistically compared with those of safety experts, and the differences are analyzed. Finally, the marketing and policy level implications for a proactive approach to consumer safety are discussed.

INTRODUCTION

With the spiraling cost of energy and the translation of these costs into increased consumer utility bills, many homeowners have turned to alternative sources of heating. Among these, coal and wood-burning stoves have become increasingly popular, principally due to their lower cost per equivalent output (BTU's).

However, numerous problems arise as this trend toward coal and wood-burning stoves continues to grow as an alternative to conventional heating. Specific problems can be generally aggregated into one of two areas: 1) direct consumption (problems here pertain to the consumers' installation, use, and maintenance of a coal and wood-burning stove within their own homes), and 2) indirect consumption (problems here include those individuals who are impacted by stove usage, yet who may or may not be stove owners themselves [i.e., pollution, fire hazards, irresponsible wood cutting, increased need for coal and wood resulting in poorly managed or relaxed conservation efforts, etc.]).

Traditional sources of home heating, such as central units, have been rasonably well-controlled through building codes so that individual users were secure in the knowledge that not only were their own homes safe, but so too was their environment (adjacent homes, air pollution directly resulting from ventilation of central heating units, etc.). Furthermore, central heating units are generally designed and installed prior/during the construction of a home, making it possible to more safely integrate these units into the home. Coal and wood-burning stoves, on the other hand, are in most cases installed in an existing home; furthermore, it is the responsibility of the stove purchaser to either arrange for installation or do it one's self.

This research was funded by a grant from the Consumer Product Safety Commission. Special thanks to Mr. William Biggs of the Consumer Product Safety Commission for his time and cooperation.

The consumer's responsibility does not end here, however. Due to the inefficient burning and general nature of the materials used within these alternative heating units, it is incumbent upon the consumer to schedule frequent maintenance-related activities. It is ironic that through building codes society has endeavored to eliminate the dangers inherent in home heating units; yet, equivalent controls have not been established with regard to alternative heating products.

The focus of this study is to investigate selected problems associated with the direct consumption of alternative sources of heating, specifically coal and wood-burning stoves. Since responsibility for installation and general stove operation has shifted from builders/contractors to the individual consumer, it is imperative that users of these products understand potential safety hazards associated with their operation. Inadequate dissemination of information regarding installation, use and maintenance of coal and wood-burning stoves may result in a corresponding increase in the rate of injuries and fatalities associated with these increasingly popular products.

BACKGROUND

From 1974 to 1979 shipments of coal and wood-burning stoves increased approximately 160 percent (Department of Commerce 1979) with over half this growth taking place in the South (U.S. Department of Energy 1980). This rise in popularity has closely paralleled a period of spiraling oil prices where the cost/benefit of alternatives to centrol heating have become increasingly attractive (Sales and Marketing Management 1979; Time 1979; and U.S. News & World Report 1980). Unfortunately, with this increased application of coal and wood-burning stoves, the number of injuries and deaths directly associated with their use have increased dramatically as well (Bylinski 1979 and Consumer Product Safety Commission 1981). Sources differ as the the relative effect of the factors which may contribute to injury; however, there appears to be some general agreement that inquiries are typically the result of improper maintenance, equipment design, operation, and installation (Peacock 1979 and Consumer Product Safety Commission 1981).

While some reactive attention (Stone 1974; New York Times 1979; and Journal of Commerce and Commercial 1980) has been devoted toward the alarming trend in injuries resulting from the use of coal and wood-burning stoves, virtually no emphasis has been placed on a proactive approach toward predicting and preventing injuries. Little is known about consumers' awareness of the potential hazards associated with these products. Therefore, this investigation is designed to assess perception of the hazard potential of cool and wood-burning stoves, both on the part of consumers and on the part of "experts" in the field, to see if indeed differences between the two exist. If such differences exist, an argument may be advanced for preventative measures to be accelerated in terms of educating, informing, and (ultimately) protecting the public.

PILOT STUDY

In April 1980, a pilot study was conducted which served as the basis for this research. A random sample of 361 metropolitan homeowners in a commonly utilized Southwestern test market were contacted via personal interview in an effort to assess consumers' perceptions of a variety of alternative sources of home heating. Respondents for this pilot study were selected to proportionately match population parameters on a variety of demographic items. The key conclusions derived from the pilot study included the following: 1) of the products studied, coal and wood-burning stoves had produced the most injuries among respondents who reported injuries, 2) respondents who owned coal and wood-burning stoves sought the least amount of product information among owners of alternative heating devices, 3) of those owners of alternative heating devices, do-it-yourself installation was most common among owners of coal and wood-burning stoves, 4) coal and wood-burning stove owners perceived less time was needed to maintain their products than was recommended by manufacturers, and 5) operating instructions for coal and wood-burning stoves were perceived as least important among the criteria for purchase of these products.

Thus, it appeared that improper installation, misuse of stove, inadequate maintenance, and stove malfunctions could serve to predict the overall perceived hazard potential of coal and wood-burning stoves. Furthermore, these factors had been identified in national studies as the most significant contributors to coal and wood-burning stove injuries.

METHODOLOGY

Simply "predicting" the perceived hazard potential based on overall consumer hazard ratings seemed inadequate, however, without a benchmark for comparison. It was decided to compare "naive" consumer hazard ratings with those of "experts"--firefighters in the same metropolitan area, hypothesizing that: H_1) A difference will be found to exist between naive consumers and experts in their perceived relationship between hazard-related characteristics and the overall hazard potential of coal and wood-burning stoves, and H_2) A difference will be found to exist between naive consumers and experts in the degree of importance of hazard-related characteristics that contribute to the overall hazard potential of coal and wood-burning stoves.

The next step was to construct two regression models, one based on consumers' responses and one of firefighters' responses, and to statistically compare the presumed discrepancy between the two. In each case, the predictor variables remained improper installation, misuse of the stove, inadequate maintenance, and stove malfunction, while the criterion variable remained the perceived hazard potential of coal and wood-burning stoves. The two models were compared via t-test, using the regression coefficients and the standard errors, to statistically assess the differences between models.

Research Design

Predictive models (multiple regression) were used to determine the relative importance of hazard ratings on an individual's assessment of the perceived hazard potential of coal or wood-burning stoves. The two sample units of naive consumers and experts were selected to determine if a comparison of the regression models representing the two groups would: 1) significantly differ in their overall predictability, and 2) significantly differ in terms of the relative importance placed upon specific hazard ratings (predictor variables). One interpretation of a resultant disparity between the two regression models would include the identification of areas where marketers or policy makers might endeavor to improve consumer information and/or investigate product modification to prevent injuries before they occur.

Sample

Two distinct populations were of interest to the researchers. One population consisted of naive consumers, and the other population was that of safety experts (firefighters) who were knowledgable of the problems with, and proper use of, home heating products.

The sample frame for the consumer population consisted of all homeowning adults within a major southwestern metropolitan area, as of the latest census. This market represented an area of heavy penetration of coal and wood-burning stoves as alternative sources of heating. To enhance the validity and generalizability of the study, the sample was selected by dividing the U.S. Census tracts into three income groups, and matching the proportions to population parameters. Two tracts were randomly selected from each of these income groups. Actual participants in this study were residents on specific blocks (which were also randomly selected) within these tracts. The consumer sample consisted 494 respondents.

The sample frame for the safety experts consisted of full-time firefighters within the same metropolitan area. The sampling procedure for selecting the experts paralleled that of the consumer sample. On-duty firefighters in fire stations adjacent to these randomly selected census treacts were identified as participants. The expert sample consisted of 102 respondents.

Instrument

The data collection instrument was a self-administered questionnaire, containing a number of hazard-related characteristics (previously identified in the pilot study and and supported by national statistics) pertaining to the perceived hazard potential in using coal and wood-burning stoves. The subjects' attitudes toward these hazard-related characteristics (independent variables) were divided into both their valence and salience components. Hence, semantic scaling questions (likely-unlikely) were used to determine the valence component of respondents' attitudes toward a potential hazard (e.g., How likely is it that a particular hazard will contribute to the unsafe use of the product?). An individual's attitude toward a particular hazard-related characteristic was determined as the product of the valence and salience components. The dependent variable for this study

consisted of responses to a 7-point agreement scale
which indicated the respondents' overall evaluation
of the perceived safety hazard in using coal or wood-
burning stoves.

A pretest of the questionnaire was conducted under
field conditions to check for both question clarity
and representativeness of the topic to be investigated. The results of the pretest contributed to a
few minor revisions in the data collection instrument.

ANALYSIS

For each group (naive consumer and expert), multiple
regression analysis was conducted. Both regression
equations were constructed from the four independent
variables (hazard-related characteristics) and one
dependent variable (perceived hazard potential of
coal and wood-burning stoves). The purpose behind
constructing the regression equations was: 1) to
determine the degree of contribution of each of the
independent variables in predicting the perceived
overall hazard potential; and 2) to determine the
difference in relative magnitude between the regression coefficients for identical independent variables
in the two predictor models. That is, the intent was
not to include all possible hazard predictors, but
only those which were both supported in the initial
pilot study and in national statistics.

It was determined that t-tests between the ratings
obtained on the hazard-related characteristics were
inadequate to accomplish the objectives stated.
Since a measure of relative contribution to overall
perceived hazard potential was intended, it was essential to assess the predictive contribution of the
hazard-related characteristics in combination.
Therefore, instead of comparing the mean hazard
ratings between the two samples, t-tests were conducted utilizing the normalized regression coefficients between each identical independent variable
across the two regression models. This was done
assuming the error terms of the two regression models
were uncorrelated (Chow 1960). That is, the entire
basis of the study was one of identifying populations
possessing unique perceptions regarding the overall
hazard potential and corresponding hazard-related
characteristics of coal and wood-burning stoves.

FINDINGS

Table 1 contains the normalized regression equations
for the naive consumer and expert groups. The analysis of variance for both regression equations resulted in an F value which was significant at the p < .01
level. Therefore, there appeared to be a statistically significant linear relationship between the
hazard-related characteristics and an individual's
perception of stove safety. The strength of this
linear relationship is critical due to the nature of
the comparative analyses which were conducted.

TABLE 1

NORMALIZED REGRESSION EQUATIONS

Naive Consumers:

$$Y = -.01722X_1 + .16299X_2 + .03957X_3 + .34224X_4$$

Experts:

$$Y = .21146X_1 + .07478X_2 + .11085X_3 + .21093X_4$$

Where: X_1 = inadequate maintenance

X_2 = stove malfunction

X_3 = misuse of stove

X_4 = improper installation

The coefficient of determination (r^2) for the regression equations was 21.7 percent and 24.7 percent for
the naive consumers and experts respectively. Although this does not represent an impressive improvement in estimation, the intent of employing these
regression models was not to <u>totally</u> predict the
overall hazard potential of coal and wood-burning
stoves, but rather to assess the relative contribution of the four hazard-related characteristics identified earlier.

T-tests were performed to assess the differences
between the normalized regression coefficients of
each of the four predictor variables across the two
regression models. The results confirmed that not
only were the two models statistically different
<u>overall</u> (p < .01), but that <u>each</u> of the four predic-
tors (regression coefficients) was also statistically
different (p < .01). The regression analysis of the
two groups (naive consumers and experts) clearly
indicated a disparity in: 1) their perceived relationship between hazard-related characteristics and
the overall hazard potential of coal and wood-burning
stoves, and 2) in the degree of importance of hazard-
related characteristics that contribute to the overall hazard potential of coal and wood-burning stoves.

Rank ordering the hazard-related characteristics for
the two groups by means of change in r^2 revealed that
naive consumers rated improper installation, misuse
of the stove, stove malfunction, and inadequate maintenance as being most to least important. The experts, however, rated inadequate maintenance, improper installation, misuse of the stove, and stove malfunction as being most to least important. In fact,
with the exception of maintenance, the rest of the
hazard-related characteristics differed by only one
rank between the two groups. The fact that the two
groups differed in their view of the importance of
inadequate maintenance clearly indicates the need for
increased consumer awareness of the vital relationship between regularly scheduled maintenance and
safety in stove use.

Further analytical support of the disparity between the two groups with regard to stove maintenance was evidenced through t-tests between regression coefficients. Again, the t-tests comparing the regression coefficients of the hazard-related characteristics was significant at the $p < .01$ level. Furthermore, visual inspection of the direction of the linear relationship indicated a negative correspondence for maintenance and safety among naive consumers, whereas this relationship was positive in the expert group. Even in other cases where the ordinal ranking was not dramatically different, the magnitude of the relationship between each hazard-related characteristic and perceived stove safety differed significantly between the two groups. Therefore, the degree of importance of each hazard-related characteristic is not shared between naive consumers and experts.

In summary, both hypotheses were accepted in that the results indicated statistically significant differences between consumers and experts both in terms of their perceptions of the relationship between the hazard-related characteristics and the overall hazard potential of coal and wood-burning stoves, and the degree of importance of each of the hazard-related characteristics. In other words, a potential problem exists in the use/purchase of coal and wood-burning stoves in that consumers appear less likely to identify possible hazards associated with stove characteristics which, as perceived by experts, are most likely to result in injury.

CONCLUSIONS

Marketers should be interested in these findings as the demand for alternative sources of heating has produced a host of new services and businesses to support growing consumer needs. Additionally, policy makers should be interested in learning that while a growing number of consumers are switching to alternative sources of heating as an energy conservation measure, they are relatively misinformed as to the hazard potential of these products. The aggregate effect of this trend may well present a need for consumer education programs, therefore, to bring naive consumer misconceptions in line with the experiences of experts in this area. The proactive approach discussed in this paper could be applied in various product areas to detect perceptual disparities between potential consumers and safety experts before injuries result.

Future research in this area should concern itself with more than the direct consumption issues discussed in this paper. That is, a variety of indirect consumption issues associated with the trend toward alternative sources of heating deserve the attention of both marketers and policy makers. Specifically, for example, air quality, multiple unit fire danger, and indiscriminant acquisition of burning materials (coal and wood) all deserve serious attention as part of this increasing national trend toward energy alternatives.

REFERENCES

Bylinski, G. (1979), "Biomass: The Self-Replacing Energy Resource," *Fortune* (September 24), 81.

Chow, G. C. (1960), "Tests for Equality Between Sets of Coefficients in Two Linear Regressions," *Econometrica*, 10, 591-605.

"Glowing Future for Forest Power," (1979) *Time* (January 22), 59.

"Health Effects of Residential Wood Combustion: A Survey of Knowledge and Research," (1980), U.S. Department of Energy.

"Label Comments Aired for Wood, Coal Stoves," (1981), *CPSC Memo* (January).

Marks, J. (1981), "A Hero of the Hot Stove League," *Journal of Insurance*, 42, 36.

"Nose-Thumbing at OPEC--With Wood Stoves," (1980), *U.S. News and World Report* (January 21), 47.

Peacock, R. D. (1979), *A Review of Fire Incidents, Model Building Codes, and Standards Related to Wood-Burning Appliances*, Center for Fire Research, National Engineering Laboratory, National Bureau of Standards.

"Selected Heating Equipment," (1979) *Current Industrial Reports*, U.S. Department of Commerce, Bureau of the Census.

Stone, W. R. (1974), "Safe Use and Hazards of Coal and Wood Stoves," *Fire Journal* (May), 87-90.

"Woodburning Stoves: The Danger Factor," (1979) *New York Times* (November 15), C13.

"Woodburning Stoves: Up From the Ashes," (1979) *Sales and Marketing Management* (February 5), 40.

"Wood Stoves Cause Major Fire Losses," (1980), *Journal of Commerce and Commercial* (October 15), 14.

CHILDRENS' COMMERCIAL CONTENT:
A LOOK AT SEXUAL ROLES AND THE USE OF ANIMATION

William C. Moncrief, Texas Christian University, Ft. Worth
Robert M. Landry, Louisiana State University, Baton Rouge

ABSTRACT

A content analysis was performed on one hundred fifty-
three (153) Saturday morning television commercials and
analyzed by a series of five judges. The study contained
variables indicating the type of product, characters in
the commericals and their roles, and other informative
items such as nutrition, jingles and special offers.
Special emphasis was placed on animation of the commercial
message and upon the decreasing dominance of male
characters.

INTRODUCTION

In recent years television commercials on Saturday morning
have become a subject of considerable debate and interest.
It has been argued that children do not have the capability of distinguishing between the commercial message and
the television program. Because of television's capability for "multi-sensory stimulation" and over representation some critics state that children, particularly
those under nine, have very little ability to process
information at an objective level (Stern & Resnik, 1978).
Because of this lack of objectivity, critics of "Saturday
Morning" advertising contend that the upcoming generation
will be more materialistic and have poorer eating habits,
leading to poor nutrition (Action for Childrens' Television, 1970).

Another concern of critics is the level of exposure that
children have to television advertising. One study found
that children between four and eight watch an average of
24 hours of television a week, or about 25,000 commercials a year (Stern, 1978). Obviously, children are being
influenced in some respect both in their learning process
and in their brand preference. Resnik and Stern in a 1977
study discovered that children preferred a brand of snack
food after viewing a snack commercial. In a similar experiment, Atkin (1975), determined that children will ask
their parents to buy a brand of cereal that they viewed
on television.

Because of the apparent influence of television commercials, the Federal Communication Commission began as early
as 1971 conducting investigations into childrens' programming as well as advertising (Doolittle and Pepper, 1974).

Recently, Gordon (1980) reports that the Federal Trade
Commission has immersed itself into what the FTC has referred to as "key questions including: 1) To what extent
can children between the ages of two and eleven distinguish between commercials and the program and 2) Can children between the ages of two and eleven defend against
persuasion.

The FTC in a 1981 hearing (Federal Register, 1981) concluded that children cannot defend against persuasion,
and that certain "techniques, focuses, and themes" do enhance the appeal of the advertised message. Furthermore,
the FTC has concluded that the only method of combating
these techniques is a total ban of Saturday morning chilrens' advertising, a method the FTC concedes is unrealistic. Thus, the FTC has proposed a total ban on rule
making in regards to childrens' capability to defend a-
gainst persuasion, and also banned rule making concerning

"sugar-products" advertised on Saturday morning. Since
marketers have all of these "themes and techniques" at
their disposal, it becomes necessary to determine the pre-
valence of these "themes and techniques" on Saturday
morning advertising.

The main purpose of this paper is to utilize the content
analysis technique to aid in determining the nature and
emphasis of "Saturday Morning Advertising." According to
Kassarjian (1977) a content analysis must be objective,
sytematic, and quantitative. It must be objective in that
the definitions of categories must be precise enough to
allow different analysts to secure the same results.

Systematization would refer to consistently applied rules.
In this research study, categories were taken from two
previous studies. The first study, Doolittle and Pepper
(1974), concentrated on role status of the actors, age,
sex and ad form (live or animated). The second study,
Cattin and Jain (1978), concentrated on 1) informative
items versus non informative items (use of central figure
to sell product), 2) copy environment (home, outdoors),
and finally 3) source participants.

Kassarjian's third requirement in content analysis is that
it be quantitative. In other words, the data should be
amenable to statistical methods for interpretation and
inference.

OBJECTIVES OF THE STUDY

While the focus of this study was a content analysis of
Saturday Morning childrens' advertising, two areas were
perceived by the authors as meriting special attention.
These areas were those involving the use of males and females in these commercials and the use of live versus
animated characters.

The first area of interest stems primarily from an earlier
study conducted by Winich, et al (1973). In this study it
was reported that males exercised authority in 72% of the
childrens commercials sampled. Similar results were found
by Doolittle and Pepper (1974). Based on these studies,
it was hypothesized that males would appear more frequently
and play a more dominant role in childrens commercials
than females. Specifically stated, the hypothesis are as
follows:
Hypothesis # 1: A major emphasis of Saturday Morning
    Childrens' Advertising is the use of significantly
    larger number of male characters than female
    characters.
Hypothesis # 2: Saturday Morning Childrens' Advertising
    emphasises the use of male characters in a dominant
    role in the commercial.

A second area of interest is the use of animation in Saturday Morning advertisements. Although animation has become popular in prime time television advertising with
SAFECO's Pink Panther, Levi's Futuristic art, and Jovan's
Frazetta (White, 1080), animation is still associated with
childrens' advertising. Psychologists have found that
animation can be an effective tool in establishing awareness and attention, particularly when dealing with children. Studies have shown that movement and animation are
effective in holding a viewers attention (Wright, Warner,

Winter, and Zeigler, 1977). On the other hand, Bush, Bush
and Hair (1981) state that the use of animation in television advertising is significant, but the effect on the
viewer is still unknown. Because of an increase in animation, and because there is some evidence to support that
animation can establish awareness and attention, one would
expect animation to be prevasive throughout Saturday
morning advertising.

> Hypothesis # 3: The nature of Saturday Morning Chil-
> drens' Advertising lends itself to the proposition
> that the majority of commercials would contain one
> or more animated characters.

RESEARCH DESIGN

Sample

In order to conduct a study of Saturday Morning Advertising, it was necessary to videotape commercials from all
three major networks. The recording of commericals took
place on Saturday, April 4, 1981 from 9:00 am to
12:00 Noon. This date was chosen as representative of
a typical weekend since it did not occur near a major
holiday. A total of 153 commercials of all types were
recorded during the three hour span. The total number includes several "duplicates" or commercials which were
aired more than once. Since it was an objective of this
study to examine the myriad of appeals made to young
consumers, all commercials were used regardless of the
number of repetitions.

Two points deserve mention at this time. First, no attempt was made to include any channels other than those
major network stations serving the market being studied.
The primary reason for this is the lack of Saturday Morning childrens' programming on many of the "pay-tv" stations. Although it was possible to monitor these stations,
this would have only served to increase the manpower requirements while making no significant contribution to
the study. Consequently, it was decided that movie
channels, sports channels, all-news channels, etc., would
not be included as part of this research project.

The second point to be made is that all commercials aired
during the aforementioned time span were videotaped and
analyzed at a later date. This procedure allowed the
judges to re-run the commercials as often as necessary so
that an accurate analysis of the ad could be made. The
use of videotaped commercials also insured that a reliability test could be conducted under controlled circumstances.

Measuring Instrument

The measuring instrument was comprised of forty-three
items divided into eight categories. Categories were
derived primarily from those used in previous studies by
Cattin and Jain (1978) and Doolittle and Pepper (1974).
The items placed into each group were drawn not only from
the two aforementioned studies, but also from a list of
items that the authors felt reflected current advertising
practices. It is important to note that a single commercial may contain only a small number of items contained
in the entire instrument. This, of course, was a result
of the fact that the measuring instrument was designed to
include a wide range of commercials. Thus, the major
categories of informative items, non-informative items,
source participant items, location items, food items, non-
food items, advertising form items, and dominance items
never all applied to the same commercial.

Another factor of the measuring instrument which must be
mentioned is that each item was operationally defined.
This was especially important to the judges, who were
allowed to continually refer to these definitions during
the analyzing process.

Analysis

The first step in analyzing the content of the "Saturday
Morning" commercials was training the judges. In this
instance, three judges were used to examine the videotaped
commercials. Trained by the authors, the judges were
taught how to analyze commercials by using a sample of
childrens' ads supplied by a local television station.
The training session continued until all three judges were
able to identically evaluate commercials. Also, during
the initial statge of the training session, different
forms of the measuring instrument were tested to determine which forms would be the easiest to use while still
providing the information desired.

Once the three judges were able to similarly analyze the
same commercial, they were then randomly assigned to analyze the commercials of one of the network stations. Since
all the commercials for a particular station were on the
same videocassette, it was most efficient to assign the
judge a "cassette" of commercials rather than use another
design. This format also allowed the individaul judges to
work at their own pace without infringing on another
judge's time. The time frame for analyzing all the commercials was one week.

Reliability

It was necessary, once the judges completed their task, to
evaluate the work they did. This was accomplished by incorporating two "expert" judges as a reliability check.
These experts were trained in the same manner as the original three judges. The major difference was that these
experts were given only twenty-five commercials to analyze. Due to the small number of commercials which they
were to analyze, these experts spent an inordinate amount
of time on each commercial. As a result of this, the results of the experts served as a basis of comparison by
which to evaluate the original judges. It is important to
point out that the commercials analyzed by the experts were
randomly selected from each of the three networks. Thus,
all three judges could be evaluated using this procedure.

The coefficient of agreement was determined by subtracting
the number of discrepancies between the judges' analysis
and the experts' analysis from the total number of items
in the experts' analysis and then dividing the remainder
by the total number items in the experts' analysis. With
a total of 180 items in the experts' analysis, only twenty-
six were different from the judges' evaluations. This
yielded a coefficient of agreement of 86% (180-26/180).
There were no significant differences among the different
judges in terms of frequency of discrepancies.

RESULTS

The frequencies of the study are presented in Table 1. Of
the 153 commercials 66% were food oriented products with
the largest category being breakfast foods(25%). Toys
were the second largest category with 22% of all commercials selling a toy product. When advertising a toy only
5% of the commercials mentioned the safety of the toy or
how to operate the toy safely.

The results indicate that the majority of the products (87%)
actually demonstrate the product regardless of category.
When a food product is presented only 29% discuss the flavor of the product. Music apparently is an important aspect of childrens' commercials in that 56% of the commercials had an identifiable jingle, 74% of those jingles
were concerned with food products.

TABLE 1

FREQUENCIES

CATEGORY	FREQUENCY	PERCENT
Informative Items		
1. Demonstration	133	88.67
2. Accessories	10	6.67
3. Safety	5	3.33
4. Claim of Nutrition	0	0
5. Flavor	44	29.33
6. Comparison with Other Products	2	1.33
7. Reference to Other Products in the Mix	19	12.67
8. Availability	25	16.67
Noninformative Items		
1. Special Offers	8	5.33
2. Jingle	84	56.00
3. Unsubstantiated Claim of Nutrition	37	24.67
4. Appeal for Social Acceptance	1	.66
Source Participants Items		
1. Male Children - Live	70	46.67
2. Male Children - Animated	7	4.67
3. Female Children - Live	69	46.00
4. Female Children - Animated	6	4.00
5. Male Teens - Live	20	13.33
6. Male Teens - Animated	1	.66
7. Female Teens - Live	23	15.33
8. Female Teens - Animated	1	.66
9. Male Adult - Live	32	21.33
10. Male Adult - Animated	12	8.00
11. Female Adult - Live	20	13.33
12. Female Adult - Animated	4	2.67
13. Father - Live	1	.66
14. Father - Animated	-	-
15. Mother - Live	1	.66
16. Mother - Animated	-	-
17. Animals - Live	20	13.07
18. Animals - Animated	30	19.61
19. Ficitious Characted - Live	25	16.34
20. Ficitious Character - Animated	26	16.99
Location Items		
1. Home	42	27.63
2. Outdoors	44	28.94
3. School	1	.66
4. Store	1	.66
5. Multiple Setting	29	19.08
6. Imaginary	10	6.57
7. Other	1	.66
8. Undetermined	24	15.78
Food Items		
1. Breakfast Foods	38	24.84
2. Sweets	19	12.42
3. Snacks	1	.66
4. Meal Food	18	9.84
5. Restaurants	17	9.28
Non Food Items		
1. Toys	33	21.56
2. Health Products	3	1.97
3. Public Service Announcements	9	5.88
4. Other	9	5.88

Table 2 concerns the first hypothesis pertaining to the number of males and the number of females appearing in the commercials. As was hypothesized, males outnumbered females by a 2 to 1 ratio. It should be noted that these figures represent the total number of participants in all commercials.

Table 3 reveals that in spite of being outnumbered, females were practically equal to males in terms of dominant roles. This is contrary to the hypothesized

TABLE 2

BREAKDOWN OF PARTICIPANTS BY SEX AND AGE

PARTICIPANTS	NUMBER	% OF TOTAL
Male Child - Live	234	34.1
Male Child - Animated	16	2.3
Male Teen - Live	67	9.8
Male Teen - Animated	6	.8
Male Adult - Live	85	12.4
Male Adult - Animated	22	3.2
MALE TOTALS	430	62.68
Female Child - Live	149	21.7
Female Child - Animated	14	2.0
Female Teen - Live	39	5.7
Female Teen - Animated	5	.7
Female Adult - Live	41	6.0
Female Adult - Animated	8	1.2
FEMALE TOTALS	256	37.32
GRAND TOTALS	686	100.00

results and could be indicative of the increasing importance of females in advertising today. These results, it should be noted, vary dramatically from previous research findings. Another noticeable difference is the number of dominant roles held by both female teens and male adults. There were no differences in dominance between the food and non-food product categories.

TABLE 3

CHARACTER DOMINANCE

CHARACTERS	NUMBER	MALE DOMINANCE	FEMALE DOMINANCE
Male Child Dominance	57	31.1%	
Female Child Dominance	52		28.4%
Male Teen Dominance	8	4.4	
Female Teen Dominance	24		13.1
Male Adult Dominance	29	15.8	
Female Adult Dominance	13		7.2
TOTALS	183	51.3%	48.7

As Table 4 shows, 56 commercials or 37% of all Saturday Morning commercials, contain one or more animated characters. Live characters appeared in 112 commercials or 73% of all Saturday Morning advertising. These figures represent those commercials which include both live and animated characters thus causing the sum of the two categories to be greater than the sample size of 153. In any case, the results are contrary to the hypothesis that animated characters would appear in a majority of Saturday Morning commercials.

Further analysis revealed that of the messages containing animation, the majority advertised food products. In fact, 75% of all animated commercials promoted food items, with breakfast foods accounting for 57% of all animation. By comparison, all food product commercials combined comprised only 59% of the commercials utilizing live characters. Table 4 provides a complete breakdown of the use of live versus animated characters.

CONCLUSIONS AND IMPLICATIONS

The use of Saturday Morning advertising has remained a controversial topic. One area of concern has been the use of male - female roles in childrens' commercials. This study found that males are used almost 2 to 1 over females in children's commercials. However, when viewing dominant

TABLE 4

ANIMATED vs. LIVE CHARACTERS

CATEGORY	Number of Commercials with Animated Characters	PERCENT	Number of Commercials with Live Characters	PERCENT
Breakfast	32	57.1	28	25.0
Sweets	3	5.4	17	15.2
Snacks	1	1.8	1	0.9
Meal Food	6	10.7	7	6.3
Restaurant	0	0.0	14	12.5
Toys	4	7.1	33	29.5
Health	1	1.8	2	1.8
Public Service	7	12.5	1	0.9
Other	2	3.6	9	8.0
TOTAL	56	100 %	112	100 %

speaking roles, the two sexes are virtually equal in number. Thus, although females are not numerically equal, they are even in the number of dominant roles.

A second finding was that animated characters appear in 37% of childrens' commercials. One important aspect is that of these animated commercials 57% appeared in breakfast foods, chiefly comprised of cereals. Animation was also important when public service announcements were aired on Saturday Morning, much more so than live characters. Animation only appeared in 4 of 33 toy commericals, while live characters appeared in all 33 commercials. Thus, animation is being used in over one-third of chilrens' commercials, but appearing primarily in the food and public service industries.

Based on the aforementioned results, several areas avail themselves for future research. These areas include an in-depth analysis of the male and female role models as presented in Saturday Morning commercials. Perhaps some explanation could be put forth to explain the use of male adults and female teenagers in Saturday Morning commercials, since categories had much higher frequencies of appearance than the same age categories of the opposite sex. A second area meriting further investigation involves the incorporation of animated characters into Saturday Morning advertising. Specifically, additional research might attempt to provide some insight into the heavy use of animated characters in breakfast food commercials.

Another topic which confronts marketing practitioners in this area results from changes in the regulatory environment. If, for example, animation is used to avoid addressing salient product issues, then prehaps a move toward increased self-regulation in childrens' advertising is advisable. Since the FTC is no longer considering the regulation of childrens' advertisements, it only seems logical that self-imposed regulations ensure that advertisements directed toward young viewers do not enhance the product solely through "techniques, focuses, and themes."

Finally, comparisons with past studies should be undertaken so as to more accurately assess the trends in Saturday Morning advertising.

REFERENCES

Atkins, Charles (1977), "Research on the Effects of Television Advertising on Children," Report, National Science Foundation.

__________, and Gary Heald (1979), "The Content of Children's Toys and Food Commercials", Journal of Communication, 27 (Winter) pp. 107-114.

Blatt, J. L. (1971), "Children's Reactions to Commercials," Journal of Advertising Research, p. 44.

Bush, Robert P. Alan J. Bush, Joseph F. Hair, Jr., (1981) "Animation in Television Advertising: An Exploratory Analysis," Southeast Aids, (In Press).

Cattin, Phillippe and Subhash C. Jain (1978), "Content Analysis of Children's Commercials" in Neil Bechwith, et al, ad., 1979 Educator's Conference Proceedings, Chicago: American Marketing Association, pp. 639-644.

Donahue, Thomas R., William A. Donahue and Lucy L. Henke (1980), "Do Kids Know What TV Commercials Intend?", Journal of Advertising Research, p. 53.

Doolittle, John and Robert Pepper (1974), "Children's TV Ad Content: 1974," Journal of Broadcasting, 19:2, (Spring 1975).

Federal Register, Vol. 46, No. 67, April 8, 1981, p. 21019.

Gordon, Richard, L. (1979), "Kid Ad Probe Down to Seven Questions," Advertising Age, (August 6).

Harris, Paul (1974), "FTC's Engman Hits Kidvid Ads, Deplores 'Heroes' and Premiums," Variety (June) p. 52.

Kassarjian, Harold H. (1977), "Content Analysis in Consumer Research," Journal of Consumer Research, 4 (June) pp. 8-18.

Reicken, Glen and A. Coskun Samli (1981), "Measuring Children's Attitudes Toward Television Commercials: Extension and Replication," Journal of Consumer Research, Vol. 8, (June), pp. 57-61.

Resnik, Alan J. and Bruce L. Stern (1977), "An Analysis of Information Content in Television Advertising," Journal of Marketing, 41 (January), pp. 50-53.

Rossiter, John R. (1977), "Reliability of a Short Test Measuring Children's Attitudes Toward TV Commercials," Journal of Consumer Research, Vol. 3 No. 4 (March), pp. 179-184.

Scammons, D. L. and C. L. Christopher, "Nutrution Education with Children via Television: A Review," Journal of Advertising, 10, No. 2, pp. 26-36.

Stern, Bruce L. and Alan J. Resnik (1978), "Children's Understanding of a Televised Commercial Disclaimed," in Subhash C. Jain, ed. Research Frontiers in Marketing: Dialogues and Direction, Proceedings of the 1978 Educator's Conference: Chicago: American Maraketing Assoc.

Ward, Scott (1972), "Children's Reaction to Commercials," Journal of Advertising Research, (April), pp. 37-45.

White, Hooper (1981), "How to Liven TV Spots: Animate," Advertising Age, (March) p. 50.

Winick, Charles, Lorne G. Williamson, Stuart F. Chuemir and Mariann Pezzella Winick, (1974), Children's Television Commercials: A Content Analysis, New York: Praeger Special Studies.

Wright, J. S. Warner, D. S., Winter, W. L., and Zeigler, S. K., Advertising, New York: McGraw-Hill, 1977.

____

Note: A list of operational definitions used in this study is available from the authors upon request.

A LABORATORY ANALYSIS OF THE EFFECTIVENESS OF THE
HOST-SELLING COMMERCIAL WHEN USED ON CHILDREN

Joseph H. Miller, Southeastern Louisiana University

ABSTRACT

The National Association of Broadcasters' Code bans the use
of the host-selling commercial. The NAB Code argues that
the host commercial appears to be too effective in encouraging children to select a given product. The American
Federation of Television and Radio Artists argue that the
host-selling rule is unreasonable because it was adopted to
prevent government regulation and to satisfy some of the
critics of this form of advertising. The courts ruled in
favor of the NAB Code even though no research evidence was
available to support either position. This paper presents
some empirical research evidence that questions the decision of the NAB Code which bans the host-selling commercial.

INTRODUCTION

The purpose of this study is to use the host-selling commercial and compare its effectiveness on children who are
familiar with the host and those children who are not.
The host-selling commercial is defined as a commercial in
which the show's personality or star appears in a commercial that is run during his program.

PUBLIC POLICY CONTROVERSY

The National Association of Broadcasters' (NAB) Code pro-
hibits the use of show personalities and stars to advertise
within the same program. Advertisers, advertising agencies, and the screen actors' guild strongly object to the
prohibition of host-selling.

In fact, the American Federation of Television and Radio
Artists (AFTRA) brought legal action against the NAB.
AFTRA sought an injunction barring enforcement of the host-
selling rule. In its suit AFTRA contended that the NAB had
restrained trade--in violation of the Sherman Antitrust
Act. AFTRA argued that the host-selling rule was unreasonable because it was adopted to prevent government regulation and to satisfy some of the critics of this form of
advertising (Broadcasting, January 26, 1976). They also
argued that there was not sufficient evidence to support
that the host-selling commercial is harmful to children.
The critics of host-selling felt that it was too effective
in motivating children to seek the purchase of the product
being promoted by the show personality.

A court decision held that the rule and broadcasters compliance with it do not violate the Sherman Act. The court
ruled that the host-selling rule showed a bona fide concern
for fair and ethical methods to be used in television advertising directed to children, regardless of whether
"scientific" evidence demonstrated actual detriment to
children (Broadcasting, January 26, 1976).

RESEARCH OBJECTIVE

In 1979, Miller and Busch published an article in the
Journal of Marketing Research that dealt with the effects
of different types of commercial formats on motivating
children to seek the selection of the advertised product.
These researchers experimented with three types of commercial formats: straight announcer commercial, host-selling
commercial, and the premium commercial.

In their research experiment, they discovered that there
was no significant difference between the effectiveness of
the host commercial and the announcer commercial. However,
their research efforts raised a very important question
that they did not address, that being, will children who
view the host television program on a regular basis respond
differently from those who do not know the host or view his
television program. (The Miller and Busch research on the
host-selling commercial was conducted on children who were
not familiar with the TV program personality.)

The main research objective of this paper is to compare the
responses of children to the host-selling commercial based
on whether a child is familiar with the host or if the
child is not familiar with the host. The responses of
these children will be measured in three different ways:
attitude towards the advertised product, recall of commercial content, and a behavioral measure (product selection).

These dependent variables are operationalized in the following ways:

1. Attitude towards the advertised product measured on a
    5-point smiling face scale.
2. Recall of the advertisement measured on an 18-item
    questionnaire.
3. A behavioral measure, i.e., selection of the advertised
    versus non-advertised brand.

METHODOLOGY

The experimental treatment--program with the host-selling
commercial--was assigned randomly to ten elementary classes.
Two classes of each grade 1-5 were used in this study. The
research was conducted in two different areas--Hammond,
Louisiana and Memphis, Tennessee. The students in Memphis
were classified as those students who were familiar with
the host since his program is run only in the Memphis area.
The students in Hammond, Louisiana were not familiar with
the host. The sample size consists of 190 children.

In discussions with the teachers and administrative personnel at the schools used in this experiment, it was decided
that the different schools whether located in Memphis or
located in Hammond were very similar based on the standardized test scores of these children.

The students were shown a color video tape presentation of
a children's show--Magicland--into which the host-selling
commercials had been spliced. The same host-selling commercial was shown twice during the program. Two showings
within the same program is the testing procedure used by
Child Research Services, Inc. of New York to test children's television commercials (Laurie 1975). Moreover, the
use of two showings is consistent with the typical advertising practice of repeated showings of ads during the TV
program. Research has shown that increasing the number of
commercials from one to three does not significantly change
either attitude or behavior (Goldbert and Gorn, 1974).

The product category selected for this study was breakfast
cereals. First, breakfast cereals are a common product
consumed by children. Second, cereals constitute a competitive market situation in which interbrand choices are
made. Third, other researchers (e.g., Rubin 1973; Shimp,
Dyer, and Divita 1976) have successfully used breakfast
cereals in studying children's reactions to commercials.

The host-selling commercial used in this research featured a hypothetical breakfast cereal, Canary Crunch. This commercial had to be custom made for the research project. The commercial was spliced into a program tape by professional production personnel at WBRT-TV in Baton Rouge, Louisiana. The professional assistance insured that the program shown to the children was as technically perfect as the TV programs they normally watched. The Magicland program consisted of the following parts: 1) Mr. Magic, the show host or personality, performing magic tricks, 2) a cartoon featuring a hunter and his dog, 3) Mr. Magic sitting in the audience and talking with the children, 4) a Bugs Bunny cartoon, and 5) Mr. Magic performing more magic tricks. The approximate time of the program was 27 minutes.

FINDINGS

Immediately after viewing the program, the students were administered a questionnaire so that the researchers could collect data on the three dependent variables. For ease of presentation, the hypotheses are stated in the null form. The statement of hypotheses is followed by a brief rationale and presentation of findings.

Hypothesis 1

H_o There is no significant difference between the mean attitude scores of children who were familiar with the host and those not familiar with the host when asked for their attitude toward the advertised product.

The attitude scores were obtained by giving each child a five-point "smiling face" scale and asking them to indicate which face showed how he felt toward the advertised product. Table I contains a summary of the mean attitude scores. Results of the t-test performed on these data show familiarity had no significant effect on the respondents' mean attitude scores. The null hypotheses, therefore, is not rejected.

TABLE I

CHILDREN'S MEAN SCORES ON ATTITUDE
TOWARD THE ADVERTISED PRODUCT

	Mean Scores
Familiar with Host	4.279
Not Familiar with Host	4.077
P=.102	

Hypothesis 2

H_o There is no significant difference based on the behavioral responses (i.e., product selection) between the children who are familiar with the host and those who are not familiar with the host.

Hypotheses 2 tests the null hypotheses that there is no significant difference between children's familiarity with the host based on how they responded behaviorally to an advertised product. After the children had viewed the entire program, the researcher told each class that he wanted to present each child with a special gift for letting him take up class time. The researcher told the children that he was going to give each one of them a box of cereal, but he did not know which each child wanted. The researcher showed the children four different boxes of cereal--Fruit Loops, Boo Berries, Kangaroo Hop, and Canary Crunch--and asked each child to select the cereal he would like to receive. Table II indicates the percentage of boys and girls who selected the advertised cereal (Canary Crunch). A test of significance of difference between two proportions was performed on the data. Based on this test of significance, the null hypotheses is not rejected.

TABLE II

THE PERCENTAGE OF CHILDREN WHO
SELECTED THE ADVERTISED CEREAL

	Selected Advertised Cereal	Selected Non-Advertised Cereal
Familiar with Host	39.6%	60.4%
Not Familiar with Host	38.0%	62.0%
P=.864		

Hypothesis 3

H_o There is no significant difference between the mean recall scores of children who are familiar with the host and those who are not familiar with the host.

Hypotheses 3 predicts that there is no significant difference between the mean recall scores of children who are familiar with the host and those not familiar with the host. (The ability of people to recall different elements of commercials is probably the most widely used measure for determining the effectiveness of commercials). This hypotheses concerns the ability of children to recall facts or information from the commercial they viewed. The dependent variable--recall--is operationalized by asking the children to answer 18 questions concerning the commercial they had just seen. The recall measure indicates the number of questions answered correctly. Table III gives the recall mean scores from this experiment. The results of the t-test indicate that familiarity with the host had a significant effect on a child's ability to identify correctly elements contained in a commercial. Based on these results, the researchers reject the null hypotheses.

TABLE III

The Mean Recall Scores of Children
Who Were Familiar and Those Who
Were Not Familiar With the Host

	Mean Scores
Familiar with Host	15.70
Not Familiar with Host	14.66
P=.001	

CONCLUSION

If the ability to recall more elements of a commercial would effect the children's desire for the product (product selection) and his attitude toward the advertised product, then I would say that the NAB is correct in arguing for the elimination of the host-selling commercial on children's program. The question now appears to be -- "should the NAB ban a commercial because it achieves significantly higher recall scores among children who are familiar with the host?"

This paper does not claim to be conclusive research on the subject of the host-selling commercial, but it does hope to stimulate further research on an important public policy question. This paper is significant because it expands the body of knowledge that is available in this subject area.

REFERENCES

Breen, Myles and Jon Powell (1973), "The Relationship
Between Attractiveness and Credibility of Television
Commercials as Perceived by Children," Central States
Speech Journal, 14 (Summer), 97-101.

Broadcasting (January 26, 1976), "Right of NAB Code to
Ban Host-Selling on Children's TV Upheld by Court," 30.

Goldberg, M.E. and G.J. Gorn (1974), "Children's
Reactions to Television Advertising: An Experimental
Approach," Journal of Consumer Research, 1 (September),
60-75.

Griffin, Emilie (1976), "What's Fair to Children? The
Policy Need for New Research on Children's Perceptions
of Advertising Content," Journal of Advertising, 5
(Spring) 15.

Laurie, Liz (1975), "Measuring Commercial Impact,"
The Journal of Advertising Research, 15 (August), 24.

Miller, Joseph H., and Paul Busch (1979), "Host
Selling vs. Premium TV Commercials: An Experimental
Evaluation of Their Influence on Children," Journal of
Marketing Research, Vol. XVI (August), 323.

Shimp, Terrence A., Robert F. Dyer, and Salvatore F.
Divita (1976), "An Experimental Test of the Harmful
Effects of Premium-Oriented Commercials on Children,"
Journal of Consumer Research, 3 (June), 3.

Ward, Scott (1974), "Kids' TV--Marketers on the Hot
Seat," Harvard Business Review (July-August), 23.

MOTHERS' SUPPORT FOR NUTRITION
EDUCATION: A SEGMENTATION ANALYSIS

Lawrence A. Crosby, University of Nebraska, Lincoln
Sanford L. Grossbart, University of Nebraska, Lincoln
Joyce L. Robb, University of Nebraska, Lincoln
Les Carlson, University of Nebraska, Lincoln

ABSTRACT

The promise of nutrition education as a partial solution to the child nutrition problem may depend on the formulation of an effective social marketing strategy that includes parents as targets. A segmentation analysis of mothers of elementary school children indicates that unique patterns of support for the objectives of nutrition education are associated with certain attitudinal and demographic characteristics. The strategy implications of these findings are discussed.

INTRODUCTION

Concern about childrens' nutrition is a multifaceted issue. This concern centers on nutrient deficiencies in children's diets thought to be associated with certain dental, health, and learning problems in childhood (FTC 1978). Also of concern are poor food habits established in childhood that lead to adult health problems (Deutsch 1976). Patterns of improper nutrition develop at an early age (Sims 1971; Caliendo and Sanjur 1978).

Poverty and the high cost of a balanced diet are factors which contribute to poor nutrition. However, the problem goes beyond the inability to purchase healthful foods and touches all segments of society. Other important factors include TV advertising to children (Leaman 1973; Clancy-Hepburn, Hickey and Nevill 1974; Atkin 1975; Robertson and Rossiter 1977), inadequate nutrition knowledge of mothers (Eppright et. al. 1970; Jacoby et. al. 1977; Caliendo and Sanjur 1978), and various aspects of the socio-cultural milieu of the United States (Bauman 1973).

Consequently, governmental response to the child nutrition problem has involved a three pronged attack. Two of these approaches, the school lunch program and the regulation of children's advertising, have been surrounded in controversy. A third approach, that of nutrition education in the schools, has been critized for a lack of effectiveness (Richmond 1977).

The Child Nutrition Act of 1966 set standards for school meals and helped states to provide a nutritious lunch and breakfast at school. While possibly benefiting all students, these programs were aimed primarily at the disadvantaged on the assumption that poverty contributes to poor nutrition which contributes to poor school performance. The major controversy over the school lunch program has been its cost (about $2.9 billion in 1979). The Reagan Administration significantly curtailed these expenditures in 1981.

In the area of children's advertising, the Federal Trade Commission brought cases against advertisers throughout the 1970's (Ward 1978). These activities culminated in a proposed ban on certain types of food commercials and the airing of nutritional messages at industry expense (FTC 1978). The proposal triggered a political storm and was withdrawn by the FTC in 1981 after being labelled "impractical."

In 1973, the Senate Select Committee on Nutrition and Human Needs heard testimony on nutrition education. The committee recommended nutrition education for all people as part of a national nutrition policy (U.S. Senate

1974). A 1975 amendment to the Child Nutrition Act provided the states with funds to develop and administer their own nutrition education programs in the schools (U.S. Senate 1975). In 1977, Congress once again amended the Child Nutrition Act thereby authorizing the Nutrition Education and Training Program or N.E.T. Program (P.L. 95-166). This amendment gave states the necessary support to present to school children "scientifically valid information about foods and nutrients...imparted in a manner that individuals receiving such information will understand the principles of nutrition and seek to maximize their well being through food consumption practices." These programs were also cutback by the Reagan Administration in 1981.

THE CASE FOR NUTRITION EDUCATION

Regardless of funding difficulties, of the three approaches to improving the nutrition of children, nutrition education may well be the most encompassing solution. Obviously, nutrition education cannot eliminate the poverty which adversely effects some children's diets. It may, however, help parents obtain the highest nutrition value for their food consumption dollar. Nutrition education cannot reduce the volume of TV food advertising aimed at children or change advertisers' promotional tactics. It may, however, provide children with necessary cognitive defenses to effectively process commercial information. Nutrition education would seem to offer considerable potential (White 1976) for raising the level of nutrition knowledge and improving consumers' understanding of the factors which influence their food choices.

Ward (1978) argues for nutrition education as a compromise solution to the "kidvid" controversy. He envisions industry and government sponsoring school based instructional programs that would teach children how to not only evaluate commercials and foods but also establish good diets. Ward correctly notes that schools would have to buy curriculum materials and textbooks on nutrition, and favors corporate sponsorship of curriculum innovations.

CAVEATS ABOUT NUTRITION EDUCATION

Certain problems are likely to be encountered when implementing school based nutrition programs. Nutrition, being a socially desirable concept, is likely to receive at least a superficial endorsement by most people. However, when it comes to actually implementing comprehensive curriculum programs in elementary schools (where real costs in terms of money, time, and effort are experienced) support for the concept is likely to wane. Sponsoring corporations may become concerned about the competitive effects of the education. Teachers may resent having to alter teaching plans, learn a new subject matter, and fit another module into the day. School administrators may balk at the financial expense. Parents may become concerned that the nutritional education is supplanting instruction in more traditional subjects and wonder about the effects of the program on next year's millage assessment. Mothers may resent being asked to modify their food purchasing and preparation practices; certainly, they would resent any implication about inadequate role performance.

These forms of resistance parallel those encountered when marketing any new product. In general, resistance to an innovation is most pronounced when risk is involved and old ways of thinking and acting are deeply ingrained and habitual (Sheth 1979). Nutrition education clearly involves a major change in beliefs, attitudes, and behavior.

SOCIAL MARKETING PERSEPCTIVE

Theory suggests that to gain acceptance of nutrition education as rapidly and efficiently as possible, marketing strategies should concentrate on key target markets. Gaining acceptance of this innovation would seem to involve "social marketing," the application of traditional marketing and diffusion concepts to the design of strategies for bringing about social change (Kotler and Zaltman 1971; Fox and Kotler 1980). The social idea or "core" product in this instance is nutrition while the tangible counterparts are the curriculum innovations themselves. The need for social marketing in the area of nutrition has been previously discussed by Fine (1980).

MOTHERS AS A KEY TARGET MARKET

The key to successfully marketing nutrition education is to recognize the role of parents. Parents exert considerable influence on curriculum matters and ultimately control the level of school funding. They provide the home environment where school lessons are (hopefully) reinforced and practiced. Mothers control the child's opportunities: to try new foods, to consume a varied and balanced diet, to assist in meal planning, and to help select and prepare foods. Without these opportunities it is very difficult to have an effective nutritional education program (Grossbart, Crosby, and Robb 1982).

We need to know how mothers view nutrition eduation because of their pivotal role in their childrens' development. However, experience in social marketing suggests that mothers' opinions about this concept are likely to be somewhat heterogeneous. Therefore we need to identify subgroups (or segments) of mothers with similar response tendencies toward the innovation. Then social marketing strategies could be devised, tailored to the needs and perceptions of these segments, that would present nutrition education in its most favorable light. The need for a segmentation perspective in the area of nutrition education has been noted (Fleming and Brown 1981; Richmond 1977; Baird and Schutz 1976).

THE STUDY

A segmentation analysis of mothers was undertaken to answer a few key questions: are there identifiable segments of mothers with similar views about nutrition education in the schools? Which objectives of nutrition education do these segments endorse and which do they oppose? What are the roots of maternal support or opposition to nutrition education? Canonical analysis was used to identify patterns of response to question items that seemed to represent groups of mothers with similar attitudes, demographics, and views about nutrition education.

The Sample

Data for the analysis were obtained from a survey of mothers of elementary school children. Eleven Nebraska schools were selected to provide a cross section of communities in the state and included urban, suburban, and rural areas. The self-administered questionnaires were distributed through the schools. The 644 returned questionnaires represented a 50% response rate. The analysis was based on a subsample of 536 cases with complete data on all variables. Cases were approximately evenly distributed by grade level of the child.

The Measures

Dependent Variables. Mothers' reactions to the four main objectives of an education program called "Experience Nutrition" served as a multivariate dependent variable in this analysis. The program was developed as a cooperative effort by the Nebraska Department of Education, Experience Education, and the Swanson Center for Nutrition, Inc., with N.E.T. Program Funds. Objectives of the program include (a) discussing food and nutrition as part of the child's education, (b) getting children to try foods they don't normally eat, (c) developing the child's understanding of what influences his or her food choices including friends, tradition, and advertising, and (d) developing more positive feelings about school lunches. Mothers were asked to indicate the extent of their agreement with each of the objectives on a five-point scale (where 1 = strongly disagree and 5 = strongly agree).

Independent Variables. Concern about children's food advertising was thought to be one of the parental attitudinal factors that might underlie a perceived need for nutrition education, especially in the area of developing children's understanding of what influences their food choices. As noted, children's food advertising is a controversial issue which has spurred government involvement in nutrition. There is also evidence indicating that children's advertising is a source of major concern to many parents (e.g. Clancy-Hepburn, Hickey, and Nevill 1974; Ward, Wackman, and Wartella 1975; Burr and Burr 1976). However, critical parents are not necessarily activists and do not necessarily support controls for advertising (Feldman, Wolf, and Warmouth 1977). This suggests that nutrition education would be an attractive alternative to these individuals. Parents who are unconcerned about children's advertising could react with indifference toward school based attempts to build children's cognitive defenses. Alternately, unconcerned parents might oppose nutrition education as unwanted interference in the child's psychological development. Concern about children's food advertising was measured with a six item CHILDAD scale (Crosby and Grossbart 1981) having a coefficient alpha reliability of .813. Higher scores indicate more concern.

The mother's attitude toward nutrition seemed to be another potentially useful predictor of support for nutrition education, particularly the aspect of discussing food and nutrition as part of the child's education. Presumably, mothers who value health and nutrition highly wish to socialize their children in a similar manner. Mothers are not likely to perceive this as an easy task, because of peer and media influence. It is understandable that such parents would seek assistance from the schools in legitimizing their views with their children. Whether nutritionally oriented mothers would endorse all the objectives of nutrition education is unclear, although this information would help to define the roles of parents and schools in this aspect of socialization. For mothers who are not nutritionally oriented, the question is how to best "position" nutrition education so as to minimize any perceived threat to their self esteem while emphasizing whatever tangental benefits may exist. In this study, the mother's attitude toward nutrition was measured with a reduced version of the ATN scale (Eppright et. al. 1970) having six items and a coefficient alpha reliability of .775. Higher scores indicate a more positive attitude.

From the teaching of evolution to sex education, the public school curriculum has always been the source of some controversy. In the late 1960's through the 1970's, schools were under pressure to expand their programs in response to changes occurring in society. Increased emphasis on contemporary subjects coupled with a purported decline in basic skills and a documented decline in S.A.T. scores led to charges that schools were no longer fulfilling their responsibility. Given this history, the possibility exists that a strong negative reaction may be provoked if schools incorporate yet another non-traditional subject into the curriculum. At a time when schools are under severe financial pressure and are attempting to adopt a more conservative posture introduction of a nontraditional subject such as nutritional education may not be expedient. To ascertain how mothers felt about nontraditional curricula, they were asked to indicate the extent of their agreement with the importance of teaching nontraditional subjects in school. This variable, denoted NONTRAD, was coded on the continuum 1 = strongly disagree and 5 = strongly agree.

Demographic variables were included to increase segment identifiability. Demographics included the mother's and father's educational level (MOMED and DADED). It was expected that educated parents would be more sensitive to the need for proper nutrition (Phillips, Bass and Yetley 1978; Sims 1976; Eppright et. al. 1970), more concerned about children's advertising (Rossiter and Robertson 1974; Robertson and Rossiter 1977; Barry 1975), and more likely to endorse educational solutions. The number of children in the family (CHILDREN) was included as socialization is more difficult in larger families, leading mothers to seek the school's assistance. Also, providing a healthful diet may be more difficult in larger families for economic and logistical reasons. Assuming mothers would endorse educational objectives in accordance with their perception of the child's stage of development (Ward 1978), the child's grade in school (GRADE) was also used. Dummy variables represented a classification of the father's occupation (FARM/NON-FARM, WHITE/BLUE). Farm mothers tend to be more knowledgeable about nutrition and better able to apply nutrition concepts (Eppright et. al. 1970); however, they may have more traditional educational preferences. Social status associated with urban occupations provides another indication of educational values and is related to nutritional orientation (Sims 1976). Another dummy variable was used to represent the mother's working status (WORKMOM). Theoretically, working mothers would seem to need the school's assistance in socialization and in monitoring and regulating their child's diet.

RESULTS AND INTERPRETATION

Variable means, standard deviations, and intercorrelations are presented in Table 1. Table 2 summarizes the canonical results with the largest loadings underlined. Three canonical variates linking the set of dependent to the set of independent variables were found to be significant ($p<.05$). Canonical correlations were .66, .26, and .18 respectively. Redundancy in the criterion set given the predictor set was .28 which is somewhat higher than other canonical applications in marketing (e.g. Shaninger, Lessig, and Panton 1980; Alpert and Peterson 1971).

The first root indicates that mothers who endorse all the objectives of nutrition education believe more in non-traditional education, have a more positive attitude toward nutrition, and express more concern about children's food advertising. Among the predictors, acceptance of non-traditional education is most strongly associated with the first canonical root. Reversing the signs indicates resistance to nutrition education is likely to come from mothers who are less supportive of non-traditional education, less nutritionally oriented, and less concerned about children's food advertising. None of the demographic variables were associated with this generalized acceptance or rejection of nutrition education.

The second canonical root indicates that some mothers have a more differentiated opinion about nutrition education that is related to a unique pattern of attitudes and demographics. Interpreting the loadings, it appears that non-working, farm mothers with a more positive attitude toward nutrition would support an instructional program that discusses food and nutrition

Table 1
Variable Descriptions and Intercorrelations

	Descriptive Stats						Intercorrelations								
---	---	---	---	---	---	---	---	---	---	---	---	---	DISCUSS FOOD & NUTRITION	TRY NEW FOODS	UNDER-STAND INFLUENCES
	Mean	SD	DADED	MOMED	CHILDREN	WORKMOM	FARM	WHITE	CHILDAD	ATN	NONTRAD	GRADE			
DADED	4.13	1.58													
MOMED	4.12	1.39	.48*												
CHILDREN	2.97	1.21	.06	.02											
WORKMOM	1.48	.56	.03	.11*	-.10*										
FARM	.34	.47	.13*	.00	.03		-.13*								
WHITE	.34	.47	.41*	.24*	.08		.11*	-.52*							
CHILDAD	22.70	3.70	.05	.00	.06	-.02	.00	-.02							
ATN	26.10	2.39	.19*	.19*	.02	.00	.08	.12*	.28*						
NONTRAD	4.20	.70	.00	-.01	-.02	.13*	-.13*	.01	.09*	.17*					
CLASS	3.01	2.00	-.11*	-.09*	.06	.02	.12*	-.14*	-.02	-1.2*	-.06				
DISCUSS FOOD & NUTRITION	4.24	.53	.02	.08	.02	.00	-.04	-.03	.20*	.35*	.05*	-.11*			
TRY NEW FOODS	4.13	.73	-.05	.03	-.01	.07	-.14*	-.02	.20*	.21*	.50*	-.10*	.56*		
UNDERSTAND INFLUENCES	3.91	.77	-.03	.14*	.02	.11*	-.11*	.02	.20*	.16*	.44*	.05	.40*	.58*	
LIKE SCHOOL LUNCH	3.94	.74	-.07	.03	.03	.10*	-.08	-.03	.10*	.09*	.43*	-.06	.37*	.59*	.63*

*p<.05

Table 2

RELATIONSHIPS BETWEEN VARIABLES AND SIGNIFICANT CANONICAL FUNCTIONS

	Canonical Loadings		
Variables	Root 1	Root 2	Root 3
Nutrition Education Objectives	Criterion Set		
Discuss food and nutrition	.87	.49	.03
Try new foods	.83	-.24	-.26
Understand influences	.74	-.55	.36
Like school lunch	.66	-.44	-.46
Attitudes	Predictor Set		
Advertising concern (CHILDAD)	.36	-.05	.44
Nutrition attitude (ATN)	.47	.66	.36
Non-traditional education (NONTRAD)	.90	-.10	-.28
Demographics			
Mother's education (MOMED)	.15	-.09	.73
Father's education (DADED)	-.02	.29	.30
Number of children (CHILDREN)	.02	.03	.00
Child's grade (GRADE)	-.17	-.15	.19
Father's occupation (FARM/NON-FARM)	-.16	.34	.04
(WHITE/BLUE)	-.03	-.10	.33
Mother's work status (WORKMOM)	.09	-.44	.01

but does not delve into food choice influences or promote
the school lunch. In this case, a reversal of the signs
does not facilitate interpretation.

The third canonical root seems to represent another group
of mothers who would also prefer to see a more limited
role for nutrition education. The results suggest an
upscale segment of mothers who are better educated, more
concerned about children's advertising and nutrition, and
have better educated husbands who tend to be employed in
white collar jobs. This pattern of association in the
predictors is linked to an endorsement of nutrition
education that helps children understand what influences
their food choices but does not promote school lunch.
The complement of this profile is a segment of lower
educated, working class mothers who are less
nutritionally oriented, less concerned about advertising,
but feel schools could do more to encourage children to
eat school lunch.

DISCUSSION

Overall, the results support the argument that proponents
of nutrition education should take a segmentation
perspective in attempting to market nutrition
education. Mothers' opinions about nutrition education
are neither uniform nor associated with a common set of
maternal characteristics. The aspects of nutrition
education which appeal to one segment may displease
others. Clearly, delivering the same nutrition
information to all groups of mothers would be a mistake.

The generalized responses of the first variate, coupled
with a lack of identifiable demographic characteristics,
may represent a formidable marketing challenge.
Designing and promoting a program that encompasses all
four objectives and has all the appearances of a major
curriculum innovation could be highly appealing to
staunch supporters while alienating everyone else. A
better positioning strategy might de-emphasize the
nontraditional aspects of nutrition education. Staunch
supporters would still find nutrition education appealing
since it addresses their concerns about children's
advertising and reinforces their nutrition socialization
efforts. At the same time, one of the strongest reasons
for opposing nutrition education is eliminated. A
strategy of this type would attempt to integrate
nutrition into the regular classroom subjects and
position nutrition education as an applications area that
reinforces basic knowledge.

The second canonical variate suggests a marketing
strategy for rural areas. This strategy should stress
the contribution of nutrition education to the child's
cognitive knowledge about food and nutrition while de-
emphasizing the children's advertising issue and school
lunch aspects. While this root implies less aversion to
nontraditional education, a more conservative positioning
of nutrition education is again indicated. The
dissemination of cognitive knowledge is, after all, the
traditional goal of education; therefore this strategy
should be appealing given the traditional value
orientation of the rural segment. Perhaps this segment's
interest in nutrition is related to their agricultural,
food production activities and therefore such knowledge
has economic utility for them.

The need to counter the influence of advertising would
appear to be an effective appeal in marketing nutrition
education to an upscale segment. This group recognizes a
need to build the child's cognitive defenses. This need
could be a result of either exposure to news sources or
as a result of child rearing styles that could involve a
heightened sensitivity to socialization influences. In
contrast, the strategy for the downscale, blue collar
segment would involve emphasizing the behavioral impact
of nutrition education especially as it relates to eating
school lunch.

An important limitation of these findings needs to be
recognized. This analysis has shown that there are
measurable segments of mothers, to whom nutrition
education might be marketed; and that some of these
segments are _accessible_ given their demographic
characteristics. What remains to be shown, however, is
that these segments are _substantial_ enough to justify a
tailored version of the marketing strategy. Also, the
polarization of opinion needs to be analyzed further to
ascertain whether there are segments who are not just
indifferent but actually hostile to nutrition
education. Additional research is currently underway,
using different analytical approaches, that will attempt
to answer these questions.

These findings have several public policy implications.
First, an all encompassing aggregated approach to
marketing nutrition education is probably not the most
efficient strategy. These results indicate existence of
population segments who hold differing beliefs regarding
attributes of a nutrition program. An aggregated
strategy, while meeting the needs and expectations of one
segment may alienate another. Disaggregated tailoring of
nutrition education to the needs and expectations of
specific population segments may ultimately increase the
acceptance of the program across the population.

A second broader implication is the effect a segmented
population may have on program evaluation. With
decreasing availability of funding, programming of all
types is likely to be required to become increasingly
accountable. Program evaluation may be confounded
because the unique influence of one segement has skewed
the results in an unnatural manner. Ignoring
segmentation effects by over-sampling from one group
could lead to unrepresentative results. Thus _before_
program evaluation begins evaluators would be _well_
advised to become familiar with the segments in a
location, their relative size, and the influence a
particular segment is likely to exert on the results.

REFERENCES

Alpert, Mark I. and Robert A. Peterson (1971), "On the Interpretation of Canonical Analysis," Journal of Marketing Research, 8, 67-70.

Atkin, Charles K. (1975), "The Effects of Television Advertising on Children: Summary Abstracts of Eight Research Investigations," Michigan State University.

Baird, Pamela C. and Howard G. Schutz (1976), "The Marketing Concept Applied to 'Selling' Good Nutrition," Journal of Nutrition Education, 8 (1), 13-17.

Barry, Thomas E. (1975), "Black Mothers Attitudes Towards Television Advertising," working paper, Southern Methodist University.

Bauman, Howard E. (1973), "What Does the Consumer Know About Nutrition," Journal of the American Medical Association, 225 (1), 61-2.

Burr, Pat L., and Richard M. Burr (1976), "Television Advertising to Children: What Parents Are Saying About Government Control," Journal of Advertising, 5 (4), 37-41.

Caliendo, Mary Alice, and Diva Sanjur (1978), "The Dietary Status of Preschool Children: An Ecological Approach," Journal of Nutrition Education, 10 (2), 69-72.

Clancy-Hepburn, Katherine, Anthony A. Hicky and Gayle Nevill (1974), "Children's Behavior Responses to TV Food Advertisements," Journal of Nutrition Education, 6, 93-96.

Crosby, Lawrence A. and Sanford L. Grossbart (1981), "Parental Concern About Child-Directed Advertising: Myth and Reality," in 1981 Educators' Conference Proceedings, Kenneth Bernhardt et al., eds., Chicago: American Marketing Association, 225-8.

Deutsch, Ronald M. (1976), Realities of Nutrition, Palo Alto, California: Bull Publishing Co.

Eppright, Ercel S., Hazel M. Fox, Beth A. Fryer, Glenna H. Lamkin, and Virginia M. Vivian (1970), "Nutrition Knowledge and Attitudes of Mothers," Journal of Home Economics, 62 (5), 327-332.

Federal Trade Commission (1978), "Staff Report on Television Advertising to Children," Office of Public Records, Federal Trade Commission, Washington, D.C.

Feldman, Shel, Abraham Wolf, and Doris Warmouth (1977), "Parental Concern About Child-Directed Commercials," Journal of Communication, 27, 125-37.

Fine, S. (1980), "Toward a Theory of Segmentation by Objectives in Social Marketing," Journal of Consumer Research, 7 (June), 1-13.

Fleming, Phyllis L. and Judith E. Brown (1981), "Using Marketing Research Approaches in Nutrition Education," Journal of Nutrition Education, 13 (1), 4-5.

Fox, Karen F. A., and Philip Kotler (1980), "The Marketing of Social Causes: The First 10 Years," Journal of Marketing, 44, 24-33.

Grossbart, Sanford, Lawrence Crosby and Joyce Robb (1982), "Parental Diffusion Roles and Children's Responses to Nutritional Education," in 1982 Educators' Conference Proceedings, Bruce J. Walker et. al., eds., Chicago: American Marketing Association.

Jacoby, Jacob, Robert W. Chestnut, and William Silberman (1977), "Consumer Use and Comprehension of Nutrition Information," Journal of Consumer Research, 4 (September), 119-28.

Kotler, Phillip, and Gerald Zaltman (1971), "Social Marketing: An Approach to Planned Social Change," Journal of Marketing, 35 (July), 3-12.

Leaman, F. A. (1973), "Nutrition: Television's Fruitless Image. A Cultivation Analysis of Children's Nutritional Knowledge and Behavior," Master's Thesis, Annenberg School of Communications, University of Pennsylvania.

Phillips, Doris E., Mary Ann Bass, and Elizabeth Yetley (1978), "Use of Food and Nutrition Knowledge by Mothers of Preschool Children," Journal of Nutrition Education, 10 (2), 73-75.

Richmond, Frederick W. (1977), "The Role of the Federal Government in Nutrition Education," Journal of Nutrition Education, 9 (4), 150-51.

Robertson, Thomas S. and John R. Rossiter (1977), "Children's Responsiveness to Commercials," Journal of Communication, 27 (1), 101-6.

Rossiter, John R. and Thomas S. Robertson (1974), "Children's TV Commercials: Testing the Defenses," Journal of Communication, (Autumn), 137-44.

Schaninger, Charles M., V. Parker Lessig, and Don B. Panton (1980), "The Complementary Use of Multivariate Procedures to Investigate Nonlinear and Interactive Relationships Between Personality and Product Usage," Journal of Marketing Research, 17, 119-124.

Sheth, Jagdish N. (1979), "Psychology of Innovation Resistance: The Less Developed Concept (LDC) in Diffusion Research," Working Paper No. 622, College of Commerce and Business Administration, University of Illinois.

Sims, Laura S. (1976), "Demographic and Attitudinal Correlates of Nutrition Knowledge," Journal of Nutrition Education, 8 (3), 122-125.

Sims, Laura S. (1971), "Nutritional Status of Preschool Children in Relation to Selected Factors Characterizing the Family Environment: An Ecological Approach," Unpublished thesis, Michigan State University.

U. S. Congress Child Nutrition Act Amendments of 1975, P. L. 94-105, 89 Stat. 528, October 7, 1975.

U. S. Senate Subpanel on Popular Nutrition Education of the Panel on Nutrition and The Consumer to the Select Committee on Nutrition and Human Needs. National Nutrition Policy Study: Report and Recommendations V, 93rd Congress, 2nd Session 1974.

Ward, Scott (1978), "Compromise in Commercials for Children," Harvard Business Review, 56 (6), 128-36.

Ward, Scott, D. B. Wackman and Ellen Wartella (1975), "Contributions of Cognitive Development Theory to Consumer Socialization Research," paper presented to the Association for Consumer Research, October.

White, Phillip L. (1976), "Why All the Fuss Over Nutrition Education?," Journal of Nutrition Education, 8 (2), 54.

Chicago: American Marketing Association.

CANONICAL CORRELATION: IS IT EVER USEFUL?

J. K. Johansson, University of Washington, Seattle
R. P. Bagozzi, Massachusetts Institute of Technology, Cambridge
Jagdish N. Sheth, University of Illinois, Champaign

ABSTRACT

Canonical analysis should be replaced by more informative techniques. The paper shows where redundancy analysis might be appropriate and where simultaneous equation systems are preferable. The role of the general linear model is briefly touched upon.

INTRODUCTION

The interpretation and use of canonical correlation has always been a difficult topic. Much has been written about the problems involved, but the constructive proposals have mostly been very guarded (Alpert and Peterson 1972, Cliff and Krus 1976, Johansson and Sheth 1977, Lambert and Durand 1975). This research note attempts to deal with the issue by identifying the cases where canonical correlation might be useful, and, in particular, by offering some guidelines as to when canonical correlation should be avoided in favor of other techniques.

A common distinction in multivariate analysis is between multiple indicator models and multiple dependent variables ("true" multivariate) models (Blalock 1971, pp. 295-298). In the former case the underlying substantive theory is couched in terms of one dependent variable with multiple operationalizations (indicators), whereas the second case is explicitly concerned with several dependent (endogenous) variables. Canonical correlation can be (and has been) employed in both instances, but our argument differs depending upon the conceptualization employed. The two cases will be discussed in order.

MULTIPLE INDICATOR MODELS

Although relatively rare in marketing research, canonical correlation could be applied in a setting where there are multiple indicators of one single dependent variable. One example is provided by Perry and Hamm (1969), who developed two measures of an individual's perception of "socioeconomic risk" and related the two variables to socioeconomic predictors using canonical correlation. An example outside marketing is provided by Van Valey (1971), where canonical correlation is employed to relate three measures of "urbanization" to three measures of "industrialization."

In the multiple indicator cases, canonical correlation is useful basically as a data reduction technique. The aim of the analysis tends to be the derivation of a single composite index summarizing the variations in the multiple operationalizations of the single theoretical construct under analysis. Of interest is, therefore, the first canonical variates alone; and where more than one canonical root is significant, the validity of the indicators is thrown into question.[1]

In developing the composite index, canonical correlation will, in general, produce a (first) linear combination of the Y-variables which correlates maximally with a linear

combination of the X-variables. As is well known, these linear combinations may or may not explain significant amounts of the variation in the original variables (Alpert and Peterson 1972). In the context of multiple indicators, this means that the composite index might not pick up very much of the variation in the chosen indicators as a function of the predictors. This is clearly an undesirable feature of canonical correlation. The recent development of an alternative to canonical correlation called redundancy analysis might provide a solution to this problem, however. The use of the redundancy index as a measure of explanatory power in canonical analysis is well documented in marketing (Alpert and Peterson 1975, Lambert and Durand 1975). A highly ingenious reformulation of the index into an operational objective function making it possible to bypass canonical correlation completely has been presented by Wollenberg (1977).

Redundancy analysis derives successively orthogonal variates of the predictors X which maximize the variance explained among the criteria Y. Starting with the objective of maximizing redundancy, Wollenberg shows how the redundancy of Y given the i'th X-variate $\hat{x}_i$ can be written:

$$R_{y_i} = \frac{1}{m_y} \mu_i f_{y\hat{y}_i}{}' f_{y\hat{y}_i} \mu_i \tag{1}$$

$$= \frac{1}{m_y} \mu_i v_i{}' R_{yy} R_{yy} v_i \mu_i \, ,$$

where m_y stands for the number of criteria, μ_i is the i'th canonical correlation, and $f_{y\hat{y}_i}{}' = v_i{}' R_{yy}$ is the vector of loadings of the variables in Y on their i'th canonical variate, v_i being the vector of the i'th Y-weights. By construction of the canonical variates, we know (Anderson 1958, p. 291)

$$R_{yx} w = \mu R_{yy} v \, . \tag{2}$$

Therefore, by substituting,

$$R_{y_i} = \frac{1}{m_y} f_{y\hat{x}_i}{}' f_{y\hat{x}_i} \, , \tag{3}$$

where $f_{y\hat{x}_i}{}' = w_i{}' R_{xy}$ is the vector of loadings of the Y variables on the i'th canonical variate of the predictors X, w_i representing the vector of the i'th X-weights.

Under the usual normalization constraint the Lagrangian can be written as

$$L = w' R_{xy} R_{yx} w - \mu(w' R_{xx} w - 1) \, . \tag{4}$$

Setting the partial derivative equal to zero produces

$$\partial L/\partial x = R_{xy} R_{yx} w - \mu R_{xx} w = 0 \, , \tag{5}$$

which translates into the general characteristic equations

$$(R_{xy} R_{yx} - \mu R_{xx}) w = 0 \, . \tag{6}$$

---

[1] In the applications mentioned, this problem is not discussed. It is faced squarely in the comprehensive formulation of the general linear model (c.f., Bagozzi 1980).

As a result, the redundancy of the criteria Y given the predictors X can be maximized without need for any canonical components of the Y's. Only the X-variates are necessary, and Wollenberg shows how these optimal X-variates differ from the variates derived through canonical correlation.

The argument in favor of redundancy analysis over canonical correlation rests simply on the fact that the variates are derived so as to directly maximize the variance explained among the chosen indicators, whereas canonical correlation maximizes a linear combination of the criterion variables.[2] In fact, in parallel with the general linear model, redundancy analysis avoids an explicit derivation of the indicators, dealing instead directly with the original measures (Bagozzi 1977, p. 217).[3]

MULTIPLE DEPENDENT VARIABLES

For the multiple indicator case, we have argued that the use of redundancy analysis might be an alternative to canonical correlation, which uses the indicators more effectively. For the more common case of multiple dependent variables (the "true" multi-variate case, as it were), we will likewise show that there are existing techniques which can yield as much or more information as canonical correlation.[4] To demonstrate this it will be useful to begin with the relationship between canonical correlation and multiple regression.

Canonical Correlation and Multiple Regression

Assume we deal with two dependent or criterion variables, y_1 and y_2, and three independent or predictor variables, x_1, x_2 and x_3.[5] These variables are all standardized with mean 0 and variance 1.

In canonical correlation we correlate a linear compound of the criterion variables with a linear compound of the predictors. These canonical correlations can be seen as regression coefficients provided the linear compounds are appropriately standardized. We know that the variables entering each compound are standardized. Accordingly, the means of the compounds will all be zero: Any linear combination of variables with mean zero will itself have a mean of zero. As for the variance, we would need a standardi-

---

[2] It might be worthwhile to point out that total redundancy is independent of rotation; hence, if one is testing the general ability of a battery of variables to predict variations in a set of multiple indicators (or even multiple constructs with multiple dependent variables), canonical analysis provides the same estimate of redundancy as does redundancy analysis. The superiority of redundancy analysis is that the typical researcher is only going to interpret the "significant" roots, and these should be extracted in such a way as to maximize the explained variation at each stage. Redundancy analysis does this, but canonical correlation might not and generally will not do so.

[3] Where a composite index is desirable, several alternative solutions are possible. One suggested by Wollenberg (1977, p. 210) is the use of the Y-variate derived through a reverse redundancy analysis of the predictors upon the criteria. Another alternative would be the derivation of the weights defining the index from a least square estimate of the coefficients in a regression of the first X-variate upon the Y-variables (Johansson 1981).

[4] For empirical studies in this category, see, for example, Farley and Ring (1974), Kernan (1968), and Sparks and Tucker (1971).

[5] The discussion that follows is directly generalizable to the case of p predictors and c criteria, $p \geq c$.

---

zation that will ensure a variance of 1. This is the standardization $a'R_{yy}a = 1$ imposed in canonical correlation.[6]

Accordingly, we can write the canonical correlation analysis as the following system of equations:

$$a_{11}y_1 + a_{21}y_2 = c_1(b_{11}x_1 + b_{21}x_2 + b_{31}x_3) + u_1$$

$$a_{12}y_1 + a_{22}y_2 = c_2(b_{12}x_1 + b_{22}x_2 + b_{32}x_3) + u_2 , \qquad (7)$$

where the $a_{i,j}$ and $b_{k,j}$, i, j = 1, 2, and k = 1, 2, 3, stand for the weights or loadings of the variables on the respective compound, and where c_i are the canonical correlations, here equal to the regression coefficients (because of the standardization, the intercepts are, of course, zero). The u_i are random disturbances with zero means and constant variances. Their covariance is zero. Define the following matrices and vectors as

$$A' = \begin{bmatrix} a_{11} & a_{21} \\ a_{12} & a_{22} \end{bmatrix}, \quad C = \begin{bmatrix} c_1 & 0 \\ 0 & c_2 \end{bmatrix}, \quad B' = \begin{bmatrix} b_{11} & b_{21} & b_{31} \\ b_{12} & b_{22} & b_{32} \end{bmatrix},$$

$$y' = \begin{bmatrix} y_1 \\ y_2 \end{bmatrix}, \quad x' = \begin{bmatrix} x_1 \\ x_2 \\ x_3 \end{bmatrix}, \quad u' = \begin{bmatrix} u_1 \\ u_2 \end{bmatrix}. \qquad (8)$$

(In estimation, the element x_1, for example, will be a column vector of observations on the first independent variable.) We can now write (7) as

$$yA = xBC + u \qquad (9)$$

so that y can be expressed as

$$y = xBCA^{-1} + uA^{-1} \qquad (10)$$

provided A^{-1} exists. But the rows of A correspond to the eigenvectors relating to each successive eigenvalue or canonical correlation.[7] Thus, A will always be nonsingular and its inverse exists.

Canonical Correlation and Simultaneous Equation System

From this development it is easy to see that canonical correlation can also be viewed as a case of simultaneous equation systems (Hannan 1967). Rewriting (9) as

$$yA - xBC - u = 0 , \qquad (11)$$

we obtain the standard version of the structural form of a simultaneous equation system (Goldberger 1964, Chapter 7). Then (10) can be seen as the reduced form of the system:

$$y = xBCA^{-1} + uA^{-1} .$$

Our basic argument in this context of multiple dependent variables is that the correspondence between canonical

---

[6] It should be emphasized that with a different normalization rule (e.g., $a'a = 1$ as in principal component analysis) the canonical analysis cannot be written as in (7). The simple correlation and regression coefficients are identical if and only if the variables have means of zero and variances equal to one.

[7] These eigenvectors are not normalized to unit length—the standardization used is the one ensuring unit variance—and thus the A matrix is not orthogonal.

correlation and simultaneous systems should be used explicitly. Stated bluntly, we think one should approach canonical correlation as a special case of simultaneous systems.
Even further, canonical correlation should not be considered until an "honest" attempt has been made to specify the
linkages between the endogenous variables on the basis of
a priori theory. The "lack of assumptions" justification
sometimes used as a rationale to favor canonical correlation is a straw-man argument and can be highly misleading.
To see why, the identification issue will be used as an
illustration.

The identification problem refers to whether distinct estimates can be derived for the parameters in (11). If we
remember that the system in (11) embodies the equations in
(7), it is clear that this is not possible. The second
equation in (7) incorporates exactly the same variables as
the first one, so that a host of linear combinations (with
at least one non-zero element) of the first equation will
be observationally indistinguishable from the second equation.

An illustration of the problem can be given with reference
to the reduced form of the system. Clearly, ordinary
least squares can be applied to the reduced form written
in (10). In this way six parameter estimates can be generated (one for each of the x-variables in each of the two
equations). As can be seen from (7), however, the number
of parameters amounts to four a's, and two c's in addition
to the six b's. Accordingly, from the reduced form estimates we cannot derive the structural form parameter esti-
mates--they are underidentified.

We need six additional independent relationships between
the parameters in order to derive the desired estimates.
These identifying restrictions are to be found in a few
arbitrary constraints routinely imposed when computing
canonical correlations. First, as was mentioned earlier,
one usually imposes a "normalizing" constraint. If a_1 and
a_2 denote the first and second column, respectively, of
the A matrix, this constraint generates the following four
equalities:

$$a_1'R_{yy}\, a_1 = 1\, , \qquad a_2'R_{yy}\, a_2 = 1\, ,$$

$$b_1'R_{xx}\, b_1 = 1\, , \qquad b_2'R_{xx}\, b_2 = 1\, . \qquad (12)$$

The last two relationships needed for identification are
to be found in the requirement that the second pair of variates be orthogonal to the first. This leads to:

$$a_1'R_{yy}\, a_2 = 0\, , \qquad b_1'R_{xx}\, b_2 = 0\, . \qquad (13)$$

Since the constraints (12) as well as (13) are quadratic
in the parameters, we still have an indeterminacy.[8] This
is reflected in the symmetry of a canonical solution,
making the first and third quadrants equivalent, as are
the second and fourth. Once the choice of direction of
axes--and thus the sign of the weights (choice of roots)--
has been made, the 12 parameters are identified.

Our argument, to reiterate, is that the arbitrary assumptions made necessary for identification should if at all
possible be replaced by more structural relationships.
In economics, the identifying restrictions derive most
often from the theoretical exclusion of some variables
from a given equation--it might be that before a canonical
analysis is applied, such a priori restrictions could be
brought out more clearly leading to results that are easier

to interpret. As one straightforward example, if one were
willing to assume $a_{21} = 0$ in (7), together with the constraints in (12), a recursive model would result with estimates of the a's and the b's easily available through ordinary least squares.[9] Such an approach becomes also feasible
if an initial canonical correlation indicates that a_{21} is
close to zero.[10] Alternatively, prior consideration might
suggest that certain of the b's on the right-hand side are
zero, serving to identify at least some of the equations
and possibly the complete model. In such cases, not forcing
these b's to zero might give incorrect parameter estimates.
This could happen when, for example, the non-excluded exogenous variables are collinear with some of the bona fide
explanatory variables, leading to unstable parameter estimates. Furthermore, once identification is complete, the
whole array of simultaneous system estimating techniques
(such as the two-stage least squares) becomes available.
The point is that without such pre-specification, ad hoc
rationalizations are frequently needed to interpret canonical results and make useful policy recommendations.

FINAL NOTE

Since it has been argued here that simultaneous systems
are preferable to canonical correlations partly because
the latter technique is a special case of the former, it
is important to note that the general linear model as
developed by Joreskog (1973) and applied to the canonical
correlations problem (Bagozzi, Fornell and Larcker 1981)
subsume both as special cases. Furthermore, the general
model handles well the multiple indicator case as demonstrated by Bagozzi (1977) whereas the simultaneous system
does not (except for the instance where the multiple indicators are obtained only for the endogenous variables).
The general linear model shares with simultaneous systems
the need for very strong prior theory. It does not perform
well, for example, where the underlying, "true" dimensionality of a construct is in doubt. The strongest disadvantage of the general linear model lies perhaps on the computational side.[11] Simultaneous systems have, of course,
been around for a long time, and estimation methods are
well established. Redundancy analysis is new, but since
the method transforms into the usual eigenvector-eigenvalue
problem (see above), the computational problems are relatively minor.[12]

The main point to emphasize, however, is that whether the
general linear model or the redundancy analysis/simultane-

---

[8]Because the original variables y and x, as well as the
derived canonical variates are standardized, the correlations between them degenerates into simple sums of cross-
products divided by the number of observations.

[9]For those estimates to be unbiased, we also require
$E(u_1\, u_2) = 0$. This is a statistical assumption, however,
not an identification constraint.

[10]In the cases where a sufficient number of observations
for a split-sample approach is available, we would argue
that one sample be used for exploratory canonical analysis. The number of significant variates and the magnitudes of the canonical weights can then be used to formulate a simultaneous system and estimate the parameters
using the hold-out sample.

[11]The LISREL program is now available at many major computer centers, and this alone should alleviate some of
the computational drawbacks. The iterations required
for the optimization routine driving the estimation may
keep the algorithm from gaining as wide acceptance as the
alternative techniques dealt with here, but with additional usage and experience this drawback should gradually diminish (Joreskog and Sorbom 1978).

[12]Wollenberg (1977) has made his algorithm available.
Alternatively, standard matrix manipulation programs are
available as subroutines in most computer installations,
and the software development takes less than a day's
work for a programmer with some experience.

ous system approach is employed, the basic features of our
argument remain unchanged. Thus, for the multiple indicator case, canonical correlation should be replaced by an
approach which more effectively employs the variations
picked by the indicators, be it in the framework of redundancy analysis or the general linear model. For the multiple dependent variable case, canonical correlation should
be relegated to only those exploratory cases where there
is not strong prior theory. Otherwise, simultaneous systems or the general linear model should be employed.

Finally, where computational issues are paramount, the new
method of partial least squares might well prove to be a
strong alternative to LISREL because of its relatively
lower complexity (Wold 1980).

REFERENCES

Alpert, M. I. and R. A. Peterson (1972), "On the Interpretation of Canonical Analysis," _Journal of Marketing
Research_, 9 (May), 187-192.

Anderson, T. W. (1958), _An Introduction to Multivariate
Statistical Analysis_, New York: Wiley.

Bagozzi, R. P. (1977), "Structural Equation Models in
Experimental Research," _Journal of Marketing Research_,
14 (May), 209-226.

___________ (1980), _Causal Models in Marketing_, New York:
Wiley.

___________, C. Fornell and D. F. Larcker (1981), "Canon-
ical Correlation Analysis as a Special Case of a Structural Relations Model," _Multivariate Behavioral Research_
(in press).

Blalock, H. M., ed. (1971), _Causal Models in the Social
Sciences_, Chicago: Aldine.

Cliff, N. and D. J. Krus (1976), "Interpretation of Canonical Analysis: Rotated vs. Unrotated Solutions," _Psycho-
metrika_, 41, No. 1 (March), 35-42.

Farley, J. U. and L. W. Ring (1974), "'Empirical' Specification of a Buyer Behavior Model," _Journal of Marketing
Research_, 11 (February), 89-96.

Goldberger, A. S. (1964), _Econometric Theory_, New York:
Wiley.

Hannan, E. J. (1967), "Canonical Correlation and Multiple
Equation Systems in Economics," _Econometrica_, 35 (January),
109-118.

Hooper, J. W. (1967), "Simultaneous Equations and Canonical
Correlation Theory," _Econometrica_, 35 (March), 245-256.

Johansson, J. K. (1981), "An Extension of Wollenberg's
Redundancy Analysis," _Psychometrika_, 46 (March), 93-103.

___________ and J. N. Sheth (1977), "Canonical Correlation
and Marketing Research," in _Multivariate Methods for Market and Survey Research_, J. N. Sheth, ed., Chicago:
American Marketing Association, 111-131.

Joreskog, K. G. (1973), "A General Method for Estimating a
Linear Structural Equation System," in _Structural Equa-
tion Models in the Social Sciences_, A. S. Goldberger and
O. D. Duncan, eds., New York: Seminar Press, 85-112.

___________ and D. Sorbom (1978), _LISREL IV: Analysis of
Linear Structural Relationships by the Method of Maximum
Likelihood_, Chicago: National Educational Resources, Inc.

Kernan, J. B. (1968), "Choice Criteria, Decision Behavior,
and Personality," _Journal of Marketing Research_, 5 (May),
155-169.

Lambert, Z. V. and R. M. Durand (1975), "Some Precautions
in Using Canonical Analysis," _Journal of Marketing
Research_, 12 (November), 468-475.

Perry, M. and B. C. Hamm (1969), "Canonical Analysis of
Relations between Socioeconomic Risk and Personal Influ-
ence in Purchase Decisions," _Journal of Marketing
Research_, 6, 351-354.

Sparks, D. L. and W. T. Tucker (1971), "A Multivariate
Analysis of Personality and Product Use," _Journal of
Marketing Research_, 8 (February), 67-70.

Van Valey, T. L. (1971), "On the Evaluation of Simple Models
Containing Multiple Indicators of Unmeasured Variables,"
in _Causal Models in the Social Sciences_, H. M. Blalock,
ed., Chicago: Aldine, 320-326.

Wold, H. (1980), "Model Construction and Evaluation When
Theoretical Knowledge is Scarce--Theory and Application
of Partial Least Squares," in _Evaluation of Econometric
Methods_, J. Kmenta and J. G. Ramsey, eds., New York:
Academic Press, 47-74.

Wollenberg, A. (1977), "Redundancy Analysis--An Alternative
for Canonical Correlation Analysis," _Psychometrika_, 42
(June), 207-219.

HETEROGENEITY AND MARKOV THEORY:
A FINITE MIXTURE APPROACH

Carsten Stig Poulsen, Aalborg University Center

ABSTRACT

The paper presents a general Markov model that takes heterogeneity in transition matrices into account. This Mixed
Markov (MM) model is a finite mixture of the well-known
Markov models. Based on panel data, ML estimators of the
model parameters and tests for various hypotheses are derived. Finally, the MM model is applied to a data set previously considered by Aaker (197o).

INTRODUCTION

Following Massy, Montgomery, and Morrison (197o) the basic
'dimensions' of stochastic models of consumer buying behavior are: (1) population heterogeneity, (2) non-stationarity of the model parameters, and (3) feed-back effect
from previous choices. When aggregate consumer data are
analyzed these three aspects are confounded. Hence, any
stochastic model applied to the data must - implicitly or
explicitly- make some assumptions with regard to all three
effects. No survey over the way this has been accomplished
in various models will be given here. The reader is referred to Massy, Montgomery, and Morrison (op.cit.), Montgomery and Ryans (1973), or Montgomery and Urban (1969).

In this paper we shall focus on Markov models. Since their
initial introduction to the marketing field, (Lipstein
1959; Herniter and Magee 1961; Maffei 1961; Harrary
and Lipstein 1962), they have seen relatively few applications. Ehrenberg (1965) has given an overly critical
appraisal of their potential value to marketing, see also
the comments by Massy and Morrison (1968). Ehrenberg was
right, however, so far as the application of Markov models
to aggregate data is not without problems.

As a statistical model the Markov model was fairly well
developed by Anderson and Goodman (1957). Unfortunately,
the theory assumed homogeneity with respect to individual
transition probabilities. Hence, when the model was applied to aggregate consumer data, one of the major dimensions
(1) was not taken properly into account.

Various efforts to adjust for heterogeneity have been seen,
viz. the mover stayer model by Blumen, Kogan, and McCarthy
(1955), Harary and Lipstein (1962), Morrison (1966), and
Blattberg and Sen (1974). All these proposals are rather
limited in their treatment of the heterogeneity.

It is the purpose of this paper to present a general Markov
chain model that allow for heterogeneity in transition matrices. The population is seen as consisting of an (unknown) number of segments, each following a separate Markov
model. We shall demonstrate how the model parameters, i.e.
the Markov model within each segment and the segment sizes, can be efficiently estimated from panel data, using
maximum likelihood methods. For hypothesis testing purposes some restricted models are considered, and conditional
likelihood-ratio tests devised. Finally, the model is applied to a data set from Aaker (197o) in order to illustrate how valuable structural and predictive information
can be obtained from the approach.

DEFINITION OF THE MM MODEL

The models we consider in this paper have the following
general characteristics:

1) The total population of individuals or consumers con-
    sists of a finite number of S segments.

2) Within each segment the consumers follow the same Mar-
    kov model in their brand choice behavior.

3) Across segments the behavioral models, i.e. their para-
    meter values, are different.

4) The segmentation variable is directly unobservable,
    and must be inferred from observed behavior.

There are two features of these assumptions that should be
noted. First, the heterogeneity is assumed to be limited.
By using a segmentation perspective on consumer heterogeneity we are expressing the view that - at least from a
practioners point-of-view - consumers are neither perfectly alike nor completely different. The problem is to find
a compromise which fits the data (Wiggins 1973). Second,
treating the segmentation variable as a latent or unobservable variable that can only be inferred from other manifest data introduces special problems of estimation associated with 'incomplete' data (Dempster, Laird, and Rubin
1977). Briefly, the model can be described as a finite
mixture of S Markov models. Hence the name mixed Markov
(MM). Also, it follows from the unobservable nature of the
segmentation that the number S will typically be unknown
a priori.

We shall now define the MM model more precisely. We concentrate on first-order models as higher-order models can
be handled as restricted first-order models (Poulsen 1982).

The parameters of the first-order MM model are:

(a) the size of each of the segments: π_s, $s = 1,\ldots,S$
     i.e. S-1 free parameters as $\sum_s \pi_s = 1$

(b) the Markov model parameters for each of the segments,
     i.e.

   (i) the initial state probabilities: $\delta_{i|s}^{(1)}$, $i \in C$,
        $s = 1,\ldots,S$, i.e. with M brands in the choice set
        C, a total of $S \cdot (M-1)$ free parameters as
        $\sum_{i \in C} \delta_{i|s}^{(1)} = 1$, all s.

   (ii) the transition probability matrix $\underset{\sim}{A}_s^{(w)} = ((\delta_{j|is}^{(w)}))$,
        containing the conditional probability for a con-
        sumer in segment s to choose $j \in C$ at purchase
        occasion w = 2,...,W, given his previous choice
        $i \in C$, i.e. (W-1)(M-1)·M·S free parameters as
        $\sum_{j \in C} \delta_{j|is}^{(w)} = 1$, all i,s, and w.

Now consider any choice sequence (ijk), where we without
loss of generality have W = 3 purchase occasions. The
probability $\theta_{ijk|s}$ of this sequence for a consumer in class
s can be calculated as

$$\theta_{ijk|s} = \delta_{i|s}^{(1)} \cdot \delta_{j|is}^{(2)} \cdot \delta_{k|js}^{(3)} \tag{1}$$

The corresponding probability θ_{ijk} for observing this choice sequence in the entire population of consumers, regardless of segment membership is then:

$$\theta_{ijk} \triangleq \sum_s \pi_s \cdot \theta_{ijk|s} = \sum_s \pi_s \cdot \delta_{i|s}^{(1)} \cdot \delta_{j|is}^{(2)} \cdot \delta_{k|js}^{(3)} \tag{2}$$

With a random sample of N consumers the number x_{ijk} with
choice sequence (ijk) will have a multinomial distributi-
on $M(N,(\theta_{ijk}))$ where θ_{ijk} is given in (2). Hence, the MM
model represents a parametric multinomial model. This observation forms the basis for the statistical results on

asymptotic tests for 'goodness-of-fit' and other hypotheses, employed in the sequel, cf. Rao (1973).

ESTIMATION AND GOODNESS-OF-FIT

The MM model will be estimated using the maximum likelihood principle. The likelihood equations for deriving the MLEs of the MM model parameters can be derived either by using Lagrange multipliers or by the EM-algorithm of Demster, Laird, and Rubin (1977). For a detailed derivation using both methods, the reader is referred to Poulsen (1982). In any case the MLEs are given as solutions to the following system of equations:

$$\hat{\pi}_s = \frac{1}{N} \sum_{ijk} x_{ijk} \cdot \hat{\pi}_{s|ijk} \tag{3}$$

$$\hat{\delta}_{i|s}^{(1)} = \frac{\sum_{jk} x_{ijk} \cdot \hat{\pi}_{s|ijk}}{\sum_{ijk} x_{ijk} \cdot \hat{\pi}_{s|ijk}} \tag{4}$$

$$\hat{\delta}_{j|is}^{(2)} = \frac{\sum_{k} x_{ijk} \cdot \hat{\pi}_{s|ijk}}{\sum_{jk} x_{ijk} \cdot \hat{\pi}_{s|ijk}} \tag{5}$$

$$\hat{\delta}_{k|js}^{(3)} = \frac{\sum_{i} x_{ijk} \cdot \hat{\pi}_{s|ijk}}{\sum_{ik} x_{ijk} \cdot \hat{\pi}_{s|ijk}} \tag{6}$$

where

$$\hat{\pi}_{s|ijk} = \frac{\hat{\pi}_s \cdot \hat{\delta}_{i|s}^{(1)} \cdot \hat{\delta}_{j|is}^{(2)} \cdot \hat{\delta}_{k|js}^{(3)}}{\sum_{s} \hat{\pi}_s \cdot \hat{\delta}_{i|s}^{(1)} \cdot \hat{\delta}_{j|is}^{(2)} \cdot \hat{\delta}_{k|js}^{(3)}} \tag{7}$$

The posterior probabilities $\hat{\pi}_{s|ijk}$ of segment membership act as weights in what would otherwise be simple frequency estimators of probabilities, see also Wolfe (1970). The equations can be solved iteratively by inserting initial estimates of the parameters in (7). Then, substituting the resulting value of $\hat{\pi}_{s|ijk}$ into (3)-(6), along with the contingency table (x_{ijk}), a new updated vector of estimates can be derived and put back into (7). This process continues until the process converges. For general results on convergence of the EM-algorithm, see Dempter, Laird, and Rubin (op.cit.).

The solution to the estimation equations cannot be proven unique. Therefore, different values to start the iterations are advised and in case of multiple solutions the one corresponding to the largest (absolute) value of the log-likelihood function is chosen.

Given the MLEs of the parameters it follows from general theory of parametric multinomial distributions that if the model is true and identified, the 'goodness-of-fit' can be evaluated by the Pearson χ^2 or likelihood ratio statistic, LR:

$$\text{Pearson } \chi^2 = \sum_{ijk} \frac{(x_{ijk} - N \cdot \hat{\theta}_{ijk})^2}{N \cdot \hat{\theta}_{ijk}} \tag{8}$$

$$\text{LR} = 2 \sum_{ijk} x_{ijk} \cdot \log \frac{x_{ijk}}{N \cdot \hat{\theta}_{ijk}} \tag{9}$$

as both statistics asymptotically as $N \to \infty$ converge to a χ^2- distribution with a df-parameter determined as

df = #cells in the contingency Table - 1

   - # estimated free parameters

i.e. $\quad df = M^W - 1 - (S - 1) - S(M - 1) \cdot (1 + M(W-1))$ (10)

A neccessary condition for identifiability of the parameters is df $\geq$ o. The neccessary and sufficient condition for identifiability is that the rank of the Jacobian of the transformation (2) from the parameter space of the unrestricted multinomial model to the space of the MM parameters is full, i.e. equal to the number of free MM parameters. For a discussion of identifiability of finite mixtures, see Teicher (1960), Blitschke (1964), and Boes (1966).

The asymptotic standard deviations of the parameters can be evaluated from the Fisher information matrix. The computations below in the application section are based on a theorem by Birch (1964) on parametric multinomial distributions. Details are given in Poulsen (1982).

RESTRICTED MM MODELS

The LR statistic has a distinctive advantage when models are compared that are hierarchically related, i.e. when one model contains the other as a special case with one or more constraints imposed on the parameters. Given that the more general (unrestricted) model fits the data, the significance of the constraints can be tested by the difference

$$\text{LR} = \text{LR}_r - \text{LR}_u \tag{11}$$

between the LR-'goodness-of-fit' statistic in the restricted and the unrestricted model. This conditional test statistic will have an asymptotic χ^2-distribution with

$$df = df_r - df_u$$
$$= \text{\# imposed constraints} \tag{12}$$

if the restricted model is true. A similar conditional break-down does not hold for the Pearson χ^2-statistic.

Poulsen (1982) demonstrates how various restrictions are easily handled by the EM-algorithm. We shall focus on two hypotheses of immediate interest. First, the hypothesis of stationary Markov models within each segments can be stated as:

$$H_o' : \Lambda_s^{(w)} = \Lambda_s, \quad \text{all } w = 2,\ldots,W \tag{13}$$

A conditional LR-test of H' will have S•M•(M-1)•(W-2) degrees of freedom. Second, the hypothesis of zero-order behavior within each segment implies:

$$H_o'' : \delta_{j|is}^{(w)} = \delta_{j|s}^{(w)}, \quad \text{all } i,j \in C, \, w = 2,\ldots,W$$

The LR-test will have df = $S(M-1)^2 \cdot (W-1)$. Under H" the MM model reduces to the latent class model (Lazarsfeld and Henry 1968), for which Goodman (1974a, 1974b) derived ML estimators, using the EM-algorithm.

APPLICATION OF THE MM MODEL

To illustrate the application of the MM model to real data, we have chosen a data set previously analyzed by Aaker (1970,1971), concerning 'new triers' of a brand A of some product group versus an 'all other' brand O. W = 5 purchase occasions are used and with two alternative, A and O, the basic manifest table (x_{ijklm}) will contain 32 cells. The input data are given as part of Table 3 below.

The ML estimation procedure of the MM model and related statistics described above have been implemented in a computer program, MLMM, (Poulsen and Juhl 1982) that forms the basis for the results reported here.

As we have no prior information on the number of segments, we fit in an exploratory manner MM models with S = 1,2,3, and 4 classes. For S = 1 and 2, we investigate non-stationary as well as stationary models, while only stationary models are estimated for S = 3 and 4. Table 1 contains the results.

TABLE 1

LR-'goodness-of-fit' for various MM models.
Brand A data from Aaker (197o).

No. of segments		LR	df	p-level
S = 1	stat.	1o2.o2	28	o.000
	non-stat.	99.o8	2o	o.000
S = 2	stat.	24.83	24	o.5oo
	non-stat.	15.21	12	o.2oo
S = 3	stat.	14.93	2o	o.8oo
S = 4	stat.	13.84	16	o.75o

S = 1 corresponds to the usual homogeneous Markov model. It is seen that the non-stationary as well as the stationary version of the one segment Markov model are handily rejected. Thus, by traditional methods the Markov modeling approach would have been refused.

Allowing for heterogeneity by letting S = 2 yields a remarkable improvement in the fit. The non-stationary two-segment model is acceptable with a p-level of o.2o. The hypothesis of stationarity can also be accepted. Using the conditional LR-test for H_o' above we obtain:

$$LR_{H_o'} = 24.83 - 15.21 = 9.62$$

$$df_{H_o'} = 12$$

which cannot be rejected at any reasonable level. The fit in separate cells of the table is provided as part of table 3 below.

Similarly, we can test the hypothesis H_o'' of zero-order behavior. We obtain:

$$LR_{H_o''} = 45.86 - 15.21 = 3o.65$$

$$df_{H_o''} = 8$$

which is significant beyond any reasonable level.

The estimated two-segment MM structure is given in Table 2.

TABLE 2

The estimated two-segment MM model.
Brand A data (Aaker 197o)
Standard deviations in parenthesis

		Segment 1		Segment 2	
Size π_s		o.188 (o.o48)		o.812 (o.o48)	
		State		State	
Initial prob.vector $\delta_{i\|s}^{(1)}$		0	A	0	A
		o.321 (o.o82)	o.679 (o.o82)	o.874 (o.o23)	o.126 (o.o23)
Transition matrix Λ_s		0	A	0	A
	0	o.498 (o.123)	o.5o2 (o.123)	o.938 (o.o1o)	o.o62 (o.o1o)
	A	o.29o (o.o42)	o.71o (o.o42)	o.792 (o.o76)	o.2o8 (o.o76)

It is clear from Table 2 that the market contains two segments with widely different switching patterns. A minor segment of less than 2o pct. has a high initial probability of choosing A and shows some loyalty toward that brand with a repeat probability of o.71o. The major segment are loyal to the 'all-other' brand.

The posterior probabilities (7) can be used to segment the consumers. One reasonable way to perform this is to assign consumers to segments according to the modal posterior probability. The segments may then be analyzed in terms of other measured characteristics of the assigned consumers.

TABLE 3

Assignment of consumers to segments.
Two segment MM model.

Purchase sequence ijklm	Actual number x_{ijklm}	Expected number $N \cdot \hat{\theta}_{ijklm}$	Modal post.prob. $\hat{\pi}_{s*\|ijklm}$	Assigned class $s*$
00000	352	348.8o	o.993	2
A0000	44	44.95	o.936	2
0A000	26	2o.78	o.934	2
AA000	14	13.44	o.693	2
00A00	2o	2o.78	o.934	2
A0A00	5	4.o5	o.581	2
0AA00	7	6.26	o.686	2
AAA00	12	7.94	o.741	1
000A0	14	2o.98	o.934	2
A00A0	5	4.o5	o.581	2
0A0A0	5	1.9o	o.573	2
AA0A0	5	2.94	o.823	1
00AA0	5	6.26	o.686	2
A0AA0	3	2.94	o.823	1
0AAA0	3	3.75	o.747	1
AAAA0	7	8.83	o.948	1
0000A	21	25.33	o.9o6	2
A000A	3	5.7o	o.511	1
0A00A	4	2.67	o.519	1
AA00A	3	4.77	o.871	1
00A0A	5	2.67	o.519	1
A0A0A	2	1.87	o.916	1
0AA0A	3	2.o6	o.874	1
AAA0A	5	6.o5	o.977	1
000AA	9	8.46	o.6o1	2
A00AA	2	4.77	o.871	1
0A0AA	o	2.26	o.874	1
AA0AA	6	6.o5	o.977	1
00AAA	5	5.93	o.81o	1
A0AAA	5	6.o5	o.977	1
0AAAA	7	7.o9	o.965	1
AAAAA	24	2o.59	o.994	1

The structural analysis above can be supplemented by a prediction of future shares of choices for brand A within each segment, $\delta_{A\|s}^{(w)}$, utilizing the stationarity of the Markov models. Then the overall share can be computed by weighting with the segment size:

$$\hat{\theta}_A^{(w)} = \sum_s \hat{\pi}_s \cdot \hat{\delta}_{A\|s}^{(w)} \qquad (17)$$

Fig. 1 is reproduced from Aaker (197o) with expected shares $\hat{\theta}_A^{(w)}$, predicted from the MM model included.

In his paper Aaker (197o) makes the point that statistical criteria for deciding the fit of a model should be supplemented by other measures such as the model's predictive power. This can be illustrated by comparing the shares predicted from the MM model with S = 2 and 3 segments, as indicated in Fig. 1. When the number of segments are increased to 3, we naturally obtain a better fit, cf. Table

1, but at the expense of degrees of freedom (statistical power).

FIGURE 1

Empirical proportions and estimated shares.
Adapted from Aaker (197o), fig. 4.

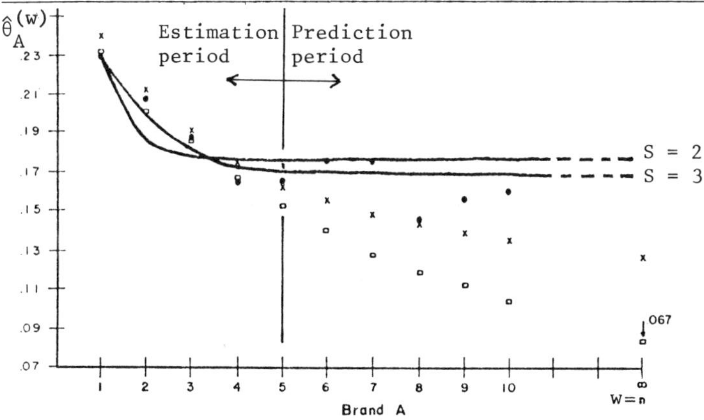

In analogy to (11) and (12), the difference in LR-'goodness -of-fit' statistics and df-parameter can be used as a guidance, when the number of segments is determined.[1] Thus, a three-segment model might be justifiable while the less parsimoneous four-class model seems unduly complicated.

Inspecting the predictions from the two MM models, however, reveals a qualitative difference between the two- and three-segment models. The predicted shares of the two-segment model can be described as 'too fast convergence towards too high a level'. The three-segment model, on the other hand, besides yielding a good fit in the estimation period, seems to capture the long-run trends somewhat better. Both MM models, however, can be seen to differ markedly from the predictions of the New Trier and the Linear Learning Model.

CONCLUSION

We have in this paper presented a direct attack on the homogeneity assumption regarding Markov transition matrices. In statistical terms the proposed model is a finite mixture of traditional Markov models. This corresponds in effect to the segmentation approach in marketing. By introducing this limited form of heterogeneity, we have obtained a generalization of the Markov theory that applied to consumer choice behavior include heterogeneity, non-stationarity, and feed-back effects. A major criticism of the traditional Markov model has been overcome.

---

[1] We hesitate to call this a LR-test for the number of classes, although some researchers seem to use it that way, see e.g. Wolfe (197o) and Forman (1978). The reason is the difficulty in interpreting an S segment model as nested in an (S + 1) segment model.

REFERENCES

Aaker, D.A. (197o), "A New Method for Evaluating Stochastic Models of Brand Choice," *Journal of Marketing Research*, 8 (August), 3oo-3o6.

__________ (1971), "The New-Trier Stochastic Model of Brand Choice," *Management Science*, Series B, 17 (April), 435-45o.

Anderson, T.W. (1954), "Probability Models for Analyzing Changes in Attitudes," in *Mathematical Thinking in the Social Sciences*, P.F. Lazarsfeld, ed., New York: The Free Press.

__________ and L.A. Goodman (1957), "Statistical Inference about Markov Chains," *Annals of Mathematical Statistics*, 28, 89-11o.

Birch, M.W. (1964), "A New Proof of the Fisher-Pearson Theorem," *Annals of Mathematical Statistics*, 35, 718-724.

Blattberg, R.C. and S.K. Sen (1976), "Market Segments and Stochastic Brand Choice Models," *Journal of Marketing Research*, 8 (February), 33-45.

Blitschke, W.R. (1964), "Estimating the Parameters of Mixtures of Binomial Distributions," *Journal of American Statistical Association*, 59, 51o-528.

Blumen, I.M., M. Kogan, and P.J. McCarthy (1955), "The Industrial Mobility of Labor as a Probability Process," Ithaca, New York: Cornell University Press.

Boes, D.C. (1966), "On the Estimation of Mixing Distributions," *Annals of Mathematical Statistics*, 37, 177-188.

Dempster, A.P., N.M. Laird, and D.B. Rubin (1977), "Maximum Likelihood from Incomplete Data via the EM-algorithm," *Journal of Royal Statistical Society*, Series B, 39, 1-22.

Ehrenberg, A.S.C. (1965), "An Appraisal of Markov Brand-Switching Models," *Journal of Marketing Research*, 2 (November), 347-62.

Formann, A.K. (1978), "The Latent Class Analysis of Polychotomous Data," *Biomedical Journal*, 2o, 755-771.

Goodman, L.A. (1961), "Statistical Methods for the Mover-Stayer Model," *Journal of American Statistical Association*, 56, 841-868.

__________ (1974a), "The Analysis of Systems of Qualitative Variables When Some of the Variables are Unobservable. Part I: A Modified Latent Structure Approach," *American Journal of Sociology*, 79 (March).

__________ (1974b), "Exploratory Latent Structure Analysis," *Biometrika*, 61, 215-231.

Harary, F. and B. Lipstein (1962), "The Dynamics of Brand Loyalty: A Markovian Approach," *Operations Research*, 1o, 19-4o.

Hasselblad, Victor (1969), "Estimation of Finite Mixtures of Distributions from the Exponential Family," *Journal of American Statistical Association*, 64, 1459-1471.

Herniter, J.D. and J.F. Magee (1961), "Customer Behavior as a Markov Process," *Operations Research*, 9 (January), 1o5-22.

Lazarsfeld, Paul F., and N.W. Henry (1968), "*Latent Structure Analysis*," Boston: Houghton Mifflin.

Lipstein, B. (1959), "The Dynamics of Brand Loyalty and Brand-Switching," Proceedings of the 5th Annual Conference, A.R.F., New York: Advertising Research Foundation.

Maffei, R.B. (196o), "Brand Preferences and Simple Markov Processes," Operations Research, 8 (March), 21o-18.

Massy, W.F. (1966), "Order and Homogeneity of Family Specific Brand-Switching Processes," Journal of Marketing Research, 3 (February), 48-54.

____________, and D.G. Morrison (1968), "Comments on Ehrenberg's Appraisal of Brand-Switching Models," Journal of Marketing Research, 5 (May), 225-29.

____________, D.B. Montgomery, and D.G. Morrison (197o), "Stochastic Models of Buying Behavior," Cambridge: The MIT Press.

Montgomery, D.B., and G.L. Urban (1969), "Management Science in Marketing," Englewood-Cliffs: Prentice-Hall.

____________, and A.B. Ryans (1973), "Stochastic Models of Consumer Choice Behavior," in Consumer Behavior: Theoretical Sources, S.Ward, and T.S. Robertson, eds., Englewood-Cliffs, New Jersey: Prentice-Hall, Inc.

Morrison, D.G. (1965), "Stochastic Models for Time Series with Applications in Marketing," Technical Report No. 8, Joint Program in Operations Research, Stanford University.

Poulsen, C.S. (1982), "Latent Structure Analysis With Choice Modeling Applications," Unpublished Ph.D. dissertation, The Wharton School, University of Pennsylvania, Philadelphia.

____________ and H.J. Juhl (1982), "MLMM - A Computer Program for Maximum Likelihood Estimation of the Mixed Markov Model," User Manual, The Århus School of Business Administration and Economics, Århus.

Rao, C.R. (1973), "Linear Statistical Inference With Applications," New York: John Wiley and Sons Inc.

Styan, G.P., and H. Smith, Jr. (1964), "Markov Chains Applied to Marketing," Journal of Marketing Research, 1, 5o-55.

Teicher, H. (196o), "On the Mixture of Distributions," Annals of Mathematical Statistics, 31, 55-73.

Wiggins, L.M. (1973), "Panel Analysis", New York: Elsevier Scientific Publishing Company.

Wolfe, John H. (197o), "Pattern Clustering by Multivariate Mixture Analysis," Multivariate Behavioral Research, 5, 329-35o.

FILLING THE GAP: A REVIEW OF THE MISSING DATA PROBLEM

David W. Stewart, Vanderbilt University

ABSTRACT

The problem of missing data in marketing research is reviewed. Procedures which have been suggested for dealing
with missing data are presented and discussed in the light
of Monte Carlo studies of their efficacy. It is concluded
that a regression approach or principal components approach
works best when the average intercorrelation of all variables is .20 or higher. When the average interitem correlation is less than .20 or when an assumption of linearity
is unwarranted, either variable mean substitution or random
assignment within groups is suggested. Problems associated
with nonrandomly missing data are also presented with some
general recommendations for dealing with these problems.
Attention is called to the need for reporting missing data
in published research.

INTRODUCTION

One of the more ubiquitous problems faced by marketing researchers is the missing data point. Whether the researcher works in a controlled laboratory environment or conducts
field surveys, the absence of one or more data points is
likely to complicate the analysis of the data and the ultimate interpretation of the results. A considerable literature on missing data now exists. Unfortunately, much of
this literature has remained in statistically and mathematically oriented publications and has not received wide application by marketing researchers.

Gappy data, as D. J. Finney (1974) refers to it, is a pervasive research phenomena and one likely to forever remain
with us. Whether it will continue to be more than a minor
irritation depends on the ability to use and improve upon
the existing techniques for handling missing data. The
presence of missing data has in the past increased the labor and expense of analyzing data. However, the computer
has made computational effort minimal, and the application
of procedures for handling missing data need not be a labo-
rious task. Indeed, examination of missing data in its own
right may well lead to some interesting findings (see for
example, Cohen, 1968, p. 438).

Even the most conscientious researcher using the most so-
phisicated research design, exercising considerable fore-
thought, and making thorough preparations, is likely to
find some data missing. Missing data creates serious problems for data analysis, particularly where the researcher
seeks to employ a multivariate statistical method. Elimination of observations with missing data, the common default
option in most computer software, often reduces the N to
such an extent that a meaningful analysis is not possible.
The data analyst must either abandon the desired statistical procedure or find a means for dealing with the missing
data problem.

PROCEDURES

A bewildering array of methods for dealing with missing data are available. These techniques fall into one of five
broad classes: 1) data elimination techniques, 2) data
substitution techniques, 3) maximum likelihood procedures,
4) principal components or factor analytic techniques, and
5) least squares or regression procedures. Table I provides a summary of some of the better known and commonly
used techniques as well as a brief discussion of the effects of the techniques on parameter estimation.

All of the techniques listed in Table I make the general
assumption that the data missing are missing at random,
that is, for reasons unrelated to other variables in the
design (Affifi and Elashoff 1966, Timm 1979, Cohen and
Cohen 1975). It is often difficult to determine whether
data are missing at random or not. One approach to making
this determination has been suggested by Kim and Curry
(1977). These authors suggest a simple test for the randomness of missing values based on the Chi Squre statistic.
Their strategy is to consider the (K+2) patterns of missing
data where K is the number of variables with a substantial
number of missing values (Kim and Curry suggest more than
20). The pattern (M_1), (M_2), . . . (M_k), (MM, missing on
two or more variables), and (NM, no missing data) is examined where M_i stands for cases on which information is missing only on the variable X_i. The significance of the deviation of the observed frequencies from the expected frequencies can be evaluated by the Chi Square test with degrees of freedom equal to the (K+1) variables involved.
This test works well when the number of missing values is
large, many variables are involved in the analysis, and the
nonrandomness can be detected by examination of the pattern
of missing values. It also works well in other circumstances, e.g., when information is missing from only one
variable or there is nonrandomness such that examining the
pattern alone is not sufficient to detect it. The latter
event is more likely to occur when the missing values are
the result of an interaction effect.

In many cases, the researcher may be left to ponder whether data are missing at random. The question certainly has
a bearing on the interpretation of research findings. However, regardless of the randomness of missing values, the
researcher must still grapple with how to plug the holes in
the data. Thus, one of the techniques provided in Table I
is likely to be used regardless of whether the assumption
of randomly missing data is met.

The amount of empirical work on the performance characteristics of these methods is small. No study, to date, has
attempted to deal with all of the techniques, nor has a
representative sample of the techniques been applied to more
than one data analytic situation in a single study. Haitovsky (1968), Kim and Curry (1977), Timm (1970), Gleason and
Staelin (1975), Chan and Dunn (1972, 1974), and Chan, Gilman,
and Dunn (1976) have conducted comparative studies of the
performance characteristics of various missing data estimation procedures. A synthesis of these studies suggests that
when the amount of missing data is small (less than 5%),
there is little real difference in the results obtained in
a statistical analysis associated with choice of a missing
data estimation procedure. When the amount of missing data
exceeds 5 percent, the choice of a missing data estimation
procedure does influence the results obtained. Monte Carlo
analysis suggests that when the average interitem correlations are low ($\bar{r} > .1$), estimating missing data with the
mean of the variable provides the most accurate results.
When the average interitem correlation is moderate to high
($\bar{r} < .3$), regression or principal components based estimation procedures appear to provide more accurate results.
The regression and principal components procedures provide
similar results, but the regression approach is computationally faster (Koopman 1976).

All of the procedures discussed above assume that data are
not present for reasons unrelated to the experimental design or to other variables in the study. The validity of
these procedures is questionable whenever the data are missing systematically. Cohen (1968) and Cohen and Cohen (1975)

suggest a particularly useful approach to this problem.
These authors maintain that each data point may carry two
pieces of information: 1) the actual value of the data
point and 2) the presence or absence of the data point.
Cohen (1968) suggests estimating the missing data point and
incorporating dummy variables reflecting the absence of data for a particular observation.

Obviously, where large numbers of variables are involved
and the amount of missing data is substantial, the number
of dummy variables can radically increase the number of
variables in the analysis. In the most extreme case, the
number of variables would double. It may be impractical to
deal with the number of variables thus created, and in some
applications the dichotomous dummy variables could produce
some methodological problems. For example, if the variances of the dummy variables were markedly smaller than
those of the original variables, method factors could be
produced by a factor analysis. This could occur even if
the data had been standardized before factoring. Recognizing these problems, Cohen and Cohen (1975) suggest the creation of a single dummy variable which would reflect the
subject's tendency toward missing data. A particular per-
centange of missing data would thus give the individual
subject a score of 1 on the dummy variable. Rummel (1970)
has suggested giving each subject a score on the dummy variable corresponding to the number of missing data points.
A subject with one missing data point would receive a score
of 1, and a subject with 20 missing data points would receive a score of 20. All of these procedures serve to pre-
serve the information that data are missing and can help in
interpreting the results of an analysis.

There are other approaches to the nonrandom missing data
problem. Finney (1974) and Rummel (1970) suggest doing a
separate analysis of the complete data and comparing the
results to that portion of the data with missing data estimated. Subjects with substantial missing data can be analyzed separately from those with complete data and results
compared. Rummel (1970) suggests including a dummy variable reflecting missing data in the data analysis. A factor analysis can be completed and the factors rotated so
that the first factor is colinear with the missing data.
Other factors could be interpreted independently of the
amount of missing data as could scores derived from these
latter factors.

Gleason and Staelin (1975) also point out that the restrictions on the use of elimination procedures with nonrandom
missing data might be relaxed if it can be assumed that the
regression of the variable in question on the remaining
variables is linear for the entire range of the variables.
Prior research may make such an assumption reasonable.

SUMMARY AND CONCLUSIONS

Missing data are a pervasive problem in marketing research.
The very nature of certain research designs ensures this
problem. Generalizability of results can be seriously affected by the presence of missing data, and computational
problems can result from the absence of data points. A review of the available techniques for dealing with missing
data and Monte Carlo work with these methods suggests that
for very small amounts of missing data, most approaches
work reasonbly well. When larger amounts of data are missing and the average intercorrelation of the variables is
.20 or less, the substitution of variable means for missing
data appears to be the procedure of choice. The economy of
the procedure easily offsets any gain involved in the use
of a more complex procedure. When the average intercorrelation exceeds .20, a regression or principal components
procedure appears best suited for the problem if linearity
may be assumed. The Gleason and Staelin and Frane approaches appear to be the best of the several regression procedures, while the Gleason and Staelin approach appears to be
the best of the principal components approaches. The re-

gression approach is slightly superior to the principal
components approach for computational speed. More precise
estimates of missing data may be obtained by iterating either the regression procedures or the principal components
procedure.

Where the assumption of linearity is not reasonable or
where regression and principal components methods cannot
otherwise be computed, the random assignment with groups
method offers an acceptable alternative. It provides somewhat less reliable results than the regression or principal
components, but in many situations may be less expensive
and time consuming. This approach may also be preferable
to the variable mean substitution approach in some circumstances: where the intercorrelations among variables are
low but the researcher wishes to use available information
from other variables and where the additional cost can be
justified. This approach is most likely to be useful with
very large data sets such as census data.

Missing data points should be estimated regardless of
whether the data are missing randomly or nonrandomly. In
some cases, it is possible to detect a nonrandom pattern of
missing data via an ordinary Chi test, but in many instances, it is impossible to determine the randomness of missing data points. For these situations or where the missing
data are clearly nonrandom, the data analyst should either
use dummy variables to indicate missing data points and incorporate these in the analysis or do separate analyses
with complete data and imcomplete data. Derived scores
should be based on estimated missing data points rather
than being obtained by adjusting derived score coefficients.

Researchers need to communicate the nature and the amount
of missing data and the procedures employed in handling the
missing data points. Such information provides preater
likelihood of replication, has a strong influence on the
generalizability of results, and may be of considerable interest in its own right. How gaps in data are handled is
an important and neglected piece of information and is an
information gap that should be filled.

TABLE ONE

PROCEDURES FOR HANDLING MISSING DATA

General Solution	Effects on Variance, Covariance & Correlation	Comments
I. Data Elimination Techniques		
A. Listwise deletion: elimination of all observations containing missing values.	Estimates may be unreliable when large amounts of data are missing. Minimal effects when amount of data missing is quite small. Estimates based on less than 85% of cases may differ significantly from estimates based on the total sample (Sharp and Feldt, 1959.	Loss of information and unreliabilty of estimates tends to increase as with number of variables. A simple, economical technique often found in statistical software packages. Generates consistent covariance matrices.
B. Deletion of items.	No parameter estimates involving the deleted items can be computed.	A simple and economical technique which may be useful when the missing data are concentrated in relatively few items. Generates consistent covariance matrices.
C. Pairwise deletion: each parameter estimate is computed using all available items (mean, variance) or pairs of items (covariance, correlation). (Glasser, 1964)	Values are same as for the full sample, but are less reliable.	For cases where bivariate correlations are moderate this technique has been found superior to listwise deletion. If sample size is small or the missing data pattern is non-random resulting covariance matrices may not be positive-definite.
II. Substitution Techniques		
A. Wilks' procedure: subsitution of the variable mean for the missing value (Wilks, 1932).	Expected value of the mean is the same as for the full sample. Estimates of variance, covariance, and correlation are conservative.	A simple, economical technique present in some statistical software packages. Use of sample mean tends to reduce the variance of variables with missing data.
B. Group means procedure: substitution of the mean of the variable for a group defined by stratification. Ordinarily the stratification variables should be unrelated to one another but highly related to a large number of variables for data are missing. (Hertel, 1976).	Expected value of the mean and covariance are the same as for full sample. Estimates of variance are deflated; estimates of correlation are inflated.	Time consuming; has little to recommend it. Homogeneity within groups is exaggerated.
C. Random assignment within groups: Identify groups via stratification. Sort cases by groups with first case in each group complete. Move through each group assigning any missing value the score for nearest preceding available nonmissing score for that item and group. (Bureau of Census, 1969; Hertel, 1976).	Expected value of variance, covariance, and correlation is the same as for full sample.	Best approach of the elimination and substitution procedures. More reliable estimates can only be obtained by estimation procedures given below. Approach is time consuming but not expensive.
III. Principal Components/Factor Analytic Approaches		
A. Dear's Procedure: Decomposition of the data matrix into known and unknown parts; use the first principal component obtained from complete submatrix to estimate values in incomplete matrix. (Dear, 1959).	Values of parameter estimates are same as for full sample if most of the information in data is represented by a single principal component.	Primary problem of approach is underfitting. Few data sets are adequately represented by a single principal component. Works best with a small, highly redundant set of variables with small amounts of missing data. Linearity assumed.

Procedure	Parameter Estimates	Comments
B. Standardize data; and substitute means for the missing values. Find first principal component of the pooled covariance matrix for entire data set. For each missing data point find the nearest point on on the first principal component. Use coordinates of point to substitute for missing coordinates. (Chan, Gilman, and Dunn, 1976).	Parameters are the same as for full sample if most of information in the data is represented buy a single component. When more than one component is present estimates may be biased.	Approach does not perform as well as II A. Underfitting is the primary problem. Linearity assumed.
C. Use pairwise deletion or mean substitution to obtain an estimate of the complete matrix. Use first k of the N principal components to estimate the missing values. The number of components used determined by a rule suggested by Horn (1965). (Gleason and Staelin, 1975).	Parameter estimates are the same as for full sample.	Best of the principal components procedures. Procedures performs well. Low cost assumed.
D. Use factor loadings rather than component loadings to estimate missing values. (Woodbury, Clelland, and Hickey, 1963; Woodbury and Siles, 1966).	If the assumption of a common factor model is warranted parameter estimates are unbiased.	Common factor model is questionable for many data sets. Approach probably works well where model holds.

IV. Last Squares/Regression Approaches

Procedure	Parameter Estimates	Comments
A. Classical Least Squares (Yates, 1933). See also Wilkinson (1958) and McDonald (1971).	Parameters are the same as for full sample. Reliability of estimates deteriorate as missing data increases. Estimates obtained without substituting values for missing data.	Assumes linearity and normality. Extensions beyond the trivariate case are limited.
B. Buck's Procedure: Partition data matrix into complete and incomplete submatrices. For each missing value use regression equations obtained by regressing that variable on all other variables in the complete submatrix (Buck, 1960; Frane, 1976).	Parameter estimates are the same as for full sample. Reliability of estimates decreases as missing data increases.	Assumes linearity. Overfitting is a problem.
C. Use pairwise deletion or means substitution to obtain first estimate of complete matrix. To estimate missing values in the jth variate, perform a multiple regression of the jth variate on the other k-1 variates using entire data set. Estimate the missing values from regression functions. (Gleason and Staelin, 1971; Chan, Gilman, and Dunn, 1976; Walsh, 1961).	Parameter estimates are same as for the full sample.	One of the better procedures. Superior to other regression methods and gives some results as III C. Assumes linearity. Iteration improves estimates. Overfitting may be a problem.

REFERENCES

Affifi, A. & Elashoff, R.M. (1966), "Missing Observations in Multivariate Statistics I. Review of the Literature," _Journal of the American Statistical Association, 61_, 595-604.

Buck, S.F. (1960), "A Method of Estimation of Missing Values in Multivariate Data Suitable for Use With an Electronic Computer," _Journal of the Royal Statistical Society Series B, 22,_ 302-307.

Chan, L.S. & Dunn, O.J. (1972), "The Treatment of Missing Values in Discriminant Analysis - 1. The sampling experiment," _Journal of the American Statistical Association, 67_, 473-477.

Chan, L.S. & Dunn, O.J. (1974), "A Note on the Asymptotic Aspect of the Treatment of Missing Values in Discriminant Analysis," _Journal of the American Statistical Association, 69_, 672-673.

Chan, L.S. & Gilman, J.A., & Dunn, O.J., (1976), "Alternative Approaches to Missing Values in Discriminant Analysis," _Journal of the American Statistical Association, 71_, 842-844.

Cohen, J. (1968), "Multiple Regression as a General Data - Analytic System," _Psychological Bulletin, 70_, 426-443.

Cohen, J. & Cohen, P. (1975), _Applied Multiple Regression/Correlation Analysis for the Behavioral Sciences._ Hillsdale, N.J.: Lawrence Erlbaum Associates, Publishers.

Dear, R.E. (1959), _A Principal Component Missing Data Method for Multiple Regression Methods._ Technical Report SP-86, Systems Development Corporation, Santa Monica, California.

Finney, D.J. (1974), "Problem, Data and Inference," _Journal of the Royal Statistical Society, Series A, 137_, 1-19.

Frane, J.W. (1976), "Some Simple Procedures for Handling Missing Data in Multivariate Analysis," _Psychometrika, 41_, 409-415.

Glasser, M. (1964), "Linear Regression Analysis with Missing Observations Among the Independent Variables," _Journal of the American Statistical Association, 59_, 834-844.

Gleason, T.C. & Staelin, R. (1975), "A Proposal for Handling Missing Data," _Psychometrika, 40_, 229-252.

Haitovsky, Y. (1968), "Missing Data in Regression Analysis," _Journal of the Royal Statistical Society, Series B, 30_, 67-82.

Hertel, B.R. (1976), "Minimizing Error Variance Introduced by Missing Data Routines in Survey Analysis," _Sociological Methods and Research, 4_, 459-474.

Horn, J.L. (1965), "A Rationale and Test for the Number of Factors in Factor Analysis," _Psychometrika, 30_, 179-185.

Koopman, R.F. (1976), "Fast Regression Estimates of Missing Data," _Psychometrika, 41_, 277.

Kim, J. & Currey, Jr. (1977), "The Treatment of Missing Data in Multivariate Analysis," _Sociological Methods and Research, 6_, 215-240.

McDonald, L. (1971), "On the Estimation of Missing Data in the Multivariate Linear Model," _Biometric, 27_, 535-543.

Rummel, R.J. (1970), _Applied Factor Analysis._ Evanston, Ill., Northwestern University Press.

Sharp, H. & Feldt, A. (1959), "Some Factors in a Probability Sample Survey of a Metropolitan Community," _American Sociological Review, 24_, 650-651.

Timm, N.H. (1970), "The Estimation of Variance - Covariance and Correlation Matrices from Incomplete Data," _Psychometrika, 35_, 417-437.

Walsh, J.E. (1961), "Computer - Feasible Method for Handling Incomplete Data in Regression Analysis," _Journal of the Association for Computer Machinery, 18_, 647-657.

Wilkinson, G.N. (1958), "Estimation of the Missing Values of the Analysis of Incomplete Data," _Biometrics, 14_, 257-286.

Wilks, S.S. (1932), "Moments and Distributions of Estimates of Population Parameters for Fragmentary Samples," _Annals of Mathematical Statistics, 3_, 163-195.

Woodbury, M.A., Clelland, R.C., & Hickey, R.J. (1963), "Applications of a Factor-Analytic Model in the Prediction of Biological Data," _Behavioral Science, 8_, 347-354.

Woodbury, M.A. & Siles, W. (1966), "Factor Analysis with Missing Data," _New York Academy of Sciences, Annals, 128_, 746-754.

Yates, F. (1933), "The Analysis of Replicated Experiments When Field Results are Incomplete," _Empire Journal of Experimental Agriculture, 1_, 129-142.

A STRUCTURAL EQUATION INVESTIGATION OF INTENTIONS TO ENGAGE IN DO-IT-YOURSELF AUTO REPAIR

Cathy A. Cole, Marquette University, Milwaukee
S. Tamer Cavusgil, University of Wisconsin-Whitewater

ABSTRACT

This paper uses structural equation modeling to isolate
the effect of situational, attitudinal, and personal characteristics on one's intentions to perform automotive repairs
oneself. The situational variables included for investigation are physical environment characteristics. The tasks
considered range in complexity from adding anti-freeze to
changing brake shoes. The relative influence of these variables is found to depend on task complexity.

INTRODUCTION

Researchers investigating situational influences on consumer behavior have focused on three basic questions: When
does a situation influence a consumer's reaction to a product or service; how strong is this influence and in what
way does this influence operate? Situational influences
on purchase behavior have been defined as including characteristics as disparate as shelf-layout, time of day,
shopping purposes and availability of excess cash (Belk
1975). These influences are distinguished from personal or
intra-individual characteristics such as attitude. Belk
(1975) observes that a consumer situation "comprises all of
those factors particular to a time and place of observation
which do not follow from a knowledge of personal and choice
alternative attributes and which have a demonstrable and
systematic effect on current behavior."

The purpose of this paper is to demonstrate the usefulness
of structural equation modeling with unobservable variables
in analyzing the strength of, and circumstances surrounding,
situational influences on consumer behavior. (For a review
of the principles of behavioral modeling and its applications in marketing, see Darden 1981.) The paper reports
on the results of a study which examined situational, attitudinal, and personal influences on consumer intentions to
perform four different do-it-yourself automotive repair
activities. Many of the situational, attitudinal, and behavioral variables were operationalized using multiple
measures.

BACKGROUND

The study of situational influences on consumer behavior
has become a fairly established area. The primary method
of analyzing such data has been analysis of variance.
Belk (1975) summarized the results of six different studies
which used analysis of variance to examine the effect of
situational, consumer and product characteristics on the
probability of consuming six different products. The major influence on behavior in all six studies was the interaction of the situation with the product. People planning
a party, for example, will purchase not more of all beverages, but more of certain beverages (e.g. beer, not milk).

A more recent paper (Harrell, Hutt and Anderson 1980)
approached situational analysis by using path analysis to
examine the impact of one situational variable, crowding,
on several aspects of shopping behavior. This study is interesting because it suggested that the effects of situational variables such as crowding on consumer's attitudes
toward a retail outlet is mediated by other variables such
as a person's strategy of adapting to crowding. By using
path analysis, the authors are able to enhance our understanding of when crowding influences consumers reactions to
a store, how strong this influence is and in what way this
influence operates.

The present study attempts to isolate the relative influence
of situational and attitudinal variables on behavioral intentions using structural equation modeling. The LISREL
(Linear Structural Relationships) program developed by
Joreskog and Sorbom (1978) is employed for this purpose.
It is hypothesized that the relative influence of situational, attitudinal and other respondent characteristics on
behavioral intentions will depend in part on the complexity
of the behavior being considered.

The particular behavior under study, willingness to repair
one's car oneself, can be viewed as an alternative to making a purchase in a service industry. A number of authors
have argued that the service industry needs to examine
factors influencing demand and the ensuing level of satisfaction in terms of task complexity (Liechty and Churchill
1979; Murdock 1981; Zeithaml 1981). For example, Murdock
suggests that the attributes which are determinant in the
selection of a lawyer may vary depending on whether the
legal issue at hand is simple, such as a name change, or
complex, such as a contested divorce.

In our study we hypothesized that when the mechanical task
is complex, one would expect attitudinal and mechanical
knowledge and variables to jointly determine behavioral
intentions. However, when the mechanical task is simple,
then situational variables should be the primary influence
on behavioral intentions.

This hypothesis is similar to previous research that found
that the relative influence of situational and attitudinal
characteristics is dependent on the level of involvement
in the purchase behavior and the situation. Clarke and
Belk (1979) examined involvement in both the situation and
the product for four product categories. They found that
when involvement in the product is low, the situation tends
to determine behavior. When product involvement is high,
the situation is not as important. In other words, the
higher the level of product involvement, the less likely it
is that situational factors will determine behavior.

METHOD

Sample

The data used to investigate the relationship between behavioral intentions, on the one hand, and attitudinal and
situational variables, on the other, are drawn from a
national mail-survey of motor vehicle owners. The purpose
of the survey was to delineate attitudes toward and actual
involvement in do-it-yourself maintenance and repair activities. A random sample of 2,000 names was systematically
selected from lists of all motor vehicle registrations in
each of 50 states. Each state is represented in the sample
in proportion to the magnitude of its motor vehicle
population.

Measures

The dependent variables used in this analysis are the self-
reported intentions of engaging in the following four auto
repairs: (1) changing anti-freeze/coolant; (2) replacing
headlights; (3) replacing brake pads/shoes, and (4) performing tune-ups. These behavioral intentions responses
were obtained on a three-point scale in response to the
following question: "If the opportunity arises in the
near future, what would be the likelihood of you performing
(one of the above four mechanical tasks) by yourself or
with the help of a friend?" The three response categories

were: Very Likely, Likely and Not Likely.[1] Changing anti-freeze and replacing headlights are generally considered to be easier tasks. Replacing brake pads/shoes and performing tune-ups, on the other hand, represent more difficult tasks.

Measures were also developed for the predictor variables--situational, attitudinal, and individual-related character-istics as potential explanations for differences in inten-tions to engage in do-it-yourself maintenance activity. The situational predictors included: access to a conven-ient area for working on a vehicle, and access to the necessary tools to work on a vehicle. The two situational variables were measured dichotomously in response to the question "Do you have access to a convenient area to work on your car? and "Do you have access to the necessary tools to work on your car?" The situational variables are thought to represent what Belk identified as the physical surrounding of a situation.

The attitudinal variable was formulated in the following way. Respondents were asked to indicate the extent of their agreement or disagreement to thirteen statements which reflected attitude toward the two basic maintenance alternatives--self-maintenance versus paying a mechanic to do the repair/maintenance work. Responses were recorded on a five-point Likert scale ranging between strongly agree and strongly disagree. Illustrative attitude statements include: "I believe I can save a lot of money by doing some work on my vehicle myself; I can rely on the work done on my vehicle when I take it to the garage to be serviced," and "I feel safer driving my vehicle because I did the work myself." An attitude score for each individual was then calculated by summing the score on all 13 statements.

Finally, the individual's self assessed mechanical know-ledge was included in the analysis as a predictor of be-havioral intentions. This is derived from the responses to an ordinal scale where the categories were as follows: None, Little , Sufficient, and Considerable. Thie predic-tor was included with the expalantion that it represents a distinct respondent characteristic, different from atti-tudes and situational characteristics.

A STRUCTURAL EQUATION MODEL

A fully recursive structural equation model of do-it-your-self car repair, built from the described variables is contained in Figure 1. Three independent unobservables impact on two dependent variables. In this figure, the unobservables, except for the error terms, are represented by circles, observables are represented by squares. The straight unidirectional arrows represent direct paths of causal influence, while the curved unidirectional arrows represent unanalyzed relationships (Duncan 1966). The system represented in Figure 1 can be written as:

$$\begin{bmatrix} 1 & 0 \\ 0 & 1 \end{bmatrix} \begin{bmatrix} \eta_1 \\ \eta_2 \end{bmatrix} = \begin{bmatrix} \gamma_{11} & \gamma_{12} & \gamma_{13} \\ \gamma_{21} & \gamma_{22} & \gamma_{23} \end{bmatrix} \begin{bmatrix} \xi_1 \\ \xi_2 \\ \xi_3 \end{bmatrix} + \begin{bmatrix} \zeta_1 \\ \zeta_2 \end{bmatrix}$$

Two other sets of equations, the measurement models, cap-ture the relationship between theoretical constructs and their indicators.

---

[1]One limitation of this research is the ordinal character of the endogenous variables. If one employs ordinal endogenous variables one must either assume that the ordinal scale approximates an interval scale (which we are assuming in this case) or treat the variables as if they have an underlying continuous distribution by estima-ting polychoric or polyserial correlations in the input data.

$$\begin{bmatrix} y_1 \\ y_2 \\ y_3 \\ y_3 \end{bmatrix} = \begin{bmatrix} \lambda_{11} & 0 \\ \lambda_{21} & 0 \\ 0 & \lambda_{32} \\ 0 & \lambda_{42} \end{bmatrix} \begin{bmatrix} \eta_1 \\ \eta_2 \end{bmatrix} + \begin{bmatrix} \varepsilon_1 \\ \varepsilon_2 \\ \varepsilon_3 \\ \varepsilon_4 \end{bmatrix}$$

and

$$\begin{bmatrix} x_1 \\ x_2 \\ x_3 \\ x_4 \end{bmatrix} = \begin{bmatrix} \lambda_{11} & 0 & 0 \\ \lambda_{21} & 0 & 0 \\ & \lambda_{32} & 0 \\ 0 & 0 & \lambda_{43} \end{bmatrix} \begin{bmatrix} \xi_1 \\ \xi_2 \\ \xi_3 \end{bmatrix} + \begin{bmatrix} \delta_1 \\ \delta_2 \\ \delta_3 \\ \delta_4 \end{bmatrix}$$

where

η=theoretical, endogenous variables that are measured with ξ error
y=theoretical, exogenous variables that are measured with error
x=measures or operationalizations of endogenous variables
  =measures or operationalizations of exogenous variables
ζ=errors in equations
ε=errors in variables for the y's
δ=errors in variables for the x's
γ=relationships between exogenous and endogenous variables
λ=relationships between the theoretical, unobserved con-structs and their operationalizations.

In the model in Figure 1, there are eight measured variables or 8(9)/2+36 variances and covariances. (The 36 correla-tions are reported in Table 1.) The model contains 24 parameters which are distributed as follows. There are three free paths from unobservables to observables, and six free error variances associated with observables. For the unobservables with single indicators, the error var-iances are fixed at zero. This procedure implies that each is a perfect indicator of its respective unobservable var-iable. The additional parameters are: six direct effects of the unobservable exogenous variables on the endogenous variables; three variances and covariances of latent endo-geneous variables and six variances and covariances of the latent exogenous variables. The chi-square statistic for this model was 23 with 12 degrees of freedom. The proba-bility is 0.02, suggesting an extremely poor fit.

The model in Figure 1 allowed no interdependence among error terms. By examining the pattern of residuals which arise because of a lack of fit in the model and by examin-ing derivatives of the error terms, an additional path representing the correlation between errors was added. (This procedure is described by Bentler 1980 and Sorbom 1975). It should be noted that, although this procedure did produce a model with a much better fit to the data, it might have been capitalizing on chance associations in the data. The new model did not also include a path from the mechanical knowledge to easy maintenance tasks since it was not statistically significant in the earlier model.

The added correlation is between ε_1 and ε_4 in Figure 1. The presence of a significant correlation among the errors in the observables of the endogenous variables suggest that there may be some unobservable not included in the model which may be indicated by both willingness to change anti-freeze and to perform a tune-up (Aaker and Bagozzi 1979). The chi-square value for the new model is 11.71 with 12 degrees of freedom. The probability level is 0.47, suggesting a much better fit to the data. Additional evi-dence that this model provides a good fit is found by examining the residuals in Table 2. It will be noted that all of the residuals are very small.

INTERPRETATION

Table 3 summarizes the relationship between the observables and the unobservables. The standardized factor loadings

401

TABLE 1

Correlation Matrix

	x_1	x_2	x_3	x_4	y_1	y_2	y_3	y_4
x_1	1.000							
x_2	.457	1.000						
x_3	.282	.491	1.000					
x_4	.313	.528	.570	1.000				
y_1	.153	.399	.529	.378	1.000			
y_2	.215	.440	.608	.420	.681	1.000		
y_3	.214	.441	.611	.483	.497	.552	1.000	
y_4	.220	.441	.628	.474	.584	.591	.728	1.000

TABLE 2

Residuals from the Fitted Model

	y_1	y_2	y_3	y_4	x_1	x_2	x_3	x_4
y_1	.002							
y_2	.002	.000						
y_3	.000	−.010	.001					
y_4	.007	.009	.002	.002				
x_1	−.064	−.030	−.025	−.027	.000			
x_2	.010	−.001	.011	−.003	.001	.000		
x_3	.018	.013	.020	−.005	.017	−.004	.000	
x_4	−.005	.002	.001	−.002	.008	−.001	.000	.000

TABLE 3

Parameter Estimates (λ's)

Endogeneous Variables	Standardized Factor Loading

Factor 1: <u>Easy and Necessary Maintenance Tasks</u>

    y_1 Changing anti-freeze/coolant   .774

    y_2 Replacing headlights   .877

Factor 2: <u>Difficult Maintenance Tasks</u>

    y_3 Replacing brake pads/shoes   .838

    y_4 Tune up   .867

<u>Exogeneous Variables</u>

Factor 1: <u>Situation Influences-Physical Surroundings</u>

    x_1 Access to convenient work area   .503

    x_2 Access to necessary tools   .905

Factor 2: <u>Mechanical Knowledge</u>

    x_3 Self-assessed mechanical knowledge   1.00*

Factor 3: <u>Attitudinal Influences</u>

    x_4 Attitude toward car repair   1.00*

Note: *Fixed parameters

from the new model (Model 2) are presented. The relative size of the factor loadings reflects how well each indicator indicates each unobservable. Both these loadings and the factor loadings in factor analysis are based on the intercorrelations among the indicators. However, in structural equation modeling, these factor loadings are also based on the links to the causal variables (Aaker and Bagozzi 1979).

Table 4 summarizes the parameter values for the earlier (Model 1) and the revised (Model 2) models. The gamma coefficients are interpretable like ordinary regression coefficients. In Model 2, intentions to perform an easy maintenance task are determined by one's physical surroundings and on one's attitudes. The respective gammas are .392 and .427. This model accounts for 52 percent of the estimated variance in the unobservable "intentions to engage in easy maintenance tasks." One's willingness to participate in fairly complex mechanical tasks, on the other hand, depends on physical surroundings, attitudes, and mechanical knowledge. The respective gammas are .323, .461 and .105. Percentage of variance in eta 2 accounted for by the model is 58 percent.

The amount of explained variance is calculated by first finding the amount of unexplained variance, which is a ratio of the unexplained error variance to the estimated variance in each eta. These figures are obtained from the regression residual covariance matrix which contains the partial covariance among the measured endogenous variables net of the unmeasured exogenous variables and from the Eta-Eta (=C) matrix which contains the estimated variance-covariances of the unmeasured endogenous variables. These are part of the LISREL output (Sewell and Hauser 1972).

IMPLICATIONS

Causal modeling can be a useful technique for analyzing the interrelationships between behavioral intentions and a variety of factors affecting them. It can help establish, for example, when a characteristic of a situation will influence consumer reaction to a product or service; the strength of this influence; and the manner in which this influence operates.

Our investigation suggests, first of all, that attitudes towards do-it-yourself activity are a strong determinant of intentions to engage in self-maintenance, regardless of whether the tasks are easy or difficult. As one would expect, mechanical knowledge plays more of a role in influencing complex mechanical tasks rather than easy tasks. There is a tendency for situational influences to have a greater impact in the instance of performing easier maintenance tasks, as hypothesized. This conclusion is not as strong as one would like to make, however.

Based upon the results of causal modeling, a tentative generalization may be offered concerning the relationship between situational variables and task complexity. For consumption activities that are relatively easy, attitudinal variables play less of a role and situational factors play more of a role in determining behavior, than for consumption activities that are relatively complex.

Other service industries, in addition to the automotive repair industry, provide the consumer with services that vary in complexity. For example, lawyers may perform routine legal tasks such as a name change or they may provide complicated legal assistance in a contested divorce. Similarly home repair businesses, travel agents and dentists offer a variety of service to the consumer. Based on this study, one could speculate that the variables influencing the demand for services depend to some extent on the difficulty of the task being considered. Structural equation modeling is an appropriate tool for understanding this demand.

REFERENCES

Aaker, David and Bagozzi, Richard (1979), "Unobservable Variables in Structural Equation Models with an Application in Industrial Selling," _Journal of Marketing Research_, 16 (May), 147-158.

Belk, Russel, W. (1975), "Situational Variables and Consumer Behavior," _Journal of Consumer Research_, 2 (December), 157-164.

- -

FIGURE 1

Situational and Attitudinal Influences on Automobile Repair Intentions

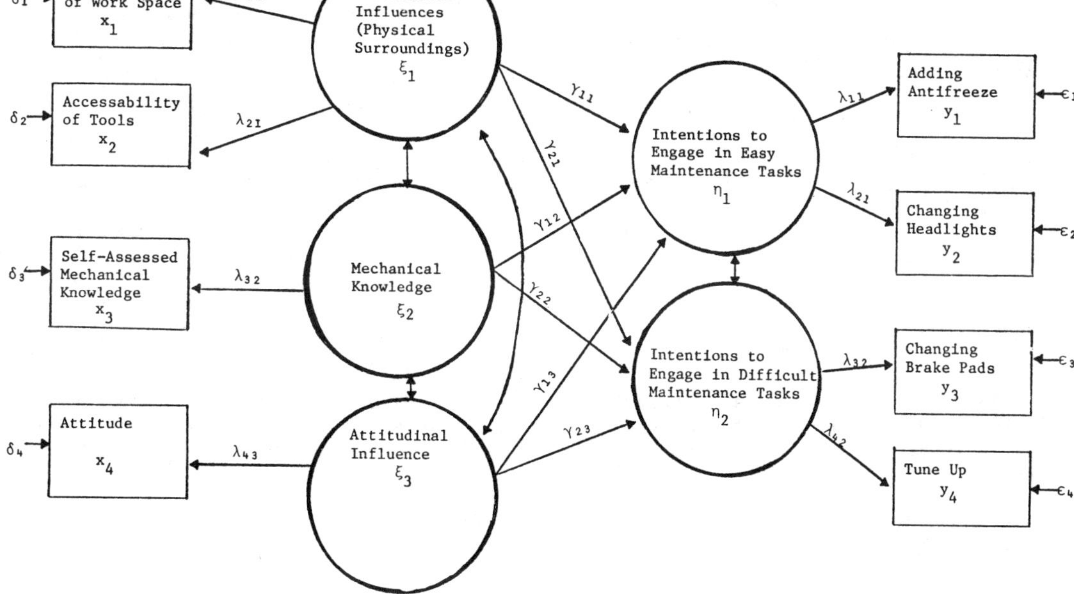

TABLE 4

Parameter Estimates

Parameter	Model 1 Parameter Estimates	T-Value	Model 2 Parameter Estimates	T-Value
γ_{11}	-.371	4.522	.392	5.367
γ_{12}	-.029	.824	.000*	--
γ_{13}	.430	12.019	.427	12.192
γ_{21}	.307	3.936	.323	4.128
γ_{22}	-.116	3.362	.105	3.299
γ_{23}	.453	13.221	.461	13.351
ϕ_{11}	.250	6.099	.253	6.193
ϕ_{21}	.290	7.967	.296	8.219
ϕ_{22}	1.00	18.668	1.00	18.668
ϕ_{31}	.270	7.770	.274	7.969
ϕ_{32}	.570	13.075	.570	13.075
ϕ_{33}	1.00	18.668	1.00	18.668
ψ_{11}	.297	10.156	.286	10.092
ψ_{21}	.159	8.543	.143	7.729
ψ_{22}	.293	10.925	.296	10.897
$\theta_{\varepsilon_{11}}$	.376	12.908	.399	13.086
$\theta_{\varepsilon_{22}}$	.256	8.946	.231	7.558
$\theta_{\varepsilon_{33}}$	.309	12.278	.296	11.625
$\theta_{\varepsilon_{44}}$	.232	9.509	.247	9.846
$\theta_{\varepsilon_{41}}$	0*	0	.063	3.458
$\theta_{\delta_{11}}$	.750	16.609	.747	16.681
$\theta_{\delta_{22}}$	.164	2.361	.180	2.801
$\theta_{\delta_{33}}$	0*	0--	.00*	--
$\theta_{\delta_{44}}$	0*	--	.000*	--
x^2	= 23.5825		11.7067	
df	= 12		12	
Probability	= .0232		.4695	

*Constrained parameter

Bentler, P. M. (1980), "Multivariate Analysis with Latent Variables: Causal Modeling," <u>Annual Review of Psychology</u>, 31, 419-456.

__________ and Spekart, George (1981), "Attitudes, 'Cause' Behaviors: A Structural Equation Analysis," <u>Journal of Personality and Social Psychology</u>, 40, 226-38.

Bielby, W. T. and Hauser, R. M. (1977), "Structural Equation Models," <u>Annual Review of Sociology</u>, 3, 137-161.

Churchill, Gilbert A. and Pecotich, Anthony (1981), "A Structural Equation Investigation of the Pay-Satisfaction-Valence Relationship Among Salespeople," Wisconsin Working Paper: Graduate School of Business: University of Wisconsin-Madison.

Clarke, Keith and Belk, Russell, W. (1979), "The Effects of Product Involvement and Task Definition on Anticipated Consumer Effort," in William L. Wilkie, (ed.), <u>Advances in Consumer Research</u>, Vol. 6 (Ann Arbor, Mich.: Association for Consumer Research), 313-318.

Darden, William R. (1981), "Review of Behavioral Modeling in Marketing," <u>Review of Marketing 1981</u>, Ben M. Enis and Kenneth T. Roering, Eds., Chicago: American Marketing Association, 21-30.

Duncan, O. D. (1966), "Path Analysis: Sociological Examples," <u>American Journal of Sociology</u>, 72 (1), (July), 1-14.

Harrell, Gilbert, Hutt, Michael D., and Anderson, James C. (1980), "Path Analysis of Buyer Behavior Under Conditions of Crowding," <u>Journal of Marketing Research</u>, 17 (February), 45-51.

Joreskog, Karl G., Sorbom, Dag (1978), <u>Analysis of Linear Structural Relationships by the Method of Maximum Likelihood: User's Guide Version LV 1978</u>: National Educational Resources, Inc., Chicago, Illinois.

Liechty, Margaret and Churchill, Gilbert A. (1979), "Conceptual Insights into Consumer Satisfaction with Services," in N. Beckwith; M. Houston; K. Monroe, S. Ward, eds., <u>1979 Educators Conference Proceedings</u>, (Chicago, Ill.: American Marketing Association), 509-515.

Murdock, Gene (1981), "The Identification of Determinant Attributes Used by Consumers of Legal Services," in Bernhardt, K.; Dolich, I.; Etzel, M.; Kehoe, W.; Kinnear, T.; Perreault, W.; Roering, K. eds., <u>The Changing Marketing Environment: New Theories and Applications</u>, (Chicago, Il: American Marketing Association), 150-153.

Sewell, William and Hauser, Robert M. (1979), "Causes and Consequences of Higher Education: Models of the Status Attainment Process," <u>American Journal of Agricultural Economics</u>, 54(5) (December), 851-861.

Sorbom, D. (19), "Detection of Correlated Errors in Longitudinal Data," <u>British Journal of Math Stat Psychology</u>, 28, 138-151.

VALIDITY ASSESSMENT:
A STRUCTURAL EQUATIONS APPROACH USING PARTIAL LEAST SQUARES

Claes Fornell, The University of Michigan, Ann Arbor
Gerard J. Tellis, The University of Michigan, Ann Arbor
George M. Zinkhan, The University of Houston, Houston

ABSTRACT

A procedure is discussed for the decomposition of trait,
method and error variance by the Partial Least Squares
method for estimating structural equation models. This
enables an assessment of construct validity that meets the
goals of the more rigorous approaches while avoiding many
of their assumptions. The advertising response-recall relationship is analyzed as an illustration.

INTRODUCTION

The development of constructs and measures to estimate them
is basic to theory building in the social sciences. Accordingly, the subject of construct validity or the degree
of correspondence between theoretical constructs and their
measures has received considerable attention in the social
science literature. In particular several methods to estimate convergent, discriminant and nomological validity have
been developed. Following the pioneering contribution of
Campbell and Fiske (1959), several alternatives have been
proposed (see Schmitt, Boyle and Saari (1977), for a review of methods and Peter (1981) for a general review).
Among these, Jöreskog's analysis of covariance structures
(1971) and more recently, his structural equation models
(1977) represent one of the more rigorous formulations.
These models use a maximum likelihood estimation (or, when
this is not possible, an unweighted Least Squares procedure) via the LISREL V computer program (Jöreskog and
Sörbom 1981).

A problem with this approach (particularly in maximum likelihood estimation) is its strong assumptions of multinor-
mality and large sample sizes. Other limitations (not specific to the estimation procedure) are:

- problems with model identification which can become more
  acute when methods factors have to be explicitly used,
- the χ^2 test, the power of which is unknown,
- the dependence of χ^2 on structural consistency which can
  lead to better χ^2 values as theory or measurement decline
  (Fornell and Larcker 1981a; 1981b),
- the problem of improper or inadmissable solutions (Fornell
  and Bookstein 1981).

What is needed is an alternative method that avoids these
problems and yet maintains about the same level of rigor.

Herman Wold's (1975; 1980a; 1980b) Partial Least Squares
(PLS) is a method which appears to satisfy these criteria.
Because it can be used to explicitly model trait, method
and error variances, it can serve as a general approach to
assess convergent, discriminant and nomological validity.

MODEL STRUCTURE

The PLS model consists of two sets of equations, the structural equations and the block structures containing the
measurement equations. The structural equation can be
written as:

$$\beta \underset{\sim}{\eta} = \Gamma \underset{\sim}{\xi} + \underset{\sim}{\zeta} \tag{1}$$

where, η = (m x 1) is a column vector of unobserved criterion variables; ξ = (n x 1) is a column vector of unobserved predictor variables; β = (m x m) is a matrix of
criterion coefficients; Γ = (m x n) is a matrix of predictor coefficients; ζ = (m x 1) is a column vector of
residuals.

The measurement equations are:

$$\underset{\sim}{y} = \Lambda_{\sim y} \underset{\sim}{\eta} + \underset{\sim}{\varepsilon} \tag{2}$$

$$\underset{\sim}{x} = \Lambda_{\sim x} \underset{\sim}{\xi} + \underset{\sim}{\delta} \tag{3}$$

where, y = (p x 1) is a column vector of criterion measures; x = (q x 1) is a column vector of predictor measures; Λ_y = (p x m) is a matrix of regression coefficients
of y on η; Λ_x = (q x n) is a matrix of regression coefficients of x on ξ; ε = (p x 1) is a column vector of criteria measurement errors; δ = (q x 1) is a column vector
of predictor measurement errors. It is assumed that the
unobservables are specified as exact linear combinations
of their respective measures and, for convenience, that all
variables are standardized.

PLS estimation requires only the basic regression by least
squares assumptions to be satisfied. It can handle fixed
variables, nonmetric data and small sample sizes. In order
to statistically evaluate the results, one can either invoke the classical assumptions on residuals, etc., or use
jackknifing in combination with a Stone-Geisser (Stone
1974; Geisser 1974) test for predictive relevance.

VALIDITY ASSESSMENT

As with Jöreskog's method, construct validity can be evaluated by partitioning variance into trait, measurement and
method components. The estimation of relative trait variance enables an assessment of discriminant validity; the
estimation of trait relative to measurement variance, an
assessment of convergent validity; the estimation of measurement and method variance, an assessment of systematic
error in the instrument; and finally partitioning of variance in the context of the structural equations, enables an
assessment of nomological validity.

Convergent Validity

Convergent validity can be defined as the degree to which
two or more attempts to measure the same construct through
maximally different methods are in agreement (Campbell and
Fiske 1959). For example, the stapel and semantic differential attitude scales are fairly similar methods, while
the stapel scale and actual observation reflect fairly different methods.

That the methods be "maximally different" is an ideal that
indicates the rigor of the empirical test rather than a
precondition of analysis. The degree of "agreement" among
the methods used can be assessed by the average variance
shared with a construct, (ρ_{vc}). Thus from equation (2),
the variance shared by the construct η_j estimated by different measures y_{ij} is given by:

$$\rho_{vc\eta_j} = \frac{\sum_{i=1}^{\ell} \lambda^2 \, y_{ij}}{\ell} \; , \text{ for } \ell \text{ measures of } \eta_j \text{ and } j = 1 \ldots m \quad (4)$$

and similarly for $\rho_{vc\xi_k}$, $k = 1 \ldots n$.

A reasonable condition for satisfying convergence is that the value of ρ_{vc} for a construct be statistically greater than 0.5, i.e., the variance shared with a construct be greater than that due to error, or else the entire measurement procedure is in doubt. The null hypothesis that $\rho_{vc}^{\frac{1}{2}} \leq 0.5^{\frac{1}{2}}$ can be tested by the t-test with N-2 degrees of freedom.

One has to be aware that this criterion becomes increasingly easy to satisfy if we increase the number of constructs. Parsimony would dictate therefore that one start with the minimum number of theoretical constructs and explore additional constructs only if it leads to a substantial and meaningful increase in the value of ρ_{vc}.

An alternate global statistic to compensate for the effect of increasing numbers of constructs is the ratio of the variance shared in the model to the number of measures and constructs, i.e.,

$$M^2 = \frac{\sum_{i=1}^{p} \lambda^2_{y_i} + \sum_{i=1}^{q} \lambda^2_{x_i}}{(p + m) + (q + n)} \quad (5)$$

By this formula, values of M^2 will range from 0 to 1 and will be high when measurement error is low and a minimum number of constructs specified. The value of M^2 can also be calculated for any subset of the measurement model.

Discriminant Validity

Discriminant validity is the degree to which a construct differs from other constructs. Since in PLS, a construct is specified as an exact linear combination of its respective measures, construct scores can be computed. Let r^2_{jk} be the squared correlation coefficient between any two constructs. A criterion for discriminant validity then, is that r^2_{jk} be statistically lower than $\rho_{vc\xi_k}$; i.e., that the variance shared between any two different constructs is less than the variance shared between a construct and its measures.

Methods Variance

A special advantage of evaluating construct validity by structural equations is that it permits partitioning of variance due to traits and measurement. In addition, by introducing a "methods" construct, it is possible to partition variance due to traits, measurement and methods, in the event that there exists a method common to subsets of the measures. In this case, the measurement variance is the random error while the method variance is the systematic error. While the estimation procedure for methods variance by LISREL has been discussed in the marketing literature (Bagozzi 1980; Phillips 1981), it is possible to estimate it also by PLS; thus from equation (2)

$$\underset{\sim}{y} = \underset{\sim y}{\Lambda} \underset{\sim}{\eta} + \underset{\sim}{\Lambda^*} \underset{\sim}{g} + \underset{\sim}{\varepsilon^*} \quad (6)$$

where, $\underset{\sim}{g} = (s \times 1)$ is a column vector of s methods factors; $\underset{\sim}{\Lambda^*} = (p \times s)$ is a matrix of coefficients for the methods; $\underset{\sim}{\varepsilon^*} = (p \times 1)$ is a vector of measurement errors. Hence $\underset{\sim}{\Lambda^*}g + \underset{\sim}{\varepsilon^*} = \underset{\sim}{\varepsilon}$ is the partitioning of the original measurement error into methods variance (or systematic error), $\underset{\sim}{\Lambda^*}$ and measurement (or random error). The partitioning of $\underset{\sim}{g}$

error variances for the x variables from equation (3), is analogous. The existence of methods factor can be inspected from the information in the residual correlation matrix, or hypothesized a priori.

Nomological Validity

Nomological validity is used here to mean the degree to which predictions of constructs in the model are verified. Thus, this definition of nomological validity is construct specific and applicable only to endogenous constructs.

A convenient means of assessing nomological validity is by extending Stewart and Love's (1968) redundancy index to redundancy between constructs (Fornell and Larcker 1981a). This type of redundancy is not based on loadings (in contrast to Stewart and Love's original formula) but simply measures the average squared multiple correlation between each construct in η and all constructs in ξ. It is written:

$$\overline{R}^2_{\sim\eta|\xi} = \frac{1}{m} \, tr \, [\underset{\sim\xi\xi}{R}^{-1} \, \underset{\sim\xi\eta}{R} \, \underset{\sim\eta\xi}{R}] \quad (7)$$

where $\underset{\sim\xi\xi}{R}$ is the (n x n) matrix of correlations between the constructs in ξ, and $\underset{\sim\xi\eta}{R}$ is the (n x m) matrix of correlations between ξ and η. The statistical significance of $\overline{R}^2_{\eta|\xi}$ can be determined by using Miller's (1975) test with $(n \cdot m)$ and $(N - n - 1) \cdot m$ degrees of freedom.

ILLUSTRATION

In our illustration of validity assessment via PLS we use preliminary data from a study on advertising recall and advertising response. Results of the analysis were intended to refine the design and analysis of the main study.

While sales is the ultimate criterion of advertising effectiveness, in practice too many factors often blur the actual causal relationship between advertising and sales. Accordingly alternate procedures have been developed to gauge advertising effectiveness. Advertising response and advertising recall are generally considered important indices of advertising effectiveness. The underlying hypothesis is that a favorable response to an advertisement leads to a favorable recall of the advertisement and of the product, and a higher probability of purchase. A sample of 111 undergraduate students was used for the experiment, yielding 105 usable cases. The respondents were subjected to a calculator advertisement (together with three others) and their response ascertained by a self-administered questionnaire. Two days later their recall of the advertisement was ascertained by a second questionnaire.

Multiple measures were used to estimate the latent constructs, response and recall. Response was estimated by six measures: how enjoyable, interesting and likable it was from an aesthetic angle and how understandable, informative and persuasive the message was. Recall was estimated from seven aided and unaided measures of recall of some aspect of the product advertised. A detailed discussion of the theory, the experiment and the rationale for the measures is provided in Zinkhan (1981).

ANALYSIS

Method

The computations were performed by iterations of explicit simple and multiple regression using the Michigan Interactive Data Analysis System (MIDAS). A general algorithm is briefly described by Fornell and Bookstein (1981). Further details are available from the authors. The methods factor was obtained by using the residuals of the regression of the observed variables on the latent variables and then running these residuals through the above PLS program. All significance tests are conducted using the standard errors available from the regression output.

Two Construct Model

The model with two constructs and thirteen measures, shown in Figure 1 was tested first. The results indicate that there is a positive link between response and recall (γ coefficient = .52). The average shared variance in the measures of the response construct is quite high (ρ_{vc} response = .63). However, all six measures do not load equally well, and the bottom measures, "information" and "understanding" in particular, have values of measurement error in excess of .5 indicating poor convergence. The shared variance in measures per construct $M^2_{2\text{-construct}}$, is .44 which is to be compared with later models.

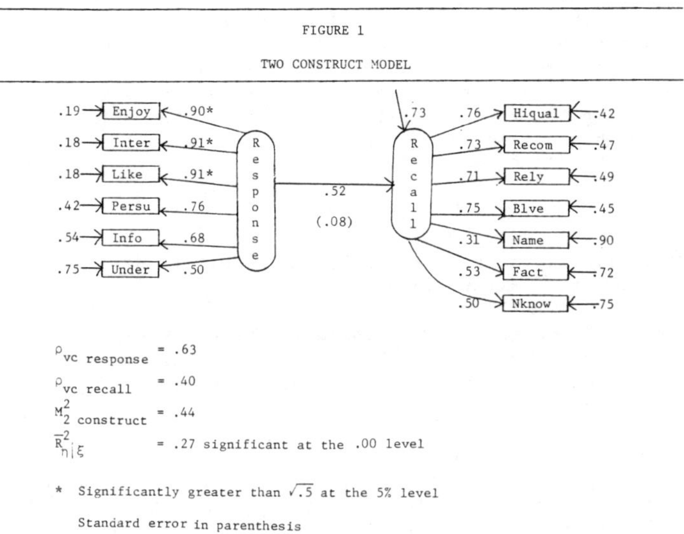

FIGURE 1

TWO CONSTRUCT MODEL

$\rho_{vc \text{ response}}$ = .63

$\rho_{vc \text{ recall}}$ = .40

$M^2_{2 \text{ construct}}$ = .44

$\overline{R}^2_{\eta | \xi}$ = .27 significant at the .00 level

* Significantly greater than $\sqrt{.5}$ at the 5% level

Standard error in parenthesis

The results for the "recall" construct are less acceptable. Shared variance in the seven measures ($\rho_{vc \text{ recall}}$) is .40, indicating average measurement error in excess of .5 for the measures as a group. A closer analysis indicates that the lower three measures, "name," "fact" and "don't know" are mainly responsible for this.

It is interesting and important to note that consistently across the thirteen indicators, the _affective_ measures load highly on their respective constructs, while the measures that load weakly on the constructs are more _cognitive_ in nature ("information," "understanding," "name," "fact" and "not know").

This leads us to three possible hypotheses to test:

- the measurement errors in the cognitive indicators are due to method variance,
- the cognitive measures are indicators of two separate constructs, "cognitive response" and "cognitive recall" as distinct from the affective constructs,
- the cognitive indicators are poorly measured in the response-recall relationship.

Each of these three hypotheses will be tested in turn.

Model with Methods Variance

In order to test the first of the above three hypotheses, a model with methods variance was specified (see Figure 2). The method construct may be labelled "cognitive method" and is formed by partitioning variance in the four measures, "information," "understanding," "fact" and "name." (The measure "unknown" was not involved as it is a component of the "fact" question and would form a separate method with "fact" distorting the analysis at this stage).

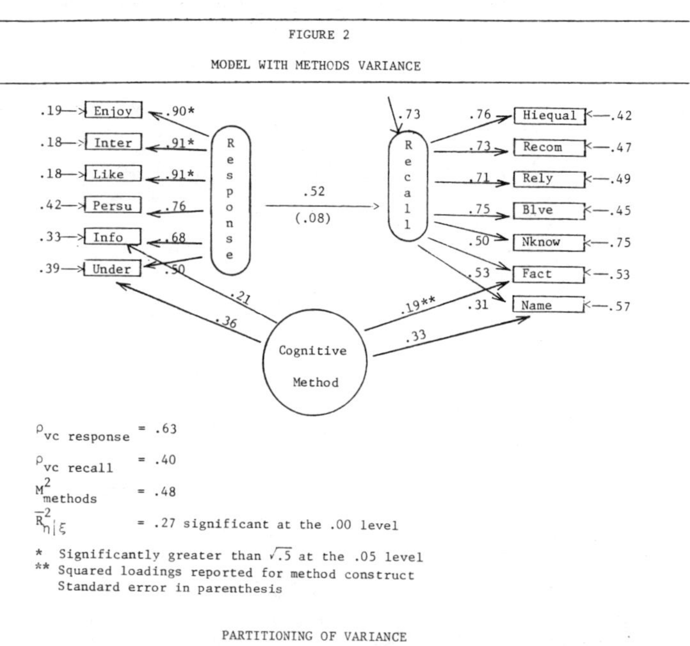

FIGURE 2

MODEL WITH METHODS VARIANCE

$\rho_{vc \text{ response}}$ = .63

$\rho_{vc \text{ recall}}$ = .40

M^2_{methods} = .48

$\overline{R}^2_{\eta | \xi}$ = .27 significant at the .00 level

* Significantly greater than $\sqrt{.5}$ at the .05 level
** Squared loadings reported for method construct
Standard error in parenthesis

PARTITIONING OF VARIANCE

Observed Measures	Trait		Method	Error
	Response	Recall	(Systematic Error)	(Random Error)
INFO	.46	---	.21	.33
UNDER	.25	---	.36	.39
FACT	---	.28	.19	.53
NAME	---	.10	.33	.57

The results partly confirm the hypothesis of the existence of a methods factor, as random error has been significantly reduced. However, there are still three indicators of recall with random error in excess of 50%. Accordingly we test for the presence of additional constructs which might capture this variance.

Model with Three Constructs

A model with three constructs was specified by separating the recall construct into two separate constructs: affective recall and cognitive recall. The results are presented in Figure 3. There is a marked improvement in convergent validity for the endogenous constructs, $\rho_{vc \text{ aff. recall}}$ = .70 and $\rho_{vc \text{ cog. recall}}$ = .69 (compared with .40 for the two construct model). Discriminant validity is also evident as the above two values of ρ_{vc} are significantly lower than $r^2_{\text{aff. recall - cog. recall}}$ = .01. The value of the shared variance in measures per construct $M^2_{3\text{-construct}}$ = .54 which is substantially higher than that for the previous two models.

Model with Four Constructs

Finally, a four construct model was specified by splitting the response construct into cognitive response and affective response. As shown in Figure 4, convergent validity is acceptable, .78 and .55 for the two response constructs. Discriminant validity for the two constructs is also acceptable (squared correlation coefficient = .47). The value of shared measure variance per construct for this model $M^2_{4 \text{ construct}}$ is .54 thus indicating that loss of parsimony compensates for gain in variance extracted relative to the model with three constructs.

FIGURE 3

THREE CONSTRUCT MODEL

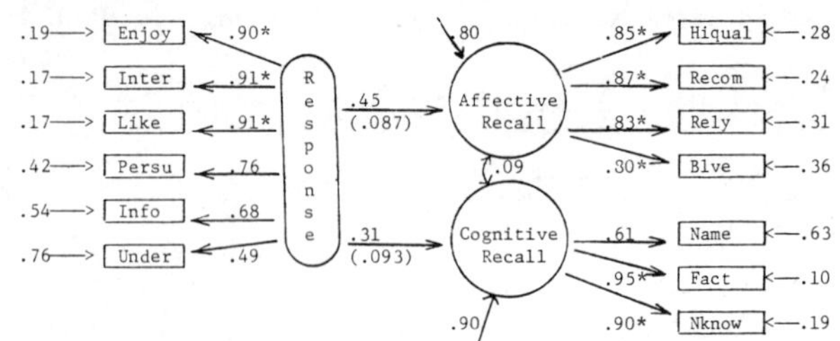

$\rho_{vc\ response}$ = .63

$\rho_{vc\ aff.\ rcll.}$ = .70

$\rho_{vc\ cog.\ rcll.}$ = .69

$M^2_{3\ construct}$ = .54

$\bar{R}^2_{\eta|\xi}$ = .15 significant at the .05 level

$r^2_{aff.\ rcll.\ -\ cog.\ rcll.}$ = .01

* Significantly greater than $\sqrt{.5}$ at the .05 level

Structural parameters significant at the .05 level

FIGURE 4

FOUR CONSTRUCT MODEL

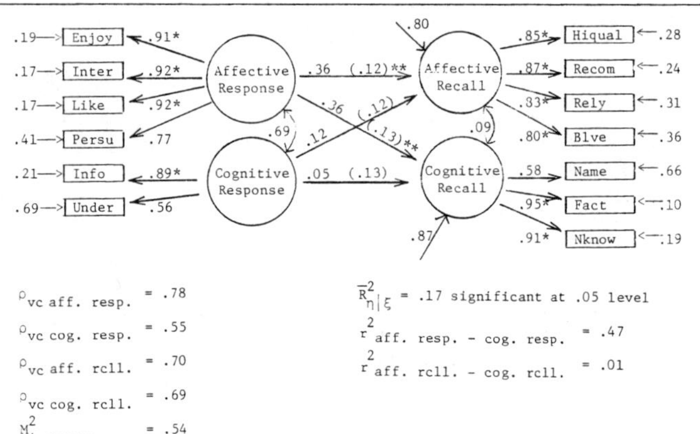

$\rho_{vc\ aff.\ resp.}$ = .78

$\rho_{vc\ cog.\ resp.}$ = .55

$\rho_{vc\ aff.\ rcll.}$ = .70

$\rho_{vc\ cog.\ rcll.}$ = .69

$M^2_{4\ constr.}$ = .54

$\bar{R}^2_{\eta|\xi}$ = .17 significant at .05 level

$r^2_{aff.\ resp.\ -\ cog.\ resp.}$ = .47

$r^2_{aff.\ rcll.\ -\ cog.\ rcll.}$ = .01

* Significantly greater than $\sqrt{.5}$ at the .05 level

** Significant at the .05 level

CONCLUSIONS

Convergent and discriminant validity are acceptable in the three- and four construct models (Figures 3 and 4). This is not the case for the two construct model (Figure 1) or for the model with method variance (Figure 2). In the three- and four construct models, there are only two indicators with excessive error vs. five in the two construct model and three in the model with method variance. These higher error levels lead to an unacceptable overall measure for the response construct, since there is more error variance than trait variance.[1] In contrast, both the three- and four construct models exhibit more trait than error variance. The price of reformulating a model such that convergent validity becomes acceptable is a reduction in predictive power of the structural model. That is, while we may obtain a satisfactory measurement model, nomological validity may not be acceptable. The reduction in predictive power is evident in comparing the first two

models (that are rejected due to inadequate measurement properties). For the first two models, the redundancy between constructs is .27; for the three construct model, .15; and for the four construct model, .17. Since convergent and discriminant (measurement) validity are necessary to even consider a model in the context of nomological validity (theory), the two construct model and the model with method variance are not subjected to further evaluation. The choice is between the three and the four construct models. The slight increase in predictive power (.15 vs. .17) in going from the three vs. the four construct model is not statistically significant or sufficient to suggest this model. Further, as shown in Figure 4, only two structural parameters (path coefficients) are statistically significant. In contrast, both structural parameters in the three construct model are significant.

In conclusion, then, the analysis suggests that the recall construct includes an affective dimension and a cognitive dimension whereas the response construct appears to be unidimensional. The reason for this is not answered by our analysis. Indeed, any substantive inferences regarding the results presented here must be subject to a closer examination of the experimental design itself.

---

[1] For "Recall" in figure 2 we have trait variance = .58 + .53 + .50 + .56 + .25 + .28 + .10 = 2.8, random error variance = .42 + .47 + .49 + .45 + .75 + .53 + .57 = 3.68 and systematic error variance = .19 + .33 = .52.

REFERENCES

Bagozzi, Richard P. (1980), _Causal Models in Marketing_ New York: Wiley and Sons.

Campbell, Donald T., and Donald W. Fiske (1959), "Convergent and Discriminant Validity by the Multitrait-Multimethod Matrix," _Psychological Bulletin_, 56 (March), 81-105.

Fornell, Claes and Fred Bookstein (1981), "A Comparative Analysis of Two Structural Equation Models: LISREL and PLS Applied to Market Data," Working Paper No. 276, The University of Michigan, Ann Arbor.

__________ and David F. Larcker (1981a), "Evaluating Structural Equation Models with Unobservable Variables and Measurement Error," _Journal of Marketing Research_, 18 (February), 39-50.

__________ and __________ (1981b), "Structural Equation Models with Unobservable Variables and Measurement Error: Algebra and Statistics," _Journal of Marketing Research_, 18 (August), 382-88.

Geisser, S. (1974), "A Predictive Approach to the Random Effect Model," _Biometrika_, 61, 101-7.

Jöreskog, K. G. (1971), "Structural Analysis of Sets of Congeneric Tests," _Psychometrika_, 36, 109-133.

__________ (1977), "Structural Equation Models in the Social Sciences: Specification, Estimation and Testing," in _Applications of Statistics_, P. R. Krishnaiah, ed., Amsterdam: North Holland, 265-287.

__________ and Dag Sörbom (1981), LISREL V: _Analysis of Linear Structural Relationships by the Method of Maximum Likelihood_, Chicago: National Educational Resources.

Miller, John K. (1975), "The Sampling Distribution and a Test for the Significance of the Bimultivariate Redundancy Statistic: A Monte Carlo Study," _Multivariate Behavioral Research_, (April), 233-44.

__________ and S. D. Farr (1971), "Bimultivariate Redundancy: A Comprehensive Measure of Interbattery Relationship," _Multivariate Behavioral Research_, 6, 313-24.

Peter, J. Paul (1981), "Construct Validity: A Review of Basic Issues and Marketing Practice, _Journal of Marketing Research_, 18 (May), 133-45.

Phillips, Lynn W. (1981), "Assessing Measurement Error in Key Informant Reports, A Methodological Note on Organizational Analysis in Marketing," _Journal of Marketing_, 18 (November), 395-415.

Schmitt, Neal, Bryan Coyle, and Bruce B. Saari (1977), "A Review and Critique of Analyses of Multitrait-Multimethod Matrices," _Multivariate Behavioral Research_, 12 (October), 447-78.

Stewart, D. and W. Love (1968), "A General Canonical Correlation Index," _Psychological Bulletin_, 70, 160-3.

Stone, M. (1974), "Cross-Validatory Choice and Assessment of Statistical Predictions," _Journal of the Royal Statistical Society_, B36, 111-33.

Wold, Herman (1975), "Path Models with Latent Variables: The NIPALS Approach," in _Quantitative Sociology: International Perspectives on Mathematical and Statistical Model Building_, H. M. Blalock et al., eds. New York: Academic Press, 307-57.

__________ (1980a), "Model Construction and Evaluation When Theoretical Knowledge is Scarce--Theory and Application of Partial Least Squares," in _Evaluation of Econometric Models_, J. Kmenta and J. G. Ramsey, eds. New York: Academic Press, 47-74.

__________ (1980b), "Soft Modelling: Intermediate between Traditional Model Building and Data Analysis," _Mathematical Statistics_, 6. 333-46.

Zinkhan, George M. (1981), "The Influence of Cognitive Complexity and Copy Structure on Advertising Effectiveness," unpublished dissertation, Ann Arbor: The University of Michigan.

THE EFFECTS OF RESPONDENT IDENTIFICATION IN A MAIL SURVEY

Nancy M. Ridgway, University of Texas at Austin
Linda L. Price, University of Texas at Austin

ABSTRACT

This research had the limited purpose of examining the impact of explicit identification of the potential respondent by the researcher on response rate, response speed and item omission in the context of a mail survey. The study used a low level of personalization and a promise of confidentiality to all respondents. Results of the research indicated that visibly identifying respondents under low personalization conditions significantly decreases response rates and slows response speed.

INTRODUCTION

Consumer researchers are increasingly concerned with non-response. At the same time there are numerous reasons to believe that respondent concerns about both confidentiality and anonymity are probable sources of non-response or low-quality responses. Research to date has failed to clarify the effect of confidentiality and anonymity on response rate and quality in common research settings. In particular, research has largely failed to differentiate identification from personalization.

PURPOSE

The purpose of this research was to examine the impact of explicit identification of the potential respondent by the researcher on response rate, response speed and item omission in the context of a mail survey. The study used a low level of personalization and a promise of confidentiality to all respondents. The sample for the study was a priori expected to come from a high income, high education population. The value of the study was expected to derive from the following research characteristics:

1. The research focused on involuntary identification as opposed to personalization.

2. The research placed an emphasis on apparent anonymity in contrast to explicit promises of anonymity.

3. The research made a promise of confidentiality to all potential respondents.

4. The sample was chosen from a population with high income and educational status. Recent findings suggest such a population may be sensitive to assurances of anonymity.

BACKGROUND

Certain terms are central to an explication of the research area, specifically: confidentiality, anonymity, personalization, and identification. For the purposes of this research the following understandings are applied. A promise of confidentiality can be taken to imply only that individually identifiable data will not be disclosed, and not the somewhat stronger assurance that the individual identity of the respondent will be unknown. Anonymity exists when the questionnaire that a respondent completes cannot be linked to the respondent because it lacks information that can be used for individual identification. There appears to be a distinction between actual anonymity and psychological "perceived" anonymity. The opposite of anonymity is identification. Identification can either be explicit, or it

can be done surreptitiously through blind coding and other techniques. Personalization makes an explicit effort to approach each potential respondent as a unique individual deserving of personal attention, rather than an arbitrarily chosen anonymous person (Shaw et al. 1979). As a consequence, personalization may threaten an individual's anonymity. Whether it does depends upon the form the personalization takes.

As indicated above, identification can be either explicit or surreptitious. The surreptitious identification of the respondent via tactics like invisible ink coding has achieved considerable public notice through articles in The National Observer, The New York Times, The Wall Street Journal and a variety of other newspapers. Similarly, blind coding has attracted the attention of market researchers (McGown 1979, Dickson, Casey and Wyckoff 1976). Despite the controversial nature of surreptitious identification, it is commonly engaged in to reduce the cost of follow-up mailings, allow for validation, and facilitate longitudinal analyses (McGown 1979). The direct benefits of identification to the market researcher are apparent. However, researchers are reluctant to use explicit identification, because of the belief that it would lead to lower response rates, lower quality data and slower response times. Despite this rather prevalent belief, results on explicit identification are inconclusive. Some researchers have found that a lack of anonymity through either personalization or identification impacts negatively the response rate and/or data quality (Andreasen 1970, Houston and Jefferson 1975, Jones 1981, Kerin and Peterson 1977). Other researchers have reported opposite or non-significant effects (Butler 1973, Futrell and Swann 1977, Kerin 1974, Kosen et al. 1970, Skinner and Childers 1980, Erdos and Regier 1977).

Prior research on anonymity has been inconclusive in part because of the interaction of anonymity with personalization, item sensitivity, confidentiality, survey sponsorship, and population characteristics. Exhibit 1 provides a depiction of general research approaches on the dimensions of anonymity and personalization.

As illustrated in Exhibit 1, anonymity and personalization should be viewed as two separate dimensions which may, or may not, appear together in a given research study. Further, they should both be conceived of as continuums along which research studies vary. The dimension of anonymity is described in terms of "apparent" anonymity because the study person may be more likely to judge anonymity by the lack of visible individual identification than by assurances of anonymity. With this definition it becomes clear that personalization can threaten anonymity if it includes the identification of the individual. For example, Kerin and Peterson (1977) report that personalization may negatively impact the accuracy of responses, and a personalized cover letter has little effect on response rates.

Anonymity can be threatened under low personalization conditions as well. For example, the potential respondent may be asked to sign the questionnaire or provide a return address. In both of these cases the lack of anonymity is in some sense voluntary in that the study person is anonymous until s/he agrees to identify her/himself. Prior research, with a few exceptions, has tended to show non-significant differences in response rate and quality in these instances (Butler 1973, Futrell and Swan 1977, Skinner and Childers 1980).

EXHIBIT 1

Anonymity and Personalization in Mail Survey Research

High Personalization

.Handwritten Message or Signature .Precontact Phone Call .Follow-up Phone Call	.Personalized Salutation on Cover Letter
Apparent Anonymity	**Explicit Identification**
.May be surreptitiously coded but appears anonymous and <u>no</u> tactic is used to make the respondent feel uniquely important	.Voluntary-Respondent signs name or provides return address .Involuntary *a. Researcher attaches name of respondent on questionnaire or return envelope <u>without</u> an explanation b. Researcher includes an explanation for the identification

Low Personalization

*Focus of Current Research

Of particular interest to this study is researcher identification of the individual on either the questionnaire or the return envelope. Houston and Jefferson (1975) affixed the potential respondent's name and address to the top of the questionnaire on half of their sample and found significant differences in response rate. On the other hand, Erdos and Regier (1977) did a study which used visible keying with an explanation of why the keying was done and a description of procedures for protecting confidentiality. They found no significant differences in response rates on visibly keyed versus unkeyed single mailings. Various types of involuntary or researcher identification of the study person are deserving of more attention since researcher identification is convenient and economical.

The population sampled may also affect the perceived importance to the potential respondent of anonymity. Preliminary findings tend to confirm that certain individuals are more likely to be concerned with anonymity than others (Shaw et al. 1979, Jones 1981). In particular, Jones (1981) used low personalization and one of two anonymity conditions (either an assurance of anonymity or no assurance). He found for higher income populations that the response rate was significantly higher with the assurance of anonymity. This could be considered a relatively weak anonymity treatment since the entire sample had <u>apparent</u> anonymity. Despite findings on population differences, there is a paucity of research on the effects of anonymity on response patterns with populations of general interest to the consumer researcher. By far the majority of studies have used students or military and other rank and file personnel (Ash and Abramson 1952, Butler 1973, Corey 1937, Dunnette and Heneman 1956, Elinson and Haines 1950, Evans 1949, Fischer 1946, Fuller 1974, Futrell and Swann 1977, Gerberich and Mason 1948, Hamel and Reif 1952, Kosen et al. 1970, Olson 1936, Pearlin 1961, Rosen 1960).

SUMMARY

Identification of the potential respondent is sometimes desirable. Surreptitious identification of the study person is highly controversial, but it is commonly employed because of the belief that explicit identification may reduce response rates or response quality. Research results on whether this is true are inconclusive. Most research has dealt with personalization, which is a separate phenomenon, or has used voluntary explicit identification techniques. In general, prior research has failed to consider the possible impact of confidentiality on the importance of anonymity for the study person. Additionally, prior studies have focused on populations which are not of direct interest to the consumer researcher. This study makes strides toward correcting these deficiencies in our understandings.

RESEARCH HYPOTHESES

This study examined the effect of identification on total response rate, response speed, total item omission, and item omission on sensitive questions. In the context of this research, questions regarding the number of pieces of art owned, the amount spent on art last year and income were defined as sensitive issues. The expectations of the researchers were, in general, that identified individuals would feel more threatened than non-identified individuals, and would therefore respond at a lower rate and a slower speed than potential respondents in the non-identified group. Because of a very weak personalization effect, it was expected that non-identified individuals who <u>did</u> answer would do so more conscientiously (via a more complete response to the questionnaire overall). On questions that were considered "sensitive," however, it was expected that identified respondents would omit answers more often than non-identified respondents. Specifically, the following research hypotheses were advanced:

H1: Subjects in the identified group will respond at a lower rate than subjects in the non-identified group.

H2: Non-identified respondents will respond more quickly than identified respondents.

H3: Identified respondents will respond with a more complete questionnaire.

H4: Identified respondents will omit answers to "sensitive" questions (art ownership, money spent on art, income) more often than non-identified respondents.

METHODOLOGY

A five-part questionnaire was mailed to a national sample of 1,108 subscribers to an art magazine. The survey was sponsored by a major Southwestern university in cooperation with the magazine publisher. The questionnaire packet included a non-personalized cover letter (addressed "Dear Subscriber") and a postage-paid return envelope. The identification treatment took the form of an address label attached to the return envelope. Half of the potential respondents were identified in this manner. The other half did not receive a label and thus were not identified. All potential respondents were told that their replies would be confidential.

The questionnaire asked the respondents about the art magazine to which they subscribed, including characteristics of the magazine liked most, characteristics of the magazine liked least, how long the subscriber intended to save the magazine, and ratings of various aspects of the magazine. Subscribers were also asked about art collecting habits, including the types of art owned, the number of pieces of each type owned, and the amount spent on art during the last year. Finally, several demographic questions were asked, including total household income, educational attainment and occupation.

RESULTS

A total of 632 responses were received, for an overall response rate of 57.3%. Hypothesis 1 stated that respondents in the identified group will respond at a lower rate than those in the non-identified group. Chi-square analysis supported this hypothesis (See Table 1). Of the 632 total responses, only 46% were from identified subjects (those receiving the address label) while 54% were from non-identified subjects. Hypothesis 2 stated that non-identified respondents will respond more quickly than identified respondents. T-tests supported hypothesis 2 (See Table 1). Mean response speed for identified respondents was 21.3 days, while mean speed for non-identified respondents was 18.7 days. Hypothesis 3, which stated that identified respondents will respond more completely overall than non-identified respondents, was not supported. The means corresponding to overall completeness were not significantly different.

TABLE 1

Response Rate and Speed by Identification Treatment

	# Responses	%	X^2 Value
Total Response Rate:			
Identified	290	26.3	10[*]
Not-Identified	342	31.0	
Total	632	57.3	
	Mean # of Days		t-Value
Response Speed:			
Identified	21.3		2.3**
Non-Identified	18.7		

*Chi Square value ρ <.005
A test for the difference between two proportions was also computed with a resulting value of 3.13 (ρ < .001).
**ρ < .025

Hypothesis 4 stated that identified respondents will omit answers to "sensitive" questions (art ownership, money spent on art, and income) more often than non-identified respondents. Analysis revealed that this hypothesis was not supported. However, based on the anonymity treatment, there were significant differences in overall spending on art and ownership of certain high visibility varieties of art such as jewelry. Identified respondents reported spending significantly less money on art and owning significantly fewer pieces of art than non-identified respondents (See Table 2). In addition, for identified respondents, comments such as "I will tell you which types of art I own, but not how many pieces of each type" and "Theft is so common these days I would be foolish to tell a stranger how many pieces of art I own" were fairly common. One possible explanation is that identified respondents may have been distorting their answers downward because they know that they are identified and may not feel that their answers will remain confidential. Another possible explanation is that identified respondents who are heavy art collectors were frightened out of responding at all to the questionnaire.

CONCLUSIONS

In this study, the overall response rate was significantly lower for potential respondents who were explicitly iden-

TABLE 2

Mean Response Difference on Sensitive Questions

	Means	t-Value*
Overall Art Spending Annually		
Identified	$ 450	2.3
Not-Identified	$1750	
Number of Pieces of Jewelry Owned		
Identified	10.8	2.7
Not-Identified	16.6	
Number of Pieces of Pottery Owned		
Identified	7.4	2.1
Not-Identified	10.4	

*All values ρ < .05

tified. Analysis revealed significant differences between identified and non-identified respondents in terms of response speed but not in terms of completeness. Although there were not significant differences in item omission to sensitive questions, significant differences were found in the mean amount reported spent on art and the number of pieces of art owned, with the identified group reporting less.

This research demonstrated that visibly identifying respondents under low personalization conditions may significantly decrease response rates. This decrease may occur despite assurances of confidentiality. In this study the individual's interest could be judged to be quite high since the magazine is an expensive special interest publication and only subscribers were sampled. Comments confirmed this high interest. With a lower interest topic, still containing sensitive questions, the effect of identification on response rates may have been even more dramatic. However, this was also a population sample expected to be sensitive to anonymity conditions. A demographic profile of the entire sample revealed an annual mean income of over $32,000 a year, with 20% of the sample making over $60,000 annually. Seventy percent of the sample are college graduates, and nearly half of the sample are in occupations best described as professional. Other lower income and education populations, of interest to the consumer researcher, might not be as sensitive to anonymity conditions.

The major implication of this study is that researchers need to explore alternatives to explicit involuntary identification as well as the effect of identification on other types of populations. Of particular interest would be a study contrasting the effects of involuntary identification without a researcher explanation with the effects of involuntary identification incorporating an explanation of the reasons for the identification. Research should also be undertaken to study involuntary identification under varying levels of personalization, survey sponsorship, and item sensitivity. Finally, this research suggests there may be an important difference in either <u>who</u> responds based on the anonymity treatment, or <u>how</u> they respond. Research on a possible distortion effect needs to be done, where a validating data base is available. This might yield valuable insights on the impact of explicit identification on the type and extent of distortion.

REFERENCES

Andreasen, Alan R. (1970), "Personalizing Mail Questionnaire Correspondence," <u>Public Opinion Quarterly</u>, 34,

273-77.

Ash, Philip, and Abramson, Edward (1952), "The Effect of Anonymity on Attitude Questionnaire Response," Journal of Abnormal and Social Psychology, 47, 722-23.

Butler, Richard P. (1973), "Effects of Signed and Unsigned Questionnaires for Both Sensitive and Nonsensitive Items," Journal of Applied Psychology, 57, 348-9.

Dickson, John, Casey, Michael, Wyckoof, Daniel (1976), "The Invisible Ink Caper--of a Watergate Mentality in Marketing Research Ethics." In Proceedings, edited by Howard C. Schneider. San Francisco: American Institute for Decision Sciences.

Dunnette, Marvin and Heneman, Herbert Jr. (1956), "Influence of Scale Administrator on Employee Attitude Responses," Journal of Applied Psychology, 40, 73-77.

Elinson, Jack and Haines, Valerie (1950), "Role of Anonymity in Attitude Surveys," American Psychologist, 5, 315.

Erdos, Paul, and Reigier, James (1977), "Visible Vs. Disguised Keying on Questionnaires," Journal of Advertising Research, 17, 13-18.

Evans, Chester E. (1949), "Item Structure Variation As A Methodological Problem in an Employee Survey," American Psychologist, 4, 280.

Fischer, Robert P. (1946), "Signed Versus Unsigned Personal Questionnaires," Journal of Applied Psychology, 30, 220-25.

Fuller, Carol (1974), "Effect of Anonymity on Return Rate and Response Bias in a Mail Survey," Journal of Applied Psychology, 59, 292-96.

Futrell, Charles M., and Swan, John E. (1977), "Anonymity and Response By Sales People To A Mail Questionnaire," Journal of Marketing Research, 14, 611-16.

Gerberich, J. B., and Mason, J. M. (1948), "Signed Versus Unsigned Questionnaires," Journal of Educational Research, 42, 122-26.

Hamel, LaVerne, and Reif, Hans G. (1952), "Should Attitude Questionnaires Be Signed?" Personnel Psychology, 5, 87-91.

Houston, Michael J. and Jefferson, Robert W. (1975), "The Negative Effects of Personalization on Response Patterns in Mail Surveys," Journal of Marketing Research, 12, 114-7.

Jones, Wesley H. (1979), "Generalizing Mail Survey Inducement Methods: Population Interactions with Anonymity and Sponsorship," Public Opinion Quarterly, 43, 102-11.

Kerin, Roger A. (1974), "Personalization Strategies, Response Rate and Response Quality In A Mail Survey," Social Science Quarterly, 175-81.

__________ and Peterson, Robert A. (1977), "Personalization, Respondent Anonymity, and Response Distortion in Mail Surveys," Journal of Applied Psychology, 62, 86-9.

Kosen, D., Kitchen, C., Kochen, M. and Stodolosky, D. (1970), "Psychological Testing By Computer: Effect on Response Bias," Educational and Psychological Measurement, 30, 803-10.

McGown, K. L. (1979), "Ethical Issues Involving The Protection of Marketing Practitioners and Respondents." In Proceedings. San Francisco: American Institute for Decision Sciences.

Olson, Willard C. (1936), "The Waiver of Signature In Personal Reports," Journal of Applied Psychology, 20, 442-50.

Pearlin, Leonard (1961), "The Appeals of Anonymity in Questionnaire Response," Public Opinion Quarterly, 25, 640-47.

Rosen, Ned A. (1960), "Anonymity and Attitude Measurement," Public Opinion Quarterly, 24, 675-79.

Shaw, William H. (Chairman), (1979). Privacy and Confidentiality As Factors In Survey Response, A Report of the Panel on Privacy and Confidentiality As Factors in Survey Research. Washington, D.C.: National Academy of Sciences.

FOOT-IN-THE DOOR FOR INCREASING MAIL QUESTIONNAIRE RETURNS: A CRITICAL REVIEW

John E. Swan, University of Alabama in Birmingham
Warren S. Martin, University of Alabama in Birmingham

ABSTRACT

A critical review found that foot-in-the door has not typically enhanced response rates more than other methods of
prenotification. A number of problems were found in the
design of "foot" studies. One study demonstrated that high
involvement "foot" was effective, thus, additional research
is warranted.

INTRODUCTION

A new method of improving mail questionnaire response rates
has been proposed and tested by several marketing scholars.
A literature review revealed five recent studies dealing
with applying the foot-in-the door technique (foot) to increase mail questionnaire response rates (see Table 1).
This technique is based upon the assumption that if a person makes a commitment to a small initial request, the
probability of later compliance with a larger task is significantly increased. A critical review of the foot method
is needed for four reasons: 1) the method is attracting
attention; 2) it holds promise for application; 3) conflicting results have been reported; and 4) the complexity
of various research designs begs for comparative treatment.
In this paper we will address each of these issues by presenting the foot technique, critically evaluating strengths
and weaknesses of foot studies, scrutinizing their results
and suggest areas for future inquiry.

BASIC FOOT PARADIGM IN SURVEY RESEARCH

The basic foot paradigm (Scott 1977) fitted to a survey research experiment (Reingen and Kernan 1979) is illustrated
in Figure 1. In the foot experimental group an <u>initial re-
quest</u> (Step 1) is made and a respondent is asked to answer
a few research questions. According to self perception
theory if the respondent <u>agrees</u> (verbal compliance) to answer some questions, upon later receipt of a questionnaire,
the individual is likely to respond (Hansen and Robinson
1980). On the other hand, if the respondent <u>refuses</u> the
initial request, a self-attribution to decline participation
in survey research takes place and the individual is less
likely to respond. Two conditions must be present for the
basic foot proposition to be judged effective. First, the
response rates should be higher in the experimental group
members who verbally complied (answered questions) compared
to those that did not comply and relative to a no initial
contact control group. Second, foot-agree should have
higher response rates than a no-initial-contact control
group. Even if the foot-agree group gave a higher response
rate than the foot disagree, the addition expenses could
not be justified unless the average response rate for both
groups did better than a control group. In order to distinguish between foot which seeks involvement from the individual (Hansen and Robinson 1980) versus <u>prenotification</u>
which simply alerts the person that a questionnaire will be
sent, a prenotification control group can be used. The
foot-agree and the foot-disagree return rates must be
higher than that of a prenotification control group in order to rule out simple prenotification as an alternative
explanation. The scope of the experimental design for foot
research has been reviewed, the next step is the application
of these ideas to published foot studies.

RESULTS OF FOOT RESEARCH

Foot research will be summarized in terms of its ability to
answer five basic questions: 1) is foot different from
prenotification? 2) Have the basic foot hypotheses been
supported? 3) Is foot effective relative to a control
group as a response inducement technique? 4) Is foot more
productive than simple prenotification? and 5) Is foot more
effective than other methods (cash-incentive or door-in-the
face) of enhancing response rates?

<u>Foot Distinguished From Prenotification</u>

Is foot distinguishable conceptually and operationally from
prenotification (Stafford 1966)? Prenotification is a general concept that involves communication designed to induce
a response and is transmitted to the respondent prior to
the attempt to administer the questionnaire. Foot would be
a specific type of prenotification and according to Hansen
and Robinson (1980), it differs from other kinds of prenotification in one critical respect: the <u>foot generates respondent involvement</u> in the survey. A conceptual distinction can thus be drawn between foot <u>vs</u> nonfoot prenotification. An example of nonfoot prenotification could be a
postcard that alerts a potential respondent to the fact
that a questionnaire will be sent.

An operational distinction between foot <u>vs</u> nonfoot prenotification (hereafter: prenotification) is difficult to
maintain. Some of the prenotification reports in the literature may have well involved an implicit foot. An example
would be Jolson's telephone prenotification (Jolson 1977,
p. 79) in which he implored members of his sample to complete a mail questionnaire that they would receive.

If the argument that the critical attribute in foot is involvement, then much of the current research on foot can be
questioned because whether or not the foot treatment generated involvement is not clear. It is also possible, but
not very likely, that the prenotification control used in
some studies may have generated involvement. The point is
that future research on foot could be strengthened by using
a pretest or manipulation check to insure that the foot generated involvement while the prenotification control did
not.

<u>Testing Foot Hypotheses</u>

Have research studies on foot found higher response rates
among foot compliers (those who comply with initial request)
than among noncompliers and a control group? The results
of five foot studies are summarized in Table 1. Only two
studies provided data to test the hypothesis that response
rates would be higher in the foot compliance than noncompliance groups. The hypothesis was supported by the Dillman and Frey (1974) study which achieved a significantly
higher response rate in the compliance than the noncompliance group. Furse, et al., (1981) did not find a significantly greater response rate among the compliers. However,
the results were in the predicted direction and the non-
complier sample size was small. The second foot hypothesis,
predicting a higher response rate among foot compliance
than control was supported by two studies (Allen, et al.,
(1980), Dillman and Frey (1974) but not by a third, Furse,
et al., (1981). Finally, the third foot hypotheses was
that the response rate among noncompliers should be lower
than the control group response rate. The results of the
Dillman and Frey (1974) and Furse, et al., (1981) studies

Table 1
FOOT-IN-DOOR STUDIES RESPONSE RATES BY GROUPS

Study	Test of Foot Hypotheses						Foot As Response Inducement Method			Foot vs Prenotification		
	Foot Compliance Group		Foot Noncompliance Group		Control Group		Net Foot Response Rate		Control Group	Net Foot Response Rate		Prenotification
	(1)	p^a (1,2)	(2)	p^b (1,3)	(3)	p^c (2,3)		P			P	
Allen, Schewe, Wijk (1980)	67.3% (66/198)	—	d	.001	22.2% (186/836)	—	55.2% (66/119.5)[e]	.001[f]	22.2% (185/836)	67.3% (66/98)	NS	69.4% (68/98)
Dillman & Frey (1974	75.2% .001[f] (185/246)		50.0% .05 (37/74)		64.5% .05[f] (224/348)		72.8% (233/320)	.05[f]	64.5% (224/348)	—		—
Furse, Steward, Rados (1981)	23% NS[f] (43/186)		14% NS[f] (14/28)		21% NS[f] (61/294)		22.0% (47/214)	NS	21.0% (61/294)	—		—
Hansen and Robinson (1980)[g]							Probe Foot					
	—	—	—	—	—	—	Short 57.6%	.005	29.7%	—		—
	—	—	—	—	—	—	Long 45.6	.005	16.6%	—		—
							Yes/No Foot					
	—	—	—	—	—	—	Short 42.8%	.09	29.7%	—		—
	—	—	—	—	—	—	Long 32.9%	.025	16.6%	—		—
Reingen & Kernan (1979)	—	—	—	—	—	—	50% (59/118)	.13	41% (24/59)	50% (59/118)	NS	44% (46/104)

[a]Probability of significant difference between foot compliance vs foot noncompliance groups.

[b]Probability of significant difference between foot compliance vs no initial request control group.

[c]Probability of significant difference between foot noncompliance vs no initial request control group.

d = Not Included; Only respondents that complied were mailed questionnaires.

[e]Only compliers were mailed questionnaires. Base is the estimated (by present authors) number of persons in the foot treatment.

[f]Calculations made by present authors.

g N = 100 each cell.

indicated a lower response rate among noncompliers than in the control group. However, the Furse, et al., (1981) result was not significant. With data from only two studies, the issue needs more research. One potential problem is that if compliance with the initial request is very high, as it was in some studies (Reingen and Kernan, (1979), 93%, Furse, et al., 87%), then the noncompliance group is rather small for a meaningful analysis. In summary, some support has been found for the basic foot paradigm that a self attribute "I answer questionnaires" can influence later behavior response to the mail questionnaire.

Effectiveness of Foot Compared To A Control Group

Some of the evidence suggests that the response rate is higher among those who comply with the initial request than those in a no initial request control group. However, the foot may not be more productive in stimulating response rates than a no initial request control group. The critical question is whether the overall response rate of the foot compliance group and the foot noncompliance group is significantly different from a control group. Comparisons with just the foot compliance group, is only part of the total evaluation. The five studies provided eight

comparisons of net foot response rates vs control (Table 1). Five of the comparisons found significantly higher response rates in foot compared to control, two results were marginal (P = .09, .13) and one found no significant difference (Furse, et al., 1981). Evidence on the productivity of foot is mixed. The three studies that did find that foot was more effective, would be subject to a number of problems noted in the next major section of this paper. The mail study with the strongest design for this question, Reingen and Kernan (1979) found a very marginal difference (p = .13) between the two groups.

Does Foot Outperform Other Methods of Prenotification?

Only two of the foot studies test foot vs prenotification. Allen, Schewe and Wijk (1980) used simple solicitation as prenotification in which the subject was asked for a commitment to fill out a questionnaire versus "foot" in which the subject was asked to respond to three open-ended questions about issues included in the study. The foot response rate 67.3% (66/98) was not significantly different from the prenotification, 69.4% (68/98). A limitation of Allen, Schewe and Wijk (1980) is that if questionnaires had been sent to noncompliers as well, the net foot response rate could have been higher. This would not change their basic finding. Reingen and Kernan (1979) used a prenotification group in which subjects were asked to respond and a foot group in which subjects were asked to perform a small task (93% agreed to do so) which consisted of answering five short marketing research questions. The prenotification response rate 44% (46/104), was not significantly different from the foot rate of 50% (59/118). It is clear that foot has not yielded better response rates than prenotification.

Foot vs Other Response Inducement Techniques

Two articles reported on a contrast between foot in comparison to alternative means of increasing response rates. Reingen and Kernan (1979) found that the door-in-the-face, in which subjects were asked to perform a very large market-research task and were sent a smaller questionnaire (same questionnaire as foot), gave a lower response rate, 38% (35/92), $p < .05$, than the foot-in-the door. Furse, Steward and Rados (1981) demonstrated that a 50¢ cash incentive (no precontact) yielded a significantly higher response rate, 36%, (106/294), $p < .01$, than foot, 22% (47/214).

THE DESIGN OF FOOT STUDIES

Three basic issues in the design of foot studies were found in our review of foot research. The first issue is that no study either contained the necessary groups and/or reported the data need to carry out all of the basic analyses (Figure 1) that would be necessary in order to thoroughly test the foot paradigm in mail survey research. The second issue involved screening only experimental subjects and the third involved a self selection bias. In order to clearly explain the major problems in foot studies, we will first present an experimental design for a comprehensive foot experiment and second discuss problems with reported foot studies.

Experimental Design For Thoroughly Testing Foot

A diagram of a before-after with two control groups experiment for foot research is presented in Figure 1. Test Group I represents the foot treatment and a resultant division of the respondents into foot-complaint and noncomplaint groups. It is hypothesized that the affect of the foot, X_1, would create a significantly different response rate between these two groups (O_{3A} and O_{3B}). A second basic hypothesis would be that the net response rate for the foot treatment ($O3C$) should be significantly greater than the response rate for prenotification, O_4, (Test Group II). A third hypothesis would be that the foot treatments, O_{3C}, would result in an average response rate that is significantly greater than a mail questionnaire without any form of prenotification (O_5), Control Group III.

Screening Experimental But Not Control Groups

A basic problem is that the experimental but not the control groups was screened in all of the foot studies cited, except Reingen and Kernan (1979). The typical design was as follows: in the foot phase of the study, telephone contact was made with all subjects in the foot treatment but not the controls. The address for controls were obtained by random sampling from sources such as telephone directories and then questionnaires were mailed to the controls. The procedure of not screening the control group while including as experimental subjects only those who answered the telephone and participated at least to the extent of answering the telephone creates two problems. First, the design of the study potentially excluded individuals who had moved or individuals who did not answer the telephone. The exclusion of people who may have moved combined with a cut-off date for replies reduces the randomization of the control group. Reingen and Kernan (1979, p. 591) using a

Figure 1
Experimental Design For Testing
The Foot-In-The Door Technique
As A Response Inducement Device

Test Group

I	Foot-test Group	O_1 X_1 O_{3A}	Complaint Group	
		O_{3B}	Noncomplaint Group	
	Net Foot Response:	$O_{3C} = (N_1 \cdot O_{3A} + N_1 \cdot O_{3B})/N$		

II	Prenotification Test Group	O_2 X_2 O_4

III	Control Group	O_5

Test Group I   The foot-test group is divided into the complaint and noncomplaint groups with the initial telephone request. It has been hypothesized that these groups (O_{3A} and O_{3B}) will have significantly different response rates.

Test Group II   The prenotification group will be a randomly selected group that will be prenotified of the questionnaire. It will be hypothesized that the response rate from this group will be significantly less than the average response rate from groups O_{3A} and O_{3B}. If this hypothesis is not accepted, the foot is not significantly better for overall response rate inducement than prenotification. Note that it is important to have comparable selection and contact procedures for the groups to yield a valid test.

Test Group III   The control group consists of a third group used to compare the effectiveness of prenotification and foot for the particular situation tested. The question is whether any of the prenotification groups induced significantly higher response rates than the no prenotification control.

similar sampling frame, reported the percentage of potential respondents who were known to have moved at over thirteen percent. Additionally, whenever a list of addresses are used as a sampling frame, there are an unknown number of people who have moved, but cannot be identified before or after the study. This limitation would tend to overstate the effectiveness of foot since the telephone contact, which was part of the foot treatment, tended to reduce the proportion of foot respondents that could not be contacted by mail.

A second difficulty with using telephone screening only for the experimental group is the handling of not-at-home households. The researchers did not state how they handled unanswered telephone numbers (aside from multiple follow-ups). If new numbers were in the sample, they systematically increased the number of people who spent more time at home for experimental groups and this action may have increased the probability of a higher response rate for the experimental groups. Additionally, the person who was contacted on the telephone may not have been the person who completed the questionnaire.

The failure to screen only the control group would have been mitigated if the foot group achieved a 100% contact rate <u>and</u> if it can be assumed that the sampling frame was equally productive for mail contact. The reported telephone contact rates were about 67% for two studies, Dillman & Frey

416

(1974), Furse, et al., (1981) that reported such data.
Reingen and Kernan (1979) reported that 13% of their potential respondents were known to have moved which gives a
single estimate of the magnitude of this bias.

A good way to handle the control group problem would be to
follow Reingen and Kernan's (1979) procedure of creating a
no foot, no prior contact control that was similar to the
other groups. This was done by using a "wrong telephone
number" technique to verify the last name of the respondent.
The questionnaire was mailed to the person who responded to
the "wrong number" making the control group accessible to
mail contact.

<u>Respondent Interest In Experimental Group Increased Returns</u>

Another problem involves the Hansen and Robinson (1980)
experiment which is of special interest because it gave the
strongest evidence of the producitivity of foot. It appears that the experimental and control groups were created
in a way that would result in more interest among experimental than control respondents in the subject matter of
Hansen and Robinson's questionnaire which was the respondent's attitudes toward their most recent new car purchase.
A control group was created by randomly selecting 200 subjects from a telephone directory and they were sent without prior contact, the same mail questionnaire as the foot-
in-the door group. All foot subjects were screened such
that the final sample contained only persons who answered
the telephone and who had purchased a new car within the
last three years. The result is that the control group
contained a mix of persons, some of whom probably purchased
a new car in the last year while others had not. The foot
group contained only new car purchasers. Recent purchase
of new cars are more likely to be interested in a mail
questionnaire on that subject than nonpurchasers. Thus,
the higher returns may simply reflect respondent interest
in the subject matter of the questionnaire and not the
foot manipulation.

CONCLUSIONS AND SUMMARY

Research to date has not provided strong encouragement to
survey researchers that foot can enhance response rates
above other methods of prenotification. It is apparent
from the literature review that little strong evidence on
the question of foot <u>vs</u> prenotification is available. We
found only two studies on that issue. Neither study found
that foot increased response rates. A reason for suggesting more research on foot is that if the key to foot is
involvement, the single study that created a high involvement foot condition did find a significantly higher response rate. Hansen and Robinson (1980) found within the
foot treatment that high involvement (51.5% response rate)
was more effective than low (38.0%, p < .01, calculation
by present authors). The design problems with their study
that this paper addressed above would not influence those
findings since the comparisons were within foot treatments.
Involvement is a new variable in foot research and the
authors should be commended for their creativity. An important criticism of foot is that the cost of administering
the "foot" by telephone may make it impractical, Furse,
et al., (1981). In view of that concern, use of a mail
foot could be a topic for future research.

REFERENCES

Allen, Chris T., Charles D. Schewe, and Gosta Wijk (1980),
    "More on Self-Perception Theory's Foot Technique in the
    Pre-Call/Mail Survey Setting," <u>Journal of Marketing
    Research</u>, 17 (November), 498-501.

Dillman, Don A. and James H. Frey (1974), "Questionnaire
    Response as an Element of a Previously Tested Method,"
    <u>Journal of Applied Psychology</u>, 59 (3), 297-301.

Furse, David H., David W. Stewart, and David L. Rados
    (1981), "Effects of Foot-in-the-Door, Cash Incentives,
    and Followups on Survey Response," <u>Journal of Marketing
    Research</u>, 18 (November), 473-478.

Hansen, Robert A. and Larry M. Robinson (1980), "Testing
    the Effectiveness of Alternative Foot-in-the-Door
    Manipulations," <u>Journal of Marketing Research</u>, 17
    (August), 359-364.

Jolson, Marvin A. (1977), "How to Double or Triple Mail-
    Survey Response Rates," <u>Journal of Marketing</u>, 41
    (October), 78-81.

Reingen, Peter H. and Jerome B. Kernan (1979), "More
    Evidence on Interpersonal Yielding," <u>Journal of Marketing
    Research</u>, 16 (November), 588-593.

Scott, Carol A. (1977), "Modifying Socially-Conscious Be-
    havior: The Foot-in-the-Door Technique," <u>Journal of
    Consumer Research</u>, 4 (December), 156-164.

Stafford, James E. (1966), "Influence of Preliminary
    Contact On Mail Returns," <u>Journal Of Marketing Research</u>,
    3 (November), 410-11.

QUESTIONNAIRE DESIGN MANIPULATIONS AND RESPONSE RATES
TO A MAIL CONSUMER FINANCES SURVEY

Valarie Veth, University of Houston
Edward Blair, University of Houston
E. Laird Landon, Jr., University of Houston

ABSTRACT

Survey design manipulations are examined for their effects
on response rates to a mail survey. The manipulations
studied are commitment, record checking, time frame, and
counting method, all of which have been associated with differences in response quality but not in response rates. The
commitment manipulation increases response rates to the mail
questionnaire. Other manipulations, which occur later in
the questionnaire, have nonsignificant effects on response
rates.

INTRODUCTION

This paper reports the effects of questionnaire design manipulations on response rates to a mail survey on checking
account attitudes and usage. The design variables studied
are: (1) the presence or absence of a request for signed
commitment by the respondent; (2) the presence or absence
of a request that respondents refer to their financial records in answering questions about checking account activity; (3) the length of the time frame for questions on checking account activity; and (4) the counting method used in
reporting frequencies and amounts of checking account activities.

All four variables have received some attention in the survey methods literature for their effects on response quality. Commitment has been found to improve the reporting of
health events in fact to face and telephone surveys (Cannell et al. 1977; Cannell et al. 1981), and recent research
has tried to extend commitment effects to non-threatening
behaviors (Berry and Cannell 1980). Ferber (1966) reports
that record checking can improve reporting of consumer financial data. Time frames have been studied from the point
of view of memory loss in consumption or health data (Sudman and Bradburn 1973; Cannell et al. 1977). Also, Calcich
and Blair (1980) show differences in store patronage data
resulting from different ways of measuring shopping frequency in a face to face interview.

In a mail survey, these variables might affect the response
rate in addition to response quality. Commonly expressed
models of response behavior propose two determinants of survey participation (Kahn and Cannell 1957; Dillman 1978); social motivation to participate (the extent to which respondents see participation as socially beneficial or a social
obligation) and costs of participation (mostly time, though
factors such as embarrassment can be important). Previous
research on response to mail surveys, summarized by Kanuk
and Berenson (1975), supports this approach. The variables
that have affected response pretty consistently, such as
providing return postage, providing incentives, and using
university auspices, all can be viewed as affecting the social motivation or costs of participating. Other design
features that may affect these variables, such as the manipulations used in this study, also are likely to impact
response rates.

A request for commitment may increase both motivation and
cost of participation. This request was operationalized in
this study through a message that stressed the importance
of the data, offered a signed promise of confidentiality,
and requested an initialled promise that the respondent
would try hard to answer fully and accurately. Such a message should increase motivation by enhancing the importance
of the research and of the respondent's answers. It also
should increase cost by asking the respondent to work hard.
In this study, the motivational benefit was expected to be
the more important influence on response because the sensitive nature of financial data and the university auspices
seemed to fit the commitment request. Also, because the
commitment request was the only manipulation to appear on
the outside of the questionnaire, the effect on response
rate was expected to be the largest of the four manipulations.

A request that respondents consult their records before
providing checking account data certainly requires more effort from the respondent than not consulting records. This
manipulation was expected to have a reasonably strong effect
because it requires the respondent to interrupt response
and leave the questionnaire, thus providing a good breakoff
opportunity (which simply produces non-response in a mail
survey). Asking about a longer time period increases the
effort of recalling events, and therefore the cost of participation. This manipulation was not expected to have a
major impact on response rate in this study because the affected questions occurred fairly late in the questionnaire
and because it was felt that the one and three month frames
used here would not greatly impact participation. The final
manipulation involved asking respondents to provide numbers
and amounts of checks either by total counts or by monthly
(and per check) averages. Averaging is the more difficult
task to do correctly because it involves totalling and then
dividing; however, it was felt that respondents could simplify the averaging task by giving a "typical" figure rather
than a true average, and that totalling therefore would be
the more costly task associated with lower response rate.
The impact of this manipulation on response rate was expected to be minor, like that of the time frame manipulation, and for similar reasons.

It also seemed possible that the four manipulations would
interact in producing response rate effects. Dillman (1978)
suggests that an important determinant of response rates is
not the disposition of individual design variables, but rather the total effect produced by all aspects of the design
considered together. Respondents might be willing to perform demanding tasks if those tasks seem necessary and appropriate to the survey. Thus, record checking might be
more acceptable in the three-month condition than in the one-
month condition, because of the increased demands that the
longer time frame places on the respondent's memory. The totalling task also might be more appropriate than averaging
in the record check condition because the records used in this
study -- account statements -- provide totals rather than
averages. Interaction effects involving the commitment manipulation would not relate as much to task appropriateness
but might be expected anyway. Respondents who received a
commitment request might have more social motivation to continue through a demanding questionnaire, so that the negative effects of record checking, totalling, and a longer time
frame all might be weaker in the commitment condition than
in the no commitment condition.

METHOD

These effects were tested in an attitude survey of bank customers that covered the respondent's satisfaction with and

awareness of various bank services, levels of checking account activity, background information about the respondent, and the respondent's subjective reaction to the survey experience. The sample for the study was drawn from customer lists of two participating banks in the Greater Houston area. One-half of the subjects were assigned to receive mail questionnaires, while the others were to be interviewed by telephone. Of the eligible cases, 426 were in the mail cell and 425 were in the telephone cell. The response rates reported in this paper are from the mail portion of the survey only.

Mail respondents received pre-notification of the survey by postcard one week in advance of receiving the questionnaire packet. Reminder postcards were sent out to respondents who had not returned a completed questionnaire within one week, and a second questionnaire was mailed out to non-respondents after another week.

Respondents were randomly assigned to either a commitment or no commitment condition, to either a record check or no record check condition, to either a three month or one month condition and to either an averaging or totalling condition. In the no commitment condition, the first page of the questionnaire contained the title of the survey, general instructions for completing the questionnaire, and the seal of the University of Houston. The version with commitment included, in addition to these things, the following paragraph:

> You are part of a small, scientifically chosen
> sample that will represent many other people,
> so the information you give must be very accu-
> rate to be useful. I've signed this question-
> naire to give you my promise that your answers
> will be held in strict confidence. In return,
> please initial your line to give me your promise
> that you will do your best to give accurate
> and complete answers.

This paragraph was followed by the principal investigator's signature and by a place for the respondent to put his or her initials.

The record check manipulation occurred about midway through the questionnaire, just before a series of questions about checking account activity. In the record check version the instructions for this series included the following paragraph:

> These questions will be easiest to answer if you
> use the checking account statement you received
> in March. Please take a minute to get this
> statement before you proceed.

This paragraph was omitted from the instructions in the no record check version.

The time frame manipulation and the counting method manipulation also affected only the series of questions on checking account activity. One-half of the sample was sent questionnaires asking about checking activity in the past three months, while the other half was asked only about the preceding one month. Those in the totalling cell were asked to total events and dollar amounts over those months, while those in the averaging cell were asked to give average numbers on a per-month or per-transaction basis. The question on dollar amount of checks written will illustrate these two manipulations. For the three-month, totalling cell, it read: "What was the total dollar amount of checks written on your checking account during those three months?" Subjects in the opposing one-month, averaging cell were asked: "What was the average dollar amount of a check written on your checking account during that month?"

RESULTS AND DISCUSSION

Response rates encountered under each of the experimental conditions are shown in Table 1. As expected because of its prominent position on the first page of the mail questionnaire, the commitment manipulation was associated with the largest difference in response rates. Including the principal investigator's signature and request for signed commitment increased response rate from 40.5% to 51.2%; this difference is significant at the .05 level. The commitment request apparently does increase social motivation to respond by showing that the researcher is vitally interested in the results and that response is important.

TABLE 1

MAIN EFFECTS

Condition	Response Rate (N)	
Commitment	51.2% (211)	$x^2 = 4.93$
No Commitment	40.5% (215)	$p < .05$
Record Check	43.0% (214)	$x^2 = 1.34$
No Record Check	48.6% (212)	
Three Month	45.1% (215)	$x^2 = .08$
One Month	46.4% (211)	
Averaging	47.4% (215)	$x^2 = .49$
Totalling	44.1% (211)	

The other three manipulations show differences that are in the expected direction but too small for statistical significance. Asking respondents to check their financial records produced a 5.6% drop in response, from 48.6% to 43.0%. The two remaining manipulations show even smaller differences in response rates; 1.3 percentage points for the time frame manipulation and 3.3 percentage points for the counting method manipulation. These small differences were in the hypothesized direction, suggesting that the three-month time frame and totalling method are more costly to the respondent than the one-month time frame and averaging method.

Overall, the pattern of main effects on response rates for the four manipulations provides support for the notions that social motivation to respond and cost of responding are determinants of participation in a mail survey, and that design manipulations within the questionnaire will not greatly affect response rate because they come after the respondent has decided to participate and sealed this decision by answering some questions. However, it is not possible to draw any strong conclusions about respondents' decision-making processes based on one study.

The response rate results for interactions of these manipulations are also statistically nonsignificant but still interesting for practitioners who must choose one design and hope to achieve the highest response rate possible. These results are reported in Table 2.

The pattern of the first three interaction effects fits the task appropriateness model of decision-making, which states that respondents are more willing to accept a higher cost of responding if the additional cost is seen as appropriate to the task. Reading across the first two lines of the table, it can be seen that the inclusion of a record check reduces response rates by only 2.1 percentage points in the three month condition compared with a reduction of 9.2 percentage points in the one month condition. It seems plausible that, as the time frame of a question is lengthened, respondents become less trusting of their own memories and are more willing to accept a record check. The next interaction shows that the totalling measure drew slightly (.6%) better than the averaging measure in the record check condition, but that averaging outdrew totalling by 7.5% in the no record check condition. This difference may reflect the fact that the records being checked contain total figures, so that totalling is a more appropriate task when records are checked. In the third interaction, the effects of averaging and totalling again switch direction. Averaging draws almost 10% higher response than totalling with a three-month time frame but totalling has about a 3% advantage with a one month time frame. This may reflect the increasing difficulty of totalling as the time frame lengthens.

TABLE 2

INTERACTION EFFECTS

	Record Check	No Record Check
Three month	44.1% (111)	46.2% (104)
One Month	41.7% (103)	50.9% (108)
	Totalling	Averaging
Record Check	43.3% (104)	42.7% (110)
No Record Check	44.9% (107)	52.4% (105)
	Totalling	Averaging
Three Month	40.2% (107)	50.0% (108)
One Month	48.1% (104)	44.9% (107)
	Totalling	Averaging
Commitment	50.5% (105)	51.9% (106)
No Commitment	37.7% (106)	43.1% (109)
	Record Check	No Record Check
Commitment	47.2% (106)	55.2% (105)
No Commitment	38.9% (108)	42.1% (107)
	Three Month	One Month
Commitment	46.3% (108)	56.3% (103)
No Commitment	43.9% (107)	37.0% (108)

The remaining three interactions all involve the commitment manipulation. Here, the beneficial effects of the commitment condition were expected to temper the negative effects of the other manipulations. This expectation is confirmed only in the commitment by counting interaction, where the reduction in response rate associated with totalling is only 1.4 percentage points in the commitment condition compared with 5.4 percentage points in the no commitment condition. The remaining two interactions do not follow the same pattern: the negative effects of including a record check requirement and of increasing the time period covered by survey questions are stronger in the commitment condition than in the no commitment condition. Thus, the commitment manipulation does not appear to have beneficial effects on response rates beyond the main effect; it does not interact positively with other manipulations.

To check the reasonableness of the tests of statistical significance for these results, two additional analyses were conducted. First, the analyses shown in Table 1 were tabulated separately for the two banks which participated in the study (no bank by condition interactions were expected). Second, these analyses were tabulated for the telephone portion of the study. These analyses showed variances in response rates as large as those seen in Tables 1 and 2. Thus, it seems reasonable that the differences shown in the tables should be regarded as interesting findings that merit further investigation, but not as statistically significant.

Additional analyses also were conducted to examine patterns of *item* non-response among the various treatments. Only the commitment manipulation had consistent effects; item response rates for sensitive questions about checking account activity generally were higher in the commitment version than in the no commitment verson for both mail and telephone interviews. Again, however, these effects did not achieve statistical significance.

CONCLUSIONS

The results of this study suggest that a commitment treatment that includes the signature of a principal investigator and a request that the respondent initial a commitment statement may be useful in increasing response rates to mail surveys on sensitive topics. Commitment also may be helpful in reducing item non-response to sensitive questions. Certainly, this approach merits further research.

Further research also will be necessary to determine whether the beneficial effects of commitment will hold up across various interviewing situations. Commitment research to date has used sensitive topics and univeristy auspices. It will be interesting to see whether commitment requests increase response rates (and/or response quality) in surveys on nonsenstive topics, where the costs of responding are lower. Another issue of interest will be whether the benefits of commitment requests are available only to a limited group of sponsoring organizations. Will the request for commitment increase social motivation to respond only if the request is made by an organization with special credibility, such as the university which sponsored this study?

Manipulations of record checking, time frame, and counting method were not found to have significant effects on response rates in this study. These results suggest that the importance of these design variables must lie in their effects on response quality, rather than response rate. The results also suggest that design variables occurring within the questionnaire generally will not affect response rate substantially. Record checking is a strong manipulation requiring task interruption, yet did not have significant effects.

The general pattern of results provide support for two models of the decision-making process that a potential respondent goes through when asked to participate in a survey. One is a cost-benefit model, in which the respondent estimates the costs of responding and weighs them against the possible benefit or obligation to himself or some social group. The other is a task appropriateness model, in which respondents are more willing to pay a high cost in responding to the survey if the cost seems appropriate to the task at hand or necessary to accomplish the goals of the study. These two models have important study design implications for market researchers: questionnaires should be designed to emphasize the social benefits of responding and de-emphasize the costs of responding, and questionnaire variables should be manipulated not individually, but as a whole, in order to produce a "total design" that is appropriate to the purposes of the study.

REFERENCES

Berry, M. M., and C. F. Cannell (1980), "Reducing Response Effects in Telephone Interviews," paper presented at meeting of American Statistical Association, Houston, TX.

Calcich, S., and E. Blair (1980), "Alternative Measures of Frequency Bias in Shopper Surveys," Proceedings of the American Marketing Association Educators' Conference, 327-329.

Cannell, C. F., R. M. Groves, and P. V. Miller (1981), "The Effects of Mode of Data Collection on Health Survey Data," 1981 Proceedings of the Section on Survey Research Methods, American Statistical Association.

__________, L. Oksenberg, and J. M. Converse (1977), "Striving for Response Accuracy: Experiments in New Interviewing Techniques," Journal of Marketing Research, 306-315.

Dillman, D. A. (1978), Mail and Telephone Surveys: The Total Design Method. New York: John Wiley & Sons, Inc.

Ferber, R. (1966), The Reliability of Consumer Reports of Financial Assets and Debts. Urbana, Ill.: The Bureau of Economic and Business Research, University of Illinois.

Kahn, R. L., and C. F. Cannell (1957), The Dynamics of Interviewing. New York: John Wiley & Sons, Inc.

Kanuk, L., and C. Berenson (1975), "Mail Surveys and Response Rates: A Literature Review," Journal of Marketing Research, 440-453.

Sudman, S., and N. Bradburn (1973), "Effects of Time and Money Factors on Response," Journal of the American Statistical Association, 805-815.

A FLEXIBLE STRATEGY FOR ANALYZING
PREFERENCE DATA

James B. Wiley, Temple University
Reza Moinpour, University of Washington
Douglas L. Maclachlan, University of Washington

ABSTRACT

This paper presents a strategy for analyzing data gathered
using Balanced and Incomplete Block Designs. A dependent
variable is developed which captures the complex nature
of the data and a weighted least squares analysis of the
variable is outlined. An application of the approach is
presented.

Conjoint analysis provides the means for significant advance in behavioral and cognitively oriented research in
marketing (Fiedler 1972; Green, Wind and Jain 1972; Green
and Devita 1975a and b; Green and Srinivasan 1978; Wind
1975). However, the newly glimpsed research opportunities
nevertheless bring practical problems of another kind. It
is clear that advances are to be purchased with very dear
coin: namely, voluminous information required from respondents. For example, there are 45 choices to be made when
evaluating 10 stimuli using the method of paired comparisons; with 25 stimuli, there are 300 choices. Single stimulus methods such as rating scales reduce respondents'
labor, but provide less information to researchers regarding the ordering of alternatives on a variable of interest.
The information loss can become pronounced when respondents
must express judgments regarding many stimuli using few
scale categories. In brief, there is a need for procedures
that enable respondents to conveniently express judgments
for large numbers of stimuli--say more than 10.

Coombs (1964) has suggested that respondent labor can be
reduced by presenting them with subsets of stimuli rather
than the full set. Balanced incomplete block designs
(BIBDs), found in experimental design texts, provide a paradigm for selecting the stimuli into subsets. The advantages and disadvantages of using BIBDs to organize concepts
in conjoint analysis research are discussed in this paper.

In addition, an approach for analyzing the resulting data
is developed and illustrated. A generalization of a method
originally suggested by Thurstone (1931) for estimating
pairwise choice probabilities from rank order data provides
a means of aggregating the multiple judgments provided by
the respondent into a single measure of preference for each
concept. Weighted regression procedures described by
Grizzle, Starmer and Koch (1969) provide a technique for
decomposing the resulting dependent variable into components (part-worths). In addition, the procedures provide a
hypothesis testing capability not offered by traditional
approaches to conjoint analysis (Kruskal 1965).

ORGANIZING STIMULI INTO SUBSETS

Durbin (1951) and Gullicksen and Tucker (1961) have suggested that balanced incomplete block designs (BIBDs) can
be used in judgmental research as a guide for systematic
organization of stimuli into subsets. Specifically, BIBDs
provide a guide for organizing stimuli into subsets or
blocks of a given size. An example of BIBD is presented in
Wiley, MacLachlan and Moinpour (1976). In this design:
   a. Each of the subsets or blocks contains the
      same number of stimuli,
   b. Each of the stimuli appears in the same number
      of subsets,
   c. Each pair of stimuli appears in the same number

of subsets.

In general, using BIBDs as an aid for systematically organizing stimuli assures that no stimulus will appear
twice in the same subset, that all will be used an equal
number of times, and finally that pairs will appear within
subsets with equal frequency (Green 1974).

Advantages

There are several advantages to BIBD data collection procedures. First, the procedures appear to increase the
rate at which information is generated (Coombs 1964; Henry
and Stumpf, 1975) and this in turn may make possible a
higher completion rate, cut interview costs, and improve
the reliability of the results (Rink and Dunn 1979).

Secondly, BIBD data collection procedures offer the opportunity to tailor the measurement procedures for judgmental
research; design constraints may be relaxed in one or more
of the following ways:

   a. the number of stimuli which often are limited can
      be increased
   b. the completeness of the preference ordering over
      stimuli, which often is weak, can be strengthened

Finally, differences in contextual factors such as number
and complexity of stimuli, the capability and motivation of
respondents, or the nature of the hypothesized decomposition rule may be accommodated in the design by varying the
number of alternatives in a single presentation and/or the
number of times each pair of stimuli appear in the same
presentation.

Disadvantages

On the other hand, organizing stimuli into subsets can introduce error, particularly stemming from a faulty organization of the study, an inability of subjects to understand
the responses required of them, and subsequent mismanage-
ment of the data collected.

Great volumes of data are generated by BIBD designs. Editing, coding, and subsequent data management become important problems in their own right. Although data management
can be facilitated by means of recent software developments
(Wiley 1978), it remains a problem especially in studies
involving repeated measures, e.g., studies of test-retest
reliability, attitude change, scenario effects, and so
forth.

There may be "block by stimulus" interactions that occur
when stimuli are organized for presentation according to
BIBDs. The choice of block size--like the choice of the
number of categories for a rating scale--arbitrarily limits
the absolute magnitude of the differences that can be observed between stimuli. Though this phenomenon generally
is not considered to be of practical consequence when analyzing rating scale data, it possibly may have practical
consequence in the context of BIBD data analysis.

Finally, the assignment of stimuli to blocks is a sampling
process. While all pairs of stimuli will occur regardless
of assignment, this is not true of all triples. If the
rank ordering of two stimuli depends upon the presence of

other intrablock stimuli, the scale value for stimuli may then depend on the way in which stimuli are assigned to blocks in the design.

When to Use the Approach

BIBD data collection procedures are likely to be useful whenever strong ordering is needed over a large number of stimuli. For example, Coombs and Huang (1970) specified three relevant factors in formulating a theory of risk preference. To test the theory, a fully crossed design with a minimum of three levels per factor was required, as was a strong ordering over the alternatives.

In marketing, concept testing often involves large numbers of multiattribute stimuli. The authors' experience suggests that BIBD data collection procedures are worth considering in any practical concept testing application; that is, in any application in which stimuli are to be described in sufficient detail to be plausibly descriptive choice alternatives of actual managerial interest. In addition, BIBD data collection organizations may also prove useful in any marketing research setting where conjoint analysis is used in connection with theory testing (Bettman, Capon and Lutz 1975a,b), model development (Green and Devita 1975a, b), and the testing of complex hypotheses, such as those relating to trends or interactions.

ANALYZING THE DATA

The numerous judgments contained in BIBD data must be aggregated before subsequent analysis is possible. Gulliksen and Tucker (1961) accomplish this by converting the rank order information on the BIBD data into a table of implied paired comparisons. They analyze the resulting data with Thurstone Case V scaling procedures. There are practical problems with their approach in marketing settings, however, where concepts are easily identified, discriminated, and recalled. Zero/one proportions in pairwise choice tables are numerous with such stimuli. The aggregation approach to be presented avoids the problems that arise with zero/one proportions when using Thurstone Case V (or logit, probit, etc.) analysis. The approach offers the following additional benefits:

    a. the dependent variable has an interpretation that is consistent with the nature of the data, viz., the probability that each of the respective concepts in the choice set will rank higher than a reference stimulus

    b. the reference stimulus is, in a sense, the average concept for the choice set, so that the proportions cluster around the value .50, thus minimizing the number of extreme values on the dependent variable

    c. standard errors for the proportions are computed and introduced in the estimation and hypothesis testing process

The Dependent Variable

The data generated within a BIBD can be represented as a (nxk) matrix, P . An element of this table, p_{ij}, represents the proportion of times alternative i is assigned to rank j, provided it appears in a block. The vector $P_i = [p_{i1}, p_{i2}, \ldots, p_{ik}]$, characterizes the individual's response to stimulus i.

The marginal row of P, $P_m = [p_{m1}, p_{m2}, \ldots, p_{mk}]$, represents the proportion of times randomly selected stimuli are assigned each of the ranks. We take as the aggregate measure of preference the probability that each of the respective stimuli in the choice set will rank higher than a hypothetical reference stimulus having choice proportions

equal to those of the marginal row. Since a BIBD is balanced and ties are not allowed, the marginal proportions will be equal.

The probability that alternative i will rank higher than the marginal alternative can be estimated by

$$P_{i>m} = \sum_j (p_{ij} \cdot p_{m<j}) + 1/2 \sum_j (p_{ij} \cdot p_{mj}) \qquad (1)$$

where p_{ij} = proportion of times i is given rank j

        $p_{m<j}$ = proportion of times reference "marginal stimulus" m is ranked lower than j on a given presentation.

The dependent variable is simply the vector of probabilities $p = \{p_{a>m}, p_{b>m}, \ldots, p_{i>m}, \ldots, p_{y>m}\}$ obtained by applying (1) to each stimulus in the choice set. This index has properties commonly posited in connection with choice processes. First, the probability that each of two equally favorable stimuli will rank highest on a single presentation is one-half. Secondly, the probability that a more favored stimulus will rank higher than a less favored one increases monotonically as the difference between their favorability increases.

<u>Decomposing the Dependent Variable into "Partworths"</u>

Estimates of partworths for multiattribute alternatives may be obtained by coding attribute levels as dummy variables (Green and Wind 1973) and then obtaining estimates of model parameters from the general linear model

$$E(p) = Xb \qquad (2)$$

where X is a design matrix and b is the vector of parameter (partworth) estimates.

However, ordinary least squares procedures are not appropriate in this setting. First, the dependent variable is a vector of proportions whose elements are estimated with unequal precision. Secondly, each element of the vector p is not a single observation but rather a composite index based on a large amount of data. Weighted least squares (WLS) procedures enable estimation to accommodate heteroscedastic variances as well as reflect the composite nature of the dependent variable.

As an approximation of the covariance matrix of p we propose:

$$\begin{array}{cccc} S & = & A & V & A' \\ (y)x(y) & & (y)x(yk) & (yk)x(yk) & (yk)x(y) \end{array} \qquad (3)$$

where A is a block diagonal matrix with y (1 by k) vectors on the main diagonal. The diagonal vectors are equal with elements equal to the vector of cumulative marginal proportions. V is a block diagonal matrix whose elements are estimated with expressions of the type:

$$Var\{v_{ij}\} = P_{ij}(1-p_{ij})/r; \quad Cov\{v_{ij}, v_{ij'}\} = P_{ij}p_{ij'}/r; \qquad (4)$$

$$Cov\{v_{ij}, v_{i'j'}\} = 0 \qquad (5)$$

where $j \neq j'$, $i \neq i'$; P_{ij} estimates the proportion of times stimulus i is assigned rank j, and r is equal to the number of times each stimulus is presented to the subject (Lehnen and Koch 1974, p.288).

Equation (4) expresses the covariance matrix for stimulus i and implies that the assignment of the stimulus to ranks can be represented with a multinomial probability model. There will be y of these (k by k) matrices arranged in block diagonal form down the main diagonal of V.

Equation (5) states that the remaining elements of V are
zero, which implies that assignment of a stimulus to ranks
is independent of the assignment of other stimuli. While
these assumptions cannot hold in a strict sense with a
ranking process, they can hold to a reasonable approximation provided that the number of stimuli in a given presentation and the number of presentations are sufficient.
Thurstone (1931) has shown with ten stimuli that estimates
of choice proportion based on this approach are almost
identical to those computed by enumeration.

A test of fit of the general linear model can be obtained
using modified chi-square methods (Grizzle, Starmer and
Koch 1969):

$$X^2 = SS[E(p) = Xb] \qquad\qquad (6)$$

$$= p'S^{-1}p - b'(X'S^{-1}X)b$$

where $b = (X'S^{-1}X)^{-1} X'S^{-1}p$, X is a design matrix in which
the j(th) row contains the coding for the j(th) alternative in dummy variable form, S is the covariance matrix of
p, (3), and $p = \{p_{a>m}, p_{b>m}, \ldots, p_{y>m}\}$.

Given the fit of the model, the test of the hypotheses
Cb = 0 is produced by:

$$X^2 = SS[Cb = 0] = b'C'[C(X'S^{-1}X)^{-1}C']^{-1} Cb \qquad (7)$$

where C is an appropriately defined contrast matrix.

AN ILLUSTRATION

The following experiment illustrates the use of BIBD designs to study the appropriateness of the two most utilized scaling models--the vector model, which posits preference to be a linear function of attribute level, and
the "distance" model, which posits preference to be a quadratic function of attribute level (Carroll 1972).

Methodology

Data was collected for two types stimuli concepts: tea
drinks and soft drinks. Twenty-four participants made preference judgements among soft drinks, 15 for tea drinks. The
judgments were replicated. Thus 78 sets were generated. A
complete description of the methodology is provided in
Wiley, Maclachlan, and Moinpour (1976).

Results

Equation 6 was employed to determine whether the hypothesized main-effect only decompositions model fitted the
individual's data. The model was rejected at the .05 level
on at least one trial for five of the 15 subjects who supplied tea drink data. Likewise, the hypothesized main effect model was rejected for six of the subjects who supplied
soft drink data. Subsequent analysis is restricted to participants for whom the additive model cannot be rejected in
either trial.

Linear and quadratic components for soft drink data and tea
drink data were calculated using equation (7). Considering
the soft drink data first, we observe evidence of a significant quadratic trend effect ($p \leq .10$) for 11 of 36 data
sets (31 percent) on the "calories" attribute, 22 of 36
(61 percent) on the "carbonation" attributes and 27 of 36
(72 percent) on the "taste" attribute. Quadratic trend accounts for the majority of variance on "calories" in 12
data sets, on "carbonation" in 21 data sets, and on "taste"
in 20 data sets.

Eleven of 20 (65 percent) of the tea drink data sets show
evidence of quadratic trend ($p \leq .10$) on "sugar." Eighteen
of 20 (90 percent) show evidence of quadratic trend ($p \leq .10$)
on "temperature." Quadratic trend accounts for the major-

ity of variance on "sugar" in six data sets, and for the
majority of variance on "temperature" in 13 data sets.

The results suggest that for most respondents the function
linking the attribute level to partworths is non-linear on
one or more attributes. Further, the strongest evidence
of non-linearity is on attributes for which the presence of
an interior ideal point has intuitive appeal. For example,
for tea drink data almost all of the respondents indicated
a negative ideal at the "lukewarm" level of the temperature
dimension. Similarly, for soft drink data, the most preferred level of taste is not extreme, neither very bitter
nor very sweet. The next stage of analysis entails a direct examination of response surface plots.

CONCLUDING REMARKS

A wide variety of opportunities exists for applying BIBD
methodology to substantive issues. A brief illustration
of such research appears in this study, i.e., the findings
relating to the form of the utility functions that link
attribute levels to preference.

Future research should attend to the tailoring of the designs to the situational determinants of success with such
methods, such as:

    a. task difficulty--itself a function of number of
        attributes, nature of attributes, and differences
        between attribute levels;
    b. subject motivation;
    c. time and model of presentation; and
    d. subject characteristics, such as tolerance for
        ambiguity and cognitive complexity.

In addition to methodological investigations, the type of
composition function--compensatory, conjunctive, lexi-
cographic, etc.--utilized by individuals in forming preferences could be studied to see if it might systematically
vary over products, with stages in a product's life cycle,
or with other factors. It appears that the flexible approach to conjoint analysis outlined in this paper can be
used to advantage when investigating a variety of methodological and substantive issues.

REFERENCES

Bettman, J.R., N. Capon and R.J. Lutz (1975a). "Multi-
    attribute Measurement Models and Multiattribute
    Theory," _Journal of Consumer Research_, 4 (March),
    81-85.

__________(1975b). "Cognitive Algebra in Multiattri-
    bute Models," _Journal of Marketing Research_, 12
    (May), 151-164.

Carroll, D. J. (1972). "Individual Differences and Multi-
    dimensional Scaling," in R. N. Shepard, A. K. Romney
    and S. B. Nerlove, (eds), _Multidimensional Scaling:
    Theory and Applications in the Behavioral Sciences_,
    New York: Seminar Press, 105-155.

Coombs, C. H. (1964). _Theory of Data_, New York: John
    Wiley, Inc.

__________ and L. Huang (1970). "Polynomial Psychophy-
    sics of Risk," _Journal of Mathematical Psychology_
    Statistical Section, 4, 85-90.

Fiedler, J. A. (1975). "Optimizing Product Design Through
    Analysis of Consumer Tradeoffs," in _Proceedings of the
    3rd Annual Conference_, Association for Consumer Re-
    search, M. Venkatesan (ed.).

Green, P. E. (1974). "On the Design of Choice Experiments

Involving Multifactor Alternatives," *Journal of Consumer Research*, 1, 61-68.

__________ and M. T. Devita (1975a). "A Complementarity Model of Consumer Utility for Item Collections," *Journal of Consumer Research*, 1 (December), 56-67.

__________ (1975b), "An Interaction Model of Consumer Utility," *Journal of Consumer Research*, 2 (September), 146-153.

__________ and V. Srinivasan (1978). "Conjoint Analysis in Consumer Research: Issues and Outlook," *Journal of Consumer Research*, 5 (September), 103-123.

__________ Y. Wind and A. K. Jain (1972). "Benefit Bundle Analysis," *Journal of Advertising Research*, 12 (April), 31-36.

__________ and Y. Wind (1973). *Multiattribute Decisions in Marketing: A Measurement Approach*, Hinsdale, IL: The Dryden Press.

Grizzle, J. E., C. F. Starmer and G. G. Koch (1969). "Analysis of Categorical Data by Linear Models," *Biometrics*, 25 (September), 489-504.

Gulliksen, H. and L. R. Tucker (1961). "A General Procedure for Obtaining Paired Comparisons from Multiple Rank Orders," *Psychometrika*, 26 (June), 173-183.

Henry, W. A. and R. W. Stumpf (1975). "Time and Accuracy Measures for Alternative Multidimensional Scaling Data Collection Methods," *Journal of Marketing Research*, 12 (May), 165-170.

Kruskal, J. B. (1965). "Analysis of Factorial Experiments by Estimating Monotone Transformations of the Data," *Journal of the Royal Statistical Society*, Series B, 27, 251-263.

Lehnen, R. G. and G. C. Koch (1974). "A General Linear Approach to the Analysis of Non-metric Data: Applications for Political Science," *American Journal of Political Science*, 18, 283-313.

Rink, D. R. and J. E. Dunn (1979). "BIB: A Solution to Analyzing Ranked Objects," American Marketing Association Educators Conference, Minneapolis, 35-40.

Thurstone, L. L. (1931), "Rank Order as a Psychophysical Method," *Journal of Experimental Psychology*, 14 (June), 187-201.

Wiley, J. B. (1978). "BIBD: A Program for Processing Order 'k/n' Choice Data," *Journal of Marketing Research*, 15 (August), 472-474.

__________, D. L. MacLachlan, and R. Moinpour (1976), "Comparison of Stated and Inferred Parameter Values in Additive Models: An Illustration of a Paradigm," in W. Perrault, Jr., ed., *Advances in Consumer Research*, vol.4, Atlanta, GA, 98-105.

QUESTION UNDERSTANDING IN SELF-REPORT DATA

Robert A. Peterson, University of Texas at Austin
Roger A. Kerin, Southern Methodist University, Dallas
Mohammad Sabertehrani, Eastern Michigan University, Ipsalanti

ABSTRACT

This study examined the assessment and implications of
question understanding in a telephone survey. Specifically, an interviewer-based evaluation technique was employed which was shown not be be interviewer specific. In
addition, it was found that question understanding is systematically related to socio-economic characteristics of
respondents and poor question understanding is associated
with a high incidence of "uncertain or no opinion" responses. Implications for the interpretation of self-
report data are discussed and recommendations for improving the quality of self-report data are suggested.

INTRODUCTION

When developing survey questions researchers have traditionally asked themselves three interrogatives about each
potential question (Peterson 1982):

> Can potential study participants understand
>   the question?
> Can potential study participants answer the
>   question?   and
> Will potential study participants answer
>   the question?

While the second and third interrogations have been widely
studied (e.g., Ferber 1956), the first--question understanding or comprehension--has only been infrequently addressed in empirical investigations. For example, in a
recent review of the literature on self-report data
quality, Peterson and Kerin (1981) found no instances in
which question understanding had been directly investigated. Indeed, Cicourel (1982) had explicitly stated that
"We need a better understanding of...the way questions are
comprehended."

All-too-often a study participant may not understand a
question, but have no opportunity to request clarification.
In mail surveys, lack of understanding could manifest itself in the unwillingness to return the questionnaire. In
a telephone or personal interview setting, however, a more
"captive" individual might participate in the survey even
though questions or question topics were not fully understood in order to be a "good" respondent (Bradburn, Sudman,
Blair and Stocking 1978).

"Question understanding" as a source of error in survey
research has not been examined explicitly in the literature, although research on question construction and interviewer effects has indirectly addressed its impact.
Question wording (e.g., Schuman and Presser 1977) and question length (e.g., Laurent 1972) in particular influence a
study participant's understanding of what is being asked.
Moreover, question difficulty has been identified as a
source of interviewer variance as well (McKenzie 1977).

Question understanding raises several issues from a data
quality perspective. First, should responses from study
participants who do not understand the questions posed,
but answer them anyway, be weighted equally with those
from study participants who do understand the questions?

This research was sponsored by the Institute for Constructive Capitalism, the University of Texas at Austin.

Second, do responses from study participants who understand
the questions posed differ from the responses of study
participants who do not understand the questions posed?
Third, is the lack of question understanding symtomatic of
certain types of survey participants? Fourth, can approaches be adopted that alert researchers to the incidence
and implications of question understanding or misunder-
standing?

Purpose

The purpose of this research was three-fold. First the
study sought to examine the applicability of an interviewer-based data quality check in telephone surveys. The
use of interviewers to assess the quality of self-report
data in personal interviews is widespread in the National
Opinion Research Center (NORC) social science surveys
(National Opinion Research Center 1980). A second objective was to determine whether "understanding of questions"
was systematically related to the socio-economic characteristics of respondents. The final objective was to
suggest how incorporating the concept of "question understanding" into the analysis of survey data can be used to
enhance the interpretation of self-report data.

METHOD

The data reported in this paper were obtained from a telephone survey of 2,041 male and female heads of households
residing in Texas. The sample was selected probabilisti-
cally in such a manner that it was representative of Texas
households with telephones in August, 1981. All interviews
were conducted by professional interviewers in centralized,
supervised telephone rooms.

The general purpose of the survey was to document attitudes, opinions, concerns and perspectives of Texas adults
with respect to selected economic, business and social
issues and problems. These issues and problems included
taxation, the role of government in the private sector, the
quality of life in Texas, and economic growth, among
others. Socio-economic characteristics of respondents
were also obtained.

Upon completion of an interview, the interviewer was asked
to assess the study participant's understanding of the
questions:

Interviewer: Was the respondent's understanding of the
                  questions...
                            Good ... 1
                            Fair ... 2
                            Poor ... 3

In addition, the interviewer was asked to assess the study
participant's attitude toward the interview:

Interviewer: In general, what was the respondent's atti-
                  tude toward the interview...
                        Friendly and Interested......1
                        Cooperative, but not
                            particularly interested...2
                        Impatient and Restless.......3
                        Hostile....................4

Both of these questions were directly drawn from the NORC

social science survey.[1]

Since "question understanding" was determined by individual interviews, an analysis of interviewer ratings was initially conducted to determine if the ratings of the eleven interviewers who conducted 50 or more interviews. These interviewers conducted 782 interviews, or 38 percent of all interviews in the study.[2] Table 1 presents the results of the analysis of variance. Even though statistically significant differences among interviewers on the "understanding" question existed, the differences were not substantively significant. Less than 1 percent of the variability in ratings was due to an interviewer effect (ω^2 = .0075). Thus, it was concluded that the measure of "question understanding" was not interviewer-specific for all practical purposes.

RESULTS

Incidence of Question Understanding

Overall, the incidence of question understanding in this study was 74.9 percent: three-fourths of the study participants were deemed to possess a "good" understanding of the questions posed. This figure is similar to the NORC mean question understanding percentage of 78.9 percent for their social surveys conducted during the 1972-1980 period using personal interviews (National Opinion Research Center 1980). It is higher than that obtained (62 percent) in a regional telephone survey relating to nuclear power issues conducted by one of the authors.

Question understanding, however, varied systematically with the socioeconomic characterisitcs of study participants. Table 2 shows the relationship between "good" understanding of the questions and selected socioeconomic characteristics of study participants. The results indicate that question understanding was related to respondent place of residence, marital status, age, education, income, ethnic group, and sex. Given the large sample size in this study, the finding of statistically significant relationships was not totally unexpected (Sawyer and Ball 1981). Therefore, Gamma was also computed to test the strength of association between question understanding and socioeconomic characteristics. This analysis indicated that respondent education and income, in particular, exhibited a relatively strong association with question understanding. Place of residence and marital status were not strongly related to question understanding.

TABLE 1
INTERVIEWER EFFECT IN RESPONDENT
UNDERSTANDING OF QUESTIONS

Source	SS	DF	MS	F	p
Between Interviewers	15.4	10	1.54	6.42	.001
Within Interviewers	184.2	771	.24		
Total	199.6	781			

---

[1]A copy of the full report, including methodology, can be obtained by writing the Institute for Constructive Capitalism, the University of Texas at Austin, Austin, Texas, 78712.

[2]Sixty-two different interviewers were involved in data collection. Thus, the average number of interviewees per interviewer was approximately 33. The distribution of interviews was, though, positively skewed.

TABLE 2
RELATIONSHIP BETWEEN QUESTION UNDERSTANDING
AND SOCIOECONOMIC CHARACTERISTICS OF RESPONDENTS[a]

Socioeconomic Characteristic	Percentage of study participants in segment with "Good" Understanding	
Place of Residence		
SMSA	76.7	χ^2 = 20.23, 4 df.
Non-SMSA (over 10,000 pop.)	66.5	p < .0005
Non-SMSA (under 10,000 pop.)	68.5	Gamma = .21
Marital Status		
Married	76.4	χ^2 = 10.27, 2 df.
Non Married	70.8	p < .006
		Gamma = .15
Respondent Age		
18-24	73.8	χ^2 = 76.01, 8 df.
25-35	79.7	p < .0001
36-49	79.7	Gamma = .17
50-64	71.2	
65+	55.7	
Respondent Education		
No Formal Education	28.3	χ^2 = 297.44, 8 df.
Some Grade School/High School	44.4	p < .0001
High School Graduate	69.6	Gamma = -.56
Some College/Trade School	81.3	
College Graduate	91.9	
Household Income		
Less than $6,000	46.3	χ^2 = 304.27, 12 df.
$6,000 - $9,900	51.6	p < .0001
$10,000 - $14,900	70.2	Gamma = -.51
$15,000 - $19,900	77.4	
$20,000 - $29,900	83.7	
$30,000 - $39,900	91.4	
$40,000+	91.0	
Ethnic Group		
White	81.1	χ^2 = 109.85, 6 df.
Black	57.6	p < .0001
Mexican-American	60.7	Gamma = .41
Other	70.4	
Sex		
Male	82.9	χ^2 = 72.28, 2 df.
Female	66.9	p < .0001
		Gamma = .40

[a]Question understanding coded as "good" understanding, "fair" understanding, and "poor" understanding.

Question Understanding and Response Behavior

The extent to which questions were understood appears to be related to the responses given by study participants. Table 3 presents illustrative question responses classified according to degree of question understanding.[3]

---

[3]Questions were posed in a Likert-type response format.

The most noteworthy observation from this table is that
study participants who exhibited "poor" understanding of
the questions were also those who gave the most <u>uncertain</u>
responses. This finding raises an interpretation issue.
Was the <u>uncertain</u> response a "true" response in that the
study participant actually had no opinion or was undertain
about his/her position, or did the respondent not understand the question and therefore elected to take a middle
ground position on the subject?

TABLE 3
RELATIONSHIP BETWEEN QUESTION UNDERSTANDING
AND RESPONSE TO SELECTED QUESTIONS

1. In general, the relationship between government and business is better now than it was 5 years ago:

| | Response[a] | | |
Question Understanding	SA	Uncert.	SD
Good	23.4%	8.5%	12.7%
Fair	17.5%	18.1%	13.8%
Poor	13.2%	28.2%	14.1%

2. Government regulation is necessary to protect and improve the quality of life:

| | Response | | |
Question Understanding	SA	Uncert.	SD
Good	27.5%	1.8%	19.2%
Fair	38.3%	4.9%	9.1%
Poor	33.9%	11.9%	6.9%

3. If the state of Texas were to provide a business with
funds for developing new energy sources, the state
should own part of the business:

| | Response | | |
Question Understanding	SA	Uncert.	SD
Good	20.8%	4.1%	35.6%
Fair	27.8%	9.9%	21.7%
Poor	19.4%	20.4%	20.2%

4. The international trading position of the United States
is better now than it was 5 years ago:

| | Response | | |
Question Understanding	SA	Uncert.	SD
Good	20.4%	16.3%	16.6%
Fair	22.3%	27.7%	12.9%
Poor	15.8%	38.6%	13.5%

5. Government and business should cooperate in developing
synthetic fuels:

| | Response | | |
Question Understanding	SA	Uncert.	SD
Good	61.9%	1.9%	7.0%
Fair	53.0%	7.2%	6.2%
Poor	39.1%	18.9%	4.5%

[a]Read: 23.4% of those respondents deemed as having a
"good" understanding of the questions strongly agreed with
the statement. A five point Likert-type scale was actually
used in the survey. Only the extreme and mid-points are
shown for illustrative purposes. All cross-tabulations
were statistically significant using χ^2 tests.

Previous research on "no opinion" or "don't know" responses in surveys offers some insight into this question.
Don't know responses have been related to study participant
education, marital status, sex, income, and cultural differences (Ziller and Long 1965; Ferber 1966; Sicinski 1970;
Francis and Busch 1975), while no opinion responses are
prevalent among study participants with limited formal education (Francis and Busch 1975; Converse 1976-77). These
same characteristics were linked to question understanding
in Table 2.[4]

A second, more global, aspect of response behavior studied
was the study participant's attitude toward the interview
itself. Table 4 shows the relationship between question
understanding and attitude toward the interview. The table
indicates that study participants who exhibited a good
understanding of questions were more friendly or interested
in the interview; study participants who exhibited a poor
understanding of the questions exhibited impatient, rest-
less, or hostile behavior. This relationship was not only
statistically significant, but substantively significant as
well (Gamma = .74).

TABLE 4
RESPONDENT UNDERSTANDING OF QUESTIONS AND
INTEREST IN THE INTERVIEW

Respondent Understanding of Questions:	Respondent Interest in Interview:[a]			
	Cooperative, Friendly/ Interested	But Not Interested	Impatient/ Restless/ Hostile	
Good	89.5%	9.4%	1.1%	100% (1527)
Fair	56.1%	37.5%	6.4%	100% (423)
Poor	33.0%	50.7%	16.3%	100% (90)

[a]χ^2 = 375.7, 4 dr, p < .0001; Gamma = .74

IMPLICATIONS OF QUESTION UNDERSTANDING
FOR THE EVALUATION OF SELF-REPORT DATA QUALITY

The approach and findings reported in this study have
several implications for the evaluation of self-report
data quality in telephone surveys. First, the use of an
interviewer-based check on question understanding appears
to be a potentially useful device for assessing the quality of self-report data in a field setting. From the
present research it appears that an interviewer-based
check is not interviewer-specific, at least when professional interviews are employed.

Second, a variable such as "question understanding" may be
used in an "explanatory" context. Consider the data below.
These data are "raw" responses to the question "Government
regulation is necessary to protect and improve the quality
of life." For ease of illustration, <u>strongly agree</u> (disagree) and <u>somewhat agree</u> (disagree) responses have been
collapsed into <u>agree</u> (disagree) while the <u>fair</u> and <u>poor</u>
question understanding categories have been combined into
a single category.

[4]For a different perspective on this issue see Coombs
and Coombs (1976-1977).

428

		Agree	Uncertain	Disagree	
Male	good	497	10	332	839
	fair/poor	128	11	33	172
Female	good	453	17	215	685
	fair/poor	248	20	72	340
		1326	58	652	2036

From these data several percentages can be calculated. For example, while 65.1 percent of the total sample agreed with the statement, 61.8 percent of the males and 68.4 percent of the females agreed with the statement. However,

- of the males whose question understanding was "good", 59.2 percent agreed with the statement

- of the males whose question understanding was "fair/poor," 74.4 percent agreed with the statement

- of the females whose question understanding was "good," 66.1 percent agreed with the statement

- of the females whose question understanding was "fair/poor," 72.9 percent agreed with the statement

Generally, the survey participants whose question understanding was "good," 62.3 percent agreed with the statement. Hence, in certain instances question understanding can be used to enhance the interpretation of, and even, to a limited extent, "explain" item responses. If, in fact, question understanding influences both location parameter and variability parameter estimates, as the current findings imply, then it is a variable well worth investigating further. For these reasons alone it should be incorporated with a personal interview or telephone survey whenever possible.

Third, the findings themselves provide new insights into response behavior. Although the finding that question understanding is systematically related to study participants' socioeconomic characteristics may be intuitively obvious, per se, the magnitude of the relationship was somewhat surprising. It may be that all study participants are not necessarily equal in terms of providing "high quality" data, or data that have identical decision implications. Thus, perhaps some sort of weighting scheme might be necessary to weight study participant answers according to question understanding. Such a scheme would, however, require more extensive investigation before even a tentative implementation.

Fourth, the use of a question understanding measure in telephone and personal interview settings could be used as an index of the difficulty of the subject matter addressed in a marketing research study. Specifically, if the percent of question understanding reported in a survey is relatively "low" (as in the nuclear power telephone survey), then the data should be viewed with caution. Because this implies that question understanding is topic-specified, determining norms for question understanding will be only obtained over time across a number of populations and survey topics.

In brief, question understanding should be investigated whenever possible in survey research. It should not be thought of as an artifact that reduces the meaningfulness of survey results, but as a means of more fully interpreting and gaining insights into the data. Merely evaluating question understanding in a pretest is not sufficient (since it only addresses question ambiguity) for improving data quality. It must be explicitly incorporated into all substantive research phases as a variable of interest.

REFERENCES

Bradburn, Norman, Seymor Sudman, Ed Blair and Carol Stocking (1978), "Question Threat and Response Bias," Public Opinion Quarterly 42 (Summer), 221-234.

Cicourel, Aaron V. (1982), "Interviews, Surveys, and the Problem of Ecological Validity," The American Sociologist 17 (February), 11-20.

Converse, Jean (1976-77), "Predicting No Opinion in the Polls," Public Opinion Quarterly 40 (Winter), 515-530.

Coombs, Clyde H. and Lolagene C. Coombs (1976-1977),"'Don't Know': Item Ambiguity or Respondent Uncertainty?" Public Opinion Quarterly 40 (Winter), 497-514.

Ferber, Robert (1956), "The Effect of Respondent Ignorance on Survey Results," Journal of the American Statistical Association 51 (December), 576-586.

___________(1966), "Item Nonresponse in a Consumer Survey," Public Opinion Quarterly 30 (Fall), 399-415

Francis, J. and L. Busch (1975), "What We Know About 'I Don't Knows,'" Public Opinion Quarterly 39 (Fall), 207-218.

Laurent, Andre (1972), "Effects of Question Length on Reporting Behavior in the Survey Interview," Journal of the American Statistical Association 67 (June), 298-305.

McKenzie, J. R. (1977), "An Investigation into Interviewer Effects in Market Research," Journal of Marketing Research 14 (August), 330-336.

National Opinion Research Center (1980), General Social Surveys Cumulative Codebook 1972-1980.

Peterson, Robert A. (1982), Marketing Research Dallas: Business Publications, Inc., 224.

Peterson, Robert and Roger Kerin (1981), "The Quality of Self-Report Data: Review and Synthesis," Review of Marketing 1981, Ben Enis and Kenneth Roering, eds. Chicago: American Marketing Association, 5-20.

Sawyer, Alan and A. Dwayne Ball (1981), "Statistical Power and Effect Size in Marketing Research," Journal of Marketing Research 18 (August), 275-290.

Schuman, Herbert and Stanley Presser (1977), "Question Wording as an Independent Variable in Survey Analysis," Sociological Methods and Research 6 (November), 151-170.

Sicinski, A. (1970), "'Don't Know' Answers in Cross-National Surveys," Public Opinion Quarterly 34 (Spring), 126-129.

Ziller, R. C. and B. H. Long (1965), "Some Correlates of Don't Know Response in Opinion Questionnaires," Journal of Social Psychology, 67, 139-147.

FOLLOW-UP TECHNIQUES: THE EFFECT OF METHOD AND SOURCE APPEAL

James M. Comer, University of Cincinnati, Cincinnati
J. Steven Kelly, DePaul University, Chicago

ABSTRACT

It is common practice for researchers using mail surveys to employ multiple waves of response solicitation. The authors, using industrial subjects, conducted a factorial design experiment testing the effects of follow-up method and source appeal on response rate, speed, and completeness. Study results indicate that the use of telephone follow-up will significantly increase response rate and speed but that no differential source effects were noted. It was also found that the simple procedure of repeat mailing of a duplicate questionnaire without cover letter produced acceptable levels of response with minimum cost.

INTRODUCTION

The problem of non-response to the initial wave of a mail survey has been the subject of considerable discussion. The broad range of remedies that have been suggested for dealing with the non-response problem may be grouped into three categories. Research in the first category suggests that the efforts to affect response should be concentrated in the first wave of solicitation. The literature of mail survey research is dominated by such first wave studies. Typically, their express purpose is to determine, primarily through factorial design methodology, the effects of certain treatments on predetermined dimensions of response (Childers, Pride and Ferrel 1980; Jones and Linda 1978; Kanuk and Berenson 1975). The second category is characterized by methodology designed to estimate the nature/direction of potential bias by investigating the characteristics of non-respondents. There is a rich history of methods designed to estimate these biases (Hansen and Hurwitz 1946; Dolde, Staelin and Yao 1980). The third category suggests that multiple waves of solicitation, often with a variety of follow-up techniques, be employed until total response rate is "sufficiently" high that non-response bias is considered insignificant (Houston and Nevin 1977). The literature in this third category is neither as rich nor diverse as exists for the first two categories.

Both the second and third category of research face a similar obstacle: How does one efficiently elicit responses from non-respondents? In an attempt to answer that question, this paper discusses a research study developed to evaluate follow-up techniques directed toward non-respondents. A factorial design was used to examine the influence of both the source of the survey and the method of contact on response rate, speed, and questionnaire completeness.

BACKGROUND

Over the years empirical studies of mail survey phenomena have accumulated into a rather sizeable body of literature (Houston and Ford 1976; Kanuk and Berenson 1975; Scott 1961). Easily the largest segment of this literature set is devoted to the study of the effects of various independent variables such as monetary inducement on questionnaire return rate, speed, and other variables. Typically, these studies have applied a factorial design methodology to the initial wave of mail survey to test the various "treatment" effects. While these results are rather well documented for the initial, or Wave 1 mailing, the effects are not so clearly defined for Wave 2 mailings.

The empirical research which has been conducted on Wave 2 solicitation falls into two well-defined categories. In the first category are studies which are essentially sequential in design where each succeeding wave of respondent solicitation is characterized by variations in method of solicitation. Donald (1960) used letter, letter plus questionnaire, and finally on the fourth wave telephone. Similarly Eckland (1965) and others (Childers, Pride and Ferrell 1980; Dillman and Frey 1974; Etze and Walker 1974; Goulet 1977) used varying combinations of letter, postcard, telegram, and telephone to increase response rate over two to four solicitation waves. Universally, and not surprisingly, they concluded that any follow-up solicitation increases response rate (Kanuk and Berenson 1975). However, since each solicitation was essentially on a different respondent subset, it is difficult to draw solid comparative conclusions on the efficacy of one technique over another. This inherent weakness of sequential design argues strongly for the use of a factorial design methodology to clearly identify follow-up effects.

Four studies were located which used a factorial design to test the effects of different follow-up techniques on certain criterion variables. Kerin (1974) found no significant differential effects of personal (telephone and personalized letter) vs. impersonal (form letter) follow-up on response rate or distortion. Peterson (1975) found that his postcard follow-up did not significantly affect response rate, speed, or quality/representativeness. Anderson and Berdie (1975) tested the effect of humorous, whimsical and formal follow-up appeals on response rate and concluded that the significance in the effect of the follow-up technique was dependent on the characteristics of the solicited group. For example, more formal groups (faculty and administrators) had significantly higher response rates to formal appeals than to humorous or whimsical appeals. Roscoe, Lang, and Sheth (1975) compared the effect of postcard reminder vs. various telephone and telephone-questionnaire combinations on response rate. Results indicated that the telephone reminder was significantly better than the other three alternatives.

There has been recent evidence that some of the sequential and factorial design studies which intended to use non-respondents may have erred in their definition of non-respondent. A study by Huxley (1980) indicates that the majority of response to a mail questionnaire occurs in Weeks 3 and 4 after the initial solicitation. In order for the researchers to receive the bulk of response in Weeks 3 and 4, the questionnaires must be completed by respondents in Week 1 or 2. This means that any follow-up stimuli in Weeks 1 or 2 are in reality applied to a heterogeneous mix of respondents and non-respondents. Not only is this potentially wasteful, it also tends to misrepresent the effect of follow-up stimuli applied in the Week 1-2 interval which are more properly classified as subject reinforcement of Wave 1 stimulus and not as Wave 2 non-respondent follow-up solicitation. Huxley's results indicate that in order to properly identify the non-respondent subset the researcher should wait until after Week 4 when the response rate drops off dramatically before applying a follow-up stimulus.

STUDY DESIGN

Subjects

The initial wave consisted of a confidential eight page multi-item questionnaire mailed to an industrial population

of 311 exhibit managers whose firms were members of the
National Trade Show Exhibitors Association (NTSEA). The
objective of the study was the traditional membership survey designed to explore current member business practices,
attitudes, expectations, etc. No incentives were extended
to subjects to respond other than a vague "good-of-the-
profession" appeal in the cover letter. One hundred eleven
subjects responded in the initial wave (36%) leaving 200
Wave 1 non-respondents for Wave 2 solicitation. In order
to insure that the follow-up study was confined solely to
non-respondents, six weeks was allowed to lapse between the
time of the initial survey and the follow-up mailing. In
addition, all follow-up questionnaires were specially coded
to insure no Wave 1 late arrivals confounded the results.
These precautions were successful since no uncoded questionnaires were returned.

Dependent Variables

Three dependent variables were investigated. The first was
response rate which was defined as the ratio of the number
of questionnaires returned divided by the number of questionnaires mailed. The second dependent variable was return speed measured in number of days from time of the receipt of the follow-up stimuls to the date the questionnaire was returned. The third dependent variable was response completeness which was measured by the ratio of completed questions to total questions.

Treatments

The 200 identified non-respondents were randomly assigned
to treatments in a 2x2 factorial design with control group
where each cell contained 40 subjects. Two treatments were
used: 1) Method of follow-up with two levels-telephone and
letter; and 2) Source also with two levels-university and
trade association. A control group was employed to provide
a base for comparison of Wave 2 treatment effects.

Procedure

In the mail treatment, 80 subjects received the questionnaire in a personally addressed typed envelope. The cover
letter were identical in content. The only difference was
that the letters to 40 subjects had a university letterhead.
The tone of the cover letter was neutral simply reminding
them that they had not responded. It was identical to the
script used in the telephone follow-up which is reproduced
as Figure 1.

FIGURE 1: Script Mail/Telephone Follow-up

"We recently sent you a questionnaire exploring your trade
show activities. In checking our records we found we have
not received a card indicating that you had completed and
returned the questionnaire. Therefore, we took the liberty
of sending you a follow-up questionnaire. We would appreciate your completing this questionnaire and returning it
to us as soon as possible."

Thank you very much for your cooperation."

The telephone follow-up involved first mailing a questionnaire without a cover letter, waiting two days for the mail
to be delivered, then making a long distance or simulated
long distance, person-to-person call soliciting response.
The only difference between the mail and telephone subject
solicitation was in the preamble to the telephone script
where the 40 subjects, when contacted, were informed that
this was "a representative from the trade association" and
then the script was read. The other 40 subjects in the
telephone treatment were informed that "Professor X from Y
University" was calling, and the script was read. The control group consisted of 40 subjects who were mailed a questionnaire without cover letters with return instructions
identical to those given in Wave 1. All other envelopes
and return procedures were identical across all treatments.

HYPOTHESES

Response Rate

<u>Method</u>. The research results from sequential studies con-
flict somewhat with that from factorial design studies.
The sequential studies observed, but did not statistically
support, that telephone follow-up increased response rate
in Waves 3 and beyond. Previous factorial design research
has incorporated the telphone either as a pre-Wave 1 alert
procedure or as a follow-up technique. Using telephone
alerts, Parsons and Medford (1972) found no significant effect on response rate, but Stafford (1966) did. As a follow-
up technique, Kerin (1974) found that personalized techniques of follow-up (telephone and personal letter) were
not differentially effective over a form letter. Roscoe,
et al. (1975) did find that telephone follow-up significantly increased response rate, but a confounding effect
may have occurred, because the telephone method was also
the same as the study source - the telephone company. Thus,
the dual source effects, if additive, would result in an
overstatement of telephone method effectiveness on response
rate. Although the evidence is not strong, the evidence
from sequential studies combined with the factorial design
results suggest that:

H_1: Telephone follow-up will produce higher response rates
than mail follow-ups.

<u>Source</u>. The existing research on the effect of sponsorship
on response rate is somewhat mixed. Although two studies
found no significant sponsor effect on response rates
(Nevin and Ford 1976; Scott 1961), the preponderance of the
studies do indicate that the university source does have a
positive differential effect on response rate as compared
to commercial or government source (Doob, Freedman and
Carlsmith 1973; Peterson 1975; Jones and Linda 1978; Jones
and Lang 1978). Member trade association as a source has
not been tested in comparison to University. Therefore:

H_2: University sponsorship will produce higher response
rates than the trade association.

Response Speed

<u>Method</u>. There have been a number of studies with response
speed as a dependent variable. Waisanen (1954) found significant improvement in response speed with advance notice
by phone vs. control. Dillman and Frey's (1974) study confirmed Waisanen's conclusion. Peterson (1975) found no
effect on response speed of a postcard follow-up.
Therefore:

H_3: Telephone follow-up will produce faster response than
mail.

<u>Source</u>. The effect of source on response speed was exam-
ined both by Peterson (1975) and Houston and Nevin (1977).
Both found that subjects tended to return the questionnaires
to the commercial sponsor faster than to the university, but
only Peterson found this difference to be significant. It
is not clear how the membership source effect will trade off
against university source. However, on the expectation that
trade association urgency will reflect commercial urgency it
is hypothesized that:

H_4: Trade association sponsorship will produce faster
response than university.

Response Completeness

<u>Method</u>. Ford (1967) found that a letter alert did not
affect item omission. Although Kerin (1974) found telephone
alert reduced item omission, the type of follow-up did not.
Therefore:

H_5: There will be no difference in the effect of telephone or letter follow-up on response completeness.

Source. Peterson (1975) and Houston and Nevin (1977) found that responses to solicitation from university sources resulted in significantly higher completion rates (lower item omission) than responses to commercials source. Therefore:

H_6: University source will produce more complete questionnaire responses than will the trade association source.

RESULTS

The overall results of the analysis of the returned questionnaire are summarized in Table 1. The treatment effects on each dependent variable-response rate, speed, and completeness are discussed separately (See Table 2 for summary).

TABLE 1
Response From Treatments

TREATMENTS		RESPONSE		
Main Effects		Rate(n)	Speed	Complete-ness
Method	Mail	33.8 (27)	12.6 days	88.6%
	Phone	46.3% (37)	8.7	88.3%
Source	University	42.5% (34)	11.3	90.1%
	Trade Assoc.	37.5% (30)	11.1	86.6%
Interactions				
	Mail/University	35% (14)	13.1	88.4%
	Mail/Trade Assoc.	32.5% (13)	12.2	88.8%
	Phone/University	50% (20)	7.7	91.3%
	Phone/Trade Assoc.	42.5% (17) 40% 64	9.7	85.9%
Control		32.5% (13)	9.9	85.7
TOTAL		38.5% 77		

Response Rate

Of the 80 questionnaires sent to subjects in the mail treatment none were returned by the post office as undeliverable. In the telephone treatment group four potential subjects were no longer with their companies and the positions were unfilled at the time of the study. However, it was decided to include these four subjects in the analysis because it was apparent that person-to-person telephone follow-up was more efficient than letter in identifying missing subjects. If they were excluded we felt it would tend to overstate the effectiveness of telephone follow-up by reducing cell "n."

The overall response rate was 38.5%. There were however significant differences across various experimental treatments.

Method. Hypothesis 1 (H_1) suggested that the response rate from telephone follow-up would be significantly better than from mail follow-up. Results of a "z" test of proportions support H_1 (z = 3.21, p < .01). The differential impact of telephone over mail in follow-up is consistent with results produced by Roscoe, et.al. (1975) but contradictory to that of Kerin (1974). In Kerin's study however, telephone and mail follow-up effects were collapsed into one category entitled "personal follow-up." The results of this study suggest that Kerin's aggregation masked the differential effect of telephone on follow-up response rate. Therefore, it appears that follow-up subjects do respond more positively to a personal telephone contact than to a personal mail contact.

TABLE 2
Summary Hypotheses Results

Response Rate*	Hypothesis*	Result*
Method (H_1)	T > M	S (p <.01)
Source (H_2)	U > TA	NS (p ~.20)
Interaction	---	TU best (p <.05)
Response Speed		
Method (H_3)	T > M	S (p <.05)
Source (H_4)	TA > U	NS (TA ~ U)
Interaction	---	TU MU, MTA (p .01)
Response Completeness		
Method (H_5)	T = M	S
Source (H_6)	U > TA	NS (p ~.40)
Interaction	---	NS

* T: Telephone; M: Mail; U: University; TA: Trade Association; TU: Telephone-University; TTA: Telephone-Trade Association; MTA: Mail-Trade Association.

\# S: Support; NS: Not Supported.

Source. H_2 could not be supported. University source did not produce significantly higher response rates than trade association source. This result agreed with Houston and Nevins results (1977) and Scotts (1961) but disagrees with the majority of the literature. It appears that these subjects do not differentiate between the trade association and university source in terms of their own response rate behavior.

Interactions. The four different combinations produced considerably different response rates. The telephone/university source combination was the best follow-up with a 50% response rate; followed by the telephone/trade association with 32.5%. Based on the Newman-Keuls test [29, 191-196] it was found that the telephone reminder from a university source (TU) is significantly better (p < .05) than the other three follow-up combinations, and that mail-trade association (MTA) is significantly worse (p < .05) than either telephone procedures in generating response.

Response Speed

Method. The mail treatment had a mean response speed of 12.6 days and telephone 8.7 days. Applying a one-tailed "t" test produced significance at p < .05. Thus H_3 can be supported leading to the conclusion that telephone follow-up will significantly increase speed of response over mail follow-up. It was also found that the control group response speed was significantly (p < .05) faster than mail treatment.

Source. Trade association response speed was faster than university (11.1 vs. 11.3) but the difference, although directionally supporting H_4, was not significant. Although this result is consistent with the existing research (Houston and Nevin 1977; Peterson 1975), that speed of return tended to be faster for commercial over university source, H_4 cannot be supported in this context.

Interactions. The telephone/university and control group produced the quickest return with an average of 7.7 days. The telephone/trade association group was not far behind at 9.7 days (Table 1). Employing a "t" test, the telephone/university (TU) group response speed was significantly (p < .01) faster than either mail group.

Response Completeness

Mean item response could not be calculated and be comparable across respondents and treatments because each subject's total number of questions depended upon their own past behavior/experiences. Thus to analyze results it was necessary to convert the response completeness measure to a proportion (expressed as percentage in Table 1).

Method. A "z" test of proportions was calculated and results indicated that method of follow-up does not affect questionnaire completeness for non-respondents. Thus H_5 is accepted that method of follow-up does not affect questionnaire completeness for non-respondents. This result agrees with findings of existing follow-up research [22, 19].

Source. Although Table 1 results indicate some source effect on response completeness, it was not significant and thus H_6 must be rejected. That is, there is insufficient evidence to conclude that a university source produces more complete questionnaire responses than does trade association source.

Interactions. The mail and telephone treatments produced 88.6% and 88.3% completeness respectively. The range for treatment groups was from a low of 85.9% for telephone/trade association to a high of 91.3% for telephone/university (Table 1). The control group had the lowest rate of completeness at 85.7%. The apparent equivalance between the control group and telephone/trade association treatment was the result of a single outlier in the treatment group with a response completeness of less than 30%. Although removal of that outlier changes treatment response completeness to a more reasonable 90.5%, it did not alter the statistical results.

CONCLUSIONS

Conclusions drawn from study results are framed in terms of the impact of method and source effects on non-respondent response characteristics.

Method. Factorial design studies employing Wave 1 subjects have found that a telephone stimulus generally increases response rate and speed but does not affect completeness. Using Wave 2 subjects: Roscoe, et.al. (1975) found telephone follow-up increased response rate; Peterson (1975) found that neither postcard nor personal follow-up affected response rate or speed. The results of this study confirm Roscoe's results and quite clearly indicate that the use of a telephone follow-up procedure is superior to mail in increasing response rate and speed although no apparent differential effect could be discerned on response completeness. It may be concluded therefore that the use of the telephone in the Wave 2 follow-up will significantly increase response rate and speed.

Response speed in both the control group and telephone treatment was superior to mail. Since the only difference between the control and mail treatments was the lack of cover letter in the control group, its superior response rate may be spurious. However it may also be true that the omission of a cover letter in the control group somewhow increased its urgency to the subject. Conversely the standardized cover letter may serve to amerliorate response urgency. Therefore, if response speed is important, but a mail follow-up is necessary, it appears that a follow-up questionnaire could be sent without cover letter. Apparently, the lack of cover letter has only a minimal effect on response rate and completeness.

Source. No factorial design studies were located which used non-respondents to test source treatment effects on response. Studies on Wave 1 subjects have variously compared university, government, and commercial source effects. Generally, they found that university source increased response rate; commercial source increases response speed; and university source increases completeness. This study using non-respondents produced similar source effects. However, these source effects were not found to be statistically significant. The lack of significance may be due to general non-respondent insensitivity to any source effects. If this is the case then subjects will respond for reasons other than source effects and no dependent variable measure will produce significant differential effects by source. The lack of significant differential effects may also be due to subject perception that no real difference exists between the sources. Since the subject population in this study was trade association member, it may be that the personal affiliation of trade association membership increased the importance of response rate, speed and completeness to the point where it compensated for the generalized impact of the university source. It is not at all clear which of these two alternatives, or some combination was operable. Hence general conclusions at this stage would at best be tenative. Future research with non-respondent subjects is needed to explore source sensitivity effects.

Control Group

Subjects in the control group were mailed a duplicate questionnaire with no cover letter. Control group response rate at 32.5% was significantly different from that of telephone (46.3%) but virtually identical with that of mail (33.8%). Furthermore control group response speed (9.9 days) was better than any treatment group except the telephone treatment group (8.7) days). However, control group response completeness was the lowest (85.7%) of any group. The implication is clear that the minimum follow-up procedures used in the control group, although probably producing a lower response rate, will produce as fast or faster return speed, and comparable completeness with all categories but telephone/university. Thus, based on the dependent variable measures the minimalism inherent in control group procedures is extremely attractive.

REFERENCES

Anderson, John F. and Douglas R. Berdie, (1975), "Effects on Response Rates of Formal and Informal Questionnaire Follow-up Techniques," Journal of Applied Psychology, 60 (April), 255-257.

Childers, Terry L., William M. Pride, and O. C. Ferrell, (1980), "A Reassessment of the Effects of Appeals on Response to Mail Surveys," Journal of Marketing Research, 17 (August), 365-370.

Dillman, Don A. and James H. Frey, (1974), "Contribution of Personalization to Mail Questionnaire Response as an Element of a Previously Tested Method," Journal of Applied Psychology, 59 (June), 297-301.

Dolde, Walter, Richard Staelin, and Tsu Yao (1980), "Estimating Response Rates for Different Market Segments from Questionnaire Data," Journal of Marketing Research, 17 (May), 245-252.

Donald, Marjorie N. (1960), "Implications of Non-Response for the Interpretation of Mail Questionnaire Data," Public Opinion Quarterly, 24 (Spring), 99-114.

Doob, Anthony N., Jonathan L. Freedman, and J. Merril Carlsmith (1973), "Effects of Sponsor and Prepayment on Compliance with a Mailed Request," Journal of Applied Psychology, 57, 346-347.

Eckland, Bruce (1965), "Effects of Prodding to Increase Mail-Back Returns," Journal of Applied Psychology, 49 (June), 165-169.

Etze, Michael J. and Bruce J. Walker (1974), "Effects of Alternative Follow-up Procedures on Mail Survey Response Rates," Journal of Applied Psychology, 59 (April), 219-221.

Ford, Neil M. (1967), "The Advance Letter in Mail Surveys," Journal of Marketing Research, 4 (May), 202-204.

Goulet, Waldemar M. (1977), "Efficacy of a Third Request Letter in Mail Surveys of Professionals," Journal of Marketing Research, 14 (February), 112-114.

Hansen, Morris H. and William N. Hurwitz (1946), "The Problem of Non-Response in Sample Surveys," Journal of the American Statistical Association, (December), 517-519.

Hochstim, Joseph R. and Demetrios A. Athanasopoulos (1970), "Personal Follow-up in a Mail Survey: Its Contribution and Cost," Public Opinion Quarterly, 34 (Spring), 69-82.

Houston, Michael J. and Neil M. Ford (1976), "Broadening the Scope of Methodological Research on Mail Surveys," Journal of Marketing Research, 13 (November), 397-403.

________________ and John R. Nevin (1977), "The Effects of Sources and Appeal on Mail Survey Response Patterns," Journal of Marketing Research, 14 (August), 374-378.

Huxley, Stephen J. (1980), "Sample Composition Bias and Response Bias in a Mail Survey: A Comparison of Inducement Methods," Journal of Marketing Research, 17 (February), 69-76.

Jones, Wesley H. and Gerald Linda (1978), "Multiple Criteria Effects in a Mail Survey Experiment," Journal of Marketing Research, 15 (May), 280-284.

________________ and James R. Lang (1978), "Sample Composition Bias and Response Bias in Mail Survey: A Comparison of Inducement Methods," Journal of Marketing Research, Vol. XVII, (February), 69-76.

Kanuk, Leslie and Conrad Berenson (1975), "Mail Surveys and Response Rates: A Literature Review, Journal of Marketing Research, 12 (November), 440-453.

Kerin, Roger A. (1974), "Personalization Strategies, Response Rate and Response Quality in a Mail Survey," Social Science Quarterly, 55 (June), 175-181.

Nevin, J. R. and N. M. Ford (1976), "Effect of a Deadline and a Vailed Threat on Mail Survey Responses," Journal of Applied Psychology, 61 (1), 116-118.

Parsons, Robert J. and Thomas S. Medford (1972), "The Effect of Advance Notice in Mail Surveys of Homogeneous Groups," Public Opinion Quarterly, 36 (Summer), 259-259.

Peterson, Robert A. (1975), "An Experimental Investigation of Mail Survey Responses," Journal of Business Research, 3 (July), 199-210.

Pressley, Milton M. and William L. Tullar (1977), "A Factor Interactive Investigation of Mail Survey Response Rates from a Commercial Population," Journal of Marketing Research, 14 (February), 108-111.

Roscoe A. Marvin, Dorothy Lang, and Jagdish N. Sheth (1975), "Follow-up Methods, Questionnaire Length, and Market Differences in Mail Surveys," Journal of Marketing, 39 (April), 20-27.

Scott, Christopher (1961), "Research on Mail Surveys," Journal of the Royal Statistical Society, 124, Series A, 2, (143-191.

Spaeth, Mary A. (1977), "Recent Publications on Survey Research Techniques," Journal of Marketing Research, 14 (August), 403-409.

Stafford, James E. (1966), "Influence of Preliminary Contact on Mail Returns," Journal of Marketing Research, 3 (November), 410-411.

Waisanen, F. B. (1954), "A Note on the Response to a Mailed Questionnaire," Public Opinion Quarterly, (Summer) 210-212.

Winter, B. J. (1971), Statistical Principles in Experimental Design, (McGraw-Hill: New York).

QUALITATIVE DATA: ASSESSING INTERCODER
RELIABILITY AND RESOLVING CODING DISCREPANCIES

John P. McDonald, Wayne State University

ABSTRACT

This paper considers two problems related to the reliability of multiple judge coding assignments. The first problem is concerned with appropriate reliability indices in the case where the assignment categories are only nominally scaled. A second problem, related to this, is once the reliability of the codings has been determined how the analyses should proceed. Several indices of reliability as well as "rules" one could impose to improve the consistency across judges, a posteriori, are discussed.

INTRODUCTION

The value of data obtained from subjects in studies where openended questions are necessary, critically depends upon the reliability with which such data are assigned to categories preceding any statistical analysis. To enhance valid interpretations, a high degree of agreement among the judges or coders of the raw data is most desirable. The assessment of the amount of agreement among judges then presents a potential problem in that most measures of reliability (i.e., intercoder reliability coefficients) are based upon the assumption of interval level properties of the data. Whereas data coded into nominal categories require different assumptions and consequently different indices of reliability.

The need to address the problem of nominal level reliability assessment has emerged as a direct result of the increase in the use of qualitative responses from subjects/ participants in marketing research. Examples include the analysis of information processing and decision processes in both the consumer and industrial buying literature (e.g., Wright 1975; Wind, Denny and Cunningham 1979; Bettman and Park 1980; Crow, Olshavsky and Summers 1980; Hansen 1980). Thus, when analyzing such data, a necessary initial step is one of data reduction. Subsequently the need for assessing, a posteriori, the reliability of such a task also emerges. Typically, the burden is placed upon a group of judges who presumably possesses the particular skills required to assign the qualitative responses or subject protocols into mutually exclusive categories. Once this task is completed, the requisite statistical analyses can be performed.

Therefore the data reduction task, involving content analysis of the responses, is crucial to the overall validity of the study's findings. A common approach to evaluating such qualitative responses is for each judge to individually assign the responses to predetermined categories. Following this activity, the evaluations are summarized and discrepancies among the judges are then resolved. Two issues that should be addressed in the process are: 1) the extent to which the judgments are consistent across judges (i.e., intercoder reliability) and 2) when complete agreement across judges does not occur, how the investigation should proceed. This paper identifies three measures for assessing the reliability of qualitative data and discusses the appropriateness of each of them. In addition, several "rules" by which the principal investigator can resolve discrepancies among the judges are offered for consideration.

RELIABILITY INDICES

The problem of determining and reporting a valid measure of reliability is considerably more complex, on theoretical grounds, than that of resolving inconsistencies among the raters of the qualitative data. The concept of measure reliability has been around since the early writings by Spearmen (Peter 1979). However, as Peter notes, the popular types of reliability measurement are for the assessment of measurement _scales_ and a particular aspect of reliability (e.g., test-retest, alternate forms, internal consistency). In the case of intercoder reliability where the coding dimensions are comprised of equal-intervals, a Pearson product-moment correlation coefficient is the most appropriate measure. Alternatively, when the data are ordered along a dimension of unknown intervals, a rank difference correlation will provide a meaningful measure of the extent of agreement among judges (Scott 1955). But when the coding dimensions are composed of nominal scales which lack the properties of higher level scales, other indices of reliability must be considered. In this section, three such indices will be discussed. While it is true that others exist, their applicability is too limited for most marketing research problems. For example, Phi, a popular measure of association, is only appropriate for dichotomous coding schemes while typically in marketing the coding schemes are considerably more complex.

Percent Agreement Method (PAM)

Often employed as an index of reliability is the percentage of the codings that all of the judges agree upon. It is simply the ratio:

$$PAM = \frac{Number\ of\ Agreements}{Number\ of\ Agreements + Number\ of\ Disagreements}$$
$$= \sum_{i=1}^{c} P_{ii}$$

where: P_{ii} = the proportion of the entire sample of responses that all judges place into the same category.

As suggested by many researchers (e.g., Yelton, Wildman, and Erickson 1977; Hartman 1977) the simple percentage of agreement index suffers from some major deficiencies. First, it is directly affected by the number of categories being utilized. Thus as the complexity of the coding scheme increases, so does the liklihood of increasing levels of disagreement among raters. Related to the first criticism is the recognition that the probability of chance agreement, rather than agreement based upon the expertise of the individual judges, increases as the number of categories decreases. And third, the PAM index fails to account for partial agreements in the case of the use of three or more judges. Even though these shortcomings exist, the literature continues to follow this traditional approach to reporting reliability (Kassarjian 1977).

Adjusted Percent Agreement Statistic (π)

An improvement over the PAM index is the measure of agreement among judges developed by Scott (1955). He proposed a measure which is adjusted for the number of categories available to the judges. Thus his statistic, π, addresses the first deficiency of the PAM cited above. In addition,

π takes into account the frequency of each category's use. The statistic, π, can be interpreted as the extent to which the evaluations of the judges exceed chance. The form of the statistic is as follows:

$$\pi = \frac{P_o - P_e}{1 - P_e}$$

where: P_o = percentage of observed agreement among judges

P_e = percentage of expected agreement among judges

and: $P_e = \sum_{i=1}^{c} P_i^2$ where c is the total number of categories and

where: P_i is the proportion of the entire sample of phrases which falls in the ith category.

While this statistic is superior to the PAM index (since it takes chance agreement into consideration), it too is deficient in that it is not generalizable beyond two judges where the assumption that both judges have identical marginal distributions of proportions has been made (Light 1971).

Chance Corrected Reliability Coefficient, Kappa (κ)

Of all the nominal level reliability statistics developed, Kappa appears to be the most popular as well as the most heavily researched (e.g., Cohen 1960, 1968; Everitt 1968; Fleiss, Cohen and Everitt 1969; Fleiss 1971; Light 1971, Hubert 1977). The difference between κ and π lies in the calculation of P_e where Cohen calculates it based upon observed margins rather than assuming symmetric marginal properties among judges (Bishop, Fienberg, and Holland 1975):

$$\kappa = \frac{P_o - P_e}{1 - P_e} = \frac{\sum_{i=1}^{c} P_{ii} - \sum_{i=1}^{c} P_{i+} P_{+i}}{1 - \sum_{i=1}^{c} P_{i+} P_{+i}}$$

where: P_{i+} = the row marginal total

P_{+i} = the column marginal total

Note: This is the form of the statistic for only two judges. The κ statistic can be extended to the case where more than two judges evaluate the data. The formula and the required computations, however, become considerably more complex as the number of judges increases (Light 1971).

The appeal of κ, as pointed out by Light (1971), is that it is a simple distance measure of agreement. Specifically, the general form of the κ statistic is $1 - \frac{d_o}{d_e}$ where d_o represents the disagreement proportion observed and d_e represents the disagreement proportion expected. Since κ is a measure of distance, it assumes interval measure properties.

As noted earlier, Kappa, is the only index of the three discussed which has stimulated research into its nature. Everitt (1968) developed the necessary computational formula for determining the moments of the Kappa statistic. As Bintig (1980) points out, κ can be tested by the t distribution:

$$t = \frac{\kappa}{\sigma_\kappa}$$

$$\text{where } \sigma_\kappa = \frac{P_o(1-P_o)}{n(1-P_o)^2} \quad \text{and df = n-1}$$

Thus κ is the only one of the three measures discussed which allows statistical inferences to be made about it.

As suggested earlier, the major disadvantage of κ is the complexity of the computations that are required for more than two judges. However, several computer programs are available for κ (e.g., Larimar and Watkins 1979; Berk and Campbell 1976; Antonak 1971) to assist the researcher in the calculation of these indices.

At this point it becomes necessary to consider the second and somewhat more pragmatic issue. Once an appropriate measure of intercoder reliability has been calculated for reporting purposes, how should the investigation proceed? Clearly, if agreement among judges is absolute, no problem exists and the analysis may continue. However, the likelihood of such an event is small. Rather the degree of agreement will most likely require a second step in the data reduction process. The reason for this is that the analysis can not proceed until all discrepancies have been resolved. Should such discrepancies be attributed to chance, this step is trivial. If on the other hand, the reliability of the judgments is low, a potentially serious problem exists. Several alternative actions are available to the researcher. One act would be for the data set to be thrown out in its entirety (although this seems unlikely). Thus, some logical and deliberate method of resolving these discrepancies among the judges must be developed. The realitites of interpreting qualitative responses force the principal investigator to apply subjective rules to such discrepancies just as the content analysts in other behavioral disciplines (e.g., clinical and social psychologists; communication researchers) are often required to do.

AGREEMENT AMONG RATERS

Once the reliability of the codings has been assessed, disagreements amongst the judges must be resolved so the data analysis can proceed. The first rule the researcher might consider imposing is referred to as the "Aggregation Rule." In the application of this rule the principal investigator has concluded that the high incidence of disagreement among judges is the result of requiring fine discriminations in the codings. The solution is simply to aggregate subcategories and to recalculate the reliability coefficient. When applying this rule, the principal investigator(s) must exercise caution to assure that the collapsing of categories does not alter the theoretical significance of the coding discriminations. While this rule assures increased agreement among the judges, discrepancies may still exist. In such cases, several alternative rules can be imposed to resolve the remaining discrepancies. These remaining approaches do not allow for the modification of the coding scheme but merely the inclusion or exclusion of a response with respect to a particular category.

The two approaches most frequently used to eliminate inconsistencies in the coding of responses can be termed "The Exclusion Rule" and "The Majority Rule." When one applies the Exclusion Rule, the effect is to exclude from further consideration any respondent whose response categorizations cannot be fully agreed upon by the raters. It can be argued that such a rule has merit, particularly in the testing of a theory related to the coding schemes themselves. However, if protocol analysis is most appropriate in the exploratory phases of theory construction, as contended by Crow et al. (1980), then varying degrees of disagreement should be expected to result among the judges. Hence, the use of the Exclusion Rule could seriously limit and thereby jeopardize the study's findings since data are being excluded from the analysis simply because they do not conform to the researcher's expectations. Thus the problem is one of category reliability rather than coder reliability (Holsti 1969). It would appear that the Exclusion Rule should only be applied when individual cases merit it. A reasonable approach would be to exclude the subject's entire set of responses, regardless of whether individual or aggregate level analyses are planned. Another approach, termed the Majority Rule, is operationalized in such a manner that any response not coded identically by all of the judges is placed into the modal rating category. Such an approach is certainly expedient although the validity of the rule is questionable since the judges may possess varying levels of expertise and the judges in the minority may be the most expert. It is difficult to identify a situation other than one requiring expediency where the use of this rule could be justified.

Two other approaches used to resolve the inconsistency in ratings can be termed the "Tie Breaker Rule" and the "Negotiation Rule." In the Tie Breaker Rule setting the principal investigator functions as an additional judge and casts a vote to resolve the disagreement. In this case, the modal category once again becomes the determinant measure. While the tie breaker judge does resolve the disagreement, the introduction of a judge for the evaluation of a select set of responses may bias the results. It is not recommended that such a rule be applied if the sole purpose is to create a modal category for selected responses. Therefore this additional judge should be required to evaluate all of the protocols (or phrases) or none at all.

The preceding rules described share the common characteristic of "one person one vote." In terms of objectivity, such a characteristic is desirable in that each judge is assured of having an equal effect on the outcome of the ratings. However, such approaches completely ignore the varying levels of expertise possessed by the individual judges. Recognition of the differential expertise among raters may be implicitly taken into account when one applies the Tie Breaker Rule , but it would be preferable to do so explicitly.

The final approach does take such expertise into consideration. The Negotiation Rule requires that every disagreement among judges be discussed and resolved. Such a task can be formidable when the coding requirements involves literally hundreds of protocols and phrases into tens of categories (e.g., Biehal and Chakravarti (1981) reportedly classified 3,026 phrases into 70 categories). However, it does allow each of the judges to participate and may result in more reliable codings in the future. The imposition of the Negotiation Rule appears more desirable than the alternative rules when the protocols are complex, the categories are not well defined, or a frequent number of disagreements emerges in the ratings (i.e., codes do not discriminate).

SUMMARY AND CONCLUSIONS

In summary, this paper has looked at two issues researchers must address in the use of qualitative data based upon nominal dimensions. It has been suggested that the determination of the degree of reliability exhibited in the data reduction procedure should include the calculation of appropriate indices of agreement. Three such indices have been identified: PAM, π, and κ. It was argued that κ is usually the most appropriate measure to use since it can accommodate multiple categories and raters as well as having its statistical significance assessed.

In addition, five rules or approaches to resolving discrepancies in the judgement process have been offered for consideration. It is not the purpose of this discussion to advocate the use of one of the methods at the expense of the others. Rather, the intent is to recognize the existence of these alternate approaches which require varying degrees of objectivity on the part of the judges making each of them more or less appropriate in a given situation. It is hoped that a particular approach be decided upon before the actual resolution of discrepancies

takes place. This procedure of resolving inconsistencies among ratings, while being extremely important, is often not reported. Instead, a statistic is presented, indicating the degree of agreement or "reliability" among the raters. It is felt that the proper assessment of the reliability of codings and an orderly procedure for eliminating disagreement amongst raters will enhance the validity of the research project.

REFERENCES

Antonak, R.F. (1977), "A Computer Program to Compute Measures of Response Agreement for Nominal Scale Data Obtained from Two Judges," Behavior Research Methods and Instrumentation, 9, 553.

Bettman, J.R. and Park, C.W. (1980), "Implications of a Constructive View of Choice for Analysis of Protocol Data: A Coding Scheme for Elements of Choice Processes," in Olson, J.C. (ed.), Advances in Consumer Research, Vol. 7, Association for Consumer Research, Ann Arbor, Michigan, 148-153.

Berk, R.A. and K.L. Campbell (1976), "A Fortran Program for Cohen's Kappa Coefficient of Observer Agreement," Behavior Research Methods and Instrumentation, 8, 396.

Biehal, G. and Chakravarti, D. (1981), "Some Experiences with the Bettman and Park Verbal Protocol Coding Scheme," Working Paper #27, Center for Consumer Research, University of Florida, Gainesville, Florida.

Bintig, A. (1980), "The Efficiency of Various Estimations of Reliability of Rating Scales," Educational and Psychological Measurement, 40, 619-643.

Bishop, Y.M.M., Fienberg, S.E. and Holland, P.W. (1975), Discrete Multivariate Analysis: Theory and Practice, MIT Press, Cambridge, MA, 397-399.

Cohen, J. (1960), "A Coefficient of Agreement for Nominal Scales," Educational and Psychological Measurement, 30, 37-46.

__________, (1968), "Weighted Kappa: Nominal Scale Agreement with Provision for Scaled Disagreement or Partial Credit," Psychological Bulletin, 70, 213-220.

Crow, L.E., Olshavsky, R.W. and Summers, J.O. (1980), "Industrial Buyers Choice Strategies: A Protocol Analysis," Journal of Marketing Research, 17, 34-44.

Everitt, B.S. (1968), "Moments of the Statistics Kappa and Weighted Kappa," The British Journal of Mathematical and Statistical Psychology, 21, 97-103.

Fleiss, J.L. (1971), "Measuring Nominal Scale Agreement Among Many Raters," Psychological Bulletin, 76, 378-382.

__________, Cohen, J. and Everitt, B.S. (1969), "Large Sample Standard Errors of Kappa and Weighted Kappa," Psychological Bulletin, 72, 323-327.

Hansen, R.A. (1980), "A Self-Perception Interpretation of the Effect of Monetary and Nonmonetary Incentives on Mail Survey Respondent Behavior," Journal of Marketing Research, 17, 77-83.

Hartmann, D.P. (1977), "Considerations in the Choice of Interobserver Reliability Estimates," Journal of Applied Behavior Analysis, 10, 103-116.

Holsti, O.R. (1969), Content Analysis for the Social Sciences and Humanities, Reading, MA: Addison-Wesley.

Hubert, L. (1977), "Kappa Revisited," <u>Psychological Bulletin</u>, 84, 289-297.

Kassarjian, H.H. (1977), "Content Analysis in Consumer Research," <u>Journal of Consumer Behavior</u>, 4, 8-18.

Larimar, L.D. and Watkins, M.W. (1979), "Computer Program for Measuring Levels of Overall and Partial Congruence Among Multiple Observers on Nominal Scales," <u>Educational and Psychological Measurement</u>, 39, 235-239.

Light, R.J. (1971), "Measures of Response Agreement for Qualitative Data: Some Generalizations and Alternatives," <u>Psychological Bulletin</u>, 76, 365-377.

Peter, J.P. (1979), "Reliability: A Review of Psychometric Basics and Recent Marketing Practices," <u>Journal of Marketing Research</u>, 16, 6-17.

Scott, W.A. (1955), "Reliability of Content Analysis: The Case of Nominal Scale Coding," <u>Public Opinion Quarterly</u>, 19, 321-325.

Yelton, A.R., Wildman, B.G., and Erickson, M.T. (1977), "A Probability-Based Formula for Calculating Interobserver Agreement," <u>Journal of Applied Behavior Analysis</u>, 10, 127-131.

Wind, Y., Denny, J. and Cunningham, A. (1979), "A Comparison of Three Brand Evaluation Procedures," <u>Public Opinion Quarterly</u>, 33, 261-269.

Wright, P.L. (1975), "Factors Affecting Cognitive Resistance to Advertising," <u>Journal of Consumer Research</u>, 2, 1-9.

ON OBTAINING MEASURES FROM RANKS

Joel H. Steckel, Columbia University

ABSTRACT

This paper proposes a methodology for the transformation of ordinal data to interval scaled data. The type of ordinal data required include a rank order of stimuli and a rank order of the differences between stimuli. Applications to data simulated from a variety of distributions as well as a field application are presented.

INTRODUCTION

In many marketing related studies consumers are asked to rank a set of stimuli according to a given variable, but cannot provide an accurate quantification of that variable. The problem of transforming ranks to measures has commanded much attention in the psychology, statistics, and marketing literatures. One major problem with simply examining ranks is that some information relating to the original variable values is lost. However this loss need not be irretrievable. Respondents are able to supply more than only a rank order of stimuli. They can often rank differences between stimuli and perhaps even differences of the differences. If we can use this information relating to successive differences in order to reconstruct intervally scaled values, we have a significant contribution.

Related to this, Kendall (1962) describes a process by which a set of n numbers is first arranged in ascending order. The ordered numbers are differenced. The n − 1 differences are ordered and differenced. The process repeats itself. Using only the rank orders of the differences at each stage, Kendall is able to recreate the numbers with a surprising degree of accuracy.

The purpose of this paper is to illustrate how Kendall's algorithm can be applied to the unidimensional scaling of ordinal data to intervally scaled measures. First we illustrate the algorithm and discuss it. We apply it to the scaling of temperature perceptions. Concluding remarks follow.

THE METHOD

We consider situations in which one can rank in order of magnitude not only the stimuli of the test but their differences as well. For example, given ten automobiles ranked on comfort from 1 to 10, we might be able to say that the biggest gap occurs between the fifth and sixth. The next biggest may be between the ninth and the tenth, and so on. Such a ranking of differences might be represented as follows:

```
Auto Comfort       1   2   3   4   5   6   7   8   9   10
Difference Ranking 6   3   9   8   1   7   4   5   2.
```

Now suppose further that these first differences can be rearranged in order of magnitude and the differences between them can be ranked. For example:

```
Differences        1   2   3   4   5   6   7   8   9
2nd Differences        6   1   7   5   2   8   4   3.
```

Theoretically, this process can be continued until we arrive at a final pair of differences that will be ranked either 1, 2 or 2, 1. It is obvious that the array of rankings of successive differences thus obtained, contains a large amount of supplementary information. The problem is how to use it.

The method itself is probably best illustrated by a numerical example. Consider Table 1. Column (1) consists of the

TABLE 1

Illustrative Example

1	2	3	4	5	6	7	8	9	10	11	12	13	14	15	16	17	18	19
104	094																	
		9	2	1														
223	103				8	2	1											
		1	1	9				7	4	1								
241	104				9	3	8				2	2	2					
		119	7	18				1	1	3				0	1½	0		
421	223				29	4	9				2	2	2				0	1
		18	3	47				20	5	5				0	1½	0		
375	241				1	1	29				2	2	2				11	2
		48	5	48				5	3	7				11	3	11		
289	289				37	6	34				13	4	13					
		85	6	85				3	2	20								
094	374				34	5	37											
		47	4	119														
103	421																	

first eight triplets taken from the Chemical Rubber Company (CRC) table of random numbers (Beyer 1971). It is these numbers that we will assume are the scale values we will try to reproduce from the appropriate rank information. Column (2) rearranges column (1) according to rank, from smallest up. Column (3) gives the first differences and column (4), the ranks of those differences. Column (5) rearranges the differences in order and their differences, the second differences, are given in column (6). Column (7) ranks these. We proceed in like manner down to column (19). In column (12) three observations are tied so we average the ranks in column (13). Similar operations occur in columns (15) and (16).

In trying to reconstruct column (1), start from column (19) and work backwards. We need an initial assumption concerning the last two differences. We use the fact that if a unit interval is broken into n parts by the random placement of n − 1 points, the expectation of the length of the parts in descending order is

$$\frac{1}{n}(\frac{1}{n} + \frac{1}{n-1} + \ldots + \frac{1}{2} + \frac{1}{1})$$

$$\frac{1}{n}(\frac{1}{n} + \frac{1}{n-1} + \ldots + \frac{1}{2})$$

$$\frac{1}{n}(\frac{1}{n} + \frac{1}{n-1} + \ldots + \frac{1}{3})$$

$$\cdots\cdots\cdots\cdots\cdots\cdots$$

$$\frac{1}{n} \cdot \frac{1}{n}. \tag{1}$$

We thus assume that our last pair of (sixth) differences have a ratio of

$$1 \text{ to } 3. \quad (n = 2) \tag{2}$$

In order to proceed to the previous differences, we make a second assumption. The "length" of the two differences is 4 with an average of 2. Assume that a piece of this average length precedes the pair in (2):

2   1   3.

The fifth differences can be constructed so as to have the

sixth differences (2),

$$2 \quad 2 + 1 \quad 2 + 1 + 3$$
$$2 \quad 3 \quad\quad 6.$$

These differences have ranks corresponding to column (16). To account for the 1½ we average 2 and 3. Arranging according to column (16) we have $\frac{5}{2}$ $\frac{5}{2}$ 6. For convenience we multiply by two to remove the fraction; 5 5 12. It is easier to consider only relative values of differences and readjust later.

Proceeding by similar assumptions, 5, 5, and 12 have average length $\frac{22}{3}$. The fourth differences are then $\frac{22}{3}$, $\frac{22}{3} + 5$, $\frac{22}{3} + 5 + 5$, $\frac{22}{3} + 5 + 5 + 12$ or proportional to 22, 37, 52, 88.

The rankings corresponding to these four are found in column (13) to be 2, 2, 2, 4. To account for the three twos we average 22, 37, and 52. Arranging according to column (13), we obtain 37, 37, 37, 88. This time the overall average is $\frac{199}{4}$. After multiplying by 4 to remove the fraction, the five third differences become proportional to 199, 347, 495, 643, 995. Rearranging according to column (10) we get 643, 199, 955, 495, 347. One can verify that the next two iterations corresponding to columns (7) and (4) will yield 1171, 1370, 2325, 528, 3167, 2820 and

3068, 1897, 13278, 4438, 7291, 10458, 6763 (total 47,193).

$$(3)$$

If our technique has been successful, these numbers (3), should be proportional to the differences between the eight original values. To compare we make the ends of the scale based on (3) correspond to the end points of column (2), 94 and 421. The range of the differences in (3) is 47,193. Therefore we multiply the values in (3) by 327/47,193 = 0.008929 and accumulate from 94. We obtain

Reconstructed Values 94 115 128 220 251 301 374 421
Original Values   94 103 104 223 241 289 374 421.

The agreement seems quite good.

Table 2 contains the results of fifteen reconstructions. The first five are of triplets of random digits (Beyer 1971). The second five come from random numbers generated from a standard normal distribution. The values were multiplied by 100 and translated by the largest negative value so that all numbers would be positive. The final five are from similar transformations of numbers generated from a normal distribution with mean zero and variance four.

DISCUSSION OF THE METHOD

The results of most of the simulated reconstructions in Table 2 are of the kind presented by the illustrative example. The only serious discrepancies occur when one end point is very distant from its neighbor (e.g. Normal (0, 1) II). This is to be expected. However that does not mean that it is not a problem.

Our example took the CRC data down to sixth differences. This is not practical for scaling purposes. Respondents can rank stimuli, usually differences between stimuli, and maybe even second differences. However one cannot imagine asking consumers questions about sixth differences in automobile handling or cakemix flavor. But the practicality of the method is not destroyed. The CRC data from the previous section is reproduced from second differences, column (7) of Table 1 as follows:

Reconstructed from 2nds 94 113 128 228 256 300 379 421.

TABLE 2

Simulated Reconstructions

									Total Absolute Deviations
Random Digits I									
Original values	94	103	104	223	241	289	374	421	
Reconstructed	94	115	128	220	251	301	374	421	61
Recon. from 2nds	94	113	128	228	256	300	379	421	70
Random Digits II									
Original values	69	143	150	368	399	409	465	483	
Reconstructed	69	159	177	304	352	376	449	483	193
Recon. from 2nds	69	159	178	316	359	382	453	483	165
Random Digits III									
Original values	15	54	62	110	225	255	433	482	
Reconstructed	15	65	84	145	246	284	415	482	136
Recon. from 2nds	15	62	82	139	247	285	421	482	121
Random Digits IV									
Original values	20	34	79	81	102	143	166	332	
Reconstructed	20	48	111	124	147	209	243	332	277
Recon. from 2nds	20	46	107	121	145	201	237	332	252
Random Digits V									
Original values	61	78	174	188	277	309	482	496	
Reconstructed	61	91	184	202	283	334	466	496	84
Recon. from 2nds	61	90	181	201	279	329	467	496	69
Normal (0, 1) I									
Original values	0	56	96	141	152	168	289	299	
Reconstructed	0	60	102	150	168	192	286	299	62
Recon. from 2nds	0	62	104	152	168	190	285	299	67
Normal (0, 1) II									
Original values	0	146	191	196	203	205	217	266	
Reconstructed	0	80	128	145	167	179	211	266	248
Recon. from 2nds	0	85	133	150	168	180	211	266	231
Normal (0, 1) III									
Original values	0	10	10	47	64	68	191	209	
Reconstructed	0	21	29	73	101	115	177	209	154
Recon. from 2nds	0	19	28	72	99	113	180	209	143
Normal (0, 1) IV									
Original values	0	13	18	64	92	102	109	184	
Reconstructed	0	20	28	70	100	115	126	184	61
Recon. from 2nds	0	19	28	69	96	111	121	184	46
Normal (0, 1) V									
Original values	0	61	61	95	100	104	110	202	
Reconstructed	0	45	53	87	105	120	141	202	84
Recon. from 2nds	0	42	51	85	102	117	137	202	81
Normal (0, 4) I									
Original values	0	237	426	460	491	518	560	575	
Reconstructed	0	165	298	364	422	468	551	575	424
Recon. from 2nds	0	172	308	369	426	474	550	575	393
Normal (0, 4) II									
Original values	0	70	145	227	322	342	360	415	
Reconstructed	0	67	143	229	333	352	367	415	35
Recon. from 2nds	0	72	149	234	333	350	364	415	36
Normal (0, 4) III									
Original values	0	270	298	352	398	406	526	657	
Reconstructed	0	183	234	313	384	410	527	657	209
Recon. from 2nds	0	191	245	320	390	417	532	657	189
Normal (0, 4) IV									
Original values	0	30	68	71	108	351	530	657	
Reconstructed	0	47	114	141	199	389	543	657	275
Recon. from 2nds	0	44	101	128	182	370	533	657	200
Normal (0, 4) V									
Original values	0	100	212	242	317	341	516	519	
Reconstructed	0	94	199	242	317	354	499	519	49
Recon. from 2nds	0	93	194	234	305	341	497	519	64

The total absolute deviation increases only from 61 to 70. Even if only first differences can be ranked, some information is gained. The last row of each entry in Table 2 reconstructs the original values based on only rankings of numbers and first and second differences. Not only do we not lose much by only going back to second differences but sometimes we may be better off in terms of total absolute deviations.

The algorithm appears to be fairly robust. It works fairly well whether the stimuli are distributed uniformly or normally (with either small or large variances).

Let's examine the number of questions asked. Suppose we ask n questions about ranked preferences, n − 1 about first differences, and n − 2 second difference questions for a total of 3n − 3. Contrast this with the $\frac{1}{2}n(n - 1)$ pairwise comparisons needed in some types of Thurstone scaling (Torgerson 1958). In the next section we will see that pairwise comparisons are the type of things we can ask.

It should be noted that as the method stands, it will separate a set of objects in such a way as to approximate a measure. It will not locate the objects on a previously determined scale unless we have among the objects a couple of "markers" which positions on the scale we already know. The relative positions of the unmarked objects can then be determined.

In the previous section, the final scaling was accomplished by fixing the endpoints. It is not obvious that this is what one wants to do. A classic example of an interval scale is temperature. Here scaling is accomplished by fixing two intermediate points, the boiling and freezing points of water. When outliers are suspected, it might be advisable to "pin" points inside the range.

To this point it has not been made clear how questions aimed at second differences etc. can be asked. That's one of the subjects of the next section.

A FIELD APPLICATION

Temperature is an interval scale that everybody is familiar with. Five months, February, April, May, July, and October, were selected at random. By interviewing nine Philadelphia residents, all employees of a major university, about their preferences of the temperatures of those five months, we tried to replicate, in each case, the average daily high temperatures in Philadelphia during those five months for the years 1936–1975. See Table 3.

Beginning with the assumption that people are most comfortable at a temperature of 72° F., we asked people for the month with the temperature they disliked the most (using temperature as the sole criterion). The assumption implies that we were asking them to pick the month with maximum deviation from 72° F., the ideal point. (Problems ensued. Not all people have this ideal point.) We then asked, "Of the four remaining months, which is your least favorite?" and so on. With five questions a preference rank order is obtained. Suppose it is May, October, April, July, February.

From this we can create the four pairs of adjacent ranked months. Here we get May-October, October-April, April-July, and July-February. The next question was phrased in a manner similar to "Between which pair are you most indifferent?" The response indicates the smallest first difference. A sequential process, as before, created a ranking of the first differences with four questions.

Second differences are tricky. Note however that if A − B and C − D are consecutive first differences, the corresponding second difference is (A − B) − (C − D) = (A + D) − (B + C). Therefore by asking about their average preferences of A and D and of B and C, we can elicit information

about second differences. It often helped when the respondent was told to think of a month, not necessarily on the list, that was intermediate in preference between A and D, and another between B and C. The problem of second differences was thereby reduced to first differences and the indifference approach was used again, this time for three questions.

The first comment relates to what was at first thought to be a problem but really isn't. Not all respondents had 72 as an ideal point. Some liked hot weather. In this case what we were measuring was not deviation from 72 but the temperatures themselves. Second, we have the benefit that an early mistake is not necessarily magnified during later rounds. The comparisons asked will be different than if no mistake occurs but it is certainly possible to rank them correctly given what is asked. (See respondent 4 of Table 3.)

TABLE 3

Field Application

	Feb	April	May	July	Oct	Total Deviations All 5	Unpinned 3
Real value	42	64	74	87	67		
Respondent 1							
Reproduced value	42	63	74	89	68	4	4
His opinion	32	64	73	79	66	21	10

Comment: Ideal point assumed to be 72°. All rankings and differences given correspond exactly to the true ones.

Respondent 2							
Reproduced value	42	64	69	88	73	12	12
His opinion	39	67	70	84	72	18	12

Comment: Ideal point was assumed to be 65°. Given this, he reversed the second and third choices with respect to smallest deviations from 65. The fourth and fifth choices as well were juxtaposed. Of the first differences asked, the two smallest were reversed from their true order. The same statement applies to the second differences. Most of these mistakes however can be traced to an imprecise opinion of October.

Respondent 3							
Reproduced value	42	58	74	87	63	10	10
His opinion	30	55	65	90	63	30	22

Comment: The hotter the better for this person. With that in mind all questions concerning ranks and ranked differences were answered correctly.

Respondent 4							
Reproduced value	42	60	74	83	65	10	10
His opinion	27	47	58	79	60	59	33

Comment: Ideal point assumed to be 72°. The only mistake was that two first differences were reversed from their true order. Note that despite his subjective estimate of October and July being closer to 72, he realized May was his favorite month.

Respondent 5							
Reproduced value	42	59	72	87	63	11	11
His opinion		Not asked for.					

Comment: The hotter the better. The largest and smallest second differences were juxtaposed by the respondent.

Respondent 6 gave the same answers as respondent 1. His opinion was not asked for.

Respondent 7							
Reproduced value	42	74	81	87	67	17	17
His opinion	32	70	80	95	65	32	14

Comment: The hotter the better. According to given preference structure the third and fourth most preferred were the reverse of the true scale values. The smallest

TABLE 3 (Contd.)

						Total Deviations	
	Feb	April	May	July	Oct	All 5	Unpinned 3
Real value	42	64	74	87	67		

Respondent 7 (Contd.)
and third first differences were also switched.

Respondent 8

Reproduced value	42	63	75	81	67	8	8
His opinion		Not asked for.					

Comment: Ideal point assumed to be 68° F. With that in mind, all answers given were correct.

Respondent 9

Reproduced value	42	69	74	88	65	9	9
His opinion	20	65	70	95	65	37	12

Comment: Ideal point is 72°. Second and third most preferred were juxtaposed from true deviations as were the two smallest first differences.

The results of the interviews are presented in Table 3, along with the real values. For each respondent we list the values reproduced from second differences. For the people with ideal points not at the high end, the final scaling was accomplished by fixing the minimum and maximum deviations from the presumed ideal and then adding the scaled deviations in the correct direction. Others were scaled by fixing the endpoints, February and July. The presumed ideal points obtained by visual inspection are included in the comments paragraph. Also in the comments paragraph is a discussion of how well each respondent answered the questions given the model implied by his/her ideal point and the assumption that preference is a linear function of distance from the ideal point.

Some respondents in Table 3 have the row "His opinion." This indicates what the respondent thought that the average daily high for that month was. The last two columns represent total absolute deviations from the true scale. The first column is for all five temperatures. The second is for the three unpinned values. This seems a desirable comparison in that people were less accurate in estimating the extremes and these were often the values that were pinned down. The last column removes the method's intrinsic advantage.

The preliminary results seem encouraging. Only one respondent, 7, was able to do better in his own estimation than by the method. Even when some questions were answered "wrong" vis-a-vis the known deviations, the results were usually still comfortable.

CONCLUSION AND FUTURE DIRECTIONS

The preliminary results presented in Tables 2 and 3 are encouraging and warrant further experimentation. The approach is an interactive one in the sense that information acquired in one round is used in preparing the set of questions used in the next round. It seems suitable to use a cathode ray tube terminal to ask the questions, process the responses, and ask the next set of questions. Indeed a function to do just that has been written in APL and was used for the temperature scaling.

Many marketing experiments have larger choice sets than five. Appropriate experiments, perhaps concerning the temperatures of all 12 months, must be run. Also when more points are being fit into a fixed interval, there is much less leeway for their placement. First differences along with ranks may provide a sufficient approximation. For example, the temperatures of the twelve months can be reproduced as follows using the correct ranks and first differences:

	Jan	Feb	Mar	Apr	May	Jun	Jul	Aug	Sep	Oct	Nov	Dec
Real	40	42	51	64	74	83	87	85	78	67	56	43
Constructed	40	41	50	63	73	82	87	86	80	64	54	41

The ideal points assumed in Table 3 were chosen from eyeballing the data. The question now is whether the ranked differences provide more information so that the ideal point can be more rationally estimated. The guess here is yes, although we have not yet investigated that problem.

In marketing problems, we usually do not have preset scales such as temperature. One might want to set up a seven point scale of detergent sudsiness, anchor two brands, and apply the method to a suitable set of responses.

The process could be generalized to higher dimensions. If we ask two sets of questions, one about sudsiness and another about cleansing power, we can construct a two-dimensional map. Two dimensions doesn't have to be the stopping point. Clearly we can represent a product by the cartesian product of its attributes.

In summary, the preliminary reports indicate that Kendall's method is worthwhile investigating as a technique of scaling. It basically can provide a quantitative measure of psychological distance (whether it be on preference or perceptions of a single attribute), something with which marketers often concern themselves.

REFERENCES

Beyer, William H., ed. (1971), CRC Basic Statistical Tables, Cleveland, OH: The Chemical Rubber Co.

Kendall, Maurice G. (1962), "Ranks and Measures," Biometrika, 49, 139-49.

Torgerson, W. S. (1958), Theory and Methods of Scaling, New York: John Wiley.

SCALING BRANDS ON THEIR ADVERTISEMENT DISTINCTIVENESS

John Keon, New York University
Terry Gleason, Bell Laboratories, Holmdel, New Jersey

ABSTRACT

Distinctiveness of a brand's advertisement depends on the amount of confusion consumers have regarding the brand, its advertisements, and competing brands and their advertisements. In this article a method is offered for scaling brands of a product class on their advertisement distinctiveness.

INTRODUCTION

The frequent objective of advertising is to differentiate the advertised brand from the competitive product offerings. Advertisers strive to give their brands distinctive or unique characters. Many advertisers, however, are not successful in their efforts at distinctiveness as witnessed by the large number of advertisements that suffer from misidentification with competitive offerings.

In a 1971 article, Harry McMahan examined Daniel Starch's data on television commercials. McMahan raised the issue that measuring only the degree of correct audience identification of a recent television commercial is an incomplete measure. Of equal importance, in establishing the distinctiveness of an ad, is the degree of audience _misidentification_ of the advertisement. As an example, McMahan referred to an Excedrin commercial which was correctly identified by 6% of the viewers but was also _misidentified_ by 18% of the viewers (who credited the advertisement to competitor brands). Such highly misidentified ads are not communicating a distinctive image and may be of more benefit to the competition than to the advertiser!

In this article we present a method for scaling the brands of a product class on the distinctiveness of their advertisements. This will be achieved by using both data regarding a brand's degree of advertisement misidentification as well as its degree of proper advertisement identification.

OVERVIEW OF PROBLEM

To scale a brand on the distinctiveness of its advertisement requires knowledge about consumer misidentification and correct identification of its advertisements. Measurement of an advertisement's misidentification can be conducted on all types of advertisements, print as well as television. For print ads, either delayed recall can be used (as is usually the case with television ads) or subjects can be shown ads with brand names and labels masked over and then asked to identify the advertiser. Once the data is collected on the proper identification and misidentification of a brand's advertisements, by whatever means, it is assembled into a misclassification or misidentification matrix.

To better understand what is meant by a misclassification matrix, let us consider the data from a print ad study. Suppose, for example, subjects are shown various print ads which have had their brand names and labels whited out. The subjects are asked to identify which of the brands (A through D) they believe the advertisement to be for. The aggregate of the data collected in this manner would look like the matrix of Table 1. Each entry in the matrix is a conditional probability that the row stimulus advertisement was identified as being an advertisement for the column

brand. For example in Table 1, 14.7% of the subjects when shown a brand A advertisement misidentified it as a brand B advertisement. The main diagonal indicates the proportion of correct identifications; the off diagonal entries indicate the misidentification proportions.

TABLE 1
MISCLASSIFICATION MATRIX

When Stimulus was:	Proportion of times classified as:				
	$\underline{A}$	$\underline{B}$	$\underline{C}$	$\underline{D}$	$\underline{E}$
A	.655	.147	.027	.056	.115
B	.345	.175	.040	.096	.345
C	.309	.172	.040	.098	.382
D	.274	.166	.040	.099	.421
E	.159	.132	.035	.094	.579

In order to scale the brands on their advertisement distinctiveness, we created our own interval scale method of analyzing misclassification data. Although two conventional scaling methods exist for scaling misclassification data, each method has deficiencies which make its use inappropriate for scaling brands on advertisement distinctiveness. To clarify what we mean by inappropriate, let us consider each of these conventional methods before introducing our new scaling method.

The first of these conventional methods of scaling the stimuli of a misclassification matrix we refer to as the _Row Method_. The Row Method translates the conditional probabilities (the proportions) into a partial ordering of distances by the rule:

ROW METHOD: $\quad P(S_j | S_r) > P(S_k | S_r) \rightarrow d_{rj} < d_{rk}$

where $P(S_j | S_r)$ is the proportion of time stimulus S_r is misclassified as stimulus S_j.

and d_{rj} is the scale distance between stimulus S_r and stimulus S_j.

An alternative method, which is a slight variation of the Row Method, is the _Column Method_. The implementation of this method requires one to compare the proportions of the matrix down each column. Application of the Column Method also realizes a partial ordering of distances between stimuli. This ordering is obtained by employing the rule that:

COLUMN METHOD: $\quad P(S_i | S_j) > P(S_i | S_k) \rightarrow d_{ij} < d_{ik}$

These two methods for scaling misclassification data suffer from three shortcomings. Both the Row and Column Methods:

● Provide only ordered metric results,
● Ignore the information along the main diagonal (i.e., ignore the data concerning proper identification).
● Require main diagonal entries to be the largest entries in their respective row (for Row Method to be valid) or in their respective column (for Column Method to be valid).

The shortcomings of these methods make their use unacceptable for the analysis of advertisement distinctiveness. To obtain a proper measure of a brand's advertisement distinctiveness requires the use of <u>both</u> the <u>misidentification</u> data and the correct identification data. Also, advertisement identification data frequently has low identification levels for some brands. When this occurs the main diagonal entries may be too small to make the use of either the Row or Column Method valid. In our sample matrix of Table 1, the main diagonal entries for brands B, C, and D are not the largest entries in their correspondint rows. Thus for our sample matrix, the Row Method's application is invalid.

The method described in this article for scaling stimuli of a misclassification matrix is especially appropriate for scaling brand advertisement distinctiveness. The method assumes a behavioral model which explains how the conditional proportions are produced and provides the user with an <u>interval scale</u> of the brands while requiring no stronger assumption than Thurstone Case V model. This scaling method uses the full information of the misclassification matrix and does not require the main diagonal entries to be larger than off diagonal entries.

Model of Behavior That Gives Rise to the Data

The Row Method is sometimes employed on conditional proportion data but never with any reference as to an underlying behavioral model which is assumed to be giving rise to the data (Green, 1968). Consequently, we shall now suggest a basic behavioral model which is similar to the model underlying Thurstone's Case V Law of Comparative Judgment (1959).

Our model, like Thurstone's Case V, postulates a psychological continuum over which the discriminal process values, associated with each stimulus, form a normal distribution. The scale value of the stimulus corresponds to the value of the mean of the discriminal process. As in Thurstone's Case V model, we assume further that the discriminal dispersion or standard deviations associated with a stimulus' distribution on the continuum are equal for all stimuli.

It is assumed that the subject will associate a certain segment of the psychological continuum with a particular stimuli. The segment of the continuum which is associated with a stimulus, say S_i, is that segment for which the discriminal processes associated with S_i yield a higher probability for S_i than for any other stimulus. We refer to the segment of the psychological continuum which a subject associates with stimulus S_i as "category S_i."

In Figure 1 below four stimuli and their respective categories are illustrated. The boundaries between categories are located at the midpoint between adjacent stimulus' means. (Boundary B_i is located between S_i and S_{i+1}, where S_{i+1} is located on the continuum to the right and adjacent to S_i.)

Having developed our consumer behavior model one can easily explain the conditional proportions or probabilities that such a model would generate. The proportion of times stimulus S_2 is mistakenly classified as S_1, $P(S_1|S_2)$, is merely the area under S_2's discriminal dispersion distribution which is located in category S_1, (See shaded area in Figure 1.)

A Method of Interval Scaling

With assumptions no stronger than Thurstone's Case V model, we can develop a scaling method which will allow us to produce interval scale data from our conditional data matrix. Let us proceed by first re-examining what a column comparison of proportions gives us assuming our Thurstone-like

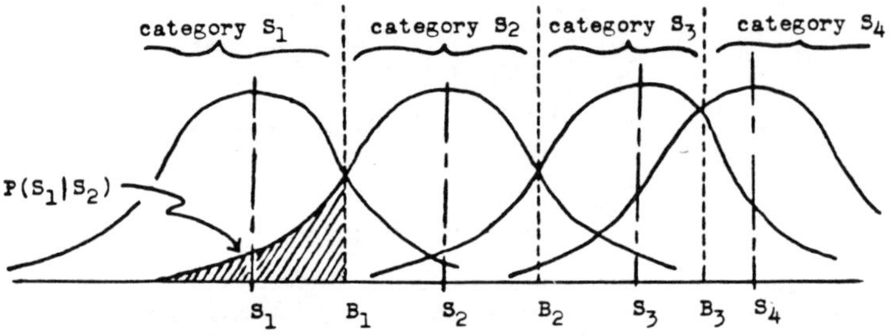

FIGURE 1

FOUR STIMULI AND THEIR RESPECTIVE CATEGORIES WITH BOUNDARIES

behavioral model.

Since we are dealing with a normal distribution, let $F_n(x)$ be the cumulative standard normal probility function. (See Figure 2 below.)

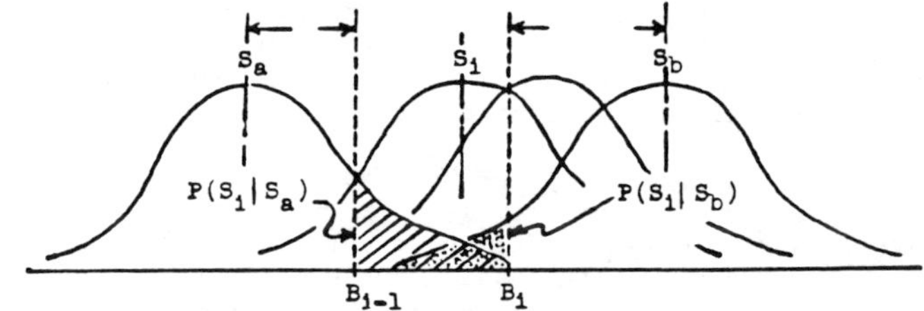

FIGURE 2

CALCULATING THE CONDITIONAL PROBABILITIES

Then

$$P(S_i|S_k) = \left| F_n\left(\frac{B_i - S_k}{\sigma}\right) - F_n\left(\frac{B_{i-1} - S_k}{\sigma}\right) \right|$$

Consequently, if we have the relationship

$$P(S_i|S_a) > P(S_i|S_b) \rightarrow \left| F_n\left(\frac{B_i - S_a}{\sigma}\right) - F_n\left(\frac{B_{i-1} - S_a}{\sigma}\right) \right| >$$

$$\left| F_n\left(\frac{B_i - S_b}{\sigma}\right) - F_n\left(\frac{B_{i-1} - S_b}{\sigma}\right) \right|$$

Letting S_i' equal the width of category S' (that is $B_{i-1} - B_i$) then $S_i' + B_i = B_{i+1}$. Substituting S_i' into the above equation we get:

$$P(S_i|S_a) > P(S_i|S_b) \rightarrow \left| F_n\left(\frac{B_i - S_a}{\sigma}\right) - F_n\left(\frac{B_i + S_i' - S_a}{\sigma}\right) \right| >$$

$$\left| F_n\left(\frac{B_i - S_b}{\sigma}\right) - F_n\left(\frac{B_i + S_i' - S_b}{\sigma}\right) \right|$$

Interpreted, the above equation suggests that S_a is closer to a boundary of category S_i. Consequently, by comparing the conditional probabilities, $P(S_i|S_k)$, over all k (down column S_i) one obtains information about how far each stimulus S_k is from its closest category S_i boundary.

The rank order of the conditional probabilities down a column (the $P(S_i|S_k)$ over all $k \neq i$) is like a folded J scale (Coombs, 1964). However the J scale is not folded at the point of stimulus S_i to obtain an I scale ranking. Rather the J scale is folded such that the boundaries of the stimulus S_i line up. In Figure 3 below is illustrated a J scale which is folded on category S_3 so that the boundaries of S_3, B_2 and B_3 coincide when folded.

FIGURE 3
FOLDING A J SCALE

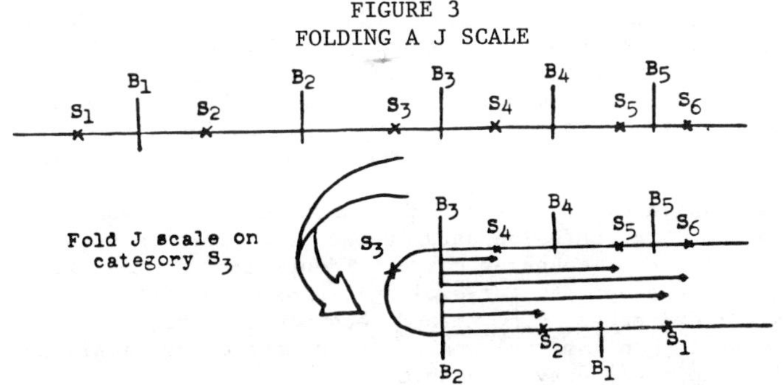

The I scale ranking for S_3 becomes the rank order of distances that the other stimuli are from the coincident boundaries of category S_3. Consequently in our illustrated example above the rank order is S_3, S_4, S_2, S_5, S_1, S_6.

As in the analysis of any I-scale only two stimuli can ever be last in the rankings of the I scales. Once these two stimuli are identified, the I scale rankings which begin with each of these stimuli should be mirror images of one another as well as being the qualitative J scale.

Imagine that the J scale ranking found is

To obtain a quantitative J scale one examines the proportions found in our data matrix along each row in the following manner.

$$P(S_1 | S_1) = F(\frac{B_1 - S_1}{\sigma}) \rightarrow z_{1,1}$$

$$P(S_1 | S_1) + P(S_2 | S_1) = F(\frac{B_2 - S_1}{\sigma}) \rightarrow z_{2,1}$$

$$P(S_1 | S_1) + P(S_2 | S_1) + P(S_3 | S_1) = F(\frac{B_3 - S_1}{\sigma}) \rightarrow z_{3,1}$$

etc.

By looking up the proportions or probabilities in a standard normal table the z_{ij} scores can be found. The z_{ij} value found then corresponds to the standard normal distance between boundary i and stimulus j.

After translating the probabilities into standard scores one has the following data:

$$z_{1,1} = (\frac{B_1 - S_1}{\sigma}) \quad z_{1,2} = (\frac{B_1 - S_2}{\sigma}) \; \cdots \; z_{1,n+1} = (\frac{B_1 - S_{n+1}}{\sigma})$$

$$z_{2,1} = (\frac{B_2 - S_1}{\sigma})$$

$$z_{3,1} = (\frac{B_3 - S_1}{\sigma})$$

$$z_{n,1} = (\frac{B_n - S_1}{\sigma}) \quad \cdots \quad z_{n,n+1} = (\frac{B_n - S_{n+1}}{\sigma})$$

When we let $\sigma = 1$ (which will in no way affect the interval scale results of our solution) z_{ij} now corresponds to the distance between boundary i and stimulus j. To find the interval scale solution of our stimuli we need only find the least squares estimate of our stimuli. This least squares solution is readily found to be:

$$S_j = \frac{1}{n} \sum_{i=1}^{n} z_{ij}$$ where there are n+1 stimuli, where we let

$$\sum_{i=1}^{n} B_i = 0 \ .$$

Comparison of Methods

A comparison of our Interval Scale Method of measuring ad distinctiveness with the other ordered metric scaling methods can be made using the data of Table 1. The results of this comparison are shown in Figure 4.

FIGURE 4
COMPARISON OF RESULTS FROM THE SCALING METHODS

Notice that the Row Method is not applicable on this data because several of the main diagonal entries of Table 1 are not larger than the other entries in their respective rows. The Column Method and Interval Scale Method, although returning similar orderings of the brands, differ in their spatial placement of the brands. For instance, the Interval Scale Method shows B, C, and D to be very close to one another and far from either E or A. The Column Method shows D to be closer to E than to B, and shows the distance between B. C. D and E to be almost the same.

Why the discrepancy between the methods? Realize that the Row and Column Methods ignore the data along the main diagonal -- that is the % of correct identification for a brand. Thus the information that B, C, and D are seldom correctly identified is lost when the Row or Column Method are applied to the data.

Empirical Application

To illustrate how to use and interpret the interval scale method of measuring advertisement distinctiveness, we apply it to some empirical cigarette data. The data was collected by showing eighty-five smokers, from two northeast universities, various cigarette print advertisements. The print advertisements had their brand identifications masked over and the subjects were asked to identify the sponsoring brand for each ad.*

Three of the ten brands used in the test showed little or no confusion. The subjects correctly identified these brands' advertisements better than 95% of the time. There was also little misclassification of these brands as being the sponsors for competing advertisements. These three brands, Benson and Hedges, Marlboro and Tareyton, were thus considered to have unique advertisement images and were dropped from any further analysis.

Formulating a misclassification matrix for the remaining brands we establish Table II. Scaling this matrix we obtain the interval scale of Figure 5.

To interpret these results requires one to examine the proximity of each brand with its neighboring brands. The relative distinctiveness of a brand depends on its distance

------

*Subjects could choose from among ten possible brands, and the presentation order for the advertisements was varied to minimize the effect it might have on the results.

TABLE II
CIGARETTE MISCLASSIFICATION MATRIX

When Stimulus was:	Proportion of times classified as:						
	True	Parliament	Merit	Camel	Kool	Salem	Winston
True	.78	.08	.11	0	.02	.01	0
Parliament	.22	.40	.28	.02	.01	.02	.04
Merit	.11	.10	.69	.01	.04	.02	.03
Camel	.01	.11	.04	.67	.09	.05	.03
Kool	0	0	.04	0	.67	.27	.02
Salem	.01	0	0	0	.05	.16	.78
Winston	.01	.02	0	.01	.04	.15	.77

FIGURE 5
CIGARETTE BRANDS SCALED ON AD DISTINCTIVENESS

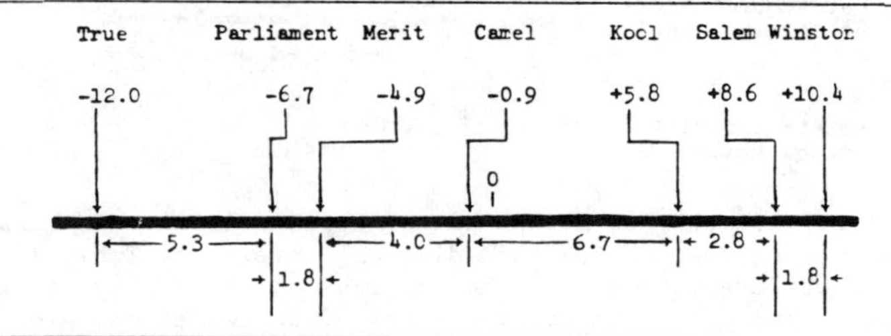

from brands. (See Table III.)

TABLE III
INTERPRETING DISTINCTIVENESS OF ADS

Distance from neighboring brand	Relative distinctive between brand	Average degree (%) confusion between brand
greater than 2.5	very distinct	less than 10%
2.0-2.5	distinct	10-15%
1.0-2.0	mildly distinct	15-30%
less than 1.0	homogenous	30+%

In this study no pairs of its brands could be considered
homogeneous as is often the case with a product class with
less distinctive brands images. Kool, Camel and True had
very distinctive advertisement images. Winston and Salem
were less than 2.0 units apart and were only mildly distinctive from one another. Likewise, Merit and Parliament
were only mildly distinctive.

In implementing this technique, a researcher first removes
from further consideration all brands which have unique or
highly identifiable advertisement image. Next the researcher formulates the misclassification matrix and establishes a unique J scale. In some instances, when confusion between brands is high, it may not be clear what
the ordering of these brands should be on the J scale. In
such cases the J scale is selected which produces the
interval scale result with the lowest least squared error.

CONCLUSION

The objective of most ad agencies is the creation of distinctive advertisement campaigns which set their brands and
their advertisement apart from the competition. Just how
distinctive an advertisement is depends on the amount of
confusion consumers have regarding the brand, its advertisement, and competing brands and their advertisements.
A brand's advertisement distinctiveness is not solely
affected by the advertisement's creativity but also by the
brand's product position, the dollar expanditure on the ad
campaign, the duration of the campaign's theme, etc.

In this article we present a way to scale brands on their
advertisement distinctiveness. The data requirements for
our scaling routine is confusion data. For television ads
the confusion data could be delayed aided recall identification; for print ads delayed aided recall could be used
or subject identifications of print ads with brand identifications masked over. With each of these methods, we
obtain data concerning consumer misidentification and
correct identification of brands and their advertisements.

As pointed out in the article, although other means exist
for scaling confusion data, these other methods ignore
the degree of consumer correct identification and are
thus inappropriate for scaling brands on advertisement
distinctiveness. The method recommended here, besides
returning an interval scale, is in most cases simple to
implement and easy to understand.

REFERENCES

Coombs, C. H., *A Theory of Data*. New York: John Wiley
and Sons, Inc., 1964.

Green, Paul E., F. J. Carmone and P. J. Robinson, "A
Comparison of Perceptual Mapping Via Confusion Data and
Direct Similarity Judgments." *American Marketing
Association Fall Conference Proceeding*, 1968, pp. 323-
333.

McMahan, Harry W., "Brand Misidentification Grows with
Clutter of :30 Spots." *Advertising Age*, May 10, 1971,
pp. 53-54.

Thurstone, L. L., *The Measurement of Values*, Chicago:
University of Chicago Press, 1959.

GENERALIZED FUNCTIONAL FORMS OF SALES RESPONSE MODELS

Randall G. Chapman, University of Chicago

ABSTRACT

This paper discusses the use of Box-Cox transformations to determine the functional form of a sales response model. These transformations involve power functions being applied to each of the variables in the sales response model. The principle features of this procedure are described. The technique is applied to constructing sales response models based on cross-sectional and time series data samples.

INTRODUCTION

When estimating econometric models to uncover the determinants of sales (or market share), marketing scientists typically employ either an additive or a logarithmic functional relationship. While marketing theory as to the expected signs of most of the independent variables in a typical sales response model tends to be quite strong (for example, price and sales will be inversely related), little a priori theoretical knowledge typically exists to support the choice of one functional form over another. Thus, it follows that marketing modelers often resort to subjective considerations, such as the principle of parsimony (ceteris paribus, simple is preferred to complex), to choose a particular functional form representation. While the true (unknown) functional relationship in a sales response model may well be non-linear, it is often the case that a linear or logarithmic approximation over the relevant range of the sample observations yields satisfactory results. Parsimony is, however, a subjective construct, and it may mean different things to different modelers. Spitzer (1978, p. 488), for example, identifies the problem associated with choosing a functional form based on considerations of parsimony: "such subjectivity leads to the construction of alternative models by different investigators, and it is difficult to discriminate between models to determine which is 'best'." To economists, for example, parsimony tends to be interpreted as corresponding to a multiplicative form (in the style of a Cobb-Douglas production function) where the parameters are conveniently interpreted directly as elasticities. (After logarithmic transformation, such a model becomes linear-in-parameters, and may be estimated with standard OLS algorithms.)

Box-Cox (1964) transformations represent one approach to generalized functional forms in econometric modeling. In the Box-Cox procedure, the functional form of the model is determined on the basis of objective, statistical criteria, and not on the basis of a priori subjectivity of the model builder. Popular functional forms, such as the additive and the logarithmic, are specific sub-cases of the more general Box-Cox class of transformations. Thus, the usual functional forms assumed within applied econometric modeling efforts are embraced within the Box-Cox procedure. A very desirable feature of this procedure is that the estimation process generates a ranking value (based on the log-likelihood function) which may be employed to evaluate the relative effectiveness of alternative models with different functional forms.

The purpose of this paper is to discuss the use of the Box-Cox transformation procedure for estimating the generalized functional form of sales response models. The theoretical basis which underlies the procedure is described in the next section. Its principle features are discussed in detail. Two applications of the Box-Cox procedure are then presented. These applications involve constructing sales response models with cross-sectional and time series data.

GENERALIZED FUNCTIONAL FORMS AND BOX-COX TRANSFORMATIONS

The Box-Cox transformation procedure is a generalized approach to choosing a functional form for an econometric model. The transformations involve power functions being applied to each of the variables in the model. Economists have employed this technique in such areas as modeling the demand for money (Zarembka 1968; White 1972; Spitzer 1977), the demand for food (Zarembka 1972; Chang 1977), the earnings-schooling relationship (Heckman and Polachek 1974), travel demand (Gaudry and Wills 1978), and air cargo demand (Wang, Maling, and McCarthy 1981).

A generalized functional form for a sales response model may be written in the following terms:

$$Y_t(\lambda) = \beta_0 + \sum_{i=1}^{I} \beta_i X_{it}(\lambda) + \varepsilon_t \tag{1}$$

where Y is the dependent variable (either sales or market share), the Xs are the relevant explanatory variables, and ε is a stochastic error term. The Box-Cox transformations of the variables in equation (1) are defined as follows:

$$Y_t(\lambda) = \begin{cases} \dfrac{Y_t^\lambda - 1}{\lambda}, & \text{when } \lambda \neq 0 \\[2ex] \log Y_t, & \text{when } \lambda = 0 \end{cases} \tag{2}$$

and

$$X_{it}(\lambda) = \begin{cases} \dfrac{X_{it}^\lambda - 1}{\lambda}, & \text{when } \lambda \neq 0 \\[2ex] \log X_{it}, & \text{when } \lambda = 0 \end{cases} \tag{3}$$

where log refers to the natural logarithm. Transformations of the independent variables were first suggested by Box and Tidwell (1962). Box and Cox (1964) focused on the transformation of the dependent variable.

These transformations are defined for all positive values of Y and X, and for all real values of λ since, by l'Hôpital's rule, $\lim_{\lambda \to 0} X(\lambda) = \log X$. Since these transformations are only defined for positive values, it follows that independent variables that are dummy variables (taking on only the values 0 or 1) would not be subject to the transformation in equation (3).

When $\lambda=1$, equation (1) simplifies to the familiar additive functional form; when $\lambda=0$, the model becomes linear in the logarithms of the variables (corresponding to a multiplicative functional form); and, when $\lambda=-1$, the model has the reciprocal functional form. Clearly, different values of λ will lead to different functional forms of the basic sales response model in equation (1). Thus, the Box-Cox functional form is "generalizable" in the sense that it includes the commonly employed forms used in applied econometric modeling.

Maximum likelihood procedures may be employed to estimate λ and the other parameters in the model. (For a complete derivation of the results which are cited below in summary form, the interested reader is referred to Box and Tidwell (1962), Box and Cox (1964), Maddala (1977, pp. 315-317), and Judge et al. (1980, pp. 308-311).) Suppose that under the appropriate λ-transformation, the ε values are independent $N(0,\sigma^2)$ random variables. Then, ignoring the extraneous constants, the kernel of the log-likelihood function is as follows:

$$L(\lambda) = -\frac{T}{2} \log \hat{\sigma}^2(\lambda) + \log J \qquad (4)$$

where: T is the total number of sample observations; log refers to the natural logarithm; $\hat{\sigma}^2(\lambda)$ is the estimated variance of the stochastic error terms when $Y_t(\lambda)$ is regressed on $X_{1t}(\lambda)$, $X_{2t}(\lambda)$, ... , $X_{It}(\lambda)$; and, J is the Jacobian of the transformation:

$$J = \prod_{t=1}^{T} \left| \frac{\partial Y_t(\lambda)}{\partial Y_t} \right| = \prod_{t=1}^{T} Y_t^{\lambda-1} . \qquad (5)$$

Substituting equation (5) into equation (4) yields the following as the kernel of the log-likelihood function:

$$L(\lambda) = -\frac{T}{2} \log \hat{\sigma}^2(\lambda) + (\lambda-1) \sum_{t=1}^{T} \log Y_t . \qquad (6)$$

Maximization of the log-likelihood function in equation (6) may be accomplished by either an iterative grid search procedure or (directly) with a non-linear optimization routine. SHAZAM (White 1978) is one available computer package which contains Box-Cox transformation capabilities.

Using large sample theory, hypotheses may be tested and confidence intervals may be constructed in straightforward fashions. To test the null hypothesis $H_0: \lambda=\lambda_0$ versus the alternative hypothesis $H_A: \lambda=\hat{\lambda}$ (where $\hat{\lambda}$ is the maximum likelihood parameter estimate), the relevant test statistic is $-2[L(\lambda_0)-L(\hat{\lambda})]$ which is asymptotically distributed χ^2 with 1 degree of freedom (Maddala 1977, pp. 316-317). A $100(1-\alpha)\%$ confidence interval on λ is given by all values of λ such that $T[\log \hat{\sigma}^2(\lambda)-\log \hat{\sigma}^2(\hat{\lambda})] < \chi^2_{1,1-\alpha}$ (Maddala 1977, pp. 316-317).

It is presumed that the error terms are approximately normally distributed and homoscedastic <u>after</u> the Box-Cox transformation procedure has been applied. Thus, it will be necessary to conduct appropriate tests on the residuals. Zarembka (1974) has studied the heteroscedasticity issue, and describes procedures for detecting and correcting it. One of his main findings is that if the error terms are heteroscedastic, the estimated value of λ will be biased in the direction required for the transformed dependent variable to yield homoscedastic residuals.

Three relevant limitations concerning the Box-Cox procedure should be noted. First, in cases where the log-likelihood function is "very flat," the Box-Cox procedure may fail to distinguish clearly among the possible functional forms. Of course, such a situation just implies that the choice of the "best" functional form does not have a large effect on the goodness-of-fit of the model to the available sample observations. Second, the statistical properties and tests associated with this model are derived from large sample distribution theory. Thus, these are asymptotic properties and in small (finite) samples care must be taken in applying and interpreting the relevant tests based on the log-likelihood function. The interested reader is referred to Spitzer (1978) for details of a Monte Carlo investigation of the small sample properties of the Box-Cox procedure. Third, by using this procedure, the modeler may obtain a functional form of a sales response model that violates the usual bounds of a parsimonious model form, since unfamiliar variable transformations may be indicated. Thus, the Box-Cox procedure may result in the marketing scientist being led to a difficult trade-off between considerations of

parsimony and the merits of statistical precision that are desirable in any econometric modeling effort.

When the sales response model is being estimated with time series data, the optimal λ-transformation may result in serial correlation being induced into the residuals. Savin and White (1978) describe a procedure for estimating λ in the presence of first order autocorrelation. Gaudry and Dagenais (1979) further extend the Box-Cox transformation procedure to situations where there is heteroscedasticity and autocorrelation in the residuals.

The model in equation (1) may be generalized further by permitting different λ values for each of the individual transformations. This is, however, at a considerable computational cost. Furthermore, such an approach leads the modeler even further afield from the usual bounds of what would be considered a parsimonious model form.

TWO SALES RESPONSE MODEL APPLICATIONS

This section is devoted to describing two applications of the Box-Cox transformation procedure for choosing the functional form of sales response models. These cross-sectional and time series applications are drawn from case studies. In both of these analyses, SHAZAM (White 1978) was used to estimate the relevant model parameters.

A Cross-Sectional Application: "Fallon Company"

In "Fallon Company" (Eskin and Montgomery 1975, pp. 29-42), the case scenario involves the construction of a cross-sectional sales response model for a leading brand of highly advertised after-shave lotion. The purpose of constructing this model is to determine the responsiveness of sales to advertising.

Available measures include sales revenues (SALES) and advertising (ADV) over a two-year period, percentage penetration of television sets (TV), and the male population (POP) for each of the 38 distributors' territories in the U.S. market. TV is relevant in this setting because most of Fallon's advertising spending is through television, so this penetration variable proxies the extent to which the presence (or lack thereof) of television sets supports (or inhibits) the reception of the advertising messages by the male population. A priori theoretical expectations are that each of the independent variables in this model will be positively related to sales.

The results of estimating this model using Box-Cox transformations are displayed in Table 1. For comparison purposes, additive and logarithmic forms were estimated and their results are also displayed in Table 1. As may be noted, the optimal value of λ for these sample observations is equal to -0.15. A 95% confidence interval for λ is approximately equal to (-0.55,0.25), a rather large range. Apparently, this log-likelihood function is quite flat in the vicinity of the MLE value. Since this confidence interval includes the point 0.0, it follows that the logarithmic functional form is consistent with these sample observations. Thus, the principle of parsimony would seem to lead the marketing scientist to the logarithmic form as a suitable model for these sample observations.

Substantively, these results suggest that the main driving force behind sales of Fallon's after-shave lotion is the size of the male population -- the larger the male population in a market area, the greater are Fallon's sales. Advertising expenditures appear to have a negligible impact on sales revenues. For the $\lambda=-0.15$ model form, the advertising elasticity (evaluated at the sample means of the relevant variables) is approximately equal to 0.093, implying that a 1% increase in advertising expenditures would lead to a 0.093% increase in sales revenues. However, a multicollinearity effect is masking the impact of the level

TABLE 1

BOX-COX ESTIMATES OF THE CROSS-SECTIONAL SALES
RESPONSE MODEL IN "FALLON COMPANY" (Asymptotic
Standard Errors in Parentheses)

	$\lambda=-0.15$ (MLE)	$\lambda=0$ (Log)	$\lambda=1$ (Linear)
Constant	2.466 (0.354)	3.421 (0.553)	-15.999 (19.761)
ADV(λ)	0.086 (0.142)	0.061 (0.163)	0.095 (0.304)
TV(λ)	0.130 (0.124)	0.134 (0.137)	0.222 (0.362)
POP(λ)	0.512 (0.086)	0.996 (0.171)	68.355 (13.844)
R^2	0.948	0.943	0.891
$\hat{\sigma}(\lambda)$	0.079	0.161	25.108
$L(\lambda)$	-163.50	-163.78	-176.40

TABLE 2

BOX-COX ESTIMATES OF THE TIME SERIES SALES RESPONSE
MODEL IN "THE STRATFORD FESTIVAL" (Asymptotic
Standard Errors in Parentheses)

	$\lambda=0.12$ (MLE)	$\lambda=0$ (Log)	$\lambda=1$ (Linear)
Constant	2.706 (1.105)	2.153 (0.655)	76.496 (102.220)
ATTEND$[-1](\lambda)$	0.440 (0.126)	0.405 (0.118)	0.661 (0.160)
WEEKS(λ)	0.899 (0.226)	0.684 (0.153)	6.475 (3.386)
PERFORMWK(λ)	0.044 (0.279)	0.047 (0.191)	1.909 (5.058)
PRICE(λ)	-0.332 (0.420)	-0.220 (0.280)	-8.730 (9.326)
R^2	0.961	0.962	0.949
$\hat{\sigma}(\lambda)$	0.162	0.082	27.736
$L(\lambda)$	-125.62	-125.66	-128.03
$\hat{\rho}$	0.065	0.085	-0.125

of advertising expenditures on sales revenues. The simple correlation between ADV and POP is 0.95, possibly reflecting an advertising expenditure decision rule in which spending is closely tied to market size (as measured by male population). In further analysis, when POP is omitted from the model, the influence of ADV on SALES shows through very clearly.

A Time Series Application: "The Stratford Festival"

In "The Stratford Festival" (Chapman 1981), the scenario concerns the construction of demand model for attendance during the season of performances of the Stratford Festival which is held annually from late-April until early-November in Stratford, Ontario. The data base in this case consists of time series measures corresponding to the available history of the Stratford Festival, from its inception in 1953 until 1980. Annual measures are available on length of season (WEEKS), total number of performances (PERFORM), total attendance during the season (ATTEND), and total box-office ticket revenues (REVENUES).

Given the available data, it is possible to construct a proxy for price (PRICE). REVENUES/ATTEND, while actually being interpreted as average revenues per attendee, is the proxy for price. Note that it is not a perfect measure of price, since it reflects both the range of ticket prices to the various performances as well as the particular demand patterns for tickets at various price levels. Other independent variables in this sales response model include WEEKS, PERFORMWK (which equals PERFORM/WEEKS, and reflects a measure of scheduling "density" of the Stratford Festival program season), and ATTEND$[-1]$, the lagged value of attendance. Note that the actual PRICE variable in the model was expressed in real 1980 Canadian dollar terms (by adjusting the nominal price level by the Canadian Consumer Price Index). Thus, this model accounts for a number of key marketing mix decision variables associated with the Stratford Festival -- price, scheduling (in terms of both length of season and "density" of the program schedule), and "reputation" (as proxied by the lagged value of attendance). A priori expectations are that WEEKS, PERFORMWK, and ATTEND$[-1]$ will exhibit a positive influence on ATTEND, while PRICE will have a negative influence on ATTEND.

The results of estimating this model using Box-Cox transformations are displayed in Table 2. For comparison purposes, additive and logarithmic forms were estimated and

their results are also displayed in Table 2. Because a lagged dependent variable was included as an independent variable in this time series sales response model, the first sample observation is lost, and the relevant data base runs from 1954 to 1980 (a total of 27 observations). The optimal value of λ is equal to 0.12. A 95% confidence interval for λ is approximately equal to (-0.77, 0.91), once again representing a fairly large range. Apparently, this log-likelihood function is also quite flat in the vicinity of the MLE value. Since this confidence interval includes the point 0.0, it follows that the logarithmic functional form is consistent with these sample observations. Thus, the principle of parsimony would seem to lead the marketing scientist to the logarithmic functional form as a suitable representation for these sample observations.

Given that this sales response model is estimated with time series data, the possible existence of serial correlation of the residuals must be considered. In Table 2, the estimated value of the first-order autocorrelation of the residuals, $\hat{\rho}$, is reported. The values are sufficiently small (i.e., near zero) that autocorrelation does not seem to be a problem with these sample observations and this model form. The inclusion of the lagged value of the dependent variable as one of the independent variables may be the cause of the apparent lack of autocorrelation of the residuals, because ATTEND$[-1]$ models out the carryover effects.

The general insignificance of the PRICE variable is the most interesting substantive result in this sales response modeling effort. Apparently, box-office ticket prices are not an inhibiting factor for attendance at the Stratford Festival. There are two possible explanations for this somewhat counter-intuitive finding. First, the total costs associated with attending a play at Stratford are substantially more than just the price of the ticket. Stratford is quite far away from major population centers (e.g., Toronto is about 100 miles distant), so that when transportation and possibly accommodation costs are accumlated with ticket prices, the ticket price may represent but a small component of the total cost of attending the Stratford Festival. Second, there was relatively little variation in the PRICE variable during the 1953-1980 time period. In real 1980 Canadian dollar terms, PRICE ranged from about $9.43 to $11.78, not a very substantial degree of variation. Thus, with regard to the price effect on attendance at the Stratford Festival, it appears that, within the relevant range of experience of price variations, price does not affect attendance in more than a minor fashion.

One final question of interest concerns the stability of the optimal λ-transformation across various sub-intervals (i.e., regimes) of the sample time series observations. Table 3 contains the results for Box-Cox estimates for two regimes: 1958-1980 and 1963-1980. As may be noted, approximate 95% confidence intervals (CI) for λ are also reported in Table 3. Once again, the flat nature of the log-likelihood function in the vicinity of the maximum likelihood estimate may be seen in the quite wide range of the 95% confidence intervals. While the optimal value of λ seems to shift somewhat as earlier years of the time series are omitted, it is important to note that in both regimes the 95% confidence interval for λ includes the point 0.0. Thus, the consistency of a logarithmic model form representation for these sample observations seems re-affirmed. The principle of parsimony would seem to lead the marketing scientist to embrace the logarithmic functional relationship for this sales response model in either of these regimes of the available time series data.

CONCLUDING REMARKS

The Box-Cox transformation procedure for choosing an appropriate functional form of an econometric model is a useful tool for the marketing scientist interested in constructing and estimating sales response models. It is interesting to note that in the two applications described in this paper, the robustness of the logarithmic functional form was affirmed. In both cases, the hypothesis that the sample observations were consistent with a logarithmic functional relationship could not be rejected at the conventional level of statistical significance. The Box-Cox procedure provided a statistically based criterion for choosing the logarithmic form over the additive form. The relatively flat nature of the log-likelihood functions in the vicinity of the maximum likelihood estimates led to rather large confidence intervals for the optimal transformation. This is perhaps attributable to the relatively small sample sizes involved and the general absence of irregular patterns (such as high degrees of skewness) in the sales response models' variables.

REFERENCES

Box, G. E. P. and C. R. Cox (1964), "An Analysis of Transformations," _Journal of the Royal Statistical Society_, 26 (Series B), 211-47.

__________ and P. W. Tidwell (1962), "Transformations of the Independent Variables," _Technometrics_, 4, 531-50.

Chang, H. S. (1977), "Functional Form and the Demand for Meat in the United States," _Review of Economics and Statistics_, 59, 355-9.

Chapman, R. G. (1981), "The Stratford Festival," Graduate School of Business, University of Chicago.

Eskin, G. J. and D. B. Montgomery (1975), _Cases in Computer and Model Assisted Marketing: Data Analysis_, Cupertino, California: Computer Curriculum, University Business Series, Hewlett-Packard Company.

Gaudry, M. J. I. and M. G. Dagenais (1979), "Heteroscedasticity and the Use of the Box-Cox Transformation," _Economics Letters_, 2 (3), 225-9.

__________ and M. J. Wills (1978), "Estimating the Functional Form of Travel Demand Models," _Transportation Research_, 12 (4), 257-89.

Heckman, J. and S. Polachek (1974), "Empirical Evidence on the Functional Form of the Earnings-Schooling Relationship," _Journal of the American Statistical Association_, 69 (June), 350-4.

Judge, G. G. et al. (1980), _The Theory and Practice of Econometrics_, New York: John Wiley and Sons, Inc.

Maddala, G. S. (1977), _Econometrics_, New York: McGraw-Hill Book Company.

Savin, N. E. and K. J. White (1978), "Estimation and Testing for Functional Form and Autocorrelation: A Simultaneous Approach," _Journal of Econometrics_, 8, 1-12.

Spitzer, J. J. (1977), "A Simultaneous Equations System of Money Demand and Supply Using Generalized Functional Forms," _Journal of Econometrics_, 5, 117-28.

__________ (1978), "A Monte Carlo Investigation of the Box-Cox Transformation in Small Samples," _Journal of the American Statistical Association_, 73 (September), 488-95.

Wang, G. H. K., W. Maling, and E. McCarthy (1981), "Functional Forms and Aggregate U.S. Domestic Air Cargo Demand: 1950-1977," _Transportation Research_, 15 (Series A), 249-56.

White, K. J. (1972), "Estimation of the Liquidity Trap With a Generalized Functional Form," _Econometrica_, 40, 193-9.

__________ (1978), "A General Computer Program for Econometric Methods - SHAZAM," _Econometrics_, 46, 239-40.

Zarembka, P. (1968), "Functional Form in the Demand for Money," _Journal of the American Statistical Association_, 63, 502-11.

__________ (1972), _Toward a Theory of Economic Development_, San Francisco: Holden-Day, Inc.

__________ (1974), "Transformation of Variables in Econometrics," in _Frontiers in Econometrics_, P. Zarembka, ed., New York: Academic Press, 81-104.

TABLE 3

BOX-COX ESTIMATES OF THE TIME SERIES SALES RESPONSE MODEL IN "THE STRATFORD FESTIVAL" FOR VARIOUS REGIMES (Asymptotic Standard Errors in Parentheses)

1958-1980: $\lambda=0.24$ (MLE)

$$\text{ATTEND}(\lambda) = 2.685 + 0.625\,\text{ATTEND}[-1](\lambda) + 0.678\,\text{WEEKS}(\lambda)$$
$$(2.164) \quad (0.169) \qquad (0.416)$$
$$+ 0.298\,\text{PERFORMWK}(\lambda) - 0.536\,\text{PRICE}(\lambda)$$
$$(0.469) \qquad (0.772)$$

$$R^2 = 0.926 \qquad \hat{\sigma}(\lambda) = 0.316 \qquad L(\lambda) = -108.80$$
$$\hat{\rho} = -0.113 \qquad 95\%\text{CI}(\lambda) = (-0.65, 1.17)$$

1963-1980: $\lambda=-1.39$ (MLE)

$$\text{ATTEND}(\lambda) = 0.408 + 0.424\,\text{ATTEND}[-1](\lambda) + 0.00756\,\text{WEEKS}(\lambda)$$
$$(0.125) \quad (0.177) \qquad (0.00268)$$
$$+ 0.00291\,\text{PERFORMWK}(\lambda) - 0.00096\,\text{PRICE}(\lambda)$$
$$(0.00200) \qquad (0.00184)$$

$$R^2 = 0.896 \qquad \hat{\sigma}(\lambda) = 0.156 \times 10^{-4} \qquad L(\lambda) = -83.66$$
$$\hat{\rho} = 0.045 \qquad 95\%\text{CI}(\lambda) = (-2.75, 0.55)$$

AN APPLICATION OF CAUSAL MODELING TO THE BUYER-SELLER
DYADIC INTERACTION PROCESS

Jeen-Su Lim, Indiana University, Bloomington
Ronald E. Michaels, Indiana University, Bloomington

ABSTRACT

A causal model of Salesperson Expert and Referent power is
constructed and tested utilizing the same experimental
paradigm used in the 1976 Busch and Wilson study. The
advantages of this approach are discussed and the results
are compared to the replicated research. Results indicate
causal modeling to be a promising methodological tool for
studying buyer-seller interaction.

INTRODUCTION

There has been much progress made in conceptualizing Buyer-
Seller interaction since Franklin B. Evans first introduced
personal selling as a dyadic relationship in 1963. Several
recent attempts have been made to model the dynamics of
the buyer-seller interaction process (Grikscheit and
Crissy 1973; Spiro, Perreault, and Reynolds 1977; Sheth
1976; Wilson 1976; Levy and Zaltman 1975; Wilson and
Bambic 1977; Taylor and Woodside 1978; Weitz 1979). In
various ways these studies model the salesperson and customer as bringing personal characteristics, role requirements and characteristics, needs and expectations, goals,
and interpersonal strategies to a dynamic interaction
process where numerous situational factors may mediate
the outcome. While there has been considerable model-
building activity in this area, methodological developments
have not kept pace, especially in the area of experimental
design. There have been notable contributions in experimental design in interaction research (Sawyer, Deutscher,
and Obermiller 1980) and in measurement (Swazy 1976), but
many of the problems associated with experimental dyadic
interaction research persist. The most commonly used
experimental method in dyadic interaction research has been
the factorial design with analysis of variance as the
analytic procedure (Woodside and Davenport 1974; Busch
and Wilson 1976). There are several reasons why this
traditional methodology may be incorrect, insufficient,
or misleading.

Differences in treatment and control groups may not be
entirely due to the treatment itself. Variation in the
dependent variable might be caused by factors such as
demand effects, evaluation apprehension, or other artifacts. In applying the ANOVA or regression models to
experimental data consisting only of measured independent
and dependent variables, the experimenter cannot determine
definitively the source of the group differences. Manipulation checks can be used to aid in inferring causality;
however, the manipulation checks are usually not modeled
explicitly in the context of the experimental design.

Another problem with traditional experimental design is
that the dependent variable is usually represented as
measured without error. In order to realize a complete
interpretation of the causal relationship among variables,
it is necessary to model the degree of measurement error
in the constructs of interest. Also in the traditional
approach there exist severe limitations for detecting
problems in any particular application or in evaluating
and comparing competing models.

The purpose of this paper is to demonstrate how a causal
modeling approach to buyer-seller interaction research can
alleviate many of the problems discussed above. In fact,
the causal modeling orientation provides the researcher
with a means for: 1) examining the existance of causal
relationships between underlying constructs; 2) determining
the magnitude of the relationships; 3) examining the
measurement error of constructs; and 4) discovering
certain problems in the particular application of an
experimental design (Bagozzi 1980). In this study, a
causal model of the relationships among salesperson expert
power, referent power, and customer attitudinal and
behavior changes will be constructed and tested.

The experimental design is a partial replication of the
1976 Busch and Wilson study. Although the causal modeling
approach does provide ways to guide theory development,
the method is predicated on the researcher beginning with
some theory to specify and test. The Busch and Wilson
study was a factorial design and the method of analysis
was ANOVA. Besides the obvious advantages of consistency
in model specification and variable operationalization,
this replication will allow the comparison of results from
two dissimilar methods of analysis.

THEORETICAL FRAMEWORK

Social Power

The theoretical framework for this study as well as the
Busch and Wilson study is the French and Raven (1959)
bases of social power which is grounded in field theory
tradition. This framework has been popular in the marketing literature (Woodside and Davenport 1974; Levy and
Zaltman 1975; Busch and Wilson 1976). Of the five bases
of social power identified by French and Raven, this study
includes only expert and referent power. Because social
power has been studied from so many perspectives, it is
understandable why a wide variety of definitions and
operationalizations exist. A basic problem in this line
of research is the absence of a proven scale for measuring
social power (Swazy 1980). Also, since social power is a
continuous construct, experimental manipulation is difficult and manipulation checks often induce demand effects.
Thus, construct validity is often threatened in this type
of experimental research. However, it is clear that the
theoretical conceptual framework so crucial to the effective use of causal modeling exists for social power.

Busch and Wilson's Findings

Exhibit 1 summarizes the basic ANOVA results of the Busch
and Wilson study. There was a definite problem in the
study concerning the manipulation of referent power. The
authors unfortunately had to report results of an ANOVA
based on a non-random assignment of subjects to the
treatment groups. As can be seen in Exhibit 1, the results
indicate significant main affects of expert power and
referent power on trust, attitude change, and behavioral
intentions. When subjects were randomly assigned, the
results show significant main effects for expert and
referent power on range of control, but only expert power
exerts a significant effect with respect to behavioral
intentions. No interactive effects were significant. The
authors performed manipulation checks on their treatments
using ANOVA and found significant differences between
treatment levels. A major conclusion drawn from the
results was that the specificity versus generality of

measurement and the degree of respondent involvement
(behavioroid measure) dramatically affect the responses
subjects make in experimental research.

EXHIBIT 1

SUMMARY OF ANOVA RESULTS IN THE BUSCH/WILSON STUDY

Non-Random Assignment of Subjects	Expert Power	Referent Power	Inter-action
Trust	S	S	NS
Attitude Change	S	S	NS*
Global Attitude (Insurance)	NS	NS	NS
Behavioral Intention	S	S	NS
Behavioroid (Commitment)	NS	NS	NS
Random Assignment of Subjects			
Behavioral Intention	S	NS	NS
Behavioroid	NS	NS	NS
Range of Control	S	S	NS

*P = .053

The Causal Model

The proposed causal model in Figure 1 is derived from
previous studies whose ANOVA results support the following
three hypotheses (Busch and Wilson 1976; Woodside and
Davenport 1974).

1) A salesperson in a high <u>referent power</u> relationship
    with a customer is more effective in producing the
    desired <u>attitudinal change</u> in the customer.
2) A salesperson in a high <u>expert power</u> relationship with
    a customer is more effective in producing an intended
    <u>attitude change</u> in the customer.
3) The more favorable the <u>attitude</u> toward the salesperson
    and the salesperson's message, the greater the likeli-
    hood of producing the intended <u>behavioral change</u> in
    the customer (McGuire 1969).

In Figure 1 and succeeding ones, the unobservable variables
(except error terms) are indicated by circles; observable
variables (i.e., indicators, measurements, operationalizations) are shown as squares, and causal relationships are
depicted as straight-line segments with arrowheads.

The model in Figure 1 may be interpreted as follows. The
manipulation of the independent variables x_1 and x_2 (expert
and referent power) ultimately causes variation in five
observables. Variation in x_1 and x_2 as stimuli will cause
a change in some psychological state in the test subjects
(e.g., an emotion or thought). This will be measured by
the manipulation checks y_1 through y_4. The manipulation
checks will be fallible indicators of theoretical con-
structs η_1 and η_2. The theoretical construct η_1 represents
the true psychological state measured by y_1 and y_2. The
correspondence between the theoretical constructs η_1 and
η_2 and the manipulation checks y_1 through y_4 is indicated
by λ_1 through λ_4. The errors in the y's are represented
by the ε's, while the errors in equations are represented
by the ζ's. The impact of the manipulation x upon the true
psychological state η is represented by γ_1. Interpretation
of parameters is similar for the true, unobserved dependent
variables η_3 and η_4. Finally, the cause-and-effect relation between theoretical terms is represented by β.

This model has the advantages of: 1) providing a direct
index of the quality of the treatment manipulation (through
the parameters γ, λ, and the variance of ε), 2) providing
a means of determining elements of construct validity, and
3) aiding in the detection of measurement error.

FIGURE 1

HYPOTHESIZED CAUSAL MODEL

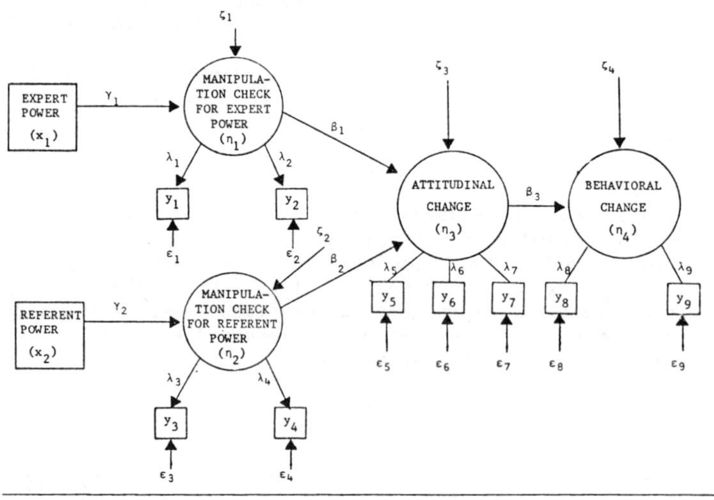

RESEARCH DESIGN AND PROCEDURE

This study followed the Busch and Wilson design and procedure as closely as possible. Subjects in this study
(as in the Busch and Wilson study) were junior level
college students. The sample size was 95, of which five
were eliminated because of incomplete instruments. From
the 90 usable responses, <u>eighty</u> (twenty randomly selected
for each treatment group) were included in the analysis.

The experimental procedure involved two separate meetings
with each subject. The first contact was made in the
classroom and subjects were provided a statement of the
study's objectives and requested to complete Byrne's
survey of attitudes questionnaire. At the second meeting
the experimental treatments were administered via a
10-minute videotaped informative sales presentation concerning life insurance. As in the Busch and Wilson study,
the use of a professional sales agent in the videotaped
presentation provided technical accuracy and also enhanced
credibility. The definitions and operationalizations of
the constructs of interest in this study are consistent
with the original Busch and Wilson study. (See Appendix)

ANALYSIS

A maximum likelihood estimation procedure for examining
linear structural equation systems (LISREL IV) was used
as the method of data analysis (Jöreskog 1973; Jöreskog
and Sörbom 1978). The use of multiple indicators of unobservable variables in structural equation models allows
for the explicit representation of measurement error in
hypothetical constructs (Aaker and Bagozzi 1979; Anderson,
Engledow, and Becker 1979; Griliches 1974).

Unlike other path or causal models, the LISREL model simultaneously evaluates the research hypotheses in terms of
both measurement and structural characteristics.

RESULTS

Goodness-of-fit

A total of 26 parameters were unknown and unconstrained
in Λ_y, Λ_x, β, Γ, Φ, Ψ, θ_δ, and θ_ε. These were estimated
by the maximum likelihood method. Because there are 66
unique elements in the observed variance-covariance matrix
among 11 observable variables, there are 40 (66-26) degrees

of freedom in the postulated model to be used in assessment of goodness-of-fit. The standardized values of Λ_y, Λ_x, β, and Γ are presented in Figure 2. The obtained chi-square is 68.9 with 40 degrees of freedom. The probability of obtaining a larger chi-square value, given that the model is correct, is only .011. Examination of the 66 discrepancies between the observed covariance and reproduced covariance matrices based on the model specification, i.e., the residuals, showed a mean absolute value of .063.

Thus, discrepancies between the variance-covariance matrix and the reproduced matrix; the chi-square ratio, and low probability value are all indicative of a relatively poor fit of the model to the data. Because of this poor fit the coefficients in the Figure 2 model were not interpreted.

FIGURE 2

CAUSAL MODEL SPECIFIED BY MAXIMUM
LIKELIHOOD ESTIMATES

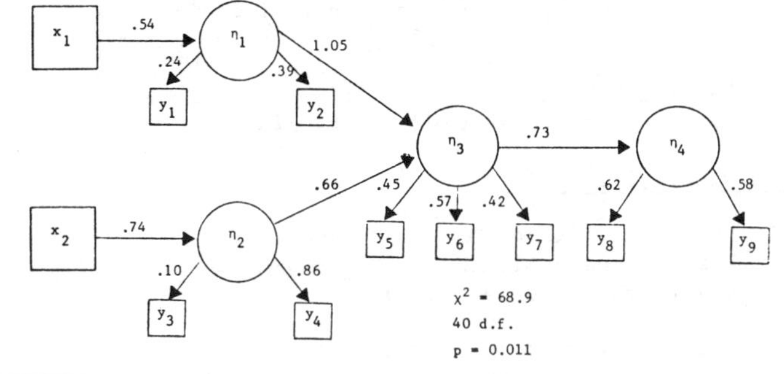

An Alternative Model

An examination of the first-order partial derivatives of the final maximum likelihood solution to the model in Figure 2 indicates an alternative specification which may improve the goodness-of-fit. Figure 3 presents a alternative model which frees γ_3, the effect of expert power on referent power manipulation. The obtained chi-square value is now 42.93 with 39 (40-1) degrees of freedom (P = 0.23). The large drop in χ^2 of 26 (68.9 - 42.9) relative to only one less degree of freedom (40-39) indicates that changes made in the original model (the inclusion of Path x_1 to η_2) represent a significant improvement in fit (Jöreskog and Sörbom 1978). In practice, values of P > 0.10 often give acceptable fits (cf., Lawley and Maxwell 1971). Examination of the 66 residuals based on the alternative model specification showed that the mean absolute value of those residuals decreased by .012 (.063 to .051). The chi-square statistic is quite sensitive to small sample sizes. Here, sample size is sufficiently large according to the rule of thumb; N - (p + q) $\geq$ 50, i.e., 80 - (9 + 2) = 69 > 50 (Bagozzi 1980).

Included in Figure 3 are the standardized values of Λ_y, Λ_x, β, and Γ. Standardized coefficients are presented because they are useful in comparing the relative contribution of independent variables to a dependent variable (Bagozzi 1977). The maximum likelihood parameter estimates for the structural equations give the direct effect of the true independent variables and the unobserved true dependent variables on the unobserved true dependent construct. An inspection of the coefficients in Figure 3 show that all are consistent with the directional hypotheses of the study. An interesting finding is the direct effect (.45) of expert power on the true independent variable referent power. Expert power is shown to be much larger in its impact on attitudinal change than referent power because of this indirect causal relationship. The indirect effect would be 0.24 (0.45 X 0.53) and, in turn, the total impact of expert power becomes 1.16 (0.929 + 0.240), compared to

0.53 for referent power. The implication of γ_3 (.45) is that referent power (perceived attractiveness) is also significantly influenced by the expertise of the salesperson. Busch and Wilson were able to allude to this in their study, but this causal model shows it explicitly.

FIGURE 3

ALTERNATIVE CAUSAL MODEL SPECIFIED BY
MAXIMUM LIKELIHOOD ESTIMATES

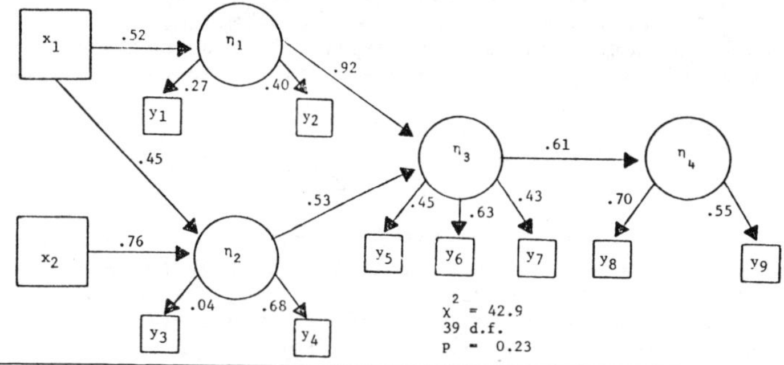

The indicator coefficients shown in Figure 3 are all significant with the exception of λ_4. The indicator associated with the manipulation check for referent power ($\lambda_3 = .04$) and the one associated with expert power ($\lambda_1 = .27$) imply problems in applying the manipulation check. In the alternative model more than half of the variance in each y_i (except for λ_8) is "unique", or specific variance not accounted for by the construct. This is indicative of interpretational confounding which can occur when the indicants of the unobserved variable have low covariance among themselves (Burt 1976, p. 10). Swazy (1980) outlined the reliability and validity problems inherent in manipulation checks in buyer-seller interaction research. Most research (Busch and Wilson 1976; Sawyer, Deutscher, and Obermiller 1980) has utilized ANOVA in analyzing manipulation check items. The ANOVA results presented in Exhibit 2 do not support the efficacy of the experimental manipulation of the four indicators (y_1, y_2, y_3, y_4). The main effect for expert power is highly significant for all four indicators, but the main effects for referent power are of questionable significance. However, the ANOVA results do not explain the inadequacy of the experimental manipulation of the four indicators.

EXHIBIT 2

SUMMARY OF ANOVA RESULTS

F-value, significance levels in parentheses

	Expert Power	Referent Power	Interaction
Knowledge (y_1)	27.75 (.001)	2.68 (.105)	0.41 (.522)
Competence (y_2)	21.95 (.001)	0.32 (.573)	6.22 (.015)
Likeability (y_3)	5.00 (.028)	5.07 (.027)	0.05 (.820)
Congeniality (y_4)	9.60 (.003)	3.69 (.058)	0.001 (.976)

A verification check of the experimental manipulation suggested by Costner (1971, p. 405) can be useful in discovering when such manipulations have incurred artifactual effects. Two separate estimates may be derived for the parameter r where

$$r = r_{xyi}/\lambda_i \text{ for } i = 1, \ldots 4, \text{ and } \lambda_i \text{ are unstandardized estimates.}$$

$$r_1 = \frac{.129}{1.0} = 0.13, \quad r_2 = \frac{.72}{1.5} = 0.48; \text{ for } \eta_1$$

$$r_1 = \frac{.24}{1.0} = 0.24, \quad r_2 = \frac{.206}{16.2} = 0.12; \text{ for } \eta_2$$

Because the estimates of r differ, one can conclude that there are some direct effects from manipulation to manipulation check such as might be produced by demand characteristics (Bagozzi 1980).

Hopefully, this discussion has shown that the proposed model does fit the data adequately. The causal relationships were found to be significant and in the expected direction. Perhaps most importantly, the causal model of Figure 3 allows the modeling of unobserved variables, provides a means of determining elements of construct validity, provides more realism because measurement error in the dependent variable is explicitly incorporated into the model, and provides for diagnosis of flaws in experimental design applications.

CONCLUSION

A causal model of buyer-seller interaction was constructed and tested with experimental data. Although there have been few marketing applications reported, the general linear structural equation model can be used for a wide range of experimental designs. The present study applied a causal modeling approach to a post-test only control group design with manipulation checks.

Despite the advantages noted earlier in this paper, a number of assumptions and limitations must be emphasized. Variables are assumed to be intervally scaled and normally distributed. It is generally suggested that three indicators are needed for each construct in order to facilitate the diagnosis of flaws in the experimental design. In some cases it might be difficult to find that number of adequate indicators. The maximum likelihood estimate and the goodness-of-fit test based on it may not perform well if a small sample is used. Finally, it must be reemphasized that the researcher needs to begin with some theory to specify and test. The present study applied the causal modeling approach to a marketing area characterized by complex constructs with difficult operationalizations. The results indicate that this approach is very promising for experimentally studying buyer-seller interaction.

APPENDIX

VARIABLES IN THE MODEL

Expert Power (X_1)

Expert Power is based upon the Influencee's Perception that the Influencer has valuable knowledge, information or skills in a relevant area. Two levels of Expert Power were manipulated by presenting the salesperson as either "above average" or "excellent" on six attributes of sales ability and experience.

Referent Power (X_2)

Referent Power is based on the perceived attraction of members in the dyad to one another. Two levels of referent power were manipulated by using Byrne's attitude similarity procedure (Byrne 1961).

Manipulation Checks for Expert Power (η_1)

1) Perceived Knowledge (y_1) – 7 point Likert-type scale with end points labeled "slightly below average" and "definitely above average."

2) Perceived Competence (y_2) – 7 point Likert-type scale with end points labeled "slightly below average" and "definitely above average."

Manipulation Checks for Referent Power (η_2)

1) Likability of Salesperson (y_3) – 7 point Likert-type scale with end points labeled "like very much" and "dislike very much."

2) Enjoy working with salesperson (y_4) – 7 point Likert-type scale with end points labeled "very much dislike" and "very much enjoy."

Attitudinal Change (η_3)

1) Trust (y_5) was measured as the sum of four Likert-type scales concerning salesperson dependability, reliability, trustworthiness and reputation.

2) Specific attitudes (y_6) toward life insurance and the sales message presented.

3) Relative range (y_7) of the Power Base refers to the various types of influencee's responses affected by the influencer. Range was operationalized via a three-step process culminated by a range score for each subject being calculated by multiplying the sum of five 7-point Likert-type scales times an importance rating for each topic measured by the Likert scales.

Behavioral Change (η_4)

1) Behavioral Intention (y_8) was measured on a 7-point Likert-type scale involving subject's willingness to meet with the salesperson.

2) The Behavioroid (y_9) measure involved a higher degree of subject commitment since level of interest was indicated on a Postcard.

Note: For a more thorough discussion of Variable Definitions and Operationalization, readers should consult Busch and Wilson 1976.

REFERENCES

Aaker, David A., and Richard P. Bagozzi (1979), "Unobservable Variables in Structural Equation Models with an Application in Industrial Selling," *Journal of Marketing Research*, 16 (May), 147-158.

Anderson, Ronald D., Jack Engledow, and Helmut Becker (1979), "Evaluating the Relationships Among Attitudes Toward Business, Product Satisfaction, Experience, and Search Effort," *Journal of Marketing Research*, 14 (August), 209-226.

Bagozzi, Richard P. (1977), "Structural Equation Models in Experimental Research," *Journal of Marketing Research*, 14, 209-226.

__________ (1980), *Causal Models in Marketing*, New York: John Wiley and Sons.

Burt, R. S. (1976), "Interpretational Confounding of Unobserved Variables in Structural Equation Models," *Sociological Methods and Research*, 5, 3-52.

Busch, Paul and David T. Wilson (1976), "An Experimental Analysis of a Salesman's Expert and Referent Bases of Social Power in the Buyer-Seller Dyad," *Journal of Marketing Research*, 13 (February), 3-11.

Byrne, D. (1961), "Interpersonal Attraction and Attitude Similarity," *Journal of Abnormal Social Psychology*, 62 (May), 713-715.

Costner, H. L. (1971), "Utilizing Causal Models to Discover Flaws in Experiments," _Sociometry_, 34 (September), 398-410.

Evans, Franklin B. (1963), "Selling as a Dyadic Relationship - A New Approach," _American Behavioral Scientist_, 6 (May), 76-79.

French, J. R. P., Jr., and B. Raven (1959), "The Bases of Social Power," in _Studies in Social Power_, D. Cartwright ed., Ann Arbor, University of Michigan.

Grikscheit, G. M., and J. E. Crissy (1973), "Improving Interpersonal Communications Skill," _M.S.U. Business Topics_, 21 (Autumn), 37-44.

Griliches, A. (1974), "Errors in Variables and Other Unobservables," _Econometrica_, 42 (November), 971-998.

Jöreskog, Karl G. (1973), "A General Method for Estimating a Linear Structural Equation System," in _Structural Equation Models in the Social Sciences_, A. S. Goldberger and O. D. Duncan, eds., New York: Seminar Press, 85-112.

__________ and D. Sörbom (1978), _LISREL IV: Analysis of Linear Structural Relationships by the Method of Maximum Likelihood_, Chicago: National Education Resources, Inc.

Lawley, D. N., and A. E. Maxwell (1971), _Factor Analysis as a Statistical Method_, 2nd ed., London: Butterworth.

Levy, Sidney J., and Gerald Zaltman (1975), _Marketing, Society, and Conflict_, Englewood Cliffs: Prentice-Hall, Inc.

McGuire, W. J. (1969), "The Nature of Attitudes and Attitude Change," in _Handbook of Social Psychology_, G. Lindzey and E. Aronson, eds., Reading, Mass.: Addison-Wesley, 136-314.

Sawyer, A., Terry Deutscher, and Carl Obermiller (1980), "Can Seller-Customer Interaction and Influence be Studied in the Laboratory," in _Advances in Consumer Research_, Jerry C. Olson, ed., San Francisco: Association for Consumer Research.

Sheth, J. N. (1976), "Buyer-Seller Interaction: A Conceptual Framework," in _Advances in Consumer Research_, Beverlee Anderson, ed., Cincinnati: Association for Consumer Research, 382-386.

Spiro, R. L., W. D. Perreault, Jr., and F. D. Reynolds, (1977), "The Personal Selling Process: A Model and a Critical Review," _Industrial Marketing Management_, 5 (December), 351-364.

Swazy, John (1976), "Measuring the Bases of Social Power," in _Advances in Consumer Research_, Beverlee Anderson, ed., Cincinnati: Association for Consumer Research, 364-369.

__________ (1980), "Comments on Buyer-Seller Research," in _Advances in Consumer Research_, Jerry C. Olson, ed., San Francisco: Association for Consumer Research, 400-404.

Taylor, J. L., and A. G. Woodside (1978), "Exchange Behavior Among Life Insurance Selling and Buying Centers in Field Settings," Center Paper #72, Research Division, College of Business Administration, University of South Carolina.

Weitz, B. A. (1979), "A Critical Review of Personal Selling Research: The Need for Contingency Approaches," in _Critical Issues in Sales Management: State of the Art and Future Research Needs_, G. Albaum and G. Churchill, Jr., eds., Eugene, Oregon: Division of Research, University of Oregon.

Wilson, D. T. (1976), "Dyadic Interaction: An Exchange Process," in _Advances in Consumer Research_, Beverlee Anderson, ed., Cincinnati: Association for Consumer Research, 394-397.

__________ and Peter J. Bambic (1977), "Conceptual Models of Buyer-Seller Interaction," paper presented at the 85th Annual Convention, American Psychological Association, San Francisco.

Woodside, A. G., and William J. Davenport (1974), "The Effect of Salesmen Similarity and Expertise on Consumer Purchasing Behavior," _Journal of Marketing Research_, 11 (May), 198-202.

INNOVATIVE BEHAVIOR AND REPEAT PURCHASE DIFFUSION MODELS

Vijay Mahajan, Southern Methodist University, Dallas
Eitan Muller, Northwestern University, Evanston

ABSTRACT

The objective of this paper is to review and synthesize
the currently available repeat purchase diffusion models
of a nondurable brand. These models have served as the
primary analytical tools for pre and early test market
forecasting. A number of issues related to the further
development and validation of these models are discussed.

INTRODUCTION

In recent years, a number of models have been proposed to
represent the first time as well as repeat buyers of a new
product. A comprehensive state-of-the-art review of the
first-purchase innovation diffusion models have been provided by Mahajan and Muller (1979). The objective of this
paper is to review and synthesize the currently available
repeat purchase diffusion models of a nondurable brand.
These models have served as the primary analytical tools
for pre and early test market forecasting (Wind, Mahajan
and Cardozo 1981).

The format of this exposition is a follows. First, the
general underlying structure employed in the development
of repeat purchase diffusion models is presented. Second,
repeat purchase diffusion models are reviewed. Finally, a
number of issues related to the further development, validation and evaluation of these models are discussed.

A GENERAL REPEAT PURCHASE
DIFFUSION MODEL STRUCTURE

Traditionally, there have been two distinct approaches to
the diffusion process of a new brand. The first is the
innovative behavior paradigm, best exemplified by Midgley
(1976), while the second is the depth of repeat purchase
approach originated by Fourt and Woodlock (1960). To put
the diffusion models of a nondurable brand in proper perspective, it is necessary to unify these approaches. Towards this, first, a brief description of these two approaches is provided. Next, a multistage diffusion model,
which unifies these two approaches, is presented. In the
following section, the repeat purchase diffusion models,
in the light of this unified approach, are reviewed.

Innovative Behavior Paradigm

The main thrust of the innovative behavior approach is that
not all consumers participate equally in the word-of-mouth
process. Some participate actively, "spreading the word"
around and can be thought of as adding a free flow of information which benefits the firm and is substitutable to
the flow generated by advertising.

A second group of consumers simply do not participate in
this social process, even though they are aware of the
brand or even have some satisfactory experience with the
brand. Moreover, a third group exists, which does participate in the process but in a negative way. The consumers
in this group diffuse information which is unfavorable to
the firm. This is composed of four types of information:
(1) brand-related adverse information such as the information about the "flammability" of the Pinto; (2) firm-
related adverse information such as the information that
the president belongs or contributes to some obscure cult;
(3) product category adverse information such as the infor-

mation about possible side effects of aspirin; (4) industry-
related adverse information such as ozone destructive capability of aerosol cans. It is clear that these flows of
information have a harmful effect on the acceptance of a
new brand.

Depth of Repeat Purchase Approach

The main point of the depth of repeat purchase approach is
that customers can be classified according to the number of
times they have purchased the product, i.e., into different
repeat classes. In this approach, first suggested by Fourt
and Woodlock (1960) and leter refined and empirically tested by Eskin (1973) and, Kalwani & Silk (1980), the model
builder is concerned with developing penetration curves for
different repeat classes. The following question is
raised:

> If $n_0(t)$ is the number of consumers who buy for the
> first time in period t, what cumulative fraction
> would have completed the first repeat by period
> t+1, t+2, and so on. Or, in general, if there are
> $n_j(t)$ number of consumers in the j-th repeat class
> at the time t, what cumulative fraction would have
> completed the (j+1)th purchase by period t+1, t+2
> and so on.

In order to model the cumulative proportion of adopters,
$P_j(t)$, who would have bought the product j-times by time t,
the following model has been proposed:

$$\Delta P_j(t) = P_j(t) - P_j(t-1) = a_j(\bar{P}_j - P_j(t-1)) \qquad (1)$$

where a_j is the penetration coefficient for the j-th repeat
class and $\bar{P}_j$ is the ceiling on the cumulative proportion of
adopters who would eventually buy the project j times.
Equation (1) suggests that the increase in the cumulative
proportion of consumers who would repeat-purchase a product
(j times) from time t-1 to t is a constant proportion of
remaining consumers who will eventually repeat-purchase the
product j times (the "untapped" jth purchasers).

The empirical studies by Eskin (1973), and Kalwani and Silk
(1980) have been concerned with the examination of the
values of a_j and $\bar{P}_j$ across the different repeat classes.
These empirical studies suggest that a_j is generally con-
tant across all the repeat classes and the ceiling $\bar{P}_j$ in-
creases with the depth of repeat, i.e., $\bar{P}_1 \leqslant \bar{P}_2 \leqslant \bar{P}_3$ and so on.

Combining the Two Approaches

The weakness of having the above two distinct approaches is
that while the first is suitable for adoption of durables,
the second is applicable to nondurables. The second approach, in fact, ignores the thesis that communicators of
the product experience may transfer favorable, unfavorable
or indifferent messages (or no messages) through word-of-
mouth. Both the approaches ignore the possiblity of impulse purchase. In addition, both the approaches do not
consider "backward" flows or decay. That is, they do not
take into account the fact that people forget or may lose
interest in the product category. Given these weaknesses,
what is now required is a comprehensive diffusion model

which (a) considers the customer flow across the untapped, potential and current market (consisting of triers or first-purchasers and second, third . . . jth repeat purchasers), (b) identifies the communicators of product and distinguishes the type of message conveyed, (c) incorporates the impulse purchase and (d) the decay. The flow diagram for such a multistage diffusion model is given in Figure 1.

FIGURE 1

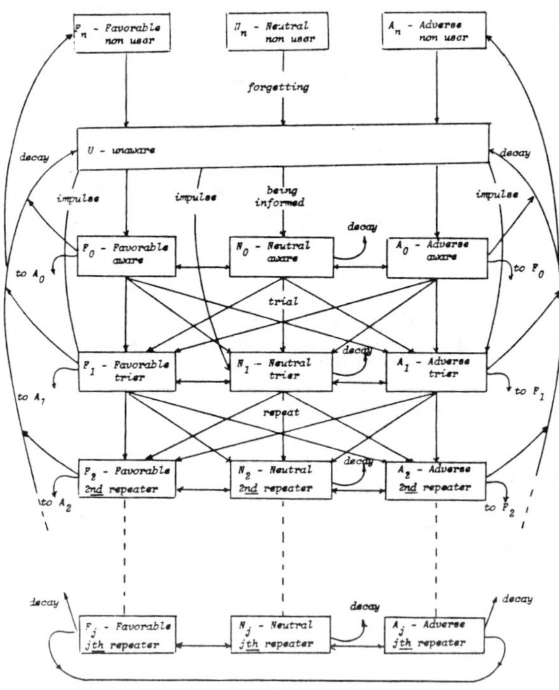

Note in Figure 1 that the total population consists of four major groups representing non-users, unawares, awares and adopters, respectively. The last group is further divided into triers and second, third . . . j-th repeaters. The type of information conveyed in the communication process is included by segmenting the non-users, awares and adopters into favorable, neutral and adverse segments. The arrows represent horizontal and vertical customer flows and interactions between segments and major groups.

The flow out of the unaware group to the aware group may be due to personal communication, advertising, samples (if they were not tried) and other marketing activities such as in-the-store displays, etc. The flow out of the unaware group to the trier group directly (denoted by "impulse" in Figure 1) is due to impulse purchase and samples which were used or consumed. Thus, impulse purchase in which awareness comes with (or after) trial is a shortcut to the usual sequence of unawareness-awareness-trial. As for the decay, two distinct processes exist: (a) <u>forgetting</u> in which a person is removed to the unaware group and ceases to participate in the word-of-mouth mechanism, (b) <u>termination of use</u> in which the person is removed to the non-user class but still participates in the word-of-mouth mechanism.

The existence of the non-user class is due to the principle of homogeneity and constancy over time of the different rates within a given segment. Had we deleted this segment, the structure of the repeat classes would have lowered the purchase rates of each repeat class. The flows from and into the different groups can be described by a set of differential equations. For the sake of brevity, we delete the precise detailing of the complex set of differential equations.

REPEAT PURCHASE MODELS

This section is a review of the multistage/repeat purchase models in the marketing literature. Since, formally, the dynamics of these models are special cases of the general multistage model just presented, no extensive discussion of the models is given. Instead, the models are reviewed briefly.

The main differences between the models are highlighted in Table 1. The models are first categorized as being deterministic (D) or stochastic (S). Second, a check mark in

TABLE 1

Table 1: Repeat Purchase Models			---Distinguishes between---			----------- includes -----------			
Model	Deterministic/Stochastic	Integrated Process	Unaware-Potential	Types of Information	Depth of Repeat	Word of Mouth	Impulse Purchase	Decay	Recycle
1. Fourt and Woodlock	D				✓				
2. Parfitt and Collins	D								
3. Calycamp and Liddy: AYER	D		✓						
4. Nakanishi	S	✓			✓			✓	
5. Massy: STEAM	S	✓			✓				
6. Assmus: NEWPROD	D		✓					partial	partial
7. Urban: SPRINTER	D	✓	✓		partial	✓		partial	✓
8. Midgley	D	✓		✓		✓			✓
9. Blattberg and Golanty: TRACKER	D		✓		✓			partial	
10. Dodson and Muller	D	✓	✓			✓		✓	✓
11. Lilien and Rao	D	✓				✓		✓	
12. Proposed Model (Figure 1)	D	✓	✓	✓	✓	✓	✓	✓	✓

the appropriate box implies that: (a) the model has one integrated process to describe the flow from and into the different groups of customers (Most depth of repeat models assume a different process for the flow from unaware to aware and for the flows between each depth of repeat class. Mostly an ad hoc assumption is made on the growth of the aware group.), (b) the model distinguishes between the group of customers who are unaware of the brand and those who are aware of the brand but have not yet purchased it ("potential customers"), (c) the model distinguishes among the three different groups of customers according to the type of information they transmit: favorable, adverse or neutral (where neutral includes transmitting no information), (d) the model distinguishes among the different depths of repeat purchases i.e., makes the distinction between triers, second-time purchasers, third-time purchasers, etc., (e) the model includes the explicit mechanism of word-of-mouth, (f) the model includes an impulse purchase rate, that is, it allows for a consumer to reverse the regular flow of awareness-trial-adoption by purchasing first and at the second stage (or at the same time) being aware of the brand, (g) the model takes into account all possible "backward" flows, that is, it takes into account that people forget, lose interest in product categories, etc. These general backward flows are denoted by "decay", (h) the model allows for horizontal flows, that is, it takes into account that people may change their opinion about the product while still remaining at the same purchase levels. They might show it by transmitting different types of information i.e., revealing directly their preferences or by revealing them indirectly, that is, purchasing a rival's brand.

It should be noted here that the above criteria have been selected based on the general multistage model presented earlier. In fact, as shown in Table 1, the proposed multistage model scores a check mark on all of the above characteristics and serves as a "bench mark" for all other models compared in Table 1. In the following paragraphs, a short description of models, compared in Table 1, is

presented. Detailed flow diagrams of these models corresponding to Figure 1 are given in the unabridged version
of this paper.

1. Fourt and Woodlock (1960): This model served as theoretical base for all later depth of repeat models. Its
flow diagram is the same as Blattberg and Golanty (1978)
where no explicit decay (to the non-user class) is assumed.

As in Blattberg and Golanty (1978) (and as opposed to
SPRINGER [1970]) the maximum depth of repeat is not externally given but is determined by the prediction period. In
the case reported every buyer group (and purchase rate)
beyond the fifth depth group (and fifth repeat rate) were
grouped together in one group (and one repeat rate). Penetration is assumed to approach an upper bound in a concave
manner. However this implicitly assumes some rather
special condition on the parameters of the underlying diffusion process (see Dodson and Muller 1978). The penetra-
tration formula fit the data rather well (with a reserva-
tion to be noted shortly). The repeat ratios are estimated
taking into account only the time between successive purchases. This was indeed a major flaw which was later corrected by Massy (1969) and Eskin (1973).

In the case reported, unlike Parfitt and Collins (1968) and
Blattberg and Golanty (1978), the prediction was made after
an observation period of a whole year. This is a relatively long period of observation since in case of product
failure, it is possible that it may be withdrawn from the
market within a shorter period of time than a year.

2. Parfitt and Collins (1968): The same model is also used
in Shoemaker and Staelin (1976). One of the problems with
the more established models such as this (or the previous)
is that the process underlying the analysis is neither explicitly discussed nor formulated. Thus our description
is of what the process should have looked like in order to
achieve the final formula discussed in the paper. The
model is on a very aggregate level. It does not distinguish between types of information nor depths of repeat
purchase. All potential triers are aggregated into one
group. Also, all those who have purchased the product are
aggregated and their purchase rates are aggregated into
one rate. The data used in application of the model were
obtained from consumer panels which is the only type of
data needed.

It is of interest to note that as in the Blattberg-Golanty
(1978) case, accurate prediction could be done after a
relatively short period of time. Parfitt and Collins
(1968) report a case in which the prediction was made 20
weeks after launch; Blattberg and Golanty (1978) report 11
cases where the predictions were made from 2 to 7 months
after launch.

3. Claycamp and Liddy: N.W. AYER (1969): This is a simple diffusion model which formalizes the following sequence of events: knowledge, trial, and repeat purchasing.
In each stage, all the marketing variables, whether controllable or not, influence the customer flows and purchase
rates. Despite its simplicity and the utilization of non-
sophisticated statistical techniques (e.g., two-stage
least squares) the model predicted well when the prediction
was made on the basis of <u>prelaunch information</u>.

4 and 5. Nakanishi (1973) and Massy: STEAM (1969): Both
of these models are stochastic depth of repeat models
based on Fourt and Woodlock (1960). The core of both
models is mathematical representation for the probability
that a consumer will make his next purchase at a given
time, given that his last purchase occurred at a particular time. Nakanishi (1973), in addition, allows for a decay, that is at any depth of repeat class, there is a positive probability that a consumer will discontinue the use
of the product (or brand).

The two models have a distinct advantage over Fourt and
Woodlock (1960) and Parfitt and Collins (1968) in that
they have one integrated model to forecast the process.
In that respect it is worthwhile to note the model developed by Eskin (1973). This is an in between model in
that it is conceptually more sophisticated than Fourt and
Woodlock model (1960) but "more understandable to the non-
technician" than STEAM (1969). However it lacks an integrated model as well. Both Eskin's and Nakanishi's models
are easier to implement as they involve simpler statistical techniques than STEAM. The latter, however, has the
advantage of yielding accurate prediction made a short time
after launch (3 to 6 months). Indeed shortening the gap
between launch and prediction time is one of the major
goals of all the diffusion models presented here.

6. Assmus: NEWPROD (1975): This is one model which is
not formally a special case of the general multistage
model. The reason is that Assmus distinguishes three types
of potential customers not according to the information
they convey about the product but according to the source
of information: advertising, sample or coupon. However,
the lack of word-of-mouth as a source of information is
surprising in such a model. The model includes segments
called skeptical trier and reluctant aware. These segments
comprise of consumers who waited one period before making
the purchase. With no mechanism of word-of-mouth, their
reluctance or skepticism adds little to the model. Decay
exists only partially. There is no decay in the repeaters
group. The model was successful in predicting sales from
prelaunch information.

7. Urban: SPRINTER Mod III (1970): The main feature of
the model is a depth of repeat model based theoretically
on Fourt and Woodlock's work (1960). The maximum depth of
repeat is externally given to be three. Repeat purchase
rates and depth of repeat consumer classes above three are
combined into a single rate (and group).

Though the full-blown flow diagram is extremely complex
the mathematical formulation allows for routine regression
techniques, both linear and nonlinear. However the data
requirements are immense and include panel data, store
audits, salesmen's reports in addition to questionnaires
regarding awareness, preference, etc. The model was
tested (apparently extensively). However a comparison of
forecasts and actual values (such as Blattberg and
golanty's Table 1) is not provided.

8. Midgley (1976): This model was the first to elaborate
on the different types of information. Although the model
is not a repeat purchase model, it does serve as a basis
to the general multistage model presented earlier. The
model was tested against data on consumer nondurables and
performed well. The problem with the model is that it requires long data series since it involves a large number
of parameters. In one extreme case, the author had to run
a regression with 20 observations and 18 parameters. This
is true with respect to the general multistage model as
well since each depth of purchase class adds a considerable number of parameters (about 15 with some symmetry
condition. The majority of those, though, will be zero
after a certain depth group).

9. Blattberg and Golanty: TRACKER (1978): This model is
also based theoretically on the depth of repeat model of
Fourt and Woodlock (1960). The maximum depth of repeat is
not externally given but is determined by the planning
(and prediction) horizon. The data inputs are obtained
from questionnaires and include information about awareness, frequency of use, time interval between uses, etc.
Both linear and nonlinear estimation procedures are used
to estimate the parameters. The model has been applied
successfully.

10. Dodson and Muller (1978): The model incorporates

advertising and word-of-mouth. One of its central results
shows the conditions under which sales will increase to a
peak or will have the characteristic single peaked profile
with sales first increasing and then decreasing to a level
below the peak. The model was tested against data on consumer nondurables and performed well. The problem with the
model, and indeed with all models which distinguish between
awareness and potential classes, is that it requires data
on awareness which is costly and cannot be "fished" out of
the panel data. The authors used grid search techniques
for obtaining the parameter estimates.

11. Lilien and Rao (1978): The model incorporates personal selling and word-of-mouth. The setting is of drug
companies selling to physicians with the help of both "de-
tailmen" who visit doctors, and advertising in trade magazines. Testing the model provided "satisfactory" fits.
As in the previous case a full solution of the model required nonlinear estimation procedures. In this case the
authors decided to linearize the model and estimate the
parameters by OLS method.

DISCUSSION AND CONCLUSIONS

After reviewing the repeat purchase models, it is important
to indicate certain key factors which have to be addressed
so that the models will become both more sound theoretically and more effective practically. The discussion
therefore will be devoted to the two areas of theory and
practice.

Theory

From the review of the models several facts are apparent.
First, several of the models do not have an integrated process in which the flows of customers from stage to stage
are treated in a unified fashion. The main discrepancy is
between the first stage (of becoming informed) and the rest
(trial and adoption). The first stage is usually formulated separately with some ad hoc assumption about the relation between advertising and awareness such as linearity
(e.g., AYER or exponential [e.g., NEWPROD]). It should be
recognized (see, for example, Urban 1970) that the awareness stage is not a separate one but instead is tied in
closely to the rest of the diffusion/adoption process.

Second, it is apparent that most models incorporate one or
two marketing variables at best (exceptions are AYER and
SPRINTER). As we have already noted elsewhere there is no
unified approach to the inclusion of marketing variables
into the diffusion process (Mahajan and Muller 1979). Moreover from the review here it is clear that there is no unified approach as to the inclusion of several market factors
such as forgetting and impulse purchase. On the other hand
the recent models reviewed here represent a major effort in
combining the diffusion process which is concerned with the
spread of the new product from the manufacturer to ultimate
user or adopter and the adoption process which is concerned
with the sequence of stages through which a consumer progresses from first awareness of an innovation to final acceptance. It is to be acknowledged, however, that increased sophistication desired in a model should be evaluated in view of such factors as model tractability, data
requirements and ease of parameter estimation.

Practice

The two main issues here are parameter estimation and empirical findings. A standard and unavoidable problem with
application of diffusion processes is the parameter estimation. If one wishes to make an accurate prediction after a
relatively short period of time, one has to work with a
few data points. The parameter estimates might then be unstable, with high standard errors. This requires consideration of approaches which adjust and update the initial

parameter estimates to change in the data patterns.

With respect to empirical findings, indeed there is a lack
of research with respect to the importance of the nonpar-
ticipants in the word-of-mouth process (the neutral group)
and the importance of the group of consumers who participate adversely in the process. Clearly the explicit inclusion of adverse information is indispensible in planning the introduction of certain new products (e.g.,
movies, plays).

In modeling the communication or word-of-mouth effect,
most of the models do not explicitly consider the intensity
of the conveyed information. It can be hypothesized that
customers who have repurchased the product a number of
times (i.e., loyal customers) may have much greater credibility (and hence influence) while informing others about
the product. Thus, the word-of-mouth effect depends on
the depth of repeat class to which the transmitter of the
information belongs. It is also desirable to empirically
test this observation.

Finally, the focus of this paper has been on the underlying structure of the repeat purchase models. It is important to compare these models on a number of other
management-oriented criteria such as diagnostic power of
the model, ease of implementation, cost of development,
data requirements and actual performance. The framework
developed by Larreche and Montgomery (1977) may serve as
a guideline for such a comparison. A subjective evaluation
of these models on some of the management-oriented criteria has been provided by Narasimhan and Sen (1981).

REFERENCES

Assmus, G. (1975), "NEWPROD: The Design and Implementation
of a New Product Model," Journal of Marketing Research,
39 (January), 16-23.

Blattberg, R. and J. Golanty (1978), "Tracker: An Early
Test Market Forecasting and Diagnostic Model for New
Product Planning," Journal of Marketing Research, 25
(May), 192-202.

Claycamp, H. J. and L. E. Liddy (1969), "Prediction of New
Product Performance: An Analytical Approach," 6 (November), 414-20.

Dodson, J. A. and E. Muller (1978), "Models of New Product
Diffusion Through Advertising and Word-ofMouth,"
Management Science, 15 (November), 1568-78.

Eskin, G. T. (1973), "Dynamic Forecasts of New Product Demand Using a Depth of Repeat Model," Journal of Marketing Research, 10 (May).

Fourt, L. A. and J. W. Woodlock (1960), "Early Prediction
of Market Success for New Grocery Products," Journal of
Marketing, 25 (October).

Kalwani, M. H. and A. J. Silk (1980), "Structure of Repeat
Buying for New Packaged Goods," Journal of Marketing
Research, 17 (August), 316-22.

Larreche, J. and D. B. Montgomery (1977), "A Framework for
the Comparison of Marketing Models: A Delphi Method,"
Journal of Marketing Research, 14 (November), 487-498.

Lilien, G. L. and A. G. Rao, "A Marketing Promotion Model
with Word-of-Mouth Effect," Working Paper 976-78, Sloan
School of Management, Massachusetts Institute of Technology, Boston.

Majahan, V. and E. Muller (1979), "Innovation Diffusion
and New Product Growth Models in Marketing," Journal of

<u>Marketing</u>, 43 (Fall), 55-68.

Massy, W. F. (1969), "Forecasting the Demand for New Convenience Products," <u>Journal of Marketing Research</u>, 6
(November), 405-12.

Midgley, D. F. (1976), "A Simple Mathematical Theory of
Innovative Behavior," <u>Journal of Consumer Research</u>, 3
(June), 31-41.

Nakanishi, M. (1973), "Advertising and Promotion Effects
on Consumer Response to New Products," <u>Journal of Marketing Research</u>, 10 (August, 242-49.

Narasimhan, C. and S. K. Sen (1981), "Test Market Models
for New Product Introduction," in <u>New Product Forecasting: Models and Applications</u>, Y. Wind, V. Mahajan and
R. Cardozo, eds., Lexington, MA: Lexington Books.

Parfitt, H. H. and B. J. K. Collins (1968), "Use of Consumer Panels for Brand Share Predictions," <u>Journal of
Marketing Research</u>, 5 (May), 131-45.

Shoemaker, R. and R. Staelin (1976), "The Effects of
Sampling Variation on Sales Forecasts for New Consumer
Products," <u>Journal of Marketing Research</u>, 13 (May), 138-
143.

Urban, G. L. (1970), "SPRINTER Mod III: A Model for the
Analysis of New Frequently Purchased Consumer Products,"
<u>Operations Research</u>, 18 (September), 805-55.

Wind, Y., V. Mahajan and R. Cardozo, eds. (1981), <u>New
Product Forecasting: Models and Applications</u>, Lexington,
MA: Lexington Books.

Keynote Session

Chair: Bruce J. Walker, Arizona State University

Speaker: Neglected Areas of Marketing Scholarship
Philip Kotler, Northwestern University

Panelists: John G. Keane, Managing Change, Inc.
Barrington, IL
William Lazer, Michigan State University

Doctoral Education in Marketing: Program Orientation, Recruiting, and Supporting Doctoral Students

Chair: Donald W. Jackson, Jr., Arizona State University

Panelists: William H. Cunningham, University of Texas –
Austin
Robert F. Lusch, University of Oklahoma
Thomas S. Robertson, University of
Pennsylvania

Electronic Shopping & Buyer Behavior

Chair: Jagdish N. Sheth, University of Illinois – Urbana

Speakers: Videotex Marketing: State of the Art
Thomas Farmer, A.T. & T., Parsippany, NJ

Impact of Electronic Shopping on Consumer
Decision Processes
Roger Blackwell, Ohio State University

Electronic Shopping: Marketer's Perspectives
Paul Dorrington, Management Horizons, Inc.,
Columbus, Ohio

Discussant: Jagdish N. Sheth, University of Illinois –
Urbana

Influence Flows Within the Organizational Buying Center: Methodological Issues and Answers

Chair: Robert E. Spekman, University of Maryland

Panelists: Bob Calder, Northwestern University
Wesley Johnston, Ohio State University
Alvin Silk, M.I.T.
Robert Thomas, University of Pennsylvania
David Wilson, Pennsylvania State University

Discussant: Yoram Wind, University of Pennsylvania

Japanese Marketing Strategies

Chair: Johny K. Johansson, University of Washington

Speakers: Japanese Export Expansion Paths
Dominique M. Hanssens, UCLA
Johny K. Johansson, University of Washington

Strategic Market Planning: The Japanese
Approach
Warren J. Keegan, New York University

The World's Champion Marketers: The Japanese?
Philip Kotler, Northwestern University
Liam Fahey, Columbia University

Japanese Companies as Competitors
John U. Farley, Columbia University
Donald Sexton, Jr., Columbia University

Discussants: Masao Nakanishi, Kwansei Gakuin University,
Japan
Yoram Wind, University of Pennsylvania

Joint Session with TIMS (The Institute of Management Science) Marketing College: Research in Managing Channel Relationships

Chair: Russell S. Winer, Columbia University

Panelists: Michael Etgar, Hebrew University, Rehovot,
Israel, and Visiting Professor, New York
University
Abel Jeuland, University of Chicago
Steven M. Shugan, University of Chicago
Richard Staelin, Duke University
Louis W. Stern, Northwestern University

Latent Structure Analysis: A Tutorial

Speakers: William R. Dillon, University of Massachusetts-
Amherst
Thomas J. Madden, University of Massachusetts-
Amherst

Marketing Education in the Information Age

Chair: Stanley M. Freedman, Old Dominion University

Speakers: Where Are We Today in Marketing Education?
William J. Lundstrom, Old Dominion University

What Is the Educational Gap?
Vico Henriques, Computer and Business Equip-
ment Manufacturers Association, Washington,
D.C.

The Need for a National Effort
Vincent Guiliana, Arthur D. Little Company,
Cambridge, MA

Marketing in Developing Economies

Chair: Philip Kotler, Northwestern University

Speakers: Marketing and Economic Development: A
Perspective
Gerald Sentell, University of Tennessee –
Knoxville

Missing Links: Marketing and the Newer
Theories of Development
Nikhilesh Dholakia, University of Rhode
Island – Kingston
Ruby R. Dholakia, University of Rhode
Island – Kingston

Adapting Marketing Theory to Different
Stages of Economic Development
Philip Kotler, Northwestern University

461

<u>The Marketing Science Institute: Business and Academic Collaboration in Research</u>

Speakers: Alden G. Clayton, Managing Director, Marketing Science Institute
           E. Raymond Corey, Harvard University and Executive Director, Marketing Science Institute

<u>Marketing Strategy: Focus, Boundaries and Directions</u>

Chair: Thomas S. Robertson, University of Pennsylvania

Speakers: The Concept of Strategy
           Bruce D. Henderson, The Boston Consulting Group

           Strategic Marketing Planning
           W. Walker Lewis, Strategic Planning Associates

           Defining New Products by Strategic Roles
           Thomas Kuczmarski, Booz, Allen and Hamilton, Inc.

           Marketing Strategy and Corporate Strategy
           Thomas S. Robertson, University of Pennsylvania
           Yoram Wind, University of Pennsylvania

<u>Marketing: The Japanese Experience</u>

Chair: Robert Holloway, University of Minnesota

Speakers: Determinants of Power in Japanese Marketing Systems
           Masanari Tamura, Kobe University, Kobe, Japan

           Trade Area Models in Public Policy Making
           Shuzo Abe, Yokohoma National University, Yokohoma, Japan

           Changing Patterns of Consumer Lifestyles in the Age of Marketing III
           Toshiaki Izeki, Keio University, Tokyo, Japan

<u>Meet the Editors of AMA-Affiliated Journals</u>

Chair: Edward W. Cundiff, Emory University
        AMA Vice President--Publications

Panelists: William H. Cunningham, University of Texas - Austin
            Editor, <u>Journal of Marketing</u>
            Harold H. Kassarjian, UCLA
            James R. Bettman, Duke University
            Co-editors, <u>Journal of Consumer Research</u>
            William D. Perreault, Jr., University of North Carolina - Chapel Hill
            Editor, <u>Journal of Marketing Research</u>

<u>Meet the Editors of New Marketing Journals</u>

Chair: O.C. Ferrell, Texas A & M University

Panelists: Philip R. Cateora, University of Colorado
            Editor, <u>Journal of Marketing Education</u>
            B.J. Dunlap, Appalachian State University
            Editor, <u>Journal of Health Care Marketing</u>
            George Fisk, Syracuse University
            Editor, <u>Journal of Macromarketing</u>

Marvin A. Jolson, University of Maryland - College Park
Editor, <u>Journal of Personal Selling and Sales Management</u>
Thomas C. Kinnear, University of Michigan - Ann Arbor
Editor, <u>Journal of Marketing and Public Policy</u>
Subrata Sen, University of Rochester
Area Editor, <u>Marketing Science</u>

<u>Presentation of Winners of AMA Doctoral Dissertation Competition</u>

Chair: Roger J. Best, University of Oregon
        Chairperson, 1981-82 AMA Doctoral Dissertation Competition

<u>Retail Productivity</u>

Chair: Dale D. Achabal, University of Santa Clara

Speakers: Joint Production in Retail
           David A. Gautschi, INSEAD, Fontainebleau, France

           The Impact of Marketing Mix Variables on Labor Productivity in Retailing
           Robert F. Lusch, University of Oklahoma
           Soo Young Moon, Import-Export Consultant

           Issues and Perspectives on Retail Productivity
           Dale D. Achabal, University of Santa Clara
           Ann Odegaard Kriewall, University of Santa Clara
           Shelby McIntyre, University of Santa Clara

           Measuring Capital Productivity at the Department Level: Implications for Management
           Hirotaka Takeuchi, Harvard University

<u>Survey Research in the Public Sector</u>

Chair: Kent Monroe, Virginia Polytechnic Institute and State University

Speakers: Thomas Maronick, Bureau of Consumer Protection, Federal Trade Commission
           Kevin McCrohan, Planning and Research, Internal Revenue Service

Discussant: James D. Smith, Institute for Social Research, University of Michigan

<u>The Use of Retail Scanning Data in Marketing Research: Current Status and Future Directions</u>

Chair: Brian Harris, University of Southern California

Panelists: Gerry Eskin, University of Iowa and Information Resources, Inc.
            John Little, M.I.T.
            C. Narasimhan, University of Chicago
            Subrata Sen, University of Rochester
            Roger Strang, New York University